World War II in Europe

VOLUME II

MILITARY HISTORY OF THE UNITED STATES (VOL. 6)
GARLAND REFERENCE LIBRARY OF THE HUMANITIES (VOL. 1254)

World War II in Europe

An Encyclopedia

Editor
David T. Zabecki

Assistant Editors
Carl O. Schuster
Paul J. Rose
William H. Van Husen

GARLAND PUBLISHING, INC.
A member of the Taylor & Francis Group
New York & London
1999

Library of Congress Cataloging-in-Publication Data

World War II in Europe : an encyclopedia / editor, David T. Zabecki ; assistant editors,
    Carl O. Schuster, Paul J. Rose, William H. Van Husen.
            p.   cm. — (Garland reference library of the humanities ; 1254.
    Military history of the United States ; v. 6)
        Includes bibliographical references and index.
        Contents: v. 1. Social and political issues and events. Leaders and individuals.
    Units and organizations — v. 2. Weapons and equipment. Strategy, tactics, and
    operational techniques. Battles, campaigns, and operations.
        ISBN 0-8240-7029-1 (alk. paper)
        1. World War, 1939-1945—Europe—Encyclopedias.   I. Zabecki, David T.
    II. Series: Garland reference library of the humanities ; vol. 1254. III. Series: Garland
    reference library of the humanities. Military history of the United States ; v. 6.
    D740.W67   1999
    940.53—dc21   98-27981
                                                                              CIP

Cover design by Lawrence Wolfson Design, New York

Printed on acid-free, 250-year-life paper
Manufactured in the United States of America

Contents

Weapons and Equipment

A

Aircraft Carriers, British

At the beginning of World War II, most British aircraft carriers were of World War I vintage. The oldest in service was the HMS *Argus,* the first flattop in the world. Converted from a passenger vessel in construction, it was completed in September 1918. The basic idea behind the *Argus* design was to provide a flight deck free from the emissions of hot furnace gases. That problem was solved initially by eliminating all the superstructure. Horizontal smoke ducts with big exhaust fans were fitted to deliver all gas and smoke out over the stern.

The old generation also included three converted battle cruisers, the HMS *Furious, Courageous,* and *Glorious.* They were the brainchildren of the then first sea lord, Sir John Fisher, conceived for the purpose of bringing battle to the German Baltic shore. Initially, the *Furious* had its original after-armament, with a flight deck mounted on the forward part of the ship. After several modifications, the *Furious* emerged as a true aircraft carrier; a flattop without funnel and mast, its smoke being discharged by vents at the after end of the hangar through cumbersome ducts. The ship had all the characteristics of a genuine fleet carrier; high speed, sufficient number of aircraft, and good range.

When the *Furious* was nearing completion, the *Courageous* and *Glorious* also underwent a similar conversion. Since the problems of smoke on the flight deck had been solved in the meantime, they were rebuilt with a side island. By 1930 all three carriers were in service. The main difference between them was the capacity of aircraft, with the *Furious* having less hangar space because of the ducts. Later, during World War II, the *Furious* also was given a small side island.

The HMS *Eagle* started its life before the war as a battleship ordered by Chile. The British government bought it on the slips for conversion in 1917. Commissioned for trials in April 1920, the *Eagle* was almost immediately sent back to the dockyard for major modifications. The additional work lasted until 1923, for a total cost of £4.6 million. Even then the results were not good. The *Eagle* could make a maximum speed of barely twenty-four knots and carried only twenty-one aircraft, compared to thirty-five for the *Furious* and forty-eight for the *Courageous.*

The world's first vessel specially designed as an aircraft carrier was the HMS *Hermes.* It was ordered in July 1917, and completed in July 1923. She compared very favorably with the larger *Eagle.* These six vessels, which constituted the Royal Navy's first generation of carriers, was the strongest carrier force in the world in the 1930s. The United States and Japan had only three carriers each, and France had only one. The aircraft carried on board were mainly of three types: fighters, reconnaissance, and attack (mainly torpedo) planes.

The first new generation carrier was ordered in 1935. Commissioned in November 1938, the HMS *Ark Royal* was a major improvement over her older sisters. The *Ark Royal* had an 800-foot flight deck that overhung the bow and the stern, hangers on two decks, three lifts, a strong antiaircraft suite, a full complement of sixty aircraft, and a maximum speed of thirty-one knots. Despite a certain similarity of appearance with other nations' aircraft carriers of the period, the *Ark Royal* was not built to the same requirements. *Ark Royal* was the only carrier built in the 1930s to have an armored flight deck. Also, the U.S. carriers, for example, were very lightly built but with bulky hangars superimposed on the hull (in order to hold the maximum possible number of aircraft), while on the *Ark Royal,* the hangar structure was part of the hull. This reduced the number of planes she could carry, but gave her a stronger hull.

When the war started in September 1939, these seven carriers were in service, and another seven were on the stocks or in planning. The *Courageous* was sunk by U-boat torpedoes while on antisubmarine patrol a fortnight after the beginning of the war. Her loss put an end, for the time being, to that type of operation. The *Glorious,* too, was an early loss when, in the spring of 1940, she was surprised and sunk by gunfire from the German battle cruisers *Scharnhorst* and *Gneisenau.* Next to be lost was the *Ark Royal,* which had served in both the Atlantic and the Mediterranean, and whose old "Stringbags" (the nickname for the Swordfish torpedo planes) had contributed to the sinking of the *Bismarck* (q.v.).

On 13 November 1941, the *Ark Royal* was torpedoed by the *U-81* off Gibraltar in the Mediterranean. Damage control was mishandled, and she capsized fourteen hours after being hit. Next on the list of war casualties came the small HMS *Hermes,* sunk by the Japanese in April 1942. The last of the grand old ladies to go to the bottom was the *Eagle,* during the Malta supply convoy Operation PEDESTAL. She was torpedoed by the *U-73* on 11 August 1942 in the western Mediterranean, north of Algiers.

Of the seven aircraft carriers on order at the outbreak of the war, four were of the Illustrious-class, and two of the Indefatigable-class. The small *Unicorn* was built as an auxiliary vessel, but during the war it was used as light fleet carrier.

The carriers of the Illustrious-class were similar to the *Ark Royal* except the first three had only one hangar deck, which limited their air wings to thirty planes. This was corrected in HMS *Indomitable,* the last ship of the class, which had two hangars. The *Illustrious* joined the fleet in July 1940 and participated in the Taranto (q.v.) attack that

November. The HMS *Victorious* played a major role in the sinking of the *Bismarck,* while HMS *Formidable* launched the torpedo planes against the Italian fleet at Matapan (q.v.).

The HMS *Indefatigable* and *Implacable* were very similar to the Illustrious-class, with several design improvements made from the experiences with the earlier ships. The *Indefatigable* was one of the carriers involved in the attacks against the *Tirpitz* in Norwegian waters.

All six of the Illustrious- and Indefatigable-class carriers survived the war. Although British carriers lacked the air wings and striking power of their foreign counterparts, they demonstrated far greater staying power. For example, the *Illustrious* was hit by several 1,000-pound bombs during one of her Malta convoys. The ship was out of action for months, but survived. No American or Japanese carrier could have survived such punishment.

The pressing need for carriers during the war gave rise to a crash building program for more economical vessels—the so-called light fleet carriers. Two classes were ordered, one begun in 1942–1943, and the other in 1944. Only four (out of sixteen ordered) of the first class, and none of the second, were completed before the end of the war. These ships were built to Lloyd's Registry rules (instead of the Admiralty's) in order to save time and money.

The idea of submarine hunter groups centered on a carrier was revived only when small specialized escort carriers were available. The first British ship of this type was a seized and converted German cargo ship, which became the HMS *Audacity.* The conversion was very simple, consisting of little more than the addition of a flight deck on the existing hull. With only six planes permanently parked on the flight deck, the *Audacity* had a brief

The fleet aircraft carrier HMS Ark Royal, *sunk by the* U–81 *and* U–205 *on 14 November 1941. (IWM A 5627)*

career. Only five other merchant ships were converted as escort carriers by Great Britain, because American shipyards were supplying newly built escort carriers at a tremendous rate. The Royal Navy acquired thirty-nine from the Americans, which were nicknamed "Woolworth carriers" (from the famous dime-store chain).

From 1944 on, the British used merchant ships with a small flight deck added to an unmodified hull. These ships flew the red ensign of the merchant fleet and were manned by civilian crews, except for pilots and aircraft maintenance staff. Called MACs (merchant aircraft carriers), they were of two types: grain carriers and oil tankers. The British had nineteen MACs. Ten of the Empire-class were grain or oil carriers, with four planes on the flight deck, and specifically built as MACs. The other nine were existing oil carriers converted to the same layout.

The MACs replaced the old CAMs (catapult merchant ships) that resulted from the early desperate need for convoys to have some sort of aerial protection against German long-range aircraft. To meet this requirement, several auxiliary and cargo ships were fitted with a catapult and a fighter plane (usually a Hurricane re-dubbed a "Hurricat") that was expendable.

Francesco Fatutta

(Refer to tables on pages 831–833)

Additional Reading

Brown, D., *Carrier Operations in World War II,* Vol. I (1975).

Roskill S.W., *White Ensign: The British Navy at War 1939–1945* (1960).

Lenton, H.T., and J.J. Colledge, *Warships of World War II,* Parts 1 and 4 (*Royal Navy Aircraft Carriers*) (1962).

Aircraft Carriers, German and Italian

Both European Axis nations suffered from their inability to provide sea-based air cover to their fleets. It was a tactical shortcoming that severely inhibited the employment of their fleets and cost them several ships. Ironically, both navies recognized the need for aircraft carriers before the war but placed a higher priority on battleship construction. The *Luftwaffe* actually developed carrier aircraft for the *Kriegsmarine* before the war, while the Italian Air Force refused to develop such planes until Premier Benito Mussolini (q.v.) directed it be done in 1941. By then it was too late, and neither the aircraft carrier nor its aircraft were

ready before Italy signed the armistice in September 1943. On the German side, it was the naval leadership that postponed and then canceled its aircraft carriers.

The Germans started carrier construction first. Germany's replacement shipbuilding program of 1934 called for three such units. The first two, *Carriers A* and *B,* were laid down on 28 December 1935 and 30 September 1936, respectively. They were scheduled to enter service by late 1939, but delays in equipment deliveries and other naval construction programs plagued the two carriers from the very beginning. By 1938, both were eleven months behind schedule and a welder shortage threatened additional delays. The limited available manpower was assigned to the higher-priority battleship and U-boat construction programs. As a result, *Carrier A* (the *Graf Zeppelin*) was not launched until December 1938, and its completion date slipped to May 1940 (thirteen months later). The completion date of *Carrier B* (the *Peter Strasser*) was set back to July 1940.

The war's start exacerbated an already serious labor shortage, as all available shipyard workers were concentrated on the *Bismarck, Prinz Eugen, Seydlitz,* and U-boats in an effort to complete them as quickly as possible. Chancellor Adolf Hitler's (q.v.) refusal to reduce steel allocations to the civilian sector meant that steel supplies had to be rationed among the services. In May 1940, Admiral Erich Raeder (q.v.) chose to scrap *Carrier B* and suspend construction on the *Graf Zeppelin*. It was 85 percent complete and its air wing had already been assembled. Instead, he allocated the navy's steel to U-boats, the new H-class battleships, scout cruisers, and destroyers. Of these, only the U-boats and destroyers were ever completed. Meanwhile, the carrier's air wing joined the *Luftwaffe* for the French campaign. The *Kriegsmarine* would never see those aircraft again.

The Italian Navy had considered converting two ocean liners into aircraft carriers in the early 1930s, but gave up on the idea in the face of Italian Air Force resistance. A 1923 royal decree had assigned all fixed-wing aircraft to the Italian Air Force, and Mussolini supported the air force's refusal to develop carrier aircraft. The navy, therefore, spent its money on modernizing older battleships. Thus, neither Axis nation had an aircraft carrier in service or under construction by the second year of the war. Events, however, were to change that situation rather quickly.

Both Hitler and Mussolini changed their minds in the face of Japanese and Allied carrier successes of 1940 and 1941. The Italians resur-

The Aquila, *the only Axis aircraft carrier completed but never put into service. (IWM C 5319)*

rected their prewar plans and requisitioned the passenger liners SS *Roma* and SS *Augustus* for conversion. They were renamed *Aquila* and *Falco,* respectively. Unfortunately, the Italians borrowed heavily from the German "experience" and adopted a heavy surface battery of eight 150mm guns in armored casements. That placed too much weight above the waterline, and 130mm guns in open mounts had to be installed instead. Their concern over stability and internal protection also led them to place a twenty-four-inch reinforced concrete bulge at the waterline. The additional weight and beam reduced the speed of the ships by two knots, but greatly increased stability and survivability. Protection was provided in other areas as well. A 3.1-inch armored deck was installed over the fuel bunkers and magazines. The air wings were supposed to consist of 36 to 51 Re.2001 aircraft, depending on whether a folding-wing variant could be developed. In its final configuration, the ships displaced nearly 32,000 tons and had a top speed of nineteen to twenty knots.

The *Aquila* was ready for sea trials when Italy signed the armistice in September 1943, and its air wing could have been ready nine months later. The *Falco* was renamed *Sparviero,* but had not progressed beyond the initial stages of work when the armistice was signed. The Germans took over both carriers, but lacked the fuel and manpower to bring them into service.

Meanwhile, Hitler ordered the *Kriegsmarine* to resume work on the *Graf Zeppelin* in August 1942. Two additional types of aircraft carriers were proposed as well, and a cruiser under construction was also allocated for modification into a carrier. Like the Italians, the Germans also set aside two passenger liners for conversion, while the *Luftwaffe* resumed work on a navalized version of the Ju-87D fighter and prepared to resume production of a naval version Bf-109. None of these plans reached fruition, however, for Germany's industry had to be applied to the more serious ground and air threats facing the nation.

There were other problems as well. The *Graf Zeppelin* turned out to be a badly balanced design and had to be rebuilt, adding some 9,000 tons to its displacement and delaying its construction even further. The completion date was moved back to late 1943 and fuel supplies were such that there was little prospect of the ship being able to operate, even if the air wing could be reassembled. Germany's carrier plans were canceled almost as quickly as they were reborn.

Interestingly enough, aircraft carrier construction was the one area where the Axis nations cooperated. The ships' elevators, arresting gear, and catapults were all provided by Germany. Both the *Graf Zeppelin* and the *Aquila* were equipped with two elevators and two catapults. The catapults were of a compressed air design, which could launch a five-ton aircraft every thirty seconds. The air reservoirs, however, needed recharging (a fifty-minute process) after only nine launches. Worse, there was no provision for radar. Also, the surface batteries were placed along the periphery of the hangar bays, a practice that reduced the number of aircraft that could be loaded or maintained at one time. The Italians found it to be a destabilizing design fault and reduced the battery's weight, while the Germans chose to retain the battery and expand hull volume. Nevertheless, neither carrier design was optimized for air wing operations and both would have been severely limited in their ability to employ their air wings either offensively or defensively.

In many ways, it is just as well that neither nation employed its aircraft carriers. By 1943, the situation in the Mediterranean and Atlantic, Allied reading of Axis naval codes, and fuel shortages virtually ensured the carriers' destruction if they went to sea. The Axis carriers would have made a significant impact on the maritime situation in 1941, but their employment after that would have been problematic. An aircraft carrier air wing requires constant practice to remain effective, and neither Axis nation had the fuel supplies to sustain that effectiveness. Moreover, neither country's air force had the resources or willingness to provide replacement aircraft or modernize their naval air arms as the war progressed, and the navies themselves placed a low priority on aircraft carrier development. Aircraft carriers are a complex amalgamation of naval and aviation technology requiring a unique and extensive resource commitment. Neither European Axis nation made that commitment in World War II.

Carl O. Schuster

(Refer to table on page 834)

Additional Reading

Chesneau, Roger, *Aircraft Carriers of the World, 1914 to Present* (1987).

Lenton, H.T., *The German Navy* (1967).

Fraccaroli, Aldo, *Italian Warships of World War II* (1968).

Aircraft Carriers, U.S.

In the years between the two world wars, the most important naval development involved fleet aviation and the integration of aircraft with sea power. Naval aviators had been among the first of the American military forces to arrive in France in World War I, and the concept of utilizing ships to house and launch aircraft was conceived early by U.S. Navy leaders. These same leaders concluded that the development of fleet aviation was of paramount importance and that "Aircraft must become an essential arm of the fleet" to insure global air supremacy. In 1919, naval aircraft proved their value in an exercise with the fleet off the coast of Cuba. Naval aviation continued to develop, resulting in 1921 with the first carrier, the USS *Langley*, a converted collier fitted with a flight deck. In July 1921, the Navy Department established the Bureau of Aeronautics, and in 1926 an assistant secretary of the navy for aviation was appointed.

When the first two ships designed as aircraft carriers, the USS *Saratoga* and USS *Lexington*, entered service, carrier tactics began to evolve. The lessons learned in these years proved invaluable during World War II. By the time of the outbreak of war in Europe, the U.S. Navy had realized the need for smaller, faster carriers, and the USS *Ranger*, USS *Yorktown*, and USS *Enterprise* were added to the fleet.

Although U.S. aircraft carriers made their biggest mark on the war in the Pacific, the Battle of the Atlantic (q.v.) did show a need for carriers in convoys to combat enemy aircraft and submarines. Before the war, Admirals William V. Pratt and J.M. Reeves were early advocates of what became known as escort carriers, initially designated auxiliary aircraft vessel (AVG), then auxiliary aircraft carrier (ACV), and finally, in July 1943, aircraft carrier, escort (CVE). But in the years leading up to World War II, the U.S. Navy had no escort carriers. After 1941, the need became apparent.

Escort carriers, nicknamed "baby flattops," were the smallest carrier class. They were capable of speeds of 18.5 knots and carried twenty-four aircraft. The first CVE was the USS *Long Island*, which entered service in June 1941. Merchant hulls converted to escort carriers were delivered to Britain under Lend-Lease (q.v.). The first converted American escort carriers were the *Sangamon, Suwannee, Chanango,* and *Santee;* all took part in Operation TORCH in November 1942.

The primary activity of escort carriers in the Battle of the Atlantic came after March 1943, and the CVEs played a significant role in convoy escort for the duration of the war in Europe. March 1943 saw the peak of the destruction by the German U-boat menace. The 600-mile stretch of the mid-Atlantic became feared as the "Black Pit." But convoys centered around escort carriers changed the face of the Battle of the Atlantic. Between March and May 1943, Allied convoy escorts claimed forty-one U-boats, and the naval battle in the Atlantic had turned the corner.

Four classes of escort carriers were either converted or constructed during the war. One of which, the aforementioned Sangamon-class, were converted oilers. The Bogue-class carriers included twenty ships, ten of which were delivered to the British under Lend-Lease. More capable than the converted oil tankers, the Bogue-class escorts helped convince the U.S. Navy of their versatility and importance. The Bogue-class carriers included the *Card, Barnes, Core, Copahee, Croatan,* and *Prince William.* These were mercantile hulls converted by the Seattle-Tacoma Shipbuilding Corporation. The Bogue-class carriers varied in appearance and armaments, but generally had one or two 5-inch guns and assorted smaller guns, twelve fighters, and nine torpedo-bombers, and were capable of 16 knots.

The largest number of CVEs built were the Casablanca-class, fifty of which were commissioned during the war. The first of the class went into service in July 1943, and all were completed within eight months by the Kaiser Company of Vancouver, Washington, or by the Oregon Shipbuilding Corporation of Portland. Considered an improvement on the Bogue-class escorts, the Casablanca-class were easier on aircraft recovery operations. Armed with one 5-inch gun and twenty-four antiaircraft guns, this class generally carried twenty-eight aircraft. Top speeds averaged 19 knots.

Henry J. Kaiser's (q.v.) company was responsible for the production of fifty escort carriers and an even more incredible total of 1,460 ships built during the war years. Kaiser's plants utilized assembly lines, prefabricated parts, and a revolutionary welding method. The Casablanca-class escort car-

riers included the *Anzio, Casablanca, Corregidor, Hoggatt, Marcus Island, Mission Bay, Rudyerd Bay, Tripoli,* and *White Plains.* Five were lost during the war.

The last of the escort carrier classes was the Commencement Bay, twenty-four of which were produced before war's end. This class was a more sophisticated ship, but production slowed as American industry geared to more offensive weaponry. A total of 118 CVEs were built during the war, with thirty-three going to the Royal Navy. The carriers ranged in length from 490 to 558 feet and averaged speeds between 16 and 20 knots. Crew sizes varied from 450 to almost 1,000 men. Six CVEs (including the five from the Casablanca-class) were sunk during the war, and the *Sangamon* was heavily damaged.

Escort carriers were versatile ships around which an escort carrier task group (TG) was organized. For example, the *Bogue,* a CVE commissioned in September 1942, was part of a TG that included seven destroyers. On subsequent missions, destroyers and destroyer escorts accompanied the *Bogue.* Antisubmarine warfare (q.v.) was an integral part of escort duty, and the *Bogue* was the nucleus of the pioneer submarine hunter-killer group of the U.S. Navy. The *Bogue* TG was responsible for sinking one U-boat on its fourth crossing, two on the fifth crossing, two more on the seventh, and three on the eighth. Another example is the TG centered on the *Croatan.* From October to December 1943, the *Croatan* ferried aircraft across the Atlantic to North Africa. In a patrol beginning 11 March 1944, her group sank two U-boats. Two

The American-built escort carrier, HMS Biter. *As the merchant ship* Rio Panama, *the* Biter *was requisitioned for conversion in December 1940 and delivered to the British in mid-1942. She was capable of a speed of 17 knots. (IWM A 12578)*

more U-boats were destroyed in another mission from 2 June to 22 July. In all cases, attacks on U-boats were the combined effort of carrier aircraft and destroyers.

Aircraft transportation was the other primary duty of the carrier groups. The *Bogue* carried fighters to the United States Army Air Forces in Europe in January and February 1944. Another escort carrier, the *Block Island,* also ferried aircraft to Ireland during the summer of 1943. In December 1943, the *Santee* left Staten Island with a hangar and flight deck packed with P-38 fighters bound for Glasgow, Scotland.

Still another important task assigned to carriers was training, both in the coordination of task group tactics and in pilot training. The USS *Guadalcanal* qualified almost 4,000 pilots before being decommissioned in July 1946. The *Card* was assigned to pilot training in March 1945. In February and March 1943, the *Core* was used for pilot training off San Diego, two months after her commissioning. Much carrier and fleet training was conducted off Guantanamo Bay, Cuba. As the ships maneuvered in surface formations, pilots and deck crews utilized the time for vital training in takeoffs and landings from carrier decks and coordination with naval surface units.

Escort carriers performed a variety of other duties in addition to the traditional carrier functions. In February 1945, the USS *Mission Bay* joined a convoy near the Mediterranean that carried President Franklin D. Roosevelt (q.v.) from the Yalta Conference. Several escort carriers, including the *Tripoli* and *Card,* served as troop transports after the end of the war in the Pacific. On 5 November 1945, the first carrier landing of a jet took place on the *Wake Island.* In June 1944, the *Guadalcanal's* crew captured an abandoned German U-boat (the *U-505*) off the African coast. The *Wake Island* earned three battle stars during the war; the *Bogue* received three battle stars and a Presidential Unit Citation; the *Block Island* two battle stars; and the *Guadalcanal* three battle stars and a Presidential Unit Citation. The CVEs were one of the decisive elements in the antisubmarine war phase of the Battle of the Atlantic.

Boyd Childress

(Refer to tables on pages 835–836)

Additional Reading

Hoyt, Edwin Palmer, *Carrier Wars: Naval Aviation from World War II to the Persian Gulf* (1989).

Jane's, *Jane's Fighting Ships of World War II* (1947).
Miller, Nathan, *Naval Air War 1939–1945* (1991).

Antiaircraft Artillery, British

As governments awoke to the bomber threat in the 1930s, antiaircraft (AA) defenses, which had been dismantled after 1918 in the belief that aircraft were the best AA weapons, were rebuilt. The essential advances necessary to make these effective lay in target finding. Progress was made in radar (q.v.), in making prediction calculations at a single location for a number of guns, and in power-laying and fuze-setting—called remote power control (RPC). Although the idea for this automation had been developed in the 1930s, it did not come into service until the war.

Military planners also came to realize that a series of guns was needed to combat different types of aircraft at various heights. The principal low-level gun for use against fast-flying aircraft below 2,000 feet was the Swedish 40mm Bofors. This was acquired in the 1930s and still in use in British service in the 1970s. Like other armies, the British had trouble finding a suitable gun for the range between 6,000 and 10,000 feet. Guns like the 6-pounder were not very successful at this task.

To attack high-level aircraft, the British produced what many at the time felt to be their best gun of the war—the 3.7-inch, first produced in 1938. It had a ceiling of 28,000 feet, and in 1944 its effectiveness was greatly enhanced by the introduction of RPC. The latter, combined with radar, predictors, and proximity fuze (q.v.) ammunition gave the gun an 82 percent success rate against the V-1 flying bombs in 1944. In retrospect, it is surprising that the British did not use the 3.7-inch piece as an antitank gun in the way that the Germans used their 88mm Flak gun. The British and other Allied ground troops were only too painfully aware of the effectiveness of the German 88mm in a ground role.

The most striking development in AA artillery was not so much in gun or gun-control equipment, but rather in the development of the proximity fuze—and even then not so much for its effect on AA operations. The proximity fuze was developed for use against aircraft, but it soon was applied to ground operations with startling success. It proved to be the forerunner of the "smart" munitions that have been the focus of munitions research ever since the end of World War II.

Jonathan B.A. Bailey

An Mk-II, 3.7-inch antiaircraft crew in action. (IWM KID 4348)

(Refer to table on page 837)

Additional Reading
Hogg, Ivan V., *British and American Artillery of World War 2* (1978).

Antiaircraft Artillery, German

Antiaircraft artillery (AAA) was primarily a *Luftwaffe* responsibility but the German Army (after 1941) and navy both acquired and trained their own AAA crews. Nonetheless, except for the navy's AAA, the *Luftwaffe* remained responsible for providing weapons, ammunition, and equipment. As a result, all German armed services used the same AAA weapons, sensors, and equipment. It greatly simplified the manufacturing and logistical support for these weapons. Naval guns differed only in that they had stabilization systems for their mountings after 1942. The army began to mount their AAA on self-propelled mountings that same year as Allied airpower began to grow in strength and effectiveness. By 1943, Germany had nearly two million personnel serving in AAA units throughout its armed forces.

The most famous of the German AAA pieces was the ubiquitous 88mm, which entered service in 1935. The "88" served not only in air defense but coastal defense, antitank, tank gun, and field artillery roles. Its larger 105mm counterpart, based on the same principles, also saw widespread service. As the Allied bombing campaign picked up in intensity, a 128mm gun was developed and introduced into service in 1942 as an interim weapon system for a 150mm super-heavy AA gun that never entered service. The 128mm gun was also mounted on trains to provide mobility, and became the basis for a naval dual-purpose gun of the same caliber.

Germany also developed a wide variety of light AAA, ranging from 20mm to 55mm. The early models were not particularly efficient, having a slow rate of fire and low velocity for the weight of the mounting. Improvements were made throughout the war, however. By 1942, Germany had a quadruple mounting for its 20mm and was introducing a rapid-fire 50mm gun into service. The former saw widespread service in the navy and in the army, which employed several towed and self-propelled variants. The 50mm system was a major disappointment and a later, improved 55mm system became operational too late to see

An 8.8cm Flak 18 mounted on an SdKfz-251 half-track. (IWM MH 9426)

extensive service, but did provide the technical foundations for the postwar Soviet 57mm AAA system.

Germany also mounted its 20mm and 37mm AAA guns on a wide array of motorized platforms. The 20mm Flak 38 was mounted on the SdKfz-10 and SdKfz-70 half-tracks, and on the PzKpfw-38(t) tank chassis. Quad Flak 38s were mounted on the SdKfz-7 half-track and the PzKpfw-IV tank chassis. The 37mm Flak 36 was mounted on the SdKfz-6 half-track, and the 37mm Flak 43 was mounted on the PzKpfw-IV.

Germany's AAA showed many technical improvements as the war progressed and the standardization of weapons offered many manufacturing and logistical advantages. Efforts to develop super-heavy AAA systems came to nought, but the muzzle velocities and rates of fire for existing systems were improved to an extent that obviated the need for such expensive systems. Nonetheless, the effectiveness of all German AAA was inhibited by the lack of precision radar fire control systems and Germany's failure to develop a radar proximity fuze (q.v.) for its AAA projectiles.

Carl O. Schuster

(Refer to table on page 838)

Additional Reading
Hogg, Ian V., *German Artillery of World War Two* (1975).

U.S. War Department, *TM-E 30–451, Handbook on German Military Forces* (1945), reprinted (1990).

Antiaircraft Artillery, Soviet

Purpose-built Soviet antiaircraft artillery (AAA) used during World War II ranged from small, lightweight pieces designed for use with mobile field armies to large, heavy guns developed for static, home defense. Many designs had their origins in foreign weapons designs. After a few modifications, the Soviets reproduced the Swedish Bofors 25mm gun as the M-1940. Similarly, they retooled the famous Bofors 40mm to fire a 37mm round.

The largest Soviet antiaircraft weapon designed for field armies, the 76.2mm M-1938, often saw service as an antitank weapon. For home defenses the Soviets relied on the 85mm M-1939. Though little more than an upscaled M-1938, this gun had considerably better performance. Produced in great numbers, the 85mm served as the principle Soviet antiaircraft gun of World War II. Like the smaller M-1938, the M-1939 also proved effective as an antitank weapon, mounted on a T-34 tank chassis.

Soviet official histories record that by the end of World War II, antiaircraft gunners shot down about 2,800 aircraft, roughly 40 percent of the total claimed by all Soviet air defense forces. The eventual success of Soviet antiaircraft crews came despite significant technical and organizational impediments. The Soviets blamed their initial inability to defend against the *Luftwaffe* on a shortage of antiaircraft guns. Soviet official histories concede that command and control failures, poor weapons performance, and marginal quality ammunition also contributed to the initial failures of antiaircraft units.

Coordination between strategic and tactical air defense proved nonexistent, hampering effective coordination between air and anti-air assets. Perhaps more importantly, the lack of radar development in the Soviet Union left the Soviets without the advantages of early warning and fire control. The failure to develop their own radars forced the Soviets to rely almost entirely on British sets obtained through Lend-Lease (q.v.). Even these imports, however, did not meet the minimum requirements of Soviet antiaircraft forces. Equally important, these failures stunted the growth of important spin-off technologies such as the proximity fuze (q.v.), which would have helped Soviet antiaircraft weapon performance.

The Soviets overcame some limitations by employing enormous quantities of guns. Between 1941 and 1945, the Soviets increased antiaircraft weapon production by eightfold. Toward the end of the war, they also finally recognized the need for ground forces to employ their own integrated air defenses, instead of relying solely on external air support. Arguably, the increasing availability of weapons, coupled with the experience of war, enabled the Soviet antiaircraft forces to better assist in the erosion of German air superiority. By no means, however, did these forces provide the key to the destruction of the *Luftwaffe*.

The experience of World War II certainly influenced Soviet thinking about air defense. Even as the Soviet forces assimilated new weapons, such as the surface-to-air missile (SAM), into their arsenals, the notions of quality and mass deployments permeated their strategy. Finally, the Cold War fostered the proliferation of large numbers of 37mm and 85mm antiaircraft guns into the hands of Soviet client states and allies around the globe. Some of these World War II–era weapons remained in service through the 1990s in Latin America, Africa, and the Middle East.

Mark R. Jacobson

(Refer to table on page 839)

Additional Reading

Hansen, James, "The Development of Soviet Tactical Air Defense," *International Defense Review* (May 1981), pp. 531–535.

Mayer, S.L. (ed.), *The Russian War Machine, 1917–1945* (1977).

Zaloga, Steven, "Soviet Air Defense Radar in the Second World War," *Journal of Soviet Military Studies,* vol. 1 no. 4 (December 1988).

Antiaircraft Artillery, U.S.

The United States entered the war with a wide variety of antiaircraft artillery (AAA) weapons in service, but few in number. The navy used different weapons from the army, a situation that would remain unchanged until both services accepted the same license-built Bofors 20mm and 40mm light antiaircraft guns. Both services were better served by their respective ordnance boards in medium and heavy AAA, with the navy's dual-purpose 5-inch guns proving particularly outstanding. More importantly, both services eventually fielded precise fire control radars and proximity fuzes (q.v.), which significantly enhanced the effectiveness of their weapon.

Both services had conducted extensive research into light, medium, and heavy AAA, but they were ultimately unhappy with the light weapons that resulted. They were either unreliable or had too low a rate of fire. Bofors was originally approached by the navy in 1937, but negotiations fell through. In 1939, the navy asked the army to approach the company to purchase the weapons. The army, for its part, was developing a similar 37mm gun, but the superiority of the Bofors weapons led to their selection for both services in 1940. The army even developed a self-propelled twin-gun system (called the Duster) for its armored divisions, and the Bofors 40mm became the most popular of the army's light AAA. Despite its popularity, however, the Bofors never completely replaced the 37mm in army service during the war, but it did become the navy's primary light AAA weapon. Only the Bofors 20mm gun served in greater numbers in the fleet.

The best U.S. AAA was its medium and heavy guns. By 1945, a fully automatic 75mm gun was entering service to replace both the earlier semi-automatic weapons and the 90mm gun that entered service in 1941. It also saw service in the U.S. Navy from 1947–1992. Although a 105mm AAA gun entered service in 1940, only a few were built, and all served in the Panama Canal Zone. The heavier 120mm gun introduced the same year was built in larger numbers but was rarely deployed overseas.

Interestingly, the U.S. Army, like its German

counterpart, based its heavy tank guns on antiaircraft guns. The Pershing tank of 1945 used the same 90mm AAA gun. In some ways, this is appropriate, for Allied air supremacy was so total after 1943 that most AAA units were either converted to infantry or employed their weapons in a ground support role. For the navy, it found its light AAA essential to the survival of its units in the Pacific, and installed increasing numbers of them on its ships as the war progressed.

Carl O. Schuster

(Refer to tables on pages 840–841)

Additional Reading
Hogg, Ian V., *British and American Artillery of World War 2* (1978).

Antitank Guns, British

British antitank guns (and some field guns too) were classified by projectile weight, not caliber. Starting the war with the 2-pounder (abbreviated pdr), they introduced the 6-pdr in 1941 and the 17-pdr in 1942. These guns were also used on British tanks and other armored fighting vehicles of the period. In general, British antitank capability lagged behind German tank armor in the first half of the war, and the 2-pdr was outranged by

German weapons. This was particularly noticeable in the desert campaign of 1941 and 1942, the most intensive armored battles fought by the British Army.

At one stage the British were not convinced of the need for a specialized antitank gun, and in the 1920s, tactical trials were held using the 3.7-inch mountain howitzer as a dual-purpose close support/antitank weapon. Eventually, however, the need was acknowledged, and the 2-pdr was introduced in 1938. An unusual feature, and one not repeated, was its cruciform firing platform, which gave a 360-degree traverse. All subsequent weapons had an orthodox split trail. The 2-pdr was the main British antitank (and tank) weapon in France and the Western Desert up until late 1941. In an attempt to improve its mobility, the 2-pdr often was carried in the backs of trucks in the desert and even on occasions fired in this fashion (a method known as "portee").

The need for a heavier weapon had been appreciated even before the 1940 *Blitzkreig* and the development of the 6-pdr was set in motion. However, so many 2-pdrs were lost at Dunkirk (q.v.) that the factories were told to produce replacements as a matter of urgency—they were tooled up for the 2-pdr and the situation was such that any weapon was better than none—but this expedient delayed the introduction of the 6-pdr until very late 1941.

An Mk-II, 6-pounder crew under fire from a German tank near El Alamien, 3 September 1942. (IWM E 16404)

Another lesson from 1940 was that the infantry needed its own antitank (AT) guns. From 1938 the 2-pdrs had been manned by the Royal Artillery, but henceforth both arms had them. Each infantry battalion had a platoon of six, and there was a Royal Artillery regiment of thirty-six in each infantry division. A standard infantry division from 1940 thus had some ninety antitank guns. The infantry's own guns concentrated on protecting its own battalions, while the artillery guarded open flanks, gaps between units, and likely tank approaches.

From 1942, the 6-pdr was the weapon of the infantry antitank platoons. Interestingly, under Lend-Lease (q.v.), the designs had been made available to the U.S. Army, which modified it slightly (mainly the road wheels and the traverse mechanism) and produced it as the 57mm M-1.

Meanwhile, an even more powerful gun, the 17-pdr, was being developed. Though it weighed almost twice as much as the 6-pdr, its ability to penetrate armor at ranges up to 1,000 yards was almost twice as great, and moreover, it was able to engage tanks with some success at 2,000 yards. The 17-pdr, mounted on the old Valentine tank chassis and dubbed the Archer, was the only British-designed self-propelled (SP) antitank gun of the war, albeit a most successful one.

From its introduction into service, the 17-pdr, towed or SP, was the weapon of the Royal Artillery antitank regiments. Two hybrids were also produced. In late 1942, to ensure that the 17-pdr was available to meet the new German Tiger tanks, 100 17-pdrs were mounted on surplus 25-pdr field gun carriages and used in Tunisia. When later carriage production outstripped gun production, some fifty obsolete 3-inch antiaircraft guns were mounted on 17-pdr carriages and used for home defense in Britain.

In parallel with increases in the size of guns went a significant development in antitank ammunition. At first the only projectiles were solid shot. Armor-piercing discarding sabot (APDS) came into service in late 1943—a device whereby the outer casing of the projectile flew away at the muzzle, leaving a small caliber tungsten shot to continue at much increased velocity. The most effective antitank ammunition to this day remains APDS.

The British Army did not use its 3.7-inch antiaircraft guns in an antitank role as the Germans did so effectively with their infamous 88mm. When the war ended, however, the design of a 32-pdr based on the 3.7-inch gun was under consideration, and two pilot models had been built.

On the other hand, one of its most prolific tank killers was the 25-pdr field gun, especially when firing armor-piercing ammunition.

In the fluid conditions of desert warfare, and with German tanks outranging British 2-pdrs, the 25-pdr batteries often found themselves facing oncoming German armor. Even without special antitank ammunition their high muzzle velocity and heavy projectile weight made them formidable opponents—sadly often at heavy cost. To give two examples: at Tobruk (q.v.) in April 1941, a battery destroyed seventeen tanks at a cost of four guns; and at Ruweisat Ridge (q.v.) in July 1942 a regiment destroyed twenty tanks while losing eight guns.

The British fielded several models of self-propelled AT guns. The 6-pdr gun mounted on a Morris armored car was called the Firefly; mounted on a Matador truck it was called the Deacon. The 17-pdr gun mounted on a U.S. M-10 gun motor carriage was called the Achilles. The most widely used British SP AT gun of the war was the Archer, mentioned earlier. A total of 665 Archers were built.

Philip Green

(Refer to table on page 842)

Additional Reading
Bidwell, Shelford, *Gunners at War* (1970).
Hogg, Ian V., *The Guns 1939–45* (1970).
———, *British and American Artillery of World War 2* (1978).

Antitank Guns, German

In the interwar period, the German Army focused considerable attention on antitank guns. Germany thus entered World War II with an edge in antitank weaponry that it maintained until 1945. In 1939, Germany's main antitank gun, the 3.7cm Pak 35/36, was an excellent weapon for its day, capable of defeating any tank then in service. (The Germans designated their weapons in centimeters, hence 3.7cm for 37mm, etc.) It exhibited features that became the hallmark of German antitank guns in World War II—low silhouette, light weight, high mobility, and proven killing power.

In 1940, the 5.0cm Pak 38 superseded the 3.7cm Pak 35/36. This gun, like its predecessor, was light, low silhouetted, and very mobile. The heavily armored Soviet T-34 tank soon rendered this gun obsolete, however. In 1941, the 7.5cm Pak 40, the premier German antitank gun of the war,

A Jagdpanzer IV (SdKfz-162) self-propelled AT gun. (IWM MH 7762)

entered service and rapidly became the mainstay of the German antitank inventory.

In early war years, the Germans experimented with taper-bore antitank guns, which produced higher muzzle velocities for greater penetration. Three main taper-bore weapons were produced: the 2.8cm sPzB 41 (actually a large antitank rifle), the 4.2cm Pak 41, and the 7.5cm Pak 41. Complexity of production, tungsten shortages, reduced accuracy, and higher barrel wear meant that few taper-bore guns saw action, and production ceased in 1943.

By 1943, it was apparent that a new generation of heavy tanks invulnerable to the 7.5cm Pak 40 would soon appear. The Germans responded with their first truly heavy antitank gun, the 8.8cm Pak 43. This weapon was probably the most formidable antitank gun produced by any nation during World War II. The Allies underestimated its lethality and assumed that the better known, but far less effective, 8.8cm Flak 41 was responsible for many of the Pak 43's kills. German design did not stop with the 8.8cm gun. In the spring of 1945, the 12.8cm Pak 44 appeared briefly on the battlefields.

A far more productive development than the taper-bore experiment was the appearance in 1943 of two personal antitank weapons for use by individual infantrymen. The first was the *Panzerfaust* (Armor Fist) series of antitank weapons, which merged principles from the recoilless gun and the rocket to propel a hollow-charge warhead from a disposable tube launcher. Cheap and easy to produce, the *Panzerfaust* was mass produced in late 1943. It was an extremely popular close combat weapon and gave German infantry a genuine antitank capability for the first time. The second design, the 8.8cm *RPzB-54 Panzerschreck* (Tank Terror) was a superior copy of the U.S. "bazooka" antitank rocket launcher, examples of which were captured in Tunisia (q.v.) in 1943. The *Panzerschreck* was an immediate success and was also produced in large numbers.

From an early date, the German Army mounted antitank guns on tank chassis to create self-propelled (SP) guns called *Panzerjäger* (Tank Hunters). The first of these, the Panzerjäger-I, appeared in 1940, mounting a Czech 47mm gun on a PzKpfw-I tank chassis. After the German invasion of the Soviet Union in June 1941, there was an urgent need for powerful SP guns. Thus, the 7.5cm Pak 40 and captured 76.2mm guns were mounted in lightly armored, open fighting compartments on French, German, and Czech chassis to form the Marder series of vehicles. These improvised SP guns, however, were vulnerable.

The success of the assault gun *Strumgeschütz,* originally designed as an infantry close support howitzer in an antitank role (*see* Artillery, German), led the Germans to develop a series of low-silhouetted tank destroyers, *Jagdpanzer,* with thick, sloping armor. In early 1944, the Jagdpanzer-IV and the Jagdpanzer-38(t) Hetzer appeared. The most impressive German tank destroyer was the Jagdpanther, based on the chassis of the Panther tank, and mounting a 88mm gun in a well-sloped, armored structure. This combination of firepower, silhouette, and armor made it practically invulnerable to Allied armor. But even the Jagdpanther was dwarfed in size by the Jagdtiger, with its 128mm gun on the Tiger II tank chassis.

Germany maintained its edge over the Allies in antitank weapons development throughout the war. This reflected the serious attention paid by the German Army to this subject in the interwar period. German doctrine called for the aggressive employment of antitank guns, in both defense and offense. While this entailed high loss rates, it was more than compensated for in terms of tactical and operational advantage. As the German Army lost the strategic initiative in 1942–1943, antitank weapons played an increasing role in the protracted defense of the Third *Reich*. Antitank units were employed as mobile fire brigades, patching the holes that appeared in ever-increasing numbers in the German lines late in the war.

Russell Hart

(Refer to table on page 843)

Additional Reading

Gander, Terry, and Peter Chamberlain, *Small Arms, Artillery, and Special Weapons of the Third Reich* (1978).
Hogg, Ian V., *German Artillery of World War Two* (1975).
McLean, Donald B. (comp. and ed.) *Illustrated Arsenal of the Third Reich* (1973).

Antitank Guns, Soviet

In 1939, the Soviet Army's standard antitank (AT) weapon was a small 37mm gun, similar in size and capability to British, U.S., and German weapons of the interwar years, and owing much in design to the German Rheinmetall Pak 35/36. Misled by their success against the brave but ill-equipped Finns in the Winter War (q.v.) of 1939–1940, the Soviets entered World War II with a 45mm gun that was merely a larger version of this. It proved pathetically inadequate against the German *Panzers*. This hard lesson, and the ever-increasing size of German tanks, led successively to guns of 57mm and 100mm caliber—the former the rough equivalent of the contemporary British 17-pdr and the U.S. 3-inch M-5.

A feature of the Soviet Army in comparison with the British, U.S., or Germans, was that as the war progressed it relied less on specialized antitank weapons, regarding its mass of close support field guns as dual purpose. Although a family of antitank guns was developed, in relative terms, few were produced. A look at muzzle velocities illustrates this point. Typically, a World War II antitank gun had a muzzle velocity of 2,600 to 3,000 feet per second, with field guns in the region of 1,600 ft/sec. The British 25-pdr, for example, had 1,700 ft/sec; the U.S. 105mm howitzer, 1,550 ft/sec; and the German le FH 18, 1,590 ft/sec. Soviet field guns, on the other hand, ran from 2,000 to 2,750 ft/sec. Such high muzzle velocities would have been a disadvantage for indirect firing artillery in more mountainous areas, but not on the plains of the western Soviet Union. Interestingly, the Germans used many captured Soviet 76.2mm field guns as antitank weapons.

Another feature of the Soviet antitank scene was the use of self-propelled (SP) tank destroyers from late 1942 onward. Learning from the way the Germans used the Jagdpanthers, and later the Elefants, the Soviets quickly developed their own equivalents. The first was the SU-76, which mated a T-70 light tank chassis with a 76.2mm M-1942 divisional gun. It proved unsuccessful as a tank destroyer because its open superstructure left its crew very vulnerable. The SU-76 was relegated to a role as an SP field gun.

The SU-76 was followed by the SU-85 and SU-100, 85mm and 100mm guns mounted on the T-34 tank chassis. The SU-85 mounted the M-1939 antiaircraft gun. These were followed in late 1944 by the ISU-122, a 122mm gun on the Josef Stalin heavy tank chassis. All, whether antitank, field, or self-propelled, fired solid shot with cased propellant. Until the very end of the war many lighter Soviet weapons were horse-drawn, or even man-drawn.

In the defense, Soviet antitank tactics were based on the establishment of antitank regions composed of mutually supporting strongpoints sited in depth covering likely tank routes. Each strongpoint, in addition to guns, contained tanks as a mobile reserve and counterattack force. When properly set up, as for example at Kursk (q.v.) in July 1943, this system could absorb, blunt, and finally defeat, the German *Blitzkreig*.

In the attack, the Soviets made great use of antitank weapons, particularly the SU tank destroyers, to give covering fire. Their main task was to engage German tanks at the maximum possible range to hinder their efforts to take on the advancing Soviet armor. A secondary task was the engagement of small but vital targets by direct fire, well-protected antitank guns, for example.

Philip Green

(Refer to table on page 844)

Additional Reading
Hogg, Ian V., *The Guns 1939–45* (1970).
Perrett, Bryan, *Tank Warfare* (1990).

Antitank Guns, U.S.

In 1939, the U.S. Army was using the 37mm M-3 gun as its main antitank (AT) weapon. Based on the German Pak 35/36, it was similar in most respects to its counterparts in other major armies of the time. Though not involved in the 1940 European campaigns, the Americans saw that one of the most obvious lessons was the inability of such light weapons to cope with modern armor.

Early in 1941, they were given the designs of the British 6-pdr gun under a Lease-Lend (q.v.) agreement. Incorporating a few modifications of their own, they produced it in quantity as the 57mm M-l, in time for the American entry into the Northwest African and European theaters. No alterations were made to the ordnance, but the wheels were changed, a new towing attachment fitted, and the British system of traversing by means of the gunner's shoulder was replaced by a more orthodox handwheel—although a later model, the M-1A2, reverted to the original British system.

As tank armor got ever thicker, even this weapon was not powerful enough, and as early as late 1940, development of its successor, the 3-inch M-5, had begun. Economy demanded that as many parts of existing weapons as possible be used. The resulting hybrid, which first saw service in December 1941, proved itself in combat to be a very effective weapon; a 105mm howitzer carriage, a 3-inch antiaircraft gun tube, and a 105mm breechblock. A 76mm variant with a shortened tube and specially designed carriage was developed. The towed version never got beyond the prototype stage, but a self-propelled (SP) version, the M-18 Hellcat, was fielded. The M-18 was unique in that its chassis originally had been designed as a tank destroyer, rather than being a chopped-down tank. A total of 2,507 M-18s were produced.

Toward the end of the war even heavier weapons were being planned, based on existing antiaircraft guns. These were the 90mm T-9 and later the 105mm T-4. Both projects were canceled when the war ended.

The U.S. Army's tactical doctrine called for its SP antitank guns to hunt enemy tanks aggressively rather than wait in defensive positions for them to approach—as the American name "tank destroyer" indicated. A great variety of these weapons were produced. Early models were the 37mm M-3 gun on a Dodge truck; the 75mm M-1897 (a World War I field gun) on an M-3 GMC (gun motor carriage) half-track; and the 57mm M-1 gun also on a half-track. Though their mobility

A

The "Wolverine," M-10 self-propelled AT gun. (IWM MH 4132)

was clearly an advantage, by the time any of these saw action their weapon was too light for the job.

Their successor was the highly effective GMC M-10, the 3-inch M-5 gun on an M-4A2 tank chassis. Toward the end of the war this was upgunned with the M-3 90mm gun. The result was the M-36, and 2,324 were built and fielded. A 17-pdr version was used by the British. The development of an even bigger equipment, the 105mm GMC T-95, was halted in 1945.

Initially all ammunition was solid shot, but technological advances led to new types as the war progressed. Using tungsten cores obtained from Britain, an armor-piercing discarding sabot (APDS) round was produced for the 90mm, but in service it became apparent that the rifling of the tube and the discarding sleeve were not compatible. Instead, a composite rigid shot was developed, the ultra-hard tungsten core being encased in a light alloy casing that was not discarded. This produced very high muzzle velocities—an essential attribute for an antitank gun—and consequently great penetration, especially at the shorter ranges.

Philip Green

(Refer to table on page 845)

Additional Reading

Hogg, Ian V., *The Guns 1939–45* (1970).
———, *British and American Artillery of World War 2* (1978).
Perrett, Bryan, *Tank Warfare* (1990).

Armored Personnel Carriers

Mechanized or armored infantry—called *Panzergrenadiers* in the German Army—were one of the major innovations in ground combat to emerge from World War II. In the years between the world wars, most armor experts came to realize that tanks operating on their own were very vulnerable. Tanks needed the close support of artillery and especially infantry. The problem was making the ground soldier as mobile and as versatile as the tank. The armored personnel carrier (APC) was thus developed to give the infantry that mobility and the protection necessary to keep up with tanks on a continuously changing battlefield.

The British started developing APCs in the closing years of World War I. In the 1920s, they experimented with one-man "tankettes." By the late 1930s, they introduced the universal tracked carrier. A full-tracked vehicle with a top speed of 32mph, the universal carrier had an open top and carried only five soldiers. Because it carried so few troops, it had a limited effectiveness as an APC. Although Britain built more than 35,000 of them, the universal carriers, also called Bren gun carriers, tended to be used mostly for reconnaissance and fire support missions. Thus, in the earlier years of World War II, British troops operating in support of tanks often were transported by truck.

In 1944, Britain and Canada began using cut-down tanks as APCs to give their troops better protection and mobility. During the fighting in Normandy (q.v.), the Canadians first used a modification of the Priest, a self-propelled 105mm howitzer mounted on a General Grant tank chassis. With the turret removed, it became a twelve-man APC, affectionately called the "Unfrocked Priest." It carried a Browning M-2 caliber .50 machine gun, which provided fire support to the infantry squad when dismounted.

In late 1944, the British introduced the Ram Kangaroo, so called because it was an eight-man APC converted from a Canadian-built Sherman tank chassis known as the Ram. It was powered by a 400 bhp Wright-Continental R-975 radial engine. At twenty-six tons, however, it had a range of only 145 miles and a top speed of 25 mph. It was armed with one Browning caliber .30 machine gun.

During the 1930s, the United States developed half-tracked APCs—vehicles with standard rubber tires on the front wheels and a tank-like tracked drive in the rear. During World War II, the most ubiquitous of these was the M-3 or M-5 half-track, which carried ten infantrymen. Its 6mm of armored plating offered some protection to its passengers, but it had an open top that afforded absolutely no protection against artillery air bursts. The M-3 had a range of 200 miles, and its White 160 AX in-line engine developed 147 bhp. It had a top speed of 45 mph and was armed with one M-2 machine gun. The M-3 chassis was highly versatile. In addition to an APC, it was used as a tank destroyer, mortar carrier, gun carriage, and artillery prime mover.

The M-39 armored carrier, developed in late 1944, was a full-tracked APC. It was based on the M-18 Hellcat tank destroyer chassis and carried twelve infantrymen. Of all the World War II APCs, the M-39 was the most similar to the modern postwar APCs. Like all the other World War II APCs, however, the M-39 had an open top.

The LVT(A)2, which the British called the Buffalo, was a full-tracked amphibious APC that could carry up to thirty men. It weighed more than fourteen tons and had a range of 150 miles on land and 100 miles in the water. It was armed with two machine guns mounted fore and aft of the troop compartment. It was widely used for amphibious operations in the Mediterranean and in Europe, as well as in the Pacific.

The Germans produced a wide variety of half-tracks *(Halbketten).* They all bore the designation SdKfz, for *Sonderkraftfahrzeug* (Special Motor Vehicle). The smallest was the SdKfz-2, which was built between 1940 and 1944. It carried only two soldiers, had a range of 150 miles, and a top speed of 70 mph. The SdKfz-10, first built in 1937, carried seven passengers plus the driver. It was the original vehicle for carrying infantrymen in the *Panzer* divisions. Later in the war it was modified as an antiaircraft gun carrier. Germany's first true APC was the SdKfz-250. It basically was

A Universal Bren Carrier passes through British positions near Cassino, 16 May 1944. (IWM NA 15047)

An M-5A1 half-track and its crew move through Avranches during the fighting in Normandy. (IWM EA 31985)

an SdKfz-10 chassis with additional armor protection and two machine guns mounted fore and aft of the crew compartment.

Germany's main APC during World War II was the SdKfz-251. It carried a driver, a vehicle commander, and ten infantrymen. Originally designed as an APC, the SdKfz-251 was highly maneuverable and versatile. It always was in great demand by branches of the *Wehrmacht* other than the *Panzergrenadiers*. As a result, the *Panzer* divisions found it difficult to maintain an adequate supply. The SdKfz-251 came in at least twenty-one variations, including an 81mm mortar carrier, a command vehicle, an assault engineer vehicle, an ambulance, a flamethrower, and a telephone exchange vehicle.

The Soviets never developed APCs during World War II, which proved a detriment to their armor units. When necessary, Soviet infantry rode on the tanks. Without any protection, these troops were highly vulnerable to both small arms and shell fire. Carrying infantrymen also restricted the tank crews by limiting the movement of their turrets, thereby limiting their range of fire. In the years following World War II, the Soviets applied those lessons with a vengeance. By the 1970s, the airborne units were virtually the only infantry in the Soviet Army that were not mounted in armored fighting vehicles.

William H. Van Husen

Additional Reading

Crow, Duncan (ed.), *British and Commonwealth AFVs: 1940–46* (1971).

Georgano, G.N., *World War II Military Vehicles: Transports and Half-Tracks* (1994).

Hogg, Ian V., and John Weeks, *The Illustrated Encyclopedia of Military Vehicles* (1980).

Senger und Etterlin, F.M. von, *German Tanks of World War II* (1968).

Vanderveen, Bart, *Historic Military Vehicles Directory* (1993).

Artificial Harbors

A harbor is a place of refuge for ships. It provides protection from the full force of a storm. A port is a place where ships can load or unload. It may or may not be located in a harbor. During World War II, a number of temporary or artificial ports were built in the European and Pacific theaters. Two artificial harbors were constructed; both were at the Normandy (q.v.) beachhead in June 1944. To sustain an invasion on occupied France, the Allies needed a port, but bitter experience proved that direct attack on established ports was very costly in casualties. The Axis also proved very capable at destroying port facilities as they retreated.

The planners of Operation OVERLORD early on decided that the only way to supply the troops after the initial assault was through a "new port." The decision was made to develop the Normandy beaches into a temporary port by building an artificial harbor. That required the construction of a breakwater to form a harbor to protect the port.

The artificial harbor was given the code name MULBERRY. The entire complex consisted of: (1) GOOSEBERRY, a shallow craft harbor formed by sinking obsolete ships in a line in four meters of water; (2) PHOENIX, a harbor formed by sinking concrete caissons varying in size up to 200 by 60 feet

Aerial photograph of the artificial harbor formed off the Normandy Coast. (IWM MH 2405)

in lines both parallel and perpendicular to the beach; (3) BOMBARDON, a floating breakwater of metal made of cruciform-shaped units 200 feet by 25 feet by 19 feet, moored in a line parallel to the beach to break the swell of the waves; (4) WHALE, a floating pier roadway extending from the shore to a spud pierhead at which a ship discharged its cargo; and (5) Lobnitz Pierheads, piers whose height could be changed mechanically to reflect the stage of the tide.

Two MULBERRY harbors were built. They were designated "A" and "B." MULBERRY "A" was located off OMAHA Beach and "B" was off GOLD Beach. Work started on these harbors on 6 June 1944. On 19 June, a storm destroyed MULBERRY "A" and damaged "B." Surviving elements from MULBERRY "A" were used to repair MULBERRY "B." Because the Axis forces damaged many of the established ports captured by the Allies, supplies continued to enter France through MULBERRY "B" into early 1945. Today, only a few scattered pieces of these two harbors remain.

Charles H. Bogart

Additional Reading

Harrison, Gordon A., *Cross-Channel Attack* (1951).
Stanford, Alfred B., *Force Mulberry: The Planning and Installation of the Artificial Harbor off U.S. Beaches in World War II* (1951).

Artillery, British

In 1939, Britain's was the only fully motorized army in the world. British field guns were towed by the Quad four-wheel-drive truck, which carried the gun detachment and ammunition. Heavier weapons were towed by the Matador or Scammel trucks, which were modified cargo vehicles.

The basic close support weapon was the 25-pdr, which played the same role as the U.S. 105mm howitzer and the German Light Field Howitzer 18 (le FH 18). The basic design of the 25-pdr had been agreed on by 1930. This consisted of a 3.45-inch barrel firing a twenty-five-pound shell. It had a box trail with a firing platform that allowed a single man to traverse the gun through 360 degrees. Early models consisted of the 25-pdr ordnance fitted to the old 18-pdr carriage, and were known as the Mark 1. These were used by the British Expeditionary Force (BEF) in France, but the carriage was too light to cope with super charge. This reduced the gun's range from 12,060 meters to 11,520 meters. The Mark 2, with its own original carriage design, was not produced until February 1940 and saw action in Norway

(q.v.) later that year. A very effective armor-piercing round was developed for the 25-pdr, which enabled it to defeat tanks when antitank guns were not available or inadequate for the task. A lightweight version was produced by the Australian Army in 1943 for service in difficult tropical terrain. A self-propelled version, named Bishop, was produced by mounting the piece on a Valentine tank chassis, but this was not deemed a success. This was superseded by the Sexton, which consisted of a 25-pdr mounted on a Canadian Ram tank. The Sexton remained in service successfully until the 1950s. The British also used the U.S. 105mm M-7 self-propelled gun, which they named the Priest.

At divisional level the British fielded medium artillery. During the first years of the war the British Army had only the 6-inch gun, the 6-inch howitzer, and the 5-inch "60-pounder," all relics of World War I. In due course, these were replaced by the 4.5-inch and then 5.5-inch guns. The original specification for a 5-inch gun weighing five and one-half tons, firing a shell of up to 100 pounds, and with a range of 16,000 yards, had been issued in the 1930s. The manufacture of a 5.5-inch gun was approved in August 1939. Production of a 4.5-inch gun sharing the same chassis was also approved. The first 4.5-inch guns saw action in Cyrenaica in 1942, and these were grouped together with 5.5-inch guns in medium artillery regiments.

It was assumed in the 1930s that heavy artillery would be unable to keep up with armor in rapid mobile operations and that the task of heavy long-range fire support would be undertaken by aircraft. However, little provision was made by the Royal Air Force to provide this support. Thus, in 1939, the field army was deficient in heavy fire support, at least by comparison with what it had been accustomed to in 1918.

At the start of the war, the British Army was equipped with 8-inch, 9.2-inch, 12-inch, and 18-inch howitzers; and 6-inch and 9.2-inch guns. These pieces were extremely ponderous and quite unsuited to the style of war to which they were committed. The majority were lost in France in 1940. Numerous experiments were conducted to produce a modern series of heavy weapons but these were abandoned once the U.S. 155mm and 8-inch pieces became available. Even so, heavy artillery never assumed the critical role and numbers it achieved in World War I, largely because the role envisaged in the 1930s for aircraft became a reality. Given the Allied air superiority in the latter years of the war, aircraft were able to deliver a

A Mk-II 25-pounder field gun in firing position. (IWM KID 4420)

heavier weight of fire at longer range than guns could have, and at less logistic cost to the land army.

The British Army grouped its batteries into "regiments," which in other armies would have been termed battalions. Each battery had eight guns and could be split into two troops each of four guns and a command post. Each regiment provided close support for a brigade, and so the standard British division of three brigades had seventy-two guns in close support. In addition, the division had a reserve of guns of a variety of calibers grouped in what was misleadingly termed the Army Group Royal Artillery (AGRA). This varied in size according to circumstances, and provided the organizational means to reinforce a division when necessary. It contained, however, a minimum of one regiment of medium guns.

The British had an unusual philosophy of command and control, which continues to this day. Most armies used junior officers to observe targets and call for fire, while more senior officers remained in immediate command of the gun line or located in artillery command posts apportioning resources to engage reported targets. The British placed their senior artillery officers with the headquarters of the unit they were supporting. Thus an infantry company, for example, would have an artillery captain as its forward observation officer, and a battalion would have an artillery major co-located with its commanding officer as his adviser. The idea was that these artillery officers should have firsthand knowledge of the situation and be empowered to order, rather than merely call for, fire. The British felt that this created a quicker and more appropriate response. The allocation of resources to observers thus became the critical issue, and this fell to the judgment of the artillery commander at divisional level. This system depended upon the widespread use of radio, which from 1940 onward became more widely available. Without radio, the development of the British command and control system, as it was refined after 1942, would not have been possible.

The British Expeditionary Force deployed to France expecting to fight a battle of maneuver in which artillery support would play only a minor part. The "Phony War" (q.v.) changed this expectation for one that envisaged positional warfare. As a result, the British reinstituted training in intricate fire planning. When war actually came, the German practice of maneuver proved devastating and the British Army was unable to coordinate its limited firepower to prevent a disaster. The most obvious disparity with the Germans was not so much in relative artillery firepower as it was in aircraft support of the land battle. Although the value of close coordination between air and ground forces had been recognized before the war, little had been done to achieve it—the RAF had preferred to devote its slender resources to building up a bomber fleet.

The British Army at this time also lacked an effective means of achieving all-arms cooperation on the battlefield. This was largely a legacy of the belief that the tank could operate effectively without the support of other arms. The deficiencies in equipment, organization, and doctrine that resulted from this were still evident in 1943.

In the early years of the war in North Africa (q.v.) against the Italians, the British enjoyed success against a relatively static enemy by using the sort of mobile tactics envisaged before the war. When these were subsequently employed against the Germans, they proved extremely costly, thanks largely to the all-arms grouping and tactics used by the Germans. Too often, British tanks attempted to attack German positions without artillery support, and were repulsed at heavy cost. At the same time, the British could not establish a coherent defense based on effective fire and maneuver to halt German attacks.

Experiments were made to remedy this. So-called Jock Columns were formed. These were all-arms groupings of about battalion size, based around artillery batteries. They would travel great distances to strike at the enemy and enjoyed some success on a broad and thinly manned front. Their total effect, however, was slight and they were unable to halt the large-scale offensive operations that the Germans were soon to mount. The British then undertook a reversal of tactic. Instead of dispersing assets in small mobile units, they grouped them in static defense by creating so-called Tobruk Boxes based around gun positions. These enjoyed mixed fortunes, but by the end of 1942, they were abandoned as well.

Too often in the early years in North Africa, British defense took the form of ad hoc groups of 25-pdr field guns trying to stave off German armor. Arguably the most significant consequence of the introduction of an effective antitank gun was that field guns were released to concentrate on their proper indirect fire role, which complemented that of the antitank gun. By 1942, the British Army was taking delivery of large quantities of field and antitank ordnance. It then undertook a complete reorganization and reappraisal of tactics, which were to prove the foundation of its successes until the end of the war.

The most important of these new equipments was the 6-pdr antitank gun, which released the 25-pdrs from antitank tasks for the indirect role. They were reinforced in this task by the arrival of the 5.5-inch guns in quantity. By 1942 and 1943, the emphasis in British antitank tactics had changed from the protection of infantry by antitank guns to the close protection of guns by infantry.

The primary architect of the new approach was General Sir Bernard L. Montgomery (q.v.),

assisted in the reform of artillery support by Brigadier Sidney Kirkman. They believed in the steady buildup of a favorable ratio of firepower and the use of artillery to provide shock in coordination with other arms. The primary tactics used were the creeping barrage and the timed concentration. These were made possible by greater technical sophistication in predicted as opposed to observed fires. As a result, at El Alamein (q.v.), 1,000 guns were able to fire 1,207,000 shells at plotted targets without adjustment in order to increase the shock effect. Whereas in the early years of the war it would be normal to support a battalion with just its own battery, by late 1942 General Montgomery had made the "seventy-two-gun battery" a standard fire mission. This used all available assets against a single target at the same time, making the most efficient use of resources.

Jonathan B.A. Bailey

(Refer to table on page 846)

Additional Reading

Bailey, J.B.A., *Field Artillery and Firepower* (1989).
Bidwell, Shelford, and Dominick Graham, *Fire-Power: British Army Weapons and Theories of War 1904–1945* (1985).
Hogg, Ian V., *The Guns, 1939–45* (1970).
———, Barrage: *The Guns in Action* (1970).

Artillery, French

In 1939, the French had a large number of Canon de 75 mle 1897 still in service. In its day, the famous "French 75" was a revolutionary weapon, being the first field gun successfully to introduce a hydraulic recoil mechanism and a breechblock that allowed a high rate of fire. It probably was the most prolific 75mm gun ever produced. After the French defeat of 1940, thousands of these pieces fell into German hands and were put into service by the Germans in low grade units. A modified version also saw service from 1942 as an antitank gun on the eastern front. The French had made various attempts to update the mle 1897, including the introduction of pneumatic tires, and a split trail.

The standard French 105mm piece was the Canon de 105 mle 1913 Schneider. It also was still in service in 1939 despite its age, and it too fell into German hands in large numbers. The French did have some modern light field guns: the Canon de 105 mle 1934S, the Canon de 105 court mle 1935 B, and the Canon de 105L mle 1936 Schneider.

Only 159 of the latter were in operation with the French Army by 1940, and they too entered German service, usually in a coastal defense role.

Large numbers of medium and heavy artillery of World War I vintage remained in French service in 1940; including 450 of the Canon de 155 Grande Puissance Filloux (Can 155 GPF). Despite their age, they were still effective weapons, so much so that the Germans issued them directly to field service. An even greater prize to the Germans was the Can 155 GPF-T, which had a carriage designed for motor transport.

In 1939, more than 1,000 105mm and 3,000 155mm pieces of World War I vintage remained in service with the French Army. Many blamed this for the failures of 1940. General V. Bourret, commanding the French Fifth Army, complained that these pieces were useless.

A French corps was supported by a regiment of horse-drawn heavy artillery consisting of four *groupes,* each of two batteries of four either 105mm or 155mm pieces. The infantry division was supported by an artillery regiment of five *groupes* of field artillery. Three of the *groupes* were composed of three batteries equipped with four 75mm guns each. The other two *groupes* contained medium artillery. One was armed with either 105mm or 155mm pieces, and the other with 155mm pieces. On mobilization the two *groupes* formed a separate regiment of horse-drawn heavy artillery, but remained a part of the divisional artillery structure. The division was also equipped with a battery of twelve 25mm antitank guns.

The French cavalry division had one regiment of artillery consisting of one *groupe* of 75mm guns and one *groupe* of 105mm short pieces. Shortly after the outbreak of war this was increased to three *groupes* totaling three batteries of 75mm and three of 105mm, giving the division twelve guns of each caliber. It also had a battery of eight 47mm antitank guns.

In 1934, France created two *Divisions Légères Mécanisees,* or light armored divisions. They later were augmented by a third. Each was supported by an artillery regiment consisting of two *groupes,* one of 75mm pieces and the other of 105mm pieces. They were also equipped with nine 47mm antitank guns. In January 1940, the French created a heavier armored division, the *Division Cuirassée.* It was supported by one artillery regiment of two *groupes.* Each contained three batteries of 105mm short pieces and one of tractor-borne 47mm antitank guns.

Arguably the greatest weakness in the French order of battle was the absence of air defense artillery at divisional level. The French Army possessed

just five antiaircraft regiments, and they were allotted one to each field army.

The modernization of French artillery after World War I was slow. Throughout the interwar years its thinking was either out of date or unduly weighted in favor of the defense. The majority of resources and technical effort was devoted to the creation of the formidable positional defenses and firepower of the Maginot Line (q.v.). The *Instruction Générale sur le Tir de l'Artillerie* of 1936 described three tasks for artillery: (1) the destruction of obstacles in preparation for the attack; (2) the support and protection of infantry and tanks in the defense; and (3) counterbattery and harassing fire. The importance of fire support in mobile offensive operations was not properly addressed. The French tactical concept of 1936 stressed the need for fire mobility and concentration of fire, but emphasized their achievement in a scenario of counterpreparation and defensive fire.

The French lacked coordinated air support and adequate air defenses. The results of this combination were seen at Sedan in May 1940, when two French divisional artilleries were routed before the Germans had even crossed the Meuse.

Jonathan B.A. Bailey

(Refer to table on page 847)

Additional Reading
Hogg, Ian V., *The Illustrated Encyclopedia of Artillery* (1987).
Hogg, Ian V., *The Guns, 1939–45* (1970).

Artillery, German

The Germans distinguished between four types of artillery equipment: the *Kanone* (gun); the *Haubitze* (gun/howitzer); the *Mörser* (howitzer firing in the upper angles of elevation only); and the *Werfer* (mortar). These were often given the overall title of *Geschütz.* German guns were generally mounted on a carriage of either box trail or split trail design.

German field artillery was based primarily on three calibers: 75mm, 105mm, and 150mm. (The Germans designated their weapons in centimeters, hence 7.5cm, 10.5cm, 15cm, etc.) By 1939 the 7.5cm pieces were obsolete and were issued only to low-grade units. The standard gun-howitzer was the towed 10.5cm leichte Feldhaubitze 18 (le FH 18). It fired all types of projectile, and in the early years on the eastern front it proved a highly effective (and at times the only effective) antitank weapon. In its self-propelled variant it was called Wespe, mounted on a PzKpfw-II chassis.

The standard flat trajectory gun at divisional level was the 100mm medium gun (10cm s K-18). The standard medium field howitzer at divisional level was the 15cm Schwere Feldhaubitze 18 (s FH 18). Its self-propelled variant was called Hummel, mounted on a PzKpfw-IV chassis. (The 15cm s FH 18 was the world's first artillery piece to be issued with a rocket-assisted projectile, which was not especially successful.) At corps and army level, the most common equipments were the 17cm K-18 gun and the 21cm Mrs 18 howitzer, both of which shared the same carriage. The German Army also possessed a range of super-heavy artillery for special tasks.

Based on their experiences in World War I, the Germans staunchly believed in the concept of providing their own infantry with organic fire support. In most armies this fire support was provided by mortars. Although the Germans had several very efficient mortars, they also included infantry guns right until the end of the war. The two basic types were the 7.5cm leichtes Infantriegeschütz 18, and the heavier 15cm schweres Infantriegeschütz 33. The latter, in fact, proved too heavy for an infantry gun.

During the course of the war the Germans developed a range of weapons for lobbing heavy projectiles onto the enemy. The most common was the 6-barreled 15cm Nebelwerfer, which was originally designed to lay smoke screens. A self-propelled version with ten barrels was also produced from 1942.

The Germans produced a wide array of self-propelled (SP) artillery pieces that fell into four basic categories: (1) SP field guns; (2) SP assault guns; (3) SP antitank guns (see Antitank Guns, German); and (4) SP antiaircraft guns (see Antiaircraft Artillery,

German). Most of these SP equipments consisted of standard towed guns mounted in various tank chassis. There were three principal exceptions— guns that did not otherwise exist in towed form. These appeared mostly on the SP assault guns. The 7.5cm Sturmkanone 40 (StuK 40) fired a 15-pound shell approximately 6,500 meters. The short-barreled 10.5cm Sturmhaubitze 42 (StuH 42) fired a 33-pound projectile 7,700 meters. And the very short-barreled (only about six feet) 15cm StuH43 fired a 95-pound shell only 4,500 meters.

The organization of the *Wehrmacht's* artillery during the war was based on its peacetime structure, although significant modifications were made in 1941–1942. *Oberkommando des Heeres* (OKH) allocated specialist forces on a semi-permanent basis to army groups, and these in turn were distributed to armies and corps. These special forces included army antiaircraft units *(Heeresflak)*, heavy artillery, 8.8cm and 12.8cm antitank units, and assault gun batteries of heavy multiple mortars and rocket projectors. Most heavy Flak units were operated and controlled by the *Luftwaffe,* but often they were allocated to the army for specific operations and tactical control. They afforded a useful addition to the army's antitank capability.

The basic self-supporting and cohesive formation in the German Army throughout the war was the division. Within the division at all levels forces were grouped in a balanced all-arms structure. Organizations varied widely depending on the theater and circumstances, but a typical *Panzer* division of 1941–1942 would have been supported by one regiment of motorized field artillery consisting of three battalions, of which two would be of 10.5cm and one of 15cm guns. Each of these battalions contained three batteries, each of four

A battery of 10.5cm le FH 18 howitzers in action near Aisne, France, May 1940. (IWM MH 9409)

The Wespe 10.5cm self-propelled howitzer (SdKfz-124 Panzerfeldhaubitze 18/Z). (IWM STT 7233)

guns. The structure was designed to ensure that immediate close fire support was available at the lowest level. This degree of dispersion, however, carried the penalty that it was often difficult to concentrate the fire of all weapons within range to achieve a decisive effect.

The need for self-propelled pieces to support fast-moving armored formations was recognized early in the war, and from about 1940 onward, self-propelled field guns, assault guns, and antitank guns began to appear in the *Panzer* divisions. By 1944, a typical *Panzer* division would have been supported by an artillery regiment of three battalions, of which one would comprise three heavy batteries each of either four guns or howitzers. This heavy battalion might also be reinforced by a battery of 100mm guns, but these sometimes operated as an independent battery together with up to six 150mm rocket projectors. The second battalion contained two batteries each of six towed 10.5cm howitzers. The third battalion contained three batteries each of six self-propelled howitzers, of which one would be a 15cm Hummel, and two would be 10.5cm Wespe. The division also would be supported by a battalion of antiaircraft guns. *Waffen*-SS (q.v.) divisions often had a complete battalion of rocket projectors and an additional battalion of assault guns. A *Panzergrenadier* division had a roughly similar organization.

The German infantry division of 1939 generally had four battalions of horse-drawn howitzers. Each comprised three batteries of four guns each. One of the battalions would have 15cm pieces and the others 10.5cm. By 1944 these battalions were motorized. Mountain divisions generally had a similar organization but with 7.5cm and 10.5cm guns rather than 10.5cm and 15cm. A parachute division was supported by a regiment of two battalions with a total of twelve recoilless guns.

The divisional artillery usually was commanded by an *Artillerieführer (Arfu),* who was the divisional commander's adviser on artillery matters. When artillery units were attached from higher formations they came with their own artillery staff, and the commander of these would become *Artillerie Kommandeur (Arko),* taking command of all artillery supporting the division to form a separate formation.

By the end of World War I, artillery had become the dominant arm in the German Army, whose tactical thinking, like that of other belligerents, had been determined by the experience of years of positional warfare. With the evolution of *Blitzkrieg* (q.v.), however, the role of artillery changed and diminished in importance. The Germans assumed that artillery, in particular its ammunition supply, would not be able to keep up with armor in a swiftly moving battle. Rather than create a force of self-propelled artillery to accompany the tanks, the Germans intended that tanks should provide their own close fire support, or even obviate the need for it through shock action.

The Germans accepted the risk that armor would at times encounter tough resistance that might slow an advance, threatening its momentum. Aircraft rather than artillery were given the task of destroying such opposition. The Germans developed a system of air-ground coordination of unprecedented sophistication to deliver timely air support to their army. In May 1940, they could concentrate as many as 2,700 aircraft under universal radio control, and available at twenty-five minutes' notice to support ground operations.

This joint service arrangement proved extremely successful in the early years of the war; but it became clear during the invasion of France in 1940 that *Panzer* forces would benefit greatly from the close support of self-propelled guns. A program of development began that would eventually result in a series of self-propelled assault, antitank, and field guns.

The tactical skills of German artillery were clearly demonstrated in North Africa (q.v.), where antitank guns rather than tanks proved to be the primary tank killers. This in turn increased the importance of field artillery in suppressing antitank guns; but by 1942, German artillery of all types found itself increasingly outnumbered and eventually overwhelmed. By 1943 in Tunisia (q.v.), and subsequently in Italy, the Germans increasingly fell back on the expedient of dispersing their guns in small groups to support small packets of infantry and tanks. These tactics met with some local success, and in part accounted for the Allies' slow progress up Italy; but they could not achieve the decisive results that the Western Allies and Soviets enjoyed by massing their artillery and concentrating its fire in enormous fire plans.

Despite the technical quality and ground-level tactical skill of German artillery, the fundamental weakness of German artillery relative to other arms and that of its opponents was never rectified. *Panzer* forces may have achieved dazzling successes in Russia in 1941; but even then the Germans found that artillery—most of it still horse-drawn—could not keep up. Once Soviet armor went onto the offensive, the Germans discovered to their horror that their antitank guns were generally ineffective, and they were forced to rely on field guns direct firing at short range to protect themselves. The *Luftwaffe* proved unable to provide reliable fire support in sustained operations, and there was no substantial body of medium and heavy artillery to take its place in what became a battle of attrition with the Soviets.

The Germans emphasized the role of artillery massed at divisional level and failed to provide the concentrations of artillery firepower at higher formation that the Soviets, by contrast, deemed decisive. By 1944, the Germans finally recognized the need for such a capability, but their efforts to create one failed in the face of Germany's overall logistic deficiencies.

Jonathan B.A. Bailey

(Refer to table on page 848)

Additional Reading

Bailey, J.B.A., *Field Artillery and Firepower* (1989).
Hogg, Ian V., Barrage: *The Guns in Action* (1970).
———, *German Artillery of World War Two* (1975).
Zabecki, David T., *Steel Wind: Colonel Georg Bruchmüller and the Birth of Modern Artillery* (1994).

Artillery, Italian

Like most European armies, the Italian Army had a large number of elderly field guns in service in 1939. However, during the 1920s, Italy had embarked on a program of rearmament ahead of its rivals. The result was that Italy's army had some advanced pieces, but they never were produced in quantity. Ironically too, they soon became relatively dated, as Italy found its designs outmatched by those of its opponents whose procurement programs began in the 1930s and bore fruit in the early years of the war.

The Cannone da 75/32 modello 37 was the product of Italy's rearmament program of the 1920s. It was an advanced weapon, but never entered full production. The same was true of the Obice da 75/18 modello 35 howitzer, of which only sixty-eight were in service by September 1942. It was, however, a successful piece and was fitted to several different self-propelled (SP) chassis.

In 1940 the Italians still had nearly 900 Cannone da 149/35 in service. It was based on a British Armstrong design from 1900 and had to be re-laid after every shot. It was due to be replaced in 1940 by the Cannone da 149/40, a gun of modern design, but which never went into mass production. The Italians also introduced an advanced howitzer, the Obice da 149/19 series. Design work on the latter began in 1930, but by 1942 only 147 had entered service. It was well regarded by the

Germans and it was kept in production for them after 1943.

Arguably the best design of this period of modernization was the Obice da 210/22 modello 35, which was an accurate and mobile piece given its heavy caliber. A total of 346 pieces were ordered, but only twenty were in service by 1942. It was also kept in service for the Germans after 1943.

Italian armies and corps were each supported by artillery regiments. They were reinforced on an ad hoc basis by additional groupings called *Raggruppamenti*. Each army was allotted one battery of heavy antiaircraft guns from the total of five regiments. A corps artillery regiment might contain from three to eight batteries of 105mm or 149mm pieces, each comprising three troops of four guns or howitzers.

By 1942 all army and corps artillery was mechanized. The division was supported by an artillery regiment consisting of one battery of howitzers and two batteries of guns. These in turn contained the standard three troops each of four pieces. In addition the division had twenty-four 20mm antiaircraft guns. At the start of the war divisional artillery was not mechanized, but by 1942, an armored division was supported by two batteries of self-propelled 75mm 75/18 howitzers on M13 tank chassis. By 1942, the British noted that the Italians were trying to strengthen their artillery at divisional level with both newer models of their own and German pieces. This was achieved at the expense of corps artillery and reflected a similar emphasis found in German organizations. The influence of German equipment and organization was particularly evident in Italian units serving in the Soviet Union.

Italian gunners had a good reputation among the British Army and performed well in a number of early engagements in North Africa; for example, at Fort Capuzzo in June 1940. They were noted for siting their guns well forward and for a willingness to engage tanks with direct fire. Despite their fine reputation they suffered the fate of the rest of the Italian Army in that theater. At the start of Operation COMPASS on 10 December 1940, which cleared the Italian Army out of Egypt, they lost 250 guns. Marshal Rudolfo Graziani (q.v.) blamed this reversal on inadequate equipment, saying that "one cannot break steel armour with finger nails alone." Bardia (q.v.) fell on 5 January 1941, with the loss of another 250 guns. By early February the Italian Army had lost more than 850 pieces.

Jonathan B.A. Bailey

(Refer to table on page 849)

Additional Reading

Hogg, Ian V., *The Illustrated Encyclopedia of Artillery* (1987).

Artillery, Railway

Railway artillery first appeared during the American Civil War, when Union forces used a 13-inch mortar mounted on a flatcar in the Richmond campaign. Subsequently, both the Confederate and Union Armies made extensive use of a wide variety of rail-mounted guns, but then the concept went into eclipse after the end of the Civil War. Following the Franco-Prussian War, the French Army started experimenting with railway artillery and by World War I both the Allies and the Germans made fairly wide use of such guns in the static environment of trench warfare on the western front.

Rail-mounted guns fell into two basic categories. Those used primarily for offensive purposes were large-caliber weapons on special mountings that enabled them to be rapidly moved from place to place, either on existing track or on track specially laid. These guns normally required some sort of special preparations to either the track or the railcar and platform before they could be fired. Rail-mounted guns used for defensive purposes were generally smaller caliber, and used to defend armored trains. During the Russian civil war, the Red Army made extensive use of such trains to move troops and as mobile patrol units. During World War II, the Soviets and the Germans both used armored trains on the eastern front to defend against partisan and guerrilla raids.

Railway guns had two basic types of mounts, usually a function of the gun's size. A pivot mount on the rail car allowed the gun to traverse and fire in any direction relative to the line of the track. Larger guns using this sort of mount required outriggers to stabilize the car and prevent the whole thing from tipping over when firing perpendicular to the track. Almost all guns larger than 200mm were rigidly aligned in their mountings. These guns were traversed for firing direction either by rotating the entire car on a track turntable, or by moving the car along a specially laid length of curved track.

Between the world wars, the Americans concentrated on using large rail-mounted guns as mobile coastal defense batteries. The British generally lost interest in railway artillery. They did retain some units from World War I, however, and the British Expeditionary Force (BEF) took them back to France in 1939. These guns were all left behind when the BEF made its evacuation from Dunkirk (q.v.). In 1943, the British briefly considered forming a railway-gun regiment for the coming invasion of the Continent. That idea was abandoned because of the overwhelming air superiority of the Allied tactical air forces, and the resulting firepower that aircraft could deliver.

Railway guns were favored by continental powers as a means of quickly transferring heavy artillery reserves from one side of the country to the other. Germany, therefore, spent the interwar years developing a fairly wide range of *Eisenbahnartillerie* (Railroad Artillery) to support ground operations and capitalize on the dense and well-developed rail infrastructure of Europe.

In the 1920s, the Krupp firm started a long-term program that focused on developing a modern family of railway guns and mounts. When it became obvious that this long-term program was proceeding too slowly and consuming too many resources, the Germans initiated a *Sofort-Programm* (Crash Program) in 1936. The *Sofort-Programm* used older, large-caliber naval guns that could be quickly pulled out of storage and placed on rail-mountings based on updated World War I designs. By the summer of 1939, the *Sofort-Programm* produced and delivered at least six different models—albeit some in very small numbers—in calibers ranging from 150mm to 280mm.

The most widely produced of the *Sofort-Programm* designs was the 215-ton 28cm Kanone 5 (E), one of the best railway guns ever made. The K 5 (E) fired a 563-pound pre-rifled shell 62,180 meters (38.6 miles), and a 547-pound rocket-assisted projectile 86,500 meters (53.8 miles). A smoothbore version, the 31cm K 5 (E) Glatt, fired the experimental *Peenemünder Pfeilgeschose* (Peenemünde Arrow Shell), a fin-stabilized, discarding sabot projectile to a phenomenal range of 151,000 meters (93.8 miles). The Germans called the K 5 (E) class of guns "Schlanke Bertha" (Thin Bertha). One of those guns, nicknamed "Leopold," was used with devastating effect against the Allied beach positions at Anzio (q.v.). The Allied troops called it "Anzio Annie." Later the gun was captured at Civitavecchia, and today it sits at the U.S. Ordnance Museum at Aberdeen Proving Grounds, Maryland.

The largest railway gun ever built was the massive 80cm K (E). The gun's official name was the "Gustav Gerät," in honor of Gustav Krupp von Bohlen and Halbach (q.v.); but its gunners called it "Dora." The preliminary work on the 800mm (31.5-inch) monster began in 1935 when the German Army asked Krupp to design a gun capable of defeating the defenses of the Maginot Line (q.v.). Full-scale development started in the summer of 1937, but the gun was not delivered until early 1942, long after the fall of France. After the gun went through acceptance firing tests, it was shipped east to Sevastopol.

Dora fired a 5.28-ton shell 47,000 meters (29.2 miles). It fired a 7.8-ton concrete-piercing shell 38,000 meters (23.6 miles). Its barrel was ninety-five feet long, and the entire gun weighed 1,329 tons. Dora was so massive that it had to be transported in sections, requiring a number of trains. In its firing configuration it was mounted on two railcars running side by side on parallel tracks. This, of course, required special tracking laid for the gun in its firing position. Normally it took three weeks to prepare the site and erect the gun. The crew totaled 1,420 men under the command of a major general.

Dora fired between only thirty-six and fifty-five rounds in support of the German siege operations at Sevastopol (q.v.). Reportedly, those few rounds caused massive damage to the Soviet positions. After Sevastopol, Dora was sent north to support the siege at Leningrad (q.v.), but the German Army started its withdrawal before it could be placed into action. Dora was hastily withdrawn to the west, where it reportedly was used to fire a few rounds into Warsaw (q.v.) during the 1944 Rising. After that, Dora disappeared from sight, presumably scrapped sometime in late 1944.

Dora remains to this day the largest gun ever built. It was a masterpiece of ordnance engineering, but militarily it was a waste of time. The time, effort, and resources that went into the gun were far out of proportion to the military effect achieved.

David T. Zabecki

(Refer to table on page 850)

Additional Reading

Hogg, Ian V., *German Artillery of World War Two* (1975).
———, and John Batchelor, *Rail Gun* (1973).

Artillery, Soviet

The excellence demonstrated by Soviet artillery in the "Great Patriotic War" owed much to the foundations laid in the 1930s. While the German Army was decentralizing its artillery organization and relying on aircraft to provide the firepower formerly provided by massed artillery, the Soviets retained their faith in the efficacy of massive artillery firepower. By the late 1930s, they had built an all-arms force with artillery as a major constituent at all levels. The Soviet artillery was equipped with an array of innovative and reliable equipment, which in many cases outclassed all rivals. Playing its part in a combined-arms tactical and operational doctrine, artillery became the dominant, and in Soviet eyes, war-winning, arm.

The Soviets were at the leading edge of artillery design throughout the war and produced outstanding equipment with a high lethality at greater range for their weight than most rival systems. Their pieces combined technical sophistication in metallurgy and design, while remaining simple to operate and extremely robust. This applied not only to guns and howitzers, but also to mortars, rockets, and recoilless rifles. The Soviets were also innovative in mass-manufacturing techniques, and managed to produce equipment cheaply and in great numbers. Through a policy of design evolution, the combining of the successful features of existing pieces, improved models were produced at very short notice. The most famous example was the production of the M-1943 D-1, by designer F.F. Petrov, in just eighteen days by combining a 152mm barrel with the carriage of the 122mm M-1938 M-30 howitzer.

While the other major combatants directed great effort into producing ever more powerful antitank guns, the Soviets virtually ignored this area of research and development. They preferred instead to rely, and successfully so, on their field guns in the direct fire role. The effectiveness of high-velocity field guns against tanks had been noted by the Soviets during the Spanish civil war (q.v.). With large quantities of these guns available, they were able both to mass indirect fire and call upon these same guns for point defense against armor if needed. That need was well demonstrated in the early years of the war, and towed field guns were responsible for the majority of German tank losses in 1941–1942.

The loss of so much equipment in the wake of the 1941 German invasion spurred the Soviets to mass-produce an array of artillery of standard design. The basis for this was the 76.2mm M-1942 ZiS-3, a long-barrelled gun with a split trail, pneumatic tires, and a range of 13,290 meters. By the end of the war versions of this "divisional gun" had been produced in calibers of 85mm and 100mm. The latter outranged all rivals, with a range of 20,700 meters, and was also fitted to the SU-100 assault gun. Soviet medium artillery was based on an excellent family of 122mm weapons, such

as the M-1931/37 A-19, and the 152mm M-1937 ML-20 and M-1943 D-1.

By 1939, Soviet doctrine required artillery firepower to maintain the impetus of an offensive throughout the depth of the enemy defense. An organization was therefore required that would provide close support for assaulting infantry, long-range artillery to destroy the enemy's artillery, and heavy artillery to smash his other defenses. Under the direction of Chief of Artillery Nikolai Voronov (q.v.), the Soviets built up a formidable inventory of artillery equipment to provide that capability. By 1937, the Soviet Union had 9,200 field and heavy guns, twice as many as Germany and three times as many as France. By June 1941 that figure had risen to 67,000, and in that year special antitank and anti-aircraft artillery categories also were created.

In 1941, a major reorganization of the Soviet artillery took place. The number of guns held at divisional level was reduced in order to make those divisions more mobile. Whereas the rifle division of 1939 had eighty-two guns and howitzers, by late 1941 it had only twenty-four. The number of mortars it possessed went up, however, from thirty to 108. Heavier pieces were grouped in special artillery reserve units, which were to be massed at the decisive point of battle. This reorganization was the precondition for Josef Stalin's (q.v.) direction in 1942 that artillery should be concentrated to achieve a breakthrough on a chosen sector, and that artillery should be made more mobile to support armored formations when that breakthrough was achieved.

By autumn 1942, the artillery reserves had been organized into artillery divisions of eight regiments each, and by 1943–1945, these had been expanded to contain up to six or seven artillery brigades. By 1945, the Soviets had more than ninety artillery divisions, each with about 288 guns and howitzers. From 1943, artillery divisions were themselves often melded into breakthrough artillery corps of perhaps two artillery divisions and one rocket launcher division, totaling more than 1,000 weapons. In 1943, guards mortar divisions were formed, with 288 mortars each, to further concentrate firepower on a main axis. This ever-greater centralization of artillery assets meant that, whereas in 1941, 8 percent of Soviet artillery was held in the high command reserve, by August 1945, the latter contained 35 percent, and of a much larger absolute total.

The dire consequences of advancing without adequate artillery support had been made clear to the Soviets in their Winter War (q.v.) against Finland in 1939–1940. As a result of this experience,

Marshal Semen Timoshenko (q.v.) ensured that his offensive of February 1940 was supported by masses of guns on a narrow front. The success of that operation confirmed the Soviet view of how artillery should be employed. Nevertheless, Soviet artillery, like the rest of the Soviet Army, suffered stunning losses following the German invasion of 1941. It has been estimated that the Soviets lost 20,000 artillery pieces in the first five months of the campaign alone. While a large number were old guns soon to be replaced with better ones, many modern Soviet pieces were captured and put into service with the *Wehrmacht*.

In winter 1941, massed artillery became the basis for the defense of Moscow (q.v.), and it is claimed that between 16 November and 10 December, artillery destroyed more than 1,400 German tanks. This successful formula was repeated at Stalingrad (q.v.), where the siting of guns in the antitank role was the foremost consideration in the deployment of Soviet forces. Guns were deployed in four belts ten kilometers deep, and tasked to fire indirectly, until tanks were in direct fire range. Self-propelled guns were held in reserve to react rapidly should the enemy succeed in breaking through. From that experience the Soviets concluded: (1) in the defense, artillery, not aircraft, was the superior form of fire support; (2) the anti-armor plan should determine the overall deployment of forces; (3) all guns should be capable of direct fire; (4) an artillery reserve was essential; (5) armor should counterattack only after a tank attack had been halted by artillery; (6) artillery must be sited in depth in prepared positions; and (7) indirect fire was only effective when massed and commanded centrally.

These principles were further refined at Kursk (q.v.) in summer 1943, where the Soviets developed their doctrine not merely for successful defense but for the launching of an offensive from it. The Soviets gave artillery three tasks in offensive operations: (1) preparation; (2) support (in the form of a rolling barrage or concentrations of aimed fire); and (3) accompaniment. Accompaniment was the task of divisional artillery and generally required direct fire support in the offense and defense. As a consequence, Soviet divisional artillery suffered approximately ten times the losses of non-divisional artillery units.

At Kursk on 5 July 1943, the Soviets used 3,000 guns in a counterpreparation role against German forces, which were poised to launch their long-awaited offensive, thereby demonstrating the power of indirect fire to preempt armored attack. The Germans learned from this bitter experience and from 1943 on, they built stronger defenses; which in turn caused the Soviets to create larger formations of heavier pieces, such as the BM-31 rocket launcher and the 160mm M-1943 mortar, to defeat them. Major General Fedor Alexandrovich Samsonov observed that "the enemy's fire weapons were so effectively protected that it was not enough to silence him. They had to be smashed to atoms."

The Soviets placed great emphasis on the careful plotting of targets prior to both offensive and defensive operations. By the end of the war, they estimated that they could locate more than 70 percent of targets before an offensive began. These would then be subjected to intense bombardment and air strikes, which over the course of the war became shorter but more intense.

The Soviets continually strove to create decisive concentrations of guns and rockets on critical sectors, and their organization was designed to provide this. It did not mean that some sectors were left without artillery support, for they ensured that at all levels units always could count on their own organic artillery units. Concentrations were achieved by allocating extra resources where needed from higher formations.

Soviet artillery concentrations grew ever more massive. On the thirty-three-kilometer breakthrough sector for the Vistula-Oder offensive (*see* Poland–East Prussia) in January 1945, the Soviets massed 7,600 guns and mortars, with 33,500 pieces deployed across the entire front. This approach continued as the basis for Soviet doctrine after the war, and was still recognizable at the beginning of the 1990s. It differed from the Western approach that saw (and still sees) the role of higher formations not so much as providing reinforcement to subordinate levels as coordinating assets, making most efficient use of them by means of ever more sophisticated and flexible fire control systems. Soviet fire control, by comparison, was unsophisticated; it was not until 1943 that artillery General Vladimir Semenov suggested that an artillery barrage could be used for covering fire during the assault, rather than stopping once the latter had started.

The Soviet system was proven successful and suited their circumstances, but it carried a number of weaknesses. It took time to assemble the concentrations of equipment required for successful operations, and that in turn called for periods of stability. Operations were characterized, therefore, by long periods of buildup, followed by surges of activity. Although these were ultimately successful at the operational level, the Germans frequently were able to achieve startling tactical successes at

A

great cost to the Soviets, thanks to the quicker reactions made possible by less cumbersome doctrine and organization. Another disadvantage of building so great a force was that training was necessarily rudimentary and did not allow Soviet artillery units to engage more than a set number of targets on a deliberate fire plan. The ability to switch fire to exploit targets of opportunity, therefore, was lacking.

There was only one part of its organization in which the Soviet Army was less well-served by artillery than its German counterpart. While by 1944 the German *Panzer* division was supported by about seventy self-propelled pieces up to 150mm, the Soviet tank corps was supported by just twenty 76mm self-propelled guns. About 70 percent of Soviet artillery was of 100mm or less, and in practice could only engage targets up to 5,000 meters away. It was at this most vulnerable range that fire support often disappeared. As a result, the Soviets often had difficulty supporting the breakthroughs that had been achieved largely thanks to the initial devastating bombardments of massed but relatively immobile guns. The Germans, therefore, frequently were able to launch rapid and ferocious counterattacks, which restored an otherwise unequal situation. The price the Germans paid for this decentralization and flexibility was that they were unable to generate the huge concentrations of artillery necessary to break through the Soviet defenses, such as they found at Kursk. Whatever local setbacks there might be overall, the Soviets achieved a ratio of forces that ultimately proved decisive. The Soviet deficiency in accompanying artillery for armored forces was corrected after the war when they devised the organizations for their tank and motorized rifle divisions.

Soviet artillery concentrations were also very vulnerable to air attack. Until 1943, the Soviets rarely were able to achieve local air superiority, but from that date they were able to amass large concentrations of artillery with relative impunity.

The Soviets built on the lessons of World War I, and throughout the 1920s and 1930s constructed the framework for an artillery arm that was to prove decisive in their "Great Patriotic War." They devised the doctrine and means to provide fire support in large-scale armored operations, and by 1945 had proved to their own satisfaction that artillery was indeed the "God of War."

Jonathan B.A. Bailey

(Refer to table on page 851)

Additional Reading
Bailey, J.B.A., *Field Artillery and Firepower* (1989).
Bellamy, Chris, *Red God of War* (1986).
Zabecki, David T., *Steel Wind: Colonel Georg Bruchmüller and the Birth of Modern Artillery* (1994).

Artillery, U.S.

America suffered the least of any of the major combatants of World War I. Nonetheless, a sense of war-weariness produced an overwhelming postwar popular sentiment to eliminate as much of the U.S. military as possible—very much the same mind-set as the end of the Cold War. In 1920, the U.S. had 174 artillery batteries in the active army. By the start of 1935, the active army was down to ninety-eight batteries, 40 percent of them still horse-drawn. Between 1926 and 1930, more than 1,000 field artillery enlisted men were involuntarily transferred to the fledgling Army Air Corps. In 1934, the Knox Trophy for the best firing battery in the U.S. Army could not be awarded because there was not enough ammunition for all eligible batteries to take part in the competition.

By the mid-1920s, the U.S. Army started to abandon many of the hard-learned artillery lessons of World War I. Lack of mobility and the resulting inability to mass rapidly were the causes of the stagnation of trench warfare. Many Western military thinkers came to regard the massive firepower of World War I as the direct cause. At the same time, the proponents of airpower in America (and in Great Britain) were making exaggerated and widely publicized claims for their arm. Yet, as in Britain (but not in Germany), those same airmen strongly resisted the idea of using their aircraft for direct support of ground troops. The result was a retarded development of close air support. In the U.S. Army, the focus of ground tactics shifted back to an infantry-centered world.

Right up to the start of World War II, the U.S. Army neglected corps-level artillery and ignored the requirements of artillery command and control above the divisional level. What corps-level artillery there was formed little more than a holding pool for firepower assets. In theory, counterbattery fire was the responsibility of the corps. In 1938, Lieutenant Colonel (later Major General) John S. Wood (q.v.) noted in an article published in the *Field Artillery Journal:* "Since . . . corps artillery exist(s) only in the imagination, counterbattery training is equally imaginary." Even as far into World War II as May 1943, the Field Artillery School at Fort Sill was still recommending that corps artillery units should be parceled out to the divisions for actual operations.

Fortunately, the U.S. Army did not go quite as far as the British, French, or even the Germans in abandoning the artillery lessons of World War I. The characteristic American propensity for technical applications prevailed, and the Field Artillery School at Fort Sill continued to experiment with all forms of fire control techniques, including aerial observation.

From the late 1920s right until the eve of World War II, the gunnery department at Fort Sill, under the successive leadership of Major (later General) Jacob L. Devers (q.v.), Major Carlos Brewer, and Major Orlando Ward (later commander of the 1st and 20th Armored Divisions in World War II), developed and refined a flexible and quick method of massing large numbers of firing units. In 1934, they introduced the first battalion fire direction center. In 1940, they developed the graphical firing table (sort of an artillery slide rule), which made the calculation of the firing solution much faster. In April 1941, Fort Sill demonstrated for Army Chief of Staff General George C. Marshall (q.v.) a divisional shoot by massing the fires of four separate battalions.

When this process started at Fort Sill, the assistant commandant of the school was Brigadier General Lesley J. McNair (q.v.), who had commanded a field artillery brigade in France during World War I. During the American buildup prior to World War II, McNair became one of the chief architects of the U.S. military machine as commander of U.S. Army Ground Forces. A strong be-liever in flexible massed fires, McNair continually pushed for the development of longer-range guns and supported all initiatives to centralize artillery command and control systems. Under his direction, non-divisional medium and heavy artillery units grew from 135 battalions for a planned 100-division army in November 1942, to 257 battalions for an actual eighty-nine-division army in July 1944.

The U.S. Army, then, entered World War II with both the means and the ability to mass widely dispersed fire units unsurpassed by any other nation. This led to an unprecedented level of coordination between infantry and artillery. American fire support capability exceeded that of the Germans throughout the war. The system was not perfect, however. The U.S. Army always had trouble coordinating above divisional level, and even between divisions. German *General der Artillerie* Karl Thoholte noted that during the Ardennes Offensive (q.v.), German forward observers usually could plot U.S. divisional boundaries by the gaps in the fires. On the whole, the German soldiers respected and feared U.S. artillery fire above almost all else.

U.S. Army doctrine specified two principal combat roles for field artillery in World War II: (1) supporting the ground-gaining (infantry, cavalry, armored) units by fire, neutralizing or destroying those targets that presented the most danger to the supported arms; and (2) giving depth to combat by counterbattery fire, by fire on enemy reserves, by restricting movement in enemy rear areas, and by disrupting enemy command and control systems.

In combat, all U.S. field artillery units were

"The Priest," a 105mm howitzer mounted on a M-3A1 tank carriage, prepares to fire during the Ardennes Offensive. (IWM EA 48119)

assigned one of three basic tactical missions. Direct support meant that an artillery unit was assigned to provide fires for a specific maneuver unit. A field artillery unit in direct support established liaison and signal communications with the supported unit and moved with it whenever necessary to ensure its guns were always within range. Normally, a field artillery battalion provided the direct support for an infantry regiment. A unit with a general support mission was responsible for providing fires for a larger unit, the subunits of which usually had their own direct support artillery. A unit with a reinforcing mission was assigned to deliver fires to reinforce those of another artillery unit. General support and reinforcing artillery units were one of the primary means divisional and higher-level commanders had of directly influencing the battle.

During World War II, the divisional artillery of a typical infantry division consisted of four battalions of three batteries each. Each battery had four guns, for a divisional total of forty-eight. Three of the battalions were armed with towed 105mm howitzers, and each generally was assigned to provide direct support for one of the division's infantry regiments. The fourth battalion was armed with towed 155mm howitzers, and had the general support mission for the division.

U.S. armored divisions were organized a little differently. The armored divisional artillery had only three battalions of three batteries, but each battery had six self-propelled 105mm howitzers. This gave the armored division a total of fifty-four guns. Two of the battalions were placed in direct support of the division's two combat commands, with the third battalion held in general support.

Almost all artillery above divisional level came under the corps artillery. The primary functions of corps artillery were counterbattery fire and long-range interdiction. Corps units generally had the tactical missions of either general support to the corps, or reinforcing to the artillery of a specific division. This latter mission usually was assigned for very specific situations; for example, when that particular division was designated to make the main effort of a corps attack.

Corps artillery organizations were flexible, usually consisting of two or more artillery groups, of two or more artillery battalions each. Artillery groups routinely were transferred from corps to corps as the tactical and operational situations required. In the final years of World War II, a typical corps artillery in Europe had an average of thirteen battalions controlled by an appropriate number of groups. Almost all corps artillery units were armed with guns of 155mm and larger caliber.

The U.S. Army classified field artillery guns and howitzers into three basic categories based on their weight; light, medium, and heavy. Light guns usually were found only in divisional artillery. The airborne divisions and the 10th Mountain Divi-

A platoon of U.S. M-2A1 105mm howitzers in firing position.

sion were armed with the 75mm M-1A1 howitzer, also called a pack howitzer. It was designed for easy disassembly, which allowed it to be airdropped or transported by mules. The 75mm pack howitzer was widely used in Italy, and also saw extensive service in the jungles of the Pacific, where its transportability made it very popular.

The workhorse of most infantry divisional artillery was the 105mm M-2A1 howitzer. Next to the World War I–era French 75mm field gun, the American 105mm was probably the most successful artillery piece in history. It was accurate, reliable, and could withstand an incredible amount of punishment and mishandling. Design work began on this weapon immediately following World War I, and originally it was intended to be towed by a team of six horses. In March 1940, the design was standardized as the M-2A1, towed by a two-and-one-half-ton truck, which also carried the gun's basic load of ammunition. Armored divisions used the same gun in a self-propelled (SP) mount; either the M-7B1 mounted on a Sherman tank chassis, or after 1945, the M-37 mounted on a Chaffee tank chassis.

In 1943, a lightened version of the M-2A1 with a shortened barrel was introduced for airborne units. The resulting M-3 was not very successful. After World War II, the M-2A1 was modified very slightly and became the M-101A1. That version remained in service with the U.S. Army through the Korean and Vietnam Wars. Between 1940 and 1953, some 10,200 M-2A1/M-101A1s were built and supplied to at least forty-five different armies. The M-101A1 was still in service with U.S. Army reserve units as late as 1990. The M-101A1 undoubtedly will remain in service in some countries well into the twenty-first century.

The standard U.S. medium artillery piece was the 155mm M-1 towed howitzer. Most of the general support battalions in the infantry divisions were armed with this piece. A self-propelled version, the M-41, was mounted on the Chaffee tank chassis, but only about 100 were ever built. The towed version was successful and popular, even though it was heavy and somewhat difficult to handle. After World War II, it too was modified very slightly and became the M-114A1. That version was supplied to twenty-eight different countries, and remained in service with some NATO armies through the mid-1990s. The cannoneers on the gun crews called these weapons "pigs"—short for pig iron.

The most widely used American heavy gun was the 155mm M-1A1 towed gun—not to be confused with the 155mm M-1 towed howitzer. The 155mm gun was two-and-one-half times as heavy as the 155mm howitzer, and could shoot a shell of the same weight (95 pounds) 60 percent farther. Being a gun, it had a very long barrel in relation to the size of its bore, and it shot its shell at a very high velocity, but in a relatively flat trajectory. The 155mm gun's nineteen-foot barrel gave it its nickname, "Long Tom." Two self-propelled versions existed: the M-12, based on a Grant tank chassis, and the M-40, based on the Sherman tank chassis.

The 8-inch M-2 towed howitzer used the same carriage as the 155mm M-1A1 towed gun. While the bore sizes of all other U.S. artillery pieces were designated in millimeters, this one was designated in inches because it originally was adopted from a British design. The 8-inch had the reputation of being the most accurate artillery piece ever invented. After World War II it was fitted to a self-propelled mount. Newer SP mounts were introduced in the 1950s, and a nuclear shell was introduced. The 8-inch underwent various modifications and improvements, and saw service in Korea, Vietnam, and the Gulf War. It was retired from U.S. service in 1992.

The heaviest U.S. artillery battalions were armed with the 240mm M-1 towed howitzer, called the "Black Dragon." It was towed by an M-6 38-ton tractor, which gave it surprisingly good mobility for a gun weighing almost twenty-one tons. It took about two hours to bring the piece into action. The 240mm howitzer saw extensive service in the Italian campaign. It remained in U.S. and British service until the late 1950s.

David T. Zabecki

(Refer to table on page 852)

Additional Reading

Bailey, J.B.A., *Field Artillery and Firepower* (1989).

Hogg, Ian V., *The Guns 1939–45* (1970).

———, *Barrage: The Guns in Action* (1970).

———, *British and American Artillery of World War 2* (1978).

Zabecki, David T., *Steel Wind: Colonel Georg Bruchmüller and the Birth of Modern Artillery* (1994).

ASDIC

See SONAR

Section IV-A
Technical Data Tables of
Weapons and Equipment

British Fleet Aircraft Carriers

	Furious	Argus	Eagle	Hermes	Courageous-Class	Ark Royal	Illustrious-Class 1st Group	Illustrious-Class 2nd Group	Indefatigable-Class	Unicorn	Collosus
Commissioned (year)	1925	1926	1923	1922	1928	1939	1940	1942	1943	1943	1945
Number Built	1	1	1	1	2	1	3	1	2	1	6
Displacement (standard tons)	22,450	14,555	22,600	10,850	22,500	22,000	23,207	24,687	1x 27,000 1x 27,700	16,510	13,190
Max. Speed (knots)	29.5	20.5	24.0	25.0	29.5	31.0	30.5	30.5	31.5	24.0	25.0
Endurance (nm) at Best Speed	8,000 nm at 12 kts	3,000 nm at 14 kts	4,000 nm at 18 kts	4,000 nm at 12 kts	7,000 nm at 14 kts	10,500 nm at 14 kts	11,000 nm at 14 kts	11,000 nm at 14 kts	11,000 nm at 14 kts	5,000 nm at 14 kts	12,000 nm at 14 kts
Number of Aircraft	33	20	21	12	48	72	36	48	54	36	48
Main Guns	12x 4-in AA	2x 4-in	9x 6-in	6x 5.5-in	16x 4.7-in AA	16x 4.5-in DP*	16x 4.5-in DP*	16x 4.5-in DP*	16x 4.5-in DP*	8x 4-in AA	None
Initial AA Battery	24x 2-pdr	4x 4-in	4x 4-in 8x 2-pdr	4x 4-in	24x 2-pdr	48x 2-pdr 32x .50 MG	48x 2-pdr 8x 20mm	48x 2-pdr 8x 20mm	1-37x20mm 1-40x20mm	48x 2-pdr 12x 2-pdr 12x 20mm	24x 2-pdr 21x 40mm
Catapults	No	No	No	1	2	2	1	1	1	1	1
Max. Armor (inches)	3	None	7	3	3	4.5	4.5	4.5	4.5	None	None
Radar	In 1940	No	In 1941	In 1940	In 1940	Yes	Yes	Yes	Yes	Yes	Yes
Sonar	No	No	No	No	No	No	No	No	No	No	No
Hydrophones	No	No	No	No	No	No	No	No	No	No	No
Crew Size	950	373	948	684	1,212	1,636	1,592	1,592	1,657	1,000	1,076
Losses	None	None	1	1	2	1	None	None	None	None	None

*DP: dual-purpose

British Escort Aircraft Carriers

	Audacity	Archer-Class	Tracker-Class	Ruler-Class	Activity	Campania
Commissioned (year)	1940	1942 Note 1	1942 Note 1	1943 Note 1	1943	1944
Number Built	1	5	11	23	1	1
Displacement (standard tons)	5,537	4x 12,150 1x 12,300	10,200	11,200	11,800	12,450
Max. Speed (knots)	16	17	18.5	18	18	17
Endurance (nm) at Best Speed	5,000 nm at 10 kts	5,000 nm at 10 kts	5,500 nm at 11 kts	7,000 nm at 11 kts	5,800 nm at 9 kts	5,800 nm at 9 kts
Number of Aircraft	6	20	20	20	15	15
Main Guns	1x 4-in	1x 5-in	2x 5-in	2x 5-in AA	2x 4-in AA	2x 4-in AA
Initial AA Battery	6x 20mm	2x 3-in 1-11x 20mm 4-10x 20mm	14x 20mm 8x 40mm	20x 20mm 16x 40mm	28x 20mm	16x 2-pdr 16x 20mm
Catapults	None	None	1	1	1	1
Max. Armor (inches)	None	None	None	None	None	None
Radar	No	Yes, 1941	Yes	Yes	Yes	Yes
Sonar	No	No	No	No	No	No
Hydrophones	No	No	No	No	No	No
Crew Size	250	556	646	646	700	700
Losses	1	2	0	2	0	0

(continued on next page)

	Nairana-Class	Pretoria Castle	Empire-Class 1st Group	Empire-Class 2nd Group	Empire-Class 3rd Group	Rapana-Class
Commissioned (year)	1944	1943	1943	1944	1944	1944
Number Built	2	1	4	2	4	9
Displacement (standard tons)	1x 13,825 1x 13,445	17,392	7,950	8,250	Note 2	8,000
Max. Speed (knots)	17	17	12.5	12.5	12.5	13
Endurance (nm) at Best Speed	5,700 nm at 9 kts	2,000 nm at 10 kts	7,000 nm at 9 kts	7,000 nm at 9 kts	7,000 nm at 9 kts	5,000 nm at 12 kts
Number of Aircraft	18	15	4	4	4	4
Main Guns	2x 4-in AA	4x 4-in AA	1x 4-in	1x 4-in	1x 4-in	1x 4-in
Initial AA Battery	16x 2-pdr 16x 20mm	16x 2-pdr 20x 20mm	4x 20mm 2x 40mm	4x 20mm 2x 40mm	8x 20mm	6x 20mm 2x 40mm
Catapults	1	1	None	None	None	None
Max. Armor (inches)	None	None	None	None	None	None
Radar	Yes	Yes	Yes	Yes	Yes	Yes
Sonar	No	No	No	No	No	No
Hydrophones	No	No	No	No	No	No
Crew Size	728	700	107	107	122	118
Losses	0	0	0	0	0	0

Notes:
1. USA built.
2. Displacements for Empire-Class, 3rd Group:
   1x 9,133 tons
   1x 8,856 tons   1x 9,249 tons
   1x 8,908 tons

Axis Aircraft Carriers

	Aquila	Graf Zeppelin
Commissioned (year/country)	1943 Italy	Germany Note 2
Number Built	Note 1	Note 2
Displacement (standard tons)	23,350	23,200
Max. Speed (knots)	30	34
Endurance (nm) at Best Speed	Unknown	6,000 nm at 19 kts
Number of Aircraft	36 type Re. 2001	Note 3
Main Guns	8 x 152mm	16 x 150mm
Initial AA Battery	104 x 37mm 12 x 90mm	28 x 20mm 22 x 37mm 12 x 105mm
Catapults	2	2
Max. Armor (mm)	Note 4	102
Radar	No	No
Sonar	No	Yes
Hydrophones	No	Yes
Crew Size	1,300	Note 2
Losses	1	Note 5

Notes:

1. The *Aquila* was completed but never saw service. The air wing was never produced. The Re. 2001 carrier program was still being developed when Italy capitulated in 1943.
2. The *Graf Zeppelin* was never completed. The air wing was formed and ready by August 1939, but carrier construction was delayed, then postponed. The program was finally canceled in 1943, and aircraft and air crews were sent to other fronts. The ship's crew was never fully completed or manned.
3. The *Graf Zeppelin* was to be equipped with 10 each Bf-109T fighters, 20 each Ju-87C dive-bombers, and 11 each Fi-167 scout/bomber aircraft.
4. The *Aquila* had 600mm of concrete in the flight deck and 60mm in the hull.
5. The semi-completed *Graf Zeppelin* was scuttled in its harbor by the Germans to prevent capture. After the war, it was refloated by the Soviets and in 1947 was being towed to Leningrad for completion when it struck a mine in the Baltic Sea and sank.

U.S. Aircraft Carriers (European Theater)

(*See* Note 1)

	Ranger	*Wasp*	Long Island-Class	Bogue-Class	Sangamon-Class	Prince William-Class	Casablanca-Class
Commissioned (year)	1934 Note 2	1941 Note 2	1942 Note 2	1942 Note 2	1942 Note 2	1943 Note 2	1943 Note 2
Number Built	1	1	2	21	4	24	50
Displacement (standard tons)	14,500	14,700	7,886	11,000	11,400	11,200	7,800
Max. Speed (knots)	29.5	29.5	Note 3	18	18	18	19
Endurance (nm) at Best Speed	7,200 nm at 15 kts	7,200 nm at 15 kts	5,000 nm at 10 kts	5,500 nm at 11 kts	7,000 nm at 12 kts	7,000 nm at 12 kts	5,800 nm at 12 kts
Number of Aircraft	86	84	21	3x 28 18x 21	30	28	28
Main Guns	8x 5-in AA	8x 5-in DP*	1x 5-in DP*	2x 5-in DP*	2x 5-in DP*	2x 5-in DP*	1x 5-in DP*
Initial AA Battery	8x .50 MG	24x .50 MG 16x 1.1-in	2x 3-in 10x 20mm	12x 20mm 8x 40mm	12x 20mm 8x 40mm	20x 20mm 20x 40mm	24x 20mm 16x 40mm
Catapults	1	4	1	Note 4	2	1	1
Max. Armor (inches)	2	4	None	None	None	None	None
Radar	Yes	Yes	Yes	Yes	Yes	Yes	Yes
Sonar	No	No	No	No	No	No	No
Hydrophones	No	No	No	No	No	No	No
Crew Size	2,000	2,367	Note 5	890	1,080	890	860
Losses	0	1	0	1	0	0	5

*DP: dual-purpose

(continued on next page)

U.S. Aircraft Carriers (*continued*)

Notes:

1. The reader will note that several famous carriers are not listed; this table lists only those carriers that had operational tours in the Atlantic Ocean or Mediterranean. *Ranger* participated in Operation TORCH (Northwest Africa), while *Wasp* resupplied the island of Malta. Eleven Bogue-class and twenty-three Prince William-class ships were provided to the Royal Navy.

2. *Ranger* and *Wasp* were main battle carriers, while the others were all categorized as escort carriers.

3. Long Island-class:
   1x 16 knots max
   1x 17 knots max

4. Bogue-class:
   Three ships had two catapults; eighteen ships had only one catapult.

5. Long Island-class:
   One ship had a crew of 970; the other had 856.

British Antiaircraft Guns

Model	Mk-I Bofors	Mk-I 6-pdr	Mk-I	Mk-I-III	Mk-VI	Mk-II	Mk-II
Caliber	40mm	57mm	3-in	3.7-in	3.7-in	4.5-in	5.25-in
Year in Service	1937	1942	1914	1938	1943	1938	1944
Sustained Rate of Fire (rounds/min)	120	70 Note 1	20	25	19	8	10
Maximum Horizontal Range (meters)	9,720	13,500	11,200	18,500	23,000	20,500	24,300
Maximum Altitude (feet)	5,000	21,000	25,200	28,000	59,300	34,500	43,000
Gun Weight (pounds)	4,368	24,650 Note 1	6,000	20,541	38,360	29,500	99,000

Note:
1. When dual mounted (normal configuration).

German Antiaircraft Guns

Model	2cm Flak 38	2cm Flak 38 Vierling*	3.7cm Flak 36, Flak 37	3.7cm Flak 43	3.7cm Flak 43 Zwilling†	8.8cm Flak 18, 36, 39	8.8cm Flak 41	10.5cm Flak 36, Flak 39	12.8cm Flak 40, Flak 45	12.8cm Flak 40 Zwilling†
Caliber	20mm	20mm	37mm	37mm	37mm	88mm	88mm	105mm	128mm	128mm
Year in Service	1940	1940	1938	1943	1944	1935–39	1941	1938	1942	1944
Sustained Rate of Fire (rounds/min)	220	800	80	180	360	15	20	15	12	25
Maximum Horizontal Range (meters)	2,700	2,700	6,600	6,600	6,600	14,800	19,700	17,600	20,500	20,500
Maximum Altitude (feet)	6,560	6,560	6,560	13,780	13,780	26,250	35,025	37,400	35,025	35,025
Gun Weight (pounds)	895	3,352	3,405	2,752	6,165	10,992	17,199	22,544	28,665	59,535

*Vierling = quad-mounted.
†Zwilling = dual-mounted.

Soviet Antiaircraft Guns

Model	M-1940 Bofors	M-1939 Bofors	M-1931	M-1938	M-1939	M-1934
Caliber	25mm	37mm	76.2mm	76.2mm	85mm	105mm
Year in Service	1940	1939	1931	1938	1939	1934
Sustained Rate of Fire (rounds/min)	80	180	10	16	15	8
Maximum Horizontal Range (meters)	6,000	8,000	14,300	14,300	15,500	18,100
Maximum Altitude (feet)	14,764	19,685	31,168	31,168	34,448	42,650
Gun Weight (pounds)	2,369	4,630	10,600	9,480	9,480	23,148

U.S. Antiaircraft Guns

Army

Model	M-55 MG (Quad)	M-1A2	M-1/M-5 Bofors	M-3	M-51	M-1A1 M-2	M-1
Caliber	0.50-in	37mm	40mm	3-in	75mm	90mm	120mm
Year in Service	1942	1939	1940	1928	1945	1941	1940
Sustained Rate of Fire (rounds/min)	450	120	120	18	45	25	12
Maximum Horizontal Range (meters)	1,500	8,000	9,800	13,300	13,000	17,600	24,800
Maximum Altitude (feet)	1,000	18,600	22,875	31,500	30,000	39,500	47,400
Gun Weight (pounds)	1,486	6,124	5,549/4,495	16,800	20,625	19,000	48,800

U.S. Antiaircraft Guns

Navy

Model	Bofors	Bofors	M-14	M-24	M-25
Caliber	20mm	40mm	3-in	3-in	5-in
Year in Service	1940	1941	1927	1945	1935
Sustained Rate of Fire (rounds/min)	240 Note 1	120 Notes 1 & 2	18	30 Note 1	12 Note 1
Maximum Horizontal Range (meters)	5,000	9,000	14,000	14,000	17,000
Maximum Altitude (feet)	5,000	11,200	32,300	32,300	23,100

Notes:
1. Double rate of fire in a dual-mount.
2. Quadruple rate of fire in a quad-mount.

British Antitank Guns

Towed Guns

Model	Mk-X	Mk-II	Mk-I	Mk-II, Note 1
Gun Caliber and Class	40mm 2-pdr	57mm 6-pdr	76.2mm 17-pdr	87mm 25-pdr
Year in Service	1936	1941	1942	1939
Maximum Range (meters)	7,200	4,950	9,000	12,250
Muzzle Velocity (ft/sec)	2,650	2,693	2,900	1,700
Penetration at 500 meters (mm)	53	75	123	62
Gun Weight (pounds)	1,757	2,521	4,624	3,968

Self-Propelled Guns

Model	Firefly	Deacon	Archer	Achilles
Gun Class	6-pdr	6-pdr	17-pdr	17-pdr
Chassis or Carrier	Note 2	Matador Truck	Valentine Tank	U.S. M-4A3 Tank
Year Placed in Service	1941	1942	1944	1944
Crew Size	2	3	4	5

Notes:
1. Field gun used in an antitank role, firing armor-piercing rounds.
2. Truck chassis was a Morris armored car.

German Antitank Guns

Towed Guns

Model	2.8cm sPzB41	3.7cm Pak 35/36	4.2cm Pak 41	5.0cm Pak 38	7.5cm Pak 40	7.5cm Pak 41	7.62cm Pak 36 (r)	8.8cm Pak 43	8.8cm Pak 43/41	12.8cm Pak 44
Caliber	28mm	37mm	Note 1	50mm	75mm	Note 2	76.2mm	88mm	88mm	128mm
Year in Service	1942	1936	1941	1940	1941	1942	1941	1943	1943	1945
Maximum Range (meters)	6,000	6,000	1,000	2,650	7,680	4,200	9,000	17,500	17,500	24,400
Muzzle Velocity (ft/sec)	4,593	2,500	4,150	2,700	2,600	3,691	2,426	3,281	3,281	3,281
Penetration at 500 meters (mm)	94	48	87	78	132	209	120	207	207	256
Gun Weight (pounds)	260	953	1,416	2,174	3,142	2,990	3,815	8,159	9,658	22,403

Self-Propelled Guns

Model	Panzerjäger-I	Marder-I	Marder-II	Marder-III	Hornisse (Nashorn)	Elefant (Ferdinand)	Jagdpanzer-IV	Jagdpanzer 38 (t)	Jagdpanther	Jagdtiger
Gun Caliber and Type	47mm Pak 36 (t)	75mm Pak 40	75mm Pak 40	76.2mm Pak 36 (r)	88mm Pak 43	88mm Pak 43	75mm Pak 40	75mm Pak 40	88mm Pak 43	128mm Pak 44
Chassis or Carrier	PzKpfw-I	Note 3	PzKpfw-II	Note 4	PzKpfw-IV	PzKpfw-VIA	PzKpfw-IV	Note 4	PzKpfw-V	PzKpfw-VIB
Year Placed in Service	1940	1942	1942	1943	1943	1943	1944	1944	1944	1944
Crew Size	4	4	4	4	6	6	4	4	5	6

Notes:
1. Taper 41.6mm/29.4mm.
2. Taper 75mm/55mm.
3. French Lorraine ammunition carrier.
4. PzKpfw-38(t).

Soviet Antitank Guns

Towed Guns

Model	M-30	M-1937	M-1942	M-1941	M-1943 ZIS-2	M-1942 ZIS-3	M-1945 D-44	M-1944 BS-3	M-1937 A-19
Caliber	37mm	45mm	45mm	57mm	57mm	76.2mm	85mm	100mm	122mm
Year in Service	1937	1937	1942	1941	1943	1942	1945	1944	1938
Maximum Range (meters)	3,000	5,000	4,400	7,700	8,400	10,980 Note 1	15,500 Note 1	20,700 Note 1	20,610 Note 1
Muzzle Velocity (ft/sec)	2,045	2,147	2,890	2,750	3,430	2,000	2,139	2,950	2,425
Penetration at 500 meters (mm)	35	40	40	140	140	92	140	195	140
Gun Weight (pounds)	952	1,125	1,250	2,400	2,530	4,900	3,795	6,800	14,000

Self-Propelled Guns

Model	SU-76	SU-85	SU-100	ISU-122	ISU-152
Gun Caliber and Type	76.2mm M-1942 ZIS-3	85mm M-1939 AA Gun	100mm M-1944 BS-3	122mm M-1937 A-19	152mm M-1937 ML-20
Chassis or Carrier	T-70 Tank	T-34 Tank	T-34 Tank	IS-1 Tank	IS-2 Tank
Year Placed in Service	1942 Note 1	1944 Note 2	1944 Note 2	1944 Note 2	1945 Note 2
Crew Size	4	4	4	5	5

Notes:
1. Field gun used in an antitank role, firing armor-piercing ammunition.
2. Assault gun used in an antitank role.

U.S. Antitank Guns

Towed Guns

Model	M-3A1	M-1	M-1	M-5	M-3
Caliber	37mm	57mm	76mm	3-in	90mm
Year in Service	1939	1941	1943	1941	1944
Maximum Range (meters)	11,560	9,230	9,000	14,490	19,260
Muzzle Velocity (ft/sec)	2,900	2,800	2,700	2,800	2,800
Penetration at 500 meters (mm)	61	82	110	135	140
Gun Weight (pounds)	912	2,810	3,820	4,875	6,700

Self-Propelled Guns

Model	GMC T-48	M-10 Wolverine	M-18 Hellcat	M-36 Jackson
Gun Caliber and Model	57mm M-1	3-in M-5	76mm M-1	90mm M-3
Chassis or Carrier	M-3 Halftrack	M-4A2 Tank	GMC T-70	M-4A3 Tank
Year Placed in Service	1942	1942	1943	1944
Crew Size	4	5	5	5

British Field Artillery Guns

Towed Guns

Model	Mk-II	Mk-II	Mk-II	Mk-III	Mk-XIX	Mk-I	Mk-VI	Mk-VII	Mk-II	Mk-IV
Caliber	87mm	114mm	127mm	140mm	152mm	152mm	183mm	203mm	234mm	305mm
Class	25-pdr	4.5-in	60-pdr	5.5-in	6-in	6-in	7.2-in	8-in	9.2-in	12-in
Type	Gun/Howitzer	Gun	Gun	Gun	Gun	Howitzer	Howitzer	Howitzer	Howitzer	Howitzer
Year in Service	1940	1939	1918	1941	1916	1915	1943	1917	1916	1917
Maximum Range (meters)	12,250	18,745	15,000	14,810	17,145	8,690	17,640	11,250	12,750	13,120
Sustained Rate of Fire (rounds/min)	5	4	2	2	2	1	1	1	1	1/2
Gun Weight (pounds)	3,968	12,880	12,048	13,646	22,792	9,262	29,060	20,048	36,288	83,800
Typical Shell Weight (pounds)	25	55	60	100	100	86	202	200	290	748

Self-Propelled Guns

Model	Bishop	Sexton	M-7 Priest
Gun Caliber and Type	25-pdr Mk-II	25-pdr Mk-II	105mm M-1
Chassis or Carrier	Valentine Tank	M-3 Ram Tank	M-3A1 U.S. Tank
Year Placed in Service	1942	1943	1942
Crew Size	4	3	6

French Field Artillery Guns

Towed Guns

Model	Canon de 75 mle 1897	Canon de 105 mle 1913	Canon de 105 mle 1934S	Canon de 105 court mle 1935B	Canon de 155 GPF	Canon de 155L mle 1932
Caliber	75mm	105mm	105mm	105mm	155mm	155mm
Year in Service	1897	1913	1934	1937	1917	1933
Maximum Range (meters)	6,850	12,700	12,000	12,000	16,200	27,000
Sustained Rate of Fire (rounds/min)	12	4	4	4	2	1
Gun Weight (pounds)	2,500	4,370	3,790	3,586	23,700	36,080
Typical Shell Weight (pounds)	13.6	22	34.5	34.5	98	110

German Field Artillery Guns

Towed Guns

Model	7.5cm le IG 18	10cm s K-18	10.5cm le FH 18	15cm s IG 33	15cm K-18	15cm s FH 18	17cmK-18 in MrsLaf	21cm Mrs 18
Caliber	75mm	100mm	105mm	150mm	150mm	150mm	170mm	201mm
Type	Infantry Gun	Gun	Howitzer	Infantry Gun	Gun	Howitzer	Gun	Heavy Howitzer
Year in Service	1927	1934	1935	1933	1938	1934	1941	1939
Maximum Range (meters)	3,375	19,075	10,675	4,700	24,825	13,250	29,600	16,700
Sustained Rate of Fire (rounds/min)	6	4	6	4	2	2	1	1
Gun Weight (pounds)	882	12,441	4,367	3,740	28,070	12,154	38,632	36,824
Typical Shell Weight (pounds)	13.2	33.4	32.7	83.8	94.8	95.2	138.5	249.2

Self-Propelled Guns

Model	Wespe	Hummel	Grille	Stug III Ausf G.	Stu Pz 43 Brumbär	Scuh 42 Ausf G.
Gun Caliber and Model	10.5cm le FH 18	15cm s FH 18	15cm s IG 33	7.5cm StuK 40	15cm StuH 43	10.5cm StuH 42
Type	SP Howitzer	SP Howitzer	SP Gun	Assault Gun	Assault Gun	Assault Gun
Chassis or Carrier	PzKpfw-II	PzKkfw-IV	PzKkfw-38(t)	PzKpfw-III	PzKpfw-IV	PzKpfw-III
Year Placed in Service	1942	1943	1943	1940	1943	1941
Crew Size	5	6	4	4	5	4

Italian Field Artillery Guns

Towed Guns

Model	Cannone da 75/32 Mo. 37	Obice da 75/18 Mo. 35	Cannone da 149/35	Cannone da 149/40 Mo. 35	Obice da 210/22 Mo. 35
Caliber	75mm	75mm	149mm	149mm	210mm
Type	Gun	Howitzer	Gun	Gun	Howitzer
Year in Service	1937	1935	1910	1935	1934
Maximum Range (meters)	12,500	9,400	9,700	22,000	16,000
Sustained Rate of Fire (rounds/min)	6	6	1	1	1/2
Gun Weight (pounds)	2,646	1,760	18,000	25,250	34,750
Typical Shell Weight (pounds)	13.9	13.9	101	112	224

Self-Propelled Guns

Model	Semoventi da 75	Semoventi da 90	Semoventi da 149
Gun Caliber and Model	75mm Howitzer 75/18 Mo. 35	90mm AA Gun 90/53 Ansaldo	149mm Gun 149/40 Mo. 35
Chassis or Carrier	M-13/40 Tank	M-15/42 Tank	M-15/42 Tank
Year Placed in Service	1942	1942	1942
Crew Size	4	4	4

German Rail-Mounted Guns

Model	24cm Th Br K (E) "Theodor Bruno"	28cm Kz Br K (E) "kurz Bruno"	28cm lg Br K (E) "Lange Bruno"	28cm K-5 (E) "Schlanke Bertha"	80cm K (E) "Gustav Gerät"
Caliber (mm)	240	280	280	280	800
Year in Service	1938	1938	1937	1940	1942
Gun Length (feet)	27.6	37.8	41.8	70.1	106.6
Gun Weight (tons)	92.5	127.0	121.1	214.6	1,328.9
Shell Weight (pounds)	327.4	529.2	626.2	563.4	10,584.0
Maximum Range (meters)	20,200	29,500	36,100	62,180	47,000
Number Built	6	8	3	28	1

Soviet Field Artillery Guns

Towed Guns

Model	M-1942 ZiS-3	M-1945 D-44	M-1944 BS-3	M-1931/37 A-19	M-1938 M-30	M-1938 M-10	M-1937 ML-20	M-1943 D-1	M-1931 B-4
Caliber	76.2mm	85mm	100mm	122mm	122mm	152mm	152mm	152mm	203mm
Type	Gun	Gun	Gun	Gun	Howitzer	Howitzer	Gun/Howitzer	Howitzer	Howitzer
Year in Service	1942	1944	1944	1938	1938	1938	1937	1943	1931
Maximum Range (meters)	13,290	16,650	20,700	20,610	11,800	12,390	17,230	12,400	18,025
Sustained Rate of Fire (rounds/min)	20	20	10	4	6	3	3	4	1/2
Gun Weight (pounds)	2,640	3,795	8,030	15,950	4,960	9,020	16,000	7,920	38,900
Typical Shell Weight (pounds)	13.7	20.9	34.3	55	48	88	96	88	220

Self-Propelled Guns

Model	SU-76	SU-85	SU-100	SU-122	ISU-122	ISU-152
Gun Caliber and Model	76.2mm M-1942 ZiS-3	85mm M-1939 AA Gun	100mm M-1944 BS-3	122mm M-1938 M-30	122mm M-1937 A-19	152mm M-1937 ML-20
Type	SP Gun	Assault Gun	Assault Gun	Assault Gun	Assault Gun	Assault Gun
Chassis or Carrier	T-70 Tank	T-34 Tank	T-34 Tank	T-34 Tank	IS-1 Tank	IS-2 Tank
Year Placed in Service	1942	1944	1944	1943	1944	1945
Crew Size	4	4	4	5	5	5

U.S. Field Artillery Guns

Towed Guns

Model	M-1A1	M-2A1	M-3	M-1918	M-1	M-1A1	M-2	M-1
Caliber	75mm	105mm	105mm	155mm	155mm	155mm	8-in	240-mm
Type	Pack Howitzer	Howitzer	Howitzer	Howitzer	Howitzer	Gun	Howitzer	Howitzer
Year in Service	1927	1940	1943	1918	1941	1938	1940	1943
Maximum Range (meters)	8,650	10,980	7,460	11,160	14,700	22,860	16,660	22,700
Sustained Rate of Fire (rounds/min)	10	8	6	2	2	1	1	1/2
Gun Weight (pounds)	1,339	4,980	2,495	8,184	11,966	30,600	31,700	41,300
Typical Shell Weight (pounds)	14	33	33	95	95	95	200	360

Self-Propelled Guns

Model	M-8	M-7	M-7B1	M-37	M-41	M-12	M-40
Gun Caliber and Model	75mm M-1A1	105mm M-2A1	105mm M-2A1	105mm M-2A1	155mm M-1	155mm M-1A1 Gun	155mm M-1A1 Gun
Chassis or Carrier	M-5 Tank	M-3A1 Tank	M-4A3 Tank	M-24 Tank	M-24 Tank	M-3A1 Tank	M-4A3 Tank
Year Placed in Service	1942	1941	1943	1945	1944	1941	1945
Crew Size	4	7	7	6	6	6	6

B

Battleships, British

Britain entered the war with twelve battleships, of which only four were "modern," and two others were being modernized. The remaining six units lacked the sensors, speed, antiaircraft armament, and armor distribution needed to survive the air-sea engagements in which they were expected to participate. As with many other navies of the period, war broke out before the Royal Navy's (RN) plans were complete. The five obsolescent Royal Sovereign-class units were to be scrapped by the mid-1940s as the new King George V-class units came into service. The even newer Lion-class had been planned as replacements for the battle cruisers.

The advent of war put these plans on hold and forced the RN to retain the older battleships even as the new units came on line. Ultimately, Great Britain suspended construction of all units that could not be completed during the war's probable duration. The only battleship laid down during the war, the HMS *Vanguard*, was an emergency program unit built as a replacement for units lost in 1941, and it was not completed until after the war ended. The lack of an opposing battlefleet, the cost of building these units, and the desperate need for convoy escorts and new merchant ship construction all mitigated against battleship construction.

The RN's battleships were a mixed lot. Wide variances in armament and speed and handling characteristics complicated their tactical employment. The King George V-class units had the same speed and handling characteristics as the battle cruisers, but used 14-inch guns instead of the 15-inch guns used by the battle cruisers. The Queen Elizabeth-class units used the same guns as the battle cruisers and could operate with either the battle cruisers or the King George V-class units. They could not, however, operate with the Royal Sovereigns, which were two to three knots too slow. The Nelsons had speed and handling characteristics that enabled them to operate with either the Queen Elizabeths or the Royal Sovereigns, but not both. The Nelsons were equipped with 16-inch guns. Levels of protection also varied, which

The battleship HMS King George V, *which was instrumental in sinking the* Bismarck *on 27 May 1941.* (IWM A 27010)

The battle cruiser HMS Hood, *shown here at Scapa Flow in 1940. The* Hood *was sunk by the* Bismarck *on 24 May 1941. Only three of her crew of 1,416 survived. (IWM A 111)*

complicated tactical employment even further. Antiaircraft protection was insufficient on all but the modernized units until late in the war. Despite these problems, however, no RN battleships were lost after 1941.

Although the war's outbreak caught the RN battleship force ill-equipped for modern warfare, this does not mean the RN's plans and leadership were faulty. The Washington Naval Treaties (*see* Conferences, Naval) had placed a ten-year moratorium on battleship construction, which had just ended when the RN began its modernization program. Also, the 1936 Washington Treaty limited new battleship construction to 35,000 tons standard displacement per unit, which placed a difficult burden on battleship designers. More significantly, the nature of the air threat was changing rapidly as newer and more capable aircraft entered service almost yearly. Building a battleship takes time and several years lay between developing the plans, initiating construction, and commissioning the ship into service. This process was exacerbated by the tight naval construction budgets imposed by successive British governments, justifiably concerned with reducing government expenditures during a time of economic depression.

It was in this atmosphere that the RN made its decision to upgrade its force primarily by new construction. Modernizing the oldest classes of battleships was expensive and offered little improvement in capability when compared to the slightly greater cost and more significant gains to be had from new construction. Nothing illustrates this better than the Italian problems with employing their modernized World War I battleships. In fact, most of the RN's battleship losses were suffered by units that had not been modernized. The destruction of the HMS *Prince of Wales* in the Pacific was a consequence of its employment in the face of overwhelming airpower, not a design fault.

Despite design deficiencies and poor armor distribution in its older units, RN battleships enjoyed a massive superiority over their opponents in the one area that counted most in World War II, that of radars. From 1941 on, RN units carried multiple radar suites, including fire control, air and surface search, as well as early warning radars. It was this equipment and Allied air supremacy at sea that most contributed to the RN's successes after 1941. It was an advantage no Axis power ever came close to matching.

Carl O. Schuster

(Refer to tables on pages 877–879)

Additional Reading

Friedman, Norman, *Naval Radar* (1981).

Lenton, H.T., *British Battleships and Aircraft Carriers* (1972).

Raven, Alan, and John Roberts, *British Battleships of World War II* (1976).

Battleships, French

The French Navy began to rebuild during the mid-to-late 1930s, primarily in response to German rearmament. The 1922 Washington Naval Treaty (*see* Conferences, Naval) limited France to 175,000 tons in capital ship (battleship/battle cruiser) displacement. This limitation remained throughout the naval treaty period and further defined French battleship design in 1936 to a standard displacement of 35,000 tons or less. The limit was raised to 45,000 tons in 1938 by a "working agreement" between France, Great Britain, and Italy. Unfortunately, the change came too late to affect French capital ships built before the war.

France inaugurated construction of new capital ships in 1931, with the Dunkerque-class battle cruisers. Although classified as battleships in French service, the two units of this class had the armor and speed of battle cruisers and lacked the side armor needed to stand up to the fire of a battleship in an extended engagement. They were the first European capital ships to employ a dual-purpose secondary battery, but the weapons suffered from unreliable loading mechanisms. Also, the antiaircraft armament was rather weak. The *Dunkerque* suffered heavily in its engagements against British forces at Mersel-Kébir (q.v.) in July 1940.

The four Richelieu-class units were the first true post–World War I battleships built by France. A relatively modern but overloaded design, these ships enjoyed good armor protection and a truly impressive primary and secondary surface-to-surface battery. Seahandling and deck wetness suffered as a result of the hull's overloading, but they were robust ships capable of absorbing heavy punishment. Unfortunately, France left the war before any of these ships could be completed. The *Richelieu* had just finished sea trials when the armistice was signed. She then withdrew to Dakar with only a small fraction of her ammunition on board. The second unit of that class, the *Jean Bart,* did not have half her engineering equipment or armament installed when she departed for Casablanca on 18 June 1940. These units never saw action against the Germans; the French colonies lacked the resources to complete the ships. Both

did see combat, however, against Allied forces. The *Richelieu* fought the Allies twice at Dakar (q.v.), while the *Jean Bart* briefly engaged the U.S. forces off Casablanca during the Allied landings on French Northwest Africa (q.v.).

France entered the war with seven modern capital ships in service and four more under construction. All enjoyed excellent underwater protection but lacked adequate antiaircraft defenses and electronic sensors—even though France had tested an early naval radar in 1937. A production-model radar was to be available for service by late 1940, but, as with so many other French developments, the armistice came before the program reached fruition. Nonetheless, Vichy France (q.v.) continued clandestine radar research and managed to install radar on four of its battleships by 1942. Nonetheless, air defense equipment remained deficient until after the war and would have led to catastrophic losses in the face of any determined air strikes.

Carl O. Schuster

(Refer to tables on pages 880–881)

Additional Reading

Couhat, Jean L., *French Warships of World War II* (1978).

Garzke, William H., *Allied Battleships of World War II* (1980).

Battleships, German

German battleship construction throughout the interwar era was influenced by international and domestic factors and can be roughly separated into three distinct periods. The Weimar Republic's (q.v.) first naval construction plan, the *Umbau* Plan, was determined by the terms of the Treaty of Versailles (q.v.). Despite Adolf Hitler's (q.v.) appointment as German chancellor in 1933, it remained in force until the signing of the Anglo-German Naval Agreement (q.v.) in June 1935. Once Germany's construction began to approach the limits of that agreement, Hitler secretly ordered his naval commanders to implement a new, vastly enlarged naval construction plan. This led to Plan Z (q.v.), for which the first ships were laid down in early 1939. The outbreak of World War II, however, effectively waylaid that program. The war also ensured that all future design projects never reached the building yards. Those units that were built included a remarkable combination of outdated and modern design features. Armor protection and speed were generally good and antiaircraft armament strong by European standards, however, the growing inferiority of German electronics placed them at an increasing disadvantage as the war went on.

The *Reichsmarine's Umbau* Plan was shaped by the strict stipulations of the Treaty of Versailles. This meant the German Navy could not begin to replace its obsolete predreadnoughts until 1926. That led to a protracted design and development program, which often verged on cancellation. After 1925, the need for a decision acted as a catalyst on the almost deadlocked design proposals. Although Germany announced its intention to embark on the construction of the first of six *Panzerschiffe* (armored ships) permitted by the Treaty of Versailles in 1926, the final design was not approved until 1927.

The designers' most difficult decisions concerned the vessels' roles and main armament. Essentially, the various design proposals alternated between the extremes of a coastal monitor and an oceangoing cruiser. *Panzerschiff A* was launched on 19 May 1931 as the *Deutschland,* and two sister ships, the *Admiral Scheer* and the larger *Admiral Graf Spee,* followed her on the stocks.

The most prominent feature of their design was the degree of weight-saving measures employed, such as welded hulls. Another example of this trend was the shallow depth of the stern aft of the second 280mm triple-gun turret. These ships tended to take on excessive amounts of water; but that was rectified in the first two ships during their 1939 and 1940 refits, respectively. They carried a useful antiaircraft armament for the period, with an adequate fire control system. Their diesel engines gave them a relatively high speed of 26 knots, and a substantial maximum range of more than 20,000 nautical miles. The *Reichsmarine* attempted to pass this feature off as an unexcepted benefit of the search for weight savings. In truth, diesels were chosen because they economized on space within the hull. The main weakness of these ships was that they were poorly protected, being especially vulnerable to long-range gunfire. The *Reichsmarine* quickly recognized that fact, and secretly increased the thickness and area of the armored belt on the third ship while she was still on the stocks, but to little avail.

The construction of the *Deutschland* created a furor in Germany and abroad. Within Germany, the Social Democratic Party railed against the construction of large warships during a time of economic crisis. In addition, the *Reichsmarine* was still under the shadow of the Lohmann affair (*see* Navy, German) which did little to encourage political support from more liberal German political factions. On the extreme right, the position of the National Socialist German Workers Party (q.v.) was more ambiguous. While it castigated the *Deutschland's* relative weakness vis-à-vis Washington-style battleships, it supported her construction as being a vital step forward for German rearmament.

Internationally, the former Allied powers were taken aback by her design. In essence, this new ship seriously undermined the uniformity of ship types painstakingly agreed to in the Washington Naval Agreement of 1922. It outgunned every cruiser, and could outrun nearly every capital ship in existence. The naval powers requested Germany to reconsider its plan to construct these ships. The *Reichsmarine* countered with a request to become a full and equal signatory to the Washington agreement, with the right to build 125,000 tons of battleships. Since that would have violated the military clauses of the Versailles Treaty, the former allies did not pursue the matter.

In an attempt to reduce the per-unit cost of their main armament, the *Reichsmarine* ordered enough guns and turrets to equip all six of the projected *Panzerschiffe*. Two developments however, forced the *Reichsmarine* to change its plan. The construction of the *Deutschland* resulted in the French refusal to extend the international moratorium on battleship building. In 1932, France laid down two battle cruisers as a counter to both the *Panzerschiffe* and Italy's heavy cruisers. A year later, Hitler's appointment as German chancellor had a major impact on Germany's rearmament programs.

Unlike his predecessors, Hitler felt no compunction about violating the restrictions of the Versailles Treaty. Consequently, the naval design staff began to formulate proposals that would ensure that the next generation of *Panzerschiffe* would exceed the limitations. These included both more and improved armor, much greater speed, and a larger main armament. Hitler was agreeable to most of the proposals, but he steadfastly refused any increase in main armament size, fearing it would overly provoke the Versailles powers. He was perfectly willing to do so in the future, however, when the political situation would permit it. Therefore, the next two ships were armed with the remaining six 280mm triple turrets that had been ordered. In anticipation of "future developments," the *Kriegsmarine* placed a development contract for 380mm guns and turrets.

Consequently, the contracts of the next two *Panzerschiffe* were canceled, and then recast along the new design lines. They were ordered in 1934, laid down in 1935, and completed as the battle

The "pocket battleship" Admiral Graf Spee. *(IWM HU 1029)*

cruisers *Scharnhorst* and *Gneisenau.* Interestingly, the newly established Nazi Labor Front diverted some of its members' funds to finance the ships' construction. The many additions and improvements made to these ships made it impossible for them to be passed off as 10,000-ton warships. Before this problem came to a head, Hitler managed to obtain a new naval agreement with Britain in 1935, which effectively legalized them. Overall, that agreement increased Germany's total battleship tonnage to 183,700 tons. In effect, Hitler had managed to obtain 50 percent more battleship tonnage than the *Reichsmarine* had dared to ask for in 1930.

According to the official tonnage figures for the three *Panzerschiffe* and the battle cruisers, Germany still had over 100,000 tons available for new construction. Theoretically, this figure allowed for the construction of three new battleships of 35,000 tons. Given the chaotic conditions of the already overextended building yards, however, only two ships were ordered immediately. Labeled as battleships "F" and "G," they emerged as the *Bismarck* and *Tirpitz.* Officially, they displaced 35,000 tons, and were to be armed with the new 380mm guns being developed by Krupp.

Although the elimination of the Versailles restrictions allowed Germany to construct bona fide battleships, all four of the post-*Panzerschiffe* battleships were seriously flawed by the consequences of the Versailles Treaty. First of all, Germany's naval designers had not designed a real battleship since 1918. In fact, they had to reach back into their archives and base their designs for these ships on World War I examples: the *Mackensen* for the *Scharnhorst,* and the *Baden* for the *Bismarck.* Considering that none of the ships of the former class had been completed, this was a major design

handicap. In regard to the *Bismarck,* at least two members of the Baden-class had seen limited active service. Furthermore, Germany had been deprived of the opportunity of testing the armor of its World War I dreadnoughts against modern shellfire. Consequently, the protection systems of all four of these ships were modeled on an obsolete pattern. Although they were well-armored, their side armor did not fully protect the vital communication areas along the upper sides of their hulls. In addition, their deck armor was divided between different decks, thus limiting its effectiveness against plunging shellfire. Underwater exploration of the wreck of the *Bismarck* has also suggested that their sterns were structurally deficient.

Despite these design flaws, however, many aspects of their design were well-conceived, though some are still quite controversial. These include the decision to equip the ships with a separate battery of secondary and heavy antiaircraft guns. Given that none of the Euroean naval powers of the period had developed an effective dual-purpose weapon, the German solution does not appear unusual. All four ships mounted a very powerful antiaircraft battery, and possessed very effective fire control systems. Like their *Panzerschiffe* predecessors, they were all modified with "Atlantic" bows during their construction or shortly after completion.

Through the Anglo-German Naval Agreement (q.v.), Germany essentially enjoyed the rights of a signatory to the Washington Naval Agreement. In 1938, a new protocol allowed the naval powers to build battleships up to a standard displacement of 45,000 tons. Although Germany probably had intended from the start not to respect the former 35,000-ton limit, that decision legalized the *Bismarck,* which displaced more than 40,000 tons.

By 1938, Hitler was beginning to realize that Germany would be confronted by Britain in another war. Consequently, he ordered his naval staff to develop a fleet construction plan that would allow the *Kriegsmarine* to fight Britain on a more even footing. The resultant Plan Z envisaged the construction of six additional battleships, and twelve vastly enlarged *Panzerschiffe*. While the designs of the former were developed quite smoothly, many problems were encountered in the development of the latter. In the end, the plans for their construction were delayed, and they were eventually replaced by three battle cruisers when Plan Z was revised in July 1939. The outbreak of World War II truncated Plan Z and the *Kriegsmarine* barely managed to complete the *Bismarck*. Although design studies for behemoth battleships were considered, none were realistically feasible under the circumstances.

Even before the outbreak of the war, *Kriegsmarine* strategy in any conflict called for the use of all of its ships in an attempt to sever Britain's extended oceanic lifelines. Commerce raiding operations by all three of the *Panzerschiffe* indicated that they were ideally suited for this type of operation. The result of the battle of the Platte River (q.v.), however, also highlighted their vulnerability to cruisers. After the *Deutschland*'s return from her first Atlantic cruise, she was renamed *Lützow,* because Hitler feared that her loss would present the Allies with a propaganda bonanza. Both of the surviving *Panzerschiffe* were reclassified as heavy cruisers in early 1940. At one point during the war the *Kriegsmarine* design staff considered plans for converting the *Lützow* and *Admiral Scheer* into aircraft carriers.

Both of the battle cruisers were also employed in commerce raiding, despite the fact that their maximum speed and endurance fell short of expectations. They were under specific orders to avoid combat with Allied heavy units. A disturbing trend in the tactical control of navy capital ships became apparent quite early in the war when the fleet commanders of two of the first sorties were sacked for exercising a large degree of tactical freedom. What is even more puzzling about this trend is that the commander of the second operation, Admiral Wilhelm Marschall (q.v.), sank a British aircraft carrier and two destroyers. There is a strong possibility that the commander of the *Bismarck* (q.v.) operation was unduly influenced by the fate of his predecessors, which may have contributed significantly to that ship's loss. After that defeat, the commanders of German surface ships were subjected to increasingly severe restrictions on their tactical freedom.

For a limited time, the *Tirpitz, Scharnhorst,* and the two surviving capital ships threatened the Allied convoy routes to Murmansk from their secluded bases in German-occupied Norway. The Allied ability to intercept and decipher the German command signals, and their marked superiority in radar, contributed to the German defeat in the battles of the Barents Sea (q.v.) and North Cape (q.v.). Germany's remaining big ships were confined to the Baltic Sea after the *Tirpitz* was sunk by the RAF in November 1944. The *Lützow* and the *Admiral Scheer* covered the retreat of the German Army from Poland in 1945. Ironically, they fired their last shells in a coastal defense role, one that the German Navy had always eschewed. Both ships were sunk by Allied aircraft just before the war ended.

Although all of these ships were well-designed, and proved capable of absorbing a tremendous amount of battle damage, all suffered from design flaws. Furthermore, they paid the price for the *Kriegsmarine*'s fatal neglect of radar. The *Kriegsmarine* also suffered from its constantly changing construction plans. It would have been better off had it managed to complete all the ships allowed under the Anglo-German Naval Treaty and then rearmed the *Scharnhorst* with 380mm guns. A consistent construction program would have led to a better balanced surface fleet, which probably would have both aided the U-boats and permitted the construction of a much larger submarine fleet before the war. Finally, the German Navy, like the political leadership it served, suffered from a critical degree of strategic shortsightedness. Even the best-built ships will be lost when they are ineffectively led and employed. Still, by their mere existance, these ships tied down as many as nine major Allied warships for every one of their own. In that respect, they made a significant contribution to Germany's strategy in the Battle of the Atlantic (q.v.).

Peter K.H. Mispelkamp

(Refer to table on page 882)

Additional Reading
Ballard, Robert D., *The Discovery of the Bismarck* (1990).

Blundel, W.D., *German Navy Warships, 1939–1945* (1972).

Lenton, H.T., *German Warships of the Second World War* (1975).

Taylor, J.C., *German Warships of World War II* (1967).

Whitley, M.J., *German Capital Ships of World War II* (1989).

Battleships, Italian

The Italian Navy had only two combat-ready battleships on 1 September 1939, with two more under construction and two being rebuilt. The situation had not changed when Italy entered the war on 10 June 1940. Much of this was due to Italy's lack of financial and natural resources. Benito Mussolini's (q.v.) foreign adventures and haphazard rearmament program had drained away much of Italy's monetary reserve. This forced the Italian Navy, which enjoyed a lower budgetary priority than the air force, to prioritize its construction plans. Destroyers, cruisers, and submarines came first because they were needed to patrol the sea lanes of Italy's new colonial empire. They had an added advantage of being cheaper to build and operate.

The 1922 Washington Naval Treaty (*see* Conferences, Naval) gave both Italy and France a total capital ship (battleship and battle cruiser) tonnage of 175,000 tons, but allowed them to build 70,000 tons of new battleships during the ten-year building moratorium. Lacking the money to build these ships, Italy chose to conduct extensive studies of new battleship designs. Those studies formed the basis of Italian battleship design and modifications for World War II. The resulting Littorio-class was a good design, comparable to other contemporary European battleships of the same period. Armor, firepower, and speed were all very good. The lack of a dual-purpose gun battery was normal for European designs of that era. (The French were the only exception). Vertical protection was also deficient but only German and U.S. battleships enjoyed better. This could not be said for the rebuilt Cavour- and Dullio-class units, which paid heavily for their inadequate protection. Like HMS *Hood,* they originally had been built for a different war. Unfortunately, all of Italy's battleships suffered from a lack of radar, night-fighting equipment, and unusually inaccurate main and secondary gun armament. It was these deficiencies and a lack of air cover that cost them so heavily in the war.

Italy came out of World War I with a force of twelve battleships, but only six were dreadnought class. A new class of Caracciolo units was under construction as the war ended. Italy's postwar economic situation and war in Libya forced some rigid naval economies. The six predreadnoughts and two of the dreadnoughts were scrapped, and the *Caracciolo* was canceled—even though its hull and main battery weapons were complete. The French decision in 1931 to build the Dunkerque-class induced the Italian Navy to respond.

Italy decided to save time by rebuilding the two Cavour-class units to modern specifications. They had their guns rebored, one turret removed to make room for additional propulsion machinery, "Pugliese cylinders" installed, additional armor added, and a stronger antiaircraft battery emplaced. The process required a 60 percent demolition of the ship and took four years to complete, but the result was a fairly successful program. The later decision to rebuild the two Duilio-class units was a mistake. They cost nearly as much as a new battleship and provided much less capability. Moreover, they were rebuilt during the same period as the Littorio-class and competed for the same resources.

In contrast to its cruiser design, the Italian Navy (*Regia Marina* or RM) recognized the need for good protection and took an innovative approach to its battleship designs. One excellent example was the "Pugliese cylinders," which consisted of cylinders placed between the armored bulkhead and the ship's hull. Subdivided into sixteen sections, the cylinders were hollow and absorbed the blast of torpedoes and mines striking the hull. Using less space than a torpedo bulkhead, the cylinders provided good protection at limited weight. Unfortunately, the cylinders placed in the rebuilt battleships were not large enough to be effective. Poor installation also reduced the cylinders' effectiveness, and those ships suffered accordingly.

Doctrinally, the RM did not anticipate night combat operations and left its units ill-equipped and untrained for night fighting, with disastrous results. Italian industry also produced poor quality powder and shells, which led to highly variable muzzle velocities that caused broad dispersion of fire at long and medium ranges. In effect, RM ships could not inflict heavy punishment on their opponents even when they could see them. Finally, the RM chose to modernize the Dullios rather than fund construction of an aircraft carrier, whose planes would have to come from the air force. Had RM doctrine and logistics support been of the same quality as its battleship designs, its reputation from World War II would have been much higher.

Carl O. Schuster

(Refer to table on page 883)

Additional Reading

Bagnasco, Erminilo, and Mark Grossman, *Regia Marina: Italian Battleships of WWII* (1986).

Fraccaroli, Aldo, *Italian Warships of World War II* (1978).

Garzke, William H., *Axis and Neutral Battleships of World War II* (1985).

Battleships, Soviet

Soviet Premier Josef Stalin (q.v.) included a massive fleet construction program in his plans for modernizing the Soviet military. Existing shipyards were expanded and new ones built as the Soviets conscripted huge levies of potential workers and forced them into industrial training programs. Foreign technicians and specialists were hired to man the shipyards and run the training programs until an indigenous shipyard industry could be developed. Stalin hoped to achieve a major balanced oceangoing fleet by the mid-1940s. Battleships were to form a major element of that fleet. The aging dreadnoughts left over from the tzar's fleet were to be modernized and two new classes of modern battleships and battle cruisers were to be built. Two factors prevented Stalin from achieving his goal: his purges (q.v.) of the late 1930s, which eliminated most of his senior naval and industrial leadership; and the German invasion of 1941, which forced the diversion of resources into the ground war.

The Soviet Union began the war with three tzarist-era battleships in service. Modernized with Italian assistance between 1928–1934, these aging behemoths were slow, equipped with obsolescent fire control systems, carried an inadequate antiaircraft suite, lacked modern electronic sensors (radar and sonar), and suffered heavily from mechanical defects. Their survivability in the face of German air supremacy was problematic, but they did have an impressive main battery that outranged anything the Germans possessed. All of this became irrelevant, however, as the Soviet Union's desperate situation on the ground forced the navy to turn over its best personnel to the army or form naval infantry brigades to participate in the ground war. That fact, the loss of repair facilities, and German air supremacy precluded the employment of these ships in anything but a static artillery support role.

The *Marat* was sunk in port at Kronstadt, and its sister ship, *Oktyabrskaya Revolutsia,* was damaged. Their artillery support, however, was critical to the Leningrad (q.v.) campaign. In the Black Sea, the *Parizhskaya Kommuna* was inhibited by both engineering defects and the *Luftwaffe.* It was withdrawn to Poti as the Germans closed in on its only major base at Sevastopol. Poti lacked the facilities and skilled labor to correct the ship's problems, so its crew was transferred into the naval infantry where they gave good service in the Caucasus and Crimea (qq.v.) campaigns.

The Soviets had one battleship under construction in Leningrad, two at Molotovsk, and two more at Nikolayev when the Germans invaded. They also had two battle cruisers under construction, one in Leningrad and one in Nikolayev. Lacking the industry to manufacture the ships' propulsion, weapons, and fire control systems, the Soviets had purchased that equipment from the Germans—but somehow it was never ready for delivery. The Soviets could not have completed the ships without German assistance and their construction was constantly delayed by material delivery and other technical problems. Thus, the ships were captured on the slips, but the Germans also lacked the materials to complete the hulls. The Soviets eventually scrapped them on the slips after the war. In many ways it was just as well, for none of the battleships were suitable for modern warfare and could not have been justified in the face of the Soviet Union's other more pressing political and economic requirements.

Stalin's plans for a fleet with battleships were ambitious and far exceeded the Soviet Union's capacity to build or support such a fleet without massive foreign assistance. Nonetheless, the facilities and cadre of trained specialists he built up before and during the war established the foundation for the Soviet shipbuilding industry that expanded so greatly and so quickly in the postwar period.

Carl O. Schuster

(Refer to table on page 884)

Additional Reading

Garzke, William H., *Allied Battleships of World War II* (1980).

Meister, Jurg, *Soviet Warships of the Second World War* (1977).

Battleships, U.S.

When Germany invaded Poland in September 1939, the United States possessed a battle fleet second only to that of Great Britain. By December 1941, the United States Navy had seventeen battleships in commission. During the war, eight more battleships were completed. Though the primary theater of operations for America's battleships was the Pacific, many served at least some part of the war supporting operations in Atlantic and European waters. American battleships bolstered the Royal Navy's Home Fleet when it was confronted with the threat of the German battleship *Tirpitz* and battle cruisers *Scharnhorst* and *Gneisenau,* and they provided gunfire support for American landings in Northwest Africa, the Mediterranean, and Normandy.

On the eve of America's entry into the war, U.S. battleships could be divided into two distinct types. The majority, fifteen, were older designs, commissioned between 1912 and 1923. The *Arkansas,* commissioned in 1912, was the oldest American battleship to see action in the war. Armed with twelve 12-inch guns, she was extensively rebuilt in 1925. This rebuild converted her to an oil burner, fitted anti-torpedo bulges, strengthened her deck armor, and added a seaplane catapult to one of her main gun turrets. In 1940, modifications to her main battery allowed an increase in gun elevation from 15 degrees to 30 degrees, and a corresponding increase in trajectory, and thus range.

The *New York* and *Texas,* both commissioned in 1914, were of the same class and mounted ten 14-inch guns in five turrets. They were originally to be powered by geared turbines, but design problems forced a return to reciprocating engines. From 1926 to 1927, both underwent rebuilds similar to that of the *Arkansas,* and their main gun elevations were increased in 1940.

Commissioned in 1916, the *Nevada* and *Oklahoma* incorporated the current theories of armor protection and propulsion. Both ships were designed with "all or nothing" protection. Armor protection was concentrated on the vital portions of the ship and the rest remaining relatively unprotected. The design also incorporated oil-burning engines and carried its ten 14-inch guns in four turrets, mounting six of its 14-inch guns in two triple-gun turrets. Modernized in the 1920s, both ships saw their secondary armament moved up one deck and the installation of two catapults, one on an aft turret and one on the fantail.

The two ships of the next class, the *Pennsylvania* and *Arizona,* were also commissioned in 1916. Similar in design to the previous class, their main battery was increased to twelve 14-inch guns by using four triple-gun turrets instead of just two. Rebuilds to both ships incorporated the raised secondary armament and catapult installation on an aft turret and the fantail.

The *New Mexico, Mississippi* and *Idaho* were commissioned between 1917 and 1919. All three ships incorporated clipper bows for better seakeeping in heavy seas. Their main armament remained at twelve 14-inch guns, but they were of an improved design. All three ships were modernized between 1930 and 1934. They were given geared turbine engines, their cage masts were replaced by tower superstructures, and catapults appeared on an aft turret and the fantail.

The *Tennessee* and *California* were commissioned in 1920 and 1921, respectively. Although the main armament was the same as the New Mexico class, they incorporated turbo-electric propulsion, eliminated all casements and recesses for secondary guns, and used two funnels instead of one. They were generally unmodified during the interwar years except for the addition of more antiaircraft guns and catapults.

The last of the older battleships in the U.S. fleet were the Colorados. Though four of this class were laid down, only three (the *Colorado, Maryland,* and *West Virginia)* were completed. Nearly identical to the Tennessees, they were commissioned between 1921 and 1923. The main difference between this and the previous class was the main armament, now eight 16-inch guns in four double turrets. Modifications during the interwar years included the addition of more antiaircraft guns and catapults.

Although modernized throughout their careers, these older battleships were the direct heirs of America's response to the British HMS *Dreadnought.* They were designed to anchor a battleline, which would destroy with gunfire any other battle fleet in the world. When the Japanese attacked Pearl Harbor the older battleships of the Pacific Fleet were their primary targets. Of these ships, the *Arizona* and *Oklahoma* were irreparably damaged in the Japanese attack. The *Nevada, California,* and *West Virginia* all required extensive reconstruction before rejoining the fleet. These reconstructions required up to two years to complete and literally transformed their appearance so as to make them unrecognizable when compared to their previous design. The *Tennessee* underwent a similar reconstruction in 1942 and emerged with an entirely new, more compact and heavily armored superstructure.

The New Mexicos, which were stationed in the Atlantic at the time of Pearl Harbor, changed relatively little from their final prewar configuration. All the older battleships received increasingly heavier antiaircraft armament as the war continued and various radar configurations were added.

Transferred back from Atlantic duty in 1942, the *New Mexico, Mississippi,* and *Idaho* joined the *Pennsylvania, Tennessee, Maryland,* and *Colorado* as protection against any Japanese attempt to attack the U.S. West Coast. With the arrival of carrier aviation as the primary offensive arm of the fleet, the older battleships formed the primary bombardment force for the amphibious landings in both the European and Central Pacific theaters. In October 1944, the *California, Maryland, Mississippi, Pennsylvania, Tennessee,* and *West Virginia* formed a classic battleline at the Surigao Strait and destroyed an attacking Japanese force.

B

The three oldest battleships, the *Arkansas, New York,* and *Texas,* spent virtually the entire war in the Atlantic where they helped escort convoys, provided gunfire support to the Northwest African (q.v.) landings, and served as gunnery training ships. Together with the *Nevada,* they supported the Normandy (q.v.) invasion and the amphibious assault into southern France (q.v.).

The second type of American battleships were those designed and built after World War I. Often referred to as fast battleships, they showed influences of interwar treaty efforts (tonnage limits affecting overall size), improved machinery, improved main armament, better secondary and antiaircraft armament, improved armor protection, and stern catapults for observation aircraft. The first two of these newer battleships, the *North Carolina* and *Washington,* joined the fleet just prior to Pearl Harbor. They mounted nine 16-inch guns and were designed to make a 28-knot top speed. They incorporated a tower foremast and a very concentrated superstructure that helped improve protection and gave their main turrets a wider arc of fire. These ships remained relatively unchanged throughout their careers except for the continued addition of antiaircraft guns.

The next four battleships, the *South Dakota, Indiana, Massachusetts,* and *Alabama,* mounted the same armament as the North Carolinas but were slightly shorter than the previous design. All were completed much more quickly than any other previous class of battleships and joined the fleet in 1942. Their main superstructure was even more compact, further increasing the firing arc of their main guns.

The final class of American battleships actually built were the Iowas. Freed from any treaty limitations, these 45,000-ton ships became the culmination of all that had been learned in American battleship design. The *Iowa, New Jersey, Missouri,* and *Wisconsin* sported longer hulls, more armor, more antiaircraft armament, and greater speed than any other American capital ship. With a 33-knot top speed, the Iowas were truly fast battleships, whose speed, armor protection, and armament made them ideal escorts for the fast carrier task forces operating in the late stages of the war.

The United States also built battle cruisers during the war but they were commissioned too late to see service. Designated CBs (cruiser, battleship), these were essentially super-large cruisers roughly equal to the German *Scharnhorst* and *Gneisenau* in capabilities. This class was named for territories, a designation between the cities reserved for cruisers, and states, used to name battleships. The *Alaska* and the *Guam* were the only units completed. They displaced 27,500 tons and carried nine 12-inch guns. With 3.25 inches of deck armor and 9.5 inches of belt armor, they were well protected, and had a design speed (33.4 knots) slightly higher than the Iowa-class battleships. They were decommissioned shortly after completion and scrapped in the late 1950s.

The fast battleships operated in all theaters of World War II. Because of the German surface threat, the *Washington, Alabama,* and *Iowa* all served some time with the British Home Fleet. The *Massachusetts* took part in the Northwest African invasion, even exchanging salvos with the incomplete French battleship *Jean Bart.* But most of the fast battleships served as escorts for the carrier task forces in the Pacific.

In World War II, U.S. battleships performed essential duties in missions far different from those envisioned by their designers. The older battleships were the essential bombardment punch in the Central Pacific and also supported landings in the European theater. The fast battleships performed escort duties for the new carrier task forces, their antiaircraft armament proving in many cases to be far more important than their main guns.

Budd Jones

(Refer to table on page 885)

Additional Reading
Friedman, Norman, *U.S. Battleships: An Illustrated Design History* (1985).
Muir, Malcom, *The Iowa Class Battleships: Iowa, New Jersey, Missouri, Wisconsin* (1987).
Terzibaschitsch, Stefan, *Battleships of the U.S. Navy in World War II* (1977).

Bazooka
See INFANTRY WEAPONS, U.S.

Bomber Aircraft, British
Britain's bomber forces entered World War II with a mixture of modern and obsolescent aircraft. Caught with its forces transitioning to more modern planes, the Royal Air Force's (RAF's) Bomber Command suffered heavy losses, particularly in France. Its bombers were too slow, too lightly built, inadequately armed, and carried insufficient bombloads to be effective in a modern air war. The RAF compensated by shifting its operational doctrine to night bombing. More significantly, it ac-

celerated design developments more attuned to modern requirements. As a result, the RAF finished the war with bombers ideally suited to the missions assigned. Few other air forces in World War II could make the same claim.

The RAF's bomber squadrons were equipped with five basic bomber variants in September 1939: the Battle, the Blenheim, the Hampden, the Wellington, and the Whitworth. The first two were light and light-to-medium bombers, normally assigned to tactical units for ground interdiction. They were deployed to France for that purpose. The other three were medium-to-heavy bombers, hence their use for daylight bombing against Germany. All five models suffered catastrophic losses during their early encounters with *Luftwaffe* fighters.

Early in the war, the RAF withdrew the

Battles and Blenheims from frontline bomber service. The Blenheim did enjoy a brief second career as a night fighter and antiship strike fighter. The Hampdens, Wellingtons, and Whitworths shifted to night bombing but their bombloads proved inadequate for that role and they finished out the war as transports. The Wellington served briefly as an airborne minesweeper using an installed magnetic coil to detonate German magnetic mines (*see* Mine Warfare, Naval).

The Beaufort medium bomber was the first new bomber introduced after the war's start. Entering squadron service in November 1939, it was intended as a dual-purpose torpedo and reconnaissance bomber for RAF Coastal Command. It was underpowered at first. After modifications that included installation of more powerful engines, Beauforts became the mainstay of Coastal

B

A Lancaster III in flight. (IWM CH 12345)

Mosquito Mk-XVI in flight, 1944. (IWM CH 14261)

Command's torpedo bomber forces. It proved very robust in that role, capable of absorbing heavy damage and still carrying its torpedoes to the target. The follow-on Botha torpedo bomber, which entered service shortly afterwards, was not as successful and was quickly withdrawn from combat duties.

The Stirling bomber became the RAF's first truly heavy bomber when it joined Bomber Command in August 1940. It was the mainstay of the Bomber Command night bombing force until the far more capable Lancaster and Halifax bombers entered service. Lacking the bombload and range of those later bombers, the Stirling served primarily in a transport role after 1942.

The RAF relied on the American A-20 Boston, Hudson, Ventura, and B-25 Mitchell for its medium bomber forces at various times in the war. Acquired through Lend-Lease (q.v.), these bombers had relatively high operational speeds, excellent range, good defensive armament, and an outstanding bombload for their size. The Hudsons were assigned to Coastal Command and used for maritime strike reconnaissance. The A-20s and B-25s were employed primarily for antishipping strikes in the Channel and for ground interdiction in North Africa (q.v.) and Italy. The Venturas served briefly with Bomber Command in 1942 but finished out the war as a short-range reconnaissance aircraft for Coastal Command.

The American B-17 and B-24 bombers also saw limited service in the RAF. The former was delivered to the British in 1942, but the early models lacked armament, self-sealing fuel tanks, and other features critical to survival in the European theater. The B-24, on the other hand, saw extensive service in some of Bomber Command's night bombing squadrons, where it was appreciated for its range, bombload, and heavy defensive armament.

The Manchester medium bomber first entered operational squadrons in November 1940, but it proved disappointing in service. Its engines were unreliable and its airframe lacked the structural integrity of the Wellington. It suffered heavily in combat, and its only claim to fame is that it formed the basis for the later and more successful Lancaster heavy bomber.

The Halifax and Lancaster heavy bombers both entered service in 1942. Essentially scaled-up medium bombers, they had the power and range to fulfill Bomber Command's stated mission of taking the war to Germany's cities and industrial centers. Intended as night bombers, they carried the heaviest bombloads of any bomber to see service in the

war. Defensive armament was light, but the internal avionics, navigational, and electronic equipment were the best available anywhere in the world. These were the first bombers to employ electronic countermeasures in combat, including "window" and deceptive jamming (*see* Electronic Warfare). Altogether, they were outstanding designs.

The most famous and impressive of the RAF's bombers in the war was the De Havilland Mosquito. This plywood twin-engine medium bomber epitomized the best of all qualities required by a wartime aircraft. It used few critical strategic materials in its construction and required little skilled labor in its manufacture. Yet, it was the fastest bomber in the European theater, and served equally well in the heavy fighter, night fighter, reconnaissance, maritime strike and ground-attack roles. It was the only bomber in the war that could actually outfly the interceptors sent against it. As a result, the Mosquito rarely flew with defensive armament. Only the later model German FW-190s and jet fighters could catch it. It undoubtedly was the most versatile aircraft design of the war.

The RAF's force structure agencies and aircraft industry served it well during the war. Its bomber designs kept pace with operational requirements, which themselves were modified to meet strategic realities. As a result, both Bomber and Coastal Command received the aircraft they required, although the latter never obtained the numbers needed before 1943.

Carl O. Schuster

(Refer to table on page 886)

Additional Reading:
Barker, Richard F., et al., *Combat Aircraft of World War II* (1977).
Bishop, Edward, *Mosquito: The Wooden Wonder* (1996).
Gurney, Gene, *The War in the Air* (1963).
Turner, John F., *British Aircraft of World War II* (1975).

Bomber Aircraft, German

Germany entered World War II with the most modern and powerful bomber force in the world. The *Luftwaffe's* deputy commander, Field Marshal Erhard Milch (q.v.), had plans to keep things that way, with faster, heavier, and higher-flying models in development. Fortunately for the Allies, the head of the *Luftwaffe,* Hermann Göring, appointed an old World War I crony, Ernst Udet

"Stuka" Ju-87 dive-bombers on their way to attack British tanks at Ghobi, 23 November 1941. (IWM MH 5591)

(qq.v.), to head the *Luftwaffe's* technical development department. Göring also undercut Milch's planning authority.

Udet proved an incompetent, technically ignorant manager. As an example, his requirement that all bombers be able to dive-bomb severely impeded development of new bomber types and virtually ensured Germany would not have a heavy bomber in service during World War II. By the time of Udet's suicide in 1942, Germany's aircraft development program was in such disarray that it took two years to sort out. Although Germany was

able to produce jet bombers before the war ended (*see* Jet Aircraft), they entered service too late to affect the outcome.

The *Luftwaffe* bomber force started World War II equipped with variants of three basic models, the Do-17, the He-111 and the Ju-87. The first of these already was approaching obsolescence, and was scheduled for replacement by the new Ju-88 entering service in 1939. The Do-17 proved disappointing in service; its range and payload were inadequate for effective employment. As the mainstay of the *Luftwaffe's* long-range reconnaissance squadrons, it suffered heavily in every campaign in which it was employed.

The He-111, on the other hand, proved robust and reliable, albeit too lightly armed for strategic bombing. Advances in aircraft design, however, made its obsolescence only a matter of time, yet it soldiered-on for the entire war, serving in antishipping and transport roles as well as for bombing. The He-111 even served as a V-1 launch platform for attacks against Britain in 1944.

The Ju-87 Stuka dive bomber, which had proved so effective in the war's early years, was approaching obsolescence. Its slow speed and light armament made it very vulnerable to enemy fighters. It could only operate in an environment of total German air supremacy. By 1944, Stuka operations were limited to the eastern front, and even there it was being rapidly replaced by FW-190F fighter-bombers.

The Ju-88, which entered production in 1939, was the *Luftwaffe's* most versatile bomber. Variants of this aircraft fulfilled night fighter, torpedo bomber, reconnaissance, and even heavy fighter roles. It also served as a missile carrier in the final months of the war. It was a sturdy, relatively well-armed design that saw minor qualitative improvements throughout the war. By 1942, however, its speed and defensive armament began to fall behind those of its opponents and it became increasingly vulnerable to enemy action. One aspect of its design that inhibited technical growth was the requirement that it conduct an 80-degree angle of dive. This ridiculous requirement led to excessive structural reinforcement and weight. The Ju-88's replacement, the Ju-188, which entered production in 1943, did away with that requirement, but the change came too late to fully replace the earlier model.

The Do-217 entered service in late 1940 as a follow-on to the Do-17. Its heavier armament, greater bombload, and longer range made it a better bomber, but like the Ju-88, it suffered a performance penalty imposed by the additional structural weight to enable a high-angle dive. The Do-217 served primarily in the long-range reconnaissance, night bomber, night fighter, and antishipping roles. It was the Do-217 that used the first guided bombs in an antishipping attack, sinking the Italian battleship *Roma* with the Fritz-X glide bomb on 9 September 1943.

The lack of long-range bomber aircraft in 1939 led the *Luftwaffe* to seek short-term improvisations for the maritime campaign. The FW-200 Kondor was a result. This modified airliner and long-range transport was first converted for its maritime role in early 1940. The first ten aircraft were transferred to Bordeaux for operational evaluation in August 1940. It proved a remarkably effective conversion. Despite their light bombload and weak airframe, the Kondors sank more than 100,000 tons of Allied shipping in the far Atlantic in 1941. They were greatly feared by merchant ships, and Kondor reconnaissance reporting and strike operations were a boon to Germany's Atlantic campaign. The Kondors proved too lightly armed to face Allied fighter opposition, however, suffering greatly whenever they encountered even single interceptors.

The Henschel aircraft company specialized in producing army support aircraft. Its Hs-126 biplane did well as a close support aircraft in Poland, and it served as a tactical reconnaissance aircraft in the French and early Russian campaigns. Henschel also developed the world's first specifically designed antitank aircraft, the Hs-129. Its development originated with a requirement drawn from the lessons of the Spanish civil war (q.v.). There the Germans discovered that bombing and conventional strafing attacks had little impact on tank units.

The *Luftwaffe* was asked to develop a cannon-armed, close support aircraft, however, the senior leadership's apathy toward that mission led to the project having a low priority. That attitude changed when Germany encountered massive Soviet tank formations in Russia. Using requisitioned French Gnome engines, the Hs-129 was suddenly rushed into service in time to make its debut during the disastrous Stalingrad (q.v.) campaign. Crippled by engine problems throughout its existence, the Hs-129 saw only limited production. Despite its extensive faults, however, it was the best antitank aircraft of the war. It is the forerunner of the American A-10 and other tank-busting aircraft of the modern era.

The only heavy bomber to enter *Luftwaffe* service was the He-177. As with so many of Germany's new bomber designs, its development and ultimate performance was severely impeded by Udet's requirement that it be able to dive-bomb. This led to the unfortunate decision to use coupled engines so the plane would have only two nacelles, thereby saving strain on the wings. The additional structural reinforcement also made for a heavily overloaded airframe. This dangerous combination had serious consequences.

Although the prototype first flew in November 1939, the He-177 was plagued by engine fires and heat-stress-related structural problems throughout its existence. Its development was delayed con-

Formation of He-111 bombers during the Battle of Britain. (IWM MH 6547)

A flight of Ju-88A4s. (IWM MH 6115)

tinuously. When finally forced into service in late 1942, it proved as dangerous to its crews as it was to the Allies. Developmental work continued even as production continued. Primarily employed for antishipping strikes in the Atlantic, the problems of the He-177 were not solved until 1944. By then, Germany's strategic situation was so perilous that no heavy bomber could have saved it.

The privately developed He-274, designed independently without *Luftwaffe* sponsorship, was a conventional four-engine bomber design that would have better suited Germany's needs. Initially flying only three months after the first He-177, the He-274 never entered service because introducing it would have disrupted the already chaotic bomber production program. With the cancellation of the He-274 program went any hopes of Germany acquiring an effective heavy bomber in World War II.

Once Germany's technical directorates recovered from Udet's disastrous mismanagement, they developed some truly revolutionary aircraft. The Arado 234 was the only jet bomber to see action in World War II, entering squadron service in November 1944. Employed primarily as a high-speed, high-altitude reconnaissance aircraft, the unarmed Arado 234 proved virtually invulnerable to Allied intercept. Its occasional bombing missions over Britain might have caused some concern had they involved more than single aircraft. As it was, the Arado 234 was introduced too late to have any significant impact on the war (*see* Jet Aircraft).

The *Luftwaffe* did have outstanding bombers in development during the war, but few reached fruition. Despite much myth-making and criticism to the contrary, the *Luftwaffe*'s faults were not in its doctrine but rather in its force development structure. Riven by internal rivalry and jealousy, and largely dominated by Göring's incompetent cronies, its technical departments neither coordinated their activities nor rationalized their requirements with unit needs in the field. All that changed after Udet's death in 1942, when all technical direction came back under Milch's management. By then, however, it was too late, and the *Luftwaffe*'s aircrews found themselves outnumbered and outgunned in the skies over Europe. Nonetheless, Germany's aviation industry made some remarkable achievements, despite it all.

Carl O. Schuster

(Refer to table on page 887)

Additional Reading:
Green, William, *War Planes of the Second World War,* Volumes 8–10 (1961–62).
———, *War Planes of the Third Reich* (1970).
Irving, David, *The Rise and Fall of the Luftwaffe* (1973).
Murray, Williamson, *Luftwaffe* (1985).

Bomber Aircraft, Italian

Like France, Italy entered the war with its bomber force approaching block obsolescence. In June 1940, its bombers were old, underarmed, and underpowered in comparison to the bombers of the remaining antagonists of the war. By the end of 1941, the Italian bomber fleet was dangerously obsolete, to the cost of its bomber crews. Although it had several modern bombers under development as it entered the war, Italy lacked the resources and industrial base to introduce them into service before leaving the war in 1943. Still,

Italy's bomber force achieved something the more highly regarded *Luftwaffe* could not, it produced an operationally effective four-engine bomber, the Piaggio 108. Its performance nearly equalled that of the American B-17F. It saw action only in limited numbers.

Italy was the only antagonist to employ three-engine bombers in World War II. The mainstays of the Italian bomber force in 1940, the Savoi Marchetti 79 and 81, were robust and stable bombing platforms. Equipped with an inadequate bombsight and carrying very little defensive armament, they proved a disappointment in the level bombing role. They excelled as torpedo bombers, but suffered heavily in the presence of Allied fighters. Newer twin-engine bombers entering service after 1940 offered little improvement in performance and never completely supplanted these triple-engine aircraft.

Italy's light bombers were disastrous failures. Poorly armed and unmaneuverable, they suffered heavily even in the face of light opposition. The worst was the Br.65, which carried only 800 pounds of bombs and could not sustain a high-angle dive. Thus, its bombing accuracy was no better than a level bomber's. It also proved vulnerable to even the lightest antiaircraft defenses. Nothing illustrates its failure more vividly than the fact that Italy began replacing them with German Ju-87 Stuka dive bombers after 1941, an entire year after the Stuka's vulnerability had been exposed over Britain.

Carl O. Schuster

(Refer to table on page 888)

Additional Reading:
Green, William, *Famous Bombers of the Second World War,* 2 vols. (1959–60).
Munson, Kenneth, *Bombers 1939–45* (1969).

Bomber Aircraft, Soviet

Soviet bombers of the 1930s were comparable to the best Western machines. The Tupolev Sb-2 was the first bomber in the world with an enclosed cockpit and retractable undercarriage to enter production. It was powered by two 830 hp M-100 inline engines, and could carry a bombload of 1,600 pounds. It first flew in 1934 and entered Soviet service in 1936. The plane's relatively high top speed of 245 mph at 13,000 feet enabled it to avoid German and Italian biplane fighters when it flew with the Republican Air Force during the Spanish civil war (q.v.). It was the main light bomber in service at the time of the German invasion of the Soviet Union, and many were destroyed by *Luftwaffe* fighters, especially when they flew without escorting fighters.

The primary long-range Soviet bomber during World War II was the twin-engine Ilyushin DB-3, which entered production in 1937. It had a maximum range of 2,280 miles with a maximum bombload of 3,300 pounds. Other long-range bombers were the twin-engine Yermolaev Yer-2, a military version of the high-performance Stal-7 transport, and the four-engine Petlyakov Pe-8.

The performance of the Pe-8 was roughly comparable to that of early models of the B-17 Flying Fortress, although the B-17, unlike the Pe-8, was designed from the outset as a high-altitude bomber. The defensive armament of the late model B-17s consisted of thirteen caliber .50 machine guns, compared to the Pe-8's two nose-mounted 7.62mm ShKAS machine guns, two 20mm ShVAK cannons (one in a dorsal turret, the other in a tail turret), and a rearward-firing 12.7mm Beresin machine gun in each inboard engine nacelle. No other World War II bomber had this latter feature.

The Soviets did not have a large strategic bomber force during World War II. Production priority went to fighters and ground-attack aircraft. Only about eighty Pe-8s and 320 Yer-2s were produced, compared to more than 12,700 B-17s. The DB-3s, Yer-2s, and Pe-8s were the first aircraft to bomb Berlin in August 1941. A Pe-8 was used to fly Soviet Foreign Minister Vyacheslav Molotov (q.v.) from the Soviet Union to London and Washington in 1942. His route included Nazi-occupied territory of the USSR.

The primary Soviet light bomber of World War II was the twin-engine Petlyakov Pe-2, with a relatively high top speed of 335 mph. When Royal Air Force (RAF) fighter units were sent to the Murmansk region in 1941, RAF pilots flying Hawker Hurricane fighters were hard-pressed to keep pace with the Pe-2s they were supposed to be escorting. The Pe-2 proved an adaptable design. In addition to its normal role as a horizontal fighter, it was successfully modified to perform as a fighter and a dive bomber. It was sometimes compared to the twin-engine De Havilland Mosquito bomber, which served the Royal Air Force so well.

The successor to the Pe-2 was the Tupolev Tu-2, which entered service in 1944. It was powered by two 1,850 hp Mikulin M-82FN radial engines, and had a range of 1,240 miles with a bombload of 6,600 pounds. Slower than the Pe-2, the Tu-2 continued in Soviet service, and in the air forces of the Soviet allies, well into the postwar years.

The most famous and numerous Soviet bomber of World War II was the Ilyushin Il-2 "Shturmovik" ground-attack aircraft, which replaced the unsuccessful Sukhoi Su-2. Large numbers of single-engine Su-2s were destroyed by the *Luftwaffe* in the first months after the German invasion. The Il-2 was powered by a 1,770 hp Mikulin AM-38F in-line engine, and had a maximum range of 475 miles with a bombload of 1,320 pounds. Alternately it could carry eight wing-mounted rockets. Two fixed forward-firing 23mm VYa cannons were mounted in the wings. The aircraft was largely invulnerable to small-caliber antiaircraft fire because its engine and cockpit were partly surrounded by armor that formed part of the aircraft's structure.

The IL-2M.3 attack bomber, called the "Flying Tank." (IWM RR 2221)

Early models of the Il-2 were vulnerable to fighter attack from above and behind. That defect was remedied by the addition of a gunner seated behind the pilot, with a rearward-firing heavy machine gun. Il-2s were extremely effective in low-level attacks against German tanks. Stalin once remarked that the Il-2 was as essential to the Soviet Army as bread. More than 36,000 Il-2s were produced. The only comparable aircraft to the Il-2 was the twin-engine Henschel Hs-129 antitank aircraft, which entered service with the *Luftwaffe* in 1943.

The only biplane bomber in Soviet service during World War II was the single-engine Polikarpov U-2, which also served as a transport and primary trainer. The U-2 was powered by a 100 hp M-11 radial engine, with a maximum speed of 92 mph. Its maximum range was 342 miles with a bombload of 330 pounds. The U-2 first flew in 1928, and more than 13,000 were produced prior to the war. In all, some 40,000 U-2s saw service. Women pilots of the Soviet Air Force flew U-2s on night bombing raids over the German front lines.

U.S. bombers supplied to the Soviet Air Force consisted of some 2,900 twin-engine Douglas A-20s, 862 twin-engine North American B-25s, and one four-engine Consolidated B-24 Liberator. The A-20s proved especially useful in Soviet service. No B-17s or four-engine B-29 Superfortresses were sent to the Soviets, but several B-29s were confiscated in 1944 after making forced landings in eastern Siberia in the course of bombing raids on Japan from bases in China and India. The Soviet version of the B-29, which entered production after World War II, was the Tupolev Tu-4.

Dennis A. Bartels

(Refer to table on page 889)

Additional Reading
Gunston, Bill, *Aircraft of the Soviet Union* (1983).
Nemeck, Vaclav, *The History of Soviet Aircraft from 1918* (1986).

Bomber Aircraft, U.S.

Following World War I, proponents of airpower stressed that the future of war would revolve around bombers. By bombing from the air, armies would spare the lives of soldiers and could shift the locus of battle, threatening enemy population centers or production facilities; cities, not trenches, would be the battlefields. Men like Hugh Trenchard of the Royal Air Force (RAF), Italian General Giulio Douhet, and American William "Billy" Mitchell (qq.v.) all believed that the extended siege warfare of World War I would be rendered obsolete by airpower. The bomber would deliver the decisive strike.

The best-known U.S. bombers of the war were the B-17 Flying Fortress, the B-24 Liberator, and, in the final stages of World War II, the B-29 Superfortress. Other bomber types, six in all, served during the war years, including the B-25 Mitchell and the B-26 Marauder. Nevertheless, the "big two," the B-17 and the B-24, were the heavy bombers that delivered thousands of tons of bombs on German industry and transportation systems, and German-occupied Europe (the B-29 was not active in the European campaign). The heavy bombers were aircraft of more than 250,000 pounds (including bombload) with greater ranges. The medium bombers, the B-25 and B-26, had less range and lower gross weight.

Before the arrival of the United States Army Air Force (USAAF) in Britain, the RAF employed an air strategy against the enemy called area bombing. Initial bombing missions began in July 1941, just prior to the Battle of Britain (q.v.). As early as 25–26 August, the RAF bombed Berlin at night, setting the RAF trend of night bombing that ensured civilians as well as military objectives would be the targets of RAF Bomber Command. That created a moral dilemma often criticized in Britain, and a trap American air leaders hoped to avoid.

By the time the USAAF joined the air war in July 1942, the RAF had held out against the *Luftwaffe* in the Battle of Britain, and had initiated its own series of bombing attacks, which, while not exclusively night bombings, included targets in Germany, German-held France, the coastal regions of Europe, and Axis shipping. In January 1942, the RAF conducted night raids on Hamburg and Bremen, as well as Cherbourg, Rotterdam, Le Harve, and Boulogne. The RAF strategy operated without mercy against German cities and industry by night, while continuing the practice of day bombing against targets in occupied France.

Night bombing missions were designed to ease the costly need for fighter support. While RAF Fighter Command could provide fighter support across the Channel to France, bombing targets in Germany required an altogether different strategy. RAF fighters lacked the fuel capacity to fly across Europe and return, a problem compounded by the fact that Germany occupied most of continental Europe. Night attacks lessened the possibility of *Luftwaffe* fighters disrupting RAF bombers. Thus Bomber Command worked feverishly to plan night attacks against Germany.

When the USAAF entered the war in mid-1942, RAF leaders tried to convince the Americans that night bombing alone was effective. This argument would eventually be solved at the Casablanca Conference in January, 1943 (*see* Conferences, Allied). USAAF General Ira C. Eaker (q.v.) felt confident that, with the British bombing by night and the Americans by day, "the devils" would get no rest. USAAF General Henry H. "Hap" Arnold (q.v.) concluded that this strategy, the Combined Bomber Offensive (*see* Strategic Bombing), would not violate U.S. principles against targeting civilians and would allow USAAF aircraft to perform within the limits for which they were designed.

The first of the devastating heavy USAAF bombers was the B-17. Designed by Boeing, the B-17 Flying Fortress was developed beginning in 1934 and entered service in 1939. It had four engines to carry bombloads at greater speeds and higher altitudes. The huge aircraft was a financial risk for the Seattle-based Boeing, but the result was the most advanced bomber in the world. Defects in armament were identified in early models supplied to the RAF. Boeing improved these problems by the time the B-17D first saw service in the Pacific. In August 1942, the Flying Fortress was introduced in the European campaign, becoming the primary USAAF heavy bomber until the advent of the B-24.

Capable of speeds up to 291 mph and a range of 3,400 miles, the B-17 could carry up to 10,496 pounds of bombs in a single load. The most significant factor in convincing the British that day bombing by the Americans could be effective was the B-17's accuracy. Experienced air observers commented that the B-17 could change the face of air warfare, and true to predictions, it had a lengthy run as the most dominant bomber of the European war. A total of 12,371 were produced by Boeing, which at one time was turning out sixteen a day at the Seattle plant. More than 8,600 were the B-17G, the last of the models built. The B-17 airframe was also used as air-sea rescue planes, transports, and radar aircraft.

The B-24 Liberator was the follow-on to the B-17 as the USAAF's primary heavy bomber. Initially, it was manufactured by the Consolidated Vultee Aircraft Corporation of San Diego after the army contracted for construction in early 1939. The first experimental model flew in December 1939, and it was put into production in the fall of 1940. Early orders came from American, British, and French sources, but the British assumed the French contracts after the fall of France. The first RAF models entered action in mid-1941, with the USAAF receiving B-24s in late 1941.

Like all other aircraft used during World War II, the B-24 was continuously refined. An armament problem centered on a blind spot was solved on the B-24D model delivered in 1943. Again, experience in the air war over Europe was a factor in aircraft design. Later models were manufactured by Douglas Aircraft Company, the Ford Motor Company, and North American Aviation. More Liberators were produced (19,203—all models) than any other aircraft in history.

The B-24 normally carried a ten-man crew, had a maximum speed of 300 mph, a ceiling of 28,000 feet, and a maximum bombload of 8,800 pounds. Armament included ten caliber .50 machine guns in four turrets. The wing design by David Davis combined for remarkable range at a high altitude. The B-24D had a range of 2,850 miles. Although many aviation experts thought the B-24 was not a marked improvement on the B-17, the "Lib's" great range was designed for bombing Germany and German-held territories. Often described as prodigious, the B-24 lived up to its name. Later models were also used as transports.

The B-25 was a medium-range bomber built by North American Aircraft. Named after controversial airpower advocate Brigadier General William L. "Billy" Mitchell, the B-25 first flew in August 1940. The aircraft carried a normal bomb load of 3,000 pounds. Early models were armed with four caliber .30 machine guns and a one caliber .50 machine gun located in the tail. Capable of a top speed of 275 mph and a range of 2,700 miles, the B-25 could climb to 23,800 feet and carried a crew of four to six men. First active in the Pacific, Mitchells from the USS *Hornet* were used on the Doolittle raid against Tokyo in April 1942. B-25s underwent continuous revision during the war; the final model was the J version. When the last B-25 was delivered in August 1945, a total of 9,816 (all models) were produced.

The B-25 was primarily active in the Pacific, but some did see service in Europe. Almost 1,000 were supplied to the Soviets and nearly 600 were transferred to the RAF. When North American Aviation designed and began production of the B-25, the corporation had no experience with this type of aircraft, but the Mitchell was produced in larger numbers than any other twin-engine combat aircraft. It was often described as the best airplane of its class in World War II. The original design was the work of Lee Atwood and Ray Rice. The USAAF ordered 184 B-25s just from the drawing board design.

The B-26 Marauder was a medium range bomber built by the Glenn M. Martin Company

A formation of B-24Gs from the Fifteenth Air Force passes over the Alps on the way to bomb targets in Germany, December 1944. (IWM TA 11321)

A B-17G of the 427th Bombardment Squadron passes through smoke from an exploded B-17 as a German FW-190 (extreme upper left) turns away during the raid on Oscherleben, 11 January 1944. (IWM EA 15850)

of Omaha. The first Marauder flew in November 1940, and Martin began serious production in early 1941. It first saw action in the Pacific in April 1942. The plane carried a five- to seven-man crew with a normal bombload of 5,200 pounds, as well as six caliber .50 machine guns. Capable of speeds of 317 mph, a range of 1,150 miles, and a ceiling of 23,500 feet, it was the primary medium bomber of the U.S. Ninth Air Force in southern Europe. Production continued into early 1945 with a total of 5,157 (all models) B-26s delivered to the USAAF and the RAF, as well as the U.S. Navy.

The Marauder had a lower rate of loss than any USAAF bomber—less than 1 percent— despite its early reputation as the "widow-maker." The B-26 won a 1939 design competition for Martin, but several problems arose when the aircraft were handled by inexperienced pilots. It was designed by the noted engineer Peyton M. Magruder, who was instrumental in the addition of a larger wing to compensate for heavier armament. Several B-26A models went to the RAF under Lend-Lease (q.v.). The B-26B first operated in Europe in May 1943, and was a mainstay of U.S. medium bombers.

The A-20 and A-26 were two additional aircraft deployed by the USAAF in Europe for bombing purposes. Both were Douglas Aircraft products. The A-20, named Havoc (Boston by the RAF), was a light fighter-bomber with twin engines refined from earlier Bostons used by the RAF. The aircraft was capable of speeds up to 350 mph and a ceiling of 28,600 feet. A three-man crew operated the Havoc, which had a bombload of 2,600 pounds and carried up to six guns (either four 20mm cannon and two caliber .50 machine guns, or six caliber .50 machine guns).

The A-26 Invader was a larger version of the A-20. The Invader first saw action with the Ninth Air Force in Europe in November 1944. An attack bomber, the A-26 was a twin-engine aircraft capable of speeds of 355 mph, a ceiling of 31,300 feet, and a range of 1,800 miles. The A-26 carried a bombload of 4,000 pounds and was armed with up to ten caliber .50 machine guns. More than 2,500 A-26s were delivered by Douglas before the end of the war. In 1948, the A-26 was redesignated the B-26, after the Martin Marauder was retired. The renamed A-26 saw extensive service in Korea and the early part of the Vietnam War.

Of the many turning points of World War II, none was more significant to Allied airpower than the introduction of long-range fighter aircraft as escorts for RAF and USAAF bombing missions into Germany. The North American Aircraft P-51

Mustang was not only a fighter superior to most the *Luftwaffe* could put into combat, the fighter was capable of escorting USAAF bombers all the way to their targets and back. The P-51 enabled the USAAF to continue daylight bombing.

Nowhere was fighter protection for bombers more vital than the U.S. bombing raids on 17 August 1943. On that day, 146 B-17s left Britain for an attack on the Messerschmitt works at Regensburg (q.v.). Within a few hours, another 230 B-17s left for an assault on the ball bearing factories at Schweinfurt (q.v.). Both were important targets, and both attack forces represented considerable numbers of aircraft, but neither had adequate fighter coverage.

The fighters accompanying the Regensburg force had to return to base early in order to support the later Schweinfurt mission. The results were devastating for the U.S. Eighth Air Force. Neither target was destroyed, but the Regensburg force lost twenty-four B-17s, while thirty-six did not return from Schweinfurt. Nearly thirty of the remaining aircraft were too severely damaged to return to action. More than 500 crewmen were killed or captured and Eighth Air Force morale took weeks to recover. The heavy losses drew attention to the need for fighter coverage and caused the USAAF leadership doubts about daylight bombing strategy.

USAAF bombing began in July 1942, and missions continued unabated until the end of the war. In September 1942, USAAF bombers dropped 188 tons of bombs on German targets. In January 1943, they began targeting sites inside Germany. In December 1943, they hit German targets with 12,000 tons of bombs. In April 1943 that figure exceeded 43,000 tons. Another 63,000 tons of bombs were dropped in May. Finally, in May 1945, they delivered 74,000 tons of bombs. Combined with RAF night attacks, USAAF heavy and medium bombers operating by day made a significant contribution to the defeat of the Axis powers.

Boyd Childress

(Refer to table on page 890)

Additional Reading

Jablonski, Edward, *Flying Fortress* (1965).

McFarland, Stephen L., *America's Pursuit of Precision Bombing* (1995).

Schaffer, Ronald, *Wings of Judgment: American Bombing in World War II* (1985).

Wilson, Stewart, *Boeing B-17, B-29, and Lancaster: The Story of the Three Classic Bombers of World War II* (1996).

B

Section IV-B
Technical Data Tables of
Weapons and Equipment

British Battleships

	Barham	Malaya	Queen Elizabeth	Valiant	Warspite	Royal Oak	Royal Sovereign	Resolution	Revenge
Commissioned (year)	1915	1915	1914	1915	1914	1915	1915	1915	1916
Displacement (tons)	31,100	31,465	31,585	31,585	30,600	29,150	29,150	29,150	29,150
Max. Speed (knots)	24	24	24	24	25	22	22	22	22
Endurance (nm) at Best Speed	4,400 nm at 10 kts	4,400 nm at 10 kts	13,500 nm at 10 kts	13,500 nm at 10 kts	12,000 nm at 10 kts	4,200 nm at 10 kts	4,200 nm at 10 kts	4,200 nm at 10 kts	4,200 nm at 10 kts
Main Armament (guns)	8x 15-in	8x 15-in	8x 15-in	8x 15-in	8x 15-in	8x 15-in	8x 15-in	8x 15-in	8x 15-in
Secondary Armament (guns)	12x 6-in Note 1	12x 6-in	20x 4.5-in DP*	20x 4.5-in DP*	8x 6-in	12x 6-in	12x 6-in	12x 6-in	12x 6-in Note 1
Initial AA Battery	8x 4-in 16x 2-pdr 16x .50 MG	8x 4-in 16x 2-pdr 16x .50 MG	32x 2-pdr 16x .50 MG	32x 2-pdr 16x .50 MG	8x 4-in 32x 2-pdr 16x .50 MG	8x 4-in 16x 2-pdr	8x 4-in 16x 2-pdr	8x 4-in 16x 2-pdr	8x 4-in 16x 2-pdr
Max. Armor (inches)	13	13	13	13	13	13	13	13	13
Radar	Yes, 1940	Yes, 1940	Yes, 1940	Yes, 1940	Yes, 1940	No	Yes, 1941	Yes, 1940	Yes, 1940
Sonar	No	No	No	No	No	No	No	No	No
Hydrophones	No	No	Yes	Yes	Yes	No	No	No	No
Crew Size	1,300	1,300	1,300	1,300	1,300	1,300	1,300	1,300	1,300
Fate	U-331 sank 25 Nov 1941	Scrapped Postwar	Scrapped Postwar	Scrapped Postwar	Foundered Postwar	U-47 sank 14 Oct 1939	Note 2	Scrapped Postwar	Scrapped Postwar

(continued on next page)

British Battleships *(continued)*

	Ramillies	Nelson	Rodney	Prince of Wales	King George V	Duke of York	Anson	Howe
Commissioned (year)	1917	1927	1927	1941	1941	1942	1942	1942
Displacement (tons)	29,150	33,950	33,950	35,000	36,380	36,380	36,380	36,380
Max. Speed (knots)	22	23	23	29	29	29	29	29
Endurance (nm) at Best Speed	4,400 nm at 10 kts	16,500 nm at 12 kts	16,500 nm at 12 kts	15,000 nm at 10 kts	15,000 nm at 10 kts	15,000 nm at 10 kts	15,000 nm at 10 kts	15,000 nm at 10 kts
Main Armament (guns)	8x 15-in	9x 16-in	9x 16-in	10x 14-in	10x 14-in	10x 14-in	10x 14-in	10x 14-in
Secondary Armament (guns)	12x 6-in	12x 6-in	12x 6-in	16x 5.25-in DP*	16x 5.25-in DP*	16x 5.25-in DP*	16x 5.25-in DP*	16x 5.25-in DP*
Initial AA Battery	8x 4-in / 16x 2-pdr	6x 4.7-in / 32x 2-pdr / 16x. 50 MG	6x 4.7-in / 32x 2-pdr / 16x. 50 MG	32x 2-pdr / 16x. 50 MG	32x 2-pdr / 16x. 50 MG	32x 2-pdr / 16x. 50 MG	32x 2-pdr / 16x. 50 MG	32x 2-pdr / 16x. 50 MG
Max. Armor (inches)	13	14	14	15	15	15	15	15
Radar	Yes, 1940	Yes, 1940	Yes, 1941	Yes	Yes	Yes	Yes	Yes
Sonar	No	No	No	No	No	No	No	No
Hydrophones	No	No	No	No	No	No	No	No
Crew Size	1,146	1,361	1,361	1,612	1,612	1,612	1,612	1,612
Fate	Scrapped Postwar	Scrapped Postwar	Scrapped Postwar	Note 3	Scrapped Postwar	Scrapped Postwar	Scrapped Postwar	Scrapped Postwar

*DP: dual purpose

Notes:
1. Also equipped with 2x 21-in torpedo tubes.
2. Transferred to the Soviet navy under Lend-Lease in 1944. Returned to the Royal Navy in 1949 and later scrapped. In Soviet service the *Royal Sovereign* was called the *Arkhangelsk*.
3. Sunk in the Pacific on 10 December 1941.

British Battle Cruisers

	Hood	Repulse	Renown
Commissioned (year)	1920	1917	1917
Displacement (tons)	42,100	32,000	31,988
Max. Speed (kts)	31	28.5	29
Endurance (nm) at Best Speed	6,300 nm at 12 kts	3,600 nm at 16 kts	4,289 nm at 16 kts
Main Armament (guns)	8x 15-in	6x 15-in	6x 15-in
Secondary Armament (guns)	12x 5.5-in Note 1	9x 4-in Note 2	20x 4.5-in DP* Note 2
Initial AA Battery	8x 4-in 24x 2-pdr 20x .50 MG	6x 4-in 24x 2-pdr 8x .50 MG	24x 2-pdr 16x .50 MG
Max. Armor (inch)	12	9	9
Radar	Yes, 1941	Yes, 1940	Yes, 1940
Sonar	No	No	No
Hydrophones	No	No	No
Crew Size	1,420	1,304	1,260
Fate	Note 3	Note 4	Scrapped Postwar

*DP: dual-purpose

Notes:
1. Also equipped with 4x 21-in torpedo tubes.
2. Also equipped with 8x 18-in torpedo tubes.
3. Sunk by the *Bismarck* in the North Atlantic on 24 May 1941.
4. Sunk by the Japanese in the Pacific on 10 December 1941 in an aerial attack.

French Battleships

	Courbet	Paris	Bretagne	Provence	Lorraine	Richelieu	Jean Bart
Commissioned (year)	1913 Note 1	1913 Note 1	1914 Note 2	1914 Note 2	1914 Note 2	1941	1940
Displacement (tons)	22,189	22,189	22,189	22,189	22,189	35,000	42,806
Max. Speed (knots)	20	20	21	21	21	30	32
Endurance (nm) at Best Speed	4,200 nm at 10 kts	4,200 nm at 10 kts	3,500 nm at 10 kts	3,500 nm at 10 kts	3,500 nm at 10 kts	5,500 nm at 18 kts	5,850 nm at 18 kts
Main Armament (guns)	12x 305mm	12x 305mm	10x 340mm	10x 340mm	8x 340mm	8x 380mm	8x 380mm
Secondary Armament (guns)	22x 139mm Note 3	22x 139mm Note 3	14x 139mm	14x 139mm	14x 139mm	9x 152mm DP*	9x 152mm DP*
Initial AA Battery	7x 75mm 2x 47mm	7x 75mm 2x 47mm	8x 75mm 12x 13.2mm	8x 75mm 12x 13.2mm	8x 90mm 12x 13.2mm	12x 90mm 16x 37mm 8x 13.2mm	24x 90mm 28x 57mm 20x 20mm
Max. Armor (mm)	320	320	400	400	400	430	430
Radar	No	No	No	No	No	No	No
Sonar	No	No	No	No	No	No	No
Hydrophones	No	No	No	No	No	No	No
Crew Size	1,068	1,068	1,133	1,133	1,133	1,550	2,134
Fate	Expended as breakwater 9 June 1944	Scrapped Postwar	Sunk by Royal Navy 3 July 1940	Scuttled Toulon 27 Nov. 1942	Scrapped Postwar	Scrapped Postwar	Scrapped Postwar

*DP: dual-purpose
Notes:
1. Refitted 1929.
2. Refitted 1935.
3. Also equipped with 4x 45.6cm torpedo tubes.

French Battle Cruisers and Other Dreadnoughts

	Dunkerque	Strasbourg	Condorcet
Commissioned (year)	1934 Note 1	1938 Note 1	1911 Note 2
Displacement (tons)	26,500	26,500	17,597
Max. Speed (knots)	29.5	29.5	19
Endurance (nm) at Best Speed	7,500 nm at 15 kts	7,500 nm at 15 kts	2,000 nm at 19 kts
Main Armament (guns)	8 x 330mm	8 x 330mm	4 x 305mm
Secondary Armament (guns)	16 x 130mm DP*	16 x 130mm DP*	16 x 75 mm 12 x 240mm
Initial AA Battery	8 x 37mm 32 x 13.2mm	8 x 37mm 32 x 13.2mm	None
Max. Armor (mm)	335	335	320
Radar	No	No	No
Sonar	No	No	No
Hydrophones	No	No	No
Crew Size	1,381	1,381	700-plus
Fate	Note 3	Note 3	Note 4

*DP: dual-purpose
Notes:
1. Commissioned as a battle cruiser.
2. Classified as a predreadnought.
3. The *Dunkerque* and *Strasbourg* were scuttled at Toulon, France, in 1942 to prevent them from falling into German hands.
4. Used as a training ship. Scrapped postwar.

German Battleships and Battle Cruisers

	Bismarck	Tripitz	Gneisenau	Scharnhorst	Deutschland (Lützow)	Admiral Graf Spee	Admiral Scheer	Schliessen	Schleswig-Holstein
Commissioned (year)	1940 Note 1	1941 Note 1	1938 Note 2	1938 Note 2	1932 Note 3	1936 Note 3	1935 Note 3	1908 Note 4	1908 Note 4
Displacement (tons)	41,700	42,900	31,800	31,800	11,700	12,100	12,100	12,100	12,100
Max. Speed (knots)	29	29	32	32	26	26	26	18	18
Endurance (nm) at Best Speed	8,100 nm at 19 kts	9,000 nm at 19 kts	10,000 nm at 19 kts	10,000 nm at 19 kts	10,000 nm at 19 kts	9,000 nm at 19 kts	9,000 nm at 19 kts	5,900 nm at 10 kts	5,900 nm at 10 kts
Main Armament (guns)	8x 380mm	8x 380mm	9x 280mm	9x 280mm	6x 280mm	6x 280mm	6x 280mm	4x 280mm	4x 280mm
Secondary Armament (guns)	12x 150mm	8x torp. 12x 150mm	6x torp. 12x 150mm	6x torp. 12x 150mm	8x torp. 8x 150mm	8x torp. 8x 150mm	8x torp. 8x 150mm	10x 150mm	10x 150mm
Initial AA Battery	16x 105mm 16x 3mm 36x 20mm	16x 105mm 16x 37mm 70x 20mm	16x 105mm 16x 37mm	16x 105mm 16x 37mm	6x 105mm 8x 37mm 10x 20mm	6x 105mm 8x 37mm 10x 20mm	6x 105mm 8x 37mm 10x 20mm	4x 88mm 4x 20mm	4x 88mm 4x 20mm
Max. Armor (mm)	350	350	350	350	140	140	140	300	300
Radar	Yes	Yes	Yes	Yes	Yes	Yes	Yes	No	No
Sonar	Yes	Yes	Yes	Yes	No	No	No	No	No
Hydrophones	Yes	Yes	Yes	Yes	Yes	Yes	Yes	No	No
Crew Size	2,200	2,530	1,800	1,800	1,150	1,150	1,150	725	725
Fate	Sunk by British 27 May 1941	RAF bombed capsized 12 Nov 1944	Scuttled Gdynia 28 Mar 1945	Sunk by British 26 Dec 1943	Scuttled 4 May 1945	Scuttled 13 Dec 1939	Destroyed by bombing 9 Apr 1945	Scuttled 4 May 1945	Scuttled 21 Mar 1945

Notes:
1. Battleship.
2. Battle cruiser.
3. Pocket battleship.
4. Obsolete predreadnought (used for training).

Italian Battleships

	Conti di Cavour	Giulio Cesare	Doria	Caio Duilio	Littorio (Italia)	Vittorio Veneto	Roma
Commissioned (year)	1915 Note 1	1914 Note 1	1916 Note 2	1915 Note 2	1940	1940	1942
Displacement (tons)	26,140	26,140	25,924	26,434	41,377	41,167	41,650
Max. Speed (knots)	28	28	27	27	31	31	30
Endurance (nm) at Best Speed	5,000 nm at 10 kts	5,000 nm at 10 kts	5,000 nm at 10 kts	5,000 nm at 10 kts	4,700 nm at 14 kts	4,700 nm at 14 kts	4,700 nm at 14 kts
Main Armament (guns)	10x 320mm	10x 320mm	10x 320mm	10x 320mm	9x 380mm	9x 380mm	9x 380mm
Secondary Armament (guns)	12x 119mm	12x 119mm	12x 135mm	12x 135mm	12x 152mm	12x 152mm	12x 152mm
Initial AA Battery	8x 100mm 8x 37mm 12x 20mm	8x 100mm 8x 37mm 12x 20mm	10x 90mm 19x 37mm 12x 20mm	10x 90mm 19x 37mm 12x 20mm	12x 90mm 20x 37mm 32x 20mm	12x 90mm 20x 37mm 28x 20mm	12x 90mm 20x 37mm 32x 20mm
Max. Armor (mm)	280	280	280	280	350	350	350
Radar	No	No	No	No	No	No	No
Sonar	No	No	No	No	No	No	No
Hydrophones	No	No	No	No	No	No	No
Crew Size	1,236	1,236	1,485	1,485	1,830	1,830	1,930
Fate	Note 3	Transferred to USSR 1944	Scrapped Postwar	Scrapped Postwar	Scrapped Postwar	Scrapped Postwar	Sunk by Germans 9 Sept 1943

Notes:
1. Refitted in 1937.
2. Refitted in 1940.
3. Sunk by Royal Navy aircraft on 12 November 1940. Salvaged and sunk again 15 February 1945.

Soviet Battleships
(*See* Note 1)

	Parizhskaya Kommuna (ex-Sevastopol)	Marat	Oktyabrskaya Revolutsia (ex-Gangut)
Commissioned (year)	1911	1911	1911
Displacement (tons)	25,464	25,000	25,464
Max. Speed (knots)	23	23	23
Endurance (nm) at Best Speed	1,290 nm at 14 kts	1,120 nm at 14 kts	1,290 nm at 14 kts
Main Armament (guns)	12x 305mm	12x 305mm	12x 305mm
Secondary Armament (guns)	16x 120mm	16x 120mm	16x 120mm
Initial AA Battery	6x 76mm 16x 13.2mm	6x 76mm 32x 13.2mm	6x 76mm 32x 13.2mm
Max. Armor (mm)	254	254	254
Radar	No	No	No
Sonar	No	No	No
Hydrophones	No	No	No
Crew Size	1,400	1,286	1,277
Fate	Scrapped Postwar	Note 2	Note 3

Notes:
1. Employed mostly as floating batteries. All ships had 4x 45.0cm torpedo tubes.
2. Sunk by German aircraft on 23 September 1941.
3. Damaged by German aircraft on 4 April 1942; scrapped in 1956.

U.S. Battleships (European Theater)

	Arkansas	New York	Texas	Nevada	Massachusetts
Commissioned (year)	1912	1914	1914	1916	1942
Displacement (tons)	26,100	27,000	27,000	29,000	38,000
Max. Speed (knots)	20.5	21	21	21	28
Endurance (nm) at Best Speed	8,000 nm at 10 kts	10,000 nm at 10 kts	10,000 nm at 10 kts	10,000 nm at 10 kts	10,000 nm at 12 kts
Main Armament (guns)	12x 12-in	10x 14-in	10x 14-in	10x 14-in	9x 16-in
Secondary Armament (guns)	16x 5-in	16x 5-in	16x 5-in	12x 5-in	20x 5-in DP*
Initial AA Battery	8x 3-in 8x .50 MG	8x 3-in 8x .50 MG	8x 3-in 8x .50 MG	8x 5-in 8x .50 MG	56x 40mm 40x 20mm
Max. Armor (inches)	12	12	12	16	17.4
Radar	Yes	Yes	Yes	Yes	Yes
Sonar	No	No	No	No	No
Hydrophones	No	No	No	No	No
Crew Size	1,650	1,530	1,530	1,500	2,235
Fate	Scrapped Postwar	Note 1	Museum Postwar	Note 2	Museum Postwar

*DP: dual-purpose

Notes:

1. Expended as a target, postwar.
2. Damaged at Pearl Harbor, Hawaii, on 7 December 1941. Salvaged. Participated in D-Day landings at Normandy, 6 June 1944. After the war, used as a target and sunk.

British Bomber Aircraft

Model	Typhoon Mk-1B Note 1	Stirling Mk-III	Wellington Mk-I	Whitley Mk-V	Lancaster Mk-I-III	Blenheim Mk-IV	Mosqueto Mk-XVI	Battle Mk-III	Hampden Mk-I	Halifax Mk-III
Service Date	1941	1941	1938	1939	1942	1939	1942	1937	1938	1941
Engines	1	4	2	2	4	2	2	1	2	4
Crew	1	7–8	5–6	5	7	2	2	3	4	7
Maximum Speed (mph)	410	270	230	230	280	260	410	260	260	280
Maximum Range (miles)	510	2,000	2,550	1,500	2,530	1,460	1,480	1,000	1,990	1,980
Gun Armament	4x 20mm	8x .303 MG	6x .303 MG	5x .303 MG	8x .303 MG	2x or 4x .303 MG	None	2x .303 MG	6x .303 MG	10x .303 MG
Maximum Bombload (pounds)	2,000 or 8x rockets	14,000	4,500	7,000	18,000 Note 2	1,000	4,000	1,000	4,000	13,000
Number Produced	3,275	875	1,519	1,737*	7,377	3,300	1,200	955	1,410	2,090
Ceiling (feet)	35,200	17,000	18,000	26,000	22,000	22,000	37,000	25,000	22,700	24,000

*All models.

Notes:

1. Ground attack.
2. A special version could carry 27,000 pounds for short-range missions.

German Bomber Aircraft

Model	FW-190F*	Ju-87B*	Ju-87D*	Hs-129B*	Do-17Z	Do-217E	Do-217M	FW-200C	He-111H	He-177A	Ju-88A
Service Date	1942	1938	1941	1943	1938	1941	1942	1942	1941	1943	1940
Engines	1	1	1	1	2	2	2	4	2	2	2
Crew	1	2	2	1	4–5	4	4	6	5	5	4
Maximum Speed (mph)	370	240	235	250	250	320	350	220	250	303	290
Maximum Rnage (miles)	330	490	950	430	930	1,740	1,550	2,175	1,200	3,400	1,700
Gun Armament	2x 20mm 2x 7.92mm MG	3x 7.92mm MG	3x 7.92mm MG	1x 30mm 2x 20mm 2x 7.92mm MG	8x 7.92mm MG	1x 15mm MG 2x 13mm MG 5x 7.92mm MG	2x 13mm MG 5x 7.92mm MG	1x 20mm MG 4x 13mm MG 1x 7.92mm MG	1x 20mm MG 1x 13mm MG 4x 7.92mm MG	1x 20mm MG 2x 13mm MG 3x 7.92mm MG	2x 13 mm MG 3x 7.92mm MG
Maximum Bombload (pounds)	2,640	1,100	4,000	770	2,200	8,818	8,818	3,750	7,200 or 2x torpedoes	13,200 or 3x torpedoes	7,900 or 2x torpedoes
Number Produced	35	1,300	3,300	400	522	300	550	276	7,300	820	7,000
Ceiling (feet)	34,780	26,150	23,900	29,500	26,900	29,500	31,200	19,000	27,900	26,200	26,900

*Ground-attack/dive bomber.

Italian Bomber Aircraft

Model	Z.1007bis	Br.20M	P.108B	S.M.79-1	S.M.81	S.M.84
Service Date	1938	1939	1942	1937	1940	1941
Engines	3	2	4	3	3	3
Crew	5	5	7	4–5	6	6
Maximum Speed (mph)	280	270	270	270	211	266
Maximum Range (miles)	1,110	1,700	2,200	1,180	1,243	1,130
Gun Armament	2x 12.7mm MG 2x 7.7mm MG	3x 12.7mm MG	6x 12.7mm MG	3x 12.7mm MG 2x 7.7mm MG	6x 7.7mm MG	6x 12.7mm MG
Maximum Bombload (pounds)	2,650 or 2x torpedoes	3,500 or 3x torpedoes	7,700	2,750 or 2x torpedoes	4,410	4,400 or 2x torpedoes
Number Produced	530	260	160	1,370	584	100
Ceiling (feet)	24,600	26,200	28,000	21,300	22,965	29,512

Soviet Bomber Aircraft

Model	Sb-2	DB-3	Pe-8	Pe-2*	Tu-2	Il-2M*	U-2*
Service Date	1936	1937	1940	1941	1944	1941	1928
Engines	2	2	4	2	2	1	1
Crew	3	3	11	3	4	2	1
Maximum Speed (mph)	245	240	272	335	340	250	92
Maximum Range (miles)	750	2,280	3,383	930	1,240	475	342
Gun Armament	5x 7.62mm MG	4x 7.62mm MG	2x 20mm 4x 7.62mm MG	1x 12.7mm MG 2x 7.62mm MG	2x 12.7mm MG	2x 23mm 1x 12.7mm MG 2x 7.62mm MG	1x 7.62mm MG
Maximum Bombload (pounds)	1,600	3,300	4,409	2,200	6,600	1,320 lbs or 8 rockets	330
Number Produced	6,967	6,800	80	11,400	1,000	36,000†	40,000
Ceiling (feet)	23,000	24,750	31,988	29,000	31,200	19,700	10,827

*Ground-attack/dive bombers.
†All models.

U.S. Bomber Aircraft

Model	A-20B	A-20G	A-26B/C	B-17C/D	B-17E/F	B-17G
Service Date	1941	1944	1944	1941	1942	1943
Engines	2	2	2	4	4	4
Crew	3	3	3	9	10	10
Maximum Speed (mph)	350	339	355	291	325	302
Maximum Range (miles)	2,300	1,090	1,800	3,400	4,420	3,400
Gun Armament	3x .50 MG 2x .30 MG	10x .50 MG	10x .50 MG or 18x .50 MG	6x .50 MG 1x .30 MG	12x .50 MG 1x .30 MG	13x .50 MG
Maximum Bombload (pounds)	2,600	4,000	4,000 int plus 2,000 ext	10,496	17,600	17,600
Number in service	999	2,850	2,446	80	3,405	8,680
Ceiling (feet)	28,600	25,800	31,300	37,000	35,000	35,600

Model	B-24D	B-24H/J	B-25C/D	B-25H/J	B-26B/C	B-26G
Service Date	1942	1943	1942	1943	1942	1943
Engines	4	4	2	2	2	2
Crew	10	8–12	5	5	7	7
Maximum Speed (mph)	303	300	264	275	317	283
Maximum Range (miles)	2,850	2,100	1,500	2,700	1,150	1,100
Gun Armament	10x .50 MG	10x .50 MG	6x .50 MG	14x .50 MG	6x .50 MG	11x .50 MG
Maximum Bombload (pounds)	8,800	8,800	3,000	3,200	5,200	4,000
Number in service	2,378	9,778	3,909	5,318	3,118	893
Ceiling (feet)	32,000	28,000	21,200	23,800	23,500	19,800

C

Carrier-Borne Aircraft, British

The Royal Navy (RN) officially regained control of its aircraft on 21 July 1937, but could not fully implement the change until it completed training its own maintenance and flight control personnel two years later. Thus, the RN's air branch or Fleet Air Arm as it was more commonly known, entered the war with second-rate aircraft and did not receive modern fully fleet-capable aviation equipment until the war's final year. Until that time, the RN's air wings made do with the obsolescent Swordfish torpedo plane, converted RAF land planes such as the Sea Gladiator, Seafire, and Sea Hurricane and American Lend-Lease (q.v.) F-4F Wildcats. Of these, the converted land planes provided the best combat capability but it came at a cost in serviceability, safety, and airframe lifespan. Nonetheless, the RN's carriers gave good service and achieved outstanding results, primarily because they faced no sea-based air opposition and rarely encountered German land-based fighter aircraft.

The Royal Navy's primary carrier planes in 1939 were the Swordfish torpedo bomber/spotting aircraft and the dual-purpose Roc and Skua fighter/dive bombers. Although sturdy and reliable, none of these aircraft were a match for the modern land-based aircraft of the day. The Swordfish, a biplane, was too slow for modern aerial operations, but it could stay in the air despite absorbing horrendous punishment. It was also the most stable torpedo plane used by any of the war's antagonists. It achieved some successes, particularly in the Mediterranean, where it was feared intensely by Italian ship commanders. The same could not be said for the RN's other aircraft, the Roc and Skua fighter/dive bombers. They were too slow and unwieldy to be effective fighters and lacked the range and bombload to be efficient dive

bombers. Still, the Skuas at least achieved distinction as the first carrier-launched aircraft to sink a warship in World War II, the German light cruiser *Königsberg*, in Bergen harbor during the Norway campaign (q.v.). These fighters' shortcomings were nonetheless apparent and the RN desperately sought a replacement. Interestingly, the Rocs never served in an active carrier air wing.

The Fairey Fulmar was the first low-wing monoplane to enter service, having been developed and ordered before the war. Entering service in early 1940, its slow speed and poor rate of climb were roundly criticized but it gave good service in the Mediterranean against Italian opposition. It was the Hawker Sea Hurricane, a derivative of the Hurricane I land-based fighter, which gave the RN its first modern carrier-based interceptor in June 1941. Ironically, a more effective variant of the Spitfire, the Seafire, had been turned down for naval service in 1939 by none other than Winston S. Churchill (q.v.), then the first sea lord. One result of his decision was to saddle the fleet air arm with second-rate aircraft until the Seafire, reordered in 1941, could enter service that summer. Unfortunately, the early versions lacked folding wings, which severely limited the number of fighters the aircraft carriers could accomodate.

Despite the serviceability problems induced by the Seafire's relatively weak undercarriage, light airframe and engine corrosion difficulties, it was the Seafire that first gave the fleet air arm a fighter that could stand up to German opposition. It remained in RN service, in various modifications and updates, until well after the war's end.

The Royal Navy's carrier air wings achieved some amazing accomplishments in the war, sinking the Italian fleet at Taranto (q.v.), damaging the *Bismarck* (q.v.) in that famous sea chase, and sinking several Italian naval units at critical times dur-

A Swordfish returns to the HMS Ark Royal *after making a torpedo attack on the* Bismarck. *(IWM A 4100)*

ing the Mediterranean campaign. In each instance, however, success was due to the high rate of training and determination of the pilots, who had to overcome enemy opposition with inferior aircraft. The price they paid is as much a testimony to their leaders' shortsightedness before the war as it is a tribute to the courage of those aircrews.

Carl O. Schuster

(Refer to tables on pages 909–910)

Additional Reading

Brown, David, *Carrier Fighters* (1975).
———, David, *The Seafire* (1973).
Green, William, *Fighters,* Vol.e II (1961).
Sturtivant, Ray, *British Naval Aviation* (1990).
Thetford, Owen, *British Naval Aircraft Since 1912* (1958).

Carrier-Borne Aircraft, German and Italian

Although neither Germany nor Italy employed an operational aircraft carrier, both nations experimented with carrier aircraft. The Germans actually formed an aircraft carrier air wing before the war (*Trägergruppe* 186). That wing has the distinction of being the first carrier air wing to sink a ship during the war (the Polish destroyer *Wicher*). Unfortunately for the *Kriegsmarine,* Germany did not complete any aircraft carriers, and these planes never took off from a carrier deck. They were absorbed into the general *Luftwaffe* order of battle in April 1940. The Italians waited longer and had only two prototypes flying when Italy signed the armistice in September 1943.

Germany started developing its carrier aircraft

in 1937, the year Hermann Göring (q.v.) assumed control over all German aircraft and aircraft development. He immediately ordered the conversion of the latest aircraft types for Germany's aircraft carriers. In many ways, this would have been fortunate for the *Kriegsmarine,* whose ever-conservative leadership had been looking at biplane fighters for its carrier air wing. Göring's orders, however, led to the Bf-109E and Ju-87A being selected for conversion into carrier aircraft. Another aircraft, the Fieseler 167 had already been chosen as the carrier *Graf Zeppelin's* reconnaissance/torpedo bomber. The *Kriegsmarine* was off to an early start in acquiring a carrier air wing.

The dive bomber squadron of *Trägergruppe* 186 was the first of the German carrier squadrons to be formed. It was stationed at Kiel-Holtenau in the fall of 1938. It was originally equipped with eight Ju-87As, but four navalized variants of the dive bomber, designated Ju-87C-0, were assigned in the summer of 1939. The Ju-87C-0 had a tail hook, a catapult attachment point, manually folding outer wing panels, and a reinforced fuselage. The C-1 production variant was to have an electrically operated folding wing. It was this squadron that participated in the attack on Poland. It never returned to the navy. The Ju-87E (a naval version Ju-87D) was considered as a carrier aircraft when carrier building was resumed in 1942, but it never progressed beyond the discussion stage.

The Messerschmitt Bf-109 carrier aircraft was next, flying for the first time in November 1939. It was essentially a naval version of the Bf-109E, designated the Bf-109T. It had a tail hook, catapult attachment point, strengthened fuselage, reinforced landing gear, and the final four feet of the wing could be folded back. The wingspan was also extended approximately two feet. Although the modification cut 4–6 mph off the plane's maximum speed, it also reduced the aircraft's turning circle and lowered its landing speed. The first squadron never embarked on a carrier, but its short takeoff and landing (STOL) capabilities were such that 750 models of a land-based version of the Bf-109T were produced and assigned to squadrons serving in Norway. The plane's STOL capabilities were ideal for that country's short runways.

Ironically, the Fieseler design was the first one approved for the carrier (in 1937) and the last one built. The first prototype flew in the summer of 1938, and was an immediate success. The design bore a striking similarity to the Fieseler Storch. It had similar handling characteristics as well. It could take off fully loaded without catapult assistance, and had a landing speed of only 25 mph. The squadron was formed with twelve aircraft in the summer of 1940 and was stationed in the Netherlands for operational trials. By 1943, the *Luftwaffe* decided that the Ju-87E would make a better torpedo bomber, and the Fieseler unit was disbanded. Some of the aircraft were assigned to experimental work, and at least four were sold to Romania.

The Italians did not start planning for carrier aircraft until late 1941. The aircraft chosen was the Falco II Re. 2001 fighter. Two were modified with reinforced airframes, landing gear, and a tail hook. The prototypes were flying by late 1942, and were available for on-board testing when Italy signed the armistice. Eventually, Italy had hoped to equip its aircraft carriers with the Falco IIG fighter/torpedo bomber, but there is no evidence the Falco IIG was ever modified for carrier operations. Since the basic Falco II carried no bombs, the initial air wing for the carrier *Aquila* would have been limited to providing defensive air cover and reconnaissance support until a carrier-based Falco IIG variant entered service. As with so many other Axis programs, aircraft carriers and carrier aircraft were another case of too little, far too late.

Carl O. Schuster

(Refer to table on page 911)

Additional Reading

Chesneau, Roger, *Aircraft Carriers of the World, 1914 to Present* (1987).
Green, William, *War Planes of the Second World War,* Vols. 1, 2, and 10 (1962–64).

Carrier-Borne Aircraft, U.S.

American naval aviation was born when the storing and launching of aircraft on a ship at sea became a viable element of the U.S. naval operations. Carriers quickly became essential to the coordinated operations of ships and airplanes after the first aircraft carrier, the USS *Langley,* proved the theory would work in 1921. U.S. carrier aviation enjoyed relatively strong support from the navy's senior leaders during the interwar years. As a result, its carrier air wings consistently received upgraded aircraft as improved engines and wing technologies came on line. Thus, although the United States had fewer carriers than the Royal Navy in 1939, its carrier aircraft were modern and capable.

American industry was quick to build aircraft carriers, both by converting existing hulls and by constructing new ships designed as carriers. By early 1943, the United States had more carriers and carrier aircraft than all the other belligerents combined.

Most of America's carriers and carrier aircraft served in the Pacific; however, American carrier aircraft were provided in large numbers to the Royal Navy and several exile navies in the European theater. American carrier aviation in Europe was primarily employed in antisubmarine warfare (ASW) (q.v.) in the Battle of the Atlantic (q.v.), but American carrier planes also saw service in the Mediterranean (q.v.) and during the TORCH landings (*see* Northwest African Landings). The primary elements of American naval airpower in Europe were the F-4F Wildcat and the TBF Avenger.

The F-4F Wildcat was first designed and produced by the Grumman Aircraft Engineering Corporation in 1939. By 1941, the F-4F4 was introduced, featuring folding wings and increased firepower. The single-seat fighter was capable of speeds of 328 mph and a ceiling of 37,000 feet. The Wildcat was the U.S. Navy's principle carrier fighter plane during America's first two and a half years of the war. Grumman stopped manufacturing the F-4F after May 1943, but the Eastern Aircraft Division of General Motors Corporation assumed production of the aircraft as the FM-1. That version and its subsequent improvements remained in production until August 1945. Total production of Wildcats (all models) reached 7,905 during the war, with 5,927 being produced by Eastern. More than 1,000 Wildcats were delivered to the British.

The other principal carrier aircraft in the Atlantic was also a Grumman creation, the TBF Avenger, a torpedo bomber. The Avenger was ordered by the U.S. Navy in 1940 and delivered in 1942. It first saw action in the Pacific at the battle of Midway in June 1942. The TBF was a three-man aircraft, carrying a pilot, bomber, and radio operator, and had two caliber .30 and two caliber .50 machine guns. It could carry a single torpedo of virtually any type, one 2,000-pound bomb, or four 500-pound bombs. The Avenger had a ceiling of 23,400 feet and a top speed of 267 mph.

By 1943, Grumman had produced 2,311 TBFs when, as with the F-4F Wildcat, Eastern Aircraft assumed production of the Avenger, redesignated TBM. A total of 7,546 TBM Avengers were manufactured by Eastern, 958 of which went to the British through Lend-Lease (q.v.). The Avenger also flew from land bases, but was considered an invaluable carrier plane because of its load-carrying capacity. It could carry either an antisubmarine torpedo, depth charges, or a full-size 22-inch-diameter torpedo, which, unlike the lighter aerial torpedoes carried by earlier torpedo planes, could penetrate any known battleship armor. The Avenger saw service in the torpedo, ground-attack, and naval-strike warfare roles in the Pacific, but was used primarily for antisubmarine operations in the Atlantic, forming the attack element of escort carrier squadrons.

Escort carrier squadrons were designated with the letters "CV-", for composite squadron, indicating a combination of fighters and torpedo bomber aircraft. The CVE (escort aircraft carrier) USS *Bogue,* for example, carried a complement of twelve F-4F Wildcats and eight TBF Avengers on her initial Atlantic crossing. From 12 April to 26 June 1944, the CVE USS *Croatan's* aircraft included nine FM-2 fighters and sixteen TBM torpedo bombers; and from 25 March to 25 April 1945, she carried three fighters and sixteen TBMs. The CVE USS *Core* carried six Wildcats and 12 Avengers on her cruises between June and November 1943; and three FM fighters and sixteen TBMs during a spring 1945 cruise. Other escort carriers were similar in aircraft composition.

Several examples serve to illustrate the success of naval aviation during the Battle of the Atlantic. Between August and November 1943, aircraft from the *Card* sank eight U-boats, two alone on 4 October. Planes from the *Core* destroyed U-boats on 13 July, 16 July, two on 24 August, and two on 20 October 1943. Fighters and torpedo bombers from the *Bogue* sank U-boats on 22 May, 5 June, 12 June, 23 July, 29 November, 13 December, and 20 December 1943. On 13 May 1944, aircraft from the *Bogue* destroyed a Japanese submarine, and on 20 August another U-boat. These examples represent only a portion of the escort carrier successes against enemy submarines. The combination of escort carriers, accompanying destroyers, and Wildcat and Avenger aircraft were the keys to the Allied victory in the Atlantic.

Boyd Childress

(Refer to tables on pages 909–910)

Additional Reading

Jane's All the World's Aircraft (1945–46).

Miller, Nathan, *Naval Air War, 1939–1945* (1991).

Morison, Samuel Eliot, *History of United States Naval Operations in World War II,* 15 vols. (1948–1962).

Commerce Raiders, German

Unlike World War I, when the German main battle fleet posed a serious threat to British naval superiority, German naval weakness in 1939 forced the *Kriegsmarine* to avoid direct combat between fleet units, and concentrate instead on disrupting and destroying British commerce. German naval strategy during World War II was to strike directly at British maritime commerce, the great source and vulnerability of British power, via submarine warfare and surface commerce raiding. During the 1920s and 1930s, Germany prepared for the latter by building fast freighters for possible use as auxiliary raiders *(Hilfskreuzers),* and the so-called pocket battleships *Deutschland, Admiral Graf Spee,* and *Admiral Scheer,* designed to either outgun (six 11-inch guns) or outrun (26 knots top speed) any possible opponent.

German commerce raiders had three primary objectives: (1) sink British commerce; (2) scatter British naval forces; and (3) disrupt British shipping patterns and schedules. The pocket battleship *Graf Spee* struck first, sinking nine ships and about 50,089 tons of shipping in the South Atlantic in late 1939, before engaging three British cruisers on 13 December 1939 in the battle of the Platte River (q.v.), near Montevideo, Uruguay. Three days later she was scuttled to avoid internment by the Uraguayans or destruction by superior British forces that the Germans erroneously believed were gathering.

The *Deutschland,* active in the North Atlantic at the start of the war, sank only two ships and captured a third before returning to Germany and being renamed *Lützow.* After the bloodletting the German Navy suffered during the invasion of Norway (q.v.) in early 1940, surface units were not active again until late 1940 and early 1941, which was the zenith of such operations.

In October 1940, the pocket battleship *Admiral Scheer* set out on a very successful 161-day cruise through the Atlantic and into the Indian Ocean that netted sixteen ships and 99,059 tons of British shipping, and caused countless delays and disruptions to British maritime commerce. During this time the heavy cruiser *Admiral Hipper* also put to sea, sinking ten ships totaling 59,960 tons (combined totals from three separate sorties). During the same period, January-February 1941, the battleships *Schornhorst* and *Gneisenau* made a successful foray into the North Atlantic, sinking twenty-two ships displacing a total of 115,622 tons.

After these successes, German surface units were systematically eliminated by British air and sea power, starting with the ill-fated voyage of the battleship *Bismarck* (q.v.), sunk 27 May 1941. The *Scharnhorst* was sunk on 26 December 1943 trying to intercept a convoy north of Norway. The last major surface unit, *Bismarck's* sister ship, *Tirpitz,* was sunk by RAF heavy bombers on 12 November 1944. The threat that these units posed from their bases in Norway to Allied convoys to Russia was demonstrated in July 1942, when convoy PQ-17 (q.v.) was virtually destroyed (twenty-four ships sunk) by German aircraft and submarines after it dispersed because of a fear that it was about to be intercepted by German surface units. Warship raiders succeeded in sinking or capturing fifty-nine ships totaling 331,692 tons.

More successful in sinking British shipping and disrupting commerce were the *Hilfskreuzers,* the German auxiliary raiders that prowled the world's ocean until 1943. Disguised to look like typical nondescript freighters, these ships were well-armed with mines, torpedos, and a main battery of six 5.9-inch guns. When they encountered British combatants they more than held their own, sinking the Australian cruiser HMAS *Sydney* (with all hands), an armed merchant cruiser, and heavily damaging two other ships while making successful escapes. Nine German auxiliary raiders operated between March 1940 and February 1943. The lightest, *Komet,* weighed only 3,200 tons, while the largest, *Kormoran,* was, at 8,700 tons, more than twice as large.

Relying on a stealthy approach and a sudden attack, these armed merchant cruisers took a steady toll of shipping, especially during their heyday in 1940 through 1942. Most ships spent long months at sea operating in isolation, broken only by an infrequent rendezvous with a German supply ship. The two most successful raiders, *Pinguin* (thirty-two ships, 154,619 tons) and *Atlantis* (twenty-two ships, 145,697 tons) were both sunk in action after being surprised by British cruisers. Overall, the nine German auxiliary cruisers sank or captured 136 merchant ships totalling over 890,000 tons, for a fraction of the expense and effort that went into equipping and sustaining the main fleet surface raiders. Despite their success in sinking and disrupting British commerce, however, they were unable to overcome the enormous advantage in naval power arrayed against them. They never posed the threat to British survival that the German U-boats did.

Daniel T. Kuehl

Additional Reading

Brennecke, H., *The Hunters and the Hunted* (1958).

Frank, Wolfgang, and Bernard Rogge, *The German Raider Atlantis* (1956).

Humble, Richard, *Hitler's High Seas Fleet* (1971).

Muggenthaler, August K., *German Raiders of World War II* (1977).

Communications Equipment

Communications have played a critical role in every war in history. World War II was the first war, however, in which technology provided instant, or real time communications on a wide scale. The success of Germany's *Blitzkrieg* (q.v.) operations was based on precise and timely coordination between the *Luftwaffe* and the army. Great Britain, on the other hand, was saved in the Battle of Britain (q.v.) by its superior communication networks.

Germany

The German military used twelve-volt radio sets extensively in the vast majority of its armor vehicles. This was the era of the vacuum tube and for German receivers, the workhorse tube was the pentode. The pentode was used for a variety of applications in the set, which reduced the variety and numbers of spares required.

German fixed-station equipment used batteries, pedal-operated or gasoline-operated generators, or line voltage (220 volts) for power. In larger mobile and fixed-station sets, component construction using plug and socket connectors facilitated maintenance.

German telephones were of standard commercial design, but constructed to withstand field conditions, including waterproofing. Field telephone exchanges ranged from simple ten-line exchanges to more complex sixty-line switchboards capable of interfacing with civilian exchanges, field phones, automatic dial, and conference call systems. With multiple jack fields, up to five additional switchboards could be added, bringing the total capacity of the field switchboard to 360 lines.

The German intelligence services used battery-operated line interceptor receivers, each capable of tapping several telephone or teletype lines simultaneously. They could only monitor one line at a time, however. No direct connection was necessary. A wire loop placed within one foot of the target circuit picked up signals through induction.

In teletype operations, the Germans used two component units separately, the teleprinter and the telewriter. The teleprinter was a versatile piece of equipment that could be adapted readily to American and British machines. It could even operate on either 110- or 220-volt power. The telewriters had a keyboard with twenty-six letters, numerals 0 to 9, and the symbols +, -, /, and ?. They, too, were similar to American and British models. Combined, the teleprinter and telewriter used telephone lines for duplex operations, which allowed them to send and receive simultaneously.

The Germans installed radio equipment in

virtually all of their multiengine aircraft, and to some extent in their single-engine fighters. Bomber radios had ranges from 300 to 500 miles. These radios, however, were too large to install in the smaller fighters. In fighter aircraft, the Germans used the smaller Fu.G16 transmitter-receiver, which had a maximum range of only 100 miles. This limited tactical command and control of the *Luftwaffe's* fighter groups.

Britain

Among the Western Allies, the British started the war with the most advanced communications technology and systems, just as they were also the most advanced with respect to radar (q.v.). By 1940, they had an elaborate system of telephone, teletype, and radios installed and operational. In September 1940, U.S. Major General Delos Emmons and Brigadier General George Strong observed that if Britain successfully avoided an invasion, it would be the direct result of their excellent communications systems.

By comparison, the U.S. lagged far behind in developing tactical communications. In August 1940, President Franklin D. Roosevelt (q.v.) enthusiastically embraced a plan to bring the United States up to date with British communications technology. The Tizard Mission—named for its British chief, Sir Henry Tizard (q.v.)—was formed to coordinate not only collaboration between Britain and America, but also collaboration between science and the military.

United States

It is hard to believe that as late as 1938, the U.S. Army Signal Corps still had the Pigeon Service in operation. By that time, the radio and the airplane had made this service obsolete, and by years' end, the Pigeon Service faded away.

A noteworthy development in telephones during World War II was the U.S. TP-3 field telephone. It used no battery, being powered from the energy of the speaker's voice. It could produce enough power to operate several miles over standard field wire. Developed by Bell Telephone Laboratories in the late 1930s, the TP-3 was never widely accepted by the U.S. Army Signal Corps.

For short-distance communication, wire was the method of choice. To help increase transmission range over field wire, loading coils were inserted at one-mile intervals. This technique could extend circuit range up to twenty miles. Loading coils used inductance to boost signal strength and required no external power sources. They were employed mainly by artillery units for contact between forward observers and the guns.

Repeater sets were also used for longer-range wire circuits. Here the theoretical distance could go in the hundreds of miles. Although spacing was done at greater intervals, the big disadvantage to repeater sets was their requirement for external power, either from line voltage or batteries.

It is important to understand that up to the eve of the Pearl Harbor attack, wire was the primary U.S. means of communications, while radio was the back-up. The Signal Corps rationale for this was that command headquarters did not move. Also, radio signals could easily be monitored and the enemy could locate the stations using direction finders.

Radio direction finders first appeared in World War I. Using two or more direction finders operating from fixed positions, enemy transmitters could be located with a fair degree of accuracy by the principal of triangulation. During World War II, the same technology was used in navigational radios. Ships or aircraft used the radio compass to align themselves with ground or shore transmitters, using that transmitter's frequency to home in on. A further development of the radio compass led to the instrument landing system, which allowed pilots to land "blind" by aligning their aircraft with radio signals aligned to runways.

U.S. teletypewriters during the early and middle years of World War II were heavy and were used only in major field headquarters. Aside from weight, their other major limitation was the requirement for a source of steady power. A shift of more than 3 percent in the cycle rate caused the loss of synchronization between sending and receiving machines. The mark/space, or current flow/current break operation was essential to teletype communications. By 1944, the PGC-1 lightweight page printer was developed for mobile use. It was light enough to be backpacked. The Americans also developed the PE-77 power supply. It too was lightweight, but more importantly, it provided stable power for synchronization. Near the end of the war, they fielded the MRC-2, a mobile duplex teletype mounted in vehicles and operated over radio.

In 1940, the U.S. Army Air Corps called for 8,000 SCR-274 air-to-ground very high frequency (VHF) radios for installation in aircraft. (Originally SCR stood for set, complete radio; later it became Signal Corps radio.) Additionally, the air corps wanted frequency meters, radio compasses, intercom phones, and command and liaison sets.

In November 1940, Major General George Brett, General Henry H. "Hap" Arnold's (q.v.) deputy, called on the Signal Corps to develop necessary radio "equipment usable under war conditions." The major immediate source of equipment design was British, but the Signal Corps had to overcome problems of differing power supply, and adapt or change British plugs, sockets, tubes, and switches for American use. By the end of 1940, the air corps had procured more than 21,000 pieces of radio equipment, much of it supplied by the British.

Early American radio and microwave sets were inferior to British sets. By 1942, however, Philco and a Canadian firm, War Supplies Limited, were producing reliable sets for use in the field.

U.S. armored forces had a huge demand for radios. As a result, by the end of 1940, the Signal Corps equipped the 1st and 2nd Armored Divisions with frequency-modulated radios. Four different models were introduced; AF-I, AF-II, AF-III, and AF-IV. The AF-I sets were long range—up to 100 miles. The AF-II radios had reliable ranges up to forty miles, but they were still too big for tanks and required tuning by the user. This proved awkward when the tank was in motion. The AF-III radios had shorter ranges of up to seven miles, but their big advantage was crystal-controlled tuning that stayed locked on once set. The AF-IV sets had even shorter ranges, but were also crystal controlled. Both the AF-III and AF-IV, developed by Bell Laboratories and Western Electric, came with models with multi-channel, pre-tuned frequencies.

U.S. armored vehicles also used the SCR-509 and SCR-510 radios, direct descendents of the Connecticut State Police car radios developed by Daniel Noble. Similar short-range radios were developed for the infantry. One in particular, the SCR-300, was an infantry walkie-talkie developed by Galvin Manufacturing Company (Motorola). It succeeded the SCR-195, the army's first walkie-talkie developed in 1937.

In February 1942, U.S. field artillery units upgraded their radios with the SCR-608. The new radio could tune up to 120 channels. The complete set measured only three cubic feet.

VHF radios are good for short-range communications, but for longer ranges (in the hundreds of miles), high frequency (HF) is required. The Federal Telegraph and Radio Corporation provided the Signal Corps with the BC-339 one-kilowatt HF transmitter and the BC-340 ten-kilowatt power amplifier. These sets were used in Iceland, Alaska, Hawaii, and Puerto Rico. The navy, which had a global communications requirement, used HF transmitters that operated on forty kilowatts of power.

In April 1942, the SCR-578 "Gibson Girl" distress radio was developed for downed airmen. Borrowing from the German *Notsender* N.S.2, the SCR-578 sent automatic distress signals by the turning of a crank. The system used two types of antenna systems, a box-like kite and an inflated balloon that carried a 300-foot antenna into the air. These radios were jointly developed by Aircraft Radio Laboratory and Bendix Aviation Limited.

The radio teletype (RTTY) was first developed in mid-1942, but a later development resulted in automatic cipher machines that encoded and decoded signals simultaneously. This allowed secure transmission over the airwaves. A perforated tape was fed into an enciphering machine for broadcast. At the receiving end, the signals were picked up, amplified, and converted into another paper tape punch in the cipher code. That tape was then passed through a decipher machine set with the same key as the encipher machine. The output was a third paper tape in plain text, which then was fed into a receive teleprinter for page copy. International Business Machines (IBM) Corporation was the primary developer. This system was first used by the weather service. RTTY was faster than radiotelegraph, which converted from message text to cipher and then to Morse code for transmission, with the reverse accomplished at the receiving station—all manually.

Although the United States lagged in communications development prior to Pearl Harbor, the necessity of war brought about a host of new innovations and equipment. New operational techniques, using coordinated air and ground forces, required reliable communications—if for no other reason than to minimize casualties from friendly fire.

Naval

All navies of World War II relied on radio electronic systems for both long- and short-range communications. As the war progressed, the accelerating pace and variety of naval operations led to an almost revolutionary change in naval communications, at least at the tactical level.

In World War I, electronic communications means were used sparingly and then only for communications between distant task groups or between task groups and shore commands. Tactical communications in that war was almost entirely by signal flag and semaphore, unless visibility limitations dictated otherwise. Although signal flags and semaphore were still used for routine formation signaling and administrative traffic within naval task groups during World War II, tactical maneuvering and engagement orders were almost entirely transmitted electronically.

Another change at the tactical level was the shift from continuous wave (CW), or Morse code, to voice, or radio, communications. This change too was dictated by the increased tempo of naval operations. With a ship under air attack, there simply was not enough time to translate the CW code into written form and get it to the ship's commander. He had to act on commands as they were transmitted. Thus, local task group communications were almost invariably "in the clear" (that is, unencrypted), or used simple unchanging code words that everyone understood.

In 1939, naval long-range communications systems were virtually unchanged from those of World War I. High frequency transmitters were used for long-distance communications, primarily using manually encrypted CW transmissions. Machine-encrypted teleprinter systems started coming into service shortly before the war began. These teleprinter systems began to supplant CW equipment on board most major combatants by 1941, but only the Germans used teleprinter systems aboard their submarines and minor combatants before 1943. Even so, CW communications remained the staple for naval long-range communications with ships and task forces at sea until well after the war.

All naval communications equipment during World War II was basically similar. The typical ship or submarine used a single 100-watt HF transmitter and receiver for long-range communications and then, as the war progressed, one or more ten-watt very high frequency (VHF) transceivers (transmitter/receiver) came into service for local electronic communications. The Allies called their VHF radio systems TBS, for "talk between ships." The Germans were the first to have their entire fleet equipped with teleprinter communications, but on the whole, Axis naval units lagged behind their Allied counterparts in the number, variety, and reliability of communications systems. Much of this was the result of the greater cooperation between Allied naval surface and air units. By 1944, it was not unusual for an Allied destroyer or convoy escort to have one or two HF and three to five VHF communications systems on board. Nonetheless, no Allied task group commander ever felt that his ships had enough communications.

William H. Van Husen
Carl O. Schuster

Additional Reading
Kahn, David, *The Code Breakers* (1973).
Terrett, Dulany, *U.S. Army in World War II: The Technical Services: The Signal Corps: The Emergency* (1956).
Thompson, George R., Dixie R. Harris, Pauline M. Oakes, and Dulany Terrett, *U.S. Army in World War II: The Technical Services: The Signal Corps: The Test* (1957).
U.S. Army Technical Manual, *TM-E 30–451, Handbook on German Military Forces* (reprinted 1990).
Winton, John, *Ultra at Sea* (1988).

Cruisers, British

The Royal Navy (RN) entered World War II still equipped with the bulk of the Emergency War Programme cruisers from World War I in their inventory. Fortunately, rising world tensions in the late 1930s led to a resurgence in the RN's shipbuilding programs and the cruiser force in particular benefited.

In general, RN cruisers of the war sacrificed firepower for good range, endurance, and protection. Antiaircraft armament proved too light during the war's early years but improved as the war went on. More significantly, the RN's cruisers enjoyed electronic supremacy over their opponents after 1941, an advantage that grew as the war progressed. Although the nature of the naval war in Europe, with its emphasis on antisubmarine warfare, offered few opportunities for the type of engagements for which these ships were designed, British cruisers performed well in every engagement from the Mediterranean to the far Arctic. It was only in the Pacific theater that their lack of firepower and inadequate antiaircraft protection placed them at a severe disadvantage.

The oldest cruisers in service in 1939 were those from World War I. The smallest of these were the C-types: the Caledon, Ceres, and Carlisle classes. They were designed as light, short-range ships for service in the North Sea. All displaced less than 4,200 tons, carried five 6-inch guns, and had a design speed of 29 knots. The Caledon-class differed from the earlier classes in having a trawler bow to allow a drier foredeck in heavy seas. The armor, speed, and design of the Dragon (D) class were similar to the Cs, but the ships were twenty feet longer to allow an additional 6-inch gun mounted forward.

The Es, the last of the Emergency War Programme cruisers, differed considerably from their predecessors. They displaced 7,550 tons and were ninety feet longer than the Ds. They carried seven 6-inch guns and five 4-inch antiaircraft guns. Their armor was the same as the earlier ships. In anticipation of the development of a fast German cruiser, they had a design speed of 32 knots. This made them the only ones of the series with enough speed to be suitable for fleet duty, but they had to carry twice as much engine power as the Ds to achieve the added three knots.

The name ship of the successor to the "alphabet" ships, the HMS *Vindictive,* was completed as an aircraft carrier and later converted back into a cruiser. As a result, the class was known in service as the Hawkins-class. The other two ships of the class displaced 9,860 tons and carried seven 7.5-inch guns as primary armament. Although their displacement and armament formed the basis of the Washington Naval Treaty limitations on capital ships, no further units were built.

The British opted for greater numbers of smaller ships rather than the larger, more heavily armed vessels favored by the United States. They did, however, proceed with one class that took advantage of the allowances of the Washington Treaty. The Counties-class heavy cruisers displaced about 10,000 tons and carried eight 8-inch guns. The design speed of these eleven ships (two types: the Kent and London series) varied from 31.5 to 32.5 knots, and they had a range of 10,400 miles at 11 knots, making them suitable for operations in the Pacific. They were well protected by 5.5-inch belt and 1.5-inch deck armor. Their primary guns could elevate to a full 70 degrees, and their powered turrets provided a high rate of fire. One of these, the *Suffolk,* became the first British ship to carry production radar in 1939; the rest of the Counties-class were similarly equipped soon after. Overall, they were quite satisfactory ships.

The preference for smaller ships reemerged with the York-class. These 8,250-ton ships carried six 8-inch guns (the minimum number needed for accurate ranging in ships without radar), three-inch belt and two-inch deck armor, and were meant solely for convoy escort. Only two examples of the class were built and both were lost during the war. The class was considered too expensive and two more planned ships were canceled.

The Arethusas of the 1930s also represented a further movement toward lighter ships. The weight reduction was partially achieved by use of electric welding and aluminum-covered plywood for inboard partitions. They displaced only 5,220 tons and carried six 6-inch guns in double mounts. They had a 12,000 nautical mile range and 32.25 knot design speed.

The Dido-class were direct descendants of the Arethusas. They were meant to fulfill two roles: light escort and antiaircraft duty. Thus they carried eight or ten dual-purpose (that is, capable of engaging either aircraft or surface ships) 5.25-inch guns, and a number of 20mm and 40mm cannons. All gunnery was radar controlled. They carried three-inch belt and one-inch deck armor. Sixteen of the class were built in two groups, which formed the backbone of the British light cruiser fleet in the war.

The Leanders, which were built concurrently with the Arethusas, displaced 7,270 tons and carried six or eight 6-inch guns in twin turrets. Their design ultimately served as a bridge between the 10,000-ton treaty cruisers and the later Town-class units. They gave good service during the war, with five of the eight surviving it.

In answer to the Japanese Mogami-class (and to a lesser extent, the American Brooklyns), the British enlarged the Leanders into the very successful Town or Southampton-class. Rather than mounting 8-inch guns, it was decided to rely on the rapid firing capability of a large bank of 6-inch guns.

The 1st Group and 2nd Group models carried nine 6-inch guns in triple turrets. It was intended to mount four quadruple turrets in the 3rd Group ships, but the turret could not be developed, thus four triple turrets were used. They displaced between 9,100 and 10,260 tons, but carried a substantial 4 to 4.5 inches of belt and 2 inches of deck armor. Their multiple directors allowed them to engage a number of targets simultaneously with controlled fire. The high rate of fire and superior protection made them more than a match for their adversaries in the Mediterranean and for the 8-inch Mogamis. Ten of these ships, starting with the *Southampton* in 1937 and ending with the *Belfast* in 1939, were built.

The need to expand the cruiser force quickly as world tensions grew led to the simplification of the Towns into the Colonies-class. The name ship, *Fiji,* was commissioned in 1940. The Swiftsures were adaptations of the Colony class built after 1943. They were the last cruisers commissioned during the war, but entered service too late to serve in the European theater.

Britain's cruiser designs were well suited for the RN's needs. Simple economic designs with good range and protection enabled the RN to have the numbers it needed with sufficient capabilities to patrol and protect its sea lanes against the likely threats they would encounter, at least in European waters. The decision to equip its ships with 6-inch guns not only simplified construction but logistics as well. Moreover, the Italian cruisers they fought had little armor protection, so the "punch" of their 6-inch guns was more than adequate.

Britain's cruiser force enjoyed many successes in the war, from the battle of the Platte River (q.v.), to the finding of the *Bismarck* (q.v.) and the engagements of the naval war in the Mediterranean (q.v.). Their performance testifies to the adequacy of their designs and the proficiency of their crews.

Jack E. McCallum

(Refer to tables on pages 912–915)

Additional Reading
Galuppini, Gino, *Warships of the World* (1989).
Jane's Fighting Ships of World War II (1989).
Lenton, H.T., *British Cruisers* (1973).

Cruisers, French

The French interwar cruiser building program was a direct response to the Italian Navy's expansion and the perceived threat to communications with France's North African colonies. Unlike the British and Americans, who viewed cruisers as smaller capital ships, the French saw them entirely as sea lane protection units. Armor protection was limited, antiaircraft armament inadequate, and they suffered from poor endurance. Moreover, they lacked radar and would not receive electronic sensors until France rejoined the Allies in 1943. Nonetheless, French cruiser designs would have been more than a match for the Italian units with which they would most likely have engaged, had France remained in the war after 1940.

The first of these new ships was the *Duguay-Trouin*, commissioned in 1923. She carried four pairs of 155mm guns. This was the standard heavy artillery caliber used by the French Army and conforming to it saved money. The use of 155mm as the limit for light cruisers in the treaty texts was a concession to the French by the British and Americans. These ships achieved a maximum trial speed of 35.7 knots but had virtually no armor.

The Tourville class was an enlarged version of the *Duguay-Trouin*, carried four pairs of 203mm guns, but was still unarmored. Their design speed was the same as the smaller ship. In exchange for a thin plate of armor over the machinery spaces, the Suffren class gave up almost two knots, while maintaining the same displacement and armament as the Tourvilles.

The French light cruiser series began with the minelaying vessel *Pluton*. She displaced 4,850 tons and carried four 140mm guns. The *Émile Bertin* was a vastly improved version, carrying three triple 152mm turrets and capable of a maximum speed of 39.8 knots in trials. She carried only one to two inches of deck armor. This failing led to the development of the La Galissonniére class, the first of which was commissioned in 1935. These six ships carried the same armament as the *Émile Bertin* but were protected by 4.7 inches of belt armor and two inches of deck armor. Predictably, their maximum trial speed was four knots slower than the *Émile Bertin*.

Additional cruisers in the French inventory at the beginning of the war included the *Jeanne d'Arc*, designed specifically for training and commissioned in 1930, and the *Algérie*, a 10,000-ton heavily armored ship built as a direct response to the Italian *Zara*. The *De Grasse* was an 8,000-ton ship under construction at Brest at the time of the armistice with Germany. She was not completed until after the war.

Few French cruisers survived the war. The *Pluton* blew up with the loss of 215 officers and men while off-loading mines in Casablanca in 1939. The *Émile Bertin* was on the way to the United States with a load of bullion to pay for war supplies at the time of the armistice. She was diverted to Martinique where she spent most of the rest of the war with the *Jeanne d'Arc* in the harbor at Fort de France.

The *Lamotte-Picquet* remained in Indochina, where she fought a single engagement in the Kho Chang archipelago against two Siamese battleships, damaging one and causing the other to run aground. She was decommissioned and sunk at anchor near Saigon by the United States in 1945.

The heavy cruisers *Algérie, Dupleix,* and *Colbert,* and the light cruisers *Marsaillaise* and *Jeanne de Vienne* were scuttled at Toulon in November 1942. The *Foch* and *La Galissonnière* were decommissioned under the armistice and also scuttled at Toulon. The *Jeanne de Vienne,* the *La Galissonnière* and the *Dupleix* were refloated by the Italians only to be sunk a second time in the Allied bombing of Toulon in November 1943. The *Georges Leygues, Gloire,* and *Montcalm* remained under French control at Dakar. The *Duquesne, Tourville, Suffren,* and *Duguay-Trouin* spent much of the war at anchor under the guns of the British fleet at Alexandria.

In 1943, when the French reentered the war on the side of the Allies, French cruisers in Alexandria were sent to Dakar. The three cruisers that had been at Dakar went to Boston to be fitted with antiaircraft weapons and radar. The two ships from Martinique were refitted in Philadelphia and

Puerto Rico. The French cruisers served out 1943 patrolling the Atlantic for German raiders and blockade runners.

Ironically, when the Italians reentered the war on the Allied side, two cruiser squadrons were formed to alternate in this duty. The first was composed of the *Duca degli Abruzzi,* the *Montcalm,* and the *Georges Leygues,* and the second of the *Duca d'Aosta,* the *Gloire,* and the *Suffren.* Later in the war, French cruisers participated in the shore bombardments at OMAHA Beach and Toulon.

Jack E. McCallum

(Refer to tables on pages 916–917)

Additional Reading
Auphan, Paul, and Jacques Mordal, *The French Navy in World War II* (1959).
Jane's Fighting Ships of World War II (1989).

Cruisers, German

The German Plan Z (q.v.) stipulated a fleet that included five heavy cruisers, twenty-two light cruisers, and twenty-two "scout" cruisers. The *Kriegsmarine* envisioned the cruisers as the outward screen elements of large raiding groups, centered around super battleships, which would sweep out across the Atlantic and prey on British sea lanes. It was an interesting concept that was never tested.

The war began before even a portion of the cruiser construction program was completed. None of the scout cruisers were finished and that program was scrapped on the slips in 1941 because steel and other resources went to higher priority systems, namely submarines and tanks. Only the Königsberg-class light cruisers reached full production. Of the Hipper-class heavy cruisers, one was sold to the Soviet Union and another was set aside for conversion to an aircraft carrier.

Germany entered the war with three heavy and six light cruisers. The heavy cruisers were all of modern design, had excellent armored protection and good speed, and were equipped with radar, sonar (qq.v.), and an outstanding hydrophone array. These units were very difficult to attack with torpedoes because their hydrophones could detect torpedo screw noises from up to 2,500 meters away. In 1939, the radar of the German cruisers was the most modern in Europe, and in contrast to the Royal Navy, all German cruisers carried it. With their superior sensor suites, armor, armament, and fire control systems, Germany's heavy cruisers probably were the most formidable in

Europe at that time. The same could not be said of the light cruisers.

The oldest of these, the *Emden,* was the first German cruiser built after World War I. As such, it suffered from an obsolete design. Originally coal fired, it was converted to oil in 1934 and was used primarily as a training ship. The other six, built in the late 1920s and early 1930s, were intended as scouts for long-range raiding squadrons operating in the far Atlantic. Their main battery was weighted astern and they employed a novel engineering arrangement—combined diesel/steam propulsion to achieve outstanding cruising range. Unfortunately, their antiaircraft armament was light and their underwater protection was very poor. More significantly, they did not originally carry radar and were never equipped with sonar or the better hydrophone arrays that came into service after the ships were built. As a result, they were very vulnerable to air and submarine attack.

The M-class "scout" cruisers were a projected design intended to operate out in front of the raiding squadrons. They had little armor, employed mixed diesel/steam propulsion, had exceptional speed, and a truly impressive operating range of 8,000 nautical miles. Nonetheless, the engine room arrangements concentrated both turbines in one space while the deck armor was thin and poorly arranged. The antiaircraft armament was clearly inadequate. It was a design that would have been very vulnerable to air and surface attack, as well as prone to a single "catastrophic" hit. Germany's economic position was such that these units never saw service.

Germany's cruisers were a mixed lot. The heavy cruisers were the best of their type in the world in 1939, while the light cruisers and their follow-ons were clearly not as well designed or built. Still, their acoustic and, later, radar suites were ahead of their opponents at war's start. By 1941, however, British advances in radar surpassed the Germans' in range, accuracy, and reliability. The Germans tried to compensate by installing radar warning receivers but that was not enough. By 1944, obsolete electronics in their cruisers made them almost helpless in night engagements against the Western Allies' radar-equipped air and surface forces.

In the final years of the war, the surviving German cruisers were moved into the Baltic to assist the army in its desperate retreat from the east. There, they retained their electronic superiority over the Soviets. The Soviets were so impressed they drafted German shipyard workers and technicians after the war and used them to build the immediate postwar Soviet Navy. The resulting heavy German influence can best be seen in the design of the Soviet Sverdlov-class heavy cruisers of that era.

Carl O. Schuster

(Refer to table on page 918)

Additional Reading

Groner, Erich, *German Warships 1815–1945* (1990).
Lenton, H.J., *German Warships of the Second World War* (1975).
Whitley, M.J., *German Cruisers* (1989).

Cruisers, Italian

Like the other major naval powers, the Italians were initially bound by the constraints of the Washington Naval Treaty of 1922. When the London Conference (*see* Conferences, Naval) extended the limitations beyond capital ships, the Italians were left on a par with the French, and neither would sign the agreement. Both were displeased with their status as equal, second-class naval powers. Ultimately, national budget constraints limited each to seven heavy cruisers. To these, the Italians added several classes of light cruisers and very light cruisers and two ships left over from World War I.

All Italian cruisers of the war were fast, but suffered from inadequate armor protection, insufficient antiaircraft armament, inaccurate main battery guns, and a total lack of electronic sensors and night vision equipment. The latter shortcoming was to prove particularly costly during the war.

The *Bari* and the *Taranto* were taken from Germany in 1920 as war reparations. The former was under construction at Danzig for the Soviets at the outbreak of World War I and was commandeered by the Germans. She proved remarkably durable, being sunk and refloated three times before finally being broken up at Livorno. The latter was in commission as the German cruiser *Strassburg* and was scuttled at La Spezia.

The first Italian building program was the 1st Group of Condottieris. These four ships were of twin-screw design with very large power plants that allowed sustained speeds of 37 knots, compared to an average of 32 to 33 knots for contemporary light cruisers of the other powers. The high speeds were obtained at the expense of range (a fault considered relatively unimportant to a Mediterranean navy) and virtually nonexistent protection. The wisdom of the latter decision may be questioned,

since all four of this group were sunk by British torpedoes, three from surface ships and one from a submarine.

Four additional groups of Condottieris were built by 1937. The main change was a gradual increase in displacement from 5,200 tons in the early models to 9,959 tons in the final group. The added weight, mostly armor, led to a loss of three knots in design speed, though the *Montecuccoli* was able to reach 39.4 knots in trials. The two ships of the fifth group mounted ten rather than the eight 153mm guns carried by the earlier groups. The evolution toward heavier armor and guns culminated in the Ciano-class. These two ships, derived from the Condottieris, were unfinished at the time of the Italian surrender.

The twelve ships of the Rogolo-class were very small (3,747 tons), fast, and essentially unarmored. Only three of the twelve were completed at the time of the armistice. Although tested without full fuel and armament, they achieved a remarkable 43 knots in sea trials. They were intended more as an answer to the French super destroyers, such as the Mogadors, than as true light cruisers.

The seven Italian heavy cruisers were wistfully named for territory sought by Italy in the armistice after World War I. The *Trento* and *Trieste* were built in 1927 in response to the French Tourville-class. Compared to the American and British heavy cruisers, they were lightly armored and constructed, but were extremely fast. The *Trento* reached 38.7 knots in trials, which were conducted without its turrets mounted, and the class had a design speed of 35 knots. The *Bolzano,* the only example of the second group of the Trento-class, carried an additional 1,000 tons of armor.

The Zara-class represented a change in emphasis. They sacrificed speed and range in favor of added armor. They were capable of a sustained 32 knots and a radius of 3,500 nautical miles at 14 knots. Both were considered adequate for the Mediterranean. They carried a 150 mm belt armor, almost equal to the American Baltimore-class.

The Italian heavy cruisers fared poorly in the war; all were lost. The *Trento* was sunk by a British submarine and the *Trieste* by aerial bombs. The *Bolzano* was scuttled at La Spezia, as was the *Gorizia*. The *Zara, Fiume,* and *Pola* were lost at Matapan (q.v.). The *Zara* and *Fiume* were caught with their 203mm guns trained fore and aft and were smothered with point-blank fire from British battleships.

The poor performance of the Italian cruisers was due, at least in part, to their lack of radar and night vision equipment, as well as the navy's failure to train in night operations, which combined to leave them essentially blind, particularly during periods of poor visibility. For whatever reasons, the Italian cruisers were among the fastest, most beautiful, and least successful ships of World War II.

Jack E. McCallum

(Refer to tables on pages 919–921)

Additional Reading

Fraccaroli, Aldo, *Italian Warships of World War II* (1968).
Jane's Fighting Ships of World War II (1989).
Maugeri, Franco, *From the Ashes of Disgrace* (1948).

Cruisers, Soviet

Stalin had planned a major seagoing-fleet for the Soviet Union, and he imported foreign technicians and equipment to build it. Unfortunately, his purges (q.v.) and the political crises of the late 1930s disrupted his plans. As a result, his fleet was stillborn. The foreign technicians, primarily Italians, went home, and the economic chaos his purges inflicted on the Soviet Union reduced the flow of steel and other supplies to his shipyards.

Despite these problems, cruisers constituted the most modern element of the Soviet surface navy in 1939. The bulk of the units were less than ten years old and all but two of the older units (which were being used as training ships) were completed after World War I. Nonetheless, it was a force penalized by obsolete sensors, archaic fire control systems, and inadequate antiaircraft weaponry. Moreover, maintenance was a problem and became even more difficult for the Black Sea Fleet units as their bases were overrun by the German ground advances of 1941.

The two oldest cruisers, *Aurora* and *Komintern,* dated from World War I and were used as training ships in the Baltic and Black Seas, respectively. The German invasion forced their operational use and both figured prominently in the city sieges conducted within their fleet areas (Leningrad [q.v.] for *Aurora,* Odessa and Sevastopol [q.v.] for *Komintern*). The two ships were heavily damaged by German bombing, which ended their active participation in the war by early 1942.

The *Krasny Krim, Chervonaya Ukraina,* and *Krasny Kavkaz* were all former tzarist navy cruisers whose construction was not completed until well after the Russian civil war ended. Although completed in the late 1920s to early 1930s, their designs were outdated, using weapons casements located just above the waterline. Moreover, they were all slow, had thin and poorly arranged armor, and provided little deck space to expand their weapons or sensor suites. Still, all gave good service in the Black Sea and only the *Chervonaya Ukraina* was sunk in the war.

The Kirov-class cruisers were the first truly modern units built for the Soviet Navy. Based on Italian designs and built with extensive Italian assistance, these units bore a marked similarity to the Italian Zara-class heavy cruisers. Like their Italian counterparts, the Kirovs and the follow-on Maksim Gorky-class units sacrificed armor for speed. This limited their ability to take punishment and made their employment a risky proposition. More significantly, the emphasis on speed led to the use of narrow, closely mounted, triple main battery turrets (to reduce beam), which severely degraded the accuracy of their main gun salvoes. Otherwise, their 180mm guns were outstanding weapons with good range and excellent individual accuracy.

The antiaircraft battery was good by prewar European standards but was inhibited by poor fire control arrangements. Antiaircraft capability was improved during the war by the addition of Lend-Lease (q.v.) antiaircraft guns and British and U.S. radar systems. Most of these units survived the war and were scrapped in the 1960s. The follow-on Frunze-class were to incorporate better antiaircraft weaponry and sensors, but were not completed until after the war.

The U.S. light cruiser USS *Milwaukee* was transferred to the Soviet Northern Fleet in April 1944 as compensation for surrendered Italian tonnage that could not be delivered. It saw little action and was returned to the U.S. Navy in 1949.

Stalin planned to buy two German Hipper-class heavy cruisers from Germany and build two more in the Soviet Union. The German invasion put an end to these plans and only one unit, the *Tallinn,* was ever delivered. It spent the war as a floating battery in Leningrad and was never commissioned. Nonetheless, it had a major influence on Soviet postwar cruiser design. The Soviets incorporated its design elements, and lessons learned from the Kirov and Frunze-classes, into the postwar Sverdlov-class heavy cruisers, which were built with German assistance. The Sverdlovs served the Soviets well into the 1980s.

Carl O. Schuster

(Refer to tables on pages 922–923)

Additional Reading

Budzbon, Prsemystaw, *Soviet Navy at War: 1941–1945* (1981).

Meister, Jurg, *Soviet Warships of the Second World War* (1977).

Cruisers, U.S.

The evolution of U.S. cruisers during World War II resulted from factors unrelated to tactical requirements. Prewar treaties sharply limited cruiser design. Because of a five- to eight-year lag between design and deployment, pre–World War II cruisers were imperfect adaptations of ships designed for other times and other missions. The designs that evolved during the war represented the lessons learned from the earlier units and combat actions in the Pacific during the war's early years. The United States built the largest, most heavily armed and electronically advanced cruisers of the war. However, no other country had the resources to build and maintain such expensive units.

The ten cruisers of the Omaha-class dated from the fleet building program of 1916. Launched in 1923 and 1924, they displaced 7,050 tons and carried ten 6-inch guns. All continued in service into the war. They were built to serve as scouts (as evidenced by their complement of two catapult-launched aircraft) and screening ships for battleship-centered fleets.

The Washington Naval Treaty of 1922 (*see* Conferences, Naval) limited the production of capital ships, defined as those of displacement greater than 10,000 tons and with guns larger than 8-inches. The 10,000-ton limit imposed severe design restrictions. In order to carry 8-inch guns and the necessary ammunition and manpower to operate them, armor had to be sacrificed.

The poorly protected Pensacola-class cruisers were appropriately dubbed the "tinclads." Although they were created to meet treaty limitations rather than tactical needs, their design dominated the rest of the World War II cruisers. It was not at all certain that the Pensacolas provided a stable enough platform to allow accuracy at the 31,000-meter maximum range of their 8-inch guns. In fact, the captain of one of the ships noted that the recoil from simultaneously firing all three guns in one mount would structurally damage the ship. Because of design miscalculations, the two Pensacolas were almost 1,000 tons below treaty limits.

The subsequent Northampton (six ships), Portland (two ships), and New Orleans (seven ships) classes progressively added weight, principally as armor. The Pensacolas had four-inch side and one-inch deck armor. By the time the New Orleans class was laid down, the sides carried five inches and the decks 2.25 inches of armor plate. Enough armor was added to protect at least the magazine and ammunition train against 8-inch shells, to which the ships had previously been entirely vulnerable.

The London Conference of 1930 extended the 5:5:3 displacement ratio for Britain, the United States, and Japan, respectively, to the 8-inch cruisers. The treaty distinguished heavy from light cruisers based on gun size, with 6.1-inch (155mm) bores being the dividing line. This allowed for the possibility, subsequently realized, of light cruisers of greater displacement than heavy cruisers. After the treaty, light cruisers were designated "CL," heavy cruisers "CA."

The seven 10,000-ton Brooklyn-class CLs carried fifteen 6-inch guns in three gun turrets. Their 8,000-mile radius at twelve knots satisfied the requirements of deployment for Pacific distances.

The USS *Wichita,* the only example of its class, was launched in 1939. Its hull was similar to the Brooklyn class, but it mounted nine 8-inch guns and was, therefore, a heavy cruiser. It was the last of the "treaty cruisers" and served as a transition to the Baltimore-class.

The London Treaty of 1936 lowered the upper limit on cruiser displacement to 8,000 tons and armament to 6-inch guns. The Atlanta-class of four 6,000-ton antiaircraft cruisers was a direct result of this agreement. Unarmored and carrying sixteen dual-purpose 5-inch guns, these ships did not do well in surface engagements. The *Atlanta* and the *Juneau* were lost in a single 24-hour period on 13 November 1942 in the naval surface engagement off Guadalcanal.

At the outbreak of the war, the first priority was production of large numbers of vessels. This precluded innovation, and both heavy and light cruisers were adaptations of previous treaty designs. The two ships of the St. Louis-class carried minor modifications of the Brooklyn's armor and power plants, and were a transition to the Cleveland-class. With twenty-seven ships in this class, the Clevelands were the largest group of cruisers of a single design ever launched, and were the standard U.S. light cruisers of the war. They carried twelve 6-inch guns and a total of forty-five 20mm and 40mm antiaircraft guns. They were protected by only 1.25-inch deck plate and a 4.4-inch belt armor. Design speed was 33.2 knots.

The Baltimore-class of CAs were linear descendants of the *Wichita.* These fourteen ships were the standard heavy cruisers of the war. They

The USS Tuscaloosa, *a New Orleans-class heavy cruiser, shown here during a 1942 convoy to Russia. (IWM A 8956)*

carried nine 8-inch guns and had deck armor of 2.5 inches and a maximum belt thickness of 8 inches. Reflecting interwar thinking about their mission as scouts, they originally were equipped with four airplanes. They had a design speed of 34 knots.

Although designed for fleet and independent action, U.S. cruisers fought their last major surface action in the Solomons, where they functioned as capital ships. After 1943, they were used almost entirely for shore bombardment and as antiaircraft screens. The change in mission and the change in perceived threat from surface to air necessitated numerous changes in the structure of the vessels as the war progressed. The need for antiaircraft ordnance and larger crews added considerable weight, compensated for by eliminating ship's boats and aircraft, cutting back masts and superstructure, and removing conning towers. Open bridges were added to allow wider observation of the skies, and 20mm and 40mm antiaircraft cannons were added. In 1942, large cruisers carried twelve of the former; by 1944, they mounted twenty-eight. Late in 1944, kamikaze attacks were such a severe problem in the Pacific that some 6-inch guns were replaced by pairs of 40mm antiaircraft cannons, while others were altered to allow 60-degree elevation for close-in fire support of shore operations.

America built the largest and most capable cruisers during the war. Most served in the Pacific and were modified or built to survive in the more intense naval warfare environment of that theater where antiaircraft protection was more important than armor. French and Italian cruisers were faster and British cruisers enjoyed heavier armor, but no navy's cruisers were more heavily armed or carried more ammunition. Most of the American cruisers employed in Europe were those of the older prewar classes, modernized only to the extent that they carried the latest radar equipment. Although they never saw significant combat against Axis naval forces in the European theater, they would have been more than a match for most of the units they would have encountered.

Jack E. McCallum

(Refer to tables on pages 924–927)

Additional Reading

Galuppini, Gino, *Warships of the World* (1989).
Jane's Fighting Ships of World War II (1989).

Section IV-C
Technical Data Tables of
Weapons and Equipment

Allied Naval Aircraft (U.S. and British)

Fighters

Model	F-4F* Wildcat	FM-1* Wildcat	F-6F Hellcat	F-4U Corsair	Sea Gladiator	Skua	Roc	Fulmar	Sea Hurricane 1	Sea Hurricane 2
Country	USA	USA	USA	USA	British	British	British	British	British	British
Service Date	1939	1943	1942	1943	1938	1938	1940	1940	1941	1943
Engines	1	1	1	1	1	1	1	1	1	1
Crew	1	1	1	1	1	1	1	2	1	1
Maximum Speed (mph)	328	332	386	417	253	225	219	280	324	342
Normal Range	770 mi	830 mi	1,090 mi	1,015 mi	410 mi	760 mi	610 mi	800 mi	425 mi	480 mi
Maximum Range	845 mi	1,310 mi	1,590 mi	1,560 mi	n/a	n/a	n/a	n/a	900 mi	985 mi
Gun Armament	6x .50 MG	4x .50 MG	6x .50 MG	6x .50 MG	4x .303 MG	5x .303 MG	4x .303 MG	8x .303 MG	8x .303 MG	12x .303 MG
Bombs or Rockets	200 lbs	500 lbs or 6x 5-in rocket	2,000 lbs or 6x 5-in rocket	2,000 lbs or 8x 5-in rocket	None	500 lbs	240 lbs	500 lbs	None	1,000 lbs
Number in Service	1,971	4,777	6,436	8,645	98	580	133	500	50	400
Ceiling (feet)	37,000	37,000	42,600	36,900	32,300	20,200	15,200	26,000	32,000	36,500

*Called Marlett I and II in British service.

(continued on next page)

Allied Naval Aircraft (U.S. and British) *(continued)*

Bombers and Dive Bombers

Model	Seafire I	Seafire II & III	SBD-5	TBF Avenger	Firefly	Swordfish	Albacore	Barracuda
Country	British	British	USA	USA	British	British	British	British
Service Date	1942	1942	1940	1942	1944	1938	1940	1943
No. of Engines	1	1	1	1	1	1	1	1
Crew	1	1	2	3	1	2–3	2–3	3
Maximum Speed (mph)	365	383	252	267	316	139	161	228
Normal Range	465 mi	430 mi	1,115 mi	1,215 mi	1,070 mi	546 mi	820 mi	684 mi
Maximum Range	725 mi*	640 mi*	n/a	2,135 mi*	1,300 mi	1,030 mi	930 mi	1,150 mi
Gun Armament	4x .303 MG 2x 20mm	4x .303 MG 2x 20mm	2x .30 MG 2x .50 MG	2x .30 MG 2x .50 MG	4x 20mm	2x .303 MG	3x .303 MG	2x .303 MG
Bombs or Other Ordnance	500 lbs	500 lbs	1,000 lbs or 2x DC†	2,000 lbs, 1x torpedo, or 4x DC†	2,000 lbs	1,500 lbs, 1x torpedo, or 2x DC†	2,000 lbs, 1x torpedo, or 2x DC†	1,500 lbs, 1x torpedo, or 4x DC†
Number in Service	156	1,571	5,937	9,839	1,623	2,393	800	2,602
Ceiling (feet)	33,800	35,500	24,300	23,400	28,000	10,700	20,700	16,600

*The normal range was extended with extra drop tanks.

†DC: depth charges

Axis Naval Aircraft (German and Italian)

All Types

Model & Type	Bf-109T Fighter	Ju-87C Dive Bomber	Fi-167 Recon/Bomber	Re. 2001 Fighter-Bomber (Carrier Version)
Country	Germany	Germany	Germany	Italy
Service Date	1939	1939	1939	1943
No. of Engines	1	1	1	1
Crew	1	2	2	1
Maximum Speed (mph)	354	238	202	337
Normal Range	412 mi	370 mi	808 mi	646 mi
Maximum Range	n/a	n/a	932 mi*	n/a
Gun Armament	2x 7.9mm MG 1x 20mm	3x 7.9mm MG	2x 7.9mm MG	2x 7.7mm MG 2x 12.7mm MG
Bombs or Torpedoes	None	1,200 lbs or 1x 45cm torpedo	2,205 lbs or 1x 53cm torpedo	2,000 lbs or 1x 53cm torpedo
Number in Service	30	24	12	2
Ceiling (feet)	34,450	26,150	26,900	36,090

*With drop tanks.

British Heavy Cruisers

	Kent-Class	London-Class	Dorsetshire-Class	York-Class
Commissioned (year)	1927	1928	1931	1931
Number Built	7	4	2	2
Displacement (tons)	4x 10,570 3x 10,800	3x 9,850 1x 10,500	1x 9,975 1x 9,925	1x 8,250 1x 8,390
Max. Speed (knots)	31.5	32	31	32
Endurance (nm) at Best Speed	10,400 nm at 11 kts	10,400 nm at 11 kts	10,400 nm at 11 kts	10,000 nm at 14 kts
Main Armament (guns)	8x 8-in	8x 8-in	8x 8-in	6x 8-in
Secondary Armament (guns)	8x 4-in AA	8x 4-in AA	8x 4-in AA	4x 4-in AA
Initial AA Battery	8x 2-pdrs 8x .50 MG	16x 2-pdrs 8x .50 MG	16x 2-pdrs 8x .50 MG	2x 2-pdrs
Mines	None	None	None	None
Torpedo Tubes	None	8x 21-in	8x 21-in	6x 21-in
Max. Armor (inches)	5.5	5.5	3	3
Radar	Yes	Yes	Yes	1-Yes, 1-No
Sonar	No	No	No	No
Hydrophones	No	No	No	No
Crew Size	685	852	819	1-623 1-630
Losses	2	None	1	2

British Light Cruisers

	Birmingham	C-Class 1st Group	C-Class 2nd Group	C-Class 3rd Group	Cavendish-Class	D-Class	E-Class	Leander-Class 1st Group	Leander-Class 2nd Group
Commissioned (year)	1916	1918	1918	1919	1919	1920	1926	1932	1936
Number Built	1	3	5	5	3	8	2	5	3
Displacement (tons)	5,100	4,180	4,190	4,290	Note 1	4,850	1x 7,550 1x 7,580	Note 2	Note 3
Max. Speed (knots)	25	29	29	29	1x 29, 2x 30	29	32	32.5	32.5
Endurance (nm) at Best Speed	2,000 nm at 20 kts	2,400 nm at 24 kts	2,240 nm at 24 kts	2,240 nm at 24 kts	5,400 nm at 14 kts	2,300 nm at 27 kts	3,850 nm at 20 kts	12,000 nm at 12 kts	7,000 nm at 14 kts
Main Armament (guns)	8x 6-in	5x 6-in	Note 4	8x 4-in AA	Note 5	6x 6-in	7x 6-in	8x 6-in	8x 6-in
Secondary Armament (guns)	3x 4-in AA	2x 3-in AA	3- 2x 3-in AA 2- None	None	Note 5	3x 4-in AA	5x 4-in AA	4- 8x 4-in AA 1- 4x 4-in AA	4x 4-in AA
Initial AA Battery	None	2x 2-pdr	3- 2x 2-pdr 2- 8x 2-pdr	4x 2-pdr 8x .50 MG	Note 5	2x 2-pdr	2x 2-pdr	12x .50 MG	12x .50 MG
Mines	None	None	None	None	None	None	None	None	None
Torpedo Tubes	None	8x 21-in	8x 21-in	8x 21-in	4x 21-in	12x 21-in	16x 21-in	8x 21-in	8x 21-in
Max. Armor (inches)	3	3	3	3	3	3	3	3.5	3.5
Radar	Yes	Yes	Yes	Yes	Yes	Yes	Yes	Yes	Yes
Sonar	No	No	No	No	No	No	No	No	No
Hydrophones	No	No	No	No	No	No	No	No	No
Crew Size	470	400	400	439	712	450	572	570	682
Losses	None	1	3	3	1	3	None	1	2

(continued on next page)

British Light Cruisers (continued)

	Arethusa-Class 1st Group	Arethusa-Class 2nd Group	Southampton-Class 1st Group	Southampton-Class 2nd Group	Southampton-Class 3rd Group	Dido-Class 1st Group	Dido-Class 2nd Group	Fiji-Class	Minotaur-Class
Commissioned (year)	1935	1937	1937	1939	1940	1940	1943	1940	1944
Number Built	2	2	5	3	2	11	5	11	3
Displacement (tons)	5,200	5,270	9,100	9,400	10,260	5,600	5,950	8- 8,525 3- 8,875	2- 8,800 1- 9,630
Max. Speed (kts)	32	32	32	32	32	33	33	33	32.5
Endurance (nm) at Best Speed	12,000 nm at 14 kts	12,000 nm at 14 kts	6,000 nm at 14 kts	6,000 nm at 14 kts	6,000 nm at 14 kts	4,240 nm at 16 kts	4,240 nm at 16 kts	5,850 nm at 16 kts	8,000 nm at 16 kts
Main Armament (guns)	6x 6-in	6x 6-in	12x 6-in	12x 6-in	12x 6-in	10x 5.25-in DP*	8x 5.25-in DP*	8- 12x 6-in 3- 9x 6-in	2- 9x 6-in 1- 6x 6-in DP*
Secondary Armament (guns)	8x 4-in AA	8x 4-in AA	8x 4-in AA	8x 4-in AA	12x 4-in AA	None	None	8x 4-in AA	2- 10x 4-in AA 1- 6x 3-in DP*
Initial AA Battery	8x .50 MG	8x .50 MG	8x 2-pdrs 8x .50 MG	8x 2-pdrs 8x .50 MG	16x 2-pdrs 8x .50 MG	8x 2-pdrs 8x .50 MG	12x 2-pdr 12x 20mm	Note 6	16x 2-pdrs 6x 40mm
Mines	None	None	None	None	None	None	None	None	None
Torpedo Tubes	6x 21-in	6x 21-in	6x 21-in	6x 21-in	6x 21-in	6x 21-in	6x 21-in	6x 21-in	Note 7
Max. Armor (inches)	3	3	4.5	4.5	4.5	3	3	3.5	3
Radar	Yes	Yes	Yes	Yes	Yes	Yes	Yes	Yes	Yes
Sonar	No	No	No	No	No	No	No	No	No
Hydrophones	No	No	No	No	No	No	No	No	No
Crew Size	500	500	930	980	990	530	530	920	2- 960 1- 900
Losses	1	1	1	2	1	4	1	2	None

*DP: dual-purpose.

Notes:

1. Displacement of Cavendish-Class:
   - 1x 9,550 tons
   - 1x 9,800 tons
   - 1x 9,860 tons

2. Displacement of Leander-Class, 1st group:
   - 1x 7,270 tons
   - 1x 7,175 tons
   - 1x 7,215 tons
   - 2x 7,030 tons

3. Displacement of Leander-Class, 2nd group:
   - 1x 6,830 tons
   - 1x 6,980 tons
   - 1x 7,105 tons

4. Main Armament for C-Class, 2nd group:
   - Three ships had 5x 6-inch guns;
   - Two ships had 10x 4-inch AA guns.

5. Armament for the Cavendish-Class cruiser consisted of:

Main Armament	Secondary Armament	Initial AA Battery
1 ship had 9x 6-in guns;	1 ship had 8x 4-in AA guns;	1 ship had 8x 2-pdrs, 12x .50 MG;
1 ship had 5x 7.5-in guns;	1 ship had 5x 4-in AA guns;	1 ship had 16x 2-pdrs, 7x 20mm cannon;
1 ship had 4x 4-in guns.	1 ship had 4x 4-in AA guns.	1 ship had 8x 2-pdrs, 8x 20mm cannon.

6. Initial AA battery for Fiji-Class cruiser:
   - 8 ships had 8x 2-pdr guns;
   - 3 ships had 16x 2-pdr guns;
   - 8 ships had 16x .50 machine guns;
   - 3 ships had 20x 20mm cannons.

7. Torpedo tubes for Minotaur-Class cruisers:
   - 2 ships had 6x 21-in tubes;
   - 1 ship had no torpedo tubes.

French Heavy Cruisers

	Tourville-Class	Suffren-Class 1st Group	Suffren-Class 2nd Group	Algérie
Commissioned (year)	1927	1930	1931	1935
Number Built	2	1	3	1
Displacement (tons)	10,000	10,000	10,000	10,000
Max. Speed (knots)	33.8	31	31	31
Endurance (nm) at Best Speed	4,500 nm at 15 kts	4,600 nm at 15 kts	5,300 nm at 15 kts	8,700 nm at 15 kts
Main Armament (guns)	8 x 203mm	8 x 203mm	8 x 203mm	8 x 203mm
Secondary Armament (guns)	8 x 75mm AA	8 x 75mm AA	8 x 90mm AA	12 x 90mm AA
Initial AA Battery	8 x 37mm 12 x 13.2mm	8 x 37mm 12 x 13.2mm	8 x 37mm 12 x 13.2mm	8 x 37mm
Mines	None	None	None	None
Torpedo Tubes	12 x 55cm	12 x 55cm	None	6 x 55cm
Max. Armor (mm)	30	50	60	110
Radar	No	No	No	No
Sonar	No	No	No	No
Hydrophones	No	No	No	No
Crew Size	605	773	752	748
Losses	None	None	3	1

French Light Cruisers

	Duquay Trovin-Class	Jeanne D'Arc	Émil Berten	La Galissonnière-Class	La Tour d'Ayveryne
Commissioned (year)	1923	1932 Note 1	1935	1935	1931
Number Built	3	1	1	6	1
Displacement (tons)	7,880	7,291	6,530	8,214	4,773
Max. Speed (knots)	33	25	34	31	30
Endurance (nm) at Best Speed	4,500 nm at 15 kts	5,200 nm at 11 kts	3,600 nm at 15 kts	7,000 nm at 12 kts	3,500 nm at 15 kts
Main Armament (guns)	8x 155mm	8x 155mm	9x 152mm	9x 152mm	4x 139mm
Secondary Armament (guns)	4x 75mm AA	4x 75mm AA	4x 90mm AA	8x 90mm AA	4x 75mm AA
Initial AA Battery	None	4x 37mm 12x 13.2mm	8x 37mm 8x 13.2mm	8x 37mm 12x 13.2mm	2x 37mm 12x 13.2mm
Mines	None	None	90	None	190
Torpedo Tubes	12x 55cm	2x 55cm	6x 55cm	4x 55cm	None
Max. Armor (mm)	30	30	80	120	None
Radar	No	No	No	No	No
Sonar	No	No	No	No	No
Hydrophones	No	No	No	No	No
Crew Size	578	648	711	540	424
Losses	2	None	None	3	1

Note:
1. Training cruiser.

German Light and Heavy Cruisers
(*See* Note 1)

	Emden	Königsberg-Class	Leipzig	Nürnberg	Admiral Hipper-Class	Prinz Eugen
Commissioned (year)	1927	1929	1932	1936	1939	1940
Number Built	1	3	1	1	2	1 Note 2
Displacement (tons)	5,600	6,650	6,710	6,980	13,900	14,800
Max. Speed (knots)	29	2x 32 1x 30	32	32	32.5	32
Endurance (nm) at Best Speed	5,300 nm at 18 kts	5,200 nm at 19 kts	5,700 nm at 19 kts	5,700 nm at 19 kts	6,800 nm at 19 kts	6,800 nm at 19 kts
Main Armament (guns)	8x 150mm	9x 150mm	9x 150mm	9x 150mm	8x 205mm	8x 205mm
Secondary Armament (guns)	3x 88mm AA	6x 88mm AA	6x 88mm AA	6x 88mm AA	12x 105mm AA	12x 105mm AA
Initial AA Battery	4x 37mm	4x 20mm 8x 37mm	10x 20mm 8x 37mm	4x 20mm 8x 37mm	4x 20mm 12x 37mm	8x 20mm 12x 37mm
Mines	120	80	80	80	None	None
Torpedo Tubes	4x 53cm	12x 53.3cm	12x 53.3cm	12x 53.3cm	12x 53.3cm	12x 53.3cm
Max. Armor (mm)	50	50	50	50	80	80
Radar	No	Yes	Yes	Yes	Yes	Yes
Sonar	No	No	No	No	Yes	Yes
Hydrophones	Yes	Yes	Yes	Yes	Yes	Yes
Crew Size	630	820	850	896	1,600	1,600
Losses	1	3	None	None	2	None

Notes:
1. The first four (the *Emden*, Königsberg-Class, *Leipzig*, and *Nürnberg*) were classified as light cruisers, while the Admiral Hipper-Class and the *Prinz Eugen* were classified as heavy cruisers.
2. The planned Prinz Eugen-Class also included the *Lützow* and *Seydlitz*, which were never completed.

Italian Heavy Cruisers

	San Giorgio	Trento-Class 1st Group	Trento-Class 2nd Group	Zara-Class
Commissioned (year)	1911	1928	1933	1931
Number Built	1	2	1	4
Displacement (tons)	9,500	10,500	11,065	11,500
Max. Speed (knots)	23	35	36	35
Endurance (nm) at Best Speed	3,000 nm at 11 kts	3,500 nm at 14 kts	3,500 nm at 14 kts	3,500 nm at 14 kts
Main Armament (guns)	4x 250mm	8x 203mm	8x 203mm	8x 203mm
Secondary Armament (guns)	8x 180mm	12x 100mm AA	12x 100mm AA	12x 100mm AA
Initial AA Battery	Note 1	8x 37mm 8x 13.2mm	8x 37mm 8x 13.2mm	8x 37mm 8x 13.2mm
Mines	None	None	None	None
Torpedo Tubes	None	8x 53.3cm	8x 53.3cm	8x 53.3cm
Max. Armor (mm)	248	100	100	150
Radar	No	No	No	No
Sonar	No	No	No	No
Hydrophones	No	No	No	No
Crew Size	300	781	788	830
Losses	1	2	1	4

Note:
1. Initial AA battery for the *San Georgio*, added in 1938:
   14x 13.7mm   6x 37mm
   12x 20mm   10x 100mm

Italian Light Cruisers

	Bari	Condottieri-Class 1st Group	Condottieri-Class 2nd Group	Condottieri-Class 3rd Group	Condottieri-Class 4th Group	Condottieri-Class 5th Group	Regolo-Class
Commissioned (year)	1914	1931	1933	1935	1935	1937	1942
Number Built	1	4	2	2	2	2	12 Note 5
Displacement (tons)	3,248	5,200	5,400	7,550	8,662	1x 9,954 1x 9,387	3,747
Max. Speed (knots)	24.5	37–42	39.6	38	37	35	43+
Endurance (nm) at Best Speed	2,000 nm at 18 kts	2,500 nm at 18 kts	2,500 nm at 18 kts	3,000 nm at 18 kts	3,000 nm at 18 kts	2,900 nm at 18 kts	2,900 nm at 18 kts
Main Armament (guns)	8x 150mm	8x 153mm	8x 153mm	8x 153mm	8x 153mm	10x 153mm	8x 130mm
Secondary Armament (guns)	None	6x 100mm AA	6x 100mm AA	6x 100mm AA	6x 100mm AA	6x 100mm AA	None
Initial AA Battery	Note 1	8x 13.2mm 8x 37mm	16x 20mm	8x 37mm 12x 20mm	8x 37mm 12x 20mm	8x 37mm 10x 20mm	8x 37mm 8x 20mm
Mines	120	Note 2	90	96	100–146	Note 3	70
Torpedo Tubes	None	4x 53.3cm	4x 53.3cm	4x 53.3cm	6x 53.3cm	6x 53.3cm	8x 53.3cm
Max. Armor (mm)	85	40	50	100	100	140	None
Radar	No	No	No	No	No	No	Note 4
Sonar	No	No	No	No	No	No	No
Hydrophones	No	No	No	No	No	No	No
Crew Size	439	521	544	648	690	892	420
Losses	1	4	1	1	None	None	None

Notes:

1. Initial AA battery for the *Bari* consisted of:
   3x 40mm AA
   6x 20mm AA
   6x 13.2mm AA

2. Number of mines for Condottiere-Class, 1st group:
   1x none
   3x 90 each

3. Condottiere-Class, 5th group, could carry 90–120 mines or 40 depth charges.

4. One ship was equipped with radar, the other two had none.

5. Only three of the Regolo-Class were completed at the time of Italy's surrender.

Soviet Light Cruisers

	Kirov-Class	Krasay Kaukaz	Krasay Krim	Chervonaya Ukraina	Komintern	Aurora
Commissioned (year)	1939	1932	1928	1927	1905	1902
Number Built	3	1	1	1	1	1
Displacement (tons)	8,800	8,030	6,934	6,934	6,338	5,622
Max. Speed (knots)	35	29	29	29.5	23	18
Endurance (nm) at Best Speed	3,000 nm at 18 kts	7,300 nm at 10 kts	3,700 nm at 18 kts	3,700 nm at 18 kts	5,300 nm at 12 kts	2,000 nm at 11 kts
Main Armament (guns)	9x 180mm	4x 180mm	15x 130mm	15x 130mm	10x 130mm	10x 130mm
Secondary Armament (guns)	6x 100mm	6x 100mm AA	4x 100mm AA	4x 76mm AA	6x 75mm	4x 75mm
Initial AA Battery	6x 45mm	Note 1	4x 45mm	12x 13mm	Note 2	2x 76mm 4x 13mm
Mines	Note 3	100	100	100	60	60
Torpedo Tubes	6x 53.3cm	6x 53.3cm	12x 53.3mm	12x 53.3cm	None	4x 45cm
Max. Armor (mm)	100	76	76	76	140	152
Radar	No	No	No	No	No	No
Sonar	No	No	No	No	No	No
Hydrophones	No	No	No	No	No	No
Crew Size	734	850	684	750	590	598
Losses	None	None	None	1	1	None

Notes:

1. Initial AA battery for the *Krasay Kaukaz* was:

   2x 76mm guns
   4x 45mm guns
   8x 37mm guns

2. Initial AA battery for the *Komintern* included:

   3x 76mm guns
   2x 47mm guns
   2x 13mm guns

3. The Kirov-class cruisers were capable of either 90 mines or 60 depth charges.

U.S. Heavy Cruisers (European Theater)

	Pensacola-Class	Northampton-Class	Portland-Class	New Orleans-Class	Wichita	Baltimore-Class
Commissioned (year)	1931	1932	1934	1935	1939	1943
Number Built	2	6	2	7	1	14
Displacement (tons)	9,100	Note 1	1x 9,800 1x 9,950	Note 2	9,324	13,400
Max. Speed (kts)	32.5	32.5	33	33	32.5	33
Endurance (nm) at Best Speed	7,900 nm at 12 kts	7,900 nm at 12 kts	7,900 nm at 12 kts	7,800 nm at 12 kts	7,700 nm at 12 kts	8,000 nm at 15 kts
Main Armament (guns)	10x 8-in	9x 8-in	9x 8-in	9x 8-in	9x 8-in	9x 8-in
Secondary Armament (guns)	8x 5-in AA	8x 5-in AA	8x 5-in AA	8x 5-in AA	8x 5-in AA	12x 5-in AA
Initial AA Battery	2x 3-pdr 8x .50 MG	2x 3-pdr 8x .50 MG	Note 3	Note 3	2x 3-pdr 8x .50 MG	48x 40mm 22–28x 20mm
Mines	No	No	No	No	No	No
Torpedo Tubes	No	No	No	No	No	No
Max. Armor (inches)	3	3	4	5	5	8
Radar	Yes	Yes	Yes	Yes	Yes	Yes
Sonar	No	No	No	No	No	No
Hydrophones	No	No	No	No	No	No
Crew Size	653	795	1,269	1,200	1,200	1,700
Losses	None	3 (Note 4)	1 (Note 4)	3 (Note 4)	None	None

Notes:

1. Displacement of Northampton-Class cruisers:
   4 each at 9,050 tons
   1 each at 9,200 tons
   1 each at 9,300 tons

2. Displacement of New Orleans-Class cruisers:
   4 each at 9,950 tons
   1 each at 9,375 tons
   1 each at 9,400 tons
   1 each at 9,975 tons

3. Initial AA battery for both Portland- and New Orleans-Class:
   2x 3-pounders
   16x 1.1-inch guns
   8x .50 machine guns

4 . All losses were in the Pacific theater of operations.

U.S. Light Cruisers (European Theater)

	Omaha-Class	Brooklyn-Class 1st Group	Brooklyn-Class 2nd Group	Atlanta-Class	Cleveland-Class	Oakland-Class 1st Group	Oakland-Class 2nd Group
Commissioned (year)	1922	1938	1939	1942	1942	1943	1945
Number Built	10	7	2	4	27	4	3
Displacement (tons)	7,050	Note 1	10,000	6,000	10,000	6,000	6,000
Max. Speed (knots)	34	32.5	32.5	33	33	33	33
Endurance (nm) at Best Speed	6,000 nm at 10 kts	8,000 nm at 12 kts	8,000 nm at 12 kts	6,000 nm at 15 kts	8,000 nm at 12 kts	6,000 nm at 15 kts	6,000 nm at 15 kts
Main Armament (guns)	7- 12x 6-in 5- 10x 6-in	15x 6-in	15x 6-in	16x 5-in DP*	12x 6-in	12x 5-in DP*	12x 5-in DP*
Secondary Armament (guns)	8x 3-in AA	8x 5-in AA	8x 5-in AA	None	12x 5-in DP*	None	None
Initial AA Battery	2x 3-pdr 8x .50 MG	Note 2	Note 2	16x 1.1-in 8x 20mm	24x 40mm 21x 20mm	16x 40mm 16x 20mm	16x 40mm 16x 20mm
Mines	None	None	None	None	None	None	None
Torpedo Tubes	6x 21-in	None	None	8x 21-in	None	8x 21-in	8x 21-in
Max. Armor (inches)	3	6.5	6.5	3.75	4.5	3.75	3.75
Radar	No	Yes	Yes	Yes	Yes	Yes	Yes
Sonar	No	No	No	No	No	No	No
Hydrophones	No	No	No	Yes	No	Yes	Yes
Crew Size	458	1,200	1,200	810	1,426	820	820
Losses	0	0	1	2	0	0	0

*DP: dual-purpose

Notes:

1. Standard displacement for Brooklyn-Class 1st group:

   2 ships 9,700 tons

   2 ships 9,475 tons

   2 ships 10,000 ton

   1 ship 9,650 tons

2. Initial AA battery for Brooklyn-Class, 1st and 2nd groups:

   4x 3-pounders

   16x 1.1-in AA

   8x .50 machine guns

3. All losses for all types of light cruisers were in the Pacific Ocean.

D

Defensively Equipped Merchant Ships (DEMS)

In anticipation of an outbreak of hostilities with Germany, the British Admiralty assumed control of all British merchant shipping on 29 August 1939. The task of managing the merchant marine was assigned to the Naval Trade Division of the Royal Naval Staff. The Admiralty created a new section within this division, the Office of Defensively Equipped Merchant Ships (DEMS), to coordinate and supervise the arming of British and neutral shipping.

The DEMS Office confronted several vital tasks. Primary emphasis went to the collection and distribution of serviceable weaponry considered useful aboard merchant ships. This included low-angle deck guns capable of combating surface attacks by U-boats as well as various weapons and devices with antiaircraft functions. Another task was training thousands of merchant seamen and naval reservists in the operation of these weapons. Finally, DEMS outfitted several liners and merchantmen for patrol duties and service as "Q-Ship" decoys similar to those of World War I.

The Admiralty succeeded in its efforts to arm the British merchant fleet. The shortage of deck guns was soon met with cannon salvaged from scrapped warships. Antiaircraft guns were in short supply and DEMS responded with a number of innovations including Holman compressed-air grenade projectors, kite and cable kits, balloons, and even fireworks. DEMS trained 24,000 Royal Navy sailors and 150,000 merchant seamen in their use. In addition, the Maritime Regiment of the Royal Artillery was created. It supplied DEMS with 14,000 army gunners for machine gun duty aboard merchant ships.

DEMS-converted liners proved effective in patrolling the Faeroe Islands, Iceland, and the Denmark Strait. Eventually, a program for converting fast merchantmen into armed merchant cruisers (AMCs) was instituted to deal with submarine "wolf pack" surface attacks (*see* Submarine and Antisubmarine Warfare). The "Q-Ship" project, however, was quickly abandoned after three of eight such decoy vessels were torpedoed soon after their launching.

By the end of the war, more than 5,500 British and Allied ships were armed. Refittings for the merchantmen occurred as vessels reached British ports and occasionally even at sea. The U.S. Navy adopted this model for the American merchant fleet, creating the Naval Armed Guard.

With a few exceptions, converted merchant ships did little to reduce British shipping losses from U-boat and air attack. Although defensive armament was distributed too widely to achieve the maximum concentrations necessary to be decisive, the presence of weaponry and trained gunners did much to strengthen the morale of merchant seamen at a time when Allied shipping losses were staggering. The DEMS project provided merchant crews with a means to strike back at attackers, stiffening resolve, which translated into tighter convoy discipline and security that significantly aided Allied success in the Battle of the Atlantic (q.v.).

Donald Frazier

Additional Reading

Kerr, J. Lennox (ed). *Touching the Adventures of Merchantman in the Second World War* (1953).
Schofield, Brian Bentham, *The Artic Convoys* (1977).

Destroyers, British

British destroyer strength was at a low ebb when

World War II broke out. Their numbers and unit capabilities were totally inadequate, and the British Merchant Marine paid the price. Few new destroyer units were built in the interwar years and the majority of those commissioned were medium-sized designs that lacked the range for a transatlantic crossing. By prewar standards, however, all were good antisubmarine warfare (ASW) platforms, equipped with sonar, and carried a fair number of depth charges. On the other hand, their antiaircraft (AA) batteries were too light to be effective. Still, British destroyers were as good as any in the world at the time. They had good all-around capabilities, handled well, and had excellent seakeeping qualities. The same could be said for the smaller escorts built during the war. More importantly, the British improved their designs as the war progressed.

Britain's destroyer strength in 1939 contrasted markedly with its situation in 1914, when the Royal Navy (RN) had the largest and most modern destroyer force in the world. The interwar years were particularly harsh, however, with more than 400 units scrapped and only 139 new units commissioned. Moreover, improvements in destroyer weapons and designs were sacrificed during the lean financial years to improve battleship systems. The most glaring example of this was the diversion of funding from dual-purpose (DP) gun development (that is, one that could engage aircraft as well as ships) to improving the secondary gun systems on battleships. As a result, British destroyers lacked the firepower to engage torpedo planes and high altitude bombers. As the RN's fleet destroyers increasingly worked within the range of the *Luftwaffe*, they suffered accordingly.

As the war progressed, many British destroyers replaced a main battery system with a single 4-inch-high-angle AA gun. The result reduced anti-surface firepower for little gain in AA defense. Still, it was an improvement, albeit small. The S-class destroyers, introduced in 1943, were the first built with a DP gun, the 4.7-inch. The Z-class destroyers, introduced in 1943, mounted a 4.5-inch DP gun. Although no longer essential in the European theater by that time, these new weapons proved absolutely vital in the Pacific.

The Admiralty's prewar decision not to acquire foreign-designed light AA guns was another error. Britain's multiple caliber .50 and 2-pounder (37mm) mounts proved less effective in combat, leaving the destroyers at a disadvantage against dive bombers. This decision was reversed in 1942, but it took more than a year to build and install the new guns. The fleet suffered in the interim, particularly in the Mediterranean.

The lack of radar (q.v.) was another shortcoming, but not a unique one. No navy had installed radar in its destroyers by 1939, and although the Germans were the first to do so, they made no technological improvements before 1944. The British made up for their late start by initiating an accelerated research and development program. New radars were designed and installed as the war progressed. By the war's end, British destroyers and escorts had better radar suites (including fire control radars) than any of their likely opponents. In fact, only the larger American destroyers had more capable radars and larger radar suites.

It was in sonar (q.v.) development (called AS-

The Lend-Lease destroyer HMS Salisbury, *formerly the USS* Claxton. *(IWM A 3160)*

DIC in British service) that Britain had the lead. The RN entered the war with the best sonars in the world, and they maintained that lead until the war's final year. British sonars had a diversity of frequencies and modulations that enabled flotilla and escort commanders to avoid mutual interference by varying each unit's operating frequencies. Axis navies had no such capability. The British were also the first to use chemical trace paper to record and examine sonar echoes, which helped the operator separate false echoes from valid contacts.

Perhaps the most important innovation British ships had after 1941, was the "operations room," which contained a plotting table that enabled the captain to see his radar, sonar, and lookout information displayed in a single location. This greatly facilitated decision making, especially during multi-threat (air, surface, and U-boat) actions.

The Admiralty recognized the urgency of its situation at war's start and ordered construction of sixty new destroyers. Ten units being built for foreign governments also were taken in hand. The older V- and W-class units were modified for convoy duty by having one boiler removed and an extra fuel tank installed. That gave them the range to reach Iceland without refueling. A new program of destroyer escort construction was also initiated. These slower and cheaper units were actually better suited for escort work because they carried more depth charges. Since sonar could not be used at high speeds, little was lost with the escort's slower speeds.

The British also built sloops and corvettes. Although they lacked the torpedoes and heavier guns of the destroyers, they had better seakeeping qualities, a stronger AA battery, and carried more ASW weapons. Derived from a prewar whaling ship design, the corvettes had particularly outstanding seakeeping qualities. More than 700 were built during the war.

The Admiralty simplified destroyer designs to increase the speed of construction. This included incorporating heavier AA suites and single main battery guns on the prewar J-class hulls. The need for larger destroyers for fleet operations was recognized in 1941, so destroyer construction from 1942 on concentrated on flotilla leaders. Although criticized for their size and expense, these larger units, with their twin DP batteries and greater operational radius, provided levels of performance comparable to the larger American destroyer designs. More significantly, these new designs had the capacity to absorb the additional weapons and sensors required in the postwar period, thus they remained in service until the early 1960s.

Britain's destroyers and escorts were the backbone of the RN's war effort. No task group or convoy went to sea without them. This put destroyers in the center of every fleet action. Britain and its dominions had 198 destroyers in service at

The Flower-class corvette HMS Columbine. *(IWM A 8422)*

the war's outbreak. Another 156 were built during the war, and fifty were obtained from the United States. More than a third (169) of the total was lost in combat. Losses among sloops and corvettes were not nearly as high overall, but those units suffered a similar loss rate in the war's early years. Their losses declined as the U-boat threat receded after mid-1943. In general, despite their flaws, Britain's destroyers, escorts, sloops, and corvettes were good overall designs that gave excellent service during the war.

Carl O. Schuster

(Refer to tables on pages 939–946)

Additional Reading

Hough, Richard, *The Longest War* (1986).
Lenton, H.T., *British Fleet and Escort Destroyers* (1970).
Roskill, S.W., *The War at Sea* (1954–57).

Destroyers, French

France entered the war with a relatively small but powerful destroyer force of thirty-two flotilla leaders (large destroyers), twenty-nine destroyers, and twelve torpedo boats, with another thirteen destroyers and flotilla leaders under construction. The flotilla leaders formed the backbone of the force.

France and Italy pioneered the construction of the large destroyer. Called *Contre-torpilleurs* (counter-torpedo boats) in France, these units were cheaper and more versatile than light cruisers and more effective than the standard destroyers of the prewar years. Their high speed, good torpedo armament, and antisubmarine warfare (ASW) equipment enabled them to be employed as destroyers, while their superior firepower and range allowed them to conduct cruiser missions. As such, they are the antecedents to modern destroyer designs, but they were not a panacea. The overloaded hulls rolled badly in heavy seas, forcing the French to remove one main battery gun from units assigned to the Atlantic.

France left the war before its radar program reached fruition, so only Free French units serving with the Allies were equipped with radar (q.v.) during the war. Some large destroyers received sonar (q.v.) before the surrender in 1940, but the smaller units were not so equipped until two years later.

Carl O. Schuster

(Refer to table on page 947)

Additional Reading

Couhat, J.L., *French Warships of World War II* (1971).
Hackmann, William, *Seek and Strike* (1989).
Masson, Henri, *The French Navy,* Vols. I and II (1969).

Destroyers, German

The German *Kriegsmarine* entered World War II with twenty-two modern destroyers, *Z.1* through *Z.22,* none of them older than three years. During the war, Germany commissioned eighteen additional destroyers built in its own yards (*Z.23* through *Z.39* and *Z.43*), while acquiring another eight from occupied countries. Of the latter, only the *Hermes* (ex-Greek) and the *ZH.1* (ex-Dutch) saw extensive service. Six former Italian destroyers (*TA.14, TA.15, TA.31, TA.32, TA.43,* and *TA.44*), booty after Italy's capitulation in 1943, fought in the Mediterranean in the closing stages of the war. Germany's wartime destroyer force was complemented by forty-eight torpedo boats of various sizes and designs, not counting vessels of this type taken from foreign navies before 1945.

German destroyer classes shared common design and performance characteristics apart from improvements over time in size, armament, electronic equipment, propulsion systems, and ocean endurance. As fleet destroyers (DDs), they resembled their British and American counterparts in appearance, fighting strength, and strategic purpose. All were two-stackers with an elevated and elongated forecastle that ran as far aft as the forward stack behind the bridge. Their silhouettes appeared comparatively low, and their main artillery was usually arranged in single superimposed turrets on the forecastle and the quarterdeck. Torpedo batteries were located at midships on both sides of the second stack.

Like their Allied counterparts, German destroyers covered a broad variety of wartime missions and, on balance, given Germany's general weakness at sea, performed satisfactorily. They acted as screens for larger ships, troop transports, minelayers, and escorts for slower surface vessels and U-boats. They deployed in coastal defense, shore bombardments, and even as floating antiaircraft batteries, not to mention other various "workhorse" assignments. As a result, Germany's destroyers saw constant action throughout the war, from the opening actions against Poland to the capitulation of the *Kriegsmarine* in May 1945.

Despite a generally solid performance record, German destroyers suffered from several handicaps.

The Z.39, a Z.23-class destroyer. (IWM HU 3302)

Their small number and early losses (no fewer than twelve fell victim to mines and direct enemy action by mid-April 1940) rendered the assembly of any strong, coherent destroyer force impossible. They were deployed piecemeal in the various theaters of the war at sea. Moreover, they encountered recurring breakdowns of their propulsion systems, leading to long overhaul periods without ever being able to eliminate the underlying design defects of their intricate high-pressure boilers and turbines.

Another problem centered on the limited ocean endurance of destroyers. The lack of mid-ocean refueling opportunities prevented them from accompanying cruisers and battleships on extended breakouts into the Atlantic. Heavy fleet units had two or three times the range of destroyers, and as in the example of the *Bismarck* and *Prinz Eugen,* they had to forgo destroyer escort on longer missions. Furthermore, German destroyers remained inferior to their Allied counterparts in radar (q.v.) and other electronic innovations. This handicap grew especially exasperating in the closing stages of the war when reliable electronic equipment became crucial in efforts to counter Allied superiority in the air as well as at sea.

German destroyer activities were limited by a conservative philosophy among the political and naval leadership, who preferred the deterrent effect of a "fleet-in-being" over a more aggressive deployment and potentially more successful use of the German surface forces at hand.

The best known and also most disastrous mission of German destroyers took place in April 1940. After carrying German troops and their equipment to the city of Narvik (q.v.) during the occupation of Norway (q.v.), no fewer than ten destroyers were trapped and sunk by superior British forces in the fjords connecting that port to the Norwegian Sea. The British suffered comparatively minor losses in the engagement.

Later in the war, German destroyers fought additional duels with Allied forces, especially in the Bay of Biscay, the English Channel, and the eastern Baltic, and against convoys in the Arctic. Their last task in the war, as was true for most of the remaining German surface units, was the evacuation of troops and civilians from the eastern front to the relative safety of Denmark and northern Germany.

Fourteen destroyers managed to survive the war and were distributed as booty to the victorious Allies. Britain received five, the Soviet Union four, France three, and the United States two. The last one, the U.S. Navy's *DD-939* (ex *Z-39*), was scrapped in 1964.

Eric C. Rust

(Refer to tables on pages 948–950)

Additional Reading

Harnack, Wolfgang, *Zerstörer unter deutscher Flagge, 1934 bis 1945* (1978).

Humble, Richard, *Hitler's High Seas Fleet* (1971).

Destroyers, Italian

Like France, Italy tried to make the most out of the relatively small tonnage it was allowed under the Washington Naval Treaties. Italy, therefore, built the most powerful destroyers it could. It also built small destroyers, called torpedo boats, whose size fell below treaty monitoring limits. In Italian service, the large destroyers were called "scouts" until May 1938 when they were reclassified as destroyers. They were not as large nor as numerous as the French units.

All Italian destroyer types were exceptionally fast and very well armed for surface combat. Unfortunately, many of the larger destroyers were overloaded and had to have their bows enlarged to improve seakeeping, which reduced their speed. All were short on range, but that was not considered a major problem, since Italy's naval strategy called for operations close to Italian possessions. The Italian destroyer force suffered heavy losses, but contrary to popular belief, it maintained high morale until Italy left the war in September 1943.

Italy had a very substantial destroyer force in service on 1 September 1939, numbering some fifteen flotilla leaders (large destroyers), sixty-three destroyers, four destroyer escorts, and forty-three torpedo boats. Italy's destroyer designs, however, clearly were framed in World War I. They lacked antiaircraft guns and sensors, both electronic and acoustic.

Although Italy did develop its own radar and sonar (qq.v.) during the war, it came too late to be widely installed before the 1943 armistice. Most of the sonars installed in 1941–1942 came from Germany, which they provided to improve the antisubmarine warfare (ASW) capabilities of units

escorting the supply convoys for the *Afrika Korps* (q.v.).

The Italians also received a few radars, but Germany did not have enough to provide more than a handful. Moreover, the Italian Navy's prewar doctrinal exclusion of night fighting left these units bereft of illumination rounds and equipment. Thus, Italy's navy was always at a disadvantage in night combat and paid heavily for it. Belated efforts were made to correct these deficiencies during the war but material shortages precluded any major new units being completed before Italy left the war.

Carl O. Schuster

(Refer to tables on pages 951–952)

Additional Reading

Fraccaroli, Aldo, *Italian Warships of World War II* (1978).

Whitley, M.J., *Destroyers of World War II* (1988).

Destroyers, Soviet

Despite Premier Josef Stalin's (q.v.) grandiose plans for a large, balanced oceangoing fleet and the high priority given to naval construction, the Soviet Navy entered World War II with an inadequate destroyer force. The shortfall was foreseen in the late 1920s, and foreign assistance was sought. His fleet expansion program called for 110 destroyers to be in service by 1945. Italian and French technicians were hired to help design the first post–World War I destroyers built in the Soviet Union. Unfortunately, progress was slow and the first unit was not laid down until 1935.

The first destroyers, Type VII, were built with extensive Italian assistance and had several design faults that degraded performance. They suffered from an overloaded hull and severe turbine vibration, which limited their sustained top speed to less than 25 knots. They also did not handle well in heavy seas. The subsequent Type VIIu corrected most of these problems, but construction did not begin until 1937. Even these units carried an inadequate antiaircraft suite and no modern electronic sensor systems until the Western Allies delivered some sonar and radar (qq.v.) sets in 1942. The German invasion caught the Soviet Navy just as it was trying to improve both the quantity and the quality of its force.

Of the forty-one destroyers and flotilla leaders (large destroyers) in service on 1 September 1939, seventeen were holdovers from World War I. Another twenty-six units were under construction in 1940, but the German invasion came before most could be completed. In addition to the sixteen World War I–era destroyers, the Soviets had six flotilla leaders, twenty-eight Type VIIs and seven Type VIIu on 22 June 1941. By omitting sea trials, they were able to rush nine more Type VIIu into service by October 1941. Several units had to be scuttled or abandoned on the slips as the German Army overran their bases and shipyards.

By November 1941, the rapid German ground advance left Stalin with only one shipyard capable of building destroyers unhindered by German air or artillery fire, the Molotovsk Shipyard near Archangel. It was there that three incomplete hulls were evacuated from Leningrad for final assembly. One unit, a totally new design, the *Ognyevoi,* was taken out of Sevastopol as German forces approached. It was towed to Batum where it was finally completed in 1943. The eighteen units of that class were completed after the war and served until the late 1950s.

The Soviets also commissioned one experimental destroyer, the *Opitny,* in Leningrad in November 1941. It was an unfortunate design that experienced heavy vibration at high speeds, which affected the accuracy of its guns. Furthermore, the hull was too lightly built to absorb the shock of firing salvoes, much less the impact of incoming shells, bombs, or even near misses. The Soviets found they could only employ it as a floating battery at Leningrad (q.v.)—a role in which it gave good service.

The Soviets also had twenty "torpedo boats," light destroyer–type vessels, in service at war's start; another eighteen were under construction. They were the first warships built after World War I, and their design and construction reflected it. They were slow, unstable, poorly armed, and suffered from mechanical defects. Only two classes of these torpedo boats saw service in the war, and their use was limited. Too slow to conduct their designed mission, torpedo attack, they lacked the antisubmarine warfare (ASW) sensors to serve as ASW escorts. Their torpedo tubes were replaced by antiaircraft batteries in 1942. All considered, it was an unsuccessful design.

The Soviets also received nine American and two British World War I destroyers in August 1944, a compensation for surrendered Italian tonnage that could not be delivered. The Western Allies also began delivering radar and sonar sets to Murmansk in 1942. The Soviet Northern Fleet's destroyers were the first to benefit from these systems, followed by the Baltic Fleet's. The Black Sea and Pacific Fleets did not see this equipment until after the war.

The deficiencies in the Soviet destroyer force imposed severe limitations on fleet deployment. Without adequate escorts, no major surface combatant could afford to face the Axis submarine threat. Thus a mere handful of submarines kept the Soviet Navy from using its naval superiority in the Black and Baltic Seas, even after the Soviets gained air supremacy. More significantly, the Soviets were never able to contribute effective escorts to the Western Allies' Murmansk convoys, which were so vital to the Soviet war effort. As a result, the Soviets made destroyer production their most important postwar naval construction priority and conscripted literally hundreds of German shipyard workers, technicians, and managers into their shipbuilding program to ensure quality production. This can best be seen in the almost "German" appearance of most Soviet surface ships built in the early postwar period.

Carl O. Schuster

(Refer to tables on pages 953–954)

Additional Reading
Budzbon, Przemysław, *Soviet Navy at War: 1941–1945* (1989).
Meister, Jurg, *Soviet Warships of World War II* (1977).
Whitley, M.J., *Destroyers of World War II* (1988).

Destroyers, U.S.
The United States entered World War II with the largest destroyer fleet in the world, and it retained that position until well into the 1970s. Unfortunately, nearly half of the units in service at the start of World War II dated back to World War I, and much of the new construction lacked the modern design features of their foreign contemporaries. American destroyers had poor seakeeping qualities in comparison to most European designs. Their guns lacked "weather shields." American sonars (q.v.) were inferior to British systems, but superior to the German and French designs.

American destroyers had several significant strengths. Virtually all carried radar (q.v.) by 1941, and their antiaircraft (AA) batteries were nearly double those of any other countries' destroyers. Moreover, American destroyers carried dual-purpose (DP) guns—that is, guns that could be used against either aircraft or surface targets. Although inadequate by Pacific theater standards, American destroyers entered European waters with more AA protection than typical European cruisers. It would serve them well. By war's end,

America had the most capable destroyers in the world, and those designs were the standard against which all other destroyers were measured.

America's immediate prewar designs incorporated lessons gained from its interwar experiences. More importantly, the new destroyers and the lighter and smaller destroyer escorts were designed for mass construction and easy modification. As a result, the Americans during the war produced a relatively small number of classes (four destroyer classes and two destroyer escort classes), but the total number of ships built was phenomenal (417 destroyers and 556 destroyer escorts).

The high volume production did not come at the expense of block obsolescence. More and improved radars, new sonars, ASW weapons, and additional AA guns were added as the war progressed. One significant innovation was the introduction of "operations rooms" (called "combat information centers" in American service). These rooms consolidated the sonar, radar, and tactical display equipment in a single space where the commander could see all the relevant tactical information he required. It greatly facilitated the captain's ability to use his ship, particularly in the multithreat environment (air, surface, and submarine) that characterized modern naval combat.

The changing nature of naval warfare also led some U.S. naval commands to make their own local modifications, but this took place mostly in the Pacific. There, the strength and intensity of Japanese air attacks, combined with the lack of close-in combat after November 1944, led many flotilla commanders to remove the torpedo tubes and install additional light AA guns (usually 20mm). This was not required in the European theater.

The greater size of the American destroyers enabled them to cross the Atlantic without refueling. Moreover, their designs facilitated underway refueling and replenishment, which gave them a greater on-station time than the destroyers of any other nation. These features and the Americans' heavier weapons suites came at the expense of other capabilities, primarily speed, seakeeping, and crew comfort. American destroyers were generally one to two knots slower than their contemporaries and were not as stable in rough weather as British destroyers. American crews often had to "hot bunk," that is, men on different watch shifts used the same bed, merely sleeping there at different times. On the other hand, American damage control equipment was also superior (but did not become markedly so until 1943). That saved many lives and ships as the war progressed.

America's destroyers were designed primarily for war in the Pacific, and in fact, that is where the overwhelming majority of the destroyers and nearly half of the destroyer escorts served. The navy's participation in the Atlantic campaign (q.v.) and the European theater was relatively small, comprising less than 20 percent of its overall war effort. Nonetheless, American destroyers made a significant contribution wherever they deployed. They proved equally effective at fleet air, antisubmarine, and anti-surface ship defense, as well as providing naval gunfire support to the troops ashore. They were the best all-purpose ships of the war.

Carl O. Schuster

(Refer to tables on pages 955–958)

Additional Reading
Hough, Richard, *The Longest War* (1986).
Jane's Fighting Ships of World War II (1989).
Lenton, H.T., *American Fleet and Escort Destroyers* (1971).
Morison, Samuel Eliot, *History of U.S. Naval Operations in World War II*, Volumes I–X (1947–56).

Section IV-D
Technical Data Tables of
Weapons and Equipment

British Destroyers

	G-Class	H-Class	H-Class converted	I-Class	Harvester-Class	Tribal-Class	J-Class	K-Class	L-Class	M-Class	N-Class
Commissioned (year)	1936	1937	1942	1937	1940	1938	1939	1939	1941	1941	1941
Number Built	9	9	2	9	8	15	9	8	8	8	8
Displacement (tons)	1- 1,465 8- 1,350	1- 1,455 8- 1,340	1,340	1- 1,544 8- 1,370	6- 1,340 2- 1,360	1,960	1,760	1,760	1,920	1,920	1,773
Max. Speed (knots)	36	36	36	36	35.5	36	36	36	36	36	36
Endurance (nm) at Best Speed	5,500 nm at 15 kts	5,500 nm at 15 kts	5,500 nm at 15 kts	5,500 nm at 15 kts	5,500 nm at 15 kts	5,700 nm at 15 kts	5,500 nm at 15 kts	5,500 nm at 15 kts	5,500 nm at 15 kts	5,500 nm at 15 kts	5,500 nm at 15 kts
Main Guns (inches)	1- 5x 4.7 8- 4x 4.7	1- 5x 4.7 8- 4x 4.7	1- 2x 4.7 1- 3x 4.7	1- 5x 4.7 8- 4x 4.7	6- 3x 4.7 2- 4x 4.7	8x 4.7	6x 4.7	6x 4.7	6x 4.7 DP*	6x 4.7 DP*	6x 4.7 DP*
Initial AA Battery	8x .50 MG 5x Lt. MG	8x .50 MG 5x Lt. MG	4x 20mm	8x .50 MG 4x Lt. MG	8x .50 MG	4x 2-pdr 8x .50 MG	4x 2-pdr 8x .50 MG	4x 2-pdr 8x .50 MG	Note 1	Note 1	Note 1
Mines	None	None	None	None	None	None	None	None	None	None	None
Torpedo Tubes	8x 21-in	8x 21-in	4x 21-in	10x 21-in	8x 21-in	4x 21-in	10x 21-in	10x 21-in	8x 21-in	4x 21-in	4x 21-in
Depth Charges	20	20	36	20	20	24	24	24	24	24	24
Depth Charge Guns	2 after 1941	None	2	2 after 1941	None	2	None	None	None	None	None
Radar	Note 2	No	Yes	Note 2	Note 2	Note 2	Note 2	Note 2	Yes	Yes	Yes
Sonar	Yes	Yes	Yes	Yes	Yes	Yes	Yes	Yes	Yes	Yes	Yes
Hydrophones	Yes	Yes	Yes	Yes	No	No	No	No	No	No	No
Crew Size	145	145	145	145	145	190	183	183	Note 3	190	183
Losses	7	7	0	6	4	12	5	6	7	3	1

(continued on next page)

British Destroyers *(continued)*

	O-Class	Campbeltown-Class U.S. 2nd Grp.	Annapolis-Class U.S. 3rd Grp.	Belmont-Class U.S. 4th Grp.	Bradford-Class U.S. 5th Grp.	Amazon-Class	A-Class	B-Class	D-Class	E-Class	F-Class
Commissioned (year)	1942	1918 Note 4	1919 Note 4	1919 Note 4	1919 Note 4	1927	1930	1931	1933	1935	1935
Number Built	8	12	15	7	13	2	9	9	9	9	9
Displacement (tons)	4- 1,540 / 4- 1,610	1,090	1,060	1,190	1,190	1- 1,352 / 1- 1,173	1- 1,540 / 8- 1,350	1- 1,400 / 8- 1,389	1- 1,400 / 8- 1,375	1- 1,495 / 8- 1,375	1- 1,475 / 8- 1,405
Max. Speed (knots)	37	32	35	35	35	37	35	35	35.5	36	36
Endurance (nm) at Best Speed	5,500 nm at 15 kts	4,300 nm at 14 kts	4,300 nm at 14 kts	4,300 nm at 14 kts	5,000 nm at 14 kts	3,300 nm at 15 kts	4,080 nm at 15 kts	4,800 nm at 15 kts	5,850 nm at 15 kts	1,275 nm at 15 kts	6,350 nm at 15 kts
Main Guns (inches)	4- 4x 4 / 4- 4x 4.7	1x 4	1x 4	1x 4	1x 4	4x 4.7	1- 5x 4.7 / 8- 4x 4.7	4x 4.7	4x 4.7	1- 5x 4.7 / 8- 4x 4.7	1- 5x 4.7 / 8- 4x 4.7
Initial AA Battery	4x 2-pdr / 4x 20mm	1x 12-pdr / 6x 20mm	1x 12-pdr / 6x 20mm	1x 12-pdr / 6x 20mm	1x 12-pdr / 6x 20mm	2x 2-pdr	2x 2-pdr / 4x .50 MG	2x 2-pdr / 5x .50 MG	2x 2-pdr / 8x .50 MG	8x .50 MG / 5x Lt. MG	8x .50 MG / 5x Lt. MG
Mines	60	None	None	None	None	None	None	None	None	2-30,7-0	None
Torpedo Tubes	8x 21-in	6x 21-in	6x 21-in	6x 21-in	6x 21-in	6x 21-in	8x 21-in	8x 21-in	8x 21-in	8x 21-in	8x 21-in
Depth Charges	24	36	36	48	48	48	12	25	24	24	20
Depth Charge Guns	None	4 Note 5	4 Note 5	4 Note 5	4 Note 5	4 Note 5	None Note 5	2 Note 5	2 Note 5	2: None 7: 2	2 Note 5
Radar	Yes	Note 2	Note 2	Note 2	Note 2	Note 2	Note 2	Note 2	Note 2	Note 2	Note 2
Sonar	Yes	Yes	Yes	Yes	Yes	Yes	Yes	Yes	Yes	Yes	Yes
Hydrophones	No	Yes	Yes	Yes	Yes	Yes	Yes	Yes	Yes	Yes	Yes
Crew Size	176	146	146	146	146	138	138	138	145	145	145
Losses	0	1	1	6	4	0	6	4	4	6	4

	Old R-Class	Old S-Class	Old V-Class	Old W-Class	Modified W-Class	V Past-Escorts	W Past-Escorts	V-Short-Rng. Esc.	W-Short-Rng. Esc.	V-Long-Rng. Esc.	W-Long-Rng. Esc.
Commissioned (year)	1917	1918	1918	1918	1920	1939	1939	1940	1940	1941	1941
Number Built	1	11	23	19	14	7	7	6	5	11	11
Displacement (tons)	900	905	2- 1,120 21- 1,090	1,120	1,120	1,120	1,120	1,120	1,120	1,112	1,112
Max. Speed (knots)	36	36	34	34	34	34	34	32	32	25	25
Endurance (nm) at Best Speed	3,440 nm at 10 kts	2,750 nm at 15 kts	3,500 nm at 15 kts	3,500 nm at 15 kts	3,200 nm at 15 kts	3,500 nm at 15 kts	3,500 nm at 15 kts	3,200 nm at 15 kts	3,200 nm at 15 kts	5,600 nm at 15 kts	5,600 nm at 15 kts
Main Guns (inches)	3x 4	9- 3x 4 2- 2x 4	4x 4	4x 4	4x 4.7	4x 4	4x 4	3x 4.7	3x 4.7	2x 4.7	2x 4.7
Initial AA Battery	1x 2-pdr 5x .50 MG	1x 2-pdr 5x .50 MG	1x 2-pdr 5x .50 MG	1x 2-pdr 5x .50 MG	2x 2-pdr 5x .50 MG	2x 20mm 6x .50 MG	2x 20mm 6x .50 MG	1x 12-pdr 2x 20mm	1x 12-pdr 2x 20mm	1x 12-pdr 2x 20mm	1x 12-pdr 2x 20mm
Mines	None	1-20 10-None	None	None	None	None	None	None	None	None	None
Torpedo Tubes	4x 21-in	4x 21-in	Note 6	6x 21-in	6x 21-in	None	Note 6	3x 21-in	3x 21-in	None	Note 6
Depth Charges	24	24	24	24	24	36	36	36	36	36	36
Depth Charge Guns	4 after 1940	8 after 1940	None	None	None	None Note 5	None Note 5	None Note 5	None Note 5	4 Note 5	4 Note 5
Radar	Note 2	Note 2	Note 2	Note 2	No	Note 2	Note 2	Note 2	Note 2	Note 2	Note 2
Sonar	Yes	Yes	Yes	Yes	Yes	Yes	Yes	Yes	Yes	Yes	Yes
Hydrophones	Yes	Yes	Yes	Yes	Yes	Yes	Yes	Yes	Yes	Yes	Yes
Crew Size	90	90	134	134	134	134	134	140	140	140	140
Losses	0	4	3	4	2	2	1	2	2	1	1

(continued on next page)

British Destroyers (continued)

	Shakespeare-Class	Scott-Class	Lewes-Class U.S. 1st Grp.	P-Class	Q-Class	R-Class	S-Class	T-Class	U-Class	V-Class	W-Class
Commissioned (year)	1919	1919	1918	1942	1942	1942	1943	1943	1943	1943	1944
Number Built	3	7	3	8	8	8	8	8	8	8	8
Displacement (tons)	1,480	1,530	1,020	1,550	1,705	1,705	1,710	1,802	1,710	1,808	1,710
Max. Speed (knots)	36.5	36.5	35	37	36	36	36	36	36	36	36
Endurance (nm) at Best Speed	5,000 nm at 15 kts	5,000 nm at 15 kts	4,000 nm at 14 kts	3,850 nm at 15 kts	4,675 nm at 20 kts	4,675 nm at 20 kts	4,675 nm at 20 kts	4,675 nm at 20 kts	4,675 nm at 20 kts	4,675 nm at 20 kts	4,675 nm at 20 kts
Main Guns (inches)	2- 5x 4.7 / 1- 4x 4	5x 4.7	3x 4	5x 4 AA	4x 4.7	4x 4.7	4x 4.5 DP*	4x 4.7 DP*	4x 4.7 DP*	4x 4.7 DP*	4x 4.7 DP*
Initial AA Battery	1x 3-in / 1x .50 MG	1x 3-in / 1x .50 MG	1x 3-in / 3x .50 MG	Note 7	Note 7	Note 7	Note 7	2x 40mm / 8x 20mm	Note 8	Note 8	Note 8
Mines	None	None	None	None	None	None	None	None	None	None	None
Torpedo Tubes	6x 21-in	6x 21-in	12x 21-in	4x 21-in	8x 21-in	8x 21-in	8x 21-in	8x 21-in	8x 21-in	8x 21-in	8x 21-in
Depth Charges	36	24	36	70	45	45	70	70	70	70	70
Depth Charge Guns	None Note 5	None	2	4 Note 5	2 Note 5	2 Note 5	4	4	4	4	4
Radar	Yes	Yes	No	Yes	Yes	Yes	Yes	Yes	Yes	Yes	Yes
Sonar	Yes	Yes	Yes	Yes	Yes	Yes	Yes	Yes	Yes	Yes	Yes
Hydrophones	Yes	Yes	No	No	No	No	No	No	No	No	No
Crew Size	164	183	146	178	176	176	225	176	176	176	179
Losses	0	1	0	5	1	1	1	0	1	1	0

	Z-Class	CA-Class	Battle Class-1st Group
Commissioned (year)	1943	1944	1944
Number Built	8	8	15
Displacement (tons)	1,710	1,710	2,315
Max. Speed (knots)	36	36	34
Endurance (nm) at Best Speed	4,675 nm at 20 kts	4,675 nm at 20 kts	4,400 nm at 20 kts
Main Guns (inches)	4x 4.5 DP*	4x 4.5 DP*	4x 4.5 DP*
Initial AA Battery	2x 40mm 6x 20mm	2x 40mm 6x 20mm	1x 4-in DP* 12x 40mm
Mines	None	None	None
Torpedo Tubes	8x 21-in	8x 21-in	8x 21-in
Depth Charges	70	70	70
Depth Charge Guns	4	4	4 Note 5
Radar	Yes	Yes	Yes
Sonar	Yes	Yes	Yes
Hydrophones	No	No	Yes
Crew Size	176	222	308
Losses	0	0	0

*DP: dual-purpose
Notes:
1. Initial antiaircraft battery:

L-Class	M-Class	N-Class
1x 4-in	1x 4-in	1x 4-in
4x 2-pdr	4x 2-pdr	4x 2-pdr
2x 20mm	2x 20mm	4x 20mm
12x 50 MG	12x 50 MG	4x 50 MG

(continued on next page)

British Destroyers *(continued)*

Notes *(continued)*:

2. Initially, most ships had no radar. Radar was installed in 1942.
3. L-Class crew size:

   3 ships had 190 crew;
   5 ships had 224 crew.
4. These ships were US-made Lend-Lease destroyers.
5. Equipped with the Hedgehog antisubmarine weapon.
6. Number of torpedo tubes for:

Old V-Class	W-Past Escort	W-Long-Range Escort
5- 5x 21-in	1- 3x 21-in	1- 3x 21-in
18- 6x 21-in	13- None	21- None

7. Initial antiaircraft battery for:

P-Class	Q-Class	R-Class	S-Class
4x 2-pdr	4x 2-pdr	4x 2-pdr	4x 2-pdr
4x 20mm	6x 20mm	6x 20mm	12x 20mm
2x Lt MG	2x Lt MG	2x Lt MG	or
			2x 40mm
			6x 20mm

8. Initial antiaircraft battery for:

U-Class	V-Class	W-Class
4x 2-pdr	1- 4x 2-pdr	4x 2-pdr
12x 20mm	8x 20mm	2x 40mm
	7- 2x 40mm	8x 20mm
	8x 20mm	

British Destroyer Escorts and Other Escort Vessels

	Hunt-Class Type 1	Hunt-Class Type 2	Hunt-Class Type 3	Hunt-Class Type 4	Evarts-Class	Buckley-Class	River-Class	Tacoma-Class	Loch/Bay Class
Commission (year)	1940	1940	1941	1942	1942	1943	1942	1943	1945
Vessel Type	Dest. Escort	Dest. Escort	Dest. Escort	Dest. Escort	Dest. Escort	Dest. Escort	Frigate	Frigate	Frigate
Number Built	23	33	28	2	30	47	69	21	69
Displacement (tons)	1,000	1,050	1,050	1,170	1,140	1,400	1,370	1,350	21- 1,435 17- 1,580
Max. Speed (knots)	27.5	27	27	27	21	24	20	24	20
Endurance (nm) at Best Speed	2,500 nm at 20 kts	2,100 nm at 20 kts	2,400 nm at 20 kts	2,350 nm at 20 kts	5,000 nm at 15 kts	5,000 nm at 15 kts	3,500 nm at 14 kts	5,500 nm at 15 kts	3,700 nm at 14 kts
Main Guns	4x 4-in AA	6x 4-in AA	4x 4-in AA	6x 4-in AA	3x 3-in DP*	3x 3-in DP*	2x 4-in	3x 3-in AA	31- 1x 4-in AA 38- 4x 4-in AA
Initial AA Battery	4x 2-pdr	4x 2-pdr 2x 20mm	4x 2-pdr 3x 20mm	4x 2-pdr 6x 20mm	2x 40mm 9x 20mm	2x 40mm 6x 40mm	2x 40mm 8x 20mm	4x 40mm 16x 20mm	2x 40mm 8x 20mm
Mines	None	None	None	None	None	None	None	None	None
Torpedo Tubes	None	None	2x 21-in	3x 21-in	None	None	None	None	None
Depth Charges	Note 1	110	110	50	48	80	70	100	70
Depth Charge Guns	2	2	2 Note 2	4	8 Note 2	8 Note 2	4 Note 2	8 Note 2	4 Note 2
Radar	Note 3	Note 3	Note 3	Yes	Yes	Yes	Yes	Yes	Yes
Sonar	Yes	Yes	Yes	Yes	Yes	Yes	Yes	Yes	Yes
Hydrophones	Yes	Yes	Yes	Yes	No	No	Yes	No	Yes
Crew Size	146	168	168	170	198	220	140	230	Note 4
Losses	2	9	11	0	6	3	4	0	4

(continued on next page)

British Destroyer Escorts and Other Escort Vessels *(continued)*

	Class	Grimsby-Class	Black Swan-Type I	Flower-Class Type II	Flower-Class Castle-Class
Commission (year)	1934	1939	1940	1943	1944
Vessel Type	Sloop	Sloop	Corvette	Corvette	Corvette
Number Built	9	37	136	10	44
Displacement (tons)	990	13- 1,300; 24- 1,350	925	980	1,010
Max. Speed (knots)	16.5	19.5	16	16	16.5
Endurance (nm) at Best Speed	3,300 nm at 10 kts	3,500 nm at 10 kts	3,500 nm at 10 kts	3,800 nm at 10 kts	3,900 nm at 10 kts
Main Guns	2x 4.7 in	6x 4-in AA	1x 4-in	1x 4-in	1x 4-in AA
Initial AA Battery	4x .50 MG 4x Lr. MG	1- 2-pdr 8x .50 MG	2- 2-pdr 8x .50 MG	2x 40mm 4x 20mm	2x 40mm 4x 20mm
Mines	None	None	None	None	None
Torpedo Tubes	None	None	None	None	None
Depth Charges	24	36	36	40	48
Depth Charge Guns	2	Squid 2	Squid 2	2 Note 2	Squid 2
Radar	No	Note 3	Note 3	Yes	Yes
Sonar	Yes	Yes	Yes	Yes	Yes
Hydrophones	Yes	Yes	No	No	Yes
Crew Size	100	100	85	110	120
Losses	2	5	21	10	3

*DP: dual-purpose

Notes:

1. Depth charges for Hunt-class, Type 1: twenty ships carried 40 charges, while three ships carried 110 charges.
2. Equipped with Hedgehog ASW system, except twenty-one ships of the Loch/Bay-class were equipped with two Squid systems.
3. Ships initially had no radar, but were so equipped in 1942.
4. Thirty-eight ships had a crew of 155; thirty-one ships had a crew of 115.

French Destroyers

	Chacal-Class	Bison-Class 1st Grp.	Bison-Class 2nd Grp.	Bison-Class 3rd Grp.	Bison-Class 4th Grp.	L'Audacieux-Class	Mogadir-Class	Bourasque-Class 1st Grp.	Bourasque-Class 2nd Grp.	Caspue-Class 1st Grp.	Torpedo Boats
Commissioned (year)	1924	1929	1931	1932	1932	1935	1934	1925	1927	1939	1936
Number Built	6	6	4	2	6	6	2	12	14	8	12
Displacement (tons)	2,126	2,436	2,441	2,441	2,441	2,569	2,990	1,378	1,378	1,772	600
Max. Speed (knots)	35	35.5	36	36	36	37	39	33	33	37	34.5
Endurance (nm) at Best Speed	3,300 nm at 13.5 kts	3,450 nm at 14.5 kts	3,650 nm at 14.5 kts	3,650 nm at 14.5 kts	3,650 nm at 14.5 kts	4,000 nm at 15 kts	4,000 nm at 18 kts	2,000 nm at 14 kts	2,000 nm at 14 kts	3,100 nm at 10 kts	1,000 nm at 10 kts
Main Guns	5x 130mm	5x 138mm	5x 138mm	5x 138mm	5x 138mm	5x 138mm	8x 138mm	4x 139mm	4x 139mm	6x 130mm DP*	2x 100mm
Initial AA Battery	2x 75mm	4x 37mm 4x 13.2mm	4x 37mm 4x 13.2mm	4x 37mm 4x 13.2mm	4x 37mm 4x 13.2mm	4x 37mm	4x 37mm 4x 13.2mm	2x 37mm 2x 13.2mm	2x 37mm 2x 13.2mm	2x 37mm 4x 13.2mm	4x 13.2mm
Mines	None	None	50	None	50	50	40	None	None	None	None
Torpedo Tubes	6x 55cm	6x 55cm	6x 55cm	7x 55cm	7x 55cm	9x 55cm	10x 55cm	6x 55cm	6x 55cm	7x 55cm	2x 55cm
Depth Charges	16	16	24	24	24	16	16	20	20	8	10
Depth Charge Guns	4	4	None	4	None	None	None	2	2	None	None
Radar	No	No	No	No	No	No	No	No	No	No	No
Sonar	No	No	No	No	No	No	No	No	No	No	No
Hydrophones	Yes	Yes	Yes	Yes	Yes	Yes	Yes	Yes	Yes	Yes	Yes
Crew Size	195	230	230	230	230	210	264	138	138	187	105
Losses	6	6	4	2	6	2	2	7	10	8	8

*DP: dual-purpose

German Destroyers

	Z.1-Class	Z.17-Class	Z.23-Class	Z.31 Class	Z.35/36-Class	Z.43-Class
Commissioned (year)	1936	1938	1940	1942	1942	1943
Number Built	16	6	8	7	2	2
Displacement (tons)	Note 1	2,411	4- 2,603 4- 2,596	2,603	2,527	2,527
Max. Speed (knots)	Note 2	38	38.5	38.5	38	38
Endurance (nm) at Best Speed	4,400 nm at 19 kts	4,850 nm at 19 kts	Note 3	5,900 nm at 19 kts	5,900 nm at 19 kts	5,900 nm at 19 kts
Main Guns	5x 127mm	5x 127mm	7- 5x 150mm 1- 4x 150mm	5x 150mm	5x 127mm	5x 127mm
Initial AA Battery	4x 37mm	4x 37mm	Note 4	6x 37mm 8x 20mm	6x 37mm 13x 20mm	6x 37mm 13x 20mm
Mines	60	60	60	60	60	76
Torpedo Tubes	8x 53cm	8x 53cm	8x 53cm	8x 53cm	8x 53cm	8x 53cm
Depth Charges	18	18	18	12	None	None
Depth Charge Guns	4	4	4	4	None	None
Radar	from 1941	from 1941	Yes	Yes	Yes	Yes
Sonar	from 1939	from 1940	Yes	Yes	Yes	Yes
Hydrophones	Yes	Yes	Yes	Yes	Yes	Yes
Crew size	315	313	321	321	321	321
Losses	10	5	5	2	2	2

Notes:

1. Displacement for Z.1-Class:

    4 ships were 2,232 tons

    4 ships were 2,178 tons

    4 ships were 2,270 tons

    4 ships were 2,239 tons

2. Maximum speed for Z.1-Class:

    4 ships could do 38.3 kts/hr

    12 ships could do 38.0 kts/hr

3. Endurance at best speed for Z.23-Class:

    5 ships 5,000 nm at 19 kts

    3 ships 5,800 nm at 19 kts

4. Initial AA battery for Z.23-Class ships: All ships had 6x 37mm guns. In addition, seven ships had 8x 20mm guns, while one ship had 7x 20mm guns.

German Torpedo Boats

	Albatross-Class	Iltis-Class	T.1-Class	T.13-Class	T.22-Class
Commissioned (year)	1926	1928	1939	1940	1942
Number Built	6	6	12	9	15
Displacement (tons)	924	933	844	853	1,294
Max. Speed (knots)	33	33	35.5	35.5	33.5
Endurance (nm) at Best Speed	3,100 nm at 17 kts	3,100 nm at 17 kts	2,400 nm at 19 kts	3,000 nm at 19 kts	5,000 nm at 19 kts
Main Guns	3x 105mm	2-3x 127mm 4-3x 105mm	1x 105mm	1x 105mm	4x 105mm
Initial AA Battery	2x 20mm	2x 20mm	3x 20mm	2x 37mm	Note 1
Mines	None	None	30	38	50
Torpedo Tubes	6x 53cm	6x 53cm	6x 53cm	6x 53cm	6x 53cm
Depth Charges	None	None	None	None	None
Depth Charge Guns	None	None	None	None	None
Radar	Note 2	No	Note 2	Note 2	Yes
Sonar	No	No	Yes	Yes	Yes
Hydrophones	Yes	Yes	Yes	Yes	Yes
Crew Size	122	123	119	119	198
Losses	6	6	8	3	13

Notes:

1. Initial antiaircraft battery for T.22-Class boats consisted of 4x 37mm guns. In addition, thirteen boats had 9x 20mm guns, while two boats had 7x 20mm guns.
2. Initially no boat of this class had radar. Radar was installed on Albatross-Class boats beginning in 1941, and on T.1 and T.13 classes beginning in 1942.

Italian Destroyers

Class	Mirabello-Class	Leone-Class	Sella-Class	Sauro-Class	Turbine-Class	Navigatori-Class	Dardo-Class	Folgore-Class	Maestrale-Class
Commissioned (year)	1916	1924	1926	1927	1927	1929	1931	1932	1934
Number Built	2	3	2	4	8	12	4	4	4
Displacement (tons)	1,811	1,742	970	1,058	1,090	1,943	1,220	1,238	1,640
Max. Speed (knots)	27	29	32	37	39.5	41.5	39.4	38.8	39.6
Endurance (nm) at Best Speed	1,200 nm at 12 kts	2,200 nm at 13 kts	1,900 nm at 10 kts	1,500 nm at 13 kts	1,500 nm at 13 kts	2,000 nm at 15 kts	1,500 nm at 13 kts	2,200 nm at 15 kts	2,000 nm at 15 kts
Main Guns	8x 102mm	8x 119mm	4x 119mm	4x 119mm	4x 119mm	6x 119mm	4x 119mm	4x 119mm	4x 119mm
Initial AA Battery	8x 20mm	2x 40mm 2x 20mm	4x 20mm 2x 13.2mm	2x 40mm 2x 13.2mm	2x 40mm 4x 13.2mm	2x 37mm 10x 20mm	8x 20mm	2x 37mm 8x 20mm	8x 20mm
Mines	100	60	32	52	52	54	54	52	56
Torpedo Tubes	4x 45cm	4x 53cm	4x 53cm	6x 53cm	6x 53cm	6x 53cm	6x 53cm	6x 53cm	6x 53cm
Depth Charges	None	None	None	None	None	None	None	None	None
Depth Charge Guns	None	None	2	None	2	2	2	2	4
Radar	No	No	No	No	No	No	No	No	No
Sonar	No	No	No	No	No	No	No	No	No
Hydrophones	No	No	Yes	Yes	Yes	Yes	Yes	Yes	Yes
Crew Size	158	206	153	156	179	222	185	180	190
Losses	0	3	2	4	8	12	4	4	3

(continued on next page)

Italian Destroyers *(continued)*

	Oriani-Class	Soldate-Class 1st Group	Soldate-Class 2nd Group
Commissioned (year)	1937	1938	1942
Number Built	4	12	5
Displacement (tons)	1,685	1,715	1,830
Max. Speed (knots)	39.6	40	39
Endurance (nm) at Best Speed	2,500 nm at 14 kts	2,100 nm at 13 kts	2,800 nm at 16 kts
Main guns	4x 119mm	4- 5x 119mm 8- 4x 119mm	1- 4x 119mm 4- 5x 119mm
Initial AA Battery	2x 37mm 12x 20mm	1x 37mm 12x 20mm	2x 37mm 10x 20mm
Mines	56	48	48
Torpedo Tubes	6x 53cm	6x 53cm	2- 3x 53cm
Depth Charges	None	None	None
Depth Charge Guns	2 to 4	4	4
Radar	No	No	No
Sonar	No	No	No
Hydrophones	Yes	Yes	Yes
Crew Size	205	217	216
Losses	3	8	2

Soviet Destroyers

	Leningrad-Class	Tashkent	Yakov Sverdlov	Frunze	Kalinin-Class	Type IV-Class	Type V-Class	Type VI-Class	Type VII-Class
Commissioned (year)	1938	1939	1913	1915	1916	1916	1915	1918	1940
Number Built	6	1	1	1	2	4	5	4	16
Displacement (tons)	2,225	2,893	1,271	1,100	1,354	1,260	1,440	1,308	1,660
Max. Speed (knots)	36	42	30	25	28	24	24	26	38
Endurance (nm) at Best Speed	2,100 nm at 20 kts	4,000 nm at 20 kts	1,800 nm at 16 kts	1,800 nm at 21 kts	1,568 nm at 16 kts	1,253 nm at 16 kts	2,800 nm at 15 kts	1,800 nm at 20 kts	2,600 nm at 19 kts
Main Guns	5x 130mm	6x 130mm	5x 102mm	4x 102mm	5x 102mm	4x 102mm	4x 102mm	4x 102mm	5x 130mm
Initial AA Battery	2x 76mm 2x 45mm	6x 45mm 8x 20mm	Note 1	Note 1	Note 1	Note 1	Note 1	Note 1	Note 1
Mines	84	80	60	60	60	60	60	None	60
Torpedo Tubes	8x 53cm	6x 53cm	9x 45cm	9x 45cm	6x 45cm	9x 45cm	6x 45cm	6x 45cm	6x 53cm
Depth Charges	32	None	21	None	80	25	None	None	15
Depth Charge Guns	None	None	None	None	None	None	None	None	None
Radar	No	No	No	No	No	No	No	No	No
Sonar	No	No	No	No	No	No	No	No	No
Hydrophones	No	No	No	No	No	No	No	No	No
Crew Size	250	250	168	160	168	168	160	160	197
Losses	4	1	1	1	2	1	5	2	11

(continued on next page)

Soviet Destroyers (continued)

	Type VIIu-Class	Opitny	Ognyevoi	Soviet Torpedo Boats	
				Yastreb-Class	Albatros
Commissioned (year)	1941	1941	1943	1941	1944
Number Built	18	1	1	3	1
Displacement (tons)	1,686	1,670	1,800	840	920
Max. Speed (kts)	36	42	36	30	25
Endurance (nm) at Best Speed	2,700 nm at 19 kts	1,000 nm at 19 kts	1,600 nm at 20 kts	800 nm at 20 kts	800 nm at 20 kts
Main Guns	4x 130mm	3x 130mm	4x 130mm	3x 100mm	3x 100mm
Initial AA Battery	Note 1	4x 45mm 3x 37mm	2x 85mm 6x 37mm	4x 37mm 8x MG	6x 37mm 8x MG
Mines	60	60	80	20	20
Torpedo Tubes	6x 53cm	8x 53cm	8x 53cm	None	3x 53cm
Depth Charges	20	25	24	10	None
Depth Charge Guns	None	None	None	2	None
Radar	No	No	No	No	No
Sonar	No	No	Yes	No	No
Hydrophones	Yes	Yes	Yes	No	No
Crew Size	207	212	250	48	92
Losses	11	0	0	0	0

Note:
1. Initial antiaircraft battery for:

Yakov Sverdlov	1x 75mm 1x 37mm 2x MG
Frunze	1x 75mm 1x 37mm 2x MG
Kalinin-Class	1x 76mm 1x 34mm 2x MG
Type IV-Class	1x 76mm 2x 45mm 2x 37mm 2x 13mm 9x MG
Type V-Class	2x 45mm 2x 37mm 3x 13mm 9x MG
Type VI-Class	2x 45mm 2x 37mm 3x 13mm
Type VII-Class	2x 76mm 4x 37mm 1x 20mm 8x MG
Type VIIu-Class	3x 76mm 6x 57mm 4x 13mm

U.S. Destroyers (European Theater)

	Wickes-Class	Clemson-Class	Farragut-Class	Porter-Class	Mahan-Class	Dunlap-Class	Gridley-Class	Benham-Class	Somers-Class
Commissioned (year)	1918 Note 1	1919 Note 1	1933	1936	1936	1937	1937	1939	1938
Number Built	39	39	8	8	16	2	10	12	5
Displacement (tons)	1,090	1,190	Note 2	1,850	Note 2	1,490	1,500	1,500	1,850
Max. Speed (knots)	35	35	36.5	37	36.5	36.5	40	38.5	Note 3
Endurance (nm) at Best Speed	4,300 nm at 14 kts	5,000 nm at 14 kts	5,000 nm at 15 kts	6,000 nm at 15 kts	6,000 nm at 15 kts	6,000 nm at 15 kts	6,000 nm at 15 kts	6,000 nm at 15 kts	6,000 nm at 15 kts
Main Guns	4x 4-in	4x 4-in	5x 5-in DP*	8x 5-in DP*	5x 5-in DP*	5x 5-in DP*	4x 5-in DP*	4x 5-in DP*	8x 5-in DP*
Initial AA Battery	1x 3-in 2x .50 MG	1x 3-in 2x .50 MG	4x .50 MG	8x 1.1-in 2x .50 MG	5x .50 MG	4x .50 MG	4x .50 MG	4x .50 MG	8x 1.1-in 2x .50 MG
Mines	None	None	None	None	None	None	None	None	None
Torpedo Tubes	12x 21-in	12x 21-in	8x 21-in	8x 21-in	12x 21-in	12x 21-in	10x 21-in	10x 21-in	Note 4
Depth Charges	None	None	12–18	12–18	12–18	12–18	12–18	12–18	12–18
Depth Charge Guns	None	None	12	12	12	12	12	12	12
Radar	Yes	Yes	Yes	Yes	Yes	Yes	Yes	Yes	Yes
Sonar	No	Yes	Yes	Yes	Yes	Yes	Yes	Yes	Yes
Hydrophones	Yes	Yes	Yes	No	No	No	No	No	No
Crew Size	153	153	250	194	172	172	158	184	270
Losses	3	9	3 Note 5	1 Note 5	9 Note 5	0	3 Note 5	2	1

(continued on next page)

U.S. Destroyers (European Theater) *(continued)*

	Sims-Class	Benson/Livermore-Class	Bristol-Class 1st Group	Bristol-Class 2nd Group	Fletcher-Class 1st Group	Allen M. Summer-Class
Commissioned (year)	1939	1940	1941	1942	1942	1943
Number Built	9	24	48	24	176	68
Displacement (tons)	1,620	9x 1,630 15x 1,620	1,630	1,620	2,050	2,200
Max. Speed (knots)	37	37.5	37.5	37.5	37	34
Endurance (nm) at Best Speed	6,000 nm at 15 kts	6,000 nm at 15 kts	6,000 nm at 15 kts	6,000 nm at 15 kts	6,000 nm at 15 kts	6,000 nm at 15 kts
Main Guns	5x 5-in DP*	5x 5-in DP*	4x 5-in DP*	4x 5-in DP*	5x 5-in DP*	6x 5-in DP*
Initial AA Battery	4x .50 MG	Note 6	Note 6	Note 6	4x 1.1-in 6x 20mm	12x 40mm
Mines	None	None	None	None	None	100
Torpedo Tubes	8x 21-in	10x 21-in	Note 7	5x 21-in	10x 21-in	10x 21-in
Depth Charges	12–18	12–18	16	16	24	24
Depth Charge Guns	12	12	None Note 8	None Note 8	None Note 8	None Note 8
Radar	Yes	Yes	Yes	Yes	Yes	Yes
Sonar	Yes	Yes	Yes	Yes	Yes	Yes
Hydrophones	No	No	No	No	No	No
Crew Size	257	276	270	270	329	350
Losses	6	5	14	2	19 Note 5	4 Note 5

*DP: dual-purpose

Notes:

1. Most were converted to fast transports. Twenty-seven ships of the Wickes-Class and twenty ships of the Clemson-Class were transferred to the Royal Navy in 1941 (Lend-Lease).

2. Standard displacements:

Farrugut-Class	Mahan-Class
4x 1,395 tons	8x 1,500 tons
1x 1,365 tons	1x 1,450 tons
1x 1,345 tons	3x 1,465 tons
1x 1,410 tons	4x 1,980 tons

3. Maximum speed for Somers-Class: 2 ships could do 35.0 knots; 3 ships could do 37.5 knots.

4. Torpedo Tubes for Somers-Class:

    2 ships 12x 21-in
    3 ships 9x 21-in

5. All losses were in the Pacific.

6. Initial antiaircraft battery:

Benson/ Livermore- Class	Bristol- Class 1st Group	Bristol- Class 2nd Group
12-6x .50MG	4x 1.1-in	4x 1.1-in
3-4x .50MG	6x .50MG	7x 20mm
2-10x .50MG	4x 20mm	4x 40mm
6-12x .50MG	4x 40mm	

7. Torpedo Tubes, Bristol-Class 1st Group:

    45- 5x 21-in
    3- 10x 21-in

8. Also equipped with the Hedgehog ASW system.

U.S. Destroyer Escorts and Frigates (European Theater)

	Evarts-Class	Buckley-Class	Cannon-Class	Edsall-Class	John C. Butler-Class	Tacoma-Class
Commissioned (year)	1942	1943	1943	1943	1944	1944
Type	Dest. Esc.	Dest. Esc.	Dest. Esc.	Dest. Esc.	Dest. Esc.	Frigate
Number Built	98	149	66	85	85	95
Displacement (tons)	1,140	1,400	1,240	1,200	1,350	1,350
Max. Speed (knots)	21	24	21	21	24	24
Endurance (nm) at Best Speed	5,000 nm at 15 kts	5,500 nm at 15 kts	11,500 nm at 11 kts	11,500 nm at 11 kts	5,500 nm at 15 kts	5,500 nm at 15 kts
Main Guns	3x 3-in DP*	3x 3-in DP*	3x 3-in DP*	3x 3-in DP*	2x 5-in DP*	3x 3-in DP*
Initial AA Battery	4x 1.1-in 9x 20mm	4x 1.1-in 6x 20mm	2x 40mm 8x 20mm	2x 40mm 8x 20mm	4x 40mm 10x 20mm	4x 40mm 16x 20mm
Mines	None	None	None	None	None	None
Torpedo Tubes	None	3x 21-in	3x 21-in	3x 21-in	3x 21-in	None
Depth Charges	48	80	80	80	80	100
Depth Charge Guns	8 Note 1	8 Note 1	8 Note 1	8 Note 1	8 Note 1	8 Note 1
Radar	Yes	Yes	Yes	Yes	Yes	Yes
Sonar	Yes	Yes	Yes	Yes	Yes	Yes
Hydrophones	No	No	No	Yes	Yes	Yes
Crew Size	198	220	220	220	220	230
Losses	5	31	0	3	4	0

*DP: dual-purpose

Notes:

1. Each ship was also equipped with the Hedgehog ASW system.
2. Thirty ships of the Evarts-class, forty-seven ships of the Buckley-class, and twenty-one ships of the Tacoma-class were transferred to the Royal Navy.

E

Enigma

The German military forces purchased a civilian cipher machine produced by *Chiffriermaschinen AG,* a company in Berlin, during the late 1920s. This machine was modified for additional security and was referred to as the Enigma G or the Mark I. By 1933, the Enigma was also adopted by the *Abwehr,* the SS, the SD, the Nazi Party (qq.v.), and other German organizations. A total of more than 200,000 machines were fielded by World War II.

The Enigma machine was a device that mechanically enciphered plain text messages. It had a twenty-six-letter keyboard and a panel with twenty-six letters illuminated by lightbulbs underneath. The main cipher components were three cipher drums or rotors and a fourth stationary reflector or reversing drum, all mounted on a single axle and mechanically geared together.

The reversing drum could be moved closer to or away from the rotors with a lever. The three rotors had twenty-six letters placed along their rims, each rotor about a half-inch wide, with the topmost letters being visible beneath the little windows in the lid. On the side of the machine, protruding slightly, were serrated disks for the manipulation of the rotors. Each rotor had twenty-six spring-loaded contacts on the other side. The fixed contacts were connected with the spring-loaded one in an irregular fashion by insulated wires passing through the ebonite heart of the rotor. The reversing drum had only spring-loaded contacts connected among themselves in pairs on one face in an irregular fashion.

The connections in those four subsystems constituted the essential ciphering part and secret of the Enigma. In front of the keyboard was the commutator, or six pairs of plugs connected with wires which made possible the interchange of twelve among the twenty-six letters of the alphabet.

Depressing a key on the keyboard caused the right-hand rotor to turn through 1/26th of a movement. At the same time, the circuit closed and current ran from the depressed key through the commutator, all three rotors, the reversing rotor, back through the rotors, and once more through the commutator, via different mazes determined by the relative positions of the rotors. That effected the encryption of each individual letter with the result being a light under one of the letters, different from the originally depressed key. Thus the Enigma transformed plain text into ciphered text—and the reverse—without any additional manipulation.

In addition to the cipher machine, the system required a daily key, which consisted of a system of settings that the cipher clerks set on the drums. It included their sequence and the connections in the plugboard. These daily keys were distributed to the cipher clerks in the form of printed tables for an entire month. During operations, the operator selected three letters, enciphered twice, and placed all six letters at the beginning of the message. If major changes to the machine were required, replacements were made of the rotors, either individually or in multiple.

The machine was not particularly fast, but the breaking of its code posed major challenges. Some of the machines had five different lettered rotors, of which any three could be used in varying order, giving sixty possible wheel alterations. Thus, there were 1,054,560 possible ways of setting up the scrambler and a further 1,547 possible jack plug settings, theoretically making 160,200,000,000,000,000 possible choices.

The Enigma machine made possible the secret German military buildup in violation of the

Treaty of Versailles (q.v.) limitations imposed after World War I. It provided secure communications support for the new doctrine of *Blitzkrieg* (q.v.). The Enigma machine led directly to the development of the world's first electronic computer, which was used to break the texts of these cipher machines. The first copies of the Enigma machines were obtained by Polish intelligence and turned over to the British in late July 1939. Intelligence the Allies recovered from broken Enigma codes was designated ULTRA (q.v.).

Alexander Molnar, Jr.

Additional Reading
Kozaczuk, Wladyslaw, *Enigma, How the German Machine Cipher Was Broken and How It Was Read by the Allies in World War II* (1984).

F

Fast Attack Boats

Whether called *Schnellbooten*, PT Boats, MAS Boats, or MTBs, fast attack boats were pound for pound the most heavily armed naval units of World War II. They operated wherever marine navigation was restricted, particularly near major straits and enemy coastlines. Relying on stealth and speed and firing torpedoes that could sink any ship afloat, these small shallow-draft boats posed a threat no naval commander could ignore.

The employment and countering of the fast attack boat threat almost became a separate element of naval warfare. Initially, the Axis countries enjoyed the advantage, but the Western Allies caught up quickly. The Soviet Union employed large numbers of fast attack craft, but their units suffered from inferior engines, poor construction, and inadequately trained crews.

By late 1943, Allied airpower and technological superiority, particularly in radar, had all but eliminated the Axis fast attack boat threat in the West. Nonetheless, their presence could never be ignored. On 26–29 April 1944, German fast attack boats in the English Channel sank three Allied landing ships, tank (LSTs), off Slapton Sands during Exercise TIGER (q.v.). More than 500 Allied soldiers and sailors perished.

Although never exerting a major influence on naval operations, except on the eastern front, fast attack boats proved a cost-effective means of deterring, or least inhibiting, an enemy's naval operations in coastal waters and straits. In that respect, they are the forerunners of the modern missile-armed coastal patrol craft that constitute such an important element of most of today's navies.

Carl O. Schuster

(Refer to tables on pages 981–982)

Additional Reading

Fock, Harald, *Fast Fighting Boats, 1870–1945* (1973).

Friedman, Norman, *U.S. Small Combatants* (1987).

Lenton, H.T., *German Surface Vessels*, Vol. II (1966).

Meister, Jurg, *Soviet Warships of the Second World War* (1977).

Fighter Aircraft, British

The Royal Air Force (RAF) entered World War II equipped with two of the best fighters in the world, the Hawker Hurricane and Supermarine Spitfire. Both enjoyed superb wing and fuselage design, which facilitated future improvements as better engines and armament became available. As with the German Bf-109 and Bf-110, they remained in first-line service to the end of the war—supplemented but never entirely replaced by later designs. The later aircraft, however, also were outstanding designs, in particular, the De Havilland Mosquito.

The RAF's research and development departments served its pilots better than its German counterparts did theirs. The RAF exploited foreign technologies gained from captured enemy aircraft more quickly and relied more readily on feedback from the "field." Moreover, access to larger oil reserves and better fuel technology enabled the RAF's fighters to use engines with high power densities (horsepower per weight of engine), since the higher octane fuels they required were available to the Western Allies. The British, in fact, built the best fighter engines of the war, including turbojets. RAF fighters benefited as a direct result.

The basic direction of British fighter development in the prewar and war periods largely paralleled that of Germany. The pursuit of more powerful engines and better wing designs was the key feature of fighter design in both countries. Britain's engine manufacturers enjoyed a substantial lead in technology in the early 1930s, producing more efficient and powerful engines. Although they lost the lead by the end of that decade, they regained it by 1942. British aircraft designers employed superior wing designs throughout the prewar period and maintained their lead until the end of the war.

The Spitfire and Hurricane reflected the influence of the prewar developments. The Hurricane was the first monoplane fighter to enter RAF service, joining its first squadron in 1937. It was a versatile design that evolved into an outstanding fighter-bomber later in the war. The Spitfire was a better aircraft, with a superior rate of climb and a higher maximum speed. The Hurricane, for its part, was more robust and easier to maintain. The two aircraft suffered from only two weaknesses in 1939: light armament and carburetor-equipped engines. The latter required the pilot to roll his aircraft before a dive, something not required of the fuel-injected plans of his German opponents. Both faults were remedied by 1941. From that point on, both aircraft underwent constant updates, which sustained them in service throughout the war.

Although not as well known today as the British monoplane fighters, the Gladiator biplane equipped thirteen of the RAF's fighter squadrons at war's start. It had been a widely exported design, equipping the Finnish, Swedish, Greek, and Portuguese Air Forces. A robust and highly maneuverable aircraft, the Gladiator saw service in Norway and France (qq.v.) before its replacement in RAF service by the Spitfire. The naval variant, the Sea Gladiator, remained with the fleet air arm until replaced by American-made F-4F Wildcats in 1941 (*see* Carrier-Borne Aircraft, British).

Not all RAF fighter designs were successful. The Defiant turret fighter was one disaster. Carrying all of its armament in a rear turret, the Defiant was significantly slower and less maneuverable than any of its contemporaries. It suffered heavily in daylight combat in 1939 and 1940 and saw service only as a night fighter thereafter. It was a reasonable night fighter, serving in nineteen squadrons until replaced in that role by the Mosquito in 1943. It was also used as a target tug and training aircraft.

The RAF also used twin-engine fighters during the war. Three designs were derived from bombers. The Blenheim was the first to see service, and the first to be equipped with radar. It served as an interim night fighter and antishipping strike fighter until replaced by the Beaufighter, an improvised conversion of the Beaufort bomber. Initially serving as a night fighter, the

A flight of Spitfire Mark-XIIs. (IWM CH 12754)

Beaufighter is best known as the heavily armed Coastal Command aircraft that preyed on German U-boats in the Bay of Biscay, and on Axis shipping in the Mediterranean.

The most successful of the converted bombers was the ubiquitous Mosquito, arguably the most versatile aircraft design of the war. Originally designed as a high-speed bomber, the Mosquito also made a truly outstanding long-range fighter, with night intruder, strike-fighter, and fighter-bomber variants all seeing service. A less successful design was the Whirlwind, the only twin-engine RAF fighter designed as such. Entering service in 1940, the Whirlwind proved a reasonably effective strike fighter but lacked the speed and maneuverability to engage or escape German fighters. Production lasted only a year, and beginning in 1942, it was replaced by the Typhoon.

The Typhoon and Tempest were the last Allied piston-engine fighters introduced into service in the European theater. The former was introduced in 1942, but suffered from a high structural failure rate, which led to numerous unnecessary casualties. It became an outstanding fighter-bomber once those problems were corrected. The Typhoon was the best Allied low-level fighter of the war. It was robust, maneuverable, and proved a remarkably stable gun and rocket platform. The closely related Tempest V and VI first entered service in 1943 and primarily was employed for home defense in Great Britain. It was a reasonable medium altitude fighter, at its best below 10,000 feet, where it could out-climb, out-turn, and outrun any other fighter in the world. Tempest-equipped squadrons became the mainstay of Britain's defense against the German V-1 flying bombs, destroying more than 600 between June and September of 1944.

Although the German Me-262 fighter is better known, Britain also introduced a jet fighter into service during World War II, the Gloster Meteor. It was a slower aircraft than the German jet, but had a better acceleration rate, more reliable engines, twice the range, and a faster rate of climb between the altitudes of 15,000 and 25,000 feet (*see* Jet Aircraft). Unfortunately, the Meteor entered service too late to see air-to-air combat, and was used primarily as a ground-attack aircraft during the war's final four weeks.

Although the RAF did not produce the variety of fighter models of most other nations, its designs were generally equal to, and occasionally superior to, those of its contemporaries in the mission areas for which they were intended. The British aviation industry proved responsive to the RAF's needs, producing the quantity and quality of aircraft required to win the war. Ultimately, that is all the RAF could have expected.

Carl O. Schuster

(Refer to table on page 983)

Additional Reading

Green, William, *War Planes of the Second World War,* Vol. 2 (1961).
Overy, R.J., *The Air War* (1988).
Turner, John F., *British Aircraft of World War II* (1975).

Fighter Aircraft, French

With the invasion of France in May 1940, the French Air Force had only 1,200 frontline aircraft, including 785 fighters. There were an additional 1,500 antiquated aircraft, including about 400 fighters. French pilots were aggressive and fought

Hawker Hurricane MK-Is of RAF No. 85 Squadron on patrol during the Battle of Britain. (IWM CH 1503)

well, but their aircraft proved inadequate in combat against the German Bf-109E.

The Morane-Saulnier M.S.406 was the French fighter available in greatest number when the war began. In August 1939, twelve groups were equipped with this aircraft. By June 1940, 1,081 M.S.406s were produced. It was the first French fighter to exceed 250 mph and could achieve speeds of 300 mph at 13,200 feet. A low-wing monoplane with retractable landing gear and enclosed cockpit, it carried a 20mm cannon and two machine guns. Although the M.S.406 was markedly inferior to the Bf-109E, only 150 Moranes were lost compared to 191 German aircraft downed and eighty-nine probables during the Battle of France. The *Luftwaffe* destroyed an additional 100 M.S.406s on the ground, and the French sabotaged 150 to prevent capture.

The best French fighter of the war was the Dewoitine D.520. This aircraft was only 25 mph slower than the Bf-109E but was less heavily armed. Mass production of the D.520 did not begin until April 1939; on 10 June 1940, only thirty-six were operational. A total of 910 were built, since production continued during the German occupation until 1942. The D.520 could reach 330 mph at an altitude of 17,100 feet and could climb to 26,300 feet in twelve minutes, fifty-three seconds. In a dive, the first prototype reached 512 mph.

A low-wing monoplane, the D.520 used a variable-pitch propeller. During the course of the war, this aircraft was also used by the *Luftwaffe,* the Italian *Regia Aeronautica,* Bulgaria, Romania, and even Free French units. After the liberation of France and the reestablishment of the French Air Force, D.520s were fitted with dual controls and used as trainers.

The Bloch MB-152 was also one of the most widely used French fighters at the time of the German invasion. Although entering service in October 1939, it was the last operational version of a series that began in 1934. Due to its awkward handling and inadequate range, the MB-152 was greatly inferior to the Bf-109E. Its design was tough and sturdy, but the plane was sluggish at higher altitudes, and its guns tended to freeze up due to a faulty heating system. Production was extremely disorganized; of the first 120 delivered, only twenty-five came with propellers and the remainder were without gun sights.

The Potez 631 appeared as a result of a project, begun in October 1934, calling for the construction of a multipurpose aircraft. An all-metal, low-wing monoplane with retractable landing gear and a twin tail, it was powered by two engines. The first prototype flew in April 1936; by June 1940, more than 1,300 were built.

The Curtiss H-75A Hawk was the export version of the American P-36. This aircraft, which met with only limited success in the United States, was eventually produced primarily for export. In the frantic effort to rearm just before the war, France ordered 1,000 of these fighters between May 1938 and October 1939. By June 1940, only 165 were in service. This aircraft first flew in May 1935 and was markedly inferior to the Bf-109E in speed and handling. On 8 September 1939, however, an H-75A scored the first French aerial victory of the war.

The Arsenal VG-33 was an all-wood monoplane fighter that first flew in the spring of 1939. Although light and compact, it was heavily armed with a 20mm cannon and four 7.5mm machine guns, and could reach speeds of 347 mph. At the time of the German invasion, only a dozen or so were operational and 160 were in various stages of assembly.

Philip C. Bechtel

(Refer to table on page 984)

Additional Reading
Angelucci, Enzo, and Paolo Matricardi, *The Complete Book of World War II Combat Aircraft* (1988).
Jane's Fighting Aircraft of World War II (1989).

Fighter Aircraft, German

As the newest branch of the German military, the *Luftwaffe* was relatively devoid of tradition. It lacked the institutional resistance of the army to Adolf Hitler's (q.v.) ideas. German leaders, including those of the *Luftwaffe,* had not foreseen a long war.

Just as Hitler failed to develop a grand strategy, the *Luftwaffe* did not establish itself in depth, and there was inadequate logistical and organizational preparation for a prolonged conflict. Also, there were fitful starts and stops in instituting production that prevented a logical program of aircraft development. The mismanagement of resources and an inconsistent policy regarding use of the air force negated the advantages of some magnificent and, for their time, highly advanced aircraft. Germany had a formidable team of designers, including Willie Messerschmitt (Bf-109, Me-163, Me-262), Ernst Heinkel (He-162), and Kurt Tank (FW-190, Ta-152).

Little consideration was given to the need for

an air defense capability, and night fighters were regarded as an unnecessary luxury in an offensive air force. The *Luftwaffe's* inability to defeat the Royal Air Force, a first-rate air force, insured that Britain would continue in the war and provide a base for future bomber streams to attack Germany day and night. Hitler's decision to invade the Soviet Union was a disaster for the *Luftwaffe,* as the eastern front relentlessly consumed German resources. All subsequent developments regarding the acquisition and use of German fighters stemmed from military and political pressures imposed by around-the-clock Allied bombing of Germany and increasing German aircraft shortages.

When confronted with the prospect of a prolonged war to be conducted with finite resources, Hermann Göring and General Ernst Udet (qq.v.) instituted Plan ELK, a program intended to discard all aircraft models that had failed under operational conditions. Industry was directed to concentrate on the manufacture of a few carefully selected models. Any new aircraft that could not be available within a year were either canceled or severely retarded in development. This resulted in the adaptation of many existing aircraft models that would blur the distinction between day fighters, night fighters, bombers, and ground-attack aircraft.

The extreme example of this is the Mistel composite bomber, which mated an FW-190 to the Ju-88. While this practice of adaptation enabled some aircraft to rise to the top in previously unforeseen roles, it tended to dilute the capabilities of certain aircraft forced into multifunctional roles. Another intrinsic weakness of the *Luftwaffe* emerged from this decision. With the sole exception of the FW-190, not a single new aircraft type was added to the *Luftwaffe* until the last year of the war.

In September 1939, the *Luftwaffe* possessed 4,300 aircraft with thirteen day-fighter wings (771 single-seat fighters) composed primarily of Bf-109Es and a few Arado Ar-68s (this latter model was rapidly phased out). More Bf-109s were produced than any other German aircraft during the war. Estimates of their numbers vary from 30,480 to 35,000. At its inception, the Bf-109 was probably the best fighter in the world. In November 1937, it set a new world speed record of 379 mph. It entered combat in Spain in June 1937. The initial production model was the B version; the C model had improved armament, and the D model, more powerful engines.

The first mass-produced version was the Bf-109E. It assumed the leading role in all *Luftwaffe* operations including the Battle of Britain (q.v.). It was consistently upgraded to confront new improved versions of the British Spitfire. The technological lead between these two aircraft alternated during the war. When armed with cannons and powered by a supercharged engine, it was the equal of the Spitfire. At high speeds, the Bf-109's controls were heavier than those of the Spitfire. Both the Hurricane and the Spitfire were more maneuverable. (The Bf-109 and Bf-110 carried the "Bf-" designation because the company's original name was *Bayerische Flugzeugwerke.* In 1938, the name changed to *Messerschmidt AG,* and all subsequent designs carried the designation "Me-.")

The most significant weakness of the Bf-109 was its short endurance. The fuselage tank held only eighty-eight gallons (imperial), providing

F

A captured Bf-109G2 with British markings. (IWM E 1375)

about one hour of flying time at maximum continuous power. During the Battle of Britain, a Bf-109 arriving over London had only ten minutes of time to fight. According to *Luftwaffe* General Adolf Galland (q.v.), this was the decisive factor in the defeat of the Germans over Britain. Newer variants of the Bf-109 carried an attachment for a long-range fuel tank.

The Bf-109H, developed in 1943 for high altitude use, possessed a larger wingspan and a supercharged engine. It had a maximum speed of 465 mph at an altitude of 32,894 feet, but structural vibration forced its abandonment. The Bf-109K was more successful and considered the best of its line. This variant used the basic airframe to its maximum advantage. It incorporated alterations in the engine housing, spinner, and tail, and the canopy allowed a greater field of vision. The final models of the K series had superb high altitude performance with a maximum speed of 451 mph at 37,500 feet. Only a few of these were delivered during the final weeks of the war.

Second in numbers to the Bf-109 was the Focke-Wulf FW-190. It made its appearance in the summer of 1941 and remained in production until the end of the war. More than 20,000 were built, with 13,367 used as interceptors and the rest as fighter-bombers. Through continuous update, this aircraft remained consistently competitive and was considered by many to be the best German fighter of World War II. Except for armament, it was superior to the Spitfire Mark V. The D model was a transitional version distinguished by a lengthened fuselage, a larger vertical tail plane, and a much more powerful engine, enabling it to reach speeds up to 426 mph at operational altitude.

With a superior rate of climb, turning radius, and enhanced maneuverability, the FW-190 was clearly superior to earlier models and proved competitive with the U.S. P-51D and the Spitfire Mark XIV. Fighter-bomber versions could carry up to 2,640 pounds of bombs and were armed with two 20mm cannons and two machine guns. Its effectiveness was neutralized in the last months of the war by a lack of skilled pilots and a shortage of fuel.

The ultimate version of the FW-190 was the Ta-152. This aircraft was designed as a high altitude interceptor in response to the potential threat of the U.S. B-29 bomber. The H version could reach speeds of 471 mph at 41,118 feet, faster than any Allied fighter. Only 150 Ta-152s were produced, and they were seldom used for their designed role.

The third major German fighter of the war was the Bf-110. At the start of the war, the *Luftwaffe* possessed ten attack wings equipped with its C version. The Bf-110 was intended as a long-range strategic escort that could also be used as a fast bomber. Its first major version, the Bf-110C, had its operational debut during the 1939 Polish campaign. Due to its lack of maneuverability, it was quite vulnerable in combat against the Spitfire and Hurricane. The Bf-110 had an operational radius of only about 300 miles, which added to its unsuitability as a fighter escort.

The Bf-110 achieved success as a fighter-bomber, reconnaissance aircraft, and particularly as a night fighter. About 6,060 (all models) Bf-110s were built between 1938 and 1945, and they served on all fronts. The Me-410 was a follow-up heavy fighter intended to succeed the Bf-110. It did not prove superior to the more reliable Bf-110 and production was halted in September 1944, after 1,160 were built.

With the Allied raids against Hamburg (q.v.) in the summer of 1943, *Luftwaffe* emphasis shifted from offensive to defensive. The punishing air raids on Germany led Göring to state that "only a strong fighter arm could save the *Reich*." The *Luftwaffe* initially deployed about 200 FW-190s and 100 Bf-109Gs for the daylight interceptor role, a number clearly inadequate to the task. The peak of day-fighter effectiveness was reached in October 1943, when thirty-six out of 230 B-17s were shot down over Schweinfurt (q.v.).

The subsequent American introduction of the P-47 and P-51 as long-range fighter escorts for bombers over Germany erected an additional buffer against German interceptors. They matched the performance of contemporary *Luftwaffe* fighters above 20,000 feet. When fitted with extra fuel tanks, the escorts had the range of heavy bombers.

Germany remained desperately short of night fighters throughout the war. The total number of twin-engine fighters available during 1943 never totaled more than 350. The initial night fighter used for operations over Germany was the Bf-110. This was supplemented by a converted dive bomber, the Ju-88, which proved remarkably adaptable. The C and G models of the Ju-88 became the standard German night fighter. A combination of a nose-mounted Lichtenstein radar and cannons on the dorsal spine of the fuselage pointing upward at an inclination of 60–70 degrees *(Schräge Musik)* proved devastating (*see* Night Operations, Air).

The only German aircraft specifically designed as a night fighter was the Heinkel He-219, judged the best German night fighter of World War II. Fewer than 300 were produced. First op-

An FW-190A3 after its pilot mistakenly landed at a British airfield, 24 June 1942. (IWM MH 4190)

erational in June 1943, this aircraft showed immediate effectiveness by achieving the destruction of twenty-five Allied aircraft during its first six missions. The two-man crew had ejection seats (the first time this feature was incorporated into an aircraft). It had formidable firepower with six 30mm and two 20mm cannons. Later models had top speeds of 434 mph.

The Dornier Do-217J-2 and N models were night-fighter versions of the bomber. Lichtenstein radar was mounted on the nose along with the armament. The N version had four 20mm cannons mounted on the back of its fuselage to shoot upward at Allied bombers.

Another role for German fighters was ground attack. The Henschel Hs-123 was the first dive bomber of the *Luftwaffe* and the last biplane to serve in the German Air Force. Although out of date by the opening actions of World War II, it saw extensive use during the early months of the conflict. It remained in service in a tactical support role up to the end of the 1940 French campaign. On the eastern front, ground support emerged as the primary fighter mission. Day-fighter versions were converted to carry bombs and were used in strafing roles.

The Ju-87G, known as the Stuka, converted for ground-attack work with the installation of heavy cannon, proved highly effective against Soviet tank formations (*see* Bomber Aircraft, German). One pilot, Hans Rudel (q.v.), destroyed 532 Soviet tanks during 2,530 combat missions flying various models of this aircraft.

The Henschel Hs-129 was designed specifically for ground attack, particularly against tanks. It had two engines for increased reliability, was heavily armored, and was considered a "flying tank." Although difficult to handle, the Hs-129 proved effective against heavy Soviet armor. A total of 879 (all models) were produced with continuous updating of its armament. In the final subseries, the Hs-129 was armed with a 75mm cannon installed in a belly mounting.

In September 1944, German fighter production reached a total of 3,013 aircraft, the highest monthly figure attained during the war. Even so, fighters were in desperately short supply. At that point, the *Luftwaffe* acquired some highly advanced aircraft that might have made a significant difference in the war if they had come into service earlier. German fighter development proceeded along three parallel but uneven lines: propeller, jet, and rocket. More advanced technology existed for some time, but Plan ELK held back development of more advanced aircraft in favor of established designs.

The Dornier Do-335 was a high-performance conventional fighter used as a day interceptor. This aircraft was unusual for its tandem engine arrangement with propellers on the nose and tail. With a maximum speed of 477 mph at 21,000 feet, it had a range of 1,280 miles. Had it been available earlier, it could well have served as the long-range penetration escort that Germany lacked. Although available in small numbers at the end of the war, it did not participate in operations.

The world's first operational jet fighter was the Me-262 (*see* Jet Aircraft). Design was started in 1938 and the first aircraft flew in 1942. Production was delayed by Hitler's insistence that it be considered primarily as a fast bomber rather than an interceptor. Final authorization for production of the Me-262 as a fighter was finally given on

November 1944. Even then, it was stipulated that it must be able to carry a 550-pound bomb. With a speed of 540 mph, it had enormous potential.

Some analysts believe that if the Me-262 had been available earlier and used in the role for which it was best suited, it could have altered the course of the war. A total of 1,433 of these aircraft were built, of which only about 100 were used in action. Some had to be reconverted from bombers back into fighters before they could be used. Opposing conventional fighters achieved some victories by exploiting the Me-262's vulnerable period of slow flight during takeoffs and landings.

The many delays in the production of the Me-262 led to a *Luftwaffe* request for an inexpensive jet fighter that could be mass-produced and rushed quickly into service in large numbers. This was the He-162. It went from design to initial flight test in sixty-nine days and was prone to many structural defects. The He-162 proved extremely difficult to handle at high speeds. Although more than 1,000 were found in various stages of con-struction in German aircraft plants at the end of the war, only 116 were delivered.

The Me-163 *Komet* marked the start of another new phase in air warfare by the use of a rocket-powered engine. It was the first aircraft of its type in the world. Its rocket engine had a total burn time of 7.5 minutes and was used during takeoff, ascent, attack, and escape. Due to its rapid closure rate with a target, there was a very short time of only three seconds during which its armament could be fired. Operational performance was further impaired because the thrust could not be varied except by turning the engine off.

The prototype for the Me-163 flew in August 1941. The first operational model flew in February 1943. It had little overall effect due to the pressure of time in developing it and in training the pilots. Allied air raids compounded these problems by causing production difficulties and magnifying the shortage of fuel. Thus, initial combat encounters did not occur until July 1944. Only about 450 Me-163s were built before production was halted by the end of the war.

Germany's fighter potential was considerable before and during the war, but it did not develop until too late to be effective. Total fighter production from 1939 through 1945 was 53,729 aircraft. During this same period, Germany lost 38,900 fighters and 9,800 night fighters. The ability of operational units steadily decreased as production and training failed to keep pace with the loss rate. New aircraft models which might have saved the *Reich* did not enter operational service until the war had already been lost.

Philip C. Bechtel

(Refer to table on page 985)

Additional Reading

Angelucci, Enzo, and Paolo Matricardi, *The Complete Book of World War II Combat Aircraft* (1988).
Jane's Fighting Aircraft of World War II (1989).
Killen, John, *A History of the Luftwaffe* (1968).
Schliephake, Hanfried, *The Birth of the Luftwaffe* (1971).

An Me-163 rocket fighter as seen in the gun camera of a P-47. (IWM EA 39083)

Fighter Aircraft, Italian

On 10 June 1940, Italy became an active participant in World War II. At that time, the *Regia Aeronautica* (*see* Air Force, Italian) had 1,796 frontline aircraft, including 594 fighters. Although these were substantial numbers, the quality of Italian fighters was quite inferior.

The CR.42 was the last biplane fighter of the *Regia Aeronautica* (RA). This aircraft was developed based on the experience of a predecessor, the CR.32, which saw service in the Spanish civil war (q.v.). The Italian military hierarchy decided to emphasize lightness and maneuverability at the expense of speed, firepower, and structural strength. First produced in February 1939, the CR.42 had an open cockpit and carried only two machine guns.

At the start of World War II, only 200 CR.42s were in service. Ultimately, Italy produced 1,781, making it the most numerous Italian combat aircraft of the war. Uninterrupted production continued from February 1939 to June 1943, at the expense of other Italian fighters that were more modern and competitive. With the eventual development of better fighters, the CR.42 was shifted to less important operational roles.

The Breda Ba.65 was a fighter-bomber already outdated by the start of the war. It originally was conceived for multiple roles, including interception, reconnaissance, and attack. Initial experience in the Spanish civil war exposed its poor handling characteristics and overall performance. This led to its later use only in attack roles. Italy had 154 Ba.65s at the start of the war. Its armament consisted of four wing-mounted machine guns. It could also carry up to 2,200 pounds of bombs. It was employed primarily in North Africa (q.v.) where it was outclassed by British fighters. It was withdrawn from service in February 1942.

The Fiat G.50bis was a transitional aircraft with an all-metal airframe, retractable landing gear, and cantilevered wings. It was the first of the RA's modern fighters. Armament was still inferior, as it had only two nose-mounted machine guns. Its overall performance could not match the British Hurricanes and Spitfires. Despite this, Italy continued producing the G.50bis, and a total of 777 were manufactured through the spring of 1942. It was eventually removed as a frontline fighter and relegated to ground attack.

The Macchi MC.200 was the best of the first generation of Italian fighters in World War II. It first flew in 1937, and 144 were in service by 1940. A total of 1,153 were produced. The MC.200 was the Italian frontline fighter throughout 1941. Although somewhat slow in level flight, it was sturdy, maneuverable, and could climb quickly. Underarmed with two 12.7mm machine guns, the MC.200 was gradually withdrawn from more hazardous areas and used as a fighter-bomber. It could carry 660 pounds of bombs.

The first World War II generation of Italian fighters proved quite inadequate against more modern aircraft. A marked advance resulted when Italian aircraft design was mated to German power plants. The Reggiane Re.2001, first produced in 1941, became operational at the end of that same year. Its service career was shortened by delays resulting from changes in production specifications and a shortage of available engines. The original fighter version carried four machine guns. About 237 were built and used in fighter-bomber and night-fighter roles. The fighter-bomber version could carry a 550-pound bomb. The night-fighter version carried two machine guns and two 20mm cannons.

The Macchi MC.202 entered service in November 1941. Powered by the Daimler-Benz D.B.601 engine, this aircraft was the best Italian fighter of World War II. Performance was excellent with a maximum speed of 370 mph. It could climb to 19,735 feet in five minutes, fifty-five seconds. Armament was limited to two 12.7mm and two 7.7mm machine guns. More than 1,100 MC.202s were produced and saw service on all fronts.

The Reggiane Re.2002 was the best Italian fighter-bomber of the war. Powered by a Piaggio radial engine, it was armed with four machine guns and carried up to 2,100 pounds of bombs. First delivered in March 1942, total production numbered 227 aircraft. Later, the Re.2002 was used by both the cobelligerent Italian Air Force that flew with the Allies, and the air force of the Italian Socialist Republic that flew with the *Luftwaffe*.

The power, armament, and overall performance of the final generation of Italian fighters proved equal to the most sophisticated aircraft of the time. This dramatic qualitative improvement over earlier Italian fighter aircraft came too late to have any significant effect. The Fiat G.55 could reach speeds of 385 mph at 23,026 feet, and was armed with two machine guns and three cannons. Fast and sturdy, it could hold its own against the Spitfire or the American P-51. Only 150 G.55s were built, and they were used almost exclusively by the Fascist forces in the north after September 1943.

The Macchi MC.205 entered service in April 1943, and was used by both the cobelligerent air force and the Fascists. Production was limited to only 177 planes. Its D.B.605A engine provided an extra 400 horsepower, boosting performance. Highly maneuverable, the MC.205 achieved speeds of 404 mph and climbed to 19,735 feet in four minutes, 52 seconds. Armament consisted of two machine guns and two 20mm cannons.

The Reggiane Re.2005 was one of the last

F

Italian fighters designed. Powered by the D.B.605 engine, the prototype could reach speeds of 421 mph at 6,578 feet. First delivered in March 1943, only thirty were produced. It was armed with three 20mm cannons and two 12.7mm machine guns, but the Re.2005 suffered from structural defects that led to its withdrawal from combat in August 1943.

Philip C. Bechtel

(Refer to table on page 986)

Additional Reading

Angelucci, Enzo, and Paolo Matricardi, *Complete Book of World War II Combat Aircraft* (1988).

Jane's Fighting Aircraft of World War II (1989).

Fighter Aircraft, Soviet

Soviet biplane fighters of the 1930s were comparable to the best Western machines. In the Spanish Republican Air Force, the gull-winged Polikarpov I-15 of 1933 performed well against German Heinkel He-51 and Italian Fiat CR.32 biplane fighters. Total I-15 production came to 3,142 machines. The successor to the I-15 was the more powerful Polikarpov I-153 biplane, with a retractable undercarriage. I-15s and I-153s were used with some success against Japanese Nakajima Ki-27 fighters during the Japanese incursions into Mongolia in 1939. About 3,430 I-153s were built.

In 1934, the Soviet Air Force began to acquire the Polikarpov I-16 monoplane fighters with enclosed cockpits and retractable undercarriages. They also performed well in Spain against early versions of the German Messerschmitt Bf-109 fighter, and against Ki-27s in Mongolia. The I-16, when it first appeared, was the most heavily armed fighter in the world. It was equipped with two wing-mounted 20mm ShVAK cannon, and two 7.62mm ShKAS machine guns mounted above the 1,000 hp Shvetsov M-62 radial engine. Production of the I-16 was halted in 1940, but briefly resumed in 1941 because of the desperate need for fighters after the German invasion.

By 1941, the I-15s, I-153s, I-16s were inferior to the improved Bf-109Es that the *Luftwaffe* used during the invasion. As soon as possible after the massive relocation of the Soviet aircraft industry, the Soviets introduced large numbers of a new generation of fighters, starting with the Mikoyan-Guervich MiG-3, powered by a Mikulin 1,350 hp AM-35A in-line engine. Although the MiG-3 had an impressive top speed of approximately 398 mph, it was inferior to the Bf-109 in the tight turns so typical of fighter combat of the era. The MiG-3 was withdrawn from frontline service in 1943.

Another inferior model was the Lavochkin LaGG-3, powered by a 1,210 hp M-105PP in-line engine. It was unpopular with pilots because of its tendency to burn after being hit by enemy fire. Like the MiG-3, the LaGG-3 was just a stopgap fighter, used simply because nothing better was available. The LaGG-3 was withdrawn from frontline service in 1942.

In 1942, the LaGG-3 was reengined with a 1,330 hp Shvetsov M-82F radial. The resulting La-5N was an outstanding fighter, which could outperform its *Luftwaffe* opponents, especially at low altitudes. Its main armament, like the earlier LaGG-3, was a 20mm ShVAK cannon mounted in the upper cowling. Minor design improvements resulted in the La-7, which served until the end of the war. Like certain Japanese aircraft of the period, the fuel tanks of the La-5 and La-7 automatically filled with a fire-retardant gas when pierced.

The other outstanding series of Soviet fighters was produced by the design bureau headed by Aleksandr Yakovlev. The prototype Yak-1 first flew in 1940. It was powered by a 1,100 hp Klimov M-105PA in-line engine, and armed with two 7.62mm ShKAS cowling-mounted machine guns and one 20mm ShVAK cannon firing through the propeller hub. The Yak-1 entered service in 1940, but large numbers were not available until 1942–1943. Essentially, it was the only Soviet fighter at the time that could meet the Bf-109E on nearly equal terms.

Reengined and redesigned, the Yak-1 resulted in the superlative Yak-3, which entered service in 1943. It was powered by a 1,300 hp Klimov VK-105PP in-line engine. Like the Yak-1, the main armament of the Yak-3 was a 20mm ShVAK cannon. The maneuverability of the Yak-3 became legendary. It was superior to the Messerschmitt Bf-109 and Focke-Wulf FW-190 in acceleration, rate of climb, and turning radius.

The Yak-3 had such a good reputation with the pilots that the Normandie-Niemen Regiment, a French unit serving in the Soviet Air Force, rejected British and American-supplied fighters—the Spitfire, Hurricane, Bell P-39 Aircobra, and Republic P-47 Thunderbolt—in favor of the Yak-3 when offered their choice. On the other hand, thirty-nine Soviet fighter regiments gave up their British Hurricanes and Spitfires as soon as the P-39s became available. Ironically, the cannon-armed P-39 was rejected by the Royal Air Force as unsuitable for combat at high altitudes.

The Yak-3 single-seater fighter, developed from the Yak-1. (IWM RR 2219)

The MiG-3 fighter-bomber. (IWM RUS 2052)

The basic Yak fighter design was extremely adaptable. It was the only World War II fighter to be redesigned as a fighter-bomber with an internal bomb bay. That version, the Yak-7, could carry 490 pounds of bombs, or six wing-mounted 82mm RS-82 air-to-ground rockets.

The Yak fighter was also produced in a long-range version, the Yak-9. The maximum range of the Yak-9 was 875 miles, less than half the maximum range of the U.S. P-51D Mustang. On the other hand, the maximum range of the FW-190A-3, a major *Luftwaffe* opponent of the

Yak-9, was only 495 miles. The Yak-9 was used by the Normandie-Niemen Regiment in 1944. In total, about 36,000 Yak fighters of all models were produced during World War II. In comparison, about 35,000 Bf-109s of all types were produced.

Like other air forces during the 1930s, the Soviet Air Force attempted development of a twin-engine fighter. Just prior to the German invasion, some units had the Yak-4 fighter-bomber, powered by two Klimov 1,100 hp M-105R in-line engines. It proved inferior in all respects to *Luftwaffe* machines and was soon withdrawn from frontline

service. Although the twin-engine Bf-110E was vastly superior to the Yak-4, it too proved vulnerable to attack by single-engine fighters during the Battle of Britain (q.v.) and the early months in the Soviet Union.

The Soviets successfully adapted the Petlyakov Pe-2, a fast twin-engine bomber, to the fighter role. The modified Pe-2, designated in Soviet service as the Pe-3, was powered by two 1,100 hp Klimov M-105R in-line engines. Its forward-firing armament consisted of two 20mm ShVAK cannons and two 12.7mm UBS machine guns. It was also equipped with three rearward-firing, flexible 12.7mm Beresin machine guns mounted in the rear cockpit and two ventral positions.

Soviet aircraft construction techniques throughout the war relied heavily on the use of wood because of a shortage of more sophisticated materials. This resulted in aircraft with relatively low fuel capacities, since wooden airframes could not support as much weight as metal. But when modern materials, like Duralumin, replaced wood in Soviet designs, the improved performance of Soviet aircraft was generally comparable to that of the best Allied and *Luftwaffe* machines.

The Soviets produced some interesting experimental fighter aircraft during World War II. An experimental version of the Pe-2, the Pe-2VI, was designed as a high altitude interceptor. Its most notable feature was a pressurized cockpit. An experimental high altitude version of the La-7 was equipped with two TK-3 turbo-superchargers. Since the Soviet Air Force did not have to counter *Luftwaffe* high altitude bombing raids, they did not actually produce high altitude interceptors until after the war. In 1942, the Soviets also tested a rocket-powered Bereznyak-Isayev BI-1 interceptor. One prototype was lost, probably due to problems of compressibility at speeds approaching Mach 1.

Soviet fighters were simple and robust in comparison with *Luftwaffe* and Western Allied machines. Those features allowed relative ease of construction and maintenance under harsh conditions, and it proved invaluable in the eastern air war (q.v.). By the end of the war, the low altitude performance of Soviet fighters outstripped that of practically all piston-engine *Luftwaffe* fighters.

Dennis A. Bartels

(Refer to table on page 987)

Additional Reading
Alexander, Jean, *Russian Aircraft Since 1940* (1975).

Green, William, and Gordon Swanborough, *Soviet Air Force Fighters,* Pts./1–2 (1977).

Fighter Aircraft, Swiss

During World War II, the Swiss Air Force was equipped with German Bf-109E and French Morane Saulnier 405 and 406 fighters. They also had two Swiss-designed fighter and reconnaissance aircraft. The official Swiss government establishment that manufactured military aircraft for the Swiss Air Force in World War II was the *Fabrique Fédérale D'Avions Emmen (Eidgenössische Flugzeug-Werke,* or EFW). In 1934, the Swiss government issued a specification for a two-seat, single-engine reconnaissance/close-support aircraft to replace earlier, foreign designs. The EFW evolved two distinctly different designs: the C-35 and the C-36. The C-35 was a biplane very similar to the type it was to replace, while the C-36 was a very clean, low-wing, all-metal monoplane. The C-35 was chosen for Switzerland's immediate needs and the first of two prototypes flew in 1936.

The first of eighty production aircraft began to reach Swiss Army Air Corps squadrons toward the end of 1937. Powered by an 860 hp Hispano-Suiza engine, and mounting a 20mm cannon between the engine's V-cylinder blocks, the C-35 also carried a 7.5mm machine gun on each lower wing, firing outside the arc of the three-bladed propeller, and a 7.5mm machine gun in a flexible mount in the rear cockpit. Provision was made for the C-35 to carry small bombs. Both cockpit positions were enclosed. The C-35 could climb to 16,400 feet in eight minutes. When war broke out, seventy-eight of the original production aircraft equipped six Army Air Corps squadrons. In 1942, a further eight aircraft were assembled from spare parts.

With the threat of war appearing more likely, the Swiss government authorized revival of the earlier C-36 design. The prototype of this new monoplane appeared with a fixed undercarriage, but production models had a fully retractable main undercarriage. Deliveries of 150 C-3603 aircraft to the *Schweizerische Flugwaffe* began during 1942. The C-36 was a single-engine, two-seat fighter and a short-range reconnaissance and bomber monoplane. Its tail unit was cantilevered with twin fin and rudders. It was armed with a 20mm Oerlikon cannon mounted in the "V" of the engine cylinders firing through the airscrew shaft, two wing-mounted 7.5mm machine guns, and a twin 7.5mm machine gun in a flexible mount in the rear cockpit. Underwing bomb racks were provided for eight 110- or four 220-pound bombs.

In August 1944, a more powerful version of the C-36 was ordered and 100 were produced. The C-3604 was nearly a ton heavier than the C-3603 and mounted a total of three Hispano-Suiza cannon in addition to the wing and rear cockpit machine guns. Considerably better performance stemmed from installation of the 1,250 hp Hispano 12Y-52 liquid-cooled V engine. Maximum speed was increased to 348 mph. Shortly after the war, production of the C-3604 ceased; only thirteen were completed.

Wes Wilson

(Refer to tables on page 988)

Additional Reading

Block, Geoffrey, *The Wings of Warfare: An Introduction to the Military Aircraft Engaged in the Western Theater of War* (1945).
Munson, Kenneth L., *Aircraft of World War II* (1062).

Fighter Aircraft, U.S.

The most versatile of all military aircraft, the fighter required speed, acceleration, agility, range, and ample armament. The role of fighter aircraft was to prevent the enemy from achieving their purposes, perform reconnaissance, provide bomber escort, provide ground forces with tactical air support, and double as a bomber when necessary. In short, the fighter had to blend the best traits of all combat aircraft. It was the most colorful instrument of World War II airpower.

When the *Luftwaffe's* airplanes began to wreak havoc on the British after 1940, neither the Royal Air Force (RAF) nor the U.S. Army Air Corps (USAAC) had a fighter equal to the German Messerschmitt Bf-109. The British attempted to keep pace with the technical developments of the German aircraft industry.

When the war began, the RAF had the Hurricane and the Spitfire, fighter aircraft with significant defensive capabilities. In the United States, however, fighter technology lagged far behind Germany and Britain. That situation set the scene for one of the significant American prewar developments, the adaptation of the aviation industry for military aircraft production, especially fighters.

Thus, 15,586 (all models) P-51 Mustangs, the most dominant U.S. fighter of the war, were produced from 1942 through the end of the war. The numbers of other aircraft that came off American assembly lines were just as remarkable. If the fighter was the most colorful instrument of the air

war, American industry was the artistic genius of its creation.

The primary fighters of the USAAC at the beginning of the war were the P-26, P-35, and P-36, three aircraft all but obsolete by 1941. The P-38, which was the first fighter introduced after 1939, was the most effective U.S. airplane of the early war years. A product of Lockheed Corporation, the P-38 Lightning was a single-seater capable of speeds up to 410 mph. Designed under the watchful eye of the legendary Clarence "Kelly" Johnson, it never measured up to its sensational introduction, as it proved to lack maneuverability in comparison to contemporary German fighters.

In 1937, the USAAC contracted for one experimental XP-38. Working closely with army officer Benjamin Kelsey, Johnson's proposed design could achieve high rates of speed and climb in a relatively large airframe with strong armament. The army ordered sixty-six in July 1940, about the same time purchasing agents for the British and French were establishing orders. Lockheed increased production to meet the army's demands, but the RAF was disappointed in the early P-38 model and they canceled their order.

The U.S. Army then assumed the British order, and by June 1941, the P-38 entered into U.S. Army Air Force (USAAF) service. The various models produced improved on earlier designs, until a total of 9,942 (all models) P-38s were produced. Despite its handling problems, the Germans labeled the P-38 the "Fork-tailed devil," due in large part to its shark-like torso and twin tail boom.

The Bell P-39 Airacobra was used in the Mediterranean, primarily in ground support, but was a disappointment as an interceptor. Later, large numbers of P-39s were sent to the Soviet Union under Lend-Lease (q.v.). In 1939, Curtiss Aircraft first produced the P-40, and it was used in every theater of the war as a fighter. In North Africa and Europe, the RAF used the P-40B Tomahawk and P-40E Kitty Hawk; the USAAF used the P-40N War Hawk. A total of 13,738 P-40s of all models were produced before it went out of production in December 1944.

The Republic P-47 Thunderbolt was the first U.S. aircraft designed using the lessons of the air war in Europe. It was a heavily armed aircraft that could reach a top speed of 430 mph. It was successful as a bomber escort with the U.S. Eighth Air Force, and also was very effective in a ground support role. The P-47 was the largest single-seat fighter produced to its time. It was conceived in 1939 by Republic's chief designer, the brilliant Alexander Kartveli.

In September 1940, the U.S. Army contracted for 773 P-47s, although the prototype was not yet completed. Designed, tested, and produced at Republic's Farmingdale, New York, facility, the Thunderbolt also went into production at a new site in Evansville, Indiana. It was first delivered in early 1943 and saw its initial combat action on 10 March over German-occupied France. Like all successful fighters, the P-47 underwent revision and improvement. A total of 15,634 of all models were built during the war.

The top-performing U.S. fighter of World War II was the P-51 Mustang, designed by North American Aviation at the request of the RAF. In October 1941, more than 800 Mustangs were delivered to the RAF, which immediately employed them as an air superiority fighter. A year after its introduction, the British replaced the original Allison engine with a more powerful Merlin. North American continued to refine the P-51 until production of the P-51H model, capable of 487

A P-51D Mustang in flight. (IWM HU 3308)

A "Thunderbolt" P-47D of the 61st Fighter Squadron, 56th Fighter Group, Eighth Air Force. (IWM HU 4036)

mph, with an operational radius that could support long-range bombers. The P-51 was a crucial element in the success of the Allied strategic bombing offensive.

The P-51 was particularly popular among USAAF pilots, as well as the bomber crews it protected. Continual refinements were made to the basic design, most under supervision of test pilot Bob Chilton of North American. He eventually accumulated more than 3,000 hours test flying Mustangs. One USAAF pilot who adored the P-51 was George Preddy. With prior experience in the Pacific, Preddy first flew a P-47 when he joined the 352nd Fighter Group in Britain in July 1943. He was one of the first USAAF pilots to fly the P-51 and became a leading American ace.

Other USAAF fighters were used mostly as either trainers or experimental aircraft. These included the Bell P-59 Aircomet, the Northrop P-61 Black Widow, and the Bell P-63 King Cobra. The P-59 saw action in the last year of the war as a training aircraft. The P-63 was used primarily as a target airplane, although the Soviet Air Force used it for ground support. Of the 3,303 P-63s produced, 2,241 went to the Soviet Union. Production ceased in early 1945. The twin-engine, twin-tail P-61 Black Widow was a fast, flexible fighter, unable to reach the higher altitudes. It was somewhat successful as a night fighter in European air operations. Only about 650 P-61s entered service.

From their arrival in Britain in early 1942, USAAF fighters saw immediate action. The first large-scale operations came in December 1942, when fighters made sweeps over German-occupied France. In July 1943, U.S. medium and light bombers and fighters equipped with bombs stepped up attacks on airfields and railroads in France.

The turning point for the role of U.S. fighters came during the bombing raids on the ball bearing factories at Schweinfurt (q.v.) and the Messerschmitt works at Regensburg (q.v.) on 17 August 1943. Without adequate fighter cover, twenty-four out of 146 bombers attacking Regensburg and thirty-six of the 230 attacking Schweinfurt never returned. More than 550 crewmen were lost and neither target was destroyed completely. The bombers had to fight their way across Europe, deliver their loads under *Luftwaffe* attack, and then fight their way back to base. While the argument of area versus precision bombing cast the larger shadow over the operation, the costly lesson was the need for fighter support of long-range bombing missions.

In November 1943, USAAF fighters carried bombs against European targets outside occupied France for the first time. Bomber raids never abated and operations involving fighters carrying bombs increased in early 1944. Most of these attacks were against German shipping.

In June 1944, all U.S. air assets were applied to the tactical support of Operation OVERLORD. Fighters of the U.S. Eighth and Ninth Air Forces flew 23,985 sorties in support of the advancing Allied troops in July. In August, Eighth Air Force fighters reported the destruction of 767 railroad oil cars carrying petroleum to German ground forces. On 11 September alone, Eighth Air Force fighters downed 116 German fighters.

In November 1944, USAAF fighters supporting bombing raids destroyed 723 *Luftwaffe* airplanes, many still on their airfields. USAAF fighters flew 13,615 sorties in January 1945. As the destruction of Germany continued, the United States continued to support long-range bombing missions. During March 1945, the Ninth Air Force sent up 55,000 total sorties, during which 33,000 tons of bombs were dropped. Among the targets destroyed were more than 10,000 vehicles and in excess of 1,000 railroad locomotives, crippling German transportation even further. In April, 2,004 German aircraft were destroyed. By 16 April 1945, the USAAF suspended all bombing operations except for tactical air support.

Almost as remarkable as the performance of aircraft like the P-47 and the P-51 was the industrial output of the American aircraft industry. Learning from experience, endless testing, necessity, technology, and the RAF's extensive use of fighter aircraft, the U.S. aviation industry responded to the USAAF's need with improved aircraft that were faster, more maneuverable, capable of higher altitudes, and more effectively armed than their predecessors.

From the beginning of the RAF and USAAF demand in 1939, American aircraft companies produced an incredible 101,500 fighters before the end of the war in Europe. Also of significance is the number of experimental fighters tested during the war years, laying the groundwork for future developments of postwar jet fighters (*see* Jet Fighters). For the U.S. aircraft industry, necessity was most surely the mother of invention.

The fighter alone did not win the World War II, but it was vital to the Allied victory. The versatility of the fighter allowed it to perform in multiple roles, including conventional air support for bomber missions and, under optimal circumstances, in a fighter-bomber role. American industry not only produced a remarkable number of fighters, but also U.S. aviation designers constantly sought to build a better aircraft. The result was an important and colorful instrument of World War II airpower, which led directly to the modern fighter aircraft of today.

Boyd Childress

(Refer to table on page 989)

Additional Reading
Jane's Fighting Aircraft of World War II (1989).
O'Leary, Michael, *USAAF Fighters of World War II in Action* (1986).

Flamethrowers

The deployment of flamethrowers on both sides was only dimly understood, if at all, by most senior commanders. Thus they were not always used effectively in the European theater, as compared to their brutal effectiveness in the Pacific. But when properly deployed in the European theater, as the Soviets and British usually did, flamethrowers were always effective.

Germany

The Germans started World War II with the Flammenwerfer 35 (Fw-35), based on the World War I–vintage M-1918 manpack flamethrower. At seventy-nine pounds, it was too heavy for one man to handle effectively in combat. They developed several others during the war, including the Fw-40, Fw-41, and Fw-42. German manpack flamethrowers ranged from twenty-five to thirty-five meters, and had a burn duration from two to about thirty seconds, with six seconds being the median.

Germany developed a towed flamethrower and flamethrowing land mines during the war. The towed flamethrower (about the size of a towed 150mm howitzer) was used almost exclusively on the eastern front, and the mines apparently only appeared in the west.

Germany adapted several armored vehicles with flame projectors based on manpack designs and on their towed model. Practically every German armored vehicle type had, at one time, a flame projector attached to it. The most successful was the PzKpfw-III *Ausf* L chassis with the main gun removed and a powder cartridge-powered projector mounted in its place, capable of five minutes of burning with a range of nearly 170 meters.

Nearly all German flame weapons used coal oil fuel, with a few rare examples using gasoline. Electric coil or spark ignition was used in manpack flame guns, and coil ignition in vehicular

units. Germany never adopted a formal flame doctrine.

Italy

Italy used vehicular flamethrowers when it invaded Ethiopia (q.v.) before the war, and it sent a few manpack units to Spain during the Spanish civil war (q.v.). The Italian models were based largely on German designs. The Italians introduced models in 1935 and in 1940. The most advanced design was the Lanciafiamme Modello 41, which weighed only forty pounds.

Soviet Union

The Soviets borrowed German designs at first, then went on to develop their own. The LPO-50, was a manpack triple-tank unit intended to be fired from the prone position, a unique weapon to this day. Other wartime models included the ROKS-2 and the ROKS-3. The Soviets developed a wide number of vehicle platforms for flame projectors, using various (mostly obsolescent) tank chassis to carry flamethrowers into combat. Nearly every mounting used a different sort of projector.

Technically, the Soviets were not innovators in flame, but they were tremendous developers. Predominantly, they used compressed gas for propellant and gasoline for fuel, with electric or cartridge ignition. Soviet flamethrower doctrine and practice integrated vehicle and manpack flamethrowers into engineer, reconnaissance, and assault units. Their sheer numbers and their tactical integration, especially useful in urban combat, made Soviet flamethrower and flame doctrine very successful.

Great Britain

Before the war Britain experimented with flame-scattering pipelines off their eastern and southern coasts, spreading a mixture of gasoline and fuel oil ignited with phosphorous bombs. The best remembered result was a much-reproduced photograph, usually captioned as taken during the war, showing the sea on fire.

Britain developed some of the most effective flame-projecting weapons of the war, including the Ack-Pak or Lifebuoy unit. This doughnut-shaped sixty-four-pound manpack flamethrower used gasoline as a fuel, nitrogen as a propellant, and a powder cartridge ignition system, with a range of about forty meters. The tank carried about five seconds of fuel.

The Crocodile flamethrower tank was the best known vehicular flamethrower of the war. The Crocodile was built on the Churchill tank chassis, replacing the main gun with the flame projector. The Crocodile carried about ten minutes of fuel internally and could tow a trailer with about thirty minutes of fuel. It was spark ignited and compressor pressurized, with a range of about seventy-five meters. The "Crocs" were so effective that German commanders issued orders that their crews were not to be taken prisoner. Three Crocodile battalions were organized in the British 79th Armoured Division, operating in platoon-sized elements attached to armored or infantry units.

Britain formed the Petroleum Warfare Board (PWB) in 1940 to develop flame weapons and doctrine. During the desperate months of 1940–1941, the PWB tested many flame-projection and scattering devices, few with any practical value, including flamethrowing antiaircraft weapons. Even though some of these were spectacular failures, these experiments did lead to some of the war's best flamethrowers and the most cohesive doctrine of any power using tactical flame in the European theater.

United States and Canada

America did not develop a flamethrower of its own until 1942, and comparatively few U.S. flamethrowers ever saw use in the European theater. The standard model was the M-1, which held four gallons of fuel and produced up to ten seconds of fire.

American vehicular flamethrowers were usually mounted on M-4 medium and M-5 light tank chassis, borrowing from the British Crocodile design. The Canadians took the American model and adapted it to some of their Ram tanks. Some U.S. M-4 tanks had entire Crocodile flame units adapted to them. U.S. and Canadian vehicular flame guns were either hull-mounted on ball joints, mounted coaxially with the main gun, or replaced the main gun altogether. For safety reasons, neither the Americans nor the Canadians ever formally adopted the Crocodile's fuel trailer.

Nearly all American and Canadian manpack and vehicular flamethrowers were built around their jointly developed Ronson electric spark flame gun series. They used gasoline for fuel, compressed air for propellant, and electric spark ignition exclusively. American tactical flame doctrine was developed almost entirely on its vast experience in the Pacific. Canadian doctrine followed both American and British practice, though without the separate British-style units.

John D. Beatty

(Refer to table on page 990)

Additional Reading
Barnes, Gladeon M., *Weapons of World War II* (1947).
U.S. War Department, *TM-E 30–451 Handbook on German Military Forces* (1945), reprinted (1990).

F

Section IV-F
Technical Data Tables of
Weapons and Equipment

Fast Attack Boats

Model/Class	Vosper 70	MTB 222	MTB 412	MGB 6	MGB 74	MGB 511	Fairmiled ML	PT 103	PT 384
Country	Britain	Britain	Britain	Britain	Britain	Britain	Britain	USA	USA
Year Entered Service	1940	1942	1942	1940	1942	1944	1940	1940	1940
Displacement (tons)	39–42	41–47	43–49	31	46	115	67	48	42
Max. Speed (knots)	37–39	35–39	34–39	23–24	35–40	31	25	37–45	40–44
Endurance (nm) at best speed	500 nm at 20 kts	500 nm at 22 kts	500 nm at 20 kts	500 nm at 20 kts	550 nm at 22 kts	700 nm at 26 kts	1,500 nm at 12 kts	481 nm at 28 kts	404 nm at 28 kts
Armament (guns)	2–3x .50 MG 2–4x .303 MG	2x .50 MG 4x .303 MG	2x .50 MG 1x 20mm	1x 20mm or 4x .303 MG 4x .50 MG	1x 37mm 2x 20mm 4x .303 MG	2x 57mm 4x 20mm	1x 3-pdr 2x .303 MG	4x .50 MG	4x .50 MG
Torpedoes	2	2	2	0	0	4	0	4	4
Mines	0	0	0	0	0	0	0	0	0
Depth Charges	2	2	2	0	0	0	12	2	2
Radar	from 1943	from 1943	Yes	from 1943	from 1943	Yes	from 1943	from 1943	from 1943
Sonar	No	No	No	No	No	No	from 1942	No	No
Hydrophones	No	No	No	No	No	Yes	Yes	No	No
Crew Size	12	12	13	12	12	30	16	14	14
Number Built	110	65	236	45	83	7	652	358	184
Losses	49	31	56	5	14	0	79	35	7

(continued on next page)

Fast Attack Boats (*continued*)

	S.6	S.14	MAS 513	Type 45	M.511	D.3	G.5
Country	Germany	Germany	Italy	Italy	Italy	Soviet	Soviet
Year Entered Service	1933	1935	1939	1941	1942	1939	1941
Displacement (tons)	86	104	30	69	68	32	17
Max. Speed (knots)	35	38.5	45	21	31–34	32–45	45–52
Endurance (nm) at best speed	750 nm at 22 kts	750 nm at 32 kts	412 nm at 12 kts	1,080 nm at 12 kts	650 nm at 12 kts	240 nm at 12 kts	240 nm at 12 kts
Armament (guns)	1x 20mm 1- 3x 13mm	1x 37mm 1x 20mm 2- 3x 13mm	1x 13.2mm	2x 20mm 2x 6.5mm	2x 20mm 2x 6.5mm	2x 12.7mm or 4x 20mm	2x 12.7mm
Torpedoes	4	4	2	2	2	2	1
Mines	0	8	0	0	4	0	4
Depth Charges	0	0	6	2	2	12	12
Radar	No	No	No	No	No	No	No
Sonar	No	No	No	No	No	No	No
Hydrophones	No	No	No	Yes	No	No	No
Crew Size	21	21	11	13	12	9–14	7
Number Built	8	236	27	45	35	130	295
Losses	0	146	11	34	15	23	35

British Fighter Aircraft

Model	Gladiator	Beaufighter IF*	Typhoon	Mosquito NF Mk-XIX†	Mosquito FB Mk-VI*	Meteor Mk-III†	Hurricane Mk-I	Hurricane Mk II-C	Tempest Mk-V	Spitfire Mk-IA	Spitfire Mk-VB	Spitfire Mk-IX	Spitfire Mk-XIV
Service Date	1936	1940	1941	1944	1943	1944	1937	1940	1944	1938	1941	1942	1944
Engines	1	2	1	2	2	2	1	1	1	1	1	1	1
Crew	1	2	1	2	2	1	1	1	1	1	1	1	1
Maximum Speed (mph)	253	306	412	380	380	410	310	330	420	360	360	410	440
Maximum Range (miles)	428	1,500	510	1,000	1,880	1,340	525	920	1,530	395	470	980	850
Gun Armament	4x 20mm 4x .303 MG	4x 20mm 6x .303 MG	4x 20mm 4x 20mm	4x 20mm	4x 20mm 4x .303 MG	4x 20mm	8x .303 MG	4x 20mm	4x 20mm	8x .303 MG	2x 20mm 4x .303 MG	2x 20mm 4x .303 MG	2x 20mm 2x .50 MG
Bombs or Rockets	None	None	2,000 lbs or 8x rocket	None	2,000 lbs	None	None	1,000 lbs or 8x rocket	2,000 lbs or 8x rocket	None	500 lbs	1000 lbs	500 lbs
Number in Service	768	553	3,270	1,799	2,720	280	3,900	6,650	800	1,500	3,920	5,700	960
Ceiling (feet)	32,800	28,900	35,200	33,000	33,000	44,000	33,400	35,660	36,500	31,900	35,500	43,000	43,000

*Night Fighter
†Jet

French Fighter Aircraft

Model	MB-152	H-75A	D.520	M.S.406C1	Potez 631
Service Date	1939	1939	1940	1939	1939
Engines	1	1	1	1	2
Crew	1	1	1	1	3
Max. Speed (mph)	316	300	330	300	224
Max. Range (miles)	336	825	550	460	758
Gun Armament	1x 20mm 2x 7.5mm MG	5x 7.5mm MG	1x 20mm 4x 7.9mm MG	1x 20mm 2x 7.9mm MG	2x 20mm 5x 7.5mm MG
Bombs or Rockets	None	None	None	None	None
Number in Service	483	165	910	1,400*	1,360
Ceiling (feet)	38,800	33,000	36,100	30,840	29,530

*All models

German Fighter Aircraft

Model	FW-190A	FW-190G	FW-190D	Ju-88C*	Ju-88G*	Bf-109E	Bf-109G	Bf-110C	Bf-110G*	Me-163†	Me-262‡
Service Date	1941	1943	1944	1940	1944	1938	1942	1939	1942	1943	1944
Engines	1	1	1	2	2	1	1	2	2	1	2
Crew	1	1	1	3	4	1	1	2–3	3	1	1
Maximum Speed (mph)	382	356	426	300	389	350	405	325	340	596	540
Maximum Range (miles)	495	395	520	1,230	1,400	410	525	680	1,300	50	525
Gun Armament	4x 20mm 2x 13mm MG	2x 20mm	2x 20mm 2x 13mm MG	3x 20mm 3x 7.92mm MG 1x 13mm MG	6x 20mm 1x 13mm MG	3x 20mm 2x 7.92mm MG	1x 20mm 2x 7.92mm MG	2x 20mm 5x 7.92mm MG	2x 20mm 5x 7.92mm MG	2x 30mm	4x 30mm
Bombs or Rockets	2x rockets	2,755 lbs	440 lbs or 2x rockets	None	None	None	550 lbs	1,100 lbs	1,100 lbs	24x rockets	500 lbs
Number in Service	(all FW-190 models) 20,000			3,200	2,800	(all Bf-190 models) 30,480		1,500	3,700	450	1,433
Ceiling (feet)	34,775	34,780	37,000	32,450	32,800	34,450	39,370	32,800	26,250	39,500	37,560

*Night fighter version
†Rocket fighter
‡Jet fighter

Italian Fighter Aircraft

Model	CR.42*	G.50bis	MC. 200	MC. 202	Re. 2001	Re. 2002
Service Date	1939	1939	1939	1941	1942	1942
Engines	1	1	1	1	1	1
Crew	1	1	1	1	1	1
Maximum Speed (mph)	280	293	310	370	337	329
Maximum Range (miles)	480	420	540	475	684	684
Gun Armament	2x 12.7mm MG	2x 12.7mm MG	2x 12.7mm MG	2x 7.7mm MG 2x 12.7mm MG	2x 7.9mm MG 2x 12.7mm MG	2x 7.9mm MG 2x 12.7mm MG
Bombs or Rockets	440 lbs	660 lbs	660 lbs	440 lbs	550 lbs	2,100 lbs
Number in Service	1,781	777	1,153	1,100	237	227
Ceiling (feet)	34,450	35,100	29,200	37,700	36,090	36,090

*Biplane

Soviet Fighter Aircraft

Model	LaGG-3	La-5	La-7	MiG-3	I-153	I-16	Yak-1	Yak-3	Yak-7	Yak-9D
Service Date	1941	1942	1943	1941	1939	1934	1940	1943	1942	1942
Engines	1	1	1	1	1	1	1	1	1	1
Crew	1	1	1	1	1	1	1	1	1	1
Max. Speed (mph)	348	402	413	398	267	326	360	403	381	363
Max. Range (miles)	497	475	394	776	560	435	528	506	513	875
Gun Armament	1x 20mm 1x 12.7 MG 2x 7.62 MG	2x 20mm	3x 20mm	1x 12.7 MG 2x 7.62 MG	4x 7.62 MG	2x 20mm 2x 7.62 MG	1x 20mm 2x 7.62 MG	1x 20mm 2x 7.62 MG	1x 20mm 2x 7.62 MG	1x 37mm 1x 12.7MG
Bombs or Rockets	440 lbs or 6x rockets	330 lbs	220 lbs or 6x rockets	440 lbs or 6x rockets	330 lbs or 6x rockets	6x rockets	440 lbs or 6x rockets	440 lbs or 6x rockets	440 lbs or 6x rockets	None
Number in Service	6,528	10,600	10,600	3,422	3,430	7,000	8,720	4,850	6,399	16,769
Ceiling (feet)	29,530	31,100	33,300	39,370	35,145	29,530	32,810	35,475	33,460	34,770

Swiss Fighter Aircraft

Model	C-35	C-3603
Service Date	1937	1942
Engines	1	1
Crew	2	2
Maximum Speed (mph)	208	240
Maximum Range (miles)	385	450
Gun Armament	1x 20mm 3x 7.5mm MG	1x 20mm 4x 7.5mm MG
Bombs or Rockets	220 lbs	880 lbs
Number in Service	86	167
Ceiling (feet)	32,810	32,970

U.S. Fighter Aircraft

Model	P-38F/G	P-38J/L	P-39Q	P-40E	P-40N	P-47D	P-51B/C	P-51D	P-61A/B*
Service Date	1942	1943	1943	1942	1944	1943	1943	1944	1944
Engines	2	2	1	1	1	1	1	1	2
Crew	1	1	1	1	1	1	1	1	3
Maximum Speed (mph)	345	410	385	335	350	430	440	440	360
Maximum Range (miles)	1,400	2,250	675	850	750	590	2,200	2,100	3,000
Gun Armament	1x 20mm 4x .50 MG	1x 20mm 4x .50 MG	1x 37mm 4x .50 MG	6x .50 MG	6x .50 MG	6x or 8x .50 MG	4x .50 MG	6x .50 MG	4x 20mm 4x .50 MG
Bombs or Rockets	2,000 lbs	3,200 lbs	500 lbs	500 lbs	1,500 lbs	2,500 lbs or 10 rockets	2,000 lbs	2,000 lbs or 6 rockets	1,600 lbs
Number in Service	1,609	6,780	4,905	2,320	5,200	12,560	3,750	7,970	650
Ceiling (feet)	39,000	44,000	29,000	29,000	31,000	42,000	42,000	41,900	33,100

*Night fighter

Portable Flame Throwers

Model	Fw-35	Fw-40	Fw-41	M-41	ROKS-2	ROKS-3	No. 1 Mk-II Marsden	No. 2 Mk-II Lifebuoy	M-1	M-1A1
Country	Germany	Germany	Germany	Italy	USSR	USSR	Britain	Britain	USA	USA
Year in Service	1935	1940	1941	1941	1943	1945	1940	1941	1942	1942
Weight (pounds)	79	47	40	40	50	75	85	64	70	70
Effective Range (meters)	25	25	35	20	35	70	30	40	25	40

G

German 88

See ANTIAIRCRAFT ARTILLERY, GERMAN

Gliders

Military gliders, one of the peculiarities of World War II, were serious military weapons that contributed significantly to the success of various airborne operations (q.v.) conducted by each side. Yet the entire history of practical military gliding is less than a dozen years, and they have not been used for military operations since the end of the war.

Military gliders evolved because of the need to deliver a load larger than what could be delivered by parachute. Unless paratroopers were able to secure a landing strip large enough to support transport aircraft, they would be left to the mercy of the defenders' armor and heavy weapons. The pattern of all early airborne attacks was a paradrop onto an airfield, seizure of the airfield, followed up by air landing of infantry and light artillery, often within an hour of the initial drop.

The concept of ferrying large loads in gliders was not new, but it was all theory. Gliders are relatively flimsy structures with long, narrow, high aspect-ratio wings that the pilot keeps aloft by seeking upward air currents. While the sport glider is slender and graceful, the military glider was large, angular, and often had struts supporting the wings and tail. Where sport gliders have a single small wheel, or light landing skids, military gliders had a full, fixed undercarriage. There was little streamlining; the fuselage was designed to carry a squad or platoon of heavily armed troops or large, bulky cargo.

Indeed, military gliders deserve that name mainly because most of them were without any independent means of power. Where a sport glider will usually "glide" around fifty feet for each foot of altitude, the military gliders were fortunate to achieve a 10:1 glide ratio. Sport gliders are launched by a variety of means. Military cargo gliders could only be launched by an aerial tow using multiengine transports or bombers modified for the purpose. A sport glider can remain aloft for several hours. A military glider, once released from the mother aircraft, had to come down immediately.

German Gliders

Germany, a leading glider nation, developed a high altitude glider for meteorological research in 1932. It was not a large step from a glider that had to carry about a ton of payload to one that might be of use to the recently established airborne forces. The first military version, the DFS-230 *(Deutsche Forschungsanstalt für Segelflug)*, appeared in 1937. Although the DFS-230 was a simplified version of its scientific forebear, it reflected certain affiliations with sport gliders. Of fabric-covered steel tubing construction, the fuselage was long and narrow, deep enough to permit headroom for a man sitting. Wings were long, tapered, made from stressed plywood and were braced by a single strut extending from the fuselage. It was equipped with a pair of wheels under the fuselage, with a long skid running from the nose about a third of the way under the belly. Later models were experimentally fitted with braking parachutes.

The DFS-230 normally carried one pilot and nine troops, with the pilot and first five facing forward, the last four facing aft. Weapons were transported in clamps beside each soldier. The man seated farthest forward could fire a machine gun through a slit in the fabric on the starboard side. Later models were fitted with a defensive machine gun mounted to fire out of the top of the fuselage. The only door was at the rear of the fuselage on the port side. It was a difficult aircraft to get into and out of.

Ten DFS-230s were deployed in the assault on Eben Emael (q.v.) in Belgium. They were also used in the invasion of Holland, and in the assault on Crete (q.v.) where they suffered heavy losses. Some DFS-230s were used by *Luftwaffe* fighter squadrons in Russia as mobile workshops and flew with a squadron to each new location carrying spares and repair equipment. Many were lost in attempts to reinforce and resupply the beleaguered troops at Stalingrad (q.v.). A total of 2,230 were built, but by the end of the war, scarcely any were left. The DFS-230 was normally towed by aircraft such as the Junkers Ju-52 (which is reported to have been able to handle two, though with difficulty), the Heinkel He-111, Henschel Hs-126, Messerschmitt Bf-110, and the Junkers Ju-87.

Limitations of the DFS-230 prompted the need for a larger, heavier-capacity glider, and they led to development of the glider produced by *Gothaer Waggonfabrik AG,* a pioneer German aviation company. The first Gotha 242s were delivered to the *Luftwaffe* in mid-1941. They were constructed with a central nacelle-fuselage and twin tail booms. The nacelle was made of fabric-covered tubular steel and the rest of the aircraft, the wing (mounted high on the fuselage) and booms and tail, were of wood. The early models had a wheeled trolley that was jettisoned on takeoff. Later models were equipped with permanent tricycle landing gear.

A large, ungainly aircraft, the Go-242 appeared in several variations. Midway in the war several Go-242s were converted into Go-244s, a twin-engine transport that was unsuccessful. Others were equipped with a primitive rocket-assisted takeoff system involving a single rocket under each wing or a battery of four on a frame at the end of the nacelle. This scheme worked well when rockets were available, which was seldom. Regular towing operations with such a large glider placed considerable strain on the tow aircraft. When long runways were unavailable, payloads had to be reduced. Tow planes were the Junkers Ju-52 or the Heinkel He-111. Cargo was loaded into the rear of the nacelle through a hinged door onto a ramp. Troops could enter and exit through doors in the forward part of the nacelle and the crew (two pilots) sat in a glassed-in nose.

The Gotha was an improvement over the DFS, but came too late for the airborne operations at the beginning of the war. Some Go-242s functioned in Russia as flying workshops and some were used as mobile field headquarters. Machine guns could be mounted as defensive armament

and the crew were protected from ground fire by floor-mounted armor plating. Total production of the Go-242 was around 1,500, including the 133 that were converted to Go-244s.

The Messerschmitt Me-321, the world's largest operational glider, resulted from the need for a large-capacity cargo and troop carrier to support the aborted Operation SEA LION (q.v.). A prototype was ready in February 1941. The crew of two pilots sat in a greenhouse on top of the forward end of the fuselage, twenty-three feet above the ground. This monster aircraft was built of steel tubing covered in fabric and weighed more than thirteen tons. Cargo capacity was 24.3 tons or 200 fully equipped troops. Passengers entered through two large clamshell doors in the nose.

Getting the Messerschmitt Me-321 off the ground was a real problem. The four-engine Ju-90 used to tow the first model (empty), needed three-fourths of a mile to get airborne. Use of three Bf-110s to tow the giant proved to be infeasible as were attempts with other aircraft and modified aircraft. Ultimately, 200 were built, but most were converted into Me-323 transports by fitting six French Gnome Rhone radial engines. The Me-323 could carry a full infantry company on a specially fitted middle deck, in addition to about five tons of cargo. The Me-323 powered version was equipped with eight pairs of wheels installed in side fairings at the forward end of the fuselage. Though stable in flight, it was very stiff and heavy in the controls.

British Gliders

The British glider program got under way early in the war. The Glider Committee of the Air Ministry originally considered the use of gliders for bombing and air-to-air refueling, in addition to troop carrying. They finally decided on troop and cargo carrying.

The Hotspur was the first military glider in use by the Allies and appeared in November 1940. Crew was a single pilot, situated in a greenhouse forward, and one infantry section of eight troops. Earlier models were awkward to get into and out of, but the Hotspur was a graceful and reasonably aerodynamic glider that bore some resemblance to the German DFS-230. Glide ratio was 24:1 for the Mk-I Hotspur. The Mk-IIs and the Mk-IIIs were somewhat steeper. This glider was used only for training.

A shoulder-wing monoplane with a large rudder, the Horsa was originally envisaged to carry paratroopers who were supposed to drop simultaneously through staggered doors on either side of the aircraft. It had a fixed, tricycle landing gear. Its huge wing flaps, awkward and difficult to operate, facilitated docile landings. Freight was loaded through a downward-hinging door on the port side just behind the cockpit.

A Royal Air Force technical team devised a system by which the entire tail section was held by six large bolts, which could be released quickly, without damage to the structure, to allow the unloading of a jeep (q.v.). The Mk-II Horsa was fitted with a hinged nose section allowing for rapid loading and unloading, but retained the tail bolts for emergencies. First production Horsas appeared in June 1942. By the end of the war, more than 5,000 were completed. They were towed by a variety of transport and bomber aircraft such as the C-47 and the Stirling Short or Whitley. Horsas figured prominently in Operations OVERLORD and MARKET-GARDEN (qq.v.).

The Hamilcar was the largest glider used by the Allies. Designed to carry armored vehicles, the Hamilcar bore external resemblance to the Me-321 though it was around half as large and carried one-third of the payload. The Hamilcar, however, could be towed by existing RAF bombers and did not need rockets to assist in takeoff. Hamilcars landed light tanks during Operation OVER-LORD. Their wing loading of nearly twenty-two pounds per square foot was only fractionally lower than that of the C-47.

Cargo was loaded through the nose that opened, hinged to starboard. Passengers could enter through small doors at the rear of the fuselage. Takeoff was assisted by a two-wheeled undercarriage that was released, once in the air, to allow the fuselage to sink down on its skids to bring the cargo floor close to the ground so that vehicles could be unloaded without ramps. The two pilots sat in a long glasshouse cockpit situated over the cargo space on top of the fuselage, forward. Controls were heavy but manageable. More than 400 were completed by 1945. The Hamilcar could carry either one light tank (M22 Locust or Tetrarch), two Universal Bren Carriers, two scout cars, or one 25-pounder gun with tractor. Since each load required different floor strengthening and fastenings, specialized equipment for the Hamilcar was needed.

U.S. Gliders

The U.S. glider effort spanned the years from early 1941 through early 1946, during which 16,000 gliders were completed. Nobody was able to decide what was needed to meet Army Air Corps chief General Henry H. "Hap" Arnold's (q.v.) request for specifications for a military glider in February 1941, but within a few months, a number of gliders were built by various contractors, each conforming to various specifications. Designs pro-

A U.S. CG-4A glider. (IWM NYF 42566)

duced by the Waco Aircraft Company of Troy, Ohio, were deemed the most suitable and contracts were let in June 1941, for an eight-seat and a fifteen-seat glider. One hundred eight-seaters were built and employed mainly for training.

The Waco CG-4 (called the Hadrian by the British) with several modifications, was utilitarian and ugly, but it was easy to fly and could accommodate fifteen fully equipped troops or a jeep and crew. A strut-braced, shoulder-wing, box-like monoplane, it could carry more than its own weight. The cockpit was situated down in the nose of the fuselage and the whole affair was hinged to swing upward to provide a clear entry and exit for passengers or cargo. It was constructed of fabric-covered steel tubing and had a plywood floor.

The first Wacos were delivered to North Africa in late 1942. The packing cases were used by the glider crews as living quarters. It had a two-wheel undercarriage and a central skid. The two pilots sat side by side in the glassed-in nose. Models completed from 1944 onward included additional steel tubing to protect the pilots in heavy landings. The tow rope, released by a lever suspended between the pilots, was attached at the top of the fuselage. The Waco was employed in large numbers during Operations OVERLORD and MARKET-GARDEN. Easily towed by the C-47, there were more than 13,900 Waco CG-4s and CG-4As completed during the war, more than 4,000 by the Ford Motor Company and a like number by Cessna.

The Waco CG-15A was an improved version of the CG-4, very similar in appearance. Delivered early in 1944, it had 40 percent less wingspan, better crash protection for the crew, and improved controls.

The Waco CG-18A was a larger version of the CG-4/CG-15 gliders, also similar in appearance to the smaller aircraft. Of the 139 CG-18s built, eighty were sent to Europe. It was used in the Rhine crossings toward the end of the war. The CG-18 was equipped with hydraulically operated wing flaps and cargo hatch. It carried thirty troops or a jeep with gun and crew.

Soviet Gliders

The Soviet glider effort differed from those of other nations in several ways. Several glider designs were produced during the war, but difficulties associated with moving factories eastward out of reach of the Germans and the need for powered operational aircraft resulted in few being completed. There was also a severe shortage of aircraft suitable to tow gliders. Unlike other nations, where glider programs ceased at the end of the war, the Soviets continued to use gliders well into the 1950s.

The A-7 glider was produced in 1939 and was similar in appearance to the German DFS-230. It was a graceful, light aircraft with good flight characteristics. It had one pilot and could carry eight troops or a ton of cargo. The A-7 was used to supply Soviet partisans (q.v.) active behind German lines.

Wes Wilson

(Refer to table on page 997)

Additional Reading

Lowden, John L., *Silent Wings: Combat Gliders in World War II* (1992).

Mrazek, James E., *Fighting Gliders of World War II* (1977).

Seth, Ronald, *Lion with Blue Wings: The Story of the Glider Regiment 1942–1945* (1955).

Wright, Lawrence, *The Wooden Sword* (1967).

Section IV-G
Technical Data Table of
Weapons and Equipment

Glider Aircraft (All Countries)   997

Glider Aircraft (All Countries)

Model	DFS-230	Go-242	Me-321	Horsa	Hamilcar	CG-4A	CG-18	A-7
Country	Germany	Germany	Germany	Britain	Britain	USA	USA	USSR
Wingspan (feet)	72.1	80.3	180.5	88.0	110.0	83.7	85.7	62.3
Length (feet)	36.9	51.9	92.4	67.0	68.0	48.3	54.3	37.8
Empty Weight (pounds)	1,896	7,055	26,896	8,370	18,400	3,790	8,900	2,200
Landing Speed (mph)	40	60	60	45	80	40	50	65
Payload (cargo, pounds)	2,800	8,000	48,600	6,900	17,500	3,750	8,500	2,000
Payload (troops)	9 troops and 600 lbs	23 troops	200 troops	25 troops	Equipment only	15 troops	32 to 40 troops	8 troops
Number in Service	2,230	1,528	200	5,000+	412	13,912	139	400

H

Helicopters

World War II saw the first operational employment of helicopters, albeit in a very limited sense. The lack of lightweight materials and the primitive power plants of the period severely limited the payload and performance of these early helicopters. Nonetheless, Germany and the Allies actively tested prototypes throughout the war and the German Navy actually employed two helicopters operationally in the Aegean Sea during the early months of 1944. Although the U.S. and Royal Navies conducted an operational test and evaluation of a Sikorski prototype, no Allied helicopters saw operational employment in the European theater.

First conceptualized by Leonardo da Vinci in 1483, rotary-winged aircraft remained little more than an amusing toy until the advent of World War I. The Austro-Hungarian Navy pushed development of a helicopter for use as ship-borne scouts but the prototype could only ascend while tethered to a rope. The U.S. Army also investigated the military uses of the helicopter in the closing days of the war and encouraged manufacturers to develop an operational model.

Despite an extensive effort by several nations, however, no successful helicopters emerged until Germany tested the Focke-Wulf 61 in 1936. It not only passed local hovering tests but test pilot Hanna Reitsch (q.v.) even took it for a 200-mile cross-country flight from Bremen to Berlin. All three German services saw the advantages of the craft and requested development of larger, more powerful models. Allied bombing destroyed the factories before production could be undertaken, so only a handful were ever produced.

The U.S. also tested several prototypes in the

A German Fa-223 Drache, one of the world's first operational military helicopters. (IWM HU 2857)

1930s, and by 1942, a working prototype was produced, the VS-300. Designed by Russian émigré Igor Sikorsky (q.v.), the single-rotor VS-300 became the core design for all U.S. and British helicopter designs in the war. Approximately 400 were built before 1945, but, except for a single operational test in the Atlantic in early 1944, service was limited to a handful used for search and rescue operations in the Burma theater during the war's final months. The Soviet Navy also tested several helicopters in the closing days of the war but none were employed operationally.

The only helicopter to see operational service in Europe was the German Navy's Flettner 282, which was deployed in the Aegean in 1943. Only two saw service and these operated from the former Yugoslav minelayer, *Drache,* which the Germans used as an antisubmarine escort for convoys supplying their Aegean Island garrisons. Their primary operating procedure called for the one-man helicopter to fly ahead of the convoy and drop a smoke float at the location where the pilot spotted a submarine. He would then fly back to the *Drache* and drop a message on the flight deck, giving his estimate of the sub's course and speed. He could also be used to mark the location of any minefields ahead of the convoy, much like U.S. helicopters did in the Persian Gulf in the late 1980s.

Although no World War II helicopter could carry anything heavier than a light machine gun, the advantages of the craft were evident and the helicopter's development was pushed aggressively in the postwar period. Today it is considered an essential element of any military force. It is used in the transport, reconnaissance, attack, and even airborne early warning roles.

Elizabeth D. Schafer
Carl O. Schuster

(Refer to table on page 1003)

Additional Reading

Morris, Charles L., *Pioneering the Helicopter* (1945).
Munson, Kenneth, and Alec Lumsden, *Combat Helicopters Since 1942* (1986).
Weal, Elke C., John A. Weal, and Richard F. Baker, *Combat Aircraft of World War II* (1977).

Hydrofoils

At least two nations conducted research into the use of hydrofoils in World War II: Great Britain and Germany. The Royal Navy conducted extensive research during the prewar period but dropped the program in 1939 because the craft's wooden foils had a tendency to come off in a seaway.

Thus Germany was the only nation to employ operational hydrofoils in the war. It was not a very large force: one squadron of six hydrofoil harbor patrol craft stationed in Bergen, Norway, and one cargo hydrofoil that saw limited service in the Baltic in 1944–1945. Germany also lost one research craft to bombing and another in a storm; both in late 1944. Germany's hydrofoils were divided among the victors after the war. The harbor craft were divided between the U.S. and Great Britain, while the cargo hydrofoil went to the Soviet Union.

Ironically, Germany's hydrofoils were developed by the army's amphibious engineering corps *(Wasser-Pionieren)* because Admiral Erich Raeder (q.v.) had terminated the *Kriegsmarine's* hydrofoil program in 1928. He felt the craft were too frail for effective use. The army took over the program because it wanted a fast transport for island assaults or to support island garrisons. Its first cargo hydrofoil, *Schell I,* was ordered in 1938. The army also contracted for a combat hydrofoil to use for harbor security. On learning of the crafts' existence, Raeder demanded that production and development be transferred to the *Kriegsmarine.* Adolf Hitler (q.v.) agreed on 20 June 1940. Raeder promptly cancelled the cargo hydrofoil project and limited development of the combat variant to one model. Six were built between 1940 and 1943.

A second cargo variant, *Schell II,* was developed at Hitler's insistence in 1943. Its mission was to run the Allied blockade into North Africa, but it was not completed until months after Tunisia (q.v.) fell. Only two were built and they both suffered from propulsion system problems. Other variants of torpedo- and mine-carrying hydrofoils were considered, but their development remained stillborn until after Raeder's resignation in January 1943. By then it was too late. Although having a large hydrofoil force would not have given Germany victory, these craft would have posed a serious threat to Allied shipping in the English Channel and North Sea had they been available in significant numbers in 1940–1941. By 1943, Allied air and sea supremacy was so great that no new surface craft could have redressed the balance.

Carl O. Schuster

Additional Reading

Bekker, Cajus, *Hitler's Naval War* (1974).
Fock, Harald, *Fast Fighting Boats 1870–1945* (1973).
Whitley, M.J., *German Coastal Forces of World War Two* (1992).

Section IV-H
Technical Data Table of
Weapons and Equipment

Helicopters (All Countries)

Model	F1-282 *Kolibri*	Fa-223 *Drache*	R-4B Hoverfly	R-5A
Country	Germany	Germany	USA	USA
Service Date	1942	1943	1944	1944
Crew	one	two	two	two
Maximum Speed (mph)	93	109	75	105
Maximum Range (miles)	186	435	130	360
Gun Armament	None	None	None	None
Number in Service	24	19	133	65
Ceiling (feet)	10,800	16,000	8,000	14,400

I

Infantry Weapons, British

In 1939, Great Britain and its Commonwealth Allies confronted the German Army with infantry weapons not unlike those their fathers had used in World War I. In the hands of the British and Commonwealth soldier, however, they were good enough to do the job.

Pistols

Many different types of handguns made their way to Commonwealth infantry troops. The most common were the Enfield Number 2 Mark I, firing a caliber .38 round, or the older Webley Number 1 Mark IV, firing a Webley caliber .455 round. These were heavy-frame, top-break revolvers with astonishing stopping power and generally good reliability and accuracy. Unfortunately, versions made in different plants did not have interchangeable parts, making for some inconvenience in logistics.

A number of Enfield revolvers in calibers .38 S&W, .380 and .38 Webley were also sometimes found in the infantry, as well as the occasional British Smith & Wesson .38 pistol (which does not fire .38 S&W ammo) that was almost indistinguishable from the standard police sidearm in the U.S. There also was a Colt .455 automatic pistol (a U.S. M-1911A1 look-alike) and a .455 Webley automatic. Many of these were issued to secondary theaters and to home guards. Canadian troops sometimes carried the FN 9mm Parabellum Browning Hi-Power, a version of the Belgian weapon of the same name.

Rifles

Arming a predominance of the British infantry units was one of ten different versions (some introduced before World War I) of the Lee Enfield bolt-action caliber .303 rifle. Most common were the Rifle Number 4 Mark I (more than five million made during the war) and the Rifle Number 1, Short Magazine, Lee Enfield Mark III (two million made from 1939–1945, also known as the SMLE). Both used a stripper-clip fed nondetachable box magazine. In the hands of the highly skilled Commonwealth soldiers, these weapons could be deadly at 300 meters, and maintained a far more accurate (though less voluminous) fire than could their American cousins with semiautomatic M-1 Garands.

In the early days of the war, however, especially during the dark days between the fall of France and the arrival of the first U.S. troops in 1942, the Home Guard (q.v.), troops in training, and soldiers in secondary theaters (including the Pacific and Asia) were armed with a polyglot of weapons, including sporting arms, American M-1917 caliber .30 Enfields, World War I–vintage Canadian Ross rifles (a poor weapon for military purposes), and specially made caliber .303 M-1903 Springfields. Most of these were replaced by more modern or suitable British equipment by 1943. Home Guard units were also issued the American M-1918 Browning Automatic Rifle (BAR), some of which found their way into regular infantry units.

Submachine Guns

The British called submachine guns "machine carbines" until the mid-1950s. For specialized troops, commandos, engineers, and some others, in 1941, the Sten gun (named after the designers Shepperd, Turpin, and the Enfield Arsenal) appeared, a 9mm miracle sometimes derisively called the "plumber's delight," and the "Stench gun." Like all submachine guns, this weapon was cheap, light, and easily made of stamped parts. Though notoriously unsafe, right-handed, and given to occasional bursting, the various marks of this revolutionary weapon could fire somewhere between 500 and 600 rounds per minute with fair accuracy.

Royal Marine (q.v.) commandos also used an adaptation of the German MP-38II, called the Lanchester Mark 1, a wooden-stocked prewar 9mm weapon. Britain also used American M-1928 Thompsons before the introduction of the Sten, and some home guards and Canadians retained Thompsons throughout the war. Australian and New Zealand troops sometimes carried the Austen, an Australian version of the Sten.

Machine Guns

Like everything else, Britain and the Commonwealth were short of machine guns at the beginning of the war, and so issued a mixture of newer weapons, older weapons, and foreign weapons to the troops. The World War I–vintage Lewis Mark I caliber .303 was issued throughout the war to second-line troops and to frontliners when the need existed. It fired the same cartridge as the infantry rifle, and some quarter million were made during the war. With a forty-seven-round drum magazine and a massive air-cooling jacket on the barrel, this twenty-seven-pound weapon fired 500 rounds a minute accurately out to about 600 meters. The strip-magazine-fed Lewis/Hotchkiss was also issued to Home Guards.

The water-cooled, belt-fed, tripod-mounted Vickers caliber .303 (another World War I veteran) equipped Home Guards and some infantry units. This heavier piece was accurate to about 1,000 meters at 250–350 rounds per minute. The lighter, air-cooled, detachable-box-magazine-fed Vickers K gun or VGO (Vickers gas-operated), originally used by the RAF as an observer's gun, was used by the Long-Range Desert Group and the SAS (qq.v.) in North Africa.

The most widely used Commonwealth infantry machine gun also was said to have been the finest light machine gun ever made. The Bren Gun was a caliber .303 detachable-box magazine-fed, gas-operated weapon first licensed to Britain from the Brno arms firm of Czechoslovakia. The various models of this twenty-two-pound weapon fired anywhere from 480 to 540 rounds per minute, with accuracy out to about 1,500 meters. The Bren was such a fine weapon that even the Germans used captured units. Practically every country in Europe and many in Asia, Africa, and South America used the Bren after World War II. More than four million were produced before the end of the war, mostly in Canada.

Grenades

British and most Commonwealth troops carried

A British 2-inch mortar crew in action in Italy, 13 September 1943. (IWM NA 6828)

the No. 36M Mills grenade, a descendent of the original Mills bomb that had been in service since 1915. It was an egg-shaped grenade weighing about a pound, containing twelve ounces of trotyl. A good thrower could hurl it about twenty-five meters, and it had a bursting radius of about ten meters. The original versions could be fitted with a steel rod for rifle launching, but in World War II that practice was abandoned. Commonwealth soldiers also carried a number of canister grenades for signaling, screening, incendiary purposes, and target marking.

Mortars

Commonwealth mortars were not unlike their cousins in America, using 2-inch, 3-inch, and 4.2-inch rounds with quite similar effects and tactics. The 2-inch platoon/section weapon with a 1.74-pound shell had a range of about 750 meters. The 3-inch company/battalion support weapon with a 10-pound shell had a range of about 2,500 meters. The 4.2-inch's massive 20-pound shell ranged about 3,750 meters, fired from brigade level or from specialized batteries for chemical smoke and incendiaries.

Antitank Weapons

Early in the war, antitank rifles that were relics of World War I had some practical use. But as armor got heavier they were relegated to limited long-range sniping. The Boys caliber .55 antitank rifle was in testing until 1943, but was never officially adopted for service. It was huge, punishing to the firer, but nonetheless accurate at nearly a mile.

By 1941, the need for a more powerful antitank weapon for Commonwealth infantry became obvious. As a result, the Blacker bombard, a large, cheap spigot mortar of dubious effectiveness (because of its indirect firing nature), was scaled down into what became known as the PIAT (projector, infantry, antitank). This awkward-looking weapon could throw a 3-pound shaped-charge grenade about 100 meters accurately, and could defeat any Axis armor from almost any aspect. The PIAT, unlike the American bazooka or the German *Panzerfaust,* could be fired inside a closed space without risk to the firer or the occupants. About 115,000 PIATs were made during the war. Canadian infantry units sometimes were equipped with the U.S. bazooka, which also was used by British and other Commonwealth troops.

Recoilless Rifles

By the end of the war, Britain had developed and deployed two recoilless rifles, a 3.45-inch man-portable model with a range of 900 meters, and a 3.7-inch vehicle-mounted weapon with a range of 1,800 meters. They appeared in small numbers, and were very similar to the American recoilless weapons.

Edged Weapons

One advantage of having an empire on which the sun never set was that some of the troops from far-off lands had colorful weapons. The Gurkhas (q.v.) carried a military version of their famous kukri knife, a scythe-shaped, slashing blade about a foot long. Sikhs sometimes carried a wavy-bladed kris or a sword-like kinjal. For more conventional troops there was the eight-inch Fairbairn-Sikes single-edged fighting knife, the double-edged dagger, or the ten-inch Enfield bayonet.

John D. Beatty

(Refer to table on page 1025)

Additional Reading

Ezell, Edward C., *Small Arms of the World* (1977).
Chamberlain, Peter, and Terry Gander, *WW2 Fact Files: Machine Guns* (1974).
Hogg, Ian V., and John Weeks, *Military Small Arms of the 20th Century* (1992).
Weeks, John, *Infantry Weapons* (1971).

Infantry Weapons, French

The French entered World War II with a mixed array of modern and obsolete infantry weapons. While most of the belligerents continued to upgrade their weapons and introduce new designs throughout the war, French small arms development virtually ended with their defeat in 1940. After that point, Free French forces were armed primarily with British and American weapons. Vichy French forces (for as long as Vichy continued to exist) retained the old prewar designs. Many of the better French designs were confiscated by the Germans and used throughout the war by their rear echelon and support troops.

Pistols

At the outbreak of World War II, the French armed forces were still using the obsolete Lebel M-1892 revolver; but the French Army was equipped with a variety of modern automatic sidearms as well. The standard service pistol was the Pistolet Automatique type Ruby, holding nine 7.65mm rounds. It remained in service until 1939, when it was largely replaced by the M-1935A and

M-1935S. These pistols were based on the U.S. Colt/Browning caliber .45 M-1911A1, but had magazine capacities of only eight rounds and were also chambered for 7.65mm. They were put in production in 1936, but did not reach large-scale production until 1938. Another pistol used was the 9mm Astra, which was adopted as a substitute sidearm.

Rifles

The *Fusil d'Infanterie* Model 1907 was the basis of a rifle made in 1934 in an attempt to give the French Army some sort of "modern" infantry weapon. The M-1907/34 fired a 7.5mm rimless round. In 1936, the *Fusil* MAS M-1936 was introduced, intended to become the standard-issue service rifle. It originally was produced in various models for the different services, but all later production was standardized. Both the MAS M-1936 and M-1907/34 had a five-round magazine. Some French units also were equipped with the old 8mm Lebel M-1886, the standard rifle issued in World War I. Some of these rifles were modernized in 1935, but still had a magazine capacity of only three rounds.

The French produced limited numbers of an automatic rifle, the 8mm *Fusil Mitrailleur* RSC M-1917. A World War I design, it was unsuited for modern warfare.

Submachine Guns

There were two models of submachine gun used by the French. The MAS M-1938 was accurate at short ranges, but fired the same light 7.65mm round as the MAS M-1935 pistol. The U.S. M-1928 Thompson was also used, chambered for caliber .45. It used a twenty-round straight magazine, or a drum magazine of 50 or 100 rounds.

Machine Guns

The French had several light machine guns, including the Hotchkiss M-1922, which fired either a 6.5mm or 8mm bullet from fifteen- or thirty-round feed strips. The 7.5mm Chatellerault M-1924 replaced several World War I models. It had design problems initially, but after these were resolved, it became very popular with French troops. The M-1924/29 version of the Chatellerault also had a 150-round drum magazine, and was designed specifically for use in the Maginot Line (q.v.). One World War I design that remained in service was the M-1914 Chauchat, which the French called an "automatic rifle." It came in 7.65mm, 7.92mm, and 8mm models.

The Hotchkiss M-1914 was the standard French heavy machine gun of World War I, and was still in service in 1939. It was heavy and bulky, but reliable. It fired a 7.92mm or 8mm round, in twenty-four- or thirty-round metal strips. It also could use a 249-round strip of belts joined together. In 1931, the French also adopted the 13.2mm Hotchkiss M-1930.

Grenades

The French used a number of hand grenades, with the *Grenade à Main* F-1 the most common. Even though it was a World War I design, it influenced the development of its American and Soviet counterparts.

Mortars

The Mortier de 60mm M-1935 entered French Army service in 1937, and eventually became the basis for the U.S. 60mm M-1 mortar. In 1939, the Lances Grenades de 50mm M-1937 entered service, but even though small and light, had too short a range to be effective. The most widely used mortar was the Mortier Brandt de 81mm M-1927/31. By 1940, the French Army had more than 8,000 in service.

Antitank Weapons

The standard French antitank rifle was the SA-L M-1934. It fired a 25mm round, but was ineffective because of its short range and light shot. The SA-L M-1937 (also known as the SA 37 APX) had the potential to be an effective antitank weapon, firing a 47mm round.

Mark Conrad

(Refer to table on page 1026)

Additional Reading

Gander T., and P. Chamberlain, *Weapons of the Third Reich* (1979).
Greenwall, Harry J., *Why France Fell* (1958).
Weeks, John, *Infantry Weapons* (1971).

Infantry Weapons, German

Germany's armed forces were known throughout the war for their superb equipment, even though weapons were almost always in short supply. Following World War I, its army had been severely restricted in size and quantity of armaments by the terms of the Versailles Treaty (q.v.). Nevertheless, Germany stockpiled and concealed as much weaponry as possible and then made agreements with foreign industrial companies for further development of desired weapons throughout the 1920s.

After 1933, the restrictions were abandoned and a period of rapid growth in the capability and number of infantry weapons began. When war broke out in 1939, most German soldiers still used stockpiled older weapons, while the elite units received the new weapons.

Pistols

The infantry weapons available during the war varied, but each was of consistently high quality. By 1939, German pistols had reached a high degree of quality and sophistication, and they retained their traditional role as a light, convenient weapon that was carried and yet permitted use of both hands and arms for other tasks. In addition, a pistol gave authority to the bearer and thereby was widely desired. Germany produced two important types. The *Pistole* 08 (P-08), known as Luger (or Parabellum outside of the *Reich)*, came into military use in World War I. By 1939, it had been improved and came in a standard 9mm version. It was, however not an ideal pistol, largely because its operating toggle breach mechanism opened upward, subjecting the mechanism to dirt and grime.

Efforts to find a replacement began in the mid-1930s, and the *Pistole* 38 (P-38) contained some improvements. It had a double-action trigger mechanism, and was also designed for mass production, an important feature as the war continued. Still, the P-38 never fully supplanted the well-established P-08, and both were widely used throughout the war. The P-38 became the standard pistol of the postwar *Bundeswehr,* and remained so to the end of the twentieth century.

Another pistol of wide usage but of a lesser quality was the Mauser C-96, the "broom handle Mauser." The C-96 existed in both 7.63mm and 9mm versions. It was bulky, awkward, complex, and difficult to produce, but the Mauser had a unique aura. The *Waffen-SS* (q.v.) preferred this pistol, and used it in anti-partisan operations because it had a twenty-round magazine and was fully automatic. In addition to these pistols, the military used some models manufactured for police use, such as the 7.65mm Walther PP and PPK.

An important source of additional weapons were the arms plants in the countries conquered by Germany. The occupation of Czechoslovakia in 1939 placed a number of plants under Nazi control and large numbers of pistols, such as the vz.24 and vz.38 came into their hands. The occupation of the Low Countries brought another famous arms manufacturer, Belgian *Fabrique Nationale d'Armes de Guerre,* which was already producing large numbers of automatic pistols, most based on Browning designs. As the German Army swept through eastern Europe, captured pistols from Poland and Hungary were also issued to the German military, but the number was never sufficient to meet the needs of the armed forces.

Rifles

The staple weapon of the infantry remained the rifle, the weapon infantrymen trained with and depended upon. German military planners responded to the recognition that most service rifles were used at relatively short distances, and improved upon the standard rifle, the *Gewehr* 98 (Gew-98) with its Mauser action, one of the most reliable bolt actions ever produced. The modified versions, known as *Karabiner* 98b (Kar-98b) and Kar-98k, incorporated several improvements, and the Kar-98k remained the standard weapon throughout the war with about 11.5 million manufactured. It also came with various accessories, including grenade launchers, winter triggers, cleaning kits, and bayonets. The Kar-98K was, moreover, the last of a number of Mauser rifles used by the German Army based on the original Mauser Gew-98.

At the outbreak of war, German forces still lacked sufficient rifles. The speed of conquest and the fact that most European arms manufacturers had adopted the Mauser action enabled the deployment of the improved Kar series to go to most of the frontline forces. By the close of the war, German production capability had been decimated by Allied air attacks and severe material shortages. Weapons were still needed, and designers came up with rifles requiring only a minimum of essential materials and production facilities. The Volkstumgewehr VG1-5, for example, was a crude but useable semi-automatic rifle.

The German infantry came to recognize the advantage of automatic-feed rifles, especially after 1941 and their encounter with Soviet automatic rifles. But low priority was given to the new models developed by German manufacturers Mauser and Walther, the Gew-41(M) and Gew-41(W). These weapons used a new cartridge, the 7.92x33mm *Infanterie kurz Patrone.* It was shorter than the standard cartridge and designed to increase infantry firepower in close-range engagements. The *kurz* version permitted more accurate and controlled semiautomatic fire than was possible in lightweight shoulder weapons using full-powered cartridges. It had a profound effect on small arms development.

Only several thousand of the Gew-41(W)

were produced, and most went to troops on the eastern front. The weapon was not well liked by the infantry, however, largely because of its poor balance and need for meticulous maintenance. When the improved Gew-43(W) came along, it was the preferred semiautomatic rifle. Even the new Gew-43(W) had disadvantages: it was heavy, and the barrel fouled easily, which meant additional care. First issued in 1943, versatile, and highly accurate, it was widely used on the eastern front. Mauser and Walther also produced a "machine carbine," the MKb-42 series, which fired the new cartridges and were welcomed by the troops.

By 1943, development of additional automatic rifles resulted in the production of assault rifles, including the *Machinenpistole* 43 (MP-43), one of the first German weapons in which production was more important than finish. This weapon offered the German infantry some considerable advantages, including a huge increase in firepower. Its semiautomatic mode, with a longer range, was used in defensive operations, and the automatic mode greatly increased the offensive impact. MP-43s were usually issued to the frontline troops, especially the *Waffen-SS,* for use on the eastern front, where it proved to be very reliable. The MP-43 was followed closely by the MP-44 and the *Sturmgewehr* 44 (StuG-44). These weapons were the first to use the 7.92mm short round, and their design influences the postwar development of the Soviet AK-47 assault rifle.

Another highly effective automatic rifle was the *Fallschirmgewehr 42* (FG-42), designed for use by paratroopers who needed the maximum firepower in the smallest possible weapon. They demanded a full-sized round, after having been targets of long-range fire by British troops. But this created problems, such as heavy recoil, which made it a difficult weapon to shoot accurately. The first use of the FG-42 was in the September 1943 Gran Sasso raid to free Benito Mussolini (qq.v.).

Submachine Guns

Some German infantry also received submachine guns, weapons that fired automatically but remained light enough for one man to handle. The ammunition for these light, burst-fire weapons was limited to pistol caliber, which also meant short-range use. Responding to the changing needs of the infantryman, the Erma-Werke produced the *Machinenpistole* 38 (MP-38). Erroneously called the "Schmeisser," the MP-38 was one of the most effective and influential designs of the war, especially its folding stock. It was mass-produced using plastic and lightweight metal. A new model, the MP-40, which came into full production in the summer of 1940, contained improvements and was produced in large numbers.

A 7.92mm MG-34 machine gun firing on French positions near Verdun, May 1940. (IWM MH 9208)

Machine Guns

Light machine guns were also deployed on the company level or lower. Most were developed out of the successful *Machinengewehr* 08 (MG-08). The MG-34, with its seventy-five-round drum magazine and bipod, was an excellent weapon widely used by all branches of the German armed forces. It was produced in large numbers until the end of the war. The need to speed up production and for improvements culminated in the MG-42, one of the finest light machine guns ever made. First issued in 1942 to the German *Afrika Korps* (q.v.), it handled well, was reliable, and was highly resistant to dust and cold, features that made it popular with the soldiers. Still, the mounting production rates could not keep up with demand, so the infantry continued to use captured guns, such as the Czech ZB-26 and the French Chatellerault.

When fighting became relatively stationary, the infantry turned to heavy machine guns with their longer range. Remarkably, German forces simply modified the MG-34 and MG-42 series. Heavier caliber machine guns were produced by the *Luftwaffe,* and some of these, such as the MG-151/20, were adopted for use by ground troops. Infantry also used heavy machine guns captured in each campaign, such as the Czech ZB-53, which remained in production and was designated the MGM-38. Polish, French, and Italian heavy machine guns were also incorporated into the German infantry arsenal.

Grenades

Hand grenades were widely used by the infantry, and the Germans had a wider range of types and used more than any of the Allies. By 1939, the two basic types included the stick grenade (*Stielhandgranate* 24—called the "potato masher" by the Allies), and the small egg grenade (*Eihandgranate* 39). Each relied on its blast effect rather than fragmentation. Several versions of the stick grenade were produced, and these could be fitted with a serrated fragmentation sleeve that enhanced antipersonnel capability.

Mortars

Mortars, as were most of the other infantry weapons, had been used during World War I, and they still offered a number of advantages, including light weight and ease and speed of firing. They could be used at close or medium range, and in offensive and defensive operations. During the 1930s, Rheinmetall produced the *Granatanwerfer* 34 (GrW-34) model and continuously improved it. One of the mortar's chief tactical advantages was its high elevation of fire, which meant that the shell fell almost vertically onto its target. Mortars were used in large numbers during the war. By 1942, the 50mm GrW-36 was abandoned in favor of larger caliber mortars, especially after encountering the Soviet Union's 120mm mortars. The Skoda *Werke* at Pilsen, Krupp, and the Gustloff *Werke* at Suhl also produced the heavy mortars such as the 120mm GrW-42.

Antitank Weapons

As early as the 1939 Polish campaign (q.v.), the German infantry used antitank rifles, including the PzB-39, which fired a tungsten-cored 7.92mm bullet. Soon, however, the armor thichness on tanks increased, thereby considerably reducing the PzB-29's effectiveness.

By late 1942, the Germans developed the first of the *Panzerfaust* (Armored Fist) series, one-man, disposable, recoilless, antitank grenade launchers. They were simple to manufacture, small, easily carried, and highly effective at short ranges, making them ideal for the ambush-type warfare in which German troops increasingly found themselves engaged. The *Panzerfaust* 30 was followed by the *Panzerfaust* 60, and the *Panzerfaust* 100. Each model could penetrate up to 200mm of armor by use of a shaped-charge warhead. Later in the war the Germans also produced the more effective *Raketenpanzerbüchse* 54. The *Panzerschreck* (Tank Terror), as it also was called, was copied after the U.S. bazooka.

Kenneth J. Swanson
Robert G. Waite

(Refer to table on page 1027)

Additional Reading
Cormack, A.J.R., *German Small Arms of World War II* (1979).
Gander, Terry, and Peter Chamberlain, *Small Arms, Artillery and Special Weapons of the Third Reich* (1978).
Hahn, Fritz, *Waffen und Geheimwaffen des deutsche Heeres 1933–1945,* 2 vols. (1986).
Markham, George, *Guns of the Reich: Firearms of the German Forces, 1939–1945* (1989).
Senich, Peter R., *The German Assault Rifle 1935–1945* (1987).

Infantry Weapons, Italian

Despite Italy's less than impressive showing in World War II, the Italian military had some first-rate infantry weapons. They also had some of the oldest and worst models, more attributable to Italian government bureaucracy than to the state of the small arms industry. Italy, in fact, has had a long tradition of excellence in weapons manufacture and design. Most of the Italian infantry weapons were well finished. Unlike the other combatant nations, Italy steadfastly refused to lower quality standards in small arms manufacturing as the war progressed. After Italy surrendered in 1943, quality standards declined in the factories the Germans seized and continued to operate.

Pistols

The M–1934 Beretta automatic was the most significant Italian pistol of the war. Chambered for the 9mm short (.380), it was an underpowered, yet excellent design. The M 1934 remained the standard side arm of the Italian Army up through the 1950s. The Italians also used several other pistols, including the 10.35mm M 1889 Bodeo revolver.

Rifles

Italian infantryman never had a truly modern rifle. The basic model was the pre–World War I Mannlicher-Parravicino Carcano Modello 91, a bolt-action piece chambered for the relatively light 6.5mm round. Based on the results of their experiences in Ethiopia (q.v.), the Italians modernized this weapon in 1938 by rechambering it for the more powerful 7.35mm round. The result was the M-1938. Many variations, including carbines, existed of both models.

Italy produced only one significant semiautomatic rifle, the 6.5mm Breda 35. It was a good design, but it was expensive and difficult to manufacture. Thus, few were ever produced, and they were issued only to specialist troops. Export models in 7.62mm and 7.92mm also existed.

Submachine Guns

Swinging back to the other extreme of the quality spectrum, the 9mm Beretta Model 1938 was one of the finest submachine guns ever made. It had two triggers. The forward one was for full-automatic fire, and the rear one was for semiautomatic (single shot) fire. The gun existed in various versions throughout the war. The Germans thought highly of it, and both the German and Romanian armies took delivery of some of the production output.

Machine Guns

The Breda M-1930 was the standard Italian light machine gun of the war. It had a blowback action and fired the light 6.5mm round. It was an odd looking weapon, with projecting parts and recesses in the most unlikely places. This feature made it especially vulnerable to dust, which caused serious problems for Italian troops in the desert. In 1938, the gun was modified somewhat and rechambered for the heavier 7.35mm round.

By 1940, many Italian units still had the World War I–era Fiat-Revelli M-1914 medium machine gun. It also shot the standard 6.5mm Italian round, which was something of a waste for a medium machine gun. It was fed from a ten-round strip-feed box magazine, which made it even more inefficient. In 1935 the Italians slightly modernized this old war-horse in an 8mm version with a belt feed. With the proper mount, the M 1935 could be used against low-flying aircraft.

Grenades

At the start of the war, the Italians had three different versions of the M-1935 hand grenade, each made by a different manufacturer—Breda, OTO, and SRC. All were of questionable reliability. In 1940, Breda brought out the more reliable M-1940, followed by the M-1942, an antitank stick grenade.

Mortars

Even today, mortars are among the simplest of all infantry weapons, but the 45mm Brixia M-1935 was a notable exception. This unnecessarily complex weapon was magazine-fed, and employed a system of adjusting gas ports to vary the range. The 81mm M-1935 was a much simpler design, and therefore much more efficient.

Antitank Weapons

Italy produced no antitank rifles or recoilless weapons during the war. They used, instead, captured stocks of the Polish Wz-35 Marosczek 7.92mm antitank rifle, a gift of the Germans in 1939. The Germans also used this surprisingly good weapon. It had a muzzle velocity of 4,200 fps, and its tungsten-cored bullet could penetrate 20mm of armor at 300 meters.

David T. Zabecki

(Refer to table on page 1028)

Additional Reading
Ezell, Edward C., *Small Arms of the World* (1977).
Hogg, Ian V., and John Weeks, *Military Small Arms of the 20th Century* (1992).
Weeks, John, *Infantry Weapons* (1971).

Infantry Weapons, Soviet

Soviet infantry weapons of World War II reflected to a large degree the nation's character and its efforts to overcome economic backwardness. The major feature of Soviet-produced small arms was their primitive and even coarse nature, especially in comparison to the weapons produced by Western European manufacturers. In the drive to produce the maximum number of effective weapons, Soviet designers and factories were not able to devote much attention to highly refined design, careful machining, or fine finishing. Factories producing small arms were also generally primitive, operating with unsophisticated machinery and tools. In addition, the weapons were used by an infantry lacking specialized training, and they therefore had to be easy to maintain and operate.

After the Nazi invasion in June 1941, and the rapid conquest of much of the western Soviet Union, new armament factories were set up farther east and moved into production very rapidly. These plants were called upon to produce enormous quantities of weapons to meet the needs of the Soviet armed forces, needs that changed as the war progressed.

Pistols

Among the Soviet infantry, pistols had never been very important. Officers were typically involved in battles and they generally carried the same weapons as their soldiers, primarily rifles. More importantly, pistols required greater training in their care and operation than did rifles, and Soviet infantry troops generally were short on training. Another factor was that production time for a pistol was about the same as for a submachine gun, a much more effective weapon.

As a result of these factors, only several pistol types were produced, all based on outdated designs. The Nagant M-1895, for example, was patterned after a nineteenth-century Belgian revolver and had a complicated mechanism. Manufactured in the Tula Arsenal at least until 1940, the M-1895 was standard issue through the end of the war.

Another pistol model was the Tokarev TT-33, a straightforward automatic handgun based on an American Browning/Colt M-1911A1 pistol. Despite its small size, the TT-33 was a powerful weapon, firing 7.62mm bottleneck cartridges. It also could chamber the Mauser 7.63mm round, which enabled the Soviets to use captured stocks of German ammunition. The TT-33 was adopted by the Soviet Army in 1933, and used throughout the war, primarily by the crews of armored vehicles and aircraft. It never was produced in large enough

quantities to make its use widespread, however. The Soviets also used pistols purchased abroad, including German Mausers.

Rifles

The staple Soviet infantry weapon, the bolt-action rifle, was the oldest design used by any belligerent in World War II. The Soviet M-1891/30 was based on the Mosin-Nagant M-1891, but with shortened barrel and other modifications. It was, however, relatively simple to manufacture and easy to maintain in the field—two big assets. The M-1891/30 rifle was also improved in the 1938 and 1944 carbine models. The standard infantry version, the M-1891/30G, had a magazine that held five 7.62x54mm rimmed cartridges. The M-1891/30G was long, heavy, and clumsy to operate. Another shortcoming was the absence of a removable bayonet; but this was remedied in the M-1944 carbine version. Some of the M-1891/30Gs were fitted with telescopes for use by snipers.

The Soviet Army recognized the need for an automatic feeding rifle well before the outbreak of war, and their interest resulted in the development of the Simonov AVS M-1936 in 7.62x54mm caliber. The weapon had problems, including a complex and weak bolt mechanism, which made the AVS M-1936 not sufficiently durable for combat. Already in the late 1930s, it was being replaced by the SVT-38, the self-loading Tokarev, which had a ten-round magazine, and to a large degree was based on the earlier AVS M-1936.

Further modifications came as a result of experience in the "Winter War" against Finland (q.v.), and the new model was the SVT-40, produced in semi- and full-automatic versions. Used primarily by special troops and snipers, the SVTs were structurally weak and lacked durability. Most were issued to NCOs who were expected to take better care of their rifles, and who also received better training than the general recruits. (The famous Soviet AK-47 assault rifle was not developed until after the war.)

Submachine Guns

The Soviet Union's arms manufacturers also began developing a submachine gun relatively early. In the early 1930s they were producing the PPD-34, a machine pistol designed by Degtyarev. Based largely on the German MP-38, the PPD-34 and PPD-34/38 used 7.62x25mm pistol bullets housed in a drum holding seventy-one rounds. Like most Soviet-made automatic weapons, it had a chromium-plated barrel, which made it more resistant to rough use, fouling, and corrosive primers. The PPD-34 was widely used in the Spanish civil war (q.v.) and in the Winter War (q.v.) against Finland. The weapon, however, proved to be too difficult to manufacture to make it a truly practical submachine gun.

During the Finnish war, Soviet officials recognized the importance of a reliable and mass-produced submachine gun. The resulting model PPD-40, however, was not produced in sufficient numbers to make it widely available, and it was not geared toward mass manufacture. Another new model, the PP Shpagin (PPSh-41), was designed to keep the number of working parts to a minimum, as production was a major concern. Factories in the Soviet Union produced about five million of the PPSh-41 submachine guns between 1941 and 1945.

Designed especially for close combat and offensive action, the PPSh-41 fit the needs of Soviet military tactics. When the Soviet Army moved on the offensive in 1942 and 1943, entire units received submachine guns. The PPSh-41 proved to be extremely valuable in the fighting at Leningrad and Stalingrad (qq.v.), and some were even issued to Soviet partisans (q.v.) fighting behind German lines. At Leningrad, a new model, the PPS-43, was developed and manufactured using more stamped parts and less metal, which allowed production to more than double. The gun went directly to the troops defending the city against the Germans. Like the PPSh-41, it fired only on automatic, and its magazine held thirty-five rounds.

Machine Guns

In the mid-1920s the Soviets developed a workable machine gun, the Degtiarev DP. It was a very simple weapon with only six moving parts. That meant that highly skilled workers or complex machinery was not necessary for its manufacture—an important consideration. The DP was a light, bipod-supported machine gun, simple to operate, with a top-mounted magazine holding forty-seven rounds. One DP was issued to each infantry section of ten men and it saw service throughout the war with only a few modifications. The effectiveness of the Degtiarev also resulted in its use on vehicles (the DT version) as well as aircraft (the DA version).

The Soviet Union's armed forces adopted the Maxim heavy machine gun, a weapon in use since 1905. The SPM-1910 model was a good design, regularly improved, and produced in large numbers. The SPM-1910 was water-cooled, which caused problems in winter combat. At more than fifty-two pounds (plus another 100 pounds for its mounting), it was a very heavy weapon. To increase its mobility, the SPM-1910 was mounted on a small wheeled carriage known as the *Sokolov.* (There also was a ski conversion for winter.) Few additional design changes were made until 1941, when there was a desperate drive for mass production. At that time the designer, Vasily Alekseevich Degtiarev (q.v.), came forward with a new version that proved to simply be a larger PM. It did offer some advantages, but it was too difficult to produce in quantity.

The SG-43 machine gun, designed by Peter Goryunov, proved effective, as well as reliable and strong. The SG-43 had a fifty-round metal link belt, and several could be linked together for nearly continuous firing. The barrel of the SG-43 was air-cooled and designed for quick changes. A further advantage was the SG-43's ease of manufacture, based on a process that relied on stamped rather than machined parts. The SG-43 also was widely used on vehicle mounts.

The largest Soviet machine gun was the 12.7mm DShK-38, designed by Degtiarev and Georgy Semenovich Shpagin. The DShK-38 saw widespread use in aircraft and vehicles. The ground mount consisted of a Sokolov-type wheeled tripod, which could be erected to form an antiaircraft platform. The modernized version of this gun, the DShK-46, remained in the Soviet inventory up through the 1980s.

Grenades

Soviet infantry forces used several different types of grenades during the war. Widely available in the early phases was the M-1914/30, a stick-type grenade first developed in 1914 and improved in 1930. As the stockpile of the M-1914/30 diminished, it was replaced by grenades that were easier to manufacture. The F-1 was a fragmentation grenade, four inches long, with an external handle and safety pin. In 1942, the F-1 was replaced by the simpler RTD-42.

Mortars

Along with their belief in the efficacy of overwhelming firepower, the Soviet Army was among the greatest exponents of mortars. Mortars provided the maximum firepower for the least expense, and their operation required only minimal training. They were cheap and easy to manufacture, as was their ammunition. Furthermore, mortars delivered a larger load of explosives for their caliber. Infantry commanders came to rely heavily on mortars, which were readily available, despite generally inadequate communications and supply lines.

Just prior to the outbreak of war, the Soviets

acquired a large number of small mortars produced by several different designers, all of whom were eager to sell their product to the army. The PM-39 fired a 50mm shell, but it was soon replaced by the more advanced PM-40. The PM-40 was also a small weapon of conventional design—a small baseplate, barrel, and steel bipod with elevating and traversing screws for sighting. It fired only at fixed elevations of 45 and 75 degrees, with the range controlled by a various number of gas ports, which bled off the propellant gasses, thereby reducing throw-weight. The PM-40 was replaced by the PM-41, a simpler version with the same range of 800 meters. The PM-41, which was easier to manufacture, eliminated the bipod, simplified the sights and gas system, and handled easily in the field.

Although mortars proved to be satisfactory weapons, their short range limited them to primarily defensive operations. By late 1944, the PM-41 models were no longer available, having been replaced by 82mm models such as the PM-41/43, which had a range of 3,050 meters. These larger mortars had been manufactured as early as 1936, but the 1941 model simplified their production, a crucial factor. In addition, the new model was easier to transport. The older models consisted of separate barrels, bipods, and baseplates, all of which had to be carried individually or together in a vehicle, thereby limiting the weapon's effectiveness for infantrymen. An improvement in the PM-41/43 was that an axle with pressed-steel wheels was attached to the end of the bipod, making the entire weapon easier to transport and maneuver. The wheels were removed for firing. In the early stages of the war, each infantry division was allocated eighty-four mortars. Later, that number increased to ninety-eight.

The Soviets also used heavy and super-heavy mortars. The 120mm HM-38 was such a successful design that the Germans copied it as their GrW-42. The Soviet 160mm M-1943 mortar, that fired a ninety-pound shell, was a breech-loading weapon, which made it almost unique among the infantry mortars of World War II.

Antitank Weapons

The Soviets started development on antitank rifles in the 1930s. Weapons designers began by using a large-bore conventional rifle firing various cartridges, including the 12.7mm heavy machine gun round, but this proved to be ineffective. The gun lacked sufficient power to penetrate even 12mm of armor at 400 meters. Two Soviet weapon designers, Degtiarev and Sergei Gavrilovich Simonov,

were given the assignment to come up with a rifle that would use the 14.5mm round and be an effective antitank gun. Simonov produced the PTRS-41, a widely used if awkward gun. It had a five-round box magazine, was eighty-four inches long, and weighed forty-six pounds. Despite these disadvantages, the PTRS-41 was issued throughout the Soviet Army.

Another antitank rifle was the Degtiarev-designed PTRD-41, a simple and reliable weapon. The PTRD-41 was a single-shot, bolt-action weapon. At thirty-eight pounds it was lighter than the PTRS-41, with a forty-eight-inch barrel, and an efficient recoil system. Beginning in 1941, one was issued to each infantry platoon. The PTRD-41 fired a square-based bullet with a tungsten-carbide core, which was effective only against lightly armored vehicles. The PTRD-41 remained in service throughout the war.

The Soviet infantry also had an antitank grenade, the RPG-43, which measured eight inches in diameter and weighed almost three pounds. According to claims of its manufacturer, its warhead could penetrate 75mm of homogeneous armor, making it effective against many German tanks. The RPG-43 was used extensively throughout the war.

The Soviet infantry continued to use primarily those weapons that were the simplest to manufacture and to deploy to their large forces in the field.

Kenneth J. Swanson
Robert G. Waite

(Refer to table on page 1029)

Additional Reading

Department of the Army, *Handbook on Soviet Ground Forces* (n.d.).

Guillaume, Augustine L., *Soviet Arms and Soviet Power* (1949).

Hogg, Ian V., *The Encyclopedia of Infantry Weapons of World War II* (1977).

Weeks, John, *World War II: Small Arms* (1979).

Infantry Weapons, U.S.

When the United States entered the war, it had a most ill-equipped army. When the war ended it was still not the best equipped, but it had one of the most powerful land organizations in the world. One factor in this transformation was the stunning success of a few small arms designs. By the end of the war a U.S. armored infantry regiment could throw more bullets at a target in one minute than a nineteenth-century regiment could in an hour. This tremendous increase in infantry power was eclipsed, however, by the even greater increases in the destructive power of the artillery and airpower.

Pistols

Handguns were carried by officers, vehicle crews, and specialists such as engineers and artillerymen. The most prevalent was the M-1911A1, caliber .45 semiautomatic pistol. Though varying wildly in accuracy, it was nonetheless a reliable, powerful weapon that provided tremendous stopping power at close range. First adopted in 1911, the M-1911A1 was finally retired from the U.S. Army inventory in 1994.

Large numbers of M-1917 Colt and Smith & Wesson revolvers, originally purchased during World War I to supplement the M-1911A1, were carried by non-infantry personnel. They fired the same ammunition as the M-1911A1, and used three-shot "half-moon" clips to hold the ammunition in place in the cylinders. These robust weapons were highly prized by their owners and envious comrades because they required less maintenance than the automatics and were generally more accurate.

Rifles

The ubiquitous "U.S. Rifle, M-1, caliber .30," was invented in 1937 by John Garand (q.v.) at the government-owned Springfield Armory in Massachusetts. It was a gas-operated, semiautomatic rifle, with an eight-shot internal magazine fed manually from a stripper clip. The M-1 used a very accurate rear peep and front leaf sighting system.

There were three main versions of the M-1 Garand. The standard infantry version could be fitted with a grenade-launching attachment to become a squad and platoon support weapon, firing colored smoke, antipersonnel, and antitank grenades. The sniper versions (M-1C and M-1D) were infrequently seen, but were built for increased long-range accuracy. A down-sized version called the "tanker Garand" was issued to some armor crews on an experimental basis, but was never used in large numbers. The Garand was the first fully semiautomatic rifle to appear in large numbers. About five million were produced by the end of 1945.

The M-1 carbine, introduced in 1942, was initially intended to arm non-infantry units. Firing a much shorter caliber .30 round than the M-1 Garand, the M-1 carbine was something of a tactical disappointment. An automatic version (M-2) was more popular and successful, and a night-fighting version (M-3) fitted with an infrared sniper scope, saw some limited service. About 6.2 million M-1 carbines were made by 1945.

During World War I the U.S. decided that the infantry squad needed a fully automatic weapon, but not a machine gun, to take advantage of the French "walking fire" tactic (which the U.S. never adopted). The M-1918 Browning Automatic Rifle (BAR), made to answer this need, fired the same .30 ammunition as the M-1 Garand. The BAR was used extensively in U.S. infantry and British Home Guard (q.v.) units, but it was not terribly popular in the field because early models were generally unmanageable and emptied magazines too fast. (Later versions had a selective fire mechanism.) Though completely outperformed by the German squad automatic weapons (the MG-34 and MG-42), and the British Bren, the BAR was an improvement over nothing at all.

Submachine Guns

Two submachine gun families were brought to Europe by U.S. troops. The M-1928A1 Thompson, had been in use with U.S. law enforcement and the marines since 1921. This weapon had a machined receiver, adjustable sights, a vertical foregrip under the barrel, and a Cutts recoil compensator at the muzzle. It used the Blish "freezing block" operating system, given to occasional failure of the system to unlock, and of questionable efficiency.

The M-1 submachine gun, based on the Thompson pattern, was designed to be manufactured out of cheaper (and faster to fabricate) stamped parts. It first appeared in 1942 and used a simple blowback system. It had a horizontal foregrip, simplified fixed sights, a detachable butt stock, and a plain muzzle. Both Thompson models (and several interim, hybrid models) appeared in Europe at different times. Both fired .45 ACP (Automatic Colt Pistol) ammunition from detachable stick or drum magazines.

The other U.S. submachine gun that appeared in Europe was the M-3, the so-called grease gun. It was an incredibly simple and quite unsafe weapon, firing .45 ACP ammunition at a low rate, intended to be carried by armored vehicle crews. The weapon was not very popular until the safer M-3A1 model was introduced.

Machine Guns

The M-1917 series water-cooled caliber .30 Browning machine gun was in service in U.S. units throughout the war. Its capacity for sustained fire was unequaled until the development of the mas-

Private Ignatz Sak (left) of Chicago and Private Carl Doskins (right) of West Virginia cleaning their water-cooled, caliber .30, M-1917 Browning machine gun. (IWM EA 25371)

sive M-2 HB. The M-1919 series caliber .30 machine guns, air-cooled outgrowths of the venerable M-1917, were the mainstay infantry machine guns throughout the war. The M-1919A4 was designed to be fired from a tripod or from a fixed mount, while the M-1919A6 version was designed to be man-carried and fired from a bipod.

The M-1921 series water-cooled caliber .50 Browning was originally intended for attacking aircraft and observation balloons. Its air-cooled descendent, the M-2 series, the "Ma Deuce," was used in every theater, in every environment, by every U.S. service. In the infantry it was vehicle or tripod mounted, feeding a linked belt of ammunition from either side of the receiver. In some cases it was used as a sniper weapon—it can be set up to fire single shots—even though international convention states that the caliber .50 round cannot be used against personnel. The M-2 HB (heavy barrel) was developed to increase the sustained rate of fire. It has a an easily detachable barrel. This weapon is still in service with U.S. forces up through the late 1990s.

Grenades

Hand grenade designs and tactics became formalized in World War I, and gave the infantryman distinct advantages, since the thrower did not give away his position, and could "fire" into areas he could not see directly. The hand grenade was the most powerful of the average U.S. infantryman's weapons. With a good arm he could throw a half-pound Mk-2 "pineapple" grenade about twenty-five meters. It killed in about a three-yard radius in an open area, and produced more casualties in a wider radius in enclosured areas. A number of other grenades with smoke, incendiary, and gas fillers were used, but the most common was the fragmentation. U.S. fragmentation grenades were developments of the British Mills bomb of 1915 vintage.

The M-7 series rifle grenade launcher at the end of the M-1 rifle fired what was really a gas-propelled grenade. Originally seen as a substitute for the light mortar, the rifle grenade was a finned projectile fired at high angles. The range of the antipersonnel/high explosive rifle grenade was about 200 meters, with a bursting radius of approximately five meters. Rifle grenades were available with the same fillers as hand grenades.

The antitank rifle grenade, fired at a shallower angle, had a range of about 120 meters, and could destroy trucks, light tanks or tracks, but could only penetrate about an inch of armor. Bigger rifle grenades were impractical because they could not be fired from a standard infantry rifle.

Mortars

The light infantry mortar, also called a "trench mortar," was a new development of World War I, having been first used in the trenches in 1915. During World War II, the U.S. had three mortars in infantry units—the 60mm, the 81mm, and the 4.2-inch. Mortars provided close support to the infantry when nothing else could.

The 60mm M-2 mortar was found at company level in small batteries of three tubes. It could throw a three-pound shell to a maximum range of about 1,800 meters. It fired high explosive (HE), illuminating, and both white phosphorous (WP) (incendiary)and normal smoke rounds. The heavy weapons company of the infantry battalion had three 81mm M-1 mortars, with a range of just over 2,900 and the same mix of ammunition. Both these weapons were man-portable.

Although originally issued to chemical units, the M-24 series 4.2-inch ("Four Deuce") mortar became common in infantry units. The 4.2-inch mortar could throw a foot-long twelve-pound high explosive round 5,400 meters, with a bursting radius of about twenty-five meters. They fired HE, WP, and normal smoke rounds. They usually were not carried by anything less than a mule or a wheeled vehicle, since the lightest of the main components weighed well over seventy pounds.

Antitank Weapons

Until the unprecedented successes of German armor in 1939–1941, artillery had been considered the primary antitank weapon. The French campaign of 1940 demonstrated the need for smaller, infantry-portable antitank weapons. Following on the development of the shaped-charge rifle grenade, the shoulder-fired rocket launcher program began in the U.S. in late 1941.

In July 1942, the M-1 antitank rocket launcher was in production. The 2.36-inch rocket used the shaped-charge Monroe effect that had been well understood since 1888. What is now known as the high explosive antitank (HEAT) warhead design is still the most effective for light-weight anti-armor weapons.

First used in Northwest Africa (q.v.) by troops almost completely untrained for it, the weapon we now call the "bazooka" (the Germans dubbed it the "Shoulder 75") had so many success stories attached to it that it is hard to separate legend from fact. It is true that they were powerful enough to blow off tank turrets at 75

meters, and impacts from near misses were once mistaken by a German tank commander (who had not seen the weapon before) for 105mm artillery splashes. The bazooka rocket was not quite powerful enough to penetrate heavy concrete, but its concussion close to bunker vision slits caused considerable casualties. The antipersonnel effect at short range was close to that of a 60mm mortar.

The bazooka was not without drawbacks, however. Its worst flaws were the relatively slow speed of the rocket and limited range. The later model, the M-9, incorporated a two-piece tube design for airborne troops. Though tactics were devised to compensate for its problems, the Bazooka was still less than perfect. More than 475,000 2.36-inch steel-tube bazookas were made before May 1945, when production was suspended to shift production to aluminum tubes.

Recoilless Rifles

Nearly parallel with rocket launcher development was the development of a truly recoilless gun such as German airborne units had been using since early in the war. The Frankford Arsenal began research in May 1943, and by 20 March 1945, the first two models were sent to U.S. airborne units in Europe. The smaller of the two, the 57mm model T-15E9, was able to easily destroy armored targets at ranges of 550 meters, and could reach nearly a 1,000 meters accurately. The larger 75mm model M-20 hit targets consistently and effectively out to 2,200 meters, thus rivaling some conventional tank guns. These weapons were so highly thought of by their crews that they seldom let them out of their sight. Even more spectacular stories were ascribed to the recoilless guns than were attached to the bazooka. Their main drawbacks were the large backblast area required behind the gun that could give away its position and made its use in confined areas somewhat problematic, and severe shortages of ammunition.

Edged Weapons

By World War II, bayonets were normally used as a knife or a cooking implement, and to instill troops with self-confidence in training environments. Rarely was the fixed bayonet used in combat. But every rifleman still carried a bayonet, and for the Americans it was usually a version of the twelve-inch M-1, descended from the eighteen-inch M-1905/M-1917 that had been carried in World War I. The M-1 carbine used the M-4 bayonet-knife, a slightly smaller (seven-inch blade) version of the M-1. A pushbutton switchblade knife (M-2) was briefly adopted for parachute troops, but this was dropped in 1943 in favor of the M-3 trench knife. The M-3 had a 6.7-inch blade, and it was dropped in late 1944 in favor of the M-4 bayonet-knife.

Personal Protection

Just as much as a rifle, the M-1 helmet, the "steel pot" was a part of an infantryman's arsenal. It replaced the "soup scuttle" M-1917 helmet in 1942 and underwent a number of modifications throughout the war. One major modification was the addition of a "blast ball" to the chin strap, so that the helmet would be blown off the head in the event of a near-miss explosion, thus leaving the head attached to the user. Another version (the M-1C, with additional webbing) was developed for use by paratroops. For the rest of the body, armor for the legs, chest, arms, and groin area was developed during the war (especially for vehicle drivers and engineers), but most of it went to the Pacific.

John D. Beatty

(Refer to table on page 1030)

Additional Reading

Ezell, Edward C., *Small Arms of the World* (1977).
Hogg, Ian V., and John Weeks, *Military Small Arms of the 20th Century* (1992).
Weeks, John, *Infantry Weapons* (1971).

Insignia, Military

Insignia usually indicate a soldier's job function, rank, unit, special skills, past achievements, or assignments. In this context, some would consider medals and decorations as a subset of insignia; these, however, are covered in their own entry (*see* Medals and Decorations). Virtually any button, piece of cloth, or metal trim has been used by one army or another as an insignia. During World War II, these devices were used to the maximum extent for their psychological impact.

Insignia of World War II were not only worn by military and naval personnel, but were also painted on vehicles, aircraft, and other military equipment to show affiliation. Insignia were also used as a general propaganda tool when worn by civilians or applied to things as diverse as letterheads and buildings. The Nazi eagle and *Swastika* are examples of widely used insignia that were applied not only to military uniforms in the traditional manner, but were also used as general insignia widely affixed to a vast number of articles.

Each country had a variety of such "national insignia," used in conjunction with uniforms and equipment. Some devices used by both sides were remarkably similar, while others were very different. Among the Allied forces, a few insignia such as selected shoulder insignia were used by more than one nation. The use of such preplanned identical insignia was rare, and usually each country designed its own insignia.

Unit insignia were widely used during World War II by U.S. and British Commonwealth armies. They ranged from army groups late in the war, down to typically battalion or regimental insignia. Most common were shoulder patches (also commonly called formation signs or flashes) usually worn on the upper sleeve just below the garment's shoulder seam. Normally these were assigned to division-sized or larger units, although special smaller units also had their own shoulder patches. In some cases, these insignia were also painted on vehicles, especially within the British Army.

The heart of the British Army was the regiment, and each regiment had its own special metal badge, which was worn on the jacket or coat lapel and on the headgear. Frequently, buttons also displayed unit insignia. British Commonwealth units also used shoulder titles to indicate regiments or corps. Previously they were made of metal, but during World War II, they appeared in cloth for the first time.

Within the U.S. Army, the main form of distinctive insignia for a regiment or battalion was a small coat of arms (commonly called a "crest"), first worn on each lapel of the dress coat, then later worn on the shoulder loops of the coat or shirt. Many newly formed units did not adopt distinctive insignia and their soldiers went through the war wearing only their divisional shoulder patch as a unique device.

During the war, insignia were created to indicate newly created ranks, such as flight officer and general of the army. The highest-ranking general officers of France (called marshals) began to carry batons during the eighteenth century to show their rank. This tradition continued, and was used by the Germans during World War II. All other ranks, i.e., enlisted persons, were indicated by cloth or metal insignia. British and U.S. Army officers usually wore rank on their shoulder, while other ranks wore them on the sleeve, usually midway between the elbow and shoulder.

French officers, as well as officers of the Royal Air Force and most of the world's navies, wore rank on the lower sleeve. In addition to these methods, officer rank was often displayed in several ways at the same time, as in the Italian Army, which used both shoulder boards and cuff marks.

The Germans, and starting in 1943 the Soviets, displayed all ranks on shoulder boards. These shoulder boards indicated not only the wearer's rank, but also his branch. German shoulder boards and other insignia were often bright gold or silver lace for dress or "walking out" uniforms, and made of duller materials for the field uniform.

For those soldiers whose job was not indicated by a colored shoulder board or collar tab, it was shown in a variety of other ways. The U.S. Army used branch insignia combined with regimental crests, while the British combined both pieces of information in the regimental badge. Most armies adopted some unique devices for certain special duties during the war. The most common were the various breast wings used by aircrews and a wide range of parachute insignia.

Badges indicated not only special skills, like aviation, but also experience in combat. Nazi Germany adopted an extensive range of such badges, including a badge to show combat wounds and combat badges for just about any conceivable situation from tank battles to motor patrol boats. The number of these badges grew during the war, as did their scope.

At first, these German badges were given for the initial participation in combat. Later, numbers appeared at the bottom of the badge to indicate the number of engagements in which the recipient had participated. Badges of this type became morale boosters for the soldiers, and something that identified a fellow soldier who had gone through the same terrible situation. Britain, unlike many other nations, did not adopt this type of insignia during World War II, while the U.S. Army adopted it only for infantry and medical combat.

Decorations can generally be divided into either awards for bravery and achievement, or for recognition of service. Many World War II awards were given to individuals, as in previous wars, but World War II saw both sides create many new awards, both for military members and for civilians. It is this latter category that was unique to World War II.

While some countries recognized selected units by giving them special designations, the recognition of units became common during World War II. The Soviets designated certain meritorious units with the title "guards," while the U.S. Army instituted "distinguished" and "meritorious" unit awards. In both cases, the countries provided the soldiers with insignia to indicate

they were members of these specially recognized units.

The Germans gave their elite units names, such as *Grossdeutschland*, and as the war wore on, many of these units were expanded in an attempt to spread the aura of their heroic accomplishments. Associated with the German forces are cuff titles, some of which recognized these honor units. Worn on the lower sleeve, German cuff titles can be divided into three categories: battle honors, elite units and training schools, and special formations.

Service medals and other service devices were created by all armies on both sides in a great array during World War II. Service on various fronts or in campaigns was recognized by medals, appurtenances, and other "veteran" devices. The U.S. Army also recognized war service overseas by allowing a small gold bar on the lower sleeve for each six months of overseas service, plus perpetual wear of the patch of a soldier's former combat unit on his right shoulder. Germany, besides issuing various campaign medals, issued eight metal shields, worn on the left upper sleeve, to commemorate selected campaigns.

Special skill or proficiency awards were greatly increased during World War II due to the large increase in technology. While marksmanship skills were recognized by most armies with various insignia, other awards came into being during the war. German and Soviet armies recognized physical fitness with badges, and the British had a special badge for physical fitness instructors. Other countries ignored this important training aspect completely.

The U.S. Army Air Force introduced a set of blue triangular cloth patches worn on the lower coat sleeve for their technical specialists. They also issued a metal proficiency badge with qualification bars for various pieces of equipment. By 1947, these air force insignia disappeared, having been brought in just for the war effort to improve morale.

Armbands or armlets were temporary devices that could easily be added to uniforms or even civilian clothes. The Nazis, as well as the Western powers, used armbands extensively, and in Germany, they served as political insignia as well as military. For partisans (q.v.), armbands were a way to quickly put on identification devices for recognition among themselves. In these cases, the armbands functioned like uniforms to bring the wearers under the protection of the laws of land warfare, although the 1929 Geneva Convention on the treatment of prisoners did not adequately cover partisans.

Regular military forces typically used armlets

to serve as supplemental insignia, so the assignment or other information carried by the armband could easily be seen from a distance. Armbands bearing the letters MP, which stands for military police, and white armbands with a large red cross worn by medical personnel, were the most common and easily recognized of these insignia.

Navy insignia, like those of the army and air force, increased greatly during World War II. The U.S. Navy brought in a few shoulder patches similar to army insignia. Rates, which showed a petty officer's rank and job specialty, became much more diversified with the growth in various military occupational specialties. Germany introduced metal pocket badges to indicate a wide range of naval combat actions.

As a result of the 1945 victory by the Allies, many of the postwar armed forces adopted U.S.-style insignia. Even the postwar West German Army initially adopted U.S.-type collar insignia, until they later reverted to their traditional branch-colored collar tabs. Military insignia served overall to reinforce individual morale and unit esprit, and at the same time, acted to identify job function, unit, and other information. From the standpoint of the historian, an ability to "read uniforms" can be an invaluable tool for interpreting photographs of the period.

William K. Emerson

Additional Reading

Emerson, William K., *Encyclopedia of United States Army Insignia and Uniforms* (1996).

Mollo, Andrew, *The Armed Forces of World War II: Uniforms, Insignia, and Organization* (1981).

Rosignoli, Guido, *Air Force Badges and Insignia of World War 2* (1976).

———, *Army Badges and Insignia of World War 2* (1972).

———, *Navy and Marine Badges and Insignia of World War 2* (1980).

I

Section IV-I
Technical Data Tables of
Weapons and Equipment

British Infantry Weapons

Individual

Model	Webley No. 1 Mk-VI	Enfield No. 2 Mk-I	No.1 SMLE Mk-III	No. 4 Mk-I	Sten
Type	Pistol	Pistol	Rifle	Rifle	Submachine Gun
Year in Service	1915	1932	1907	1931	1941
Caliber	0.455	0.38	0.303	0.303	9mm
Weight (pounds)	2.4	1.58	8.6	8.8	7.8
Rate of Fire (rounds per min)	24	24	15	15	500–600
Effective Range (meters)	50	30	500	500	150

Crew-served

Model	Bren	Vickers Mk-I	Lewis Mk-I	M.L. 2-in Mk-II	M.L. 3-in Mk-II	S.B. 4.2-in	PIAT	Mk-I	Mk-I
Type	Machine Gun	Machine Gun	Machine Gun	Mortar	Mortar	Mortar	Antitank Launcher	Recoilless Rifle	Recoilless Rifle
Year in Service	1938	1912	1916	1938	1932	1941	1942	1945	1945
Caliber	0.303	0.303	0.303	2-in	3-in	4.2-in	3.45-in	3.45-in	3.7-in
Weight (pounds)	22.3	40.0	27.0	10.5	126.0	1,210	32.0	75.0	375.0
Rate of Fire (rounds per min)	500	450–550	500	10	10	12	4	8	8
Effective Range (meters)	1,500	1,000	600	750	2,500	3,750	100	900	1,800
Crew Size	2	3	2	2	3	4	2	2	3

French Infantry Weapons

Individual

Model	Lebel M-1892	MAS M-1935A	Lebel M-1886	M-1907/34	MAS M-1936	RSC M-1917	MAS M-1938
Type	Pistol	Pistol	Rifle	Rifle	Rifle	Auto Rifle	Submachine Gun
Year in Service	1892	1936	1886	1934	1936	1917	1938
Caliber	8mm	7.65mm	8mm	7.5mm	7.5mm	8mm	7.65mm
Weight (pounds)	1.8	1.6	8.3	7.9	8.3	18	6.3
Rate of Fire (rounds per min)	24	30	8	10	10	500	700
Effective Range (meters)	35	40	400	450	500	600	150

Crew-served

Model	M-1924/29	Horchkiss M-1914	M-1930	M-1935	M-1927/31	SA-L M-1934	SA 37 APX
Type	Machine Gun	Machine Gun	Machine Gun	Mortar	Mortar	Antitank Rifle	Antitank Gun
Year in Service	1929	1914	1931	1937	1931	1934	1937
Caliber	7.5mm	8mm	13.2mm	60mm	81mm	25mm	47mm
Weight (pounds)	24.5	55.7	90	39.3	40.8	1,093	962
Rate of Fire (rounds per min)	550	450	600	25	20	6	12
Effective Range (meters)	600	1,100	1,800	1,700	2,850	1,500	3,000
Crew Size	2	3	3	3	3	3	4

German Infantry Weapons

IndMual

Model	P-08 *Luger*	P-38 *Walther*	C-96 *Mauser*	Gew-98	Kar-98k	FG-42	Gew-43	MP-40	StuG-44	*Panzer-faust*
Type	Pistol	Pistol	Pistol	Rifle	Carbine	Rifle	Rifle	Submachine Gun	Assault Rifle	Rocket Launcher
Year in Service	1908	1938	1932	1898	1935	1942	1943	1940	1944	1942
Caliber	9mm	9mm	7.63mm	7.92mm	7.92mm	7.92mm	7.92mm	9mm	7.92mm	150mm
Weight (pounds)	1.9	2.1	2.93	8.8	8.6	9.9	9.5	8.9	11.5	11
Rate of Fire (rounds per min)	32	32	24	15	20	600	30	500/120	500	Single Shot
Effective Range (meters)	50	50	50	500	450	500	450	150	350	80

Crew-served

Model	MG-34	MG-42	MG-151/20	GrW-36	GrW-34	GrW-42	RPzB-54 *Panzerschreck*	LG-40	LG-42	LG-240
Type	Machine Gun	Machine Gun	Machine Gun	Mortar	Mortar	Mortar	Rocket Launcher	Recoilless Rifle	Recoilless Rifle	Recoilless Rifle
Year in Service	1934	1942	1934	1936	1934	1942	1943	1940	1942	1943
Caliber	7.92mm	7.92mm	20mm	50mm	81mm	120mm	88mm	75mm	105mm	150mm
Weight (pounds)	26.5	25.5	93.5	31	124	616	20.5	321	1,217	1,875
Rate of Fire (rounds per min)	900	1,200	800	20	12	8	8	8	6	4
Effective Range (meters)	1,200	1,250	3,000	500	2,300	5,900	120	7,400	8,700	5,750
Crew Size	2	2	3	2	3	6	2	3	4	4

Italian Infantry Weapons

Individual

Model	M-1934	M-1891	M-1938	M-1938
Type	Pistol	Rifle	Rifle	Submachine Gun
Year in Service	1934	1891	1938	1938
Caliber	9mm	6.5mm	7.35mm	9mm
Weight (pounds)	1.3	8.6	7.5	9.25
Rate of Fire (rounds per min)	28	10	10	600
Effective Range (meters)	40	350	500	160

Crew-served

Model	M-1930	M-1938	M-1914	M-1935	M-1931	M-1935	M-1935
Type	Machine Gun	Machine Gun	Machine Gun	Machine Gun	Machine Gun	Mortar	Mortar
Year in Service	1930	1938	1914	1935	1931	1938	1935
Caliber	6.5mm	7.35mm	6.5mm	8mm	13.2mm	45mm	81mm
Weight (pounds)	22.8	27.8	49.5	41.5	90	34.2	130
Rate of Fire (rounds per min)	450	450	500	500	500	25	20
Effective Range (meters)	600	800	500	800	1,600	550	4,050
Crew Size	2	2	3	3	3	2	4

Soviet Infantry Weapons

Individual

Model	M-1895	TT-33	M-1891/30G	M-1944	SVT-38	SVT-40	PPSh-41	PPS-43	RPG-43
Type	Pistol	Pistol	Rifle	Carbine	Rifle	Rifle	Submachine Gun	Submachine Gun	Rocket Launcher
Year in Service	1895	1933	1930	1944	1938	1940	1941	1943	1943
Caliber	7.62mm	7.62mm	7.62mm	7.62mm	7.62mm	7.62mm	7.62mm	7.62mm	200mm
Weight (pounds)	1.7	1.9	8.7	8.9	8.7	8.6	9.3	8	3
Rate of Fire (rounds per min)	24	32	10	10	25	25	900	650	2
Effective Range (meters)	50	50	500	360	500	500	100	100	400

Crew-served

Model	DP	SPM-1910	SG-43	DShK-38	PM-41	PM-41/43	HM-38	M-1943	PTRS-41	PTRD-41
Type	Machine Gun	Machine Gun	Machine Gun	Machine Gun	Mortar	Mortar	Mortar	Mortar	Antitank Rifle	Antitank Rifle
Year in Service	1928	1910	1943	1938	1941	1941	1938	1943	1941	1941
Caliber	7.62mm	7.62mm	7.62mm	12.7mm	50mm	82mm	120mm	160mm	14.5mm	14.5mm
Weight (pounds)	28.5	52.5	29.8	80	20	99.2	1,110	2,840	46	38
Rate of Fire (rounds per min)	550	550	600-700	500	25	25	12	3	10	5
Effective Range (meters)	600	1,200	1,000	1,500	800	3,050	5,850	5,150	1,000	500
Crew Size	2	2	2	3	3	5	6	7	2	2

U.S. Infantry Weapons

Individual

Model	M-1911A1	M-1917	M-1 Garand	M-1 Carbine	M-2	M-1918A2 BAR	M-1 Thompson	M-3
Type	Pistol	Pistol	Rifle	Carbine	Carbine	Auto Rifle	Submachine Gun	Submachine Gun
Year in Service	1911	1917	1936	1942	1943	1939	1942	1942
Caliber	0.45	0.45	0.30	0.30	0.30	0.30	0.45	0.45
Weight (pounds)	2.4	2.3	9.5	5.5	5.5	19.4	10.5	8.2
Rate of Fire (rounds per min)	35	24	30–50	40–70	750	550	700	400
Effective Range (meters)	50	50	460	300	300	600	170	150

Crew-served

Model	M-1919	M-2	M-2	M-1	M-24	M-1 Bazooka	M-9 Bazooka	T-15E9	M-20
Type	Machine Gun	Machine Gun	Mortar	Mortar	Mortar	Rocket Launcher	Rocket Launcher	Recoilless Rifle	Recoilless Rifle
Year in Service	1919	1933	1938	1938	1940	1942	1943	1945	1945
Caliber	0.30	0.50	60mm	81mm	4.2-in	2.36-in	2.36-in	57mm	75mm
Weight (pounds)	33	84	42	136	650	14	16	49	165
Rate of Fire (rounds per min)	400–500	450–550	18	18	20	10	10	8	6
Effective Range (meters)	1,100	2,000	1,800	2,900	5,400	300	300	1,000	2,200
Crew Size	3	3	3	3	7	2	2	2	4

J

Jeep

The jeep was a U.S.-manufactured, four-wheel-drive, light utility vehicle that became almost universally known during World War II. Motorized movement finally became recognized by almost all military theorists during the 1930s as the way of the future. Consequently, the U.S. War Department started considering the purchase and use of a light reconnaissance car. Among the requirements was the capability to negotiate such varied terrain as hills, deserts, and swamps.

The Bantam Car Corporation developed a four-wheel-drive vehicle that was tested and approved by the Ordnance Department. In 1940, procurement was initiated, but the ability of Bantam to meet their forecasted output was questioned. At that point, the Ford Motor Company and the Willys-Overland Company were allowed to submit vehicles for testing and the Willys version was standardized as the new army vehicle. As it turned out, only Willys and Ford ended up producing the vehicle.

The name is a shortened version of the general purpose (GP) label. Originally, the half-ton version was called the jeep and the quarter-ton version was the peep, but even after the larger truck was discontinued, its name stuck. Almost one million jeeps were produced between 1940 and 1945. The jeep was used for command and control, reconnaissance, carrying litters, mounting (or towing) weapons, carrying (or towing) equipment, and moving personnel. Its uses were only limited by imagination. The venerable jeep, although it underwent several revisions, stayed in active U.S. Army service until the mid-1980s.

Steven D. Cage

Additional Reading
Thomson, Harry, and Linda Mayo, *The Ordnance Department: Procurement and Supply* (1960).

Jet Aircraft

Jet aircraft form the biggest "might-have-been" of World War II. If the Germans had employed this technological breakthrough as fighters, they might have been able to thwart the Allied bomber offensive and give their industry and infrastructure a much needed break. While Great Britain and the United States were vigorously pursuing jet combat planes, the Germans had a superior technical lead. Fortunately for the Anglo-Americans, German bureaucratic ineptitude squandered this advantage (*see* Fighter Aircraft, German).

By the mid-1930s, many in the international aviation community realized that piston-driven propeller aircraft would soon reach a performance plateau. Pure physics provided a solid barrier: the phenomenon of compressibility. When a moving body approaches the speed of sound, shock waves build up around the body and degrade performance. Compressibility problems first surfaced with propellers. Propeller tips of late 1930s high-performance engines often approached near-sonic speeds, causing shock waves to form and producing performance-inhibiting drag. Other parts of aircraft, such as engine cowling, canopies, and fuselages, were also affected by compressibility.

Moreover, piston engines had other drawbacks for increased aircraft performance. They were noisy with power-to-weight ratios that were too low for high subsonic and supersonic speeds. They increased in mechanical complexity, weight, size, maintenance requirements, fuel consumption, and cost. In other words, piston-powered aircraft were reaching their ultimate limits for military applications.

During the late 1930s, theorists, designers, and engineers in several countries looked for alternate solutions for high-speed flight. Several bright minds pursued turbojet technology, which offered several theoretical advantages. Careful design of this power plant can avoid compressibility problems. Equally important, the turbojet is smaller than its piston-engine counterpart but is much more powerful. Finally, it has fewer moving parts and lower maintenance requirements. While turbojets offered the means to reach better performance, aircraft designers of the period did not understand all the effects of compressibility, and thus were unable to produce machines that took full advantage of this new power plant.

Germany was the most successful combatant to capitalize on the turbojet concept. A brilliant young engineer, Hans von Ohain, began work on turbojets in the mid-1930s. In April 1936, iconoclastic aircraft manufacturer Ernst Heinkel gave von Ohain's research generous financial support. By 1938, von Ohain's progress spurred the German Air Ministry to press other engine makers to develop their own turbojets. Heinkel gained fame for the first turbojet flight in the experimental He-178 on 27 August 1939. Unfortunately, he never realized his goals of adding engines to his airframe business or of fielding operational jet aircraft.

The Aviation Ministry decided to back Messerschmitt's effort, the Me-262. Powered by two Junker Jumo 004 turbojets, the *Schwalbe* (Swallow) sported swept-back wings, which improved its performance over straight-wing designs. Its top speed was 540 mph and it mounted a devastating quartet of four 30mm MK-108 cannons. By the spring of 1943, many in the *Luftwaffe* were convinced that the Me-262 would give them the technological edge in the skies.

At that point, Adolf Hitler (q.v.) intervened. Technical and industrial problems delayed initial production to the fall of 1943. In November 1943, he decreed that the Me-262 be used as a fast bomber to blunt the anticipated Allied invasion of France. *Luftwaffe* commanders, notably fighter chief Major General Adolf Galland (q.v.), tried to circumvent the directive. On learning of this in May 1944, Hitler insisted that future turbojet development be devoted to bombers.

With the June 1944 invasion of Normandy (q.v.), few Me-262 bombers were ready. Some sorties were flown against Allied forces in France in July and August of 1944, but they were too few and too late. Ironically, Hitler became impressed with several Me-262 fighter successes, and allowed renewed activity along this line, but too much time was lost pursuing the bomber variant. Moreover, tactics developed for the *Schwalbe* may not have been the best. They were deployed to a string of bases in the Low Countries and northern France to defeat Allied fighter escorts, leaving the bombers prey to German conventional fighters.

When the Me-262 bases were overrun in late 1944 and early 1945, this strategy could not be sustained. Despite their technical lead and the production of 1,433 planes, the Germans had little to show. The *Luftwaffe* was able to field a straight-wing jet bomber, the Arado 234 *Blitz*, which was powered by two BMW 003 jets for a top speed of 460 mph. The *Blitz* was flown by a small number of bomber and reconnaissance units. Its most prominent use was for near-suicidal

A captured German Me-262A jet fighter, with British markings. (IWM MH 4909)

attacks on the captured Ludendorff Bridge on the Rhine at Remagen (q.v.).

The only other German jet produced in some numbers but never used operationally was the interesting Heinkel 162 Salamander. Winner of the *Volksjäger* (People's Fighter) competition, the He-162 was constructed from nonstrategic materials and designed to be flown by novice fliers, namely Hitler Youth (q.v.). A small, lightweight throwaway fighter in every sense, the He-162 was to have been constructed in the thousands and would counter Allied numerical superiority. Designed and flown in three months (September–December 1944), the BMW 003-powered Salamander proved difficult to fly even for experienced pilots. The He-162 was never flown operationally, despite the fact that close to 1,000 were in various stages of completion at war's end.

Allied material superiority and German logistical inferiority ultimately counted more than technical supremacy. Opposing fliers found that the jets were sluggish at low altitudes and slow speeds. Jet bases became magnets for Allied fighters that would pounce on vulnerable Me-262s and AR-234s that were taking off or landing. While Albert Speer's (q.v.) manufacturing apparatus produced wonders in building jet aircraft, lack of fuel grounded most of them. Moreover, German designers had a perverse tendency to put inordinate effort into pursuing variant models of a design rather than concentrating on a single one.

Finally, it must be pointed out that wartime demands forced the Germans to employ their jets before the turbojets were technically and operationally developed. In the final analysis, the *Luftwaffe's* technical brilliance could not compete against the numerical advantages of its foes and Germany's inferior strategic position in a two-front war.

Great Britain was the leading Allied power in turbojet development. In 1936, Royal Air Force officer Frank Whittle was placed on special detachment to the newly established Power Jets Company to perfect a workable turbojet. His labors were rewarded in May 1941 with the first flight of the experimental Gloster E.28/39. A fighter jet, the Gloster Meteor Mk-I, was designed around a pair of Whittle/Rolls Royce W.2B Welland turbojets and mounted four 20mm Hispano cannons to perform high altitude interceptions.

The first flight of the Gloster Meteor was 5 March 1943, and it became operational in July of that year with Number 616 Squadron. It was used for interceptions against V-1s, with Flying Officer T.D. Dean scoring its first victory on 4 August 1944 by tipping over the flying bomb with his wing tip. The straight-wing Gloster Meteor was not a successful counter to its German rival, being 130 mph slower (top speed 410 mph). The Gloster Meteor subsequently was used for ground strafing.

The United States started behind in the turbojet field. In the late 1930s, a navy investigation in this area was aborted on the advice of a high-level advisory committee that the project would not be worth the trouble. In 1941, the British conveniently supplied Whittle W.2B engines to the General Electric Company for development for the Army Air Forces. Derivatives of these engines were used in the straight-wing Bell P-59A Aircomet (first flight 1 October 1942), which had a disappointing top speed of 413 mph and was relegated to training duties.

Frantic development produced success on 8 January 1944, with the first flight of the Lockheed P-80. Designed by Clarence "Kelly" Johnson's "Skunk Works," and powered by a single Allison J33 turbojet, the Shooting Star had a top speed of 558 mph. Teething troubles, especially those involving engines and parts, prevented the P-80 from seeing combat during the war. Four prototypes were sent to the European Theater of Operations for tactical duty under the so-called EXTRAVERSION project that ended in May 1945.

The other warring powers made little progress on turbojet development during the war. Germany, the country with the biggest technical lead, faltered in the political and bureaucratic translation of technology into power. The numerical superiority of the Allied air forces negated much of the Me-262's advantages and enabled them to capitalize on the turbojet's weaknesses: sluggish performance at low speeds and limited endurance.

Michael E. Unsworth

(Refer to table on page 1037)

Additional Reading

Boyne, Walter, and Donald S. Lopez, *The Jet Age: Forty Years of Jet Aviation* (1979).
Masters, David, *German Jet Genesis* (1982).
Wooldridge, E.T., Jr., *The P-80 Shooting Star: Evolution of a Jet Fighter* (1979).

Section IV-J
Technical Data Table of
Weapons and Equipment

Jet Aircraft (All Countries)

Model	Me-262	He-162A	AR-234B	AR-234C	Meteor
Country	Germany	Germany	Germany	Germany	Britain
Service Date	1944	1945	1944	1945	1944
Type	Fighter*	Fighter	Bomber	Bomber	Fighter
Engines	2	1	2	4	2
Crew	1	1	1	1	1
Maximum Speed (mph)	540	522	460	542	410
Maximum Range (miles)	525	410	1,013	920	1,340
Gun Armament	4x 30mm	2x 30mm	None	2x 20mm	4x 20mm
Bombs or Rockets	500 lbs†		3,300 lbs	3,300 lbs	
Number in Service	1,433*	116	274	14	280
Ceiling (feet)	37,560	39,500	32,810	39,370	44,000

*Approximately 400 of the fighter-bomber variant were built.
†The fighter-bomber variant carried 2,200 pounds of bombs or 24 rockets.

L

Landing Craft

Amphibious warfare is as old as man's use of the sea. The history of Greek and Roman warfare contains various accounts of amphibious warfare. The Viking raids were amphibious attacks. Amphibious raids were carried out in the Napoleonic wars. In World War I, the Germans took the Russian Baltic islands, the Russians assaulted the Turkish Black Sea coast, and the British tried to take Gallipoli with amphibious assaults. In these landings, troops were transported to the objective area in either modified or unmodified merchant ships or warships. Specialized ships or boats for amphibious landings were the exception and, when used, were usually converted obsolete warships or merchant ships.

During World War II, both the Allies and the Axis carried out amphibious assaults and landings. The Italians took Ethiopia and Albania (qq.v.) with amphibious landings. Denmark and Norway (qq.v.) were captured by German amphibious operations. The taking of the Greek islands was by amphibious attack. No special landing craft were used in these early operations. Although the German *Wasser-Pionieren* (Water Engineers) studied and developed small-scale landing craft before the war, Germany's senior leadership did not see the need for specialized landing craft for assaulting and holding a beachhead until they began to plan Operation SEA LION (q.v.), the aborted invasion of Great Britain.

While warships or merchant ships carrying troops could be used against undefended ports and beaches, such targets were extremely rare by the summer of 1940. Putting troops ashore on a hostile beach required craft capable of operating in unsheltered waters, carrying significant loads of troops and supplies, and off-loading over an unprepared beach. They also had to be easy to operate and inexpensive to build, as losses would be high.

The problem of landing troops on a hostile shore was investigated by Great Britain and the United States between the wars. The U.S. Marine Corps (USMC) gave considerable study to the problem. In 1935, it issued its *Tentative Landing Operation Manual,* and conducted Fleet Landing Exercise Number 1 at Culebra, Puerto Rico. The USMC conducted fleet landing exercises every year thereafter until 1940.

With the exception of Japan, no nation produced a specialized landing craft during this period. Specialized landing craft only became a military priority when Germany wanted to invade Britain and Prime Minister Winston S. Churchill (q.v.) wanted to strike blows against the German forces on the European coast. In the United States, fear that European possessions in the Caribbean and South America would be turned over to the Germans by the nations they had conquered led the United States to plan to capture these territories by amphibious assault. The need for specialized landing craft arose during that planning.

Landing craft can be divided into various classes: assault or supply, screw- or track-driven, personnel- or vehicle-carrying, armored or unarmored, seagoing or sheltered water operations, bow ramp or fixed bow, and capable of operating on both land and in water (amphibious) or restricted to water-borne operations. The most common features of a landing craft are a blunt bow, diesel engines, twin screws, stern anchors, shallow draft forward, flat bottom, and a bow ramp. The bow ramp allows loading and unloading without the necessity of cranes to hoist materiel on or off. Only the United States built large numbers of amphibious wheeled and tracked vehicles capable of carrying their loads from offshore, over the beach, and then inland.

British soldiers in Tripoli board a troop ship from an LCM in preparation for the landings at Salerno, 5 September 1943. (IWM NA 6675)

Landing craft give the attacker certain advantages. They allow him to consider a wider area over which to make the landing, thereby forcing the defender to spread his forces to cover all potential landing sites. That means the attacker can concentrate his forces while the defender's are dispersed. With properly designed landing craft, the landing force need not consist of only light infantry. Heavy equipment, including tanks and artillery, can be brought ashore during the assault. Landing craft also mean that a harbor is not an immediate necessity, since considerable follow-up supplies can be brought to the beachhead, allowing the assault force to hold and consolidate its position.

The Germans built more than 1,000 landing craft during the war. These vessels ranged in size from 150 tons to 280 tons in displacement. They were used mainly for supply operations in the Adriatic, Aegean, Black, Baltic, and Mediterranean seas, and for evacuation of German forces as they retreated from the Soviet advance.

The main builders of landing craft during the war were the Americans and British. From May 1942 to April 1943, the U.S. alone produced 8,719 landing craft totaling 512,000 tons. In 1943, U.S. long-term war production goals called for the building of more than 100,000 landing craft of all types by 1946. Allied landing craft ranged in displacement from four tons to 8,000 tons. Often, the larger landing ships carried smaller landing craft on their decks. Unlike other warships, landing craft seldom carried names. Almost all were designated by a series of letters followed by numbers, usually starting with LS or LC. The most common designations were

LSD	Landing Ship, Dock
LSV	Landing Ship, Vehicle
LST	Landing Ship, Tank
LSM	Landing Ship, Medium
LCI(L)	Landing Craft, Infantry (Large)
LCS(L)	Landing Craft, Support (Large)
LCT	Landing Craft, Tank
LCM	Landing Craft, Mechanized
LCVP	Landing Craft, Vehicle or Personnel

Manning these craft was a major problem. Crews not only had to be trained how to navigate landing craft, but also how to run them ashore and then back them off into deep water. The crews of the landing craft were sometimes looked down upon by the warship sailors as not being real fighting men. In reality, landing craft crews often suffered heavier combat losses than warship crews. It was the landing craft sailor who brought the Allied invading armies to the shores of Northwest Africa, Italy, Sicily, and France (qq.v.).

Throughout the war, construction of landing craft vastly complicated the allocation of shipbuilding resources. Given a lower priority at the start of the war, landing craft within one year became one of the highest priority weapon systems. General George C. Marshall (q.v.) stated in 1943: "Prior to the present war I never heard of landing craft except as a rubber boat. Now I think of little else." British Prime Minister Winston S. Churchill wrote in 1944:

> The whole of this difficult question, how to divide military resources between the Normandy invasion and the invasion of southern France, only arises out of the absurd shortage of the LSTs. How is it that the plans of two great empires like Britain and the United States should be so hamstrung and limited by a hundred or so of these vessels will never be understood by history.

Landing craft were viewed by war planners as expendable and assumed to be good for use in only one landing. It was expected that landing craft would be lost during the assault to enemy fire or natural hazards, or be so damaged in running ashore as to be unrepairable. Amazingly, many were able to participate in multiple assault landings and make numerous supply runs from ships offshore to the beachhead.

Confounding the estimates of the naval experts, some of these little vessels served for many years after the war in the various colonial wars and police actions of the Cold War. Other landing craft were converted to merchant shipping use. World War II landing craft also served as the design basis for the modern Roll-on/Roll-off (RoRo) merchant ship and the seagoing auto ferry.

Charles H. Bogart

(Refer to tables on pages 1045–1046)

Additional Reading

U.S. Naval Institute Press, *Allied Landing Craft of World War II* (1985).

Bartlett, Merrill L. (ed.), *Assault from the Sea* (1983).

Coakley, Robert W., and Richard M. Leighton, *Global Logistics and Strategy* (1968).

L

Liberty Ships

Originally designed to meet wartime supply requirements and expedite victory, 2,695 Liberty ships, known as the "workhorses of World War II," reliably delivered myriad cargoes to all major theaters of the war. The first of these gray cargo ships were launched at fourteen different shipyards on Liberty Fleet Day, 27 September 1941. Built to facilitate rapid construction, these stable, efficient cargo ships ensured the Allied victory in World War II.

Designated by the Maritime Commission as ECL (representing emergency, cargo, and large capacity), Liberty ships were derived from blueprints for the reliable British tramp ships. They were similar in design, with tonnage varying slightly with each ship. This standardization was implemented to enable quick production.

Liberty ships were produced by eighty companies located in coastal states. Workers fitted together prefabricated parts, quickly assembling a ship in the short span of several weeks. The employees, including women, attended training schools to receive instruction for construction.

These simple cargo ships were manned by American merchant mariners. Their basic duty was to transport supplies and replace ships destroyed by German submarines. Each ship could carry approximately 10,000 tons of cargo. The freight varied, depending on war theater and mission. They transported troops, carried food, stored ammunition, housed mules, hauled tanks, and ferried jeeps. For efficiency, most Liberty ships returned with raw materials after delivering their finished goods. They were easily converted for both the navy and the army for use in a wide range of roles. They were used to shelter wounded in floating hospitals, to move prisoners of war, to shuttle fuel to ships and airplanes, and to deliver relief cargo.

Liberty ships faced their greatest risks in the Battle of the Atlantic (q.v.) in the Murmansk run, the sea route used to supply the Soviets. The Germans attacked twenty-four hours a day when the ships were at sea, even risking daylight air raids against the Soviet ports while the crews unloaded the ships. In supplying the Soviet Union, ninety-seven Liberty ships were lost. They also hazarded the other Atlantic sea lanes, and more than 1,000 were present at the Normandy (q.v.) invasion, where they provided shelter, protected unloading transactions, and supplied the soldiers after they reached shore.

Overseen by the War Shipping Administration, each Liberty ship crew consisted of approximately fifty merchant mariners, one-fourth being officers. Each crew member had a specialization, such as operating the radio or serving as an engineer. Crew members included veterans, Allied foreigners, and new recruits. During the war, the age limit of Liberty ship recruits was reduced to sixteen years old in order to staff all the ships produced.

Most Liberty ships were named in honor of American heroes, leaders, veterans, war correspondents, and authors. A few ships were dedicated in honor of merchant marine heroes in order to enhance crew morale. Usually, a member of the na-

val auxiliary WAVES (q.v.) christened each new Liberty ship.

As the war waned, Liberty ships were overhauled for other uses. They were dismantled for scrap, refitted for transport of postwar supplies, or sunk—filled with surplus chemicals and ammunition—to eliminate undesirable war residue. They enabled postwar American industry and commerce to rebuild by providing abundant, cheap, reliable transport. They were sold at reduced rates to other nations for industrial transport, as well as dispersed to Allies though the Lend-Lease program (q.v.). As part of the reserve fleet, they transported supplies from American to Asian ports in the Korean and Vietnam Wars. The last Liberty ship officially retired from service in 1972.

Elizabeth D. Schafer

Additional Reading

Bunker, John Gorley, *Liberty Ships: The Ugly Ducklings of World War II* (1972).
Chell, Randolph A., *Troopship* (1948).

Section IV-L
Technical Data Tables of Weapons and Equipment

Allied Landing Craft (British and American)

Type	LSD	LSV	LST	LSM	LCI(L)	LCS(L)	LCT	LCM	LCVP
Year First Built	1943	1944	1942	1944	1942	1944	1942	1941	1941
Number Built	27	6	1,040	539	920	130	1,465	11,350	23,358
Displacement (tons)	4,500	5,875	1,653	490	246	380	320	60	11
Max. Speed (kts)	15	18.5	10	10	15	15	10	10	10
Dimensions (feet)	458 x 72	453 x 60	327 x 50	204 x 34	157 x 23	157 x 23	120 x 32	56 x 14	36 x 11

German Landing Craft

Type	SF	MFP 1-626	MFP 627-2000	MNL
Year First Built	1940	1942	1942	1942
Number Built	50 +	200 +	150 +	100 +
Displacement (tons)	143	200	280	154
Max. Speed (kts)	7.5	10	8	10
Dimensions (feet)	106 x 48	163 x 22	163 x 22	131 x 27

M

Medals and Decorations

Military medals generally fall into four broad categories. Decorations are individual awards given to specific people for heroism, outstanding achievement, or for meritorious service over a period of time. Campaign and service medals denote participation in a campaign or other specified service. Good conduct medals are based on the length and quality of an individual's service. Finally, qualification medals denote skill or achievement in a specific field (i.e., marksmanship). Decorations carry the greatest prestige because they represent achievement above and beyond what is ordinarily expected.

Military decorations (especially those open to all ranks) did not gain widespread popularity until the nineteenth century. Before then, they were generally few in number and limited to senior officers. The trend toward recognizing enlisted ranks began in 1802 when Napoleon Bonaparte created the Legion of Honor to reward distinguished service in both military and civil life. Although the Legion of Honor could be granted to all members of the military, it was given to privates and noncommissioned officers only under exceptional circumstances. To recognize noncommissioned officers, corporals, privates, or marines in time of war, France created the *Médaille Militaire* in 1852.

Following Napoleon's lead, King Friedrich-Wilhelm III of Prussia created the Iron Cross in 1813 and made it available to all ranks. From its inception, the Iron Cross was intended as a temporary award, to be given only during time of war, when it would replace various other state decorations. The value of a senior combat decoration open to all ranks was also recognized by the British, who were frequently involved in military hostilities during the nineteenth century as they tried to maintain order in their far-flung empire. In the

last year of the Crimean War (1853–1856), Queen Victoria established the Victoria Cross as the highest honor for combat heroism that could be conferred by the sovereign on any member of the armed forces. In 1940, King George VI (q.v.) established the George Cross as Britain's highest decoration for non-combat heroism. Both civilians and military personnel were eligible for the George Cross.

In 1861, during the American Civil War, the United States established its Medal of Honor. Originally, the army version was open to all ranks, while the Navy version was available only to enlisted men. Just before World War I, naval officers finally became eligible for the decoration. Up until the beginning of World War II, the Army Medal of Honor could only be awarded for combat heroism, while the Navy Medal of Honor could be awarded for both combat and non-combat actions. At the beginning of America's involvement in the war, the criteria were standardized, with the Medal of Honor becoming a combat decoration only.

Because of widespread racial discrimination in American society of the time, no black soldiers received the Medal of Honor during the war. Almost fifty years later, the U.S. government attempted to redress that injustice by having a panel of military historians review and analyze the wartime awards records. As a result, eight American black soldiers received the Medal of Honor in January 1997. Only one of the eight was still living at the time.

In the years leading up through the end of World War I, the U.S. and other major nations of the world established other decorations of lesser precedence, and eventually a hierarchy of decorations emerged in each nation.

The practice of awarding campaign medals probably began with the British when Elizabeth I

Great Britain	Victoria Cross	182
	Victoria Cross and Bar	1
	George Cross	158
	Distinguished Service Order	5,444
Germany	Knight's Cross of the Iron Cross	
	Grand Cross	1
	Gold Oak Leaves	1
	Diamonds	27
	Swords	159
	Oak Leaves	890
Poland	*Virtuti Militari*	
	Grand Cross	13
	Commander	24
	Cavalier	74
	Gold Cross	442
	Silver Cross	10,658
Soviet Union	Hero of the Soviet Union	11,066
	2nd Award	104
	3rd Award	3
United States	Medal of Honor	440
	Distinguished Service Cross	5,057
	Navy Cross	3,958
France	Legion of Honor	21,000
	Medaille Militarie	222,000

By the time World War II began, most of the belligerent nations already had well-established systems of decorations and medals. In most cases, they used existing decorations (sometimes with modifications), although a number of new ones were created. Campaign medals were established to denote participation in major campaigns or battles, and these were the primary medals of World War II. In the sections that follow, the primary medals of each major belligerent are discussed, but for the most part, the emphasis is on their campaign medals.

United States

The American campaign and service medals for World War II were recognized by geographic participation and the specific component in which the recipient served. Armed forces campaign medals were similar for each branch, but the merchant marine had its own distinctive medals. U.S. military medals included:

American Defense Service Medal: Established on 28 June 1941 for service in the armed forces between 8 September 1939 and 7 December 1941.

American Campaign Medal: Established on 6 November 1942 for thirty days of service outside the continental United States but within the American theater of operations between 7 December 1941 and 2 March 1946, or an aggregate of one year of service within the continental United States during the same period.

Asiatic-Pacific Campaign Medal: Established on 6 November 1942 for thirty days of service within the Asiatic-Pacific theater between 7 December 1942 and 2 March 1946.

European-African-Middle Eastern Campaign Medal: Established on 6 November 1942 for thirty days of service within the European-African-Middle Eastern theater of operations between 7 December 1941 and 2 March 1946.

Women's Army Corps Medal: Established on 29 July 1943 for service in the Women's Army Auxiliary Corps (WAAC) (q.v.) between 10 July 1942 and 31 August 1943, or for service in the Women's Army Corps between 1 September 1943 and 2 September 1945.

World War II Victory Medal: Established on 6 July 1945 to commemorate service during World War II. It was awarded to all members of the armed forces of the United States or the Philippines who served on active duty at any time between 7 December 1941 and 31 December 1946.

Army of Occupation Medal: Established in 1946 for military service in one of the occupied territories (Germany, Austria, Berlin, Italy, Japan,

authorized a medal for the defeat of the Spanish Armada. The first actual campaign medal was probably the Dunbar Medal, which commemorated Cromwell's success at Dunbar on 3 September 1650. This was the first medal that could be given to both officers and men (although not all participants received it). The first campaign medal awarded to all participants was the Waterloo Medal. It is also the first campaign medal awarded to the next of kin of those killed in battle.

The first "modern" British campaign medal was the Military General Service Medal (1793–1814), which was authorized in 1847, struck in 1848, and awarded to all soldiers who participated in the Peninsular campaign. This medal employed twenty-nine bars that denoted specific campaigns (not all of which were part of the Peninsular campaign). From that point forward, Britain has awarded campaign medals to all participants in major military or naval actions. British campaign medals were widely noted in Europe and encouraged a similar practice in other nations so that by World War I, campaign and service medals were employed extensively by all participating nations.

or Korea) after World War II. This medal was awarded to U.S. forces serving in Berlin through 1990.

Naval Occupation Service Medal: Established on 22 January 1947 for military service in one of the occupied territories or afloat in their home waters after World War II.

United Kingdom

Great Britain's participation in World War II was global in nature, and this is reflected in its campaign medals:

Defence Medal (3 September 1939–2 September 1945): Awarded to a wide range of individuals in both military and civil defense organizations, but primarily for those serving in nonoperational areas.

War Medal (3 September 1939–2 September 1945): Awarded to all full-time personnel of the armed forces who served at least twenty-eight days.

1939–1945 Star (3 September 1939–2 September 1945): Awarded to members of the armed forces, generally for six months of service in operational areas.

Atlantic Star (3 September 1939–8 May 1945): Awarded to those who participated in the Battle of the Atlantic. This is primarily a naval campaign medal, although members of the other services could receive it if they met its requirements, which consisted of six months of service afloat in the Atlantic.

Air Crew Europe Star (3 September 1939–5 June 1944): Awarded for four months of service as a member of an aircrew in an operational unit, any two months of which qualified for the Air Crew Europe Star.

Africa Star (10 June 1940–12 May 1943): Awarded for one or more days service in North Africa between the inclusive dates.

Pacific Star (8 December 1941–2 September 1945): Awarded for service in the Pacific.

Burma Star (11 December 1941–2 September 1945): Awarded for service in the Burma campaign.

Italy Star (11 June 1943–8 May 1945): Awarded for operational service in Italy. Royal Navy and merchant navy personnel had to qualify for the 1939–1945 Star before eligibility for the Italy Star could begin.

France and Germany Star (6 June 1944–8 May 1945): Awarded for service in France, Belgium, Holland, or Germany between D-Day and the surrender of Germany, provided the service was directly concerned with military operations.

British Commonwealth

The Commonwealth nations augmented the British awards by establishing their own service medals. These medals are distinctive in design, purpose, and criteria:

Indian Service Medal (3 September 1939–2 September 1945): Awarded to Indian forces for three years of nonoperational service in India (and certain other places). It could not be awarded to those who qualified for the Defence Medal. Those serving with United Kingdom forces in India were not eligible, nor were those who were recruited from outside India, but who served with the Indian Army.

Canadian Volunteer Service Medal (2 September 1939–1 March 1947): Awarded to members of Canadian fighting forces and the Nursing Service upon completion of eighteen months of voluntary service. A service bar denoted overseas service.

South African Service Medal. Awarded to those who signed either the Africa Oath acknowledging liability for service or the General Service Oath acknowledging liability for service with the Union Defence Forces. It was also awarded to personnel of such uniformed services as the Protection Corps, South African Military Nursing Services, the South African Police, etc.

South African Medal for War Services (6 September 1939–15 February 1946): Awarded for a minimum of two years of service, one of which was continuous, rendered voluntarily and without pay, in one or more of the officially recognized voluntary organizations, providing five or more hours were worked each week.

Australia Service Medal (3 September 1939–

Table 2

Relative Precedence of American Military Decorations of World War II

1. Navy Medal of Honor (1861)
   Army Medal of Honor (1862)
2. Distinguished Service Cross (1918)
   Navy Cross (1919)
3. Army Distinguished Service Medal (1918)
   Navy Distinguished Service Medal (1918)
4. Silver Star (1918)
5. Legion of Merit (1942)
6. Distinguished Flying Cross (1926)
7. Soldier's Medal (1926)
   Navy and Marine Corps Medal (1942)
8. Bronze Star (1942)
9. Air Medal (1942)
10. Navy Commendation Medal (1944)
    Army Commendation Medal (1945)
11. Purple Heart (1932)

TABLE 3

Relative Precedence of British Orders and Decorations of World War II

1. Victoria Cross (1856)
2. George Cross (1940)
3. Order of the Garter (1348)
4. Order of the Thistle (1687)
5. Order of the Bath (three classes) (1399)
6. Order of Merit (1902)
7. Order of St. Michael and St. George (1818)
8. Royal Victorian Order (1st–3rd Class) (1896)
9. Order of the British Empire (1st–3rd Class) (1917)
10. Order of the Companions of Honour (1917)
11. Distinguished Service Order (1886)
12. Royal Victorian Order (4th Class) (1896)
13. Order of the British Empire (4th Class) (1917)
14. Imperial Service Order (1902)
15. Royal Victorian Order (5th Class) (1896)
16. Order of the British Empire (5th Class) (1917)
17. Distinguished Service Cross (1914)
18. Military Cross (1914)
19. Distinguished Flying Cross (1918)
20. Air Force Cross (1918)
21. Distinguished Conduct Medal (1854)
22. Conspicuous Gallantry Medal (1855)
23. George Medal (1940)
24. Distinguished Service Medal (1914)
25. Military Medal (1916)
26. Distinguished Flying Medal (1918)
27. Air Force Medal (1918)
28. British Empire Medal (1917)

2 September 1945): Awarded to all members of the Australian armed forces and the Australian merchant marine who served overseas for at least eighteen months.

New Zealand War Service Medal (3 September 1939–2 September 1945): Awarded to personnel of the New Zealand armed forces and under certain conditions to members of the New Zealand Home Guard, merchant navy, and civilian air lines for twenty-eight days of full-time service or six months of part-time service.

Southern Rhodesia War Service Medal (1939–1945): Awarded to those who served at home. It was not issued to anyone qualifying for any of the campaign medals or service stars.

Newfoundland Volunteer War Service Medal (1939–1945): Awarded by the Canadian province of Newfoundland to any person from the province who served overseas in any of the British imperial forces, and who was ineligible for (or did not re-ceive) a volunteer service medal from any other country, and to every veteran from Newfoundland who for various reasons did not participate in overseas duty.

Soviet Union

During World War II, the Soviet Union had a rich array of decorations, service medals, and campaign medals reflecting the full range of its military efforts. The principal campaign medals fell into the following categories:

Defense Medals: These medals were awarded to both military personnel and civilians who took an active part in the defense of certain cities, including those who worked on the defensive fortifications of those places.

Medal for the Defense of	Established on	Inclusive Qualifying Dates
Leningrad	22 Dec 42	08 Sep 41–27 Jan 44
Moscow	01 May 44	19 Oct 41–25 Jan 42
Odessa	22 Dec 42	10 Aug 41–16 Oct 41
Sevastopol	22 Dec 42	05 Nov 41–04 Jul 42
Stalingrad	22 Dec 42	12 Jul 42–19 Nov 42
Kiev	21 Jun 61	07 Jul 41–26 Sep 41
The Caucasus	01 May 44	Jun 42–Oct 43
The Soviet Arctic	05 Dec 44	Jun 41–Nov 44

Capture Medals: These medals were awarded to military personnel who took part in the assault on and capture of the cities indicated below, during the inclusive dates shown for each city.

Medal for the Capture of	Established on	Inclusive Qualifying Dates
Budapest	09 Jun 45	20 Dec 44–15 Feb 45
Königsberg	09 Jun 45	23 Jan 45–10 Apr 45
Vienna	09 Jun 45	16 Mar 45–13 Apr 45
Berlin	09 Jun 45	22 Apr 45–02 May 45

Liberation Medals: These medals were awarded to military personnel who took an active part in the liberation of the following cities during the dates indicated:

Medal for the Liberation of	Established On	Inclusive Qualifying Dates
Belgrade	09 Jun 45	29 Sep 44–22 Oct 44
Warsaw	09 Jun 45	14 Jan 45–17 Jan 45
Prague	09 Jun 45	03 May 45–09 May 45

Victory Medals: The Soviets issued two victory medals. The first was the Medal for Victory over Germany, which was established on 9 May 1945, and was awarded to all military personnel who took

TABLE 4

Relative Precedence of Soviet Orders and Decorations of World War II

1. Hero of the Soviet Union (1934)
2. Hero of Socialist Labor (1938)
3. Order of Lenin (1930)
4. Order of Victory (1943)
5. Order of the Red Banner (1924)
6. Order of Suvorov (Army, three classes) (1942)
7. Order of Ushakov (Navy, two classes) (1944)
8. Order of Kutuzov (Army, three classes) (1942–1943)
9. Order of Nakhimov (Navy, two classes) (1944)
10. Order of Bogdan Khmelnitsky (three classes) (1943)
11. Order of Alexander Nevsky (Army and Air Force) (1942)
12. Order of the Patriotic War (two classes) (1942)
13. Order of the Red Star (1930)
14. Order of the Badge of Honor (Civilians) (1935)
15. Order of Glory (Army and Air Force, three classes) (1943)
16. Order of Mother Heroine (Civilians) (1944)
17. Order of the Glory of Motherhood (Civilians) (1944)
18. For Valor (1938)
19. For Meritorious Service in Battle (1938)
20. Ushakov Medal (Navy, two classes) (1944)
21. Nakhimov Medal (Navy, two classes) (1944)

part in "The Great Patriotic War" from 22 June 1941 until the defeat of Germany. The other was the Medal for Victory over Japan, which was authorized on 30 September 1945, and awarded to all military personnel who served with units that operated against the Japanese between 2–23 August 1945. Civilians who served with Soviet armed forces units were also eligible to receive these medals.

Anniversary Medals: The Soviets also issued two anniversary medals commemorating service during World War II. The first was the Twentieth Anniversary of Victory in the Great Patriotic War 1941–1945 Medal, which was established on 7 May 1965, and issued to all military personnel and civilians (including partisans) who took part in the war. The second anniversary medal was the Thirtieth Anniversary of Victory in the Great Patriotic War Medal 1941–1945 Medal, established on 25 April 1975. It was issued to all Twentieth Anniversary Medal recipients, as well as to civilians who worked in the rear during the war. It was issued in two versions: one for "war veterans" and the other for "home front veterans."

France

Although France fell on 17 June 1940, its government-in-exile under General Charles de Gaulle (q.v.) continued to fight. The unique nature of France's participation in the war limited the scope of the medals it could award. Since the country was occupied by the Germans, much of its focus was on activities resulting from occupation: resistance and volunteering for combat. A number of new awards and decorations were authorized during and after the war. The following awards are among the chief French awards for World War II:

Croix de Guerre (1939–1945): Established on 26 September 1939, this decoration is a continuation of the *Croix de Guerre* first established during World War I and was awarded on the basis of individual and unit citations.

Order of Liberation: Founded on 16 November 1940 by de Gaulle as a reward to those who provided exceptional service in the liberation of France.

Medal of the French Resistance: Established on 9 February 1943 by de Gaulle to recognize gallantry by members of the resistance.

Free French Forces Medal: Established on 4 April 1946 for those who volunteered to serve in the Free French Forces before 1 August 1943, or who served in territories under the authority of the French National Committee before 3 June 1943.

War Medal (1939–1945): Established on 21 May 1946 for award to all Frenchmen serving in a recognized French unit (including those who were part of Allied armies).

Medal of Liberated France: Established on 12 September 1947, this medal recognized both French and Allied personnel who made a notable contribution to the liberation of France.

Medal for Those Deported or Interned for Acts of Resistance: Established on 6 August 1948, this medal was awarded to those who were imprisoned in France or deported from the country for their service in the resistance.

Medal for Those Deported or Interned for Political Reasons: Established on 9 September 1948, this medal was awarded to those deported or interned as political prisoners.

Cross for Combat Volunteers (1939–1945): Established on 4 February 1953, this cross was similar to its World War I predecessor and was awarded for those who had volunteered to serve in a combat unit.

Italian Campaign Medal (1943–1944): Established on 1 April 1953, this medal was awarded to all members of the French Expeditionary Corps who served in Italy between 1 December 1943 and 25 July 1944.

Cross for Combatant Volunteers in the Resistance: Established on 15 April 1954 for those who had served in one of the resistance organizations for at least three months in an occupied zone before 6 June 1944.

Medal for Patriots in Forced Labor: Established on 27 December 1954, this medal was awarded to French citizens who lived in Haut-Rhin, Bas-Rhin, and Moselle, and who were arrested by the Germans and interned for at least three months.

Belgium

Like France, Belgium was occupied by the Germans for most of the war and therefore its awards focused either on activities involving occupation and resistance or on the service of those who escaped from Belgium and fought in exile. The Belgian medals are, in general, quite similar in purpose and scope to French medals:

Maritime Medal (1940–1945): Established on 17 July 1941 for Belgian seamen serving with the Allies from 3 September 1939 to the end of the war.

Croix de Guerre (1940): Established on 20 July 1941, this medal was created to recognize heroism in combat. A bronze lion indicates a mention in the dispatches of a regiment; a silver lion denotes a mention in the dispatches of a brigade; and a bronze tower denotes "civic virtue on duty."

Escapee's Cross: Established on 20 February 1944 by the Belgian government-in-exile, this medal was awarded to those who escaped from Belgium and subsequently served in some capacity in the war effort against Germany.

Civil Decoration (1940–1945): Established on 21 July 1944, this medal was awarded to civilians who distinguished themselves by their service to Belgium during the war. It was awarded in five classes.

Medal of Belgian Gratitude (1940–1945): Established on 1 August 1945, it was created to recognize services by Belgians and foreigners, particularly those who served in a humanitarian, charitable, or philanthropic capacity. The medal was awarded in three classes.

Medal for Volunteers (1940–1945): Established on 16 February 1946 for volunteers who entered the armed forces prior to 8 May 1945.

Commemorative War Medal (1940–1945): Established on 16 February 1946 for Belgians and foreigners for service during the war. It included a variety of devices for the ribbon that denoted the specific nature of the recipient's contribution.

Medal for Armed Resistance (1940–1945): Established on 16 February 1946 to recognize the heroism of members of the Belgian resistance.

Medal for the Abyssinian Campaign (1941): Established on 30 January 1947 for participation in the campaign to liberate Ethiopia between 6 March and 3 July 1941.

African War Medal (1940–1945): Established on 30 January 1947 for those who served at least twelve months between 10 May 1940 and 7 May 1945. It has campaign bars for *Nigerie, Moyen-Orient* (Middle East), and *Madagascar.*

Medal for Efforts in the Colonial War (1940–1945): Established on 30 January 1947 for government officials, magistrates, volunteers, missionaries, settlers, and others who gave honorable service of at least one year.

Prisoner of War Medal (1940–1945): Established on 1 October 1947 as the Prisoner of War Card. The medal was later authorized on 20 October 1947.

Political Prisoners Cross (1940–1945): Established on 13 November 1947 for Belgians confined as political prisoners by the Germans during the war. A silver bar with a silver star indicates each six months of imprisonment.

Medal for Non-Collaboration (1940–1945): Established 12 February 1951 for those who refused to cooperate in military service or to work for the German occupation forces in Belgium.

Medal for Civil Resistance: Established on 21 March 1951 for civilians who served or assisted in armed resistance against the German occupation.

Medal for the Military Fighter of the War (1940–1945): Established on 19 December 1967 for active duty military personnel who served in the war, including foreigners who served with Belgian forces.

Germany

During World War II, Germany had an enormous array of awards, decorations, and qualification badges. This article only addresses the most significant awards and is limited for the most part to military awards.

The premier German decoration during World War II was the Iron Cross. Originally established by King Friedrich-Wilhelm III in 1813, it was reinstituted during the Franco-Prussian War (1870–1871), and again during World War I (1914–1918). The Iron Cross was a purely Prussian decoration until World War I. On 1 September 1939, Adolf Hitler (q.v.) reinstated the Iron Cross, but changed its grades and altered its ribbon. The 1939 version of the Iron Cross was originally established in four grades: Second Class (worn as a ribbon in the second buttonhole), First Class (worn as a one-sided pin-back badge on the left breast), Knight's Cross (worn on a neck ribbon), and the Grand Cross (larger than the Knight's Cross and worn on 57mm-wide neck ribbon). The medal followed its traditional design but contained a *swastika* in the center of the obverse.

During World War II, the Knight's Cross was expanded to include higher grades, with Oak Leaves (1940), Oak Leaves and Swords (1941), Oak Leaves with Swords and Diamonds (1941), and Golden Oak Leaves with Swords and Diamonds (1944). For those who received the Iron Cross during World War I, a bar was authorized to indicate subsequent award of the World War II version. The lower grades of the Iron Cross were awarded in large numbers, but the Knight's Cross was given to only 6,973 recipients. Its higher

grades were likewise awarded in limited numbers: 890 received the Knight's Cross with Oak Leaves, 159 received it with Oak Leaves and Swords, and twenty-seven received it with Oak Leaves, Swords, and Diamonds. Hermann Göring (q.v.) was the only recipient of the Grand Cross. Stuka pilot Hans-Ulrich Rudel (q.v.) was the only recipient of the Golden Oak Leaves, and in fact that grade was created specifically for him.

A companion decoration, the War Merit Cross, was established on 18 October 1939 to reward contributions to the war effort under circumstances other than those for which the Iron Cross could be awarded. It was initially established in two classes, but in August 1940, it was expanded to include a Knight's Cross and a War Merit Medal, which ranked below the War Merit Cross Second Class, and could only be awarded to civilians. Finally, in 1944, Hitler expanded the War Merit Cross to include a Golden Knight's Cross (which was awarded only twice). The War Merit Cross could be awarded with or without crossed swords. It was awarded with swords if earned in support of military objectives or for bravery other than in combat.

In September 1941, Hitler established a new decoration, known as the German Cross, that ranked between the Iron Cross First Class and the Knight's Cross of the Iron Cross. It was awarded in two grades: Gold for acts of bravery in the field and Silver for outstanding military merit. It was not awarded to civilians, although it could be awarded to uniformed formations such as the police, railways, and so on. The German Cross was a double eight-pointed star with a *swastika* in the middle.

Although the Germans did not establish a system of campaign medals, they did create several medals that effectively served that purpose. Perhaps the best known was the Medal for the Winter Campaign in the East (1941–1942), also known as the East Front Medal, but among soldiers, it was referred to as "the Order of the Frozen Flesh." It was established on 26 May 1942 for combatants who served on the Russian front for at least two weeks, and for noncombatants who served at least sixty days between 15 May 1941 and 15 April 1942.

The Germans also instituted an award that was a combination decoration and campaign medal for service in the Spanish civil war from 1936 to 1939. Known as the Spanish Cross, it was awarded in six grades. It was awarded without swords to noncombatants who served at least three months in Spain (in bronze or silver, depending on the recipient's rank). It was awarded with swords to combatants in

TABLE 5

Relative Precedence of German Military Decorations of World War II

1. Grand Cross of the Iron Cross (1813/1939)
2. Knight's Cross of the Iron Cross with Gold Oak Leaves, Swords, and Diamonds (1944)
3. Knight's Cross of the Iron Cross with Oak Leaves, Swords, and Diamonds (1941)
4. Knight's Cross of the Iron Cross with Oak Leaves and Swords (1941)
5. *Pour le Mérite* with Oak Leaves (1810–1918)[*]
6. Knight's Cross of the Iron Cross with Oak Leaves (1940)
7. *Pour le Mérite* (1740-1918)[*]
8. Knight's Cross of the Iron Cross (1939)
9. War Order of the German Cross in Gold (1941)
10. Knight's Cross of the War Cross of Merit in Gold (1944)[†]
11. Knight's Cross of the War Cross of Merit in Silver (1940)[†]
12. War Order of the German Cross in Silver (1941)
13. Iron Cross First Class (1813/1939)
14. War Cross of Merit First Class (1939)[†]
15. Iron Cross Second Class (1813/1939)
16. War Cross of Merit Second Class (1939)[†]
17. War Medal for Merit (Civilians) (1940)

Notes:

[*] Not awarded after 1918 but still worn on German uniforms during World War II.

[†] Awarded with or without swords to indicate a direct connection to military operations.

bronze, silver, or gold according to their rank and duties. In July 1942, the Germans also established the Decoration for Bravery and Merit for the Associated Eastern Peoples. These awards were made in five grades to citizens of eastern European countries who joined the German Army.

Italy

Italy's participation in the war was somewhat complex, and this is reflected in its medals and decorations. Italy entered the war in 1940 as one of the Axis powers, but fell in 1943, after which the liberated portions joined with the Allies. This was complicated by the existence of the Italian Social Republic in the north, which continued from 1943 to 1945 under German domination. Thus, the Italians had awards of the Kingdom of Italy, the Republic of Italy, and the Social Republic of Italy.

Three primary Italian decorations were either "updated" or established during the war. The Medal for Military Valor was continued by the Italian Social Republic in gold, silver, and bronze. The War Merit Cross, originally established in 1918, was likewise modified for use during the war. A new award, the Order of the Roman Eagle, was established on 14 March 1942 for foreigners who made noteworthy contributions to Italy. It was awarded in five classes. Although this order was abolished in 1944, the Social Republic of Italy continued to award a modified version until 1945.

The Italians established several campaign and service medals. The Medal for the Campaign Against France was a bronze medal that commemorated the short campaign along the Riviera and in the alpine passes in June of 1940. The War Commemorative Medal (1940–1943) was established on 17 March 1948 for members of the armed forces and certain others for service between 11 June 1940 and 8 September 1943. The Medal for War Volunteers (1940–1945) was established on 21 April 1948 for those who volunteered for service during the war. The Medal for the War of Liberation was established on 4 April 1950, and is similar in purpose to the War Commemorative Medal, but is for services rendered after 9 September 1943.

Charles McDowell

Additional Reading

Braun, Saul M., *Seven Heroes: Medal of Honor Stories of the War in the Pacific*, (1965).

Hare-Scott, K.B., *For Valour: Biographical Sketches of Some of World War II's Winners of the Victoria Cross*, (1949).

Philips, Cecil E.L., *Victoria Cross Battles of the Second World War*, (1973).

Scott, Jay (pseud.), *America's War Heroes: Dramatic True Tales of Courageous Marines, Army, Air Force, and Navy Men Whose Exploits Won Them the Congressional Medal of Honor*, (1961).

Missiles, Guided

Scientists in the Soviet Union, Germany, and the United States began experimenting with rocket propulsion and guidance systems in the 1920s and made considerable progress by the late 1930s. There was, however, little continuity or direction in these efforts. The outbreak of World War II ushered in an era of rapid development and deployment. Every major belligerent power undertook a significant research and development program, resulting in major technological advances.

The weapons that resulted fell into three general categories. Rockets, sometimes called free-flight rockets, are self-propelled explosive weapons with no guidance systems. Like a cannon-fired projectile, they go where they are pointed. Unlike an artillery round, the rocket's warhead and the propulsion system are contained in a single unit (*see* Rockets, British, German, Soviet, and U.S.). Guided bombs have a warhead and a guidance system, but no propulsion system. Dropped from aircraft, they rely on gravity to carry them to their targets. Missiles, also called guided missiles, consist of a warhead, a propulsion system, and a guidance system. The propulsion system usually is a rocket motor, but it can be a jet engine.

The United States experimented with a number of guided bombs. The GB-1 was developed in early 1941, entered into production in May 1943, and was used against Cologne in May 1944. Weighing 2,000 pounds, the GB-1 was equipped with wings and a television guidance system. Another such weapon was the VB, a vertical bomb dropped in clusters and guided by bombardiers from their aircraft. A single bombardier could guide clusters of five VB-1s (called Azons), if weather and flying conditions were good. The last of this series, the VB-13, weighed 12,000 pounds and was more than twenty feet long. Several other larger guided bombs, such as the Razon and the Bat, were deployed late in the war.

Germany developed the Fritz-X (also known as the FX-400 and the SD-1400), a 3,000-pound armor-piercing glide bomb with wings and a small tail unit. Radio signals caused spoilers on the tail surface to raise and lower, modifying the bomb's trajectory. The Fritz X was developed between 1939 and 1942. Its most significant operational employment came on 9 September 1943 when three Fritz-Xs were used to sink the Italian battleship *Roma.*

Germany introduced the world's first operational wire-guided missiles, the X-series, developed by Ruhrstahl AG of Düsseldorf. The X-4 was an air-to-air missile that carried bobbins of wire in its wing tips. The wire unwound as the missile flew. The wires carried guidance signals that operated spoiler tabs on the missile's wing surface. The warhead was triggered by a proximity fuze. After tests in 1944 showed that the wire link between the missile and the launch aircraft was too restricting, design modifications were tested using both radio guidance and acoustic homing systems. Neither made it out of the development stage before the war ended.

The wire guidance system of the X-4 was also used in the X-7, a ground-to-ground antitank missile. Armed with a shaped charge warhead and an impact fuze, the twenty-two-pound X-7 was capable of penetrating 200mm of armor at ranges up to 1,000 meters. The war ended before the X-7 could be brought into production, but it became the prototype of the wire-guided antitank missile that is standard in all armies of the 1990s.

Germany's infamous V-series (standing for *Vergeltung,* the German word for reprisal) were the world's first operational guided surface-to-surface missiles (SSMs). The V-1 "Buzz Bomb" was the forerunner of the modern cruise missile, and the V-2 was the forerunner of the modern intercontinental ballistic missile (ICBM). These weapons were designed to wreak havoc and destruction on the cities of Britian.

Both the German Army and the *Luftwaffe* conducted guided missile research and development programs in the years before the war. The German Army set up its research facility at Kummersdorf-West in 1932. That establishment was responsible for coordinating rocket research throughout the *Reich.* It was led by Captain Walter Dornberger (q.v.), who remained in charge until 1945 (by which time he had become a major general). He gathered under him a team of outstanding scientists, including Wernher von Braun (q.v.), Walter Riedel, Heinrich Gruenow, and Walter Thiel. Together they were responsible for the development of both solid-fuel artillery rockets and long-range liquid-fuel rockets.

The first long-range rocket from the Kummersdorf-West team was the *Aggregat* 1 (A-1), which used a motor fueled by liquid oxygen and alcohol. The next model, the A-2, had a better weight distribution and was successfully fired from Borkum on the Baltic coast in 1934. By 1936, both the army and the *Luftwaffe* had moved their research to an elaborate new complex on the coast at Peenemünde.

German V-1s (minus wings) in an underground factory at Nordhausen. (IWM OWIL 64355)

In 1937, testing began on a new model, the A-3, which used advanced graphite rudders in the rocket exhaust to improve stability during takeoff. It was the success of this model that convinced the Germans that a military rocket was within their grasp. To this end the A-4 (later designated the V-2) was developed with a guidance system and a 2,200-pound warhead. Further research into stability problems was conducted using the A-5. The first firings of the A-4 motor began in 1940, but by that time it seemed to many in Germany that the war was already won.

Rocket research, because of its high cost, was regarded as something of a technical novelty and it was given a low priority for funding. It was not until October 1942 that the A-4 achieved a successful launching and flew 115 miles. In December of that year Dornberger received the support of Chancellor Adolf Hitler and Armaments Minister Albert Speer (qq.v.) to go ahead with mass production.

The *Luftwaffe* was alarmed by this development, which would give the army a long-range strike capability. They therefore intensified the development of their own jet-propelled rocket, the Fi 103 (FZG-76), later designated as the V-1 Flying Bomb, which the Allies dubbed the "Buzz Bomb." Simpler and cheaper than the A-4, it carried a similar warhead. The *Luftwaffe* planned to produce 3,000 a month by the time it became operational in December 1943.

The army intensified its efforts in the face of this competition, planning an output of 900 A-4s per month. In May 1943, Hitler personally gave the project his highest priority for the allocation of resources, and massive launching bunkers were soon constructed in northern France for launches against Britain. Both the A-4 and FZG-76 programs received major setbacks on 17–18 August 1943 when severe damage was caused to the Peenemünde (q.v.) facilities by RAF bombing (Operation HYDRA). Continued bombing of dispersed sites eventually led to most production being moved to underground factories such as those at Nordhausen in Thurungia.

The initial testing of the V-1 began at Peenemünde in December 1941. Basically, the missile was a pilotless single-wing plane driven by a pulse-jet engine. It was 25.4 feet long, thirty-three inches in diameter, and it weighed 4,858 pounds—including the 1,870-pound warhead. The V-1's wingspan was 17.5 feet, and it carried 150 gallons of fuel. The guidance was set into the Asksania autopilot prior to launch, which made it secure from electronic jamming during flight. The V-1 was launched from a fixed ramp roughly 45

meters long. Launch speed was about 200 mph, and cruising speed once in the air was 350 mph. The V-1 cruised at altitudes between 3,500 and 4,000 feet. Maximum range was about 140 miles. Eighty percent of the missiles landed within an eight-mile radius of their intended targets.

Mass production of the V-1 started in September 1943, with monthly production rates increasing to 1,400 by January 1944 and 8,000 by September. Originally, the V-1 assault on Britain was scheduled to begin on 15 February 1944, when about 12,000 were ready for use. The actual barrage did not start until June 1944, however. A total of 9,251 V-1s were launched against Britain before the end of the war. Thousands more were launched from 100 sites in northern France against Allied targets throughout Europe, including 6,551 against Antwerp. Casualties caused by the V-1 totaled 7,810 killed and 44,435 injured.

Most of the V-1 launch sites were identified by Allied intelligence and became bombing targets, especially under Operation CROSSBOW (q.v.), which began on 5 December 1943. By June 1944, almost 40 percent of the Allied air effort was being directed against the V-1 threat. However, it was only when the Allied ground advance overran the launch sites that the V-1 threat to Britain ended. The Germans then turned the V-1s on Antwerp.

The V-1 experienced several operational problems. Its slow 350-mph speed made it a vulnerable target, especially to Allied fighters. Of the totals launched against Britain and Antwerp, 4,621 and 2,455, respectively, were destroyed before they reached their targets. The V-1 also suffered reliability problems.

The need for greater range to hit Britain revived interest in the V-2. The V-2 was more than forty-six feet long, weighed 27,000 pounds, carried a 2,200 pound payload, and had a range of 180 to 210 miles. It used a bi-fuel motor, burning alcohol and liquid oxygen. The warhead, which was triggered by a simple impact fuze, consisted of a TNT and ammonium nitrate mixture called amatol. It was a relatively weak explosive. Several attempts were made to use more powerful fillers, but heating of the missile body from air friction often caused premature explosions.

When full production of the V-2 began at Peenemünde, plans called for a production rate of 300 in October 1943, increasing to 900 a month by December. After the RAF HYDRA attack put production back by about six months, manufacturing was relocated to the underground site near Nordhausen. By December 1943, the first V-2s were completed, and the rate of their production increased to nearly 900 a month. Using concentration camp prisoners as forced laborers, the Nazis produced a total of more than 10,000 V-2s. By the fall of 1944, the program of constructing launch sites was also well advanced.

One of the major advantages of the V-2 was that because it was launched vertically, it could be launched from just about any location with a few square yards of clearance. Although less accurate than the V-1, the V-2 was more deadly. It was almost impossible to defend against. The V-1 was slow and its engine made a loud noise. The V-2 was silent as it dropped from about sixty miles up at a speed of 2,200 mph.

The first V-2 landed in Britain on 8 September 1944. By 27 March 1945, 1,359 V-2s had been fired against thirteen British cities. The Germans also fired 1,341 V-2s against Antwerp; sixty-five against Brussels; ninety-eight against Liege; fifteen against Paris; and five into Luxembourg. Eleven V-2s were fired in a attempt to destroy the Remagen Bridge (q.v.) over the Rhine after it fell into Allied hands. Casualties from the V-2 totaled 4,148 killed and 8,477 wounded.

The Germans started development work on several other ballistic missile models that never saw completion. The potentially most devastating was the A-10, a two-stage missile first conceived in 1940 as a transatlantic weapon. The A-10 was to be the booster, with a V-2 as the second stage. The projected range for the system was 3,000 miles. They also had plans for another missile that could be launched from a submarine to hit the United States. Fortunately, none of these designs ever got off the drawing board.

The Germans also experimented with various designs of guided surface-to-air missiles (SAMs). In 1943–1944, Germany deployed limited numbers of the Enzian. Carrying a 1,000-pound warhead with a proximity fuze, it was powered by four solid-fuel rocket boosters. The missile was guided by a ground operator using a radio link and either radar or optical tracking. Once the missile was in the target area, an infrared homing device took control for the final approach. The Germans considered modifying the Enzian for a surface-to-surface, and even for an antitank role. About sixty of the missiles were built in various stages; thirty-eight actually flew, sixteen with radio guidance.

In 1943–1945, experiments were also made with the Rheintochter, another solid-fueled SAM. It was guided by radio control, and optically tracked by flares attached to its fins. It had a 330-pound warhead and was capable of altitudes of 26,000 feet.

Work on the Rheintochter was suspended in 1944 when the *Luftwaffe* decided it needed greater range. The Rheintochter 3 was redesigned for a liquid-fuel engine, but only six were built and fired before the program was suspended in January 1945.

Another radio-guided missile, the 8–117C, was ordered and ready to enter service when the war ended. More advanced and expensive than any of these was the Wasserfall, a liquid-propelled, radar-controlled Flak missile, which carried a massive 670-pound warhead. Resources, however, were diverted to the V-2 project, and production planned for March 1945 never went ahead.

The V-2 was an instrument of technical brilliance, but it required an enormous diversion of precious resources to produce a weapon that could deliver a warhead weighing only about one ton. The program owed more to the irrational expectations of its political masters than to objective military analysis. While the V-l and V-2 programs yielded little benefit to their originators, the long-term dividends fell to the Allies.

When the final collapse came for Germany, Dornberger, von Braun, and the other remaining senior staff from Peenemünde, along with their most important files, fled to southern Germany to escape the advancing Soviet forces. Many of these German scientists and technicians, von Braun and Dornberger foremost among them, later went to the United States and played key roles in starting the U.S. space program. Other German scientists captured by the Soviets were instrumental in the Soviet space program.

Jonathan B.A. Bailey
Robert G. Waite

(Refer to table on page 1061)

Additional Reading
Baker, David, *The Rocket: History and Development of Rocket and Missile Technology,* (1978).
Cooksley, Peter G. *Flying Bomb: The Story of Hitler's V-Weapons in World War II,* (1979).
Dornberger, Walter, *Peenemünde: Die Geschichte der V-Waffen,* (1981).
Henshall, Philip, *Hitler's Rocket Sites,* (1985).
von Braun, Wernher, and Frederick I. Ordway, III, *History of Rocketry and Space Travel,* (1951).

Mulberries
See ARTIFICIAL HARBORS

Section IV-M
Technical Data Table of
Weapons and Equipment

German Guided Missiles

Model	V-1	V-2	Enzian	Rheintochter 1	Wasserfall	X-4	X-7
Type	SSM	SSM	SAM	SAM	SAM	AAM	Antitank
Year in Service	1943	1943	1944	1944	1944	1944	1945
Power Source	Pulse-Jet Engine	Liquid Fuel Rocket Motor	Solid Fuel Rocket Motor	Solid Fuel Rocket Motor	Solid Fuel Rocket Motor	Liquid Fuel Rocket Motor	Solid Fuel Rocket Motor
Guidance System	Askania Autopilot	Gyroscope	Radio Link Radar Track	Radio Link Optical Track	Radar	Wire Guided	Gyro Stable Wire Guided
Length (feet)	25	46	12.3	33.8	26	2.5	6.5
Maximum Speed (miles per hour)	350	3,600	1,980	3,465	1,663	550	212
Maximum Range	140 miles	190 miles	Note 1	Note 1	Note 1	6,000 meters	1,000 meters
Maximum Altitude (feet)	4,000	320,000	44,550	26,000	65,000	Note 1	Note 1
Warhead Weight (pounds)	1,870	2,200	1,000	330	670	44	0.3
Number Built	35,000	10,000	60	82	50	1,300 Note 2	None

SSM = Surface-to-surface missile
SAM = Surface-to-air missile
AAM = Air-to-air missile
Notes:
1. Not applicable.
2. Number in production on 6 February 1945.

N

Norden Bombsight

Carl Norden invented his bombsight for the U.S. Navy in the 1920s, perfecting it during the 1930s. The U.S. Army Air Corps tested the device between 1933 and 1936. During World War II, nearly all U.S. bombers and all naval patrol planes were equipped with the Norden bombsight (NBS).

The NBS had a computing device that was set for wind speed, altitude, ballistic data, and the aircraft's movements over the ground, generating course corrections, so the bombardier could control lateral movements of the aircraft via the automatic flight control system ("automatic pilot"). With the bomb bay doors open, the bombardier flew the plane, lining up the crosshairs on the NBS and making level corrections by knobs on the sight, one for lateral movement, the other for altitude. The bombs dropped automatically at the release angle calculated by the sight's computer. The bombardier then returned control of the aircraft to the pilot.

The NBS was a significant improvement over previous horizontal bombing sights, which were limited in altitude (10,000 feet) and accuracy. The NBS was capable of pinpoint accuracy at altitudes up to 26,000 feet in a peacetime training environment. In actual combat over Europe, however, the skies were thick with cloud cover, haze, and smoke of industry, and the results were not as good. During one four-month period in 1944, the Allies flew 55,950 sorties, with 4,145 aborted due to cloud cover or weather conditions. Additional effects of cold, fear, antiaircraft fire, and searchlights also limited the NBS's accuracy. Other problems included inaccurate instruction books, vibrations of the sight mounting, crosshairs that were too thick (incompatible with accurate aiming), and sight calibration in knots instead of miles per hour. NBS production was slower than aircraft production. Originally it was designed to meet the navy's requirements, not those of the air corps. The air corps's automatic pilot was not compatible with the sight.

The initial combat mission results in 1942 allowed U.S. air commanders to predict that 10 percent of the bombs dropped would be dead on target, and 90 percent would be within a mile radius. By comparison, the best that night area bombing was achieving was 5 percent of the bombs within a mile of the target. Even with the NBS and the other technologies that emerged during the war, only one in twenty-nine Allied bombs hit structures essential to Axis wartime production.

The difficulties in pinpoint bombing led to the development of other improved bombing sights, radio, radar navigation aids, and modern sighting optics, as well as the television and laser-guided smart weapons of today. The experience with the Norden bombsight illustrated many lessons that remain valid today. Some of these same lessons resurfaced during the high-tech Persian Gulf War of 1991.

Rapid development in science and technology often outpaces tactics and doctrine. Each new development must be introduced with consideration for potential enemy countermeasures. Joint service weapons procurement can prevent redundant systems, costly mistakes, and the loss of valuable time. Weather, cloud cover, and other obscurities can still confound ordnance delivery, even with precision guided munitions. Finally, post-strike reconnaissance and bomb damage assessment are still required for evaluating bombing accuracy and producing reliable intelligence estimates of remaining enemy capabilities.

Alexander Molnar, Jr.

Additional Reading

Cross, Robin, *The Bombers: The Illustrated Story of Offensive Strategy and Tactics in the Twentieth Century* (1987).

Hansell, Haywood S., Jr., *The Air Plan That Defeated Hitler* (1972).

P

Panzerfaust

See INFANTRY WEAPONS, GERMAN

Proximity Fuze

The development of the proximity fuze was the major technical development in artillery in World War II, comparable in its way to the introduction of the point detonating fuze for high explosive rounds in World War I. The VT fuze (as it is called today) gave field artillery greatly increased lethality against infantry and soft-skinned vehicles at a time when indirect fire artillery was becoming less effective against the tank.

The idea for the fuze may have occurred to German scientists in the 1930s, but certainly British scientists working on the use of radar (q.v.) in antiaircraft gun control understood such possibilities at that time. They were aware that the benefits of radar control were likely to be wasted by the inaccuracy of fuzes. They toyed with the idea of making the fuze detect radar reflections from the target aircraft, which was being illuminated by the gun directing radar, but the technology at that time could not compress a radar receiver into a fuze.

The idea developed into providing the fuze with both its own transmitter and receiver, so that it sent out a signal in flight and detonated on receiving an echo from its target. Production of such a fuze was dependent on producing very small vacuum tubes, condensers, resistors, and a powerful battery that could be stored for years if necessary and yet still produce full power seconds after firing. In 1940, the British electronics industry was overstretched and could not take on research and development of such components. In August 1940, the Tizard (q.v.) Mission went to the United States to enlist scientific aid and handed over the theoretical work on the proximity fuze. This was based on a Doppler effect radar developed by Sir Robert Watson-Watt (q.v.).

The United States assumed responsibility for work on the fuze under the direction of the newly established National Defense Research Committee, working with the Office of Scientific Research and Development and the National Bureau of Standards. Responsibility for the project was given to the U.S. Navy. Section V of the Bureau of Ordnance took charge of the program, assisted by Johns Hopkins University. It was allotted the code letter "T." The fuze, therefore, came to be known as the VT fuze, and mistakenly, it was believed that this stood for variable time. The fuze was also at times known as "Pozit," "Peter," or "Special." Eastman Kodak was awarded the development contract, and it awarded a number of subcontracts, for example, for vacuum tubes to Sylvania, and the battery to the National Carbide Company (Exide).

Proximity fuzes entered production and the first Japanese aircraft was shot down by one fired by the USS *Helena* in June 1943. The British Mark 33 VT fuzes for the 3.7-inch antiaircraft gun were used with great success in 1944 against V-1 flying bombs over southern England.

An official request for modification of the fuze for use with howitzer shells was made in April 1943, and it was decided to develop fuzes for a variety of shells, because the size of the shell and the rate of its spin affected radio emissions. Fuzes for howitzers also needed more powerful batteries for their longer flight times. The army version of the VT fuze, therefore, required a radical redesign, and the responsibility was given to Colonel H.S. Horton and a completely new research team.

Trials were conducted on the sensitivity of the fuze over different types of terrain, and the first trials were conducted at Romney Creek on Aberdeen Proving Ground in April 1943 using a 90mm gun. In June, a five-second arming delay was introduced to improve troop safety and lessen the risk of muzzle burst. The first 155mm VT fuze was fired on 16 June 1943 and an 8-inch version followed soon after. It was the enthusiastic report of Colonel M.R. Cox of the Army War College on the 8-inch firing that probably persuaded the Joint Chiefs of Staff to raise the development priority of the fuze. Soon after, a single standard fuze was designed for all howitzer calibers.

Manufacture of howitzer VT fuzes by RCA and Eastman Kodak began in late 1943, with the U.S. Army Signal Corps responsible for quality control. By 1945, the fuzes were being produced in more than 120 plants. VT fuzes were issued to U.S. Army units in September 1944. The first reported use of VT fuzes in the land battle was by U.S. 1st Field Artillery, a 12th Army Group unit, on 18 December 1944 near St. Vith (q.v.) during the German Ardennes offensive (q.v.).

VT fuzes frequently provided effective airburst fire in misty conditions and at night. A report on 23 December 1944 stated: "It is hard to believe, but cumulative figures indicate 2,000 dead which could be observed and counted . . . VT ammunition is most deadly." General George S. Patton (q.v.) wrote to Lieutenant General Levin H. Campbell: "The new shell with the funny fuze is devastating. The other night we caught a German battalion which was trying to cross the Sauer River, with a battalion concentration and killed by actual count 702. I think that when all armies get this we will have to devise some new method of warfare. I am glad you all thought of it first, it is a really wonderful achievement." The VT fuze became very popular and soon accounted for about 25 percent of fuzes fired. The outstanding performance of these fuzes of the 1940s is evidenced by their design remaining substantially unchanged forty years later.

Jonathan B.A. Bailey

Additional Reading
Baldwin, Ralph, *The Deadly Fuze* (1980).

R

Radar

Radar, the Allied acronym for radio detection and ranging, was first developed in the 1930s. Scientists in the U.S., Britain, and Germany pursued secret developmental work, bouncing radio signals into the upper atmosphere. In the process they noticed the phenomena of nearby airplanes and boats interfering with those waves. The resulting ability to produce and guide ultrashort electromagnetic waves was a pivotal factor in the Allied victory in the war.

Britain, preparing for possible German bombing attacks, developed radar as a defense measure. Originally called RDF (radio direction finding), radar was refined with data developed by Edward Appleton, a physicist who studied the ionosphere, and Robert Watson-Watt (q.v.), the director of the radio research station at Slough. Watson-Watt used this information to detect movement by aiming radio transmitter waves at objects with electrically conductive surfaces.

In December 1934, Sir Henry Tizard (q.v.), rector of Imperial College in London, and Watson-Watt sought to establish scientific air defense procedures. Noting that aircraft reflected energy from ground transmitters, they stated that the resulting echo could detect enemy aircraft hundreds of miles away, even to the point of determining numbers, altitude, and direction of travel.

In February 1935, Watson-Watt conducted a successful demonstration of the system for Air Marshal Sir Hugh Dowding (q.v.), who at that time was the head of research and development for the Air Ministry. Dowding immediately recommended the Air Ministry give the project full support. This one action by Dowding probably did more than any other to influence the outcome of the Battle of Britain (q.v.).

The Air Ministry organized a radar system headquartered at Bawdsey Manor to monitor the British coast. Radar research continued there from 1936 to 1939. The initial detection system had radar stations along the east and southern coasts. The system was known as IFF (identification friend or foe), but it was not entirely accurate. The first British operational radar, Airborne Interception (AI) Mark II, also was ineffective. In October 1939, the Mark III was introduced, but it too failed to detect objects as accurately as expected. In order to achieve accuracy and range, both shorter wavelengths and higher power were needed, but no transmitters could produce both.

In 1940, researchers at Birmingham University developed the magnetron, a cavity resonator that combined high power and the transmission of high frequencies. This technology enabled smaller radar units to be produced and installed in airplanes. Pilots could use the radio waves at night to locate targets and to navigate. Stations on the ground tracked planes with radar, and aided pilots in the exact release of bombs.

Once ground radar stations detected approaching enemy planes, orders were issued to waiting fighter groups to defend or attack. Radar was economical, saving the costs of organizing and manning continuous patrol systems. Also, planes were not deployed unless necessary, saving fuel and related maintenance costs. During the Battle of Britain, radar helped the British deny the Germans the element of surprise.

By the summer of 1940, Britain was protected by a system of radar defenses called CHAIN HOME (q.v.). Each radar station was mounted on a 240-foot wooden tower and had a range of about 120 miles. The CHAIN HOME sets had a minimum operating altitude of 3,000 feet, under which low-flying fighters could slip. To plug this gap, the British deployed a second line of low-level but shorter range radars called CHAIN HOME LOW. Both systems proved to be critical elements in the coming Battle of Britain.

Early on, the Germans suspected that the British might have a functioning radar system, especially with the erection of the tall towers along the coast. In 1939, the airship *Graf Zeppelin* was sent on several electronic intelligence reconnaissance missions to the British coast. The airship, however, was such a big target on the British radar scopes that the British simply shut down their systems whenever it appeared. Thus the Germans started the Battle of Britain knowing that the British had some sort of radar, but assumed it to be technically inferior to what the Germans were developing to that point. It was a deadly mistake.

Radar range and precision in detecting enemy craft improved throughout the war. Technical cooperation between Allied scientific institutions, including the Massachusetts Institute of Technology and the Bell Laboratories, generated new ideas and techniques. A series of Mark IV to Mark X radars improved range from 100 feet to 100 miles. Precision also improved. The transition from meter to centimeter-long waves enabled higher performance standards from the radar. Tizard encouraged scientists to experiment

Lichtenstein radar antennas on a Bf-110G-4 night fighter. (IWM CL 3299)

with variations of the basic radar sets to make British bombing raids over Germany more successful.

Beginning in 1942, the British employed the TR-1335, or Gee, radar to direct RAF bombers to their targets. Using one master and two slave ground transmitter stations on a 200-mile baseline, Gee measured distance by the time it took for a signal to travel to a specific point and return. The differences between the signals from the master and each slave were indicated on a cathode ray tube (CRT) in the aircraft. The system, which had a 400-mile line-of-sight effective range, was instrumental in bombing missions against German industry in the Ruhr district. The Rebecca-Eureka radar also was used to direct planes, with the Eureka being the beacon on the ground and the Rebecca unit attached to the plane.

As the war progressed, Allied radars became more sophisticated and specialized, with self-contained radars (not requiring ground stations) carried in the aircraft. The British Oboe radar was carried by Mosquito aircraft acting as pathfinders for the main force. The planes were guided from two stations, called "Cat" and "Mouse." The distance from the aircraft to the target was indicated by signals of dots (short) and dashes (long), indicating when to drop the bombs.

The downward-looking H2S radar had a transmitter-receiver with rotating antennas. Reflections from the ground showed as blips on a screen in the plane's cockpit, providing the flight crews with topographical information. Monica, introduced in 1943, was a back-looking radar that warned the bombers of approaching German night fighters. Monica, however, had difficulty distinguishing between enemy and friendly aircraft.

The Allies also developed passive radar detection systems, which detected transmissions from German radars, but did not emit any signal of their own. Boozer was a system that detected both ground-based and aerial intercept radars. Indicator lamps inside the cockpit used yellow lights to warn the crews of AI radar from night fighters, and red lights to warn of detection from ground-based defenses.

Although German radar research was less organized than the Allies', they were the first to introduce an operational radar directional system, the Knickebein (Crooked Leg). By 1939, the Germans had their own long-range, ground-based detection radar called Freya. It was designed with more naval applications than the British system. Freya's main problem was that it was not very accurate in determining altitudes. The Germans then supplemented the Freyas with shorter range Würzburg radars. These two systems became the mainstay of the Kammhuber Line (q.v.).

AI radar systems carried by German night fighters included the Fu-220 Lichtenstein and the Neptun. The later versions of the highly effective Lichtenstein had a range of about five kilometers, projecting its waves in a conical pattern 60 degrees right, left, above, and below the nose of the fighter. The Neptun was a rear-looking radar designed to warn the German night fighters of approaching night-fighting Mosquitoes accompanying the RAF bombers. The sophisticated Neptun displayed a target's range, azimuth, and altitude on a single screen.

The Germans also mounted passive detection systems on their night fighters. The FuG-350 Naxos was designed specifically to home onto the British H2S system. It had an effective range of about thirty miles. The Germans started using it in late 1943, but the British only became aware of its existence in July 1944 when a Ju-88 mistakenly landed in Britain. The FuG-227 Flensburg was designed to detect the British Monica. The Flensburg had an effective range of up to 130 miles.

In order to circumvent radar, both sides developed methods to confuse it. These countermeasures included dropping metal strips known as "window," or "chaff," and creating false blips on radar screens by altering transmission frequencies. Radar had its limitations. It was not able to detect airplanes obscured by hills or flying at extremely low altitudes.

Radar changed the nature of warfare at sea in World War II. As early as 1936, the Germans had fire control radar operational on the *Admiral Graf Spee*. The first naval action using radar was fought by the *Graf Spee* during the battle of the Platte River (q.v.) in September 1939. In December 1943, the battle of North Cape (q.v.) between the British Home Fleet and the *Scharnhorst* was the first sea battle fought entirely by means of radar plots.

While the Germans concentrated most of their efforts on fire control radars, they virtually ignored air-warning and surface search radars. This was a mistake the Allied navies did not make. By 1941, the Type 291 surface search radar was installed on British escort vessels, and soon proved invaluable against German U-boats that conducted the majority of their attacks on the surface at night. As early as November 1940, a British Sunderland Flying Boat equipped with ASV (air-sea vessel) radar detected a German U-boat.

The main application of radar in land warfare was the development of the proximity fuze (q.v.) for artillery. Originally developed for antiaircraft artillery, the fuze was equipped with a transmitter-receiver that beamed consecutive waves, triggering the round at its closest approach to the target. Near the end of the war these fuzes were used for field artillery in order to produce a perfect twenty-meter high air burst.

Radar helped the Allies defeat Germany by alerting defense forces of eminent attacks. It also served as an offensive weapon, providing navigation information, pinpointing enemy targets, and directing bombs to their detonation points. Radar today has become the basis of all modern military defense systems throughout the world. It also has benefited civilian spheres by assisting in such daily activities as course plotting for ships and aircraft, and in meteorology.

Elizabeth D. Schafer

Additional Reading
Fisher, David E., *A Race on the Edge of Time: Radar—the Decisive Weapon of World War II* (1988).
Guerlac, Henry E., *Radar in World War II* (1987).
Jones, R.V., *The Wizard War* (1978).

Rockets, British

During World War II, Dr. Isaac Lubbock suggested to the British government that a solid-fuel rocket should be developed for cross-channel bombardment, but his idea was dismissed and he was told to concentrate on liquid propellants. By 1942, he had developed liquid propellant engines, but they were not harnessed to a weapon system and he thereafter was employed primarily to monitor German designs.

The British did, however, maintain an interest in solid-fuel designs, and produced a number of important tactical battlefield systems. Research at first focused on antiaircraft weapons, and by 1939, more than 2,000 rounds of a 3-inch rocket had been test-fired under the direction of A.D. Crow. By 1941, the weapon, designated UP-3, was capable of intercepting aircraft at a height of 21,000 feet, and by 1942, 5,800 nine-barrelled UP-3 launchers were deployed. The UP-3 was used to supplement the fire of guns and proved effective in deterring low-level attackers. By 1944, a larger rocket, called Stooge, had been developed to counter faster aircraft. It had a speed of more than 480 mph, a range of up to 13,000 meters, and contained a radio guidance system in its nose.

By 1942, the British also had developed a 5-inch rocket that could be fired from a portable frame or from a truck, six at a time. With a range of about 3,000 meters, it was intended to be a short-range battlefield system, but was seldom used. Development of the system was taken up by the Royal Navy in 1943 and its range was increased to about 8,000 meters. It was mounted on specially designed landing craft, tank (rocket)—LCT(R)—vessels, from which 800 rockets could be fired in about thirty seconds. This proved highly successful in the Mediterranean and it was also used in October and November 1944 for the assault on Walcheren (see Scheldt). These successes rekindled the army's interest. A new mount, named Land Mattress, was designed for the back of a truck, allowing rockets to be fired in salvoes of thirty. The system was used successfully in northwest Europe in 1944 and 1945, most notably at Venlo and Breda. A battery could cover an area 800 by 800 meters, but was less accurate than a gun battery. After the operation at Venlo on 3 December 1944, British XII Corps recorded that the effect of the system was out of all proportion to the size of the firing unit, and that it should be made available to support all corps. It was never produced in sufficient numbers to make a major impact, however. A single-round projector, called Lilo, was also developed to counter Japanese bunker positions in the Far East, but it too was never mass-produced.

The British took a keen interest in German long-range rocket development from 1943–1945. The British efforts were assisted by the recovery of two errant V-2s (see Missiles, Guided), one of which had fallen in Sweden and the other in Poland. The remnants of these were assembled into a virtually complete rocket, but it was not until the end of the war, and the capture of the scientists behind Germany's rocket program, that the technology of these weapons was fully understood.

The British had neglected rocket design before the outbreak of the war. They did appreciate that rockets could be effective in the air, on the ground, and at sea, and they produced some effective weapons, but with resources stretched to the limit to produce proven systems, they did not have the means to develop and exploit the new technology once the war started.

Jonathan B.A. Bailey

(Refer to table on page 1077)

Additional Reading
Bailey, J.B.A., *Field Artillery and Firepower* (1989).

Baker, David, *The Rocket: History and Development of Rocket and Missile Technology* (1978).
Chamberlain, Peter, and Terry Gander, *Mortars and Rockets* (1975).

Rockets, German

Advances in propellant technology during World War I enabled German scientists to produce large-grain, slow-burning propellant, suitable for use in rockets. As a result, all three of the German military services set up programs in the 1930s to develop rockets.

The army set up its research facility at Kummersdorf-West in 1932. That establishment was responsible for coordinating rocket research all over the *Reich*. It was led by Captain Walter Dornberger (q.v.), who remained in charge until 1945 (by which time he had become a major general). He gathered under him a team of outstanding scientists, such as Wernher von Braun (q.v.), Walter Riedel, Heinrich Gruenow, and Walter Thiel. Together, they were responsible for the development of solid-fuel artillery rockets and long-range, liquid-fuel rockets (see Missiles, Guided).

During the 1930s, the German Army produced 15cm and 28/32cm rockets that were accepted into service in 1940. The 15cm *Wurfgranate* 41 (15cm Wgr-41) was an artillery missile designed to saturate an area with high explosive (HE), smoke, or chemical agents. It was spin-stabilized and designed to detonate above the ground as the nose struck the target. It was fired electrically in a ripple from the 15cm *Nebelwerfer* 41 (15cm NbW-41), which consisted of six tubes mounted on a simple two-wheeled carriage. The system left a clear firing signature and it was essential to bring it out of action quickly after firing. Although the system was primarily intended to provide tactical smoke screens (hence those manning it were called *Nebeltruppen*—Smoke Troops), it was in practice more often used to deliver HE. It was first used on the eastern front in 1941 and in North Africa (q.v.) by 1942. They proved effective weapons, not least because of the effect on morale of their shock and blast.

The 28/32cm rockets, which also entered service in 1940, shared the same motor but carried different warheads. The 28cm *Wurfkörper Spreng* (28cm Wk Spr) had a large HE warhead, while the 32cm Wk Fl was an incendiary. The rockets could be fired directly from their crates, or from a frame carrying four crates. They could also be fired from a two-wheeled trailer that carried six rockets. These systems were deemed to lack the mobility required for the support of *Panzer* formations, and in late 1940, a half-track, the *schwere Wurfrahmen 40* (sWuR-40), was produced. It could fire six rockets and proved highly successful, earning the nickname *"Stuka-zu-Fuss"* (Foot Stukas). A 21cm rocket, the 21cm Wgr-42, was produced in 1941–1942. It was a more advanced system with a range of 10,500 meters. It had an HE warhead and was also fired from a trailer. A 30cm rocket, the 30cm *Wurfkörper* 42, entered service in 1942.

Unlike Allied rockets, which used fin-stabilization, German rockets were spin-stabilized. This was a more effective method, but was technically more difficult to achieve. In 1941, the Germans encountered Soviet rockets, which were easy to produce and easy to launch from rails. The Germans wondered if they had selected the best method, but by that time their own production lines were in full flow. A disagreement emerged between the SS (q.v.) and the army, with the former favoring the Soviet rocket and setting up factories in Germany to produce them privately. In March 1944, Chancellor Adolf Hitler (q.v.) had to intervene personally on behalf of the army to prevent the SS equipment being foisted on it. By the end of the war, however, the German army had come to admit that the spin technology was too expensive and difficult to produce.

The most advanced solid-fuel rocket produced by the Germans was the RSpr 4831, *Rheinbote*. It was a four-stage, unguided ballistic rocket with a range in excess of 120 miles, achieving a speed of Mach 5.5. More than 200 were fired in 1944 against Antwerp, but with a warhead of only about 90 pounds, it had limited military use. Development continued on the personal insistence of Hitler, despite advice to the contrary from General Dornberger.

The Germans also developed a number of specialized rockets. In 1941, they produced the 7.3cm *Propagandagranate* 41 for dispensing propaganda leaflets. By the end of the war they had developed a 38cm rocket mounted on top of a PzKpfw-VI Tiger tank, designed to demolish strong points during street fighting.

Early rocket designs were intended for an antiaircraft role, but they achieved only limited success. The Hecht and Feuerlilie ground-to-air rockets were developed but never entered service. It was not until 1945 that the RZ-73 was used in the air defense of Berlin. A shoulder-launched *Luftfaust* was in production by the end of the war, but never entered service. The Germans also experimented with several designs for liquid-fueled guided missiles. In the closing months of the war, however, all resources were diverted to the V-2 project.

Jonathan B.A. Bailey

(Refer to table on page 1078)

Additional Reading

Baker, David, *The Rocket: History and Development of Rocket and Missile Technology* (1978).

Ford, Brian, *German Secret Weapons: Blueprint for Mars* (1969).

Gander, Terry, and Peter Chamberlain, *Small Arms, Artillery, and Special Weapons of the Third Reich* (1978).

Rockets, Soviet

The Soviets set up a research laboratory to study rocket propulsion in 1921. By 1931, research was progressing on booster rockets for aircraft, solid-propellant rockets, and liquid-propellant rocket motors. In 1932, military research was started at the Gas Dynamic Laboratory at Leningrad, and by 1937, the Soviets had produced the ORM-65 motor, which could have been used to power a rocket similar to the German V-1. Project 212, a flying bomb powered by the ORM-65, was flown in 1939, but it never came into service.

By 1938, the Soviet Union was committed to a massive armaments buildup to rival Germany's, but although the Soviets made great progress in developing the technology for long-range, liquid-propelled rockets, the military emphasis switched to smaller solid-propellant weapons. The German invasion reinforced that trend, as all resources were harnessed to produce systems of immediate military use.

Soviet rocket research was shrouded in mystery, with Soviet launchers even manned by police or NKVD (q.v.) troops. The obsession with secrecy meant that few were aware of Soviet interest in the subject, and even today little is known of the early Soviet work.

In June 1941, the Soviets began production of the BM-13, Katyusha multiple rocket launcher. Known as the "Stalin Organ," original work on the design was started by B.S. Petrapovlovsky. On his death in 1935, it was taken up by Andre Kostikov, and for a time the system was known as the "Kostikov Gun." The BM-13 could fire a ripple salvo of sixteen fin-stabilized 132mm rockets from rails on the back of a truck. The entire system could be reloaded in six to ten minutes. It was first used on 15 July 1941 at Orszy and came to be greatly respected by the Germans, who even made copies of it. It normally carried a high explosive (HE) warhead, but fragmentation warheads were also made, as were leaflet-carrying rounds.

Numerous vehicles were eventually used to carry the system, including Lend-Lease (q.v.) trucks, and even tanks. The rocket was very similar to the British UP-3 and the U.S. 4.5-inch M-8 rocket. It proved the basis for a series of successful weapons for use on land and sea and in the air. The success of the weapon led to the introduction of 300mm and 310mm rockets shortly afterward.

By the end of 1941, the Soviets were using an air-to-ground rocket, the 82mm RS-82, to attack German troops. It had been tested in 1937 and became a standard armament for Soviet fighters throughout the war. Aircraft carried three or four RS-82 rockets under each wing. In contrast to other air forces, Soviet fighters carried these in preference to bombs. A variant, the RBS-82, was fitted to bombers, and a 132mm armor-piercing version, the ROFS-132, was used to attack hardened targets.

Experiments continued with liquid propulsion as a means of powering conventional aircraft and gliders, culminating in designs for a rocket-powered aircraft, the BI-1, intended as an interceptor outpacing German opponents. Test flights were conducted in May 1942, but the aircraft suffered from short range and low endurance. It crashed on its third flight and the project was abandoned.

The Soviets followed German rocket research as closely as they could and made elaborate plans to exploit the technological windfall that was expected to come to them with victory. When the Soviet Nineteenth Army occupied Peenemünde, however, it found little of value; the research facilities having been evacuated to Nordhausen in the Harz Mountains. The Soviets soon appreciated the scale of German research and production techniques, and in the postwar era they shifted their emphasis once more to liquid-propelled rockets.

The Soviet Union's greatest contribution to rocketry was the development of rugged, solid-propellant systems, which became the mainstay of Soviet fighter aircraft armament. They also provided the weight of fire and shock effect that characterized the artillery bombardments, which the Soviets credited with winning the ground war. After 1945, ground-to-ground rocket systems were largely ignored by Western armies. It was not until the 1980s that their successors re-emerged in the West, carrying hi-tech warheads,

to provide the weight of firepower at long range that their Soviet predecessors had been designed to deliver in World War II.

Jonathan B.A. Bailey

(Refer to table on page 1079)

Additional Reading
Baker, David, *The Rocket: History and Development of Rocket and Missile Technology* (1978).
Chamberlain, Peter, and Terry Gander, *Mortars and Rockets* (1975).

Rockets, U.S.

No specific date can be discovered for the invention of rockets. Some authorities hold that the Chinese developed the first practical rockets for military use around 1232. What is certain is they were known for several centuries and were used in combat during the Napoleonic Wars and the War of 1812 (hence the reference in the *Star-Spangled Banner* to "the rockets' red glare").

During World War II, rockets were a form of "unguided" missile used as signals and weapons. They were inexpensive, lightweight, and relatively effective for use by land, air, and naval forces.

The work of Dr. Robert H. Goddard underlies all modern development of rocketry and space flight. A rocket is larger and heavier than a gun-fired projectile of equivalent explosive power. The rocket lacks recoil, which makes it ideal as an aircraft weapon for air-to-air or air-to-ground combat.

The Soviets were the first of the World War II Allies to show interest in rockets. They developed an 82mm rocket carrying a 6.5-pound high explosive warhead, launched from a 2.5-ton truck bed, with a range of 5,500 meters. The weapon was manned by NKVD (q.v.) troops to keep it secret. Later, a 132mm version, carrying a ninety-three pound warhead, entered Soviet service.

Beginning in the 1930s, the Germans developed an ingenious rocket design that carried the propulsion in the nose and the explosive charge in the rear. Other advanced versions were developed but were not used until the Russian campaign. The Germans made great progress on rockets during the war, and by 1945, they had a lead of approximately ten years over all other nations as a result of experimental work at Peenemünde. In the U.S. little work was done on rockets until 1940, when research was started on a spin-stabilized rocket

T-34 rocket launcher mounted on a Sherman tank, capable of firing 60 4.5-inch rockets. (IWM EA 56517)

carrying the warhead in the nose and the engine in the tail. The engine was vented through rings of angled, short tubes with constricted necks, creating pressure, thrust, and spinning action to power and stabilize the rocket in flight. Other rockets were generally fired from a tube or rail-type launcher.

The United States also adapted rockets for firing from airplanes. Lacking precision, rockets could not be used for close support of ground troops, but they were valuable for attacking ground or water targets where better accuracy was required than bombs could provide. Proximity fuzes (q.v.) were developed for use with aerial rockets. This gave airplanes much greater gunnery power than was provided by conventional guns.

The truck-mounted T-27 was one of the earliest U.S multiple rocket launchers of the war. It fired eight 4.5-inch M-8 rockets. The T-34 "Calliope" was a sixty-tube launcher mounted atop a Sherman tank. It fired its rockets independently or in salvos. Its use did not affect the tank's other functions. The M-17 rocket launcher, which also was mounted on a tank, fired twenty 7.2-inch rockets. Originally, the M-17 fired the T-37 rocket,

which was directly adopted from the navy's anti-submarine "Hedgehog," and had only a very short range. Later, the M-17 was used to launch the longer-range T-57 and M-25 rockets. The tank-mounted launchers could not traverse, but could be elevated from +45 to -5 degrees.

U.S. fighter aircraft employed five-inch rockets with a fifty-pound explosive warhead, which was particularly effective against ground targets. A later version, designated HVAR (high-velocity aircraft rocket), was popularly referred to as the "Holy Moses." Near the end of the war, the U.S. Navy developed a 298.5mm aircraft rocket, popularly referred to as "Tiny Tim." It carried a potent 150-pound warhead for use against ground targets.

Paul J. Rose

(Refer to table on page 1080)

Additional Reading

Emme, Eugene M. (ed.), *The History of Rocket Technology* (1964).
Sutton, George P., *Rocket Propulsion Elements: An Introduction to the Engineering of Rockets*, 3rd ed. (1963).

Section IV-R
Technical Data Tables of
Weapons and Equipment

British Rocket Artillery

Rockets

Model	UP-3	Land Mattress
Caliber	3-inch	5-inch
Year in Service	1939	1944
Maximum Range (meters)	3,700	8,000
Rocket Weight (pounds)	54	67

Rocket Launchers

Model	No. 1, Mk-I	No. 2, Mk-I	No. 4, Mk-I	No. 6, Mk-I	No. 8, Mk-I
Launcher Type	Rail	Rail	Rail	Rail	Barrel
Year in Service	1940	1940	1941	1944	1945
Number of Rockets	1	2	9	20	30
Type of Rockets	UP-3	UP-3	UP-3	UP-3	Land Mattress

German Rocket Artillery

Rockets

Model	15cm Wgr-41	RSpr 4831	21cm Wgr-42	28cm Wk Spr	30cm Wk-42	32cm Wk Fl
Caliber	150mm	190mm	210mm	280mm	300mm	320mm
Year in Service	1940	1942	1942	1940	1942	1940
Maximum Range (meters)	6,900	634,000	10,500	1,900	4,600	2,200
Rocket Weight (pounds)	75	3,773	248	189	280	174

Rocket Launchers

Model	15cm NbW-41	15cm PzW-42	21cm NbW-42	28/32cm NbW-41	28/32cm sWuR-40	30cm NbW-42
Launcher Type	Towed	Half-track Mounted	Towed	Towed	Half-track Mounted	Towed
Year in Service	1941	1942	1942	1941	1942	1942
Number of Rockets	6	10	5	6	6	6
Type of Rockets	150mm	150mm	210mm	280/320mm	280/320mm	300mm

Soviet Rocket Artillery

Rockets

Model	RS-82	M-13	M-30
Caliber	82mm	132mm	300mm
Year in Service	1941	1941	1942
Maximum Range (meters)	5,500	8,500	4,320
Rocket Weight (pounds)	17.6	93.5	158.4

Rocket Launchers

Model	BM-13 Katyusha	BM 31–12	M-8	M-30
Launcher Type	Truck Mounted	Truck Mounted	Truck or Ground Mounted	Ground Rack
Year in Service	1941	1942	1941	1942
Number of Rockets	16	12	36	4
Type of Rockets	M-13 132mm	M-30 300mm	RS-82 82mm	M-30 300mm

U.S. Rocket Artillery

Rockets

Model	M-8	M-16	T-37	T-57	M-25*
Caliber	4.5-in	4.5-in	7.2-in	7.2-in	7.2-in
Year in Service	1943	1945	1944	1945	1945
Maximum Range (meters)	3,600	5,250	230	1,200	3,430
Rocket Weight (pounds)	38.5	42.5	61	70	52

*Smoke warhead only

Rocket Launchers

Model	M-17	T-34 Calliope	T-27	T-66	M-12*
Launcher Type	M-4A3 Tank Mounted	M-4A3 Tank Mounted	Truck Mounted	Towed	Tripod
Year in Service	1944	1944	1943	1945	1943
Number of Rockets	20	60	8	24	1
Type of Rockets	T-37, T-57 M-25	M-8	M-8	M-16	M-8

*Expendable

S

Signals Equipment
See COMMUNICATIONS EQUIPMENT

Sonar

The submarine's success in World War I prompted all the major naval powers to develop antisubmarine detection devices. The earliest of the detection devices was the hydrophone, an underwater listening device installed below a ship's waterline. Unfortunately, although the hydrophone gave the direction to the submarine's location, it could not determine range. Only an active echo-ranging system could provide that, and every major fleet except that of the Soviet Union pursued the development of such a system during the interwar period. By 1937, all but the Soviet and Italian Navies had working echo-ranging sound equipment. The antisubmarine capabilities of those two navies suffered accordingly.

The British called the system ASDIC (Allied Submarine Detection Investigation Committee), while the Americans dubbed it sonar, an acronym for sound navigation and ranging. The Germans called their system *S-Gerät* (Sound Device). Sonar, as it is now almost universally known, was housed in a streamlined, retractable dome on the ship's bottom and was used in one of two different ways. It could be operated passively, as a hydrophone to detect a submarine's propulsion noise; or it could be operated actively, to transmit a sound wave to echo off the submarine. The active mode was that most commonly used by Allied naval forces because it gave a better detection range than passive listening, and more importantly, provided an instantly accurate target position (bearing and range). Moreover, because of the Doppler effect, the echo reached the operator with varying degrees of pitch, which gave the operator an idea of the

target's course and relative speed, vital information for a successful attack. Axis navies preferred to use their hydrophones, which were far superior to Allied ones, to detect enemy submarines. They only used active sonar when they felt submarines were in the immediate vicinity.

The British and U.S. Navies were the first to install sonar on their ships. The Royal Navy installed the first ASDIC on the patrol craft of the 1st Antisubmarine Flotilla in 1922, and continued development throughout the interwar period. The U.S. installed sonar on the ships of Destroyer Division 20 and on two submarines in 1934. The U.S. Navy also installed it on the old four-stack destroyers when they were recommissioned in 1939. By September 1939, the U.S. had about sixty old and new destroyers fitted with the device, while the Royal Navy had ASDIC on 165 destroyers and fifty-four other craft. Germany began installing *S-Gerät* on its submarines in 1937, but did not install it on a surface ship until 1939. France also developed a sonar by that time, but it was not ready for operational service until after the German invasion. Italy did not develop its own sonar until 1943, relying instead on German sonars provided from late 1941 on.

Using sonar required a high degree of training. Both the U.S. and Royal Navies established schools to train their operators, while their Axis counterparts learned "on the job." The Allies also established strict mental and physical requirements for their operators, which paid dividends in reduced training time and improved operator efficiency. Allied sonar equipment also facilitated operator performance by providing a persistence scope presentation and strip chart recorder, which recorded the target's position relative to the ship. This equipment gave the operator more time to analyze his sound data, as well as enabling him to determine the submarine's depth and the best time to drop depth charges.

Sonar equipment and its trained operators were a vital component of the antisubmarine warfare effort in World War II. This was particularly true for the Allies, who faced a greater underwater threat; but the Italo-German effort to supply their armies in Africa was greatly hindered by the Italian Navy's lack of sonars and skilled operators. Still, sonar was not a panacea. Sonar operators often mistook schools of fish, whales, wrecks, even coral reefs, for submarines. Echoes from these could be distinguished from those from submarines only with extreme concentration and experience. As a countermeasure, submarines often hid below thermal layers—areas of water with a different temperature from the water on the surface. After 1941, German submarines often employed false echo generators, called *Pillenwerfer,* and other deceptive tactics to fool Allied sonar operators. The extensive German effort to defeat Allied sonars testifies to its effectiveness and vital importance in the Battle of the Atlantic (q.v.).

Robert F. Pace
Carl O. Schuster

Additional Reading

Keegan, John, *The Price of Admiralty* (1989).
Hackman, Willem, *Seek and Strike* (1984).
Morison, Samuel Eliot, *The Battle of the Atlantic: History of United States Naval Operations in World War II,* Vol. 1 (1947).

Submarines, British

According to British Prime Minister Winston S. Churchill (q.v.), the achievements of British submarines during World War II can be considered as unsurpassed by those of any other service, land, sea, or air. This sentiment was more an acknowledgment of the gallantry of the British submariners than of their successes against the enemy. In fact, Great Britain was the world's greatest naval power at the start of the war, but from the very beginning of submarine warfare, the Royal Navy had considered it more of a nuisance weapon than anything else.

At the end of the nineteenth century, torpedoes and submarines were regarded in most Royal Navy circles as distinctly "un-British," because of their stealthy nature. British diplomacy, therefore, had continuously tried to limit, if not forbid, the use of submarines in every disarmament conference convened, but always with little results. Thus the Admiralty, while suspecting that the submarine would never be a truly strategic weapon, gave some attention to its development and generally procured the most modern versions available for the fleet.

During World War I, the Royal Navy built several so-called strategic models. Among them were the big and speedy, but dangerous and ineffective, steam turbine-driven K-class, also called fleet submarines. The last three of this class were converted to diesel-driven monitor submarines, the M-class, armed with huge twelve-inch pre-dreadnought vintage guns. When this idea proved unworkable, these three boats became the subjects of many experiments during their remaining careers.

During the 1920s, after the wholesale demobilizing and scrapping of large numbers of naval vessels that followed the end of the war, Great Britain maintained a constant number of about sixty submarines in service. As newer models were developed, they phased out the war-vintage boats and replaced them with the more advanced types. These included a coastal, an oceanic, a minelayer, and a new model fleet submarine.

The first new type of craft were the oceanic O-class, developed from the World War I–era L-class. In order to operate more effectively in the Pacific Ocean, they had more range than their predecessors. They were not, however, a great success. The most remarkable fact about the O-class was that the HMS *Oberon,* the first of the class, was also the first submarine to carry the new ASDIC submarine detection device, today better known as sonar (q.v.). The boats of the O-class suffered from several technical problems, including oil leakage from fuel tanks.

The O-class was followed by the P-class, the R-class, the cruiser (or fleet) submarines, the River-class, and the Porpoise-class. This last class represented the last specially built minelayer submarines. They carried the mines on rails on a deck built between the outer hull and the pressure hull, and delivered them through a large porthole in the stern. All submarines after them launched mines from torpedo tubes. Five of the six Porpoise-class submarines built were lost during World War II. One of them, the HMS *Seal,* was the only British submarine captured by the Germans. From 1940, it fought nearly the whole war as the *U-B,* flying the *swastika.*

Three classes developed during the 1930s resulted in a large number of craft that bore the brunt of World War II operations: the S-class, the T-class, and the U-class. The HMS *Swordfish,* the first S, was launched in 1931—roughly in the same period the *Porpoise* was developed. Simplicity was the key to the *Swordfish* design. Medium-sized, she and her thirteen sisters built between 1932 and 1938 were so successful they were followed during the war by thirty-seven more S-class boats built almost without modification.

The T-class was perhaps the single greatest success of the Admiralty's naval architects in the submarine field. The first boat of this class, the HMS *Triton,* was commissioned in December 1938, and was followed by fifty-one others. Classified as "patrol submarines," they were sturdy and handy boats with good range and a strong underwater armament of ten or eleven torpedo tubes. The second unit in the class, the HMS *Thetis,* sank in the River Mersey while running her trials in 1938. The unsuccessful attempts to rescue her ill-fated crew made worldwide headlines. The same boat, raised and renamed the HMS *Thunderbolt,* was lost again in 1943.

The small coastal U-class initially was developed only as unarmed training submarines to replace the H-class boats, but as the political situation worsened at the approach of the war, they were converted to fighting craft. Even though they lacked the Royal Navy's standards for range, they were very successful in the Mediterranean, proving themselves more capable than their larger sisters (because of their sturdiness) of withstanding severe depth-charging. Simple, quick to build, and inexpensive, the Us (and later the Vs) were produced in large numbers with very few modifications.

At the outbreak of the war, the Royal Navy had about a dozen old and outdated training submarines in service, about twenty old but still capable boats, and not more than twenty first-line boats. The Admiralty immediately decided to increase the rate of construction of the most current models, without sacrificing the time required to introduce improvements. The only exception to this policy was the introduction of a new A-class, especially designed to intercept the virtually unescorted (and therefore vulnerable) Japanese merchant traffic. The As were large, fast, had good range, and were heavily armed, but they were not as simple and handy as the Ts. Only two A-class boats were completed before the end of the war.

In September 1939, all British submarines were designated with a pennant number (for optical recognition) preceded by the class letter. In 1940 the system was changed. All prewar submarines were designated with the letter N followed by a two-digit number. All British submarines built during the war were designated by the letter P with a two- or three-digit number. At the same time the decision was made to no longer give names to the war-built boats, just the pennant number. This policy remained in force up through early 1943, when all British submarines built after 1939 were given names.

On the outbreak of World War II, most British submarines deployed outside the immediate theater of war were quickly recalled to the North Sea. The first boat to see action was the HMS *Spearfish,* which managed to dodge a torpedo salvo from a German U-boat only four minutes after the

The X-25, *a midget submarine of the type used to attack the* Tirpitz. *(IWM A 22903)*

official start of the war. On 20 November 1939, the HMS *Sturgeon,* operating in the Skagerrak, an arm of the North Sea, became the first boat to sink an enemy vessel, a small antisubmarine craft. It was not until the 1940 Norway campaign that British submarines produced significant results, sinking twenty-one German naval and merchant ships, including the light cruiser *Karlsruhe.* During the course of the war only a few German vessels were sunk by British submarines in the northern theater. For the most part, the Germans managed to close the Baltic to the British, and very few noteworthy targets were to be found along the North Sea's European coasts. The Mediterranean, therefore, became the British submariners' primary strategic theater of the war, particularly after Italy's entry into the conflict made it the only sector where Axis merchant traffic could be found in any numbers. Italy's primary line of communications with its army in Lybia was by sea, and British submarines attacked it mercilessly.

The Royal Navy enjoyed significant technological advantages over its enemy. The Italian Navy had no radar, no sonar before 1942, almost no night-fighting capability, and very poor coordination with the Italian Air Force. Thus many Italian vessels went to the bottom at the hands of British submarines. It was not, however, entirely a one-way struggle. British submarines in the Mediterranean also suffered a high casualty rate. In just thirty-eight months of operations there, the British lost forty-five boats out of a total loss of seventy-five for all theaters for the entire war. By comparison, they lost only three submarines to the Japanese in the Indian and Pacific Oceans.

During the war several navies-in-exile operated their submarines under the control of the Royal Navy. Although they were manned by their own crews and sailed under their own national flags, the Royal Navy was effectively reinforced by five Polish, four Norwegian, seventeen Dutch, eighteen Free French, one Yugoslav, and eight Greek boats. After September 1943, twelve Italian submarines also operated under the control of their former enemies.

Other important underwater weapons used by the Royal Navy during the war included manned torpedoes and midget submarines. The British manned torpedoes (dubbed "Chariots") were, with minor improvements, copies of Italian models captured at Gibraltar. The Italian manned torpedos sank several British vessels, including the battleships HMS *Queen Elizabeth* and HMS *Valiant* in Alexandria (q.v.). The British Chariots, on the other hand, had only limited success in the

Mediterranean, usually against ships moored in dock for repairs.

The British enjoyed greater success with their midget submarines (called "X-craft"). Instead of torpedoes, these small boats placed huge explosive charges under the keels of moored vessels. Their major success (with the help of ULTRA intercepts) was the mining of the German battleship *Tirpitz.* Incapacitated by the attack, the *Tirpitz* became an easy target for bombers.

During World War II, British submarines sank 493 merchant and 169 naval vessels, including thirty-five Axis submarines. They also damaged 109 merchant and fifty-five naval vessels. Most of these victories were achieved in the Mediterranean (361 merchant vessels sunk, as opposed to eighty-four in North Sea and the Atlantic). The Royal Navy, in turn, lost seventy-five submarines out of about 215 deployed in actual combat operations. Close to 3,500 men were lost with their boats. It was to their bravery that Churchill dedicated his words.

Francesco Fatutta

(Refer to tables on pages 1095–1096)

Additional Reading
Lenton, H.T., *British Submarines* (1973).
Lipscomb, F.W., *The British Submarine* (1975).
Poolman, Kenneth, *Allied Submarines of World War II* (1990).

Submarines, German

On 29 June 1935, the Third *Reich's Kriegsmarine* commissioned the *U-1* in Kiel, Germany's first new U-boat in seventeen years. The Versailles Treaty (q.v.) had forbidden Germany to have submarines, but the Anglo-German Naval Agreement of 1935 (q.v.) with Great Britain allowed 45 percent of the German fleet to consist of submarines. The new U-1 was only a small 354-ton coastal craft, derived from the U-BII Series of World War I.

By 3 September 1939, Germany had fifty-six submarines commissioned, some thirty under construction, and many more in planning. Fortunately for the Allies, *Kriegsmarine* commander Admiral Erich Raeder (q.v.) froze submarine design and research shortly after the war started and did not change his decision until late 1942. By then it was too late, and German U-boats fought most of World War II with submarine designs and propulsion systems little different from those of World War I.

Type VIIb U-boat U-52. (IWM HU 1008)

The majority of German U-boats were of four types. Types I and IX were oceangoing boats with minelaying capabilities. The Type II was coastal, and the Type VII was a medium-sized oceanic boat. The Type VII and Type IX accounted for 70 percent of the entire World War II U-boat fleet. Of the 1,240 U-boats completed (including experimental models), 685 were Type VII and 187 were Type IX. The Germans also built ten Type XIV supply submarines, nicknamed *Milch Kühe* (milk cows), that gave operational groups of U-boats greater range and on-station time. A type of cruiser submarine was planned but never built because it did not fit the envisaged tactics.

The German building program was influenced greatly by the submarine warfare theories of the chief of the submarine branch of the German Navy, then Captain Karl Dönitz (q.v.). Having had substantial submarine experience during World War I, Dönitz was convinced that in a future conflict against Great Britain, German submarines should primarily target merchant vessels in order to sever the maritime routes, the so-called bridge of ships across the Atlantic that would provide Great Britain with vital supplies. To do this, German submarines had to attack convoys en masse, as "wolf packs," hunting on the surface at night as normal torpedo boats, and diving only for defensive measures. Such a system required radio direction from a single command and control center able to collect the needed information and transmit directions to the boats at sea. Big submarines did not fit in with these tactics because they dived too slowly and lacked maneuverability.

The execution of these tactics required a mass of U-boats in numbers sufficient to sink ships at a faster rate than the Allied shipyards could replace them. Admiral Raeder, however, only partially accepted Dönitz's ideas. As a result, the German Navy entered the war far short of the number of submarines it required.

The main effort of the German submarine campaign was the Battle of the Atlantic (q.v.). Although that battle lasted from the outbreak of the war right up to May 1945, the German Navy had lost it for all practical purposes by 1943. During the very early days of the campaign, U-boat operations were limited by their small numbers and by legal and political restrictions that inhibited their use. Perhaps the most spectacular U-boat exploit of the entire war came on 14 October 1939 when the *U-47*, under the command of Lieutenant Günther Prien (q.v.), penetrated the main British naval base at Scapa Flow (q.v.), sank the battleship HMS *Royal Oak*, and succeeded in making it back to Germany unscathed. Nonetheless, by the first months of 1940, the rate of Allied merchant ships sunk actually declined because many of the U-boats were committed to the Norway (q.v.) campaign. Torpedo (q.v.) malfunctions also limited U-boat success rates. Thus, by the end of April 1940, the loss rate for Allied merchant shipping was almost nil. But with the correction of the torpedo defects, the end of the Norway campaign, the acquisition of French Atlantic coast bases, and the increased numbers of new U-boats delivered, the *Kriegsmarine* was able to start the Battle of the Atlantic in earnest.

In November 1940, the Germans established a submarine command and control center in Paris, and the U-boats began night attacks against the Allied convoys. By April 1941, the wolf pack tactics were being employed on a large scale with great success. Throughout 1940 and 1941, the ratio of merchant ships sank to U-boats lost ran strongly in favor of the Germans, with peaks of more than sixty Allied ships lost for each submarine. The total tonnage sank in the early years grew exponentially: 103,544 gross register tons (grt) the last three months of 1939; 2,171,890 grt for 1941; and almost six million grt in 1942.

Despite this apparently successful trend, it

was only in 1941 that the German Navy finally reached the level of 300 operational U-boats originally considered necessary for successful application of the wolf pack strategy. In 1940, this might have been sufficient, but by 1941, the submarine countermeasures initiated by the Royal Navy and the RAF Coastal Command had been improved and refined. More escort vessels and aircraft with greater range were brought into use against the U-boats. The mass-produced Flower-class corvettes and Hunt-class destroyer escorts carried increasingly efficient sonar (q.v.) systems and depth charge launchers. After January 1941, aircraft like the Avro Anson, the Lockheed Hudson, the Short Sunderland, and the Consolidated Catalina and Liberator carried small but efficient radars that could detect targets and guide attacks by night and in foul weather. Thus, the German U-boats were increasingly compelled to attack their targets farther and farther from the western approaches to Britain. This, of course, made the U-boat task more difficult.

When the United States entered the war on 9 December 1941, everything changed. At that point the Battle of the Atlantic had almost brought Britain to its knees. Suddenly now, the U-boats had new and very profitable hunting fields on the east coast of the United States and in the Gulf of Mexico because the U.S. Navy was relatively unprepared for the new submarine warfare methods. In these sectors, the best results were obtained by the Type IX U-boats, with their torpedo capacity and range much greater than Type VIIs. But in the long run, the U.S. in the war meant that the huge American industrial capacity was now turned against Germany. For the U-boats, this meant a continuously growing capacity for the Allies to hunt and destroy them everywhere, plus an unceasingly growing number of merchant vessels to replace the lost ships.

Even as the tide started to shift away from the Germans in 1942, the U-boats achieved their highest success rates of the war with 1,094 merchant ships sunk. The peak came in November with 118 ships for 743,321 grt. By the end of 1942, the U-boats were a menace to Allied shipping from the Arctic Sea to South Africa to the Indian Ocean. Nonetheless, by the start of 1943, the Germans were starting to loose ground. By July, the Germans were losing U-boats faster than they were building them. These trends clearly indicated that the prewar U-boat designs were now obsolete against the new weapons and tactics used by the Allies—especially the new escort aircraft carriers. The *Kriegsmarine* tried to extend the effective operational lives of the old types by intro-

A crew from the USS Guadalcanal *prepares to take a German submarine under tow. The U-505, a Type IXc U-boat, is now on display at the Museum of Science and Industry in Chicago. (IWM NYF 71314)*

ducing new subsystems and upgrading old ones. They introduced the Metox radar range finder; the *Zaunkönig* acoustic torpedo, activated by the sound of the engines or screws of the target; and most importantly, the *Schnorchel,* which allowed a submerged U-boat to pull in air from the surface and remain submerged for long periods.

The new additions were not enough. As soon as a new device became operational, the Allies found the right countermeasures. Thus the *Kriegsmarine* was compelled to accelerate the development of the new types of boats. They had three basic types under development. The first operated on a closed-cycle diesel engine, in which the fuel burned using compressed oxygen stored in special tanks. It never reached operational status. The second type operated on the experimental Walter gas turbine, which exploited the chemical phenomena that highly compressed hydrogen dioxide in the presence of calcium permanganate released oxygen and a great quantity of heat, thereby allowing the combustion of almost any type of fuel. The initial experiments were promising, but this type of engine finally proved unsuitable for submarines because it was very noisy, not easily controllable, and used huge quantities of fuel.

The third developmental type, using a special streamlined hull and enlarged battery capacity, was a great success. Dubbed *Elektro-Boote* by the Germans, the key to the design was a new type of very light and high capacity battery that gave the electric motors an output equal to that of the diesel engines. This drive system, combined with the *Schnorchel* for the periscope-depth operation and the streamlined shape of the hulls, gave the new models a very high submerged speed, which made them almost impossible to track by the then current escort ships.

Two types of *Elektro-Boote* were actually commissioned. The Type XXI was oceangoing, the Type XXIII was coastal. These two types were the world's first modern conventional submarines. Every nonnuclear submarine built after World War II embodied the ideas and the technical solutions developed by their designers, the naval architects of the *Gluckauf Ingenierburo.* The construction of the Types XXI and XXIII was handled by *Organisation Todt* (q.v.), which was responsible for all submarine construction after 1941. About 230 of both types were commissioned.

The final war years were very hard for the *Kriegsmarine,* losing more U-boats than were commissioned. When Admiral Dönitz signed the armistice on 8 May 1945, 360 U-boats were still in commission and many more were still under various stages of construction by the collapsing shipyard industry. About 230 of the surviving U-boats were scuttled by their own crews. The remainder surrendered to Allied forces.

Besides the conventional submarines, the *Kriegsmarine* also developed small underwater craft and manned torpedoes similar to those of the Italians, British, and Japanese. Even though the technical solutions were often interesting and sometimes brilliant, the results obtained by the German midgets never compared with those of the Italian or British Navies. Their major recorded success was the sinking of the old Polish cruiser, the *Dragon,* and some landing vessels on the beaches of Normandy. Their boldest action would have been the planned but later canceled attack against the Russian battleship *Arkhangelsk* (Archangel) in the waters of Murmansk. These somewhat feeble efforts were among the last attempts made by the *Kriegsmarine* to use a weapon, the submarine, that just might have given Germany its greatest potential for winning World War II.

Francesco Fatutta

(Refer to tables on pages 1097–1099)

Additional Reading

Brennecke, Hans J., *The Hunters and the Hunted* (1958).
Dallies-Labourdette, Jean-Phillippe, *U-Boat, 1939–1945* (1996).
Mason, David, *U-Boat: The Secret Menace* (1968).
Raeder, Erich, *Struggle for the Sea* (1959).
Showell, J.P.M., *U-Boats Under the Swastika,* 2nd ed. (1987).

Submarines, Italian

Italy entered World War II with the world's second largest submarine fleet. Only the Soviet Union had a larger submersible force and the Royal Navy viewed both with great concern. The British even considered Italy's 100 submarines a more serious threat than Germany's small submarine force. Events were to prove those fears misplaced. Of the 115 boats in Italian service, most suffered from technical and mechanical deficiencies that inhibited their effective employment. The most serious of these were the unreliability of their engines and their poor underwater stability. These factors adversely affected the morale of the crews and their captains, and in the end, they prevented the Italian submarine fleet from achieving its mission.

Individual submarines, however, enjoyed notable successes. The Italian midget submarine force, in particular, set the tone for naval special warfare operations during the war (*see* 10th Light Flotilla, Italian).

The Italian submarine fleet had been designed to fight the last war. Some thirty Italian submarines served in the Battle of the Atlantic (q.v.), sinking approximately 500,000 tons of shipping there. The boats' superstructures were too large for them to conduct night surface attacks effectively. They also dived slowly, were very unstable once submerged, and maneuvered poorly underwater. They were too noisy to approach a convoy protected by any but the most lax of escorts. More significantly, the Italian submarines lacked fire control equipment to assist their captains in calculating torpedo attack angles. They had to judge the best aim point themselves. It is little wonder then, that only the most determined and skilled Italian submarine captains achieved any successes in the war.

Carl O. Schuster

(Refer to tables on pages 1100–1103)

Additional Reading

Fraccaroli, Aldo, *Italian Warships of World War II* (1968).
MacIntyre, Donald, *The Battle for the Mediterranean* (1964).
Van der Vat, Dan, *The Atlantic Campaign* (1988).

Submarines, Soviet

The Soviet Navy had the largest submarine force in the world in 1939, numbering more than 168 units. More than two-thirds of the force was stationed in European waters. By the time of the German invasion, the Soviets had 215 submarines in service and another 100 undergoing sea trials or in various stages of construction; an impressive force total. The poor quality of the units and disappointing performance of their crews, however, reflected the hurried nature of the Soviet submarine program. The Soviet submarine force suffered heavily as a result.

Nonetheless, Josef Stalin's (q.v.) efforts ensured that the Soviet Union entered the war with the newest, as well as the largest, submarine force in the world. All but a handful of units had been built since 1931. Construction centered around five classes of submarines from small coastal units to large *Kreyser* (cruiser) boats. Manning the boats

was a problem, however, since more than two-thirds of the navy's senior officers had been purged by 1939. Theoretically, a submarine commander was a graduate of a Soviet naval academy and had served four to five years in various positions on several submarines. Stalin's purges (q.v.) and the rapid expansion of the submarine force, however, made this impossible. This led to short-term expedients.

Experienced officers were drafted out of the merchant marine and given a quick course in submarines, followed by a short tour as an executive officer. Those who "qualified" were then given command. It virtually guaranteed a limited experience level and the Soviets attempted to compensate for this by assigning a "staff rider" to go out with new commanders on their first few cruises and periodically thereafter. The Soviets also established very restrictive rules on diving and the conduct of attacks, probably to prevent the commander from attempting more than his crew could handle. Combat gave the Soviets an intensive training crucible that ultimately provided them with a cadre of very experienced commanders by late 1944. It was a painful process, however, with losses far out of proportion to results.

Soviet prewar submarines were noteworthy for their unreliability, slow diving capability, and noisy machinery. The first post–World War I Soviet submarines were the Dekabrist, or D-class units. Commissioned between 1930 and 1932, they were medium-displacement, double-hull submarines derived from the tzarist-era B-class. The Ds were very unstable during diving and had a tendency for the quick-dive tank to open while submerged, with fatal consequences on at least one occasion. Only six boats were in service at war's start. The *D-1* was lost during a training accident in 1940, and the other five were stationed in the Baltic, where they primarily conducted supply missions. Only one D-class unit survived the war, and it did so in a damaged state.

The next units to enter service were the much smaller Malyutka, or M-class coastal submarines. The first boats of the class were slow and had a tendency to surface after firing their torpedoes, but these defects were corrected in subsequent units. Essentially an improved tzarist-era A-class design, the single-hull Ms were built in sections at Gorky and transported by rail to the shipyards in Leningrad, Nikolayev, and Vladivostok for completion. The Ms were the first Soviet units to use welded construction and were built in series' of approximately thirty boats, each series an improvement on its predecessors. They were fast diving, maneuverable, and relatively quiet. More than 100 Ms were built before and during the war, but losses (thirty-five) were heavy. Construction of the fifth series of the M-class continued throughout the mid-1950s, and the units remained in service until the middle of the 1960s.

The slightly larger SHCH (Shchuka)-class units were also inspired by the American Holland design, but were slightly larger. They were popular with their crews because of their easy handling, quick diving, and good speed. Approximately ninety were built in four successive series between 1933 and 1942. They saw service in all three western fleets and achieved some modest success. Of the eighty-eight units that saw service in the war, thirty-two were lost. The surviving boats remained in service until the mid-1950s.

The next units built were the Pravda, or P-class. The Ps were the first true oceangoing submarines built in the Soviet Union. Built in Leningrad between 1933 and 1937, these double-hulled units had good range, carried two 100mm guns, and were designed for surface combat. They were, however, an unfortunate design, with noisy and unreliable machinery. They also proved awkward and slow diving in service. Only three were built, and all were sunk by January 1943.

The K-class followed the P-class and were the largest Soviet submarines to see service in the war. The K design corrected most of the faults found in the P design, featuring increased speed, reliability, and range. Entering service in 1938, the Ks were intended for long-range operations against an enemy's sea lines of communications. Their size and complexity, however, made them very difficult to build under wartime conditions. Only thirteen were commissioned, of which five were sunk. They were equally divided between the Baltic and Northern Fleets.

The Leninets, or L-class units, were next in size. Built as a follow-on to the D-class, the Ls were more reliable, more stable, and carried more mines. They were evenly distributed between the Baltic and Black Sea Fleets, where they were employed primarily for minelaying. Construction of the Ls began in 1933, and twenty-four were built before the war's end. Of those, six were lost, mostly in German minefields.

The most successful Soviet submarine design to see service in the war was the Stalinets, or S-class. Designed with German assistance, the S-class was based on the German Type Ia U-boat, which saw service with the Spanish, Finnish, and Turkish Navies. These medium-displacement submarines were faster and stronger than their German prede-

cessor. They were well armed, relatively quiet, very reliable, and quite maneuverable. Only thirty-three were built and nearly half (fifteen) were lost by war's end. Nonetheless, the S-class saw extensive employment in all theaters and scored several of the few successes obtained by the Soviet submarines force.

The oldest group of Soviet submarines in service at war's start were the boats dating from World War I. The best of the group was the former British *L-55*, which was sunk by a Soviet destroyer in 1919 and recovered in 1928. The tzarist-era A- and B-class units (five each) were based on the American Holland design and were suitable only for training. The Soviets withdrew the *L-55* and B-class boats in 1940, converting them to battery-charging units. The A class remained in service and three were lost in combat.

About one-third of the Soviet Navy's submarines (fifty-five units) were stationed in the Baltic on 1 September 1939. Despite having first pick of submarines and crews, the Baltic Fleet Submarine Force failed to execute its first wartime mission— the covert sinking of the Soviet tanker *Metallist* to provide a justification for the Soviet invasion of Poland. The submarine *SHCH-303* missed, and the tanker had to be sunk by a Soviet torpedo boat. It was not an auspicious beginning, and the Soviet submarine force had not improved much by the Winter War (q.v.) with Finland. Operating in pairs, Soviet submarines gave their positions away by frequent communications, and managed to sink only one Finnish merchant ship, two neutrals, and a few small Finnish coastal craft.

The German invasion caught the Baltic Fleet with sixty-nine operational submarines. Of these, only thirty-seven were operationally ready and ten were on patrol. Losses were heavy and immediate. Of the units on patrol, four were sunk in the first three days of the war. Another eight Baltic Fleet submarines were lost by 29 June 1941. Other units had to be scuttled as German ground forces approached their bases. By September, the Baltic Fleet was blockaded within its base and incomplete units had to be evacuated to the Northern and Black Sea Fleets via the Soviet river and canal system.

The Black Sea and Northern Fleets had forty-four and fifteen operational submarines, respectively, on 22 June 1941. Both fleets had newly established shipyards in their areas, but only the Black Sea had any submarines under construction. Neither fleet made contact with Axis forces until mid-July and the resulting actions were inconclusive. Soviet losses in the Black Sea were confined to four units abandoned in the newly built and now overrun Nikolayev shipyard east of Odessa. The newly reestablished (in 1933) Northern Fleet had no submarines under construction, but received six new units from the Baltic Fleet in August. The Black Sea Fleet also received several units from the Baltic by early fall. Despite the reinforcements, however, neither of the fleets achieved any significant submarine successes.

By October 1941, the Soviets controlled only two fully functional shipyards—in Leningrad and Sevastopol—and they were under German air attack and artillery fire. As with his civilian industry, however, Stalin's submarine force benefited from his prewar planning for industrial dispersal. Shipyard workers were transferred to new shipyards such as the Severodvinsk Naval Shipyard near Archangel and the Krasnoye Sormovo Naval Shipyard in Gorky southeast of Moscow. These two shipyards teamed up to produce nearly fifty submarines between 1941 and 1945. The basic hulls were complete in Gorky and then transported to Severodvinsk for completion. It was a surprisingly innovative approach to a difficult construction problem.

The Soviets went on to produce fifty-seven new submarines during the war, as well as repairing damage to more than thirty others. Production was centered around five basic types: the K-, L-, SHCH-, S-, and M-classes. Refinements were added to new units and improvements made on units entering the yards for repairs. Two experimental submarines were launched during the war but only one was ever completed, the *M-401*. It used a closed cycle diesel for propulsion and was tested successfully in the Caspian Sea, but never saw operational service. A submerged stabilization system that enabled a submarine to hover at a given depth was also tested during the war and was used operationally in 1944. Other improvements noted on Soviet submarines included quieter propulsion, and better hydrophones and sonar. Despite testing a primitive snorkel-like device before the war, the Soviets did not pursue development of the snorkel, waiting instead until after the war to install a copy of the German *Schnorchel* on their units.

Although the Soviet submarine force achieved only limited results during the war, its efforts were not entirely without benefit. Soviet submarine crews pressed home their attacks in the face of heavy losses and often overwhelming odds. They got better as the war progressed and they attempted increasingly complex tactics, involving cooperation with surface units, fast patrol boats, and even aircraft. Although these new tactics were generally ineffective, they caused the Germans much concern, particularly in the final days of the war. If nothing else, they diverted German resources from other potential military endeavors. In that respect, perhaps, the Soviet submarine campaign was successful.

Carl O. Schuster

(Refer to table on page 1104)

Additional Reading

Meister, Jurg, *The Soviet Navy* (1972).
Polmar, Norman, *Submarines of the Russian and Soviet Navies, 1718–1990* (1990).
Ruge, Friedrich, *The Soviet Navy As Opponents* (1979).

Submarines, U.S.

The United States Navy ended World War I with a fleet of submarines constructed for operations along the North American continental shelf. While some of these boats had deployed to Europe during the war, they compared unfavorably with the German U-boats in range and armament. The 1920s were thus a period of reevaluation for the U.S. submarine force. Instead of being viewed as the outer defense of the United States, the submarine was recast in the role of an offensive weapon to carry the war to the enemy's doorstep—the most probable enemy being Japan. The U.S. Navy therefore adopted long-range, sustained fighting power, and good crew habitat as the characteristics for their submarine fleet.

The U.S. Navy constructed only three submarines in the 1920s, but during the 1930s, six different classes of submarines totaling thirty-two boats were built. An additional thirteen boats of three different classes entered service by the end of 1941. During World War II an additional 230 boats were added to the fleet. The average U.S. submarine displaced 1,500 tons surfaced, was 310 feet long, had a surface speed of twenty-one knots, a sustained submerged speed of four knots, and was armed with ten twenty-one-inch torpedo tubes carrying twenty-four torpedos total. The major prewar submarine bases were Portsmouth, New Hampshire; Colon, Canal Zone; Mare Island, California; Pearl Harbor, Hawaii; and Manila Bay, Philippines.

When war broke out in Europe in September 1939, the U.S. government remained aloof from the conflict. As the Nazi war machine gained control of Western Europe, the U.S. adopted a pro-British stance and started to shift naval units to the

Atlantic from the Pacific. Ships commissioned on the East Coast were held there. The only exceptions were the submarines, which sailed for the Pacific as soon as they were considered operationally ready. The majority of the new boats were based at Pearl Harbor and Manila, along with some World War I–era S-class boats. Older boats based at Panama as part of canal defense served as training boats for new submariners, or acted as targets for sonar (q.v.) training.

When Japan attacked Pearl Harbor on 7 December 1941, the U.S. Navy's submarine force was a combination of obsolete, obsolescent, and modern boats. The obsolete units included six O-class and eighteen R-class boats used for training. The obsolescent units were thirty-eight S-class boats, suitable only for continental defense; but many were deployed in forward areas due to the lack of modern boats.

The modern units consisted of thirty-two boats, of which twenty-nine were front line. The U.S. Navy suffered its first World War II–era submarine loss on 20 June 1941 when the *S-70* sank in a training dive off New London, Connecticut. The first U.S. submarines to enter the war were the *S-80* and *S-130,* which were transferred to the Royal Navy as HMS *P-511* and HMS *P-551.* The *P-511* was later lost as the Polish *Jastrzab.* During 1942, six more R- and S-class boats were transferred to the Royal Navy for use as trainers to free more modern boats for war patrols.

War came to the U.S. submarine force on 7 December at Pearl Harbor and 8 December at Manila. The Japanese attack at Pearl Harbor focused on the battleships and inflicted no damage on the submarine base. At Manila's Cavite Naval Yard, the target was the submarine base, which was destroyed. The U.S. Navy had anticipated a war starting with Japan sometime around April 1942, thus several submarines were at Cavite undergoing repairs in December. Lost in the attack was the USS *Sealion,* the first of fifty-two U.S. submarines destroyed in the war.

With the exception of the few aircraft carriers, the submarine force was the only striking power the U.S. Navy had left in December 1941 to carry the war to Japan. Unfortunately, the force was flawed due to poorly designed torpedoes (q.v.) that, to save money, had never been tested during peacetime. U.S. submarines fought the first two years of the war with a torpedo that ran ten feet deeper than set, because the depth settings had been calculated on practice torpedoes that were much lighter than the war torpedo. The firing trigger of the magnetically armed torpedo, which was supposed to explode under the hull of the target ship, was too sensitive and exploded before reaching lethal range of the target. The contact-triggered torpedo had a mechanical firing pin that traveled vertically instead of horizontally. On contact, the pin often was pinched in place by the crushing of the torpedo's nose cap against the side of the target, thus preventing warhead detonation. The gyroscope control of the torpedoes was unreliable and sometimes caused the torpedo to curve back on the firing boat. The problem was compounded by the blind refusal of the staff ashore to examine the torpedoes, instead blaming the failures on the men using the weapons. This torpedo problem emasculated the submarines based at Manila at the start of the war, and contributed heavily to the ease of the Japanese conquest of the Philippines, Malaya, and the Netherlands East Indies.

The U.S. submarine force also entered the war with a faulty torpedo attack doctrine that emphasized defense over aggressive action in launching attacks, combined with a policy of attacking only combat ships. As the war actually played out, the prime targets for submarines on all sides were the enemy's merchant ships. With the correction of the mechanical problems in the torpedoes, the introduction of the wakeless electric torpedo, the addition of radar (q.v.), and a change of attack doctrine, U.S. submarines grew into a potent force.

U.S. submarines were deployed mainly in the Pacific, but some operated in the Atlantic in 1942 and 1943. Their commitment was the result of the U.S. policy of engaging the Germans in offensive operations on all fronts. The deployment plan adopted by the U.S. Navy was to base Submarine Squadron 50 (SubRon 50), consisting of six Gato-class boats and their tender, the USS *Beaver,* at Roseneath, Scotland. That allowed the Royal Navy to redeploy six of its submarines to the Mediterranean. SubRon 50's boats sailing for Scotland were first ordered to operate off the Atlantic coast of French Northwest Africa. Their mission was to reconnoiter the area, provide meteorological data, and act as beacons off the beaches that the Allied forces would invade on 8 November 1942. In carrying out that mission the USS *Herring* sank the French cargo ship *Ville de Havce.*

Once the invasion of the French Northwest African ports started, SubRon 50 sailed for Scotland. From there they patrolled the Bay of Biscay. Since the boats were in a war zone as soon as they left Scotland, their war patrols consisted of alternating fifty and thirty days at sea, as opposed to the Pacific war patrols, which lasted a standard sixty days.

In the Pacific, part of the patrol time was spent passing through Allied-controlled waters.

Patrolling the Bay of Biscay was nonproductive, but not because of a lack of shipping. The problem was too many ships and an inability to distinguish Axis from neutral Spanish and Portuguese ships. An attack by the USS *Barb* on what she identified as an Axis tanker hit the Spanish tanker *Campomanes*. The USS *Shad* on 4 January 1943 sank the German minesweeper *M-4242* and a barge in a surface gunnery attack. The USS *Blackfish* sank the German patrol boat *V-408* on 19 February 1943. On 1 April 1943, the *Shad* damaged the blockade runner *Pietro Orselo*.

Based on their lack of success in the Bay of Biscay, the boats of SubRon 50 were redeployed to the waters off northern Norway to hunt German U-boats. During the months of April and June 1943, patrols in those waters produced no contacts, so the U.S. Navy redeployed the boats to the Pacific. SubRon 50 made twenty-seven war patrols in European waters, sank three ships, and damaged three more. Other U.S. submarines conducted eighty-seven war patrols in the Atlantic and Caribbean, hunting German U-boats with no success.

The main battleground for the U.S. submarine force was the western Pacific. During World War II, U.S. submarines sank 1,150 Japanese merchant ships totaling 4,852,000 tons. That amounted to 54.5 percent of the Japanese merchant fleet lost from all causes during the war. U.S. submarines also sank one Japanese battleship, nine aircraft carriers, thirteen cruisers, and many smaller ships.

Of the fifty-three U.S. submarines lost during the war, three were lost in the Atlantic. One was destroyed inadvertently by U.S. fire, and two were lost in noncombat accidents. The overall loss rate for U.S. submarine crews in World War II was 14 percent.

Charles H. Bogart

(Refer to table on page 1105)

Additional Reading

Alden, John D., *The Fleet Submarine in the U.S. Navy* (1979).

Holmes, W.J., *Underseas Victory* (1966).

Poolman, Kenneth, *Allied Submarines of World War II* (1990).

Roscoe, Theodore, *U.S. Submarine Operations in World War II* (1949).

Section IV-S
Technical Data Tables of
Weapons and Equipment

British Submarines

	H-Class	L-Class	U.S. R-Class	U.S. S-Class	Oberon-Class	O-Class	P-Class	R-Class
Commissioned (year)	1918	1920	1919 (1941)	1919 (1941)	1927	1929	1930	1930
Total Number in Service	9	3	3	6	3	6	10	10
Displacement Surfaced (tons)	410	760	530	854	1,350	1,475	1,475	1,475
Max. Speed Submerged (knots)	9	10.5	10.5	11	9	9	9	9
Max. Speed Surfaced (knots)	11.5	17.5	13.5	14.5	15	17.5	17.5	17.5
Max. Range (miles)	2,985	3,800	3,700	5,000	6,500	8,500	8,500	8,500
Torpedo Tubes	4	4	4	4	8	8	8	8
Torpedoes/Mines Carried	6/None	8/None	8/None	12/None	16/None	16/None	16/None	16/None
Radar	No	No	No	No	No	No	No	No
Sonar	No	No	No	No	No	No	No	No
Hydrophones	Yes	Yes	Yes	Yes	Yes	Yes	Yes	Yes
Guns	None	1x 4-in	1x 3-in	1x 4-in	1x 4-in	1x 4-in	1x 4-in	1x 4-in
Crew Size	22	35	33	42	56	56	56	56
Losses	2	None	1	1	1	4	8	8

(continued on next page)

British Submarines *(continued)*

	River-Class	Porpoise-Class	S-Class	T-Class	U-Class	V-Class	X-Class Midget Subs
Commissioned (year)	1933	1933	1932	1938	1939	1944	1943
Total Number in Service	3	6	51	52	49	11	10
Displacement Surfaced (tons)	1,850	1,520	12x 670 39x 715	1,040	15x 540 34x 545	545	27
Max. Speed Submerged (knots)	10	9	9	9	9	9	5.5
Max Speed Surfaced (knots)	21.5	16	15	15	12	13	6.5
Max. Range (miles)	10,000	7,400	6,000	8,000	4,050	4,700	100
Torpedo Tubes	6	6	4x 6 47x 7	15x 10 37x 11	8x 4 41x 6	4	None
Torpedoes/Mines Carried	12/none	12/50	4x 13/none 47x 12/none	15x 16/none 37x 17/none	8x 8/none 41x 10/none	8/none	None
Radar	No	No	Yes, after 1943	Yes, after 1943	Yes, after 1944	Yes	No
Sonar	No	No	No	No	No	No	No
Hydrophones	Yes	Yes	Yes	Yes	Yes	Yes	Yes
Guns	1x 4-in	1x 4-in	38ea 1x 3-in 13ea 1x 4-in	1x 4-in	15ea 1x 3-in or 1x 12-pdr; 34ea none	1x 3-in	None
Crew Size	61	59	36–48	56–61	27–33	37	4
Losses	1	5	19	16	20	None	7

German Submarines

	Type I	Type II	Type VIIa	Type VIIb	Type VIIc	Type VIId	Type VIIf	Type IXa	Type IXb	Type IXc
Commissioned (year)	1937 Note 1	1936 Note 1	1937	1939	1941 Note 2	1942 Note 2	1942 Note 4	1939 Note 2	1940	1941 Note 2
Total Number in Service	2	50	10	24	603	6	4	8	14	146
Displacement Surfaced (tons)	862	Note 3	626	753	769	965	1,084	1,032	1,051	1,120
Max. Speed Submerged (knots)	8	7	8	8	7.5	7	8	8	7	7
Max. Speed Surfaced (knots)	18	13	16	17	17	16	17	18	18	18
Max. Range (miles)	6,700	1,300	4,300	6,500	6,500	8,100	9,500	8,100	8,700	11,000
Torpedo Tubes (front & rear)	6	3	5	5	5	5	5	6	6	6
Torpedoes/Mines Carried	14/none	6/8	11/none	12/14	14/14	14/14 or none/39	14/none Note 6	22/42	22/42	22/none
Radar	No	No	No	No	Yes, 1944–1945	No	No	No	No	Yes, 1944–1945
Sonar	No	No	Yes	Yes	Yes	Yes	Yes	Yes	Yes	Yes
Hydrophones	Yes	Yes	Yes	Yes	Yes	Yes	Yes	Yes	Yes	Yes
Guns	1x 20mm 1x 105mm	Note 7	1x 20mm 1x 90mm	1x 20mm 1x 90mm	1x 20mm 1x 90mm	2x 20mm 1x 37mm	2x 20mm 1x 37mm	1x 20mm 1x 37mm 1x 105mm	1x 20mm 1x 37mm 1x 105mm	1x 20mm 1x 37mm 1x 105mm
Crew Size	43	25	44	44	44	44	46	48	48	48
Losses	2	29	10	24	482	5	3	8	13	117

(continued on next page)

German Submarines (continued)

	Type IXd	Type Xb	Type XIV	Type XVIIa	Type XVIIb	Type XXI	Type XXIII	Type XXVIIa	Type XXVIIb
Commissioned (year)	1943 Notes 2, 5	1942 Note 2	1942 Note 8	1944 Note 9	1945	1944	1945	1944 Note 10	1944 Note 10
Total Number in Service	42	8	10	3	3	124	63	5	100
Displacement Surfaced (tons)	1,616	1,763	1,688	236	312	1,621	232	12	15
Max. Speed Submerged (knots)	7	7	6	9	5	15.5	10	6	3
Max. Speed Surfaced (knots)	19	16.5	14	26	21.5	16	12	6	7
Max. Range (miles)	23,700	14,550	9,300	1,840	3,000	11,150	1,350	38	300
Torpedo Tubes	6	2	None	2	2	6	2	1	2
Torpedoes/Mines Carried	24/32	15/66	4 torp. as cargo	4/none	4/none	23/12	2	1	2
Radar	No	No	No	No	No	Yes	No	No	No
Sonar	Yes	Yes	Yes	No	No	Yes	No	No	No
Hydrophones	Yes	Yes	Yes	Yes	Yes	Yes	Yes	No	No
Guns	1x 20mm 1x 37mm 1x 105mm	1x 20mm 1x 37mm 1x 105mm	1x 20mm 2x 37mm	None	None	4x 20mm or 4x 30mm	None	None	None
Crew Size	57	52	53	12	19	57	14	2	2
Losses	38	7	10	3	3	26	6	None	80

Notes:

1. Primarily training boats.
2. *Schmorchel* added beginning in 1943.
3. Surface displacements:
   - 6 subs: 259 tons
   - 20 subs: 279 tons
   - 6 subs: 314 tons
   - 8 subs: 291 tons
4. Supply boat.
5. Used as submarine tanker.
6. This model could carry fourteen torpedoes as resupply to the tubes, plus an additional fourteen torpedoes as cargo. This sub carried no mines.
7. Armament consisted of:
   - 20 subs: 1x 20mm cannon
   - 30 subs: 4x 20mm cannon
8. Cargo sub, nicknamed the "Milk Cow."
9. First Walter boat.
10. Midget submarines:
   Type XXVIIa was used for training; Type XXVIIb was used by *Kleinkampfverband* (Small Combat Units).

Italian Large Submarines

	Balilla-Class	Fieramosca	Archimede-Class	Glauco-Class	Pietra Mica	Calvi-Class
Commissioned (year)	1928	1930	1935	1935	1935	1935
Total Number in Service	4	1	2	2	1	3
Displacement Surfaced (tons)	1,368	1,400	880	977	1,371	1,331
Max. Speed Submerged (knots)	7	7	8.5	8.6	7.3	7.4
Max. Speed Surfaced (knots)	16	14	17	17	15.5	17
Max. Range (miles)	8,000	8,000	8,000	8,000	8,000	8,000
Torpedo Tubes	6	8	8	8	6	8
Torpedoes/Mines Carried	16/none	14/none	16/none	14/none	10/20	16/none
Radar	No	No	No	No	No	No
Sonar	No	No	No	No	No	No
Hydrophones	Yes	Yes	Yes	Yes	Yes	Yes
Guns	1x 119mm	1x 119mm	2x 100mm	2x 100mm	2x 119mm	2x 119mm
Crew Size	78	78	55	59	72	77
Losses	1	None	2	1	1	3

(continued on next page)

	Foca-Class	Marcello-Class	Cappellini-Class	Brin-Class	Luizei-Class	Marconi-Class
Commissioned (year)	1937	1938	1939	1938	1939	1940
Total Number in Service	3	9	2	6	4	6
Displacement Surfaced (tons)	1,200	962	955	913	1,031	1,036
Max. Speed Submerged (knots)	8	8	8	8	8	8
Max. Speed Surfaced (knots)	16	18	18	17	18	18
Max. Range (miles)	8,000	6,500	6,500	5,600	7,500	8,000
Torpedo Tubes	6	8	8	8	8	8
Torpedoes/Mines Carried	8/36	16/none	16/none	14/none	12/none	12/none
Radar	No	No	No	No	No	No
Sonar	No	No	No	No	No	No
Hydrophones	Yes	Yes	Yes	Yes	Yes	Yes
Guns	1x 100mm	2x 100mm	2x 100mm	1x 100mm	1x 100mm	1x 100mm
Crew Size	61	58	58	58	58	58
Losses	1	7	1	4	4	6

Italian Medium and Small Submarines

	Mameli-Class	Pisuni-Class	Bandiera-Class	Squala-Class	Bragadin-Class	Argonauta-Class	Semttembrini-Class	Sirena-Class	Perla-Class	Adua-Class	Argo-Class
Commissioned (year)	1929	1929 Note 1	1930	1930	1931	1932	1932	1933	1936	1936	1937
Total Number in Service	4	4	4	4	2	8	2	12	10	17	2
Displacement Surfaced (tons)	786	807	858	857	833	611	872	617	622	623	689
Max. Speed Submerged (knots)	8	8	8	8	7	8	8	8	8	8	8
Max. Speed Surfaced (knots)	17	15	15	15	12	14	17.5	14	14	14	14
Max. Range (miles)	5,000	5,000	5,000	5,000	5,000	4,500	5,100	4,600	4,600	4,800	5,500
Torpedo Tubes	6	6	8	8	4	6	8	6	6	6	6
Torpedoes/Mines Carried	10/none	9/none	12/none	12/none	6/24	12/none	12/none	12/none	12/none	12/none	10/none
Radar	No	No	No	No	No	No	No	No	No	No	No
Sonar	No	No	No	No	No	No	No	No	No	No	No
Hydrophones	Yes	Yes	Yes	Yes	Yes	Yes	Yes	Yes	Yes	Yes	Yes
Guns	1x 102mm	1x 102mm	1x 102mm	1x 102mm	1x 102mm	1x 102mm	1x 102mm	1x 100mm	1x 100mm	1x 100mm	1x 100mm
Crew Size	49	49	52	52	55	44	56	45	45	46	46
Losses	1	None	1	3	None	6	1	11	7	16	2

	Acciaio-Class	Flutto-Class	Type VIIc	H-Class	CA-Class	CB-Class
Commissioned (year)	1942	1942	1943 Note 2	1916 Note 3	1938 Note 4	1941 Note 5
Total Number in Service	13	8	9	5	4	22
Displacement Surfaced (tons)	629	746	769	342	12	25
Max. Speed Submerged (knots)	6.7	8.5	7.5	11	6	7
Max. Speed Surfaced (knots)	14	16	17	12	7	7.5
Max. Range (miles)	5,000	5,600	6,500	200	100	200
Torpedo Tubes	6	6	5	4	None	None
Torpedoes/Mines Carried	8/none	12/none	14/14	6/none	2/2 Note 6	2/2
Radar	No	No	No	No	No	No
Sonar	No	No	Yes	No	No	No
Hydrophones	Yes	Yes	Yes	No	No	No
Guns	1x 20mm 1x 100mm	1x 20mm 1x 100mm	2x 20mm 1x 37mm	1x 30mm	None	None
Crew Size	44	53	44	27	3	4
Losses	10	5	7	2	4	11

Notes:
1. Laid up as hulks in 1942.
2. German small submarine provided to Italy.
3. Made by Germany and bought by Italy after World War I.
4. Italian midget submarine.
5. Italian midget submarine. Five subs were sold to Romania in 1943.
6. Carried explosive charges or two torpedoes.

Soviet Submarines

	A-Class	B-Class	D-Class	K-Class	L-Class	M-Class	P-Class	S-Class	SHCH-Class
Commissioned (year)	1921	1916 Note 1	1930	1938	1933 Note 2	1933	1936	1936	1933
Total Number in Service	5	6	5	13	24	100+	3	33	90
Displacement Surfaced (tons)	356	664	920	1,480	1x 1,040 23x 1,200	206	950	840	577
Max. Speed Submerged (knots)	8	9	8.4	10	9	8	7.7	9	8
Max. Speed Surfaced (knots)	12	11.4	15	22.5	14	14	19	19.5	14
Max. Range (miles)	1,500	3,700	7,000	15,000	7,400	1,660	5,750	9,800	3,250
Torpedo Tubes	4	4	8	8	6	4	6	6	6
Torpedoes/Mines Carried	4/none	6/none	10/8	22/20	12/14	4/4	10/none	12/none	10/none
Radar	No	No	No	No	No	No	No	No	No
Sonar	No	No	No	No	No	No	No	No	No
Hydrophones	No	No	No	Yes	?	Yes	Yes	Yes	Yes
Guns	None	1x 45mm 2x 76mm	2x 45mm 1x 102mm	2x 45mm 2x 100mm	1x 45mm 1x 100mm	1x 45mm	2x 45mm 2x 100mm	1x 45mm 1x 100mm	1x 45mm
Crew Size	22	25	60	65	54	18	54	50	38
Losses	3	None	4	5	6	35	3	15	32

Notes:
1. Decommissioned in 1940.
2. Twelve subs served in the Pacific Fleet.

U.S. Submarines (European Theater)

	S-Class	Dolphin-Class	Gato-Class
Commissioned (year)	1919 Note 1	1933 Note 2	1942
Number in Service (year)	38 (1939)	1 (1939)	74 (1943)
Displacement Surfaced (tons)	low 854 high 906	1,560	1,526
Max. Speed Submerged (knots)	11	8	9
Max. Speed Surfaced (knots)	14.5	17	20
Max. Range (miles)	2,500	3,500	10,000
Torpedo Tubes	4	6	10
Torpedoes/Mines Carried	12/none	18/none	24/Note 3
Radar	No	No	Note 4
Sonar	No	No	Note 4
Hydrophones	Yes	Yes	Yes
Guns (type)	1x 4-in	1x 4-in	1x 3-in
Crew Size	42	60	80
Losses	4	0	18

Notes:
1. Provided to the Royal Navy in 1941; used for training sub crews.
2. Training boat.
3. Mines could be carried in lieu of torpedoes at the rate of two mines per torpedo for a maximum of forty-eight mines.
4. Yes, from 1943 onward.

T

Tanks, British

When the war broke out in September 1939, Britain's tank force consisted of only seventy-nine modern medium tanks, sixty-five small and heavily armored infantry support vehicles, 1,000 machine gun light tanks, and 160 medium tanks from the 1920s. Originally the pioneer in tank warfare, Great Britain now had a tank force that was seriously lacking. A variety of strategic and political factors contributed to this situation.

In the 1920s, the British Army resumed its traditional role as a colonial police force, where tanks had little importance. Increasingly, however, interest and military planning did turn to mechanized forces, and a large number of tracked carriers for the infantry and heavily armored tanks were built. In 1937, the 1st Mobile Division was formed, and in 1939, the force was increased to two regular and four reserve armored divisions.

When British armored forces entered combat in France in 1940 the results were mixed. On the western front the British lost more than 700 tanks. In North Africa (q.v.), the Western Desert Force (31,000 troops and 275 tanks) smashed the Italian forces in Egypt, destroying or capturing more than 380 tanks. But when German armored forces entered combat in North Africa, the situation changed quickly. Learning from these early lessons, Britain established more armored divisions and British industry mobilized to begin production of the needed tanks. By 1942, the British manufactured 8,611 tanks, double the number of Germany. Still, the need exceeded the capability of British manufacturers. After 1941, U.S. tanks, self-propelled guns, and tank destroyers were imported.

In September 1939, the majority of the 1,300 armored vehicles in the Royal Tank Corps were light tanks, mechanized machine gun vehicles or infantry carriers. These tanks, mostly Marks VIs, had first been developed in 1927–1928 by Vickers as highly mobile and sturdy vehicles. The Mark VI, the last and most highly developed of this series, had a larger turret, thicker armor, wider tracks, and a better machine gun than its predecessors. The Mark VIB, the most common version, was thirteen feet, two inches long and six feet, ten inches wide. It weighed about 5.4 tons, carried a crew of three, was covered with armor between 10mm and 14mm in thickness, and was armed with caliber .303 and caliber .50 Vickers machine guns. Since they were relatively cheap to produce, the British had large numbers of Mark VIs in service in 1939. During the early period of the war, British light tanks were outgunned and under-armored, but their speed allowed them to perform useful scouting missions.

Another light tank, the Mark VII (also known as the Tetrach) was developed in 1937. Though lightly armored (16mm thickness), it carried the main armament of the contemporary British Cruiser tank, a 2-pounder (40mm) gun with a coaxial 7.92mm Besa machine gun. The Tetrachs were first used in action in 1942, and most were reserved for airborne operations. About a half-dozen were glider-landed in Normandy (q.v.) on D-Day.

Heavier tanks were available in 1939, although in much smaller numbers. Among these, the Infantry Tank Marks I and II Matilda, had been developed in the mid-1930s. The Matilda Mark II weighed 29.7 tons, had a speed of 15 mph, was armed with a 2-pounder (40mm) Mark IX or X gun and a 7.92mm Besa machine gun, and carried armor 40mm to 70mm thick on the sides and 75mm on the turret. At eighteen feet, five inches long and eight feet, six inches wide, the Matilda was a much larger vehicle than the Mark VI. Conceived for use in direct support of infantry, the

A Crusader tank passes a burning German PzKpfw-IV during Operation CRUSADER, 27 November 1941. (IWM E 6751)

Matilda emphasized protection rather than speed. The first models were very slow but armed with machine guns capable of shooting up enemy infantry or light defenses.

Fifty Matildas were sent to France in May 1940 and they played an important role in the battle against the invading German forces. Virtually impervious to the standard German antitank gun, the 3.7cm Pak 35, the Matilda's armor could only be penetrated by field howitzers. Development on the Matilda models continued and they were sent to join the Western Desert Force in September 1940. There, the Matilda gained the reputation as the "Queen of the Battlefield," as they proved themselves superior to German armor in battle. Still, the Matilda's gun lacked long-range, high explosive shells. With its reliability and mobility, the Matilda also fought in the Pacific theater.

Another infantry tank, the Mark III Valentine, was in service by late 1940. The Valentine II (seventeen feet, nine inches long and eight feet, seven inches wide) weighed 19.5 tons, had a maximum speed of 15 mph, and was armed with a 40mm main gun and a 7.92mm Besa machine gun. Its hull armor was 60mm thick. Compared to the Matilda, the Valentine was lighter, had a shorter range, and was protected by less armor, but it had certain advantages. It was easier to build and

required fully one-third less man-hours in production. The original Valentines were improved by the time they saw combat in 1941 in North Africa and later in the Pacific theater. More powerful engines and heavier guns were added before production of the Valentine ended in 1944 with the Mark XI. The Valentine chassis was also used to carry two other types of self-propelled guns: a 17-pounder antitank gun, called the Archer, and a 25-pounder self-propelled gun/howitzer, known as the Bishop. Valentines were also used as amphibious vehicles, as flamethrower carriers, and for mine clearing. By the end of the war, 8,280 Valentine tank chassis had been built—more than any other British type. The ease of construction and reliability made up for its low speed, poor crew layout, and, later, insufficient firepower and armor.

The last and best of the British infantry tanks was the Churchill line. Introduced to replace the Matilda, the Churchill's armor was thicker and its engine more powerful. The Churchill Mark IV (43.7 tons, twenty-four feet, five inches long, and nine feet wide) had a 40mm main gun and two 7.92mm machine guns, a top speed of 15 mph, and a range of ninety miles. The first fourteen production models were completed in June 1941. By the middle of 1942 production amounted to forty per week.

The Churchills first saw action in the Dieppe

(q.v.) raid in August 1942, when about thirty were used in support. Mechanical problems prevented their deployment to Africa until the battle of El Alamein (q.v.). It was there they proved their worth. Two brigades also were deployed to Tunisia (q.v.). In combat, the Churchill was a formidable opponent, with armor able to deflect 50mm and even 75mm antitank rounds. Its weakness was a lack of firepower, which was remedied in the Churchill Mark V with the introduction of a 95mm gun. Production of the Churchill Mark VI, an interim design with a 75mm gun, began in November 1943. It was replaced by the Churchill Mark VII, which incorporated many improvements, including 152mm armor in some places.

Before the outbreak of the war, designs for medium tanks had already been worked up. The A-9, Cruiser Tank Mark I, which weighed 14.4 tons, carried 14mm armor, and had a top speed of 25 mph. It was first produced in 1937. It was updated a year later by the A-10, and together these tanks constituted half the available number of Cruiser tanks in the early months of the war. Cruiser Marks I and II served in France and Egypt as did updated versions, the Marks III and IV. All suffered from mechanical problems, however.

The heavier Cruiser Mark VI weighed 22.1 tons and was armed with a 40mm 2-pounder Mark IX or X gun and two 7.92mm machine guns. With a top speed of 26.7 mph, the Mark VI was not fast, but it had a range of 124 miles. Dubbed the Crusader, it first saw combat in Egypt in 1941, and it compared well with its main German opponent, even though its gun was relatively light. The Crusaders also performed other specialized roles as recovery vehicles, bulldozers, and command vehicles. About 5,300 Crusaders were built after 1940, and they served as Britain's major operational battle tank during 1941–1942.

Early combat in France and North Africa revealed the need for more reliable, more heavily armored and armed tanks. Production of 500 model A-24 tanks, based on the Crusader design, began in June 1941 and were designated the Cavalier, but they saw only limited action. Another tank, the Centaur, appeared in June 1942, but was used for specialized roles such as antiaircraft tanks and observation post vehicles.

In 1943, mass production of the reliable Cromwell Mark I began, with other versions following quickly. The Cromwell Mark IV weighed 30.8 tons, was armed with a 75mm Mark V or VA main gun and two 7.92mm machine guns, and had a speed of 32 mph and range of 173 miles.

Out of the Cromwell was developed the last and most powerful British tank to see combat, the Comet, which was not available for service until November 1944.

The British also used large numbers of the U.S. M-4 medium tank, the Sherman (*see* Tanks, U.S.). About 600 Shermans of various models were modified by removing the 75mm or 76mm main gun and replacing it with the British 17-pounder. The result was called the Sherman "Firefly," which saw extensive action in northwest Europe.

Kenneth J. Swanson
Robert G. Waite

(Refer to table on page 1131)

Additional Reading

Forty, George, *World War II Tanks* (1995).
Gander, Terry, and Peter Chamberlain, *British Tanks of World War 2* (1976).
Grove, Eric, *World War II Tanks* (1976).
Murland, J.R.W., *The Royal Armoured Corps* (1943).

Tanks, French

"Tanks assist the advance of the infantry by breaking static obstacles and active resistance." This 1921 quote from France's commander in chief, Marshal Henri Philippe Pétain (q.v.), fairly well summed up the problems of his nation's interwar tank designs. Despite some innovative efforts and high quality construction, 1940 saw this section of the French Army unprepared for modern war.

A major reason for such was the basic thrust of national strategy. While certainly not passive, France's military men saw the offensive as a slow, methodical buildup, with the need for massive artillery support to reduce enemy resistance. With these parameters in mind, it was unnecessary to build either fast-moving tanks, or vehicles specifically designed to kill other tanks.

The result was a collection of heavy "breakthrough" models like the Char B1 and Char B1-bis. With a 75mm hull-mounted gun, plus a 47mm turret gun, they packed considerable firepower, but had a top speed of only 17 mph. Even more ponderous was the seventy-four-ton Char FCM2c-bis with its 155mm gun. Large and slow moving, these tanks were easy targets that could be easily penetrated by Germany's primary antitank gun, the 3.7cm Pak 35.

By 1936, France had slightly more than 200

medium and heavy tanks. On 7 September 1936, General Maurice Gamelin (q.v.) launched an ambitious four-year program to improve the French armed forces. With 14 percent of the budget allocated for mechanization, many new armored fighting vehicles were slated for production. These included the fast-moving Panhard AMD 178 armored car with its 25mm gun, plus a variety of light and medium tanks like the H-39, R-35, and S-35. The latter, sometimes called the "Somua," had a 47mm gun and a top speed of 25 mph. It was the best of the lot, with more than 400 produced by March 1940. Like all other French tank designs, however, it suffered from poor crew distribution, most notably in its one-man turret.

This was a serious flaw. The turret crewman served as the vehicle's commander. As the French design placed him there alone, he doubled as gunner and loader for the main armament. It was simply too much to expect one person to successfully accomplish all these missions. The German tanks were not only faster, but featured two-man turret crews, which gave them an important edge over their French opponents.

Production slowdowns compounded these problems. The French national armaments industry was partially nationalized in order to meet the four-year plan. Strikes and labor unrest drastically reduced output in 1937 and 1938, sometimes by as much as 50 percent. When the war began, fac-tories were unable to gear up to full production before the German invasion.

In the summer of 1940, France had 2,285 modern tanks. While the crews fought well and scored some local victories, the overall story was one of defeat by faster, better designed, and better directed German vehicles. Typical of such was the fate of a column of monster FCM2c-bis tanks destroyed by airpower while still on railway flat-cars, having never fired in battle.

After 1940, many French tanks were taken over by the *Wehrmacht*. Numerous German assault guns used captured H-39 and R-35 chassis for their motive power. Other tanks, including the antiquated Renault FT-17 of World War I fame, were used by German police, security, and anti-partisan units. In addition, some of the better models were handed over to the Italian and Romanian armies.

John Dunn

(Refer to table on page 1132)

Additional Reading

Boucher, J., *L'Arme Blinde dans la Guerre* (1954).
Forty, George, *World War II Tanks* (1995).
Frankenstein, Robert, *Le Prix du Réarmement Français (1935–1939)* (1982).
Goutard, Adolphe, *The Battle of France, 1940* (1958).

A Char B1 heavy tank. (IWM MH 224)

Tanks, German

Of all the belligerent nations, the Germans had the greatest success with armored fighting vehicles, and most of their early victories depended upon the skillful use of tanks. This expertise came slowly, after the other European powers had developed their own tanks. Germany's armed forces were severely reduced by the Versailles Peace Treaty (q.v.), but this also gave German military figures like Heinz Guderian (q.v.) an opportunity to substitute technology for manpower.

Because the treaty prohibited Germany from possessing tanks, the first developments were done secretly, in cooperation with Swedish and Soviet forces. After Guderian's appointment as chief of staff to the Inspectorate of Motorized Troops in 1934, planning for new light and medium tanks began. This, too, remained secret, and some vehicles were disguised as tractors. The Nazi takeover and the renunciation of the Versailles restrictions led to the formation of three *Panzer* divisions. The first test of Germany's tanks came with the occupation of Austria in 1938, when both their mechanical weaknesses and their impressive long-range mobility were demonstrated.

Much of the German armor used early in World War II were light tanks, the PzKpfw (Armored Fighting Vehicle) I and II. First developed as "light and heavy tractors" to evade treaty restrictions and then adopted as training vehicles, the PzKpfw-I came into production by several firms in 1934. The early models were armed with two MG-13 machine guns mounted in a turret. These vehicles proved to be underpowered, and changes were made, including increases in weight and size. They saw their first combat during the Spanish Civil War (q.v.). About 3,000 of all models of the PzKpfw-I were manufactured. Production continued until 1941, largely because of delays in the production of the new PzKpfw-III and IV. In fact, a large number of the undersized PzKpfw-I tanks fought in Poland (q.v.) in 1939 and were later deployed in the Norway (q.v.) campaign. About 520 were involved in the 1940 invasion of France (q.v.), and some even saw combat against the Soviet Union (q.v.). By late 1941, most had been reassigned to training duties.

Development of the PzKpfw-II began in 1935 when the need for an improved light tank was recognized. Different models were successively manufactured and each received improvements, such as new chassis, heavier armor, and larger engines. The first of the PzKpfw-IIs weighed 7.2 tons and was powered by a six-cylinder engine with a top speed of 25 mph. By 1939, some 1,226 PzKpfw-IIs were in service, although their deficiencies like thin armor and a lightweight 20mm gun, were well known. These vehicles proved their

A PzKpfw-III advances through the desert during Rommel's drive on Bir Hacheim. (IWM MH 5852)

A *PzKpfw-I, Ausf. B, in France, May 1940. (IWM MH 9196)*

worth in combat against Poland and France. They remained in production through 1941 when 233 of the *Ausführung* F (Model F), with heavier armor and guns were produced.

More than 1,060 PzKpfw-IIs fought in the invasion of the Soviet Union, but their effectiveness against the heavier Soviet tanks proved less than expected. The chassis of the PzKpfw-II was then adopted for 75mm self-propelled antitank guns. Called *Panzerjäger* (Tank Hunters), they were widely used in 1942 and 1943. The PzKpfw-II chassis was also used as a base for other fighting vehicles, including a reconnaissance vehicle, a mobile flamethrower, and the Wespe 10.5cm self-propelled howitzer.

In 1935, the need for a heavier tank was recognized and development of the PzKpfw-III commenced. It was to be a fifteen-ton armored vehicle, and the core of the new armored divisions. Armed with a 37mm gun, improvements were introduced with each new model. By 1939, ninety-eight of the Ausf. D and E were ready for combat. Production was accelerated and by the end of the year, 157 were manufactured.

At the time of the invasion of France, 349 PzKpfw-III-series tanks were available and the bulk of these saw duty under Guderian's command. Their guns proved inadequate, however, and a rush was made to add more firepower in the form of a new 50mm gun. Improved armor protection came with the Ausf. H, available in late 1940. Extra 30mm plates were added to the front and wider tracks were adopted.

When Germany invaded the Soviet Union, 1,440 PzKpfw-III tanks were in service. They proved adequate against the older Soviet tanks, but the newer Soviet KV-1 and T-34 tanks were harder to destroy. Improvements came with Ausf. J, which had 50mm armor and the new 50mm L-60 main gun. With improved effectiveness of armored vehicles and the prolonging of the conflict on the Soviet front came the demand for more tanks, something that strained the capability of German industry. In 1941, 1,173 PzKpfw-III tanks were manufactured. That number went up to 2,605 in 1942. By the end of 1942, the PzKpfw-III was really out of date and the Ausf. N was the last of the line. Production ceased in order to devote resources to the manufacture of assault guns.

The only German battle tank to remain in production throughout the war was the PzKpfw-IV, development of which began in 1934. During its development, this vehicle was to be a medium-weight tank of about seventeen tons, with a 75mm main gun and a MG-34 machine gun. Production began slowly, and in 1936 only thirty-five were manufactured. The PzKpfw-IV performed well in combat, although the need for additional armor became apparent during the invasion of Poland. The armor thickness on the front was increased to 60mm and on the side to 40mm. By the time of the invasion of France, 278 PzKpfw-IVs of various models were available to ten *Panzer* divisions. Production continued and about 580 were ready to participate in the attack against the Soviet Union. As more German tank factories were built, production of the PzKpfw-IV increased to 480 in 1941 and 964 in 1942. More were desperately needed, especially when the Germans recognized that its gun was their only tank gun that could penetrate the armor of the Soviet T-34s and KV-1s.

Production of the PzKpfw-IV came to an end in June 1944 when Adolf Hitler (q.v.) ordered resources to be devoted to the series' tank destroyer derivative, the *Jagdpanzer*-IV. Development of that system actually began in 1942 when a need for a heavily armored assault gun was recognized. Such a vehicle also was to be used against the well-protected buildings and fortifications encountered during the urban fighting in the Soviet Union during 1941 and 1942.

One version of the *Jagdpanzer*, the III/IV, was a formidable armored vehicle, weighing more than twenty-three tons, well armored, and equipped with an 88mm Pak 43/1 gun. Other adaptations of the PzKpfw-IV chassis were made. In 1943, one version became an antiaircraft vehicle with two 37mm guns. Another, the Whirlwind, appeared in December 1943. Also in 1943, the 150mm self-propelled assault gun, the Stu Pz 43, *Brumbär*, was

The Tiger-E, PzKpfw-VI, Ausf. E, (Sd.Kfz.181), one of the best tanks of the war. (IWM STT 4877)

based on the PzKpfw-IV chassis. The PzKpfw-IV series proved to be one of the best German tanks produced. Throughout the war, more than 10,500 combat vehicles were manufactured on its chassis, including about 9,000 tanks.

The Germans gained two additional tanks with the defeat of Czechoslovakia. That nation's well-established munitions industry produced the LT-35 in 1936, a 9.0-ton light tank armed with the 37mm A-3 tank gun. Comparable to the PzKpfw-III, the LT-35s were taken over by the Nazis and used as the PzKpfw-35(t) in combat against Poland, France, and the Soviet Union.

The major Czech tank used by the German forces was the LT-38 designated by the Germans as the PzKpfw-38(t). Initially successful in France, their effectiveness did not last against the more powerful Soviet tanks. The PzKpfw-38(t) chassis was, however, reliable and easy to maintain, and the Germans used it for the 150mm self-propelled infantry support gun, *Grille*. Beginning in March 1942, the Germans fitted captured Soviet 76.2mm guns, which the Germans designated the Pak 36(r), to the chassis of the PzKpfw-38(t) to form the Marder-III self-propelled antitank gun. About 120 Marder-IIIs were built within two months at the Prague munitions works. Most went to North Africa to combat the British Matilda tanks. An additional 344 were produced in 1942 and saw combat in the Soviet Union. The Marder-IIIs were

basically stopgap measures, but their effectiveness prompted the Germans to redesign and manufacture a new model of tank destroyer based on the PzKpfw-38(t) chassis. The *Jagdpanzer*-38(t) mounted a 7.5cm Pak 40 antitank gun. The prototype of the *Jagdpanzer*-38(t) appeared in 1943 and production began a year later.

Among German tanks, the heavy PzKpfw-VI Tiger became the best known and most widely feared armored vehicle of the war. Development began in 1937 for a thirty-ton tank, one powerful enough to break through enemy lines. A number of models and designs emerged, and in May 1941, Hitler called for a still more powerful version. The PzKpfw-VI, Ausf. H was the result. When introduced, it was the most powerfully armed and best protected tank in the world. It did, however, have some limitations. The weight, more than sixty tons, meant that its range and speed were limited. Because the turret traverse was low-geared (and therefore slow), skillfully handled Allied tanks could maneuver around the Tiger to hit its vulnerable rear.

Tigers were intended for use in independent three-company battalions of thirty tanks to support various units, but Hitler's eagerness to get them into action meant they were initially poorly deployed. They were overwhelmed in their first offensive combat, near Leningrad (q.v.) in the fall of 1942. The fighting at Kursk (q.v.) in July 1943 was also disastrous for the Tigers. Still, if deployed from camouflaged positions and supported by other tanks, the Tiger was very formidable and attracted a disproportionate amount of Allied attention.

Germany's armored forces faced ferocious opponents. The mauling received in early October 1941 from the new Soviet T-34 led Guderian to ask for the development of a new tank. The specifications called for a thirty-five-ton vehicle with a 75mm main gun, a coaxial machine gun, hull armor of 60mm (turret 100mm), and a speed of 37 mph.

In January 1943, the PzKpfw-V Panther came off the production lines, and it saw its first major combat at Kursk. The results were disappointing, with 160 of 200 knocked out of action by the end of the first day. Improved models followed quickly, however, and during 1944 and 1945, more than 4,800 Panthers were produced. Two models, the Ausf. A and G, were important in the large-scale defensive battles at Normandy (q.v.), where Allied air superiority prevailed.

Taking cognizance of the sloped armor of the Soviet T-34, specifications for a modified and larger Tiger were issued in August 1942. The first of the PzKpfw-VI, Tiger II (Ausf. B) appeared only in late 1943. By February 1944, the first eight were completed. It saw its first combat on the eastern front in May 1944. The *Königstiger* (King Tiger) was a formidable weapon, one of the heaviest, most powerful, and well-armored main battle tanks of the war. Its gun could penetrate 182mm of 30-degree sloped armor at a range of 500 meters, which made even the heaviest Soviet IS-2 tanks vulnerable. The Tiger II, however, weighed more than seventy tons. That might not have mattered much in defensive combat, but it certainly made it an ineffective offensive weapon, as demonstrated during the Ardennes (q.v.) offensive. A derivative of the Tiger II, the *Jagdtiger*, with its 12.8cm Pak 44 main gun, was the war's most powerful armored vehicle and saw duty in tank destroyer battalions, particularly those of the *Waffen-SS* (q.v.).

Even with the superior fighting power of the Panther and Tiger tanks, German production was simply inadequate. Between 1939 and 1945, Germany manufactured about 27,872 tanks and 17,445 other armored fighting vehicles—most after 1942. With the opening of a second front in Western Europe, German forces faced two opponents well equipped with armored vehicles. Increased production in 1944 and 1945—when 8,328 tanks and 10,659 other armored vehicles came off of German assembly lines—failed to prevent the German forces from being overwhelmed

by the Allies. Nazi Germany had not prepared for a war of long duration because Hitler had firmly believed that lightning strikes and surgical actions would win his war.

Paul W. Johnson
Robert G. Waite

(Refer to table on page 1133)

Additional Reading

Chamberlain, Peter, and Hilary Doyle, *Encyclopedia of German Tanks of World War Two* (1993).

Forty, George, *German Tanks of World War II "In Action"* (1987).

Guderian, Heinz, *Die Panzerwaffe. Ihre Entwicklung, Ihre Kampftaktik und Ihre Operativen Moeglichkeiten bis zum Beginn des Grossdeutschen Freiheitskampfes* (1943).

Senger und Etterlin, F.M. von, *German Tanks of World War II: The Complete Illustrated History of German Armored Fighting Vehicles* (1969).

Tanks, Polish

Despite the fabled reputation of its cavalry, Poland possessed 1,000 armored fighting vehicles in 1939. While most of these were armored cars, tankettes, or the antique Renault FT-17, Poland did have some were first-rate models. This heterogeneous collection was the result, not so much of short-sighted military planners, but what Polish writer Stanisław Litynski described as "the real Polish military doctrine—the doctrine of poverty."

With a weak economy and limited industrial base, Polish tank design did not start until the 1930s. The first production model was the TK, a tankette based on the British Carden-Lloyd Mark VI chassis. A slightly better version, the TKS, was soon fielded. Although a few were armed with tank-killing 20mm cannon, most of the 700 produced had but a 7.92mm machine gun. Lightly armored and slow, these were little better than mobile machine gun platforms.

Vastly superior Polish models existed in the form of the 7TP. Based on the Vicker's E six-ton design, these vehicles were state of the art in 1939. Well armored, capable of 23 mph, and armed with a tank-busting 37mm Bofors gun, they were equal to any contemporary tank. Unfortunately, less than 100 were available by 1 September 1939.

John Dunn

(Refer to table on page 1134)

Additional Reading

Barbarski, Krzysztof, *Polish Armour, 1939–45* (1982).

Forty, George, *World War II Tanks* (1995).

Zebrowski, Marian W., *Zarys Historii Polskiej Broni Pancernej 1918–1947* (1971).

Tanks, Soviet

The development of tracked armored vehicles for the Soviet armed forces began during World War I. The real boost in tank development and production came in 1929 with the first five-year plan. It included measures for mechanizing the Red Army and providing a range of tanks in the various tactical categories. A number of new designs appeared, but the Soviet armed forces continued to depend upon another well-proven tactic, buying and adopting weapons from abroad.

A Soviet commission traveled to Great Britain, purchased several Vickers light and medium tank designs along with a license for production in the Soviet Union. This arrangement gave the Soviet Army the foundation for a series of light and medium tanks. The T-26, T-27, and T-37 were all essentially British types, and the BT series was patterned after the American Christie design. Even the medium T-28 and heavy T-38 designs, although entirely Soviet, included some features from British and German designs.

A result of these efforts was that during the 1930s, the Soviet Army greatly increased its armored strength. About thirty factories began mass production of tanks and other armored vehicles and production rates soared. By 1935–1936, the Soviet Union possessed the largest tank force in the world, with more than 10,000 tracked armored vehicles. Toward the end of the decade, the emphasis was on improving the quality as well as the number of Soviet tanks. In addition, observers were impressed by the tactical handling of armored formations. Tank units could operate over wide areas in conjunction with other mobilized forces, and they were capable of independent offensive action.

Soviet tank forces gained important experience during the Winter War (q.v.) with Finland in 1939–1940. Initial Soviet operations included the deployment of T-37, T-26, BT-5, and T-28 tanks. Medium and heavy tanks were used in support of infantry units, and they attacked Finnish fortifications in an effort to break through the defensive lines. The experience gained also revealed the weaknesses of Soviet tanks and armored tactics. Reforms were introduced by newly appointed Marshal Pavel Rotmistrov (q.v.). Increasingly, the focus was on production and expansion of tank forces. Efforts were made to increase the operating range of the tanks and to improve their armament.

When German forces invaded in June 1941, the Soviet Army had some 20,000 tanks organized into armored divisions on the German model. At the time of the invasion, reorganization was not completed, command experience was lacking, and most of the tanks were of prewar design. Production of replacement vehicles had not gone on long enough to provide the necessary number of medium and heavy tanks.

German forces devastated the Soviet tanks, destroying about 17,000 in the early months of the campaign. In addition, the rapid advances of the German Army forced the evacuation of the majority of the western tank plants, which were relocated in the Urals and Siberia. Despite these setbacks, new Soviet tanks continued to be developed and manufactured, and they came with improved armor, armament, and engines.

The winter of 1941–1942 provided an essential respite for Soviets. This break, combined with the introduction of new tanks (the T-34 and an improved version of the KV-1), the arrival of large numbers of Lend-Lease (q.v.) tanks, and the use of captured German tanks, enabled the Soviets to regain the initiative. With the enormous losses early in the campaign, Soviet premier Josef Stalin (q.v.) ordered the production of the maximum number of tanks possible. Beginning in the summer of 1942, armored formations received large numbers of tanks, and during that year, production reached 24,446 tanks. In addition, Great Britain supplied about 5,000 tanks (including 3,780 Valentines and 1,080 Matildas) and the United States supplied about 7,000 (including 1,670 Stuarts, 1,385 Grants, and 4,100 Shermans).

In 1941, the Soviet arsenal included a number of light tanks. Several models, T-27, T-37 and T-26, were developed on the Vickers designs purchased earlier. The T-27 first appeared in 1931 and was quickly updated in the T-27A and B models. About 4,000 were produced, and they saw action in the Winter War, but even by then they were already obsolete.

The T-37 came into service in 1931, and it too, was improved with a new turret and thicker armor. Deployed against Finland, the T-37 was used in reconnaissance units. The T-26 series, adopted in 1931 and continuously improved, took the brunt of the German invasion in 1941. The final production model, the T-26S, had thicker armor, weighed 11.6 tons, and carried a 45mm main gun plus two machine guns.

Soviet forces gained several new light tanks after the outbreak of war. The T-40 amphibious tank, an improvement on earlier amphibious tanks with completely new superstructure and suspension, entered service in 1941. Its armor was thin and it carried only one machine gun. Only a limited number were manufactured in 1942. The T-60, a completely new series, entered production in 1941. Armed with a 20mm aircraft cannon and protected by thick armor, it filled the need of replacing the now obsolete light tanks. T-60s were assigned to reconnaissance units until 1943 when that function was taken over by armored cars and U.S. Lend-Lease half-tracks. More than 6,000 T-60s were manufactured.

In early 1942, the T-70 came into production as a light tank with increased armor and a more powerful gun designed to counter the new German tanks. It also was designed to surpass the T-60's limitations of armor and firepower. The T-70's hull armor was increased, and it carried a 45mm main gun plus a machine gun. During the war, 8,226 were manufactured. A version with thicker armor and an improved engine, known as the T-80, came out in mid-1943, but production was halted later that year as light tanks were withdrawn from service with reconnaissance battalions.

The Soviet Army's medium tanks were first developed in the early 1930s and many were in use when the German Army invaded. The T-28 was developed in 1932 as a breakthrough tank, and during the decade, this series was continuously improved. Even with extra armor and a top speed of 23 mph, many were easily destroyed by German tanks in the summer of 1941.

The BT (Fast Tank) series emerged in 1931 on the basis of the American Christie designs. The BTs were intended for an independent role as mechanized cavalry. By the end of the 1930s, however, Soviet strategy relegated all tanks to infantry support. Still, the BT-5 was the most important Soviet tank between 1939 and 1941, and with the T-26s, they amounted to 75 percent of Soviet tank strength.

Developed in the late 1930s, the T-34 series was a major advancement, with many mechanical improvements, including wider tracks, improved transmission, more powerful guns and better suspension. After the experiences with older tanks in the Winter War, great efforts were made to speed up production of the T-34. Prototypes were tested in 1940 and the model was hurried into production. The first production model carried a 76.2mm L/30.3 M-1938 tank gun, and was protected with 45mm of armor on the front and 40mm on the sides.

German forces first encountered this formidable opponent in September 1941, when it demonstrated its ability to outshoot, outrun, and outlast German tanks. The T-34 was the most successful tank design to date, and it set many trends for future designs. Even Nazi Germany adopted many of its features into the Tiger and Panther

A T-34/76 tank, perhaps the best tank of the war. (IWM STT 5316)

tanks. In 1943, the Soviets introduced an up-gunned version of the T-34, with a 85mm main gun.

Among the Soviet heavy tanks, the T-35 was developed and produced from 1933 to 1939, but only about sixty vehicles of this fifty-ton behemoth were manufactured. The T-35 evolved out of the T-32 models and had better armor and improved transmission and suspension. Like its forerunner, the T-35 was created as a combat vehicle capable of breaking through heavily fortified positions. The main turret carried a 76.2mm gun and two auxiliary turrets had 37mm guns. The T-35 was handled by a crew of eleven. At the end of the decade, two new multi-turret designs, the T-100 and the SMK, were built in small numbers. Intended as replacements for the T-35, these new models had similar bulk and size, but the prototypes used in the war against Finland proved unsuitable and never went into full production.

A genuine improvement was the KV series, a modified T-100, with the smaller front turret removed. The savings in weight and length made for a more compact vehicle with thicker 90mm armor. Originally called the Kotin-Stalin, after the chief engineer of the Kirov-Zavod Tank Factory who designed it in 1938, and Stalin who called for changes, its name was officially changed to KV, in honor of General Kliment Voroshilov (q.v.). Production of the KV-1 began in December 1939, and it proved to be an excellent tank, bigger and better armed than the heaviest German tanks of 1941. Throughout the war, the KV was continuously improved, and the final production version came out in early 1943.

To counter the increased use of heavy 88mm tank and antitank guns by the German forces, the Soviets needed a faster tank with better maneuverability and a heavier gun. A modified version of the KV-85 provided the best solution. Production began in late 1943. Named after Stalin, it was designated the IS-1. An up-gunned version was soon introduced as the IS-100, and finally, in 1943, the design was finalized as the IS-122, later designated the IS-2. It carried a new 122mm gun and featured sloping armor all around.

Deployed in late 1943, the IS-1 first saw combat in early 1944. Improved models, including the completely redesigned IS-2, followed in 1944. By the end of 1944, 2,250 IS-2s were produced and quickly gained a high reputation in combat. The last improved model, the IS-3, was an excellent tank with sloped armor and a ballistically superior turret, but it did not reach the field until January 1945. The IS-3 was the most powerfully armed tank in full production. It continued in service after the war.

Throughout World War II, the quality of Soviet tanks increased, as did the ability of industry to mass-produce them. During the last three years of war, annual production rates exceeded 25,000 tanks and armored vehicles. In 1944, the figures were 28,963 tanks and self-propelled guns, and 122,400 guns of other types. By June 1944, the Soviet Army had a reserve of 9,500 tanks.

The Soviets used their tanks effectively. The offensive operations of 1943–1944 demonstrated conclusively the value of tanks in support of attacking infantry. The Soviet armed forces used tanks most frequently as breakthrough weapons. In the final stages of the conflict, Soviet tactics used tanks only when their overwhelming force went against a numerically inferior or badly shattered enemy. The heavy tanks would strike first, followed by waves of medium tanks, self-propelled guns, and finally, light tanks and infantry. In the decisive battles of the war the effectiveness of Soviet tanks was shown, especially with their ability to break through enemy lines.

Paul W. Johnson
Robert G. Waite

(Refer to table on page 1135)

Additional Reading
Chamberlain, Peter, and Chris Ellis, *Soviet Combat Tanks, 1939–1945* (1970).
Grove, Eric, *World War II Tanks* (1976).
Milson, John, *Russian Tanks, 1900–1970* (1971).
Orgill, Douglas, *T-34: Russian Armor* (1971).

Tanks, Special

Special purpose armored vehicles were a British development for the most part. Based on their early experiences in the North African campaign (q.v.), the British identified two primary types of requirements for which the specialized equipment was needed. The first was the clearance of minefields and the breaching of a variety of obstacles while under heavy fire. The second was the recovery of armored vehicles on the battlefield, again while under heavy fire.

The results of the disastrous Dieppe (q.v.) raid in August 1942 also pointed to the requirement for armored vehicles with amphibious capabilities. With all these lessons in mind, the British formed the 79th Armoured Division specifically to provide specialized armored support for the Normandy invasion. The new division was commanded by

Major General Sir Percy Hobart (q.v.), one of Britain's early tank pioneers. Almost all the specialized tanks developed were modifications of existing designs—standard-model tank chassis with special attachments. Hobart's special tanks soon became known affectionately as "Hobby's Funnies."

One of the earliest British modified tanks was a 1940 antiaircraft version of the Mark VI light tank. It carried four 7.92mm Besa machine guns in a rotating turret, making it an effective and mobile weapon system. It was designated the Light Tank AA Mark I or Mark II. Other antiaircraft tanks included versions of the Crusader tank, which carried a 40mm Bofors gun or twin 20mm Oerlikon antiaircraft guns.

Later model British tanks were designed to facilitate specialized conversion and modification. The Churchill tank was one of the most successful. One variant was an armored recovery vehicle (ARV) used to clear stranded tanks from the battlefield. An even more specialized beach armored recovery vehicle (BARV) was designed to clear tanks from landing areas, thereby preventing congestion on the beachhead. The armored vehicle Royal Engineers (AVRE) was a modified Churchill used to breach obstacles such as ditches and hedgerows. The AVRE could carry and deploy a scissors bridge, a small box girder bridge (SBG), or fascines to fill in antitank ditches. The Churchill AVRE was armed with a powerful, short-range 165mm gun for blasting strong points.

Another modification of the Churchill carried a track or carpet layer attached to the tank's front end. It unrolled a mat as it moved forward, which allowed other tanks to follow over wet and soggy ground. The Churchill Crocodile had a flamethrower mounted in the turret in place of its main gun. The self-propelled flamethrower was not an Allied innovation. The Italians used flamethrowers mounted on their light tanks in campaigns throughout the 1930s. The specialized Churchills proved to be the most successful vehicles used by the 79th Armoured Division on D-Day.

The variants of the Cromwell tank included one called the Prong, which carried a device for tearing through the hedgerows in the *bocage* country of Normandy. The Centaur tank was modified with a dozer blade attached to the front, making it an armored bulldozer. The Matilda tank was modified by replacing its main turret gun with a powerful searchlight to provide battlefield illumination. The result was called the CDL Tank, for canal defense light.

The Valentine Snake used a towed explosive device to clear minefields. The Valentine Scorpion had a revolving cylinder with chains attached to the front. The flailing chains would detonate mines, clearing a path through the minefield for other vehicles and troops. The Valentine duplex drive (DD) was capable of swimming short distances. This made it particularly useful for amphibious operations. It used a canvas screen attached to the tank chassis. When the screen was raised, it gave the tank enough buoyancy to float. The Valentine had a small external propeller to push the tank through the water. However, it was highly susceptible to floating mines, underwater objects, and high waves.

Although the U.S. Army was at first skeptical about specialized tanks, they eventually adopted a wide range of variants. One of the first was the M-19, twin 40mm guns mounted on the Chaffee light tank chassis. It was effective as both an antiaircraft and an antitank weapon. The M-4 Sherman tank was modified to operate as a bulldozer, a flamethrower, a rocket launcher, a duplex drive, and a mine detonator. The Sherman Crab was a flail tank similar to the British Scorpion. The Sherman Crocodile flamethrower could shoot a flame 100 yards.

The British adapted Sherman tanks for rocket launchers and ARVs. The Sherman duplex drive operated similarly to the Valentine DD, and it was vulnerable to the same hazards. The Sherman was also waterproofed by installing extension cowlings over the exhaust and intake ports and sealing all other openings. The tank could then drive through the surf while submerged up to its turret. The cowlings and tape were designed for easy removal once ashore.

Another special purpose "tank" was made from inflatable rubber. The pneumatic dummy tanks were designed by the British, built by the Americans, and used extensively by both. Their first widespread use was during Operation FORTITUDE (q.v.) as a deception device prior to the Normany (q.v.) invasion. When real tanks in Britain moved out of their staging areas in preparation for loading for D-Day, pneumatic tanks were set up and camouflaged in their place. This produced two effects. It led German intelligence to estimate that the Allies had more tanks than they really did, and it served to conceal the final movements in preparation for the invasion.

The Italians mounted their antiaircraft guns in trucks, but they employed flamethrower and command post/operations center variants of their light tanks. The command post tanks were fitted with turrets with dummy guns so they would appear indistinguishable to an enemy in battle.

The Soviets employed very few special purpose tanks. The most significant was the SU-37, single or twin 37mm M-1939 antiaircraft guns mounted on a T-70 light tank chassis.

Earlier in the war, German antiaircraft guns were mounted on half-tracks, but their first fully tracked antiaircraft gun did not come out until 1943. The *Leichter Flakpanzer* 38(t) Sd Kfz-140 was based on the old Czech PzKpfw-38(t) chassis. It carried a single 2cm Flak 38 gun. The *Flakpanzer IV* was much larger at twenty-five tons. Based on the PzKpfw-IV chassis, it carried four 2.0cm *Flakvierling* 38 guns. It was an effective system that could lay down a barrage of 800 rounds per minute and had 85mm armor protection.

During the planning for the aborted Operation SEA LION (q.v.), the German Army wrestled with the problem of how to provide armored support to its troops that would be assaulting the beaches of Britain. The Germans tried to modify their existing tanks to make them amphibious, which would give them the ability to float and power themselves through the water from the landing craft offshore (like the Allies' later DD tanks). Only the PzKpfw-II proved light enough to become a *Schwimm-Panzer*, but it was too lightly armed to provide the required support. The more powerful PzKpfw-III and PzKpfw-IV were too heavy for the flotation kits then available. As a result, the German Navy was given the task of quickly developing submersible variants.

The initial conversions were carried out at the Wilhelmshaven naval shipyard. The tanks' turret rings, hatches, drive trains, and engine compartments were all fitted with rubber seals made from bicycle inner tubes. The main guns also were fitted with pneumatic seals and plugs, but in such a way that they could be blown open quickly as the tank broke the water's surface. The engines received air via a sixty-foot rubber hose that attached to a *schnorchel* mounted on a rubber float. The *schnorchel* stood about one meter above the float, which also carried the tank's radio antenna. The tank had a gyroscope driving mechanism and a simple navigation system that permitted blind steering. Essentially, the driver drove the tank along a prescribed course from the landing craft, plotting his position on a chart based on the direction and duration of the underwater voyage.

Tests on the *Unterwasser-Panzer* or *U-Panzer* were completed in six weeks. About 270 *U-Panzers* of various models were converted, and the tanks were declared operationally ready by mid-July 1940. The SEA LION plan called for a battalion of *U-Panzers* to be attached to the first wave of

each infantry division going ashore. When SEA LION was canceled, the *U-Panzers* were absorbed into the German Army's *Panzer* divisions. In November 1940, three of the battalions were formed into the 18th *Panzer* Regiment and assigned to the 18th *Panzer* Division. The fourth battalion joined the 3rd *Panzer* Division's 6th *Panzer* Regiment. In January 1941, both divisions were assigned to the preparations for Operation BARBAROSSA.

The *U-Panzers* proved valuable during the Second *Panzer* Group's crossing of the Bug River during the early stages of BARBAROSSA. On 22 June 1941, the 18th *Panzer* Regiment's 1st Battalion made a submerged crossing of the fifteen-foot deep river and hit the opposite bank with a phalanx of eighty tanks. For this operations the tanks' *schnorchels* were replaced with 10-foot steel breathing tubes. The crossing was a complete success. The surprised Soviet defenders were quickly overwhelmed and the bridgehead was secured in minutes with no *Panzer* losses.

The 18th *Panzer* Regiment's submerged crossing of the Bug was the first and last of its kind in military history. It was a remarkable technical and operational achievement. Late in the war the Soviets attempted to produce a submersible tank by modifying their standard T-34. During the Cold War years, the Soviet Army continued to experiment with submersible tanks and conducted many such operations in training.

William H. Van Husen
Carl O. Schuster

Additional Reading

Carell, Paul, *Hitler's War on Russia* (1987).
Crow, Duncan (ed.), *British and Commonwealth AFVs: 1940–46* (1971).
Hahn, Fritz, *Waffen und Geheimwaffen des Deutschen Heeres 1933–1945* (1992).
Harris, J.P. and J.P. Toase, *Armoured Warfare* (1990).
Hogg, Ian V., and John Weeks, *The Illustrated Encyclopedia of Military Vehicles* (1980).
Schenk, Peter, *Invasion of England 1940* (1990).
Speilberger, Walter J., and Uwe, Feist, *Sonderpanzer: German Special Purpose Vehicles* (1968).
Vanderveen, Bart, *Historic Military Vehicles Directory* (1993).

Tanks, U.S.

Only after the German victories in 1940 did the United States begin to fund a massive increase in its armored forces. America, in fact, had lagged well behind the other powers, neglecting armor almost completely during the interwar period. Committed to isolationism, it saw little need for powerful (and expensive) mechanized units. Until just shortly prior to the start of the war, a U.S. tank corps did not exist, and control of the tanks lay with the infantry, which preferred lightly armored (and armed) vehicles. In July 1940, the newly created U.S. Armored Force under Brigadier General Adna R. Chaffee (q.v.) began to be developed, with an initial strength of two armored divisions and one independent tank battalion. Each division was to have three regiments of 381 tanks, but initially a total of only 464 serviceable tanks and combat cars were available. More armored vehicles were desperately needed.

The response of American industry to the military's needs was phenomenal, with production rising from 330 new tanks in 1940 to 4,052 in 1941, 24,997 in 1942, and 29,487 in 1943. Between July 1940 and the end of the war, the United States produced 88,276 tanks—2,330 heavy, 28,919 light, and 57,027 medium. America's expertise in vehicle mass production, plus the construction of two new tank arsenals—completed within months—led to the jump in production. In part, this resulted from the decision to manufacture a few standard types, such as the M-4 medium tank. During the war, one armored division (the 1st), and eight tank battalions fought in Italy. A further six armored divisions were at Normandy (q.v.), and their importance was confirmed after Allied forces broke out from the beachhead. General George S. Patton's (q.v.) advance across France was only halted by the needs of supply and inter-Allied politics. An additional nine armored divisions were available for the final defeat of Germany, and about thirty-nine separate tank battalions fought in northwest Europe.

The success of the German campaign in France (q.v.) in June 1940 led to a major redesign of the American light tank and the application of thicker armor. At the start of the war, the U.S. had four types of tanks, the infantry's medium M-2A1 and light M-2A4, and the cavalry's combat cars, the M-1 and M-2. These models had all been developed from the T-2 tank series that dated back to 1933. The new M-3 light tank weighed twelve tons, and these were developed largely from the M-2A4s. They carried a 37mm gun in a fully rotating turret, had thicker armor (38mm on the front and 38mm on the nose). Production began in July 1940, and over the next two years, 5,811 were manufactured. During these two years numerous technical changes were made.

One version, the General Stuart, was sent to Britain after the passing of Lend-Lease (q.v.) in March 1941, and the first U.S. tanks arrived in North Africa (q.v.) in July 1941. British forces were the first to use the Stuart in combat, and as a result of these experiences, other modifications were made. The Stuart carried a 37mm M-5 gun and three caliber .30 Browning M-1919A4 machine guns. The M-3 and M-5 light tanks were also important in the American armed forces, even though they were quickly replaced by medium tanks. The M-3s were, incidentally, the first American tanks to see combat against the Japanese. The first of the M-5s, the final model in this series, came off the production line in March 1942, and this tank saw its first action near Casablanca, and more combat in France.

Another version of the light tank was the M-22 Locust, produced as a vehicle that could be brought in by airborne forces. Several hundred were shipped to British and U.S. forces after December 1942 when it first came off the production line. The M-22 carried a 37mm M-6 main gun and a caliber .30 machine gun. Mechanical defects, its thin armor, concerns about the effectiveness of an eight-ton vehicle and the absence of a means of transporting it into combat effectively doomed the M-22 among American forces.

Early in the war, the need for better armed and armored tanks than the Stuart became quickly apparent. Work on an improvement of the M-5 began in April 1943, and the T-24 was the result. The light tank T-24 carried one 75mm M-6 main gun, two caliber .30 machine guns, and one caliber .50 machine gun. Its success led to the production figures being increased from 1,000 to 5,000. Production began in April 1944, and in May it was standardized as the M-24. Used in light tank companies and cavalry reconnaissance units in northwest Europe and Italy, the M-24 Chaffee saw its first action in late 1944 during the Ardennes offensive (q.v.). Although lightly armored, its maneuverability and agility made it a good reconnaissance vehicle. Several variations were produced.

In May 1940, the United States armed forces had only eighteen modern medium tanks, all of the M-2 type developed in the late 1930s for infantry support. The M-2 medium tank weighed nineteen tons, carried 25mm-thick armor, and was armed with six machine guns. The swift German victory over France forced a radical shift in American tank policy. Battlefield experience showed the need for thicker armor and a gun capable of firing both armor-piercing and high explosive ammunition. The immediate call was for 1,741 medium tanks, and plans were approved for a $21 million tank arsenal to be established by Chrysler at Detroit. Further German successes led to the call for a medium tank with a 75mm main gun, and by April 1941, three manufacturers had produced prototypes of the M-3. Production began in August. The M-3 weighed 30.0 tons, was armed with 75mm and 37mm guns, as well as three caliber .30 Browning machine guns. Relatively simple in design, the M-3 had armor up to 57mm thick, and a top speed of 26 mph. The guns were major improvements, with the high velocity of the 75mm gun and a gyroscopic system of stabilization that allowed the tank to fire while moving, and to accurately sight the gun as soon as the tank stopped. Six different models of the Generals Lee and Grant tanks were produced, the last being the M-3A5, which was produced from January to November 1942.

Modified M-3s were sent to the British after passage of the Lend-Lease act. They desperately needed armored vehicles, and the Grants saw combat in North Africa in 1942. U.S. forces first used the M-3 in combat in Northwest Africa (q.v.) in November 1942. Production of the M-3 continued until late 1942, with about 6,200 of various models having been built. The M-3 chassis also served as the basis for a number of specialized vehicles (*see* Tanks, Special), including recovery vehicles, tractors for heavy artillery, minesweeping tanks, and self-propelled artillery.

From the beginning, the M-3 was viewed as an interim vehicle, and development of a replacement, based on the M-3, started in March 1941. By the following September, a prototype of the M-4 Sherman had been assembled, and a production target of 2,000 a month established. The first came off the assembly line in February 1942, and it first saw combat with British forces in North Africa. During the course of the war more M-4s were produced than any other type of tank. A total of 48,347 Sherman tanks of all types were produced—a figure that is more than the total combined tank output of Germany during the entire war.

Although not up to the firepower level of the best German tanks, the Sherman clearly was the most important Allied tank of the war. The Sherman made up for its defects not only in sheer numbers, but also in ease of maintenance, ruggedness, and reliability. It was simple to operate and manufacture. The Sherman's 75mm guns were equal to the firepower of most existing German tanks, but as Nazi Germany introduced more powerful tanks, improvements in the M-4 were called for. The Sherman had an early reputation for combustibil-

A Sherman M-4A3 tank, armed with a 76mm M-1A2 main gun. This variant was designated the Medium Tank, M-4A1 (76mm). The turret machine gun is an M-2 caliber .50. (IWM KID 6033)

ity when hit, and was nicknamed the "Ronson Lighter" by the troops. By early 1944, improved versions came into service, with larger guns (the 76mm M-1A1) and heavier armor. The last modification, improved spring suspension, was made in late 1944.

During the war several versions of the M-4 were used, with the M-4A3 being the most common. A special assault version, designed hurriedly in 1944, was a heavily armed infantry support vehicle used in northwest Europe, the location where the greatest number of Shermans were deployed. Its nose armor was increased to 140mm, the side armor to 76mm, and the weight went to forty-two tons. Speed was reduced, however, to 22 mph. Many M-4s were modified for special purposes, including two flamethrower models, a rocket launcher model that fired 4.5-inch rockets, and a mine exploder. Some were fitted with bulldozer blades and others were used as minesweepers. The chassis also served as the basis for a self-propelled gun and mobile antitank weapons.

The Sherman also became a standard battle tank of the British Army. In the fall of 1942, M-4s fought at El Alamein (q.v.). Late in the war the British modified about 600 M-4s of various models by replacing the 75mm or 76mm main gun with the British 17-pounder. The resulting "Sherman Firefly" saw extensive action in northwest Europe. Production of the Sherman ended in June 1945, although development did resume after the war.

The success of German *Panzers* in May 1940 also revealed the need for a heavy tank. The M-6, a sixty-ton vehicle with 76mm armor, was produced, but then canceled because of difficulty shipping it overseas and concerns over its reliability. Opinion changed when Allied forces encountered the heavily armed Panther and Tiger tanks, and as a result, the U.S. developed several new tank models with greater firepower, battlefield maneuverability, and armored protection.

Experimental models included the T-22, T-23, T-25, and T-26. Priority for development of the T-26 came in June 1944, and 250 were ordered. The first twenty were shipped to the European theater in January 1945. The new tank (at twenty-eight feet, ten inches long and eleven feet, six inches wide) was standardized as the M-26 "General Pershing." It carried a 90mm main gun, almost equal to the German 88mm in performance, and weighed just over forty-six tons. The Pershing could reach a top speed of 30 mph and had a range of ninety-two miles. Because of its relatively late deployment, the M-26 saw only limited use with the 3rd and 9th Armored Divisions. Only 310 reached the European theater before V-E day, and of these only twenty actually engaged in combat.

Kenneth J. Swanson
Robert G. Waite

(Refer to table on page 1136)

Additional Reading
Forty, George, *United States Tanks of World War II in Action* (1983).
Grove, Eric, *World War II Tanks* (1976).
Hunnicut, R.P., *Firepower: A History of the American Heavy Tank* (1988).
———, *Sherman: A History of the American Medium Tank* (1978).
Macksey, Kenneth, *Tank Force: Allied Armor in World War II* (1970).

Torpedoes

Torpedoes were the deadliest naval weapons of World War II, sinking more than 17 million tons of ships and shipping in the European theater alone. In fact, torpedoes sank or damaged more ships than all other weapons combined, primarily because they were used by submarines. Although carried by ships and aircraft as well, the advent of radar (q.v.), combined with the torpedo's short range compared to other naval weapons, made the torpedo increasingly hazardous for surface ships and aircraft to employ as the war progressed. In terms of range, the torpedoes of 1939 were little better than those of 1918. Yet they had become so important to naval warfare by 1940 that all the major belligerents conducted sustained efforts to improve them. As a result, the torpedoes of 1945 had more in common with those of today than they did with their predecessors of World War I.

The most promising advances in torpedo design during the interwar years were in guidance systems, propulsion, and warhead fuzing. During World War I, all torpedoes had to be physically aimed down the bearing they were to take to the target. Moreover, their steam propulsion systems left a visible wake which not only warned the target of their impending approach but more critically for submarines, could be traced back to the launch point. These torpedoes also used contact fuzes, requiring a direct hit on the target for detonation. Most of the major naval powers undertook programs to correct these problems during the interwar period.

By 1939, all the major powers except France

had developed torpedoes that could have their courses offset by as much as 90 degrees from the direction of launch. This negated the necessity to maneuver the launching unit into position. France was also the only major power that had not installed automated fire control systems on its ships and submarines, although they had one almost ready to enter service as the war began. All the major navies, except the Soviet Union, had wakeless electric torpedoes entering service as the war began, but quantities were limited.

One of the most promising developments at the start of the war was the magnetic fuze. Designed to detonate upon encountering a ship's magnetic signature, that is, the disruption in the earth's magnetic pattern brought on by the ship's metal hull, the magnetic fuze promised to make the torpedo even deadlier. Since a direct hit was no longer necessary, the torpedo could be set to break a ship's back by exploding under the hull. Unfortunately, a torpedo's speed gave the fuze little time to adjust to local magnetic conditions. This and the introduction of degaussing equipment on surface ships rendered the magnetic fuze unreliable. None were in service after 1942.

Only three countries entered the war with torpedoes incorporating all of these advances: Germany, Great Britain, and the United States. Interestingly, their torpedoes all initially suffered problems in service. The newly introduced magnetic fuzes proved unreliable and the depth-setting mechanisms were faulty. Only Britain's Royal Navy responded quickly, correcting the depth-setting problem within weeks of the war's start. The United States and Germany reacted more slowly, not even testing their torpedoes until nearly a year after they entered the war. Thus, they did not correct their respective depth-setting problems until late 1941 (Germany) and 1942 (United States). (see Submarines, U.S.) None of these countries were able to fix their magnetic fuzes and ultimately returned to contact fuzing. As with the depth-setting mechanisms, both Germany and the United States had difficulties with their contact fuzes and took more than a year to correct those as well.

Despite their simplicity, French torpedoes also performed poorly in combat, while the Soviet Union and Italy produced the simplest and most reliable torpedoes of the war. In fact, Italy's air-delivered torpedoes were so much better than Germany's that the *Luftwaffe* used Italian torpedoes until improved German ones could enter production.

Surface ship-and submarine-delivered torpedoes were remarkably similar during the war, differing only in the supporting fire control and launch systems. Air-delivered torpedoes of the early war years were of lighter construction, employing a smaller propulsion section and a smaller warhead to reduce the weight by nearly 600 pounds. Most aircraft of 1938–1940 lacked the lifting capacity to carry the one-ton weight of a standard torpedo. By 1941, this no longer held true, and differences between naval and aerial torpedo range and hitting power gradually diminished. By war's end, they differed only in guidance and launch systems, but radar-controlled antiaircraft fire with the deadly proximity fuze (q.v.) made aerial torpedo attack against surface ships an almost suicidal affair. Few countries continued the practice in the postwar period, except for antisubmarine warfare (q.v.).

Germany's Navy, the *Kriegsmarine,* developed the most technologically advanced torpedoes of the war. Facing increasingly powerful Allied escort forces, Germany placed a high priority on improving the guidance systems, range, and hitting power of its submarine-launched torpedoes. By 1942, Germany introduced the T-4 electric acoustic homing torpedo. Equipped with two acoustic receivers in its nose, the T-series homed in on the noise put in the water by an escort vessel's propulsion system. Since the torpedo was guided by its target's propulsion noise, it promised a high hit probability despite any evasive maneuvers the target might take. The Allies developed acoustic deception devices to defeat these weapons, and the Germans produced increasingly sophisticated models as they discovered the Allied countermeasures.

The Germans also introduced long-range, pattern-running torpedoes, allowing their submarines to attack from outside the convoy's escort and still have a fair hit probability. Other technological avenues were pursued as U-boat losses continued to mount. They were testing a wire-guided torpedo and preparing a prototype "wake homing" model when the war ended. As with so many other weapon developments of the war, however, it was another case of too little, too late.

Faced with a less overpowering and resilient antisubmarine warfare campaign in Europe, the Western Allies concentrated on producing large numbers of reliable wakeless antiship torpedoes, rather than developing exotic guided systems. For the Allies, destroying submarines was the primary research goal, and by 1943, the U.S. introduced the Mark 24 antisubmarine mine, an active sonar guided, airdropped, antisubmarine torpedo. Theoretically employable from ship, its use was limited to aerial dropping because of the potential for it to home in on the propulsion noises of the ship that launched it. Using a more sensitive acoustic receiver than the German T-series, the Mk-24 moved at less than 12 knots, and tracked the lower propulsion noises of a slow-moving electrically driven submarine. Employed almost exclusively by the hunter-killer task groups in the war's final year, the Mk-24 was one of the lesser-known but most successful of the Allied antisubmarine warfare weapons of World War II.

The torpedo experienced revolutionary development during World War II. It evolved from a simple straight-running "self-propelled mine" to an underwater guided missile. Moreover, it emerged from the war with its basic mission changed. No longer restricted to antiship operations, the torpedo today is the central weapon of choice in the war between naval forces operating on and above, versus below, the water's surface.

Carl O. Schuster

Additional Reading
Campbell, John, *Naval Weapons of World War II* (1985).
Hough, Richard, *The Longest Battle* (1986).
Piekalkiewicz, Janusz, *Sea War 1939–1945* (1980).

Transport Aircraft, British
Britain entered the war with no aerial transport fleet. Faced with limited funding and foreseeing no requirement for air transport, the Royal Air Force (RAF) concentrated on building fighters and bombers. As a result, Britain was forced to rely on modified obsolete bombers and American-built Lend-Lease (q.v.) aircraft for its air transport fleet. Although it was a useful expedient that worked during the war, it placed the country's aviation industry in a poor position to compete in the postwar air transport production market—a position from which it has never recovered.

The inadequacy of the RAF's transport fleet first became apparent in 1940, when Prime Minister Winston S. Churchill (q.v.) directed the formation of Britain's first airborne units. Having no air transports other than small army liaison aircraft in its inventory, the RAF could only provide six old and obsolescent Whitley bombers to Britain's budding airborne establishment. The Whitley, which could only carry six paratroopers, remained the backbone of the RAF transport force until 1942. It initially was superseded by the slightly larger Whitworth bomber, while redundant Stirling and Halifax bombers served as long-range transports in some circumstances.

The American-built C-47, which the British called the Dakota, was the mainstay of the RAF transport service from mid-1942 until several years after the war. Simple, robust and reliable, the C-47 and its civilian counterpart, the DC-3, were outstanding transport aircraft. Many continued flying in Africa, Asia, and Latin America well into the 1990s.

Carl O. Schuster

(Refer to table on page 1137)

Additional Reading
Gregory, Barry, *British Airborne Troops* (1974).
Turner, John, *British Aircraft of World War II* (1975).
Weal, Elke, et al., *Combat Aircraft of World War Two* (1977).

Transport Aircraft, German
Under the terms of the Versailles Treaty (q.v.), the post–World War I *Reichswehr* was forbidden aircraft. Thus, during the first phase of the military rebuilding of the Third *Reich* in 1934–1935, the *Luftwaffe* planned on using commercial aircraft of the state-owned Lufthansa airline for military air transport. When paratroops units were added to the *Wehrmacht* in 1936–1937, special transport aircraft became indispensable.

The Germans turned to the Soviet Union for a model. During the fall maneuvers of 1936, the Red Army managed to fly 1,500 men, 150 machine guns, and eighteen artillery pieces with their basic loads of ammunition to the operations area in the Byelorussian military district with just two TB-3 aircraft. Additional ideas for building up air transport units came from Great Britain. In order to quickly suppress revolts in the colonies Britain converted bombers into transports. Thus at the beginning of 1936, when the first German paratrooper battalion was built from the General Göring Regiment, the air transportation group *Kampfgruppe z.b.V.1* was equipped with converted Ju-52 bombers, in models Ju-52/3M and Ju-53 G3E for transporting the troops. Four squadrons with twelve planes each could transport the whole battalion at once.

The Ju-52 faced its first operational test as transport during the Spanish civil war (q.v.). On 27 July 1936, the first transport planes took off from Berlin's Tempelhof Airport and headed for

Spanish Morocco. From there, the German squadron transported 15,000 soldiers of the Spanish Foreign Legion and 270 tons of war materiel to Spain in support of General Francisco Franco (q.v.). This mission was the first major air transport operation in military history.

After the *Anschluss* (q.v.) with Austria in March 1938, the number of paratroop units increased in anticipation of a military conflict with Czechoslovakia. At the end of 1938, the 7th Air Division had five air transport groups with 250 Ju-52 transports. For transport, courier, and training purposes, the *Luftwaffe* had 552 Ju-52s at the beginning of World War II. In accordance with the operational requirements of *Blitzkrieg* (q.v.), air transport units were expected to support any specific campaign. The occupations of Denmark and Norway (qq.v.) in April 1940, surfaced a certain lack of coordination between the army and air transport operations.

At the beginning of the invasion of Western Europe on 10 May 1940, a special unit of paratroops caused a sensation when they landed in DFS 230 gliders on top of Eben Emael (q.v.), and took the Belgian fort in relatively short order. With that operation and similar landings against Dutch fortresses, an entirely new era of airborne warfare came into being.

After the armistice with France in June 1940, Hermann Göring (q.v.) established a central command post for all air transport operations at *Luftwaffe* high command headquarters. The new section was headed by an air transport commander (*Lufttransportführer),* but he actually exercised very little control because the air transport units were assigned to the air corps of the various air fleets. Air transport task groupings were also specially formed for specific operations. During the 1941 attack on Crete (q.v.), for example, all transports came under the command of the XI Air Corps.

In the years following Crete, German air transport resources became increasingly dispersed. In the Mediterranean area, transport units had to conduct numerous flights to supply the *Africa Korps* (q.v.). The eastern front also needed an increasing number of planes to transport important supplies (engines for planes and tanks, spare parts, fuel, ammunition) for the provision of isolated and sometimes encircled units, and to transport the wounded out.

Often, the number and capacity of the available aircraft was insufficient. Purposeful and efficient mission planning, cooperation between the army and air force, and an efficient ground organization did not exist. In attempting to supply the German forces at Stalingrad (q.v.), the transport pilots lost 495 planes in just nine weeks of operations; 269 were Ju-52s and 169 were He-111s, which were used for additional support. All together, the *Luftwaffe* lost 1,240 transport planes between 1 December 1942 and 30 April 1943.

The German aircraft industry was not able to keep pace with the demand placed by the *Luftwaffe* general staff for more and better planes. The immense use of materials, the high numbers required in the workforce, and the mostly hand-crafted production methods caused long production lead times, high costs, and differing levels of quality. The conversion to mass production methods occurred only in 1943–1944. By that time, German transport aircraft were almost helpless and at the mercy of the Allied tactical air forces.

Even though it was built in great numbers, the Ju-52 was technically obsolete. Between 1939 and 1944, 2,804 Ju-52s were delivered to the *Luftwaffe* (1939: 145; 1940: 388; 1941: 502; 1942: 503; 1943: 887; and 1944: 379). The Ju-52 was an open fuselage, three-engine plane with a corrugated metal skin. It could carry eighteen fully equipped soldiers, or twelve stretchers when used as an air ambulance. Transported material was loaded and unloaded through side doors. Air-dropped supplies were jettisoned through two double chutes; paratroopers jumped through the side doors.

High losses of aircraft and the increasing lack of fuel by the end of 1943 led to the dissolution of some air transport units. On 1 May 1944, the *Luftwaffe* had only two air transport command staffs, six wing staffs, twenty-four air transport groups, an additional mixed group, and five independent squadrons. The planes themselves were a mixture. Besides the Ju-52, they were using the He-111, Ar-232B, Ju-290A1, Ju-352, Go-244B, Me-323D, BV-222A, P-108C, and the SM-82.

By the beginning of 1945, air superiority of the Allies reduced the German air transport fleet to seven groups of Ju-52s, a partial group of Ju-352s, two groups of He-111s, and five glider squadrons. During the 1945 operations to supply the German troops encircled at Breslau, the *Luftwaffe* lost another 165 Ju-52s and He-111s. When Germany finally surrendered on 8 May 1945, only 150 more-or-less functioning Ju-52s were left.

Franz W. Seidler

(Refer to table on page 1138)

Additional Reading
Deichmann, Paul, *German Air Force Operations in Support of the Army* (1968).
Morzik, Fritz, *German Air Force Airlift Operations* (1961).

Transport Aircraft, Soviet

In the 1930s, the Soviet aircraft industry produced several gigantic transports for the Maxim Gorky Squadron, whose task was the support of pro-Communist cinema performances, lectures, and public functions throughout the Soviet Union. The five-engine Tupolev Ant-14 first flew in 1931, and the eight-engine Ant-20 "Maxim Gorky" first flew in 1934. After the Maxim Gorky was destroyed in an accident in 1935, it was replaced by the more powerful Ant-20bis. Only single examples of these machines were built, but they provided valuable experience for the fledgling Soviet aircraft industry. Another prewar type, the trimotor Ant-9, had persistent engine problems, and was redesigned as the twin-engine passenger aircraft PS-9. The PS-9 was more successful, and sixty were built by 1934. They served as frontline transports at the battles of Stalingrad and Kursk during World War II.

The four-engine Tb-3 bomber, originally produced in 1931, was used as a transport during World War II. Eleven Tb-3s were used to fly ball bearings directly to tank plants. They were also used to carry paratroops. A few were specially modified for Arctic conditions and remained in service until the 1950s.

The significant twin-engine Soviet transports of the prewar period were the Stal-7 and the Ant-35, both low-wing monoplanes. Although the Stal-7 and the Ant-35 had good performance, their cargo and passenger capacity was limited. The Stal-7 could carry twelve passengers, and the Ant-35 could carry only ten. In comparison, the American DC-3 could carry twenty-eight passengers. Consequently, the Stal-7 and the Ant-35 were not ordered into production.

Instead, Soviet production of a licensed version of the DC-3 began in 1939. Modification of the DC-3 was carried out by the Soviet designer Lisunov, and the resulting aircraft was designated as the Lisunov Li-2. During World War II, some Li-2s were fitted with a dorsal turret, that mounted a flexible ShKAS machine gun. Apertures in fuselage windows allowed troops to fire their rifles at enemy aircraft. In all, about 2,000 Li-2s were built by the Soviets. In addition, the U.S. supplied some 700 C-47s (the military version of the DC-3).

The most notable single-engine Soviet transport of World War II was the Polikarpov U-2 biplane, which was used for liaison, reconnaissance, VIP transport, ambulance duties, supply flights (including clandestine operations behind enemy lines), propaganda operations, and light bombing. More than 13,000 were built before the June 1941 German invasion. Modified U-2s included a short takeoff and landing (STOL) version, and a four-place passenger model. U-2s were used to transport molybdenum ore from Siberian mines to railway stations.

In 1942, some 400 Antonov A-7 cargo gliders were built for the Soviet Air Force. These clean, high-wing aircraft were usually towed by Sb-2 bombers, and sometimes were used to supply Soviet partisans (q.v.). Twin-engine Yak-6 and Shcherbakov Ts-1 light transports were also used for supply flights to the partisans. The Ts-1 was constructed almost entirely of wood.

Although the Soviets led the world in experimental airborne operations during the 1930s, Soviet paratroopers were not used to any great extent during World War II. This was due in part to problems of air superiority in the first years after the invasion, and to a lack of transport aircraft that persisted throughout the war. In 1945, Soviet transports were used in airborne attacks on Japanese-held areas in Manchuria.

The transport arm of the Soviet Air Force, supplemented by aircraft and personnel from the Aeroflot airline, were active in supply operations at all the crucial battles on the eastern front: Moscow, Leningrad, Stalingrad, Kursk, Berlin, and Byelorussia (qq.v.).

Dennis A. Bartel

(Refer to table on page 1139)

Additional Reading
Alexander, Jean, *Russian Aircraft Since 1940* (1975).
Nemecek, Vaclav, *The History of Soviet Aircraft from 1918* (1986).

Transport Aircraft, U.S.

World War II in Europe posed no larger problem for the Allies than that of logistics. Transports those large, relatively slow, long-range aircraft proved to be the lifeline of Allied military operations. Transports were used to move supplies, equipment, munitions, and troops. Responsibility for aerial transportation during the early stages of the war fell to commercial airlines under contract

The U.S. Army established a temporary transport group in 1932 and made it permanent in 1937. In 1941, the U.S. Air Corps Ferrying Command was created to deliver aircraft to the British under Lend-Lease (q.v.). After America's entry in the war, the transportation arm of the United States Army Air Force (USAAF) was renamed the Air Transport Command (ATC) under the command of Brigadier General Harold George.

The primary transport aircraft used by the USAAF were the C-45, C-46, C-47, C-53, C-54, and C-60. The "C" designation for transports stood for cargo. Most World War II transports were military adaptations of commercial aircraft already in service. Modified B-17 and B-24 bombers were also used as transports. The Douglas C-47 Skytrain and the Douglas C-54 Skymaster were the mainstays of ATC operations in Europe.

The C-47 was manufactured by Douglas Aircraft as a military version of the DC-3, a widely successful commercial transport. The Skytrain had a five-ton cargo or twenty-eight-troop capacity, a large loading door, a range of 1,500 miles, but was capable of speeds of only 229 mph. It was unarmed. Another version of the basic DC-3 was the Douglas C-53 Skytrooper, which had a greater range but a smaller cargo capacity than the C-47.

The C-53 first entered USAAF service in late 1941 as a troop carrier.

The C-47, lovingly called the "Gooney Bird" by the pilots who flew it, saw its initial service in the late 1930s. It was also used by the Royal Air Force (RAF), which called it the Dakota. In all, a total of 10,123 DC-3s were produced for military use, with 1,200 going to the British. On two occasions in 1942, American production of C-47s was revived because of the British need for proven aircraft.

General Dwight D. Eisenhower (q.v.) called the C-47 one of the four weapons that contributed the most to winning the war; the others were the bazooka, the jeep, and the atomic bomb. The C-47 remained in active status with the U.S. Air Force up through the 1970s. During the Vietnam War, some of the old C-47s were fitted with a 20mm electric Gatling gun and used in a ground-attack role. The AC-47, as it was designated, was called "Puff, the Magic Dragon" by U.S. troops on the ground. The DC-3/C-47 was one of the most successful and reliable designs in aviation history.

The C-54 was also a major player in European operations, although only 1,242 Skymasters were built. The C-54, which was later popular as the DC-4 commercial aircraft, had a range of 3,900 miles, more than twice the C-47. The

A C-47 in flight, the workhorse transport of the Allies. The RAF also used the C-47, designating it the "Dakota." (IWM E 1266)

C-54 had a maximum speed of 239 mph and a capacity of 28,500 pounds or fifty passengers. Only a handful were loaned to the British. They made a combined total of 79,642 ocean crossings during the war and only three were lost. The C-54 was also one of the mainstays of the postwar Berlin Airlift (q.v.).

During the war, the USAAF also purchased 3,341 Curtis C-46 Commandos. Manufactured by Curtis Aircraft, it had a bigger payload than the C-47 and was capable of higher altitudes. It was used primarily in the India-China-Burma Theater.

The C-82 was the first aircraft designed specifically as a military transport. Manufactured by Fairchild Engine and Airplane Corporation, the C-82 had ground-level cargo access. After the aircraft first flew in 1944, the USAAF ordered 100, but the new planes arrived too late for service in the war.

During the first years of the war most military transport was handled by contract with the commercial airlines, with Pan American Airlines flying the most miles. Cyrus R. Smith of American Airlines became the deputy commander of ATC, and many other airline executives assumed ATC administrative functions. The list of contributing airlines reads like a "Who's Who" of commercial airways. In the months immediately following the beginning of America's involvement, most of the transport aircrews were airline employees. After a high of 88 percent in 1941, commercial airlines still contracted for 68 percent of military transport in 1943, and 33 percent in 1944.

After ATC was formed in June 1942, it assumed the mission of the Ferrying Command, but its primary responsibility was moving men and equipment. Transports headed for Europe followed an often hazardous route across the North Atlantic, beginning from the supply base at Presque Isle, Maine, then flying to Goose Bay, Labrador. The route continued to Iceland and/or Greenland before reaching Prestwick, Scotland.

Supplies were then sent by rail to parts of Britain or even flown into the London area.

The northern route was susceptible to bad weather and sudden climatic changes that made flying difficult. Fog, storms, heavy snows, and unpredictable ice created nightmares for transport crews. Although airfields were excellent and constantly maintained, conditions caused hazardous landings and takeoffs. Aircraft sometimes were forced down by weather changes or in-flight engine problems. Icing of windshields, inside and out, caused vision problems and the cold often was unbearable. Rescue operations were a vital part of maintaining the North Atlantic route. To allow for greater cargo capacity, fuel loads were reduced, thus creating the necessity for repeated landings and refueling.

U.S. transports also played a direct combat role carrying troops. During the first fifty hours of Operation OVERLORD, C-47s delivered most of the 30,000 Allied paratroopers and glider-borne troops dropped behind German lines.

When the ground fighting ended in Europe, transport aircraft became even more active, as supplies, equipment, and men were moved deeper into Europe. In August 1945, ATC evacuated almost 9,000 medical patients by air. That same month, 85,191 other passengers were carried, along with 11,040 tons of cargo. ATC also had the mission of rapidly shifting U.S. troops from Europe to the Pacific. When the global war finally ended, ships carried the bulk of U.S. troops back home, although some did return by air.

Boyd Childress

(Refer to table on page 1140)

Additional Reading

Cleveland, Reginald M., *Air Transport at War* (1946).

Jane's All the World's Aircraft (1945–46).

La Farge, Oliver, *The Eagle and the Egg* (1949).

Section IV-T
Technical Data Tables of
Weapons and Equipment

British Tanks

Model	Mk-VI	Tetrarch	Cruiser	Crusader	Cromwell	Matilda	Valentine	Churchill Mk-IV	Churchill Mk-VII	Comet
Year in Service	1928	1937	1937	1941	1943	1939	1940	1942	1944	1944
Number Built	1,210	177	655	5,300	3,000	2,990	8,280	Note 1	Note 1	1,186
Combat Weight (tons)	5.4	8.4	16.5	22.1	30.8	29.7	19.5	43.7	44.8	39.4
Maximum Speed (miles per hour)	35	40	30	27	32	15	15	15	13	29
Cruising Range (miles)	125	140	93	124	173	160	90	90	217	123
Main Gun(s) Caliber	.50 MG	40mm	40mm	57mm	75mm	40mm	40mm	40mm	75mm	76.2mm
Number of Machine Guns	2	1	2	2	2	1	1	2	2	2
Maximum Hull Armor	12mm	16mm	30mm	40mm	63mm	70mm	60mm	101mm	152mm	76mm
Maximum Turret Armor	14mm	16mm	14mm	49mm	76mm	75mm	65mm	90mm	90mm	101mm
Crew Size	3	3	6	5	5	4	3	5	5	5

Note:
1. A total of 5,640 Churchill tanks of all Marks were built.

French Tanks

Model	Renault R-35	Char B1-bis	Somua S-35	Hotchkiss H-39
Year in Service	1934	1929	1935	1939
Number Built	2,000	400	430	1,100
Combat Weight (tons)	11.7	34.7	21.5	13.3
Max. Speed (miles per hour)	13	17	25	23
Cruising Range (miles)	87	93	143	74.5
Main Gun(s) Caliber	37mm	47mm, 75mm	47mm	37mm
Number of Machine Guns	1	2	1	1
Maximum Hull Armor	40mm	60mm	40mm	34mm
Maximum Turret Armor	45mm	56mm	56mm	45mm
Crew Size	2	4	3	2

German Tanks

Model	PzKpfw-I	PzKpfw-II	PzKpfw-III	PzKpfw-IV	PzKpfw-V Panther	PzKpfw-VI Tiger	PzKpfw-VIB Tiger II	PzKpfw-35(t)	PzKpfw-38(t)
Year in Service	1934	1936	1937	1936	1943	1942	1944	1935	1938
Number Built	3,000	3,580	5,644	9,000	4,814	1,354	489	190	1,400
Combat Weight (tons)	6.5	10.5	21.8	27.6	50.2	62.8	75	9.0	10.9
Maximum Speed (miles per hour)	25	25	25	24	28	23	22	19	26
Cruising Range (miles)	90	125	102	130	124	87	106	68	155
Main Gun(s) Caliber	MG	20mm	37mm	75mm	75mm	88mm	88mm	37mm	37mm
Number of Machine Guns	2	1	2	2	2	2	3	2	2
Maximum Hull Armor	15mm	30mm	30mm	60mm	80mm	102mm	150mm	25mm	25mm
Maximum Turret Armor	15mm	30mm	57mm	40mm	110mm	100mm	180mm	25mm	30mm
Crew Size	2	3	5	5	5	5	5	3	4

Polish Tanks

Model	TKS	Vickers Mk-E	7TP
Year in Service	1933	1938	1936
Number Built	700	38	95
Combat Weight (tons)	2.6	7.3	10.4
Maximum Speed (miles per hour)	28	22	23
Cruising Range (miles)	80	130	93
Main Gun(s) Caliber	Note 1	47mm	37mm
Number of Machine Guns	1	2	2
Maximum Hull Armor	10mm	13mm	17mm
Maximum Turret Armor	10mm	13mm	17mm
Crew Size	2	3	3

Note

1. The majority of the *TKS* tanks were armed only with a machine gun; however, some twenty tanks were equipped with 20mm cannon.

Soviet Tanks

Model	T-26	BT-5	T-70	T-60	T-34/76	T34/85	KV-1	KV-85	IS-1	IS-2
Year in Service	1931	1935	1942	1941	1941	1943	1939	1943	1943	1944
Number Built	12,000	7,000	8,226	6,000+	Note 1	Note 1	3,010	130	100+	2,250
Combat Weight (tons)	11.6	12.7	10.1	6.4	28.7	35.3	47.4	46	50.7	50.7
Maximum Speed (miles per hour)	18	44	28	27	34	34	22	21	25	23
Cruising Range (miles)	139	124	223	279	186	224	208	150	155	150
Main Gun(s) Caliber	45mm	45mm	45mm	20mm	76.2mm	85mm	76.2mm	85mm	85mm	122mm
Number of Machine Guns	2	2	1	1	2	2	3	3	2	3
Maximum Hull Armor	25mm	13mm	60mm	20mm	45mm	60mm	130mm	110mm	110mm	120mm
Maximum Turret Armor	15mm	13mm	60mm	20mm	65mm	90mm	120mm	116mm	160mm	160mm
Crew Size	3	3	2	2	4	5	5	4	4	4

Note:
1. A total of more than 40,000 T-34s of all models were produced.

U.S. Tanks

Model	M-2A4	M-3/M-5 Stuart	M-22 Locust	M-24 Chaffee	M-3 Lee/Grant	M-4 Sherman	M-26 Pershing
Year in Service	1940	1941/1942	1943	1944	1941	1942	1945
Number Built	365	14,000+	830	4,415	6,258	48,347	2,500*
Combat Weight (tons)	11.5	14.2/16.9	8.2	20.2	30.0	33.3	46.0
Maximum Speed (miles per hour)	30	37	40	35	26	24	30
Cruising Range (miles)	124	68/99	130	100	120	100	92
Main Gun(s) Caliber	37mm	37mm	37mm	75mm	37mm 75mm	75mm	90mm
Number of Machine Guns	4	3	1	3	3	3	3
Maximum Hull Armor	20mm	38/61mm	25mm	25mm	50mm	51mm	102mm
Maximum Turret Armor	25mm	38/44mm	25mm	25mm	57mm	76mm	102mm
Crew Size	4	4	3	5	6	5	5

*Only 20 M-26 Pershings engaged in combat in Europe.

British Transport Aircraft

Model	Whitley Mk-V	Halifax Mk VI-VIII	Stirling Mk IV-V
Service Date	1942	1944	1944
Engines	2	4	4
Crew	5	5	5
Maximum Speed (mph)	230	280	280
Maximum Range (miles)	2,400	2,000	3,000
Gun Armament	None	None	None
Maximum Cargo	7,000 lbs or 6 troops	8,000 lbs or 24 troops	14,000 lbs or 40 troops
Number in Service	1,737*	834	739
Ceiling (feet)	26,000	24,000	17,000

*All models

German Transport Aircraft

Model	Fi-156 Storch	Ar-232B	Go-244B	Ju-52/3M	Ju-290A5	Ju-352	Me-323E
Service Date	1936	1941	1942	1935	1943	1944	1942
Engines	1	4	2	3	4	3	6
Crew	1	4–5	2	3	9	5	7
Maximum Speed (mph)	109	191	290	180	273	205	177
Maximum Range (miles)	200	830	435	808	4,620	1,832	630
Gun Armament	1x 7.92mm MG	1x 13mm MG 1x 20mm	4x 7.92mm MG	3x 7.92mm MG	1x 13mm MG 6x 20mm	2x 13mm MG 1x 20mm	7x 13mm MG 2x 20mm
Maximum Cargo	600 lbs	10,097 lbs	7,900 lbs or 21 troops	3,300 lb or 18 troops	18,000 lbs or 48 troops	9,500 lbs	48,000 lbs or 120 troops
Number in Service	2,900	180	169	4,845	45	31	201
Ceiling (feet)	16,900	22,640	25,100	18,000	19,685	19,685	14,760

Soviet Transport Aircraft

Model	Li-2	U-2
Service Date	1942 Note 1	1928
Engines	2	1
Crew	3	1
Maximum Speed (mph)	170	92
Maximum Range (miles)	1,500	342
Gun Armament	1 x 7.62mm MG	1 x 7.62mm MG
Maximum Cargo	8,200 lbs or 28 troops	550 lbs or 4 troops
Number in Service	2,000	40,000+
Ceiling (feet)	23,200	10,827

Notes:
1. The Li-2 was a copy of the U.S. C-47 cargo aircraft licensed for manufacture in the Soviet Union. Soviet-manufactured engines were used.

U.S. Transport Aircraft

Model	C-45	C-46	C-47	C-53	C-54	C-60
Service Date	1938	1940	1938	1941	1941	1941
Engines	2	2	2	2	4	2
Crew	2	4	3	3	6	2
Maximum Speed (mph)	215	269	229	229	239	266
Maximum Range (miles)	700	1,600	1,500	2,125	3,900	1,660
Gun Armament	None	None	None	None	None	None
Maximum Cargo	6–8 troops	10,000 lbs or 40 troops	10,000 lbs or 28 troops	7,500 lbs or 28 troops	28,500 lbs or 30–50 troops	21 troops
Number in Service	9,100	3,341	9,185	337	1,242	560+
Ceiling (feet)	20,000	27,600	23,200	23,200	22,000	27,000

U

Uniforms

Military uniforms evolved during the sixteenth and early seventeenth centuries as standardized clothing to help instill discipline and cause immediate recognition by friend and foe alike. By World War II, uniforms not only served these historic purposes, but also instilled individual and unit pride. Further, uniforms served as an identification for those captured on the battlefield to help ensure treatment in accordance with international standards. Aircrews in particular wore heavy outer clothing for warmth at high altitudes, and there was concern by some aviators that the leather clothing worn would not be recognized as a uniform in the legal sense. Thus, conventional uniforms were usually worn under flight clothing to insure treatment as prisoners of war (*see* Prisoner of War Operations).

The Geneva Convention of July 1929 dictated the identification and treatment of prisoners. After the war, it was replaced by the Geneva Convention of 1949, which was revised particularly to recognize partisans who spontaneously took up arms in an organized manner, and who were not protected by the wearing of uniforms in the traditional sense.

Uniforms also served as propaganda and morale devices, both within the armed forces and for the civilian populace. Through the appearance of huge numbers of uniformed men and women, everyone was continuously reminded of the war effort and the work required to win the war. This psychological advantage was used by both sides throughout the war. Within an armed force, different uniforms, accoutrements, and insignia (q.v.) served to reinforce the esprit de corps of various units and skills. This was an especially new tool for the United States during World War II, while other countries previously had employed the technique widely.

Uniforms carried insignia, decorations, and other rewards for service (*see* Medals and Decorations). Insignia typically indicated the wearer's job function, rank, and unit, with additional insignia indicating special skills and past achievements and assignments. As the war progressed, more and more such devices were created by both sides. Generally, the Axis powers created more badges and insignia for their soldiers than did the Allies, and the Axis and the Soviet servicemen typically wore these in a field environment. The U.S., British, and other Western allies, in contrast, generally did not wear medals or ribbons in combat.

By the early 1930s, the uniforms of most of the future World War II belligerent armed forces had evolved so that a wide variety of specialized clothing was in use. Names of the various categories of uniforms varied from country to country, and even within a single nation's army, navy, or flying arm. The designation of a particular uniform may have changed during World War II. During the 1930s, the Germans introduced new uniforms to bolster the military image and appeal, while Allied changes were generally slower and more evolutionary. This lag in adapting to new conditions caused the U.S., in particular, to make radical changes during the war.

While all of the belligerents started World War II with a substantial variety of uniforms, during the war a large number of new clothing styles were introduced, and for some countries these new styles far exceeded the prewar range. The Axis powers generally introduced revised uniforms before the start of the conflict, and thus made fewer changes during the war itself. By contrast, the Americans, in particular, entered their 1939 prewar buildup with few sets of clothing and ended the war in 1945 with virtually all new designs.

Globally, uniform changes were made to improve morale. During the 1939–1945 period, the Allied powers brought out a large number of uniforms. The Axis powers tended to introduce special uniforms first, while the Allies played catch-up. Ground troops often identified the nationality of infantrymen by the silhouette of their helmets.

Even uniform colors can not totally be ascribed to one country or another. Various camouflage battle clothing was used by both sides. Germany is remembered for the grey-green wool uniforms that buttoned to the neck with turndown collars, but they also used browns, tans, and black, sometimes made into lapel-type coats. The U.S. adopted olive drab, but more than fifty official shades of "O.D." and brown were used. British Commonwealth forces used olive drab shades more consistently than the U.S., but the Royal Air Force had its own separate uniform colors.

New forms of warfare or improvements in existing equipment also resulted in new uniforms. Tank and parachute troops of all the major powers adopted distinctive clothing for the first time during the war. Aircraft flew longer and higher, and the vast increase in the number of aircrew personnel caused an entire new stock of clothing, although the forerunners of these new uniforms were developed during the 1920s and 1930s. Prior to World War II, soldiers generally were issued a single, heavy overcoat for winter use. U.S. and British forces began to use the layer principle during the war, thus replacing one heavy winter coat with several lighter layers that could be added or taken off to keep the soldier comfortable. This wartime innovation was widely adopted during and after the war.

The U.S. Army introduced a lapel service coat in 1925 for the air service and in 1926 for the rest of the army. The transition from the World War I–style high collar coat was completed by 1930 and made for both comfort and style. This was primarily influenced by the exposure to the British during World War I. This lapel-type coat was used throughout the war. A new U.S. combat helmet came out during 1941, and the popular style was adopted by many Allied armies-in-exile. The garrison cap, similar to the World War I overseas cap, was phased in just prior to World War II as common U.S. headgear.

Olive drab work uniforms made of herringbone twill replaced the pre–World War I U.S. blue denim versions in 1941. These so-called fatigue uniforms became widely used during the war, replacing the olive drab wool service coats and trousers. Accompanying field jackets were also introduced to replace heavy single-layer garments. In the winter of 1944–1945, however, the army had to revert to issuing long wool overcoats to men in combat because of a shortage of field jackets.

Britain started to replace their service dress uniforms in 1939 with a new battle dress, which included a waist-length jacket. This new British garment influenced the U.S. Army to adopt the so-called "Eisenhower" jacket in 1943. For use in North Africa, tropical clothing was used, including khaki shirts, jackets, and long and short trousers.

British regiments retained distinctive dress uniforms, and especially local headgear, such as the glengarry cap used by Scottish highland units. Although minor changes were instituted during the war, the British, along with the Germans, made relatively few changes in the general cut of their uniforms. Initially, the Canadians had British-type uniforms of a slightly more greenish hue, but as the war progressed, the standard British clothing was adopted. Australian and New Zealand units had their unique uniforms, each with a different pattern broad-brimmed hat that was recognized as a symbol of the troops from down under. The World War I–pattern helmet, with a low crown and wide brim, remained the standard British Commonwealth combat headgear throughout the war.

France started the war with a khaki uniform adopted in 1935, which replaced the 1915 horizon blue uniform. The Vichy government retained the 1935 uniforms, while the Free French adopted a combination of British and American uniforms. The French forces had two unique types of headgear: the beret and the kepi, a rigid circular cap with a short bill. While many nations later adopted the beret, the kepi, adopted in 1919, remained (and remains) distinctively French. The French also retained their World War I Adrian helmet, with the comb down the top. Vichy forces also used the Adrian helmet, while the Free French adopted the American "steel pot."

The Soviets started the war with 1935-style uniforms that buttoned up to the neck with turndown collars. In early 1943, these German-style coats, with colored collar patches, were replaced by coats with standing collars and shoulder boards.

The Germans adopted new uniforms in 1935 as part of their consolidation of political power, replacing the older World War I–style clothing from the kaiser's era. Germany had a greater variety of uniforms than any other country. *Waffen-SS* (q.v.), mountain, and other special troops adopted unique uniforms. In addition, within Germany, a broad section of the citizenry was uniformed, ranging from Nazi Party officials to such diverse groups as railroad workers and coal miners.

The large number of German uniform styles and their association with the war effort is one of the interesting features of World War II. Volumes have been written just on the many uniforms worn within Nazi Germany. In addition, German-occupied countries adopted German-style uniforms for police, armed forces, and other government agencies. The many colors and cuts of uniform coats authorized between 1935 and 1945 preclude any generalization about them, except to note that cloth collar patches of various colors were widely used. The German helmet retained its general World War I "coal scuttle" shape, although it was modified for parachute troops.

Italy, like Germany, adopted several additional uniform styles at different times during World War II. The most distinctive part of the Italian uniform was the variety of headgear, which included historically based caps and hats.

The smaller belligerent armies, like the major powers, made significant uniform modifications and changes during the war, sometimes even taking a major power's uniform design directly and adding only special insignia. This especially was true for the many armies-in-exile that operated from Great Britain, including the Poles, Norwegians, and Czechs. Following the 1939 Polish defeat, the Free Polish Army went through several uniforms, but by 1941, they were wearing British uniforms with their own native insignia.

Native forces from Yugoslavia reflected the complex political situation within that country. Some units fought alongside the Soviets on the eastern front and wore Soviet uniforms, while Yugoslav forces within the country wore modified German-style uniforms, prewar monarchist uniforms, or captured uniforms.

During World War II, uniforms changed significantly. Insignia, equipment, medals and awards, and various articles of clothing came into being or were modified greatly. In the United States, the layer clothing principle came into wide use, and in the postwar years these uniforms and the insignia concept became very influential among emerging armies.

William K. Emerson

Additional Reading
Davis, Brian L., and Pierre Turner, *German Uniforms of the Third Reich: 1933–1945* (1980).
Emerson, William K. *Encyclopedia of United States Army Insignia and Uniforms* (1996).
Mollo, Andrew, and Malcolm McGregor, *Army Uniforms of World War 2* (1973).
———, *Naval, Marine, and Air Force Uniforms of World War 2* (1975).

V-Weapons
See Missiles, Guided

Wonder Weapons

In the realm of science, there are three general fields: theoretical, experimental, and applied. All these fields are closely related, and it is nearly impossible to separate them. Theoretical science takes an idea from an observed phenomenon or a hypothesis and establishes a repeatable mechanism and an explanation for it. Experimental science refines or tests the phenomenon or thing that creates the phenomenon. Applied science makes the phenomenon or thing useful to society or humankind—or in the case of World War II, for the war effort. Both sides strove mightily to outdo the other in applied science in what British prime minister Winston S. Churchill (q.v.) called "the wizard war."

Applied science, in general, requires three factors to succeed: (1) a political and ideological climate that nurtures, or at least allows, work with little or no constraint; (2) the resources to perform the work, whether the resources are raw materials, equipment, or people; and (3) a place where the work can be performed and the apparatus derived tested in a controlled, safe environment.

Great Britain and the Commonwealth

Great Britain and its Commonwealth enjoyed all three required factors in some abundance, and used them almost from the moment the war began. Arguably, the very survival of Britain depended on how long and how well its science could stay one step ahead of its enemies.

Air Defense: Britain developed the first successful integrated air defense network, gathering together the early warning system of CHAIN HOME (q.v.) radar stations with ground observers, the plotting and vectoring of interceptors, and the targeting of large formations of enemy aircraft for antiaircraft artillery. The success of this integra-

tion was evident in the Battle of Britain (q.v.) in the fall of 1940. Air defense radar work continued throughout the war. Barrage balloons and captive rockets were also used with some success.

Air: Fighter and bomber development in Britain and the Commonwealth yielded some remarkable achievements, including the Mosquito bomber, built mostly out of plywood, the 12,000-pound and 20,000-pound penetrating bombs used to destroy submarine facilities and other large structures, the Gloster Meteor jet fighter, the Hawker Fury fighter series, the ungainly but effective Bristol Beaufighter, continual improvement of the Supermarine Spitfire throughout the war, and the Avro Lancaster and Hanley-Page Halifax bombers, with records of success exceeded only by the U.S.

Tactically, the RAF developed the fighter sweep to a fine art over the French coast, and the idea of the fighter/bomber "cab rank" for close ground support over the battlefield. Strategically, Bomber Command introduced area or "transportation" bombing of urban areas at night, as well as the near-perfection of incendiary bombing (q.v.) techniques and "dam-busting" with specially designed bombs.

Night bombing missions guided by radio beams and onboard navigational radar became commonplace for both the RAF and the *Luftwaffe,* as was jamming and misdirecting the similar radio and radar guidance systems used by both sides. Even more important, the development of "chaff" or "window" radar-blinding materials made German intercept almost impossible.

Land: Britain was not the true innovator on land that it was elsewhere, but still, the country did have its moments. Britain's love affair with the horse ended in World War II and its new love, the tank, was more successful in German hands.

Nonetheless, British tank development continued, albeit slightly behind Germany and the Soviet Union. A number of British tanks carried flamethrowers, notably the Churchill Crocodile series, and tanks were adapted to a number of different specialized tasks, including gap-bridging, mine clearing, and other field engineering tasks.

In small arms, Britain made some genuine strides. The PIAT antitank grenade launcher, an adaptation of a prewar spigot mortar, placed a light, practical antitank weapon in the hands of the infantry that could be fired from inside buildings without the distinctive backblast of the bazooka and the recoilless rifle. The Sten submachine gun was an inexpensive, high rate of fire weapon that became the favored weapon with the resistance movements in occupied Europe.

Sea: At sea, Great Britain had the most real work to do, inasmuch as the German submarine threat early in the war nearly killed the country. Sonar (q.v.) (or ASDIC) was a prewar development, but it was refined and reworked until it became quite effective in the hands of skilled operators. Antisubmarine warfare (q.v.) weapons also included improvements in aircraft patrolling and station time, the use of millimeter-wave radar to detect submarines on the surface or their periscopes, and the adaptation of American developments, such as the shaped-charge depth bomb ("Hedgehogs") and directional control of depth-bomb projection. Also, at sea, Britain was the first to dismantle and develop countermeasures for the German magnetic mines and acoustic-homing torpedoes. Britain also worked extensively on the U.S. magnetic anomaly detector (MAD) used for submarine detection in restricted waters.

Other: The entire Commonwealth contributed in one way or another to nuclear weapons development. Nearly all sent at least one scientist, engineer, or technician to either the American MANHATTAN Project (q.v.) or the British TUBE ALLOYS project. Much of the low-grade pitchblende used for the research came from Canadian mines.

On the less deadly side, British code breakers became so proficient that by 1944, there was hardly any operational communication into or out of Germany that they could not intercept and make some sense of. The German Enigma (q.v.) machine, captured by Poles and smuggled out of Europe in 1939, made the Allied cryptanalytic attack on German tactical ciphers a constant cat-and-mouse game. Communications intercept, jamming, spoofing, and direction finding were developed at Britain's Bletchley Park (q.v.) throughout the war, and were especially useful for finding German U-boats.

On the medical front, British medical science gave the world perhaps the most miraculous of the miracle drugs—penicillin. Sir Alexander Fleming, Dr. Ernst B. Chain, and Dr. Howard W. Florey searching for wide-spectrum antibiotics that were less toxic than the sulfanilamides then available, resurrected prewar work on penicillin and developed cost-effective production methods. Their work earned them the Nobel Prize for medicine in 1945. This "wonder drug," which revolutionized medicine, was used on more than 100,000 wounded soldiers during the 1944 Normandy (q.v.) campaign alone. Australian doctors developed antimalarial drugs, and an effective immunization against tetanus was first tested on the evacuees from Dunkirk (q.v.) in May–June 1940.

Germany

Germany enjoyed almost none of the factors required for successful application of applied science, and it is remarkable that many of the innovations that it did accomplish actually occurred. To cripple German science even further, the Nazis expelled or forced many of its leading scientists—many of whom were Jews—to flee before the war even started. Some of these refugees would later work on the MANHATTAN Project.

Air: In the air, German science enjoyed the most freedom, largely because Hermann Göring (q.v.), a former pilot and titular head of the *Luftwaffe,* was also the plenipotentiary for the five-year plan and was thus in virtual charge of all German industry. Fighters were Germany's most important innovations in the air, with the introduction of the FW-190 piston-engined fighter, the Me-262 jet fighter, the Me-163 rocket interceptor, and the He-219, the first aircraft in the world designed as a night fighter.

The V-1 flying bomb and the V-2 trans-atmospheric missile were important as technical innovations, even if they failed to fulfill their early destructive promise. In support of the ground mission, Germany was a pioneer in using aircraft as "airborne artillery" to support fast-moving armor and infantry. Germany also had operational helicopters (q.v.) as early as 1942, but their value was not foreseen and they never got beyond the experimental phases.

Land: On land, Germany reintroduced mobile warfare with the tank/infantry team, and led the world in tank design throughout the war. The Tiger and Panther series were arguably the finest of the period. The super-heavy *König* series tanks and tank destroyers, practically rolling forts, never appeared in large enough numbers to affect the course of the war. However, these nearly indestructible monsters were threat enough to become legends out of all proportion to their actual effect. By the time the super-heavy tank came into vogue, the personal antitank weapon and airpower, both ironically developed by the Germans themselves, had sounded the death knell for the heavy tank.

To keep up with the fast-moving tank columns, Germany built a number of assault guns and self-propelled howitzers on tank chassis. These deadly innovations were quickly copied by the Allies, but in very few cases were they as effective.

In artillery, the *Nebelwerfer* multibarrel rocket launcher demonstrated that mass indirect fire could also be cheap and movable. The excellent World War I–vintage 8.8cm Flak 18 gun was developed into at least thirty different models, in addition to its original antiaircraft role. Tank guns such as the 75/L50 and the 88/L35 were superior to almost all Allied weapons. Later, squeeze bore antitank guns, personal shaped-charge, and wire-guided missile antitank weapons, all introduced too late, were copied by all belligerents.

The *Wehrmacht* caught up to the U. S. M-1 Garand rifle with the Gew-43 semiautomatic rifle, albeit in small numbers. They excelled, however, in the field of light machine guns with the MG-34 and the later MG-42.

Sea: At sea, Germany spent much of its effort in keeping up with the Allies' rapidly accelerating ASW capabilities. The radar detector, the acoustic homing and pattern-running torpedoes, the hydrogen peroxide submarine engine, and the *Schnorchel* were all responses to the increasing deadliness of the Allied navies against them. As with many other developments, few arrived in service soon enough to make much difference in the outcome.

Also at sea, Germany's relentless attack on Allied shipping lanes (a development of tactics originally seen in the Baltic and Mediterranean in World War I) by submarines and by commerce raiders introduced a new form of warfare—that of true attrition. The much-vaunted "wolf packs" wreaked havoc on Allied shipping until Allied countermeasures and code breaking finally tipped the scales.

Besides submarines, Germany developed the "pocket battleship" before the war. It seemed at the time to be the perfect commerce raider, powered with diesel engines and armed like a small battleship. Unfortunately, they were too few in number to have much of an influence. The entire small, but remarkable, German surface fleet was something of an innovation. The Bismarck-class battleships were the heaviest battleships in the world until the U.S. Iowa-class, although their hull protection was poor. The *Scharnhorst* and *Gneisenau* heavy fleet units (they have always defied classification) were the fastest of their type. Although they were equipped with technically excellent vessels, the German surface navy lacked free open-sea access and escort vessels.

Other: In other efforts, Germany usually lagged behind its enemies, but that was in large part because the political climate was not the best for anything that did not quickly produce an obvious weapon. In nuclear research, quantum physics—an understanding of which is required for the study of the atom—was labeled "Jewish physics" by the Nazis, and could not be taught in schools, nor was it funded.

Despite this, Nobel-laureate Dr. Walter Heisenberg, Germany's leading resident nuclear physicist, proceeded with nuclear research. Assisted by such notables as Ernst Mach and Hans Geiger, Heisenberg became convinced by 1941 that nuclear weapons were not feasible. When the Allied ALSOS Mission (q.v.) technical intelligence personnel interrogated them about their research prior to Hiroshima, they expressed their confidence that if Germany could not do it, no one could. They had, however, begun construction of a nuclear pile by the time the war ended.

Despite the blindness of Naxi ideology, Germany made tremendous strides in nerve gas research, the extraction of synthetic petroleum and rubber products from coal, trace metal and gas recovery from sea water, radar and radio beam detection, and other physics and high-pressure chemistry work. The Nazi data in sterilization techniques, genetics, human exposure to extreme cold, pressure, and oxygen starvation has, for the most part, never been used by the scientific world because of the taint of the inhuman practices associated with its collection.

Italy

Italy started the war at something of a disadvantage, inasmuch as applied science was not thought to be necessary in Fascist ideology. Most of the theoretical work done by Italian scientists could not be brought to fruition in Italy's political climate and with its limited resources. What they did accomplish in the realm of science is limited to the development (slow and incomplete) at Caproni of jet aircraft, which were never operational, and the development of small manned torpedoes, which did serious damage to the British fleets at Alexandria (q.v.) and at Gibraltar. Italy did have, however, one of the best land-based torpedo bombers of the war, the three-engine Savoia-Marchetti S.M.79. Italy also produced some high-level ciphers that were nearly impossible to break without keys.

Soviet Union

The Soviet Union began the war with something of a problem: many of its finest scientists and engineers were in prison. This problems was rectified in part by creating "prison design bureaus" or by outright release. The problem was compounded when most of its centers of higher learning and research were destroyed, captured, or moved in the initial months of the war. Nonetheless, Soviet science provided some genuine surprises, as much by pure stubbornness as by design.

Air: The Soviets demonstrated that aircraft need not be complex to be effective. The Yakovlev Design Bureau created the Soviets' first fighter, the Yak-1, that could at least match German aircraft, followed by the Yak-3 and Yak-9. The Petlyakov Pe-2 was arguably the best light bomber of the war, and was adapted to ground-attack and reconnaissance roles. The Soviets also built a series of aircraft collectively called the *Sturmoviks,* usually the Ilushyn Il-2, that dominated the ground support role by 1944.

Land: Since the Soviet Union was largely a land power, it is not surprising that most of its applied science work went into the ground war effort. The Soviets built some of the finest tanks of the period, including the ubiquitous T-34 series, the KV series, and the IS series. Soviet science also produced the remarkable Kalashnikov automatic rifle, even though it was designed by an army NCO with little scientific training and did not see service before the war ended; twenty-five years later this weapon was the famous AK-47 of the Vietnam War. Doctrinally, the Soviet Red Army adapted German ground warfare methods to Red Army capabilities and developed effective doctrine, specializing in the "unbalanced front" strategic offensive.

Sea: The almost landlocked Soviet Union made some strides in riverine/amphibious warfare. Its deep-water fleet was largely negated by German air superiority and the superiority of German submarines, but lighter units operated on Russian and eastern European rivers throughout the conflict. The series of amphibious raids and assaults in the Crimea (q.v.) campaign of 1942–1943 was a remarkable achievement of adaptation. In deeper waters, Soviet mine detection and minesweeping became quite effective against the million or so mines that the Soviets themselves and the Germans laid in the Baltic and Black seas.

Other: The Soviets became masters of "reverse engineering," also known as copying. They learned to copy practically everything they came across, from German hand grenades to the U.S. B-29 bomber. They began the war with nearly unbreakable ciphers based on the time-proven "one-time pad," which improved throughout the conflict. Soviet communications intercept and code breaking, among the best in the world at the beginning of the war, also steadily improved. The Soviets became aware that the United States and Great Britain were performing nuclear weapons research through espionage and by another feat of reverse engineering: they noticed that American and British scientists had stopped publishing on the subject in late 1940. The Soviets began their research in 1942, but it would not come to fruition until 1949.

In medicine, Soviet scientists developed the first practical skin-grafting techniques for burn patients, and performed extensive research on biogenic agents (chemicals that encourage healing and tissue regeneration). They also had unprecedented opportunities to observe and to amass comprehensive data on the physiological effects of cannibalism on humans, using large numbers of Axis prisoners as research subjects. This work, however, was tainted in the same way as the Nazi's experimental work on humans in the concentration camps.

United States

The United States had a virtual monopoly on all the prerequisites to make applied science work. Added to its virtually infinite resources were a united home front not under steady, direct attack and cities full of refugees willing and able to wreak vengeance on their enemies.

Air Defense: The United States approached the problem of hitting flying targets from the ground with an entirely different philosophy from most everyone else: "If it doesn't come close enough, don't make it go off." This philosophy led to the early electric eye, and later the radar proximity fuze (q.v.), probably the most important single air defense tool other than early warning radar.

Air: The United States had a considerable aircraft industry before the war started, and a fairly large air force that was largely destroyed in Hawaii and in the Philippines in the first few days. What was left was stretched so thin to cover ship losses that for all intents the country had to start over. U.S. plants produced such innovations as the P-51, the P-38, and the P-47 fighter-bombers, and the P-61 night fighter. Medium bombers, including the A-20, the B-25, and the B-26, were improved throughout the war. The stalwart B-17 heavy bomber was continuously upgraded, as was the B-24.

The major U.S. innovations in the air were the advent of the truly strategic bomber, the B-29, and the mutual defense "combat box" formation. The U.S. also perfected area bombing with incendiaries, laying waste to large areas with limited air losses. Finally, the principle of precision bombing was tested and unfortunately found wanting.

Land: The United States had virtually no land forces worth mentioning at the beginning of the war but by its end had built one of the largest and most efficient. Tactically, the U.S. idea of trading ordnance rather than lives resulted in the world's most efficient field artillery arm. Supported by the artillery, a vehicular-mobile land force armed almost entirely with the gas-operated M-1 Garand semiautomatic rifle, was built up from a unique "pool" system of specialist units added to major units as needed. Amphibious operations (q.v.), driven and guided by U.S. Army and Marine Corps experience in the Pacific, became almost uniquely American flavored. Practically every type and class of landing craft (q.v.) used by the Allies in World War II originated in the U.S.

The M-1 Garand, described by General George S. Patton (q.v.) as "the finest battle instrument ever devised," changed infantry combat so radically that it is hard to assess its true impact. The concept of giving every infantryman more firepower than a company of infantry from a century before was at the time quite revolutionary. By World War II, the role of infantry small arms was so diminished by the crushing power of artillery and the machine gun that this revolution went practically unnoticed.

The revolutionary M-3 submachine gun was an American response to the British Sten gun, lightweight and easily mass-produced. The 57mm and 75mm recoilless rifles were the first man-portable weapons of that type extensively used in combat.

Sea: As with Britain, America's first priority at sea was the U-boat menace. The "hunter-killer" antisubmarine group, formed around escort aircraft carriers, probably did more to turn the tide in the Battle of the Atlantic (q.v.) than any other innovation. The shaped-charge depth bomb, launched at a target and only exploding when it

hit, also helped to stem the U-boat menace. Furthermore, the advent of airborne millimeter-wave radar that could detect a submarine conning tower or even its periscope on the surface made the seas increasingly unsafe for hostile submarines. Other submarine detection tools included the sonobuoy and the magnetic anomaly detector (MAD).

Radar-guided naval gunnery was hardly a U.S. invention, but the country's experience with it in the Pacific provided much-needed guidance and improvements. The aircraft carrier, initially invented in Britain, was carried to a logical extreme by the Americans, who built more than seventy of four different types during the war. Another U.S. development was the antiaircraft ship, deployed solely to protect the rest of the force from air attack.

Other: Domestically, the Americans used their superabundance of resources to produce synthetic rubber in usable quantities, develop safe blood transfusions and plasma separation techniques, enact effective rationing systems for precious resources, use electrolytic separation for various minerals and chemicals from sea water, apply mass production techniques to nearly every aspect of manufacturing, and introduce a myriad of other innovations.

The bulk of the Allied work on chemical and biological weapons was performed in the United States, as was most of the work on countermeasures. Rocketry, long a British specialty, came to have a distinctly American flavor by 1945. Development of guided and unguided missiles included such developments as the bazooka and the recoilless rifle.

The crowning technical achievement of the war, however, was the MANHATTAN Project developing the first atomic bomb. This technical marvel was the equivalent of virtually inventing an entire industry in just four years.

John D. Beatty

Additional Reading
Amrine, Michael, *The Great Decision: The Secret History of the Atomic Bomb* (1960).
Eggleston, Wilfrid, *Scientists at War* (1951).
Goudsmit, Samuel, *ALSOS* (1947).
———, *The Failure of German Science* (1947).
Hartcup, Guy, *The Challenge of War: Scientific and Engineering Contributions to World War II* (1970).
Stewart, Irvin, *Organizing Scientific Research for War* (1948).

Z

Zyklon B

In the summer of 1941, Rudolf Höss (q.v.), camp commandant of Auschwitz (Oswiecim), toured the concentration camp at Treblinka to see its "Final Solution" (q.v.) methods. In six months, Treblinka had exterminated 80,000 people by shooting or carbon monoxide gassing from vehicle exhaust fumes. Höss claimed he could do better.

At Auschwitz, Höss had four large gas chambers built to accommodate up to 2,000 people at a time. Instead of using exhaust fumes, he used Zyklon B, or prussic acid. Originally, Zyklon B was a commercial pesticide. It was so toxic that manufacturers added an irritant to warn users to stay clear. The version used at the concentration camps had no irritants added, and in most cases the victims were unaware they were being gassed until near death.

Höss was guaranteed a steady supply of Zyklon B from its primary manufacturer, *Degesch* (*Deutsche Gesellschaft zur Schädlingsbekämpfung*— German Company for Pest Control). The gassing was carried out by pouring Zyklon B crystals down hollow sheet metal pillars. The pillars were perforated at regular intervals for gas to enter the chamber. Inside the pillars, spiral slides ensured an even distribution of crystals. Sealed Zyklon B was safe to handle. When exposed to the air, however, the blue crystals turned into hydrocyanic (HCN) gas.

After the victims had died, ventilators in the gas chamber walls dispersed the gas for safe removal of the corpses. Initially, the corpses were buried in mass graves, but by November 1942, burial space was exhausted. As a result, four crematoria were built and co-located with the gas chambers at the Auschwitz II–Birkenau camp. Once completed, up to 18,000 people could be gassed and cremated in a twenty-four-hour period. By late 1943, with an increasing tide of "enemies of the *Reich*" flowing into concentration camps, Jews and Gypsies were gassed, while all others were either hanged, shot, or given lethal injections. Upon seeing Höss's operation, Adolf Eichmann (q.v.) praised him for his ingenuity.

William H. Van Husen

Additional Reading

Gilbert, Martin, *The Second World War: A Complete History* (1989).

Hart, Kitty, *Return to Auschwitz* (1981).

Müller, Filip, *Eyewitness Auschwitz* (1979).

Strategy, Tactics, and Operational Techniques

A

Airborne Operations

In World War II, the concept of airborne operations was new, and doctrine emerged with each succeeding commitment of airborne troops to battle. The popular perception of the paratrooper is one of a near-superman, his unit capable of undertaking any mission regardless of the dangers and difficulties.

While certainly the airborne soldier, by nature of his training and obvious high morale and esprit de corps, stands out as a model of the highly motivated fighter, the fact still remains that once on the ground he is an infantryman or artilleryman. He has to fight with certain disadvantages, not the least being severe problems with supply and reinforcement, since that too must come by air.

The number of airborne divisions in World War II in Europe was quite small in comparison to other infantry divisions, but their feats and reputations far outdistance their ground-oriented comrades-in-arms. Ironically, the U.S. 101st Airborne Division is perhaps best known as the "Bloody Bastards of Bastogne," although the battle was a classic infantry defense.

The advantages of using parachute or glider forces were obvious. If landed successfully, a commander could achieve surprise and psychological advantage. This is particularly important when airborne formations are landed behind enemy lines and can disrupt the enemy's lines of communication and supply. Critical objectives for airborne can be bridges, road junctions, enemy command and communication centers, supply bases, and railways.

If airborne forces are used properly, their operations are short in duration and marked by surprise and by short, violent combat action. Once these missions are complete and an airborne division becomes part of the regular order of battle,

they can fight as regular infantry. However, continually using airborne units as regular infantry is a waste of a unique weapon in the commander's offensive arsenal. Airborne units so used are then at a disadvantage because of their special qualifications. Supply systems are adapted to dealing with regular ground combat problems, and in World War II, airborne forces were small, compact, and maneuverable. Heavy artillery simply could not be factored into an airborne operation because of the initial difficulties in delivering heavyweight artillery by air.

For the United States in World War II in Europe, there was a constant tension between traditional infantry commanders and airborne commanders as to the utilization of the units and the length of time an airborne unit could remain committed to battle. At one point in 1942 prior to Operation TORCH, there were discussions of disbanding the two newly formed U.S. airborne divisions, the 82nd and the 101st, and converting them into light infantry divisions.

While this conflict was resolved in favor of keeping the airborne divisional formations, it does show that a gulf existed between traditionalists, many of whom served in the very heavy 28,000-man divisions of World War I, and innovators who saw possibilities for these highly mobile units. The innovators were never totally successful in achieving all that they had hoped for with airborne, but the traditionalists were forced to give way. The problem again surfaced after World War II, as the traditionalists tried to end such things as distinctive airborne insignia and to do away with the "jump boot" as a distinctive item of military apparel.

In World War II, the airborne picture was further complicated by the fact that an airborne division needed extra training time, and training time was a very precious commodity for an army at war.

The individual must be trained as a parachutist or a glider team member. Jump masters and glider pilots required even more time to master these skills. Once individual training was completed, collective training began. This required teams to jump as units and to train for airborne commitment to the battlefield. The time required for training an airborne unit was always an aggravation for those who saw the need to train entire combat divisions quickly for widespread operations.

The airborne had to have close coordination with the air force, which would transport the parachutists and glider troops to the areas over their drop and landing zones. This meant bringing together two very different branches having very different sets of combat priorities. For the airborne soldier, it was a question of getting on the ground with a minimum of jump or landing casualties and being ready to engage in mortal combat. For the air force, it was a question of navigating to the drop areas, perhaps through antiaircraft fire, and then returning as many planes as possible back to base to continue air missions. Weather certainly had to be factored into the coordination equation.

There was also a cost factor to consider in war. Usually, a large number of parachutes were lost, special equipment was used, gliders had a high attrition rate, and resupply could be very costly for the air force because of enemy antiaircraft fire and other combat-related losses. Medical evacuation was extraordinarily difficult, as was medical support once the airborne soldiers were on the ground. The psychological factor of knowing that many paratroopers and glider troops could never be treated properly for their wounds, and that many would be left behind or die because they could not be evacuated to medical field hospitals, weighed heavily on the commanders, and certainly on the troops as well.

With all the difficulties involved, the United States pressed forward with the formation of airborne units. By the time the United States entered the war, there were spectacular airborne successes. Most European countries were far in advance of the U.S. in combat parachute and glider deployment.

The Soviet Union led the way in the development of parachute forces and after some false starts, was writing airborne operational doctrine by 1936. The French established a parachute school in southern France near Avignon and formed two small airborne infantry units. The Italians followed in 1938, first with a school in Libya and then in Italy proper.

The Germans placed their embryonic parachute force under the *Luftwaffe*, believing air-delivered troops belonged to the air arm and coordination between the paratroopers and the aircraft planners and flyers would be easier. Interservice or interbranch rivalries could then be kept to a minimum, and there would be less likelihood of wasteful "turf battles" between army and air. Colonel Kurt Student (q.v.), who was a highly decorated flyer in World War I, was selected to command the airborne forces, and his selection was a key factor in the development of German paratroopers as a force to be reckoned with on any battlefield.

The first test for the German airborne came on 10 May 1940, when paratroopers landed in Holland with total tactical and operational surprise. Student had only 4,500 trained airborne soldiers available for the drops in Holland, but the shock value was enough to make them effective. In Belgium, on 11 May, another small airborne force captured the powerful fort of Eben Emael (q.v.), and the Germans landed airborne forces west of the critical Albert Canal. The psychological effect of the Holland and Belgium drops far outweighed the small number of airborne soldiers involved.

The value of paratroops on the battlefield, as far as shock and speed was concerned, was clear. What was not clear, however, was the sustainability of such forces. The German spring 1940 campaign moved with speed, and the airborne forces were not required to maintain continual combat operations with resupply. American military planners certainly took note of the headline-catching airborne forces, and moved to establish their own airborne units.

On 26 June 1940, the first American experimental parachute unit was formed for training at Fort Benning, Georgia. From that meager start with only fifty men, the army was soon in the process of putting together two airborne divisions. There was opposition to parachute troops, however, because the results of training maneuvers were not totally positive. Despite calls to do away with airborne divisions, the Americans continued to develop their airborne forces.

In May 1942, the United States formed its first glider regiment at Fort Bragg, North Carolina, and American airborne forces become a mix of paratroopers and glider soldiers. Actually, gliders offered some advantage in that the front was hinged and small vehicles and artillery pieces could be placed in the glider along with troops. The glider did give a certain amount of airlift capability to the airborne. If the glider did not crash on landing, there was the advantage of having artillery landing simultaneously with the paratroopers. Typically,

British airborne forces landing on the outskirts of Arnhem, 17 September 1944. During World War II, airborne operations typically included landings by both parachute and glider. (IWM BU 1163)

glider "landings" in actual operations were controlled crashes, and few gliders ever flew again.

On 20 May 1942, the Germans employed 13,000 glider and parachute troops in an operation against a British garrison on the island of Crete (q.v.). Since the British commander knew the Royal Navy controlled the waters around the island and the rugged mountainous terrain mitigated against the attackers, he was able to deploy his defenses and inflict heavy casualties on the descending troops. Whole companies of paratroopers were wiped out and gliders were hit by antiaircraft fire. The operation almost failed. Due to communications difficulties, British officers believed the German paratroop forces had achieved all of their major objectives, namely the seizing of three key airfields, and they withdrew from the battle. The Germans took quick advantage of the opportunity. They captured the airfields and called in waiting German troops who were delivered by aircraft.

More than 5,000 German paratroopers and glider troops were killed during the operation. Adolf Hitler (q.v.) decided against using airborne forces again in such large numbers, but as in Belgium and Holland, the psychological advantage of using such forces was clear. Highly trained and motivated German paratroopers blew ancient hunting horns while descending onto the drop zones. Their élan was superb, and while the Germans opted against further large deployments of airborne

forces by parachute drop, the Americans hurried their own formations and training along.

By 15 August 1942, two American airborne divisions were formed. With a little over 8,000 men, the American formations had two parachute regiments and one glider regiment with a mix of artillery and other units necessary for combat operations. The 82nd Division (redesignated Airborne) had a long and distinguished history from World War I, where its legendary Sergeant Alvin York won the Medal of Honor in the Meuse-Argonne offensive of 1918. The 101st Airborne Division was relatively new, with little combat heritage. Both divisions became well known for their state of training, high morale, esprit de corps, and leadership.

The first use of American paratroopers came when a battalion task force from the 82nd Airborne was dropped in Algeria as part of Operation TORCH. The Northwest African drop was a fiasco, mainly due to lack of experience and to the long distances involved in getting the paratroop forces to Northwest Africa.

The next major operation for U.S. airborne forces came in Sicily (q.v.), and again there were severe problems in finding their drop zones. At this point, American military planners began to complain that large formations of paratroopers simply could not be used on the battlefield. Calmer heads prevailed and U.S. plans moved along to train the two divisions in Britain in preparation for Operation OVERLORD, the cross-channel invasion.

A number of difficulties surrounded Allied airborne operations. The one that seemed to be insurmountable was the fact that in two drops, jumpers failed to hit their drop zones. This was due in part to the length of the flight from air bases to the drop zones, and was also due in part to the aircraft. In the case of the parachute drops in southern France (q.v.), in 1944 (Operation ANVIL), many pilots and aircrews, under the stress of long hours and antiaircraft fire, dropped their paratroopers too soon. The aircraft commander commanded the actual timing of the drop, and during Operation ANVIL, many Allied paratroopers were dropped into the Mediterranean Sea.

Another problem was the extraordinary weight of the jumper's load. German paratroops dropped without weapons and this proved a mistake. Once on the ground, they were defenseless until they located the bundles containing weapons. American and British jumpers carried everything and often jumped with well over 100 pounds of equipment. Also adding to weight, the safety-conscious Americans carried a chest-mounted reserve parachute, the only Allied paratroopers to do so.

The Normandy (q.v.) landings on the night of 5–6 June 1944 again saw misdrops. However, this time the soldiers of the 82nd and 101st Airborne Divisions caused a great deal of confusion in the German ranks and in the enemy command and communication structure, and contributed greatly to the successes of Operation OVERLORD.

In 1944, the Americans reorganized their airborne units under the XVIII Airborne Corps, and all Allied paratroop forces came under the First Allied Airborne Army. It was this army that Field Marshal Bernard L. Montgomery (q.v.) planned to use in Operation MARKET-GARDEN (q.v.). The plan was a good one, but intelligence and execution were faulty. An "airborne carpet, fifty miles long," was to be dropped in Holland to open the way for Sir Brian Horrocks's (q.v.) XXX Corps tanks to make a dash for the Rhine River bridges at Arnheim, Holland. The operation failed despite extraordinary heroism and effort by American, British, and Polish paratroops.

The last major airborne operation of the war was Operation VARSITY (q.v.), a drop of the U.S. 17th Airborne Division and the British 6th Airborne Division across the Rhine River on 24 March 1945. As far as troops, planes, and gliders were concerned, Operation VARSITY was a larger single day's drop than Operation MARKET-GARDEN

in Holland a few months earlier. While casualties were severe in men and aircraft, Operation VARSITY did have a number of pinpoint drops despite a heavy ground fog, mist, and German resistance. Quickly off the drop and landing zones, the airborne forces pushed deeper into Germany. During the operation, General Student was captured.

With German resistance crumbling and the end of the war in sight, tentative plans were made for the 82nd Airborne to be dropped near Templehof Airport in Berlin. However, as Soviet forces closed in on Adolf Hitler's beleaguered capital, this operation was scrubbed.

The performance of airborne forces in World War II was a mixture of successes and failures. No one doubted the superior élan and training of the paratroopers and glider soldiers. They emerged from the war with a reputation for fighting that overshadowed the misdrops and failures such as Operation MARKET-GARDEN.

Immediately after the war, the XVIII Airborne Corps was deactivated and attempts were made to disband the 82nd and 101st Airborne Divisions. The opponents of airborne claimed their record in World War II was marred by their failure to hit drop zones, inconsistent resupply, and inability to sustain combat operations over long periods of time.

Once on the ground, by parachute or glider, the airborne soldier was a formidable fighter. German paratroop formations maintained their solid combat reputation despite the defeat of Nazi Germany. The problem of having enough aircraft to deliver paratroops remained a serious question, and planners pondered just exactly what kind of mission was right for airborne forces.

Gliders were abandoned as a method of bringing troops to the battlefield. The emerging helicopter took the place of the glider. Helicopters were controllable, faster, and able to land and take off from untenable landing zones. The course of airborne operations in World War II in Europe was not smooth, but as armies analyzed the lessons learned, paratroop divisions, now minus the glider regiments, were maintained as a viable postwar force.

James J. Cooke

Additional Reading

Ambrose, Stephen E., *Pegasus Bridge, June 6, 1944* (1985).

Blair, Clay, *Ridgeway's Paratroopers: The American Airborne in World War II* (1985).

Devlin, Gerard M., *Paratrooper* (1979).

Gavin, James, *Airborne Warfare* (1947).

Hickey, Michael, *Out of the Sky: A History of Airborne Warfare* (1979).

MacDonald, Charles B., *Airborne* (1970).

McGuirl, Thomas, and Uwe Feist, *Fallschirmjäger: History of German Parachute Troops* (1993).

Ryan, Cornelius, *A Bridge Too Far* (1974).

Air Defense Operations

Of all the types of operations common to military organizations in 1939, the very concept of "air defense" was probably the newest. Like almost all else in the war, what started out to be the first primitive attempts using ineffectual equipment and useless, sometimes bizarre tactics, ended in well-oiled military machines capable of meeting, if not defeating, nearly any air threat. Air defense in World War II, for the sake of convenience, can be divided into two types—passive (observers, radars, and guns) and active (fighters and, arguably, bombers).

Passive Air Defense

The defense of ground troops was the main reason for light and most medium air defense weapons. Heavier weapons, being by their nature larger and more complex, were developed to defend fixed sites, cities, and important military and industrial targets. No side developed tactical (ground troop) air defense operations (not to say the weapons) to any high degree during the war, but strategic passive defense advanced considerably from its crude beginnings. Tactical ground force defense, until the development of the guided missile, largely was best at making the attacker miss the target.

Though ground fire accounted for a fair number of downed airplanes, the total was minuscule compared to the enormous number of kills scored by the hunters of the skies—the fighter-interceptors. While passive air defense was vital, in truth, tactical and strategic air environments changed in World War II because of the activities of a more active, strategic nature.

Germany held a near-monopoly on tactical air support for ground operations early in the ground war, having been one of the few countries to have actually practiced coordinated air-ground operations. Accordingly, few of the Allied powers even had an idea of what needed to be done to protect their ground forces in a tactical environment. The Western Allies found out early that tactical air defense operations protecting ground forces and fixed ground targets was an essential part of warfare. Gradually, tactical air defense improved while the Germans' ability to attack Allied targets on the ground and at sea diminished.

Common to most Western Allied forces, barrage balloons were the simplest of systems that kept Axis aircraft at higher altitudes and decreased their already marginal accuracy. Normally filled with helium or simple hot air (hydrogen's flammable nature made that gas a poor choice), American balloons were either tethered low to the ground and released over slow-moving ships and stationary ground targets during diving attacks, or kept at altitudes where their tether wires posed a grave danger to the unwary pilot.

Allied fleet defense improved steadily from the early days of the war, when better early warning radars and the proximity fuze (qq.v.) made almost all Western Allied ships at sea formidable targets by 1944.

The British Commonwealth nations began the war with only a dim idea of how to defend ground forces from air attack, and this was reflected in their casualty rates and their difficulties early in the war. Initially, machine guns and automatic cannon were employed in a variety of mounts and vehicles, intended to engage attacking aircraft with streams of bullets. All Commonwealth industrial powers developed at least one mount or specialized vehicle for ground defense.

Defending larger, strategic targets, however, was a different matter. Spurred by the dreaded zeppelin and Gotha bomber raids of World War I, British strategic air defense was probably the most sophisticated in Europe. This defense integrated the CHAIN HOME (q.v.) radar net (providing early warning of air attacks), the Ground Observer Corps (picking up target tracking duties after the target was over Britain, and providing much-needed altitude and target count information that CHAIN HOME could not provide), the guns themselves, and the Royal Air Force (RAF) interceptors (usually the first to engage the inbound targets).

The guns belonged to the army, which served all air defense batteries in Britain. Commonwealth strategic air defense depended on the same kind of weapons as all the other powers: high-velocity, flat trajectory, high-explosive shells. Unlike the Germans and Soviets, however, the Western Allies had proximity fuzes that greatly increased the accuracy of antiaircraft artillery (AAA). They also developed better target acquisition, tracking, and height-finding radar than their Soviet allies.

In response to increasing German radar sophistication, the RAF and the United States Army Air Forces (USAAF) developed a variety of electronic and mechanical countermeasures to protect their bombers on raids over Germany. The most famous was the strips of light metal and metallic paper dropped to mask aircraft movement from radars. These strips were called "window" by the RAF and "chaff" by their American counterparts. Other passive measures intended to confound, confuse, and redirect German electronic communications, alert, guidance, and control systems were employed almost from the beginning of the war, including communications spoofing, radar jamming, and radar blanking.

The Soviets employed the simplest forms of passive air defense by launching ground offensives and counterthrusts during periods when the Germans could not effectively use their considerable airpower—at night or during bad weather. This simple stratagem met with success where it could be used, and it was the best the ill-prepared Soviets could do for the first few months of the war.

To defend their troops, the Soviets modified their already successful weapon designs, notably the 12.7mm, 14.5mm, and 20mm heavy machine guns for forward air defense roles. These weapons, deployed in the lead elements of the ground forces, engaged low-level air targets using visual sights, and were usually at least as successful as any other weapon of that nature. Heavier pieces included versions of the 45mm and larger field and antitank guns.

Major Soviet cities, airfields, industrial plants, and railheads, however, were defended by large numbers of antiaircraft artillery. German pilots flying on air raids over Moscow said the city had the highest concentration of the deadliest antiaircraft artillery in the world, and they were probably right. What the Soviets lacked in sophistication they could make up for in sheer numbers, for in passive air defense it is volume of fire that determines the effectiveness of any barrage. At one time, Moscow was defended by as many as 2,500 pieces of medium and heavy antiaircraft artillery.

The Soviets, lacking height-finding radar and other means of pinpointing target altitude accurately early in the war, would merely blanket the airspace with fire. Later, with better coordination between searchlight batteries and guns, they wasted less ammunition and provided even denser fire at attack altitudes. Radar direction of Soviet air defense was slow in coming due largely to the lack of Soviet technological development. Eventually, it did include the same sorts of early warning and target tracking capabilities as the Germans and Western Allies employed, though on a cruder scale.

The U.S. Army adopted a surprisingly sophisticated passive air defense doctrine and a number of fairly advanced weapons systems for tactical air defense by 1941. Every American combat vehicle was intended to be self-defending against attacking enemy aircraft with machine guns. American infantrymen were also trained to engage low-

Allied anti-aircraft fire over Algiers on the night of 23 November 1942. (IWM NA 176)

flying aircraft with anything at hand. Though in practice the effects of the tremendous volume of American ground fire was not apparent in terms of real kills, ground fire did usually make the Axis attackers more careful.

The specialized American air defense vehicles had a more impressive record, especially the quadruple M-16 caliber .50 half-track-mounted machine gun. Though appearing lethal, it had a less impressive (but still respectable) real-kill record than desired. Heavier artillery included 90mm and larger guns with fairly sophisticated target tracking equipment.

Air defense artillery was entirely an army operation in the U.S. forces, except for fleet defense. Specialized antiaircraft artillery was usually formed into batteries, battalions, and brigade groups, with larger units providing early warning and communications. AAA assets were distributed down to the combat command and even regimental level in ground forces, as well as assigned to fixed points.

Germany by far developed the best passive air defense systems of all the Axis powers in Europe, but it was never as effective as that of the Allies. Germany remained a step behind the Allies largely because of the lack of resources and time for development.

The light (forward) antiaircraft assets were controlled by the ground forces. These included heavy machine guns and automatic cannons. By 1943, the Germans developed the *Wirbelwind* (whirlwind) quad-antiaircraft gun system mounted on a turret affixed to the Sfz-251 half-track, as well as other versions of the same system on trailers and full-tracked chassis. This weapon, while effective at extremely low-level and predictable flight paths, suffered from a lack of sophisticated target tracking and early warning systems. The 88mm/L35 "barn door" was the largest antiaircraft piece appearing at the front lines, but enjoyed far more success as an antitank gun than a plane killer.

The construction of "*Flak* towers" in strategic areas was inspired by the disastrous AAA crew casualties caused by the massed raids early in the war. These structures usually stood above the surrounding terrain by several stories and were armed with a combination of light and heavy guns. The sides and roofs of these circular concrete obelisks sloped down toward the ground to deflect falling bombs, and the walls at their bases were as much as twenty feet thick. Testimony of the durability of these structures was that the zoo tower in Berlin was the last fortified point to fall in May 1945.

At strategic, fixed points, antiaircraft guns were manned by the *Luftwaffe*, some from the same organizations as the intercepting fighters. While deadly effective, German static antiaircraft suffered from shortages of manpower, adequate early warning and alert systems, and guns too light to reach high altitude bombers effectively. The heavier caliber guns, generally those larger than 100mm, were simply too few.

The German strategic early warning system, operational at the beginning of the war, was wholly inadequate for the task required of it, and spent most of the war catching up to the increasing sophistication of Allied air attack tactics. Very large raids easily overwhelmed the reporting networks and alerting systems with multiple, large penetrations. That the *Luftwaffe* coped as well as it did was a tribute to the dedication and tenacity of the leaders of the systems.

Active Air Defense

The Western Allies were doctrinally prepared for sustained air offensive operations, but were woefully unprepared for the tenacity of the *Luftwaffe*. Defending both the battlefield and the industrial base from air attack was possible only through an effort aimed at destroying the *Luftwaffe* itself.

The Western Allies used only one common tactic to defend their bombers from *Luftwaffe* fighters. Very large raids were usually preceded by light and medium bomber attacks on Axis interceptor fields, communications centers, and radar sites along the flight routes. This proactive strategy may have alerted the defenders that something big was coming, but it did decrease their ability to respond.

The Royal Air Force was prepared, by dint of very secret and sustained effort, to meet the German air onslaughts with the CHAIN HOME stationary-array radar that could detect groups of aircraft over the Continent and, through a telephone network, report the approach of enemy aircraft. Ground observers, sound-locator stations, and other reporting means gave more information based on CHAIN HOME's rough bearings. Once reported, the RAF scrambled fighters from forward dispersal fields to intercept the attackers.

Generally, RAF fighters would look for a height or light advantage over the attacking formations. Then the Spitfires would attempt to engage the escorting fighter aircraft and draw them away from the bombers, which would then be attacked by the Hurricanes and other less nimble planes. When the engaging planes ran out of fuel or ammunition, the forward squadrons were relieved by subsequent units to maintain a continuous attack on the bombers.

A

While this meant that many German bombers got through to their targets, it was thought to be a moderate trade-off for the advantages, however dubious, of presenting continuous resistance. This technique was moderately successful, but the RAF lacked the aircraft to sustain the operation for very long. During the V-weapon offensives, techniques were augmented by Bomber Command and the USAAF bombing of Germany's Peenemünde missile facilities and other launch sites.

Early USAAF doctrine stated that heavy bombers could defend themselves from enemy fighters. As it recognized that this did not work, the fighter escort concept was born. Initially, escorts were hampered by a lack of range, so protection all the way to the target was not possible. By early 1944, drop tanks allowed the fighters to provide penetration, target, and withdrawal support for the bombers.

Beginning in 1942, Allied planners realized that any landings in northwest Europe would require air superiority over not only the North Sea but also much of northwestern Europe. To that end, bomber targets were suppliers of aircraft components and fuel, while fighters not escorting bombers were expected to prowl the Continent in "fighter sweeps," looking for the *Luftwaffe* to rise up to meet them. The *Luftwaffe* defended the bomber targets with great zeal that seemingly increased as time went on, while it practically ignored the fighters.

By late 1943 and early 1944, the Allies decided that the fighter sweeps were not working, and the fighters were committed to escort duties. But rather than the traditional "close" escort, where fighters and bombers could always see each other, the fighters would hang back, waiting for the interceptors to rise. This concept of using the heavy bombers as bait for the fighters was far more successful in reducing the *Luftwaffe* to near nonexistence by late 1944. In the end, the U.S. active air defense, that of attacking the *Luftwaffe* first, worked because of superior depth of training, and because the U.S. had more operational aircraft more often than the Germans.

The *Luftwaffe* started the war nearly at its peak strength. Originally, it was equipped essentially to support ground operations. Beginning in 1939, the Germans practiced the most active kind of air defense—destroy the enemy on the ground. The Polish, Yugoslav, Belgian, Greek, Dutch, and Soviet air forces were decimated hours after the beginning of hostilities.

During the Battle of Britain (q.v.), the *Luftwaffe* attacked the RAF at its airfields and factories in an effort to clear the way for Operation SEA LION (q.v.), the invasion of the British Isles. Unfortunately, the *Luftwaffe* was not an instrument designed for such activities and the Messerschmitt Bf-109 fighters expected to take on the RAF in the air lacked the dwell-time over Britain to protect the bombers adequately. The Bf-110s were too slow and clumsy to match the Spitfires or even the Hurricanes. Despite these limitations, the German fighters nearly achieved their goal of knocking out effective British airpower over southern England. When the Germans switched targets late in 1940 to concentrate on British cities, the RAF won a reprieve, from which the *Luftwaffe* never recovered.

The *Luftwaffe*'s home defense was always a weak link in the defensive chain, in part because experienced airmen were often fewer in number than the planes on hand. *Luftwaffe* pilots, on average, had only a quarter of the flying training time (especially instrument flying) that their Allied counterparts had. As a result, the *Luftwaffe* suffered from what *Luftwaffe* commander Herman Göring (q.v.) himself called "the plague"—numerous accidents caused by simple inexperience. On more than one occasion, the *Luftwaffe* lost more interceptors to bad weather flying and midair collisions than to Allied fighters and bombers. The problem was compounded by the German tendency to strip flight training units of experienced instructor-pilots to replace losses in front-line units. That ensured there would never be enough pilots to man the defenses of the *Reich*.

Despite all its shortcomings, the *Luftwaffe* accounted for hundreds of Allied aircraft in the air battles over Germany. Its tactics were simple enough, and greatly resembled the RAF's in many respects. One group of fighters (generally the lighter Bf-109s) would engage the Allied escorts, while the heavier-armed fighters would attack the bombers—preferring head-on attacks against USAAF daylight bombers and belly attacks on the Bomber Command's night bombers.

More daring and skilled pilots would fly into a bomber formation, pump a few rounds into an aircraft's vulnerable wing roots, and speed away before the gunners could react. A more successful tactic was for heavy twin-engine aircraft to fire 210mm rockets into bomber formations from beyond machine gun range, causing the defensive formations to break up. That enabled the more nimble single-engine fighters to avoid the interlocking defensive fires provided by the tightly packed bomber formations.

At night just finding the incoming bombers

was a problem. Vectored by ground radar or by large radar-carrying aircraft to the vicinity of a target, single-engine fighters were expected to find their targets by luck and by looking for engine exhausts. Night intercepts were the most dangerous of all *Luftwaffe* missions.

By June 1944, the *Luftwaffe* could not contest any ground attacks and was having a hard time contesting the nearly incessant pounding from the air. Late technological innovations, including jet and rocket fighters, were too little, too late.

John D. Beatty

Additional Reading

Anderton, David A., *The Aggressors*, Vol. 3: *Interceptor vs Heavy Bomber* (1991).

Arcangelis, Mario de, *Electronic Warfare* (1985).

Crabtree, James D., *On Air Defense* (1994).

McFarland, Stephen L., and Wesley P. Newton, *To Command the Sky: The Battle for Air Superiority over Germany, 1942–1944* (1991).

Pile, Frederick, *Ack Ack: Britain's Defense Against Air Attack During the Second World War* (1949).

Routledge, N.W., *Anti-Aircraft Artillery, 1914–1955* (1994).

Air-Sea Rescue

The idea of establishing a specialized and elite force for the rescue of downed aircrews grew out of three interlocked circumstances just before World War II: (1) a deep-seated European belief in the sanctity of life; (2) the high expense of training replacement aircrews for those lost in combat; and (3) the greater effectiveness of aircrews who believed there was a reasonable expectation of surviving a bail out or crash landing.

In 1935, these factors led the German *Luftwaffe* to establish a sea-based unit, named the *Seenotdienst* (Sea Emergency Service), under the command of Lieutenant Colonel Konrad Glotz, at Kiel for the sole purpose of recovering aircrews from the ocean. By 1939, the *Luftwaffe* expanded his rescue force by adding Heinkel-59 float aircraft specifically modified for this mission.

The Germans pioneered the development of equipment and techniques during the years before 1940. Their Heinkels were equipped with medical supplies, respirators, electrically heated sleeping bags, a floor hatch with a collapsible ladder, and a hoist to lift injured aircrew members. The exteriors were painted white and sported a red cross to distinguish them from combat aircraft.

The Germans introduced unmanned large buoy-type floats, outfitting them with all manner of equipment that could be used by downed flyers of all nations. Additionally, each *Luftwaffe* aircraft contained inflatable dinghies, survival equipment, and green dye that could be released in the ocean to aid in spotting survivors. By the Battle of Britain (q.v.) in 1940, the Germans had in place, for the English Channel and the North Atlantic, a rescue system in which a downed aircrew member had a reasonable chance of survival.

The British efforts early in the war were haphazard. The Royal Air Force (RAF) relied on its coastal defense force for the rescue of crewmen, although by March 1940 a communications system was established to give priority to distress signals. In July 1940, with the heavy attrition in men and materiel wrought by the Battle of Britain, Air Vice Marshal Keith R. Park (q.v.), commanding Number 11 Group of Fighter Command, acquired twelve Lysander patrol aircraft and the services of sea craft to search and recover downed airmen. The next month, the British formalized this arrangement by creating the Directorate of Air-Sea Rescue at the Air Ministry to coordinate rescue efforts.

In August 1941, executive control of all rescue operations was vested in the commander of RAF Coastal Command. From this beginning, rescue operations became increasingly efficient throughout the remainder of the war, at least for airmen lost in areas other than those held by the enemy.

Like its allies, the United States entered the war without any organized air-sea rescue capability. As casualties from the bombing campaign began to mount, General Henry H. "Hap" Arnold (q.v.), the commanding general of the U.S. Army Air Forces, made rescue a priority. In September 1942, British and American forces agreed to cooperate and coordinate rescue operations. Although the British dominated the rescue program in the European Theater of Operations (ETO), the U.S. assisted and made special efforts to properly equip aircrews and train them for survival in a crash or bail out.

They also employed seaplanes for search and rescue over water, even though the PBY-1 Catalina's short 800-mile radius of action limited its effectiveness. Later, other aircraft, such as modified bombers, were used for rescue operations. The U.S., for instance, modified some of its B-17s to carry mahogany-laminated, plywood boats under their fuselages that could be dropped to airmen in the water. The boats were stocked with food, water, clothing, supplies, and two small motors to allow the airmen to travel home. The SB-17 was the first American aircraft modified and used specifically for rescue. Its first operational mission took place in April 1945, just as the war in Europe was about to end.

The success of air-sea rescue operations in the ETO was sufficient to elicit excited response from most airmen. A total of 1,972 American airmen were saved in the waters around Britain through March 1945. As a measure of its development, the U.S. Eighth Air Force's rescue efforts saw only a 28 percent save rate in 1942, compared to a 43 percent rate by April 1943. Indeed, by the end of the war, Allied combat aircrews from all theaters could reasonably expect to be picked up if downed in the water.

Roger D. Launius

Additional Reading
Barker, Ralph, *Down in the Drink: True Stories of the Gold Fish Club* (1955).
Richards, Denis, *Royal Air Force, 1939–1945,* Vol. 1: *The Fight at Odds* (1953).

Amphibious Operations

Amphibious warfare, that is, the projection of sea-based ground forces onto land, was more widely conducted in World War II than in any previous conflict and on a greater scale than ever before or since. Involving all aspects of naval and military operations from mine warfare (q.v.) to air and ground combat, amphibious warfare represented the most complex and dangerous of all military activities.

Ironically, the basic principles were established in the post–World War I period, but the lessons were largely ignored by most military leaders except in the Soviet Union, the United States Marine Corps (USMC), and Germany's *Landungspionieren* (Landing Pioneers). The combined nature of such operations were therefore not widely understood, and only the USMC, which played no part in the European theater, proposed procedures for conducting them. By 1942, however, the Allies in particular had special procedures, equipment, and even ships designed and built specifically for amphibious operations.

Although not a maritime power, Germany initiated the war's first amphibious operation when it invaded Norway (q.v.) in April 1940. It was the Allies, however, who demonstrated the true mastery of the amphibious art in the end, landing more than four million troops in more than five major amphibious assaults, dozens of tactical landings, and countless amphibious raids along occupied Europe's vulnerable coasts. In fact, it was through amphibious warfare that the Western Allies were able to regain their foothold on the continent and participate in the final victory over the Third *Reich*.

Amphibious operations can be broken down into four categories: a raid, a full assault, an evacuation, and an administrative (noncombat) landing. The first of these is the most dangerous since it generally occurs in an area of enemy superiority and involves elements of both an assault and an evacuation. An administrative landing is the safest, being conducted in a benign environment without enemy ground or naval forces present. Assaults and evacuations face varying levels of risk, depending on the enemy's forces in the area. The German invasion of Norway is an example of an assault, although most of its troops landed under circumstances approaching that of an administrative landing. Britain's Dunkirk (q.v.) evacuation represents the war's first major combat evacuation.

The German invasion of Norway was a well-planned but improvised affair. No specialized equipment or troops were employed. However, the unpreparedness of the Norwegian defenses and lack of Allied response to the invasion made such arrangements unnecessary. As a result, Germany learned few lessons from its success and remained inadequately prepared for amphibious operations when it began the planning process for Operation SEA LION (q.v.).

Germany's *Landungspionieren* had studied amphibious operations before the war and had advocated the construction of specialized landing craft (q.v.), assault boats, amphibious vehicles, and high-speed hydrofoil transports. Lack of resources and the low priority given to such missions resulted in none of these projects reaching fruition before the war. In fact, Operation SEA LION was long-since canceled before any of this equipment was introduced into service. The assault boats, however, were used in the German amphibious raid on Spitzbergen Island (q.v.) in 1943, while the landing craft were used in the successful assaults on the Dodecanese Islands (q.v.) that same year. They also saw widespread usage in river crossing operations (q.v.) in the Soviet Union. Nonetheless, Germany never developed a true amphibious doctrine and had no capacity to land troops in the face of determined opposition until well into 1942. By then, Germany's strategic situation denied such operations, except in very limited and special circumstances.

As for the Allies, only the Soviet Union had a specialized amphibious force—its naval infantry—

at war's start, but it lacked adequate equipment and training. It, like Britain's Royal Marines (q.v.), expected to land on the beach using ships' boats or other improvised transport. Still, the Soviets had studied the lessons of Britain's Gallipoli campaign and Imperial Russia's amphibious operations from World War I. What the Soviets lacked was adequate resources to apply those lessons fully. The same could not be said of Great Britain.

Driven by the will of Prime Minister Winston S. Churchill (q.v.), Britain formed a command for raiding operations and later Combined Operations (q.v.). This organization was responsible for planning and executing the commando raids (q.v.) that wreaked such havoc in occupied Europe. Landing craft were improvised from RAF air-sea rescue boats. The first two Allied amphibious operations, or commando raids, were conducted against German targets in occupied France in June and July 1940. Gradually, the Allied amphibious raids became more effective as lessons were learned, expertise expanded, and training improved. As Allied power increased, preparations were made for full amphibious assaults.

Meanwhile, on the eastern front, the Soviet Union found itself facing an overwhelming German onslaught in Operation BARBAROSSA. It was there that the Allies conducted their first amphibious assault on 23 September 1941, when a Soviet Black Sea Fleet element under Captain First Rank Sergei Gorshkov (q.v.) landed a naval infantry regiment against the coastal flanks of the Romanian army besieging the city of Odessa. Preceded by extensive naval gunfire and an airborne special forces unit that attacked the local Romanian headquarters, the Soviet landing force quickly drove the defenders away from the beach. Nearly 2,000 Romanians and much of their equipment were captured, eliminating the Romanian threat to the city's harbor.

The Soviets successfully evacuated the defenders from Odessa to Sevastopol when the German advance threatened that more important Soviet naval base. Amphibious raids and assaults figured prominently in Soviet naval operations along Germany's Black and Arctic Sea flanks during the war in the east (see Eastern Naval War). They conducted more than 150 amphibious raids and assaults during the war.

Soviet doctrine called for the naval infantry to conduct amphibious raids, but all assaults were to be joint operations. The naval infantry conducted the initial assault and then held the beachhead while conventional army troops disembarked behind it. Although this approach economized on the number of troops requiring specialized amphibious assault training, it proved costly in combat as any delays in the follow-on landing left the naval infantry dangerously exposed to counterattacks. As a result, the Soviet naval infantry suffered heavy casualties in its amphibious assaults. Consequently, the Soviet Navy of the 1960s pushed heavily to provide amphibious tanks, mechanized vehicles, and fast-moving air cushion vehicles for its naval landing forces in an effort to reduce their vulnerability to enemy defenses.

The unsuccessful Allied raid on Dieppe (q.v.) in August 1942 was intended to test German defenses and provide lessons that might be applied to conducting full amphibious assaults on the Continent. For the British, those lessons included a need for specialized vehicles and equipment to remove beach obstacles and defenses. Those vehicles, which the British called "funnies," were ready by the Normandy (q.v.) landings in 1944; but the earlier Allied landings in Northwest Africa (q.v.) and Italy were conducted without those specialized vehicles.

The Northwest Africa landings in November 1942 were the Western Allies' first amphibious assaults. The Americans employed specialized amphibious "scouts and rangers" in those landings, or, as they were known later, "frogmen" (see Underwater Demolition Teams [UDTs]). The Operation TORCH landings also saw the first employment of the specialized amphibious landing ships that were so critical to getting forces ashore quickly. The landing ships, tank, or LSTs, were particularly important since they allowed the landing of tanks directly onto the beach during an assault. Although many mistakes were made in the planning and execution of Operation TORCH, the basic foundations for all future Allied assaults in the west were established during the Northwest Africa landings.

All subsequent landings were preceded by special forces, such as UDTs and commandos, to remove obstacles and seize key terrain and defensive features before the main assault force approached the beach. They also included airborne drops to seal the assault area from enemy reinforcement. Additional lessons about air and naval support were gained from the Sicily and Salerno (qq.v.) landings. Everything was done to isolate the beach defenders from their reinforcements until the landing force established itself ashore. More significantly, procedures and equipment, particularly specialized landing ships and craft, were developed to accelerate the pace of force buildup ashore. That it was a successful effort can best be measured by the success of the Normandy landings that placed six divisions ashore in less than twenty-four hours, and nearly a million men and their equipment into France in less than a week—a phenomenal accomplishment.

Amphibious operations were critical to the Allied war effort. They enabled the Soviets to threaten the Axis extreme flanks throughout the eastern campaign; a factor they employed to divert Axis forces away from the front and facilitate Soviet offensive efforts in the war's final two years. The Western Allies could never have contributed to Germany's defeat had they not mastered amphibious operations, the most complex of all military activities. Doctrinally, they established the procedures that are used by all Western nations to this day.

Carl O. Schuster

Additional Reading

Achkasov, V.I., and N.B. Pavlovich, *Soviet Naval Operations in the Great Patriotic War, 1941–1945* (1981).

Jones, Vincent, *Operation Torch* (1972).

Mason, David, *Salerno* (1972).

Morrison, Samuel Elliot, *History of United States Naval Operations in World War II*, Vols. II, IX, and XI (1947–1952).

Ruge, Friedrich, *The Soviets As Naval Opponents, 1941–1945* (1979).

Schmitt, Pietr, *Operation Sea Lion* (1992).

Thompson, R.W., *D-Day* (1968).

Young, Peter, *Commando* (1969).

Antisubmarine Warfare

See Submarine and Antisubmarine Warfare

Antitank Warfare

The tank first appeared on the battlefield in World War I. By 1917, the Allies had an overwhelming superiority in tanks on the western front, leaving the Germans to develop the first antitank (AT) warfare measures. The immediate German response to Allied tanks was to designate all artillery as antitank weapons. The earliest force with a specific antitank role consisted of batteries of infantry guns, light artillery pieces that were man-handled forward by their crews and modified to fire only in the direct-fire mode.

The search for effective antitank warfare in World War II was a balancing act between technology and tactical doctrine. By the start of the war, most armies saw the tank as the primary antitank

weapon. To their horror, the light guns on most tanks proved as ineffective as the light antitank guns that were supposed to be the backup system. As a result, between 1941 and 1942, on the eastern front and in North Africa (q.v.), field artillery in the direct-fire mode was the primary antitank system. Only with the arrival of large numbers of heavier AT weapons in later 1942 could the field artillery return to concentrating on its proper task.

Additional antitank fire was supposed to be provided by infantry equipped with AT rifles. The infantry AT rifles also quickly proved mostly worthless, and gave way to projector-type weapons, such as the bazooka, the PIAT (projector, infantry, antitank), or the *Panzerfaust* (*see* Infantry Weapons).

In North Africa, the Germans did not use their tanks in a primary antitank role. They quickly discovered that their high-velocity 8.8cm *Flak* guns were devastatingly effective against British tanks. Many Soviets also believed that tanks should focus on the destruction of enemy manpower rather than fighting other tanks. Thus, in 1942, the Soviets fell back on the German tactic of 1917 and declared all artillery weapons as antitank. As the war moved into 1943 and 1944, the Germans could not match the Soviet production rates for guns, and the balance tipped against the Germans.

High-velocity antitank guns were manned by artillery crews in many armies. As the war progressed, antitank guns (q.v.) became larger and more powerful, and many were mounted on self-propelled (SP) carriages to give them mobility equal to the tank. The Germans pioneered in the offensive use of SP antitank guns on the eastern front. By the end of the war, German SPs had destroyed some 30,000 Soviet armored vehicles, and Soviet tanks generally had orders to avoid direct combat with them.

The Soviets responded by developing a wide range of SP guns, and the distinctions between SP field guns, SP assault guns, and SP antitank guns blurred as the war progressed. While U.S. SP antitank guns were almost all turret-mounted, the German, and particularly the Soviet, SPs were based on turretless vehicles, which were simpler and cheaper to design and build. The lack of a turret gave these vehicles a lower profile and made them smaller targets on the open battlefields in the east. The disadvantage was that the entire vehicle had to turn to traverse the gun more than a few degrees. These weapons were most effective against tanks when firing from an ambush position.

Because they spent the first two years of the war on the defensive, the Soviets excelled in the development of antitank tactics in the defense. At Stalingrad (q.v.), for example, they deployed four sets of antitank belts ten kilometers deep. One of the basic principles was that Soviet tanks would only counterattack after an enemy tank attack was stopped with artillery—all forms of artillery. The lessons learned at Stalingrad were refined and applied with a vengeance later at Kursk (q.v.), the graveyard of the *Panzers.*

The United States organized AT guns into tank destroyer (TD) battalions. In 1942, a TD battalion was organized around three companies of three platoons of four self-propelled guns each. TD battalions also had a reconnaissance company and a combat engineer platoon. In the event of an enemy armored penetration, the doctrine called for the TD battalion to conduct massed ambushes throughout the depth of the defensive zone.

American tank destroyers did not do well in Northwest Africa (q.v.). The combat area was too vast for the guns to mass effectively, and the terrain was too open for the vehicles to find the hull-down positions necessary for their survival. As a result, many American commanders tended to favor the British system of towed antitank guns. When the fighting shifted to Western Europe, the towed guns proved far less effective in the more restricted terrain—they moved too slowly and they were too close to the ground to shoot over the hedgerows. In July 1944, the U.S. Army started reequipping all TD battalions with SP guns. For the most part, however, the TD battalions were not employed en masse because by the end of 1944 the limited *Panzer* threat tended to be very thinly dispersed. This situation allowed Allied tanks in the west to advance relying largely on their own armament for defense against German tanks and antitank guns.

World War II was a continuous tug of war between the size and power of AT and tank guns, and the thickness and strength of tank armor. The challenge for tank designers was to develop a tank with a gun large enough to defeat the armor of other tanks, but with armor strong enough to withstand other tank guns. Thicker armor meant heavier vehicle, and a larger gun meant greater recoil, which required a larger turret and a larger hull to support it. Heavier tanks had less mobility, and larger tanks were bigger targets. World War II designs tended to place heavier armor on the tank's front and sides, the areas most likely to be attacked. Crews also placed spare tread links on the outside areas of their tanks to give them an extra edge.

A tank can be defeated in several different degrees." The most effective is called a "total kill," in which the crew is killed and the tank is utterly destroyed. This accomplishes two things: the killing of the crew eliminates the tank as an immediate threat, while the destruction of the vehicle means it cannot be put back into service at some future time. A "mobility kill" is a much less desirable effect. A mobility kill results when a tank is stopped because of damage to its engine or drivetrain, or to its treads. In such cases, the tank can no longer maneuver and advance, but it is still dangerous because it can fire. Depending on the degree of the damage, it can also be placed back in service. Tanks that hit land mines suffered mobility kills for the most part. The advantage of a mobility kill, of course, is that the tank becomes much more vulnerable to subsequent attack.

In World War II, as today, antitank projectiles fell into two basic categories, kinetic energy and chemical energy. Kinetic energy rounds are solid shot that depend on mass and velocity to defeat the target's armor. The heavier the round and the faster it travels, the more armor it can penetrate. Range from the gun to the target also is a factor, as the projectile loses velocity the farther it travels. The German 8.8cm Pak 43 could penetrate 207mm of armor at a range of 500 meters, but only 159mm at a range of 2,000 meters. The round's angle of impact is a factor as well. At a 30-degree angle of impact, the penetration of the Pak 43 at 500 meters dropped to 182mm.

The earlier kinetic energy rounds had a tendency to ricochet unless they hit the target at just the right angle. The solution to this problem was the addition of an armor-piercing cap, a soft metal nose cone that absorbed the shock of the initial impact and stuck to the outer skin of the armor just long enough for the round to start to penetrate. The armor-piercing cap, however, gave the projectile an overall blunt shape, which reduced its velocity, and thus its penetrating power. The solution to that problem was the addition of a second ballistic cap, a streamlined nose cone of light metal that shattered on impact and fell away, allowing the armor-piercing cap to do its job.

Tapering the bore of the gun itself was another way of increasing the velocity of kinetic energy rounds. This "squeeze bore" technique employed a projectile with a plastic front driving band that wore away as the round moved down the bore. As the bore narrowed, the pressure behind the round increased. Near the muzzle the round's rear driving band engaged the barrel's rifling. Once the round emerged, the remnants of the rotating band fell away. The Germans used this technique on their 4.2cm and 7.5cm Pak 41 antitank guns.

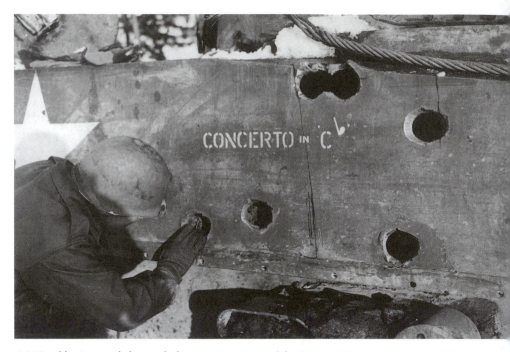

A U.S. soldier inspects holes punched into an American tank by German 8.8cm antitank guns at Monde St. Etienne, Belgium, 16 January 1945. (IWM EA 50516)

Technical problems made the squeeze bore technique difficult to apply to larger calibers.

The most effective kinetic energy rounds were made from dense materials such as tungsten carbide, which has a density about 1.4 times that of steel. Full-size projectiles made from tungsten were impossible, however, because their weight and hardness would quickly wear out any gun that fired them. By 1944, the British solved that problem with the development of the armor-piercing discarding sabot (APDS) round, a solid shot in a plastic casing that fell away as soon as the round left the bore. The advantage of this system is that the high pressures that are generated by a large-bore gun are placed behind a much smaller projectile, giving it far greater velocity and penetrating power. APDS remains the primary antitank round today, with cores made of such materiel as depleted uranium.

Chemical energy rounds depend on explosive effect to defeat armor. The effectiveness of a chemical energy round is a function of the size, composition, and arrangement of its explosive charge, rather than of its velocity. Because they tend to travel slower and at a more arched trajectory than kinetic energy rounds, an accurate range to the target is necessary to achieve the all-vital first-round hit that can mean the difference between life and death in armored warfare.

Chemical energy rounds that produced only a high explosive (HE) or blast effect, were only effective early in the war against tanks with riveted as opposed to welded or cast armor. A far more effective round was based on the Monroe effect—also known as the hollow charge or shaped charge effect. In such rounds, the leading end of the explosive charge has a cone-shaped recess that is lined with some light metal such as copper. When the round strikes the target, the explosive charge i detonated from the rear. The hollow cone has the effect of channeling the entire force of the explosion into a small spot opposite the apex of the cone. The result is a jet of very hot and very fast (up to 20,000 ft/sec) explosive gas that punches hole through the target's armor. Hollow charge antitank rounds received the designation high explosive antitank (HEAT).

A second type of chemical energy round, the plastic, or "squash-head" round, uses a plastic explosive charge and a base-detonating fuze surrounded by a thin metal casing. When the round strikes, the charge pancakes onto the armor like a blob of modeling clay. The detonation sends shock wave through the armor that produces flaking effect on the far side, sending chunks of steel into the tank's inner compartments. Quite often a squash-head round does not penetrate the target's armor, but the tank's crew is killed by piece of its own armor. Squash-head projectiles were developed during World War II, but they did not enter service until after the war.

The main disadvantage to firing HEAT projectiles from guns is that the stabilizing spin imparted by the rifling tends to degrade the penetrating effect. This led to the development of fin-stabilized projectiles launched from close range, low-velocity infantry weapons such as the bazooka, the *Panzerfaust,* and the recoilless rifle. Since HEAT rounds do not depend on velocity, they can be launched very effectively from such light weapons.

Today, tanks mostly use APDS rounds for antitank fire. Helicopter and ground-launched AT guide missiles, and shoulder-fired infantry AT rockets (the successors of the bazooka and *Panzerfaust*) fire projectiles with HEAT warheads.

Taken over the entire course of World War II, no single system stood out as the overwhelming tank killer—although during certain periods and in certain theaters some systems predominated. Overall figures for British tanks show roughly 30 percent of the casualties caused by antitank guns; 25 percent caused by enemy tanks; 22 percent caused by mines; 20 percent caused by indirect artillery fire and aircraft; and the remaining 3 percent caused by infantry AT weapons. In North Africa, however, 40 percent of the British tank casualties were caused by Axis AT guns, while in Italy that rate was only 16 percent. Because German tanks tended to be more powerful and better armed, Allied tanks most likely destroyed far fewer *Panzers* than the other way around.

J.B.A. Bailey
David T. Zabecki

Additional Reading

Bailey, J.B.A., *Field Artillery and Firepower* (1989).

Gabel, Christopher R., *Seek, Strike, and Destroy: U.S. Army Tank Destroyer Doctrine in World War II* (1986).

Hogg, Ian V., *German Artillery of World War Two* (1975).

House, Jonathan, *Toward Combined Arms Warfare: A Survey of 20th Century Tactics, Doctrine, and Organization* (1984).

Weeks, John S., *Men Against Tanks: A History of Antitank Warfare* (1975).

Armored Operations

For the most part, World War II was a foot soldier's war. Despite that fact, the period 1939 to 1945 saw the maturation of modern armored and mechanized operations in Europe and North Africa. While the presence of tanks in a given action is usually what classifies it as an "armored" engagement, the essence of armored operations is characterized by more than just the commitment of a large number of tanks. Even in its infancy in World War I, the tank was never designed as a stand-alone weapon, although some of the more extreme theorists of the 1920s and 1930s argued so. Thus the integration of the tank with other arms and services is one of the main themes in World War II's tactical development, and a great part of that conflict's legacy to subsequent military theory and practice.

The character of armored and mechanized operations in the war depended largely on the changing concepts and means of the combatants. To a large extent, this was a reflection of the various national prewar military and political decisions that were modified by the changing means at hand as the war progressed. The development of interwar mechanized theory sprang from a deep-rooted desire to avoid the stagnation of the trench warfare that characterized the great battles of World War I. The speed, mobility, and comparative protection of the tank were seen as essential to restoring mobility on the battlefield. While each of the various national military establishments generally recognized these advantages at the tactical level, acceptance of the concept to the point where operational results could be expected was far from universal.

In the years before the war, only the Germans, and to some extent the Soviets (before the 1937–1938 purges), saw enough potential in tanks to commit them to large-scale force structures and equipment changes within their armies.

The British, French, and Americans were plagued by intraservice and interservice rivalries and competition for scarce funding. Two of the major feuds concerned the comparative roles and missions of tanks versus cavalry, and the relative importance of the close air support from each nation's air force. As a result, their late moves toward modernization had not produced much in the way of combat-capable formations before the outbreak of the war. Generally, they had neither organized large mechanized units nor adopted doctrine on how to fight with or against such formations. The French and British in particular reaped the bitter benefits of their failure in the summer of 1940.

At the beginning of the war, both the British and American postures for armored combat were ambivalent at best. While doctrinal proponents in both nations wrote extensively about tactical concepts and their implications for equipping, manning, and controlling the force, the reality was that the tank was seen as primarily an infantry support weapon and a reconnaissance means.

Some efforts at experimentation with small (and usually provisional) armored units were made by both armies in the interwar period, but these did not lead to much. On top of the interbranch rivalries, the only major use of armor (in the Spanish civil war) (q.v.) led many to believe that the tactical value of the tank was overstated. Advances in antitank technology led many to the conclusion that massed armor was as vulnerable as massed infantry had been to the machine gun in World War I. Finally, neither nation made the commitment of scarce, Depression-era resources to equip an expensive armored force. The military leadership of both nations understood all too well that they were limited to the means at hand.

Most proponents of armored warfare saw the German model as the one to emulate. In order to produce tactically significant mass, they organized their tanks into divisions, the heart of which was two regiments of tanks. In France (q.v.) in 1940, the Allies actually had more tanks than the Germans, but they dispersed them in support of their dismounted infantry, while the Germans concentrated theirs in powerful strike units. Throughout the war, the strength of a *Panzer* division varied greatly. The authorized strength, which was rarely achieved, never exceeded 250 tanks. By contrast, when the U.S. Army finally organized armored divisions, they had up to 390 tanks of various types. British armored divisions varied between 290 and 336. The equivalent Soviet unit was a tank corps, with between 160 and 200 armored vehicles.

The German *Panzer* division was supposed to be equipped in such a way that the division's other units could keep up with the tanks. Doctrinally, the pace of combat was supposed to be geared to the fastest weapon as opposed to the infantry direct-support role where operations were paced to the slowest weapon, which was the foot soldier. The principal use of the *Panzer* division was in offensive action, rapidly achieving tactical initiative by massing force on enemy weak points while fixing and bypassing enemy strength. At critical points, the firepower of the various arms (tanks, infantry, artillery, engineers, and close-support aircraft) were massed to achieve overwhelming superiority. The reduction of resistance at decisive points was necessary to maintain the momentum of the attack.

The synchronization of this effort was made possible by a leadership style characterized by all elements operating under a single commander who frequently controlled the action from a forward position where he could actually see the battle. This commander, in turn, was guided by his higher commander's intent, usually issued in broad mission-type orders rather than lists of detailed tasks. The Germans called this technique *Auftragstaktik*. At the operational level, this approach allowed for maintenance of the initiative by continuous combat constantly adjusted to focus on the enemy's weakness, and paced faster than the enemy commander could react effectively. When it all worked, it took on the character of an unstoppable juggernaut. It was, however, a risky business.

Much could (and often did) go wrong. The system required superbly trained junior commanders, operating in essential agreement with their commander's intent. Decentralization was fine as long as things went well, but it imposed severe strains on communications when things went awry. The real-world shortfall in tactical mobility within the division could turn local success into dangerous gaps in the all-around security of the force as a whole. The very psychological confusion one wanted to impose on the enemy could act on one's own senior leadership as well. The increases in pace and distance typical of armored operations required senior leaders who could accommodate rapid change, and who would neither attempt to over-control field commanders, nor panic in the absence of reports from subordinates.

The rapid pace and increased lethality of armored operations could overwhelm command structures where leadership was done by committee or where operational control was withheld at the national level. This required that before the start of an operation the national leader form and clearly communicate their complete strategic intent and the extent to which they were willing to risk the force. The loss of the German Sixth Army at Stalingrad (q.v.) and the failure to maneuver armor against the Normandy (q.v.) beachhead are classic examples of failures to do this.

Logistics paced armored maneuver more than anything else. Both the production and distribution of supplies had as great an influence on the outcome of large-scale armored operations as enemy action. As German Field Marshal Erwin Rommel (q.v.) once noted, before the first shot of the battle is fired, "the quartermaster has already decided the outcome." Both sides had problems with logistics. The Germans had enormous difficulty with both tactical resupply and reconstituting depleted units. By the end of the war, most of their *Panzer* units were armored in name only. On the Allied side, even the huge buildup of supplies prior to the Normandy invasion could not prevent the "either/or" choice between continuing British General Bernard L. Montgomery's or U.S. General Omar N. Bradley's (qq.v.) advance owing to supply shortages.

The Soviets (who spent much of the 1920s training with the future leadership of the *Wehrmacht*) adopted concepts similar to those of the Germans and began the process of fielding the required equipment as part of the early five-year plans. Unlike the Germans, the Soviets focused initial investment almost exclusively on tanks and artillery. Throughout the war, most Soviet infantry and engineers operating with tanks had little or no organic transport. Other technical adjuncts to armored warfare, like tactical radio communication, were likewise distant seconds to tanks and guns in procurement priority.

At the beginning of the war, the Soviets also were hamstrung by the loss of trained leadership from the 1937–1938 purges (q.v.). Driven largely by the extensive space available for maneuver in the Soviet Union, the Soviets primarily saw armor in an operational sense. Tactics were rudimentary and fairly rigid, but they were optimized for success at the higher operational levels. Absent was the reliance on subordinate commander initiative so important to the Germans, or the intricate communications and cross talk by which the U.S. Army was able to mass artillery fires with batteries widely dispersed. Instead, Soviet maneuver tactics trusted that mass, courage, and tenacity would prevail. They raised and equipped huge armored forces, then employed them in massive counterattacks that usually resulted in the surrender or destruction of a completely enveloped enemy.

The hard lessons of 1941 lead the Soviets to develop and refine the most effective defensive tactics against the German combined arms attack. These tactics called for placing infantry, artillery, and antitank weapons in mutually supporting positions in great depth along the attacker's avenue of approach, while holding one's own armor as a mobile reserve to counterattack locally between defensive positions as the enemy became extended and dispersed. While all this was in progress, the higher operational commander (usually at the front level) would constitute and position a massive reserve for a larger-scale counterattack timed to envelop the enemy as his momentum was expended. It was brutally costly in casualties, but it worked.

As the war progressed, both sides learned from their own weaknesses and their enemy's strengths. The extent to which these lessons had an impact on the war was largely a function of the means to put them into effect. Unfortunately for the *Wehrmacht*, those means were seldom available. Its once diverse and capable units lost much of their combat power through continual reorganizations.

While the Germans faced increasingly restrictive decisions about weapon production priorities, the British and Americans developed and fielded armored and mechanized divisions of increasing diversity and power. Organic-tracked transport for mechanized infantry and engineers, self-propelled artillery, and direct ground-to-air communications all made their appearance. In reaction to the highly successful German 88mm gun, the British and Americans pursued the development of a high-velocity tank cannon that would overmatch an opponent's armor protection. Thus they began to abandon the notion of antitank guns.

By the war's end, the significance of mass in armored warfare, the role of the tank as the primary antitank weapon, the importance of equal mobility within the combined arms team, and the importance of logistics all spurred the organizational and equipment changes that would influence the major armies of the world for decades to come.

Raymond J. Leisner

Additional Reading

Brooks, Stephen, *Armored Warfare* (1980).
Fuller, J.F.C., *Armoured Warfare* (1943).
House, Jonathan M., *Toward Combined Arms Warfare: A Survey of 20th Century Tactics, Doctrine, and Organization* (1984).
Mackesy, Kenneth, *Tank Versus Tank: The Illustrated History of Armored Battlefield Conflict in the Twentieth Century* (1988).
———, *Tank Warfare: A History of Tanks in Battle* (1972).
Weeks, John, *Men Against Tanks: A History of Antitank Warfare* (1975).

Artillery
See FIRE SUPPORT OPERATIONS

Atlantic Wall
On 14 December 1941, the *Wehrmacht* high command gave orders to build defensive constructions along the Norwegian, Danish, German, Dutch, Belgian, and French coastlines in order to protect conquered Europe. In his Führer Directive 40,

issued on 23 March 1942, Adolf Hitler (q.v.) himself gave detailed orders for the coastal constructions. This chain of fortifications was at first supposed to be called the "New West Wall," but later was named the *Atlantikwall* to "prove" to the Germans and the rest of the world the invincibility of Fortress Europe (q.v.). The Atlantic Wall became the last big defensive line constructed on the European continent, and it was fashioned after the Maginot Line and the West Wall (qq.v.).

The goal of the project was to put fifteen to twenty bunkers along each kilometer of the coastline, with priority going to the western-most coasts. Between the Pas de Calais and Brittany, 15,000 fortified positions were to be built within one year. These installations were to be manned by 300,000 soldiers, securing the coast against Allied landings. But no central concept existed for the construction, and three different building periods produced rather differing results.

The German Navy was the first to secure the most important harbors and waterways with coastal artillery and an extensive building program right after the conquest of the West European countries. In the fall of 1942, a second building period started aimed at positioning infantry defenses along the coast as well. The army's fortification pioneers built these installations. In the third period, German Field Marshal Erwin Rommel (q.v.) tied the loosely connected defensive positions into one complete system. At the end of 1943, he was given the task of determining the preparedness of the Atlantic coast defenses against the anticipated Allied landings.

The army and navy, in the meantime, had various types of bunkers developed and built according to their own specific needs. The coastal batteries of the navy were the outstanding fortifications. Each consisted of a gun position, an ammunition bunker, and command and observation posts. They also had billets for soldiers and positions for searchlights for night firing. The coastal guns ranged in caliber from 75mm to 406mm. The main problem was that there were twenty-eight different calibers in use because the guns came from ships and captured weapons from all over Europe. The navy protected the harbors with heavy antiaircraft batteries. The army did the same with the airfields close to the coast.

The core of the Atlantic Wall defenses, however, consisted of smaller bunkers, which were supposed to be the backbone of the defense during the main battle. They were of the "Tobruk" type, tested for their efficiency in North Africa.

Each bunker complex consisted of an observation post, a machine gun position, mortars, and flamethrowers. The protection of the troops in the area of their bunkers was provided by tens of thousands of nonstandardized smaller bunkers. The construction was done both by private companies and by military fortification engineers.

The heaviest fortifications along the coast, which still can be seen today, were built by the *Organisation Todt* (q.v.). Between July 1940 and July 1944, some 17.3 million cubic meters of concrete and 1.2 million metric tons of steel were used in them. The work was done by 400,000 people, mainly forced laborers from all over Europe.

By January 1944, only those buildings under actual construction were completed, because Rommel favored measures intended to prevent the adversary from reaching the coast, rather than fighting him on the beach. These measures included extensive obstacles off the coast that were supposed to prevent the landing of ships of any kind. Along the coast from Pas de Calais were placed some 900,000 blocking units along the waterline. They were built from posts, concrete dragon teeth, and cut iron girders, and were reinforced with 6,756,000 mines. Along the coastline they also set up poles connected with wire, called "Rommel's asparagus," that were supposed to entrap enemy paratroops and block glider landings.

The huge amount of material and great number of workers necessary for these construction projects were far out of proportion to the results achieved. The final result was a linear defense line without sufficient depth and without main strategic points. The Allies broke through several positions in the Atlantic Wall on the first day of the 6 June 1944 landings using their superior air and sea power. They took the major fortified harbors of Cherbourg and Le Havre from the land side after linking up their two landing bridgeheads.

The building of the Atlantic Wall was a big step backward, both tactically and technically, in German operational thinking. It was a measure that ultimately did not justify the cost of undertaking it.

Ekkehart Guth

Additional Reading

Gresser, K., and J. Stahlmann, *Westwall, Maginotlinie, Atlantikwall* (1983).
Harrison, Gordon A., *Cross-Channel Attack* (1951).
Wilt, Alan F., *The Atlantic Wall: Hitler's Defense in the West, 1941–1945* (1975).

B

Blitzkrieg (Lightning War)

In May 1940, the German *Wehrmacht* and *Luftwaffe* unleashed their great offensive in the west and in a few weeks destroyed the French and British forces opposing them. The French sued for an armistice, while the British desperately tried to remove as many soldiers as possible from the ever-shrinking Allied pocket at Dunkirk (q.v.). The smashing victory in the west was seen as a vindication of the German doctrine of the *Blitzkrieg*, or lightning war, a triumph of combined arms operations, with ground and air working together as a well-oiled military machine.

The idea of the *Blitzkrieg* as official doctrine of the German Army became fixed in the minds of public and military thinkers alike. Doctrine, however, has been defined as: "The fundamental principles by which the military forces or elements thereof guide their actions in support of national objectives. It is authoritative . . ." (U.S. Department of Defense, 1989). *Blitzkrieg* was not a set of fundamental principles, nor was it written down as an authoritative document.

The term *Blitzkrieg* describes a set of results, not a formalized, published doctrine. During the war, the Germans became focused on the results of the lightning war in the west and failed to see the weaknesses in the operations in the spring of 1940, especially in the area of the employment of German artillery and in the availability of aircraft for operations over a vast amount of terrain. The campaign in France used concentrated airpower, while Russia, with its huge land expanses, made concentration of air assets a near-impossibility. Many German military planners became victims of what Carl von Clausewitz described as the "fog of war," with the inherent dangers of adopting a concept and then trying to apply it where it could not be effectively used. When the Germans needed masses of aircraft, they were not available, and when they needed artillery, guns were too few.

The much reduced German Army of the immediate post–World War I period studied the causes of its defeat in 1918 and concluded that a lack of traditional mobile, maneuverable warfare sapped the vitality of the army and produced the war of attrition that eventually spelled the doom of Imperial Germany on the battlefield. Unlike the French, who were building their Maginot Line (q.v.), the Germans came to believe that the next war would be of short duration, built on maneuver warfare in the classical sense.

The search for a usable doctrine in Germany in the interwar period focused on mobility and maneuverability as the keys to the victory that eluded the army in the Great War. Under an agreement between Germany and the Soviet Union in the 1920s, German officers traveled to Russia to study the emerging technology of the tank on the battlefield. Tank warfare in World War I offered some possibilities in achieving penetration of enemy lines, allowing for maneuver combat to then take place. However, the restrictions of the Versailles Treaty (q.v.) meant that what the Germans learned could not actually be put into practical training or the building of a mobile army.

Mobility advocates read widely and were enthusiastic over works by J.F.C. Fuller, Charles de Gaulle, and Basil Liddell Hart (qq.v.), all leading theoreticians of mechanized, mobile combat. German officers then engaged in intellectual debates, with little real hard evidence that a tank force could alter the outcome of battles.

Many older officers in the Germany Army resisted the notion that the tank could be a decisive combat arm because they remembered the grave difficulties armor encountered in World War I. British tanks did well initially at Cambrai in

November 1917, but because the British failed to exploit their initial successes, the Cambrai operation came to be seen as a raid rather than as an offensive to achieve penetration and allow for the infantry to assume maneuver operations. The American use of tanks in the St. Mihiel and Meuse-Argonne offensives of 1918 had not produced much due to the condition of the terrain over which the tanks crossed. It is not surprising that German senior officers were skeptical of the tank and more than a little irritated with the more vocal exponents of the tank such as Colonel Heinz Guderian (q.v.).

The German field service regulations of 1921 (*Command and Combat of the Combined Arms*), was an infantry-oriented document that cast tank and air assets in a strictly infantry-support role. While this document, which was doctrine for the German Army, emphasized traditional German thinking on mobility, it did allow for a decentralization of control and offered latitude for changes within the German force structure. It was also not tied to specific operational doctrine to the exclusion of all others. There were possibilities, given the right set of political and technological circumstances.

The circumstances came together when Adolf Hitler (q.v.) came to power in Germany in 1933. From the beginning of Hitler's rule, it was clear he intended to rearm Germany, and that he was interested in the iconoclastic ideas of younger members of the German Army. In June 1934, Guderian was made chief of staff of a newly formed motorized troop command. In a little over a year, an experimental *Panzer* division was in operation. In October 1935, still only a colonel, he was given command of one of three new *Panzer* divisions, and immediately set out to convince the still traditional, infantry-oriented German General Staff (q.v.) to accept his concepts of armored warfare. While Guderian received little support from many of his superiors, Hitler, already distrustful of the staid, conservative senior officer corps, encouraged Guderian and his aggressive concepts.

While ground forces were examining their operations, the German air force, the *Luftwaffe*, was undergoing important changes. Prior to the German intervention in the Spanish civil war (q.v.), most *Luftwaffe* officers favored long-range strategic bombing and achieving air superiority over the battlefield. This was little different from any other air force at that time, but the successes of the Germans in air-ground operations in Spain convinced a number of high-ranking air force officers to reconsider air support for ground operations.

General Ernst Udet (q.v.), in charge of the *Luftwaffe*'s development section after 1936, argued for and got a dive bomber, the Ju-87 *Stuka*, which was extremely accurate and very mobile and was developed to support ground forces. While Guderian labored to make the armored force the mailed fist of the German Army, the *Luftwaffe* had the plane that would add the critical air dimension to the *Blitzkrieg*.

Guderian continued to press for special manuals and publications for a large armored force, but the army, still basically a foot-infantry, animal-drawn transport system, resisted. Tanks would not fit into the traditional framework of the revitalized German Army. On the surface, the Poland campaign of 1939 was completed in a short time with a dazzling German success of arms. The so-called *Blitzkrieg* doctrine was not applied, and *Panzer* units were allocated to the various armies.

The *Luftwaffe* was primarily concerned with establishing air superiority and striking deep at Polish lines of communications. Close air support and liaison between ground and air units became secondary to what the *Luftwaffe* planners saw as the more traditional role of the air arm. Tank maintenance was a severe problem, and too often the German system of resupply was unequal to the tasks assigned to it. Of primary importance was the fact that Germany crushed Poland in rapid order, and this obscured the grave operational and tactical difficulties the *Wehrmacht* encountered during the Polish operation.

Between the end of the Polish campaign and the main attack in the west against France and Britain in May–June 1940, the German Army underwent some basic changes. *Panzer* units were consolidated into a corps under the ever-aggressive Guderian, and while the number of tanks increased only slightly in the German inventory, the number of *Panzer* divisions grew.

Consequently, and out of necessity rather than doctrinal dictum, the *Panzer* divisions became combined arms units with a balance between tanks, infantry, artillery, engineers, and other arms. Because artillery units were in short supply, tactical air, especially the highly effective and psychologically terrifying *Stuka*, became an important part of the combined arms mix. For the Germans, this was a mixed blessing in that the use of tactical air was so successful against France that it obscured the problem of a shortage of artillery in the German Army. Against the poorly arrayed French and British, this would present no problem, but later, against the artillery-conscientious Soviets, the effects would prove devastating.

The defeat of France was the result of a large number of critical factors ranging from superior German operational planning, to poor Franco-British assessment of intelligence, to the excellent physical conditioning of the *Wehrmacht* soldier in the ranks. Additional factors for France's defeat included weak French leadership and inadequate French-British airpower. For those observing the campaign of May–June 1940, the results were spectacular—a lightning victory. It is at this point that the term *Blitzkrieg* became a part of the common lexicon, but in Germany it was not doctrine, for it was never written down as a set of authoritative principles.

Guderian, commanding the XIX *Panzer Korps,* prearranged for tactical air support and concentrated his armor. The *Panzer* divisions were followed up by five motorized infantry divisions. All struck through the supposedly impenetrable Ardennes Forest toward the Meuse River at a time when the British and French believed that the main German assault was farther to the north.

In reviewing the operation later, Guderian stated, "The assault proceeded as if it had been a training exercise." Certainly Guderian's XIX *Korps* and Major General Wolfram von Richthofen's (q.v.) VIII *Fliegerkorps* had every reason to be pleased with the results. The euphoria of the victory over France hid the fact that the *Stukas* of the VIII *Fliegerkorps* took the place of artillery, and this was done for a purpose. Guderian wanted less reliance on the slow-moving artillery and the equally ponderous methods of resupply of artillery ammunition. This fact was overlooked as German planners evaluated the lessons learned from the French campaign.

The *Blitzkrieg* is most associated with the German campaign in the west in the spring of 1940. It was an operational concept limited to a particular time and place in the war. The rapidity of the German advance, the terrifying scream of the *Stuka* dive bomber, the concentration of seemingly unstoppable armor, and the use of every member of the combined arms team captured the imagination of journalists and overwhelmed military planners in Europe and America.

In a recent article on the *Wehrmacht,* Roger A. Beaumont wrote: "In World War II, the Nazis' early successes with the *Blitzkrieg* sprang from tactical fusion of various weapons through radio networking, and a general emphasis on mobility and maneuver. As the Allies got the measure of it, the result was often grim indeed, such as the destruction of the massed *Panzers* at Kursk and Mortain, and of German and Italian armor at 'Snipe' in North Africa." What the Allies did was to examine their own doctrine, operational concepts, and weapons systems, and adapt them to the war they had to fight.

The confusion over the *Blitzkrieg* is basically that it was not doctrine, not authoritative at all, and most importantly, it was more noticeable for the results produced than for its influence on future German operations. The *Blitzkrieg* obscured flaws in the German war machine (transport, maintenance, deterioration of artillery, etc.), and this proved very costly to German military planners as the war progressed. As the war dragged on, the *Luftwaffe* would be incapable of supporting such operations. The *Blitzkrieg,* while spectacular, was dependent on many factors. As the Allies grew stronger in the course of the war, such an operational concept became increasingly difficult, if not impossible, to implement on a very lethal battlefield.

James J. Cooke

Additional Reading

Beaumont, Roger A., "Wehrmacht Mystique Revisited," *Military Review,* LXX, 2 (February 1990), 64–75.

Dupuy, T.N., *A Genius for War* (1977).

Guderian, Heinz, *Panzer Leader* (1952).

Horne, Alistair, *To Lose a Battle: France, 1940* (1969).

Blockade Running

Both sides in World War II smuggled critical high value–low volume war materials through the other's blockades. For the British, it was the Swedish steel bearings so essential to production machinery and precision instruments. For the Axis countries, it was either key raw materials unavailable in Europe, such as tungsten (used in armor), tin, and rubber, or medicines such as quinine and opium. Most of these materials had to be brought in from Asia. Both sides employed special vessels to conduct the smuggling and were successful, despite suffering heavy losses. For the Axis, blockade running became increasingly difficult as the war progressed, while Britain's difficulties decreased proportionately with the rise in Allied fortunes. In all cases, these operations stand out as prime indicators of the growing, indeed critical, importance of high value materials to modern war machines.

The Germans initially brought ships and cargo in from Latin America, running a gauntlet of British and supposedly neutral American patrols. These ships brought their normal peacetime cargoes of oil, beef, margarine, and timber. Most of the ships that departed North and Central America were intercepted because of American assistance, but the majority of those coming from South America got through in 1939 and 1940. Critical materials, including industrial diamonds, were routed through Italy or the Soviet Union, but these routes became unavailable after 10 June 1940 and 22 June 1941, respectively. At that point, Germany and Italy began to run their cargoes out of Japan, which had joined the Axis in September 1940.

Britain initiated its smuggling of special steel materials after the German seizure of Norway and Denmark (qq.v.) cut off the normal routes to the sources in Sweden. The first operation was successfully conducted in December 1940, using regular merchant ships. The Germans were ready for the second attempt four months later and destroyed six of the eight ships. All subsequent British blockade running was conducted by high-speed motor gunboats running at night. The Germans established extensive air and naval patrols, pressured Sweden diplomatically, and employed spies and saboteurs against the British "blockade busters," but they never seriously threatened Anglo-Swedish trade after 1941.

The Allies also had little luck in intercepting the German blockade runners from Asia prior to 1943. The Japanese presence in the Indian Ocean throughout 1942 inhibited patrolling that ocean. The German surface ships steamed in radio silence and all communications were conducted using "one-time pads." They generally pulled into Spanish ports or into Bordeaux. Their effectiveness in getting through so frustrated the British that they mounted a costly commando raid against the German ships in December 1942, and conducted bombing raids against them whenever they could catch the ships in port.

Most Allied successes in intercepting the Axis trade with Asia came about as a result of Allied code breaking efforts (see Cryptography). Since the Axis countries did not want their submarines to sink their own blockade runners, the ships' routes were broadcast to the respective submarines, and the submarines were ordered to stay clear. Reading the codes enabled Allied naval patrols to intercept the blockade runners along routes that had been cleared of Axis submarines by the Axis themselves. As a result, only one of five Axis merchant ships despatched from Asia reached Europe in the winter of 1943–1944. At that point, Germany's leaders decided to shift to submarine transport, using oceangoing submarines returning from the Far East. Those submarines continued to run their critical cargoes to Germany until the very end of the war, but the last effective deliveries actually ended with the isolation of the French ports in August 1944.

Blockade running was essential to the war efforts of both sides. Britain's manufacturing industries, operating old machinery that had been poorly serviced during the Great Depression, could not have sustained wartime production without new bearings. Moreover, importing Sweden's unique precision bearings relieved Britain from having to invest in developing a new industry to support its war effort at a time when all production capacity was already overtaxed.

The Axis countries' blockade running provided materials either unavailable or not easily obtainable in Europe. Their blockade runners brought in 43,891 tons of natural rubber and more than 68,000 tons of tungsten, molybdenum, tin, quinine, and opium during the war. The Axis war effort would have been crippled without those materials. If nothing else, the World War II blockade-running operations illustrate the lengths and risks countries will undertake to obtain essential materials in the face of blockades and economic sanctions. This is a pattern that can still be seen clearly in the postwar period.

Carl O. Schuster

Additional Reading
Barker, Ralph, *The Blockade Busters* (1976).
Brice, Martin, *Axis Blockade Runners of World War II* (1981).
Piekalkiewicz, Januscz, *The Sea War 1939–1945* (1986).

C

Carpet Bombing

Initially, carpet bombing was a tactic for aiming a "carpet" of bombs at a target to inundate the area with bombs and compensate for the inaccuracy of high altitude bombing. After the Normandy (q.v.) invasion it became a tactic for using aerial bombing in close air support of ground forces to break up strong enemy concentrations.

The effort involved thousands of tons of relatively small bombs dropped in high concentrations on German forces confronting American and British units to disrupt German formations and communications, devastate their morale, destroy vehicles, and open an avenue for large-scale Allied movements. The technique proved less effective than hoped, especially against dug-in personnel. Field Marshal Günther von Kluge (q.v.) wrote German chancellor Adolf Hitler (q.v.) of the psychological impact of "bombs raining down on them with all the force of elemental nature."

Craters and debris, especially at Caen (q.v.), impeded Allied advances after the bombings. Delays between the bombings and the advance of Allied ground forces also gave German forces time to reorganize.

Used first to destroy the Benedictine abbey at Monte Cassino (q.v.) on 15 February 1944, carpet bombing was also employed at Cassino a month later, Caen on 7–8 and 18 July 1944, Caumont on 30 July, and Falaise (q.v.) in August. Most famous was Operation COBRA on 24–25 July 1944, when 2,446 American medium, heavy, and fighter-bombers dropped 4,169 tons of high explosives, fragmentation bombs, and napalm in the area around St. Lo (q.v.) to facilitate Lieutenant General Omar N. Bradley's (q.v.) breakout from the bocage country of Normandy. Short bomb drops killed several hundred Allied soldiers at Caen, St. Lô, and Falaise, including U.S. Lieutenant General Lesley J. McNair (q.v.).

Stephen L. McFarland

Additional Reading
Dickens, Sir Gerald C., *Bombing and Strategy: The Fallacy of Total War* (1947).
Hallion, Richard P., *Strike from the Sky: The History of Battlefield Air Attack, 1911–1945* (1989).

Cavalry Operations

The images of World War II–era ground combat often conjure up tanks, jeeps, or self-propelled artillery. While such visions are quite appropriate for American or British forces, most other nations were unable to reach a status of complete mechanization. Often, such a handicap was overcome by the use of horse-mounted forces. Indeed, on the eastern front, cavalrymen were sometimes more useful than motorized units.

Though some use of cavalry forces might include tradition, economic or tactical considerations were the main reasons for employment of cavalry during World War II. The second point is worthy of note. Mounted troops could operate in mountains or swamps—terrain features that severely restricted rapid deployment of motorized forces. Also, they were less affected by the mud and primitive road networks of Eastern Europe.

Employment of such formations was usually sound. The horse soldier was a mounted infantryman. While spectacular charges were part of this story, like that of Italy's *Savoia Cavalleria* at Chebotarevsky on 12 August 1942, or the sabre-to-sabre combat of Polish and German *Uhlans* (lancers) along the Ulatkowka River on 1 September 1939, doctrine recognized that horses were just transportation, not weapons.

The Poland (q.v.) campaign presents good examples of extensive use of cavalry by both sides. The Germans allocated squadron-sized reconnaissance units to most of their divisions, and retained one cavalry brigade for use in East Prussia. The Poles made a similar distribution, but they had many more brigades. The latter proved rather useful, and contrary to popular myth, they did not "charge German tanks, lance in hand." There were certainly a few cases when Polish cavalrymen were caught in the open by German armor; however, the results of such combat were of no surprise to either party. Tactical doctrine in both armies was very clear as to the vulnerability of mounted targets.

Lances, of course, were out of the question, but Polish cavalrymen found their "UR" antitank rifles and 37mm Bofors guns quite capable of destroying any *Panzer* in range. An excellent example is the battle of Morka. Slightly north of Czestochowa, the terrain features of this hamlet, combined with a mobile defense, allowed the Wolynska Cavalry Brigade to halt attacks by the 4th *Panzer* Division. Three days later, the brigade withdrew, but only after knocking out eighty tanks and armored cars.

The lessons of 1939 convinced the *Wehrmacht* to expand its mounted formations. By 1940, in addition to reconnaissance units, they also had the 1st Cavalry Division. During the invasion of France (q.v.), it covered 1,200 action-filled miles, moving from the Dutch border to La Rochelle. The French opposition included regular and colonial cavalrymen. The former, which included the 1st Brigade of Spahis were among the most formidable units in the entire French Army.

The invasion of the Soviet Union (q.v.) provided scope for even larger cavalry actions. The vast areas involved created a need for mobility that neither side could meet through motorization. Soviet leadership recognized this from the start. The Soviets created large cavalry formations with significant artillery, automatic weapons, and support units. Germany's mounted forces were also upgraded. By 1944, the *Wehrmacht* contained five regular and SS cavalry divisions. In addition, the Nazis benefited from the Soviets' ethnic and political problems. Numerous volunteers came from groups of traditional horsemen, like the Kalmucks and Cossacks. The latter were organized into a corps, which gives some idea as to the scope of cavalry action on this front.

Cavalrymen were also employed in many of World War II's partisan campaigns. This led to some interesting situations, such as Cossack squadrons fighting the French *Maquis*, or U.S. cavalry officers advising their counterparts in the Greek ELAS movement. In the Soviet Union, mounted partisan actions often pitted Russian against Russian.

Soviet mounted guerrillas were very active in the Ukraine. As this region featured large tracts of forest and swamps, cavalry forces could combine concealment with mobility to evade German mechanized and aerial counterstrikes. Although most actions were small, there were notable exceptions such as the 2,000-man raid against the Galician oil fields in 1943.

In 1945, corps-sized cavalry units fought on the eastern front. Yugoslavia and Italy also fielded

A Cossack cavalry unit crossing a stream during the Soviet 1942–1943 Winter Offensive. (IWM RUS 4229)

large formations. Mounted troops maintained their usefulness to the very end.

John Dunn

Additional Reading

Piekalkiewicz, Janusz, *The Cavalry of World War II* (1979).

Rudnicki, K.S., *The Last of the War Horses* (1974).

CHAIN HOME

The CHAIN HOME system was a radar (q.v.) defensive network established around the eastern and southern coasts of Britain between 1936 and 1939. Each of the radar stations operated on a broad frequency band of 22–30 mHz and was mounted on a 240-foot wooden tower. The system had a range of about 120 miles. That range allowed it to detect *Luftwaffe* units forming up along the northern French coast, giving Royal Air Force (RAF) Fighter Command enough time to scramble its aircraft for interception.

The CHAIN HOME stations had a minimum operating altitude of 3,000 feet, under which low-flying aircraft could easily slip. To plug this gap the British deployed a second line of low-level but shorter range radars called CHAIN HOME LOW. These operated on the much shorter wavelength of 200 mHz.

The CHAIN HOME system was one of the decisive elements in the Battle of Britain (q.v.). The information provided by the radar, however, was only one of three key sets of variables in the equation. The second set of variables consisted of what the British did with the information and how fast they did it. This was the Ground Controlled Intercept (GCI) system, developed by Air Chief Marshal Sir Hugh Dowding (q.v.), the head of RAF Fighter Command.

The early CHAIN HOME radars had to be located as close to the coast as possible, because the first generations of the equipment were very susceptible to ground clutter. That meant that as soon as incoming aircraft crossed the coast they had to be tracked by visual or acoustical means by ground observers. This required the establishment of an extensive Ground Observer Corps and a supporting communications network. The Royal Mail was given the responsibility for establishing and maintaining the phone lines, and local police forces assumed administrative control of the observers.

Initial inputs to the GCI system came from both the CHAIN HOME radars and the RAF's "Y Service," which monitored *Luftwaffe* radio transmissions. The directions, distances, numbers, and altitudes of the incoming German planes were fed simultaneously to Fighter Command headquarters, and the headquarters of the fighter group re-

The CHAIN HOME radar station at Dover. CHAIN HOME was a critical element in British defenses during the Battle of Britain. (IWM CH 15173)

sponsible for the region. Throughout the Battle of Britain, the responsible group almost always was Air Marshal Sir Keith Park's Number 11 Group.

At group headquarters, all incoming information on enemy forces, as well as on all friendly forces, was maintained on a large table-like plotting board. Operations officers at group then decided which squadrons to launch against the attackers, and when to launch them. Once the aircraft were in the air, operational control passed to the ground controller at the appropriate sector station. The sector station operations room also maintained a horizontal plotting board for its sector.

The sector station controller was responsible for issuing climbing, vector, and recall orders. When the interceptors established visual contact with their targets, tactical control passed to the commander in the air and the fighters operated on visual means. Once the fight was over, control reverted back to the ground controller, who directed the planes back to their recovery bases. Often, these were not the same bases from which they had been launched.

For the most part, neither Dowding nor Fighter Command headquarters played any direct role in controlling the battle. The key players were the fighter groups and their respective sector stations. Each fighter group had operational control over the antiaircraft artillery (AAA) batteries in its area, even though these were army units. This was necessary to assure the proper control of the AAA weapons in the intercept areas. On some occasions, when Number 11 Group was overwhelmed, Fighter Command intervened to send in reinforcements. As the battle progressed, Dowding delegated to Park the authority to task directly other group commanders for reinforcements.

The third variable in the equation was the aircraft themselves. Fortunately, the British Hurricanes and Spitfires could stand up reasonably well to the Messerschmitt Bf-109Es. Although the Bf-109E had generally better performance characteristics, the British had two clear advantages. First, operating over their own territory, they had a much longer endurance time than the Germans. Second, the British airplanes had far superior radios. The Bf-109Es had only adequate air-to-air communications, and poor air-to-ground. The British radios were excellent in both cases. This enabled British pilots to make maximum use of the information being fed into the front end of the equation by the CHAIN HOME system. All three variables, radar, GCI, and the airplanes—including, of course, the pilots—combined to produce the decisive results of the Battle of Britain.

David T. Zabecki

Additional Reading
Deighton, Len, *Fighter: The True Story of the Battle of Britain* (1977).
Fisher, David E., *A Race on the Edge of Time: Radar—the Decisive Weapon of World War II* (1988).
Hough, Richard and Denis Richards, *The Battle of Britain: The Greatest Air Battle of World War II* (1989).

Chaplain Support Operations
With the rapid buildup of American forces during the early days of World War II, a call went out to clergy of all denominations to accompany their nation's troops as they embarked to uncertain destinies on foreign shores. Many responded, and by July 1945, 8,171 chaplains were on active duty with the U.S. Army—up from a 1941 total of 1,478. The U.S. Navy Chaplain Corps swelled from 192 to 2,811 during the same period. During the war, 164 U.S. Army chaplains died in uniform, 63 of whom were killed in action. Twenty-four U.S. Navy chaplains suffered a similar fate, ten of whom perished in action.

The contribution of chaplains to the American military dates to the colonial era. During the American Revolution, chaplains played a key role, not always as noncombatants. During World War II, thousands of clergy left their civilian ministries to don uniforms and serve beside the soldiers, sailors, airmen, and marines wherever the fortunes of war took them. The chaplains shared the deprivations and dangers of conflict and gained the respect of the men and women they served. Many of their duties were similar to those of their civilian counterparts. They preached and conducted worship, occasionally performed marriages, and all too often, buried the troops they served.

Some of their responsibilities, however, differed remarkably from those of civilian ministers. Military chaplains rendered aid to the wounded on the battlefield and suffered beside their fellow service members as prisoners of war (POWs). Chaplains during World War II represented three faith groups: Jewish, Protestant, and Roman Catholic. The ability of clergy from these different traditions to so effectively work together is one of their proudest accomplishments of the war. This interfaith harmony was immortalized by the Four Chaplains (q.v.) who gave away their own life preservers and heroically went down with the USS *Dorchester* on 2 February 1943.

The goal of Army Chief of Chaplains Major General William R. Arnold was to maintain a ratio of one chaplain per 1,000 troops. In this he was quite successful. Recognizing that soldiers far from home and daily facing death required intimate contact and encouragement, the army initiated an aggressive chaplain recruiting campaign. This was made more difficult by the fact that many churches initially held isolationist views. As late as 1941, a Gallup poll reported that 55 percent of Americans did not want to hear about American participation in the war effort from their pulpits. The tragedy of Pearl Harbor, however, caused a dramatic reversal of national feeling.

Because of their status, clergymen were exempt from Selective Service. Clergy holding reserve commissions as line officers were allowed to resign them. Pastor James Tull was one of a number of chaplains originally called from their pastorates to serve as line officers, only later to be recommissioned as chaplains. In the summer of 1940, 770 of approximately 1,000 reserve chaplains were found eligible for active duty. Of this number, 145 already were serving with the army, and an additional 100 with the Civilian Conservation Corps.

Unlike most army corps or branches, civilian seminaries produced graduates with no additional need for military training in their specialty. Hundreds of thousands of seminary and rabbinical school graduates were technically available for service with only a brief orientation to ministry within a military setting required. Unlike the medical and legal branches, whose quotas were administered by draft boards, the chaplaincy had a purely civilian agency endorsing men to serve in its ranks. The three major faith-group endorsing agencies were the Jewish Welfare Board, the General Commission on Army and Navy Chaplains, and the Roman Catholic Military Ordinariate.

In December 1941, army regulations established the requirements for appointment to the army as a chaplain: (1) a male citizen of the United States (later expanded to allow appointment of citizens of cobelligerent and friendly powers); (2) between twenty-three and thirty-four years of age; (3) regularly ordained and in good standing with a religious body holding an apportionment of chaplains' appointments in accordance with the needs of the service; (4) a graduate of both four-year college and three-year seminary programs (later reduced in particular instances); and (5) three years of experience in civilian ministry. Navy requirements for commissioning as a chaplain were similar.

The Jewish Welfare Board labored effectively to ensure that the particular needs of Jewish military personnel were met. Its chaplaincy committee consisted of twenty-five members drawn from Orthodox, Conservative, and Reform traditions. At the passage of the Selective Service Act, seventeen rabbis held reserve commissions in the army, along with two in the navy. While eight were disqualified from service for various reasons, the other eleven served during the war. The largest number of Jewish chaplains on duty at any one time was 245.

In 1939, Pope Pius XII (q.v.) appointed Bishop Francis J. Spellman to be military vicar for the United States, with jurisdiction over Roman Catholic chaplains and members of the armed forces. Under his leadership, the Military Ordinariate expanded from a total of fifty-five chaplains to more than 3,000. Despite this phenomenal growth, the church was unable to supply the full number of priests sought by the army. In reaching 88 percent of its quota, by the close of the war nearly 6 percent of all Roman Catholic priests in America were serving in the army. They were assisted by more than 1,700 auxiliary Catholic chaplains, who served the military as civilians.

Racial factors were also considered. In addition to commissioning a number of minority chaplains representing various major denominations, the army sought representation from predominantly black denominations. To enhance effectiveness and sense of community, the goal was to assign black chaplains to minister to black troops. Unfortunately, while these denominations authorized 790 chaplains, only 174 were on active duty at the war's end. The primary reason for this disparity was differing educational requirements from church to church. Even when these requirements were modified to enable some previously barred clergy to qualify for commissioning, quotas fell short.

During World War II, the gender of chaplains was not a major issue. All of the clergy who served in uniform were male. The only occasion on which this was questioned was with the formation of the Women's Army Auxiliary Corps (WAAC) (q.v.). A civilian organization of female ministers and their supporters urged that female chaplains be assigned to serve at WAAC training bases, and at any locations with a large WAAC contingent. The matter was dropped after a survey revealed that very few of the women involved desired female chaplains. During the course of the war, many women did serve with distinction as chaplain's assistants and religious education coordinators in all branches of the armed forces.

The military also made attempts to include chaplains from other than the three largest denominations. After the War Department organized an all-Greek battalion in 1942, it took a year before a suitable Greek Orthodox priest could be found. In 1943, a Buddhist chaplain was sought for the Japanese-American 442nd Infantry Regiment. After the Buddhist Mission of North America was unable to produce a qualified candidate, a Christian chaplain of Japanese descent was assigned to the regiment.

In 1942, the Chaplain School at Fort Leavenworth, Kansas, which had graduated its last class in 1928, was reactivated. Seventy-five chaplains were in the initial class, which lasted twenty-eight days. Within the year, class size had grown to 450. When expanded mission requirements outgrew the facilities, several universities offered to house the school. Harvard was selected and the government paid the university $10.50 for each chaplaincy student. By 1944, class sizes had decreased to 200, and the school was relocated to Fort Devens, Massachusetts.

In 1942, the U.S. Navy established a chaplain school at Norfolk, Virginia. Prior to that, new chaplains typically were assigned to a large base where they were supervised by a more experienced chaplain for several months before being given independent duty. In 1942, the navy also began the process of establishing the chaplain's specialist rating. A primary responsibility of these specialists, identified with a "W" for welfare, was to provide music for worship services. During the war, 350 men and women were trained in this specialty, which was restricted to stateside duty.

Chaplains went wherever the troops were. Chaplain Raymond S. Hall was the first airborne chaplain. He explained his desire to jump with the soldiers by saying that "it increases attendance at church, and the men can talk to me now." Donald Burgett, recalling his days as a private at Fort Benning, wrote of a man who fell from the sky with an unopened chute. As Burgett was limping toward the waiting trucks after his own jump, he saw the man hit the ground with a muffled thud. Burgett was shocked when the soldier opened his eyes and asked, "what happened?" Despite a broken leg and some internal injuries, he had survived. Noticing the cross on the soldier's collar, Burgett thought, "Who else but a chaplain could fall a thousand feet with an unopened chute and live?"

Early in the war, it became apparent that ministry within the Army Air Forces was somewhat different than with ground troops. In order to match men suitable to work with air units, Chaplain Charles I. Carpenter was appointed to serve as air chaplain. Since he was only a captain and would be working directly with senior chaplains in the field, he was promoted about every three months until he attained the rank of full colonel. Carpenter served in this position throughout most of the war, eventually becoming chief of chaplains of the U.S. Army Air Forces (USAAF).

In 1944, the USAAF opened its own school for chaplains at San Antonio, Texas. It provided a two-week supplement for graduates of the army school selected for assignment to air units. The air corps was so committed to the importance of the enlisted members of the chaplain service team that a parallel course was developed for chaplain assistants.

Chaplains rendered service wherever the need existed, from the chapels at the training fields to the foxholes and temporary cemeteries of the battlefield. At the outset of the war, only seventeen of the 160 army posts requiring a chapel possessed one. President Franklin D. Roosevelt (q.v.) authorized the rapid construction of 604 regimental cantonment chapels during the next six months. Many of these remained in service for years, and at least one, at Fort Benning, Georgia, has been designated a historical site. At the dedication of the first such chapel, Quartermaster General Edmund B. Gregory affirmed its unique design: "There is nothing in construction that could stamp it as so distinctively American as this altar, because only in a free country could you find a church built to be used for worship by Catholic, Protestant, and Jew alike."

Many of the duties of the chaplain were self-evident. They conducted worship, counseled and encouraged the troubled, advised their commanders on morale issues, and comforted the injured and dying. Other duties were occasionally more exotic, such as the seeking of divine intervention on behalf of Allied military efforts. One such episode was immortalized, albeit rather inaccurately, in the epic film *Patton*. During the German Ardennes offensive, General George S. Patton (qq.v.), called Chaplain James H. O'Neill and asked, "Do you have a good prayer for weather? We must do something about these rains if we are to win the war."

Another area in which the chaplains were essential was work with displaced persons and other civilian victims of the war. Here the Jewish rabbis frequently took the lead, particularly where the members of their own faith were concerned. Thirty-two rabbis were among the chaplains who entered Germany with the invading forces. Ironically, four of these men were born in Germany and Hungary, but had fled Nazi tyranny. Chaplain Emanuel Schenk was with the 4th Armored Division when it liberated Buchenwald. The following day, Chaplain Herschel Schacter of VIII Corps arrived to join him in his efforts to save the lives of 4,500 Jews, including 1,000 children. For many of these chaplains the emotions were overwhelming. One, Rabbi David M. Eichhorn, resolutely remained at Dachau, rejoining his advancing unit only when he received a direct order to do so. Naturally, chaplains of all faiths labored with equal fervor to preserve and restore the well-being of the war's countless victims.

Many chaplains served as ministers to POWs from the German, Italian, and Japanese armies. Chaplain Arthur J. Doege, who worked with German POWs at Camp Edwards between 1943 and 1945, recorded full services and nearly 1,800 baptisms. Despite the fact that not all of the chaplains involved volunteered for these duties, they performed them conscientiously. The experiences of chaplains assigned to the defendants at the Nuremberg trials (see American Military Tribunals) were especially challenging. Many prisoners were extremely grateful for the ministry provided by their captors. Even some of those convicted of crimes resulting in their execution publicly expressed gratitude for the compassionate service of the American chaplains.

Motivated by compassion, American chaplains frequently risked their lives to attend to enemy soldiers as well as their own troops. William E. King crawled through the midst of a raging tank battle to bandage the wounds of an enemy soldier whose leg had been shattered by machine gun fire. Later, an interpreter related that the grateful young German had been told that Americans mutilated their prisoners. Chaplain Eugene L. Daniel was captured by the *Afrika Korps* when he elected to remain behind retreating American forces to care for wounded prisoners they were forced to leave behind in Tunisia (q.v.). The officer commanding the German unit that captured him gave him a letter of commendation, and during his twenty-six-month confinement, he was allowed significant freedom to minister to Allied troops in captivity.

Other Allied nations, notably the United Kingdom, possessed a proud tradition of chaplaincy ministry in their own ranks. Of the 3,000 chaplains who served with the British Army, ninety-six were killed in action or died of combat wounds. British chaplain numbers grew from a prewar 169 to a peak of 3,052. Because Britain had an official state church, the majority of the British clergy came from the Church of England itself. Most of the remainder came from the Church of Scotland, Methodist, Presbyterian, Baptist, Congregational, and Roman Catholic Churches.

Many British chaplains were captured and continued their ministries as POWs. Chaplain G.F. Miller was taken prisoner shortly before Dunkirk (q.v.). With regularity during the days that followed, he was assured that he would be repatriated in accordance with the Geneva Convention; yet it was five years before he finally was released in April 1945. Due to the early success of the German *Blitzkrieg*, thirty-one British chaplains fell into enemy hands within a single month. Generally, the Germans were very reluctant to allow the transfer of chaplains to enlisted POW camps, which otherwise had no ministerial coverage.

Among the Allies, little distinction between nationalities existed when it came time to serve. Chaplain John W. Foote led his fellow Canadians in sharing their meager resources with 1,000 tattered Americans who joined them as fellow prisoners in Stuttgart. One midnight mass on Christmas 1943 found American, British, and French chaplains jointly presiding at a service in Algiers. While democratic nations included chaplains within their military forces, the Soviets numbered no chaplains in their ranks, as befitted an officially atheistic state. Some writers have argued for parallels between the Soviet political officers and the chaplains of their allies. However, even a superficial examination reveals the enormous differences between the two groups. Moreover, since the collapse of the Warsaw Pact and the crumbling of its Communist foundations, many Eastern European states have moved toward the restoration of the military chaplaincy in their forces. Although the Soviets stopped short of reestablishing their chaplaincy during World War II, they recognized the patriotic potential of the Orthodox Church, and Premier Josef Stalin (q.v.) loosened restrictions on the faith.

The military chaplaincy within the Axis forces provides an intriguing contrast to that of the Allies. In their case, comparisons with the Soviet political officers might possess more validity. These men were often erstwhile proponents of Nazism and Fascism. Chaplain John T. Byrne reported that "when Italian POWs became 'friendly co-belligerents,' attitudes changed; only one POW remained adamant in his Fascism—you guessed it. He was a chaplain!" As for Germany, the history of the church there is fascinating. With some success, the National Socialists were able to reshape a portion of the Evangelical Church into a patriotic movement labeled the "German Christians" (*Deutsche Christen*). While some clergy supported the movement, and many acquiesced in the face of intimidation, others rallied to form a "Confessing

Church" *(Bekennende Kirche)*. The best-known member of this communion was Pastor Dietrich Bonhoeffer (q.v.), who was executed on 9 April 1945 for his role in the failed plot to assassinate Adolf Hitler (q.v.).

Not all Axis chaplains were devout disciples of their governments; many answered the call to serve inspired by genuine patriotism and a recognition that their brothers-in-arms would require the same compassionate ministry and encouragement as Allied soldiers. A German chaplain, Anton Egger, held by Americans as a prisoner at Camp Maxey, Texas, expressed his gratitude to American chaplains after the war. After coming into contact "with many who had to undergo the same misfortune of capture, but in other hands and at other places—I really learned to appreciate how fortunate I was."

As to their daily duties during the conflict, the role of chaplains did not differ dramatically, whatever uniform they wore.

Robert C. Stroud

Additional Reading

Barish, Louis, *Rabbis In Uniform* (1962).
Crosby, Donald F., *Battlefield Chaplains: Catholic Priests in World War II* (1995).
Drury, Clifford, *The History of the Chaplain Corps, United States Navy*, Vol. 2, 1939–1949 (n.d.).
Gushwa, Robert, *The Best and Worst of Times: The United States Army Chaplaincy, 1920–1945* (1977).
Jorgensen, Daniel, *The Service of Chaplains to Army Air Units, 1919–1946* (n.d.).
Smyth, Sir John, *In This Sign Conquer* (1968).

Civil Defense

Civil defense is a term that came into existence with bomber aircraft. The concept of civil defense, however, is as old as humankind. During a war, civil defense involves civilians taking shelter or evacuating to a safe place under direction of a civilian volunteer organization, following national government direction but under local government control. The primary responsibilities of civil defense are to mitigate loss of life and property, respond to incidents in an organized, responsible manner, and return the area of incident to normal conditions as soon as possible.

During World War I, rear-area civilians and economic infrastructures came under attack by aircraft and zeppelins. Since the means of defense against air attack were almost nonexistent at that

An Air Raid Warden comforts a child who was rescued from her house by firemen after it was struck by a V-1 on 23 June 1944. (IWM HU 36227)

time, the belief grew in many quarters during the interwar years that the bomber would always reach its target, causing tremendous loss of life and property damage. Continued bombing would so destroy civilian morale that a country could be forced to surrender within weeks. A minority held that improvements in air defense and the organization of civilians to prepare to respond to aerial bombings could reduce the bombing threat to acceptable levels and prevent the breakdown in civilian morale.

The concept of civil defense gained the support of some governments during the late 1930s. Their reasons for adopting civil defense were based on humanitarian principles, the need to protect the civilian population from harm, and the need to show that the country could survive a bombing attack and continue to fight. Critics of civil defense centered around the propositions that civil defense gave false hopes to a country's civilians by encouraging them to believe that they could survive bombing attacks. That false assumption, the critics concluded, made war more likely as governments prepared their total populations for total war.

During World War II, all the belligerent countries and many of the neutrals put civil defense programs in place. These programs normally consisted of moving the young and old to the countryside away from potential target areas, and providing shelters and training for those remaining behind. Shelters were facilities built or modified to provide various degrees of protection from the direct or indirect effects of a bomb burst for a family, neighborhood, or facility. Training encompassed first aid, fire suppression, law enforcement support, search and rescue, feeding, minimizing damage to structures and equipment, damage assessment, and casualty evacuation.

The World War II experience showed that where local governments had taken the concept of civil defense seriously, personnel casualties were reduced, structural damage was lessened, infrastructures were restored faster, and civilian morale did not break. When attacks caused high casualties and massive damage, it was often due to an ineffectual civil defense program. Civil defense provided a means by which all citizens could participate in the war effort. It also provided an organization that could respond to natural disasters that continue to occur during war or peace.

Charles H. Bogart

Additional Reading
Collier, Basil, *The Defence of the United Kingdom* (1957).
Conn, Stetson, *Guarding the United States and Its Outposts* (1964).
Depuy, Richard E., and Hodding Carter, *The Civil Defense of the U.S.* (1942).
O'Brien, T.H., *Civil Defense* (1953).

Combined Bomber Offensive

See STRATEGIC BOMBING AND GERMANY AIR CAMPAIGN

Convoys, Naval

German U-boat operations in World War II began with the sinking of the British liner *Athenia* on 3 September 1939. These attacks inflicted their most serious damage on Allied merchant navies, which were so crucial to Britain's survival during the war.

Having defeated the U-boats through convoying in World War I, the Royal Navy (RN) instituted mercantile convoys three days before World War II began. Under this system, merchant ships waited in port until a group of ten to twenty ships of similar speed and destination gathered. The group, called a convoy, then departed port together for its destination. In the war's early years, convoys were not always under the protection of warships, called es-

corts. Convoys increasingly were provided such protection as more escorts vessels entered service.

By 1943, the typical convoy had an escort consisting of at least one aircraft carrier and six to eight other warships. Many convoys also had one or two hunter-killer groups, composed of an escort carrier and several destroyer escorts, in close support. Although convoys reduced the efficiency of merchant shipping, the rapid introduction of convoying, with a corresponding growth in escort strength (in both numbers and technology), ultimately defeated the German U-boat threat in World War II. After some early disasters with submarine hunting operations, British (and later Allied) tactics came to center on the protection of the convoys.

Convoys gained their effectiveness from two factors. First, they imposed large gaps in mercantile traffic on the sea lanes. Unless the U-boats had the convoys' routes and arrival and departure times, they spent the bulk of their patrols searching empty ocean. Thus, the U-boats had fewer opportunities to attack in a given patrol area or time. Second, convoys allowed the antisubmarine forces to concentrate in the area where they knew the U-boats must come to achieve their mission—in close proximity to the convoy. British and later Allied convoys were organized and controlled by the British Control of Shipping Section, and received a sequential alphanumeric designation based on the convoy's speed, point of origin, and destination (*see* table of allied convoy designation codes).

British escort tactics called for the escort group to patrol a wide front along the perimeter of the convoy. As Prime Minister Winston S. Churchill (q.v.) envisioned it, they worked like a cavalry screen on the approaches, while maintaining the standard convoy speed of between 9 and 15 knots. The senior leadership of the Royal Navy expected its sonar-equipped escort ships to make short work of any submerged U-boat daring to attack a convoy, and no one seriously expected the U-boats to even approach on the surface.

The Royal Navy's leaders felt only those merchant ships too fast or too slow for convoys (about 10 percent of the world's merchant shipping) faced any risk of U-boat attack. Events proved them right—but only in the long run. Vessels with speeds above or below convoy range sailed unescorted and independently. Although much effort was expended trying to route these ships around known U-boat patrol areas, "independently routed" ships suffered far more heavily than ships in convoy. Losses were also heavy among ships whose convoys

Allied Convoy Designation Codes

Code	Origin	Destination	Starting Dates
AT	United States	Britain	January 1942
HG	Gibralter	Britain	September 1939
HX	Halifax	Britain	September 1939
HX	New York	Britain	September 1942
JW	Scotland	Russia	December 1942
KM	Britain	North Africa	October 1942
ME	Malta	Alexandria	July 1940
MG	Malta	Gibralter	December 1940
MK	North Africa	Britain	November 1942
MW	Alexandria	Malta	July 1940
OB	Liverpool	North America	September 1939
OG	Britain	Gibralter	October 1939
ON	Liverpool	North America	July 1941
OS	Britain	West Africa	July 1941
PQ	Iceland	Russia	September 1941
QP	Russia	Britain and Iceland	September 1941
RA	Russia	Scotland	December 1942
SC	Halifax	Britain	August 1940
SC	New York	Britain	September 1942
SL	Sierra Leone	Britain	September 1939
SW	Suez	South Africa	June 1940
TA	Britain	United States	January 1942
WS	Britain	Middle East via South Africa	June 1940

had to disperse before reaching their destinations, a common situation early in the war caused by the Allies' shortage of escort vessels.

Unfortunately for Britain, Germany's U-boat commander, Admiral Karl Dönitz (q.v.), also learned some lessons from World War I. Recognizing that no single submarine could devastate a convoy, he modified the "group tactics" that some U-boat commanders had developed in the later stages of 1918. The resulting "wolf pack" tactics called for the U-boat sighting a convoy to follow and report its movements, acting as a beacon until a group of three to twenty U-boats could mass for an attack. Conducting night surface attacks, much like torpedo boats, wolf packs often ranged up and down a convoy's length, choosing the best targets. These tactics were nearly a perfect counter to the Royal Navy's tactics.

By operating on the surface, and therefore above sonar's (q.v.) subsurface search area, wolf pack tactics enabled the U-boats to ravage convoys almost at will—particularly since the U-boat's low surface silhouette made it virtually undetectable at night in the years before radar (q.v.) came into wide use. These devastating tactics often overwhelmed the numerically weaker escort groups in the war's early years.

In September 1940, U-boats penetrated Con-

voy SC-7's escort screen and sank seventeen ships nearly half the convoy. To both the victims and the overwhelmed escorts, the attacks seemed to come unseen from every direction, all at once. The German U-boat commanders called the period from June to October 1940, "The Happy Time," when they sank 274 ships—a total of 1,395,000 tons—at the price of only six U-boats. Most of those ships sunk, however, were sailing independently at the time they were attacked. They were either independently routed ships, or members of dispersed convoys in the far eastern Atlantic.

To achieve maximum effectiveness, wolf pack tactics required good intelligence and reliable communications between the U-boats and U-boat Command headquarters. The former came from the German Navy's code breaking organization which was able to read the Royal Navy's Main Operating Broadcast (1939–1940) and Merchant Convoy Broadcast (1939–early 1943). This enabled U-boat Command to concentrate its U-boats efficiently by providing convoy routes and arrival and departure points. The intelligence gathered via code breaking was supplemented in 1940, and again in 1942, by aerial reconnaissance support provided by the *Luftwaffe*'s KG-40, which used Kondor patrol bombers to home the wolf packs onto Allied convoys. Fortunately for the Allies,

An Atlantic convoy. Picture taken from an RAF Coastal Command aircraft. (IWM C 2647)

neither the air support nor the code breaking successes were consistently available to U-boat Command. More significantly, the wolf packs' reliance on communications became their major vulnerability, as Allied code breakers came to read the U-boat Command's Main Operational Broadcast for most of the war. (*See* Atlantic Campaign and ULTRA).

As the war progressed the wolf packs began to encounter other problems. By mid-1941, the number of Allied escorts, particularly those equipped with radar, reached a level where the U-boats were no longer "stealth" platforms at night. Moreover, by July 1941, there were enough long-range escorts to provide protection for the entire length of a convoy's North Atlantic transit. This "end-to-end" escort reduced losses by providing extended convoy protection to ships that previously had to complete their voyages independently after their convoys were dispersed in the North Atlantic. Large wolf packs still had the ability to overwhelm an escort group and inflict losses on its convoy, but it came at an increasingly heavy cost.

Few incidents demonstrate the effectiveness of convoying better than the U-boats' devastation of America's coastal shipping during that country's first six months in the war. Designated Operation DRUMBEAT (q.v.), U-boat Command deployed six U-boats off America's eastern seaboard beginning January 1942. Hobbled with inexperienced crews, few escorts, and even fewer aircraft, the U.S. Atlantic Fleet decided not to implement convoying, concentrating instead on roving antisubmarine patrols and active hunting. The result was an unmitigated disaster. Some 444 unescorted ships of nearly two million tons of cargo-carrying capac-

ity were sunk by less than a dozen U-boats in American waters between January and June 1942. Germany in return lost only one U-boat. Germany's U-boat captains called this their "Second Happy Time," which ended with the implementation of coastal convoying in American waters in late June 1942.

The effectiveness of U-boats continued to decline as convoy escorts and their supporting air and naval forces became increasingly stronger and more technologically advanced. Despite its early successes, the German Navy could not keep up with the new technology and tactics that the Allies developed, nor were the Germans even fully aware of them. Code breaking enabled the Allies to divert convoys away from U-boat concentrations, and to reinforce escort groups as necessary. The growing number of escort carriers, particularly after March 1943, also meant that U-boats operating near convoys did so under the constant threat of air attack. The introduction of new and more sensitive radars, sonars, and other submarine detection equipment virtually eliminated the U-boats' stealthfulness.

By April 1943, U-boats attacking a convoy ran a gauntlet of air patrols, as well as an inner and outer screen of escort ships, before getting within effective torpedo range. By that stage of the war, the average survival rate of a U-boat crew was two patrols. Although U-boats continued to operate against Allied shipping until the end of the war, Dönitz conceded to the "overwhelming superiority achieved by the enemy defense." On 24 May 1943, he suspended further submarine operations on the convoy routes in the North Atlantic. For the Allies, the Battle of the Atlantic had been won.

Although the Royal Navy had overestimated

its ability to contain the U-boat threat in World War II, there is no doubt that the early decision to establish convoying was a key factor in the Allied victory in the Battle of the Atlantic. Moreover, the Allies established the Operational Evaluation Group to study convoy battles and tactics. The resulting analysis enabled the Allies to optimize the size of their convoys and the tactics and equipment to protect them. The Germans never established any similar group. In effect, the Battle of the Atlantic was between convoys and wolf packs. It was a closely run contest, but the convoys won in the end.

Donald P. Doumitt
Carl O. Schuster

Additional Reading
Coale, Griffith B., *North Atlantic Patrol* (1942).
Irving, David, *The Destruction of Convoy PQ-17* (1969).
MacIntyre, Donald G., *U-Boat Killer* (1956).
Middlebrook, Martin, *Convoy* (1976).

Counterintelligence Operations
Counterintelligence (CI) aims at neutralizing or destroying the effectiveness of the enemy's intelligence systems. It is an essential element in the success of any military operation. By denying information to the enemy and thereby decreasing his ability to use his combat power effectively, counterintelligence aids in reducing the risks of a military operation.

CI operations take two basic forms. Defensive CI measures are designed to conceal information from the enemy. They include such techniques as operational security, personnel security, security of classified documents, movement control, signal security, censorship (q.v.), camouflage, electronic counter-countermeasures, and light and noise discipline in tactical units in the forward areas of the battle zone. Defensive CI measures are readily standardized regardless of a unit's particular mission. Offensive CI measures actively block the enemy's attempt to gain information or to carry out sabotage (q.v.) or subversion. They include electronic countermeasures, counterreconnaissance, counterespionage, deception (q.v.), and the use of smoke by forward tactical units to mask their movements. Offensive CI measures vary with the threat and the mission of the unit.

Like military intelligence itself, most armies only started to develop formal CI structures in the early twentieth century. During World War I, the U.S. Army called CI "negative intelligence," while all other intelligence activities were classified as "positive intelligence." The first official CI structure in the U.S. Army came with the creation of the Counterintelligence Police (CIP) in 1917. Between the wars, CI suffered the same neglect as the other intelligence functions. By 1934, the U.S. Army had only fifteen active CIP agents. The CIP was revitalized with the start of World War II. In 1942, it was reorganized into the Counterintelligence Corps (CIC), which during the course of the war trained and fielded 13,000 agents in more than 300 CIC detachments. Inside the continental United States, the main task of the CIC units was conducting background investigations on candidates for security clearances. Overseas, tactical CIC detachments supported the field army. Each U.S. division in Europe had a seventeen-man CIC detachment.

Like the broader intelligence operations (q.v.), counterintelligence operations can encompass the entire scope of a nation's activities and capabilities—political, social, economic, and military. At the national level, each of the major participants in World War II had at least one organization that conducted counterintelligence. In some cases a country had more than one, which usually resulted in overlapping activities, and even competition. In Britain, MI-5 (q.v.) was responsible for counterintelligence, although MI-6 (q.v.) handled any CI activities outside British territory. In the United States, the Federal Bureau of Investigation (FBI) was primarily responsible for counterintelligence, but the CI organizations of the military services also worked in that area. In Germany, the *Gestapo* (q.v.) was responsible for all internal state security, while the *Abwehr* (q.v.), was supposed to handle all military intelligence. The Nazi Party, however, also had its own security service, the *Sicherheitsdienst (SD)* (q.v.), which was a rival organization to the *Abwehr*. In the Soviet Union, CI functions were split between the NKVD (q.v.)—the forerunner of the KGB—and Soviet military intelligence, the GRU. Later, the Soviets established an organization called *Smersh* (q.v.), whose primary mission was to detect and eliminate spies and other "counterrevolutionaries."

At the start of the war, Germany's main CI focus was on the Soviet Union. As the war progressed, German efforts increasingly focused on penetrating western European resistance groups and frustrating the efforts of OSS and SOE (qq.v.) agents to support and direct those groups. Soviet CI was concerned with both the Germans and the Western Allies. As the war progressed, the main CI task of the Western Allies became defeating German efforts to discover the time and the place of the invasion of the Continent. Thus Britain, the base of the cross-channel attack, was the location of the greatest Allied CI activity. German CI activity, likewise, increasingly focused on those countries with coastlines on the English Channel or the North Sea.

German intelligence operations in the Western Hemisphere centered in Mexico and Brazil. As early as 1936, Dr. Heinrich Norte arrived at the German embassy in Mexico City with the mission of establishing an *Abwehr* network. The FBI responded by assigning throughout the war 360 agents to the CI effort south of the border. Norte, however, was able to place a source inside the office of Mexico's prosecutor general. The Germans were thus able to obtain a forty-seven-page memo from J. Edgar Hoover (q.v.) himself detailing FBI counterintelligence operations in Mexico.

Closer to the enemy's center, the Germans managed to place Simon Emil Koedel, one of their most effective agents. Koedel first arrived in the United States in 1906, became an American citizen, and actually served in the U.S. Army. Sometime around 1937 Koedel became an active agent for the *Abwehr*. He became a member of the American Ordnance Association (AOA), a defense industry professional group. Membership in the AOA gained him access to many otherwise restricted defense sites. Koedel, who was finally apprehended by the FBI on 23 October 1944, spent a great deal of his time around east coast ports, watching the comings and goings of U.S. merchant and warships. His information was then passed to German U-boats through the *Abwehr's H-Dienst* (*Hafen-Dienst,* or Harbor Service).

Both sides relied heavily on radio intercepts to detect and locate enemy intelligence agents. Radio was an agent's principal means of reporting information, but clandestine transmissions were vulnerable to detection through triangulation using multiple radio direction finders. This vulnerability required agents to change locations frequently, often more than once a day. The British were aided in their CI effort by the *Abwehr's* failure to use one-time cypher key pads, which enabled MI-5 to decrypt its messages. Many agents who were caught were summarily executed, but many were forced to work for their captors. The Western Allies had a built-in security measure against such an event. Allied agents were supposed to include a prearranged coding error in their transmissions. Any message received by London without this error would be an indication that the message was phony and that the agent or his codes had fallen into German hands.

This security check was not foolproof. In one case it's failure contributed to the success of the German Operation NORTH POLE, which effectively neutralized all Allied intelligence and covert operations in occupied Holland. On 6 March 1942, *Abwehr* Major Hermann Giskes captured Hubertus Lauwers, a young Dutch SOE agent. When Giskes forced Lauwers to transmit a message requesting an airdrop of supplies, Lauwers left out the required coding error, which should have notified London that he had been captured. The supplies were still dropped. Over the course of the next two years, the Dutch section of SOE in London continually ignored indications that Lauwers was compromised. They even ignored the reports of Pieter Dourlein, another SOE agent who was captured by Giskes but escaped. As a result of Operation NORTH POLE, forty-seven of the fifty-two SOE agents who dropped into Holland were captured and shot; and 1,200 Dutch resistance fighters also lost their lives.

The British became the war's undisputed masters at turning captured enemy agents to their own use. What became known as the Double-Cross, or "XX" System, was first conceived by Thomas Robertson, a Scottish infantry officer. After seven German agents were executed in 1940, it occurred to the economically-minded Scot that this was a waste of real talent. Robertson convinced officials at MI-5 that using the captured agents would be far more effective. Double agents, after all, were the mainstay of counterintelligence operations since the days of Sun Tzu, the ancient Chinese military writer.

Captured agents, when faced with certain death by shooting or hanging, could usually be counted on to serve the British and double-cross their former German masters. The operation came under the direction of Sir John Masterman and the XX Committee (qq.v.). Central to the success of the whole system was the use of the agents to send genuine but only marginally valuable information back to the *Abwehr*. This required information concocted with supreme ingenuity. In some cases, the information fed back through the controlled agents put in jeopardy the lives of British subjects. During the 1940 Battle of Britain (q.v.), for example, the controlled information was geared to fending off *Luftwaffe* attacks on strategic targets, but sometimes resulted in the German bombers targeting London residential areas. The Double-Cross System was ultimately effective, eventually snaring and turning most, if not all, of the German agents operating in Britain.

John F. Murphy, Jr.

Additional Reading

Bennett, Ralph, *Behind the Battle: Intelligence in the War with Germany, 1939–1945* (1994).

Farago, Ladislas, *The Game of Foxes* (1971).

Hinsley, F.H., and Alan Stripp, *The Codebreakers* (1993).

Kahn, David, *Hitler's Spies* (1979).

Masterman, John C., *The Double-Cross System in the War of 1939–1945* (1972).

Payne, Lawrence, *German Military Intelligence* (1970).

West, Nigel, *The Secret War* (1993).

Wark, W., *The Ultimate Enemy* (1985).

Cryptography

Almost as soon as writing was invented, humans began to use secret writing, or cryptography, to conceal information. Of course, those who were not supposed to have access to the information began to look for ways to read the secret writing—a process called cryptanalysis.

Two kinds of secret writings evolved: codes and ciphers. In codes, words or numbers stand for plain language. For example, the number 1029 could stand for the word "artillery." Ciphers are concerned only with letters and have two basic operations: transposition and substitution. In transposition, the letters are rearranged so that the message looks like nonsense to an uninitiated person. In substitution, letters of the message are replaced by other letters or numbers, or occasionally by shapes of one kind or another. (Readers of Sherlock Holmes will recall the cipher in the "Adventure of the Dancing Men.")

The simplest substitution cipher is merely a shift of the plain text alphabet. Julius Caesar, according to tradition, devised a simple one, known as the Caesar cipher, in which A is designated as B, B as C, and so on. A cipher that uses one letter for another throughout the message is termed a monoalphabetic cipher.

Cryptographers in the Renaissance hit upon the idea of using a more complex cipher, in which a letter is encrypted by one letter at one point, another letter at another point, and so on. Such ciphers are called polyalphabetic ciphers. In the Vigenere cipher, for example, a classic polyalphabetic cipher invented in the sixteenth century by Blaise de Vigenere, there are twenty-six alphabets formed by shifting the letters by one unit to the left in each new alphabet. The displaced letter or letters move to the end of the alphabet. Thus, the first alphabet is A through Z; the second, B through Z, with A placed at the end; the third is C through Z, with A and B at the end; until the twenty-sixth alphabet is Z through Y. The alphabets are named for their initial letters. To make it even harder for the enemy, the message is sent out in groups of five letters, so that the word division is concealed.

In the 1920s, cipher machines were invented, which, using rotors that moved at varying rates, could speedily encipher messages using polyalphabetic ciphers of great complexity. Until the modern computer revolution, all ciphers could, at least in theory, be broken, except for the one-time cypher key pad system invented by Major Joseph O. Mauborgne of the U.S. Army during World War I. In this system, letters of the alphabet are assigned numbers and then the letters of the message are added, in noncarrying arithmetic, to numbers of a sequence that is absolutely random. The recipient of the message has in hand the random sequence of numbers and simply performs the necessary subtraction to get the message. Both sender and receiver then discard the random number sequence so that it is used only once. This process completely obliterates the frequency characteristics of language and so makes it impossible for cryptanalysts to break the cipher.

Why then would armies and navies not use the one-time pad for all their messages? It was in fact used in World War II for the most important kinds of messages, but was far too cumbersome to use for ordinary traffic. The huge volume of traffic in World War II (General Dwight D. Eisenhower's [q.v.] headquarters was sending the equivalent of a shelf of twenty books a day before the Normandy invasion) made necessary the use of cipher machines.

Cryptanalysts begin with the fact that each language has its own frequency patterns. In English, for example, "e" is the most frequently appearing letter; "t" the second most frequent; "z" the least frequent, and so on. There are other characteristics: "th" is the most frequent diagraph; the vowels "a," "o," and "i" are rarely found in junction; "n" follows a vowel in 80 percent of its appearances; the letter most frequently preceding vowel is "h"; and there are many more such characteristics, all laid out conveniently in tables. These characteristics can be concealed in greater or lesser degree, hardly at all by a monoalphabetic cipher, quite cleverly by a polyalphabetic cipher, but never completely. The cryptanalyst can crack polyalphabetic cipher using techniques pioneered by nineteenth-century cryptanalysts Friedrich Kasiski and Auguste Kerckhoffs.

Cryptanalysts have other tools besides frequency tables. A very important one is looking for what are called "probable words." Military messages, in the nature of things having a certain stereotyped quality, are replete with phrases like "the convoy will sail," or "we have sustained heavy bombardment," or "need fuel urgently."

Also, careless enemy code clerks and radio operators can be the cryptanalyst's best friend by not observing communications security procedures. For example, a routine procedure is to break a message in half, putting the last half first and the first half last when it is transmitted, in order to conceal the standard beginnings and endings of a message. Careless clerks, neglecting to follow this procedure, give the enemy cryptanalyst a good way to break the cipher, because he can see how the standard beginnings and endings of the message were enciphered. There are other errors easily fallen into by sloppy communications personnel. Also, since cryptography partakes of mathematics, use of mathematics, especially statistics and group theory, can crack the ciphers.

Additionally, cryptanalysts are not above stealing the other side's codes and ciphers where possible. If the theft can be kept secret, then there is no need to refer to frequency tables or hope for careless code clerks, because the enemy communication system has fallen intact into the other side's hands. Such thievery happened more than once in World War II.

Both sides in World War II enjoyed victories and sustained defeats in the code and cipher war. The Germans, for example, had detailed information about British military operations in North Africa (q.v.). This intelligence resulted from the Italian theft of the main American diplomatic code from the American embassy in Rome in August 1941, before America's entry into the war.

The American military attache in Cairo regularly reported the British military situation to Washington. The Germans intercepted the radio messages, decoded the material with the purloined code books, and sent the information on to Field Marshal Erwin Rommel (q.v.). He therefore had exhaustive information about the British supply situation, about upcoming commando operations, and even about British defense plans. This whole intelligence coup was important enough for German Chancellor Adolf Hitler (q.v.) to mention it in his "table talk." One historian wrote, "It was the broadest and clearest picture of enemy forces and intentions available to any Axis commander

throughout the whole war." The Americans later changed their code, abruptly closing the curtain for the Germans.

The Germans enjoyed other successes, most notably in the Battle of the Atlantic (q.v.). For a time, until the Allies improved their ciphers, the Germans could locate Allied convoys by reading Allied messages.

German successes notwithstanding, the victory in the code and cipher war unquestionably went to the Allies. The British were able to read most of the German radio traffic because they mastered the German Enigma (q.v.) cipher machine, a feat designated ULTRA (q.v.), for ultrasecret. It was essential to keep the breakthrough a secret so the Germans would not know their messages were being read—often by Winston Churchill (q.v.)—at the same time as the German recipients were reading their copies.

The basis of the British success was the information obtained by the French from a German informer who worked in the German Army enciphering division in the early 1930s. He supplied essential information about the Enigma machine to the French, who turned it over to the Poles, who then built on the information until they were able to read the German messages. Fortunately for the Allied war effort, the Poles were able to get their secrets to the British before the Polish collapse in 1939.

It is impossible to overestimate the value to the Allies of their knowledge of German ciphers. That knowledge played a key role in the German defeat in the Battle of the Atlantic. The Allies could follow precisely the paths of the German U-boats and could move in at the most vulnerable moment in a U-boat's life, when it is being refueled by a supply submarine. There were many other successes; for example, the exact knowledge possessed by the Allies about German plans to counterattack the Normandy beachhead, which greatly simplified Allied planning.

Separate from the ULTRA success was the American breaking of the Japanese PURPLE code by William F. Friedman, still regarded as probably the most astonishing feat in the history of cryptanalysis. The American knowledge helped mightily in the Pacific war, but was also of great value in the European theater, because the Japanese military attache regularly reported to Tokyo in detail about German plans. The attache even made a lengthy report about his inspection of the Atlantic Wall (q.v.) which General Eisenhower and his staff used in planning the invasion.

Why were the Allies so superior to the Germans in cryptanalysis? First of all, the Germans used the same cipher machine throughout the war, while the Allies used several machines. The sole use of the Enigma by the Germans meant the Allies could concentrate all their efforts on one type. Moreover, Allied machines were superior to the German machine, in that they had more rotors, thereby producing more complex ciphers.

Secondly, the Germans were sloppy in their communications security, regularly making all the blunders that radio operators and cipher clerks are trained not to make.

Third, the Germans fragmented their cryptanalysis efforts among several groups, quite in harmony with Hitler's abhorrence of good organization. The Americans and British by contrast, kept their cryptanalysis in one place, Washington, D.C., and Bletchley Park (a stately home north of London) (q.v.), respectively. The two groups cooperated closely.

Fourth, the Germans advanced only to electromechanical devices, while the Allies had protocomputers—the British "Colossus" and the American "Madame X." These were electronic devices that vastly speeded up the process of deciphering German communications.

Finally, the Germans could not face up to reality. Even a modicum of reflection would have told them that their ciphers had been broken; but because they believed that their ciphers were "unbreakable," they neither changed them nor bothered to observe elementary security procedures. Perhaps in this as in so much else, Nazism had made the Germans complacent.

Historians have tried to quantify just how much the successes in cryptanalysis helped the Allied cause. One historian calculated that it shortened the war by a year. But in the nature of things it is impossible to say more than that it was of tremendous assistance to the Allies to know so much about the enemy. All the Allied commanders, from General George C. Marshall (q.v.) on down, gave copious credit to the cryptanalysts for their brilliant work.

It should be noted too that cryptanalysts do not win wars. Wars are won by good generals, by well-trained personnel with high morale, by the quality and quantity of equipment, and by a measure of luck. The best information in the world will not produce a victory unless the wherewithal is present to exploit that information and defeat the enemy. But certainly no Allied leader would have wanted to be without the information that ULTRA provided.

New advances in technology have revolutionized cryptography and cryptanalysis since World War II. Not only does the modern computer create ciphers of mind-boggling complexity, but also the nature of radio transmission has been radically altered.

One new method of transmission, called "spread spectrum communications," sends the message over different wavelengths and at different times, making it hard to intercept. Messages can also be sent by "high-speed burst transmission," which gives the enemy only seconds to catch the transmission. Also, computers can transmit continuously (as compared with World War II transmitters, which operated only when a message was being sent) so that the real message is hidden within hours of nonsense. This system is called "constant key," referring to the fact that the cryptographic machine constantly sends keying pulses of random characters in between messages.

Today, it is probable that enciphered messages can no longer be read by an enemy, bringing to an end the long struggle between cryptographers and cryptanalysts. More than one student of cryptanalysis, while bemused by these advances, has complained that the romance has gone out of the field, for technology has pushed human ingenuity aside.

Ronald V. Layton, Jr.

Additional Reading

Deavors, C.A., and L. Kruh, *Machine Cryptography and Modern Cryptanalysis* (1985).

Gaines, Helen Fouche, *Cryptanalysis: A Study of Ciphers and Their Solution* (1939).

Kahn, David, *The Codebreakers: The Story of Secret Writing* (1967).

D

Deception Operations

The use of deception in military operations is as old as war itself. Deception is used to mislead and confuse the enemy about the true nature of the opposing force's intent, and it is used on all three levels of warfare—strategic, operational, and tactical.

Contrary to popular perceptions, deception is the result of detailed planning done in conjunction with other plans, and is fully integrated into all plans. It is not the result of a group of highly inventive, highly imaginative persons removed from the actual conduct of war or from war planning. The use by an organization of deception plans, regardless of the level, is a building block in the overall concept and implementation of plans and operations leading to victory. Deception, then, does not and cannot exist in a vacuum apart from all other military considerations.

Deception plans can be confusing in that they cover a wide range of operations, from simple battlefield deception such as a few men occupying dug-in positions using fake weapons to give the impression that part of the line is heavily defended, to an elaborate scheme to convince the enemy's high command that a major sea and airborne operation is about to take place hundreds of kilometers from the actual landing zone. Carefully planned bogus radio traffic can also deceive the enemy. It can appear that deception is a haphazard, opportunistic set of unrelated actions.

Deception plans and operations are used to support military actions, not to be conducted without fitting into the overall set of strategic, operational, or tactical objectives, and they must be agreed upon by the overall commanders and staffs prior to implementation. In World War II, it was critical that all deception operations be coordinated at the highest levels. There could have been a tendency for each ally to conduct his own operational and strategic deceptions that could very well have, in the long run, been a disaster.

The most massive deception operation for the Allies occurred with the preparations for Operation OVERLORD (q.v.), the cross-channel invasion of occupied France in 1944. Obviously, there was no way Allied planners could keep German intelligence from knowing that a massive buildup of forces was taking place in Britain, and the continual arrival of men and supplies there could mean only one thing—invasion. The Germans countered with their own plan, which painted the Pas de Calais area on the French north coast as heavily fortified and as an invasion area that offered the least chance of success.

Throughout southern England, fake bases were set up with barracks and mess halls that actually had smoke coming from the chimneys and aircraft, tanks, and other large pieces of war materiel that were either wooden or canvas mock-ups or discarded pieces of equipment. From the air or from a distance, it would be impossible to tell the bases were not operational. Military and civilian police guarded these phony bases to keep unwanted eyes from looking too closely.

All military intelligence systems have sections devoted to the study of enemy order of battle. They inform commanders what enemy troops are where, in what strength, and with what capabilities. To deceive German order of battle specialists, the Allies created divisions, known as ghost or phantom divisions, each with its own distinctive shoulder insignia, but with few staff and no line troops. These patches, both regular and airborne infantry and others, could be seen in Britain. They gave the impression that Allied combat power was more massive than it really was, and they confused the important intelligence questions of when and where those divisions would be deployed.

Flamboyant American general George S. Patton (q.v.) was seen in and around the fake bases. It was rumored that Patton, who had been in disgrace and obscurity since an incident in 1943, would lead an invasion army into Europe. The Germans were deceived by the plan into thinking that two separate invasion plans were at work with so much usable combat power.

All of these long-term and well thought-out deceptions supported the major objective of Operation OVERLORD: the successful landing of Allied forces at Normandy. These plans were carried out over a long period of time, and had to be carefully orchestrated.

Of immediate value to Operation OVERLORD, and of short-term existence, was the dropping of thousands of small dummies by parachute in the early minutes of 6 June 1944, on drop zones far away from where the actual paratroop drops would be made. This deception, of very limited duration, caused confusion among the German commanders, before three Allied airborne divisions were parachuted into France at other sites several hours prior to the actual beach invasion. The integration of the dummy drops into the overall operational plan was critical in that the actual drop zones had to be avoided, and bogus sites had to be selected for distance from the actual zones and for dispersion over the French countryside to further confuse the countermeasures of the German defenders.

Not all successful deception operations in World War II were carried out by the Allies. In the winter of 1944, the Germans were able to totally deceive the Allies about their plans for a major offensive in the Ardennes (q.v.). Adolf Hitler's (q.v.) daring gamble for a major attack on the American front in December 1944 required careful, meticulous preparation to deploy the armor and infantry tactical units that would make the attack on 16 December. To do this, in the face of Allied air superiority, a complete and comprehensive deception plan with stringent security measures was part of the overall operational plan. When the Germans smashed into Allied lines before dawn on 16 December, surprise was complete.

The German planners integrated deception and tight security into their plans and imposed a strict radio silence on their troops. The lack of radio communications gave Allied intelligence officers the impression that the Ardennes was a quiet sector and that little was going on. Just the opposite was true, as the Germans brought vast quantities of men, material, and equipment into the dense forest. They made extraordinarily good use of overhead tree cover in the thick forest, and air observation reports reflected the success of this deception. There was heavy use of camouflaging equipment to keep observations at a minimum. Concealment techniques were enforced at every level of the German command, and Allied reports reflected a view that there were few German troops in the wooded area to their front.

Rumors were leaked by Germans that some units already in their attack positions were in reality in the lines facing the Soviet Army. Whole divisions were lost by Allied order of battle analysts due to this well-constructed deception plan. The result of this was a tactical and operational plan that achieved surprise and inflicted heavy losses in manpower, equipment, and territory on the defenders.

It is also possible that one highly successful deception operation can bring about unplanned benefits later. In 1943, the British naval intelligence section responsible for strategic deception planning totally fooled the Germans over the upcoming invasion of Sicily (q.v.). They placed a body in waters off Spain that contained documents indicating that major Allied attacks in the spring of 1943 would come in Greece and Sardinia, rather than Sicily, hoping to divert German planning elsewhere. Pro-Nazi Spanish authorities gave copies of the documents to German intelligence agents who immediately sent them to Berlin. These carefully faked documents convinced Hitler and his planners that Greece and Sardinia were the areas for invasion, and they ignored Sicily, where the Allies successfully landed. It took a full two weeks for the Germans to realize that they were the victims of a complex Allied deception operation (see Operation MINCEMEAT).

In the fall of 1943, the Germans were contacted by a man claiming to be valet to the British ambassador to Turkey, who offered to sell highly classified and important documents that he photographed. As the ambassador's valet, he had access to a safe containing critical information about Allied-Turkish relations, reports of such high-level meetings as the Teheran Conference, and other top-secret military information pointing to the eventual implementation of Operation OVERLORD. The Germans paid the agent, code named "Cicero," a large sum of money for these documents, but there were suspicions that "Cicero's" activities and information could indeed be part of another Allied deception plan to fool the German as they had before the invasion of Sicily.

Hitler and his generals and diplomats were skeptical about "Cicero's" information. The *Führe* nsisted that all manner of tests be run on the documents provided by "Cicero," who claimed to be working alone. Questions arose about his ability to hold and photograph material singlehandedly and doubts were cast on his veracity. The fear of another deception operation paralyzed the Germans when they did indeed have vital information before them.

Regardless of "Cicero's" motivations (greed, ideological, etc.), the fact remains that the German high command, including Hitler, were fearful of another deception. This is an example of one plan that worked, reaping unexpected benefits later.

The basic principles of deception plans and operations have not changed since the beginning of warfare. Deceptions alone do not win wars, but it would be extremely difficult not to have a plan and then place it into operation. During the Persian Gulf War in 1991, the Iraqis tried the use of dummy aircraft and tanks plus other measures. The sending of false messages, the digging of trenches never meant for combat use, and other measures limited only by the planners' imagination, are constants in warfare.

As the many operations of World War II show, one principle remains fixed and cannot be violated. Deception plans and operations must be an integral part of the overall offensive or defensive plan. Deception cannot stand alone. Once deception operations become an end unto themselves, the dangers of confusion and misspent efforts increase and they can become a detractor. The commander must insist that the deception plan and deception operations be integrated at all levels and be known to himself, his staff, and his subordinates on the battlefield.

James J. Cooke

Additional Reading

Breuer, William B., *The Secret War with Germany: Deception, Espionage, and Dirty Tricks* (1988).

Brown, Anthony C., *Bodyguard of Lies* (1975).

Cruickshank, Charles, *Deception in World War II* (1980).

Dewar, Michael, *The Art of Deception in Warfare* (1989).

Glantz, David M., *Soviet Military Deception in the Second World War* (1989).

Perrault, Gilles, *The Secret of D-Day* (1965).

Desert Operations

The desert operations of World War II were unlike those of World War I in that the employment of tanks, mechanized and motorized infantry, and airpower added new dimensions to old problems. Traditional perceptions of defensive positions became obsolete and new concepts of offensive maneuver warfare had to be developed. All of this was dictated by the nature of the terrain, the effects of weather, the lack of roads, and the vast distances to be covered by opposing forces.

The effective desert generals—Rommel, Montgomery, O'Connor (qq.v.) and the like—found out there had to be an unbreakable marriage between speed and mobility and logistics in combat operations. The commanders also discovered that human lessons from the past were valuable. Troops in the desert faced a difficult set of physical and mental pressures and tensions, and the effective commander had to be aware of the sense of isolation, the effects of widely varying degrees of heat and cold, and the general debilitation caused by those effects.

Desert terrain offered to the soldiers of World War II a bewildering set of problems. The great expanses of the desert seemed more like an ocean than a piece of ground over which to fight. In Europe, soldiers trained where the ground and foliage offered cover from fire and concealment from observation. Trees, gullies, hills, creeks and rivers, and even mountains were the usual setting for military maneuvers. The desert is basically flat, with slightly undulating sands. There are few trees, if any, for many miles, and it is possible to observe the movements of the enemy because of the great clouds of dust raised by tanks and motorized transport.

Desert maneuvers in World War II were more like naval engagements. Battles were fought in great sweeps, and traditional methods of military map reading gave way to more nautical expressions. New gunnery skills were learned because tankers and artillerymen tended to engage targets at hundreds or thousands of meters beyond the maximum effective range of their guns. Artillery and infantry observation also suffered from the distance factor, and often adjustments were learned by trial and error. While commanders adjusted to an extended battlefield of hundreds or thousands of kilometers, their armor, infantry, and artillery had to remember not to be fooled by distance and begin firing at impossible ranges.

German Field Marshall Erwin Rommel learned the hard way that traditional infantry really had no place in a desert environment. Tanks and mechanized infantry could move with speed over the vastness of the desert. Nonmechanized infantry were a hindrance to operations because tanks and motorized infantry became tied down waiting for the walking infantry. Rommel saw this during the retreat from Cyrenaica in the winter of 1941–1942, when the entire Italian infantry and a good portion of the German infantry had no transport, and the retreat became agonizingly slow.

Rommel observed that the stress placed on walking infantry by the heat and cold and the need for water wore down the combat capability of the troops. As anticipated, the primary role for them was in prepared defensive positions; but if forced to move or retreat, they again posed a threat to the speed of the overall operation. What one can gather from Rommel and the other generals of the desert is that only motorized units should be considered for desert deployment.

The British learned quickly that combat operations in the desert were based on combined arms, with the artillery forming an important part of any offensive or defensive scheme. Rommel observed that for artillery to be effective in desert offensive operations, it had to be, "mobile in the highest degree, including its ammunition in large quantities."

Engaging an enemy at maximum effective range with artillery was critical in the desert because of the speed of armor and the lack of natural obstacles. The tank also needed a ". . . long range gun, for the side which has the more powerful gun has the longer arm and can earlier engage the enemy." Since an army fought over vast tracts of land and cover and concealment were at a premium, it was vital that boldness and rapidity be the hallmarks of an offensive force. In the long run Rommel believed, it was the clash of tank against tank in the desert that would decide the outcome of the battle.

Since desert warfare is rapid and covers such distances, the command and staff elements of the army must be flexible and quick to respond to any change in the tactical situation. Everything in desert warfare, Rommel posited, was boldness and speed, ". . . for the side which makes the greater effort is the faster, and the faster side wins the battle."

What Rommel could have added was his concern for the logistics flow during desert combat which placed greater strains on the supply systems of the contestants than ever experienced in European warfare. The supply of ammunition, fuel repair parts, food, and water must keep up with the rapidity of the battle in the desert. Because of speed, vast distances, and the constant problem of dust and sand, the supply chain could not be in fixed logistic bases, but had to follow the tanks and the motorized infantry and artillery.

Rommel never achieved his supply goals, but eventually the British, under commanders such as General Sir Harold Alexander and General Bernard L. Montgomery (qq.v.), certainly did. Rommel wrote later that one of the quickest ways to force an enemy to give up the fight was to get armored forces into his supply areas. Fixed logistic bases invited certain disaster in high-speed, mobile desert warfare.

A Long Range Desert Group truck being dug out from the soft sand, 25 May 1942. Note the Pierced Steel Plates (PSP) for placing under the truck's wheels. (IWM E 12391)

Also of concern to Rommel was the emergence of air superiority as a deciding combat factor, especially in the desert. Unlike Europe, there was little cover and concealment, and this necessitated night moves by combat and supply units that could be very difficult due to terrain, weather conditions (sandstorms and the like), and the degree of light from the moon.

Rommel believed that the superior British Royal Air Force (RAF) gave his opponents three advantages: it provided rapid and complete reconnaissance, slowed down German advances, and allowed the Allies to achieve the desired goal of speed and maneuver in the desert. "(The enemies') bombs," Rommel wrote, "will be particularly effective against the motorized forces standing still without cover in the open desert." When Rommel wrote these observations in late 1942, he stated that by restricting movement to night moves by tactical and supply units, his *Afrika Korps* (q.v.) lost time, and the decisive element of speed was denied to him.

The conduct of desert operations in World War II offered some perplexing situations for men who were trained to fight in the wooded or urbanized terrain of Europe. Faced with vast expanses of flat desert that was either very sandy or very rocky, the commanders had to concern themselves with the dual problem of achieving speed and maneuverability on one hand, and finding an answer to the lack of cover and concealment on the other.

Both Axis and Allied generals faced logistic problems that were nightmares, and they became worse for Rommel as he lost command of the air. Maneuvering tanks with speed and boldness was the key to victory, and all other assets such as infantry, artillery, and especially supply had to be motorized to keep up with the armor. Nonmechanized infantry was nearly worthless in the desert because of its lack of mobility, and, in fact, as the Italians had shown, it could be a hindrance to either offensive or defensive operations. The desert generals of World War II broke new ground. As he looked back over his experiences in North Africa (q.v.), Rommel realized the lessons learned there would be guiding principles for desert warfare for generations to come.

James J. Cooke

Additional Reading

Barnett, Correlli, *The Desert Generals* (1961).
Carver, Michael, *Dilemmas of the Desert War* (1986).

Douhet Doctrine

Giulio Douhet (q.v.) was an Italian Army general who studied World War I in a attempt to draw lessons for future conflicts. In 1921, he published his book, *The Command of the Air,* in which he stressed the vital role airpower would play in a future war.

Douhet argued that aerial bombardment of the unarmed populations of cities and industrial centers would cause a breakdown in the social order and fatally undermine the will to continue the war. He took particular note of the panic in London caused by the Zeppelin and *Gotha* bomber raids of World War I. In short, one could bomb an enemy into defeat. He regarded this as "inhuman and atrocious," but a fact nonetheless.

On the other hand, he ascribed the victories in World War I to the performances of the armies in the field more than anything else. Indeed, the crucial point about his work is that he did not advocate strategic "terror" bombing as a tool on its own to secure victory, as some strategists in Britain did. He saw airpower as a vital contribution to a combined effort, believing that command of the air could only be fully exploited by the other services.

In the post–World War I era, aerial bombing was an attractive idea to those still recovering from the prolonged horrors of trench warfare. The Italians were actually the first to use aircraft in this manner when they bombed Turkish positions on Libya in 1911. In 1915, Douhet, an artillery officer, requested an independent bomber force with which to attack the Austro-Hungarians.

Douhet's writings led directly to the establishment of the *Regia Aeronautica* (the Italian Air Force [q.v.]) in 1923 as an independent service. Benito Mussolini (q.v.) was attracted to the whole idea as a new and very Italian form of warfare. But he never gave Douhet any real opportunity to develop his combined-force theories, despite the experiences during the Spanish civil war (q.v.) that tended to confirm the theories of the combined approach.

As events actually played out, technology held the bomber back from being as fearsome a weapon as predicted. Strategic bombing accounted for a relatively minor portion (about 3 percent) of the casualties of World War II. It was, however, the most technologically advanced countries, with sufficient resources to build a full range of desired weapons, that took the idea the farthest. Britain and the United States designed and flew large four-engine bombers. They became the exponents of the "art," dropping an incredible amount of ordnance on Axis targets.

In 1942, when Air Marshal Arthur T. Harris (q.v.) took over control of the RAF's Bomber Command, the emphasis switched from industrial targets to the specified mass bombing of cities. This trend actually marked a distinct divergence from the work of Douhet in that the bomber came to be regarded as the sole instrument capable of victory. Douhet had seen it as merely one weapon among many. Post–World War II bombing surveys suggest that much of the resources spent on city bombing were not effectively used.

Strategic bombing (q.v.) did not fatally undermine civilian morale; it did not even significantly cut into industrial production. It became a high-tech example of trench warfare, doling out destruction in a war of seemingly endless attrition. Douhet was prophetic enough to foresee the awesome threat posed by airpower (as indeed it exists today), but much of what he argued was proved wrong during the war. The bomber was not unstoppable, as fighter defenses and radar (q.v.) proved. Command of the air was not won or lost when one side was forced onto the defensive, as the RAF proved in the Battle of Britain (q.v.).

Douhet has been classed as a strategic theorist on the strength of his mentions of civilians becoming targets. In fact, much of what he advocated were tactical and operational concepts, like troop concentrations and attacks on supply lines. In reality, he wished to combine the two, but with the Italian Air Force, he lacked the means to do so. His ideas remain influential theories from aviation's early years.

Chris Westhorp

Additional Reading
Douhet, Giulio, *The Command of the Air* (1921).

E

Economic Warfare

To wage economic warfare is to organize one's own economy so that it can produce the armaments and food necessary to carry the war through to victory. At the same time, it harms the enemy's economy so that it cannot produce the armaments and food necessary for its own victory. Although the term came into use only in the 1930s, economic warfare is as old as war itself, in that even the most primitive ancient economy had to produce shields and spears and food.

Economic warfare looms very large in twentieth-century conflicts, because modern technology makes possible a plenitude of weapons of boundless complexity. One of the central principles of a correct strategy requires clear thinking and wise decisions about what one's economy can do.

When World War II broke out in 1939, British and French leaders assumed Germany was fully prepared for a major war and that its economy was mobilized for a total and prolonged conflict. In fact, the German economy was not geared for modern warfare. Adolf Hitler (q.v.) believed the war would consist of a series of short *Blitzkriegs* (q.v.), each gaining a quick victory, so that Germany could simply expropriate the armaments of the crushed opponent. With the captured booty, there would be no need to cut back on the production of consumer goods.

Hitler did not proclaim sacrifice to German civilians until after Stalingrad (q.v.), and far into the war the production of consumer goods was maintained at prewar levels. Hitler also refused to allow German women to work in the factories, preferring that they remain at home producing new "Aryan" children. In an especially bizarre twist, the Nazis imported untold numbers of Ukrainian girls to work as maids in German middle-class households.

In the area of economic warfare as elsewhere, Hitler helped ensure Germany's defeat.

When Germany began to suffer reverses, Hitler was finally prevailed upon to mobilize the economy for total war. Albert Speer (q.v.), one of the most remarkable figures of World War II, was placed at the head of the German production effort. Knowing Germany could never match in quantity the production of its enemies, he stressed "qualitative superiority."

German armaments on the whole were of very high quality, but the difference between them and Allied weaponry was not great enough to be really significant. Speer accomplished miracles in the face of tremendous difficulties, both from Allied air attacks and from the opposition of his fellow Nazis. His "party comrades," jealous of Speer's closeness to the *Führer,* actually sabotaged some of Speer's efforts, trying to discredit him in Hitler's eyes. The SS (q.v.), among other inane activities, employed a large labor force quarrying stones for the cities of the new Germany.

In spite of every difficulty, Speer's organizational genius and the productive capacity, which a highly developed economy retains in the face of every imaginable hindrance, caused Germany's production to rise steadily until the last months of the war. It was at this point that the whole German war effort disintegrated in the face of the Allied onslaught.

The British had a much better understanding of economic warfare than the Germans. In the beginning, they ascribed a far larger importance to it than events would justify. They believed a blockade would strangle Germany, bringing it to its knees without the need for large-scale bloodletting. When it became clear in 1940 that a traditional blockade alone would not bring victory, Britain turned to total mobilization of its economy. Supreme authority to direct the economy and to mobilize the population, both men and women, was given to the Lord President's Committee, which, its quaint name notwithstanding, did its job very well. British production rose steadily, and because of the stress on research, a host of new weapons was developed.

It was the American entry into the war that sealed Germany's fate. America had a huge industrial capacity, all of it beyond the reach of the *Luftwaffe*. Its steel production in 1939 easily outdistanced Germany's, and its coal output was almost double Germany's. Hitler was unimpressed. For him, the important fact was that the Americans were a "mongrel race" without a military tradition. However, in Roosevelt's happy phrase, the United States became the "Arsenal of Democracy" (q.v.).

Government boards, headed by the Office of War Mobilization, allotted raw materials, organized labor, set quotas, opened bottlenecks, contained inflation, and raised the money to finance the whole gigantic effort. The American economy not only produced the armaments, but actually increased the output of consumer goods and services by about 12 percent during the war. Anyone perusing old copies of *LIFE* magazine from this era will quickly realize that the gods of war excused the American civilian population from any real suffering. America never had to make the traditional choice between guns and butter.

If we look at actual Allied warfare waged against the German economy, we see that the results were not as decisive as the proponents of economic warfare had promised. To strangle the German economy, the Allies engaged in various tactics. In addition to a traditional blockade, the Allies practiced "preemptive buying," or the buying of key raw materials from neutrals to keep them out of German hands, and also brought pressure on neutrals not to trade at all with Germany. The Germans made use of reserve stockpiles and invented substitutes such as synthetic oil and rubber from coal.

Finally, Allied bombing, which reduced Germany's ancient cities to rubble and killed hundreds of thousands of German civilians, was surprisingly ineffective in reducing Germany's production. The Germans under Speer's leadership quickly put bombed factories back into production. Allied destruction of German oil and transportation facilities did play a major role in the collapse of the German war effort, but it was the most time-tested of military techniques—occupation of the enemy's territory—that finally brought Germany's surrender.

Not much is known about the Soviet economy as compared to the other wartime economies. Because of Josef Stalin's (q.v.) five-year-plans, it was already on a war footing when Germany attacked in 1941. Huge areas fell under German occupation, including most of the productive farmland, causing food shortages. For a period, Soviet production fell to almost nothing.

One of the great feats of World War II was the moving of Soviet factories from the path of the advancing Germans to the center of the country. Factory workers, functioning on very poor diets, without adequate shelter in the cold Russian climate, and without medical care, steadily raised Soviet production until the country was manufacturing more tanks and guns than Germany. American Lend-Lease (q.v.) helped, but the Soviets performed great prodigies on their own. Their achievement in World War II is more a tribute to their loyalty to "Mother Russia" than to Stalin's dictatorship or to Communism.

If Allied attempts to bring the German economy to a halt did not succeed, at least until the German armed forces had already been defeated on the field of battle, it is one of the major facts of World War II that the Allies managed their own economies in such a way as to overwhelm their enemies with a torrent of production. One of the interesting results of this management was the realization that people need not be helpless victims of economic forces. If an economy could be managed for warfare, it could be managed for human welfare. One of the most beneficial results of the Allied victory in World War II was that the Western economies, including Germany's, were managed in such a way in the postwar period as to provide a long era of prosperity for the Western world.

Ronald V. Layton

Additional Reading

Hancock, W.K., and M.M. Gowing, *British War Economy* (1949).

Kennedy, Paul, *The Rise and Fall of the Great Powers: Economic Change and Military Conflict from 1500–2000* (1987).

Medicott, W.N., *The Economic Blockade*, 2 vols. (1952, 1959).

Milward, Alan S., *The German Economy at War* (1965).

———, *War, Economy, and Society, 1939–1945* (1977)

Electronic Warfare

World War II brought about dramatic advances in

many areas of technology. One of the most important was electronics, which became a little known but bitterly contested battleground between the Allies and the Axis. The term electronic warfare, commonly called EW, originated in these battles for control of the electromagnetic spectrum. The terminology itself is somewhat esoteric and imprecise, and most nations define EW somewhat differently. The American definition centers on those military actions to "detect, deny, analyze, and hinder enemy use" of electronics.

Although not limited to radar (q.v.), the battle for radar superiority was acute, and the Allies' success in exploiting both radar and antiradar technology (then called radar countermeasures, or RCM; now called electronic countermeasures, or ECM) was a critical element in the Allied victory. Although EW is related to activities such as electronic intelligence gathering (ELINT), this discussion centers on the battle for radar superiority.

At the outset of World War II, the Germans and British had roughly comparable radar and electronic capabilities. German naval radar was more advanced, while the British ability to spoof and mislead the *Luftwaffe*'s electronic navigational aids *(Knickebein)* during the Battle of Britain's (q.v.) "Battle of the Beams" was a key reason for the British victory.

While both sides worked to improve their radar technology, the Germans halted all research in radar jamming while the British pushed forward. As a result, when the Royal Air Force (RAF) surprised the German air defenses during the attacks on Hamburg (q.v.) in July 1943 by dropping chaff (called "window"), small pieces of tinfoil or wire that reflected radar waves to present an indecipherable set of radar returns, the German air defenses were crippled, contributing to the destruction of that city. Not only was the night fighter force nullified, searchlight and *Flak*-control radars were also put out of action by this new device.

By early 1944, the *Luftwaffe* night fighters, equipped with advanced airborne intercept *Lichtenstein* radars, had regained the upper hand. During the disastrous (for the British) raid on Nuremburg (q.v.) in March 1944, more than 100 RAF bombers were shot down, most by *Luftwaffe* night fighters. Until the end of the war, British bombers and German night fighters fought an intense electronic battle for ownership of the nighttime skies over Europe.

American bombers faced a different problem. It was impossible to blind early warning radars to prevent knowledge of an attack, because the very act of jamming those radars would have announced the attack. The radars that controlled German *Flak,* however, were prime targets. By 1945, virtually every American heavy bomber carried transmitters to jam German radar. As the *Luftwaffe* declined and *Flak* became the greatest threat to American bombers, the need to degrade *Flak* control radars grew increasingly important.

Other jammers were used to block German voice communications and fighter control nets. A postwar assessment indicated that American use of RCM had saved upwards of 600 heavy bombers from destruction by German *Flak.*

World War II was the birthplace of electronic warfare, which has become a key element of virtually every aspect of modern warfare. Every warship and combat aircraft is now equipped with a variety of electronic warfare systems and capabilities. Although current technologies have far outstripped those of 1939–1945, many tactics, doctrines, and procedures trace their roots back to that war's bitter struggles for control of the ether.

Daniel T. Kuehl

Additional Reading
Dickens, Sir Gerald P., *Bombing and Strategy: The Fallacy of Total War* (1947).
Gordon, Don E., *Electronic Warfare* (1981).
Price, Alfred, *History of U.S. Electronic Warfare: The Years of Innovation—Beginnings to 1946* (1984).
———, *Instruments of Darkness: The History of Electronic Warfare* (1977).

Engineer Operations

The mechanization of land warfare, which began midway through World War I and became most apparent in World War II, brought to the battlefield ever-heavier equipment, such as tanks, and required ever-sturdier bridges and hard-standing roads. With the increased firepower offered by tanks and quick-firing artillery, defensive positions needed substantial excavation and reinforcement with concrete and steel. Ensuring the mobility of one's own formations, denying that mobility to the enemy, and preparing adequate defenses were the tasks of military engineers.

For engineers, perhaps the most hazardous type of combat operation—because of the much greater chance of being captured—was the withdrawal. Their main role, whether they were British or French engineers in the opening phases of the war or Soviet and German engineers later on, was to delay the enemy by destroying bridges, roads, railway lines, and in a war where airpower grew increasingly important, airfields. In the North Africa (q.v.) campaigns, the destruction of water sources was also a high priority.

As much as possible, engineers destroyed bridges with explosives. In cratering roads, they could also use an excavator, the latter proving especially useful in destroying sections of causeway. In their many retreats from Soviet forces, the Germans destroyed railway lines by having a locomotive pull a large cutting device that severed the ties and rendered the track useless. In their withdrawal through northwest Europe, the Germans often resorted to abatis, cutting down trees so their upper branches would intertwine to block roadways.

Explosives could serve another purpose in the form of mines or booby traps. Antitank mines (which could also be set off by trucks and automobiles) could force an enemy to delay an advance in order to clear them. Antipersonnel mines could make enemy infantry wary of treading on more accessible paths and tracks, forcing it along slower avenues of approach. In North Africa, mines perhaps played a more important role than in any other theater, as hard-standing areas suitable for vehicles were rare. One of the more interesting aspects of a withdrawal was the reserved demolition, where explosives were affixed to the target, usually a bridge, but not detonated until an order arrived from higher headquarters or the area was in imminent danger of being overrun.

Reserved demolitions could also be part of a defensive position, where mines, booby traps, and barbed wire also figured prominently. Army engineers carried out those middle tasks that were more complicated than the infantry's trench digging and wiring, but less capital and labor intensive than fortresses or their equivalent, which were often the responsibility of civilian contractors or formations like *Organisation Todt* (q.v.) in German-occupied Europe. Placing minefields, putting up large barbed-wire obstacles, excavating command post bunkers, and the like were the main tasks for army engineers in the defense.

Engineers faced perhaps their greatest challenges when supporting an assault or advance. They had to open roads the enemy had cratered or blocked, prepare airfields, clear minefields and booby traps, and build bridges, all while trying to keep up with the infantry and armored formations they were supporting. Filling craters required building them up from the bottom the same way the road was constructed, or they would simply become large depressions after the first few vehicles crossed. Heavy equipment, the bulldozer being

prominent, was often used in filling craters or clearing roads and airfields.

Mines and booby traps, in spite of the development of the flail tank and similar devices, were usually cleared by hand. First they were located using metal detectors, prodders, and educated guesswork; then they were disarmed or destroyed.

To get tanks and other vehicles across gaps required rafting or bridging equipment. In both cases, engineers relied heavily on prefabricated structures that could be carried to the front on trucks and put together at the chosen site in a few hours. Sometimes such equipment was lacking and engineers had to rely on local resources, usually timber, to get the job done. Rafts were a temporary measure to get the forward elements of one's forces across a river, often in the latter stages of an assault water crossing. Their main advantage lay in the speed with which they could be assembled and put into operation.

It is tempting to concentrate on the complexity of engineering operations in World War II, but infantry and armored operations were no less complicated. The need for large engineering organizations in all the modern armies of that conflict was symptomatic of the ever-growing reliance on the products of industrial production for making war.

William Rawling

Additional Reading

Bell, Frank F., *The 373rd Engineer Service Regiment in World War II* (1947).
Coll, Blanche, et al., *The Corps of Engineers: Troops and Equipment* (1958).
Duggan, Thomas V., *History of the 234th Engineer Combat Battalion* (1947).

Escape and Evasion (E+E)

Escape is when a prisoner breaks away from his captors. Evasion is the methods employed to avoid capture, normally used by military personnel stranded behind enemy lines or by escapees.

During World War II, Axis occupation policies, coupled with their brutal suppression of human rights, the large number of captured Allied prisoners of war (POWs) (7 million by 1945) (*see* Prisoner of War Operations), and the Axis forced labor programs (300,000 in 1939; 7.5 million by September 1944), led to large numbers of individuals trying to flee Axis-held territory.

E+E personnel were assisted by individuals, their friends, families, and later by organized escape lines. Eventually, various governments sponsored these networks because some of the E+E personnel (both civilian and military) in occupied Europe were considered critical war assets. The demands of the Allied air campaign, for example, increased daily.

Trained aircrews needed significant reinforcements, especially when the losses increased between 1942 and 1945, and the Allied air forces lost more than 143,000 aircrew members. Technical changes and the constant introduction of new aircraft and equipment meant constant retraining for aircrews. Successfully returning E+E aircrews did not have to be trained in the basics of airmanship, only on new improvements; a substantial saving in money and especially time.

The initial crisis that forced government sponsorship occurred with the British evacuation of Dunkirk (q.v.) in 1940, where 4,000 Allied troops were left behind to fend for themselves. Dunkirk presented an unforeseen and unprecedented problem: how to rescue thousands of cut-off or trapped troops in occupied territories. Within the British War Office, MI-9 was charged with setting up an organization responsible for establishing an official escape system using all available means, including aircraft pickups, fast patrol boats, and submarines.

On the Continent, meanwhile, the first unofficial E+E organizations were formed by small groups of patriots of all ages and walks of life, without money or outside aid. These groups conducted parties of Allied soldiers and airmen through safe havens and eventually to neutral territory. Unofficial E+E organizations became numerous and continued to expand, and soon were supported by the Allies and the various governments-in-exile.

Eventually, both official and unofficial escape lines formed tentacle-like outstations that kept watch for E+E personnel, escorted and transported them to safe houses, and equipped them with forged papers, disguises, and local clothing. They then moved these people along to other safe houses in the network, which covered a good portion of occupied Europe. Some of the more famous lines were the Pat O'Leary Line, based in Marseille; the Comet Line, in Brussels; and the Trix Line, in Holland. Not all E+E networks were strictly land routes. The Shelburne route among others, employed fast patrol boats, assault craft, fishing boats, and submarines to retrieve E+E personnel from the regions along the Brittany and Mediterranean coastlines. Operation PEGASUS I employed small assault boats to rescue 138 Allied personnel from the vicinity of Arnheim. Others were extracted via Lysander flying boat.

The escape networks and E+E personnel had to deal with a wide range of problems including language differences, penalties for aiding escapees, mass reprisals against civilians, scarcity of foodstuffs and other consumer goods, lack of clothing, lack of transportation, bombing destruction, constantly policed checkpoints and roving patrols, necessary official forms and passes, inquisitive local citizens, and the weather.

Then there were the official Axis security forces. At first, the German military counterespionage service, the *Abwehr* (q.v.), had the responsibility for detecting and destroying escape routes. Later that mission was taken over by the *Gestapo* (q.v.). These and the other official security organizations (gendarmerie, criminal and special police, militia, etc.) numbered more than 3.5 million. A significant number of local nationals also volunteered (collaborated) to assist the Axis powers. Tens of thousands of frightened civilians provided information to these organizations.

The E+E networks faced other problems as well. Quite often there was a lack of coordination and cooperation between all the various escape agencies and networks. They lacked trained security screening personnel and procedures. Even if the escapees were successful in reaching neutral territory, such as Spain or Switzerland, they stood a good chance of being interned there.

The entire E+E effort provided Allied forces with proven methods to facilitate escaping POWs and other Allied personnel. It also forced the employment of enemy manpower (police, military, home and forest guards) into rear-area duties. On 3 June 1943, a mass escape by sixty-five Allied POWs caused more than 50,000 Axis soldiers, police, and home guards to spend up to two weeks rounding up the escapees.

At the *Stalag Luft III* POW camp during a twenty-two month period, Allied POWs attempted 262 escapes via some 100 tunnels. Returning POWs often collected and brought with them information on enemy troop movements, bomb damage assessment, rail schedules, locations of enemy units, order of battle, life in the occupied territories, weather, and data on other POWs. The entire E+E effort also gave a tremendous morale lift to Allied soldiers and aircrews. By 1943, Allied air force officials believed that if a crewman landed by parachute in occupied territory, he had a 50 percent chance of getting home safely.

The total number of individuals who attempted E+E in Europe is unknown, but it is believed to exceed 200,000. Successful escapes by civilians and military personnel possibly number

E

85,000, with 30,000 reaching Spain, 50,000 Sweden, 5,000 the Soviet Union. Perhaps 120,000 attempted escapes failed. Among Allied military personnel, 26,923 successful escapes were made (4,477 officers and 22,446 enlisted).

German and Italian POWs also made numerous escape attempts, but many were sent to America for internment, which made escape and return to Europe far more difficult. In the words of *Gefreiter* Fritz Schweigler held at Camp Gordon, Georgia, "If we did escape from the camp, where could we go?" The fairly humane treatment Axis POWs received from their Allied captors also reduced much of the incentive to escape. Quite often they were fed better as POWs than by their own armies.

No formal Axis escape networks existed until after the war, when ODESSA (q.v.) was set up to arrange the escape from Germany of SS (q.v.) personnel from prosecution for war crimes. Similar networks, such as *Kameradenwerk* and *Die Spinne,* as well as those actually set up by Allied intelligence agencies for various political reasons, and even by the Catholic Church, helped many avoid war crimes prosecution after the war.

Some German and Austrian priests were fanatically nationalistic and sympathized with former Nazi officials. After the war, with the Allies seeking former SS members for war crimes, these priests helped establish escape routes for many SS members from the western zones of occupation to the Middle East and South America. Their aim was to preserve a nationalist entity to continue the struggle against the anti-Christian, communist regimes in eastern Europe. Also, some Catholics viewed the holocaust as a crusade against the Jewish "Christ killers" and, therefore, felt justification in aiding the instruments of that crusade.

The E+E operations and their results led to the development of specialized equipment, such as escape kits, flexible hacksaws, silk maps, compasses, and beacon transmitters. The World War II experience also resulted in the search and rescue operational methods used in modern combat.

Overall, E+E operations provided the Allies with significant intelligence information, higher morale, and vital manpower resources. But the cost to the operators of the E+E networks remains unknown. One source suggests that for every successful escapee to reach neutral territory, one French, Belgian, or Dutch helper lost his or her life.

Alexander Molnar, Jr.

Additional Reading

Foot, M.R., and J.M. Langley, *MI-9 Escape and Evasion 1939–1945* (1979).

Heaps, Leo, *The Evaders: The Story of the Most Annoying Mass Escape of World War II* (1976).

F

Fire Support Operations

Artillery had proven itself the dominant arm in all armies in World War I. By 1918, the starting point for operational planning was an assessment of the number of guns available, and logistic planning was essentially a matter of the supply of artillery ammunition. From this, the breadth and depth of an offensive was determined by what was virtually a mathematical calculation. The advent of the tank affected the ability to break through enemy defenses, but the fundamental and dominant role of artillery was scarcely affected. The tank was generally no more than a means of supporting assault troops.

Given the relatively static World War I battlefield, the mobility of guns was less important than the weight of shells they could fire, and these were delivered with ever-greater accuracy as the science of predicted indirect fire (that is, fire delivered to an unseen target without adjustment of the fall of shot) was developed in ideal conditions. The ability to mass guns and fire them at targets beyond their immediate line of sight was matched by the centralizing of command and control. Guns would typically fire lengthy, deliberate fire plans programmed at high level to a set timetable. These were of necessity inflexible since radio communications, the means to alter them to reflect the fortunes of battle, had yet to be mastered. The 1918 victory eventually went to the Allies, thanks largely to the overwhelming artillery firepower that they could deploy.

Between the wars, the Germans evolved the doctrine of *Blitzkrieg* (q.v.), which sought to avoid an expensive war of attrition, and a style of operation was planned that did not risk a set-piece positional battle with the outcome determined by weight of fire. Operations were intended to remain fluid and not to slow down lest firepower be concentrated in defense. Shock action by armor would replace the massive artillery bombardment as the primary means of breakthrough, and where this was in danger of being thwarted, aircraft controlled from the ground by radio would deliver the heavy, long-range firepower to smash resistance.

In this scenario there was little role for artillery, if only because it could not keep up with offensive operations, and in the German Army, artillery was consigned once more to the merely supporting role it had before 1914. In Britain in the 1920s, the need for artillery to support the tank, which Britain had pioneered, was recognized and the first self-propelled field gun, the Birch gun, was developed. But by the 1930s, while the British artillery was motorized, the idea that artillery could support tanks in mobile operations was abandoned. The Soviets, on the other hand, were constructing an artillery arm on a massive scale, replicating the structures developed during World War I in the West. For them, all offensive and defensive operations relied on massive artillery support.

The primary challenge for all armies in the opening years of World War II was to provide fire support in mobile armored operations. Until 1942, the German formula generally proved triumphant but not decisive, allowing the Allies to devise new organizations and tactics to defeat them. In defense, the tank was the primary threat. In the early years of the war, antitank guns proved wanting against the improved armor of newer models of tanks. In the German, Soviet, and British armies, field guns were pressed into service as antitank guns in the direct-fire role, often at the expense of other tasks.

Prior to 1942, the British struggled to find a way to check the Germans. They experimented in North Africa (q.v.) with decentralizing artillery command and control and conducting small-scale mobile operations. Then, in a complete reversal of approach, they concentrated their resources in "islands" of positional defense.

By 1942, they believed they had found a formula for successful operations based largely on a new handling of artillery. The introduction of large quantities of new, modern antitank guns meant that in the defense, field artillery could concentrate on destroying enemy artillery prior to an attack, thus protecting friendly antitank guns from destruction. Once enemy tanks were halted, field guns could destroy opposing antitank guns in preliminary bombardments characterized by massive concentrations on sequential targets to ensure that resources were used most efficiently. This opened the way for friendly tanks to break through, supported by infantry behind a moving barrage of fire.

Just as in World War I, command and control became increasingly centralized at a higher level, so the widespread use of effective radios meant that fire could be switched rapidly from one target to another. Thus an entire fire plan could be modified instantly by a single observer as the battle developed. These tactics would not have been possible without technical developments in target location, survey, and ballistic computation, based on the foundations laid down in World War I, which made predicted fire even more accurate.

What artillery could not do was hit critical headquarters and logistic targets in depth. It had neither the range nor the accuracy to reach into what became a greatly extended battlefield compared to that of World War I. The Allies, however, enjoyed an increasingly favorable air situation as the war progressed. As the balance turned against Germany, they used their airpower not merely in the close support of leading troops, but with medium and heavy bombers, for massive bombardments of enemy positions in depth as part of deliberate fire plans coordinated with artillery. Thus, in many operations from 1943 onward in Tunisia, Italy, and France, Allied airpower took over the role that might otherwise have fallen to heavy artillery. This accounts for the relative paucity of such equipment in Allied forces, compared to the latter years of World War I.

From 1942, Allied successes in the west were based on a superior artillery logistic capability and carefully planned tactics, which owed much to the lessons of World War I artillery fire planning, brought up to date with significant advances in command and control and equipment mobility.

For the Germans, the problem was rather different. The *Wehrmacht* was designed to win a war quickly without reliance on massive artillery fire support. By 1941, it was clear that tanks did need artillery support, that towed equipment could not provide it, and that aircraft could not be relied upon as a substitute for artillery firepower in close support. At the same time, the balance of logistic capability was tilting against Germany. Despite this, the Germans produced some excellent pieces and increasingly mounted these on self-propelled vehicles, not merely to keep pace with tanks in the offense but to react swiftly in the defense across thinly manned fronts.

The Germans decentralized their artillery command and control with the emphasis on divisional-level operations. They never managed to produce enough guns to build artillery formations at higher levels to match those of the Soviets. Under growing pressure on all fronts, German artillery tactics became increasingly decentralized, while their opponents achieved a decisive advantage through concentrating assets under higher levels of command.

In Italy in 1943–1944, German guns were often dispersed and grouped with small detachments of armor and infantry, achieving small tactical successes but at the expense of the possibility of major triumphs. The need for firepower was not ignored, rather it became logistically unattainable. Cheaper expedients such as rocket launchers and mortars increasingly took the place of guns, to the extent that in the Normandy (q.v.) campaign, they caused more Allied casualties than did guns.

When the Germans did, with great effort, achieve a significant concentration of guns, they could not provide them with sufficient ammunition and fuel to exploit it. For example, when the Germans massed a large number of guns for their Ardennes offensive (q.v.) of December 1944, the majority were unable to move from their original positions and were severely rationed in ammunition expenditure.

For the Soviets, the challenge became one of generating a decisive superiority in firepower. Tactics amounted to the calculation of relative strengths, the marshaling of masses of guns and ammunition, the careful plotting of targets, and the destruction of the enemy, simultaneously across a decisive sector and, if possible, in depth along the chosen axis. There was little sophistication or flexibility in Soviet fire planning, but the organization and scale of forces deployed made this deficiency virtually irrelevant.

The U.S. Army's experience was in many respects similar to that of its Allies. As the war progressed, the American logistic advantage became increasingly decisive. This was matched by a greater emphasis on the corps-level of command, joint operations, and airpower. The latter were

A British 25-pounder firing at night during the massive preparation that opened the British attack at El Alamein, 23 October 1942. (IWM E 18470)

especially evident in the Far East where amphibious operations and jungle terrain militated against the massing of artillery to support the sort of mobile armored operations experienced in the western theaters.

Equally, artillery in the Far East was not obliged to focus on antitank operations. Where firepower was required, it was usually preferable to use the more mobile and heavier punch of aircraft and naval guns to destroy enemy positions. As a result, U.S. forces developed the most sophisticated amphibious fire support techniques yet seen.

In conclusion, it is ironic that Allied fire support tactics in World War II owed more to the lessons of artillery from World War I than from the ideas of mobile armored warfare developed between the wars.

Jonathan B.A. Bailey

Additional Reading

Bailey, J.B.A., *Field Artillery and Firepower* (1989).
Bidwell, Shelford, *Artillery Tactics 1939–45* (1976).
Hogg, Ian V., *The Guns: 1939–45* (1969).
Zabecki, David T., *Steel Wind: Colonel Georg Bruchmüller and the Birth of Modern Artillery* (1994).

Führer Directives

German strategy (q.v.) in World War II was as much a reflection of Adolf Hitler's (q.v.) vision as it was Germany's strategic requirements. Nothing depicts that better than the *Führer* Directives *(Weisungen)* he issued during the war. Intended to guide the military execution of his policies, they also revealed Germany's evolving strategic situation and Hitler's changing relationship with his military. Those issued during the war's early years when Germany had the initiative were numbered, assigned general goals and guidelines, and generally were optimistic in tone. As Germany's fortunes waned, the directives became more detailed, reactive, and pessimistic. They no longer were numbered after 1943 and they took on an almost surreal quality and tone after 1944—as if Hitler felt the need to reassure the recipients that all was well despite contrary evidence. As such, his directives stand out as a barometer of Germany's fortunes and strategic direction throughout the war.

In many ways, World War II was Hitler's war. He wanted it, he prepared for it, and he orchestrated events to bring it about. More importantly, he started it, albeit a few years earlier than he originally intended. The attack on Poland (q.v.) represented the culmination of Hitler's efforts to bring all aspects of Germany's policy and strategic decision making into his hands. The German General Staff (q.v.) resisted all of his earlier expansionist efforts, from the reoccupation of the Saarland (q.v.) to the seizure of Czechoslovakia (*see* Bohemia and Moravia). Yet Hitler won over his opposition via a combination of flattery, astute political maneuvering, scandal mongering, and outright intimidation.

The *Führer* Directives

Number	Subject	Date
1	Plan of Attack on Poland (Case WHITE)	31 Aug 1939
2	Hostilities in the West	3 Sep 1939
3	Transfer of Forces from Poland to the West	9 Sep 1939
4	Conclusion of the War in Poland	25 Sep 1939
5	The Partition of Poland	30 Sep 1939
6	Plans for Offensive in the West	9 Oct 1939
7	Preparations for Attack in the West	18 Oct 1939
8	Additional Preparations for Attack in the West	20 Nov 1939
9	Instructions for Warfare Against the Enemy's Economy	29 Nov 1939
10	Concentration of Forces for Case YELLOW	19 Jan 1940
10a	The Invasion of Denmark and Norway	1 Mar 1940
11	The Offensive in the West	14 May 1940
12	Prosecution of the Attack in the West	18 May 1940
13	Next Objective in the West	24 May 1940
14	Continuation of the Offensive	8 June 1940
15	Advance on the Loire River	14 Jun 1940
16	Preparations for Invading Britain	16 Jul 1940
17	The Conduct of Air and Sea Warfare Against Britain	1 Aug 1940
18	Plans to Take Gibraltar Through Spain	12 Nov 1940
19	The Occupation of Vichy France	10 Dec 1940
20	War in the Balkans	13 Dec 1940
21	BARBAROSSA: Assault on the Soviet Union	18 Dec 1940
22	German Support to Mediterranean Campaign	11 Jan 1941
23	Operations Against the British Economy	6 Feb 1941
24	Cooperation with Japan	5 Mar 1941
25	Plans for Invading Yugoslavia	27 Mar 1941
26	Cooperation with the Balkan Allies	3 Apr 1941
27	Plans for Invading Greece	4 Apr 1941
28	MERCURY: The Invasion of Crete	25 Apr 1941
29	Proposed Military Government of Greece	17 May 1941
30	German Intervention in Iraq	23 May 1941
31	German Military Organization in the Balkans	9 Jun 1941
32	Plans for After the Victory in the Soviet Union	11 Jun 1941
32a	Supplement to Directive 32: Reduction of the Army After the Victory over the Soviet Union	14 Jul 1941
33	Continuation of the War in the East	19 Jul 1941
33a	Supplemental Instructions to Directive 33	23 Jul 1941
34	Change of Strategy in the Soviet Union	30 Jul 1941
34a	Supplemental Instructions to Directive 34	12 Aug 1941
35	Army Group Center Placed on the Defensive	6 Sep 1941
36	Objectives in the Arctic Theater	22 Sep 1941
37	Reorganization of Forces in the Arctic Theater	10 Oct 1941
38	The Air War in the Mediterranean	2 Dec 1941
39	Defense on the Eastern Front	8 Dec 1941
40	Operational Instructions for Coastal Defense	23 Mar 1942
41	The Spring Offensive in the Soviet Union	5 Apr 1942
42	Invasion of Vichy France and the Iberian Peninsula	29 May 1942
43	Continuation of Operations in the Crimean Peninsula	11 Jul 1942
44	Operations in Northern Finland	21 Jul 1942
45	Continuation of the Caucasus Offensive	23 Jul 1942

(continued next page)

By 1938, Hitler had firmly established himself as the dominant authority over Germany's policy and war-making machinery. The *Oberkommando der Wehrmacht* (OKW) (q.v.) replaced the general staff as the preeminent war-planning organization, and its reins rested clearly in Hitler's hands. Hitler's directives were drafted by Field Marshal Wilhelm Keitel (q.v.), chief of the OKW staff, for Hitler's approval. They represented Hitler's personal guidance to the planning staffs and the military commanders in executing the campaigns and operations that would achieve his latest strategic objective, such as defeating France or the Soviet Union.

It is clear that Hitler originally intended his directives to be general long-term orders of a prophetic nature. As such, they also represented the ideological foundation for the operations they guided and their wartime issuance indicated the Nazis' ideological victory over the pragmatic military strategists of the general staff. It also is apparent that Hitler's personal belief in his control over the forces of history dictated the system by which the directives were issued and recorded. They were numbered whenever he felt he was dictating the course of events and wanted an easily accountable method of recalling them.

Hitler's first directives were actually issued before the war and even before he had fully established his authority over the military. The first came in 1933 and pertained to armed forces preparations in the event the League of Nations imposed sanctions against the Nazi regime. Others related to precautions ordered in the event that war broke out in reaction to Hitler's foreign policy initiatives, such as the occupation of the Saarland or the formal repudiation of the Versailles Treaty (q.v.).

The first numbered directive was issued on 11

March 1938 for the occupation of Austria (*see Anschluss*). Directive 2 followed later that same day, ordering the actual invasion of the country. A second "Directive 1" was issued for the occupation of Memel, ordering precautions to be taken should Poland go to war over that action. The plan for the invasion of Czechoslovakia was covered by an unnumbered directive, followed by several more unnumbered ones and Directive 4, all of which concerned the invasion of Czechoslovakia. The bloodless occupation of that country rendered continuation of the series unnecessary.

The series was resumed when Hitler turned his attention to Poland in August 1939. The first directive ordering the armed forces to be prepared to invade Poland was not numbered, but when Poland showed signs of going to war over Danzig (q.v.), Hitler felt that another moment in history was coming and began a new system of numbering. This time, however, the crisis never ended, so the series continued until Hitler dropped the numbering system after Directive 51, which ordered the strengthening of defenses in the west.

This last numbered directive, issued on 3 November 1943, is noteworthy for its length in comparison to its predecessors and for its demanding tone. Hitler knew instinctively that he had lost the strategic initiative. The crushing German defeats at Stalingrad and Kursk (qq.v.) made it clear his armies were stuck for another frozen winter in the Soviet Union. The Allies were ashore in Italy and building up their forces in Great Britain for a cross-channel attack. Believing himself to be another Frederick the Great, Hitler felt that he alone could guide Germany's forces in this, its hour of need. Directive 51 froze all forces in their present locations and prohibited any redeployments without Hitler's personal approval. Since he was no longer able to dominate events, the serialization of the directives lost its purpose. Although he did not call his subsequent orders directives, but rather "special instructions," they nonetheless were treated the same by his subordinates.

Hitler continued to issue these orders but the old confidence was gone. Moreover, they lost their unity, both in purpose and in organization. Their tone and content became threatening as he began to view the war as one of survival, not just for Germany but for National Socialism as well. Trusting only his own judgment, many of these later orders reminded commanders to send all their orders, even tactical ones, to him so he would have time to intervene if the commanders made a mistake. Thus, Hitler exacerbated Germany's already difficult strategic situation through his "stand fast" and "attack at all costs" orders. He continued that line almost to the very end. His last supplemental order was issued on 15 April 1945, as the Soviet armies prepared to launch their final drive on Berlin (q.v.).

Hitler's directives and later supplemental orders provide a broad outline of Germany's strategy in the war. They show in a crude but clear fashion that he directed Germany's war effort from its early successes to its ultimate failure. They show how he envisaged that war and directed Germany through all of its stages. They also reveal his changing personality and altering mental state, particularly in the war's final year. In that respect, perhaps, the *Führer* Directives are central to understanding what went wrong with the German war effort.

Carl O. Schuster

Additional Reading

Hubatsch, Walther (ed.), *Hitler's Weisungen für die Kriegführung, 1939–1945* (1983).
Irving, David, *Hitler's War* (1977).
———, *The Path to War* (1972).
Trevor-Roper, Hugh R. (ed.), *Blitzkrieg to Defeat: Hitler's War Directives 1939–1945* (1964).

I

Incendiary Bombing

Firebombing was a strategic bombing technique intended to destroy industrial machinery and large-area targets quickly. Unless hit directly, industrial machinery is difficult to knock out with high explosive (HE) bombs. Incendiary bombs, whether they hit the target directly or not, heat precision machinery enough to ruin its accuracy. On this premise, most industrial targets were attacked by both sides with a bomb mix of approximately 25 percent incendiaries.

Allied firebombing of large-area targets in Europe employed a mix of high explosive bombs and incendiaries. The HE-heavy bomb mix in the leading aircraft would block city streets with rubble, break water mains, and raise clouds of dust. Following aircraft dropped increasingly larger numbers of incendiaries. Firefighters could not pass the blocked streets. With water mains broken, the fires could not be fought. The incendiaries set the airborne dust on fire. The result was tremendous firestorms with cyclonic winds, tremendous drafts, and extremely high temperatures.

Although Warsaw, Rotterdam, and Leningrad (qq.v.) had large fires started by *Luftwaffe* raids, these were mostly secondary fires. Germany did use firebombing techniques on London, Coventry (q.v.), Birmingham, and Manchester, but they never gained the capacity the Allies had for large-scale incendiary raids. Against large urban targets such as Dresden, Cologne, Hamburg, and Berlin (qq.v.), the Allies used firebombing techniques with tremendous, yet terrible success.

European firebombing techniques were adapted by the Americans in the Pacific theater, where they were effective in destroying widely scattered Japanese industrial targets.

John D. Beatty

Additional Reading

Bushby, John, *Gunner's Moon: A Memoir of the RAF Night Assault on Germany* (1972).
Frankland, Noble, *Bomber Offensive: The Devastation of Europe* (1969).

Infantry Tactics

The dictionary defines infantry as, "The branch of an army made up of units trained to fight on foot." The infantry refers to itself as "The Queen of Battle." Despite the appearance of large-scale mechanization in World War II, infantry dominated the battlefield, as it has since the dawn of human history, and as it is likely to do well into the high-tech future. The nineteenth-century German military theorist, Carl von Clausewitz, wrote, "The end for which a soldier is recruited, clothed, armed, and trained, the whole object of his sleeping, eating, drinking, and marching is simply that he should fight at the right place and the right time." Clausewitz was talking primarily about the infantryman.

In some respects, the World War II infantryman was little different than his counterpart in the Roman legions 2,000 years earlier; in other respects, they were vastly different. In both eras, the individual infantryman lived and fought on the ground, day or night, in all weather, on all types of terrain. In both eras he fought with hand-held weapons, and his main function was to close with and destroy the enemy. The World War II infantryman, however, had far greater destructive power, reach, and staying power than his ancient counterpart. A World War II infantry company was a more lethal organization than an entire infantry regiment of Napoleon's era. This was a function of not only the reach and rate of fire of modern weapons, but also of communications technology that could put the fire of an entire divisional artillery or air force fighter-bombers at the fingertips of the company commander.

During World War II the American infantryman was the best equipped. The German infantryman was arguably the best led. The Soviet infantryman was probably the toughest and most inured to physical hardship. The question of who had the best infantrymen overall is open to debate, but the consistent battlefield performance of three groups in particular stand in the forefront—the Australians, the New Zealanders, and the Gurkhas (q.v.).

The two basic elements of applied combat power are firepower and maneuver. Firepower provides the destructive force essential in defeating an enemy's ability and will to fight. Maneuver is the movement of combat forces to gain positional advantage, usually in order to deliver, or to threaten to deliver, fire by direct or indirect means. On the modern battlefield firepower is delivered by artillery and aircraft. The tank, while considered a maneuver weapon, really combines both fire and maneuver. The infantry is primarily a maneuver force.

Like the tactics of the other arms of service, infantry tactics are very much a function of the technology and culture of the times. Most armies entered World War I advocating highly mobile and aggressive tactical doctrines. When the fighting actually started in 1914, the infantrymen in the front lines encountered previously unimaginable levels of firepower delivered by the then new technologies of quick firing artillery, the magazine-fed rifle, and above all, the machine gun. Unable to survive on the surface of the earth, the troops started digging. The result was the stagnation and horror of trench warfare. Throughout World War I, tactical planners struggled with various methods of breaking the deadlock and restoring mobility to the battlefield. They were on the verge of achieving the solution when the war ended in 1918.

Contrary to widely held belief, most armies did not spend the period between the two world wars training and organizing for a repetition of trench warfare. Most professional soldiers concluded fairly early that the positional warfare had been an anomaly. In general, however, advancements in military technology and doctrine were retarded by social, political, and economic factors, including a worldwide revulsion with all things military. This particularly was true in France, which had suffered the most of all the Western Allies.

The Western armies ended World War I with massive supplies of weapons and equipment. This also impeded technological advancements because political leaders insisted for economic reasons that existing stocks be consumed before new weapons were developed and purchased. Germany was different in this respect. Ironically, the provisions of the Versailles Treaty (q.v.) worked to Germany's long-range military advantage. Deprived of all its armaments in 1919, Germany was forced to make a fresh start, technologically and doctrinally.

Many of the technologies that had their primitive origins in World War I matured in the interwar years and radically altered the face of combat in World War II. The modern concept of combined arms operations was born in World War I. Combined arms—the British term is "all arms"—operations are those where the effects of infantry, artillery, armor, air support, engineers, and the like are all brought to bear on an objective in a coordinated and synchronized manner that produces a multiplier effect greater than the sum of its parts. Each of the combat arms has particular strengths and weaknesses. In a combined arms effort, the strength of one arm is used to protect the weakness of another. Tanks, for example, are vulnerable to light infantry antitank weapons like the bazooka or *Panzerfaust* (qq.v.). By combining infantry with tanks, the infantry can protect the tanks from enemy infantry. The tanks, in turn, give their own infantry added firepower and mobility.

One of the greatest technological differences between World War I and War II was motorization. During World War I the prime source of motive power was the horse, as it had been for thousands of years. During World War II the American and the British armies were completely motorized, while the Soviet and the German armies were partially motorized, but continued to use horse transport on a large scale.

The need for infantry to keep up with tanks in fast-moving situations resulted in the development of first motorized infantry, and then mechanized—or armored—infantry. Motorized infantry was transported to the scene of the fight in trucks. Mechanized infantry was transported in various forms of armored personnel carriers (q.v.) that usually were tracked or half-tracked vehicles. The armored personnel carriers usually carried machine guns, which provided the infantry with additional firepower. Both motorized and mechanized infantry dismounted from their vehicles to fight.

Infantry, in its mobile role as *Panzergrenadiers,* played a key role within the German concept of *Blitzkrieg* (q.v.). If at all possible, German commanders avoided fixed frontal attacks, which are always the most costly form of combat. The Germans preferred to attack around an enemy's flanks using the operational principles articulated by Count Helmut von Moltke in the late nineteenth century—*umfassen, einschliessen, vernichten*—fix, encircle, destroy. When a deliberate attack was unavoidable, the Germans usually chose to conduct a penetration with conventional infantry supported closely by engineers, artillery, and tactical air support.

Once a penetration or flanking movement succeeded, German tank forces exploited by encircling the enemy, from two directions in a pincer, if possible. After the jaws of the pincer closed, the attacking force formed two concentric rings, one facing inward to hold and destroy the trapped enemy force, the other facing outward to prevent any relief efforts. The Germans called this tactic a *Kesselschlacht*—a cauldron battle—and used it very successfully in many of the early battles in Russia in the summer of 1941. Later, on the western front, the Germans themselves were the victims of *Kesselschlacht* at Falaise and the Ruhr pocket (qq.v.).

Another characteristic of German operations was the concept of *Auftragstaktik*—mission tactics. Contrary to the popular notion of the rigid German mentality, German military leaders down to the most junior officers and even NCOs were encouraged to be flexible and innovative in their approach to accomplishing their assigned missions. German operations orders generally described what subordinate units had to accomplish and when they had to accomplish it. The question of how to accomplish the task was left to the subordinate leaders, who were supposed to understand the overall intentions of their commanders at least two levels up. The result was that German units, even large units like divisions, could react quickly to changes in the tactical situation, often acting on verbal orders only.

For all its operational and tactical sophistication, the German Army eventually was worn down and overcome by the requirements of a two-front war. In order to maintain their massive armies in the field, the Germans were forced to progressively decrease training times and even to commit training units to combat during emergencies. The decline in infantry quality meant that infantry units survived for shorter periods in combat, and thus had to be replaced at a faster rate. It was a vicious circle. In response, German commanders tended to rely more heavily on firepower as the war progressed.

The fighting in Russia was more infantry intensive than in North Africa (q.v.) or on the western front. After the initial successes of 1941, the *Blitzkrieg* concept began to fail the Germans because their *Panzer* forces and, even more so, the *Luftwaffe,* became increasingly thinly spread over the vast spaces in the east. In such an environment, the advantage slowly shifted to the Soviets, with their vast numbers of infantry divisions. While some battles like Kursk (q.v.) were classic clashes of armor, the set-piece urban fight for Stalingrad (q.v.) was dominated by the foot soldier.

During the early part of the war, the Soviets' main problem in conducting an attack was to break through the German defenses. The Soviet solution was to put the majority of their combat power up front. In a typical division attack, up to nineteen of the division's twenty-seven infantry companies would form the front line for a deliberate attack. Later in the war, as the Germans were being pushed back, their defenses developed much greater depth. The Soviet response was to echelon their attacks.

Infantrymen do not fight as individuals; they fight as part of a team, and each member of that team performs a specialized function. The basic infantry tactical unit is a squad—or section—usually consisting of eight to fifteen soldiers commanded by a junior ranking NCO. The squad is the "largest unit that a leader can command by direct personal influence on the individual soldier." The organization and structure of these units usually reflected the tactical beliefs of the larger army.

At the start of World War II, the German infantry section consisted of ten men organized into two groups. The four-man machine gun group (including two ammunition bearers) was armed with the excellent MG-34 light machine gun. The machine gun group was supported by a five-man rifle group. The two groups advanced by fire and movement, with their actions coordinated and synchronized by the section leader, an *Obergefreiter* (corporal). The Germans placed particular emphasis on selecting and training their section leaders. By 1943, manpower shortages forced the Germans to reduce the infantry section to nine men.

The organization of the French infantry squad *(groupe de combat)* was superficially similar to the German section. Its manner of operating, however, reflected the overwhelming defensive mentality of the French Army. Whereas the Germans believed that fire and movement complemented each other, the French believed that movement was only possible once superiority of fire was established. The *groupe* consisted of twelve men,

I

subdivided into a six-man light machine gun/ automatic rifle team, and a five-man rifle team. Rather than being capable of individual maneuver and providing mutual support to each other, the two teams were linked rigidly to the machine gun. The function of each member of the group was defined in terms of the gun—fire it, move it, feed it, protect it.

The Soviets and the British had the smallest infantry squads. The Soviet section consisted of nine men and a light machine gun. Following organizational reforms in 1936, the British infantry section consisted of a corporal, seven men, and the Czech-designed Bren gun as the automatic weapon. The Bren, which was much lighter than the Lewis gun it replaced, facilitated an increased emphasis on fire and movement within the British infantry.

The U.S. Army did not become involved in ground combat operations until late 1942. The American infantryman, armed with the outstanding semiautomatic M-1 rifle, could produce a far greater rate of fire than either his Axis enemies, or his Canadian and British allies, all of whom generally were armed with bolt-action rifles. The twelve-man American infantry squad was organized into three teams. The squad leader (a sergeant) usually traveled with the two-man scout (Able) team. Once an enemy objective was located, the squad leader ordered the four-man fire (Baker) team, which was armed with a Browning automatic rifle (BAR), to lay down a base of fire. The five-man maneuver (Charlie) team then attacked the objective in short rushes. In practice, the unbalanced teams, and especially the low rate of fire of the BAR, made the American infantry squad particularly vulnerable to casualties. After World War II, American infantry squads were reconfigured into two evenly balanced teams.

Many popular beliefs about the infantry and infantrymen are false. Infantrymen, for example, are not the intellectual underclass of an army. Modern infantry combat has become so technical, so fast-paced, and so lethal, that only the quick-witted, physically fit, and highly trained can survive it. Nor did the infantry suffer the highest casualty rates in World War II. Combat aircrews and above all, submarine crews had higher casualty rates. Few would argue, however, that the "poor bloody infantry"—as the British called them—led the hardest lives in the war. Regardless of the overall scheme of maneuver of the larger unit, at the level of the individual infantry soldier, every attack is a frontal attack.

David T. Zabecki

Additional Reading

Bidwell, Shelford, and Dominick Graham, *Firepower: British Army Weapons and Theories of War, 1904–1945* (1982).

Clausewitz, Carl von, *On War,* edited and translated by Michael Howard and Peter Paret (1976).

Doubler, Michael, *Closing with the Enemy: How GIs Fought the War in Europe, 1944–1945* (1996)

English, John A., *On Infantry* (1981).

Gajkowski, Matthew, *German Squad Tactics in World War II* (1995).

House, Jonathan M., *Toward Combined Arms Warfare: A Survey of 20th Century Tactics, Doctrine, and Organization* (1984).

Liddell Hart, Basil H., *The Future of Infantry* (1933).

Marshall, S.L.A., *Men Against Fire* (1947).

United States War Department, *FM 100–5 Field Service Regulations, Operations* (15 June 1944).

Wynne, Graeme C., *If Germany Attacks* (1940).

Intelligence Operations

Intelligence operations involve the collection, analysis, and interpretation of information about an enemy for the purpose of predicting his capabilities, vulnerabilities, and intentions. There is a difference between information and intelligence. Information is unevaluated material of every description and from every source, including direct observation, communications, reports, photography, and even rumors. The information may be true or false, accurate or inaccurate, confirmed or unconfirmed, important or unimportant, or positive or negative. Intelligence is the product that results from the process of subjecting various elements of information to collection, analysis, and interpretation.

Most Western intelligence organizations categorize intelligence by the source of the original information. During World War II, there were three primary categories. Human intelligence (HUMINT) came from human sources, which included informants, agents, reconnaissance patrols, and the interrogation of POWs (*see* Prisoner of War Operations). Communications intelligence (COMINT) came from monitoring the enemy's communications transmissions. Often the most important transmissions were encoded, which required code breaking, or cryptography (q.v.). The most successful example in World War II was the Allies' ULTRA (q.v.) effort. In some cases, good intelligence could be gleaned from monitoring the enemy's lower-level uncoded (also called "clear") transmissions. The third major source of intelligence was from photographic images (PHOTINT), primarily aerial photography.

Intelligence operations can encompass the entire scope of a nation's activities and capabilities: political, social, economic, and military. Military intelligence operations are further divided into two broad areas: strategic and combat. Strategic intelligence, which is long-term in its focus, is required for the formulation of policy and military plans at the national and international levels. Combat, or tactical intelligence, is more immediate. Its primary objective is to minimize uncertainty by providing tactical and operational commanders with knowledge of the terrain, weather, and the enemy. Intelligence on enemy strength and organization is also called order of battle.

At the national level, intelligence organizations engage in three broad categories of activities: intelligence, counterintelligence (q.v.), and covert operations. During World War II, each of the major participants had various organizations that conducted one or more of these activities, often with a fair degree of overlap.

As Britain entered the war, MI-5 (q.v.) was responsible for counterintelligence, while MI-6 (q.v.) handled intelligence. As the war progressed, covert operations behind enemy lines came under the Special Operations Executive (SOE) (q.v.), while propaganda and other political actions came under the Political Warfare Executive (q.v.). In the United States, the Federal Bureau of Investigation was responsible for counterintelligence, while the newly formed Office of Strategic Services (OSS) (q.v.) handled foreign intelligence and covert operations.

In Germany, the *Gestapo* (q.v.), a police organization, was responsible for all internal state security, while the *Abwehr* (q.v.), a military organization, was supposed to handle all military intelligence. The Nazi Party, however, also had its own security service, the *Sicherheitsdienst* (q.v.), which was a rival organization to the *Abwehr*.

In the Soviet Union, the NKVD (q.v.)—the forerunner of the KGB—was at first responsible for internal security only. Later it acquired a foreign intelligence mission, which overlapped with Soviet military intelligence, the GRU. The Soviet structure was even further complicated by the establishment of *Smersh* (q.v.), whose mission was to detect and eliminate spies and other "counterrevolutionaries," mostly behind enemy lines. In both the Soviet Union and Germany, the overlapping and competing intelligence organizations, combined with the internal paranoia typical of totalitarian states (they spent almost as much time collecting information on each other as on the enemy) seriously compromised the quality of the intelligence product.

Military intelligence has existed in one form or another since biblical times. It began to take on a formal structure after the Congress of Vienna in 1815, when military, naval, and later air attachés were routinely assigned to embassies. These attachés served the dual functions of being legitimate information gatherers, as well as conduits for any information the host country wished to channel. Most countries did not start to develop military intelligence organizations in their armies until the twentieth century. This development coincided with the evolution of military staffs.

During World War I, France's general staff structure, with intelligence in the *Deuxième Bureau*, provided the prototype for U.S. staffs. As a result, during World War II (and to the present day), intelligence officers on battalion and brigade staffs are known as the S-2. At division level and above, they are known as the G-2. The Germans organized things a little differently, with operations, intelligence, and supply being subsections of their first staff section.

During World War I, the United States had to build up a military intelligence organization almost from scratch. As soon as the war ended, it dismantled it with as much speed. In the years just before World War II, military intelligence was neither a separate branch nor a recognized specialty, and assignment as a G-2 or S-2 was something most officers avoided. By the end of World War II, the army established and fielded an effective Military Intelligence Service, Counterintelligence Corps, and Signals Intelligence Service.

Reconnaissance (also called recce) is one of the primary sources of combat information on the enemy and terrain. Ground recce units usually worked ahead of their parent units to maintain contact with the enemy by working through gaps in the lines, and around the enemy's flanks and rear. Air recce assets extended the zone covered by ground reconnaissance to give greater depth to the combat commander. Aerial photography was a primary air recce technique in World War II.

Germany entered the war with supremacy in all three intelligence categories: HUMINT, COMINT, and PHOTINT. As early as 1939, all German divisions had a recce battalion. The German mobile divisions each had six recce aircraft assigned. German combat intelligence was organized around the simple principle of getting the information to the commander on the spot as soon as possible. Within one hour after a recce aircraft landed from a mission, the division commander had the photo negatives. When General Heinz Guderian (q.v.) reached the Meuse River in 1940, he had information on the French troop dispositions in less than three hours. His French counterpart had information more than twenty-four hours old.

One of the reasons German combat intelligence could produce results with such speed was that they ignored the use of stereoscopic photography. While monoscopic photography is much faster than stereoscopic, it also is very susceptible to camouflage and deception. The Western Allies concentrated on stereoscopic aerial photography throughout the war. In the long run, this paid dividends, especially after they acquired air superiority. The Soviets had an air recce doctrine very similar to the Germans, except that they too used stereoscopic photography. Both the Germans and the Western Allies used night aerial photography.

German air recce was very effective, but it also was very costly. Divisional recce aircraft suffered high loss rates, which mounted steadily as the Germans lost control of the skies. By 1942, the *Luftwaffe* consolidated all recce aircraft and the army lost control. By the time of the battle for Stalingrad (q.v.), German divisional commanders had no recce air support at all.

In the area of communications intelligence, Poland had one of the most effective operations in the 1920s and 1930s. The initial Polish work on the German codes and the Enigma (q.v.) machine ultimately led to Western successes with ULTRA (q.v.). Britain's "Y" Service (*see* Signals Intelligence) gleaned intelligence from monitoring open circuit transmissions and commercial radio broadcasts. Germany too had very effective communications intelligence. Even before the start of the war, the German Navy's *B-Dienst* (Naval Intercept Service) had broken the codes of most of its neighbors. The *Luftwaffe* concentrated on the air and diplomatic codes of potential opponents. The Germans, however, made one fatal mistake; they used the same basic code for all intelligence reporting. Once that code was broken, German intelligence operations became almost an open book.

At the tactical level, most countries during the war introduced signals intelligence units. By the time World War II ended, for example, each of the fourteen U.S. corps under General Dwight D. Eisenhower's (q.v.) command was supported by its own signals service company, which included intercept, direction finding, and analytic sections. At the army group and field army levels, cryptologic support came from signals radio intelligence companies supported by analytical detachments from the theater signals intelligence service.

At the tactical level, the Germans and the Soviets had a preference for direct observation, and both sides mounted a massive HUMINT effort on the eastern front. HUMINT, however, can be a double-edged sword. While it is one of the most direct sources of information, it is also the most susceptible to deception techniques. For that reason, HUMINT generally is considered unreliable, and intelligence analysts generally require corroborating information from multiple sources before they will give it serious consideration. Sometimes a too cautious approach can produce negative results. In December 1944, U.S. intelligence officer Colonel Benjamin Dickson concluded, based on his interrogation of POWs, that the Germans were preparing a massive offensive through the Ardennes (q.v.). Unfortunately, his report was rejected.

Carl O. Schuster
David T. Zabecki

Additional Reading

Bennett, Ralph, *Behind the Battle: Intelligence in the War with Germany, 1939–1945* (1994).

Finnegan, John P., *Military Intelligence: A Picture History* (1985).

Hinsley, F.H., and Alan Stripp, *The Codebreakers* (1993).

Jones, R.V., *The Wizard War: British Scientific Intelligence, 1939–1945* (1978).

Kahn, David, *Hitler's Spies* (1979).

Payne, Lawrence, *German Military Intelligence* (1970).

Van der Rhoer, Edward, *Deadly Magic: An Account of Communications Intelligence in World War II* (1978).

Wark, W., *The Ultimate Enemy* (1985).

West, Nigel, *The Secret War* (1993).

K

Kammhuber Line

The Kammhuber Line, named after *Luftwaffe* General Josef Kammhuber (q.v.), was a German version of the British CHAIN HOME (q.v.). It was a defense system composed of radars, searchlights, antiaircraft *Flak* artillery, and night fighters. It consisted of nearly 750 stations stretching from Denmark to Ostend, Belgium, and around the principal German industrial centers. There were so many stations that the Allies were unable to knock enough of them out to effectively penetrate the line. Construction began in June 1940, and by March 1941, a line was completed from Denmark to the Rhine Estuary in the Netherlands. The Kammhuber Line accounted for 75 percent of Allied bomber losses over Europe.

The line was divided into "boxes," areas roughly twenty miles square under the direction of a control center. Each "box" had a *Freya* long-range search radar used for air surveillance and early warning detection of incoming bombers. The *Freyas* were not very accurate, particularly in determining altitude. Thus, two short-range (twenty miles) *Würzburg* radars also were used: one to track the bombers and the other to guide the fighter aircraft—usually Bf-110Gs or later Ju-88Gs. Radar information was fed to the control centers that would then plot the movement of the bombers and fighters.

Each "box" had searchlights and *Flak* batteries. Since most Allied bombing missions flew at 15,000 feet or lower, Flak rounds were fuzed to explode at 15,000. Also, by setting the fuzes for that altitude, the *Flak* artillerymen avoided hitting their own fighters, which flew at much higher altitudes.

Behind the line of coastal radars was a second defensive line of *Henaja* sectors, arrayed roughly around the borders of Germany itself. Each sixty-mile-long *Henaja* sector was covered by a search-light regiment. The final lines of defense were called *Konaja* zones, established around major German cities and industrial areas. The *Konaja* zones were defended by both *Flak* artillery and night fighters. In addition to being a *Konaja* zone, Berlin also was defended by its own *Henaja* sector, northwest and west of the city.

The Kammhuber Line had one flaw. Each "box" was assigned only one fighter. The control center also was limited in controlling the fighter interceptors. This was sufficient defense when the Royal Air Force launched relatively few bombers. To overcome this beginning in 1942, the Allies concentrated their raids through a single "box" and launched massive attacks to saturate the German defenses. Since it took one fighter roughly ten minutes to intercept each bomber, a massive attack would result in relatively few Allied losses. To counter this Allied tactic, Kammhuber established additional "boxes" in depth to continuously intercept bombers from the North Sea and English Channel coast to deep inside Europe.

In late July 1943, the Allies started using "window," or "chaff," small strips of tinfoil to give false radar images. When the tinfoil spread out, it gave a strong echo return on German radar screens. Fighters were dispatched to chase these false images. By the time fighter pilots realized the ruse, the bombers were hundreds of miles away. "Window" cut Allied bomber losses in half.

Kammhuber wanted to couple his defensive tactics with an offensive technique of his own. He called for intruder operations against British airfields to attack bombers when they were most vulnerable, during take-offs and landings. In 1940 and 1941, his Ju-88 fighters inflicted two-thirds of British bomber losses using this tactic. In October 1941, Chancellor Adolf Hitler (q.v.) ordered Kammhuber to halt the intruder missions and use the fighters to defend German skies only. This proved disastrous for the *Luftwaffe*. Once the Allied bombers were airborne and in tight formation, they defended much more effectively against German fighter attacks. This is only one of many examples of Hitler's mismanagement of his armed forces to the benefit of the Allies.

William H. Van Husen

Additional Reading
Churchill, Winston S., *The Hinge of Fate* (1950).
Deighton, Len, *Blood, Tears, and Folly: An Objective Look at World War II* (1993).
Hastings, Max, *Bomber Command* (1979).

L

Logistics Operations

The word *logistics* comes from the Greek word *logistikos,* which means calculating. The first known use of the term was by the Romans to refer to a military administrative official known as *Logista.* That usage contained an implied skill in the science of mathematical computation.

The first apparent use of the term *logistics* as part of the modern science of war was by French writer A. H. Jomini in his 1838 book, *The Art of War.* Jomini's military science was based on a trinity of "strategy, ground tactics, and logistics." Jomini defined logistics as "the practical art of moving armies," which involved "providing for the successive arrival of convoys of supplies" and "establishing and organizing lines of supply."

Today, as in World War II, logistics provides the foundation for combat power. It can be thought of as the bridge connecting a nation's economy to that nation's war-fighting forces. Logistics is the process of planning and executing the movement and sustainment of operating forces in the execution of a military strategy and operations. Logistics includes the design and development, acquisition, storage, movement, distribution, maintenance, and evacuation of materiel. It also includes the movement, feeding, equipping, sheltering, and evacuation of personnel. The relative combat power a military force can bring to bear against an enemy is a direct function of a nation's ability to deliver forces and materiel to the decisive point at the decisive time.

Logistics is often viewed as the unpopular stepchild of the more glamorous game of military strategy and operations. Military strategy and its analysis possess the attractive and stimulating qualities of an intellectual contest. Logistics is seen more as the pedestrian exercise of providing the means to carry out a given strategy. But one can-

not be separated from the other. The U.S. Army Historical Series volume on logistics states, "To the question of whether there can be a strategic decision distinct from logistical decision, the answer is no . . ." Strategy, not unlike politics, is often reduced to the art of the possible. Without an adequate logistical strategy, a sound operational policy is impossible.

Early in World War II, Britain and the United States decided to press for the early defeat of Germany while fighting a holding action against Japan. The European war would receive priority in all logistical matters. This policy was easier stated than implemented. The decision was unpopular with the American public because of anti-Japanese feelings and it was difficult to implement because of widespread disagreement with the policy. This debate was never fully resolved.

American logistic planners had to operate without strategic plans approved far enough in advance to provide a solid basis for production programs. They found it necessary to estimate what the strategic plans would be and plan accordingly. Troops often were mobilized long before weapons and supplies were available, and on occasion, supplies were produced that had no immediate use. This is often the price that necessity pays to expediency when a great nation goes to war as unprepared as the United States was in 1941.

The objective was to outproduce the enemy through a production program based not on strategic plans, but rather on producing an arsenal of weapons to equip army, navy, and air force units to implement unknown future strategic plans. This thinking led to the munitions program of 1940 and to President Franklin D. Roosevelt's plan to make the United States the "Arsenal of Democracy" (qq.v.). Undersecretary of War Robert Patterson wrote a memorandum to the effect that the total amount of production was more important than was the purpose it might ultimately serve. In the same vein, Roosevelt issued a directive requiring that an estimate of equipment and supplies needed should "exceed by an appropriate amount that available to our potential enemies."

Not surprising, overproduction, underproduction, and misproduction occurred. But the system functioned to the extent that the United States and its allies ultimately possessed a quantitative, if not always a qualitative, superiority in almost every category of weapons and supplies needed to wage war. The Western Allies controlled the oceans of the world and had access to resources on a global scale, while the Axis powers had to fight a war with increasingly limited resources. The outcome of the war hinged on this factor.

The United States provided the Allied coalition with more than 50 percent of its armaments. This included 35 percent of the arms used against Germany, and 86 percent of those used to defeat Japan. In addition, America mobilized 16 million military personnel and equipped and supplied more than five million troops fighting thousands of miles from home in every operational theater except eastern Europe.

American production, almost three times greater before the war than its nearest rival, doubled during the war, while standards of living also increased. The traditional choice between "guns and butter" was never faced by Americans. This was accomplished without making any fundamental changes in economic theory or structure. By 1943, the United States was producing more materials than the three Axis powers combined.

The voracious maw of war consumed all sorts of materials at an incredible rate. In one month alone, June 1940, $43 million worth of planes, tanks, guns, and shells were rushed to Britain, which stood alone against the military might of Nazi Germany. Lacking cash reserves to pay for such quantities of arms, Britain was unable to fulfill its war needs under the existing "cash and carry" American policy. A new method for financing the war had to be found.

Roosevelt had long searched for a way to aid Britain without demanding cash payment. In one of his "fireside chat" radio broadcasts, he reasoned that in case of a fire, a person would naturally lend his garden hose to his neighbor, with the understanding that it would be returned after the fire had been extinguished—but without first trying to sell it to him. This was the idea of the Lend-Lease (q.v.) program that Congress approved in March 1941. The law authorized the president to manufacture,

transfer, sell, lease, or exchange any war material to "the government of any country whose defense the President deemed vital for the defense of the United States."

Congress immediately authorized an initial appropriation of $7 billion of Lend-Lease funds. By the end of the war, an astronomical sum of $50 billion was spent on a program that British prime minister Winston S. Churchill (q.v.) called "an inspiring act of faith" and "the most unsordid act in history."

Often overlooked was an aspect of Allied cooperation known as "reverse Lend-Lease." This involved the practice of procuring local facilities and supplies for U.S. forces that did not involve cash transactions. The general purchasing boards organized in Britain and Australia became the model for such programs around the world. In Australia and New Zealand, for example, American forces obtained most of their food and some other supplies under this agreement. While the total amount of reverse Lend-Lease never approached the quantity of materiel flowing from America, it did amount to almost $8 billion, or approximately one-sixth of total Lend-Lease aid.

In 1941, after the United States entered the war, the Allies faced almost unimaginable obstacles. Japan, a formidable enemy with access to natural resources in China, Manchuria, southeast Asia, and much of the western Pacific, had been converting its industrial production toward war since 1928. After the devastation of the U.S. Pacific Fleet at Pearl Harbor, the Japanese enjoyed a substantial naval and a two-to-one air superiority over the United States in the Pacific. Supplying the war in the Pacific was a formidable task and is mentioned here only because of the impact it had on keeping to the established priority of defeating Germany first.

Pushing the Japanese back to their homeland involved tremendous logistical problems for the United States because of the distances involved. Often, thousands of miles separated one island supply base from another. For all of the dangers of submarine attacks, however, sea supply routes were safer than land routes. One need only compare the U.S. logistical successes in the Pacific with initial Allied supply problems in France, and with the German problems supplying their forces over land in Russia to realize the truth of this observation.

After the sea voyage was completed, supplies were taken ashore and moved up to where the troops were located. Once a bridgehead was secured, resupplying was needed quickly and on a regular basis. However, until a major port could be taken, all supplies and follow-on units were funneled across the beach. The potential for a large logjam was obvious. The Americans learned at such Pacific landings as Guadalcanal in 1942 that specialized beach groups, joint army-navy units, had to be trained to police and organize the landing beach, evacuate the sick and wounded, and ensure that incoming supplies, equipment, and replacement personnel kept moving inland.

The radical improvement in mechanization of weapons and equipment for World War II created enormous logistical problems. In North Africa (q.v.) and the eastern front, the attacker was invariably forced to halt and wait for supplies to catch up. Likewise, the Allies ran out of many types of supplies, particularly fuel, during the drive across France. In some areas of rough terrain, supplies had to be airdropped.

The more sophisticated the army, both in equipment and in living standards, the more elaborate its logistical system had to be. Thus, the Western Allies required many more men to support the soldier at the front line than did the Soviets or Japanese.

To meet these needs, the British worked out a resupply system known as "through running." Maintaining a force in the field as large as a corps required a flexible system. It had to be as simple as possible while employing economy of effort and good cooperation among all involved agencies. Logistic planners needed foresight and anticipation to support the commander's objectives.

To accomplish this, supplies were brought forward in relays. First-line transport was provided by the actual combat battalions. They went back to supply and fuel points to pick up supplies that were dumped there by second-line transport organized at division levels. Corps (third-line) transport brought stocks forward to each division. Usually railroads could not be used because they either did not exist, as in Africa or parts of Russia, or were destroyed, as in Italy and France. Hence additional transport (fourth-line) was organized. This included a large number of trucks, for example the American Red Ball Express (q.v.), to bring supplies from ports to the corps area. This was an enormous task since a typical Allied division needed 650 tons of supplies daily.

Before the war, Germany was the second-greatest industrial power in the world. By 1941, Germany had conquered the natural resources and manpower of most of Europe, and the *Wehrmacht* was hammering at the gates of Moscow. The highly developed German railways and *Autobahns* facilitated the movement of armies and supplies, and

German U-boats were threatening to sever supply links between the United States and Europe.

German industrial genius produced a wide range of war supplies including many synthetics and motor fuels. German military industrialization, however, was carried out in breadth rather than in depth. Due mainly to overconfidence, production of tanks, planes, self-propelled guns, trucks, and other war materials ran well below Germany's industrial capacity until 1943.

In 1940, 1941, and 1942, British production of war materials exceeded that of Germany. The Germans reached full-scale production for war only after the United States entered the war, and after the German defeat at Stalingrad (q.v.). Then, even with heavy Allied bombing, production dramatically increased until 1944.

During the Russian campaign, the *Wehrmacht* never had sufficient logistical resources. This was especially true of reserve stocks and means of transport. The Soviet wide-gauged rails were only one of many problems. The German *Eisenbahntruppen* (railroad units) were not sufficiently numerous, well-equipped, or adequately trained for the task at hand. The railways were not flexible enough to support *Blitzkrieg* (q.v.) warfare.

The war in the Soviet Union (q.v.) was the greatest military operation in history. The quantity of supplies required staggers the imagination. The *Wehrmacht* was never adequately supplied. German successes were owed mainly to extremely brave troops and superb commanders willing to suffer appalling hardships and make do with whatever supplies they had or could find. Contrary to German Chancellor Adolf Hitler's (q.v.) expectations, German efficiency and National Socialist élan, without adequate material preparation, proved inadequate to the task.

The natural resources of the Soviet Union were enormous and potential military production was great. In 1940, the Soviets produced 30 million tons of steel, 18 million tons of cast iron, 166 million tons of coal, 31 million tons of oil, and 50 million kilowatts of electricity. Sufficient armaments, however, were not being produced to meet the wartime needs of the Red Army. In 1940, the Soviet Union produced a few hundred aircraft compared to more than 10,000 by Germany. Production of tanks in 1940 was better, nearly 3,000, but much less than needed to sustain protracted war. Soviet Premier Josef Stalin (q.v.) did not order full mobilization of war production until after the German invasion.

Soviet wartime production can be divided into two phases. In 1941, great effort was exerted evacuating factories to the east, resulting in low levels of production. "General Winter," and German supply inadequacies saved the Soviet Union from what appeared to be certain defeat. In the second phase beginning in 1942, evacuations continued but production steadily increased. Soviet factories produced more than 25,000 aircraft, 24,000 tanks, and 30,000 field guns in 1942, compared to a German production of 15,000, 9,000, and 12,000, respectively. By 1944, Soviet production figures rose to 40,000 aircraft, 29,000 tanks, and 122,000 guns annually, at a point when German production began to taper off.

The Soviets won the battle of logistics against their more highly industrialized enemy. But the immense size and climate of the Soviet Union saved the Soviets from being smashed by the German *Blitzkrieg* as Poland and France had been. Instead, the *Wehrmacht* suffered its greatest defeats on the steppes of Russia; 75 percent of Germany's effective strength was on the eastern front at all times, and 75 percent of its casualties were suffered there. British historian A.J.P Taylor maintained that the Soviets alone could have defeated Germany, difficult though it would have been, because of their superior manpower and natural resources.

The Western Allies won the battle of logistics, and therefore the war, thanks in large measure to the industrial productivity of the United States. None of the Axis powers could afford to fight a protracted war, primarily because of their lack of resources—and their leaders knew it. They had to win quickly or ultimately lose any war. Yet both Germany and Japan allowed their early successes to lead to overconfidence, which delayed full eco-

nomic mobilization for war. When they did finally mobilize their industrial capacity, it was a case of too little and too late.

America's greatest contribution to victory was its logistical effort. When American troops invaded Western Europe and then defeated the Japanese a half a world away in the Pacific, American logistical support reached its ultimate level of accomplishment. In landing such great numbers of men on hostile shores from 3,000 to 6,000 miles from home and more than 10,000 miles from each other, with their own supplies and equipment arriving from home in their own ships, the American military accomplished what no other force in history had ever done. Nothing in the history of the world before or since can be compared to it. This accomplishment may never be equaled. World War II, in fact, may well be one of a kind. One can not imagine ever seeing its like again.

Paul J. Ros

Additional Reading

Jomini, A.H., *The Art of War* (1838).

Richardson, Endora, and Sherman Allan, *Quartermaster Supply in the European Theater of Operations in World War II* (1948).

Ruppenthal, Roland G., *Logistical Support of the Armies* (2 vols.) (1953–58).

United States Army Historical Series, *The Sinew of War: Army Logistics 1775–1953* (1966).

Van Creveld, Martin, *Supplying War: Logistics from Wallenstein to Patton* (1977).

Weeks, Sir Ronald M., *Organization and Equipment for War* (1950).

M

Maginot Line

The French military lacked the experience with a mobile and fluid campaign gained by the Germans in the east and they underestimated the mobile potential of the tank. Believing that France could not endure another bloodbath like that experienced from 1914 through 1918, it placed its hope for a future war in defense. The lesson belatedly learned by the French military in World War I was that the side that remained on the defensive suffered fewer casualties than the side that attacked.

The proposal for a system of border fortifications was prepared by commissions, which began their work in May 1920. While Marshal Ferdinand Foch continued to argue the virtue of the offensive, Marshal Joseph Jacques Joffre, impressed by the performance of the Verdun defenses, argued for a series of fortified zones running from the North Sea to the Alps. Marshal Henri Philippe Pétain (q.v.), who was appointed inspector general of the French army in 1921, prevailed.

Pétain favored a continuous battlefield prepared in advance stretching along the Rhine and then to Thionville on the Moselle. The rest of the frontier he preferred to defend from inside Belgium. In February 1927, War Minister Paul Painlevé won parliamentary authorization for the first three of the planned twenty sections of defended front. Parliamentary approval was gained for the remaining monumental expense on 28 December 1929 while André Maginot (q.v.) was minister of war.

The Maginot project, which eventually cost $1 billion, stretched along the Franco-German frontier area from Longwy, near the juncture of the French, Belgian, and Luxembourgian borders to the Swiss border near Basel. The strength and depth of the defensive network was not uniform. Two strongly developed sections or "fortified re-gions" covered potential invasion routes: the approach to Metz and Nancy from the Moselle north of Thionville to Longuyon, and the path to the plains of lower Alsace between Bitche and the Rhine. These two major fortified regions were linked by fortified points that complemented and strengthened the barrier of the Rhine River, the Rhine Canal, and the Vosges Mountains. Interval casements between Teting and the Saar were begun only in 1938 and remained uncompleted in 1940.

At the frontier were fortified barracks, *maisons fortes*. Their purpose was to provide warning of a surprise attack and to slow the enemy's advance. The fortified regions, which lay a kilometer or two to the rear, consisted of three fortified belts. The front position consisted of antitank emplacements, barbed-wire entanglements, antitank and antipersonnel mines, pillboxes, and reinforced barracks. The second position was formed by a deep antitank ditch, more barbed wire, and artillery casements.

The casements, protected by three meters of concrete, contained antitank guns, machine guns, and 50mm mortars. Each casement was manned by a crew of twelve to thirty, housed in subterranean quarters. The spacing of the casements varied according to the terrain. Some were built back to back to cover two sides of a hill. Others were separated by 1,800 meters. The final belt consisted of forts at intervals of five to eight kilometers. Their conceptualization drew heavily on the fortifications constructed by the Germans from the 1890s at Mutzig in the Vosges and around Metz and Thionville.

The forts, connected by tunnels to fortified entrance blocks two to three kilometers to the rear, were designed to operate independent of external support for three months. Twenty to ninety meters beneath the surface were barracks and canteens;

stores of food, water, fuel, and ammunition; power stations; compressors to provide ventilation and protect the defenders against poison gas by keeping the interior air pressure higher than that outside; and electric trains for transportation. There were series of armored doors covered by firing ports, and seventeen-ton automatic doors were designed to seal off magazines from the rest of the fort in case of an explosion. Elevators connected various levels of the complex structures.

The biggest forts possessed fifteen to eighteen concrete blocks armed with retractable armored turrets mounting armament from 37mm to 155mm, and manned by up to 1,200 troops. Each fortress consisted of two independent sections connected by deep tunnels. Each was able to bring fire to bear on its neighbor and its defending casements. To prevent infiltration from above, "interval troops" were positioned above to provide mobile defense to threatened forts.

The system, impressive as it was, had flaws and negative repercussions. The thin one-and-one-half-meter concrete of the rear walls of the blocks proved vulnerable to German units outflanking the line. The periscopes on the turrets presented a vulnerable weak point endangering those inside. At its most developed points, the defensive line was only twelve miles deep. Its fatal flaw was its limited length. It did not extend along the 250-mile frontier with Belgium. Cost and the developed nature of France's northern frontier were considerations. More important, however, was the desire not to alienate France's ally, Belgium, or, after Belgium's retreat again into neutrality in 1937, not to write it off.

The French, who saw northern France fought over, occupied, and devastated in World War I, wished to see the fighting in a future conflict occur inside Belgium and intended to counter the Germans with a swift advance into that country. They also expected the Belgians to develop their own defensive system to complement the Maginot Line. Nevertheless, after 1937, perhaps for the sake of morale, several thousand small bunkers were constructed between Dunkirk and Longuyon. Many had been fitted with embrasure shields by 1940. Due to the enormous expense, which far exceeded original estimates, plus the burdensome cost of maintenance, the Maginot system denuded the rest of the French military and left it strapped by fiscal restraint and internal opposition. The Maginot Line has also been blamed for infecting France and the French military with a false sense of security.

When the German attack in the west came on 10 May 1940, the Maginot Line could have played a decisive role by threatening the flank of the Germans preparing their assault through the Ardennes. A French light cavalry division did move out from the Metz fortified region, but when it ran into German armored units moving through Luxembourg, it withdrew.

The Germans on 12 May pressed the Maginot Line advanced posts in the Longwy salient to counter a potential flank thrust, but the move had the added advantage of confirming General Maurice Gustave Gamelin's (q.v.) belief that a German attack against the line was in the offing. On 13 May, after silencing most of the French bunkers on the west bank of the Meuse with *Stuka* dive bombers and artillery, General Heinz Guderian's (q.v.) men were able to force the crossing and outflank the Maginot Line. The potential effectiveness of the line was demonstrated by the temporary success of the imperfectly developed defensive works to the west of the Montmedy bridgehead, La Ferte (o 505). Though they lacked emplacement laced artillery, they held until their interval troops were withdrawn to defend Paris.

On 14 June, two days after the remaining interval troops were ordered from the line proper, the Germans attacked between Saaralbe and St Avold. The next day, they attacked across the Rhine at three points. The Rhine defenses proved feeble and the attackers pushed through Colmar and into the Vosges within two days. The withdrawal of the interval troops was fatal, but the major forts proved their worth by holding out until the capitulation of France and the cease-fire in the early morning of 25 June.

Bernard A. Coo

Additional Reading

Horne, Alistair, *To Lose a Battle: France 1940* (1979).
Hughes, Judith M., *To the Maginot Line: The Politics of French Military Preparation in the 1920s* (1971).
Kemp. Anthony, *The Maginot Line: Myth and Reality* (1981).

Master Bomber Technique

First used by Guy Gibson (q.v.) of Number 61 Squadron during the low altitude raid of 16–1 May 1943 against the German Möhne, Ede Sorpe, and Schwelme Dams, master bombers were highly experienced RAF officers orchestrating bombing mission through radio-telephone communications. Arriving early over the target, th master bomber evaluated the accuracy of markers and target indicators dropped by pathfinders. Orbiting the target, he directed the crews of the main force when and where to drop their bombs.

Perfected by Number 5 Group, master bombers first guided Bomber Command at Friedrichshafen on 20–21 June 1943. They accounted for the successful bombing of the rocket facilities at Peenemünde (q.v.) on 17–18 August 1943. The technique was critical in limiting French civilian casualties during Bomber Command's participation in the Transportation Plan (q.v.) in support of the Normandy (q.v.) invasion. Air Commodore Ralph Cochrane of Number 8 Group achieved accuracies in night bombing of less than 300 yards by directing his master bombers to fly at low altitudes, ensuring proper target identification.

In the U.S. Army Air Force, master bombers, usually called lead crews, led bomber formations to their targets and determined the bomb release point. A group's bombardiers served as "toggliers," who released (toggled) their bombs on the lead bombardier's signal. The technique guaranteed tight bombing patterns of special accuracy when the lead bombardier was on target, but eliminated the law of averages when off target, leading to occasional total misses.

Stephen L. McFarland

Additional Reading
Harris, Sir Arthur, *Bomber Offensive* (1947).
Verrier, Anthony, *The Bomber Offensive* (1968).

Medical Support Operations, Allied

Total war on the scale of World War II presents unique challenges for medical personnel. Casualties are not only produced in vast numbers, but new and difficult problems are encountered. In fact, it may be said that from a medical standpoint, wars provide a vast laboratory filled with the victims of disease and injury.

Civilians were injured through air attacks and the bombing of cities. Starvation through sieges and blockades caused problems on a scale never previously imagined. In a sense, every man, woman, and child was potentially in the front line of battle. In addition to the size of the problem, there were new terrors for the medical services. The possibility that noxious gases might be used created the need for study into suitable defensive measures. New and more deadly explosives in aerial bombs gave rise to blast injuries of a nature previously unknown.

In addition to specific problems tackled by the scientific medical community, there were administrative problems caused by total war. Medical organizations had to be reorganized from the simplistic treatment of wounds at the battlefront to a much more complicated comprehensive structure. Facilities for blood transfusion, which were only used to a limited extent in previous wars, were organized on a large scale. The principle of "medical treatment in stages," which has a modern spin-off in the management of civilian natural disasters such as earthquakes and airplane crashes, was perfected.

Because of the high rate of casualties in a limited area over a short time, it became essential to evacuate the wounded. Airplane ambulances, first used as a routine by the Germans during the invasion of Poland, were a new innovation. The process of evacuation, however, endangers the condition of the patient. Hence medical treatment had to be provided in stages. In addition, adequate and clear categorization and sorting according to priority became necessary.

First aid is provided on the battlefield. Then the casualty is taken to a regimental aid post, perhaps by an armored ambulance, to be seen by a doctor. From here, further evacuation by field ambulances to field hospitals at the rear takes place where specialized assistance ensures a high rate of

Two U.S. medics administer blood plasma to a wounded GI on the Normandy beachhead, 6 June 1944. (IWM OWIL 44977)

survival. To ensure continuity, standard treatment regimes were devised. Regardless of the stage, every doctor knew exactly what type of treatment was provided to each casualty at the preceding stage and could continue with the same treatment. This was especially necessary when Allied forces were fighting alongside each other and casualties were often evacuated through each other's medical services.

Medical specialties, such as plastic surgery, were at first overwhelmed by the influx of casualties caused by the awesome firepower of the new weaponry. Burn victims from tanks, and aircrews who escaped from burning airplanes, often by parachute, provided a new challenge to specialists who had to reconstruct from horrific injuries. This was achieved by collecting patients and expertise together in special centers where new techniques of skin grafting were developed. It may be said that modern-day victims of traffic accidents are now benefiting from the experience and expertise derived from battle casualties of World War II.

The stresses of total war were recognized by military psychiatrists, who coined the term "battle shock." Prompt removal of the soldier from the firing line and careful counseling and treatment enabled many to be returned very shortly to full duty. Recognizing and treating these psychiatric casualties in an appropriate manner not only spared the fighting force a loss of trained personnel, but also prevented many from suffering long-term psychiatric problems, as happened in previous wars.

World War II saw many other medical innovations. Sulfonamide was used to treat septic infections, and toward the end of the war, the use of the new antibiotic penicillin transformed the outcome of what had previously been hopeless cases. Compound fractures were treated with the closed plaster method that allowed the patient to be safely evacuated over long distances. The Tobruk splint incorporated a plaster cast with a traction splint and allowed limbs that would previously have been lost to be saved. New forms of litters to carry casualties away from the battlefield were developed, and a variety of vehicles, including the ubiquitous jeep (q.v.) were employed as ambulances. Nevertheless, the casualty lists in World War II were appalling.

Combatant armies strove to squeeze every last drop of fighting strength out of their men. Battle casualties not only depleted the fighting force but were a drain on resources, as the wounded had to be cared for many miles away from the home base. Hospitals and a long, complicated chain of evacuation proved a brake on the efficiency of the fighting machine. It was thus important for army commanders not only to minimize the number of casualties, but also to ensure that they could be evacuated and treated and, where possible, returned to the front line as speedily and efficiently as possible.

Medical help contributed in World War II as never before to improve the fighting efficiency of the troops. Fighting took place around the clock, in extremes of temperature. High altitude flying, fighting in armored vehicles, and parachuting caused types of injury and stresses to the human body not previously experienced. Just as science was used to develop new machines of war, it was also used to develop the means by which these machines could be operated by troops more efficiently and with the minimum number of casualties. When casualties did occur they were evacuated and treated in an efficient, scientific manner the benefits of which we are still reaping.

John D.C. Bennet

Additional Reading

Andrus, Edwin, et al. (eds.), *Advances in Military Medicine* (2 vols.) (1948).
Hutchinson, R.H., *War and Disease* (1946).
Laffin, John, *Surgeons in the Field* (1970).

Medical Support Operations, German

The medical services of the *Wehrmacht* started World War II with high goals. Their objective was to maintain a high standard of medical care based on thorough preparation during peacetime. Despite extraordinary achievements on all fronts during the war, they fell short of that goal. The war cost the *Reich* 3.25 million dead *Wehrmacht* soldiers, and 10 million sick and wounded. During the war the medical services treated a combined total of 52.4 million individual cases.

The army, *Luftwaffe*, and *Kriegsmarine* each had its own medical services. The command of each rested in the hands of an inspector general of the medical service. Each service had its own institutions for training, research, and care. In the case of unexplainable health problems, they had access to teams of specialist consultants.

Every army group was staffed with military hospitals, units for transportation of the sick and wounded, medical parks, and institutions for medical research. The field armies had their own medical units in the rear areas of the combat zone or were allocated to directly support the divisions. The most important service provided by the field armies were the mobile hospitals, which wer equipped for 500 heavily wounded. The field armies also had teams of specialist consultants. Each team consisted of three surgeons and their assistants, plus specialists for internal medicine, psychiatry, hygiene, pathology, and bacteriology.

In preparation for mobile warfare, the German Army developed a chain of transport that led from the point the soldier was wounded to the battalion dressing station; to the main dressing station of the medical company; to the field hospital of the division; to the mobile hospital of the field army; and finally to a reserve hospital back in Germany. The German military developed special vehicles for medical transport, including hospital trains, hospital ships, and medical air transport.

On the front lines, medical attention at the battalion level focused on first aid. On average, each division had two medical companies and one field hospital. The main dressing station of the medical company had two surgical teams whose primary objective was to prepare the wounded for transport. The divisional field hospital sat ten to fifteen kilometers behind the front lines. It had 200 beds, several large surgery rooms, and specialized diagnostic and therapy facilities. It offered services comparable to a good county hospital.

The *Luftwaffe* had a medical service organized similar to the army's, but adapted to the special structure of that service. The doctors at *Luftflotte* (Air Fleet) level had overall management of the system in the field. For major surgery, each *Luftflotte* had a medical standby service with four specialized surgeons.

The *Luftwaffe's* most important innovation was a standby medical flight service. It consisted of five to six Ju-52 transports, each of which could transport twelve wounded on stretchers and four sitting wounded. The *Luftwaffe* also used the Fieseler *Storch* liaison aircraft to transport wounded directly from the front. Each plane could carry two wounded. Regular air transport units were used as well, and in Russia they transported 80 percent of the wounded.

The *Luftwaffe* established an air-sea rescue (q.v.) service to save aircrews who had to ditch in the water. They used He-59s, Do-18s, and Do-24s, as well as different types of ships. The *Luftwaffe's* airborne units also had a medical corps of parachutists, who jumped immediately following the paratroopers.

The medical service of the *Kriegsmarine* had a central office at Kiel on the Baltic Sea, and another at Wilhelmshaven on the North Sea. Combat ships at sea had hospitals and their own doctors, depending on the size of the ship. For the most part, smaller ships carried only medical stores cases containing bandaging material. For the transport of the wounded and sick at sea, the Germans had ten large hospital ships with 600 beds each, twenty-five smaller hospital ships with 350–400 beds each, and thirty-five medical transport ships. Contrary to the requirements of the Geneva Convention, almost half of the German hospital ships and 25 percent of the medical transport ships were sunk during the war through direct enemy action.

On 28 July 1942, the office of chief of the *Wehrmacht* medical service was established in order to increase the efficiency of the different medical services working independently of each other. That office was supposed to combine all the functions of the three medical services, and to allocate the material and manpower available to the different elements of the *Wehrmacht*. Despite the central position of the new office, very little actually changed in the way the three different medical services operated.

From the standpoint of the German medical services, there were three separate phases to World War II, each with its own unique set of problems. During Phase 1, the years of mobile warfare, 1939–1941, the medical services of the army, *Luftwaffe*, and navy managed their tasks fairly well. They followed the quickly moving forces and dealt with the more conventional medical problems. During the 1939 campaign in Poland (q.v.), a combination of disease and combat wounds produced fairly high losses. A dysentery epidemic hit up to 50 percent of the combat troops. The transportation system worked well, however, and the sick and wounded were returned to rear areas very quickly.

During the occupation of Denmark and Norway (q.v.) in April 1940, the medical services had to deal with frostbite, which caused 40 percent of all injuries. In the northern sectors frostbite remained a major problem during the entire war.

During the campaign in France (q.v.) in May 1940, the experiences of the medical services to that point served them well. As in Poland, a similar percentage of the wounds were caused by rifle shot and grenade splinters. Whenever possible, the wounded were cared for on the spot, but transport to the reserve hospitals along the border operated efficiently as well. In occupied France, great attention was given to maintaining the health of the troops, as well as of civilians, in order to prevent epidemics.

The war in North Africa (q.v.) between 1940 and 1943 confronted the German medical services with far bigger problems. In that theater, six times as many soldiers fell sick as were wounded. The tropical climate, the solitude and desolation of the desert, combined with supply and transport problems, had devastating effects on the health of the *Afrika Korps* (q.v.). The tropical heat multiplied the cases of dysentery, diphtheria, and jaundice, as well as a variety of abscesses.

Operations in the Balkans after April 1940 brought unexpected medical problems. Actual combat losses were not all that high—except for German paratroopers at Crete (q.v.)—but the transport of the wounded proved very difficult. The medical services were forced to rely increasingly on aircraft for evacuation. The many swamps in the Macedonian mountains and the humid river valleys were hotbeds for malaria and other fever-causing diseases.

The first few months of the campaign in Russia brought no changes in the operational methods of the German medical services. The winter of 1941–1942, however, with heavy snows and temperatures as low as -57 degrees Celsius, produced many cases of frostbite of all types, and many other complications.

In 1942, the increasing resistance of the Red Army introduced Phase 2 of the war, from a medical standpoint. Large-scale Soviet use of field artillery and rockets led to drastic increases in the number of seriously wounded German soldiers. Transport of the wounded to rear areas became increasingly difficult throughout the winter. The activities of Soviet partisans (q.v.) also played havoc with the medical transport system. When the Soviets started launching their major counteroffensives, many of the German frontline medical elements were lost in the turmoil of retreat.

Increasingly, the system of organizing the wounded for transport based on medical criteria failed, and the death rate on the transports increased. Hygiene became increasingly worse. This led to epidemics of spotted fever and other infectious diseases, including typhus, jaundice, and diphtheria, which put increasingly high demands on German medical services.

The *Luftwaffe* and the navy experienced some medical problems that were unique to them. Aircrew members who were shot down or had flying accidents often suffered from facial or brain wounds. The injuries of sailors at sea were caused by shell fire, aerial bombardment, machine gun fire, torpedo and mine explosions, or burns. Swallowing floating oil caused severe poisoning for shipwrecked sailors.

In an attempt to develop new treatments, some military doctors experimented on concentration camp inmates, testing medications, making transplants, and conducting tests on low air pres-

sure and exposure to low temperature. Many prisoners died as a consequence of these criminal experiments. In 1946 and 1947, the offending medical personnel who could be identified were tried at Nuremberg (*see* American Military Tribunals).

During the period of the German large-scale defensive operations in 1944–1945, the war entered medical Phase 3. The severity of the fighting during the withdrawal in Italy, the fierce struggles in Normandy and northern France (qq.v.), and the collapse of Army Group Center on the eastern front produced a new magnitude of combat losses. The German surgeons were hopelessly overwhelmed. Often they had to operate for two or three days without a break. The number of dead and wounded in this phase of the war was higher than in all the years before.

In the final days of the war, the increasingly improvised structure of the German medical services collapsed. Many medical facilities and resources were lost during the Allied bombing campaign. On 8 May 1945, the medical services of the *Wehrmacht*, like the *Reich* itself, ceased to exist.

Ekkehart Guth

Additional Reading

Fischer, H., *Der deutsche Sanitätsdienst 1921–1945,* 5 vols. (1982).

Guth, Ekkehart (ed.), *Sanitätswesen im Zweiten Weltkrieg* (1990).

Ring, F., *Zur Geschichte der Militärmedizin in Deutschland* (1995).

Medical Support Operations, Soviet

In World War II, the basic operational unit of the Soviet Military Medical Service was the "organic medical platoon." Care of the sick and wounded was based on a system of "treatment and evacuation by stages," first developed by the pioneer surgeon Dr. Nicholas I. Pirogov during the Crimean War in the mid-19th century. The system was based on five stages of treatment: (1) first aid, (2) premedical treatment, (3) preliminary treatment, (4) full medical treatment, and (5) specialized treatment.

First aid was administered on site by either the injured soldier himself or a comrade. Premedical treatment consisted of dressing or redressing wounds, setting splints, and applying tourniquets at the battle site by company medics. In preliminary medical treatment, the sick or wounded soldier was moved to an advanced field hospital a few miles from the battle front where he was treated by regimental medical personnel based on a classification of either immediate or delayed treat-nent. Delayed treatment included both initial examinations for evacuation from the front and treatment of minor wounds for return to duty. Immediate treatment included emergency life-saving procedures, such as amputations. Full medical treatment and specialized medical treatment required further evacuation from the front for more extensive care in permanent hospitals.

During the war, the Soviet Military Medical Service proved relatively effective, despite having many poorly trained personnel and inadequate supplies. Of those Soviet soldiers wounded in battle, an impressive 73 percent returned to duty. This is surprisingly high considering that the more than 8,000 doctors who staffed the advanced field hospitals generally had only a three-month surgical training course. Their problems were compounded by a primitive and over-extended supply system that resulted in extreme shortages in medical supplies. Soviet medical personnel routinely were forced to reuse bandages, X-ray film, and splints, and to resort to the use of herbs for the treatment of infections and diseases. Moss and linden tree shavings often served as a substitute for cotton.

Significantly, women made up the majority of the staff members in the hospitals behind the front lines. Women in the Soviet Military Medical Service included doctors, nurses, technicians, and front-line medics. Their contributions were so significant that immediately after the war, 80 percent of the medical students in the Soviet Union were women.

Karl Van Husen

Additional Reading

Knaus, William A., *Inside Russian Medicine* (1981).

Mine Warfare, Land

Throughout the war, and especially in the last two years, the armed forces of the belligerent nations made extensive use of a variety of antipersonnel weapons, particularly land mines. Often used as effective defensive weapons or to deny the enemy access to additional territory, mines were used largely to cover defensive actions and retreats or as flank protection for an offensive action. Germany was one of the largest users, laying extensive minefields along the Atlantic coast, in North Africa (q.v.), and on the eastern front.

German units carefully placed the mines, usually in front of the primary line of resistance. Engineers used reference points so that their troops could

A combat engineer from the U.S. First Army plants an antitank mine in a Belgian road to impede German movement during the Ardennes Offensive. (IWM EA 47933)

readily identify a minefield, and a variety of signal techniques marked the specific fields. In addition, maps of the fields, showing all necessary technical details, were also prepared for use by the troops.

In order to effectively deploy the mines, engineers laid out minefields in specific patterns, but they also placed mines randomly in sectors where no offensive action was planned. A common pattern was to place two rows of mines in an area of approximately 80 by 105 feet, except in special sectors where more rows were added. Mines were also randomly placed in front of the regular fields, and lanes were left open for patrols or use by assault troops. Most minefields were located adjacent to or on roads, on airfields and railways, and along telegraph lines. Dummy minefields were also laid out to slow enemy advances.

The various armed forces deployed both antitank and antipersonnel mines, placing them carefully to avoid detection. Antitank mines, designed to disable a tank by damaging its tracks but not destroying it, were set for specific pressures, and usually buried two feet below the road. They would detonate only after much traffic had passed and compacted the roadway. Tire prints might be rolled over a mine to disguise it. Antipersonnel mines were placed in ditches or at sites where soldiers would have to step out of their vehicles to check a road sign, or where troops would be advancing against a defensive position.

Among the belligerent forces, a number of different mines were used. The Germans, for example, had about forty types of antitank mines, with *Teller* mines being the most common. Shaped like a dinner plate, several inches thick, about a foot in diameter, and equipped with a pressure-sensitive detonator, the *Teller* mines were filled with TNT and weighed about eighteen pounds. Most other antitank mines contained less explosive and included the *L.Pz.*, *Riegel* R.Mi. 43 *Topfholz* mine, French light antitank mine, and the *Topfholz* mine.

Antipersonnel mines were frequently deployed in conjunction with antitank mines, but the size and explosive charge were much smaller. The larger of the German antipersonnel mines, the S-mines, held upwards of a pound of TNT. Most were detonated by direct pressure or by an attached trip wire. Other mines, such as the S-mine 35 and 44, had igniters that propelled the mine several feet into the air before exploding, spraying shrapnel over a wide area. American GIs dreaded this one and called it the "Bouncing Betty."

Robert G. Waite

Additional Reading
Stiff, Peter, *Taming the Land Mine* (1986).
U.S. War Department, *Handbook on German Military Forces* (reprint of March 1945 edition) (1990).

Mine Warfare, Naval

Hidden, unseen, and inflicting their damage below the waterline, mines were one of the most feared naval weapons of World War II. Worldwide, mines sank 534 ships, accounting for some 1.4 million tons. Only torpedoes sank more ships than mines. The same had held true in World War I, and yet most of the great naval powers entered World War II poorly prepared to deal with mines. Only Germany and the Soviet Union included strong mine countermeasures forces in their fleets, no doubt because of their mutually bad experiences with each others' mines in World War I. They also had the largest mine inventories at war's start.

More significantly, Germany exploited British magnetic mine technology from World War I to produce a magnetic mine of its own. It was a technical surprise that cost the British dearly in the war's early months, but fortunately the Germans had few in stock and their production had a low priority. Moreover, the German Navy commander, Grand Admiral Erich Raeder (q.v.), wasted the opportunity by using them in small numbers instead of concentrating them for a decisive effect.

The British implemented countermeasures by mid-1940 and began to develop advanced mines of their own. Thus began a technological war between the Western Allies' mine and mine-countermeasure experts and their German counterparts. It was a war the Allies eventually won, but not without difficulty or pitfalls.

Although seemingly unglamorous and unexciting, mine warfare was a critical element of naval operations in World War II. By 1943, for example, mine-countermeasure forces constituted nearly 60 percent of the German Navy, while their Allied counterparts had grown to more than 1,100 ships and boats from a force of only two dozen at war's start.

German minefields were the deciding factor in Russo-German naval operations in the Baltic Sea, and a major hazard to Allied shipping. Axis minefields affected Allied planning for every amphibious operation in the war except Operation TORCH in Northwest Africa (q.v.). The Western Allies, on the other hand, used mine warfare to choke German Baltic coastal and river commerce during the war's final years, while Soviet minefields severely inhibited Axis naval operations in Soviet coastal waters. In each instance, the country employing mines found them to be a cost-effective weapon, particularly in circumstances and areas where the opposition had naval supremacy.

Mines can be used either offensively or defensively, with the latter being the most common. Laying defensive minefields around key ports and coastal areas was one of the first naval actions undertaken by nations entering the war. This activity also highlights where a country either felt most vulnerable or most expected an enemy attack. These minefields served to restrict maritime movements within the mined areas to "transit lanes"— areas within the minefields, or between them, in which no mines were present.

Since mines, particularly moored mines, often drift with the tide and current and are indiscriminate in what they destroy, transit lanes had to be maintained by constant clearing. Hiding the locations of the transit lanes from the enemy was a major concern as well, since he might use the land to penetrate the minefield or lay mines within it.

Mines are classified by how they are detonated (contact or influence) or deployed (moored, bottom, or free-floating). Contact mines explode when the target makes contact with the mine. Influence mines detonate as a result of the target's influence on the local environment—either due to the noise it makes (acoustic mines), its effect on local water pressure (pressure mines), or magnetic attraction (magnetic mines). Moored mines are secured by cable to a casing that lies on the bottom. As the name implies, bottom mines rest on the bottom, while free-floating mines float just below the surface. There are three types of free-floating mines: drifting mines drift in the surface current; creeping mines drift at a fixed depth in the subsurface current; and oscillating mines drift at varying depths within the subsurface current.

Each type of mine has its own strengths and weaknesses. All bottom mines, for example, are influence mines and must be laid in waters less than 100 fathoms deep. Otherwise, the targets may not pass close enough to detonate the mines, or they may be too far away for the blast to be effective.

Influence mines were the most difficult to detect and counter. They also drifted less than the other types of mines, and therefore were easier to "reseed" (that is, lay additional mines in the field) and sustain. Moored mines could be either contact or influence and could be laid almost without depth restrictions. They were the easiest to detect and remove, however, and had a tendency to drift with wind and current over time. This made moored minefields more difficult to maintain.

All free-floating mines of World War II were contact mines. Almost totally random weapons, they were rarely laid in fields but generally were employed near enemy harbors or staging areas, where current and tides would preclude their becoming a threat to friendly forces. They are the most difficult mines to defeat and they are such a random hazard that international law requires free-floating mines to sink within eight hours of being laid.

The mine's primary effectiveness is in its psychological impact. Mines can be laid by any platform (ship, plane, or submarine), encountered anywhere, and they are virtually undetectable. Thus, prudent mariners avoid known or suspected minefields. More significantly, mines require more effort to clear than they do to deploy. The best minefields include a mixture of moored and bottom, contact and influence mines, but such fields are exceptionally difficult and dangerous to lay. Whatever that difficulty, however, it is little compared to what is required to clear such a minefield.

Minesweeping was the only available method of clearing mines in World War II. So-called because the original mine-clearing equipment employed a steel cable towed behind the sweeping ship to "sweep" away the mines' mooring cables so they would float to the surface for destruction, minesweeping was a tedious and dangerous task.

The ships that carried the gear were called minesweepers.

The only available mine-countermeasures equipment at war's start was the Oropesa sweep from World War I. Essentially a "wire sweep" that trailed behind the minesweeper, the Oropesa sweep cut cables out to about eighty meters from the sweeper. Each sweeper could conduct two sweeps, one to a side, per sweep run. The lead ship in a sweep formation had to literally "lead" the unit through the minefield. The position was normally rotated since losses among lead ships exceeded 10 percent. The trail ships also faced danger because they had to avoid, as well as destroy, the mines the lead ships released. Unfortunately, the Oropesa gear could only be used against moored mines. The introduction of German bottom magnetic mines in 1939 came as a total surprise and ultimately led to the development of influence sweep gear and degaussing equipment.

The introduction of influence sweep gear in mid-1940 marked the beginning of the technology race in the mine war. The British LL magnetic sweep used alternating electric current, pulsed through a cable towed behind the minesweeper, to detonate magnetic mines at a safe distance by simulating the passage of a ship. The Germans and the British also modified aircraft, the Ju-52 and Wellington bomber respectively, to conduct influence sweeping. Carrying huge electric coils in rings attached to their fuselage and wings, these aircraft cleared suspected minefields by flying over them at altitudes of less than forty meters. Such aircraft swept large areas of influence mines but proved vulnerable to enemy fighter aircraft.

One other countermeasure to magnetic mines that all sides used after 1940 was the elimination of ships' magnetic signatures. Since all metal ships acquire the magnetic signature of the area in which they are built, they need a major deperming or signature removal effort to reduce their magnetic vulnerability. Maintaining that magnetically neutral signature requires the installation of electric cables along the ship's hull. Passing electric current through those cables "degaussed" the ship (that is, prevented its developing a local magnetic signature). Degaussing equipment is a major design feature of all warships to this day.

The Germans got the mine warfare lead again later in 1940 when they introduced acoustic mines. However, Raeder employed them before they were available in large numbers. The British recovered one in August 1940, and one month later put a mechanical acoustic sweep into service that could defeat the German acoustic mine. Unfortunately, sound dampening the equipment on British ships proved too expensive to implement during the war, although they did do it in minesweeping units. The Germans countered by producing a combined acoustic/magnetic mine, but the British soon developed minesweeping tactics to counter it as well.

The Allies were not idle in mine development. Great Britain developed magnetic mines in World War I and employed them again beginning in April 1940. The Germans countered by developing their own magnetic influence sweeps. They also built a specific class of magnetic sweep ships, called *Sperrbrecher*. Equipped with huge electric coils in their bows to project a strong magnetic field ahead of them, these specially reinforced ships had shock-mounted equipment and other damage reducing features to survive mine detonations. The Germans used these units to lead coastal convoys through suspected and likely enemy minefields. They became increasingly important in the war's final two years, as the Western Allies, in particular, laid more and larger minefields.

The Germans began to employ mines with arming delay mechanisms in late 1941. The mines could also be set to arm from six hours to twelve days after they were laid. Hence, a field thought safe after multiple sweeps could suddenly become active. The Germans also introduced refinements in their acoustic mine sensors, lowering the frequencies monitored and targeting specific ship equipment, making it more difficult for Allied sweep gear to simulate. They also began to employ multiple polarity magnetic mines and finally, ship counters to complicate sweep efforts—that is, the mines required a variety of magnetic phenomena to detonate and allowed a preset number of ships to pass by safely before they would detonate. Thus, an area was not truly clear until the entire field had been swept to the maximum "number" that an enemy mine could be set. Moreover, the sweep gear had to simulate a wider variety of magnetic signatures to detonate the mine.

Both the Germans and Western Allies had combined acoustic/magnetic mines with ship counters and variable arming delays in service by late 1943, when the Germans introduced their latest technical innovation, the bottom pressure or "oyster" mine. These mines were detonated by the pressure wave a ship generated as it moved through the water. No minesweeper could simulate that wave since each pressure wave was unique to the size and speed of a ship.

Determined not to repeat Raeder's mistakes from earlier in the war, Grand Admiral Karl Dönitz (q.v.) waited until the Allied Normandy landings (q.v.) to employ oyster mines. By then, however, he lacked the means to lay the mines in the invasion area. Only a handful could be deployed. Had they been laid in the invasion fleet's assembly areas, they would have had a devastating effect. As it was, after some nasty surprises, the Allies easily avoided the few areas where these mines were laid. A few were recovered and the technology incorporated into Allied mines used against the Germans in the war's closing months.

Although the Germans developed the most technologically advanced mines of the European theater, they did not employ mines to their maximum effect. Missing several opportunities to exploit their advantages both early and late in the war, the German mine warfare effort was further weakened because it supported only naval operations. Allied mine warfare operations were more opportunistic and better integrated into their overall war effort. Thus, they employed mines effectively to cut German commerce on the Danube and other river systems critical to the German economy as part of the overall Allied strategy of attacking Germany's infrastructure.

Allied mining was also geared to support the Allied ground campaign in Italy by interdicting German coastal convoys supporting German ground forces. A similar German mining effort directed at the Soviet river and coastal navigation system would have paid huge dividends for the German war effort on that most critical front. As it was, naval mine warfare represents yet another area in which the Germans wasted their initial lead and regained it too late to affect the war.

Carl O. Schuster

Additional Reading
Bekker, Cajus, *Hitler's Naval War* (1974).
Campbell, John, *Naval Weapons of World War II* (1985).
Hartmann, Gregory K., *Weapons That Wait* (1979).
Hough, Richard, *The Longest Battle* (1986).

Mountain Operations

Mountain operations have been carried out since ancient times, but specialized mountain units did not come into their own until World War I, mainly on the Italian front. During World War II, mountain operations were largely support, secondary operations, or independent actions dictated by terrain constraints, again as in the Italian campaign. The

Italian campaign saw the heaviest use of mountain troops, both in the German and Allied armies.

The most common organizational unit was the mountain division, which was more lightly equipped than regular line infantry divisions. This sometimes created problems when mountain units were used in a conventional role. This was especially apparent during the German assault on Tuapse, in the Caucasus (q.v.), in 1942. Two divisions of the XLIV *Jäger Korps* were too lightly armed and equipped to dislodge the Soviet defenders. Mountain troops were brought in but were still unable to break the defenders. This was partly a result of the lack of heavy formations in mountain units.

Mountain formations were used primarily in Italy, the Caucasus region of the Soviet Union, and Yugoslavia and Greece. Although mountain troops served in nearly every theater, these were the areas where they were actually used as mountain troops. The United States, Germany, Soviet Union, Italy, Greece, France, and Poland all used mountain troops varying from battalions to corps-sized units. During the costly German airborne assault on Crete (q.v.), the 5th Mountain Division was flown into captured airfields by Ju-52 transports to support the airborne units. As with modern airborne operations (q.v.), the parachutists seized the objective to be occupied later by other units. Although they were technically not trained for this task, these mountain troops became one of the first air mobile units in history, made possible by the lighter equipment loads they carried.

One of the most famous feats of mountain troops took place on 21 August 1942, during the German advance south to seize the oil fields of the Caucasus. Elements of the German 1st and 4th Mountain Divisions climbed the summit of Mount Elbrus, the highest peak in the Soviet Union. The world knew of their feat by the 23rd of August, but ironically it only enraged Adolf Hitler (q.v.), as it was an accomplishment of no military value.

For the United States, the 10th Mountain Division was the premier mountain unit operating in the difficult and well-defended terrain in Italy. The 10th Mountain Division was often used as a spearhead unit and was instrumental in breaking through the Gothic Line (q.v.) in late 1944. This was accomplished, however, with ample support from heavier artillery and air formations, something the Germans usually lacked. The Germans also fielded mountain divisions in Italy. The French had several divisions of North African troops, mainly Algerians and Moroccans, who were excellent mountain troops because many of them had been mountain-dwellers originally.

The British 52nd Lowland Division, was trained in mountain tactics, as well as in glider operations. There were plans to use them in Operation MARKET-GARDEN (q.v.) in Holland in 1944, but these never materialized.

Timothy Wilson

Additional Reading

Gregory, Barry, *Mountain and Arctic Warfare: From Alexander to Afghanistan* (1989).
Lockwood, Theodore, *Mountaineers* (1950).
Lucas, James, *Alpine Elite: German Mountain Troops of World War II* (1980).

M

N

Naval Gunfire Shore Support

Ship-based gunfire against land targets has existed since ships mounted guns; for various technical reasons, however, it was generally ineffective. During the interwar period, the U.S. Marine Corps investigated amphibious warfare and in 1935 published its *Tentative Manual for Landing Operations.* This manual contains a chapter on naval gunfire support. It was the first formalization of the concept of naval shore bombardment in support of a landing force. The manual was tested during the annual fleet landing exercises held between 1935 and 1940. These exercises pointed out several key needs: a shell designed for shore bombardment; concentrated sustained force on the target; close integration of landing force movement and naval gunfire; and radio-equipped fire control parties with the landing force to direct the ships' fire.

A warship assigned to shore gunfire support faced five problems: (1) a limited load of ammunition; (2) the allocation of the ammunition between the surface battle, antisubmarine operations, and air defense; (3) the firing solution had to consider the movement of the ship; (4) the bombardment ship was restricted to a small area near the target, making it vulnerable to air, surface, and subsurface attack; and (5) the targets ashore generally were hidden and well protected.

The war in Europe started in 1939 with the German battleship *Schleswig-Holstein* firing on the Polish defensive positions at Danzig, and ended in 1945 with the cruiser *Prinz Eugen* covering German troops retreating along the Baltic coast. In between, Soviet warship guns helped defend Leningrad and retake the Crimea (qq.v.), while Allied warship guns made possible the successful assault landings on Northwest Africa, Sicily, Salerno, Anzio, Normandy, southern France (qq.v.) and the Dutch islands guarding the mouth of the Rhine River. Without naval gunfire support there would have been no second front in Europe.

Charles H. Bogart

Additional Reading
Heinl, Robert D., *Naval Gunfire: Scourge of the Beaches* (1954).
McMillian, Ira E., *The Development of Naval Gunfire Support of Amphibious Operations* (1948).

Naval Gunnery

Naval gunnery in World War II was a complex and technologically challenging affair, and it became increasingly more so as the war progressed. All navies had expended extensive research on improving the effectiveness of naval gunnery during the interwar years as they tried to deal with the evolving nature of modern war at sea. World War I had demonstrated that engagement ranges as well as speed and variety of targets had grown to the point that firing over an open sight was as impractical as it was inefficient. By the end of World War I, nearly every major navy employed centralized fire control procedures to concentrate multiple guns against long-range targets.

Between the wars, virtually every aspect of naval gunnery was examined and modified to increase the probability of hitting fast-moving targets at long ranges. In addition to centralized fire control, more accurate rangefinders, improved optics, better gun designs, and more precise ammunition manufacturing techniques were introduced. The navies most advanced in those technologies entered World War II with an advantage. At the start of the war, German gunnery was the best in the European theater, while the Italian and Soviet navies probably had the worst. By 1943, however, the Western Allies began to gain the advantage as their newer and more accurate fire control radars entered service, and Allied crews became more experienced in using radar for gunnery.

Naval gunnery is both technically and tactically demanding. In an engagement between units at sea, both the firing ship and its target are moving in all three axes in a fluid environment. The aiming systems of the respective guns must take these simultaneous movements into account. At longer ranges, it can take from twenty-five to fifty-five seconds for shells to reach their target. A ship moving at 30 knots can travel more than half a mile and almost turn completely around in that time. Hitting such a target requires a combination of accurate gunnery and the selection of a shot pattern that gives a good probability of hitting the target as it maneuvers through the water.

The first step in this process involved gaining an accurate range (distance) and bearing (direction) to the target and accurately determining its course (direction of movement) and speed. Since the firing ship's course and speed were known, accurately measuring the range and bearing of the target gave its course and speed as well. The target's aspect (facing) also could be used to determine its course, but this generally was an impractical technique at long ranges under all but the most ideal conditions. If the target was an aircraft, its angle above the horizon was used in combination with its range to determine its altitude. Regardless of the nature of the target, the accuracy of the measurements determined the accuracy of the gunnery aim point and, in the case of antiaircraft gunnery, the time setting of the shell's fuze to produce a detonation close enough to inflict shrapnel damage.

In 1939, range and bearing measurements were determined visually using optical rangefinders. The bearing was first determined by centering the target in the optical sight's crosshairs. The rangefinder operator then fed the bearing data into a primitive analog computer. Range was determined by focusing the target's image in the sight. Visual rangefinders used two sets of lenses with a known separating distance. Focusing both lenses on the target enabled the analog computer to calculate the range via a trigonometric function. Special "high angle" directors were developed during the war for antiaircraft fire control, because the standard "low angle" directors could not elevate high enough to engage dive bombers. Under ideal conditions, visual rangefinders had a nominal accuracy of 99 percent for range, and plus or minus one degree in bearing and angle above the horizon.

Ideal conditions, however, were rarely realized in combat, and the gunnery process was difficult under the best of conditions. Even the largest ships appear little bigger than a dot on the horizon at ranges beyond 20,000 yards, and the rangefinder operator had to take his readings while both ships were moving up and down with the motion of the ocean, shaking from the blasts of their own guns, making smoke screens to hide behind, and taking evasive action by zig-zagging. It took a highly skilled operator to make accurate measurements under such conditions.

Of the major navies in World War II, Germany expended the most effort in the prewar period, training its operators to a high level by forcing them to take measurements under the worst of conditions. The Italians and the Americans took the opposite approach, training and testing their personnel under ideal conditions. Royal Navy training fell somewhere in-between, which made its gunnery inferior to Germany's but better than the Italians and Americans. The Soviet Navy's operators were the least trained. Combined with the Soviets' other problems, their navy had the worst gunnery of the war.

Radar (q.v.) eliminated most of the problems of visually controlled gunnery. With radar, the target's position could be determined accurately at virtually any range, and under all but the worst of conditions. Radar had a profound impact on naval gunnery, nearly doubling the percentage of hits achieved at ranges beyond 20,000 yards. The effect on gunnery inside that range was even more significant, and it was the Allies' growing superiority in radar that ultimately shifted the balance against the Germans.

Although accurate fire control was the most important element of the gunnery equation, it was not the sole factor. The motion of the firing ships also had a significant effect on accuracy. Most modern ships of the World War II period were equipped with gun stabilization systems to ensure the guns remained level throughout the ship's range of motion. For those ships lacking such systems—including all Soviet ships and the prewar destroyers of most nations—the individual gunner fired when he believed his ship was level. Since all fire control solutions were based on the premise that the gun's elevation in relation to the ship's hull was the same as its angle above the horizon, the accuracy of the gunner's judgment could make a difference of 2,000 to 3,000 yards between a shell's predicted versus its actual splash (surface target) or burst (air target) point. It was that element of the gunnery equation that gave the American and newer British destroyers (those built after

1939) the advantage over their Axis counterparts. The Germans did not install gun stabilization on their destroyers until 1940; and the Italians never did.

The spacing between the individual gun barrels of a turret or gun mount also could affect accuracy, unless an interrupter mechanism was employed to prevent simultaneous firings. If the barrels were placed too closely, the shells had a tendency to collide because of the venturi effect—the phenomena of two high-speed bodies being drawn together when traveling in close proximity along parallel paths. This could be avoided by introducing a brief interval between the firing of the guns to ensure that the shells neither traveled side by side nor through each other's shock wave. This was especially critical in the narrow turrets used by some navies—e.g. the French, Italian, and Soviet—to reduce the beams of their ships in order to increase speed.

The final part of the fire control solution was the predicted behavior of the shell, based on the calculated performance of the guns and ammunition under the environmental conditions at the time of firing. The only elements that could be modified directly by man were the quality of the guns and the quality of the ammunition. The higher the velocity of the shell, the straighter its flight path, the shorter its time of flight, and therefore, the smaller the shot pattern required to hit the target.

The determination of the aim point was as much a function of the speed of the projectile as it was the movements of the target. Thus, a precise knowledge of shell velocity was critical. The rifling inside the barrel had to be consistent, and that consistency had to be maintained—or at least deteriorate at a predictable rate—throughout repetitive firings. Deterioration in the rifling reduced the shell's velocity and the stability of its flight path, which in turn degraded accuracy.

Ammunition quality, particularly with respect to shell shape and propellant powder consistency, also affected accuracy. For that reason, ammunition was manufactured in controlled lots with the weight of the shells and powder measured as precisely as possible so that velocity and flight stability could be predicted under varying climatic and estimated barrel conditions. The condition of the barrel and the predicted flight characteristics of the ammunition were entered into the fire control computer every morning and rechecked before every engagement.

The shell's flight path also was affected by atmospheric conditions. High humidity reduced a shell's velocity and increased its deceleration rate. Increases in air temperature increased shell velocity. The shell's flight path also was influenced by surface wind speed and direction for engagements at all ranges, or by "ballistic" (high altitude) winds for long-range targets—i.e., engagements beyond 16,000 yards for surface targets and above 10,000 feet for airborne targets.

The Coriolus effect—shell versus target movement in relation to the earth's rotation—also had to be taken into account when firing at surface targets more than 20,000 yards away. Ignoring this phenomena could result in an error up to 400 yards or greater at the point of impact.

The final factor was the "art" or tactics of gunnery. Against surface ships, the gunner generally fired at a pattern of overlapping aim points along the target's likely path of movement. Since range was the most variable of the shells' flight characteristics, the gunner generally fired a "walking ladder" pattern, with some rounds landing beyond and others short of the target. He then corrected the two sets of aim points inward toward the target until it was "straddled"—surrounded by close-in shell splashes. Once the target was straddled, the gunner concentrated all fire at the "corrected" aim point. If the target reduced speed or took a sharp turn, it ran the risk of being hit by the "back of the ladder"—the shells fired behind the aim point. If the target accelerated or traveled in a straight line, it hit the "front of the ladder." Many ship commanders tried to defeat this tactic by "chasing salvoes"— steering into the shell splashes—hoping the enemy gunner would not fire at the same aim point twice. Most of the time this evasion technique worked.

Choosing the correct aim points and right "shot pattern" determined the effectiveness of a ship's gunnery. As a general rule, it took a salvo of six guns to achieve a reasonable probability of hitting a high-speed maneuvering ship at ranges beyond 16,000 yards. A hit rate of 5 percent at that range was considered outstanding gunnery using visual fire control. The *Bismarck*'s (q.v.) 10 percent hit rate at 15,000 to 25,000 yards during its engagement with the British battle cruiser HMS *Hood* was truly exceptional for 1941. By 1943, however, it was not unusual for American battleships to achieve 10 to 14 percent hit rates at those ranges when using radar fire control.

The poor gunnery of the Italian and Soviet Navies was the result of several factors. In addition to poor training and doctrine, they both also suffered from inconsistent propellent powder and shell quality, and narrow turrets with tight barrel

The Bismarck *fires on the HMS* Hood, *24 May 1941. Photograph taken from the* Prinz Eugen. *(IWM HU 381)*

spacing. Their ships lacked the necessary interrupter mechanisms in their main battle turrets, which degraded the effectiveness of their long-range shell patterns. The French also suffered from poor long-range gunnery, as did the Americans early in the war. Germany started with superior gunnery, but reduced training and the advent of Allied fire control radars gradually eroded the German advantages. By 1943, the Western Allies had virtually unchallenged supremacy in both surface and antiaircraft gunnery.

In contrast to the Pacific theater, surface gunnery continued to play a significant role in naval warfare in the European theater. As in the Pacific, however, antiaircraft gunnery gained in importance as the war went on. By 1943, both types of gunnery had shifted to centralized fire control for long-range engagements. Only self-defense weapons (40mm and smaller) were fired under the direct control of their gun crews. From 1943 on, only the smallest and oldest naval combat units continued the now obsolete practice of individual gun crews aiming and firing their guns independently—except as an emergency procedure.

Carl O. Schuster

Additional Reading
U.S. Navy Bureau of Ordnance, *Principles of Naval Gunnery* (1963).
U.S. Navy Bureau of Personnel, *Blue Jacket's Manual, 1944* (1944).

Night Operations, Air

Toward the end of September 1940, the *Luftwaffe* switched its bombing raids from daylight to the cover of darkness. This shift in tactics was the result of the heavy losses sustained during the Battle of Britain (q.v.). With the shift in tactics by the *Luftwaffe,* the British found themselves hard pressed to stem the flow of German bombers crossing the English Channel almost every night.

When the Royal Air Force (RAF) initiated similar night bombing missions against Germany, primarily in the industrialized areas of the Ruhr Valley, the *Luftwaffe* in turn intensified its nightly bombing of British cities throughout the winter of 1940–1941. Owing to German advances in radio-navigational technology, the *Luftwaffe* was able to locate its targets in the dark with uncanny accuracy.

After having lagged behind in night operational capabilities, the British rushed to improve whatever means they possessed to defend and strike back at the Germans. In early 1941, the RAF hurried into production several new bomber and fighter models. The British also made many advances in their ground-based and airborne intercept (AI) radars (q.v.), enabling them to score some successes against the nightly German intruders. As the spring of 1941 approached, the British discovered that by jamming the *Luftwaffe*'s radio frequencies they could prevent many of the German bombers from locating their targets.

The most dramatic blow to the *Luftwaffe* was

the introduction of airborne radar into RAF night fighters. Built into the twin-engine Bristol Beaufighter, these radar-equipped fighters proved to be highly lethal against the lumbering *Luftwaffe* bombers.

As the cost of the ill-conceived air campaign rose, Adolf Hitler (q.v.) lost interest in an invasion of the British Isles and shifted his attention to other fronts. The main force of *Luftwaffe* bombers was transferred to the east, but the British still were determined to mount an all-out bombing offensive aimed at the German homeland and Axis-controlled areas. By the beginning of summer 1941, RAF Bomber Command was attempting to inflict heavy damage on the Germans, but the results were somewhat less than anticipated. Logistical and operational delays within Bomber Command also gave the Germans ample time to improve their own air defenses.

By the end of the summer of 1941, the Germans completed construction of their own air defenses, the Kammhuber Line (q.v.). These defenses were arranged in a belt that stretched from Belgium to Denmark. They were composed of radar-directed antiaircraft batteries, searchlights, and specially designed night fighters such as the Bf-110G and the Ju-88G. All these elements combined into a deadly killing ground for RAF bombers, which needed to pass through the zone to reach their targets in Germany.

Flight controllers on the Kammhuber Line directed the German night fighters to their targets by use of a device called a Seeburg table. The table consisted of a translucent gridded surface, with each grid representing 2.5 square kilometers. One radar set on the ground tracked the incoming Allied bomber, while another radar tracked the intercepting night fighter. Using different colored lights, two operators tracked the course of the bomber and fighter on the underside of the table based on information from the radars. A flight controller, viewing the table from above, was able to guide the fighter close enough to the bomber for the fighter's on-board radar to acquire it.

By autumn 1941, the true measure of the German air defensives were being felt by the RAF, as the mortality rate sometimes rose to almost 10 percent for any given raid. Faced with such losses, Bomber Command began to question the validity of continued night bombing. At the end of 1941, however, the U.S. entered the war, and by early 1942, Air Marshal Arthur Harris (q.v.) became the head of Bomber Command.

That spring, Bomber Command started to concentrate the objectives of its bombing efforts.

At that time, Bomber Command had an ever-expanding number and variety of assets. Harris opted to try to overwhelm the German air defenses with sheer weight of numbers, and thus were born the "1,000 plane raids." Harris's strategy ultimately worked. Armed with the latest in night navigational aids, state-of-the-art heavy bombers, and incendiary bombs, the RAF rained destruction down upon Germany.

At the height of the air campaign over Germany, British night bombing raids were guided to their targets by the ground-based Gee or Oboe radar systems. The H2S radar carried by the bomber gave the plane's navigator information about the ground he was flying over. Passive radar detection systems, such as Boozer and Monica, warned Allied aircraft when they were being scanned by German ground-based or AI radars. The British also had a device called Serrate, a passive system to detect standard radio transmissions from the German night fighters.

Each British bombing force was accompanied by a number of specially equipped bombers (usually Lancasters) called ABC aircraft, or "airborne cigars." These aircraft essentially were airborne jammers, whose mission was to interfere with the radio transmissions of the German night fighters.

Being on the strategic defensive from 1942 on, the *Luftwaffe* developed and fielded increasingly sophisticated systems for its night fighters. The forward-looking Fu-220 Lichtenstein and rearward-looking Neptun radars were particularly effective. The FuG-350 Naxos radar homed in on the H2S radar carried on the British bombers. The FuG-227 Flensburg was a passive system that detected the emissions from the British rearward-looking Monica radar.

In May 1943, Major Rudolf Schönert, a German night-fighter pilot, developed a system called *Schräge Musik* (Jazz music). It was an upward-firing 20mm cannon, designed to attack bombers from their relatively unprotected underside. Schönert first used the system in a Do-217. Later it was mounted in the Bf-110G and Ju-88G night fighters.

From 1943 until the Normandy (q.v.) landings in 1944, the combined air forces of the Allies bombed transportation and other communications targets in order to set the stage. After the invasion, Bomber Command shifted its focus back to the industrial centers of Germany. With increased pressure on their cities, interservice rivalries and political infighting raged within Germany. The Kammhuber Line was cannibalized and its antiaircraft guns and searchlights were shifted back into Germany, as every sector of German society sought to protect itself from the Allied bombing. Then, with the introduction of Allied long-range escort fighters to combat what was left of a dwindling *Luftwaffe* fighter force, the Allies began to achieve relative air superiority.

The initial shift in tactics to night air operations altered the face of aerial warfare and spurred technological advances that continue to the present. Prior to World War II, aerial night combat was quite literally a "shot in the dark." Today, most modern air forces can operate with equal effectiveness in both day and night.

Rob Nadeau

Additional Reading

Held, Werner, and Holger Nauroth, *The Defense of the Reich: Hitler's Nightfighter Planes and Pilots* (1982).

Johnen, Wilhelm, *Duel Under the Stars: A German Night Fighter Pilot in the Second World War* (1957).

Rawnsley, C.F., and Robert Wright, *Night Fighter* (1957).

Night Operations, Land

Periods of poor visibility, especially during the night, became increasingly more important for the fighting forces as the war continued. Combatants became more adept at taking advantage of nightfall when air assaults and long-range surveillance were effectively thwarted. Advantage was gained by those forces able to continue fighting at night, and crucial to this was the ability of the soldiers to overcome their concerns with night combat, the recognition of the unique elements of night actions, and a commitment to exploit the available technology as an aid in night operations.

Night combat also gained further significance, particularly on the eastern front, where more individual and unit training for this type of operation took place than in other theaters of operation. For successful night operations, commanders had to be thoroughly familiar with the terrain, as well as with enemy resources, tactics, and deployment. Troops also required careful training.

Throughout the war, Soviet soldiers proved themselves to be particularly adept at night operations, which they adopted to changing military objectives, circumstances, and methods of execution. Unit commanders improved their nighttime effectiveness after 1941 as they fought at night more often in order to take advantage of the halt of the German ground forces. This was especially true

during winter months when the shortness of the days meant that most engagements continued into darkness. Many of the night assaults, however, involved untrained infantry replacements deployed for massive attacks. These tactics proved to be ineffective. Additional training and the use of calvary and tanks improved the effectiveness of night operations for the Soviet forces, but they characteristically did not exploit their initial breakthroughs.

In 1942–1943, large-scale Soviet assaults continued after dark with tanks used frequently now that the threat from air attack had diminished. By 1944, Soviet tactics shifted as attack methods improved and the objectives tended to be more distant. Tanks always led the way, but the progress was usually slow, and that allowed German commanders adequate time to respond. In most instances the attacks stalled, and by the summer of 1944, new Soviet methods were adopted, such as the use of diversionary tactics and the selection of well-defined and limited targets. The overall goal was to split and paralyze German defensive lines. Throughout the war, Soviet partisans (q.v.) remained active at night as they moved from their hideouts to strike at the German forces.

Night operations gained significance for the German armed forces during the Russian campaign. German military principles, as contained in *Army Manual 300, Troop Command,* were updated and included a special supplement on night combat that was based largely on the lessons learned on the eastern front. Commanders recognized that, for example, moving their troops at night would cut losses, but these operations faced problems such as poor roads, sudden changes in the weather, and attacks from enemy troops or partisans.

Crucial to effective night operations was good reconnaissance, and for this the German forces often used tracer ammunition, star shells, or searchlights. German troops also continued their assaults into the night, if commanders believed that would maximize their gains. The nighttime assaults took place only after careful preparations.

Soviet terrain was ill-suited to these actions and the enemy's defensive preparations were difficult to observe. A successful attack had to be well planned, launched from an unexpected direction with proper timing, and had to be completed by daybreak. The use of seasoned and well-trained troops was important.

German commanders applied the same principles to defensive actions, although additional preparations were made at night. For example, outposts were strengthened and moved as far forward as possible. Reconnaissance activities carried out by light infantrymen were also increased, and several defensive lines established in order to thwart the massive Soviet assaults. By late in the war, as German troops became more depleted, commanders relied on a system of widely separated strong points that were also more vulnerable to Soviet night operations.

Robert G. Waite

Additional Reading

Detweiler, Donald S. (ed.), "Night Combat," *Department of the Army Pamphlet* No. 20–236 (June 1953), reprinted in *World War II German Military Studies* (1979).

Toppe, Alfred, et al., "Night Combat," *Foreign Military Studies* (12 May 1950).

Oil Plan

In early 1944, the Economic Objectives Unit of the American Embassy in London identified fifty-four oil targets concentrated in the Ruhr Valley in Germany and around Ploesti, Romania (q.v.), as part of a comprehensive strategic bombing plan to find the elusive choke point in the German industrial economy.

The commander of U.S. Strategic Air Forces in Europe, Lieutenant General Carl Spaatz (q.v.), presented the plan to Supreme Allied Commander Dwight D. Eisenhower (q.v.) on 5 March 1944 as "the most far-reaching use of strategic air power that has been attempted in this war." Spaatz believed oil to be Germany's Achilles' heel, attacks against which would force the *Luftwaffe* to expose itself to attrition and allow the Allies to gain air superiority in time for Operation OVERLORD. It was also intended as an alternative to Air Chief Marshal Trafford Leigh-Mallory's Transportation Plan (qq.v.).

Eisenhower's 26 March compromise sent Spaatz's bombers after what U.S. Major General Frederick Anderson called Leigh-Mallory's "God-damn rail targets," but allowed a limited offensive against oil. The U.S. Fifteenth Air Force circumvented the Transportation Plan by striking against Balkan railroad facilities in April, chosen because they were adjacent to oil refineries. Its effort combined with three Eighth Air Force strikes against synthetic oil plants in Germany in May cut German gasoline production in half by D-Day. The ULTRA (q.v.) network immediately revealed that Germany had suffered a mortal wound and Armaments Minister Albert Speer (q.v.) later admitted a "new era" in the air war had begun. Continued attacks in June encouraged Speer to tell Adolf Hitler (q.v.) that "from this time onward there will be an unbridgeable deficit [between fuel production and consumption] which must lead to tragic consequences."

Stephen L. McFarland

Additional Reading

Cooke, Ronald C., and Roy C. Nesbit, *Target: Hitler's Oil* (1985).

Rostow, W.W., *Pre-invasion Bombing Strategy* (1981).

Tedder, Arthur, *With Prejudice* (1966).

P

Pathfinder Technique

A product of the struggle within the Royal Air Forces's (RAF) Bomber Command between advocates of area and precision bombing, the pathfinder technique employed a force of experienced bomber crews to mark aiming points for night bombing with sky and ground target indicators. The strongest advocate was Group Captain Sidney Bufton. The technique was worked out by Number 8 Group's Air Vice-Marshal Donald Bennett (q.v.), who formed the Pathfinder Force (PFF) beginning on 15 August 1942 over the objections of Bomber Command commander in chief Air Marshal Arthur Harris (q.v.).

When visual bombing conditions existed, PFF used flares to illuminate the target area for aiming their ground markers, which served as aiming points for the main force. PFF also employed blind-bombing radio and radar techniques, including Gee, Oboe, and H2S airborne radar (*see* Night Operations, Air). At its best, Air Vice-Marshal Ralph Cochrane's Number 5 Group, using a low-altitude offset tactic to drop ground indicators away from the dust and smoke obscuring the target, could achieve accuracies within 300 yards. At its worst, the PFF misidentified Pilsen, Czechoslovakia, on 16–17 April 1943, and the main force bombed an asylum seven miles from the target. The pathfinder technique provided for greater bomb concentrations, but only if the PFF found and identified the correct aiming point.

In American use, the pathfinder technique allowed daylight bombers to bomb through undercast. Equipments included H2S/H2X and Micro-H (a modified Gee system), accounting for more than half of the bomb tonnage dropped in the last two years of the war. Where the Eighth Air Force achieved 30 percent of its bombs within 1,000 feet of the assigned aiming points in late 1944 using visual aiming, PFF techniques using Micro-H achieved 5 percent and H2X only 0.2 percent.

Stephen L. McFarland

Additional Reading

Harris, Sir Arthur, *Bomber Offensive* (1947).
Verrier, Anthony, *The Bomber Offensive* (1968).
Webster, Charles, and Arthur Noble Frankland, *The Strategic Air Offensive Against Germany, 1939–1945,* 4 vols. (1961).

Plan Z

Many historians of World War II have argued that Germany might have won the war at sea if only Hitler had waited until 1942–1944 to start the war. That assessment is based on Germany completing the so-called Plan Z, which was approved on 27 January 1939 (*see* table). Plan Z was intended to establish a fleet that fell within the basic parameters of the 1935 Anglo-German Naval Agreement (q.v.), and yet provide Germany with the naval strength needed to dominate the Baltic Sea and deter Britain from joining the war against Germany.

The fact remains, however, that Germany did not have the economic base needed to support such a construction program, nor did it have the resources to fuel the fleet once war broke out. Even the truncated German fleet that entered the war faced fuel restrictions as early as 1941. Moreover, shortages of steel, copper, and skilled labor forced serious delays on ship construction that would have prevented the bulk of the plan from reaching fruition on time.

Adolf Hitler (q.v.) approved Plan Z with the hope that it would provide a fleet superior to France and able to deter Britain. Admiral Erich Raeder

Plan Z

Approval Date: 27 January 1939
Scheduled Completion Date: 1 December 1948

Ship Type	Planned Number	In Service 1 Sept 1939
Large Battleships	10	0
Fast Battleships (20,000 tons)	12	0
Battlecruisers (29,000 tons)	3	2
Pocket Battleships	3	3
Large Aircraft Carrriers	2	0
Small Aircraft Carriers	2	0
Heavy Cruisers	5	2
Light Cruisers	6	6
Scout Cruisers	22	0
Destroyers	68	22
Torpedo Boats	90	11
Type IX U-Boats	62	6
Type VII U-Boats	100	23
Type II U-Boats	60	34

(q.v.) used the plan to argue for a higher raw materials priority for the *Kriegsmarine,* whose shipbuilding plans were already in difficulty. By 1937, virtually every ship under construction, except submarines, was suffering construction delays and cost overruns. The destroyer, cruiser, and aircraft carrier programs were three, eleven, and sixteen months behind schedule, respectively. Shortages of skilled labor, raw materials, and experienced program managers all contributed to the problem. The situation was so bad that the *Kriegsmarine* ordered no new ships in 1937, and would not do so in 1938 until the backlog was cleared. Even so, the German shipbuilding program was twelve months behind schedule when the war began.

In many ways, Germany's shipbuilding problems were induced by the rapidity of its naval buildup. The German Navy's shipbuilding budget grew twelvefold in less than six years. Although orders never exceeded the shipbuilding industry's maximum theoretical capacity, Germany's shipbuilders were idle for nearly a decade before the buildup began. The Weimar Republic's (q.v.) navy was small and old (*see* table), requiring the annual construction of only a few relatively small ships to maintain its strength.

The rapid construction of a greater number of larger units strained the managerial expertise of the shipyards and naval construction bureaus. The new warships of the 1930s also used new technologies not commonly employed in merchant ship construction. For example, Germany's new warships used welding instead of rivets in construc-

tion. Although this development accelerated the rate of construction and provided a stronger and lighter hull, it required a larger number of skilled welders—a class of laborer in short supply until the mid-1940s.

The new warships also used steam boilers and turbines that were a major technological improvement over those used in merchant ships. Although the new technologies provided a steam plant with greater power density (horsepower per weight and volume of machinery) and better fuel economy (steaming miles per ton of fuel), they also required a higher quality of steel, closer tolerances in construction, more maintenance, and a more highly trained operating crew. More importantly, Admiral Raeder ordered the construction and installation of these steam plants into new construction units before the test program was completed. Thus, many of the power plants required modification as the ships were being built, thereby delaying final ship delivery.

The most important impediment to Germany's naval dreams, however, was oil. Germany simply did not have the fuel sources needed to support a Plan Z fleet. The *Reich*'s total annual oil resources (imports and synthetic and domestic oil production) never exceeded 10 million tons. Less than two million tons of that was available for naval purposes—approximately one-third of what a Plan Z fleet would have required. Not much more would have been forthcoming, even if oil production were significantly higher. Germany's wartime emergency plans called for synthetic oil production equivalent to more than six million tons of petroleum per year. The overwhelming majority of that increased production was destined for the *Luftwaffe* and the army, not the *Kriegsmarine*. Barring the defeat of the Soviet Union and control of its oil fields, the Plan Z was merely a dream looking for a fuel station. Germany was a continental power facing a large ground and air threat in a modern war with limited fuel resources.

The Weimar Fleet
1932

Ship Type	Number Allowed	Number in Service	Tonnage
Battle Crusiers	6	3	28,000
Light Cruisers	6	6	30,000
Destroyers	12	0	0
Torpedo Boats	12	12	10,800
Minesweepers	24	20	10,000
Auxiliaries	20	14	20,000
Reserve Units	12	0	0

It was this reality and not the timing of the war's start that terminated the Plan Z at birth.

Carl O. Schuster

Additional Reading

Cooke, Ronald C., and Roy Nesbit, *Target: Hitler's Oil* (1985).

Deist, Wilhelm, *The Wehrmacht and German Rearmament* (1981).

Goralski, Robert, and Russel W. Freeburg, *Oil and War* (1987).

Madej, Victor, *German War Economy* (1984).

Principles of War

The principles of war are a collection of fundamental war-fighting considerations that make up the bedrock of military doctrine in most modern armies. The principles have existed in one form or another for centuries. The current version was developed after World War I by British Major General J.F.C. Fuller (q.v.), who drew heavily from the work of Major General Carl von Clausewitz, the nineteenth-century German military theorist. The U.S. Army first included them in its 1921 *War Department Training Regulation 10–5*.

The principles of war are not immutable physical laws, nor are they hard and fast rules that guarantee results. Every principle does not necessarily apply to every situation, and in some cases they may even appear antithetical. The relative importance of each principle is entirely dependent on the situation, which itself is influenced by five primary elements: (1) the mission to be accomplished; (2) the strength and position of the enemy; (3) the strength and position of one's own troops; (4) the terrain and weather; and (5) the available time. In many situations it may be impossible to adhere to one principle without violating another.

Another factor influencing the relative value of the principles is the level of war at which they are applied. Generally, there are three levels of war, the strategic, the operational, and the tactical. The objective of the tactical level is to win battles. The objective of the strategic level is to win wars. The objective of the operational level is to win campaigns. The operational level is the critical link between the tactical and the strategic. Wars consist of a series of campaigns, just as campaigns consist of a series of battles. During World War II, U.S. military doctrine did not recognize the operational as a distinct level of war. The Soviets recognized the operational level well before World War II, and the U.S. finally recognized it after Vietnam. Since each level has a different focus, the applica-

tion of the principles of war can be quite different at each level.

During World War II, U.S. military doctrine recognized nine principles of war:

Objective: The ultimate military purpose of war is the destruction of the enemy's armed forces and will to fight. Every military operation should be directed toward a clearly defined, decisive, and attainable objective.

Offensive: The most effective and decisive way to attain an objective is to seize, retain, and exploit the initiative.

Mass: The concentration of the effects of overwhelming combat power at the decisive place and time.

Economy of Force: The judicious employment and distribution of forces. All combat power available should be employed in the most effective way possible. Minimum essential combat power should be allocated to secondary efforts.

Maneuver: The movement of forces in relation to the enemy to gain positional advantage.

Coordination: Unity of purpose, effort, and command.

Security: The enhancement of freedom of action by reducing vulnerability to hostile acts, influence, or surprise.

Surprise: Striking the enemy at a time or place or in a manner for which he is unprepared.

Simplicity: The preparation of clear, uncomplicated plans and concise orders to ensure thorough understanding.

Not all armies use the exact same list. Some recognize the same principles under different names, while others recognize entirely different principles. The British, for example, use the word *concentration* instead of *mass.* They also include the principles of flexibility, administration, and morale. The British do not recognize maneuver as a specific principle of war. Maneuver for them is one of the two basic elements of combat power—the other being firepower. U.S. doctrine considers maneuver to be both a principle of war and an element of combat power.

The Soviets have only five principles of war, a list quite different from the American. The Soviet principles are (1) Morale; (2) Quantity/Quality of Divisions; (3) Armament; (4) Ability of Commanders; and (5) Stability of the Rear.

The lists of the principles of war are not even necessarily the same for the different services of the same country. After World War II, when the U.S. Army Air Force was separated from the army to become the U.S. Air Force, the army modified the principle of coordination to unity of command, which requires that all forces are under one responsible commander. The air force, however, retained coordination on its list.

Despite their lack of absoluteness and the different ways of articulating them, the principles of war are still a practical and valuable checklist for military planners. Any commander who ignores them does so at the peril of his force and his mission.

David T. Zabecki

Additional Reading

Collins, John M., *Grand Strategy: Principles and Practices* (1973).

Fuller, J.F.C., *The Foundations of the Science of War* (1925).

U.S. War Department, *FM 100–5 Field Service Regulations: Operations* (1944).

Prisoner of War Operations

The concept of prisoners of war (POWs) as we know it now was relatively new in 1939. In the earliest days of organized warfare, captives were ransomed, put to death, or used as slaves. By the seventeenth century, a system of parole-release and exchange was adopted by most European military institutions. The American Civil War (1861–1865) was the last major conflict where prisoner parole and exchange were commonly practiced. Prisoner treatment and conduct in World War II were based on the Law of Land Warfare, developed at a number of conferences and conventions held at The Hague, Netherlands, and at Geneva, Switzerland, from 1896 up until just before World War II.

Prisoner of war operations were conducted, for the most part, by military police and military intelligence units given the responsibility of guarding and administering the camps. Many of the personnel involved in these operations were unfit for frontline duty because of physical disabilities, but in no case is there any documentary evidence that this was a cause for abuse of prisoners. For the most part, POWs were treated as humanely and as fairly as the captor nations could manage, but regardless of treatment, the most salient feature of all belligerents' POW operations was a rather benign neglect.

By 1939, mechanized units moved so swiftly over such large areas, and the foot-infantry moved so slowly, that POWs in large numbers were taken by all belligerents. While being taken prisoner is never psychologically easy, in many cases taking prisoners can be equally traumatic for the captors.

In the heat of combat, surrendering enemy personnel are sometimes killed or wounded simply because the captor does not understand that his enemy just wants to give up. The language barrier was sometimes extraordinarily difficult to overcome, and in some cases impossible. Captive Russian "volunteer helpers" in German service, captured in turn by the Allies in the Normandy area in 1944, had a tremendous problem, as did the odd Ethiopian, Senegalese, or Indian in Allied uniform in Northwest Africa (q.v.), simply because their captors were not expecting to find them there.

After a certain point in a losing situation, any reasonable commander worth his rank will recognize that further resistance is futile and will surrender his command. In the cases of airmen escaping from destroyed aircraft or sailors leaving sinking vessels, fighting resistance (other than just evasion) was almost unheard of. The physiological strain of combat, ending with the relative exhilaration of knowing that he survived the ordeal, was usually enough to convince the soldier that resistance was really futile, regardless of whether he faced organized troops or local farmers armed with pitchforks.

In 1943, Adolf Hitler (q.v.) decreed that escaping Allied airmen were to be treated as spies and summarily executed, but this was honored more in the breach than the observance by German armed forces. Such treatment, they knew, would be met with similar retaliation on the part of the Allies.

Under international law, neutral countries have to treat belligerents within their territorial boundaries and sea areas in a similar fashion to POWs, calling them "internees." Every neutral in Europe dealt with at least a few escaped POWs or downed airmen who couldn't make it all the way back home.

The Hague Convention requires POWs to be removed from the combat zone as quickly as practicable. During the war, this rule was usually well observed. Germans captured by Commonwealth troops were often shipped off to Canada. Allied troops in Axis hands were removed to their host countries as soon as it was practical. Safeguarding POWs during transit was sometimes problematic, as inevitably all means of transport were targets. Commonwealth ships carrying POWs were sometimes torpedoed. Axis trains and ships were attacked from the air. When practiced, large "PW" signs were usually protection against such attacks, but they could not safeguard POWs from angry civilians or vengeful soldiers. By and large, the transporting units went to some lengths to protect their charges from attack, but were not always successful.

Toward the end of the war, Allied POWs in German hands were at a great deal of risk from marauding Allied fighter-bombers that shot at anything that looked worthy. One marching column of about 3,000 POWs was attacked several times as they tried to get away from the battle zone. Because they did not wish to invite return visits, the German guards of POW columns were ordered not to shoot back at their attackers. This caused some dissension and resentment among the guards, but the fighters eventually lost interest in targets that did not defend themselves.

Not all POWs were truly interrogated, as not all POWs knew anything that was of any real value. Enlisted personnel and junior officers in the combat branches were infrequently asked about anything more than the usual name, rank, and service number. Senior officers and their staffs and aides, communications specialists, transport drivers, and military intelligence personnel were of particular value as POWs and usually were subjected to real interrogation.

Selecting POWs for interrogation (a process called screening) is the first thing that all captors do after a POW is handed over to the prisoner handling system. Occasionally, POWs who may have had some tactical information, information

valuable for only forty-eight hours or so, were subjected to interrogations outside of the regular system. Usually these were quick affairs, over in a matter of minutes. POWs usually gave up what they knew after a few simple, direct questions. If the prisoner demonstrated any resistance that could not be overcome in a few minutes, they were normally passed into the system.

It is well understood by interrogators that physical torture will yield little valuable information, but it will yield a great deal of enmity from the POW, as well as answers to the questions that might be true or not. In the interests of fairness, it must be said that both Axis and Allies were equally guilty of occasionally brutal interrogation (usually in tactical situations), but beatings and torture were the exceptions rather than the rule. Both Allied and Axis intelligence services reported after the war that all persons subjected to active, intense interrogation "broke" eventually, revealing at least some of what they knew.

The first thing most prisoners want to do is escape from captivity, so the first priority for captors is detention. Prison camps for Western Allied and Axis POWs were essentially the same: buildings surrounded by barbed wire, and the segregation of ranks (and where required, sexes) from each other

Sergeant Leroy Cook of St. Louis, Missouri, searches a German officer for hidden weapons. The Germans were captured outside Gavray, France. (IWM OWIL 52270)

to prevent any one leader from emerging easily. Food was usually edible, but not always palatable. Under the Geneva rules, captor nations must provide food that the prisoner is accustomed to, but this was not always possible. Each prison camp had rules as to where prisoners could go and not go, what they could do and not do, and so on.

Given these conditions, the second priority for captors was to provide diversion for their charges. Americans played baseball; Europeans played soccer; all planted gardens for their own use. Gambling, illegal in most camps, was endemic but usually tolerated. Some camps put on plays and burlesques, occasionally with POWs and guards interacting. Many others held classes in whatever fields of expertise were on hand, from accounting to ornithology to zoology and languages. All these activities were intended to prevent the inevitable boredom caused by so many men, most in the prime of their lives, who were engaged in a war and who were suddenly faced with doing absolutely nothing. Both captors and POWs spent a great deal of energy trying to keep their minds off things such as escape and the impossibility of escape.

POWs' performing actual productive work for their captors was legal, as long as such work did not further the captor nation's war efforts and did not endanger the prisoners. In at least one instance in the United States, where German POWs were put to work making terrain models for army training, the POWs protested and were removed from the job. Since escape was difficult, many Axis POWs in the Western Hemisphere were allowed to work outside the camps and even live outside the wire. Most such work was agricultural, harvesting crops or tending stock. Many Axis POWs were allowed to stay in the United States and Canada after the war as a reward for the work they had performed.

Allied POWs infrequently worked outside their camps, and when they did, it was of questionable legality. POWs were used to clean up bomb damage in cities, including Hamburg and Dresden, but there are no records of successful protests.

Disease (most commonly dysentery), deaths from wounds inflicted in capture, starvation, and malnutrition were common in Axis-run camps, especially during the final months of the war.

Punishment for rules violations was always severe. Isolation from fellow POWs (the "cooler") was a common punishment for minor infractions. Execution was also common for assaulting or killing guards, or for unsuccessful escape attempts. Crimes against other POWs were sometimes never discovered by the captor authorities. These usually

Prisoner Nationality	Captor Nation	Total Captured*
France	Germany	1,450,000
Italy	Germany	550,000
Commonwealth of Great Britian	Germany	200,000
Greece	Germany/Italy	270,000
United States	Germany	90,000
Yugoslavia	Germany	125,000
Soviet Union	Germany	5,500,000
Italy	Western Allies	430,000
Germany	Western Allies	8,035,920†
Germany	Soviet Union	3,060,000

Notes:
* Most POW numbers are approximations at best.
† 630,000 German prisoners prior to the German surrender.

were dealt with by the POWs, with loss of privileges meted out as punishment. Occasionally POWs killed each other, and the guilty were dealt with by the captors. Sometimes, for major crimes (such as informing on other POWs), punishment was delayed until release, but usually major crimes were dealt with severely by the POWs themselves, with strangulation or severe beating as the punishment.

Though all treatment of internees in neutral countries was to be equal, Allied internees generally received better treatment in Switzerland and Sweden, and the Germans received better treatment in Turkey and Spain. Nonetheless, all internees in neutral countries were better off than their comrades in enemy hands.

Because of the tremendous ideological differences between Germany, Italy, and the Allies, proselytizing among the POWs was infrequent, but did occur. A few American and British POWs joined the German *Waffen-SS* (q.v.) as a part of a large propaganda move. After the Italian surrender in September 1943, many Italian soldiers applied to fight the Germans, but few were accepted. A minute number of Germans expressed any desire to fight their countrymen, though many were interested in fighting the Soviets.

The defection and surrender of Axis allies occasioned a most unusual situation for the Germans. Technically, the Italians became neutrals, but most of the Italians that the Germans could lay their hands on were either executed or imprisoned if they would not swear oaths to Benito Mussolini's (q.v.) rump government. Other Axis allies that surrendered (except Finland) received similar treatment.

Allied POWs in Italian hands were another problem, however. In theory, when Italy became a nonbelligerent the POWs became "internees." Some broke out of their pens, only to be swiftly recaptured by the Germans and sent to Germany. Most only exchanged guards.

Inevitably, POWs are to be returned to their home countries after the end of hostilities. Most Allied POWs were liberated by the time the Germans surrendered. The few that were not were quickly turned over to their home nations. Axis POWs, however, were not so lucky, some being held in forced labor until 1948. Internees in neutral states were usually returned through the Red Cross (q.v.).

The International Red Cross monitored the entire prisoner handling process, making regular inspections of as many camps as possible on both sides. It often protested about unsanitary conditions, bad clothing, bad food, or whatever else it could find that was against the Geneva rules. Toward the end of the war, however, the Red Cross recognized that the worsening food situation in Axis camps was unavoidable because food supplies were so short and poor everywhere. It did ensure that the Red Cross parcels were distributed when it could, but the number of Red Cross observer teams was extremely limited.

None of what has thus far been said can be generally true about the war in the Soviet Union, and generally, in eastern Europe. POWs were slaughtered wholesale before or immediately after capture by both sides. Soviet political commissars and German SS members were specifically singled out for execution. Rather than being treated as POWs, Soviets were put into forced labor camps along with political prisoners, Jews, and other "undesirables." German and other Axis POWs were sent to Siberia and the Soviet Far East, never to be heard from again.

POW transportation in the east was either on foot or on open rail car, regardless of weather. One account mentions stacks of bodies used as a windbreak in front of open rail gondolas in sub-zero weather; another of washing corn and other undigested food from fecal matter for reconsumption. There were numerous accounts of cannibalism.

Defection was rampant. Soviet General A.A. Vlasov (q.v.) captured at Sevastopol (q.v.) in May 1942, made propaganda broadcasts and raised an army of fellow Soviet POWs to fight for the Germans. Soviet ethnic minorities (notably Balts and Ukrainians) were singled out from the prison pens

and made trustees, guards, and executioners in the German-run prison and concentration camps. Ordinary Soviet soldiers sometimes volunteered for heavy labor on the western front.

Repatriation of prisoners in the east was not a normal event. As late as the mid-1950s, Germans were identified as still in the Soviet penal system. Many Soviet POWs who returned (most against their will) were ordered executed or imprisoned by Premier Josef Stalin (q.v.), fearing their "Western influence," or that they "had not fought hard enough." The collapse of the Soviet Union in 1991 resulted in the release of information from KGB files, and is shedding new light on the treatment of Axis POWs.

Though exact numbers are hard to come by, POWs in World War II were treated as humanely as possible, but they still died by the thousands due to neglect, starvation, disease, and brutality—in roughly that order. Although the systems in place by 1939 were better than they had been previously, they were still not good. Generally, the Soviets and the Germans bore the brunt of it, with close to 60 percent of all Soviets and 40 percent of all Germans captured in the east not returning home.

John D. Beatty

Additional Reading

Baker, A.J., *Prisoners of War* (1975).

Reid, Pat, and Maurice Michael, *Prisoner of War: The Inside Story of the POW from the Ancient World to Colditz and After* (1984).

Sajer, Guy, *The Forgotten Soldier* (1965).

Psychological Operations

Psychological warfare ("sykewar") endeavors to sustain one's own morale and the morale of one's allies, turn neutrals against the enemy and bring them to one's own side, and above all, undermine the enemy's will to fight. Psychological warfare can consist of "terror tactics" against the enemy, as when teams circulate at night behind enemy lines slitting throats and setting off explosions. The German distribution throughout Europe in 1939–1940 of pictures of blitzed Polish cities constituted terror tactics, as did their attachment of "screamers" to their *Stuka* dive bombers.

By far, the main part of psychological warfare is the conduct of propaganda (q.v.). Propaganda against the enemy is divided into "strategic" propaganda directed against the whole enemy nation, and "tactical" or "combat" propaganda directed against enemy troops on the front lines.

The Anglo-Americans used several instruments to send their tactical propaganda to the enemy. Radio was used, but not extensively, simply because Axis soldiers did not have many radios with which to listen. Loudspeakers, especially in a static situation, were used to blast propaganda at the enemy. ("Sykewar" memoir writers after the war took great pride in their "talking tank"—loudspeakers mounted on a tank that gave the loudspeakers the mobility of their host vehicle.)

By far the most used instrument of combat propaganda was the printed word—leaflets especially, and also newspapers, delivered to the enemy lines by artillery or from planes dropping the "Monroe bomb" (named for the inventor, Captain James L. Monroe), which was activated by a barometric fuze, exploding at a set height to send the reading material floating down on enemy troops. Artillerymen and airmen generally resisted using their tools of war for sending leaflets instead of explosives to the enemy. (Lovers of Bill Mauldin's [q.v.] cartoons will recall the one in which Willie refuses to fire the leaflet shells, saying, "Tell them leaflet people th' Krauts ain't got time fer readin' today.") This difficulty, however, was regularly overcome, for millions of leaflets and newspapers were dispatched to the enemy during the war.

Anglo-American propaganda from the beginning adopted as its basic principle the axiom that truth makes the best propaganda, not so much because the Anglo-Americans were virtuous, but because they knew what would work. It was not, to be sure, "the truth, the whole truth, and nothing but the truth." Propagandists were selective in their choice of the truth. It was, however, far closer to the whole truth than the German soldiers heard from their own side. A sampling of German POWs in August 1944 showed that 92 percent of them felt they could believe what they read in the Allied leaflets.

Various themes were present in the leaflets sent to the Germans. One major theme was to shake the myth of German invincibility by describing in a simple, factual way German defeats on the battlefield and the failure of the *Luftwaffe* to prevent the steady destruction of German cities in the Allied strategic bombing offensive. Another theme tried to divide the army and the Nazi Party, the soldier and the SS man. Almost all the themes tried to create a picture of a "war gone wrong"; one the Germans could not win because of the preponderance of Allied power.

If the certainty of German defeat could be planted in the German soldier's mind, then it was only a small step (or so the "sykewarriors" hoped) to having him come over to the Allied lines to surrender. Accordingly, Allied tactical propaganda made great efforts to show that surrender was not dishonorable, that the German Army had done its duty, and that further resistance was equivalent to suicide. Huge numbers of "safe-conduct passes" were sent to the Germans. High quality paper and printing, U.S. and British Army seals, and General Dwight D. Eisenhower's (q.v.) signature made them look "official."

Accompanying leaflets stressed the good Allied treatment of POWs; they were given the same rations of food and cigarettes as the "GIs," and were quickly moved to the rear to safe, warm places. They could send and receive mail, and would be sent home after the war. In harmony with the Anglo-American stress on truth, the leaflets repeatedly affirmed that "being a POW is no fun," but it was preferable to death.

Besides the leaflets, the Allies sent a daily newspaper to the Germans, beginning even before D-Day and continuing to the German collapse. Entitled *Nachrichten für die Truppe,* it featured objective news, features, sports, a pin-up picture, and in the enigmatic words of a "sykewarrior" writing after the war, "humor of a German type." Propaganda nuggets were, of course, inserted into the paper.

Working against Allied combat propaganda were such factors as the traditionally high level of discipline of the German Army, its professional pride, and the comradely feelings within individual units. Desertions were far less than the Allied "sykewarriors" hoped for, at least until the last weeks of the war when the *Wehrmacht*'s discipline fell apart and mass surrenders, at least in the west, occurred.

Some German soldiers, bearing the safe-conduct passes that had been dropped in their lines and influenced no doubt by Anglo-American combat propaganda, came over to Allied lines in the months and years before the collapse at the end. Better to have some than none, but certainly the numbers were not high enough to constitute a success story for Allied combat propaganda. Nor was the "will to fight" of those soldiers who did not desert undermined in any significant way, as can be testified by the ferocity with which the Germans fought on all fronts well into 1945.

After the war, Eisenhower bestowed lavish praise on the Anglo-American "sykewarriors," and no doubt it was better to have them than not to have them. In a total war, all fronts must be manned. Given the tenacity of the German soldier in World War II, they had a tough mission.

The German psychological warfare operatives, considering the nature of the Nazi message together with the steadily falling German fortunes, had a truly hopeless task. They did, however, send their own quota of leaflets to the Allied lines, where they had little or no impact.

Roland V. Layton

Additional Reading
Cruichshank, Charles, *The Fourth Arm: Psychological Warfare 1938–1945* (1977).
Lerner, Daniel, *Sykewar: Psychological Warfare Against Germany, D-Day to VE-Day* (1949).
Margolin, Leo J., *Paper Bullets: A Brief Story of Psychological Warfare in World War II* (1946).

R

RAINBOW Plans

The RAINBOW war plans were developed in 1938–1939 by the U.S. Joint Planning Board. As the European situation rapidly changed in the 1930s, U.S. planners tried to bring strategic planning up to date. All RAINBOW plans assumed a coalition of Germany, Italy, and Japan as the potential enemy. These plans became the foundation for U.S. strategy during World War II. Eventually, there were five different variations of RAINBOW.

The joint board outlined the plan as follows: RAINBOW-1 assumed the United States would fight without allies, with enforcement of the Monroe Doctrine and protection of the Western Hemisphere paramount. The Pacific was to be a defensive theater.

RAINBOW-2 assumed the U.S. would be allied with France and Great Britain, with limited involvement in continental Europe. There would be an offensive posture in the Pacific from the outset.

RAINBOW-3 was similar to RAINBOW-2, but with the assumption that the U.S. would fight without allies.

RAINBOW-4 again assumed a war without major allies, with an emphasis on the Western Hemisphere, and involved ground presence in South America in conjunction with operations in the eastern Atlantic. The Pacific would be a defensive zone.

RAINBOW-5 entailed a U.S., French, and British coalition with Western Hemisphere defense, but with early projection of U.S. forces into the eastern Atlantic, possibly operating in both Europe and Africa. Quick defeat of European enemies was the primary goal with the Pacific remaining a defensive theater until after Germany and Italy were subdued.

RAINBOW-5, also known as Plan DOG, formed the basis of U.S. strategy at the start of the war. In March 1941, the British agreed to the general outlines of the plan at the American-British Conversations (ABC-1). British prime minister Winston S. Churchill (q.v.) and his advisors also agreed to the basic concept at the Arcadia Conference (*see* Conferences, Allied).

Timothy Wilson

Additional Reading

Davis, Forrest and E.K. Lindley, *How War Came: An American White Paper from the Fall of France to Pearl Harbor* (1942).
Ross, Steven T., *American War Plans, 1941–1945* (1997).

Red Ball Express

The rapid Allied advance after the breakout at St. Lô (q.v.) caused serious strains to the U.S. logistical system. On 24 August 1944, the Allies reached the Seine River, eleven days ahead of schedule. The original invasion plans had called for the U.S. communications zone to support twelve American divisions at the Seine on D+90 (4 September), but by that date, there already were sixteen U.S. Divisions some 200 kilometers beyond the Seine. Although the Allies existing port facilities were inadequate to support any sustained advance at that rate, a large amount of supplies did exist in depots near the Normandy beaches some 600 kilometers behind the Allied front lines.

The main problem was transportation. Allied logistical planners had anticipated moving supplies forward using the rebuilt French railroad network, but the rate of advance had proceeded far faster than the ability to rebuild the railroads. Air transport capability was limited too, placing the bulk of the transport load on the road network. The logistical plans, however, called for trucks to work only within 250 kilometers of the railheads. Thus there were not enough trucks in the theater, and the majority of them were light trucks rather than the heavy vehicles needed for long hauls.

The short-term solution became known as the Red Ball Express. Designed as an emergency expedient to support the Seine crossing, the Red Ball used parallel sets of French main roads for one-way traffic in each direction, with the trucks running twenty hours a day and ignoring the blackout rules at night.

The first trucks started rolling on 25 August, delivering 4,482 tons of supplies to depots in the Chartres-Dreux area. By 29 August, the Red Ball Express consisted of 132 truck companies operating 5,958 vehicles, and delivering 12,342 tons of supplies. That was the peak for the Red Ball, and it proved impossible to sustain. When it finally suspended operations in November, the Red Ball Express had averaged 7,000 tons of supplies a day. Originally, it was not supposed to operate east of the Seine, but after mid-September it did.

The Red Ball Express was not an orderly, well-conducted operation, and not without cost. In addition to the 300,000 gallons of gasoline the Red Ball itself consumed each day, wear and tear on the vehicles and accidents caused by driver fatigue took a high toll. The loosely regulated roads were often chaos, with shipments often getting lost. Many shipments were hijacked by other supply-starved U.S. units along the way, and a dismally high percentage of the supplies wound up on the French black market. The Red Ball Express was a temporary and imperfect fix at best, but it did deliver 89,939 tons of supplies to the American armies during the critical eight days between 25 August and 6 September.

A. Gregory Gutgsell, Jr.

Additional Reading
Blumenson, Martin, *Breakout and Pursuit* (1961).
Ellis, Chris, *Military Transport of World War II* (1971).
Rose, Joseph R., *American Wartime Transportation* (1953).
Weigley, Russell F., *Eisenhower's Lieutenants: The Campaigns of France and Germany, 1944–1945* (1981).

River Crossing Operations
Because of the large number of rivers in Europe, river crossing operations took place on all fronts in World War II. Although the armies of different nations used techniques that varied slightly in de-

tail, the same basic problems confronted all river crossing operations during the war, as they do to this day.

As with any operation, a force attempting to cross a river considers the enemy and friendly situations, weather and terrain, and its mission. Since river crossings are inherently complicated and risky, and troops conducting the crossing are vulnerable, places where a favorable force ratio can be achieved are best. Other important factors are the level of training of one's own troops and the availability of bridging equipment or boats. River width, current velocity, riverbank conditions, and any existing bridges must be accounted for. Weather can have considerable effects as well; rivers swollen by rain or full of ice floes further complicate planning. The time available to the crossing force also has an impact on the operation. Considerations for a hasty crossing attempted from the march differ from a deliberate crossing characterized by centralized planning and substantial time for rehearsal.

A hasty crossing is the preferred method. Ideally in this case, the situation is developing so quickly that the defending enemy is either unsure of the proposed crossing site or at least not firmly in position and therefore unprepared or unable to react. Here, initiative and decisive leadership on the part of the attacker are essential. This is not to say that hasty crossings are not planned. Anticipating the obstacle and preparing to cross it, such as placing bridging equipment near the front of a march column, are prerequisites for a successful hasty operation.

One of the best examples of a hasty, albeit planned and well-rehearsed, river crossing took place on 13–14 May 1940, when Colonel Hermann Balck's (q.v.) regiment of the 1st *Panzer* Division crossed the Meuse at Sedan. Balck's unit contributed significantly to the German success in spring of 1940 by crossing a defended major river in broad daylight, working all night to expand and reinforce the bridgehead, and finally defending that bridgehead against a combined arms attack barely twelve hours after seizing it.

Deliberate crossings are much more set-piece affairs. Once a crossing location is chosen, serious preparations begin. The crossing force surveys the site, lays in any supporting fires and close air support, plans for smoke screens, and brings crossing equipment forward. The actual crossing operation generally begins with suppressive fires to cover one's own attacking forces while simultaneously softening up the defenders. If possible, the assault itself is obscured by darkness or smoke. Once the

Waffen SS *troops practice river crossing techniques in rubber assault craft. (IWM GER 604)*

assault force has secured the far bank, follow-on forces cross to further clear away any defenders and proceed to exploit the breach.

The 20–22 January 1944 attempt to cross the Rapido River (q.v.) is an example of a poorly planned and executed deliberate river crossing. During the crossing, the U.S. 36th Infantry Division (ID) had to deal with a sixty-foot-wide river, winter mud, 88mm guns sited in bunkers, and overwatching German positions atop Monte Cassino and Monte Majo. The commander of the 36th ID, Major General Fred L. Walker, wanted to try a more indirect approach by outflanking Monte Cassino (q.v.) to the north; but he could not dissuade his superiors. Planning time for the 36th ID was practically nonexistent. Walker received the order from U.S. II Corps only four days before the assault's start date. Out of a five-battalion assault force of 3,000 men, 1,681 were either killed, wounded, or missing. In the end, poor leadership at the corps and army levels, inadequate planning time, and being forced to attack into the enemy's strength condemned Walker's river crossing to failure.

River crossings should adhere to the principles of mass and synchronization (*see* Principles of War). Mass is achieved through concentrating at a specific point to cross a river and rupture the defense. Attacking forces want to direct their combat power against enemy weaknesses. If a natural weakness cannot be found, one is created by attacking an isolated enemy force. The commander must balance the need for massing his crossing assets against the need to use those same assets elsewhere.

Support, assault, and exploitation forces must act in a synchronized manner. The supporting force's direct and indirect fires are massed in concert with assault force's maneuver. Engineers must be sensitive to premature exhaustion of resources needed to punch through subsequent obstacles once across the river. Synchronization is achieved through detailed planning, clear instructions, effective command and control, and well-rehearsed forces.

There were some occasions in World War II where a crossing was forced through a *coup de main,* such as capturing a bridge intact. In these cases, luck played as big a role as planning: a bridge or fording site was either lightly defended or not defended at all, explosives meant to demolish a bridge failed to explode, or the soldiers detailed to blow up the bridge did not. Remagen (q.v.) is an example of such a crossing, but such instances were rare in World War II.

Robert Kirchubel

Additional Reading
Coll, Blanchard, et al., *The Corps of Engineers: Troops and Equipment* (1958).

S

Sabotage

The word *sabotage* probably comes from the French word *sabots* (wooden shoes), which workers reputedly jammed into machinery to disrupt rail movement during the French railroad strike of 1910. During World War II, anti-Axis resistance and partisan movements in Europe practiced both passive and active sabotage against factories, military installations, railroads, bridges, and military forces.

Passive sabotage efforts are those that cannot always be pinpointed as real or actual sabotage, and the persons who commit the acts cannot be directly implicated. Passive methods include malingering, working at a slow pace, turning out flawed or incorrect parts, introducing abrasives into complicated machines and lubricating oils, neglecting maintenance, misdirecting shipments, switching road signs, losing or misplacing paperwork, and issuing wrong or conflicting orders.

During the first six months of 1944, the French resistance (q.v.) sabotaged more than 100 factories producing war materiel for the Axis. Some were disabled by raids, but most were put out of action through the complicity of workers and management. Allied undercover agents requested assistance or permission from factory managers to conduct sabotage. If the management failed to agree, they were threatened with Allied bombing of the factory with its risk of massive loss of life. If that approach failed, the French trade union was approached, and then the individual workers. The British Broadcasting Corporation (BBC) (q.v.) and Radio Moscow made repeated appeals to all foreign workers in and out of Germany to sabotage the plants where they worked.

European railroad workers outside Germany used these passive methods and baffled the Germans, who lacked the manpower to run all the conquered rail lines by themselves. The workers disruptive actions included switching bills of lading, misdirecting cars and whole trains, losing empty freight cars (resulting in shortages of cars), minor yard accidents (causing timetable delays), misrouting shipments, and dropping fragile articles.

Doctors in the occupied territories often used their positions to issue certificates showing the bearer was suffering from a disease like tuberculosis or leukemia. They also used their automobiles to move messages, POWs, and weapons. They set up private clinics for wounded resistance members and ran secure meeting centers.

Postmen set up and ran a secret communications system, distributing messages and packages and providing a warning service to the resistance by telephone. They also furnished copies of German telegrams and letters that might contain information of interest to the resistance.

Another form of passive sabotage was the counter-scorch operation, which prevented the Axis occupation forces from destroying important structures to impede the Allied advances. During the advance of General George S. Patton's U.S Third Army (q.v.), for example, his forces were able to move several divisions across two critical bridges in less than one week because both bridges were seized from the occupation forces in counter-scorch strikes by the resistance.

Active sabotage is the direct destruction of the enemy's means to function as an occupation power and war machine. This type of sabotage involved the work of individuals and organizations (networks) that ambushed convoys; derailed trains; cut communications lines; blocked roads and rail lines; destroyed bridges, factories, power stations, locomotives, vehicles, barracks, ammunition and oil storage sites, and military equipment; conducted assassinations of commanders and couriers; and stole their papers. One important example was the destruction of the telephone systems in France, Belgium, and the Netherlands, which forced the Germans to do most of their business by radio, resulting in considerable opportunity for Allied intelligence-gathering systems like ULTRA (q.v.).

One night in early 1944, a group of saboteurs executed what they called the "great cut-off," involving the destruction of fifty electric towers and halting production in a number of industrial plants in Belgium and the Ruhr. This act also cut the rail communications between Germany and the Belgian coast. That one night's work cost the Axis approximately 10 million man hours of lost work.

General Dwight D. Eisenhower (q.v.) reported that the combined resistance efforts in France accomplished the following from sabotage operations between June and August 1944: 885 railroad cuts, 140 telecommunications cuts, seventy-five road and waterway cuts, forty-four industrial incidents, 322 locomotives destroyed, twenty-four convoys ambushed, and seven aircraft destroyed. Another report stated that during the week of D-Day (6 June 1944), more than 800 strategic targets in France were destroyed.

In Greece, according to one report, resistance groups by November 1944 sabotaged and destroyed fifteen bridges, including the Svilengrad and Alexandropdu bridges; ambushed fourteen trains; destroyed sixty-one trucks; blew up six miles of rail line; and inflicted more than 500 Axis casualties.

In Norway, the resistance sabotaged the Norsk Hydro (q.v.) plant, which produced heavy water, as well as the Lake Tinnsjoe ferry that transported the last known reserves of heavy water. Other targets included German naval vessels, tanker trucks, engineer equipment, and the entire supply of torpedoes in Norway.

In the Netherlands, a resistance organization destroyed the provincial registers in Amsterdam, which disrupted the Axis roundups of Jews and other wanted civilians.

In Italy, German Field Marshal Albert Kesselring (q.v.), commander in chief of the Italian front, stated that the destruction of rail bridges by the resistance made German operations almost impossible. During the German withdrawal, the resistance blew up seven major highway and rail bridges.

In Denmark, the resistance severely damaged the German air base at Aalborg. As the Allies approached, the railroads were put completely out of action, as were all tugboats (which were sent to Sweden, making their ports unusable). The resistance also destroyed the Charlottenland factory that made radio parts for the V-2 rockets.

In Romania, the resistance struck the Ploesti petroleum refineries and oil wells and destroyed the Tirgoviste arsenal and the Miras ammunition plant warehouse.

As the war progressed, the Allies' Supreme Headquarters Allied Expeditionary Force (SHAEF) (q.v.) made a determined effort to coordinate the sabotage activity with military operations. In July 1944 in Brittany, as Patton's Third Army swung southeast, resistance groups fed intelligence to the advancing forces, while others, on specific orders from SHAEF, performed acts of sabotage immediately ahead of the leading Allied troops. Eventually, this type of coordination was incorporated into the operations of all the advancing Allied field armies.

Throughout the war, the resistance had to contend with intrafaction rivalry, political constraints, collaborators, and the Axis occupation forces. In one operation alone, the Germans neutralized more than 50 percent of the Allied sabotage agents in Holland. In the French village of Oradour-sur-Glane (q.v.), on 10 June 1944, German reprisals for a resistance raid cost the lives of 642 men, women, and children. On 24 March 1944, at the Ardeatine Caves (q.v.) in Italy, the Germans executed 335 political prisoners and Jewish civilians in retaliation for an attack by the Italian resistance.

The successes achieved by sabotage operations against the Axis occupation forces and their collaborators strengthened the various resistance movements, but as a result, large segments of the populations learned clandestine methods and guerrilla tactics. This training was frequently used after the war to continue the struggle for control of postwar governments, which led to intense conflicts between various political factions and nationalities, and in some cases caused civil wars. Sabotage also became a basic weapon of insurgent groups associated with the anticolonial, separatist, and Communist-backed movements of the Cold War era.

Alexander Molnar, Jr.

Additional Reading

Blake, Ehrlich, *Resistance: France 1940–1945* (1965).

Brown, Anthony Cave, *The Secret War Report of the OSS* (1976).

Michel, Henri, *The Shadow War: European Resistance 1939–1945* (1972).

Schlieffen Plan

Fall GELB (Case YELLOW), the war plan Germany used for the 1940 invasion of France (q.v.), has often mistakenly been identified as just an improvement over the Schlieffen Plan of World War I. Operationally and tactically there were similarities. Strategically, the two plans were different.

General Alfred *Graf* von Schlieffen became Germany's chief of the general staff in 1891, and remained in that post until his retirement in December 1905. During that period, he developed the war plan that bore his name and became, despite subsequent changes, the operational blueprint for German planning in case of war with both Russia and France.

The Schlieffen Plan, in development since 1897, was based on several considerations. The first was Germany's geographical location in central Europe. The second was the growing prospect of having to wage war against both Russia and France, which had been drawing closer together since 1892, and the imperatives this imposed on maintaining German security. The third consideration was the necessity of ensuring a short war because of Germany's insufficient raw material base and the threat of a longer war becoming a widening war.

These assumptions were consonant with the age of imperialism and social Darwinism: competition for empire; growing national antagonisms; the inexorable progress of science and technology and their military implications; increasing international anarchy; and the political repercussions of Germany's *Weltpolitik*. Germany's foreign policy after the turn of the century alienated several counties and left only one ally, the declining Austro-Hungarian Empire, itself at odds with Russia and the southern Slav nationalism emanating from Serbia.

Von Schlieffen, like his counterparts elsewhere, believed that war was probable and preparation necessary. He assumed Germany's main task was to defeat France quickly in order to free German forces to halt the more backward and slower to mobilize "Russian steamroller." Hence, Germany had to assume the offensive against France, even if its attitude toward war with Germany was ambiguous, while taking up a defensive position toward Russia, aided by Austria-Hungary.

Given the importance of time, mobilization schedules, and the balance of forces, the only way to obtain this quick victory against France was to outflank French fortifications (which pivoted on Verdun), by passing through Luxembourg and Belgium. The main thrust would be made with the bulk of the German Army, fifty-three divisions. Simultaneously, holding actions would be conducted on the southern front, with ten division against the fulcrum of Verdun and another nine against Lorraine. Based on precise timetables mobilization by either opponent, France or Russia, would necessitate immediate recourse to war by Germany.

Von Schlieffen's plan was a radical departure from that devised by Field Marshal Helmut von Moltke, who envisaged defensive actions against France while launching a limited offensive against Russia. Von Schlieffen's successor, Helmut von Moltke (the younger), chief of staff from 1906 to September 1914, made significant changes in von Schlieffen's plan. He excluded Holland from attack and changed the ratio of troops allocated to the northern and southern sectors of the western front. Once World War I commenced, von Moltke reinforced the southern sector of the front when France implemented its Plan XVII. He attacked in force, resisting the French Army rather than drawing it into Germany and completing the "wheeling operation" of the Schlieffen Plan. Several corps were withdrawn from the northern front, not only to augment the screening actions against Belgian fortresses, but also to assist the German Eighth Army in the east against the earlier than anticipated Russian advances into East Prussia. Furthermore, in neither von Schlieffen's plan nor von Moltke's modification were British intervention on the Continent or the effect of British sea power given a great role; a costly mistake in view of Germany's known vulnerable resource base.

The Schlieffen Plan has been the subject of much debate, analysis, and controversy. Its rigidity was blamed for making World War I inevitable. Certainly the violation of Belgian neutrality made the likelihood of Great Britain's entry into the war with Germany much greater. Whether or not the implementation of the original plan would have achieved Germany's victory on the western front is still debatable, even after the experience of 1940. There is general agreement, however, that von Moltke's modifications compounded Germany's strategic and logistical problems.

Strategically, *Fall GELB* was different. The original Schlieffen Plan was designed to defeat the French Army in one decisive operation because of the necessity to then turn east and face Russia. *Fall GELB* had no such objective, since Germany was not contemplating a two-front war at that point. The original version of *Fall GELB*, developed in October 1939, had two operational similarities with the Schlieffen Plan: (1) the advance through

Belgium, and (2) the main attack on the right. Based on proposals by General Erich von Manstein (q.v.) and others, *Fall GELB* underwent several modifications before it was put into action.

By February 1940, the drastically revised *Fall GELB*, with von Manstein's "sickle cut" of armored forces through the Ardennes, now had the decisive objective of cutting off the Allied forces north and west of Sedan, France. That decisive objective was necessary because in 1940 the Allies expected Germany to advance through Belgium, whereas in 1914 the Allies were surprised by the size of the German force in Belgium. Likewise, in 1940, the Germans had to plan on dealing with a British force on the Continent, something that had not been a major planning factor in 1914. Thus *Fall GELB* had the operational objective of seizing the Channel coast.

In the final analysis, however, *Fall GELB* lacked the overriding imperative of quickly having to shift toward the east that was the hallmark of the Schlieffen Plan.

N.H. Gaworek

Additional Reading

Griess, Thomas E. (ed.), *The West Point Military History Series: The Second World War: Europe and the Mediterranean* (1984).

Ritter, Gerhard, *The Schlieffen Plan: Critique of a Myth* (1958).

Second Front

See STRATEGY, ANGLO-AMERICAN AND STRATEGY, SOVIET

Siegfried Line

See WEST WALL

Signals Intelligence

Signals intelligence, the intercept and analysis of electronic signals, had its birth just before World War I as telecommunications became increasingly important in diplomacy and military operations. In many European countries, the monitoring of this new communications system came under the same bureaus (called "black chambers") that previously had intercepted and read foreign mail. Their contributions to military operations in that war and the importance of intercepting and analyzing a likely opponent's communications (called signals at that time) were widely recognized during the interwar period.

By 1939, virtually every power in Europe had a signals intelligence agency within its foreign ministries and, more often than not, within its military departments as well. Signals intelligence (called SIGINT) was expanded during World War II to include the intercept and analysis of electronic signals not related to communications. This reflected the growing importance of radar (q.v.) and electronic systems in warfare. Winning the electronic war determined the outcome in the Battle of the Atlantic (q.v.) and contributed to the success of the Allied bombing campaign. Signals intelligence played a key role in every military campaign in World War II.

The more spectacular code breaking or cryptographic (*see* Cryptography) aspects of signals intelligence are well known if not well understood. Successful code breaking can have an immediate strategic impact on a country's activities, both military and diplomatic. With it, one can read an enemy's actual thoughts and plans and prepare one's own countermeasures or reactions accordingly. For that reason, every major SIGINT agency had a code breaking section, and those of the respective foreign ministries generally had the largest and best funded.

The U.S. State Department was the only major foreign ministry that did not maintain a signals intercept service during the interwar period. Even minor European countries, such as Romania and Hungary, had such services. Fortunately for the United States, its military services retained their SIGINT agencies after World War I and had begun to expand their capabilities as World War II approached. At first, the U.S. military's focus on protecting America's territories in the Pacific limited its code breaking successes to the major countries in that theater, but with British assistance, the Americans were able to make a significant contribution to the Allied SIGINT effort in Europe after 1943.

Although spectacular in its impact, code breaking is neither the only element of signals intelligence nor the most important. Much can be gained from analyzing the nature of the signal itself, as well as from whom and to whom the signal is directed. Individual Morse code operators tap out their messages in a unique way that can be identified. This "fist" could be used to track the operator's movements. Since many military and political leaders of the period used their own personal communicators, the leaders or their units could be located by finding the communicators. Also, unit call signs or the code names that units and commanders used to identify themselves in electronic communications provided a means by which to track the movements and activities of those units. For that reason, many successful deception plans of World War II revolved around the placement and activities of communications personnel and the exchanging of call signs.

Determining with whom units and agencies are communicating can do much to identify the intentions, capabilities, and likely missions of those units or their leaders. For example, communications between a major enemy ground component commander's headquarters and most of the enemy's armored or mobile divisions in the area might indicate an impending offensive in that sector. The addition of a major air force HQ communicating with that commander's HQ would be an additional indicator. Indeed, those were exactly the SIGINT indicators available to the Allied ground commanders in France on 8–9 May 1940, some twenty-four hours prior to the German invasion of Belgium.

Denying this sort of information to an opponent was as important as gaining it from them. Hence, SIGINT was very much a chess game between those collecting the signals and their opponents' efforts to protect their own communications from interception or deny the collectors the details required to analyze those communications. This was called communications security. The communications security effort had to be balanced against the likely impact on one's own forces. Using a permanent call sign, for example, simplified friendly force identification on the net, but also made it easier for hostile SIGINT services to do the same. Thus, most nations rotated their call signs periodically, except where speed of identification or communications outweighed the need for security—such as for aircraft, individual minor combatants, or tactical communications among units in combat.

Another aspect of SIGINT was direction finding, or DF. This technique used directional antennas to determine the azimuth or direction from which a signal emanated. Two or more intercept stations operating in concert against a single transmitting station (or emitter) could triangulate its position. In other words, they could fix the emitter's location by plotting the respective azimuths on a map or chart. The emitter's location, or fix, was where the azimuths intersected. The closer the angle of intersection was to 90 degrees (a "cross bearing"), the more accurate the fix. The fix's accuracy also improved with the number of azimuths, since the primitive directional antennas of the period required the operator to judge the azimuth himself by deciding from which direction

the signal was strongest. The more experienced the intercept operator, the more accurate his judgment. A larger number of azimuths also enabled the plotter to discard the most inconsistent azimuths, or to determine an area of probability if no clear fix emerged.

The transmitter's frequency also affected the accuracy of a DF fix. Higher frequency systems had narrower beams and were easier to judge. Lower frequencies could be detected at longer ranges since their signals often traveled along the earth's surface beyond the horizon (ground wave) or reflected off the stratosphere back onto the earth's surface (sky wave). Radars, airborne navigation systems, and the higher frequency communications systems—such as very high frequency (VHF) air and tactical ground communications—could only be intercepted if the receiver was located within a direct line of sight of the transmitter. When detected by multiple intercept stations, however, an emitter's position could be fixed very accurately and within a very short time.

Proximity to the transmitter was another consideration. The closer the intercept station was to the transmitter, the more accurate the azimuth was likely to be. That was why Allied naval authorities wanted high frequency DF (HF/DF) systems installed on destroyers escorting convoys. It enabled the escorts to locate the U-boat reporting the convoy's location more accurately, significantly improving the chances of destroying the U-boat.

High frequency communications were so important to naval operations, because of the vast distances involved, that all nations employed huge naval SIGINT infrastructures with numerous HF/DF sites to track hostile and neutral naval forces. The Western Allies had the most extensive and effective networks, with SIGINT stations at virtually every British and American overseas base. The Italians and Soviets had networks that enabled them to track naval units operating in the waters near their shores. The Germans had only a limited capability to track naval units in the Atlantic accurately until they established HF/DF sites in France and Norway. Even then, the lack of "cross bearings" inhibited the accuracy of their fixes against units in the South Atlantic and Indian Oceans.

Britain had the world's largest and most capable SIGINT organization at the start of World War II. All military and diplomatic SIGINT activities theoretically came under its umbrella, but in practice, the tactical and operational SIGINT collection of the military services came under the service chiefs. Still, Britain's SIGINT effort was better coordinated than that of any of the war's participants. Britain entered the war at a slight disadvantage since most of its SIGINT efforts had been directed against the Soviet Union during the interwar period—Germany had been identified as a threat only in the late 1930s. Britain did benefit from its good relations and cooperation with France, and from 1939 on, with Poland.

The French had a good picture of the German military communications networks, much of it gained from the Czech intelligence services that transferred many of their files to the French just before the German occupation in 1938.

The activities of Bletchley Park (q.v.) and its decoding successes are generally well known, but the British military SIGINT services also made a significant contribution to the Allied war effort. The Anglo-American HF/DF sites greatly facilitated the Allies' antisubmarine efforts, particularly after HF/DF equipment was installed aboard Allied escort ships. The British Army assigned signals intelligence companies, called special wireless sections (SWS), to each British field army HQ. Equipped primarily with HF intercept equipment and lacking DF capability at war's start, these units became more mobile as the war progressed. The doctrine changed as well. In 1940, British SWS units in France detected the movement of the *Panzer* divisions up to the border and into the Ardennes. British commanders, however, did not accept their reports, waiting instead for confirmation by aerial reconnaissance. The resulting forty-eight-hour delay was an important element in the Allied defeat in France. Afterward, such reports of "immediate significance" went directly to the British field army commander.

The British "Y" Service, or voice intercept service, intercepted uncoded German voice communications—primarily the *Luftwaffe*'s, but those of the German Army as well. Field Marshall Sir Bernard L. Montgomery (q.v.) recognized and exploited the capabilities of the Y Service better perhaps than any other senior British commander.

Initially employed against German fighter and bomber communications to supplement data obtained from radar plots, the RAF's Y Service took on a broader role as the British shifted to the offensive after 1942. Assigned to disrupt the German air defense system, Y Service operators actively intruded in the German night fighter and later on day fighter communications circuits. British operators would call the German pilots or HQ controller on the radio, issue false orders, request operational information, or question orders and otherwise disrupt communications. Beginning in 1942, every bomber raid

included a specially modified bomber carrying Y Service operators who provided warning of German fighter activities and disrupted German communications as necessary. Since the German Army used tactical codes in their voice circuits, the British rarely used the Y Service operators to intrude on German ground communications.

To be effective, Y Service operators required an extensive knowledge of German communications procedures and call signs, as well as near native fluency in the language. Intrusion can be countered, however, by the use of regularly changing tactical codes and tight communications discipline. Since air operations occurred at a speed that precluded the extensive use of codes, air control nets were the most likely to suffer intrusion. The Germans countered the RAF's Y Service by using female communicators, but the British introduced female operators of their own. Although the Y Service never completely disrupted the German air defense command and control system, it certainly reduced its effectiveness.

The Polish security service was much smaller than that of its allies and opponents, but it still managed to obtain copies of the German Enigma (q.v.) encryption machine and made significant inroads toward breaking Germany's codes—particularly those of the *Luftwaffe*. The Poles also reportedly broke some of the lower tactical Soviet code systems. They shared their results with their Anglo-French allies, even smuggling the files and equipment to France after Warsaw's fall in 1939. This collaboration was the foundation of the Allies' successful and widespread penetration of the German Enigma encryption systems (*see* ULTRA). Cooperation and collaboration between the United States and Great Britain only began after Dunkirk, and accelerated after the Battle of Britain (qq.v.).

Little is known about the Soviet SIGINT services, but given the lack of cooperation between the state security organs (*see* NKVD) and military intelligence before the war, it is reasonable to assume that each of those agencies operated its own separate SIGINT services. Although the extent of Soviet SIGINT capabilities in World War II probably will never be known, the Germans discovered during their early offensives that the Soviets had extensive knowledge of the German communications networks and command structure. Finland's SIGINT services discovered in November 1939 that the Soviets had been monitoring their air defense and army communications for some time. The Finns also believed that they had discovered several instances of Soviet operators intruding on Finnish communications networks.

The Germans reported similar experiences during the battle for Stalingrad (q.v.) and the later campaigns on the eastern front. At the very least, this suggests that the Soviets had a significant capability to operate against the communications of its two most important European foes.

Germany entered the war with three separate military SIGINT organizations: the *Abwehr*'s (q.v.) *Chiffrierwesen*; the *Kriegsmarine*'s *Beobachdienst* or *B-Dienst*; and the *Luftwaffe*'s *Forschungsamt*. The *Gestapo* (q.v.) had a SIGINT service as well, but used it primarily for counterintelligence. Each agency operated independently after 1938, and rarely shared information, much less cooperated with each other. The German military service chiefs, in fact, often used their SIGINT agency's reports to curry favor with Adolf Hitler (q.v.). The resulting dispersal of effort inhibited the overall effectiveness of Germany's SIGINT effort. The *Luftwaffe*, for example, would not ask the *Kriegsmarine* to collect information about Allied land and air radars and electronic systems, nor would the *Kriegsmarine* ask the *Luftwaffe* for information about Allied sea-based systems. Conversely, neither service was enthusiastic about sharing what it knew about these systems. Both services had to collect against all possible Allied systems, and given the limited resources available, neither obtained all the information it needed to support its respective war efforts.

Nonetheless, all the German SIGINT services enjoyed some successes, particularly early in the war. The Germans concentrated on operational and tactical signals intelligence—that is, the rapid dissemination of SIGINT information directly and immediately to the operational-level commander. German Army SIGINT units were assigned to each army corps and contributed greatly to the successful ground offensives of 1939 and 1941. Detecting the movements of Allied ground units far ahead of the German advance, they provided timely warning of Allied countermoves that enabled German mobile units to outmaneuver their slower Allied opponents, who received their own SIGINT reports much more slowly. The German SIGINT equipment was also light and mobile and the units were totally motorized so they could keep up with the *Panzer* units. General Erwin Rommel's (q.v.) signals intelligence company is probably the most famous of these units, and he credited much of his success to its efforts. That company was so good that Field Marshall Montgomery specifically targeted the unit for destruction before launching the El Alamein (q.v.) offensive.

The *Luftwaffe* used the same equipment and employed a structure similar to the army's, providing each *Luftflotte* (Air Fleet) with a radio reconnaissance battalion. These battalions monitored enemy air force and ground service communications to provide warning of enemy air movements, locate enemy operating bases, and locate enemy air headquarters and command posts. The radio reconnaissance battalions in Germany and on the western front were consolidated in May 1944 to concentrate against the Allied bombing campaign. They provided warning of Allied bombing raids by intercepting the prelaunch testing of electronic systems aboard the bombers. They also helped to track night bomber streams by monitoring the bombers' navigation systems and radar emissions.

The *Kriegsmarine* primarily employed permanent HF/DF sites located near its major bases in Germany and the occupied countries in the west. These sites enabled the *B-Dienst* to provide accurate locating data on enemy ship movements in the North Sea and northern Atlantic to German naval units involved in the Battle of the Atlantic. The data were disseminated immediately to naval and U-boat operational headquarters and disseminated regularly to units at sea. The accuracy was not very good on shipping in the Mediterranean, South Atlantic, and Indian Oceans, but it did give German naval units an idea of what they might encounter. Also, the *B-Dienst* was able to decrypt Allied convoy and Royal Navy operational communications during much of the war's early years. That was critical to Germany's success in Norway (q.v.) and contributed to the effectiveness of U-boat operations during early phases of the Battle of the Atlantic.

The *Kriegsmarine* also assigned *B-Dienst* detachments to Germany's surface raiders and major surface combatants. Thus, every flagship and surface raider had the ability to detect Allied naval formations and convoys in their operating area. In some cases, the *B-Deinst* detachments also did local decoding of enemy communications, particularly merchant shipping and aerial reconnaissance reporting. Transmission security was provided by the use of "one-time" pads to protect against enemy decoding.

Italy's state and military intelligence services had SIGINT units. Targeted mostly against the French and Yugoslavs, the Italians had a reasonably effective decoding service, which successfully broke the Yugoslavian Army and the French and British naval codes during the interwar period. The Italians, however, were similar to the French in that they relied on permanent signals-monitoring sta-ions. The Italian services were totally dependent upon SIGINT sites in Italy and Albania. This not only inhibited the interception of Allied communications in North Africa (q.v.) and the more distant waters of the Mediterranean, but it delayed dissemination of the reporting. It also prevented the rapport and mutual understanding between the intelligence services and the supported commanders that are so essential to effective intelligence support.

The Italians' most prominent success came during the invasion of Yugoslavia when Italian radio operators in Albania regularly intruded on the encrypted Yugoslav command net, countermanding attack orders and misdirecting Yugoslav units and logistics support.

In contrast to the cooperative Anglo-American SIGINT effort, the Axis countries did not trust each other enough to share information, much less coordinate their SIGINT efforts. Finland had the best SIGINT service of the minor countries, decrypting Soviet naval and other communications at various times during the Winter War (q.v.). Monitoring of Soviet Air Force and army communications also provided the Finns with key information about Soviet intentions and preparations well in advance of actual attacks and bombing raids. Unfortunately, it was not enough to know when, where, and with what your opponent was attacking. One had to have the resources to defeat the attack, and such resources were what the Finns most acutely lacked. The Romanians and Hungarians also had fairly large and effective SIGINT services, but their efforts were directed more against each other, so they contributed very little to the overall Axis war effort.

SIGINT has become one of the most important elements of modern intelligence operations in a world of fast-moving, mobile military forces. Electronic signals are the means by which every modern commander sees and controls his forces, which are themselves dependent upon electronic systems to conduct their missions. SIGINT became an increasingly technological and complex affair as World War II progressed. The ability to read an enemy's communications or know which of his units were in contact with each other provided insights into his operations and intentions. Knowing an enemy's electronic sensor and navigation systems led to the development of effective countermeasures and the ability to blind him at a critical time, or just to avoid his forces when necessary. The Anglo-American cooperation in SIGINT enabled both countries to make the most of their SIGINT efforts and virtually guaranteed

the Allied victory once the war-fighting forces had the resources to exploit the insights the SIGINT services developed.

Carl O. Schuster

Additional Reading

Andrew, Christopher, *Codebreaking and Signals Intelligence* (1986).
Clayton, Aileen, *The Enemy Is Listening* (1980).
Irving, David, *Breach of Security* (1968).
Kahn, David, *The Codebreakers* (1972).
Norman, Bruce, *Secret Warfare: The Battle of Codes and Ciphers* (1973).
West, Nigel, *The SIGINT Secrets* (1986).

SOFT Underbelly

See STRATEGY, ANGLO-AMERICAN

Special Operations

Special operations are military actions conducted by specially organized, trained, and equipped forces to achieve military, political, economic, or psychological objectives by nonconventional means in enemy-held or politically sensitive areas. Although special operations of one sort or another have been used by military commanders for hundreds of years, the basic framework of special operations and special operations forces (SOFs) as we know them today emerged during World War II. Virtually every country that fought in the war employed specially trained elite forces to conduct missions where stealth, shock, and surprise provided results far out of proportion to the forces involved.

Contrary to the position espoused in many postwar writings, the idea of special operations did not originate in Great Britain, Rather, it appears to have been a common theme among pioneering military thinkers in several countries during the interwar period. Drawing from the lessons of similar operations in World War I, these analysts saw the emerging technologies of the airplane, the submarine, and the motorcar as enabling commanders to avoid the stalemate of trench warfare by striking at targets deep within an enemy's rear. Although mostly ignored by traditional military leaders, their ideas found fruit among political leaders seeking economical ways of striking at more powerful neighbors.

Germany, Italy, and the Soviet Union, which all saw themselves as surrounded by more powerful and threatening neighbors, developed SOFs before the war. Facing a seemingly desperate strategic situation following the fall of France, Great Britain followed suit in 1940. It was Britain's spectacular special operations successes in World War II that established the standard for the world's elite special forces of today.

In every country, highly motivated and capable personnel who had exceptional physical and mental capabilities were recruited for SOF units. Independence, initiative, intelligence, and a broad range of specialized knowledge were all required of personnel assigned to these units. SOF personnel had to be able to enter and depart a target area stealthily, have the patience to await developments, and yet be capable of decisive action under rapidly changing circumstances. SOF units also had to maintain combat cohesion and effectiveness despite casualties or other losses. As a result, their personnel also had to be nearly impervious to adversity.

Special operations had exceptional requirements that gave these units and their training an almost dichotomous quality. The units had to be small, yet powerful and self-sufficient. That led to a proclivity for automatic weapons and demolition equipment. Since most of their combat was conducted at close range, these troops tended to carry submachine guns. They were essentially light infantry units, yet it was not unusual for each team's member to carry more than 100 pounds of equipment into action. Most of that load was special weapons and ordnance employed in the destruction of the target.

Although flexibility was the key to success, SOF units rehearsed their operations meticulously, learning each step almost by rote. This was done so that all team members would be as familiar with each other's parts in the operation as with their own. One never could predict when another unit would fail to arrive at a designated point, or when a plan might go awry. Discipline, therefore, was tight but not rigid. Only the most dedicated personnel could be included. Anyone with doubts had to be left behind. Surprise was their primary advantage and hesitation generally led to casualties and defeat.

These principles guided the formation and development of all special operations forces in the war. Germany was the first country to employ SOFs, infiltrating special teams of *Brandenburgers* (q.v.) into Poland (q.v.) more than a week before actually invading that country. The *Brandenburgers* not only seized key bridges and military objectives along Germany's projected lines of advance into Poland, they also sabotaged critical communications centers and logistics facilities to disrupt

Poland's mobilization and ability to control it forces. More significantly, these teams occupie and protected Polish factories and resource center considered vital to Germany's long-term wa effort.

The successes of the *Brandenburgers* led t their employment as the lead elements to ever German invasion thereafter. They seized bridges i Holland, Belgium, France, and even the Sovie Union. General Erwin Rommel's (q.v.) disapprova of such operations inhibited their employment i North Africa, where he used them primarily fo long-range reconnaissance. The *Brandenburger* performed their greatest services on the Russia front, operating as far as 400 kilometers behin Soviet lines. The overall effectiveness of Germa SOF units declined, however, as the war went on

Assigned to the *Abwehr* (q.v.), the *Branden burgers* suffered in consonance with that agency declining fortunes. As their operational codes wer broken by Allied intelligence and their resource were drawn off by the indifference of the Germa Army's leadership and Adolf Hitler's (q.v.) prefer ence for Nazi Party or SS-affiliated special units the surviving personnel of the *Brandenburgers* in creasingly were malemployed as Germany shifte to the strategic defensive.

By 1944, the *Brandenburgers* were either in corporated into conventional army units, siphone off to specialized conventional formations, or re cruited into SS (q.v.) special forces units. Thes units, led by the redoubtable Otto Skorzeny (q.v.) enjoyed some spectacular successes of their own i the war's final two years, but on the whole the suffered inordinate casualties in the majority o their operations.

German special forces also suffered fron the navy's apathy. Admiral Erich Raeder (q.v. openly opposed such units, forbidding naval in volvement in special operations until the final day of his tenure as commander in chief. Admiral Ka Dönitz (q.v.) had a different point of view. H advocated such operations and supported ther once he assumed command of the German Nav on 31 January 1943. Unfortunately, it was too lat by then. The German naval special forces, th *Kleinkampfverbände* (q.v.), suffered the fate of al such units thrown into the fray with inadequat training and support; but not before they dre considerable Allied resources toward their defea

In late 1939, the British started experimen ing with special forces, establishing "independen companies" from territorial units. These units wer badly misused during the Norway (q.v.) campaig It was only through Prime Minister Winston

Churchill's vision and aggressive stewardship that Britain became the primary advocate and most successful practitioner of special operations in World War II.

Following the disaster at Dunkirk (q.v.), the British formed their first commando (q.v.) units, initially drawing personnel from the earlier independent companies and from other free spirits entering the British armed forces. Churchill avoided the German mistake by organizing British SOFs under one command, Combined Operations (q.v.). Although other British SOF units were raised in various theaters and services, Combined Operations served as the focal point for developing special operations equipment, concepts, and tactics. Thus, British SOFs obtained special equipment and support more easily than the SOFs of their allies and opponents.

Despite some rough starts and early failures, Britain's SOFs became a threat feared by all Italian and German troops in occupied Europe and North Africa and an inspiration to the Allies and occupied peoples. British SOFs struck critical resource centers, stole radars and other secret equipment, and kidnapped senior German officers. In so doing, they tied down more than 150,000 Axis troops at a time when the British SOFs themselves never numbered more than 5,000.

The British also were quick to adapt good ideas and equipment from others. After suffering at the hands of Italian special naval units, the British developed their own miniature submarines from captured Italian models. These units were then used to make attacks on the German battleship *Tirpitz* on 31 October 1942 and on 22 September 1943. The latter raid at Alten Fjord (q.v.) was successful, putting the battleship out of action for several months.

Britain's SOF evolved from a raiding force to a specialized reconnaissance and assault force as the Allies shifted to the strategic offensive. These units now conducted preinvasion reconnaissance, destroyed obstacles, marked channels and transit lanes, and seized key facilities in advance and along the flanks of Allied beachheads. Once the Allied armies were established ashore throughout western Europe, the British SOFs were employed more and more as specialized reconnaissance or assault units, operating ahead of the Allied advance.

After the war, Britain consolidated its many SOF units into two main components, the Special Air Service (SAS) and the Special Boat Service (SBS) (qq.v.). Those units continue to serve Great Britain to this day.

Having enjoyed some success with special operations in World War I, the Italian Navy formed two special purpose squadrons for naval operations, the 1st and 10th Light Flotillas. Using specially modified "sleds" or miniature submarines, these units struck at Allied shipping and warships in their supposedly safe operating bases in the far reaches of the Mediterranean. Interestingly, the commander of the 10th Light Flotilla (q.v.) refused to accept missions transmitted to him via radio. He felt that any code could be broken. As a result, all of his operations achieved surprise. His force sank merchant ships in Gibraltar and crippled the British battle fleet at key points during the Mediterranean campaign.

The Italian 1st Light Flotilla was very similar, employing miniature submarines and remote-controlled Lentl boats to attack Allied ships and shipping in Malta and along Italy's coast. Following the Italian surrender in September 1943, the two units split up, with the 10th Light Flotilla staying with Benito Mussolini's (q.v.) Italian Social Republic, and the 1st Light Flotilla going over to the Allies.

The Soviet Union had the largest special operations force structure before the war, having learned of the utility of such units during the Russian civil war. Soviet doctrine at the start of World War II required so-called diversionary forces to operate throughout the enemy's operational depth, disrupting his command and control, logistics, and force structure. In the early stages of the war, however, the Soviets suffered more at the hands of German SOFs than the other way around.

The Soviets learned from their mistakes and were quick to react. The first known employment of Soviet SOFs came during the amphibious assault on the Romanian Army's coastal flank at Odessa on 22 September 1941. A Soviet naval SOF unit attacked the headquarters of the Romanian 13th Division, killing many key staff officers and paralyzing the Romanian defenses.

As the war progressed, Soviet SOFs and specialized "engineer" units acted as advisors to partisan (q.v.) units, assassinated Axis military leaders in rear areas, protected intelligence agents, and acted as forward reconnaissance detachments deep in the German rear. Soviet naval SOF units also conducted raids against German coastal defenses and facilities on the Black and Arctic seas, operating much like Allied Special Boat Section (SBS) and UDT (q.v.) personnel. Soviet SOF losses were much heavier because they lacked the specialized equipment or support of their Allied counterparts. Nonetheless, Soviet SOFs were a major distraction to the Germans, even if their successes were not fully exploited.

The Americans were the last to get into special operations, forming the rangers (q.v.) and scouts and rangers (later named UDT) in 1942. The rangers operated in a fashion similar to the British commandos, although being established as the Allies made the transition to the offensive meant that the rangers were employed more as forward reconnaissance and special assault units than as raiding forces.

The scouts and rangers evolved into the "frogmen" or underwater demolition teams that combined with the army's explosive ordnance disposal (EOD) teams to conduct pre-landing reconnaissance and obstacle clearing operations for every Allied landing after Operation TORCH. Landing with the first wave, the rangers and frogmen assaulted the most critical positions in the enemy's defenses or cleared away the dense minefields and obstructions that protected those defenses. They suffered heavy casualties in the process.

The Office of Strategic Services (OSS) (q.v.) also employed specially trained personnel as forward agents and saboteurs in the German rear, primarily in France, Italy, and Yugoslavia. Their operations enjoyed mixed success, but established the doctrinal foundations for modern American special forces.

By their nature, special operations were risky and potentially expensive affairs. When successful, however, they provided a payoff that far exceeded the expense of maintaining the forces involved. The very existence of such units forced every nation to divert thousands of troops from the conventional front lines. Special operations proved cost effective from that perspective alone. Moreover, the surgical nature of such operations, which could be targeted against even the smallest facility with little danger to the surrounding area, made them all the more attractive in a world increasingly dominated by weapons of massive and seemingly random destructiveness. Thus, special operations gained in importance after World War II, and remain so today.

Carl O. Schuster

Additional Reading

Dwyer, John B., *Scouts and Rangers* (1993).
Leonov, Viktor, *Blood on the Shores* (1993).
Lucas, James, *Kommando: Germany's Special Forces of World War II* (1985).
Schofield, Carey, *The Russian Elite* (1993).
Seymour, William, *British Special Forces* (1986).
Warren, C.E.T., *The Midget Raiders* (1954).

Strategic Bombing

Time has not abated the controversies surrounding the strategic bombardment campaign of 1940–1945. Critics like J.F.C. Fuller (q.v.) argue that a least up to the spring of 1944, the campaign starved the Allied armies of necessary air support promoted an unhealthy imbalance in armament production, and its costs, in terms of raw materials and industrial manpower, actually prolonged hostilities.

The costs were indeed high; more than 2 million Germans experienced the Allied assault which included multiple attacks on sixty-one cities with a population of more than 100,000 people. Between 305,000 and 593,000 German civilians died, an estimated 20 percent of whom were children, while 7.5 million people were left homeless. In contrast, it cost Great Britain and the United States more than 98,000 airmen killed o missing, and 40,000 aircraft damaged or destroyed, to decrease overall German war production by 15 to 20 percent. In the case of RAF Bomber Command, the typical airman completed only fourteen of thirty required missions. Such statistics do suggest, at least in part, that the effort may not have been worth the costs.

Critics like Robert Leckie and Ronald Schaffer argue that strategic bombardment was largely immoral. Great Britain and the United States may have invested 35 to 50 percent of their war production on modern air forces, but their return on investment, particularly in the case of strategic air attack, was a growing absence of proportionality, target discrimination, and respect for noncombatant immunity. Sound strategy was thus not a synonym for fair play, regardless of the desperate demands of total war. (That pundits often confuse the entire Combined Bomber Offensive with costly British area attacks is undeniable. It explains as does the bitter memory of the Vietnam War, the retroactive moral discomfort some now feel toward strategic bombardment in World War II.)

Moral issues aside, it is true that the strategic air campaign did not break the will of the German people, waive the need for a massed land invasion and thus win the war by itself. On the other hand, few Allied leaders expected the campaign to win the war alone or avert a necessary invasion of the Continent. They largely saw strategic bombardment as a preparatory action and did not hesitate to divert resources elsewhere: 46 percent of the U.S. Eighth Air Force's sorties, for example, participated in air support and defensive operations to include antisubmarine and V-weapon activities rather than in the strategic air campaign proper.

Despite its limitations, strategic bombardment did make substantial contributions to the defeat of Nazi Germany, especially from the spring of 1944 onward. (One must remember that the Eighth Air Force dropped 72 percent of its total bomb tonnage after the Normandy [q.v.] invasion.)

The British entered World War II with an air doctrine designed to destroy an enemy nation's morale. There was, however, a chasm between doctrine and capability. Through 1941, Bomber Command was a ramshackle organization that had poor aircraft and puny munitions. Primitive navigation skills and the decision to bomb at night yielded yet another problem: by August 1941, only 33 percent of the bombs released by Bomber Command crews landed within five miles of the target. As a result, the British lost 700 aircraft in 1941 in order to "crater the countryside."

A solution appeared with Air Marshal Arthur "Bomber" Harris (q.v.), who became the leader of Bomber Command in February 1942. Harris's view was that if 40 to 50 percent of the principal cities of Germany were exposed to repeated and indiscriminate area attacks at night, the Nazi regime would surrender by April 1944. Further, He wanted to avenge the deaths of those who fell in the Battle of Britain (q.v.). In British Prime Minister Winston S. Churchill's (q.v.) words, he wanted to "light a fire in the belly of the Nazi beast and burn his black heart."

Harris knew that the technology required for precision bombardment was then unavailable. If, on the other hand, Bomber Command attacked worker housing and public works projects, he hoped to hamper German production as badly as if he had assaulted enemy factories directly. He further believed German civilians were not tough enough to endure a sustained aerial assault, just as their resolve had crumbled under the hunger-inducing Allied blockade of World War I. There was, however, a major flaw in Harris's doctrine of area night bombardment: it ignored the need to establish command of the air by defeating enemy air defenses.

The first true British area attack occurred against Lubeck on 28 March 1942, and quickly escalated to the 30–31 May bombardment of Cologne (q.v.), where a 1,000-airplane armada destroyed 600 acres of the city and left 45,000 people homeless.

Emerging new technologies further supported the Harris doctrine. "Gee" allowed aircraft to plot their approximate position within German air space. "Oboe" provided attacking bombers a primitive electronic picture of their targets, while the workhorse Avro Lancaster, a heavy four-engine bomber that could carry a 18,000-pound load up to 2,500 miles, began to appear in large numbers. The stage was now set for a combined bomber offensive with the U.S. Eighth and Fifteenth Air Forces.

The Casablanca Conference of January 1943 formalized a new direction in the strategic air war. It loosely combined British and American efforts together in Operation POINTBLANK, the Allied Combined Bomber Offensive (CBO) (see Germany Air Campaign). Bomber Command would continue its nocturnal area assaults against enemy cities, while the Eighth Air Force would conduct high altitude precision daylight bombardment against the following primary targets: submarine construction yards, aircraft production facilities, ball bearing plants, transportation centers, and enemy oil facilities. By either destroying or disrupting these key targets, American airmen thought the German economy would collapse like a house of cards. They further believed that mass formations of B-17s and B-24s provided a level of mutual fire support that made daylight attacks largely unstoppable.

Additionally, the Norden bombsight (q.v.), which remained top secret until 1955, would provide the necessary accuracy required to strike specific targets. Unfortunately, and as in the case of Bomber Command, the Americans decided to send their unescorted bombers deep into German territory before they established air superiority. The immediate results were costly.

In 1943, Bomber Command and Eighth Air Force began a series of strategic air attacks that ultimately ended in failure. Bomber Command began with the Ruhr air campaign (q.v.), which lasted from March to June 1943. In forty-three major attacks, and at the cost of 872 aircraft, the British flew 18,506 sorties, dropped 58,000 tons of munitions, and cost Germany the equivalent of 1.5 months of war production.

Air attacks against Hamburg (q.v.) then followed from 24 July through 2 August. The city was a logical target because of its shipyards, which eventually built one-third of the German U-boat fleet, and its oil refineries, which represented 28 percent of Germany's production capacity. The Allies dropped 8,334 tons of munitions on Hamburg and triggered a firestorm that reached 1,500 degrees Fahrenheit. The attacks killed 40,000 people, burned more than 62,000 acres, thwarted the construction of twenty to twenty-seven U-boats, and cost Germany the equivalent of 1.8 months of war production.

S

Lastly, the British conducted the Berlin air campaign from November 1943 through March 1944. In thirty-five Hamburg-type raids, sixteen of which centered on the German capital, Bomber Command lost a whopping 1,047 aircraft, while driving 1.5 million people from their homes.

Like the British, the Eighth Air Force suffered serious losses. It lost fifty-four out of the 177 B-24s that attacked the Ploesti (q.v.) oil fields on 1 August 1943, and it lost 16 percent of the aircraft that assaulted the ball bearing facilities at Schweinfurt on 17 August. (The latter provided 42 percent of Germany's needs.) Only thirty-three aircraft returned undamaged from both raids, and the loss rate was an intolerable 18 percent.

The worst was yet to come. During the week of 8–14 October 1943, Eighth Air Force lost 152 bombers (11.3 percent of those that attacked) in four giant raids. On Black Thursday (14 October), German defenders shot down sixty of the 291 B-17s dispatched yet again to Schweinfurt (q.v.). For the entire month, the U.S. Army's strategic air arm experienced a loss rate of 10 percent (214 bombers) and a damage rate of 42 percent. The conclusion was obvious: at such a pace the U.S. would require a new bombardment force every three months. They had no choice but to cease operations and stand down.

Why did the British and American offensives fail? First, they unnecessarily dispersed their efforts. Generalized attacks scattered against four major target groups failed to adequately burden the German people and economy. Second, neither the British nor the Americans had enough aircraft to inflict sufficient damage. Eighth Air Force had only 200 heavy bombers by June 1943, while the British averaged only 350 aircraft per raid.

Third, the German economy could absorb the punishment. From 1941 to 1944, the percentage of the German GNP devoted to the war grew from a modest 49 percent to just 64 percent.

Last, the *Luftwaffe* succeeded in seriously depleting the number of Allied bombers. The P-47 fighter, even with detachable drop tanks, could escort bomber formations only up to the German border. As a result, by the summer of 1943, unescorted bombardment missions experienced seven times the losses of those protected by fighter escorts.

The turnabout came in February 1944. American airmen now had the P-51 Mustang, which had an effective escort range of 1,500 miles. They had twice the number of bombers than were available just four months before. The Fifteenth Air Force now assumed the heavy responsibility of attacking the south of Germany, and air planners had fixed their sights on just one target—the German *Luftwaffe*. The resulting Allied push occurred during BIG WEEK (q.v.) (20–25 February 1944). For six straight days, massive attacks against enemy aircraft facilities and twelve synthetic oil plants resulted in 225 *Luftwaffe* pilots dead and 141 wounded. P-51s and P-47s now provided long-range escort for bombers and went far afield in search and destroy missions against enemy fighters. As a result, the *Luftwaffe* lost 3,450 aircraft in the first quarter of 1944 alone. Its resistance soon crumbled and the Allies had air supremacy by April 1944.

After supporting the Normandy (q.v.) invasion, Allied strategic air forces conducted the most concentrated and devastating air assaults of the war. Sixty percent of the munitions dropped during the strategic bombing campaign fell from September 1944 through April 1945. With German air space now undefended, the Allies focused on oil and transportation targets. As a result, available German aviation fuel totaled 175,000 tons in April 1944 but plummeted to 5,000 tons five months later. In turn, by December 1944, the number of available German railroad cars shrunk precipitously from 900,000 to 214,000 a week. Without the economic sinews of war, Germany's fate was sealed.

Ultimately, what did the Allied strategic air war accomplish? First, it represented a victory of improvisation. The defeat of the *Luftwaffe* by the escort fighters ensured Allied air superiority during the Normandy invasion. When ground troops waded ashore there were only eighty operational German aircraft in the immediate area. A total of 8,722 Allied sorties eventually supported the invasion, while the *Luftwaffe* mustered only a paltry 250 sorties in trying to fend it off. Admittedly, the defeat of the *Luftwaffe* did not stem from strategic bombardment proper, but from a counterforce strategy used in a war of attrition. Bombardment did, however, have an indirect economic impact.

Second, the air campaign diverted 1.5 million German soldiers and civilians to home defense. Rather than aggressively supporting offensive operations in the Soviet Union and the Mediterranean, this manpower performed the largely passive role of rebuilding and protecting the *Reich*.

Third, strategic bombardment did slow the growth of German arms production, perhaps by 9 percent in 1943 and 17 percent in 1944.

Fourth, the assaults conducted against German oil and transportation targets during the latter stages of the war severely restricted Germany's ability to fight. The 3,031 German aircraft produced in September 1944 may have been a wartime high, but with oil production running only 12 percent of previous totals there was little aviation fuel available for poorly trained *Luftwaffe* pilots to mount limited defensive operations. In turn, the disruption of the German transportation system stymied the *Wehrmacht*'s battlefield mobility, and it totally isolated critical Ruhr Valley industries dedicated to the production of explosives, rubber, and oil.

Finally, by 1944, the damage caused by strategic bombardment forced the *Luftwaffe* to regroup on German soil. The *Wehrmacht* was not only increasingly immobile, it could no longer expect the close air support that was part and parcel of its fighting doctrine. As a result, *Wehrmacht* operations increasingly became a series of desperate improvisations.

Ultimately, strategic bombardment may not have fulfilled its prewar billing as a comparatively painless alternative to total war, but the relentless pressure it exerted on Germany did yield the above-mentioned benefits. Perhaps most importantly, it also helped inculcate in a militaristic society a distaste for war that still survives today.

Peter R. Faber

Additional Reading

Brooks, Stephen, *Bomber: Strategic Air Power in Twentieth Century Conflict* (1983).
Clark, Ronald W., *The Role of the Bomber* (1977).
Hastings, Max, *Bomber Command* (1979).
Middlebrook, Martin, and Chris Everitt, *Bomber Command Diaries: An Operational Reference Book, 1939–45* (1995).
Verrier, Anthony, *The Bomber Offensive* (1968).

Strategy, Anglo-American

From 1939 to 1941, Britain and the United States built an unofficial strategic alliance. Expelled from the Continent in France, Norway, and Greece in 1940–1941, Britain endured German bombardment and threatened invasion. British troops defending the Suez Canal fought Axis troops to a standstill but did not win a decisive battle. Prime Minister Winston S. Churchill (q.v.) aimed to involve the United States in the war against Fascism and National Socialism (qq.v.).

American neutrality sentiment of the 1930s, meanwhile, gave way under the shock of Nazi aggression and the fall of France. President Franklin D. Roosevelt considered Adolf Hitler (qq.v.) so reprehensible and dangerous to American security that he gradually made an unofficial but working alliance with London. Roosevelt allowed British pilots to train in America, and traded fifty destroyers to Britain in exchange for leases at British bases in the Western Hemisphere. He secured Lend-Lease (q.v.) legislation authorizing him to arm Britain for war against Germany. He issued the Atlantic Charter (q.v.), a joint Anglo-American statement of postwar aims, and ordered the U.S. Navy to escort supply ships to the British Isles, even at risk of combat. After German units rolled into the Soviet Union (q.v.) in June 1941, he extended Lend-Lease to the Soviet Union as well.

In 1941, Britain and America made their alliance formal. Before Pearl Harbor, military officers secretly planned joint allocation of scarce resources and productivity and agreed that, in the event of American belligerency, the two states should devote themselves to the defeat of Germany first and Japan second.

Roosevelt and Churchill affirmed this "Germany first" strategy in August 1941. After Pearl Harbor, they established the mechanisms of joint war making by integrating the American Joint Chiefs of Staff and the British Imperial General Staff into the Combined Chiefs of Staff (q.v.) to devise military strategy. They also created joint boards to allocate munitions, raw materials, shipping, food, and production, and reiterated the principles of the Atlantic Charter in the Declaration of United Nations of 1 January 1942. Finally, the two agreed two months later to spheres of wartime responsibility. The United States became responsible for the Pacific and the Western Hemisphere; Britain for Africa, the Middle East, and southern Asia; and both for Europe.

Consistent with the doctrine of Germany first, the United States and Britain sought to defeat Nazi Germany through three broad strategies. Their first and most urgent task was the Battle of the Atlantic (q.v.), which the Axis initially dominated. Germany benefited from its acquisition of naval and air bases in France and Norway, access to Italian ports and submarines after June 1940, and an intense construction program that led to deployment of 249 U-boats in 1942 and 393 the next year.

American efforts to supply the Soviet Union after June 1941 provided the Germans ample North Atlantic convoys to prey upon. The damage suffered at Pearl Harbor forced the United States to divert ships to the Pacific, which enabled German U-boats to patrol the western Atlantic. German submarines took a large toll on Allied shipping in the Atlantic and Mediterranean, sinking eight million tons of Allied shipping by December 1941, 4.5 million tons in January–June 1942, and 3.3 million tons in July–December 1942. One-third of the British merchant marine sank between June 1940 and December 1942, and a German surge in March 1943 sent ninety-seven vessels (500,000 tons) to the bottom. Because the Allied nations could not produce crews or ships as fast as they sank, the German attacks prevented the buildup of the forces in Britain needed to invade the Continent.

Alarmed, Roosevelt and Churchill ordered resources diverted from other efforts to antisubmarine warfare in January 1943, and countermeasures implemented by the Allies gradually turned the tide of battle. American shipbuilders accelerated production so that ships were added faster than they were sunk. Carrier and land-based aircraft, especially long-range PB4Y Liberator bombers, preyed efficiently on U-boats. Elaborate support groups of ships and improved sonar, radar (qq.v.), and depth charges enabled naval forces to do likewise. In May 1943, the Allies sank forty-one U-boats, nearly a third of Germany's operational fleet, forcing Hitler to restrict submarine operations. Never again did U-boats challenge the Allied buildup in Britain.

A second and more divisive strategy in the war against Germany involved the question of a second front against German armies in Europe. Although American and British officials had agreed to the doctrine of Germany first, they vigorously debated how to achieve that end. In July 1941, Josef Stalin (q.v.) called for an attack by the Western powers in France to relieve Soviet troops suffering the brunt of a German offensive.

After Pearl Harbor, American strategists including General George C. Marshall (q.v.) urged an Anglo-American cross-channel invasion in 1943 at the latest, and preparations for an assault in September 1942 if needed to rescue the Soviets from utter defeat. Marshall deemed it essential to Western security to keep the Soviets fighting. British officials refused to approve an early invasion. They were haunted by the memory of trench warfare during World War I and believed that six Allied divisions, all that could be sent to France given the availability of landing craft (q.v.), would not dislodge the thirty-three German divisions defending the coast. They questioned whether an invasion certain to fail would assist the Soviets, doubted American capabilities for major operations, and wanted to protect their African and Middle East empires. British officials advocated action in North-

west Africa (q.v.), where Americans could gain experience in a less risky theater and where Allied forces could threaten Hitler's southern flank.

At a Combined Chiefs of Staff meeting in London in July 1942, the British rejected Marshall's argument that the Western Allies launch a suicidal assault at La Havre in September. British insistence on action in North Africa produced a deadlock, and briefly, American strategists advised Roosevelt to abandon the Germany first strategy and concentrate on the defeat of Japan. Having committed to the Soviets in May 1942 that a second front would be opened that year, however, Roosevelt broke the deadlock by siding with the British.

Committed to the Germany first policy, but prevented by London from invading France, Roosevelt approved operations in Northwest Africa for political reasons, to thrust American soldiers into action against Germany before 1943, and to reassure Soviet premier Josef Stalin. Churchill ventured to Moscow in August 1942 to convince Stalin that operations in North Africa would be a genuine second front and not a diversion. He sketched a crocodile to depict how those operations would enable the Western powers to stab the enemy's "soft underbelly" as well as its head in France.

Operation TORCH, the Northwest African offensive, ultimately succeeded. In November 1942, British troops in Egypt began a steady march to the west and Anglo-American units under General Dwight D. Eisenhower (q.v.) occupied Algeria and Morocco and pushed to the east. These twin offensives conquered Axis territory, improved the naval situation in the Mediterranean, and provided bases for offensives into southern Europe.

Operation TORCH was not entirely successful, however. Because German forces defended Tunisia (q.v.) until May 1943, the Allies had to postpone the invasion of France until 1944. Because the offensive had little effect on German strength on the eastern front, it left Stalin dissatisfied. He complained that the Soviet Army engaged 180 German divisions while the Western Allies engaged a mere twelve.

Operation TORCH also had strategic repercussions because Eisenhower negotiated a deal with Admiral Jean Darlan (q.v.), an avowed Fascist, to ease the task of occupying French North Africa. The Darlan deal ended Vichy resistance to American landings, saved an estimated 16,000 American casualties, and prompted the defection of the Vichy fleet at Dakar. However, it failed to deliver the French fleet at Toulon or end Vichy resistance in Tunisia. It also irritated the Free

French, devastated the morale of resistance groups in Europe, made Stalin suspicious of Western willingness to make peace with Fascists, and thus forced Roosevelt to announce the policy of unconditional surrender.

Unconditional surrender (q.v.) remains one of the war's more controversial policies. It was born of Roosevelt's concern that Stalin was losing confidence in the alliance in 1942. Roosevelt had agreed to a second front in Africa only, although Stalin had interpreted his May 1942 pledge to mean an attack in Europe. Roosevelt also refused to recognize Soviet territorial demands in the Baltic region. Stalin blamed the late 1942 German move on Stalingrad (q.v.) on Western inactivity and remained unhappy with the quantity of Lend-Lease supplies reaching Soviet ports. The Darlan deal compelled Roosevelt to reassure Stalin that the Western Allies would not make separate peace agreements with Axis powers. Therefore, he announced the doctrine of unconditional surrender at the Casablanca Conference, and Churchill reluctantly agreed. Unconditional surrender also promised to avoid the indecisiveness of the 1918 armistice, about whether Germany had been defeated, and it distinguished the noble Western war ideals from the evil Axis aims.

Some scholars argue that the doctrine of unconditional surrender damaged Western interests by stimulating tenacious fighting by German soldiers. Propaganda Minister Joseph Goebbels (q.v.) certainly publicized it to motivate Germans to fight. Others point out that the United States applied the doctrine unevenly in Italy in 1943, making a deal with Marshal Pietro Badoglio (q.v.) that turned Italy from the Axis to the alliance in six weeks. On the other hand, it remains plausible that the doctrine did reassure Stalin and thus keep Soviet troops actively fighting Germany. The United States applied the policy rigidly toward Berlin, rejecting an early May 1945 request from Admiral Karl Dönitz (q.v.) for a separate peace with the West, and forcing him to surrender unconditionally on 7 May 1945.

When the policy of unconditional surrender was announced in 1943, American and British strategists had to decide where to attack the Axis once North Africa was liberated. At the May 1943 Trident Conference in Washington, the Americans approved a British demand that North African operations be extended to invasions of Sicily (q.v.) and Italy, but they refused Churchill's suggestion that subsequent operations target the Balkans. At American insistence, the British agreed to a 1 May 1944 target date for the cross-channel attack.

In August 1943 at the Quebec Conference, the Americans again rejected Churchill's bid for action in the eastern Mediterranean and convinced the British to reaffirm a cross-channel assault. At the Teheran Conference in November, Churchill tried again to promote operations in the Balkans, but Roosevelt and Stalin refused, confirmed plans for a cross-channel invasion, and planned a Soviet offensive to assist. Anglo-American meetings at the Cairo Conference in December ironed out the strategic discrepancies for the cross-channel attack.

Operation OVERLORD, the invasion of France, was jointly planned by British and American officers commanded by General Eisenhower, chief of Supreme Headquarters, Allied Expeditionary Force (SHAEF) (q.v.). British and American contingency documents were integrated into a plan to attack five beaches in Normandy (q.v.). Deception, aerial bombardments, sabotage by resistance fighters, and airborne assaults behind enemy lines were also planned.

By May 1944, Eisenhower presided over 150,000 men poised for invasion. Weather, tide, and moon conditions determined the invasion date of 6 June. After some tense moments on D-Day, Operation OVERLORD succeeded. Beachheads were secured within days, and the Allies landed 1.4 million men by 23 July. Allied forces broke out of the coastal region in late July, halted a German counterthrust at Mortain (q.v.) in August, and liberated Paris (q.v.) on 25 August. American and British units bridged the Rhine in March 1945 and accepted a German unconditional surrender in May.

The Allied offensive did not lack problems. The rapid advance thinned reinforcements and gasoline supplies, and British and American commanders vied for such scarce resources. German troops demonstrated a determination not to surrender, erasing early hopes for a victory in 1944. Eisenhower and British Field Marshal Bernard L. Montgomery (q.v.) seriously erred in September when they ordered an airborne assault at Arnheim (q.v.), a premature, poorly conceived, and utterly unsuccessful effort to breach the Rhine.

In December 1944, Hitler finally ordered a counterattack against the thinned Allied center in the Ardennes, resulting in the Battle of the Bulge (see Ardennes Offensive). Eisenhower ordered a flanking attack on the German penetration, and after clear skies enabled Allied aircraft to enter the fray, the German assault was repulsed. Yet the battle cost the Allies casualties, delay, and some embarrassment.

The third Anglo-American strategy, the

bombing of Germany, remains the most controversial. In the 1930s, the Royal Air Force (RAF) had ascribed to the theory that strategic bombing (q.v.), including terror bombings of cities, would shatter civilian morale and thus determine the course of future wars. In 1939–1940, fear of retaliation and aircraft shortages deterred the British from launching any noteworthy aerial attacks against Germany.

After surviving the Battle of Britain (q.v.), however, Britain turned to strategic bombing against Germany. Initially deeming indiscriminate bombing as immoral and ineffective in breaking morale, British strategists tried precision bombing—daytime attacks on targets such as oil facilities believed vital to the Axis war effort. Daytime raids were costly and studies revealed that precision bombing was inaccurate. One report found that only 20 percent of bombs landed within five miles of their target. In 1941, therefore, the British turned to indiscriminate nighttime raids, called "area bombing." Its advocates sought revenge for attacks on British cities and argued that German morale, unlike the British spirit in 1940, would crumble under a sustained onslaught.

British strategists implemented a "de-housing" campaign, targeting fifty-eight German cities in an effort to render homeless one-third of Germans. Some British officials criticized area bombing as ineffective and a waste of resources needed for the Battle of the Atlantic (*see* Atlantic Campaign), but Churchill disagreed and allowed the raids to continue. Area bombing often produced spectacular destruction, but it neither broke German morale nor slowed war production.

American air strategists, who entered the scene in January 1943, viewed area bombing as wasteful and militarily ineffective. American bombers, therefore, engaged in daytime precision bombing, with little coordination with British efforts in 1943. The American plan was initially costly. In October 1943 raids on a ball bearing plant at Schweinfurt (q.v.), sixty bombers were downed, so great a loss that the U.S. suspended daylight raids. Rather than adopt the British approach, however, the Americans deployed the P-51 Mustang, a long-range fighter escort that could limit bomber losses. Daytime bombing resumed in February 1944.

Only during the last year of the war did the Anglo-American dual bombing strategy clearly contribute to the defeat of Germany. In 1944, American and British strategists finally coordinated their efforts to attack German oil facilities and provoked a shortage of gasoline that crippled

the *Luftwaffe* in 1944–1945. Moreover, Allied warplanes gained complete mastery of the skies and used it relentlessly to pummel German cities; 72 percent of the 2.7 million tons of bombs dropped on Germany during the war fell after 1 July 1944. The complete destruction of Hamburg in July-August 1944 and Dresden (q.v.) in February 1945 proved Allied absolute mastery of the skies. German morale finally began to collapse.

In addition to the ethical questions of attacking civilians, controversy surrounds the Anglo-American bombing strategy on military grounds. Some suggest that the bombings, by depleting manpower and materials, hurt the Allies more than Germany, while others argue that the raids prevented Allied casualties and shortened the war. In retrospect, the bombings did not destroy morale and may have stiffened it through 1944. They did not ruin German industrial productivity, and they consumed resources needed in the Battle of the Atlantic and Operation OVERLORD.

On the other hand, the attacks undeniably destroyed many industrial facilities and forced skilled workers to spend time rebuilding instead of producing, thereby limiting German industrial output. German officials later testified that the American precision bombing took a large toll on Germany's industrial might. The raids also forced the *Luftwaffe* into a defensive posture, securing the buildup in Britain from attack and gaining the Allies command of the skies over the battlefields in France. Whatever it did to German morale, the death and destruction inflicted from the sky certainly sapped Germany's war-making potential.

Peter L. Hahn

Additional Reading

Eisenhower, John S.D., *Allies: Pearl Harbor to D-Day* (1982).

Leighton, Richard M., and Robert W. Coakley, *Global Logistics and Strategy, 1940–1943* (1955).

Liddell Hart, B.H., *History of the Second World War* (1970).

Wright, Gordon, *The Ordeal of Total War, 1939–1945* (1968).

Strategy, German

During the interwar period, a group of "Young Turks" within the German General Staff (q.v.) sought to exploit the independent use of mobile tank units to disrupt and paralyze an opposing force. Although their analysis was based on a careful study of the last year of World War I, their conclusions were not universally accepted. Adherents of traditional operational thinking considered the newly developed mobile units as subordinate support units, which were to aid massed infantry to encircle and annihilate an opposing force.

Despite their disagreements, both the proponents of the new tactics and the more conservative generals ultimately agreed that operational superiority alone would not be sufficient to offset Germany's military deficiencies. What was needed was more arms and men. At that juncture, Adolf Hitler (q.v.) and the traditional military elite found common ground. He promised the military a large army, something the Weimar Republic (q.v.) was unwilling and unable to do. The military in turn granted the Nazi regime its guarded support.

From the beginning, however, the military elite and the National Socialists disagreed fundamentally about the ultimate rationale and structure for conducting war. The professional soldiers sought to preserve the military's identity and safeguard its autonomy of command structure. During the six months following Hitler's rise to power, the officer corps enjoyed almost complete autonomy in rebuilding the army and became the exclusive body for the development of strategic and operational planning for the next several years. Even so, National Socialist leaders never accepted the prospect of a war planned and executed by the military. Instead, they saw the military as an instrument in the social and political mobilization of the German nation in its fateful mission of expansion and greatness. As long as the military's expertise could be harnessed to that end, the military would be allowed to serve the nation unhindered.

The General Staff achieved the initial buildup within the framework of traditional military planning. By the summer of 1935, they were ready to give serious consideration to plans for upgrading the army from a purely defensive military to a mobilized force capable of offensive operations. Strategic considerations and operational tactics were once again argued and discussed between the different branches of the armed forces within the context of a rapidly changing international situation, the militarization of the Rhineland (q.v.), and the economic constraints of the four-year plan. From 1936 on, the General Staff issued directives that marked the progress toward the ultimate goal of achieving the offensive capability in a two-front war by 1940.

Even the continued expansion of Germany's military capabilities could not fully overcome Germany's logistical and demographic weaknesses.

As the first deployment plans were being elaborated in 1935, Hitler and the military leadership began to question whether Germany would ever be sufficiently prepared to fight a war according to the conventional standards of military calculus. It was at this point that Hitler, through the political offices of the *Oberkommando der Wehrmacht* or OKW (q.v.) (Armed Forces High Command), began to challenge the prerogatives of the General Staff. Contingency plans were requested and subsequently prepared, but these plans were not part of the General Staff's strategy for a European war. Instead, they were the military component of Hitler's opportunistic foreign politics.

The first of these plans dealt with the possibility of a surprise attack against Czechoslovakia. Arguments over its execution increased tensions between the OKW and the *Oberkommando des Heeres* or OKH (Army High Command). On 5 November 1937, Hitler decided to use this intra-military rancor to offer his own critical evaluation of the entire rationale of the General Staff's deployment planning. He once again questioned whether the military would ever be adequately prepared for a European war and defended the exploitation of national and international situations even at the risk of having to shelve the carefully crafted deployment plans of the General Staff in favor of improvised military force.

General Ludwig Beck (q.v.), the chief of the General Staff, opposed such an approach and presented the generally held military opinion that the National Socialist leadership should avoid unnecessary risks, which would expose Germany to precipitous and ill-conceived military involvement. His cautions were so well argued that he basically substantiated Hitler's contention that the military would never be sufficiently prepared to fight a war of German expansion. Thus Hitler concluded he had been right all along: the military could not control all the factors necessary to secure an advantageous military result. Instead, it would have to follow the same type of opportunistic posturing and maneuvering Hitler used so effectively during the Rhineland remilitarization in 1936 and in achieving the *Anschluss* (q.v.) of Austria in March 1938.

Beck resigned as chief of staff in August 1938, largely because of his disagreement with Hitler over the timing of a proposed attack on Czechoslovakia. His departure marked an end to the old-style strategic planning, controlled and directed according to the principles of an autonomous military structure.

A younger generation of officers, who were

more attuned to the possibilities of Hitler's opportunistic tactics, came to the forefront. In general, these men were more technocrats than strategists. They favored maximizing the use of weapons to achieve military objectives over the carefully calculated approach of the traditional strategists. Improvisation, speed, mobility, and use of crushing force offset, or so they believed, the need for the elaborate planning and calculations of the old-style strategists. These men proved to be the chief proponents of *Blitzkrieg* (q.v.), an operational-level technique for massing force to quickly overwhelm an enemy. Although not fully worked out until 1941, it appeared to offer the type of operational flexibility needed to once again make war a viable option for a Germany incapable of a World War I–style European war.

Hitler found this new arrangement much better suited to his leadership style. As within the Nazi Party, he preferred to encourage a certain amount of rivalry. This allowed him to remain the ultimate arbitrator in disputes, lessened the chances of a coalition forming against him, and fitted well into the overall social Darwinist and racist mind-set of the Nazis. Struggle was good, essential, and natural in the contest for survival of the race. War would glorify and strengthen the German people, or so he believed.

Having bypassed the old strategic control of the General Staff, Hitler used the internal divisions over planning and objectives to become the final arbitrator of German strategy. Working in Hitler's favor was the tendency of his officers to think in operational rather than strategic terms and his own vaunted reputation after the fall of France.

Hitler's vision of an expanded German *Reich* led him and his advisors to consider a variety of operational-level plans to exploit the prevailing international situation. In April and May 1939, Hitler decided to attack Poland. In August, he concluded his secret nonaggression pact with the Stalin, thus removing the only immediate military threat to German aggression. Britain and France were reluctant to come to the aid of Austria or Czechoslovakia, and Hitler now surmised that once they were presented with a *fait accompli,* they would probably come to accept this new German thrust as well. War with the Western powers was simply a calculated risk he was willing to take.

Poland (q.v.) fell quickly to the combined force of the German *Blitzkrieg* and the might of the Soviet Red Army. When Britain and France refused to acquiesce and declared war on Germany, Hitler then faced the reality of a general European war for which Germany was ill-prepared. The air and naval buildups, scheduled for completion in 1944–1946, had barely begun.

For Hitler, the strategic problem was to find a way to free up German materiel in the west so that he could once again turn to the east, where the new German *Reich* was to find its *Lebensraum* (q.v.). He was convinced that Britain was the key, since its global resources and island status made it a more dangerous enemy than France. His main strategic objective was to convince the British that further hostilities were futile. To do this, the Germans planned to strip Britain of its continental bases and allies.

In keeping with this strategy, the Germans felt obliged to respond to the well-founded fears of a British landing in Norway by drawing up ad hoc plans for the invasion of Denmark and Norway (qq.v.). Danish airfields were deemed necessary to extend the reach of the *Luftwaffe* for the Norwegian campaign, and the conquest of Norway would deny the British naval bases and provide the German Navy with additional anchorages. On 9 April 1940, the German attack began. Denmark fell without a fight, and within two months, most of Norway. The success of these operations was due as much to the irresolute action of the British and French as to the skill of the German forces.

With the Scandinavian operations successfully underway, Hitler turned his attention to France. Plans for the invasion of France (q.v.) were in place ever since the autumn of 1939, but difficulties in providing the necessary men and materiel postponed the attack until 10 May 1940. To facilitate the attack on France, neutral Luxembourg, Belgium, and the Netherlands were overrun. A powerful thrust through the Ardennes sealed the fate of France within six weeks. Even before the invasion, Hitler decreed that northern France, Belgium, and the Netherlands would be occupied "for the successful prosecution of an air and sea war against England."

Hitler hoped that Britain would agree to a compromise settlement, since his main concern remained the Soviet Union. But the British, buoyed by Commonwealth and U.S. support, refused his overtures. The decision was then made to invade Britain, but only if the *Luftwaffe* could secure the necessary control of the air to protect an invasion fleet against the powerful British Navy. The Battle of Britain (q.v.) began on 10 July and ended officially on 13 October, a disappointment for the Germans, who failed to overwhelm the British air defenses.

Even as he attacked Britain, Hitler continued to consider his options. Increased naval activity in the Atlantic would interrupt vital British trade and project German power into an area where he envisioned German expansion after the war. The negotiations for bases with Spain and Portugal, however, never came to fruition. Another possibility was an attack on the Soviet Union. The Nazis had singled out the Soviet Union as the chief ideological and racial enemy. From a strategic perspective, the defeat of the USSR would end British hopes for an alliance, free Germany from its dependence on Russian oil and other important materials, remove the threat of a Soviet attack should the war in the west turn against the Germans, and offset any advantage the British would gain from future U.S. involvement.

Hitler ordered the army to plan the campaign on 31 July 1940, and by December, the plans were substantially complete. German attention was momentarily distracted when Italian premier Benito Mussolini's (q.v.) forces ran into trouble in the Balkans (q.v.) and in North and East Africa (qq.v.). Hitler felt obligated to aid his ally for "strategic, political, and psychological reasons." Mussolini's defeat could have seriously compromised his government in Italy, and strengthened British resolve. Moreover, the British were sending air units to Greece (q.v.), and eventually those forces could pose a threat to economic targets. German forces arrived in North Africa in February (Hitler had already sent an air corps to Sicily), and took over Yugoslavia, Greece, and Crete (q.v.) in April and May 1941.

The campaign against the Soviet Union (q.v.) was again delayed, for which Hitler's Balkan campaign has been blamed, though it appears that German industrial and procurement problems were chiefly responsible. Hitler envisioned a typical *Blitzkrieg* campaign of no more than four months in duration. Once victory was obtained, he believed, Germany would be able to challenge British interests on a global scale.

When the attack began on 22 June, the *Wehrmacht*'s spectacular early successes seemed to bear out Hitler's optimism, but again, without any coherent strategy, he and his generals were unable to agree on how to best exploit their successes. As the year ended, the German advance bogged down outside of Moscow (q.v.), hampered by increased Soviet resistance, indecisive strategy, lack of needed reserves, and the Russian winter. Throughout the winter, Soviet forces counterattacked, but the Germans, under Hitler's directives, stubbornly refused to give ground and finally fought the Soviets to a standstill.

Despite remarkable early success, Germany's strategic position was becoming increasingly difficult. Military units were tied down to control and administer vast areas, lessening Germany's ability to concentrate the necessary force to achieve future victories. Hitler's strategic gambles, despite their operational brilliance, did not force Britain or the Soviet Union out of the war. Germany had to respond to the almost inexhaustible resources of the United States and the indomitable resilience of the USSR, otherwise, attrition would continue to erode Germany's military capabilities.

In December 1941, Hitler himself questioned whether the war had been lost, but by February 1942 his confidence had returned. A quick, decisive thrust against the Soviet Union was now impossible, but it was still possible to make the war so costly that the Soviets would withdraw, particularly if a vital "artery" were severed.

Bold, but unrealizable, plans were drawn up for cooperation and a possible linkup with the Japanese in the Indian Ocean. More realistic plans called for scaled-down German initiatives in North Africa. The Soviet Union, however, remained the primary focus of Hitler's attention.

Instead of engaging the massed Red Army before Moscow, which would have been in keeping with von Clausewitz's fundamental rule that the defeat of the enemy's military forces must precede political and economic objectives, Hitler decided to attack economic targets. His decision was, at least in part, an admission of the *Wehrmacht*'s declining resources and the need to weaken the fighting ability of the Red Army before attempting a head-on confrontation.

After "retiring" several of his generals, Hitler pushed through plans for a four-stage attack on the Soviet southern flank with a possible new thrust against Leningrad (q.v.) once those operations were completed. The campaign sought to eliminate Soviet forces north of the Don River, force the Red Army back toward Stalingrad (q.v.), and then proceed to the primary objective, the Caucasus (q.v.). The goal was to cut off the rich Caucasian oil-producing areas from the Soviet industrial base and to open the possibility of a linkup with General Erwin Rommel's (q.v.) offensive in North Africa, crushing the British Middle Eastern forces between them.

Early successes and the fall of Sevastopol (q.v.), convinced Hitler that he could accelerate the original plan. Forces were diverted from the thrust against Stalingrad and sent on a drive to the Caucasus, while reserves were sent north for a future attack against Leningrad. German forces were now overextended and Hitler's continued shifting of forces between the two operations succeeded in weakening them both. The German offensive flagged at the foothills of the Caucasus, unable to reach most of its objectives, while Hitler adamantly sought to take Stalingrad. He believed that he was bleeding the Soviet Army at Stalingrad, but in reality his fixation with Stalin's namesake and his refusal to allow a withdrawal in the face of a massive Soviet counterattack greatly weakened the *Wehrmacht*'s offensive abilities in the east. On 14 October 1942, Hitler called off all offensive operations in the east except for the Stalingrad battle and some local operations. The German soldiers were to stand on the defensive.

A number of generals urged Hitler to adopt an elastic defense in the hope that the *Wehrmacht* might wear down the Red Army to the point that the Soviet people would loose the will to fight. Such a strategy sought to exploit any rash moves the overzealous Soviet generals might make in their desire to drive out the invader. German forces might then execute a counterstroke that would radically change the situation, but Hitler remained convinced that the war could only be won through determined offensive action.

On 2 February 1943, the starving and decimated German Sixth Army surrendered at Stalingrad. After staving off the subsequent Soviet counteroffensives, the Germans attempted to demonstrate their ability to take up the offensive by eliminating the Red Army salient west of Kursk (q.v.). That campaign was a dismal failure. The Soviets, aided by excellent intelligence, blunted the attack and counterattacked. By mid-July, Germany was no longer able to mount a major offensive in the east.

In Africa, meanwhile, Germany's fortunes initially looked bright in 1942, despite the fact that the African theater was only of secondary importance to Hitler. Rommel's offensive had routed the Allied forces to within sixty miles of Alexandria. Undersupplied and inadequately supported, Rommel halted operations on 23 July. When a subsequent offensive in August and September was blunted by the British at Alam el Halfa (q.v.), Rommel was too weakened to renew hostilities. In October and early November, reinforced British and Commonwealth forces attacked the badly outnumbered and outgunned Rommel at El Alamein (q.v.). Though Rommel's force escaped, the *Afrika Korps* (q.v.) suffered irreversible losses. Allied landings in Northwest Africa (q.v.) in November made recovery impossible despite Hitler's belated efforts to shore up the front by dispatching fresh troops and supplies. In May 1943, the Allies captured Tunisia (q.v.), thus eliminating the Axis presence in Africa.

From mid-1943 until Germany's defeat in March 1945, Hitler and his staff faced increasingly fewer options as the initiative had decidedly passed to the Allies. In July 1943, Anglo-American forces invaded Sicily (q.v.) and precipitated Mussolini's fall from power. In response, Hitler had to transfer a number of *Panzer* divisions west from Russia, where they were critically needed.

The first three months of 1943 had shown great promise for German U-boats in the Atlantic, but by early summer 1943, the Allies had decisively turned the tide. Admiral Karl Dönitz (q.v.) was forced to call off his U-boat wolf packs in the Atlantic because of prohibitive losses. By year's end, Allied kills of U-boats exceeded the ability of the Germans to replace them. In every category of military production, Germany was now lagging far behind the Allies, which translated on the battlefield as an ever-increasing disparity in war-making capacity. By 1943, for example, Allied air forces in the Mediterranean theater alone outnumbered the entire operational strength of the *Luftwaffe*.

Hitler had little choice but to intensify the holding strategy that he had adopted in October 1942 and to continue hoping that the "unnatural alliance" of his enemies would collapse. Stubborn defensive resistance and limited offensives, such as Kursk, Mortain, and the Ardennes (qq.v.), were supposed to convince the Allies of the *Reich*'s continued viability and to test their common resolve.

In 1944, Hitler shifted attention from the east and south to shore up and expand defenses in the west in an ill-fated attempt to preserve Fortress Europe (q.v.) from further Anglo-American gains in Italy and to prevent the Normandy (q.v.) invasion. New air attacks were prepared against Britain, and V-1 flying bombs struck London shortly after the Normandy landings. Although the V-1s and later the V-2 rockets shook British morale, the new weapons did not weaken their resolve.

During the last twenty-one months of the European war, Hitler attempted unsuccessfully to fend off the Allies, while telling the German people that defeat would mean horrible reprisals at the hands of their enemies. On the battlefield, the contradictions of Hitler's strategy became apparent. His refusal to see war in terms of men and materiel, according to traditional strategic thinking, led him to spend the lives of German soldiers in useless attempts to hold indefensible territory. War, for Hitler, was primarily a contest of wills. What he failed to appreciate was that the will of his enemies could be just as tenacious as his own.

In the end, the overwhelming resources and determination of Germany's enemies proved the bankruptcy of Hitler's strategy. As Soviet forces closed in on his Berlin bunker, he and his staff were still deploying depleted units and nonexistent divisions to hold the line.

Hitler attempted to change the nature of strategy to overcome Germany's military limitations and provide himself with an instrument capable of gaining *Lebensraum* in the east. Strategy for him was not a systematic, rational calculation of the use of force, but a series of gambles marked by cunning. Hitler's "new strategy," however, had miscalculated in 1939, when Germany was not sufficiently ready for war. Fearing an erosion of his popularity at home if he overtaxed the German people with extensive war preparations, Hitler did not have sufficient resources to accomplish all his aims when the war began. Island Britain remained beyond the reach of the *Wehrmacht,* and even the great victories in the east during 1941 failed to reach any critical areas that might have incapacitated the Soviets. Moscow was not taken, nor was Leningrad. The Soviets maintained their control of the vital Murmansk supply route, through which their allies poured massive amounts of supplies, without which the Soviets would have been unable to take the offensive in 1942.

Hitler's strategy, rather than a lack of resources, kept the oil fields in the Caucasus out of German hands and frustrated Rommel's attempt to seize the Suez Canal in 1942. Nonetheless, even had the *Wehrmacht* gained control over one or more of these important objectives, the Allies could have managed to carry on. In short, the Germans simply did not have sufficient force to overwhelm their enemies.

As that fact became increasingly obvious, Hitler had no recourse but to escalate the level of conflict with new weapons and terror. But even terror has its limitations. As he stated in 1941: "one cannot beat the Russian with operational successes . . . because he simply does not acknowledge defeat." His use of excessive brutality was supposed to wear down the Soviet will, which he assumed was inferior to his own. Instead, the unbridled use of terror inspired unflinching resistance. Had Hitler been willing to lessen his ideological and racist views, he might have accommodated some of the opposition groups to the Soviet government, making them important allies rather than loyal partisans.

German strategy failed to win the war because it was based on a political and military gamble that assumed a lack of will and preparedness on the part of Germany's potential enemies. Once a coalition of great powers mustered its forces against Hitler, Germany's defeat was assured by the same laws of attrition that led it to defeat in World War I.

Robert Gerlich

Additional Reading

Förster, Jürgen, "The Dynamics of *Volksgemeinschaft*: The Effectiveness of the German Military Establishment in the Second World War," in *Makers of Modern Strategy: From Machiavelli to the Nuclear Age,* pp. 527–597, edited by Peter Paret (1986).

Leach, Barry A., *German Strategy Against Russia, 1939–1941* (1973).

Liddell Hart, B.H. *Strategy* (1954).

Trevor-Roper, H.R. (ed.), *Blitzkrieg to Defeat: Hitler's War Directives 1939–1945* (1964).

Wilt, Alan F., *War from the Top: German and British Military Decision Making During World War II* (1990).

Strategy, Soviet

There is no overall comprehensive definition of military strategy. The nineteenth-century German military theorist, Carl von Clausewitz, defined it as "the use of combat, or the threat of combat, for the purpose of the war in which it takes place." A modern historian has characterized Clausewitz's formulation as "both revolutionary, and defiantly simplistic" because "it can be amended and expanded without difficulty." Count Helmuth von Moltke called strategy simply "a system of expedients." This suggests that strategy is a highly pragmatic science and any strategic theory would have to be more applied than pure reason.

The word *strategy* derives from the French *strategie,* which in turn comes from Greek *strategos* (general). A dictionary definition is "the science or art of military command as applied to overall planning and conduct of large-scale combat operations." A practical, modern theory of military strategy is "the use of armed forces to achieve military objectives in support of political purposes."

Great sacrifices in war could never be justified if victory was nothing more than an end in itself. Able strategic thinkers will always look beyond the end of the current war to see what political conditions they wish to achieve. It is the anticipation of these improved conditions that makes war a rational exercise. Soviet wartime leaders were nothing if not adept at the art of looking ahead and anticipating postwar political conditions. In this capacity, they proved superior to their Western allies. Later, Western leaders had reasons to regret not having paid more attention to their own political interests.

Soviet military strategy is complex since it flows from the holistic nature of Marxism, which rejects the idea of compartmentalization of human experience. No narrow definition, neatly separating war and peace or the military and society at large, is accepted. War is total and personal commitment is total. No one can be neutral. People not wholeheartedly supporting the war are enemies to be liquidated. There are no fronts and no frontiers. The Communist Party, the army, and the people make up one monolithic entity.

Soviet leaders were faithful to the Clausewitzian dictum that war is politics by other means. Consistent with this practice, military strategy was subordinated to, or fused with, political strategy in ways few Western leaders would understand or accept. American leaders, for example, have long viewed war as a purely technical operation divorced from larger political considerations. In their view, political matters were something to take up after the war was over. Victory was an end in itself. Not so with Soviet leaders. The two went hand in hand, with political concerns dominant.

A sound approach to analyzing Soviet strategy in World War II is to examine particular Soviet actions and ask what motivated them. For example, why did they sign the Molotov Ribbentrop Pact (q.v.); why were they so suspicious of their allies, so eager to expand their borders, so fearful of domestic enemies; why did they fight the war the way they did; why did they agree to enter the war against Japan in 1945; and why did they feel the need to establish Communist regimes in Eastern Europe after the war?

Soviet leaders had no overall, conspiratorial strategy during World War II. They responded to their hopes and fears and reacted to problems and opportunities as they arose. Close scrutiny of Soviet strategy will reveal that they, like most other nations, behaved aggressively when they could and defensively when they could not do otherwise.

The centuries-old methods used by Russia's rulers to maintain power in a huge, backward, and unwieldy empire institutionalized repression on a scale seldom seen elsewhere. At the same time, anarchy became an integral part of, and endemic to, Soviet society. Both Russian and Soviet history have been one of continual crises.

Russian awareness of its own backwardness has produced a tragic and pessimistic view of human beings' role in society and Russia's place in the world. Outward manifestations to the contrary, the Soviet Union needed constant reassurances it really was a great power. These special experiences produced a feeling of insecurity resulting in a constant push beyond its borders for the establishment of "Friendly Brother States" (i.e., Eastern Europe). Any understanding of Soviet military strategy must consider this suspicious and paranoid outlook.

George F. Kennan (q.v.), in his famous "X" article of 1947, compared the Soviet expansionistic urge to a fluid stream constantly pushing onward filling every "nook and cranny" of world power available to it. Soviet officials once admitted to Henry Kissinger that they were incapable of policing themselves. They needed limits established and enforced by others if they were to resist expansion into border states. Kennan recognized this tendency when he called for an American policy of "containment" of Soviet expansion until the internal dynamics of Soviet Communism changed, which finally occurred in the 1980s.

World War II brought the Soviet motherland to the verge of extinction. Until December 1941, the very existence of the Soviet Union was in doubt. The margin by which the German advance was halted was very narrow. The Germans occupied territory inhabited by more than 40 percent of the Soviet people and contained a large part of the USSR's aluminum, pig iron, coal, and food supply.

Only the Russian climate, geography, and vast manpower saved the Soviet Union from complete annihilation. Soviet leaders could and did trade space and lives for time. No human cost was considered too high in achieving their overriding goal of preserving the Soviet Union. Measures of extreme ruthlessness, even against their own people, characterized all of their war efforts. The role of the "super" Soviet soldier in defeating the *Wehrmacht,* although significant, was greatly exaggerated by Soviet writers eager to extol Communist virtues.

More threatening to the Soviet Union and Communist Party control was that so many people, particularly in the Ukraine and border republics, welcomed the German invaders as liberators. Hitler might have won the war by the simple expedient of treating these people decently. Soviet leaders were painfully aware of Hitler's missed opportunity and were eager to prevent future internal betrayal. This realization added to their already high degree of anxiety and dominated their military and political thinking throughout the war.

The Soviets wanted, of course, to win the war, but that was not an end in itself. It was important that the war be won in such a way as to achieve two important political objectives. These two objectives dominated Soviet political and military strategy throughout the war.

The first was an overriding concern to insure maintenance of power by the elite, that is, the Communist Party. The enemy within was always more feared than the enemy without. In their view, winning the war against an external enemy would avail them nothing if the Communist Party lost power in the process. Stalin was paranoid about challenges to his position. The fear of a Napoleon-like figure on a white horse was one of his worst nightmares.

While going about the task of defeating the German enemy, great care was taken to strengthen the internal controls of the Communist Party over the people. In this task they succeeded grandly. The war was a catastrophe for the Soviet people but not for the Soviet state, which emerged stronger than ever.

The second objective, desire to expand their territorial boundaries, was a constant in Soviet strategic thinking. The same urge for territorial aggrandizement was present from the earliest days of the tsars. Russia began as a very small country in the ninth century and constantly pushed outward until it occupied one-sixth of the earth's land surface. The twentieth-century Marxist imperative to carry Communism to the world's toiling masses brought increased urgency to this tendency, but territorial expansion was not a Communist invention.

These two objectives, maintenance of power by the Communist Party and territorial expansion, drove Soviet strategic thinking. In pursuing them, Soviet officials were very successful. Internal controls were strengthened and the Soviet Union emerged as a truly great power by gaining control over more land and more people than ever before.

After the German invasion, Stalin was so desperate that he pleaded for British and American troops to be sent to the Soviet Union to fight under their own command. He soon realized his mistake and never again repeated this request, wanting all Western troops to remain in Western Europe, far from the USSR and Eastern Europe. Eastern Europe was the only front on which Americans did not fight and Soviet distrust kept them out.

In view of Stalin's double-dealing with Hitler over Poland and the Baltic states, Allied aid may have been conceded too easily. Perhaps as then Senator Harry S Truman (q.v.) suggested, the Nazis and Communists should have been allowed to destroy each other, but Western fears of an early German victory paralleled those of the Soviets, and early, limited aid was extended. After the

Japanese attack on Pearl Harbor in December 1941, the United States became the third member of the anti-Axis coalition and started massive aid to the USSR.

In all negotiations with his Western allies, Soviet Premier Josef Stalin's (q.v.) main objective was to keep what territory he gained in the German-Soviet nonaggression pact, plus acquire other territory Hitler had denied him. Basic Soviet interest had not changed one iota, merely the men with whom they bargained had changed.

The American focus was to defeat the Axis and win the war. After victory, "normalcy" would be restored. In characteristic American fashion, President Franklin D. Roosevelt (q.v.) felt most political concerns could be delayed until after the war. Some of his major subordinates, such as Generals Dwight D. Eisenhower and George C. Marshall (qq.v.) were often heard to say, "I will not play politics," when asked to take certain measures to head off Soviet advances into Western Europe. One can only wonder what they thought they were doing all along. Being less artless than their American allies, the Soviets acted differently. They saw the need to beat and shape the iron during the crucibles of war, while it was still hot. They knew that *how* they fought the war would determine *what* the world would look like, and *how* the spoils would be divided once it was over.

The irony of the Roosevelt-Stalin relationship was amazing. While Roosevelt naively viewed Stalin as a Russian Roosevelt, Stalin cynically saw Roosevelt as an American Stalin. Roosevelt felt that through the power of his gregarious personality, he could influence and manage Stalin, whom he called "Uncle Joe."

As an "imperialist" leader of a capitalist nation, Roosevelt was viewed as an implacable and deceitful enemy of the Soviet Union. As a fellow capitalist state leader, he was no better than German dictator Adolf Hitler (q.v.). All capitalists were hostile to Soviet interests. Hitler was simply more hostile and more aggressive than the others. In the desperate situation in which he found himself, Stalin sought and used capitalist aid, but basic political differences and antagonisms were never forgotten. "Uncle Joe" was well aware, even if Roosevelt was not, that he who sups with the devil must use a long spoon.

Stalin never viewed Soviet interests as static. He understood that the war opened new vistas for Soviet expansion he meant to exploit. The ultimate defeat of Germany, Italy, and Japan would leave vast political and military vacuums to be filled. This Stalin never overlooked. He was aware that the Bolshevik opportunity to seize power in 1917 arose directly from the weakness of the tsarist government brought on by protracted war. He was eager to exploit similar opportunities sure to arise during the current war.

Soviet leaders justified their territorial expansion by reference to Leninist doctrine. Lenin taught that Soviet military force must be used whenever possible to advance Marxian world political objectives. They realized they could not rely on spontaneous revolutions to achieve their goals. Western leaders might, and often did, confuse these political and military priorities, but never Soviet leaders. During the darkest days of the war, they continued to press for Western recognition of Soviet territorial gains under the Molotov-Ribbentrop Pact, the recovery of former tsarist territory, plus the acquisition of as much enemy land as possible.

Stalin never let himself forget that more was at stake than mere military victory. June 1941 was a turning point in Soviet history. Hitler's gratuitous aggression opened the door for Soviet emergence as a world power and provided justification for any territorial expansion.

Soviet leaders felt the Soviet Union could survive after the war only when surrounded by friendly, "democratic" states. "Democratic" states meant states controlled internally by loyal, Soviet-style Communist Parties. Stalin warned his Western Allies at Potsdam that any freely elected government in Eastern Europe "would be anti-Soviet, and that we cannot allow."

To alleviate Allied fears, Stalin deemphasized international Communist ambitions and stressed nationalism at home. The tsars were praised, the Russian Orthodox Church was reinstated, and the Comintern (q.v.) was officially disbanded; (actually, put in a "deep freeze" until after the war when it reappeared as the Cominform). Stalin understood that tradition, nationalism, "Mother Russia," and even religion had greater appeal to the people than Communism. This approach also had useful propaganda value abroad.

One month after the German invasion, the Soviets began to clamor for a second front in Western Europe to take the pressure off the hard-pressed Red Army. Many problems, including Anglo-American disagreement over timing and location, U.S. involvement in the Pacific war, and lack of shipping (including specialized landing craft), caused postponement of a second front from 1942 to 1943 to ultimately 6 June 1944. Soviet leaders saw these delays as a manifest desire by Western leaders to have Hitler destroy the So-

viet Union. The failure to launch a second front in 1942 or 1943 was a constant irritant in all Western conversations with Soviet leaders.

Stalin understood that, at least in the short term, he would have to fight the Germans alone. Once the *Wehrmacht* was halted in the fall of 1941, the Soviets slowly took the offensive. By this time, no perceptive German officer on the eastern front could have had any illusions about a German victory. The Germans had already lost 750,000 men—23 percent of the original number committed to the Russian front. Soviet losses were far greater, but it was clear the Soviets could trade lives at the rate of five to one and make up their losses from a much larger population.

To pursue the offensive, the Soviets produced massive quantities of field artillery weapons and small arms. They also employed a cavalry force of 600,000 men who, at a shocking cost in human lives, constantly harassed the Germans by infiltrating through the snowbound forests or suddenly appearing out of the fog at dawn.

The snow, so dreaded by the Germans, was a Russian ally. Historian Louis L. Snyder writes of the Soviet soldier: "camouflaged in white cloth, wrapping his weapon in white cloth, carefully smoothing his tracks, he could sink at night into the snowy background and then suddenly emerge to wreck havoc on the enemy's flanks and rear."

Augmented by recently brought up Siberian divisions, Marshal Georgy Zhukov (q.v.) took the offensive on 6 December 1941 with 100 divisions. The overextended and poorly equipped Germans were thrown back, causing General Franz Halder (q.v.) to later write, "The myth of the invincibility of the German Army was broken."

The Russian campaign was the greatest military conflict in all history. In 1945, the Soviets arrived in the west with one of the strangest armies ever seen. It consisted of three main elements. Up front were elite, hard-hitting guard units to break through German lines, followed by illiterate infantry soldiers who annihilated the German infantry. Carrying only a rifle and some provisions in a small rucksack, these peasant soldiers lived off the land. Often the Germans cut their supply line only to realize they had no supply line. Following them in the rear came NKVD (q.v.) units with orders to shoot stragglers on sight. As Zhukov told Eisenhower, it took a braver Soviet soldier to turn back than to go forward and face the enemy.

Of crucial importance in considering Soviet military strategy was the massive increase in the size and mission of state security organizations brought on by the war. Soviet obsession about the need to conduct counterinsurgency, counterintelligence, and counter-guerrilla operations against suspected anti-Soviet elements among their own people placed a premium on the use of state security forces.

Thousands of state security officers were sent behind enemy lines to recruit, train, and command partisan (q.v.) forces. No independence on the part of these units was tolerated. Partisan, special detachments, NKVD, *Spetsnaz* (q.v.), extermination, hunter, and special control units, all operating under the central direction of *Smersh* (q.v.), and controlled in Moscow by the *Stavka* (q.v.), were organized behind German lines.

Whatever else these state security units may have accomplished—and they accomplished much—they maintained a Soviet presence in the occupied territories. A proclamation broadcast in June 1942 stated: "Those who remain in hiding or stay at home in order to save their skins . . . or those who . . . desert to the Fascist army . . . will be liquidated by us sooner or later." This same warning was repeated hundreds of times in official Communist bulletins. Thus, Soviet citizens everywhere were poignantly reminded that they ultimately would be held accountable for their wartime behavior. Using these weapons of fear and intimidation, effective recruiting campaigns were conducted in the occupied territories with the recruits filtered back through gaps in the German lines.

As the Red Army pursued the retreating Germans after victory at Stalingrad (q.v.), plans were laid for absorption of liberated areas into the Soviet orbit. During the last two years of the war, specific plans were developed to absorb Albania, Bulgaria, Hungary, Poland, eastern Germany, Yugoslavia, and Romania into the Soviet bloc. In pursuing these goals, the Soviets generally operated in three stages. First, a genuine anti-Nazi resistance movement was established by Soviet-trained Communists in cooperation with local peasant and socialist parties. Next, the Communist Party endeavored to split parties by exploiting religious, ethnic, and regional jealousies, transforming the coalition into a Communist-controlled alliance. Finally, timed with the arrival of the Red Army, a coup d'etat established complete Communist control.

In negotiations with his allies, Stalin knew now to exploit his strong military position. He made forceful economic claims against Germany during the Yalta Conference in February 1945. He demanded $10 billion in reparations, plus a massive transfer of German industrial plants to the Soviet Union. He repeated a demand, made earlier at the Teheran Conference, to have three million Germans taken to the Soviet Union for ten years to rebuild the war-damaged economy.

The overly eager and ill-advised American effort to obtain a Soviet second front against Japan made it rather simple for the Soviets to realize their ambition to reclaim lost territory in Asia. Stalin at first seemed reluctant to commit Soviet troops against Japan, arguing that Soviet public opinion—as if such a thing really mattered—would not understand this sacrifice unless the Soviet Union received compensation. The Americans were all too willing to sweeten the offer at someone else's expense. Stalin wanted to maintain the "status quo" in Outer Mongolia, which meant it became a Soviet satellite. Additionally, he demanded and obtained the southern half of Sakhalin Island (lost to Japan in 1905), the Kurile Islands (ceded to Japan in 1875), the lease on Port Arthur as a Soviet naval base, and joint interest with China in the foreign-built Manchurian Railway.

Soviet ambitions greatly exceeded their acquisitions. Stalin demanded control over the Turkish Straits and return from Turkey of the provinces of Kars and Ardahan, which a "weak Soviet government had been forced to cede to Turkey in 1921." The British refused and Roosevelt equivocated. At the Potsdam Conference, however, Truman firmly put his foot down and refused to allow it. Stalin also sought a United Nations trusteeship for the USSR over the Italian colony of Tripolitania, the western and most prosperous part of Libya.

The Soviets were thwarted in their claim to the Turkish Straits, the provinces of Kars and Ardahan, reparations, and Tripolitania, but the Western powers also failed, among other things, to influence events in Eastern Europe. Truman left Potsdam determined not to share atom bomb secrets with the Soviets and to deny them an occupation role in Japan. He drew the line and made it clear the Soviet challenge would be met. In Truman, Josef Stalin met his match.

The power and momentum of the Red Army's advance into Western Europe could not be halted short of its objectives. Stalin's tough, even brilliant diplomacy brought the Soviet Union many gains. In the most critical days of the war, he never forgot what he was fighting for. In advancing the national goals of the Soviet Union, he furthered the cause of international Communism. To him they were one and the same. Lenin had been right: Soviet military power accomplished what revolutions had never been able to do. At the end of the war, the Red Army controlled more than half of Europe and reclaimed lost territories in Asia.

Paul J. Rose

Additional Reading

Armstrong, John A. (ed.), *Soviet Partisans in World War II* (1964).

Garthof, Raymond L., *Soviet Military Policy* (1966).

Mastny, Vojtech, *Russia's Road to the Cold War* (1979).

More, Barrington, Jr, *Soviet Politics—the Dilemma of Power* (1950).

Paret, Peter (ed.), *Makers of Modern Strategy* (1986).

Seaton, Albert, *The Russo-German War 1941–1945* (1971).

Submarine and Antisubmarine Warfare

In contrast to the Pacific theater, naval warfare in Europe was not one of major fleet actions fought in the ocean's vast expanses. In Europe, the naval war was mainly one between submarines and those trying to stop them. From the Battle of the Atlantic through the Mediterranean (qq.v.) to the far Arctic and Black Seas, the objective was to eliminate the enemy's commerce or logistical support to his military forces.

Merchant ships were the primary targets in this struggle and all nations went to great lengths to attack their opponents' shipping while protecting their own. The enemy's surface warships were also major targets. Submarines were the premier weapon of attack and a vast array of air and naval forces had to be employed against them. No surface ship larger than a destroyer went to sea without an escort of antisubmarine-capable ships.

For the Western Allies, defeating the German submarine or U-boat menace was the driving factor in their naval operations, and that goal consumed a major portion of their research and production effort. It was this effort and the overwhelming Allied superiority in resources and material that gave their antisubmarine forces victory.

This reliance on submarines as the primary strike arm made the European naval war one of stealth, punch, and, counterpunch. All nations relied on convoys (q.v.) to protect their shipping—that is, one or more merchant ships were gathered together under the protection of one or more specialized escort vessels. These vessels were generally equipped with underwater detection gear and carried depth charges (underwater explosive devices that detonated at a preset depth). Because of their effect on underwater detection equipment and threat to the surface ship's hull, depth charges could only be deployed behind and away from surface ships. This left the escort commander temporarily "blind" after an attack and many submarine commanders exploited this to escape subsequent attacks.

Radar (q.v.) generally was not available early in the war and was found only on Western escort vessels after 1941. The escort vessels generally operated in a "screen" around the ships they were protecting and the entire formation zigzagged to complicate the submarine's torpedo firing solution. The same principles applied when the unit to be protected was a major warship, such as a battleship, cruiser, or aircraft carrier, only the group moved at higher speed. A submarine versus escort engagement, therefore, consisted of submarines trying to penetrate the escort's screen to attack the ships under protection.

The submarines of the period were little improved over those of World War I. Most had a good surface speed but were slow and unwieldy when submerged. Their underwater endurance was also poor. Moreover, a submerged submarine had only a limited ability to detect and track targets. In effect, it was little more than a slightly mobile minefield with a reach no greater than that of its periscope's horizon, about three nautical miles. This disadvantage was offset by the stealth that underwater operations provided. Few nations had effective underwater detection gear, although the Royal Navy (RN) placed great faith in its ASDIC or sonar (q.v.). Thus, a submerged submarine had a good chance of approaching a ship or group of ships undetected. It also had a good chance of escaping after its attack.

Mitigating against this was the requirement by international law that the submarine observe prize rules in attacking merchant ships. That is, the submarine was supposed to surface and challenge the ship, board it, and examine its cargo before taking action. Given that a submarine could rarely match the gun armament of the merchant ships and their escorts, it was a rare submarine commander who could observe these rules for long and survive. In fact, all the combatants ceased to observe prize rules very early in the conflict.

Another hazard for submarines was the mutual interference problem—the risk of two friendly submarines interfering with each other. Given the primitive nature of communications, sensors, and navigation equipment of that period, there was a great risk that submarines operating in close proximity might encounter each other with deadly consequences. In fact, the first Royal Navy submarine sunk in World War II, HMS *Oxley*, was sunk by another RN submarine, HMS *Triton*. The victim had unknowingly intruded into its attacker's patrol area.

Thus, most nations, except Germany, employed their submarines individually to conduct their attacks submerged. Only Germany's submarine arm under Admiral Karl Dönitz (q.v.) considered night surface attacks using group or wolf pack tactics. He recognized that operating on the surface expanded the submarine's horizons, reach, and striking power. He saw sonar as a threat but also realized that a surfaced submarine was difficult to detect at night and could use its speed to dart in and out of the escort screen to conduct multiple attacks. These proved effective tactics for most of the war.

Ironically, Germany was the only major participant in World War II that entered the war without a major submarine fleet. Only forty-six of its sixty-three U-boats were operational at war's start, and more than half of those were small coastal submarines, incapable of attacking the Allies' oceanic sea trade. Lacking the numbers to initiate wolf pack tactics, German U-boats attacked individually, preferring night surface attacks. Losses were heavy during the war's early months because the RN was prepared. They quickly established convoys, and the U-boats' limited reach, a result of the need to circumnavigate Great Britain to reach the ocean sea lanes, enabled the RN to concentrate its escorts most effectively.

The Western Allies and Germany entered World War II much better prepared to conduct antisubmarine warfare (ASW) than they did in World War I. They established ASW escort groups before the war, using ships equipped with sonar. Among the major combatants, only Italy, France, and the Soviet Union entered the war with ships lacking sonar.

Of the participating nations, Great Britain was the best equipped to conduct ASW. It had stockpiled more than 200 sonars for installation in requisitioned civilian craft, and another 200 were installed in destroyers, sloops, and ASW trawlers. The RN also had prepared plans for the rapid construction of specialized convoy escort vessels based on an existing British whaling ship design. Their only shortfall was in radar and air reconnaissance support. Indeed, the Royal Navy was so confident in its ASW capabilities that it feared German surface raiders more than it did U-boats. That emphasis seemed well placed in the war's early months. German mines sank more ships in that period than did U-boats. It was not to last, however.

The fall of Norway and France (qq.v.), combined with Germany's accelerated construction of U-boats, changed the situation by August 1940. The U-boats began to reach farther out, beyond the range of most convoy escorts. U-boats began to conduct surface attacks in daylight. This was followed by the first wolf pack attacks in late 1940. The convoy escorts were quickly in danger of being overwhelmed. They lacked air support, and radar was only just beginning to be installed on ASW ships. About the same time, the Allies began to break the U-boat communications codes through ULTRA (q.v.). This allowed the British to route convoys evasively to avoid U-boat concentrations. Still, the advantage rested with the U-boats.

Dönitz's wolf pack tactics required a centralized direction of the U-boat effort. As such, it was communications dependent. The U-boats were deployed in long patrol lines. The first U-boat to detect a convoy took station behind it and reported its position and movements to Dönitz's operations center. The nearest available boats were then directed in to intercept. The senior U-boat commander took command of the "pack" and conducted the actual attack, which consisted of a series of individual hit-and-run raids against all quarters of the convoy. The effect stretched the escorts' capabilities to the maximum and exhausted their crews. It was a very successful technique; its only weakness was its heavy reliance on communications.

Until the ULTRA breakthrough, the Allies' only method of locating U-boats prior to their attacks was via aerial surveillance or high frequency direction finding (HF/DF). The former required the aircraft to spot a single submarine in a vast expanse of ocean—a difficult task at best except in areas close to the U-boats' target. An early war tactic of using open-ocean "hunter-killer" groups centered around an aircraft carrier was unsuccessful because of this. Only an aircraft carrier operating in proximity to a convoy (an escort carrier) had a high probability of detecting U-boats. The RN never felt it had enough air cover for its convoys until escort carriers were available in large numbers in 1943. Thus, HF/DF was the primary means of monitoring U-boat dispositions.

HF/DF employed several sensitive high frequency receivers with directional antennas to detect and determine the location of a U-boat transmitting its reports. Unfortunately, the primitive antennas of the time could only provide an approximate position, accurate only to within a couple of hundred miles at long range. Generally, the closer the transmitter to the receiver, the more accurate the fix. If within range, aircraft could be dispatched to the general area to determine the U-boat's actual position. The U-boats continued to flourish, however, in the areas where aircraft could not reach.

S

The Western Allies won their antisubmarine war by taking a series of initiatives to improve the technological and tactical efficiency of their ASW forces. All intelligence information on enemy submarines was channeled into the Operational Command Center for immediate analysis and action. This consolidation of intelligence from all sources, photo reconnaissance, ship, aircraft, agent reports, HF/DF, and ULTRA was critical to the effective management of the ASW war.

The Royal and U.S. Navies also established standardized tactics and training in 1942 to improve the proficiency of their sensor operators and escort commanders. The RN organized its escort groups into tactical units, which trained and operated together. The greater cohesion gained from this team concept was directly responsible for the escort groups' increased effectiveness after mid-1942. Thus, the entire operational chain of command improved in efficiency as the war went on.

There was a technical side to this as well. The RN developed tactical plotting tables and installed them on destroyers and major combatant vessels before the war. These tables enabled ship commanders to maintain a moving plot of the tactical situation around their ship or group. All visual sightings, as well as radar, aircraft, and sonar reports could be plotted on the table. The RN also began to install such tables on all ASW vessels in late 1941. This small innovation enabled escort and convoy commanders to visualize the U-boat situation around them more quickly and to react faster and more effectively.

The installation of HF/DF on escort ships and the integration with shore-based HF/DF systems was another major step. It significantly improved the escort commander's ability to locate and attack the trailing U-boat guiding the rest of the wolf pack onto his convoy. The survivability of the trailing U-boat drastically decreased as more escort ships and escort carriers became available after late 1941. By mid-1943, it was almost suicidal for a trailing U-boat to make its reports.

Ship sonars also improved in range and accuracy. The introduction of chemical trace paper recorders also helped sonar operators by recording U-boat positions and analyzing a potential target's sound echo. This reduced the operators' susceptibility to U-boat countermeasures and other false indicators. The introduction of magnetic anomaly detection (MAD) gear for Allied aircraft in 1943 gave them the ability to detect submerged as well as surfaced submarines. Finally, improvements in radar, particularly the shift to centimetric radar, sounded the death knell for Germany's wolf pack

tactics. Night and the vast ocean no longer provided much security to a slow-moving U-boat.

Another innovation was the establishment of British and American operational research groups (ORGs), organizations that analyzed the entire spectrum of naval operations and tactics. By studying ASW action reports, they identified the most efficient convoy size and determined that it was the number of escorts and not the size of the convoy that determined convoy vulnerability. It also helped determine which tactics would work and which were not successful, for example, the best depth charge patterns. One of the key judgments noted by the ORGs was that the presence of aircraft significantly degraded U-boat effectiveness. This led to the development of escort carriers.

ASW weapons also improved significantly during the war. The first of these was the air-dropped depth charge. Initially deployed in 1940, it gave Allied aircraft the ability to attack submerging submarines. The design of air- and surface-dropped depth charges was streamlined to accelerate descent into the depths, and their explosive power was increased.

The Hedgehog, a rocket-thrown projectile that exploded only on impact, was introduced in late 1941. Fired in patterns of twenty-four rockets, it provided ASW units with the capability to engage submarines ahead of them, enabling them to track a U-boat continuously while conducting their attacks. (An escort versus submarine engagement is called a prosecution.) A modified version of these weapons, mounted backward on aircraft wings, was introduced in late 1942, enabling MAD-equipped aircraft to attack U-boats they detected underneath them.

The final weapons development was the introduction of ASW torpedoes, originally called mines, which used their own active sonar to detect and attack U-boats. Introduced in mid-1942, they were the deadliest and most effective weapons facing U-boats in the war, although they were too slow to engage the German Type XXI U-boats that entered service in the war's final month.

The Allies employed these innovations effectively, using radar-equipped aircraft to attack U-boats as they transited to and from their bases in France and Norway. The Allies also reestablished hunter-killer groups in 1943, using ULTRA and integrated HF/DF information to track down and destroy U-boats in the open ocean. U-boat survival became increasingly problematic after May 1943, and by August, Dönitz had to withdraw them from the campaign. They were never a serious threat after that.

The Germans' unsuccessful efforts to counter these developments also relied on a combination of technology and tactics. They developed radar warning receivers in 1941 to detect airborne radars, but Allied superiority in electronic research enabled them to stay ahead for most of the war.

In 1940–1941, Adolf Hitler (q.v.) imposed a ban on short-term research, and thus Dönitz found himself in a weak competitive position. Although he commanded the U-boat force, he had no influence on the German Navy's research and development efforts. As a result, German U-boat design essentially stagnated during the critical 1940–1942 period when the Allies introduced most of their major advances in ASW technology. Although after 1941, they did have the *Pillenwerfer*, a sonar deception device, German technology remained a step behind Allied efforts until the end of the war.

German submarines did not obtain radar until 1942, and the *Schnorchel,* which allowed them to recharge their batteries submerged, did not come into service until 1943. The installation of radar- and sonar-absorbent materials onto superstructures and *Schnorchels* also came too late. Finally, the high-speed Type XXI and XXIII U-boats, which could have defeated any Allied ASW system available, did not enter service until the war was already lost. The extent of the German failure is best indicated by the greater than 80 percent death rate of the U-boat crews who served in combat.

German U-boat tactics also lagged. Faced with increasing air attacks in their transits to and from their bases, Dönitz had them armed with stronger antiaircraft batteries. He also had them transit in groups. Both tactics enjoyed initial success, but quickly proved a costly mistake. The *Schnorchel* enabled the U-boats to make their transits submerged, but even that became hazardous as Allied radars acquired the capability to detect *Schnorchels.*

U-boats employed their T-series acoustic homing torpedoes specifically to attack the convoy escorts, but the Allies soon developed effective countermeasures. Lacking anything similar to the Allied ORGs, Dönitz found himself groping for a solution. He abandoned wolf pack tactics in December of 1943, but a year would pass before new tactics were adopted. As with the introduction of new U-boats, they came too late as well.

The Soviet Navy was the only other European fleet to even attempt submarine group tactics, albeit to little effect. By 1944, the Soviets were using coordinated air, surface, and submarine attacks against German convoys in the Black and Baltic Seas, and the Arctic Ocean. Although these attacks generally overwhelmed the German convoy escorts, convoy losses did not increase significantly.

The Soviet concentration on tactical training came at the expense of technical proficiency. They neglected the primary requirement of naval warfare—putting ordnance on the target. Most of their torpedoes and bombs missed their targets. Hence, although the Germans found the Soviet naval threat to be increasingly worrisome, it never interrupted their sea commerce in the east—not even in the war's final month.

Neither the Axis countries nor the Soviet Union mounted anything like the Western Allies' ASW effort. Blessed with shorter maritime lines of communications, these countries emphasized deterring submarine attack over destroying the submarine.

Until 1940, German ASW doctrine relied primarily on passive hydrophones to detect submarines, using active sonar only for the final attack. The Germans also employed ship-borne helicopters (q.v.) in ASW in the Aegean Sea in 1943. Interestingly, the *Luftwaffe* employed air-dropped depth bombs from the war's beginning, but otherwise the Germans introduced no new or innovative ASW weapons or tactics during the war. Generally, the Germans preferred to use defensive ASW minefields to protect their convoys whenever possible, employing them to good effect on the eastern front and in the North and Aegean Seas.

The Italians faced a serious British submarine threat in the Mediterranean, and found themselves ill-equipped to deal with it. Italian destroyers and escorts had no active sonars until late 1942, and most of those came from Germany. The only doctrine Italy employed was to use active-sonar-equipped units to lead the convoy, leaving it up to the individual initiative of ship commanders to determine how best to prosecute any submarines they encountered. Still, some Italian escort commanders proved very effective. The RN's submarine force suffered nearly 20 percent casualties in the Mediterranean.

The Soviet Union never developed an effective ASW doctrine, relying on Lend-Lease–provided radars and sonars to equip their units during the war. The result was that a handful of small Axis submarines severely inhibited Soviet surface ship employment.

Submarines had a decisive impact on the war's outcome and paid high dividends to those who employed them effectively. Basically, destroying a submarine required ten times the economic and military effort of commissioning and deploying one. Still, as the Western Allies proved so convincingly, it could be done if one dedicated the resources and effort to the task. The Allied victory, however, was as dependent on the very limited technical advances made by their opponents, the U-boats, as it was on their own efforts. Had the more capable Type XXI and XXIII U-boats entered service a year earlier, the outcome may well have been different. Still, the impact of the submarine versus antisubmarine war remains with us into modern times. The tactics, technology, and strategies of today all have their foundations in World War II.

Carl O. Schuster

Additional Reading

Achkasov, V.I. and N.B. Pavlovich, *Soviet Naval Operations in the Great Patriotic War, 1941–1945* (1981).

Dönitz, Karl, *Ten Years and Twenty Days* (1964).

Frank, Wolfgang, *The Seawolves* (1955).

Hackman, Willem, *Seek and Strike* (1984).

Hough, Richard, *The Longest Battle* (1986).

Kahn, David, *Seizing the Enigma: The Race to Break the German U-Boat Codes, 1939–1943* (1991).

Piekalkiewicz, Janusz, *Sea War 1939–1945* (1980).

Polmar, Norman, *Imperial Russian and Soviet Submarines 1917–1987* (1990).

Poolman, Kenneth, *Allied Escort Carriers of World War II* (1988).

Ruge, Friedrich, *Der Seekrieg 1939–1945* (1958).

———, *The Soviets As Naval Opponents, 1941–45* (1979).

T

Tactical Air Support

A major role of air forces is support of ground forces. Such support is both offensive and defensive in nature. Airpower is postured to seek out enemy air forces both in the air and on the ground in order to eliminate the enemy. Air forces are expected to attack enemy ground forces to delay, disrupt, or destroy them. Also, air forces protect the movement of ground forces by maintaining air superiority. The basic objective of air forces is to win the air battle, to gain and maintain control of the operational environment, and to take decisive action directly against an enemy's war-fighting capacity.

The success of ground operations depends upon massing airpower at decisive points so the theater commander can seize the initiative. Tactical air operations are carried out in coordination with land forces to attain and maintain air superiority, to prevent movement of enemy forces, and to seek out and destroy these forces and their supporting installations. Tactical air support is most effective when used in the preplanned role that is designed to break through enemy defenses or to stop a penetration. Battles are fought and won by land and air forces working together. The interaction and cooperation between them extends into almost every function of modern combat, and this was very true in Europe during World War II.

The early years of 1941 and 1942 were less decisive than originally hoped for by the Allies. By mid-1943, however, the British and the American air forces had seized the lead in developing air-ground tactical air support techniques once held by the Germans. Tactical airpower, the use of airplanes to directly support the ground forces rather than for the strategic purpose of undermining the overall war-making ability (called interdiction), was employed by the Allies in three deadly phases.

First, aircraft were ranged well ahead of the ground units to attack *Luftwaffe* bases and aircraft on the ground to gain local air superiority. Next, airpower was used to isolate the enemy forces in the battle area. Finally, tactical airpower was used to hit enemy forces that stood in the way of the advancing ground troops.

Tactical airpower was pioneered by the German Air Force. The *Luftwaffe* massed thousands of its airplanes, and in coordination with the armored and infantry units, lent terrifying potency to the German juggernaut that rolled across Europe in 1939 and 1940.

The first period of the war, up to 1941, saw little strategic bombardment and numerous operations in direct support of the land forces. To the Germans, the *Blitzkrieg* (q.v.) was proof that aircraft used in support of land forces was key to successful operations. Adolf Hitler (q.v.) was convinced that the *Luftwaffe* was needed for tailored air support and that victory could be achieved in this manner.

The British air minister observed, after noting the success of the German close air support aircraft early in the war, that strong airpower must be met by "stronger" airpower. The Royal Air Force (RAF) was convinced of the wisdom of tying aircraft to a tactical role with the army. RAF losses were light compared to *Luftwaffe* losses only because fewer aircraft were committed to the tactical air support role. The RAF kept its aircraft at home for air defense, while the French were holding their aircraft for the expected attack in the west. The prudence of that move was manifested in the Battle of Britain (q.v.), where the RAF successfully thwarted Hitler's strategic bombing campaign prior to a planned invasion of the British Isles.

In 1941, the Germans invaded the Soviet Union (q.v.) and the *Luftwaffe* was again dedicated to tactical support of ground forces. Thus, the eastern front saw airpower predominantly employed by the Germans and the Soviets in direct support of their ground armies. Soviet premier Josef Stalin (q.v.) too believed air forces should be used in a tactical air role. Although some planning in a limited way was done for long-range bombing activities, the bulk of airpower on the eastern front was in direct support of ground forces and in achieving air superiority over the battlefield.

The Western Allied air strategy was less than clear from the very beginning of the war. The first attempts by the Allied air forces, primarily the RAF, were concentrated attacks on troop movements from forces stationed in France, while forces in Britain harassed German communication facilities. Both had little success. Allied effort was fragmented over a number of objectives.

The Soviet Air Force learned valuable lessons from the eastern front operations. It was reorganized to take advantage of its new doctrine of "air offensive." This doctrine had two purposes: first, to prepare the way for ground attack by massive preparatory strikes; and second, to give immediate support, with large concentrations of aircraft, to the ground armies. When the Soviet counteroffensive was finally launched in 1942, it confirmed the new Soviet doctrine of air offensive. The Soviet Army, which drew heavily on airpower for long-range fire support, drove the German armies back across central Europe. The Soviet ground and air forces proved a mighty combination.

The RAF reorganized on 14 June 1943 by creating a tactical air force whose mission was to achieve even closer cooperation with the ground forces. The London *Times* described it as the "most significant reform by the RAF since the war began." This combined use of aircraft with the other services gave the RAF its first real opportunity for testing the "tactical" use of airpower. The U.S. Army Air Force, meanwhile, began its buildup in the Mediterranean. By joining forces, the combined British and American air forces provided a strong tactical air force in that theater of operations.

American use of tactical airpower supported the air strategy "to conduct a sustained and unremitting air offense against Germany and Italy to destroy their will and capability to continue the war." The most important task was to provide "for the close and direct support of the surface forces in the invasion of the Continent and for major land battles thereafter."

Throughout the war, there were constant discussions over the "proper" role of airpower: close support of the armies versus the wider role of strategic bombardment. A compromise was reached whereby Allied airpower was used in a more flexible combat role where air forces were directed from a central air headquarters working closely with the ground armies but not subordinate to them.

Out of the Casablanca Conference in 1943 came the policy to obtain complete air mastery over the Axis. The first need was to apply continuous aerial warfare, what U.S. General Henry H "Hap" Arnold (q.v.) called the "continuous application of massed airpower against critical objectives," and to keep up a constant war of attrition in order to wear down all resistance. The second need was for a large tactical air force to achieve mastery over the battlefield.

General Dwight D. Eisenhower (q.v.), as the commander in chief of Allied forces in northern Africa, established the Northwest African Air Forces. That organization worked with the Allied 18th Army Group. This air command organization was unique at the time, and it was specifically tasked to provide tactical air support to ground units. Allied support of the army by air forces in World War II began in Africa and was refined on the European continent.

The most successful tactical air operation was the support of the Normandy (q.v.) invasion in June 1944. By the time Operation OVERLORD was executed, the tactical use of air forces conformed to the operational experience of earlier campaigns, and working with strategic bombing (q.v.), ensured permanent air superiority.

The basic objective of air forces is to win the air battle. A general strategy toward meeting that objective involves the pursuit of all major aspects of air doctrine: air defense, strategic bombardment, support of naval operations, and close support of ground forces. A limited strategy forces upon the enemy only one or two of those doctrines. The United States and Great Britain practiced a general air strategy. Germany and the Soviet Union adopted a more limited strategy.

Thomas A. Cardwell, III

Additional Reading
Coleman, John M., *The Development of Tactical Services in the Army Air Force* (1950).
Hallion, Richard P., *Strike from the Sky* (1989).
Rust, Kenn C., et al., *The Ninth Air Force in World War II* (1967).

Transportation Plan

The Transportation Plan was an air plan authored

y Professor Solly Zuckerman on 3 March 1944 to create a "railway desert" in France in support of Operation OVERLORD. Zuckerman believed all Allied air resources should be used against rail facilities in France and western Germany to isolate the Normandy (q.v.) landing area. Support came mainly from Air Chief Marshal Sir Trafford Leigh-Mallory (q.v.), in charge of tactical air forces for Operation OVERLORD.

Opposition was strong. Prime Minister Winston S. Churchill (q.v.) feared the political costs of high casualties among French civilians. RAF Bomber Command's Air Marshal Sir Arthur Harris (q.v.) opposed any diversion from his city-busting campaign. U.S. Strategic Air Forces in Europe commander General Carl Spaatz (q.v.) favored a campaign against oil targets to strike directly at the sources of German power and wear down the *Luftwaffe*. President Franklin D. Roosevelt's (q.v.) determination that the controversy should be a military matter freed Supreme Allied Commander General Dwight D. Eisenhower (q.v.) to decide in favor of the Transportation Plan on 26 March 1944.

The effort accelerated on 17 April 1944, continuing until D-Day and after. RAF Bomber Command had noteworthy success at night against marshalling yards, while Allied tactical air forces and U.S. strategic air forces struck at targets during the day. A key factor was the late addition of bridges over the Seine River and the use of fighters to attack trains. Allied aircraft dropped more than 75,000 tons of bombs and stopped two-thirds of French railway traffic. The accomplishments of the campaign remain subject to debate today, but the effort clearly contributed to the successful interdiction of German troop movements in the critical weeks following D-Day.

Stephen L. McFarland

Additional Reading

Rostow, W.W., *Pre-invasion Bombing Strategy* (1981).
Tedder, Arthur, *With Prejudice* (1966).
Webster, Charles, and Arthur Noble Frankland, *The Strategic Air Offensive Against Germany, 1939–1945* (1961).

U

ULTRA

The most carefully concealed intelligence triumph of World War II was the Allied ability to read Germany's most secret communications encrypted by the Enigma (q.v.) cipher machines. These wireless signals were intercepted by various special receiving stations. Sent by teleprinter to Bletchley Park (BP) (q.v.) outside of London, they were deciphered and distributed to special liaison units (SLUs) attached to the major Allied field commands. The deciphered product was known as "special intelligence," and was marked Most Secret-U (which stood for ULTRA), later known as Top Secret-U.

Any document or message so marked was only circulated to selected individuals on a very restricted list. For wider usage, the information was paraphrased and disguised as to the method of its collection. The SLUs (fifty by the war's end) normally received ULTRA traffic four times a day, except during operations when critical material was provided immediately to the appropriate commands.

ULTRA provided the Allies with the ability to read the German orders, which the latter believed remained secure. The ULTRA intelligence revealed the German leaders' hopes and anxieties, resources and prospects, vulnerabilities and strong points. It told of actual plans and of planned contingencies should things go wrong. This insider knowledge gave a priceless advantage to the Allied commanders. ULTRA provided a database built through close observation over a prolonged period that allowed Allied analysts to develop profiles of the German commanders' personal traits, thoughts, and relations with colleagues.

ULTRA diplomatic intercepts provided the technical reports of the Japanese naval attache in Berlin on German aircraft performance and pro-duction. Finally, ULTRA provided the Allies with German intentions and capabilities of new weapons like V-1, V-2, rocket planes, and new model of U-boats.

During the France (q.v.) campaign, the Allies learned that speed was a critical factor in exploiting the ULTRA advantage. Deciphering had to be swift and reasonably continuous if there was to be a payoff in the field. Even the best of secret intelligence diminished in value when the enemy was overwhelmingly superior.

During the Battle of Britain (q.v.), ULTRA enabled RAF Fighter Command to understand the Germans' main strategy. It kept them informed of the enemy strength, locations, and readiness of individual *Luftwaffe* units. It supplied the British with invaluable advance warning about impending air raids.

The information received through ULTRA included advanced warnings on German plans to invade the Soviet Union, and their intentions to invade the Balkans. Also included were German diplomatic relations and negotiations with other countries, German appreciations of Allied intentions and their plans to counter them, and German measures for the invasion of France and plans for counterattacks if any other power intervened. The Allies learned of German plans and movements of troops from one front to another, information on the internal disintegration in Germany, and information on the attempted assassination of Adolf Hitler (q.v.).

When the fighting returned to the European mainland, the Allies discovered that the Germans conducted much of their internal military communications by telephone and telex, which are far less vulnerable to intercept than radio. Nevertheless, various German headquarters did find the need to talk to each other by radio. ULTRA's strength lay n identifying those headquarters and the units they called, revealing the German order of battle. Prior to the D-Day landings the Allied forces had thorough knowledge of the German formations and defensive preparations they faced across the Channel, including the groupings of German *Panzer* units. On D-Day, ULTRA intelligence showed the way through the German naval minefields off the French coastline. The Allies suffered only seven losses to mines.

In the air war, ULTRA gave relatively little direct targeting information for strategic bombing because high grade military ciphers were not the normal communications channel for industrial facilities. Most industrial communications took place by telephone and teleprinter. Occasionally, however, ULTRA did present new and valuable targets, such as the Walke-Wecke plant at Kiel, which made power units for the new rocket aircraft. ULTRA was still the base for tactical and strategic air targeting intelligence because of the in-depth knowledge of strength, disposition, composition, production, wastage, reserves, and serviceability of the *Luftwaffe*. ULTRA proved indispensable as a chronicle of the day-to-day and hour-to-hour movements of operational units of all German services and the supplies on which they depended.

In the war at sea, ULTRA eventually gave the Allied naval commanders an unprecedented overview of German operations and intentions. Among its major successes, ULTRA contributed to the destruction of the Italian Navy. ULTRA also allowed the Allies to track German ships around the Atlantic, choosing the best time and suitable means to strike. Within one period of a few weeks, the Allies were able to sink fifteen German surface raiders.

As the war progressed, Allied commanders came to rely more and more on ULTRA, as they eliminated one question mark after another about their opponents. Thousands of operational decisions by Allied commanders were assisted by the tremendous volume of material ULTRA provided, and that in turn helped to optimize the use of the sometimes thin Allied resources. The ULTRA system, of course, did not have control over the messages it intercepted; nor could it influence whether the entire message or only a fragment was caught.

At first many Allied leaders thought ULTRA was too good to be true, and the system had to overcome the prejudices military commanders had against intelligence from so startling a medium. Once accepted, ULTRA threatened to become the taskmaster that would not be denied. Whenever ULTRA was wrong, either through misreading or misinterpretation, or simply because the enemy commander did not follow orders or changed his mind, ULTRA was considered guilty.

Once accepted, the main problem with ULTRA became one of overreliance, which sometimes had dire consequences. Overreliance led to a neglect of other basic intelligence sources. ULTRA came to be expected to cover all significant aspects of a situation, which actually was far beyond its capabilities. ULTRA information often came in bits and pieces, at intervals, out of chronological sequence, and had to be fitted into the big picture. Often there were cases where a subordinate Allied analyst, intimidated by his superior and eager to please, tailored the reports to the wishful thinking of the commander. This, of course, is a traditional pitfall with any intelligence system.

In the beginning, BP had only a small staff, inexperienced at its craft. Another major problem was that the analysts at BP had virtually no knowledge of the current military situation, except for the German view. They knew nothing about Allied intentions or plans. Thus, they were unable to focus the information they processed on the basis of understanding what was needed.

The Enigma machine and the efforts to decipher its messages through the "Bombe," an electromechanical device built at BP to decrypt Enigma messages, contributed to the development of modern computer systems. The standard terminology of modern code breaking also developed. These include signals intelligence (SIGINT) (q.v.), the general term used for all processes and for any intelligence produced from intercepted communications traffic, traffic analysis (TA), and direction finding (DF).

Today, all modern military forces have become highly dependent upon rapid secure communications. Intercepting and breaking hostile communications codes is a major activity of most intelligence agencies, as is communication security and the protection of such systems. Even today, SIGINT cannot be relied upon totally to answer critical questions explicitly. Normally, SIGINT information must be confirmed by other intelligence collection means, and the SIGINT data must be disguised to prevent compromise. Databases are critical in developing targets and enemy orders of battle. Virtually all countries today have the capability to intercept some level of military communications and gain similar information on their opponent's operations.

Alexander Molnar, Jr.

Additional Reading

Kahn, David, *Seizing the Enigma: The Race to Break the German U-Boat Codes, 1939–1943* (1991).

Lewin, Ronald, *ULTRA Goes to War* (1978).

Montagu, Ewen, *Beyond Top Secret ULTRA* (1977).

Winterbotham, F.W., *The ULTRA Secret* (1974).

Winton, John, *ULTRA at Sea* (1988).

V

Veterinary Services

During World War II, a total of 5,650 Allied and Axis veterinarians provided necessary services for food inspection and care of cavalry horses and military dogs. Most of the major armies used horses and mules to pull artillery, carry radios, transport supplies, serve as battle mounts, carry dispatches, and scout on reconnaissance missions. Dogs were used for tracking and scouting as well as transporting supplies and messages.

The Soviet Union used approximately 3.5 million horses and mules, while Germany had at least 2.7 million in service. Poland, which relied heavily on cavalry, employed almost 100,000 horses for military duty. Approximately 13,000 soldiers were attached to Allied and Axis veterinary companies as assistants. In a war where horses faced attacks launched by mechanized vehicles and airplanes, the carnage sometimes was devastating.

Horse fatalities resulted mainly from battle wounds (75 percent) and heart failure or exhaustion (17 percent). German veterinarians executed 10,000 cavalry horses at the Bay of Severnaya to prevent the Soviets from capturing them. Allied officers such as General George S. Patton (q.v.) ordered veterinarians to assist the evacuation of valuable European breeding stock, mostly Arabians, Trakehners, and Lipizzans, for use in postwar remount breeding programs. Horses were useless without proper hoof and leg care, so all armies had blacksmiths; approximately 3,700 served in World War II.

American military veterinarians were trained the Army Veterinary School and at branches located near military veterinary hospitals in every war theater. Classes stressed meat and food inspection as well as forage examination, and they offered lessons on military protocol and operations. Veterinarians from Allied nations also attended these schools, standardizing practices on the European front.

Unlike other medical officials, the veterinarians were not protected by the Geneva Convention. During the war, seventeen American veterinary officers were killed. Many veterinary personnel were cited for bravery. In the autumn of 1942, the first woman veterinary assistant, a member of the Women's Auxiliary Army Corps (WAAC) (q.v.), began service. In August 1945, she was joined by the first female veterinary officer.

Veterinarians had three primary tasks: (1) inspect slaughtered animals and the resulting food product; (2) provide service to military animals by tending wounds and destroying severely injured animals; and (3) engage in laboratory research to investigate possible animal disease prevention measures. All three objectives were undertaken in order to protect human and animal health and to eradicate contagions.

Veterinary duties varied. Veterinarians at the front tended to cavalry and artillery mounts injured in battle, provided immunizations against diseases, performed surgery, and cared for convalescing patients in veterinary hospitals. They aided in evacuations, quarantining, and examining captured animals. They also performed unofficial tasks such as taking care of soldiers' pets. In food production, they supervised meat, dairy, and poultry operations and the process of canning food. They operated in emergency veterinary hospitals, using portable equipment. When hospitals were unavailable, soldiers often relied on local women to nurture sick horses, or had to act as their own veterinarians, caring for their wounded mounts at the battle site.

Military horse hospitals were located in the interior where severely sick or wounded animals could recuperate or be operated on in specially designed operating rooms outfitted with state-of-the-art technology. These hospitals had X-ray machines, slings to remove stress from legs, and steam baths to debug the animals. Dental care was provided to ensure that horses could eat their rations. The Soviets built underground stables to protect their ill horses, as well as to provide a safe shelter for broodmares and foals to replenish the supply. During the first years of the war, animals were allowed to convalesce before returning to the front. As the war progressed and fewer mounts were available, these horses were returned to the front as relief mounts.

When Allied veterinarians entered Germany after the capitulation, they tried to standardize the veterinary medicine practiced by Soviet, French, British, and American practitioners as much as possible. In the chaotic occupation period, they published multilingual health certificates and dictionaries of animal diseases. They also printed this material in German and emphasized the importance of preventive animal health care to the German people. Primarily, they were concerned with checking the dispersion of contagious livestock diseases; there was fear that saboteurs would intentionally contaminate the Allied occupiers and local populations.

In what will probably be the last major war using horses, veterinarians were effective in regulating foodstuffs, controlling epidemics, and providing crucial health care and maintenance for the troops' horses.

Elizabeth D. Schafer

Additional Reading

Brereton, John M., *The Horse in War* (1976).
Miller, Everett B., *United States Army Veterinary Service in World War II* (1961).

West Wall

The West Wall was the first of Nazi Germany's programs of constructing fortifications and bomb-proof shelters. Its origins stem from German defensive experience on the western front during World War I. During World War II, the Allies referred to the West Wall as the "Siegfried Line," derived from the sector of the World War I Hindenburg Line that ran from Dracourt, near Lille, to just south of Saint-Quentin. The Germans never called the West Wall the "Siegfried Line."

The army started construction on the West Wall in 1936 as an attempt to defend the Saar industrial area after Germany reoccupied the Rhineland. As construction continued, the line's stated purpose was to be a defensive position that supplemented the attributes of the mobile German Army. The West Wall was to slow down and break up an enemy attack, while strong mobile reserves prepared and delivered the crushing counterattack.

Work intensified in May of 1938 as Fritz Todt (q.v.), architect of the *Reichsautobahnen,* was directed by Adolf Hitler (q.v.) to take charge of the project. By 1939, more than 500,000 men from the *Reichsarbeitsdienst* (RAD), civilian contracting firms, army engineers, and various army personnel came under the direction of *Organisation Todt* (q.v.). At the height of construction, the West Wall took up one-third of all cement production in Germany—350 trainloads, and an equal amount of materials transported by vehicles, arrived each month. Six million tons of concrete and three million rolls of barbed wire were laid in an eighteen-month period. In total, more than 3,000 pillboxes, among a total approaching 22,000 individual constructions, were completed.

In 1938, the intention was to complete 560 kilometers of the West Wall from Lörrach, near Basel on the Swiss border, to the point where the Rhine flows into the Netherlands. The original plans called for two lines: an army line twenty to thirty kilometers in depth, and the air defense zone *(Luftwaffe West)* of thirty to fifty kilometers. *Luftwaffe West* was to provide a "wall of fire several kilometers high." Designs were submitted to contractors according to army requirements, but no standard design ever was implemented. A great variety of designs were approved and construction started, creating a lack of economy and inefficiency in materials.

Depth and strength of the West Wall depended on geography. To the south, behind the natural barrier of the Rhine, only a single band was established. The strongest fortifications ran from the Rhine through the Saar as far as Trier. Near Saarbrücken, the double-belt (eleven kilometers apart) was backed up by a third belt sixteen kilometers behind the first two. Only a single line ran from Trier northward along the Ardennes. Farther northward, a double belt (Schill and Scharnhorst Lines) began in the Hürtgen Forest and encircled Aachen (eight kilometers between the belts), protecting the southern avenues of approach to the Ruhr industrial area. North of Aachen, the fortifications became thinner as they neared Holland. The line was to be permanently manned by only a skeleton force with fixed weapons and equipment kept to a minimum. During an actual attack, a single infantry division was to man eight kilometers of front.

Pillboxes on the line were built in cluster patterns, each sited in consideration of cover, concealment, and mutual support of antitank and machine gun fire. To their front, a continuous antitank barrier was formed either by natural or man-made obstacles and backed by barbed wire and mines. The most common antitank obstacles were "dragon's teeth"—concrete pyramids placed four to five rows deep. These devices typically were eighty to 100 centimeters high in the front row, increasing to 140 to 175 centimeters in the back rows. The dragon's teeth normally were reinforced by steel rods, with half the assembly buried in the ground. Pillboxes were situated to cover the obstacles by fire and observation. Nearby foxholes and trenches further strengthened the pillboxes when enough infantry personnel were available.

Pillboxes generally were six to ten meters wide, twelve to eighteen meters long, and five to seven meters high. Usually at least half of a pillbox was underground. Most installations were designed for self-sufficiency with a fighting room; ammunition, tool, and storage rooms; sleeping quarters; food preparation and storage rooms; washing facilities; and lighting and electricity provided via underground cables.

Most pillboxes had chemical protection and ventilation devices. Few had indoor toilets. The walls and roofs were one to three meters thick, usually made of concrete reinforced with steel wire mesh, steel rods, or steel beams. Later in the war some of the thinner walls were thickened with another layer of concrete. Few had more than two firing embrasures, one of which was sited to cover the entrance. Most firing embrasures were designed for the 37mm antitank gun and the MG-34 machine gun. This was a real problem in 1944 when the modern 75mm and 88mm antitank guns, and more critically, the MG-42 machine gun could not be accommodated. The normal complement of men was twenty to forty—five to seven per firing embrasure, plus support troops. Fields of fire were normally limited, typically to an arc of fire of 50 degrees, and seldom more than 90 degrees.

Supporting the pillboxes were various designs of bunkers (for local reserves), bomb shelters, observation posts, and command posts. An installation of one of these kinds normally had only a single rifle port, to cover its own entrance. Bunkers and bomb shelters were mostly located well to the rear of pillboxes.

Construction on the West Wall came to a virtual halt after Germany's victory over Belgium and France (qq.v.) in May 1940. Afterward, the West Wall progressively was stripped to provide needed materials for Germany's other theaters of war—although the next four years of neglect gave a very realistic camouflaged appearance to the installations. Nonetheless, the West Wall served as a very effective propaganda instrument. Joseph Goebbels's (q.v.) propaganda campaign contributed to discouraging the Allies from fulfilling their obligations to Czechoslovakia and Poland. In 1944, General Dwight D. Eisenhower (q.v.) halted his armies to reequip before proceeding into the West Wall in earnest. Since the West Wall at that moment was virtually bare, his decision gave the Germans vital time to prepare, and possibly prolonged the war by several months.

Samuel J. Doss

Additional Reading

Kumpf, Walter, "Organisation Todt im Krieg," in *Bilanz des Zweiten Weltkrieges: Erkenntnisse und Verpflichtungen für die Zukunft,* edited by Helmut Arntz (1953).
MacDonald, Charles B., *The Siegfried Line Campaign* (1963).

Winter Operations

The severe winter conditions of northern Europe and the Soviet Union had a major impact on the conduct of the war for all the combatants. German troops, in particular, suffered from a lack of sufficient preparation for winter warfare, while the Soviet forces lacked supplies. The cold, snow, and ice of winter came hard and fast to these areas on the eastern front where winter lasted five to six months. These conditions severely affected troop movements and combat.

The winter of 1941–1942 was most severe on the eastern front, with the temperature remaining well below zero degrees Fahrenheit. The sudden fall of temperature, in early December 1941, was partially responsible for the halt of the German 6th *Panzer* Division only nine miles from Moscow (q.v.). German troops were unable to fire their rifles because the mechanisms jammed or even shattered in the severe cold. Machine guns and artillery became encrusted in ice and snow, thereby minimizing their effectiveness.

Only by the next winter had cold-resistant lubricants been developed and distributed among the various units. Similar problems affected motor vehicles whose grease and oil froze solid. At first the troops simply towed the vehicles, but that severely damaged the motors. The vehicles had to be warmed before they could be moved.

The clothing worn by the German soldier was totally inadequate during the winter of 1941, especially as the troops had to march and bivouac in the open and defend positions fully exposed to the winter elements. Footgear was the most difficult problem. Only in the spring of 1942 did the German troops receive appropriate clothing. Other problems were caused by the harsh weather.

American troops in winter camouflage use sleds during the Ardennes Offensive. The line of sleds on the left is moving supplies to the forward areas. The line on the right is moving wounded to the rear. (IWM KY 50716)

Mortar rounds and artillery shells sank into the snow, muffling the blast effects. German tanks also faced difficulties, as their narrow tracks sank into the snow. The harsh weather also meant that about 15 percent of German casualties during the first winter along the eastern front came from frostbite, especially among drivers and troops moving long distances in open vehicles.

German aircraft held up well in the winter weather, but as temperatures fell, they too faced problems. Oil became more viscous and excessive engine wear resulted. Some planes were kept in heated hangers, and runways had to be kept clear of drifting snow. Furthermore, the short days meant that night flying was part of most missions. Orientation on the featureless snow-covered terrain was often very difficult.

During the winter of 1942–1943, snow did

not fall along the lower Don River until December and had little impact on troop mobility. Farther to the north, however, snowfalls were much greater.

Throughout the eastern front, troop movements were severely affected by winter weather. Marching in the snow exhausted the soldiers. In deep snow, German forces took turns packing it down, while the Russian forces used the T-34 tank whose wide tracks worked well in the snow. Civilian labor was also used. The heavy weapons became bogged down in the snow and covered with ice. Movement on hard-packed snow also had a disadvantage—it was noisy. To facilitate troop movements, the German forces established relay stations where soldiers could warm themselves and be fed. Heavy snowfalls and harsh weather also disrupted rail traffic, and in the winter of 1941–1942, for example, only one-third of the twenty-eight trains needed daily arrived at Army Group Center.

Winter also affected tactics. German forces tried to avoid launching major offenses during the winter months, often delaying important operations. Often, as German vehicles became bogged down, they were simply abandoned. Soviet commanders used their ski troops for assaults, and the infantry followed closely behind tanks. Increasingly, they used infiltration tactics against the German forces and these proved effective in the winter.

Robert G. Waite

Additional Reading
Clothing and Equipment in Snow and Extreme Cold, Department of the Army, Office of the Chief of Military History, D-019.
Effects of Climate on Combat in European Russia, Department of the Army Pamphlet No. 20–291 (February 1952).
Rendulic, Eric, *The Effect of Extreme Cold on Weapons, Wheeled Vehicles, and Track Vehicles,* Headquarters, European Command, D-035 (24 February 1947).

Wolf Pack Tactics
See SUBMARINE AND ANTISUBMARINE WARFARE

Battles, Campaigns, and Operations

Geographical and Chronological Index
of Battles, Campaigns, and Operations
by Encyclopedia Entry Name

The Preliminaries

Russo-Polish War	1919–1921
Ethiopia	1935–1936
Spanish Civil War	1936–1939
Guernica Air Raid	26 April 1937
Albania	7–10 April 1939

Intelligence and Deception

HAIFISCH [SHARK], Operation	April–August 1941
PASTORIUS, Operation	12–27 June 1942
BERTRAM, Operation	26 September–23 October 1942
MINCEMEAT, Operation	Spring 1943
FORTITUDE, Operation	1943–1944

Air Actions

Malta Air Campaign	June 1940–June 1943
Britain, Air Campaign	13 August–12 October 1940
Coventry Air Raid	14–15 November 1940
Baedeker Air Raids	April 1942
Germany Air Campaign	September 1939–May 1945
Berlin, Air Raids	25 August 1940–21 April 1945
SICKLE, Operation	1942
Cologne, Air Raid	30–31 May 1942
Ruhr Air Campaign	March–June 1943
Ruhr Dams Air Raid	16–17 May 1943
Hamburg Air Raids	24–30 July 1943
Regensburg Air Raid	17 August 1943
Peenemünde Air Raid	17–18 August 1943
Schweinfurt Air Raid	14 October 1943
CROSSBOW, Operation	5 December 1943–29 March 1945
DIVER, Operation	June 1944–March 1945
BIG WEEK, Operation	20–27 February 1944
Nuremberg Air Raid	30–31 March 1944
FRANTIC, Operation	June–September 1944
Freiburg Air Raid	27 November 1944
Dresden Air Raid	13–14 February 1945
CLARION, Operation	22–23 February 1945

Eastern Air War	June 1941–May 1945
Ploeşti Air Raid	1 August 1943
Bari Air Raid	2 December 1943
V-1/V-2 Offensive	June 1944–April 1945
Aarhus Air Raid	31 October 1944
BODENPLATTE [BASEPLATE], Operation	1 January 1945
Berlin Airlift	26 June 1948–31 October 1949

Naval Actions

Atlantic Campaign	1939–1945
Scapa Flow	13 October 1939
Platte River	13–17 December 1939
Altmark Raid	16 February 1940
German Raiders	1940–1943
Atlantis Raids	31 March 1940–22 November 1941
DYNAMO, Operation	26 May–4 June 1940
Dakar	23–25 September 1940
Convoy Battle in the North Channel	17–20 October 1940
Bismarck	23–27 May 1941
Convoy Battle off Portugal	14–23 December 1941
DRUMBEAT, Operation	January–July 1942
Channel Dash	11–12 February 1942
Convoy PQ-17	1–9 July 1942
Convoy PQ-18	12–20 September 1942
Barents Sea	30–31 December 1942
Convoys HX-229 and SC-122	14–20 March 1943
Alten Fjord Raid	22 September 1943
North Cape	26 December 1943
Granville Raid	8–9 March 1945
Mediterranean Campaign	1940–1944
Mers el-Kébir	3 July 1940
Calabria	9 July 1940
Malta Relief Convoys	August 1940–December 1942
Malta Convoy PEDESTAL	10–15 August 1942
Taranto	11 November 1940
Matapan	28–29 March 1941
Sirte I	17 December 1941
Alexandria	18–19 December 1941
Sirte II	22 March 1942
Toulon	27 November 1942
Eastern Naval War	June 1941–May 1945
WUNDERLAND [WONDERLAND], Operations	Summers 1942 & 1943

Land and Combined Actions
North Europe

Finnish Winter War	30 November 1939–12 March 1940
Mannerheim Line	6 December 1939–15 February 1940
Suomussalmi	11 December 1939–6 January 1940
Denmark	9 April 1940
Norway	9 April–9 June 1940
Narvik	9 April–9 June 1940
Iceland	10 May 1940–1945
IKARUS, Operation	June 1940

Strategic Maps of World War II Military Operations

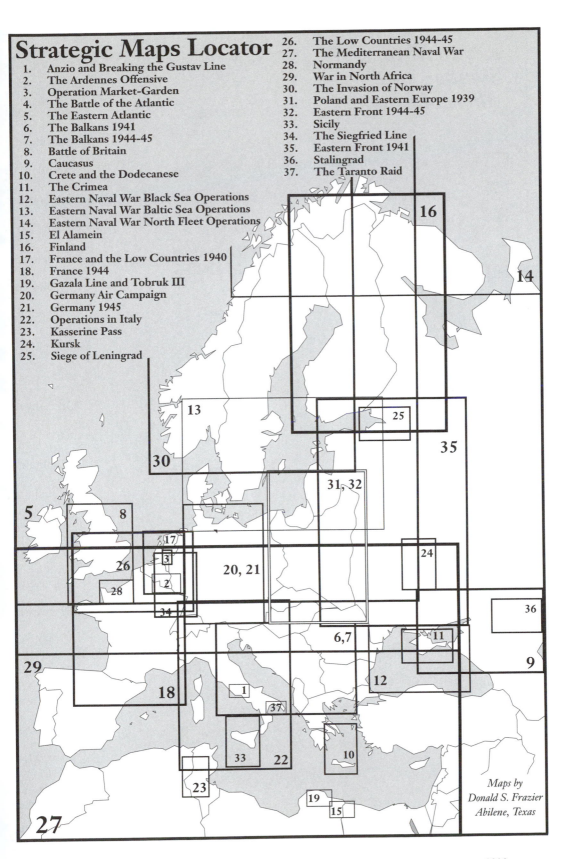

Strategic Maps Locator

1. Anzio and Breaking the Gustav Line
2. The Ardennes Offensive
3. Operation Market-Garden
4. The Battle of the Atlantic
5. The Eastern Atlantic
6. The Balkans 1941
7. The Balkans 1944-45
8. Battle of Britain
9. Caucasus
10. Crete and the Dodecanese
11. The Crimea
12. Eastern Naval War Black Sea Operations
13. Eastern Naval War Baltic Sea Operations
14. Eastern Naval War North Fleet Operations
15. El Alamein
16. Finland
17. France and the Low Countries 1940
18. France 1944
19. Gazala Line and Tobruk III
20. Germany Air Campaign
21. Germany 1945
22. Operations in Italy
23. Kasserine Pass
24. Kursk
25. Siege of Leningrad

26. The Low Countries 1944-45
27. The Mediterranean Naval War
28. Normandy
29. War in North Africa
30. The Invasion of Norway
31. Poland and Eastern Europe 1939
32. Eastern Front 1944-45
33. Sicily
34. The Siegfried Line
35. Eastern Front 1941
36. Stalingrad
37. The Taranto Raid

Maps by
Donald S. Frazier
Abilene, Texas

Key to Map Symbols and Abbreviations:

Allied Infantry
Axis Infantry
Axis Motorized Infantry
Allied Armor
Axis Armor
SF — Special Service Unit
U.S. Ninth Army — Allied Army
FIFTH PANZER ARMY — Axis Army
Army Group E (Löhr) — Army Group
Pol — Polish Units
It — Italian Units
US — United States Units
Can — Canadian Units
Br — British Units
Abn — Airborne Units
SS — Schutzstaffeln Units
Armd — Allied Armored Units
Bde — Brigade
Grds — Soviet Guards Units
Pz — German Panzer Units

Army Group E (Löhr)   Army Group

Pol   Polish Units

It   Italian Units

US   United States Units

Can   Canadian Units

Br   British Units

Abn   Airborne Units

SS   Schutzstaffeln Units

Armd   Allied Armored Units

Bde   Brigade

Grds   Soviet Guards Units

Pz   German Panzer Units

 Allied "Mulberries"

Airbases and Airfields

Bombing Raids

Axis Minefield

Allied Minefield

Ship Losses

Sub Operations

Paratroop Drops

Operation **MARITA**   Codenames

Engagements

Aircraft Industry

Other Industry

Strategic Railway

Oil Industry

Submarine Pens

Missile Base

Barrage Balloons

Capital Ship

Escort Ship

Oil Field

Fortifications

Bridges

Mountains

Rivers

Roads

Trees

Maps by
Donald S. Frazier, PhD.
McMurry University
Abilene, Texas

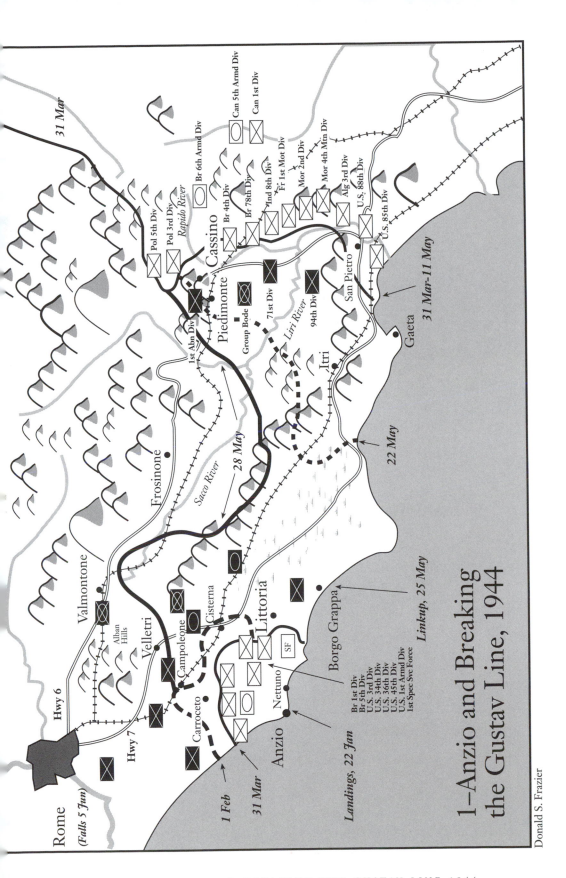

1–Anzio and Breaking the Gustav Line, 1944

Rome
(Falls 5 Jun)

31 Mar

Hwy 6

Hwy 7

Valmontone

Alban Hills

Velletri

Frosinone

Campoleone

Carroceto

Cisterna

1 Feb

31 Mar

Anzio

Nettuno

Littoria

SF

Borgo Grappa

Saco River

28 May

1st Abn Div

Piedimonte

Cassino

Pol 5th Div

Pol 3rd Div

Rapido River

Br 6th Armd Div

Can 5th Armd Div

Can 1st Div

Br 4th Div

Br 78th Div

Ind 8th Div

Fr 1st Mot Div

Mor 2nd Div

Mor 4th Mtn Div

Alg 3rd Div

U.S. 88th Div

U.S. 85th Div

Group Bode

71st Div

Liri River

94th Div

Itri

San Pietro

Gaeta

31 Mar–11 May

22 May

Linkup, 25 May

Landings, 22 Jun

Br 1st Div
Br 5th Div
U.S. 3rd Div
U.S. 34th Div
U.S. 36th Div
U.S. 45th Div
U.S. 1st Armd Div
1st Spec Svce Force

Donald S. Frazier

ANZIO AND BREAKING THE GUSTAV LINE 1944

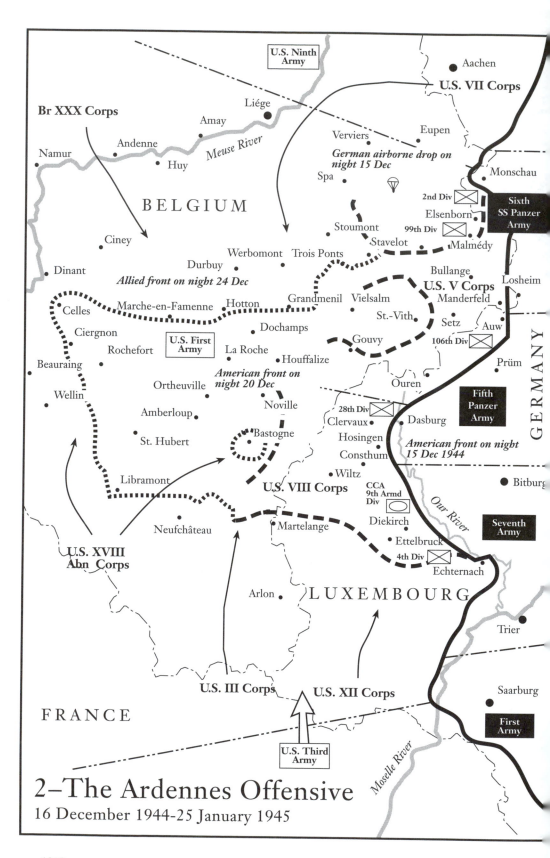

2–The Ardennes Offensive

16 December 1944-25 January 1945

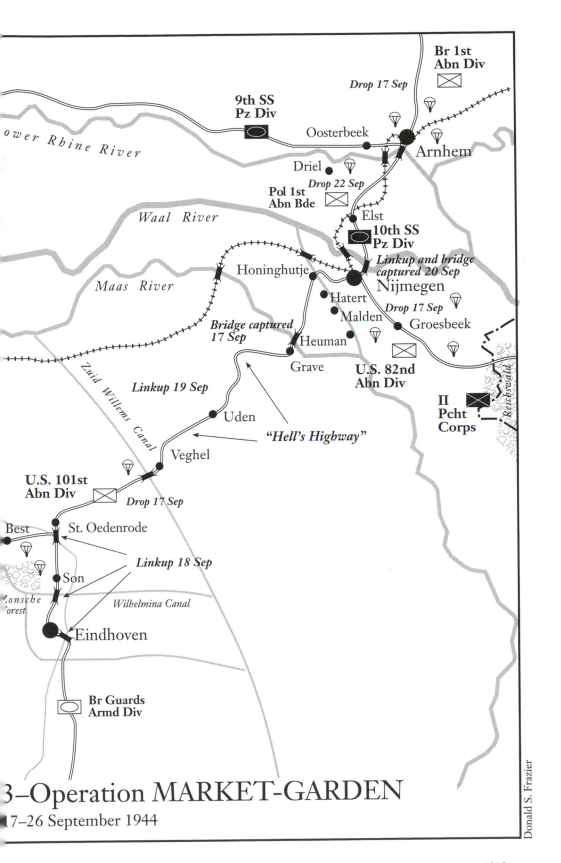

Br 1st Abn Div ⊠

Drop 17 Sep

9th SS Pz Div

Oosterbeek

ower Rhine River

Arnhem

Driel

Drop 22 Sep

Pol 1st Abn Bde ⊠

Waal River

Elst

10th SS Pz Div

Honinghutje

Linkup and bridge captured 20 Sep

Nijmegen

Maas River

Hatert

Malden

Drop 17 Sep

Groesbeek

Bridge captured 17 Sep

Heuman

Grave

U.S. 82nd Abn Div ⊠

II Pcht Corps ⊠

Reichswald

Linkup 19 Sep

Zuid Willems Canal

Uden

"Hell's Highway"

Veghel

U.S. 101st Abn Div ⊠

Drop 17 Sep

Best

St. Oedenrode

Linkup 18 Sep

Son

Zonsche Forest

Wilhelmina Canal

Eindhoven

Br Guards Armd Div

3–Operation MARKET-GARDEN

17–26 September 1944

Donald S. Frazier

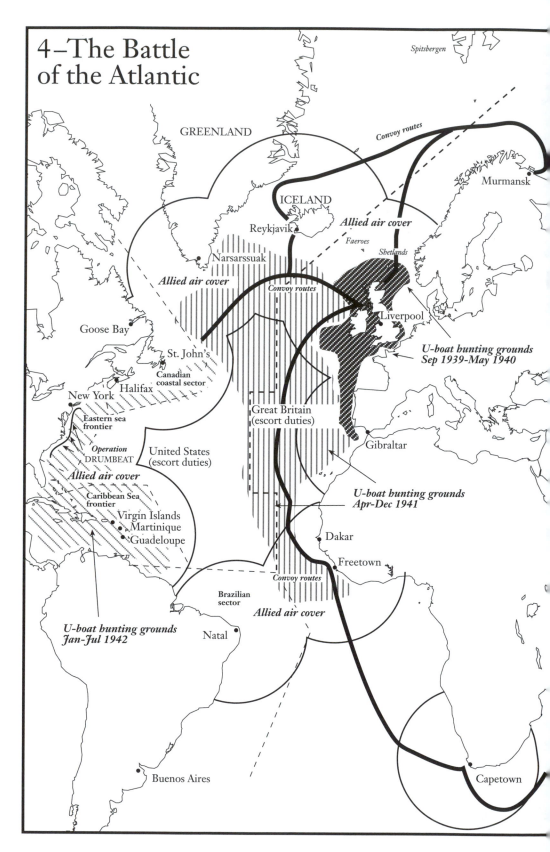

4–The Battle of the Atlantic

Spitsbergen

GREENLAND

Convoy routes

Murmansk

ICELAND

Reykjavik

Allied air cover

Faeroes

Shetlands

Narsarssuak

Allied air cover

Convoy routes

Liverpool

U-boat hunting grounds Sep 1939-May 1940

Goose Bay

St. John's

Canadian coastal sector

Halifax

New York

Eastern sea frontier

Operation DRUMBEAT

United States (escort duties)

Allied air cover

Great Britain (escort duties)

Gibraltar

U-boat hunting grounds Apr-Dec 1941

Caribbean Sea frontier

Virgin Islands

Martinique

Guadeloupe

Dakar

Freetown

Brazilian sector

Convoy routes

U-boat hunting grounds Jan-Jul 1942

Natal

Allied air cover

Buenos Aires

Capetown

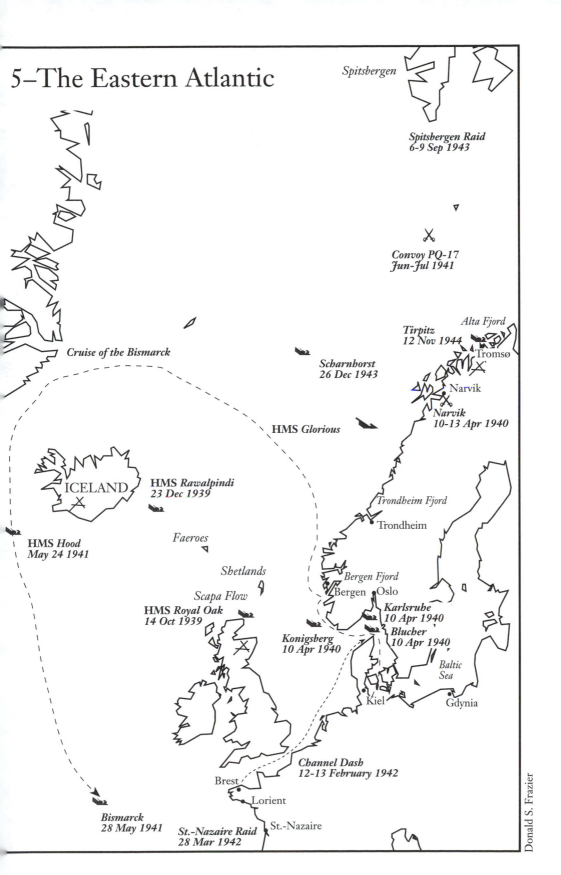

5–The Eastern Atlantic

Spitsbergen

Spitsbergen Raid
6-9 Sep 1943

Convoy PQ-17
Jun-Jul 1941

Alta Fjord

Tirpitz
12 Nov 1944

Tromsø

Cruise of the Bismarck

Scharnhorst
26 Dec 1943

Narvik

Narvik
10-13 Apr 1940

HMS *Glorious*

Trondheim Fjord

Trondheim

HMS *Rawalpindi*
23 Dec 1939

ICELAND

Faeroes

HMS Hood
May 24 1941

Shetlands

Bergen Fjord

Bergen Oslo

Karlsruhe
10 Apr 1940

Blucher
10 Apr 1940

Scapa Flow

HMS Royal Oak
14 Oct 1939

Konigsberg
10 Apr 1940

Baltic Sea

Kiel

Gdynia

Channel Dash
12-13 February 1942

Brest

Lorient

Bismarck
28 May 1941

St.-Nazaire Raid
28 Mar 1942

St.-Nazaire

Donald S. Frazier

TURKEY

German Twelfth Army

Operation MARITA

ROMANIA

Ploesti •

Bucharest •

BULGARIA

First Panzer Group

Sofia •

XL Panzer Corps

XVIII Mtn Corps

Captured and annexed 11-12 Apr

XLI SS Motorized Corps

12 Apr

Yugoslav Fifth Army

Niš

Skopje

7 Apr

Monastir

9 Apr

Salonika

Aliákmon Line

Metaxis Line

XXX Corps

Greek Second Army

Surrendered

Aegean Sea

Hungarian Third Army

Yugoslav Third Army

Belgrade

YUGOSLAVIA

Sarajevo

Dubrovnik

Scutari

Italian Ninth Army

Italian Eleventh Army

Greek First Army

British W Force

20 Apr

Thermopylae

GREECE

HUNGARY

Pécs •

Zagreb

Operation "25"

10 Apr

Trieste

German Second Army

Italian Third Army

Venice •

ALBANIA

Surrendered 20 Apr

Ionian Sea

Adriatic Sea

ITALY

Rome •

Naples •

6–The Balkans 1941

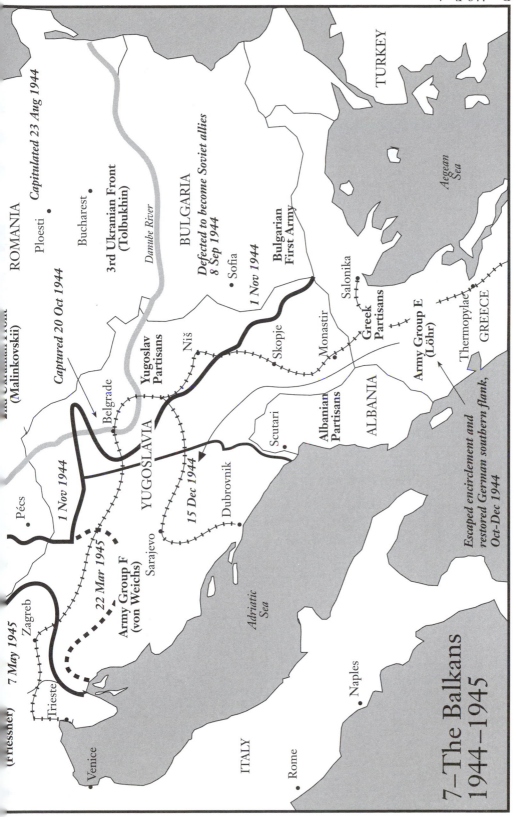

ROMANIA

Capitulated 23 Aug 1944

Ploesti

Bucharest

**3rd Ukranian Front
(Tolbukhin)**

Danube River

BULGARIA

*Defected to become Soviet allies
8 Sep 1944*

Sofia

1 Nov 1944

**Bulgarian
First Army**

(Malinkovskii)

Captured 20 Oct 1944

Niš

Skopje

Monastir

Salonika

**Greek
Partisans**

**Army Group E
(Löhr)**

Thermopylae

GREECE

**Yugoslav
Partisans**

Belgrade

Pécs

1 Nov 1944

YUGOSLAVIA

15 Dec 1944

Dubrovnik

Scutari

**Albanian
Partisans**

ALBANIA

*Aegean
Sea*

TURKEY

*Escaped encirclement and
restored German southern flank,
Oct–Dec 1944*

Sarajevo

22 Mar 1945

**Army Group F
(von Weichs)**

Zagreb

7 May 1945

Trieste

(Friessner)

Venice

*Adriatic
Sea*

ITALY

Rome

Naples

7–The Balkans
1944–1945

8–Battle of Britain

Towns Bombed
Group Boundary
Fighter Base
Bomber Base
Stuka Base
Luftflotte Boundary

SCOTLAND

Glasgow

Fighter Command 13 Group (Saul)

Belfast

IRELAND

Newcastle
Sunderland

Middlesbrough

Cover of Chain Home radar (15,000 ft.)

Luftflotte 5 (Stumpff)
From Norway and Demark

North Sea

Liverpool

Manchester

Hull

Sheffield

ENGLAND

Fighter Command 12 Group (Leigh-Mallory)

Cover of Chain Home Low radar (500 ft.)

Nottingham

Swansea

Birmingham

Cardiff

Coventry

Norwich

Fighter Command 10 Group (Brand)

Bristol

Bath

London

Luftflotte 2 (Kesselring)

Exeter

Southampton

Ipswich
Thames Estuary
Canterbury

Rotterdam

Plymouth

Portsmouth

Antw

English Channel

Cherbourg

Fighter Command 11 Group (Park)

Calais

Lille

BELGIU

Luftflotte 3 (Seperrle)

Le Havre

Amiens

Paris

Rennes

FRANC

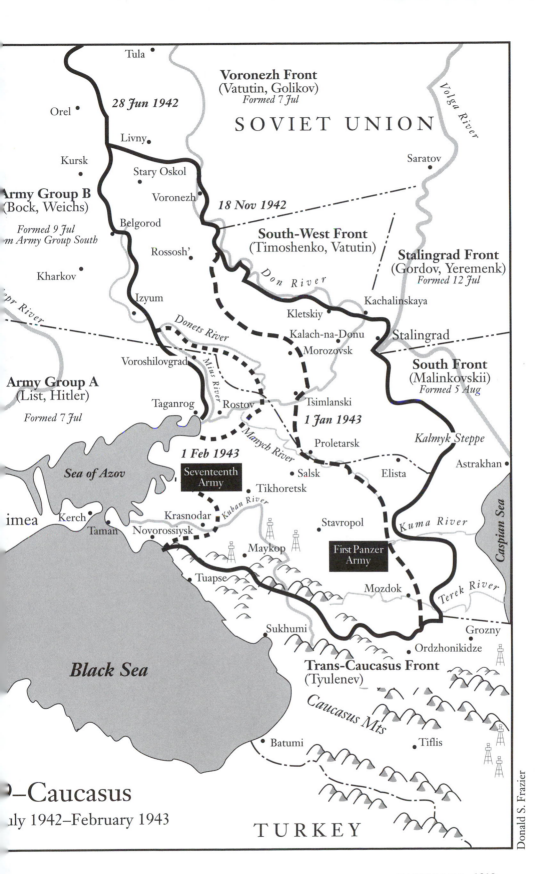

Tula

Voronezh Front
(Vatutin, Golikov)
Formed 7 Jul

Orel

28 Jun 1942

Livny

SOVIET UNION

Volga River

Kursk

Saratov

Stary Oskol

Army Group B
(Bock, Weichs)

Formed 9 Jul
m Army Group South

Voronezh

18 Nov 1942

Belgorod

Don River

Rossosh'

South-West Front
(Timoshenko, Vatutin)

Stalingrad Front
(Gordov, Yeremenk)
Formed 12 Jul

Kharkov

Izyum

Kachalinskaya

Donets River

Kletskiy

Kalach-na-Donu

Stalingrad

Voroshilovgrad

Mius River

Morozovsk

Army Group A
(List, Hitler)

Formed 7 Jul

Taganrog

Rostov

Tsimlanski

South Front
(Malinkovskii)
Formed 5 Aug

1 Jan 1943

Proletarsk

Kalmyk Steppe

Manych River

1 Feb 1943

Astrakhan

Sea of Azov

Seventeenth
Army

Salsk

Elista

Caspian Sea

imea

Kerch

Tikhoretsk

Stavropol

Kuma River

Taman

Novorossiysk

Krasnodar

Kuban River

First Panzer
Army

Maykop

Tuapse

Mozdok

Terek River

Black Sea

Sukhumi

Grozny

Ordzhonikidze

Trans-Caucasus Front
(Tyulenev)

Caucasus Mts

Tiflis

Batumi

–Caucasus

uly 1942–February 1943

TURKEY

Donald S. Frazier

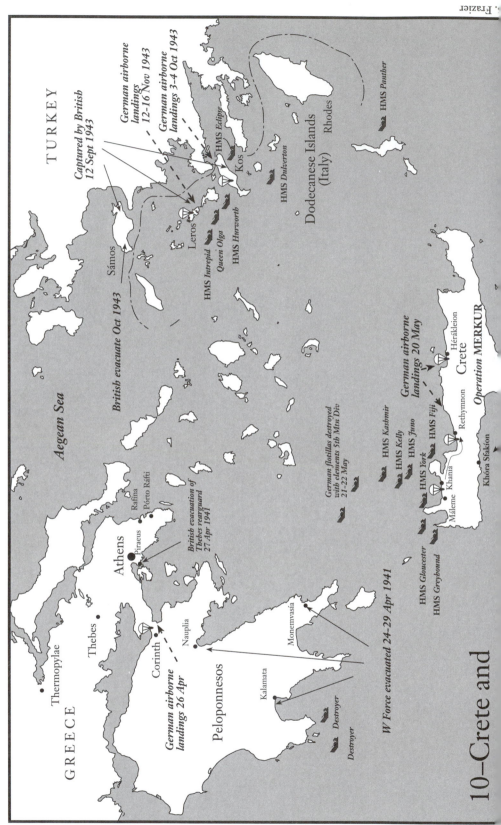

GREECE

Thermopylae

Thebes

Athens

Piraeus

Rafina
Pórto Ráfti

*British evacuation of
Thebes rearguard
27 Apr 1941*

*German airborne
landings 26 Apr*

Corinth

Nauplia

Monemvasía

Kalamata

Destroyer

Destroyer

Peloponnesos

W Force evacuated 24–29 Apr 1941

Aegean Sea

Sámos

British evacuate Oct 1943

TURKEY

*Captured by British
12 Sept 1943*

*German airborne
landings
12–16 Nov 1943*

German airborne landings 3–4 Oct 1943

HMS *Eclipse*

Kos

Leros

HMS *Dulverton*

HMS *Intrepid*
Queen *Olga*
HMS *Hurworth*

**Dodecanese Islands
(Italy)** Rhodes

HMS *Panther*

*German flotillas destroyed
with elements 5th Mtn Div
21–22 May*

HMS *Kashmir*
HMS *Kelly*
HMS *Juno*
HMS *York*
HMS *Fiji*

HMS *Gloucester*
HMS *Greyhound*

Máleme
Khaniá
Rethymnon

*German airborne
landings 20 May*

Herákleion

Crete

Khóra Sfakíon

Operation **MERKUR**

10–Crete and

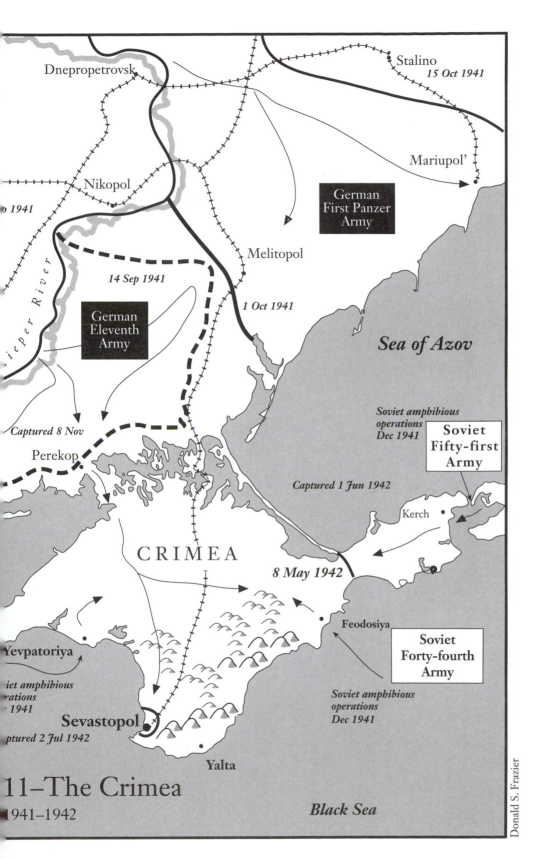

Dnepropetrovsk

Stalino
15 Oct 1941

Mariupol'

Nikopol

1941

German
First Panzer
Army

Melitopol

14 Sep 1941

1 Oct 1941

German
Eleventh
Army

Sea of Azov

Dnieper River

Captured 8 Nov

Perekop

*Soviet amphibious
operations
Dec 1941*

Soviet
Fifty-first
Army

Captured 1 Jun 1942

Kerch

CRIMEA

8 May 1942

Feodosiya

Soviet
Forty-fourth
Army

Yevpatoriya

*iet amphibious
rations
1941*

*Soviet amphibious
operations
Dec 1941*

Sevastopol

ptured 2 Jul 1942

Yalta

11–The Crimea

1941–1942

Black Sea

Donald S. Frazier

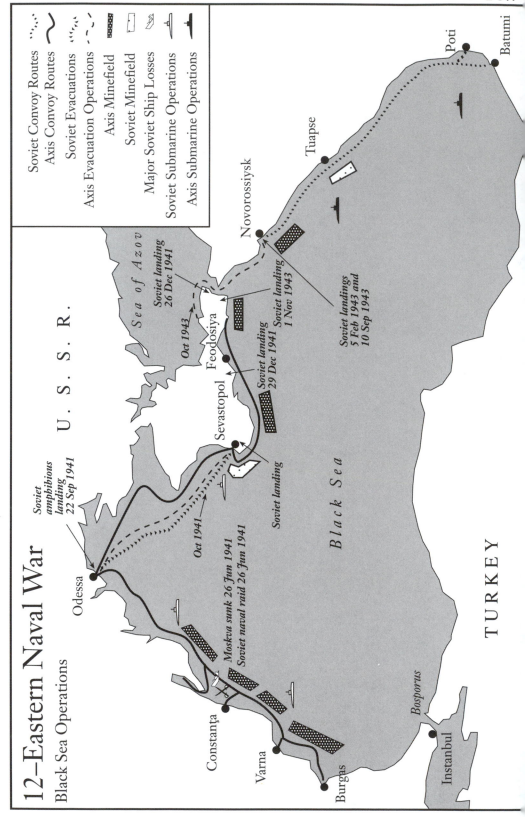

12–Eastern Naval War
Black Sea Operations

Legend:
- ∴∴∴ Soviet Convoy Routes
- 〰 Axis Convoy Routes
- ⌒⌒⌒ Soviet Evacuations
- - - - Axis Evacuation Operations
- Axis Minefield
- Soviet Minefield
- Major Soviet Ship Losses
- Soviet Submarine Operations
- Axis Submarine Operations

U. S. S. R.

Sea of Azov

Black Sea

TURKEY

Odessa

Soviet amphibious landing 22 Sep 1941

Oct 1941

Sevastopol

Feodosiya

Oct 1943

Soviet landing 26 Dec 1941

Soviet landing 29 Dec 1941

Soviet landing 1 Nov 1943

Novorossiysk

Soviet landings 5 Feb 1943 and 10 Sep 1943

Tuapse

Poti

Batumi

Soviet landing

Moskva sunk 26 Jun 1941
Soviet naval raid 26 Jun 1941

Constanţa

Varna

Burgas

Bosporus

Instanbul

Baltic Sea Operations

Legend:
- Axis Convoy Routes
- Axis Evacuation Operations
- Axis Minefield
- ASW Net Barrier
- Soviet Minefield
- Axis Ship Losses
- Major Soviet Ship Losses
- Soviet Submarine Operations

Leningrad

Marat sunk 23 Sep 1941

Failed German landing on
Hogland Island 15 Sep 1944

U. S. S. R.

Helsinki

ESTONIA

Riga

Windau

LATVIA

Libau

LITHUANIA

Memel

Ilmarinen
13 Sep 1941

Gotland

Königsberg

Schleswig-Holstein
sunk 18 Dec 1944

Öland

Gustloff 30 Jan 1945

Goya 17 Apr 1945

Hel

Gneisenau scuttled
4 May 1945

Danzig

POLAND

Steuben 9 Feb 1945

Stockholm

SWEDEN

Schlesien scuttled
4 May 1945

Copenhagen

Bornholm

Leutzow sunk
5 May 1945

GERMANY

DENMARK

Kiel

Admiral Scheer
sunk
9 Apr 1945

NORWAY

Oslo

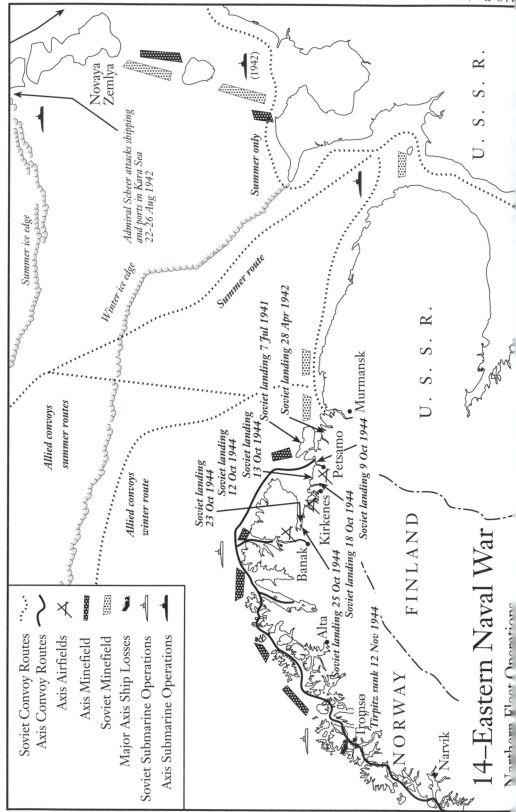

14—Eastern Naval War

Northern Fleet Operations

Soviet Convoy Routes
Axis Convoy Routes
Axis Airfields
Axis Minefield
Soviet Minefield
Major Axis Ship Losses
Soviet Submarine Operations
Axis Submarine Operations

Summer ice edge

Winter ice edge

Allied convoys
summer routes

Allied convoys
winter route

Summer route

Summer only

(1942)

Novaya
Zemlya

Admiral Scheer attacks shipping
and ports in Kara Sea
22–26 Aug 1942

U. S. S. R.

U. S. S. R.

Murmansk

Petsamo

Soviet landing 7 Jul 1941

Soviet landing 28 Apr 1942

Soviet landing 9 Oct 1944

Soviet landing 13 Oct 1944

Soviet landing
12 Oct 1944

Soviet landing
23 Oct 1944

Kirkenes

Soviet landing 18 Oct 1944

Soviet landing 25 Oct 1944

Banak

Alta

FINLAND

NORWAY

Tirpitz sunk 12 Nov 1944

Tromsø

Narvik

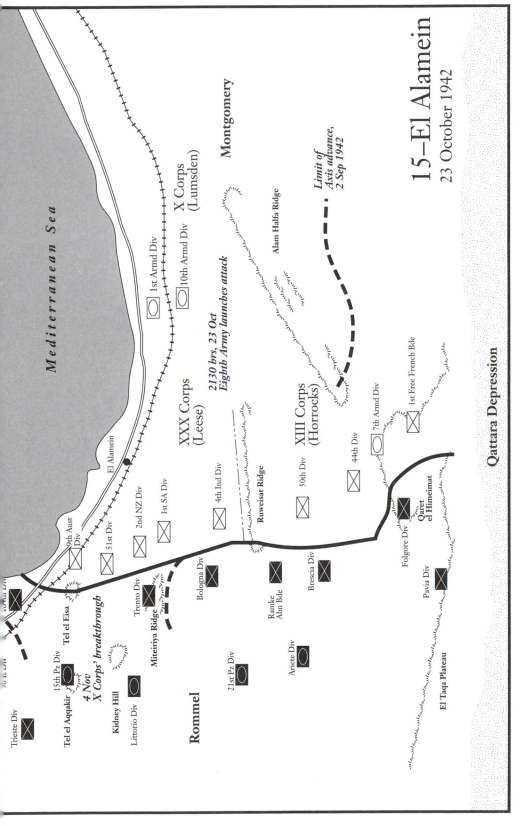

15—El Alamein

23 October 1942

Mediterranean Sea

Montgomery

X Corps
(Lumsden)

1st Armd Div

10th Armd Div

*Limit of
Axis advance,
2 Sep 1942*

Alam Halfa Ridge

El Alamein

2130 hrs, 23 Oct
Eighth Army launches attack

XXX Corps
(Leese)

4th Ind Div

Ruweisat Ridge

XIII Corps
(Horrocks)

50th Div

44th Div

7th Armd Div

1st Free French Bde

9th Aust
Div

51st Div

2nd NZ Div

1st SA Div

Trento Div

Miteiriya Ridge

Bologna Div

Brescia Div

Ramke
Abn Bde

Qaret
el Himeimat

Folgore Div

Pavia Div

Qattara Depression

Trieste Div

15th Pz Div

Tel el Aqqakir Tel el Eisa

**4 Nov
X Corps' breakthrough**

Kidney Hill

Littorio Div

21st Pz Div

Ariete Div

El Taqa Plateau

Rommel

16–Finland

0   Miles   100

NORWAY

Rybachi Peninsula

Petsamo

Salmijärvi

Murmansk

Nautsi

Areas ceded to Soviet Union by Russo–Finnish Treaty 12 Mar 1940

Kuolayarvi

Kandalaksha

Markajarvi

Salla

Kemijärvi

SWEDEN

Rovaniemi

Front lines 10 Jun 1944

Tornio

Kemi

Kuusamo

White S

Front lines 12 Mar 1940

Oulu

Suomussalmi

Hyrynsalmi

Kuhmo

Repola

Gulf of Bothnia

FINLAND

Nurmes

Vaasa

Areas ceded to Soviet Union by Russo–Finnish Treaty 12 Mar 1940

Porajarvi

Ilomantsi

Joensuu

Tolvajarvi

Vaptsila

Suoyarvi

Leppasilta

Pitkyaranta

Tampere

Sortavala

Salmi   Aunus

Lake Ladoga

Ahvenanmaa Islands

Turku

Helsinki

Porvoo

Vilpuri

Koivisto

Mannerheim Line

Summa

Hangö

Gulf of Finland

Karelian Isthmus

Leningrad

Soviet amphibious operations 1939–1940

ESTONIA

SOVIET UNIO

1326 FINLAND

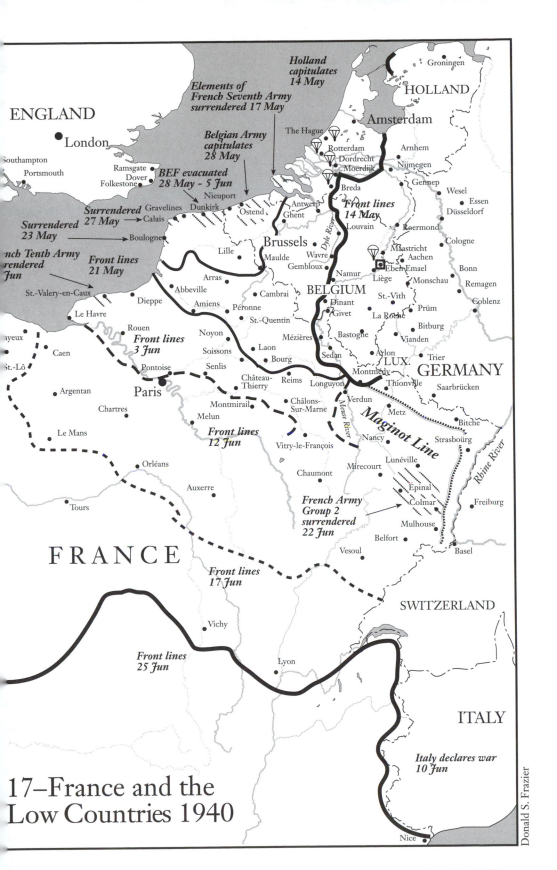

ENGLAND

London

Southampton
Portsmouth

Ramsgate
Dover
Folkestone

**BEF evacuated
28 May – 5 Jun**

Nieuport

**Surrendered
27 May** → Gravelines

**Surrendered
23 May** → Calais

Dunkirk

**nch Tenth Army
rendered
Jun** →

Boulogne

**Front lines
21 May**

St.-Valery-en-Caux

ayeux

St.-Lô

Caen

Le Havre

Dieppe

Rouen

**Front lines
3 Jun**

Pontoise

Argentan

Chartres

Paris

Le Mans

Melun

Orléans

Montmirail

**Front lines
12 Jun**

Auxerre

Tours

**Front lines
17 Jun**

FRANCE

Vichy

**Front lines
25 Jun**

Lyon

**Holland
capitulates
14 May**

**Elements of
French Seventh Army
surrendered 17 May**

**Belgian Army
capitulates
28 May**

The Hague

Rotterdam
Dordrecht
Moerdijk

HOLLAND

Amsterdam

Groningen

Arnhem

Nijmegen

Gennep

Wesel

Essen
Düsseldorf

Breda

**Front lines
14 May**

Ostend
Ghent

Antwerp

Lille

Maulde

Brussels

Wavre
Gembloux

Louvain

Roermond

Maastricht
Aachen

Cologne

Bonn

Arras

Abbeville

Amiens

Cambrai

Péronne

St.-Quentin

Namur

Eben Emael
Liège

Monschau

Remagen

BELGIUM

Dinant
Givet

St.-Vith

Prüm

Coblenz

Noyon

Soissons

Laon

Bourg

Mézières

Sedan

La Roche

Bastogne

Bitburg

Vianden

Senlis

Reims

Château-
Thierry

Longuyon

Arlon

Trier

LUX.

GERMANY

Montmédy

Thionville

Saarbrücken

Châlons-
Sur-Marne

Verdun

Metz

Vitry-le-François

Nancy

Maginot Line

Bitche

Strasbourg

Chaumont

Mirecourt

Lunéville

Epinal

**French Army
Group 2
surrendered
22 Jun**

Colmar

Freiburg

Mulhouse

Belfort

Vesoul

Basel

SWITZERLAND

ITALY

**Italy declares war
10 Jun**

Nice

Donald S. Frazier

17–France and the
Low Countries 1940

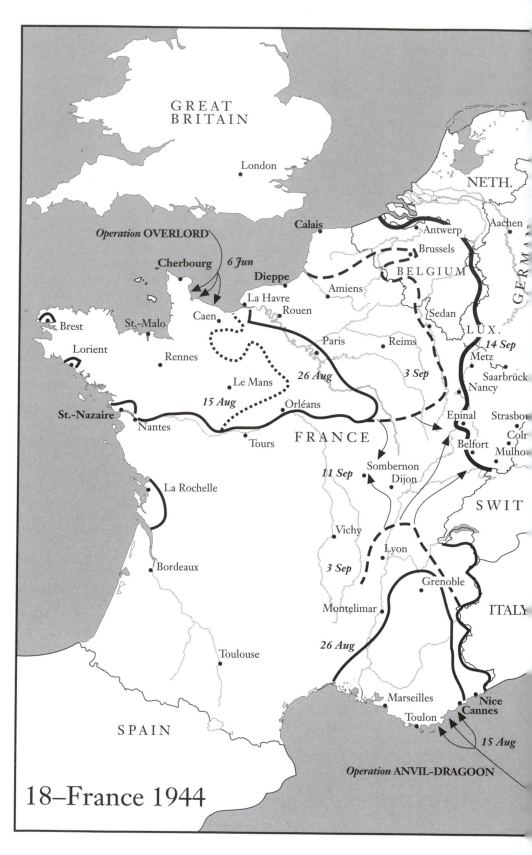

18–France 1944

17 Gazala Line and Tobruk III
26 May–21 June 1942

Ritchie

Tobruk

Garrison
surrenders
21 Jun

Three armored divisions
make coordinated assault
on S.E. corner
20 Jun

5th Ind Div

2nd SA Div

90th Div

El Adem

Bir al Gobi

British units
withdraw
13 Jun

Sidra Ridge

7th Armd Div

21st Pz Div

27 May

Heavy tank battles
in this area 30 May–2 Jun

1st Armd Div

British armor and Afrika Korps
engage in this area 27–30 May

3rd Ind Bde

Knightsbridge

Bir el Harmat

15th Pz Div

1st Free French Bde

27 May

Axis forces repel
attacks on the
"Cauldron"
2–10 Jun

50th Div

Sidi Muftah

Bir Hacheim

Gazala

1st SA Div

26 May

It

It

Trieste Div

27 May

27 May – 10 June

Ariete Div

It

It

Rommel

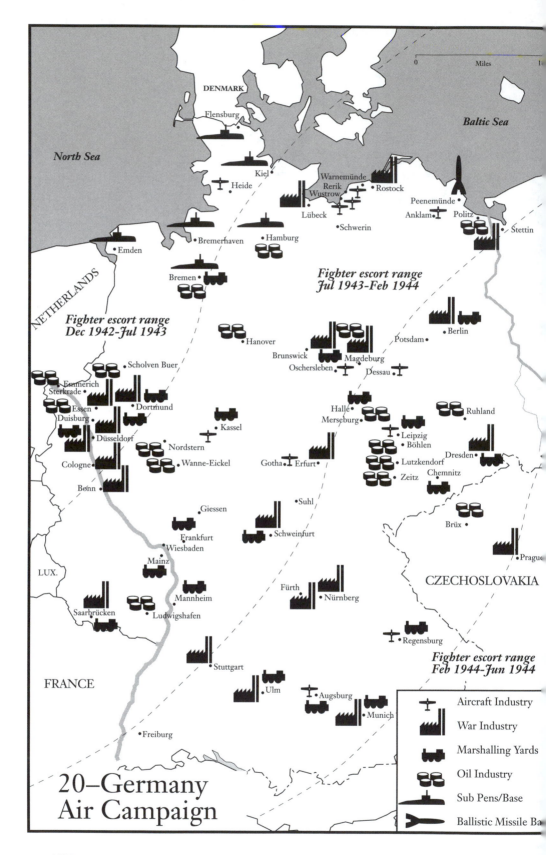

DENMARK

Flensburg

North Sea

Kiel

Heide

Baltic Sea

Warnemünde
Rerik
Wustrow
Rostock

Peenemünde

Anklam
Politz

Lübeck

Schwerin

Stettin

Bremerhaven

Hamburg

Emden

Bremen

*Fighter escort range
Jul 1943-Feb 1944*

NETHERLANDS

*Fighter escort range
Dec 1942-Jul 1943*

Hanover

Potsdam
Berlin

Scholven Buer

Brunswick
Magdeburg

Emmerich
Sterkrade

Oschersleben
Dessau

Essen
Duisburg

Dortmund

Ruhland

Düsseldorf

Kassel

Halle
Merseburg

Leipzig
Böhlen

Nordstern

Cologne

Wanne-Eickel

Gotha
Erfurt

Dresden

Lutzkendorf

Chemnitz

Bonn

Zeitz

Giessen

Suhl

Brüx

Frankfurt

Schweinfurt

Prague

Wiesbaden

Mainz

CZECHOSLOVAKIA

LUX.

Fürth
Nürnberg

Mannheim

Saarbrücken

Ludwigshafen

Regensburg

*Fighter escort range
Feb 1944-Jun 1944*

Stuttgart

FRANCE

Ulm

Augsburg

Munich

Freiburg

20–Germany
Air Campaign

✈	Aircraft Industry
🏭	War Industry
	Marshalling Yards
	Oil Industry
	Sub Pens/Base
	Ballistic Missile Ba

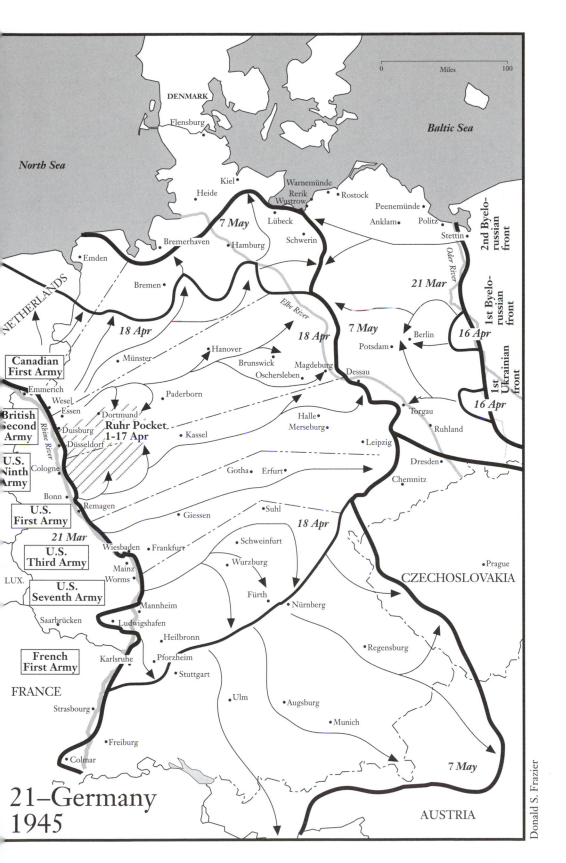

DENMARK

North Sea

Baltic Sea

Flensburg

Kiel
Heide

Warnemünde
Rerik
Wüstrow

Rostock

Peenemünde
Anklam
Politz

Stettin

7 May

Lübeck
Schwerin

2nd Byelo-russian front

Bremerhaven
Hamburg

Oder River

Emden

21 Mar

1st Byelo-russian front

NETHERLANDS

Bremen

18 Apr

Elbe River

18 Apr

7 May

Berlin

16 Apr

1st Ukrainian front

Canadian First Army

Münster

Hanover

Brunswick
Oschersleben

Magdeburg

Potsdam

Dessau

Emmerich

Wesel
Essen

Paderborn

16 Apr

Duisburg

Düsseldorf

Dortmund

Ruhr Pocket 1-17 Apr

Kassel

Halle
Merseburg

Torgau

Ruhland

British Second Army

Rhine River

Leipzig

U.S. Ninth Army

Cologne

Gotha

Erfurt

Dresden

Chemnitz

Bonn

Remagen

Giessen

Suhl

U.S. First Army

21 Mar

18 Apr

Wiesbaden
Frankfurt

Schweinfurt

CZECHOSLOVAKIA

Prague

U.S. Third Army

Mainz
Worms

Würzburg

LUX.

Fürth

Nürnberg

U.S. Seventh Army

Mannheim

Ludwigshafen

Saarbrücken

Heilbronn

Regensburg

French First Army

Karlsruhe

Pforzheim

Stuttgart

FRANCE

Strasbourg

Ulm

Augsburg

Munich

Freiburg

Colmar

7 May

21–Germany 1945

AUSTRIA

Donald S. Frazier

SWITZ-
ERLAND

*Line reached by Allied
forces in Western
Europe 7 May 1945*

AUSTRIA

*Line reached by
Soviet forces
7 May 1945*

HUNGARY

Bolzano

7 May

Sondrio

Belluno

Udine

Aosta

Varese

Como

Trento

Pordenone

Gorizia

Novara

Milan

Brescia

Vicenza

Treviso

Trieste

Vercelli

Verona

Padova

Venice

*Line reached by
Yugoslav partisans
7 May 1945*

Turin

Pavia

Cremona

Mantova

Rovigo

Asti

Piacenza

Parma

Ferrara

30 Apr

Cuneo

Genoa

Modena

23 Apr

Bologna

15 Jan – 8 Apr 1945

YUGOSLAVIA

Savona

La Spezia

Ravenna
Rimini

Gothic Line

Imperia

Massa

4 Aug

Lucca

Pesaro

Ligurian Sea

Pisa
Leghorn

Florence

Arezzo

Ancona

Siena

17 Jun

Grosseto

Ascoli Piceno

9 Jun

Teramo

**Gustav
Line**

CORSICA
(FRANCE)

*Evacuated by
German forces
18 Sep–Oct 1943*

Pescara

15 Jan – 11 May 1944

Viterbo

5 Jun

28 Sept

Adriatic Sea

Rome

Isernia

25 Sep

Cassino

8 Oct

Foggia

14 Sep

*Allies enter Rome
4 Jun 1944*

Anzio

Capua

Benevento

Bari

Gaeta

Brin

Sassari

**SHINGLE
22 Jan 1944**

Naples

Potenza

Matera

Taranto

Lecce

Nuoro

Salerno

**SLAPSTICK
9 Sep 1943**

Oristano

Tyrrhenian Sea

**AVALANCHE
9 Sep 1943**

SARDINIA

Cagliari

**Italy surrenders
3 Sep 1943**

Cosenza

Catanzaro

9 Sep

*Evacuated by
German forces
18 Sep 1943*

Messina

Reggio di Calabria

Palermo

Trapani

**BAYTOWN
3 Sep 1943**

Caltanissetta

Enna

Catania

Agrigento

SICILY

Strait of Sicily

Siracusa

Ragusa

0   Miles   100

**HUSKY
10 Jul 1943**

MALTA

Mediterranean Sea

22–Operations in Italy

1943–1945

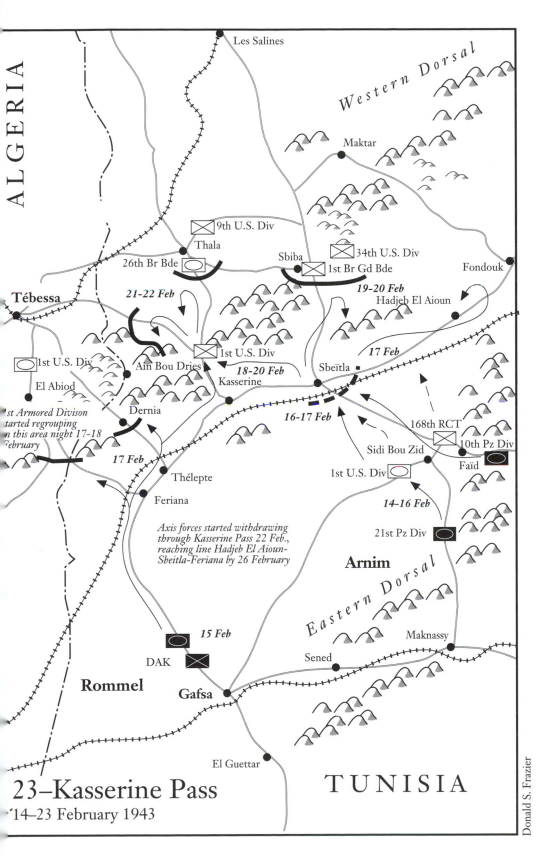

Western Dorsal

ALGERIA

Les Salines

Maktar

9th U.S. Div

Thala

26th Br Bde

Sbiba

34th U.S. Div

1st Br Gd Bde

Fondouk

21-22 Feb

19-20 Feb

Hadjeb El Aioun

Tébessa

1st U.S. Div

Ain Bou Dries

1st U.S. Div

18-20 Feb

Kasserine

Sbeïtla

17 Feb

El Abiod

1st Armored Divison started regrouping in this area night 17-18 February

Dernia

16-17 Feb

168th RCT

Sidi Bou Zid

10th Pz Div

Faïd

17 Feb

Thélepte

1st U.S. Div

Feriana

14-16 Feb

Axis forces started withdrawing through Kasserine Pass 22 Feb., reaching line Hadjeb El Aioun-Sbeitla-Feriana by 26 February

21st Pz Div

Arnim

Eastern Dorsal

Maknassy

15 Feb

Sened

Rommel

DAK

Gafsa

El Guettar

TUNISIA

23—Kasserine Pass

14–23 February 1943

Donald S. Frazier

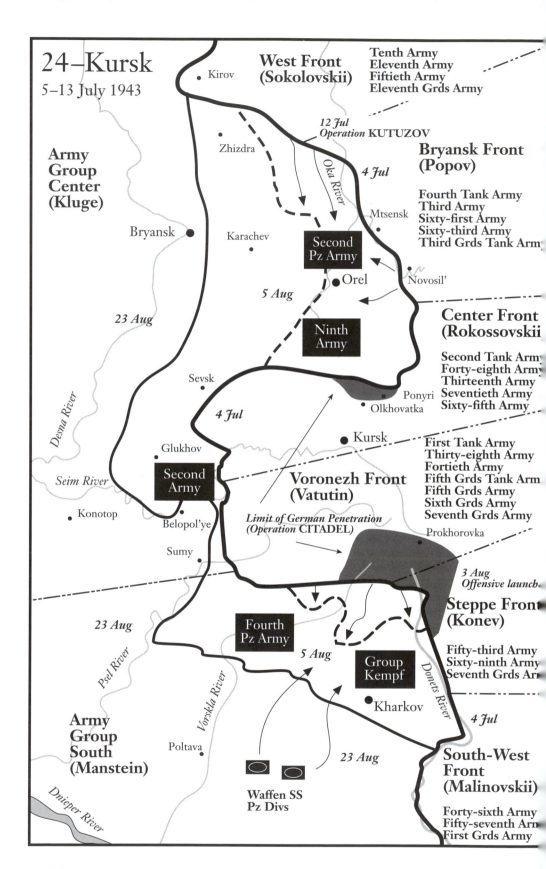

24–Kursk
5–13 July 1943

Kirov

West Front
(Sokolovskii)

Tenth Army
Eleventh Army
Fiftieth Army
Eleventh Grds Army

Zhizdra

12 Jul
Operation KUTUZOV

Oka River

4 Jul

Bryansk Front
(Popov)

Army
Group
Center
(Kluge)

Bryansk

Karachev

Mtsensk

Fourth Tank Army
Third Army
Sixty-first Army
Sixty-third Army
Third Grds Tank Army

Second
Pz Army

Orel

Novosil'

5 Aug

23 Aug

Ninth
Army

Center Front
(Rokossovskii)

Desna River

Sevsk

4 Jul

Ponyri
Olkhovatka

Second Tank Army
Forty-eighth Army
Thirteenth Army
Seventieth Army
Sixty-fifth Army

Glukhov

Kursk

First Tank Army
Thirty-eighth Army
Fortieth Army
Fifth Grds Tank Army
Fifth Grds Army
Sixth Grds Army
Seventh Grds Army

Seim River

Second
Army

Konotop

Belopol'ye

Voronezh Front
(Vatutin)

Limit of German Penetration
(Operation CITADEL)

Prokhorovka

Sumy

3 Aug
Offensive launch

Steppe Front
(Konev)

23 Aug

Fourth
Pz Army

5 Aug

Group
Kempf

Fifty-third Army
Sixty-ninth Army
Seventh Grds Army

Psel River

Vorskla River

Donets River

Army
Group
South
(Manstein)

Poltava

Kharkov

4 Jul

South-West
Front
(Malinovskii)

23 Aug

Waffen SS
Pz Divs

Forty-sixth Army
Fifty-seventh Army
First Grds Army

Dnieper River

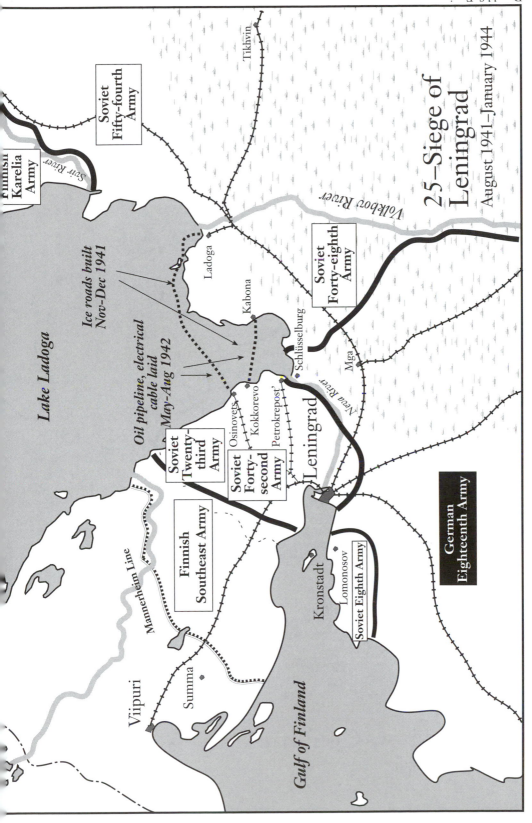

25–Siege of Leningrad
August 1941–January 1944

Donald S. Frazier

Tikhvin

Soviet Fifty-fourth Army

Suir River

Finnish Karelia Army

Volkhov River

Ladoga

Soviet Forty-eighth Army

Ice roads built Nov–Dec 1941

Lake Ladoga

Kabona

Schlüsselburg

Mga

Oil pipeline, electrical cable laid May–Aug 1942

Osinovets

Kokkorevo

Petrokrepost'

Neva River

Soviet Twenty-third Army

Soviet Forty-second Army

Leningrad

Kronstadt

Finnish Southeast Army

Mannerheim Line

German Eighteenth Army

Lomonosov

Soviet Eighth Army

Viipuri

Summa

Gulf of Finland

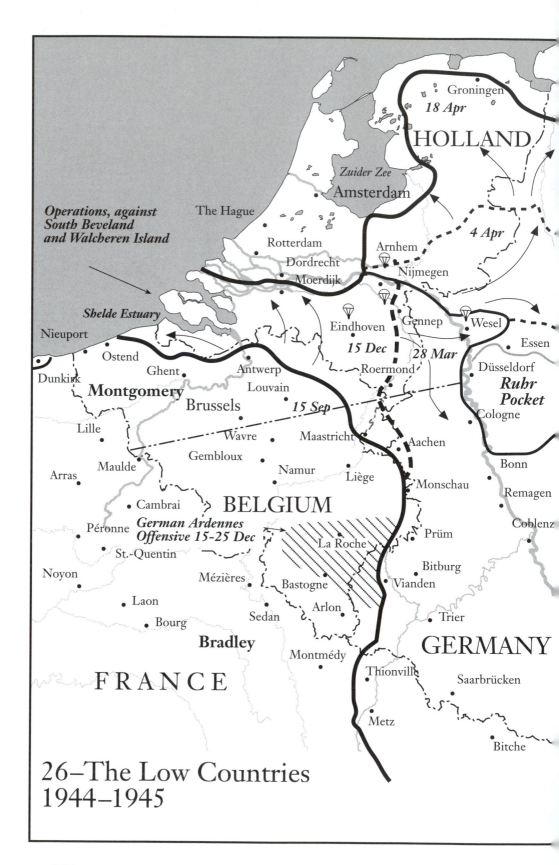

Operations, against South Beveland and Walcheren Island

Shelde Estuary

Groningen
18 Apr

HOLLAND

Zuider Zee
Amsterdam

The Hague

Rotterdam
Dordrecht
Moerdijk

Arnhem
Nijmegen

4 Apr

Nieuport
Ostend
Dunkirk
Montgomery
Ghent
Antwerp
Louvain
Brussels
Lille
Wavre
Maastricht
Gembloux
Maulde
Namur
Liège
Arras
Cambrai
Péronne
BELGIUM
St.-Quentin
Noyon
Mézières
Bastogne
Laon
Sedan
Arlon
Bourg
Bradley
Montmédy

German Ardennes Offensive 15-25 Dec
La Roche
Vianden

Eindhoven
15 Dec
Gennep
Wesel
28 Mar
Roermond
Essen
Düsseldorf
Ruhr Pocket
Cologne
Aachen
Bonn
Monschau
Remagen
Prüm
Coblenz
Bitburg
Trier
GERMANY
Thionville
Saarbrücken
Metz
Bitche

15 Sep

F R A N C E

26–The Low Countries 1944–1945

27–The Mediterranean Naval War

North Atlantic Ocean

SPAIN

PORTUGAL

MOROCCO

Casablanca

Gibraltar

Force H (Somerville)

Oran

French fleet destroyed 3 Jul 1940

Algiers

ALGERIA

HMS *Ark Royal* Nov 1941

Mediterranean Sea

SARDINIA

Cagliari

French fleet scuttled 27 Nov 1942

Toulon

Marseilles

FRANCE

Roma 9 Sep 1943

Genoa

Spezia

Venice

Trieste

Adriatic Sea

ITALY

Rome

Naples

Tyrrhenian Sea

SICILY

Bombardment 9 Feb 1941

Shipping lanes

Malta Convoy PEDESTAL 11–13 Aug 1942

Tunis

TUNISIA

Tripoli

MALTA

HMS *Southampton* 11 Jan 1941

Shipping lanes

Taranto

Air raid 11 Nov 1940

ALBANIA

GREECE

Action off Calabria 9 Jul 1940

Battle of Cape Matapan 28 Mar 1941

Colleoni 19 Jul 1940

HMS *Barham* 25 Dec 1941

Sirte I 17 Dec 1941

Sirte II 22 Mar 1942

Shipping lanes

Benghazi

LIBYA

Aegean Sea

LEROS

KOS

SAMOS

CRETE

German convoys destroyed 21–22 May 1941

CYPRUS

LEBANON

Port Said

Suez Canal

Alexandria

Med. Fleet (Cuningham)

Sub raid 19 Dec 1941

EGYPT

Istanbul

TURKEY

Black Sea

BULGARIA

ROMANIA

YUGOSLAVIA

HUNGARY

GERMANY

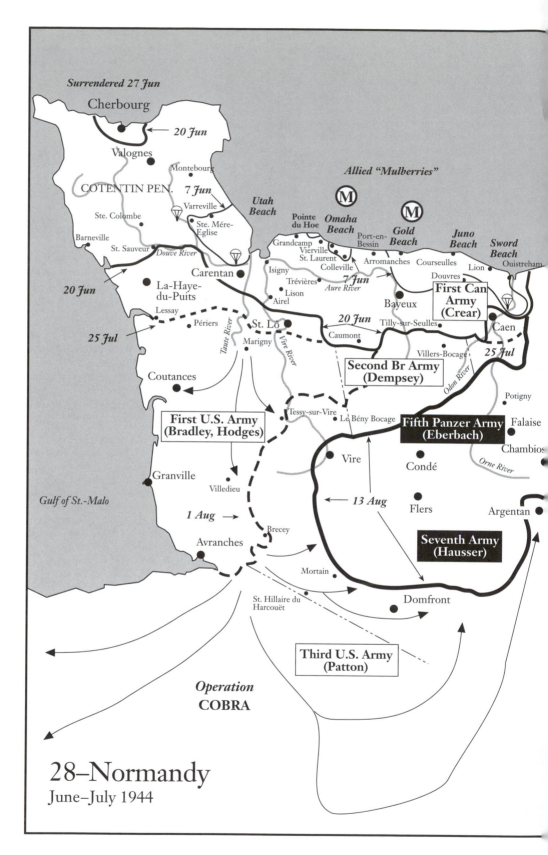

Surrendered 27 Jun

Cherbourg

← 20 Jun

Valognes

Montebourg

COTENTIN PEN.   7 Jun

Varreville

Utah Beach

Allied "Mulberries"

Ste. Colombe

Ste. Mére-Eglise

Barneville

St. Sauveur

Douve River

Carentan

La-Haye-du-Puits

Lessay

20 Jun

Périers

Taute River

25 Jul

Coutances

Pointe du Hoe

Omaha Beach

Grandcamp

Vierville
St. Laurent

Isigny

Trévières

Airel

Lison

St. Lô

Marigny

Vire River

Port-en-Bessin

Colleville

7 Jun

Aure River

Gold Beach

Arromanches

Courseulles

Bayeux

20 Jun

Tilly-sur-Seulles

Caumont

Juno Beach

Douvres

Lion

Sword Beach

Ouistreham

First Can Army (Crear)

Caen

25 Jul

Second Br Army (Dempsey)

Villers-Bocage

Odon River

Potigny

First U.S. Army (Bradley, Hodges)

Tessy-sur-Vire

Le Bény Bocage

Fifth Panzer Army (Eberbach)

Falaise

Chambios

Granville

Gulf of St.-Malo

Villedieu

Vire

Condé

Orne River

Flers

Argentan

1 Aug →

Brecey

Avranches

Mortain

St. Hillaire du Harcouët

13 Aug

Seventh Army (Hausser)

Domfront

Third U.S. Army (Patton)

Operation COBRA

28–Normandy
June–July 1944

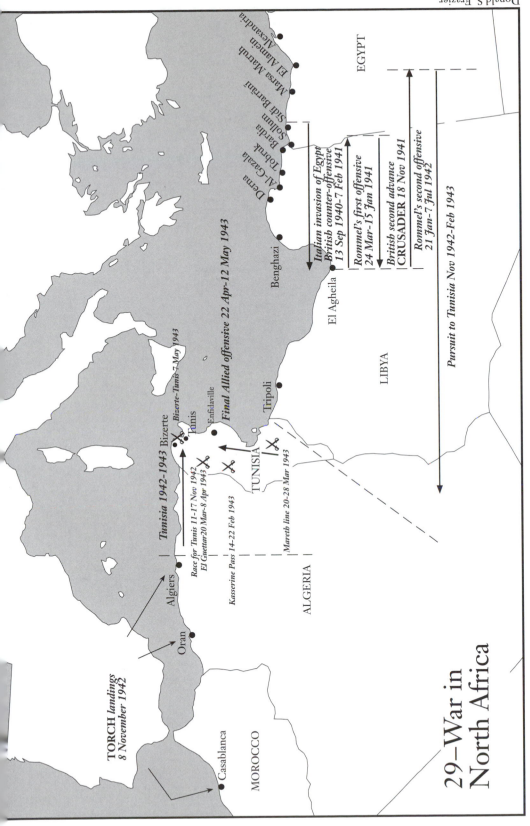

Alexandria
El Alamein
Marsa Matruh
Sidi Barrani
Sollum
Bardia
Tobruk
Al-Gazala
Derna

EGYPT

Italian invasion of Egypt
British counter-offensive
13 Sep 1940–7 Feb 1941

Rommel's first offensive
24 Mar–15 Jan 1941

British second advance
CRUSADER 18 Nov 1941

Rommel's second offensive
21 Jan–7 Jul 1942

Benghazi

El Agheila

LIBYA

Pursuit to Tunisia Nov 1942–Feb 1943

Final Allied offensive 22 Apr–12 May 1943

Bizerte–Tunis 7 May 1943

Tunisia 1942–1943 Bizerte

Tunis

Enfidaville

Tripoli

Race for Tunis 11–17 Nov 1942
El Guettar 20 Mar–8 Apr 1943

Kasserine Pass 14–22 Feb 1943

TUNISIA

Mareth line 20–28 Mar 1943

Algiers

ALGERIA

Oran

MOROCCO

Casablanca

TORCH landings
8 November 1942

29–War in
North Africa

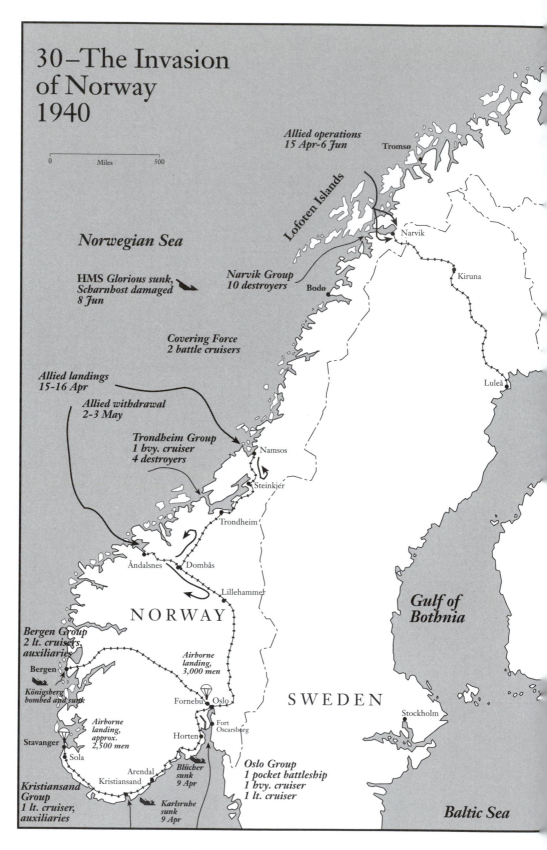

30–The Invasion of Norway 1940

0 — Miles — 500

Norwegian Sea

Allied operations 15 Apr-6 Jun

Tromsø

Lofoten Islands

Narvik

HMS Glorious sunk, Scharnhost damaged 8 Jun

Narvik Group 10 destroyers

Kiruna

Bodø

Covering Force 2 battle cruisers

Luleå

Allied landings 15-16 Apr

Allied withdrawal 2-3 May

Trondheim Group 1 hvy. cruiser 4 destroyers

Namsos

Steinkjer

Trondheim

Åndalsnes

Dombås

Lillehammer

N O R W A Y

Gulf of Bothnia

Bergen Group 2 lt. cruisers, auxiliaries

Bergen

Airborne landing, 3,000 men

Königsberg bombed and sunk

Fornebu — Oslo

S W E D E N

Airborne landing, approx. 2,500 men

Stockholm

Stavanger

Sola

Horten

Fort Oscarsborg

Arendal

Kristiansand

Blücher sunk 9 Apr

Oslo Group 1 pocket battleship 1 hvy. cruiser 1 lt. cruiser

Kristiansand Group 1 lt. cruiser, auxiliaries

Karlsruhe sunk 9 Apr

Baltic Sea

31–Poland and Eastern Europe 1939–1940

Gulf of Finland

Leningrad

ESTONIA
*(Occupied by Soviets
15–16 Jun 1940)*

LATVIA
*(Occupied by Soviets
15–16 Jun 1940)*

Riga

Dvina River

Velikiye Luki

Dvinsk

Smolensk

Baltic Sea

LITHUANIA
*(Occupied by Soviets
15–16 Jun 1940)*

Memel

Tilsit

Kovno

Niemen River

Vilna

Minsk

**Army Group North
(Bock)**

Hel

Königsberg

EAST PRUSSIA

Grodno

Pripet Marshes

Dnieper River

Danzig

**Narew
Group**

**Fourth Army
(Kluge)**

**Third Army
(Kuchler)**

**Modlin
Army**

Biatystok

**Pomeranian
Army**

Toruń

5 Sep 1939

Modlin

**Wyszkow
Group**

**S O V I E T
U N I O N**

Poznań

Vistula River

Warsaw

Bug River

Brest

**Kutno
Group**

Kutno

**Poznań
Army**

Warta River

Bzura River

Kock

**Prusy
Army**

Lublin

*Pockets of resistence
eliminated by 6 Oct 1939*

Kiev

Lodz

5 Sep 1939

**Limit of Soviet advance
20 Sep 1939**

Breslau

Oder River

Piotrków

P O L A N D

Brody

**Eighth Army
(Blaskowitz)**

**Łódź
Army**

San River

Rawa
Russka

**Tenth Army
(Reichenau)**

**Kraków
Army**

Kraców

Tarnów

5 Sep 1939

Przemyśl

Lwów

**Army Group South
(Rundsted)**

Gorlice

CarpathianArmy

Drohobycz

Dniester River

SLOVAKIA

**Fourteenth Army
(List)**

Cernăuţi

Vienna

Danube River

H U N G A R Y

Budapest

Theiss River

*Annexed by
Hungary 1940*

*Survivors flee
through Romania*

*Annexed by
Soviet Union
1940*

ROMANIA

Donald S. Frazier

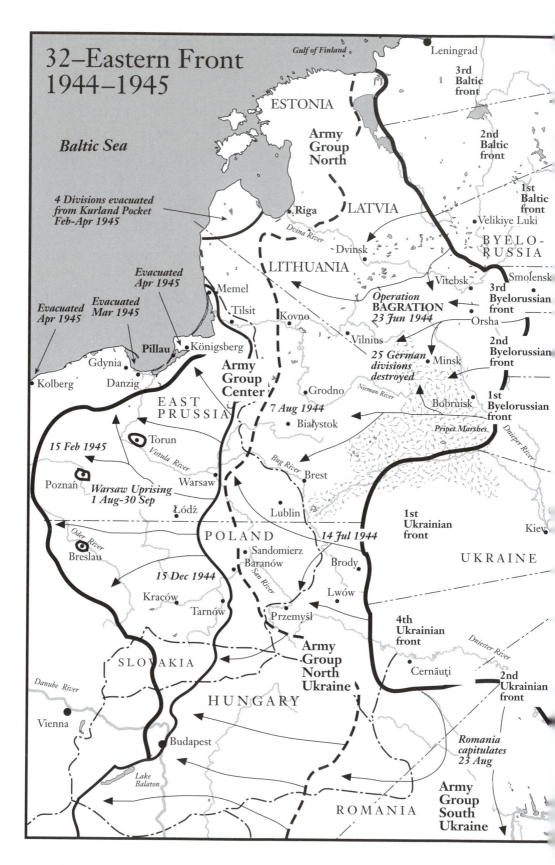

32–Eastern Front 1944–1945

Baltic Sea

Gulf of Finland

Leningrad

3rd Baltic front

ESTONIA

Army Group North

2nd Baltic front

LATVIA

1st Baltic front

4 Divisions evacuated from Kurland Pocket Feb–Apr 1945

Riga

Velikiye Luki

Dvina River

BYELO-RUSSIA

Dvinsk

Smolensk

LITHUANIA

Vitebsk

3rd Byelorussian front

Evacuated Apr 1945

Memel

Operation BAGRATION *23 Jun 1944*

Orsha

2nd Byelorussian front

Evacuated Mar 1945

Tilsit

Kovno

Vilnius

Evacuated Apr 1945

Pillau

Königsberg

25 German divisions destroyed

Minsk

1st Byelorussian front

Gdynia

Army Group Center

Grodno

Nieman River

Bobruisk

Kolberg

Danzig

EAST PRUSSIA

7 Aug 1944

Białystok

Pripet Marshes

Dnieper River

15 Feb 1945

Toruń

Vistula River

Bug River

Brest

Poznań

Warsaw Uprising 1 Aug–30 Sep

Warsaw

1st Ukrainian front

Łódź

Lublin

Kiev

Oder River

POLAND

14 Jul 1944

Breslau

Sandomierz

Baranów

Brody

UKRAINE

15 Dec 1944

San River

Lwów

4th Ukrainian front

Kraców

Tarnów

Przemyśl

Dniester River

SLOVAKIA

Army Group North Ukraine

Cernăuţi

2nd Ukrainian front

Danube River

HUNGARY

Vienna

Budapest

Romania capitulates 23 Aug

Lake Balaton

Army Group South Ukraine

ROMANIA

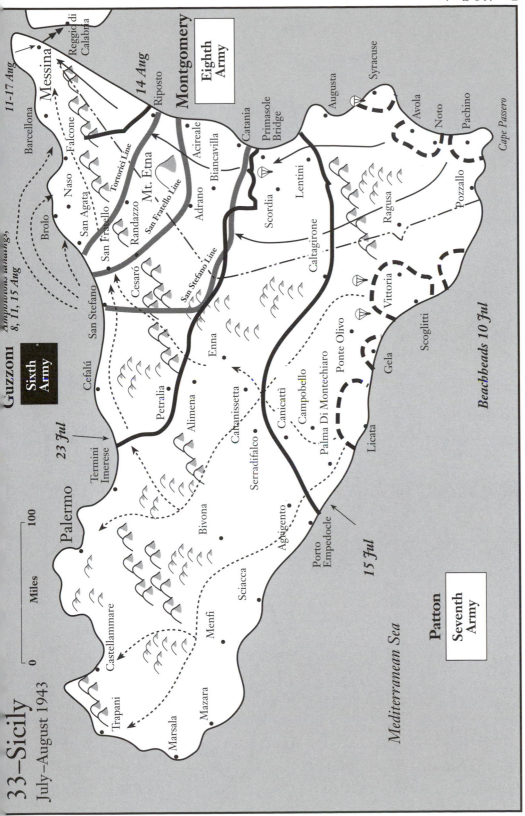

33–Sicily
July–August 1943

Donald S. Frazier

Guzzoni
Sixth Army

Montgomery
Eighth Army

Patton
Seventh Army

Miles
0   100

Mediterranean Sea

Cape Passero

Beachheads 10 Jul

11–17 Aug

Amphibious landings,
8, 11, 15 Aug

14 Aug

23 Jul

15 Jul

Messina

Reggio di Calabria

Barcellona
Falcone
Riposto
Naso
Acireale
Biancavilla
Brolo
San Agata
Tortorici Line
Mt. Etna
Adrano
Catania
Augusta
Syracuse
Avola
Noto
Pachino
San Fratello
Randazzo
San Fratello Line
Cesarò
San Stefano Line
Scordia
Lentini
Primasole Bridge
Pozzallo
San Stefano
Enna
Caltagirone
Ragusa
Vittoria
Cefalù
Petralia
Alimena
Caltanissetta
Ponte Olivo
Scoglitti
Termini Imerese
Palermo
Serradifalco
Canicatti
Campobello
Palma Di Montechiaro
Gela
Licata
Bivona
Agrigento
Porto Empedocle
Sciacca
Castellammare
Menfi
Mazara
Trapani
Marsala

Rotterdam

Dordrecht

Moerdijk

Front lines 15 Dec 1944

Operation MARKET-GARDEN
17 Sep 1944

Arnhem

Nijmegen

Reichswald

Operation VARSITY
24 Mar 1945

Wesel

Essen

Front lines 10 Mar 1945

Ruhr River

Eindhoven

Venlo

Roermond

Düsseldorf

THE RUHR

Antwerp

Ghent

Louvain

Neerpelt

Brussels

Front lines 15 Sep 1944

Wavre

Maastricht

Roer River

Aachen

Schmidt

Hurtgen Forest

Cologne

GERMANY

Bonn

Remagen

Front lines 21 Mar 1945

Gembloux

Namur

Meuse River

Liège

BELGIUM

St.-Vith

Front lines 15 Dec 1944

Prüm

Bitburg

Coblenz

Moselle River

German Ardennes offensive 16-26 Dec

Givet

La Roche

Bastogne

Mézières

Mainz

Bourg

Sedan

LUX.

Trier

Front lines 10 Mar 1945

THE RHEINLAND

Rhine River

Reims

Montmédy

Saarbrücken

Châlons-sur-Marne

Verdun

Thionville

Metz

Bitche

Vitry-le-François

Nancy

Front lines 15 Dec 1944

Strasbourg

Karlsruhe

Lunéville

Chaumont

Mirecourt

Épinal

The Siegfried Line

Front lines 15 Sep

Colmar

34–The Siegfried Line

and the Advance to the Rhine

September 1944–March 1945

Mulhouse

Belfort

Front lines 21 Mar 1945

SWITZERLAND

35–Eastern Front 1941

Donald S. Frazier

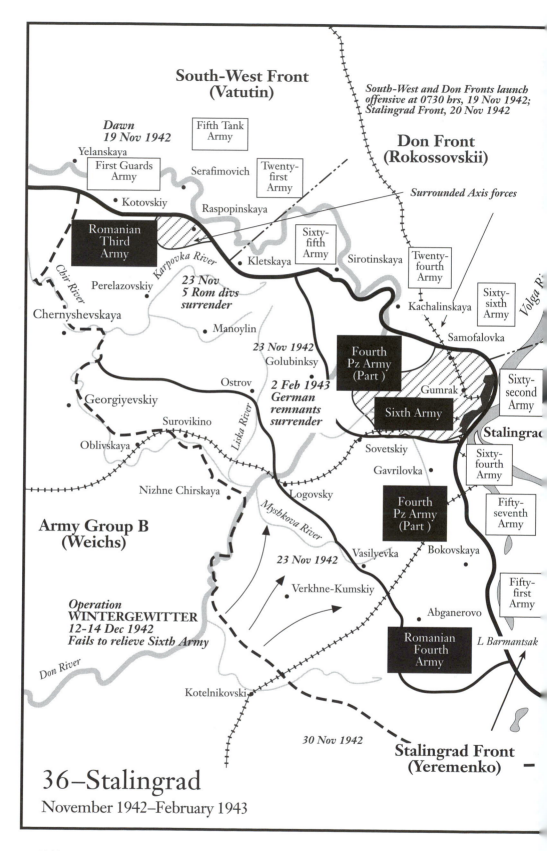

South-West Front
(Vatutin)

South-West and Don Fronts launch offensive at 0730 hrs, 19 Nov 1942; Stalingrad Front, 20 Nov 1942

Don Front
(Rokossovskii)

Dawn 19 Nov 1942

Fifth Tank Army

Yelanskaya

First Guards Army

Serafimovich

Twenty-first Army

Surrounded Axis forces

Kotovskiy

Raspopinskaya

Romanian Third Army

Karpovka River

Kletskaya

Sixty-fifth Army

Sirotinskaya

Twenty-fourth Army

Sixty-sixth Army

Chir River

Perelazovskiy

23 Nov 5 Rom divs surrender

Kachalinskaya

Volga R.

Chernyshevskaya

Manoylin

Samofalovka

23 Nov 1942 Golubinksy

Fourth Pz Army (Part)

Gumrak

Sixty-second Army

Ostrov

2 Feb 1943 German remnants surrender

Liska River

Georgiyevskiy

Sixth Army

Stalingrad

Surovikino

Sovetskiy

Sixty-fourth Army

Oblivskaya

Gavrilovka

Myshkova River

Nizhne Chirskaya

Logovsky

Fourth Pz Army (Part)

Fifty-seventh Army

Army Group B
(Weichs)

Vasilyevka

Bokovskaya

23 Nov 1942

Verkhne-Kumskiy

Fifty-first Army

Abganerovo

Operation WINTERGEWITTER *12–14 Dec 1942 Fails to relieve Sixth Army*

Romanian Fourth Army

L Barmantsak

Don River

Kotelnikovski

30 Nov 1942

Stalingrad Front
(Yeremenko)

36–Stalingrad

November 1942–February 1943

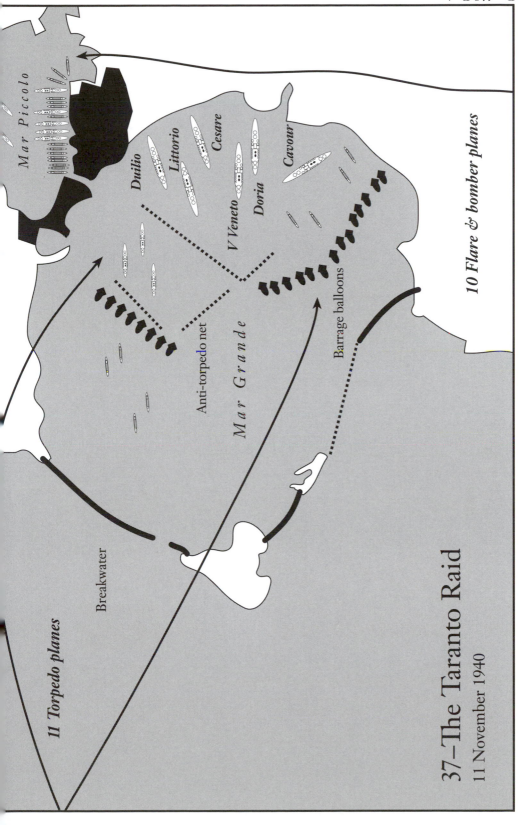

Mar Piccolo

Duilio

Littorio

Cesare

V Veneto

Doria

Cavour

Anti-torpedo net

Mar Grande

Barrage balloons

10 Flare & bomber planes

Breakwater

11 Torpedo planes

37–The Taranto Raid
11 November 1940

A

Aachen (13 September–21 October 1944)
Aix-la-Chapelle, later Aachen, was the capital city of the Holy Roman Empire, the city in which Charlemagne was crowned Holy Roman Emperor on Christmas Day 800. Over the next 500 years, thirty-two kings and emperors were crowned in the city. Since Adolf Hitler (q.v.) considered Charlemagne the founder of the First *Reich,* the city of Aachen on Germany's western border had near-sacred status for the *Führer.*

By late September and early October 1944, the Allied situation on the western front had stabilized. To the north, British General Bernard L. Montgomery's (q.v.) 21st Army Group was tasked with skirting the Siegfried Line (q.v.) and encircling the German industrial heartland, the Ruhr. Attacking along the southern end of the Siegfried Line—also known as the West Wall—was Lieutenant General Jacob L. Dever's (q.v.) 6th Army Group. To his north and in the middle of the Allied forces was Lieutenant General Omar N. Bradley's (q.v.) 12th Army Group. On Bradley's southern flank was Lieutenant General George S. Patton's (q.v.) Third Army, besieging Metz (q.v.). The rest of Bradley's sector was held by Lieutenant General Courtney H. Hodges' (q.v.) First Army.

Supreme Allied commander General Dwight D. Eisenhower's (q.v.) staff had estimated that it would take eleven months after the Normandy (q.v.) landings to reach the German border. Yet on 11 September 1944, American patrols from the First Army crossed the Our River at several points along the Belgian-German border. Hodges' immediate objective was the high ground overlooking Aachen rather than the city itself. The ultimate objective was the second line of the Siegfried fortifications that stood east-southeast of the city.

The German unit defending Aachen was the 116th *Panzer* Division, commanded by Lieuten-

ant General Gerhard von Schwerin. In reality, the 116th *Panzer* Division consisted of little more than two understrength *Panzergrenadier* regiments. While trying to organize his fragmented forces, Schwerin entered Aachen on 12 September and encountered a panicked civilian populace. Although Hitler had ordered the historic city evacuated, von Schwerin decided Aachen was lost anyway and halted the evacuation. Unbeknownst to Hodges, only local defense forces stood in the way of an American occupation of Aachen on the morning of 13 September.

Unaware that Aachen was his for the taking, U.S. VII Corps commander Major General J. Lawton Collins (q.v.) opted to continue his assault on the Siegfried Line rather than occupy the city. On the evening of 15 September, Major General Clarence R. Huebner's (q.v.) 1st Infantry Division started moving to surround the city from the south and southeast.

Hitler ordered the city evacuated, by force if necessary. Von Schwerin, however, refused and was relieved of command. Leaving a letter in the hands of a civilian official, addressed to any responsible U.S. commander, von Schwerin noted that he had stopped the "absurd" evacuation of the city and asked the Americans to care for the populace. After von Schwerin's departure, German forces allowed the civilians still in Aachen to leave before the battle for the city started, and 145,000 of the city's original 165,000 residents fled.

On 17 September, the Allies' Operation MARKET-GARDEN (*see* Arnhem) started, and all other operations along the Siegfried Line came to a standstill. During that pause, the Germans used the time to reorganize and strengthen their defenses at Aachen. By the end of September, MARKET-GARDEN had failed and the focus of operations shifted back to the Aachen area.

From 7 to 20 October, elements of the U.S. VII and XIX Corps, particularly the 1st and 30th Infantry Divisions, tightened their hold around the city. With the additional forces the Germans had moved up, Aachen was now defended by elements of the I SS *Panzer Korps* (which included the 116th *Panzer* Division and the 3rd *Panzergrenadier* Division), and the 246th *Volksgrenadier* Division. The latter unit was commanded by Colonel Gerhard Wilck. The still relatively weak German defenses were intended to hold only until the arrival of reinforcements promised by the commander in chief west, Field Marshal Gerd von Rundstedt (q.v.).

On 8 October, Huebner ordered a pre-dawn attack on the city. Two days later, he delivered an ultimatum to Lieutenant Colonel Maximilian Leyherr, a regimental commander of the 246th *Volksgrenadier* Division, instructing him to surrender unconditionally or the city would be reduced to rubble by U.S. artillery and aerial bombardment. Leyherr rejected the ultimatum on 11 October, whereupon 300 P-38s and P-47s of the IX Tactical Air Command dropped sixty-two tons of bombs on the city. Ground-based U.S. artillery followed up with another 169 tons of explosives.

The following day, Wilck arrived in the town and assumed command of the approximately 5,000 German troops inside the city. The same day, U.S. fighter-bombers dropped another sixty-nine tons of bombs, and U.S. artillery fired an additional 5,000 shells. On 13 October, two battalions of the U.S. 26th Infantry Regiment began a direct attack on the city proper. They soon learned that the only way to advance was by pairing infantry with tanks or tank destroyers. The Americans fought doggedly from house to house and from one storm cellar or sewer to another, using flamethrowers, demolition charges, and grenades.

In an example of American ingenuity, 1st Infantry Division soldiers developed a makeshift weapon for the assault on the city dubbed the "V-13." Using captured trolley cars, the soldiers packed them with explosives, painted a large "13" on the side of the cars, and rolled them downhill into the city. Each trolley car exploded with the force of a 2,000-pound bomb.

Wilck ordered a counterattack on 15 October, but the offensive was stopped by a bombing and strafing run by P-47s. German forces launched a renewed assault before daybreak on 16 October, but the attacking force had lost one-third of its manpower in two days and was compelled to withdraw and regroup. That same day, U.S. units working their way around the city linked up, completing Aachen's encirclement. The city, with its 20,000 remaining inhabitants, was surrounded.

Wilck, defending what was left of the city, asked permission to withdraw. Field Marshal Walter Model (q.v.), the commander of German Army Group B, cabled in reply: "Fight to the last man! If necessary, have yourself buried under the ruins!" When two German breakout attempts on 18 and 19 October failed, the German high command abandoned the defenders to their fate. Wilck then asked for volunteers from a group of thirty U.S. prisoners of war to convey his surrender to the Americans.

The assistant division commander of 1st Infantry Division, Brigadier General George A. Taylor, accepted the surrender on 21 October. In taking the city, U.S. forces captured approximately 12,000 Germans. In the process, the Americans suffered 3,600 casualties—3,100 from the 30th and 500 from the 1st Infantry Divisions. Aachen was the first German city to fall to the Allies, but U.S. forces discovered that the city was an empty prize. There was no electricity in the city, all the water mains and sewers had burst, and the city streets were littered with shattered glass, dead animals, and wrecked civilian cars and military vehicles. As one American observer noted, "The city is as dead as a Roman ruin . . . but it has none of the grace of gradual decay." Remarkably, the city's magnificent ancient cathedral, in which a succession of German kings and emperors had been crowned, emerged unscathed.

David A. Foy

Additional Reading
MacDonald, Charles B., *The Siegfried Line Campaign* (1963).
Polmar, Norman, and Thomas B. Allen, *World War II: America at War, 1941–1945* (1991).

Aarhus Air Raid (31 October 1944)
The Aarhus raid was a daring, low-level precision bombing attack on the *Gestapo* (q.v.) headquarters in Denmark. On 31 October 1944, in broad daylight, twenty-five Mosquitoes from Number 140 Wing of the Second Tactical Air Force launched the raid. The wing had three squadrons: Number 21 of the RAF, Number 464 of the Royal Australian Air Force, and Number 487 of the Royal New Zealand Air Force.

The raid was mounted in response to an urgent request from the Danish resistance (q.v.). At the time, Pastor Harald Sandbaek, a resistance leader, was being held at Aarhus and tortured for information by the *Gestapo.* The attack was led by Wing Commander Bob Reynolds. His aircrews managed to place their bomb loads in the dead center of the building that had once housed the University of Aarhus. All aircraft returned safely; 200 *Gestapo* personnel were killed, and all files on the Danish resistance were destroyed.

In carrying out the raid, the Mosquitoes flew so low, in order to ensure no civilians were injured by near misses, that one plane lost its tail wheel when it clipped the front of the building. After the building was destroyed, members of the resistance dug Pastor Sandbaek out of the rubble—still alive. To prevent his further capture, they smuggled him to Sweden.

Chris Westhorp

Additional Reading

Johnston, Frank (ed.), *R.A.A.F. over Europe* (1946).

Ross, J.M.S., *The Royal New Zealand Air Force* (1955).

ACHSE (AXIS), Operation (9 September–October 1943)

Following the removal of Benito Mussolini (q.v.) from power on 25 July 1943, King Victor Emmanuel (q.v.) and the new head of the Italian government, Marshal Pietro Badoglio (q.v.), publicly announced that the country would continue to fight on Germany's side until final victory had been won. Adolf Hitler (q.v.) and many of his advisors, however, suspected from the start that the new regime in Rome was, in fact, trying to take Italy out of the war as soon as possible.

Accordingly, German military commanders in Italy and adjacent regions were instructed to prepare for that eventuality. Based on an earlier contingency plan (Operation *ALARICH*), the German response to the disappearance of Fascism and the likelihood of Italy's defection was embodied in a new plan, code named Operation *ACHSE* (AXIS). Between 28 July and 30 August, the later plan went through several modifications. Originally, Operation *ACHSE* just dealt with the capture of the Italian fleet, while Operation *SCHWARZ* covered the military occupation of Italy. In the end, both operations were combined into a coordinated effort. Under the plan, Field Marshal Erwin Rommel (q.v.) was assigned a key role as commander of a newly formed Army Group B.

When Italy's surrender to the Allies was announced on 8 September, the *Wehrmacht* implemented *ACHSE* on 9 September with great speed and energy. In central and northern Italy, German troops immediately occupied strategic points and proceeded to disarm and round up the Italian armed forces. Wherever the Italians resisted, as in the vicinity of Rome, Milan, Turin, Florence, and elsewhere, they were either subdued by force or eventually persuaded to surrender. On 21 September, Army Group B notified the German high command that in northern Italy alone more than 415,000 Italian soldiers had so far laid down their arms, and almost 184,000 were sent off to Germany as prisoners.

Resistance by Italian Army units was more pronounced and also more prolonged in the Balkans. On the Ionian island of Cephalonia, for instance, the *Acqui* Division under General Antonio Gandin put up a fight for almost two weeks. When its resistance was finally broken on 23 September, a large portion of those captured, including Gandin, were shot on Hitler's orders. In Albania, the *Perugia* Division likewise proved troublesome, and eventually handed some of its equipment over to Tito's partisans (qq.v.). In Montenegro, the *Taurinense* Division held out against the Germans until the beginning of October, and German records indicate that skirmishes with Italian troops, particularly those from the *Firenze* and *Venezia* Divisions, dragged on in some Balkan areas until the middle of October.

Most of the Italian fleet, which had long been the object of German suspicion, managed to escape from its ports and sail to Allied waters. *Luftwaffe* bombers caught up with some of the ships on the afternoon of 9 September and sank the battleship *Roma.* Approximately 1,200 Italian sailors, including the fleet commander, Admiral Carlo Bergamini, were killed. The Germans also captured two older battleships and two heavy cruisers (all under repair in port), as well as five light cruisers, five destroyers, and seven submarines.

Three days after the *Roma* was sunk, German glider-borne commandos liberated Mussolini from his place of internment on the Gran Sasso (q.v.), an operation for which exaggerated credit was later given to a small SS detachment under Otto Skorzeny (q.v.). The rescue of the deposed *Il Duce* was a personal triumph for Hitler and allowed him to reestablish a Fascist regime, the Italian Social Republic, in the northern half of Italy.

Ulrich Trumpener

Additional Reading

Deakin, F.W., *The Brutal Friendship: Mussolini, Hitler, and the Fall of Italian Fascism* (1962).

Alam el Halfa (30 August–5 September 1942)

By July 1942, the British Eighth Army had been pushed back after a series of defeats by German Field Marshal Erwin Rommel (q.v.) into a defensive position sixty miles west of Cairo. The position ran north to south between El Alamein, a railway halt near the sea, and the Qattara Depression, an impassable area thirty miles south. The British were preparing for an Axis offensive in a final bid to gain the Nile Delta and evict them from Egypt.

Aware of imminent disaster, British Prime Minister Winston S. Churchill (q.v.) in early August relieved General Sir Claude Auchinleck (q.v.) as commander in chief of the Middle East, and replaced him with General Sir Harold Alexander (q.v.). As the new commander of the Eighth Army, Churchill selected General William Gott (q.v.). Unfortunately, Gott's aircraft was shot down and he was killed on 7 August while on his way to Cairo. With Gott dead, Churchill's second choice was the relatively unknown Lieutenant General Bernard L. Montgomery (q.v.). Adopting the plan already worked out by Auchinleck, Montgomery was determined to fight a purely defensive battle to husband his resources for the offensive he planned for later in the fall.

The keys to the British position were two dominant ridges that ran roughly east and west; Ruweisat Ridge just south of El Alamein, and Alam el Halfa Ridge ten miles farther east. The British had four and a half divisions on the main line running twenty miles south from the sea. Ruweisat Ridge was held by a complete division, backed by an armored division, and another infantry division was dug in on Alam el Halfa Ridge. The gap of some ten miles between the southern end of the British position and the Qattara Depression was held by a light armored division as a delaying force.

Rommel's plan was to make diversionary attacks in the north while his armor moved south through the gap and then moved north to roll up the defenders. After that he would break out to the east. On the night of 30 August 1942, feint attacks in the north and center covered the movements of Rommel's *Panzer* divisions south and then east. In the gap, however, the German tanks encountered minefields of a depth and concentration unsuspected by Rommel. Thus, at first light on 31 August, the German tanks were just emerging from the minefields, having been subjected to continuous British air attack throughout the night. That morning Rommel directed

the *Panzers* to wheel north and secure Alam e Halfa Ridge.

A sandstorm during the day grounded all aircraft, enabling the German armor to make good progress and close the approaches to the ridge by late afternoon. At 1700 hours they were engaged by the British 22nd Armoured Brigade, fighting from defensive positions some two miles south of the main ridge. This brigade was equipped with U.S.-built Grant tanks, the only tank at the time capable of holding its own against the German PzKpfw-III and -IV tanks. Failing to dislodge the 22nd Brigade, the Germans withdrew at nightfall into defensive positions, where, for a second night they were subjected to continuous air and artillery attack.

Having identified Rommel's axis of advance Montgomery tried to concentrate an entire armored division on the 22nd Brigade's positions but he was only partially successful. Throughout 1 September, Rommel made sporadic and limited attacks to find weak spots in the defenses and to lure the British armor out of their positions and into a counterattack. Once his enemy was in the open, Rommel was confident he would again win the day in a fluid tank battle. Montgomery did not take the bait and kept his armor under tight control. He was adamant that it should stay put and not be loosed against the *Panzers*, a tactic that hitherto had led to disastrous British tank losses. He was, however, anxious to wrest the initiative from Rommel and break the stalemate.

On 2 September, Montgomery ordered the division holding Ruweisat Ridge to move south east and threaten the neck of the Axis salient. For various reasons, this move did not start until 2200 hours that day, and then it proceeded slowly and cautiously. Rommel, worried about his fuel supplies, and aware that he could not overcome the British in the north and east, nor bypass them in the south, had already ordered a withdrawal. He put out a strong flank guard of seasoned troops to cover the retrograde move of his tanks. This flank guard successfully held the advancing British division throughout 3 September and on 4 September counterattacked it, allowing the *Panzers* to successfully withdraw.

By 5 September, apart from a small rear guard, Rommel's *Panzerarmee Afrika* was back behind its own minefields, counting its losses and surveying damage. The battle of Alam el Halfa known to the Germans as "The Six-Day Race, was over. It was the turning point in the war in North Africa. The Axis forces suffered 3,000 casualties and lost fifty tanks, fifteen field guns, thirty ive antitank guns, and 400 trucks. The Allies suffered 1,640 casualties and lost sixty-eight tanks. Rommel had made unusual errors—lack of reconnaissance, loss of surprise, and an uncharacteristic hesitation on 31 August. Montgomery's handling of the battle became a model. More importantly, it stamped his personality, tactical thinking, and art of command on the Eighth Army, rejuvenating them and laying a sound foundation for the offensive battle of El Alamein (q.v.), which followed.

B.K. Warner

Additional Reading

Carver, Michael, *El Alamein* (1962).
Lucas, James S., *War in the Desert: The Eighth Army at El Alamein* (1982).
Messenger, Charles, *The Unknown Alamein* (1982).
Pitt, Barrie, *The Crucible of War: Year of Alamein, 1942* (1982).

Albania (7–10 April 1939)

The invasion of Albania in April 1939 was not a spontaneous act on the part of Benito Mussolini (q.v.). As early as the Munich Conference in late September 1938, he ordered operational plans drawn up for the occupation of Albania. With Albania's population at just over one million, it also gave Italy "living space" to ease it's overpopulation. Mussolini's rationale for the invasion was to forestall a takeover by Yugoslavia and the formation of a greater Balkan federation. Yugoslav Prime Minister Milan Stojadinović, however, had repeatedly expressed no interest whatsoever in Albania.

On 25 March 1939, *Il Duce* delivered an ultimatum to King Zog I (formerly Ahmed Zogu, a Muslim military chieftain who proclaimed himself king of Albania). Simply stated, Mussolini demanded the recognition of a formal Italian protectorate over Albania and the stationing of Italian troops on Albania, or risk war. Zog refused to acknowledge the ultimatum.

At dawn on 7 April, Good Friday, Italian General Alfredo Guzzoni launched the invasion from Bari and Brindisi and quickly occupied the Albanian port cities of San Giovanni di Medua, Durazzo, Valona, and Santi Quaranta. The invasion force consisted of four infantry regiments, three mechanized battalions, and an assortment of other ground units supported by nearly 400 aircraft. That afternoon, a regiment of grenadiers landed at Tirana airport, seized the capital, and quickly joined up with the landing force coming up from the coast. By 10 April, Easter Monday, all

the major Albanian cities were occupied. Only sporadic fighting in several mountainous regions persisted after 10 April.

Resistance was mild. In seizing the ports, the Italians encountered significant resistance only at Durazzo, where several machine gun placements held them up for nearly two hours. King Zog was not very popular with the Albanians. In fact, the Italians sent Giovanni Giro to Albania early to organize a rebellion, He found little difficulty locating Albanians anxious to help the Italians. Realizing his country was about to be overrun, Zog abdicated on 8 April and fled to Greece.

In official Italian press releases, the invasion was requested by Albanians desiring the overthrow of King Zog's mismanaged government, and by Italians in Albania to protect their lives and property threatened by armed bands. Mussolini did not consult Adolf Hitler (q.v.) prior to the invasion. This was in retaliation to Hitler's failure to inform Mussolini on the former's occupation of the remainder of Czechoslovakia on 15 March 1939.

Strategically, the seizure of Albania was a huge asset for Italy. With Albania, Italy controlled both sides of the Strait of Ottranto making the Adriatic an "Italian lake." Also, Italy acquired the foothold in the Balkans from which it launched its hapless attack on Greece (q.v.) in October 1940.

To favorably influence world opinion, Italy established an interim government run by Albanians. Italian officials, however, were posted at various levels to oversee the government institutions. On 15 April, King Victor Emmanuel III (q.v.) assumed the crown of Albania and became "King of Italy and of Albania, Emperor of Ethiopia." Representing the king as vice regent was General Francesco Jacomoni di Sanlavino, formerly the Italian minister to Albania.

World reaction to the invasion was the continuation of a pattern that started with the *Anschluss* (q.v.) and continued up to the invasion of Poland (q.v.) in September 1939—apathy. The world gave verbal support to the oppressed states, but took no action against the aggressors. The League of Nations (q.v.) was helpless, as were the world's democracies, in preventing aggression by the dictatorships. Great Britain, which three months earlier had signed an agreement with Italy acknowledging the status quo in the Mediterranean, was angry. In the end, however, Britain and France ultimately accepted the *fait accompli* in Albania.

William H. Van Husen

Additional Reading

Craig, Gordon A., *Europe since 1914* (1961).

Kee, Robert, *1939: In the Shadow of War* (1984).

Rothschild, Joseph, *East Central Europe between the Two World Wars* (1974).

Toynbee, Arnold, and Veronica M. Toynbee, *The Eve of War, 1939* (1958).

Alexandria (18–19 December 1941)

[See map 27 on page 1337]

At 0555 hours on 19 December 1941, the British tanker *Sargona* and the nearby destroyer HMS *Jervis* each suffered crippling damage from an underwater explosion. Ten minutes later, the battleship HMS *Valiant* also went down from an underwater blast; and ten minutes after that, the battleship HMS *Queen Elizabeth* suffered a similar fate. Struck down by Italian "human torpedoes," the loss of the British ships in the harbor at Alexandria, Egypt, marked the high point of Axis fortunes in the Mediterranean during World War II. At the cost of only six prisoners of war, the Italian 10th Light Flotilla (q.v.) struck a potentially decisive blow, by sinking all of the Royal Navy's (RN) battleships in the Mediterranean.

The Alexandria raid had its roots in the 10th Light Flotilla's earlier successes at Scuda Bay in March 1941, and at Gibraltar that September. For the commander of the 10th Light Flotilla, Commander Valerio Borghese (q.v.), the successes of his unit, combined with the German sinking of the aircraft carrier HMS *Ark Royal* and the battleship HMS *Barham* the previous month, meant that the RN's choices for safe anchorages had been reduced. The Axis now had the opportunity to achieve naval supremacy in the Mediterranean.

Planning for the Alexandria raid began in November, when Commander Ernesto Forza was given direct command of the operation. He and Borghese selected Alexandria as the target for their next attack, reasoning that the British would regard it as a safe port, far from Axis bases. They gathered aerial photographs from German high altitude reconnaissance aircraft, agent reports about the harbor and its defenses, and prewar charts. They examined the Italian signals intelligence assessment of the RN's activities in and around the port. They then deployed the "mother submarine" the *Scire*, to the island of Leros, near Rhodes, while the six "sled" (human torpedo) operators conducted their training in Brindisi. The operators and the sleds were then flown to Kos and transported by ship to Leros. The final planning and briefings were conducted aboard the ship *Asmara*. Once the final details were confirmed, the sleds and operators boarded the *Scire,* which transported them to a point 1.3 nautical miles off Alexandria.

All went well until the sleds entered the harbor shortly after sunset on 18 December. They entered by following a small group of ships through the harbor nets, moved past the Free French ships interned in the main port area, and then began to seek out their targets. It was at that point that the problems set in. The first team, under Lieutenant Luigi Durand de la Penne, sought the *Valiant,* but their sleds and breathing equipment failed as they were making the final approach. De la Penne and his partner had to manhandle their explosive charge into position under the battleship. They were successful in this exhausting effort, but later were captured as a result.

Meanwhile, another team under Gunner Captain Vincenzo Martellotta, could not find their target, the aircraft carrier HMS *Eagle,* because it had departed Alexandria earlier that evening. Desperate to find a target before the batteries on their sleds died, they located the 16,000-ton oiler *Sargona,* and placed their explosives. The *Jervis* later came alongside to refuel and in the process also fell victim to the Italian explosives. Martellotta and his partner successfully exfiltrated from the oiler's anchorage, but were arrested later that morning before they could make their way to the coast.

The third and final team, under Engineer Captain Antonio Marceglia, encountered no problems. They easily found their target, the *Queen Elizabeth,* in her assigned anchorage. They made an undetected approach, placed their explosives, and successfully made it ashore. They were the only team to witness their success, listening to the explosions from a train station in the city. They were arrested the next day, however, when they tried to pass one of the counterfeit five-pound notes they had been issued.

The Italian raid on Alexandria epitomized naval special operations in World War II. It was economical, precise, and for a short time altered the strategic naval balance in Italy's favor by removing the RN's only remaining capital ships in the Mediterranean. Yet the raid failed to have a decisive effect on the overall course of the campaign because Italy's naval leadership refused to risk their fleet without conclusive evidence that the battleships at Alexandria had been taken out of action. This was one of many examples in the war of the success of a bold stroke being wasted by a later failure to exploit it. The Alexandria raid, nonetheless, inspired many imitations, including the British Alten Fjord raid q.v.) that crippled the German battleship *Tirpitz* in March 1944.

Carl O. Schuster

Additional Reading

Borghese, Valerio, *The Sea Devils* (1952).
Carisella, P.J., and William Schofield, *Frogman: First Battles* (1987).

Alten Fjord Raid (22 September 1943)

[See map 5 on page 1315]

During World War II, German air and naval units positioned at Alten Fjord, on Norway's North Cape, attacked Allied convoys bound for northern Russia. Heavy Allied naval and maritime losses in 1943 prompted the British Admiralty to launch Operation SOURCE in an effort to cripple a good portion of Germany's naval strength at Alten Fjord. This effort consisted of six thirty-ton midget submarines identified as *X-5* through *X-10,* with crews of four men each. The entire force was commanded by Rear Admiral C.B. Barry. The force was towed from Scotland by conventional submarines across 1,000 miles of North Sea and Norwegian Sea toward Alten Fjord.

From the start, the operation seemed bedeviled as the *X-9* sank with its crew in heavy seas during the long passage. The *X-8* suffered mechanical failures and was scuttled. Four other submarines had compass problems, periscope troubles, and electrical problems caused by water leakage. The *X-5* was shelled by German fire and sunk, and its crew was taken prisoner. The *X-10*'s mission was to sink the battleship *Scharnhorst,* which, when the British arrived, was at sea for gunnery practice.

On entering Alten Fjord on 22 September 1943, the *X-6,* under the command of Lieutenant Donald Cameron, and the *X-7,* commanded by Lieutenant Basil Place (qq.v.), planted their mines below the *Tirpitz,* damaging its engine and two of the main gun turrets. The *X-6* was discovered when it accidently surfaced. The *X-7* was damaged in the attack and had to be abandoned. With its primary target gone, the *X-10* attacked the *Tirpitz* after the *X-6.* The *X-10,* however, was not as successful, and was sunk with all hands.

Both commanders of the *X-6* and *X-7* and four of the six other crew members survived and were taken prisoner aboard the *Tirpitz.* Although the British midget submarines crippled the *Tirpitz* for several months, Operation SOURCE failed to achieve its objective of sinking or damaging a sizeable portion of the German Navy using Alten Fjord as a northern base. That mission was later accomplished in April 1944 by British torpedo bombers from aircraft carriers. Irrespective of its many misfortunes, the British midget submarine action at Alten Fjord was noteworthy in its conception, imagination, and courage.

Donald P. Doumitt

Additional Reading

Gallager, Thomas, *The X-Craft Raid* (1971).
Middleton, Drew, *Submarine: The Ultimate Naval Weapon: Its Past, Present, and Future* (1976).

Altmark Raid (16 February 1940)

While disguised as a tanker, the *Altmark,* a 12,000-ton German auxiliary warship armed with three 6-inch guns and capable of cruising at 25 knots, served as the supply ship for the pocket battleship *Graf Spee.* The *Altmark* also acted as a prisoner-of-war (POW) transport for British sailors captured by the *Graf Spee* when she sank British ships. After the *Graf Spee* was scuttled at Montevideo on 17 December 1939 (*see* Platte River), the *Altmark,* which separated from the ill-fated *Graf Spee* on

The German prison ship Altmark *aground in Jøssing Fjord, Norway, after the rescue of 299 British sailors by a boarding party from the HMS* Cossack. *(IWM HU 27803)*

6 December, vanished into the vast expanse of the Atlantic. Her captain waited until the British forces had dispersed, then headed for home on 24 January 1940. He managed to move undetected through British convoy routes until sighted in Norwegian waters on 14 February.

British Admiral Sir Charles Forbes (q.v.) learned from intelligence sources that the wanted ship had passed Bergen moving southward on 15 February. The British, suspecting that she carried POWs, protested that it was a breach of neutrality to allow passage of POWs through neutral waters.

On 16 February 1940, the British light cruiser HMS *Arethusa* and five destroyers led by the HMS *Cossack,* commanded by Captain Phillip Vian (q.v.), sighted the *Altmark* in Norwegian waters escorted by two Norwegian patrol boats. Two British destroyers attempted to board her, but the *Altmark* refused to stop, and the Norwegians intervened. The *Altmark* put into Jøssing Fjord. Vian followed and ordered the Norwegians to release the British POWs. The Norwegians replied that the *Altmark* was boarded off Bergen the previous day and no POWs were found. Vian realized he needed Admiralty permission to proceed further and withdrew outside territorial waters to contact his superiors.

Winston S. Churchill (q.v.), then first sea lord, ordered Vian to offer to accompany the Norwegians and the *Altmark* back to Bergen. If this offer was refused, Vian should board the *Altmark.* At 2200 hours, Vian reentered the fjord. The Norwegians refused to cooperate but remained passive while the HMS *Cossack* put alongside the *Altmark* and boarded her. Little resistance was offered and the incident was over by midnight. The British rescued 299 of their sailors from the secret holds of the *Altmark,* and the HMS *Cossack* returned to Rosyth on 17 February with battleships sailing out from Britain to provide cover. In the bleak early hours of the war for Britain, the HMS *Cossack* and her captain became national heroes. The boarding of the *Altmark* enraged Adolf Hitler (q.v.) and precipitated the German attack on Norway (q.v.).

Laura Matysek Wood

Additional Reading

Frischauer, Willi, and Robert Jackson, *The Navy's Here: The Altmark Affair* (1955).
Roskill, Stephen W., *The War at Sea 1939–45.* Vol. I: *The Defensive* (1954).
Wiggan, Richard, *Hunt the Altmark* (1990).

Antwerp (4 September–2 October 1944)

Following the Allied breakout and pursuit north of the Seine in the last week of August 1944, the capture of a major port closer to the battlefront became imperative, as 20,000 tons of supplies daily had to be transported overland with considerable difficulty from the Normandy beachhead.

The Canadian First Army was detailed to clear the Channel ports. Held as "fortresses" by the Germans, most of these ports were heavily damaged in the subsequent fighting, or had inadequate handling capacity to start with. Meanwhile, the British Second Army, spearheaded by XXX Corps, advanced in a spectacular six-day, 250-mile thrust to the vital port of Antwerp, Belgium. The city was captured by the 11th Armoured Division on 4 September with its harbor facilities virtually intact—facilities capable of unloading 60,000 tons of supplies daily. This powerful armored drive opened a seventy-mile gap in the front and isolated the German Fifteenth Army along the Channel coast and in the Scheldt estuary. The Rhine crossings and the outflanking of the Ruhr were within the Allies' immediate grasp.

The Germans were so surprised by the speed of the British advance they were unable to put into operation their plans for the destruction of the port of Antwerp with its twenty-six miles of quays, drydocks, locks, 625 cranes, warehouses, oil storage facilities, marshalling yards, and sluice gates. Most of the credit for the successful capture of the undamaged port facilities goes to the Belgian resistance, especially the *Mouvement National Royaliste,* which for three years had made plans to save the port from German demolition. Using a force of 600 men hand-picked for their knowledge of the dock area, the resistance accomplished this feat with only minimal British assistance. Yet, despite the pleas of the resistance fighters, the small and relatively unsupported British armored force in place was not ordered to advance beyond the docks. Thus the Germans tenaciously retained control of the important canal system and power station in the northeast suburb of Merksem, which were not captured until 2 October.

On 4 September, in one of the more controversial Allied strategic decisions of the war, Field Marshal Bernard L. Montgomery (q.v.) ordered XXX Corps to "rest and refit," despite the fact that an eighteen-mile advance farther northward toward Woensdrecht, the Netherlands, would have trapped the German Fifteenth Army. Moreover, only the weak 719th Infantry Division stood between the XXX Corps and the Rhine. The Germans recovered quickly, however, and

Colonel General Kurt Student's (q.v.) First Parachute Army, including the crack 6th Parachute Regiment, was redeployed in the Antwerp–Leopold Canal sector by 5–6 September.

Simultaneously, the Canadian First Army, tied down in the Channel ports and effectively halted for lack of logistic support, might have struck at Breskens, the Netherlands, to seal the final escape route of the Fifteenth Army. Notwithstanding Allied knowledge of the German evacuation, more than 80,000 troops with vehicles and guns were able to escape over the next two weeks via the Breskens-Walcheren-South Beveland route. That would have a disastrous effect on the forthcoming Operation MARKET-GARDEN (q.v.).

Though a great coup in itself, the capture of Antwerp proved an incomplete victory. Without a speedy concurrent advance to trap the Fifteenth Army and eject the Germans from the forty-five-mile-long Scheldt estuary, which controlled the entrance to Antwerp, use of the port was impossible and no immediate easing of the Allies' supply problem was achieved. This point seemingly was disregarded by Montgomery while planning for Operation MARKET-GARDEN monopolized his attention. As Admiral Sir Bertram Ramsay (q.v.) wrote on the day the port was captured, "Antwerp is useless unless the Scheldt estuary is cleared of the enemy."

If available resources were used to continue the advance, perhaps Operation MARKET-GARDEN would have been unnecessary. Not until the failure of this latter operation were serious efforts undertaken to clear the Scheldt (q.v.). Following a costly campaign and an extensive minesweeping operation, Antwerp was opened to Allied shipping on 28 November, nearly three months after its capture. The use of Antwerp proved key in determining the timing of the end of the war in the west.

Previously near the launch sites of V-1 and V-2 rocket strikes against London, Antwerp itself was the target of 1,214 V-weapon attacks during October and November 1944. Though these only lightly damaged the harbor installations, 3,000 people were killed and 12,000 were injured. In further recognition of its importance in sustaining the Allied advance, Antwerp was fixed as the main objective of the ill-fated German Ardennes offensive (q.v.) in December 1944.

Serge M. Durflinger

Additional Reading
Horrocks, Brian, *Corps Commander* (1977).
Moulton, J.L., *Battle for Antwerp* (1978).

Vogel, R., and T. Copp, *Maple Leaf Route: Victory* (1984).

ANVIL, Operation
See FRANCE, SOUTHERN

Anzio (22 January–25 May 1944)
[See map 1 on page 1311]

On 22 January 1944, the Allies achieved at Anzio, Italy, what was probably the most complete tactical surprise of World War II. Starting just after midnight, they landed some 40,000 troops and 5,200 vehicles and secured a beachhead only thirty-seven miles from Rome. But the initial success of Operation SHINGLE was not exploited. The Germans were able not only to surround the beachhead, but also to launch a series of counterattacks that almost eliminated it. The standoff was locked into a stalemate that lasted until late May, when the Allies finally broke out of the beachhead. By then, the Allied force had grown to seven divisions.

Anzio was not the first Allied amphibious assault on Italy. The Allied army, under General Mark W. Clark (q.v.) had landed at Salerno (q.v.) just south of Naples on 9 September 1943. They just narrowly avoided being pushed back into the sea. That close brush with disaster created a "Salerno mentality" that would affect the planners of the Anzio landings. In the minds of American commanders, the first essential step in an amphibious operation was to establish a secure beachhead with a complete concentration of troops, tanks, and artillery, before any attempt was made to exploit inland. This philosophy caused the Allies to hesitate in exploiting their initial success at Anzio.

After Salerno, Clark led the Fifth Army to Naples while the British Eighth Army, commanded by General Sir Oliver Leese (q.v.), moved up the Italian east coast to Foggia. Both armies came under the command of British General Harold Alexander's (q.v.) 15th Army Group. From the very start of the Anzio planning, Alexander had trouble communicating his intent to Clark. Alexander's plan was to land an amphibious force at Anzio "to cut the enemy's main communications in the *Colli Laziali* [the Alban Hills] area southeast of Rome, and then to threaten the [German] rear." Such a landing would force the Germans to weaken their Gustav Line defenses, currently under assault from the front by 15th Army Group, and thus allow the Allies to break through and make quick contact with the beachhead.

Clark put General John Lucas (q.v.), commander of the U.S.-British VI Corps, in charge of the amphibious force. Lucas was not the man for the job. On being told of his mission, Lucas wrote in his diary, "this whole affair had a strong odor of Gallipoli and apparently the same amateur was still on the coach's bench," a disparaging reference to Prime Minister Winston S. Churchill (q.v.). To make matters worse, Clark gave Lucas a directive that was considerably watered down from Alexander's original order.

Clark merely required Lucas to "seize and secure a beachhead in the vicinity of Anzio" and then to "advance on the *Colli Laziali.*" This distinction between advancing *to,* versus advancing *on* the Alban Hills was critical. He added one more bit of advice: "Don't stick your neck out like I did at Salerno." Clark recommended that VI Corps make immediate defensive preparations upon landing and that a strong reserve be kept in readiness in case of a German counterattack.

Lucas's landing force consisted of the U.S. 3rd Infantry Division, commanded by General Lucian Truscott (q.v.), and the British 1st Division, commanded by Major General W.R.C. Penney. The U.S. 1st Armored and 45th Infantry Divisions would follow from Naples as soon as the landing was consolidated. The Americans landed on the beaches south of Anzio, and the British landed to the north. Once the landing was made, VI Corps was to take action based on the level of enemy resistance.

If, as Clark expected, the Germans reacted violently by committing the two divisions believed to be held in reserve in Rome, Lucas had only to seize and secure a beachhead. If, contrary to Clark's estimate, resistance was light, Lucas was to advance "on" the Alban Hills by one of two routes: either up the Albano Road to cut Highway 7, or through Cisterna to cut Highway 7 there and Highway 6 at Valmontone, near the head of the Liri Valley. Since VI Corps was most vulnerable at the port and on the beaches, Clark primarily was interested in holding the beachhead.

The primary German defenses in southern Italy comprised the Gustav Line, under the overall command of Field Marshal Albert Kesselring (q.v.). These substantial works ran from Ortona to Cassino to Gaeta and were manned by 90,000 soldiers from XIV *Panzer Korps* and an additional 60,000 from LXXVI *Panzer Korps.* The true strength of the defenses lay in Kesselring's contingency plans. He made a careful study of all possible landing sites and developed a plan to meet each situation. Each plan was assigned a code word, and he merely had to transmit the signal *"Fall RICH-*

*ARD" f*or six divisions and a corps headquarters t converge on Anzio. The Germans thought the were ready.

Early on 21 January, the Allied amphibiou force left Naples commanded by Rear Admira Frank Lowry. Shortly after midnight, the vessel dropped anchor off Anzio and the assault craft wer lowered into the water. Just before 0200 hours o 22 January, the first wave headed toward th beaches. The assault was spearheaded by the U.S 1st, 3rd, and 4th Ranger Battalions, and the Brit ish Number 9 and 43 Commandos. The ranger landed virtually unopposed, finding only a smat tering of German engineers who were positione to destroy the port if the Allies tried to seize it. Th rangers captured the bulk of these defenders sti in their pajamas, and then dug in along a perimete

The 3rd Infantry Division landed south o Anzio almost unopposed and advanced three mile by mid-morning with all its artillery and tank ashore. They destroyed four bridges along th Mussolini Canal to protect their right flank, an then dug in to prepare for the anticipated counter attack. To the north, the British 1st Divisio moved only slightly more slowly, gaining two mile by midday. The commandos cut the road leadin to Albano and established a roadblock just nort of Anzio. The bulk of the landing force's action was defensive in nature.

By early afternoon of the first day, the port o Anzio was open. The British beaches proved to shallow for effective unloading operations, s Lucas directed the British into the port. By mid night, VI Corps had unloaded 90 percent of it force. The only casualties were eleven killed ninety-seven wounded, and forty-four missing 127 Germans were captured. This unprecedente success did not change the defensive frame of min with which Lucas had come ashore. Between 2 and 28 January, Lucas did little more than buil his logistical base, send out reconnaissance patrol receive more troops, and cautiously advance t within three miles of Cisterna. Entirely frustrate Churchill wrote to Alexander, "I expected to see wildcat roaring into the mountains—and what d I find? A whale wallowing on the beaches."

Kesselring learned of the Allied landing a hour after it started. The operation caught th Germans by surprise, as their attention was focuse on the British X Corps attack across the Garglian Kesselring correctly feared the Allies wanted t seize the Alban Hills, cut the German line of com munications, and force a withdrawal from th Gustav Line. At 0500 hours on 22 Januar Kesselring ordered 4th Parachute Division an

Captured German paratroopers carry a wounded British infantryman at Anzio, 21 May 1944. (IWM NA 15295)

several nearby replacement units of the Hermann Göring *Panzer* Division to block the roads leading from Anzio to the Alban Hills. An hour later, Kesselring requested help from the OKW (q.v.).

Later that day, the OKW mobilized the 715th Division from southern France, the 114th Division from the Balkans, and additional miscellaneous units from Germany amounting to roughly a division. The OKW also authorized Kesselring to activate a new division, the 92nd, from several replacement battalions in northern Italy.

By nightfall, Kesselring also had the 65th Division (less one regiment), elements of 16th SS *Panzergrenadier* Division, 3rd *Panzergrenadier* Division, 71st Division, additional elements of the Hermann Göring *Panzer* Division, 26th *Panzer* Division, and elements of 1st Parachute Division all heading toward Anzio. A thin defensive line formed quickly around the beachhead, and he began to regain his optimism. The Allies apparently were not going to launch a large-scale attack toward the Alban Hills, although Kesselring still

felt this axis would be vulnerable for the next two days. Beyond the Alban Hills, Rome lay virtually undefended.

During the two-day period of German vulnerability, the Allies only slightly expanded their beachhead. German reinforcements continued to stream into the area. Siegfried Westphal (q.v.), Kesselring's chief of staff, noted "on 22 January and even the following day, an audacious and enterprising formation of enemy troops . . . could have penetrated into the city of Rome itself without having to overcome any serious opposition . . . but the landed enemy forces lost time and hesitated."

Kesselring took full advantage of the delay to formulate a plan to eliminate the beachhead. On 15 January, General Eberhard von Mackensen (q.v.) and his Fourteenth Army headquarters arrived at Anzio and took command of now eight divisions deployed there in defense. Kesselring made it clear to him that the primary mission was to counterattack as quickly as possible. On 28 January, von Mackensen submitted a plan for a 1 February attack. The plan was delayed by one day, but before it could be executed, the Allies launched an attack of their own.

On 29 January, the eighth day of the invasion, Lucas finally felt strong enough to conduct a major attack. By this time, the initial landing force had been joined by the U.S. 45th Infantry Division and 1st Armored Division. Both Clark and Alexander had visited the beachhead. They expressed initial satisfaction, but they were also getting anxious for Lucas to act. Lucas's attack plan called for the British 1st Division and Combat Command A (CCA) of the 1st Armored Division to make the main drive toward Albano. The tanks would exploit initial British gains by passing through and attacking the Alban Hills from the west. A supporting attack on Cisterna would also be conducted by the 3rd Infantry Division, spearheaded by the rangers and the 504th Parachute Infantry Regiment.

The British, in an initial success, seized the Rome-Cisterna railroad embankment and continued on to Campoleone, which they took on 31 January. The 1st Armored Division was unable to exploit the gains, however. Muddy roads and a lack of cover stalled the tank attack along the railroad. On the night of 31 January, Lucas relegated the 1st Armored Division back to the corps reserve. The main Allied attack created a two-mile-wide gap in the German defenses around Campoleone but could advance no farther.

The right flank of VI Corps, where Kesselring concentrated his efforts, was in even more serious trouble. Truscott instructed Colonel William O. Darby (q.v.) to infiltrate two of his three ranger battalions down the road to Cisterna. The movement began at 0130 hours on 30 January. Within twelve hours all but six of the 767-man force were either dead or captured. The units following the rangers did not arrive in time to relieve them, and by late afternoon, the 3rd Infantry Division had gained only a mile and a half. The 504th's diversionary attack routed the Germans from the Mussolini Canal, but not before the defenders had destroyed key bridges across Cisterna Creek, creating an obstacle for Allied armor. Truscott launched renewed attacks over the next two days, but he could not reach Cisterna. The initiative passed to the Germans. On 2 February, Alexander and Clark, fearing a counterattack, instructed Lucas to resume the defensive.

Early on 4 February, von Mackensen launched his first attack against the Allied salient around Campoleone. The salient held, but Lucas felt his forward units were dangerously exposed and ordered a withdrawal to a more defensible line.

This final perimeter was strongly fortified with mines and barbed wire. It also coincided with the beachhead line the Allies occupied on 24 January, just two days after the landing.

On the night of 7 February, von Mackensen struck again with an artillery preparation, followed by infantry infiltration, and then a concentrated assault. At first, the British line held, but on 9 February, von Mackensen gained his objective, the factory at Aprilia. By the next day, the Germans held the surrounding ground necessary for a decisive attack. Both the Germans and the Allies had suffered heavy casualties and had to call for reinforcements. von Mackensen's push to the sea had to wait.

In the interim, Clark launched the rest of Fifth Army in a massive attack against Cassino to try to break through the Gustav Line and link up with the Anzio beachhead. The effort was entirely unsuccessful and the initiative once again passed back to Kesselring.

On the morning of 16 February, the Germans launched two diversionary attacks with the Hermann Göring *Panzer* Division and the 4th Parachute Division. Then they launched a two-wave main attack. The first wave included the elite *Infantrie-Lehr Regiment* and parts of 3rd *Panzergrenadier*, 114th, and 715th Divisions. They attacked along a six-mile front just east of the Albano-Anzio Road. The attack hit the boundary between the 157th and 179th Infantry Regiments of the U.S. 45th Infantry Division. Commitment of reserve battalions halted the German drive. Despite the heavy casualties, von Mackensen insisted on keeping heavy pressure on the Allies. He continued his first-wave attacks throughout the night. By the afternoon of 17 February, he stretched Lucas's final beachhead line to the breaking point.

At dawn on 17 February, von Mackensen committed his second wave. The 29th *Panzergrenadier* and 26th *Panzer* Divisions made a serious penetration against the 179th Infantry Regiment. They were on the verge of achieving a breakthrough when the German drive shifted inexplicably to the right. There they struck the relatively fresh 180th Infantry Regiment, and after four hours of desperate fighting the German attack stalled. For the next two days, the Germans launched several ineffective attacks that merely confirmed the beachhead would hold. Although the entire Allied position was within range of German artillery, the Germans were short on ammunition for the big guns, and the Allies still had air superiority.

Von Mackensen had not accomplished his objective, but his offensive had serious repercussions for the Allies. The five-day attack inflicted approximately 5,000 Allied casualties, bringing the total for the operation to almost 19,000. The Germans, however, suffered nearly identical losses, and both sides had to stop to reorganize. On the Allied side, this involved a change of leadership. One month to the day after the start of the operation Clark relieved an exhausted Lucas and appointed Truscott commander of VI Corps.

Truscott had a fighting reputation, and he quickly set out to abate the feeling of despair along the beachhead. Under him, the Allies repulsed the last of the German attacks at Anzio. After suffering more than 3,000 additional casualties, Kesselring decided to break off operations. With Adolf Hitler's (q.v.) concurrence, Kesselring started to withdraw to the Caesar Line, which ran from the mouth of the Tiber, through Cisterna, Valmontone, and Avezzano, to Pescara.

Alexander, meanwhile, reorganized his forces for Operation DIADEM, the final assault on the Gustav Line. At Anzio, 34th Infantry Division relieved 3rd Infantry Division which, after sixty-seven days of frontline fighting, was placed in corps reserve. Truscott's force now consisted of the British 1st and 5th Divisions; the U.S. 3rd, 34th, and 45th Infantry and 1st Armored Divisions; the newly arrived U.S. 36th Division; and the brigade-size U.S.-Canadian 1st Special Services Force (q.v.).

Operation DIADEM started on 11 May and got off to a slow start. On 18 May, the German strong point at the Monte Cassino (q.v.) monastery finally fell to the Polish 3rd Carpathian Division. Even before this loss, Kesselring knew he was in trouble and began pulling reinforcements from his forces around Anzio. On 16 May, he ordered 29th *Panzergrenadier* Division to move south and advised von Mackensen to be prepared to provide additional support. They arrived too late to halt the Allied advance and Kesselring had to pull 26th *Panzer* Division from Anzio as well. The situation at the beachhead was now very favorable for a breakout.

With Allied forces within forty miles of Anzio and the German forces severely weakened, Alexander ordered Clark to prepare to break out and seize the town of Valmontone, east of the Alban Hills, in order to cut off the escape of General Heinrich von Vietinghoff's (q.v.) Tenth Army. Alexander, with access to intelligence from ULTRA (q.v.), knew that the Tenth Army was close to falling apart. Clark, however, was obsessed with capturing Rome, and he concocted a plan to penetrate the Caesar Line before it was fully manned by the German forces withdrawing to the north.

On the evening of 22 May, elements of British divisions at Anzio began a diversionary attack from the left flank of VI Corps. At 0630 hours the following morning, American forces launched the main attack on the right, but the attack ran up against extensive minefields and the going was slow. By the end of the first day, the Americans reached the line of the Cisterna-Rome railroad but were unable to take Cisterna.

On 24 May, U.S. II Corps units moving up from the south captured Terracina, only 30 miles from Cisterna. Kesselring then started a full-scale pullback to the Caesar Line. The next day, units from II and VI Corps made contact, and 125 days after the first landings, Anzio was no longer a beachhead. Clark, meanwhile, sent four divisions racing northeast toward Rome and one division toward Valmontone. The drive was stopped in its tracks by three German divisions. Clark's Fifth Army entered Rome on 4 June 1944; but as a result of Clark's obsession for Rome, most of the German Tenth Army escaped.

Anzio was a costly adventure for the Allies. During the first month, the casualty toll reached 19,000. The Allies failed to destroy Kesselring's forces, and months of tough fighting in Italy lay ahead. Anzio had, however, shown that the Germans were vulnerable to an amphibious assault. Allied planners also drew a very valuable lesson from Anzio; an amphibious operation required a strong initial landing followed by an immediate drive to key points inland. This lesson was not forgotten by those who planned the Normandy (q.v.) landings; and therein, perhaps, lies the greatest significance of Anzio.

Kevin Dougherty

Additional Reading
Allen, William L., *Anzio: Edge of Disaster* (1978).
Blumenson, Martin, *Anzio, The Gamble That Failed* (1963).
———, *Salerno to Cassino* (1969).
Graham, Dominick, and Shelford Bidwell, *Tug of War: The Battle for Italy 1943–1945* (1986).
United States Army, Historical Division, *Anzio Beachhead (22 January–25 May, 1944)* (1948).

Ardennes Offensive (16 December 1944–30 January 1945)
[See map 2 on page 1312]

In the fall of 1944, the German leadership knew

A

that the broad Allied advance was slowing down in front of the West Wall (q.v.) and that the Allied lines were only weakly held in the Ardennes sector. Thus, sometime in September, Adolf Hitler (q.v.) decided that the *Wehrmacht* should go on the offensive in the west in November, when the probability of bad weather would reduce Allied air support.

The planned German offensive was to be launched between Monschau and Echternach, through the northern part of the Ardennes Forest. Part of the reason for the choice of that sector was the fact that in May 1940 a rapid thrust toward France had succeeded there. Moreover, east of that sector lay the heavily forested Eifel region, where large units could be massed in relative secrecy.

In order to prevent the Allies from detecting the preparations for the attack, the highest levels of operational security measures were implemented. Even the *Oberbefehlshaber-West* (commander in chief West, or *OB-West*), Field Marshal Gerd von Rundstedt (q.v.), the commander in chief of German Army Group B, Field Marshal Walter Model (q.v.), and the commanders of the attacking field armies were only informed of the plan at the end of October. The participating corps and divisional commanders were not informed until 8 December.

Hitler's plan, known as the "Big Solution," was to cut off the American and British units south of the line Bastogne-Brussels-Antwerp, to destroy those units, and to take Antwerp and its harbor. Antwerp, about 160 kilometers away, was the principal Allied port. At that stage in the war, however, even Hitler could not have believed in a German *Endsieg* (final victory) anymore. He, as well as the high military leaders, knew that the war could not be won after the successful invasion of the Allies in the west.

The two senior commanders in the west and the three generals who were supposed to command the attacking armies did not agree with the goal for the offensive. They had grave doubts about the possibility of success because of the German lack of men and materiel. They suggested instead, a "Small Solution." With a double attack from the Eifel and the area of Roermond, they wanted to destroy the Allied forces in the area of Aachen. Hitler, as usual, imposed his own views.

Originally, the attack was scheduled for 25 November. The generals, however, did not think they could have their units ready soon enough, and managed to win several delays. Finally, the attack date for Operation *WACHT AM RHEIN* (WATCH ON THE RHINE) was set for 16 December 1944.

Even with the extra few weeks to prepare, the activities were intense. The Germans had to replace the materiel they lost during the retreat from France, they had to reconstitute units that had been decimated in previous fighting, and they had to shore up the morale of the troops. The last task was the most difficult. By that point, the German soldier had lost all faith in the continuous string of announcements about fresh reserves, new positions, and "miracle weapons." Particularly demoralizing to the ground troops was the overwhelming superiority of the Allied air forces, coupled with the disappearance of the *Luftwaffe* from the skies overhead.

In the end, it proved impossible by the start of the offensive to build up the forces of Army Group B as much as the planners had hoped. The tank units of the Fifth *Panzer* and Sixth *Panzer* Armies were in fair shape, generally well equipped and high in morale. Most of Army Group B's other units, however, consisted of *Volksgrenadiers*, recently drafted. They were poorly armed, supplied and trained.

Terrain would be another problem. The Germans would have to negotiate rivers with high water levels and snowy mountain areas. The Eifel and Ardennes Mountains had few roads, none of them good. The difficult grades, steep banks, and winter road conditions would cause severe difficulties for the attacking units with vehicles.

Von Rundstedt had a total of twelve *Volksgrenadier* divisions, seven *Panzer* divisions, two airborne divisions, and Hitler's escort brigade for the Ardennes offensive. The Sixth *Panzer* Army commanded by *SS-Oberstgruppenführer* Josef Dietrich (q.v.), was positioned in the north; the Fifth *Panzer* Army, commanded by General Hasso von Manteuffel (q.v.) was in the center; and the Seventh Army, commanded by General Erich Brandenberger (q.v.), was in the south. The reserves, which were brought up after the start of the offensive, consisted of two more *Panzer* divisions, four infantry divisions, and two *Panzergrenadier* divisions. The attacking units had 420 tanks and assault guns, 1,900 artillery pieces, and 240,000 troops.

The *Luftwaffe* also made extensive preparations to support the operation. A *Luftwaffe* West Command was set up especially for the offensive. That command was assigned the remaining combat groups from the *Luftflotte Reich*, including groups located at Duisburg, Vogelsang, Trier, Frankfurt, Lippe, Soesterburg, and Quakenbrück. The III *Flak-Korps* was assigned to Army Group B to provide air defense coverage to the ground forces.

The *Luftwaffe* had three primary missions: (1) destroy a large portion of the Allied fighter-bomber force by conducting attack missions on all Allied bases close to the front; (2) provide air cover to the units on the ground; and (3) protect the German bridgeheads across the Meuse River. To support the offensive, the *Luftwaffe* had a total of 1,492 fighters, 171 bombers, ninety-one attack planes, and forty reconnaissance aircraft.

The staff of *OB-West* was sceptical about the ability of the *Luftwaffe* to carry out its assigned missions. At best, the Germans could only hope to obtain temporary and local air superiority during the first phase of the attack. The general opinion was that despite the careful preparations, the *Luftwaffe* most likely was not going to be able to influence the action or protect the ground forces against air attack.

During the course of the preparations, the generals tasked with leading the attack realized that their initial assessments concerning the low probability of success were justified. It just was not possible to reconstitute all the units and to establish them in the necessary attack positions. The Sixth *Panzer* Army, which was supposed to carry the main effort against Antwerp, seemed to be the only really powerful unit the Germans could muster. Nonetheless, the preparations proceeded, and by the morning of 16 December, 240,000 troops and their air support were in position. It was, however, the last such military force the Third *Reich* would assemble.

The high command of the German armed forces (OKW) (q.v.), under the direction of its operations chief, Colonel General Alfred Jodl (q.v.), knew that only absolute secrecy in the preparations would insure the surprise necessary to get through the Allied lines without encountering strong resistance. On 5 November, the *OKW* issued a secrecy order. Everyone concerned with the plans and preparations had to read the order and sign a statement that he understood that violation of the order could be punishable by death. All files and communications were transported by special couriers only. The couriers were not allowed to fly, and no information concerning the operation could be passed by phone or any other form of telecommunications. The security plan even concealed the object of the preparations from the average German soldier until the very hour of the attack. They, as well as the Allies, were supposed to believe that they were forming groups to counterattack into the Allied flanks in case of a breakthrough toward the Rhine.

Similar measures were taken at the tactical level. The Germans cut back on reconnaissance patrols, and completely abandoned them after 1 December to prevent deserters from compromising the operation. This resulted in some serious disadvantages. At the start of the attack, the Germans did not have a complete picture of the Allied situation in front of them and the assault companies did not have explicit intelligence on the terrain.

The Germans also planned two special operations in support of the offensive. Operation *GREIF* involved 2,000 English- and "American"-speaking troops in Allied uniforms under the command of SS-*Obersturmbannführer* Otto Skorzeny (q.v.). Their mission was to occupy the Meuse passages between Liège and Namur and cause confusion. Operation *STÖSSER* involved twenty transport gliders and 300 to 400 airborne troops under the command of Lieutenant Colonel Friederich von der Heydt. Their mission was to drop in at Hohe Venn on the northern flank of the penetration and open two important passes.

Like all other preparations, planning for the two special operations went unnoticed. The ban on telecommunications traffic also meant that no indicators of the attack came through ULTRA (q.v.) intercepts. Ironically, at that point in the war, higher-level Allied intelligence had become so dependent on ULTRA that it is doubtful they would have believed other indicators without ULTRA conformation.

At the beginning of December, three Allied army groups with seven field armies stood ready for the final assault on the *Reich*. Field Marshal Bernard L. Montgomery's (q.v.) 21st Army Group covered the north of the line, the Brussels-Maastricht-Mönchengladbach sector. His force included the Canadian First and the British Second Armies. Lieutenant General Omar N. Bradley's (q.v.) 12th Army Group held the Allied center, Troyes-Nancy-Kaiserslautern. Bradley's Ninth Army was centered around Aachen, his First Army between Eupen and Luxembourg, and his Third Army south of the Saarland. General Jacob Devers's (q.v.) 6th Army Group held the Allied southern sector.

The Allies considered their situation stable at the start of December. Things were quiet in the Netherlands, as well as between Aachen and Arnhem. In the Ruhr, they tried to push back the German bridgehead west of Düren. Recently, heavy fighting had taken place only in the Hürtgen Forest (q.v.). The Ardennes sector was very quiet. On the evening of 15 December, the American front between Echternach and Monschau was only lightly held. Three divisions had just moved into the sector, the 9th Armored Division, the experienced but tired 28th Infantry Division, and the green 106th Infantry Division. On the south end of the line stood the veteran 4th Infantry Division. In the north were the veteran 2nd Infantry Division, and the relatively new, but reliable, 99th Infantry Division, respectively.

There were few reserves in this part of the front. The American troops believed the war was over and they hoped to be back home by Christmas. They did little reconnaissance to their front. Bradley accepted the relatively weak position of this sector of the line as a calculated risk. He considered the Ardennes to be an obstacle for tanks and he did not expect further fighting there. The six divisions on the 120-kilometer-long line had about 85,000 soldiers and 400 artillery pieces. They were far inferior to the strength the Germans had massed.

Operation *WACHT AM RHEIN* started at 0530 hours on 16 December. In four different phases the fight would last until 10 January 1945. Army Group B attacked the American positions with the Sixth *Panzer* Army spearheading, the Fifth *Panzer* Army on the left, and the Seventh Army providing cover on the southern flank. North flank security also was provided by the Fifteenth Army, which was not attacking. The plan called for the Sixth *Panzer* Army to reach Antwerp in seven days.

During the first four days, the German forces broke through the weak American positions and reached the line Monschau-Malmédy-St. Vith-Houffalize-Bastogne-Echternach. The ground they took, however, was less than what they had expected. American resistance developed quickly, weather and road conditions were unfavorable, and the German supply situation was extremely bad.

The Sixth *Panzer* Army advanced between Monschau and Losheim toward Liège. It was held up, however at Elsenborn by the U.S. V Corps, and particularly, the 99th Infantry Division. The Sixth *Panzer* Army could not deploy all its forces adequately because it was bound to five main roads, which were crowded with traffic. On 18 December, the *Panzer* units finally broke through to Stavelot, where they were stopped temporarily by the first American counterattack. The Germans did not manage to make another significant penetration into the V Corps sector until 19 December.

The Fifth *Panzer* Army attacked the U.S. VIII Corps positions between St. Vith and Posingen. By 19 December, it advanced past St. Vith (q.v.), trapping two U.S. divisions in a pocket. The LVIII and XLVII *Panzer Korps* were able to deploy their forces, but they were not able to fight effectively because of strong American resistance. The Fifth *Panzer* Army finally achieved a major breakthrough when it reached the Houffalize-Wiltz Line on 19 December. The Germans, however, had not reached the Meuse within two days as originally planned. The German advance had been held up long enough for the Americans to assemble and commit their reserves.

The German Seventh Army had orders to cross the Our and Sauer Rivers between Vianden and Echternach and to reach the Gedinne-Libramont-Marte-Wasserbillig Line. Instead of one day, the Seventh Army needed four days to overcome American resistance and pass the rivers. The slow advance, however, did not disrupt the link with the Fifth *Panzer* Army on the right. The Sixth *Panzer* Army, trying to avoid American strength, managed to reach Salm with its *Kampfgruppe* Peiper; but the Sixth *SS Panzer* also bogged down along the line Basse-Badeux-Vaux-Chavanne-Sadzot.

On 19 December, senior Allied commanders met at Verdun to consider how to deal with the German offensive. Their plan called for a counterattack from the south by General George S. Patton's (q.v.) Third Army. Patton, who was scheduled to launch his own major offensive toward the Saarland on 19 December, was to leave one of his three corps in the line, and attack north with the other two by 22 December. Meanwhile, the German penetration had driven so deep that the U.S. First and Ninth Armies were effectively cut off from Bradley's 12th Army Group headquarters. Late that day, the Allies made the decision to transfer operational control of those two armies to Montgomery's 21st Army Group, until the Germans could be pushed back and normal communications restored.

Four days after the start of the attack, Army Group B still was not at the Meuse. That schedule, of course, had been unrealistic. The planners severely underestimated the difficulties caused by the weather and the enemy. On the average, the Germans had advanced twenty kilometers into Allied terrain. Contrary to the plan, the Fifth *Panzer* Army had reached the farthest, approaching Bastogne. Meanwhile, airborne Operation *STÖSSER* and Operation *GREIF* had failed.

Despite its only limited success, the German offensive continued. Hitler shifted the main effort of the operation from the Sixth *Panzer* Army to the Fifth *Panzer* Army, which now was supposed to advance toward Antwerp. Accordingly, the Fifth

Panzer was allocated all available reserves. It succeeded in moving farther west, with elements of the 2nd *Panzer* Division reaching Celles on 24 December. Once more, however, the German supply problem contributed to the advance stalling. With the Fifth *Panzer* Army at a standstill, von Manteuffel turned his attention to the encircled American position at Bastogne (q.v.), deep in his rear.

Until about 18 December, the Seventh Army was successful in screening the left flank of the Fifth *Panzer* Army. From that point, American counterattacks became stronger, and the Germans lost the bridgeheads on the far side of the Sauer.

By Christmas Day 1944, the Germans had gained as much ground as they were ever going to. Lack of transportation resources and especially fuel made their situation worse. Their existing reserves could not move up. At that point, they had lost so many men and so much materiel that the OKW considered the "Big Solution" a failure. On 24 December, the Allies assumed the initiative. They blocked the Meuse passages and started to move in on the German flanks, placing their main concentration in the southern flank of the "Bulge."

On 24 December, *OB-West* asked Hitler for permission to halt the offensive. As witnessed so

many times in the past, Hitler insisted on "continuing the fighting." The operations plan was changed, however. Now all Allied forces east of the Meuse were to be destroyed—essentially the "Small Solution." The events after Christmas, however, were dominated completely by Allied initiatives. The British attacked with the 21st Army Group from the north; the Americans with the 12th Army Group's Third Army from the south. The German counterattacks in the north were unsuccessful, and on 28 December the Sixth *Panzer* Army went over to the defensive. The Fifth *Panzer* Army's 2nd *Panzer* Division, which penetrated the farthest west, was caught in a pocket near Celles (q.v.) and virtually destroyed. From that point on, the path was now wide open for Allied counterattacks into the Bulge from the west.

The situation was especially bad for the Germans on the left flank of the Seventh Army. There, the Americans were vastly superior in men and materiel. Patton's Third Army, for example, used more than 133,000 vehicles to transport troops, materiel, and ammunition north for the counterattack. The Third Army broke through to Bastogne on 26 December and threatened the rear of the Fifth *Panzer* Army.

The Allies were not in position to mount a

A U.S. infantryman from the 424th Infantry Regiment, 106th Infantry Division, kneels at the edge of a snow-blanketed field near Medell, Belgium, December 1944. He wears a white camouflage suit and carries an M-1 rifle. (IWM EA 51089)

major counterattack until 3 January. Up to that point, the main weight of the Allied counterstrikes was carried by their air forces. Starting on 24 December, the first day of good flying weather, they committed 10,000 aircraft against the German ground forces. For days, German units were exposed to uninterrupted attack from Allied fighters and bombers. The *Luftwaffe* was almost helpless to prevent the attacks. The German Army now was forced to do all its moving by night.

On New Year's Day 1945, the *Luftwaffe* used what aircraft it could muster to conduct Operation *BODENPLATTE* (BASEPLATE) (q.v.) against seventeen Allied air bases in Belgium, Holland, and northern France. The attack was a complete surprise to the Allies. The attackers destroyed airports and aircraft and caused major losses in men and materiel. The return flight, however, turned into a disaster for the *Luftwaffe*. Because of a lack of coordination with their own air defenses, the Germans shot down 300 of their own planes, losing 280 pilots. The *Luftwaffe*, in effect, had committed suicide.

The last phase of the Ardennes battle started on 3 January 1945. The Allies launched major attacks against the German lines, intending to link up the U.S. First and Third Armies at Houffalize, in the center of the Bulge. Such a move would put the German units in the west end of the Bulge in a pocket. At that point, the German high command suddenly decided to shift their attention to Alsace, at the extreme southern end of the Allied line. With little regard for the overall military situation, Army Group B was ordered to hold their positions. As a prestige objective, Bastogne, also was to be retaken. Operation *NORDWIND* (NORTH WIND) (q.v.), against Devers' 6th Army Group, was launched on New Year's Eve 1944. Even though the Allies were weak in that sector, that attack failed too.

Because of bad weather, snow, and low temperatures, the Allied counterattack into the Bulge made slow progress. The Germans, however, were systematically pushed back to the east. When it became obvious that the German units west of Houffalize were in danger of being cut off, Hitler allowed Army Group B to withdraw to the line Vielsalm-Dechamps-Wiltz. That retreat was completed on 13 January. On 17 January, the Germans started to withdraw to their original West Wall positions. By 30 January, they were back where they had started on 16 December.

The Ardennes offensive had failed. The costs were heavy on both sides. The Germans lost 17,200 killed, 34,000 wounded, and about 50,000

captured. The Americans suffered 10,276 killed, 47,493 wounded, and 23,218 missing. British casualties were 1,400. Even with the high losses, however, there still remained four million Allied troops in three army groups ready to move into Germany. The Ardennes offensive was the last desperate major German operation on the western front before the final collapse of the Third *Reich*.

Ekkehart Guth

Additional Reading

Cole, Hugh M., *The Ardennes: Battle of the Bulge* (1965).

Dupuy, Trevor N., David L. Bongard, and Richard C. Anderson, Jr., *Hitler's Last Gamble: The Battle of the Bulge, December 1944–January 1945* (1995).

Eisenhower, John S.D., *The Bitter Woods* (1969).

Elstob, Peter, *Bastogne: The Road Block* (1968).

Jung, H., *Die Ardennenoffensive 1944/45* (1971).

MacDonald, Charles B., *A Time for Trumpets: The Untold Story of the Battle of the Bulge* (1985).

Arnhem (17–26 September 1944)

[See map 3 on page 1313]

The long-awaited cross-channel invasion began on 6 June 1944, and after hard fighting, the Allies had broken out of the Normandy peninsula as German troops fled back to the Rhine River. By late August, Paris (q.v.) had been liberated and the Allies were deep into eastern France and approaching Belgium. Critical supplies began to run short for the Allies, however, and the offensive that had produced such spectacular results ground to a halt. At that point, there developed an intense debate between two of General Dwight D. Eisenhower's chief subordinates, Generals George S. Patton and Bernard L. Montgomery (qq.v.).

Basically, Eisenhower favored a broad front approach to defeating the Germans. This meant there would be an equal allocation of supplies, especially gasoline, to all units in contact with the enemy. Patton put a great deal of pressure on his commander to allow his U.S. Third Army to continue its highly successful advance, while Montgomery favored what he called a "dagger thrust" into the industrial Ruhr Valley of Germany. Pressures began to build on Eisenhower to consider Montgomery's plan for a narrow thrust across Holland, breaching the Rhine, moving into the Ruhr, and thereby depriving the Germans of their industrial heartland. Montgomery proposed an audacious plan involving three airborne divisions seizing key terrain in Holland, opening the roads to the Rhine River bridge at Arnhem, Holland, and passing a large armored force through the paratroops.

The plan, Operation MARKET-GARDEN, was an excellent concept, except that Montgomery had never been known for anything but caution. His proposed armored force, the British XXX Corps, under Lieutenant General Sir Brian Horrocks (q.v.), had seen extensive combat, was understrength, and had tired, battle-weary troops. Yet, there were political reasons to listen to Montgomery. He was persuasive, and his plan offered to end the war quickly and keep casualties down, a proposition that appealed to Eisenhower.

For airborne divisions, Montgomery proposed the use of the U.S. 82nd Airborne under Brigadier General James Gavin (q.v.), and the U.S. 101st Airborne under Major General Maxwell Taylor (q.v.), both experienced paratroop commanders. The British 1st Airborne Division was basically untested and was led by Major General Robert Urquhart (q.v.), a non-airborne general. The Polish 1st Parachute Brigade, commanded by the competent Major General Stanisław Sosabowski (q.v.), would reinforce the British.

Strategy consists in having an objective that is clear and obtainable and then formulating a plan to reach that objective based on the resources at hand. Eisenhower's strategic objective was simply to defeat Nazi Germany with as few casualties as possible. Montgomery's Operation MARKET-GARDEN, if properly executed, could advance that objective. The planning for Operation MARKET-GARDEN fell to the British, who allocated the key objectives to either relatively green forces, as in the case of the British 1st Airborne Division, or to tired and battle-spent troops, like XXX Corps. There was a shortage of aircraft to deliver the para- and glider troops and to resupply the force by air.

The British were assigned drop zones almost ten miles from their objective at Arnhem, which meant that the key element of tactical surprise would be missing. Also, intelligence was building a picture of German forces in the area. From aerial photographs and information from the Dutch resistance, a picture emerged that should have given cause for reconsideration, but headquarters planners chose not to believe what they saw.

The plan did not get all combat forces on the ground quickly. As the events played out, the Polish 1st Parachute Brigade did not arrive on the battlefield until after the battle was lost. To make matters worse, the road assigned to Lieutenant General Brian Horrock's XXX Corps was an old,

narrow, two-lane road that was elevated. That meant German antitank gunners would have clear targets. Montgomery's headquarters, however, discounted German resistance and the plan went ahead.

Eisenhower also was under pressure from Generals George C. Marshall and Henry H. "Hap" Arnold (qq.v.) to make good use of airborne troops for strategic operations. The Allied supreme commander agreed to Montgomery's plan, and the date for Operation MARKET-GARDEN was set for 17 September 1944. The initial briefing was conducted by Lieutenant General Frederick M. "Boy" Browning (q.v.), commanding British I Airborne Corps, who represented Montgomery's plan forcefully. The Americans and Poles, however, were aghast at the short time for preparation, the lack of intelligence, and the uncertainty about follow-up airlift for troops, gliders, and resupply. Urquhart, who was not very familiar with either paratroops or glider operations, accepted drop zones for the British that were eight to ten miles from their objective, the Arnhem Bridge. The fate of the operation was sealed.

The U.S. 82nd and 101st Airborne Divisions made good drops, even though the operation was conducted during daylight. The British, however, dropped too far from the Arnhem Bridge, and critical supplies and equipment were lost when gliders crashed. To make matters worse, the Germans recovered a complete set of plans for Operation MARKET-GARDEN from one of the crash sites, and they therefore knew from the outset what the Allies would do.

To compound the impending disaster, only a few kilometers to the north and east of Arnhem were the 9th and 10th *SS Panzer* Divisions. The Germans were fortunate enough to have three dynamic and experienced *Waffen-SS* commanders in charge. The 9th *SS Panzer (Hohenstauffen)* Division, was commanded by Colonel Walter Harzer, and the 10th *SS Panzer (Frundsberg)* Division, by Major General Heinz Harmel. Despite the fact they were understrength from continual combat, their morale was high and they were commanded by the proficient II *SS Panzer Korps* commander, General Willi Bittrich. To complicate matters for the Allies, the newly formed German First Parachute Army was being assembled and rushed to General Walter Model (q.v.), commander in chief west. The Allies had no idea of the growing might of the enemy in and around Arnhem. As British para- and glider troops were landing on their drop zones, they came under heavy small arms and artillery fire from the *Waffen-SS* soldiers.

Communications between British Airborne forces on the ground were nearly nonexistent, and a battalion of parachute infantry sent to seize and hold the key objective of the Arnhem Bridge could not be contacted. The *SS Panzer* troops continued to hit the British near the drop zones. Bittrich immediately sent SS forces against the lone British battalion near the bridge. Instead of achieving surprise, the British paratroops now found themselves besieged. Lieutenant Colonel John D. Frost (q.v.), commanding the 2nd Battalion, 1st Parachute Brigade, held out until he was wounded and the houses used by the British were literally burning around them. With Allied troops only a few miles from Arnhem, Frost surrendered what was left of his command.

The 101st Airborne Division engaged in sharp fighting north of Eindhoven, and the 82nd Airborne Division was attacked by German forces that had taken up positions in the *Reichswald* to the east of Nijmegen. The critical task assigned to the 82nd Airborne Division, seizing the Nijmegen Bridge over the Waal River, was slowed down by fierce SS resistance. To complicate the operational picture, Horrock's XXX Corps discovered that the Germans were in front of them in force and were determined to contest every kilometer of the exposed highway. Elements of the German Fifteenth Army, which had been tied down in the Pas de Calais because of the Allied deception plan known as Operation FORTITUDE (q.v.), had escaped into Holland and now began to appear on the battlefield.

Bad weather began to hinder resupply and reinforcement efforts, especially to the battered British forces. There were two separate agendas for the forces engaged in Operation MARKET-GARDEN. The ground forces believed that their requirements for men and materiel should take first priority. The air arm, however, was equally concerned with the preservation of aircraft, of which there was a shortage. Since it was unclear where units were—especially the British 1st Airborne Division—due to a lack of communications, the air force was reluctant to fly missions that, in their opinion, had little chance of success and endangered crews and the dwindling supply of airplanes.

XXX Corps' advance up the road to link up with the paratroopers continually fell behind schedule because of fierce German resistance, the nature of the road, and the tendency to fight each engagement as a set-piece battle. The advancing infantry should have been supported by tanks and artillery, but bringing the proper support over such crowded,

congested roads made the going slow. The Germans blew up a number of critical small bridges, which required engineer units to move bridging equipment from the rear of the column to the front against scattered but effective German resistance.

Montgomery's objective was to "bounce" across the Rhine River with as much speed as possible, but he failed to achieve that objective, which was the key to Operation MARKET-GARDEN. All he got was the near-destruction of the 1st Airborne Division. Had it not been for heroic efforts by Urquhart and his embattled staff, the Germans could very well have totally annihilated the unit. As it was, when the British were withdrawn they were only able to bring out about 2,000 paratroopers, having to leave many of their wounded behind.

The 82nd and 101st Airborne Divisions suffered almost 25 percent casualties, and the British XXX Corps suffered a similar fate. The Polish 1st Parachute Brigade suffered as badly as the British paratroopers, although they were dropped into a cauldron after the contest was clearly lost. Allied troops would not cross the Arnhem bridge until late in the war.

After such successful fighting across France and into Belgium, why did the Allies fail so badly at Arnhem? The operation was conceived to deliver a lightning blow and take the Rhine River bridge. There appears to have been an air of overconfidence at Montgomery's headquarters that would not allow the planners to believe what intelligence was telling them about the condition and the strength of the Germans in Holland. The German Army was battered, but it was not beaten. By the luck of the draw, the well-commanded 9th and 10th *SS Panzer* Divisions were resting very near the British drop zones and the ultimate objective.

There were not enough aircraft to bring in the troops the first day, and despite heroic sacrifices by aircrews, the British simply could not be resupplied with critical materiel. Too much of the needed equipment for the British was destroyed or rendered useless in the first drop. Then there was the road that ran from the Belgian border for almost 100 miles to Arnhem. It simply was unsuitable for the timetable set by Montgomery's planners. It was narrow and elevated, and had too many bridges. There was almost no maneuver room, and that cost the British time. Although Horrock's XXX Corps certainly did not lack experience or bravery, it was a fought-out unit.

The error rested with Montgomery's planning and selection of objectives for the units involved. What should have taken three days dragged on, and time was on the side of the German defenders. Operation MARKET-GARDEN lasted from 17 to 26 September 1944. Regardless of what post-war apologists have written, it was a stinging Allied defeat that bolstered the Germans' confidence and paved the way for their December counteroffensive. The defeat also consolidated the Allies' wiser broad front strategy for the final push into Nazi Germany.

James J. Cooke

Additional Reading

Bauer, Cornelius, *The Battle of Arnhem: The Betrayal Myth Refuted* (1966).

Cholewczynski, George F., *Poles Apart: The Polish Airborne at the Battle of Arnhem* (1993).

Gavin, James M., *On to Berlin: Battles of an Airborne Commander* (1978).

Greenfield, Kent R. (ed.), *Command Decisions* (1987).

Hibbert, C., *The Battle of Arnhem* (1984).

Lewin, Ronald, *Montgomery as Military Commander* (1971).

Ryan, Cornelius, *A Bridge Too Far* (1974).

Atlantic Campaign (1939–1945)

[See maps 4 and 5 on pages 1314 and 1315]

The "Battle of the Atlantic," as it was called then, was the longest campaign of World War II. For the Western Allies, particularly Great Britain, it was the most crucial. Virtually all of Great Britain's raw materials and all of the Western Allies' supplies to their forces had to transit the Atlantic Ocean. Defeat in the Atlantic, therefore, meant defeat for that country, while it was their success in the Atlantic that enabled the Western Allies to conduct the amphibious landings that opened the "Second Front."

For that reason, it was the Atlantic campaign that offered Germany's best hope for defeating Great Britain and preventing an American landing in Europe. Thus, the stage was set for a desperate struggle—one in which no quarter was requested and none granted, and one in which more than 162.8 million tons of shipping and 70,000 lives would be lost.

The Atlantic campaign began on the evening of 3 September 1939, when the German U-boat *U-30* sunk the liner *Athenia,* less than ten hours after Britain declared war on Germany. The campaign ended three days after the German surrender when *U-2336* sank the Canadian merchant ship *Avondale Park.* The battles fought in between stretched across the full length and expanse of the Atlantic Ocean. Most of them took place in the open ocean and involved groups of submarines and groups of antisubmarine escorts fighting over merchant ships in convoys. That was the essence of the Atlantic campaign—a war of attrition.

For Germany, every merchant ship sunk not only destroyed the ship and its cargo, but ensured that no other cargo would be carried in that ship. For the Allies, every U-boat sunk not only prevented the attack of the moment but also prevented future attacks by that unit. In that context, it was a race between the German "ship sinkers" (primarily submarines) and Allied shipbuilders on the one hand, and between the "U-boat sinkers" and the "U-boat builders" on the other. It was a race in which technology and tactics played a decisive supporting role. It was the application of these tactics and technology that ultimately determined victory.

Germany entered the campaign with a limited technical but significant intelligence superiority. Its Type VII U-boats were the state of the art, with the world's best hydrophones, periscope optics, and underwater performance. Unfortunately, they were limited in numbers and saddled with defective torpedoes. Moreover, the commander of the U-boat force, Admiral Karl Dönitz (q.v.), had no control of and only limited influence over the U-boat design, construction, and modification programs. He had even less influence over the Navy's overall naval construction program (*see* Plan Z). Grand Admiral Erich Raeder (q.v.), commander of the *Kriegsmarine* (German Navy), was the man who controlled these things, and his views on naval strategy were quite different from Dönitz's—at least initially.

Although Raeder agreed that any war with Britain would necessitate a naval campaign against its commerce, he felt that surface raiders, not U-boats, would be the predominant instrument in that campaign. He even established a clandestine overseas logistics system to support his raiders. The U-boats would have an important supporting role, in the same way aircraft would, but they clearly would be subordinate to the surface forces.

Germany started the war with battleships having a higher construction priority than U-boats. Aircraft carrier construction was slowed and then halted. The events of the war's early months would change Raeder's views on U-boats, but an important early lead was squandered. Germany entered the war with only forty-six operational U-boats out of a total force of sixty-three. Few were under construction, and the force mix was not optimized for the campaign ahead.

Raeder wanted a "balanced submarine force" and thus the pace of construction did not increase during the first several months of the war. More significantly, his basic conservatism and skepticism about new technology and submarines led him to restrict research and development into new technologies. The result was that the *Kriegsmarine* in general, and the U-boat arm in particular, achieved little technical progress during the course of the war. By late 1942, Germany faced an enemy at sea that was technically as well as numerically superior.

Dönitz tried to redress the balance after he assumed command of the *Kriegsmarine* in January 1943. By bringing both the technicians and fleet commanders together, he tried to rationalize the research and development effort to satisfy operational requirements. He streamlined the bureaucracy and prioritized programs in an effort to accelerate development. He was partially successful. *Schnorchels* (snorkels) and improved batteries gave his U-boats better underwater performance. Torpedo performance improved and work on the new streamlined Type XXI boats began. The high-speed Walter boat program (using a hydrogen-peroxide catalyst propulsion system) was accelerated. As a result, Germany ended the war with the most technically advanced submarines to see service until the introduction of nuclear submarines in the mid-1950s. By the time the new U-boats entered service in the war's final weeks, they were too few in number and Germany's strategic situation too perilous for them to alter the outcome. It was another case of too little, too late.

The Allies, too, were unprepared for the Atlantic campaign as it came to be fought. The Royal Navy (RN) entered the war with a dangerous overconfidence in its capability to defeat the U-boat threat. With all of its destroyers and the small escort force equipped with sonar (q.v.), the RN believed that U-boat attacks would be deterred by convoys (which proved so effective in World War I), while sonar-equipped antisubmarine "hunting groups" tracked the U-boats down and destroyed them. Given the expected ease with which the RN expected to defeat the U-boats, its leaders saw the German surface fleet as the primary threat to Britain's commerce.

The RN also ignored evidence of the U-boats' preference for surfaced night attacks and "wolf pack" tactics. Even though prewar exercises with its own submarines demonstrated the effectiveness of submarine night attacks, the RN was surprised by the German tactics. Additionally, training in antisubmarine warfare (ASW) (q.v.) received low priority during the interwar years. As a result, not many officers understood ASW tactics, even fewer were trained in it, and worse, few sonar operators had the requisite degree of training. Moreover, at war's start, convoy escort ships had an even lower priority in the RN's construction program than U-boats did in the German. Unlike Raeder, however, the British quickly changed their construction priorities to meet the situation.

The British also entered the war at a technological disadvantage, caused principally by their overreliance on sonars for U-boat detection in the first two years of the war. Sonar was their only electronic sensor and it could not detect a surfaced submarine. The only ASW weapon the British had in service was the depth charge. Nonetheless, the British recovered quickly and initiated a massive ASW research effort, which the Americans later joined. This led to the introduction of new ASW sensors (sonobuoys, radar, and high frequency direction finding or HF/DF equipment) and weapons such as Hedgehogs and Mark 24 ASW torpedoes. The Allies had technological superiority by late 1942, and they would not lose it until the war's closing weeks.

Neither fleet entered the campaign with adequate air support, but each enjoyed airpower advantages in its respective operating areas. The *Luftwaffe* made it hazardous for the RN to operate near German waters, while the RN's aircraft carriers posed a significant, albeit not truly appreciated, threat to Germany's naval units. Moreover, Royal Air Force (RAF) Coastal Command provided some long-range air reconnaissance support to the RN, but it lacked sufficient numbers to be truly effective. Still, it was an air reconnaissance capability Germany lacked for most of the war.

Measured against this was the significant superiority the *Kriegsmarine* had in intelligence support during the war's early months. The German *B-Dienst* (Naval Intercept Service) broke the RN's operational codes before the war. As a result, the *Kriegsmarine* knew the convoys' routes, route changes, and intentions for most of the war's first four years. It also was reading portions of the British submarine and main battle fleet codes during the first year of the war. This greatly facilitated the German effort to evade the Allied blockade, break its surface raiders out into the ocean, and deploy its submarines against Allied convoys. The *Kriegsmarine* lacked the forces, however, to fully exploit this advantage. By the time it had the forces, its intelligence superiority was gone.

This was the situation at war's start. While the British fleet sat at anchor in Scapa Flow on 3 September, the *Kriegsmarine* had forty-six U-boats and two surface raiders (the pocket battleships *Deutschland* and *Graf Spee)* at sea. These units carried the bulk of Germany's initial fight to the high seas, sinking 230 ships before Adolf Hitler (q.v.) diverted the U-boats to support his Norway (q.v.) campaign. By that time, the *Deutschland* was recalled home after sinking only two ships and the *Graf Spee* was sunk in the mouth of the Platte River (q.v.) after a brief but fairly successful career in the southern Atlantic and Indian Oceans.

The battle cruisers *Scharnhorst* and *Gneisenau* also made a sortie during this period, sinking the auxiliary cruiser *Rawalpindi* in November but missing a nearby convoy. The ten ships sunk or captured by the surface raiders paled in comparison to the U-boats' score of 222. The *Luftwaffe's* attacks on Allied coastal shipping and the *Kriegsmarine's* mining of British coastal waters sunk another twelve and twenty-seven ships, respectively.

At the start of the war, all German naval units were ordered to observe the Hague Convention prize rules for intercepting shipping; that is, to give warning before attacking and allow the crew and passengers time to abandon the ship. *U-30,* however, conducted an attack against an unarmed passenger liner without the required warning. It proved a major embarrassment for Germany and forced Hitler to reemphasize adhering to international law. The impracticality of carrying out that requirement, however, led to rescinding the order within three months. By December 1939, the U-boats resumed attacking without warning.

Initially, the RN was confident, but concerned. Most U-boat attacks were conducted against unescorted ships sailing individually or straggling behind convoys. Moreover, the RN fulfilled its primary mission of delivering the British Army to France without loss. Escort forces would be reinforced as soon as more units became available, and countermeasures for the new German magnetic mines were developed and deployed rapidly. Hunter groups were on the high seas seeking out the German surface and subsurface raiders. The first lord of the Admiralty, Winston S. Churchill (q.v.), had faith that the RN would soon have the measure of its foe, despite losses that included the aircraft carrier HMS *Courageous,* sunk by the *U-29* on 17 September. Churchill, in fact, deployed his submarines against German shipping to Norway and planned to penetrate the Baltic to attack the Swedish-German iron ore trade.

To the British public, the early losses seemed all too similar to those of World War I. Nothing, however, prepared them for the sudden loss of the battleship HMS *Royal Oak* in the RN's main base at Scapa Flow (q.v.) on 14 October 1939. Coming so early in the war and at a time of heavy shipping losses, the attack devastated British morale. It seemed no British port was safe. If the RN could not defend itself, what could it defend? Churchill rode out the storm, organizing a board of inquiry to determine what went wrong, but it was the December sinking of the *Graf Spee* that restored British morale and the RN's reputation.

More significantly for the Atlantic campaign, Hitler delivered a reprieve in the trade war by diverting fifteen of his precious U-boats to the Norwegian campaign. There, hindered by their poor mobility and unreliable magnetic torpedoes, the U-boats accomplished almost nothing at a cost of two boats. Germany's other naval losses in that battle were more significant: ten destroyers and two cruisers sunk and a pocket battleship, another cruiser, and the battle cruiser *Scharnhorst* damaged. Thus it would be months before the German antishipping campaign could begin anew.

Despite the losses, the *Kriegsmarine* acquired an important advantage from the Norwegian and the subsequent French campaigns. These victories provided the navy with bases some 450 nautical miles closer to the Atlantic shipping lanes, and eliminated the need to transit around Great Britain to reach them. This not only gave the U-boats more reach, but nearly doubled their on-station time, while the loss of French ports lengthened Allied convoy transits by 30 to 40 percent. It could not have come at a better time for the Germans. Increased production had more U-boats entering service just as the French bases became available. Thus began the first "Happy Time" for the German U-boats. It would run from July 1940 to December 1941.

By September, Dönitz had enough U-boats to initiate wolf pack tactics, first employing them against convoy SC-2. The convoy battle in the North Channel (q.v.) against convoys SC-7 and HX-79 was the first full-scale application of the devastating new tactics. In a four-day fight beginning on 17 October 1940, twelve German U-boats sank thirty-two of the total of seventy-nine ships from the two convoys. For the British, it was the worst four days of the war. The Germans would never again sink so much tonnage so quickly.

The U-boats' "Happy Time" also coincided with the *Luftwaffe's* entry into the campaign and Raeder's second attempt to prove his surface raiding strategy. Deploying seaplanes to Bergen and FW-200 Kondors to Bordeaux, France, the *Luftwaffe* began to range out over the Atlantic, attacking ships and providing aerial reconnaissance support to the *Kriegsmarine.* The combination of aerial attacks and reconnaissance reporting enabled the *Kriegsmarine* to dispatch its units through the many holes in Britain's air and naval patrol coverage in the Atlantic.

While the U-boats and the *Luftwaffe* were going from success to success, Raeder dispatched his surface ships into the Atlantic that September. The heavy cruiser *Hipper* was the first to try, but her boilers proved troublesome and the attempt was postponed. In her absence, the pocket battleship *Admiral Scheer,* and four converted merchant ships broke out into the Atlantic, followed by the battle cruisers *Scharnhorst* and *Gneisenau* in December 1940. The *Hipper* finally was able to make two sorties before engine problems forced her into overhaul in March 1941. That was the high-water mark of German surface raider operations, sinking more than 162,000 tons of shipping in four months. The *Luftwaffe's* twelve Kondors, based in France, sank an additional 160,000 tons of shipping during that same period. The U-boats, meanwhile, were destroying more than 250,000 tons a month. The combined campaign was devastatingly effective, and placed Great Britain within six weeks of losing the war.

British fortunes were at their lowest ebb. Most convoys had no more than one or two escort vessels and efforts to acquire additional maritime patrol aircraft were complicated as Britain husbanded its aerial resources for the expected German invasion. Despite seizing Iceland in April of 1940, British convoys still had no air cover in the middle Atlantic. Shipyards were pushed to produce more escorts but it was 1942 before appreciable numbers were ready.

The American offer in March 1941 of fifty obsolescent destroyers in exchange for bases on Bermuda and in the Caribbean was welcomed enthusiastically. More significantly, President Franklin D. Roosevelt (q.v.) assumed responsibility for protecting shipping in the Western Hemisphere and for the defense of Iceland. Thus the RN's burden was suddenly cut in half. By September 1941, a de facto undeclared war (q.v.) was being waged in the Atlantic between the U.S. Navy and the *Kriegsmarine.* The RN desperately needed the help.

Another element helped turned the tide against the Germans at this time—the Allies began to gain intelligence superiority. The British started to break the German naval codes in April 1941. Coming just before the fateful *Bismarck* (q.v.) sortie into the Atlantic, that success provided the Allies with German unit locations, plans, and intentions. German U-boat losses began to climb. Although merchant ship sinkings continued, the now-increasing U-boat casualties ate into Dönitz's reserve of trained crews, even as more U-boats were entering service. Allied losses in the Atlantic began to decline, but U.S. entry into the war handed Dönitz another opportunity to score.

Anticipating America's entry into the war in Europe, Dönitz initiated planning to dispatch a dozen U-boats to raid America's coastal waters before its defenses could be prepared. Operation DRUMBEAT (q.v.) was a brilliant stroke. Although Hitler only approved the dispatch of five boats, Dönitz was able to sink more than two million tons of Allied shipping between January and July 1942. Only one U-boat was lost. Successes came so fast and so easily that the U-boat men called it their second "Happy Time." This unequaled disaster for the Allies helped make 1942 Dönitz's most successful year, with more than six million tons sunk.

That also was the year the Allies started sending convoys to the Soviet Union. These PQ-series convoys suffered particularly heavy losses. The most serious losses were suffered by Convoy PQ-17 (q.v.), which lost nearly every ship to U-boat and *Luftwaffe* attacks in July 1942. The blow was so devastating that Churchill canceled Arctic convoys until 1943. On the other hand, U-boat losses for 1942 reached sixty-six. Growing Allied airpower, stationed in Iceland and western Britain, forced Dönitz's U-boats further out into the central Atlantic. Nonetheless, Dönitz was pleased overall. By year's end, he had about 200 boats in service with nearly twenty new units being produced each month.

At this critical point, the Allies lost access to Germany's naval codes. Dönitz became suspicious of his communications security by the end of 1941 and ordered a change in the codes and the encryption system. That change was completed by the end of July 1942. The Allies did not break the new codes until April 1943. In many ways, the tide of the Atlantic campaign reflected that of the contenders' intelligence war. The Germans greatest relative success (sinkings per submarine) came when their intelligence superiority was highest; and their highest losses came when the Allies had intelligence superiority.

Thus the stage was set for what would become the decisive period of the Atlantic campaign, the last two months of 1942 and the first three months of 1943. Both sides were approaching their numerical and technological apogees. The German *Schnorchel* boats were just entering production and U-boat strength was reaching its peak. The *Luftwaffe* returned to the skies to provide aerial reconnaissance support, and the Italians provided additional submarines, with some thirty serving in the Atlantic between July 1942 and September 1943. At the same time, however, Allied escort carriers were entering service in increasing numbers, and enough long-range patrol bombers became available to cover all but the very central areas of the Atlantic. New Allied aerial radars operated in frequencies the German radar receivers could not detect, while German U-boats were just beginning to receive radar and sonar-deception equipment.

The Germans also introduced the new acoustic homing torpedo, which could be used against escorts to clear a path into the convoy. German logistics support submarines, the so-called *Milch Kuhe* (Milk Cows) extended the on-station time of the combat U-boats. The number of Allied escort vessels entering service skyrocketed, and their crews were better trained and equipped than ever before. These escorts carried the new rocket-thrown Hedgehogs, and every one of them carried radar and sonar. Other escorts had HF/DF installed enabling them to detect and locate the U-boats that tracked and reported on the convoys.

More significantly, Allied aircraft were beginning to carry sonobuoys and the new ASW torpedoes. Diving would no longer offer sanctuary from air attack. Dönitz's initial reaction to this latest development was to equip his U-boats with massive antiaircraft batteries and tell them to fight it out with the aircraft, but heavy losses eventually forced him to abandon that tactic.

The initial round of this last phase of the struggle went to the Germans, when they sank more than 740,000 tons of shipping in November 1942. Churchill recognized that Great Britain could not afford losses on that scale to continue. The Allies reacted by attacking the U-boats throughout the full range of their existence, at the point of construction, at their bases, in the transit lanes to and from their bases, and in their operating patrol zones. Shipping losses fell briefly when Hitler ordered Dönitz to send U-boats against the Allied invasion force off Northwest Africa (q.v.), but Dönitz returned to the Atlantic in February 1943, sinking another 380,000 tons.

March 1943 marked the German final high-water mark in the campaign. The U-boats sank nearly 600,000 tons of shipping. Dönitz realized he was at a decisive point in the war. More U-boats were rushed out into the fray, but they were not able to sustain the former levels of success. The three months following March saw nearly 100 U-boats go down.

By that point, the Allies had enough escorts and escort carriers to establish "hunter-killer" groups. Using information drawn from Allied code breaking and HF/DF information, these groups ranged freely across the convoy lanes, seeking out and destroying U-boats in their patrol areas. Portugal began to ease its neutrality, allowing the United States to station patrol aircraft in the Azores. The "air gap" where U-boats could operate without fear of air attack all but disappeared.

By August 1943, Dönitz realized the battle was lost and began to withdraw his U-boats, reporting to Hitler that the Allied technical and numerical edge was more than the U-boats could overcome. Hitler ordered the campaign continued while newer and more powerful U-boats and weapons were produced. He told Dönitz that the U-boats tied down forces that might otherwise be employed against Germany itself. Thus, the U-boat force continued to fight for two years after it had been decisively beaten. The price was phenomenal; some 785 of Germany's total 908 U-boats in service were lost.

The Atlantic campaign was fought primarily between the British and German Navies. The United States provided aircraft, weapons, merchant ships, and some escorts, but for the most part, it was a British and Canadian operation. The German U-boat service carried the burden for the Axis with a little assistance from the Italian submarine and German surface forces. For the Allies, it was a war of close calls and courageous decisions. For Germany it was one of wasted opportunities.

Still, the U-boat arm proved exceptionally cost effective. For an expenditure of less than 15 percent of Germany's total war effort, the U-boat arm tied down Allied forces nearly six times its size and forced the Allies to expend nearly 40 percent of their much larger war effort to its defeat. It was a remarkable achievement. Fortunately for the world, it failed in its purpose.

Carl O. Schuster

Additional Reading

Allen, Kenneth, *Battle of the Atlantic* (1973).
Goulter, Christina J.M., *A Forgotten Offensive: Royal Air Force Coastal Command's Anti-Shipping Campaign, 1940–1945* (1995).
Hessler, Gunter, *The U-Boat War in the Atlantic, 1939–1945* (1989).
Hough, Richard, *The Longest Battle: The War at Sea, 1939–1945* (1987).

Kemp, Paul, *Friend or Foe: Friendly Fire at Sea, 1939–1945* (1995).

Middlebrook, Martin, *Convoy* (1976).

Raeder, Erich, *The Struggle for the Sea* (1959).

Smith, Peter C., *Hold the Narrow Sea: Naval Warfare in the English Channel, 1939–1945* (1984).

Van der Vat, Dan, *The Atlantic Campaign* (1988).

Atlantis Raids (31 March 1940– 22 November 1941)

The German merchant raider *Atlantis* (also known as *Schiff* 16 or *Raider C*) undertook a highly successful cruise in the Atlantic, Indian, and Pacific Oceans between March 1940 and November 1941. It captured or destroyed twenty-two vessels with a combined displacement of 145,697 tons. It greatly disrupted Allied shipping at a time when Allied countermeasures were limited because of priorities in the North Atlantic.

Launched in 1937 as a sister ship of the raider *Pinguin* (*see* German Surface Raiders 1940–1942), the *Atlantis* displaced 7,862 tons, carried a wartime crew of 347, and reached a speed of 17 knots. Her concealed armament included six 150mm, one 75mm, one twin 37mm, and four 20mm guns, four 21-inch torpedo tubes, ninety-two mines, and two seaplanes.

Under Captain Bernhard Rogge (q.v.), the *Atlantis* left German waters disguised as a Soviet freighter on 31 March 1940 and headed for the South Atlantic and the Indian Ocean. Later she changed disguises repeatedly to confuse victims and hunters. In early May, having penetrated the British blockade and cornering a British vessel south of the equator, Rogge dropped his mines off Cape Agulhas as he entered the Indian Ocean. There the *Atlantis* captured or sank thirteen vessels before year's end. She also obtained valuable intelligence as well as fuel and provisions from her prey. Prisoners were sent to France or Japan. The absence of an Allied convoy system or regular aerial surveillance, and frequent changes of his operational areas, facilitated Rogge's work.

After spending Christmas at the remote Kerguelen Islands and capturing three more victims in early 1941, Rogge paid another visit to the South Atlantic. By summer, the *Atlantis* had taken five more vessels before heading east again well to the south of the Cape of Good Hope. The *Silvaplana,* with a rich cargo of rubber, tin, copper, coffee, and spices, became her last victim in the Pacific Ocean northeast of New Zealand. Still well-supplied, Rogge decided to return home by way of Cape Horn.

The *Atlantis* may have made it home safely had it not been for orders to resupply German submarines in the South Atlantic. On 22 November 1941, while servicing the *U-126* northwest of Ascension Island, she was recognized and surprised by the British heavy cruiser HMS *Devonshire,* commanded by Captain R.D. Oliver. While the U-boat dived to safety, the *Atlantis* was quickly sunk, unable to even return fire.

The raider's survivors then faced another odyssey. First picked up by friendly submarines or placed in lifeboats, they eventually were transferred to the supply ship *Python,* only to be shipwrecked one week later as the *Python* was sunk by HMS *Dorsetshire.* Again German and Italian submarines came to the rescue. The last of her crew reached France on 29 December 1941, after 655 days and 110,000 miles at sea. Rogge, highly decorated and later promoted to vice admiral, survived the war and retired in 1962 from the West German Navy.

Eric C. Rust

Additional Reading

Muggenthaler, August K., *German Raiders of World War II* (1977).

Rogge, Bernhard, and Wolfgang Frank, *Schiff 16* (1960).

Austria (March–May 1945)

The end-phase of the military campaign for Austria really began in late 1943. Two independent developments combined to create the conditions under which Austrians would struggle for the last part of the war. One of these developments was the Moscow Declaration, issued by the Allied foreign ministers in November 1943. The declaration was intentionally ambiguous; it stated that Austria was on the one hand a "victim" of Adolf Hitler's (q.v.) and German aggression; on the other hand, Austrians were reminded of their cooperation with Hitler's regime and encouraged to contribute to their own liberation. The Moscow Declaration reflected in outline form all of the various attitudes of Austrians toward Nazism: capitulation, collaboration, resignation, and resistance. From November 1943 until the end of the war in May 1945, Austrians would have opportunities to demonstrate each of these attitudes.

The other development of 1943 which conditioned the end of the war in Austria was the Allied invasion of Italy. After 1943, Allied bombers operating out of Italian bases struck Austrian targets. The first major raid on Vienna came in April 1944, and other industrial centers such as Wiener Neustadt and Linz were heavily damaged between 1943 and 1945. The aerial destruction of much of the transportation network and many armaments factories created chaotic economic conditions within Austria, and shattered German hopes for creating a bomb-free zone for the production of military goods in Austria and Bohemia. By the winter of 1944–1945, the Allies stepped up their bombing to almost nonstop raids.

In the last phase of the war, it was clear that the important task of taking Vienna would fall to the Soviets. Soviet troops approached the Austrian frontier in late 1944, but did not actually move into Austrian territory until 20 March 1945. This development caused a rash of activity among Austrian political and military leaders. The representatives of former political parties tried to devise a plan for the inevitable Soviet occupation. Some Austrian military leaders, in an attempt to spare their country needless destruction, formed an underground anti-Nazi organization known as O5. This group made contact with the Allies through Switzerland and Italy. Unfortunately, elements of the O5 organization were uncovered by the *Gestapo* (q.v.) and liquidated.

As the Soviet 2nd and 3rd Ukrainian Fronts (army groups) closed on Vienna (q.v.) in early April 1945, Hitler ordered that the city be used as a last line of defense. The futile military effort of the combined German and Austrian forces succeeded only in causing needless destruction to the city and resulted in the inevitable Soviet victory and occupation. By 14 April, the Soviets were in control of the Austrian capital, but it took somewhat longer to restore order to the streets and to put in place a new civilian government.

Although Vienna was the most important battle in Austria in the last year of the war, other key military encounters took place in various parts of the country. In Lower Austria outside of Vienna, Soviet and German forces engaged in bitter fighting, especially in the oil territory north of the Danube River. As Nazi officials desperately sought refuge in the towns of the Lower Austrian countryside, a provisional government for the territory was established in Vienna.

Throughout Austria, the formation of provisional governments at the territorial level aided the Allies in occupying the country and eased, to a certain extent, the transition to postwar administration. Nevertheless, the de-Nazification of the Austrian government and bureaucracy was conducted unevenly in the various territories occupied by the different Allies, and became a disputed issue in the postwar period.

In western Austria the Allies, especially the United States, feared that Hitler planned to build an alpine fortress where his best soldiers would fight to their last breath. Although Hitler did give orders on 28 April 1945 to establish officially an alpine military refuge, the plan had no real substance. The German forces had neither the time nor the wherewithal for such an undertaking. With the capitulation of the German armies in Italy in early May, any such maneuver was rendered completely untenable. In the end, there was little resistance from German or Austrian troops in the west. Austrian forces preferred to surrender to U.S. or French units rather than to Soviet forces, from whom they feared reprisals. On 7 May 1945, German Army Group South surrendered to the U.S. Third Army, which was approaching from the east.

World War II was over in Austria. The country, like Germany, was occupied by the four primary Allied Powers: the Soviet Union, the United States, Great Britain, and France. Austria would become disputed territory between East and West—a part of the Cold War—for the next ten years. In 1955, Austria was reconstituted as the Second Republic, given complete sovereignty, and declared itself neutral—in accordance with the treaty ending the occupation. Largely because of World War II, Austrians drew the conclusion that military nonalignment was the best policy for a small, central European nation. With the end of the Cold War, however, Austria became a full member of the European Union on 1 January 1995.

William D. Bowman

Additional Reading
Jelavich, Barbara, *Modern Austria: Empire and Republic* (1987).
Shtemenko, S.M., *The Last Six Months: Russia's Final Battles with Hitler's Armies* (1977).

B

Baedecker Air Raids (April 1942)

During the night of 28–29 March 1942, the Royal Air Force (RAF), perfecting its raiding technique of mounting a heavy attack on one objective in a short period of time, bombed Lübeck, causing very heavy damage. The city was a leading member of the old Hanseatic League. It contained many architectural treasures and was an important center for German literature (it was the birthplace of Thomas Mann and the setting of some of his greatest works). The city also was almost totally without military significance.

The German popular uproar, led by Adolf Hitler and Joseph Goebbels (qq.v.), called for reprisal strikes on British cities. Hitler boasted, in a speech on 26 April 1942, that he would take his *Baedecker's Guide* (the famous guide for European tourists in the nineteenth and early twentieth centuries) and mark each British city off the guidebook as it was destroyed. Accordingly, the raids became known as the "Baedecker Raids."

The *Luftwaffe*, then busy in the Soviet Union, did not have enough planes in France to mount such attacks, but some squadrons were soon brought from the eastern front to soothe Hitler's rage. Raids were carried out on a number of British cities of historic and artistic importance. Exeter, Bath, Norwich, and York were hit in April. The British, by this time, had improved their fighter defenses even above the level of the Battle of Britain (q.v.), and German losses were proportionally higher than in 1940. The losses included flight instructor crews who were thrown into the attack. The mission of these crews was to train *Luftwaffe* combat crews at home, not in the skies above Britain, and they could not be spared. The attacks were broken off until later in 1942, when much smaller raids were made on Newcastle, Sunderland, and Canterbury.

The Baedecker raids caused extensive damage and heavy loss of life, especially in Bath. Fortunately, most of the damage could be repaired, and the whole episode, including the British raid on Lübeck, takes its place alongside the other horrors of World War II.

Roland V. Layton

Additional Reading
Harris, Arthur, *Bomber Command* (1947).
Lyall, Gavin, *The War in the Air, 1939–1945* (1968).
Rothnie, Niall, *Baedeker Blitz: Hitler's Attack on Britain's Historic Cities* (1992).

Balkans (April 1941)
[See map 6 on page 1316]
The German invasion of Greece (Operation *MARITA*) and Yugoslavia (Operation "25") began on the morning of 6 April 1941. The first major thrusts were delivered by units of the German Twelfth Army, commanded by Field Marshal Wilhelm List (q.v.). Advancing from their staging areas in southern and western Bulgaria, three divisions of the XVIII Mountain Corps struck at the Greek Metaxas Line. Two divisions from the XXX Infantry Corps pushed their way into the eastern reaches of Greek Macedonia and Thrace, while five other divisions (belonging either to the XL Motorized or the XVIII Mountain Corps) swung through southern Yugoslavia on their way into Greece. The latter operation made rapid progress and was also far less costly than the attack on the Metaxas Line. By 7 April, the Germans took Skopje. Two days later their tanks rumbled into Thessaloniki. With their supply lines cut, the Greek East Macedonia Army under General Nikos Bakopoulos surrendered shortly thereafter.

Because German military action against Yugoslavia from the north had to be improvised, no major operations in that region were feasible on 6 April. To express his wrath over the recent political changes in Yugoslavia, Adolf Hitler (q.v.) ordered massive air strikes against Belgrade (q.v.). These attacks, carried out under the direction of Colonel General Alexander Löhr (q.v.), caused high civilian casualties and seriously disrupted the country's communications and control system.

On 8 April, the First *Panzer* Group, commanded by Colonel General Ewald von Kleist (q.v.), advanced from Bulgaria into the Morava Valley, and after crushing resistance from the Yugoslav Fifth Army, entered Nis the next day. Here, as in many other encounters during the Balkan campaign, German ground forces were massively supported by air strikes from various *Luftwaffe* units.

During the following days, divisions from Kleist's *Panzer* Group fought their way northward, toward the Belgrade area, with varying degrees of success. On 11 April, Colonel General Georg-Hans Reinhardt's (q.v.) XLI Motorized *Korps* entered Yugoslavia from its staging area in western Romania and reached the vicinity of Belgrade within twenty-four hours.

Even before this direct threat against their capital had materialized, the Yugoslavs found themselves assaulted from the north by three additional field armies: the Italian Second Army, headed by General Vittorio Ambrosio (q.v.); the hastily assembled German Second Army, commanded by Colonel General Maximilian von Weichs (q.v.); and the Hungarian Third Army, a force of more than 140,000 men. The Italians first occupied Slovenia, then pushed south along the Dalmatian coast. Von Weichs quickly overran Croatia and then penetrated into Bosnia-Herzegovina. The Hungarians occupied the northeastern corner of Yugoslavia, gaining more than 11,000 square kilometers and a million people in the process.

With its armies disintegrating in many areas, Yugoslavia's leadership split. While the king and his prime minister, General Dušan Simović (q.v.), left the country, others assumed the onerous task of securing an end to the hostilities. On 17 April, a formal surrender document was signed in Belgrade by Aleksander Cincar-Marković (a former foreign minister) and Lieutenant General Momcilo Janković (of the Yugoslav general staff).

In the meantime, List's Twelfth Army pushed farther into Greece, although it encountered fierce resistance from both British Commonwealth and Greek troops in a number of places. In a wide swing to the west, some German divisions sliced into the rear echelons of Greece's West Macedonia and Epirus Armies, which had hitherto played havoc with Benito Mussolini's (q.v.) legions in southern Albania.

With the Germans in their flank and rear, the Greek commanders in that region eventually decided to surrender their sixteen divisions to the *Wehrmacht.* On 21 April, List accepted the Greek capitulation, but the Italians insisted that their exclusion from the process was unacceptable. As a result, a second surrender was staged two days later at Thessaloniki under the direction of General Alfred Jodl of the OKW (qq.v.) and in the presence of Italian representatives.

Faced with the steady advance of the Germans, Greek Prime Minister Alexandros Koryzis took his own life on 18 April. His successor, Emanuel Tsouderos, was committed to the continuation of the war on Britain's side, but made it clear that Greek troops would henceforth only help with the evacuation of General Henry Maitland Wilson's (q.v.) Commonwealth force from the mainland. On 23 April, King George II (q.v.) and the Tsouderos cabinet left for Crete. The following day, the last Royal Air Force (RAF) planes left Greece.

Despite gallant rear guard action by Australian, British, and New Zealand troops, List's advance during the following days made rapid progress. On 26 April, German paratroopers took Corinth. The following morning, German tanks rumbled into Athens. During the next three days, several German columns overran the entire Peloponnesus. Most of Wilson's troops, more than 50,000 men, were evacuated by that time, but they left all of their heavy weapons and equipment behind. The Germans also captured more than 8,000 Commonwealth troops, along with almost 250,000 Greek soldiers, but most of the latter were soon released.

While Axis casualties during the conquest of Yugoslavia were remarkably light, German losses in the Greek campaign were significantly higher, particularly during their opening moves against the Metaxas Line (*see* Greece). Altogether, the Balkan campaign in April 1941 cost the *Wehrmacht* close to 12,000 men, including 2,559 dead and 5,820 wounded. It caused considerable wear and tear on tanks and other vehicles, but neither these losses nor the temporary diversion of German troops and air force units to the Balkan peninsula in April 1941 had much of an impact on the Axis buildup against the Soviet Union. Most historians are agreed today that Operation BARBAROSSA was not seriously affected by the Balkan interlude.

Ulrich Trumpener

Additional Reading

Blau, George E., *The German Campaign in the Balkans, Spring 1941* (1953).

Buchner, Alex, *Der Deutsche Griechenlandfeldzug: Operationen der 12. Armee* (1957).

Van Creveld, Martin, *Hitler's Strategy 1940–1941: The Balkan Clue* (1973).

Balkans (March 1944–March 1945)

[See map 7 on page 1317]

At the outset of 1944, what fighting there was in the Balkans was between German forces and guerrilla groups. On 22 February 1944, Prime Minister Winston S. Churchill (q.v.) told the British Parliament that Marshal Tito's Yugoslavian partisans (qq.v.) were the only effective guerrilla group remaining in Yugoslavia and that they were tying down fourteen of the twenty German occupation divisions in the Balkans. In Greece, the Communist ELAS was completing the elimination of all military rivals except the nationalist EDES, while limiting the German occupiers to control of the larger towns, cities, and transportation routes. The other Balkan nations were Axis satellites with relatively small resistance movements.

In March 1944, the spearhead of Soviet General Ivan Konev's (q.v.) 2nd Ukrainian Front thrust across the Prut River and menaced Jassy, Romania, while Marshal Georgy Zhukov's (q.v.) 1st Ukrainian Front seized Cernauti, prompting Adolf Hitler (q.v.) to order the German Army into Hungary. In early May, Konev's attack down the banks of the Siret River west of Jassy was thwarted and that front remained static through most of the summer.

The task of defending the Balkans against a Soviet attack fell to Colonel General Johannes Friessner (q.v.) and the 800,000 troops of his Army Group South Ukraine. The left flank of the army group was held by the fourteen German and seven Romanian divisions of the German Eighth and Romanian Fourth Armies. Both armies came under the operational control of General Otto Wöhler (q.v.), the Eighth Army commander. Wöhler's force was responsible for barring access to Transylvania via Targu-Mures and to Ploesti and Bucharest via the Focsani gap. The right flank of the army group, from Husi to the Black Sea at Ovidiopol, was held by the seventeen German and seven Romanian divisions of the German Sixth and Romanian Third Armies. This force was under the operational control of Colonel General Petre Dumitrescu (q.v.), commander of the Romanian Third Army. Friessner could also call on about 57,000 assorted troops from police, SS, air defense, and naval infantry units, and about 120 tanks and 800 aircraft.

Against this force, the Soviets on 20 August 1944 launched nearly 900,000 troops, 1,700 aircraft, and 1,400 tanks. The 2nd Ukrainian Front, now commanded by Marshal Rodion Malinkovsky (q.v.), attacked northwest of Jassy, moving west toward Tirgu-Mures, southwest toward the Focsani gap, and east toward Husi. The 3rd Ukrainian Front, commanded by Marshal Fedor Tolbukhin (q.v.), thrust into the Moldavian salient westward toward Chisinau and Husi, southwest toward Ceadar-Lunga.

By 23 August, what was left of Army Group South Ukraine faced a catastrophic situation. The Romanian government abruptly capitulated, ordering all of its troops immediately to cease hostilities with the Soviets. Most of the German troops were trapped. The Soviets swept into Galati on 27 August, Ploesti on 30 August, and Bucharest on 31 August. The German Army lost twenty divisions, at least 180,000 troops. Another 380,000 Germans, taken prisoner by the Romanians, were handed over to the Soviets. Surviving units of the Romanian Army also attacked the Hungarians in Transylvania. The armistice of 12 September gave Transylvania to Romania, but returned Bessarabia and northern Bukovina to the Soviet Union, which had seized them in 1939.

Germany's Bulgarian allies learned the lesson from Romania's collapse. On 26 August the Bulgarians announced their withdrawal from the war and ordered the disarmament of all German troops in Bulgaria. This did not prevent the Soviet Union from declaring war on Bulgaria on 5 September. The Red Army entered the country on 8 September and Bulgarian leftists seized the government. Following an October armistice, the 450,000-man Bulgarian Army was employed under Soviet leadership against the Germans in Yugoslavia and Hungary.

The way now stood clear for the Soviets to develop a strong attack through Romania into Yugoslavia and Hungary. By 19 September, lead elements of the 2nd Ukrainian Front moving from Bucharest had skirted the southern flank of the Carpathians and reached Timişoara in western Transylvania. Three days later they were in Arad, only 150 miles from Budapest. They got to within sixty miles of Budapest by 11 October, when the rest of the 2nd Ukrainian Front took Cluj, the capital of Transylvania, 170 miles to their rear.

Meanwhile, the 3rd Ukrainian Front, in addition to marching into Bulgaria, moved along the north bank of the Danube, linked up with Tito's partisans, and entered Belgrade on 20 October after a stiff fight. German Army Group E had begun to evacuate Greece on 12 October, the last of its units crossing into Yugoslavia on 2 November. Its rear was attacked by elements of the 3rd Ukrainian Front and the Bulgarian Army, and its eastern flank was hit by other elements of the 3rd Ukrainian Front in the vicinity of Belgrade. The surviving German forces were incorporated into Army Group F, which deployed on a line from Belgrade to the Albanian border.

To the north, Admiral Miklós Horthy (q.v.), the Hungarian regent, announced on 11 October his intention to surrender to the Allies. By 13 October, the Germans had taken Budapest, arrested him, and were preparing to defend the city. The 2nd Ukrainian Front attacked from the march with sixty-four divisions (including fourteen Romanian) on 29 October. The twelve German divisions guarding the eastern approaches to the city halted the assault in the suburbs on 4 November. The thirty-five divisions of the 3rd Ukrainian Front launched an attack from 130 miles south of Budapest (q.v.) in late November. At the beginning of December, the 2nd Ukrainian Front attacked in the northwest to surround the city. Completely surrounded by 26 December, Budapest held out until 13 February 1945, at a cost of 50,000 dead and 138,000 captured.

The final tragedy for the Balkans was the outbreak of civil war in Greece (q.v.) around Christmas. As the year ended, the British 2nd Parachute Brigade intervened on the side of the nationalists and was fighting the ELAS in Athens and elsewhere.

Joseph M. McCarthy

Additional Reading

Allen, W.E.D., and Paul Muratoff, *The Russian Campaigns of 1944–45* (1946).
Erickson, John, *The Road to Berlin* (1983).
Maclean, Fitzroy, *Disputed Barricade: The Life and Times of Josip Broz-Tito* (1983).
Seaton, Albert, *The Russo-German War, 1941–45* (1971).

BARBAROSSA, Operation

See SOVIET UNION

Bardia (3–5 January 1941)

In 1941, Bardia, along with Tobruk, stood as the guardian to the eastern approaches to Libya, which the Italians had finally conquered after a long war in 1911. As part of the old Roman Empire, Libya was the jewel of Benito Mussolini's (q.v.) overseas possessions. On 9 December 1940, General Richard O'Connor's (q.v.) Western Desert Force launched Operation COMPASS, originally conceived as a "nine-days' raid" to push the Italians out of Egypt. The rapid collapse of Italian resistance, however, led to a British attempt to take all of Libya. The coastal fortress of Bardia, just inside the Libyan border, then became a British prime objective.

Mussolini, leaving no doubt as to the importance of holding Bardia, cabled the port's commander, General Annibale Bergonzoli: "I have given you a difficult task, but one well suited to your courage and experience as an old and intrepid soldier—the task of defending Bardia to the last." Bergonzoli responded: "In Bardia we are and here we stay."

To defend against the British attack, the Italians had Bardia well-fortified. The city was ringed with minefields (an important part of every North African desert battle), antitank ditches, and two lines of mutually supporting reinforced bunkers, 800 yards apart. Dug in for a siege, Bergonzoli had 45,000 troops and 400 guns. The defenses, however, did not deter the ambitious O'Connor, who wrote; "I thought we should take Bardia all right, although of course it would require quite different tactics." What O'Connor meant was tactics quite different from those the British had used in earlier attacks against the Italians, largely in open country. Only three weeks after his major victory at Sidi Barrani (q.v.), and despite supply problems and the withdrawal of the Indian 4th Division, O'Connor was ready to try for Bardia.

To spearhead the attack, O'Connor planned to use the fresh Australian 6th Division. He believed infantry units were better suited to overcome Bardia's fixed defenses than the tanks of his "Desert Rats," the 7th Armoured Division. Once the Australians cleared a path, the Matilda tanks could roar ahead and exploit the breakthrough.

At 0530 hours on 3 January 1941, the North African sky was lit up by a furious British artillery preparation against the Bardia defenses. Soon after, the Australians advanced, singing "South of the Border, Down Mexico Way." They broke through the Italian barbed wire, using Bangalore torpedoes and wire cutters. Tearing a gap through the Italian lines, the infantry opened the way for the tanks. By noon, the attackers captured some 30,000 stunned Italian prisoners. In the southern defensive sector, however, the Australians met stiff resistance, which led to bitter fighting that slowed the Australian push.

In the mid-morning hours the next day, the Australians turned toward the road to Tobruk and the port of Bardia itself. Once inside the main defensive perimeter, the Australians, closely supported by the tanks, rampaged at will. According to John Strawson, the blueprint for the Bardia operation had been classic O'Connor: clean and simple. The penetrating forces turned both left and right and began to clear the perimeter, while follow-on units penetrated deeper into the center. O'Connor also held a force in reserve to deal with unforeseen resistance. On the second day, the Italian garrison was cut in half by the Australians.

Italian resistance continued in the northern and southern sections of the battlefront, but for all practical purposes, the battle for Bardia was over by 5 January. There have been few instances of the combined operations of armor and infantry as well orchestrated and as well executed as O'Connor's capture of Bardia. Both during the initial assault and then inside the defensive positions the tanks and the infantry fought as one. The Italians lost more than 40,000 troops, many guns, nearly 130 tanks, and 700 Lancia trucks, which helped provide O'Connor with vital mobility. Bergonzoli, who prudently left west toward Tobruk early in the course of the battle, was not among the Italians captured.

With the unexpectedly easy fall of Bardia, O'Connor cast his net even farther. His successes even forestalled, at least for a time, the British government's sending more troops to the quicksand war in Greece. O'Connor immediately planned to exploit his success with the seizure of Tobruk (*see* Tobruk I), the strongest bastion in Mussolini's Libyan colony. Within twenty-four hours of the surrender of Bardia, the untried Australian 19th Brigade was blocking the eastern defenses of Tobruk. O'Connor, however, continued to be plagued by the chronic problems of operating over a slim and extended supply line, compounded by the never-ending problem of insufficient transport. The battle for Tobruk was not launched until 21 January.

Bardia was the key battle of Operation COMPASS. The vigorous fire preparation, the swift attack by the infantry, the surely coordinated use of infantry and armor, and the vigorous exploitation represented one of the first uses of true combined arms tactics by the British. Tragically, at the very time that O'Connor was preparing to make a clean sweep of Libya, Prime Minister Winston S. Churchill (q.v.) ordered some of his best units off to the Greece (q.v.) campaign, robbing O'Connor of his striking force at a critical time.

John F. Murphy

Additional Reading
Barnett, Correlli, *The Desert Generals* (1964).
Keegan, John (ed.), *Churchill's Generals* (1991).
Strawson, John, *The Battle for North Africa* (1969).

Barents Sea (30–31 December 1942)
After the costly voyages of Convoys PQ-17 and PQ-18 (qq.v.) in the summer of 1942, the British temporarily suspended convoy sailings to the northern Soviet Union. Only merchantmen proceeding singly kept open the Allied supply link to Murmansk and Archangel. The suspension also was due in part to the Allied landings in Northwest Africa (q.v.) in November, with their attendant demand on transports and escorts. Once Operation TORCH succeeded, and with long Arctic nights promising safer passage, the convoys resumed in December under the new "JW" designation.

German naval forces in Norway remained as eager as ever to intercept Allied supplies to the Soviets. While the *Luftwaffe*'s strength was reduced since September, the German Navy still maintained a formidable force ready to take on the Allies. By late 1942, ships commanded by Vice Admiral Oskar Kummetz included the pocket battleship *Lützow (Deutschland)*, the heavy cruiser *Admiral Hipper* (the force flagship), and the six fleet destroyers: *Friedrich Eckoldt, Richard Beitzen, Theodor Riedel, Z.29, Z.30,* and *Z.31.* They were based in Alten Fjord near Norway's North Cape ready to engage convoys in the Barents Sea. Germany also operated twenty-three U-boats in Arctic waters. Successes against Soviet-bound convoys seemed especially crucial since they meant relief for the German Sixth Army, then surrounded at Stalingrad (q.v.).

On 24 December 1942, German aircraft spotted Convoy JW-51B, two days out of Scotland. German naval commanders welcomed the news. The convoy's first section, JW-51A, proceeded separately and reached Murmansk intact on 25 December. JW-51B was less fortunate. At noon on 30 December, the *U-354* reported the convoy fifty miles south of Bear Island, within striking distance of Kummetz's force at Alten Fjord. The submarine's skipper added significantly, "Convoy weakly escorted."

At that juncture stormy weather and poor visibility caused JW-51B to separate into several segments. Its core was reduced to nine merchantmen, their immediate escort, under Captain Robert S. Sherbrooke, consisting of the destroyers *Onslow* (flag), *Obedient, Obdurate, Orwell,* and *Achates,* two corvettes, *Hyderabad* and *Rhododendron,* and the armed trawler *Northern Gem.* Stragglers included five merchant vessels, the destroyer *Oribi,* and the trawler *Vizalma.* The minesweeper *Bramble* managed to reunite three of the missing merchantmen with the main body by 31 December. Providing distant cover for the convoy was the Royal Navy's Force R, consisting of the two light cruisers *Sheffield* and *Jamaica,* under Rear Admiral Robert Burnett, which recently had delivered JW-51A to Murmansk. Sherbrooke assumed Force R to be somewhere to his north, when it actually was positioned ahead of the convoy. Weather conditions throughout the events of 30–31 December posed challenges to both sides with freezing temperatures, inadequate and frequently changing visibility, extremely short daylight hours, snow showers, and stormy seas.

The Germans initiated Operation *REGENBOGEN* (RAINBOW) shortly after noon on 30 December. The move against JW-51B meant a welcome opportunity to demonstrate that Germany's surface ships were not useless liabilities, as Adolf Hitler (q.v.) had sometimes claimed, and could strike against the enemy as readily as U-boats. Kummetz, however, had to obey the long-standing order not to engage superior enemy forces so Germany could keep a "fleet-in-being" in Norwegian waters. This notion was reinforced by a message Kummetz received as he put to sea and headed north at 1840 hours on 30 December. It read in part, "Use caution even against enemy of equal strength; accepting undue risks for cruisers undesirable." Kummetz's tactical decisions would thus reflect his superiors' somewhat ambiguous instructions to press his attack against the enemy, but not to place his forces in jeopardy.

As they headed north from Alten Fjord into the Arctic winter night, the German units formed a long column with the *Hipper* in the lead, followed by the *Lützow* and the destroyers. At 0240 hours on 31 December, Kummetz divided his force into two sections: the *Hipper, Eckoldt, Beitzen* and *Z.29* spread out to the north and west of the convoy's projected route, while the *Lützow* and the other destroyers remained to the south in anticipation of a southward evasive maneuver by the convoy once it was being attacked from the north and rear. By this time, JW-51B was headed east at about 10 knots, the British 0-class destroyers guarding its van and flanks, and the *Achates* bringing up the rear. The *Sheffield* and *Jamaica* meanwhile were gradually gaining a position about thirty miles to the north.

A lookout on the *Hipper* first established contact with the convoy at 0718 hours, reporting "two shadows bearing 60 degrees, distance eight miles" in the faint light of the Arctic dawn. While the cruiser continued its northward sweep for a while, Kummetz sent the *Eckoldt* to investigate. Joined by the *Z.29* and the *Beitzen,* the *Eckoldt* soon approached the convoy from the west. At the same time, the *Lützow* and her destroyer companions reacted to Kummetz's report by increasing speed to 26 knots and veering to the northeast to cut off the convoy from a possible escape to the south. Everything looked perfect for a pincer attack by the Germans, the convoy and its out-gunned escorts seemingly at their mercy.

JW-51B got its first hint of trouble when the *Hyderabad* and later the *Obdurate* reported two destroyers to the southwest at 0830 hours. Not sure whether these were Soviet reinforcements or German warships, Sherbrooke detached the *Obdurate* to find out. Doubts ceased at 0920 hours when the *Eckoldt* and her two companions opened fire on a British destroyer. The *Hipper,* meanwhile, swung around to the east and southeast to bear down on the convoy from the northwest. The *Sheffield* and *Jamaica,* still many miles to the north, temporarily mistook the convoy's stragglers for the main body and thereby delayed their appearance on the scene, even though they observed gunfire to the south.

Realizing that the *Obdurate* had come under attack, Sherbrooke ordered the other 0-class destroyers to join her in action against the three German warships, while the smaller *Achates* laid a smoke screen to obscure visibility for the enemy. The merchantmen and their three remaining escorts turned south away from any immediate threat. Before long, however, the *Hipper's* approach from the northwest suspended the developing destroyer battle. Kummetz, irritated by poor visibility and the difficulty of telling friend from foe, had the three German destroyers join him while his cruiser opened fire on the *Achates,* damaging her badly. Sherbrooke responded by releasing the *Obdurate* and *Obedient* to guard the merchantmen, while the *Onslow* and the *Orwell* endeavored to frustrate the moves of the German force. Shortly after 1000 hours, the *Hipper* found the range of the two British destroyers and scored several hits on the *Onslow,* wounding Sherbrooke so severely that he had to turn over command to Lieutenant Commander D.C. Kinloch. Soon, however, the *Hipper* and three destroyers shifted attention to the mine-sweeper *Bramble* on their port quarter, while the *Onslow* and *Orwell* retreated behind the *Achates'* smoke screen and rejoined the convoy. None of the *Bramble*'s eighty crewmen survived the unequal duel.

While Kummetz was crowding JW-51B from the north and west, the *Lützow* and her escorts inadvertently crossed three miles in front of the convoy on northeasterly courses without getting more than a dim glimpse of a vessel on their port beam. The *Lützow* thus missed a golden opportunity to complete the envelopment maneuver Kummetz had intended, and moved on harmlessly to the north and later to the west for a rendezvous with the *Hipper*.

It was now 1100 hours with little more than an hour of daylight remaining. By that time, Burnett realized his mistake and was bearing down on the convoy from the north at 31 knots. Before long his radar picked up the *Hipper*. Once visual contact was established with the German cruiser silhouetted against the southern horizon, the *Sheffield* and *Jamaica* opened fire at 1131 hours, scoring hits on the *Hipper* that reduced her speed and set her aircraft hangar ablaze. Six minutes after British shells began falling around him, Kummetz ordered his entire force to retreat to the west.

That move came too late to save the *Friedrich Eckoldt*. She was busy finishing off the *Bramble* when the *Sheffield*, mistaking the *Friedrich Eckoldt* for the *Hipper*, opened fire at close range. The German destroyer sank within minutes with her entire crew. As the Arctic dusk settled over the scene shortly after noon, Kummetz was headed home on westerly courses, distantly shadowed by Force R. The *Achates* became the last casualty of the engagement. Heavily damaged, she sank shortly after 1315 hours, taking 100 men down with her. Convoy JW-51B, to whose survival the *Achates* had contributed so valiantly, resumed an otherwise uneventful voyage to Murmansk.

The safe arrival of convoy JW-51B was a remarkable victory for the Allies. Kummetz failed to take advantage of his superior strength and the element of surprise. In the confused duel with the convoy's escort forces, he threw away too many good chances to press his attack home. The failure of Operation REGENBOGEN would contribute, within three weeks, to the downfall of Grand Admiral Erich Raeder (q.v.) as the German overall naval commander, and his replacement by the leader of the U-boats, Grand Admiral Karl Dönitz (q.v.).

Eric C. Rust

Additional Reading
Carmichael, Thomas N., *The Ninety Days* (1971).
Pope, Dudley, *73 North: The Defeat of Hitler's Navy* (1959).

Bari Air Raid (2 December 1943)

On 10 July 1943, Allied forces landed in Italy and began the slow, hard drive up the Axis-held Italian peninsula. In August, alerted by reports of possible use of chemical agents by the Germans, President Franklin D. Roosevelt (q.v.) promised "full and swift retaliation in kind." This stern warning failed to stem the rumors that the Germans were stockpiling chemical weapons in Italy. After careful consideration, Roosevelt approved the shipment to the Mediterranean theater of chemical munitions containing liquid mustard agent.

On 18 November 1943, the American liberty ship *John Harvey*, commanded by Captain Elwin F. Knowles, set out from Oran, Algeria, carrying 2,000 M-47A1 one-hundred-pound, World War I–type mustard bombs to Italy. A nervous crew had maneuvered the *John Harvey* around several German U-boat wolf packs while crossing the Atlantic. The convoy with the *John Harvey* stopped at Augusta, Sicily, on 25 November. The next day, after 1st Lieutenant Howard D. Beckstrom of the 7th Chemical Ordnance Company had inspected the cargo, the *John Harvey* moved carefully out of Augusta. It sailed through the Strait of Otranto, and arrived at the Italian port of Bari, which was then occupied by the British 1st Airborne Division.

Bari was jammed with thirty merchant ships and tankers waiting to be unloaded. The *John Harvey* had to wait several days, in plain sight of any *Luftwaffe* aircraft that might overfly the area. Knowles wanted to tell the British port director about his dangerous cargo and request expeditious unloading, but secrecy prevented his doing so. On the sixth day in port, a *Luftwaffe* reconnaissance plane, piloted by *Oberleutnant* Werner Hahn, spotted the large number of merchant vessels jammed in the harbor and quickly returned to his base in northern Italy to inform Field Marshal Wolfram von Richthofen (q.v.), commander of the Second *Luftflotte*. Von Richthofen was under orders to find any way to slow down the American and British advance. Now, in Bari harbor, he saw an opportunity to accomplish his mission.

On 2 December 1943, eighty-eight German bombers attacked Bari harbor, killing over 1,000 people, sinking seventeen ships, and damaging eight others. One of the badly damaged ships was the *John Harvey,* which caught fire from exploding debris. In the chaos of the attack, no one paid any special attention to the chemical-laden vessel which, even before the crew could evacuate, flamed out of control and exploded. A huge fountain of multicolored gas jets spewed in all directions, shooting more than a thousand feet in the air. Knowles, the only man who could have told the British authorities about his deadly cargo, was killed. The mustard weapons caused 430 casualties among military personnel. No record is available on the number of civilian casualties.

Not knowing the source of the many blisters and burning eyes sustained by their patients, Allied medical personnel were stunned by the mysterious ailments that failed to respond to standard treatments. Emergency medical personnel were flown in from Algiers. On 11 December, a British diver recovered one of the shell casings that had contained the mustard agent. Little by little and piece by piece, local military authorities learned what had happened, but too late to respond effectively to many of the sick and dying.

The Germans learned earlier what had happened. Three German agents, headed by Dieter Gollob and living under cover in Bari, obtained a piece of metal casing brought up from the bottom by an Italian diver. Within hours they had identified it. It was not difficult to do because, as Gollob said later, "the marking M-47A1 was on the metal casing and a call to our headquarters in the north soon verified that it was a hundred-pound bomb that was used by the Americans for carrying liquid mustard." By 5 December, SS General Karl Wolff (q.v.), German military governor for northern Italy, knew exactly what was causing the many Allied deaths. He urged Heinrich Himmler (q.v.) to exploit the incident for propaganda purposes. For reasons not entirely clear, the Nazi government failed to do so.

From the stand point of surprise and shock effect, Bari was a merchant marine disaster reminiscent of Pearl Harbor, and a catastrophic loss of human lives, shipping, and supplies. Much mystery still surrounds this affair. For many years after the war, American authorities were less than forthcoming in releasing information. The Bari incident was the only confirmed major event involving poison gas during World War II in Europe.

Paul J. Rose

Additional Reading
Gleichauf, Justin F., *Unsung Heroes: The Naval Armed Guard in World War II* (1990).
Infield, Glen B., *Disaster at Bari* (1971).
———, *Secrets of the SS* (1982).

B

Bastogne (19 December 1944–9 January 1945)

[See map 2 on page 1312]

During the Ardennes offensive (q.v.), the initial German attack in the early morning hours of 16 December 1944 surprised the Allies completely. The Fifth *Panzer* Army under General Hasso von Manteuffel (q.v.) formed the southern thrust of the German drive on Antwerp. The spearhead of the Fifth *Panzer* Army was General Heinrich von Lüttwitz's XLVII *Panzer Korps,* consisting of the *Panzer-Lehr* Division, the 2nd *Panzer* Division, and the 26th *Volksgrenadier* Division.

Initially, the XLVII *Panzer Korps* headed directly toward the city of Bastogne, an important traffic junction. Seven main roads, a railway, and several minor roads met there. The *Panzer-Lehr* Division had orders to approach the city from the south and to occupy the undefended town before 18 December, if possible. Bad road conditions and misleading information from the Belgian population prevented them from getting there before midnight 18 December.

In the meantime, the Allies finally realized that the German attacks were the start of a major offensive, rather than just spoiling attacks, as they originally thought. All along the front, they quickly started pulling back in order to buy time to organize a more effective defense. The first American forces to arrive in Bastogne, thirty kilometers from the initial German line of attack, were elements of the 10th Armored Division, commanded by Colonel William L. Roberts. They reached the city at sunset on 18 December and immediately blocked the roads running east and northeast from Bastogne.

The *Panzer-Lehr* Division, under General Fritz Bayerlein (q.v.), arrived at Bastogne shortly after midnight on 19 December. They attacked immediately, because they knew from radio intercepts that the U.S. 101st Airborne Division was on its way to the city. Elements of that division, however, had already reached Bastogne late at night on 18 December. The U.S. 501st Parachute Infantry Regiment occupied the hills east of the city. The fighting for this high ground and the entrance of the city only lasted three hours on the morning of 19 December. Bayerlein gave up because he sustained high losses and the terrain was not suitable for his *Panzers.* Thus, the first German attack stopped two kilometers outside the city.

That same day, von Manteuffel decided that in order to continue the westward momentum of the offensive, he would not commit all of the XLVII *Panzer Korps* to the fight for Bastogne. He ordered the *Panzer-Lehr* to leave its 902nd *Panzer* Regiment behind and to continue moving south of Bastogne. He also sent Colonel Meinrad von Lauchert's 2nd *Panzer* Division north of Bastogne, so that both would reach the Meuse without delay.

Colonel Heinz Kokott's 26th *Volksgrenadier* Division moved up and joined the 902nd *Panzer-Lehr* Regiment in the fight for Bastogne. With three infantry regiments in the north and a reinforced reconnaissance battalion in the south, the city was almost completely surrounded, except for one small gap in the west between Champs and Senonchamps.

The defending forces at Bastogne had increased as well, with the 101st Airborne Division arriving in strength. The north approaches to the city were defended by the 705th Tank Battalion, whose Sherman tanks were armed with the high-velocity 76mm main gun. By the evening of 21 December, the Germans had completely encircled Bastogne, cutting off the American defenders in a pocket eight kilometers in diameter.

For two days there was almost no action while the Germans extended their positions and brought up supplies. On 22 December, von Lüttwitz sent a surrender ultimatum to Brigadier General Anthony McAuliffe (q.v.), the acting commander of the 101st Airborne Division. Knowing General George S. Patton's (q.v.) U.S. Third Army was on its way to Bastogne, McAuliffe reportedly replied with the cryptic statement, "Nuts"—an answer that somewhat confused the Germans at first.

The encircled American troops were supplied by air with ammunition, food, and medicine. That helped them get through the German attack of 23 December, one of the most critical periods of the whole siege. The 26th *Volksgrenadier* Division, the *Panzer-Lehr* units, and the Seventh Army's Fifth Parachute Division then tried to break the defenses from the southeast and the northwest. Even though the *Luftwaffe* provided support with two heavy attacks, they failed on 24 and again on 25 December. During those attacks, the Germans sustained heavy losses in tanks, materiel, and men. Those also turned out to be the last and the strongest of the attacks directed against the defenders in the city itself.

In the meantime, the Third Army was heading for Bastogne. General Erich Brandenberger's (q.v.) Seventh Army was supposed to screen the left flank of the Ardennes offensive, but with only four divisions and no tanks there was little they could do to stop the Third Army. On 26 December, elements of the 4th Armored Division's 37th Tank Battalion, commanded by Lieutenant Colonel Creighton W. Abrams (q.v.), reached Bastogne. It had taken the 4th Armored Division five days, and they lost 1,000 men during the heavy fighting along the route of the march. They succeeded, however, in breaking open the German ring around Bastogne. At first, they opened a narrow passage to the city, then they enlarged it. The fight for Bastogne now consisted of enlarging that corridor.

The Germans pulled in more forces. Contrary to the original operational plans, but in accordance with Adolf Hitler's (q.v.) orders, the Fifth *Panzer* Army now made Bastogne their main effort. Colonel Otto Remer's *Führer* Escort Brigade and elements of the 15th *Panzergrenadier* Division attacked to close the corridor on 27 December. The attacking force was not strong enough to accomplish the mission. Next, the 3rd *Panzergrenadier* Division and the 167th *Volksgrenadier* Division joined the fight. Command of the German operations at Bastogne passed to Lieutenant General Karl Decker of the XXXIX *Panzer Korps*. On 29 December, Decker received as reinforcements the 1st *SS Panzer* Division from the Sixth *Panzer* Army.

Hitler still insisted on taking Bastogne as quickly as possible. On the evening of 29 December, German units assembled around Bastogne for a renewed attack. The XLVII *Panzer Korps* was upgraded to *Armeegruppe* Lüttwitz; and the XXXIX *Panzer Korps*, which had been leading the fight, came under the group's command.

The next attack started at 0625 hours on 30 December. The *Führer* Escort Brigade and elements of the 3rd and 15th *Panzergrenadier* Divisions headed for Sibret from the west, while in the east, the 167th *Volksgrenadier* Division and the 1st *SS Panzer* Division went for the road connecting Bastogne and Martelange. The Germans gained some ground until the afternoon, but then the attack faltered. To the west of the city, the *Führer* Escort Brigade and the 15th *Volksgrenadier* Division were checked by units of the Third Army.

In the final days of December, the Germans shifted the entire thrust of the Ardennes offensive. The planned drive to the Meuse River and Antwerp turned into a battle over Bastogne, which devoured one German division after the other. The Germans made almost no progress against the strong American resistance. On 31 December, the Germans committed additional units, including the 12th *SS Panzer* Division of the I *SS Panzer Korps*, and the

40th Division. When those attacks failed, *Armeegruppe* Lüttwitz was dissolved, and its units reverted back to the control of the Fifth *Panzer* Army.

The German commander in chief in the west, Field Marshal Gerd von Rundstedt (q.v.), knew that if the Germans failed to destroy all the Allied forces at Bastogne, the Germans would be forced into waging a defensive battle of attrition that they could never win. Hitler, too, steadfastly opposed any halts or rearward movements. Thus the Germans prepared to mount another major attack on 1 January 1945. In the meantime, the Germans had to fend off heavy American attacks along the southern flank of the XLVII *Panzer Korps*.

As the Americans continued to move reinforcements into the area, they grew increasingly strong in artillery. Also, the Allied air forces were attacking the Germans continuously since the weather had cleared on 24 December. The German positions east of Bastogne were pushed so far back that the attack plans had to be changed completely. Now, instead of attacking from the southeast, the 9th and 12th *SS Panzer* Divisions, together with the *Führer* Escort Brigade, were to attack from the north, northeast, and east.

Why did the Germans have to commit an increasingly larger number of divisions as the Ardennes offensive wore on? At the beginning of 1945, the typical German division only had a fraction of its former strength. The 9th *SS Panzer* Division, for example, started the offensive with 120 tanks and assault guns. Now it had only thirty left. The division's grenadier battalions were down to only 150 to 175 men. The 12th *SS Panzer* Division was in no better shape. It had only twenty-five of its 100 tanks left, and its grenadier battalions had only 100 to 125 men. The battalions of the 340th *Volksgrenadier* Division had 150 to 175 men. At that rate, German strength would soon wither away to nothing. The American units, on the other hand, were in much better condition. They could obtain almost immediate replacements for losses of materiel and men.

The last major German attack began on 4 January and stalled very quickly. Further small actions continued until 8 January. The German hold on Bastogne was broken finally by the Third Army on 9 January 1945. The fight for Bastogne was over. The losses were considerable. The city of Bastogne lost 782 civilians. The Americans lost about 2,700 troops, the Germans about 3,000.

Some 6,785 German soldiers killed in the battles between Malmedy, St. Vith (qq.v.), and Bastogne are buried in the German military cemetery close to Bastogne. The American dead lie in the Henri-Chapelle Cemetery between Liège and Aachen.

Ekkehart Guth

Additional Reading
Cole, Hugh M., *The Ardennes: Battle of the Bulge* (1965).
Dupuy, Trevor N., David L. Bongard, and Richard C. Anderson, Jr., *Hitler's Last Gamble: The Battle of the Bulge, December 1944–January 1945* (1995).
Eisenhower, John S.D., *The Bitter Woods* (1969).
Elstob, Peter, *Bastogne, The Road Block* (1968).
Jung, H., *Die Ardennenoffensive 1944/45* (1971).
MacDonald, Charles B., *A Time for Trumpets: The Untold Story of the Battle of the Bulge* (1985).

Battle of Britain

See BRITAIN, AIR CAMPAIGN

Battle of the Atlantic

See ATLANTIC CAMPAIGN

Battle of the Bulge

See ARDENNES OFFENSIVE

Beda Fomm (5–7 February 1941)

After the British capture of Tobruk (*see* Tobruk I), General Richard O'Connor (q.v.) was anxious to clear the Italians out of Libya before the British campaign in Greece (q.v.) severely crippled his offensive capability by drawing off more resources. "Like a terrier ratting," in the words of General Eric Dorman-Smith (q.v.), O'Connor sought a decisive victory over Benito Mussolini's retreating Tenth Army.

At dawn on 4 February 1941, the 7th Armoured Division, O'Connor's spearhead, set out to find the Italians and destroy them. O'Connor was so intent on cutting off the retreating Italians that he sent the 7th Armoured on a detour march south, through the hard desert terrain, abandoning the coastal highway. With orders from O'Connor to cut the coastal road, the 7th Armoured Division's commander, Major General Sir Michael O'Moore Creagh, told his men, "the code word is Gallop."

In order to block the retreat of the Italians under General Annibale Bergonzoli, the 7th

Armoured Division dispatched an advanced guard, called "Combeforce" (named for its commander, Lieutenant Colonel John Combe), to take up forward positions across the coastal road on 5 February. By noon that day, Combeforce reached the main road at Beda Fomm. Within thirty minutes of their arrival, an Italian convoy retiring from Benghazi, the main base still in Italian hands, was stopped fast by Combe.

At 1500 hours on 5 February, an Italian convoy tried to break through the British lines and was captured. At 1700 hours, another column met the same fate. Desperately, the Italians poured more men and equipment into the battle, determined to overcome Combe's roadblock with frontal attacks and retreat to safety in the west. As the Italian pressure continued to increase, the British 4th Armoured Brigade, sent forward over the rough desert terrain by Creagh, arrived just in time to strengthen the hard-pressed Combeforce.

Arriving as dusk began to settle over the North African landscape, the tanks of 4th Armoured Brigade immediately engaged the lightly armored Italian tanks. The 7th Hussars, the leading element of 4th Armoured Brigade, crashed into the surprised Italians, and shortly the battle was fought by the light of burning armored vehicles. Only the coming of night saved the Italians from complete destruction. Throughout that night, the British maintained their hold on the Italians, preventing a breakout under cover of darkness.

The next day was stormy. Buffeted by rain, however, the Italians kept up the pressure to break out, hammering at the southern British positions. The Italian efforts were repulsed by British artillery used in a defensive role. Throughout 6 February, Bergonzoli's troops struck against at the restraining British cordon. By mid-day, the Italians had lost some forty tanks, as British antitank guns engaged Italian armor at almost point-blank range through the driving rain. Despite the severe mauling, the Italians still had almost fifty tanks, against fifteen for the British. So desperate was the combat that a British officer, seeing a tank with a damaged main gun barrel, ordered the tank's commander to "look dangerous."

Throughout the night of 6 February Bergonzoli's troops tried to breach the British lines. The Rifle Brigade alone repulsed at least nine determined Italian attempts to cut through its position.

On the morning of 7 February, Bergonzoli mounted his last desperate attempt to break out of the British ring by hurling his last thirty tanks at the British. Aiming at the depleted Rifle Brigade,

the Italian column punched a hole in the position. At one critical moment it seemed that the Italians would break out. To stem the Italian rush, the gunners of the Royal Artillery received the unprecedented order to fire into the Italians as they were intermingled with the soldiers of the Rifle Brigade. O'Connor, meanwhile, drove the Australian 6th Infantry Division into the Italian rear. The last Italian tank was knocked out just before it reached the tent housing the British officers' mess.

That was the end of the Italian Tenth Army. A handful of Italian troops tried to escape into the desert, only to be picked up by Combeforce. By the time the Tenth Army surrendered to O'Connor, its commander, General Giuseppe Tellera, had been killed. General Bergonzoli, however, was captured alive. O'Connor later commented, "I think this may be termed a complete victory, as none of the enemy escaped." The Italians lost eighty-four tanks and some 20,000 troops surrendered. The British also captured 112 medium tanks, 216 guns, and 1,500 wheeled vehicles, a bonanza for the transportation-starved O'Connor. British losses were only nine killed and fifteen wounded.

With the Italian catastrophe at Beda Fomm nothing lay before O'Connor and a triumphant British advance on into Italian Tripolitania, the westernmost province of Libya and the last part of Mussolini's new Roman Empire in North Africa. Combining a seaborne landing behind Italian lines near Tripoli with an overland push from Beda Fomm, O'Connor intended to crush the last remnants of the Italian forces in Libya. O'Connor later reflected: "In my opinion the operation would not only have been possible, but would have had every chance of success provided all three services gave their maximum support and were not deflected by other commitments."

The "other commitments" that O'Connor feared became reality. Prime Minister Winston S. Churchill (q.v.), believing that saving Greece was essential, diverted vital forces from O'Connor that could have ensured the final victory over the Italians in Libya. The gutting of the Western Desert Force (which later became the British Eighth Army) was a major factor in prolonging the war in North Africa for two more years.

Although Adolf Hitler (q.v.) already approved plans to reinforce the Italians in Tripolitania with the nucleus of Lieutenant General Erwin Rommel's *Afrika Korps* (qq.v.), it seems unlikely, with German campaigns already approved for the Balkans and Russia, that he would have committed sizable numbers of troops to retake a Tripolitania already largely in O'Connor's grip. As General Archibald

Wavell (q.v.), the theater commander, noted later, "I am still sure that my instinct, to fight as far forward in defence of the Middle East, was correct."

On 13 February 1941, Wavell received orders from Churchill to abandon the advance on Tripoli in favor of reinforcing the Greeks. That previous day, Rommel landed in Tripoli with the German 5th Light Division and forward elements of the *Afrika Korps*. The tide of war in North Africa was again turning against the British.

John F. Murphy

Additional Reading

Barnett, Correlli, *The Desert Generals* (1964).
Keegan, John (ed.), *Churchill's Generals* (1991).
Strawson, John, *The Battle for North Africa* (1969).

Belgium and Flanders (10 May–4 June 1940)

[See map 17 on page 1327]

Flanders is a region of the Low Countries traditionally defined by the North Sea, the Scheldt or Escaut River, and the hills of Artois. On 10 May 1940, the same day Winston S. Churchill (q.v.) became Britain's prime minister, the Germans launched a *Blitzkrieg* offensive through the area. In less than a month, Holland and Belgium surrendered, the British retreated across the Channel, and the French were on the verge of collapse.

The Allies, particularly the French, were convinced that any German attack would roughly parallel the Schlieffen Plan (q.v.) of 1914. The Allies, therefore, planned to focus the bulk of their efforts in the north. In the south, they relied on the strength of the Maginot Line (q.v.), and in the center, they depended on the natural defensibility of the Ardennes Forest. As the Germans struck across the Low Countries, the French and British would dash through Belgium to link up with Belgian and Dutch units along a defensive line that ran from Antwerp to Namur. A major portion of that line ran along the Dyle River, east of Brussels.

The initial 19 October 1939 version of Germany's *Fall GELB* (Case YELLOW) was, in fact, somewhat similar to what the Allies anticipated. General Erich von Manstein (q.v.), however, recognized that such a course of action most probably would attack the Allies' strength. Instead, he recommended a *Sichelschnitt* (sickle cut) maneuver. The sickle would be General Gerd von Rundstedt's (q.v.) Army Group A (forty-five divisions), slicing through the Ardennes where the French line was weakest. General Heinz Guderian (q.v.), who had

assured von Manstein the Ardennes were passable with tanks, would lead his XIX *Panzer Korps* in the main effort toward Sedan. Meanwhile, General Feodor von Bock's (q.v.) Army Group B (thirty divisions) would conduct a supporting attack in the north in order to draw the Allies' main strength into northern Belgium and Holland. There they could be enveloped by von Rundstedt. General Wilhelm von Leeb's (q.v.) Army Group C (nineteen divisions) would conduct a holding attack to fix the Allied forces in the south.

On 10 January 1940, a German liaison plane carrying a portion of the *Fall GELB* plan made a forced landing near Mechelen, Belgium. Based on the captured plans, General Maurice Gamelin (q.v.), chief of the French General Staff, issued a change to the Dyle Plan, known as the Berda Variant, which extended the Allied defensive line to Berda, Holland. Now, instead of the ten French divisions and the British Expeditionary Force (BEF) previously allocated to the Belgian operation, a total of thirty divisions would be involved. General Henri Giraud's (q.v.) French Seventh Army (seven divisions) was committed to the Allies' extreme northern flank. The Seventh Army was supposed to race through Belgium and link up with the Dutch Army at Berda to defend "Fortress Holland." Previously, the Seventh Army was to have been the bulk of the Allies' mobile strategic reserve. Its commitment into Holland would prove to have grave consequences for the Allies.

A modified version of the compromised *Fall GELB* plan was signed on 24 February 1940. Adolf Hitler (q.v.) was profoundly affected by the breach in security, and he ordered strict measures to safeguard the revisions. Even commanders of the spearhead units were kept in the dark as to the exact timing of the attack. These internal security precautions were complimented by extensive intelligence and sabotage efforts by German sympathizers in the Low Countries and France. In the end, it was German *Panzers* and not the Fifth Columnists that defeated the Allies in Flanders, but the panic and doubt spread by exaggerated reports helped to distract the defenders and undermine morale.

The German offensive began just after midnight on 10 May with well-coordinated *Luftwaffe* attacks. Bombers laid mines off the Dutch and British coasts, hit airfields in Holland, Belgium, and France, and struck key transportation centers deep in France. The main *Luftwaffe* effort was concentrated over the Netherlands (q.v.), which masked the true location of the sickle cut through the Ardennes.

General Georg von Kuchler's Eighteenth Army struck north through the Netherlands, forcing the Dutch to surrender in just five days. On his southern flank, General Walther von Reichenau's (q.v.) Sixth Army pierced into Belgium. On this axis, von Reichenau had to contend with the formidable Albert Canal and the powerful Fort Eban Emael.

The fort controlled two bridges over the canal critical to von Reichenau's advance. In order to maintain his momentum, he had to capture these bridges intact. In continuing his drive, he would cause the Allies to deploy to shore up the Belgian line. The task of securing the bridges was accomplished with an ingenious glider-borne assault on Fort Eben Emael (q.v.). By 11 May, the 3rd and 4th *Panzer* Divisions were across the bridges and spreading out over the plains to the fort's west. In the wake of this onslaught, Belgian King Léopold (q.v.) ordered his forces to begin a general withdrawal.

At approximately 0700 hours on the morning of the attack, Gamelin, the Allied commander in chief, ordered his troops to the Dyle Line. Five armies totaling 600,000 troops moved forward, but the Allies had no standing reserve as a result of the Berda Variant. As his forces were hurrying to the aid of the Belgians, they were about to become decisively engaged with the German supporting attack, rather than the main effort.

Gamelin also faced command and control problems. His headquarters in Vincennes (in Paris) lacked radio transmitting capability, and his commander in chief on the northeast front, General Alphonse Georges (q.v.), was more than forty miles away at La Ferté-sous-Jouarre. This command relationship proved too remote to handle the rapidly unraveling situation.

Two more problems confronted Gamelin. The first was that his own subordinate commanders were less than unanimous in their support for the modified Dyle Plan. Many felt the line of defense should be established along the Scheldt River, requiring a shorter move for French forces, but a larger forfeiture of territory for the Belgians. Whatever the line, Gamelin assumed his troops would arrive at prepared fortifications ready to be occupied. That was not the case, which was Gamelin's other big problem. The positions offered by the Belgians were scratchy and unfinished at best.

Despite these difficulties, Gamelin committed himself to the modified Dyle Plan. His most forward unit was General René Prioux's French Cavalry Corps, whose mission was to screen the arrival of the French First Army. After a march of

between seventy-five and ninety-five miles, Prioux reached the Dyle and established his defense in the scant positions. He arrived just in time, because the forward Belgian defense did not last nearly as long as expected. As early as 11 May, the Germans breached the Meuse-Albert Canal Line, and the Belgians were retiring to the Antwerp-Louvain Line, with the Germans in close pursuit. The first clashes between General Erich Hoepner's (q.v.) XVI *Panzer Korps* and the French cavalry occurred on 12 May.

Prioux's efforts bought the Allies valuable time. By the evening of 11 May, the II Corps of the British Expeditionary Force (BEF), commanded by General Alan Brooke (q.v.), occupied the Louvain to Wavre section of the Dyle Line. On the north flank, Giraud's Seventh Army was advancing toward Breda. Giraud had 145 miles to cover, a far greater distance than what faced the Germans. To compound this disadvantage Giraud was further hamstrung by the weak resistance of the Dutch forces. The whole reason for the move to Breda was for Seventh Army to link up with Fortress Holland, but the Dutch effort was so negligible Giraud never had a chance (*see* Netherlands). Thus, the entire move of the Seventh Army was in vain, and with it, Gamelin forfeited his option to maintain a reserve. On the afternoon of 12 May, Giraud was ordered to regroup his forces west of the Scheldt.

To the south of the BEF, the French First Army, commanded by General J.C.N. Blanchard, advanced slowly, impeded by swarms of Belgian refugees heading for France. This delay and the unexpectedly weak Belgian defensive efforts put increased pressure on Prioux and his cavalry to slow the German advance. Thanks to Prioux's efforts, the First Army reached its positions on the morning of 15 May, occupying a line from Wavre to Namur.

With the arrival of Blanchard, Gamelin now had forty divisions on the line in the north. This strength was more than sufficient to repel the attack of the German Sixth Army. Von Reichenau, therefore, elected to concentrate his forces and suspend further assaults until 17 May. The Allies brought the situation under control in the north, but they also played directly into the German trap. The situation farther south was entirely different.

While the Allies were reacting to the northern thrust, Guderian's XIX *Panzer* Korps, spearheading the main German effort, was conducting an uneventful passage through Luxembourg. The country had no defense to speak of, and it was overrun in a matter of hours. By 11 May, Guderian's 1st and 2nd *Panzer* Divisions advanced o the Semois River, a distance of sixty miles in forty-eight hours. The next day, he closed up his divisions in preparation for the assault. The decisive action came on 13 May, when he crossed the Meuse River, and that bridgehead expanded into a raging torrent.

On breaching the Meuse and breaking through at Sedan, Guderian swung his corps west toward Abbeville and the English Channel. The 1st and 2nd *Panzer* Divisions pushed across the River Bar and the Ardennes Canal, and then sliced through the southern flank of the French Ninth Army. In the process, the French 1st Armored Division, designated to be the Allied counterattack force, was caught by surprise while refueling and virtually destroyed. On 14 May, the German Army high command (OKH) pulled von Bock's armor units to reinforce Army Group A's advance. By the morning of 16 May, the advance elements of the XIX and XLI *Panzer Korps* met at Montcornet, deep in the rear of the French XLI Corps. The threat of an even more encompassing envelopment was too great for the Allies to bear. General Gaston Billotte (q.v.) ordered his 1st Army Group to abandon the Dyle Line and withdraw under cover of darkness to the Escaut.

On 17 May, OKH and Army Group A, fearing a French counterattack from the Verdun-Chalons area, ordered a halt to the *Panzer* advance. Guderian vigorously protested the order. After a heated confrontation with General Paul von Kleist (q.v.), commander of the *Panzer* group (actually a *Panzer* army), Guderian was allowed to conduct a "reconnaissance in force."

During that advance, the French Ninth Army made its last attempt to halt the Germans, including a counterattack against Guderian's southern flank by Brigadier General Charles de Gaulle's (q.v.) 4th Armored Division. De Gaulle's division was too weak to do any real damage to the Germans. On 19 May, OKH lifted the restrictions on Kleist's armor. With General Georg-Hans Reinhardt's (q.v.) XLI *Panzer Korps* running on a roughly parallel course in the north, Guderian's corps moved rapidly to the west along the Somme River. On 20 May, they took Abbeville, completing the "*Panzer* Corridor" to the sea. The BEF was cut off.

The advance on Army Group A's north flank was slower. General Hermann Hoth's (q.v.) XV *Panzer Korps,* spearheaded by Major General Erwin Rommel's (q.v.) 7th *Panzer* Division, crossed the Meuse and had to fight through defensive positions prepared the previous winter. Rommel's division moved to Cambrai rapidly

enough, but the following infantry of the German Fourth Army had a tough time. The French First Army put up a good resistance. On 19 May, Hoth ordered Rommel to hold at Cambrai until the German infantry could close up. The following day, Rommel resumed his westward advance, and reached the vicinity of Arras. He stopped briefly to close up his division but then resumed the advance on the afternoon of 21 May.

Meanwhile, dissatisfaction with Gamelin's leadership was running high. On 17 May, General Maxime Weygand (q.v.) was summoned to Paris, and three days later, he assumed the duties as Allied commander in chief. His first priority was to reestablish communications among the various Allied armies. His plan to accomplish this involved simultaneous attacks toward Bapaume, south from Arras and north from the Somme River Line.

On 21 May, the British counterattacked at Arras with Frankforce, an ad hoc group composed of parts of two infantry divisions and a tank brigade. The counterattack also had the mission of blocking the roads to the south of Arras to halt the German advance, but "Frankforce" proved to be too weak to cause more than a temporary inconvenience to the Germans. Hoth moved up his other units and forced the British back into Arras by 22 May, and to Bethune by 23 May. The British attack, however, did shake up the OKH and may have contributed to the decision to halt the *Panzer*s, ultimately allowing the British to escape from Dunkirk (q.v.).

On 23 May, the French launched their counterattack from the Somme River into the southern flank of the "*Panzer* Corridor." They attacked without complete knowledge of the failure of the Frankforce attack, and with inadequate intelligence of the vast German combat power now concentrated west of Cambrai. To add to the Allies' confusion, Billotte was killed in an automobile crash in the middle of the battle. The French attacks failed.

The setback at Arras convinced Field Marshal John Gort (q.v.) he had to take independent action to save the BEF. At that point, he was receiving no specific instructions from Weygand, and he was becoming increasingly frustrated with the lack of French leadership following Billotte's untimely death. Churchill was committed to Anglo-French cooperation, but even he was becoming disillusioned with the French lack of initiative. In this confused climate, Gort decided to withdraw the BEF behind the Haute Deule Canal in preparation for a retirement to Dunkirk. Gort's decision was made with only the BEF in mind, and the withdrawal put the French and Belgians in even greater jeopardy. Gort acted without informing the French, and as a result, they later felt abandoned by the British.

For King Léopold, the order to abandon the Dyle Line was a bitter pill. It meant the loss of Belgium's principal cities, including Brussels. Nonetheless, he complied. The failure of the BEF counterattack at Arras caused the Belgians to thin their defenses along the Scheldt and establish a new line along the Lys River, a front of sixty miles. On 24 May, Reichenau's Sixth Army struck at Courtrai and isolated the Belgians from the BEF. The British refused to counterattack the flank of the German penetration toward Ypres, and continued their withdrawal to Dunkirk. Leopold did not even learn of the British decision to evacuate until 27 May. That same day, he dispatched an envoy to the German lines in order to discuss surrender terms. On 28 May, after only eighteen days of fighting, Leopold accepted Hitler's demand for unconditional surrender.

With the Belgians out of the war and the French on the verge of collapse, the BEF continued withdrawing to Dunkirk. Between 26 May and 4 June, the British evacuated 338,226 British and French soldiers in one of the most incredible feats of the war; but the success of Operation DYNAMO (q.v.) doomed what remained of the Allied force on the Continent. The Allies were left with only seventy-one divisions to face 143 German divisions, many of which were still fresh. The battle for France (q.v.) started on 5 June 1940, one day after the British completed the Dunkirk evacuation.

The battle for Flanders destroyed the Belgians and Dutch, sealed the fate of the French, and forced the British back across the Channel. An even far more decisive success had lain within Germany's grasp. Their most critical error was the failure to destroy the BEF. Even with this missed opportunity, the Germans were still in an excellent position to continue the momentum of their drive with a cross-channel invasion of Britain.

Apparently the remarkable success of the German offensive surprised even Hitler. At that time, there were no plans to continue the drive across the channel. On 21 May, Grand Admiral Erich Raeder (q.v.), commander in chief of the German Navy, approached Hitler with the idea, but he was coolly received. Hitler at that point was still obsessed with the heady prospects of quickly conquering France. The German victory in Flanders was impressive, but it fell short of its potential.

Kevin Dougherty

Additional Reading

Baldwin, Hanson, *The Crucial Years: 1939–1940* (1976).
Guderian, Heinz, *Panzer Leader* (1952).
Horne, Alistair, *To Lose a Battle: France 1940* (1969).
Jacobsen, H.A., and J. Rohwer, *Decisive Battles of World War II: The German View* (1965).

Belgrade (6–12 April 1941)

Following the 26–27 March 1941 overthrow of the Yugoslav government and the termination of Prince Paul's regency by a group of Serbian military men, Adolf Hitler (q.v.) furiously ordered his subordinates to "make all preparations to destroy Yugoslavia militarily and as a national unit, without waiting for any possible declaration of loyalty from the new government." The invasion of Yugoslavia by German troops began early on 6 April. It was accompanied by the bombing of Belgrade by close to 500 planes of General Alexander Löhr's (q.v.) Fourth *Luftflotte*.

Contrary to Hitler's wishes, the air attacks (which were repeated on a smaller scale the next day) were aimed primarily at military, administrative, and transportation centers, though some residential areas in the city were hit as well. The attack persuaded the Simović government to leave the capital immediately, and they thoroughly disrupted the entire command and control system of the country. Also exposed to the bombing, it appears, were several members of the German legation in Belgrade, including the military attaché Colonel Rudolf Toussaint, and his colleague from the *Luftwaffe*, Colonel Arthur Laumann. Total casualties attributable to the German bombing of Belgrade are still a matter of controversy, with figures ranging from 1,500 civilian deaths to more than 10,000. Some earlier claims of 30,000 victims are no longer considered realistic.

Starting about 8 April, three separate German forces converged on Belgrade from different directions. The Twelfth Army's First *Panzer* Group struck northwest from Bulgaria; the Second Army's XLVI *Panzer Korps* came from the opposite direction from Hungary; and the XLI *Panzer Korps* came from Romania in the northeast. The lead units reached the outskirts of Belgrade on 12 April. They took control of the undefended city on the following day. A general surrender of the Yugoslav armed forces was signed in Belgrade on 17 April and came into effect the next day. The Soviet 3rd Ukrainian Front recaptured Belgrade on 20 October 1944.

Ulrich Trumpener

Additional Reading

Blau, George E., *The German Campaign in the Balkans, Spring 1941* (1953).

Olshausen, Klaus, *Zwischenspiel auf dem Balkan* (1973).

Berlin (16 April–2 May 1945)

[See map 21 on page 1331]

In January 1945, much of Berlin lay in rubble. The city was littered with bombed-out structures, the result of years of air attacks and saturation bombing. The city, in fact, endured more than 450 bombing raids and was the target of 45,517 tons of bombs dropped during the war. Beginning in mid-February 1945, Berlin experienced almost continual aerial bombardment from the U.S. and Royal Air Forces for thirty days and nights. Many of the ruins, however, were cleared out and the lots used to raise a few crops as the populace attempted to survive until the end of the conflict.

With the almost complete destruction of the social and economic system, black markets flourished, as did a variety of other illegal war-related activities, such as theft, break-ins, and roving teenage gangs. Transportation lines within the city and interconnecting with other cities lay in ruins, and the city was increasingly isolated. Berlin was vulnerable to the final onslaught and conquest.

The Allies decided to have the Soviet Union conquer and occupy Berlin. The planning for the final assault on the German capital began in April, although the Soviet armies began redeployment for the attack a month earlier. Aerial surveys of the city were taken, captured documents analyzed, and POWs interrogated on the defense of the city, all of which were crucial to the preparation of detailed assault plans. Soviet engineers made a large model of the city and its suburbs. In preparation for the operation, more than two and a half million Soviet troops under the command of Marshals Georgy Zhukov and Ivan Konev (qq.v.) were assembled outside of the city. Responding to the imminent Soviet threat, Nazi leaders declared Berlin to be a "Defensive Area," on 1 February 1945, when the Soviet soldiers had already reached the Oder River. Lieutenant General Helmuth Reymann took over as commander of the Berlin Defense Area and began issuing immediate orders for blockading the major road junctions north and south of the city. Three defensive rings were set up around the city, one along the sixty-mile-long city boundary, a second following the city's rail lines, and a third around a core area encompassing the more important government buildings. The arrangements and preparations at each of these defensive lines depended heavily on local commanders.

The German defensive forces consisted of the Ninth Army, elements of the Third and Fourth *Panzer* Armies, the *Grossdeutschland* Guard Regi-

The courtyard of Hitler's Chancellery in Berlin shortly after the fall of the city. (IWM S&G 72829)

ment, and an assortment of other forces, including about 200 *Volkssturm* (q.v.) battalions. All of these units had one order from Adolf Hitler (q.v.): "The capital of the *Reich* is to be defended to the last man and until the last bullet." The overriding objective was to prolong the war.

From February to April 1945, Soviet forces pushed toward Berlin, overrunning locations on the west bank of the Oder River and advancing on the city from the northeast. The final battle was to be a lopsided fight. The Red Army had an overwhelming superiority, including 40,000 artillery pieces, 6,000 tanks, and 7,500 aircraft. The *Wehrmacht* could muster only 10,000 artillery pieces, 1,500 tanks, and 3,000 aircraft.

The operation for Berlin began at 0430 hours on 16 April. Following an intense artillery preparation delivered by 20,000 guns, Zhukov's 1st Byelorussian Front (army group) attacked the north part of the city, and Konev's 1st Ukrainian Front attacked directly into the city center. On 20 April, General Konstantin Rokossovsky's (q.v.) 2nd Byelorussian Front joined the attack to neutralize what was left of Colonel General Gotthard Heinrici's (q.v.) German Army Group Vistula along the Baltic coast. By 21 April the Red Army occupied the outlying areas of the city. Nazi leaders rejected a demand to surrender, hoping that troops from the western front, particularly the Twelfth Army, would come to the city's aid. On 23 April, Hitler made General Helmuth Weidling the defense commandant of Berlin. Two days later, Berlin was completely surrounded, with nine Soviet armies positioned for the final assault.

The advance proceeded methodically. By the end of April, only the area around the *Reich* Chancellery and the zoo remained in German hands. With the final defeat clearly imminent, Hitler and Joseph Goebbels (q.v.) took their lives on 30 April. On 1 May, Zhukov's troops raised the Red Flag over the ruined *Reichstag* building. The following day, the last of the defenders put down their arms in response to Weidling's order to surrender. The victorious Red Army took 134,000 German soldiers and officers prisoner.

To a certain degree, the battle for Berlin was simply a gigantic mopping up operation. In the face of overwhelming Soviet military superiority the defensive rings were not manned sufficiently to be effective and the suburbs were thinly defended. Pockets of resistance did exist, but these were either destroyed by artillery or bypassed and isolated until supplies ran out.

Resistance was strongest in the center of Berlin as the German forces—often bolstered by the on-the-spot courts-martial operated by the SS—defended their positions vigorously. The fighting in that part of the city was intense, and early efforts by the Red Army to penetrate the city's center in armored columns were abandoned when the vehicles were destroyed by German infantry armed with antitank weapons. The Red Army also had difficulty using artillery in the city because of the lack of open spaces. The Soviets, therefore, relied heavily on short-range mortars and rockets. Much of the fighting was led by Soviet infantry combat teams armed with automatic weapons, grenades, and flamethrowers. Supported by snipers, mortars, and tanks, these units cleared the center city block by block.

Soviet retribution was immediate and severe once Berlin was conquered. The initial wave of Soviet troops were not, however, the barbarians loudly predicted by Goebbels. They were battle-hardened, experienced, highly trained soldiers who were also determined to destroy Nazism and avenge the devastation of parts of the Soviet Union. The support troops and reserves of the second wave were not as disciplined. They principally were the ones who looted and raped at will for at least a week. Within two weeks, however, discipline was restored.

By the end of June, the combat troops were replaced by the first garrison regiments with orders to make Berlin a four-power city in accordance with the agreement reached at Yalta in February 1945 (*see* Conferences, Allied). During the final battle for Berlin, the Soviets began building an administrative system in Berlin based on the Soviet model. House, street, and block foremen were introduced into conquered parts of the city in late April.

The administrative structure of the city came into the hands of the Ulbricht Group, German Communist functionaries who returned from exile in Moscow on 30 April. One of its first actions was to issue a directive that while governing ought to appear democratic, control must remain in Communist hands. Although individuals from the traditional parties gained positions, the key posts were held by Communists. Gradually, the Communists gained control of the twenty administrative districts through the newly established Magisrat. From the signing of the capitulation on 2 May until the arrival of Allied forces in early June, control of Berlin lay in Soviet hands, and they used that time to strengthen their grip.

The arrival of the Western Allies in early July was welcomed by many Berliners as a virtual liberation. On 11 July 1945, the Allied commanders took control of Berlin, and held their first meeting. One decision was to permit all of the Soviet orders and decrees for Berlin to remain in effect. At the same meeting, the boundaries of the four sectors were identified and confirmed. The Western allies controlled 481 square kilometers and a population of 2.1 million, and the Soviet Union controlled an area of 403 square kilometers with a population of 1.1 million.

The destruction in the city was extensive. More than half of the total living area had been destroyed and transportation lines, as well as gas, water, and electricity lines were devastated. Conditions throughout the city remained desperate. Water supply, sewage, and electricity had been restored, yet starvation was widespread. There was, moreover, a desperate shortage of housing as a large number of "displaced persons" from former German territories in Eastern Europe flocked to the city. Berliners living in the Soviet sector had access to some farm and garden produce from the outer areas. In the western sectors, some food supplies from these areas were made available. It was not enough to meet the demand, resulting in the introduction of food rationing.

A number of Berlin residents turned to black marketeering and prostitution. Conditions during the winter of 1945–1946, one of the coldest on record, were particularly severe. The populace survived the initial turmoil and despair, but the conflicting aims of the four occupation powers—with the West wanting the city quickly rebuilt and financially stable and the Soviets wanting a reliable Communist administration and political loyalty—were to cause tension and future difficulties (*see* Occupation, Berlin).

Robert G. Waite

Additional Reading

Chuikov, Vasily, *The Battle of Berlin* (1968).
Kubig, Erich, *The Russians and Berlin, 1945* (1968).
Le Tissier, Tony, *The Battle of Berlin 1945* (1988).
Ryan, Cornelius, *The Last Battle* (New York: 1966).
Slowe, Peter, and Richard Woods, *Battlefield Berlin: Siege, Surrender, and Occupation, 1945* (1988).
Strawson, John, *The Battle for Berlin* (1974).
Zeimke, Earl F., *Battle for Berlin* (1968).

Berlin Air Campaign (25 August 1940– 21 April 1945)

[See map 20 on page 1330]

The air campaign against Berlin began in the summer of 1940 and continued intermittently for the rest of the war. The first attack took place on 25 August, when eighty-one Royal Air Force (RAF) bombers made a night raid on the Berlin suburb of Richleben. This attack stunned the German people and *Luftwaffe* chief Hermann Göring promised Adolf Hitler (qq.v.) that it would never happen again. He was wrong. Within two weeks RAF Bomber Command conducted four more night raids on the city.

These air strikes infuriated Hitler and provoked him to change German strategy in the Battle of Britain (q.v.). Instead of continuing its assaults against British airfields and supply depots, the *Luftwaffe* would concentrate its efforts on London. This shift in priorities gave RAF Fighter Command a much needed respite, which it used to regroup its forces. Because it knew where the *Luftwaffe* was focusing its attack, Fighter Command could be ready and waiting. The RAF was able to inflict a serious blow on its enemy.

In 1941, Bomber Command launched a limited number of raids on Berlin, but for several reasons they were not very successful. RAF did not have a sufficient number of bombers. This prohibited Bomber Command from initiating any large-scale raids against the city. Also, every raid into Germany cost the RAF more bombers than it could afford to lose. Lack of fighter escort was another reason why air strikes on Berlin were unsuccessful. RAF had a limited number of fighters and few, if any, could be spared for offensive operations. Moreover, at this point in the war, Berlin was beyond the range of effective fighter support. Berlin's air defenses also limited the success of RAF bomber attacks. Radar (q.v.) alerted defense fighters long before the bombers reached the target, giving them plenty of time to intercept. In addition, the searchlight belt surrounding Berlin was sixty miles wide, and a network of antiaircraft guns ringed the city for a distance of forty miles.

The RAF ignored Berlin throughout 1942, choosing instead to build up its forces for an offensive the following year. The long-expected campaign, known as the Air Battle of Berlin, began on 23 August 1943 and lasted until 25 March 1944. During this ten-month interval Bomber Command launched nineteen major attacks on the German capital. All told, more than 10,000 bomber sorties dropped more than 33,000 tons of bombs on Berlin. Furthermore, these raids produced more successful bombing results and were less costly in men and aircraft. This increased rate of success was due to advances in military technology. The British recently developed a device, called "window," which enabled them to jam German radar. As a result, German night fighters could only intercept the enemy by visual means. Germany countered by developing a new radar system for its night fighter, but it took more than five months to produce.

Before 1944, the U.S. Army Air Force did not initiate any raids on Berlin, preferring to concentrate its efforts on other industrial targets. In the three months before the Normandy (q.v.) invasion, U.S. heavy bombers, accompanied by long-range P-51 fighter escorts, delivered a series of devastating attacks on Berlin. There were two motives behind these raids. They forced Germany to defend its capital at a cost intolerable to the *Luftwaffe*, while creating havoc in Berlin just prior to the Allied landings. After Normandy the U.S. Eighth Air Force did not fly another mission against Berlin until 3 February 1945, when more than 900 B-17s attacked the city, killing an estimated 25,000 civilians.

RAF Bomber Command resumed its attacks on Berlin in 1945, but these raids were not of the same magnitude. In these air strikes, RAF employed Mosquito bombers, fast twin-engine planes that could carry a maximum bomb load of only 4,000 pounds. During February and March, Mosquitoes flew thirty-six successive night raids on Berlin. Joseph Goebbels (q.v.) noted in his diary: "Mosquito raids have become so heavy that they are almost comparable to a raid by a small force of heavy bombers . . . millions of people in the *Reich* capital are steadily becoming nervous and hysterical."

The RAF continued its attacks on Berlin until 21 April 1945, when all bombing stopped as the Soviet Army was about to enter the city.

Michael G. Mahon

Additional Reading

Harris, Sir Arthur, *Bomber Offensive* (1947).
Hastings, Max, *Bomber Command* (1979).
Middlebrook, Martin, *The Berlin Raids, RAF Bomber Command Winter 1943–44* (1988).
Schaffer, Ronald, *Wings of Judgment: American Bombing in World War II* (1985).

Berlin Airlift (26 June 1948–31 October 1949)

The Berlin Blockade (q.v.) and Airlift arose from the unique situation in Europe at the end of World War II. The victorious Allies divided Germany and Berlin into four zones, one each for France, Great Britain, the United States, and the Soviet Union.

As Soviet-American relations deteriorated in 1946 and 1947, jointly occupied Berlin, which was deep inside the Soviet zone, became the focus of confrontation between the two ideologies. In early 1948, the Soviets began to exploit the vulnerability of the Western Allies' position in Berlin by stopping coal deliveries to the Western-controlled sections of the city.

A larger crisis arose in April when the Soviets restricted rail traffic into Berlin in a "mini-blockade" to protest the development of a proposed West German state. The Western Allies responded with what became known as the "Little Airlift," as local transport aircraft, mostly C-47s, carried enough supplies into Berlin to overcome the short-lived blockade. All of this portended and foreshadowed the blockade and airlift that followed between June 1948 and May 1949.

During the spring of 1948, the Allies persisted with the establishment of an independent West German state. As a result, the Soviets cut off all supply of food and electricity to Berlin on 24 June 1948, making the excuse that it was the result of "technical difficulties." The blockade represented an opportunity for the Soviets to gain a valuable prize, Berlin, with very little risk.

The alternatives open to the Western powers appeared inadequate. If they remained in Berlin they would be unable to supply their sectors of the city. If they tried to force a supply convoy through the Soviet occupation zone, war could result.

The Soviets believed the Allies would not risk war (a correct assumption as it turned out), and if they did, world opinion would label them responsible for a third world war. Moreover, Soviet officials believed they had sufficient forces in the area to quickly expel the Allies from Germany if fighting began. Finally, the Soviets, as well as many Western observers, believed that air transport could not meet the needs of two million Berliners for 4,500 tons of coal and food per day. The Soviet Union concluded that the Allies could never win this confrontation.

General Lucius Clay (q.v.), U.S. forces commander in Germany, and other leaders immediately considered using aircraft to overcome an effort to blockade Berlin. When the Soviets slammed the doors to the city, he ordered Lieutenant General Curtis LeMay (q.v.), commander of United States Air Forces in Europe, to organize his fleet of C-47 transports into a massive airlift to resupply Berlin. LeMay designated Brigadier General Joseph Smith to command the first airlift flights using 102 C-47s and two newer C-54s from the 60th and 61st Troop Carrier Groups on 26 June

1948. The British also furnished some Dakota transports to carry a share of the tonnage.

On the first day of the airlift, dubbed Operation VITTLES, American crews took eighty tons of milk, flour, medicine, and other high priority cargo to the city on thirty-two C-47 flights. They began operating daily between Wiesbaden and Rhein-Main Air Bases and Tempelhof Air Field in Berlin.

Within a month, the airlift proved successful, but not spectacularly so. Clay early estimated that 4,500 tons of supplies would be needed each day to sustain Berlin's population. At that time, Americans were moving about 1,000 tons and the British about 750 tons per day. To achieve the minimum tonnage necessary, the airlift required an increased rate of delivery. To do that, Clay and other leaders created an expanded organization that could manage the aircraft and squeeze the maximum capacity out of resources. To improve operations, the U.S. Air Force assigned Brigadier General William H. Tunner, a proven airlift expert, to command the operation.

With the wholehearted support of numerous other military and civilian leaders, Tunner expanded the number of bases from which airlift missions flew, phased out the small C-47s for larger C-54 transports, raised the number of aircraft and personnel assigned to the airlift, streamlined the size and complexity of the airlift support system, and most importantly, greatly increased the efficiency of the operation through a number of management innovations.

Tunner wanted to use all 1,440 minutes of the day for the Airlift. His goal was to have an airplane land every minute. Although this was an impossible rate in 1948, it indicated the degree of proficiency he sought. He settled for the more practical, yet still efficient, rate of one every three minutes his predecessor had established. This rate, he noted, "provided the ideal cadence of operations with the control equipment available at the time." He explained, "At three-minute intervals, this meant 480 landings at, say, Tempelhof, in a 24-hour period. The planes that came in had to go out again, of course, and with the takeoff interval also set at three minutes, this meant that a plane either landed or took off every 90 seconds." In an understatement, he noted, "There was little time wasted sitting at the ends of the runways."

Early in the operation, the Royal Air Force (RAF) permanently attached three representatives to the task force to coordinate the efforts of the two nations. On 14 October 1948, the RAF was incorporated more directly into the headquarters when the United States and the United Kingdom created the Combined Airlift Task Force (CATF). The two air forces merged under a single commander, Tunner, with RAF Air Commodore J.W.F. Merer as his deputy.

All of these diverse elements came together to establish the Berlin Airlift as an operation that could continue indefinitely. Milestones along the way reflected the airlift's success. On 7 July 1948, during the command of Smith and before the arrival of the C-54s, tonnage exceeded 1,000 tons for one twenty-four-hour period. This was especially important when compared with the seemingly insurmountable goal of 10,000 tons per month for the "Hump" airlift between India and China during World War II. The airlift set another record of 1,918 tons on 30 July 1948, but that record was broken the following day, and almost every other day until winter set in. The harsh weather did not end the airlift, and by 5 November, the total amount delivered had reached 300,000 tons.

The tonnage records climaxed with the "Easter Parade" on 16 April 1949. Wanting to stretch the potential of the airlift force and to send a message to the Soviet Union that the blockade would not succeed, Tunner ordered a maximum effort for twenty-four hours. His goal was one completed mission for each of the 1,440 minutes of the day. The Task Force did not reach that goal. It did complete 1,398 missions, delivered 12,941 tons of food, coal, and other supplies, and flew 78,954,500 miles with no accidents or injuries. Colonel William Bunker, an army transportation officer, put this effort into perspective. He told Tunner, "You guys have hauled the equivalent of 600 cars of coal into Berlin today. Have you ever seen a fifty-car coal train? Well, you've just equaled twelve of them."

One project, dubbed Operation LITTLE VITTLES, was an especially important contribution to the morale of the airlift. First Lieutenant Gail S. Halvorsen, a transport pilot, decided to supplement Berlin's children's meager supply of candy. In June 1948, he was struck by the thought that, unlike other European children he had met, the Berliners did not ask him for gum or candy when he was on the street. He handed out some sweets anyway. The next day he dropped three handkerchief "parachutes" with candy from the flare chute in the bottom of his aircraft. Thereafter, he made daily drops.

At first, Halvorsen was concerned that Tunner might disapprove, but the Task Force commander immediately grasped the morale benefit of the action for both the aircrews and the Berliners.

Tunner institutionalized the LITTLE VITTLES airdrops by establishing collection points for candy and handkerchiefs and by arranging special flights for Halvorsen to circle the city dropping candy, even to children in the Soviet Zone. It was a tour de force as a morale booster, a unifying effort, and a means of ensuring Allied cooperation. Halvorsen became known to history as the "Candy Bomber."

From the beginning of the airlift, American diplomats worked feverishly to resolve the blockade, at first with little success. The Soviets were positive that the airlift would fail, that Berlin would starve or freeze, or both, and that the Western Allies would vacate the city. The airlift's success during the winter of 1948–1949, however, began to erode Soviet resolve. After months of negotiation, on 4 May 1949, officials from both sides announced that the blockade would end on 12 May. As promised, the Soviets reopened the rail lines and highways from the West into Berlin.

Fearing the Soviets might reinstate the blockade after the Allies deactivated the Combined Airlift Task Force, Clay continued the operation throughout the summer to stockpile a reserve food and coal supply. On 30 July 1949, the Allies announced that the airlift would officially end on 31 October. The Combined Airlift Task Force headquarters was inactivated on 1 September 1949, and on 31 October, the phase-out was complete.

In terms of sheer numbers, it would be an understatement to call the Berlin Airlift impressive. It delivered a total of 2,325,509.6 tons of food, fuel, and supplies to Berlin in fifteen months, and transported 227,655 passengers either into or out of the city aboard 189,963 American and 87,606 British missions. There were 126 American aircraft accidents and thirty-one fatalities during the airlift.

The Berlin Airlift was significant for many reasons. In foreign relations it demonstrated the U.S. resolve to meet a Soviet challenge. America's allies around the world regarded the airlift as a triumph of will, and it built the resistance and raised the morale of Berliners. It also was a significant tool to impress the Soviet Union. At no time in their history prior to 1948 could the Soviets have mounted such an extensive operation. The size and extent of the airlift, the requirement for close coordination, and the resourcefulness of Allied leadership impressed the Soviet leadership.

The Berlin Airlift affected U.S. Air Force doctrine as well. The airlift demonstrated, for example, that virtually any amount of cargo could be moved anywhere in the world with little concern for geography or weather, if proper support were available. It provided valuable experience in operational techniques, air traffic control, and aircraft maintenance and reconditioning. Furthermore, as the editor of *Air Force Magazine* reflected in September 1948, "For the first time in history, the United States is employing its Air Force as a diplomatic weapon."

The Berlin Airlift proved for the first time what has been confirmed many times since: airlift is a more flexible tool for executing national policy than either fighter or bomber aircraft. The Berlin Airlift was thus a significant outgrowth of World War II and in one of the first major confrontations of the Cold War. It overcame the Soviet Union's blockade of Berlin without provoking war.

Roger D. Launius

Additional Reading

Collier, Richard, *Bridge across the Sky: The Berlin Blockade and Airlift, 1948–1949* (1978).
Giangreco, D.M., and Robert E. Griffin, *Airbridge to Berlin: The Berlin Crisis of 1948, Its Origin, and Aftermath* (1988).
Launius, Roger D., and Coy F. Cross, *MAC and the Legacy of the Berlin Airlift* (1989).

BERTRAM, Operation (26 September–23 October 1942)

As the British Eighth Army prepared to launch its offensive at El Alamein (q.v.) in late 1942, it faced a problem that was unusual in the desert campaign, though quite normal in other theaters of war. In previous encounters, the Mediterranean provided a firm northern flank, while the southern flank was normally imprecise and open. Here, however, the Quattara Depression, an impassable area forty-five miles inland, provided a clearly defined southern flank, and thus the two armies faced each other along a narrow front with little room for maneuver. Moreover, it was obvious to Field Marshal Erwin Rommel and his *Afrika Korps* (qq.v.) that a British attack was inevitable, and he was preparing defenses of a strength previously unknown in the desert.

At a very early stage of planning, General Bernard L. Montgomery (q.v.) knew that a deception plan of some magnitude would be needed. Code named BERTRAM, this plan was of sufficient importance to be controlled at Eighth Army headquarters, and considerable quantities of men and material were used. The task, difficult enough in any case, was made even harder by the complete lack of cover in the desert terrain. In Montgomery's own words the twofold aims of BERTRAM were:

1. To conceal from the enemy as long as possible the British intention to take the offensive.
2. When this could no longer be concealed, to mislead him about both the date and the sector in which the main thrust was to be made.

The British plan called for the main thrust to be made in the north in late October. In the south, the task of XIII Corps was to engage the Germans with sufficient effort to prevent them from reinforcing the north once the British attack began. The deception plan, therefore, had to make the Germans think that the main effort was in the south, and also to mislead them about the date. There were two key parts.

A dummy water pipeline, twenty miles long and sunk in a trench, was laid toward the southern flank from the real water point at Bir Sadi. To increase the realism, five miles of railway track were laid, three "pumping stations" were constructed, and as each section was completed, the trench was filled in. To deceive the Germans as to the timing of the attack, the speed of the work, which began on 26 September, appeared to indicate completion in early November, two weeks after the real attack was due to begin.

In the north, where the real attack was due, dummy vehicles and guns were put in position by 1 October, exactly where their genuine counterparts for the offensive were due to concentrate. The real equipment was kept further back, where training and other preparations could continue in relative safety. A few days before the attack, real and dummy equipments were exchanged under the cover of darkness. Thus, German air photography disclosed no change in the apparent strength of British forces.

The deception plan was completed by stringent attention to secrecy and camouflage, the latter no easy matter in the open desert. Yet, near the railway station at El Alamein a supply point containing 2,000 tons of fuel, 600 tons of general supplies, and 400 tons of engineer stores, all intended to support the major attack in the north, remained successfully hidden.

The battle of El Alamein, which lasted from 23 October to 4 November, was one of the most significant British victories of the war. What part did Operation BERTRAM play? The evidence indicates that *Afrika Korps* was taken by surprise. With Rommel absent on sick leave, his stand-in, General Georg Stumme, was not even at the front when the attack was launched—he died of a heart

attack on his way forward. Montgomery had no doubt about BERTRAM. "Those responsible for it deserve the highest praise: for it succeeded," he wrote.

Philip Green

Additional Reading
Barnett, Correlli, *The Battle of El Alamein: Decision in the Desert* (1964).
Carver, Michael, *El Alamein* (1962).
Montgomery, Bernard L., *Memoirs* (1958).

BIG WEEK, Operation (20–27 February 1944)

Operation ARGUMENT, commonly known as BIG WEEK, was a series of coordinated precision attacks by the U.S. Eighth and Fifteenth Air Forces against ball bearing manufacturing, aircraft production, and final assembly operations for single and twin-engine German fighter planes in a triangle bounded by Brussels, Rostock, and Poland. It had been planned since November 1943 and scheduled many times during the winter months but postponed due to weather conditions. In February 1944, improving weather and the urgency of the task persuaded General Carl Spaatz (q.v.) to order completion of the operation by 1 March.

The Royal Air Force (RAF) began a series of night attacks to coincide with the American daylight raids by bombing Leipzig on the night of 19–20 February 1944. Despite the commitment of the Fifteenth Air Force to support the Anzio (q.v.) beachhead and fears of problems to bombers and fighter escorts alike from icing, the Eighth Air Force began the attacks on 20 February. Sixteen bomber wings flew 941 sorties protected by thirteen P-47 groups, two P-38 groups, and two P-51 groups from the VIII Fighter Command and the Ninth Air Force, as well as sixteen RAF fighter squadrons.

It was the largest force assembled to that time by the American strategic air forces. Ten bomber wings attacked major plants in the Brunswick-Leipzig area; all of the fighters were assigned to protect them. The remaining six bomber wings were directed without fighter escort against two plants in Poland and one at Tutow. Anticipated problems with icing and visibility never materialized and the raids proceeded according to plan. Only twenty-one bombers were lost, about 10 percent of the projected losses. Severe structural damage was done to plants producing Ju-88s and Bf-109s as well as damage to machine tools and to completed aircraft.

B

On the night of 20–21 February, RAF Bomber Command mounted a 600-plane raid on Stuttgart. On 21 February, the Eighth Air Force carried out another massive raid, doing damage to some airfields and bombing Braunschweig through heavy cloud cover without damaging the aircraft factories that were targeted. Unfavorable weather on 22 February led to the recall of the Eighth Air Force's 2nd and 3rd Air Divisions, leaving the 1st Division to attack targets shrouded in clouds. As a result, only 255 of 466 planes bombed any targets—with 156 attacking only targets of opportunity. Serious damage was done at Ascherleben and Bernberg.

At the same time, Fifteenth Air Force bombers from Italy attacked the Messerschmitt factory at Regensburg. Since German fighters were now attacking well before bombers approached the target area where escort was thickest, and because of the dispersion of bomber groups in search of targets of opportunity, the Eighth Air Force lost forty-one bombers while the Fifteenth Air Force lost only fourteen. Fighter escorts shot down sixty German fighters at a cost of eleven of their own.

On 23 February, visibility problems kept the Eighth Air Force from mounting a mission, while 102 bombers from the Fifteenth Air Force hit a ballbearing plant at Steyr in Austria. Better weather on 24 February permitted Eighth Air Force to send five combat wings to bomb FW-190 factories at Tutow and at Kreising and Posen in Poland. Three combat wings also attacked the largest producer of Bf-110s at Gotha, and five more bombed the ball bearing plants at Schweinfurt.

At the same time, the Fifteenth Air Force once again attacked Steyr. While the force attacking North Germany and Poland met little opposition, the Schweinfurt and Gotha groups lost forty-four planes and the Steyr force lost seventeen. Claims were made of 145 German fighters shot down. Half of the Gotha plant was destroyed. Severe damage done at Schweinfurt was augmented by an RAF bombing of the industrial areas of the city that night.

On 25 February, 176 Fifteenth Air Force planes attacked the Messerschmitt components plant at Regensburg-Obertraubling. The Eighth Air Force launched 738 planes at Messerschmitt plants in Regensburg-Obertraubling, Regensburg-Prüfening, and Augsburg; a ball bearing plant at Stuttgart; and the Bf-110 assembly plant at Fürth. Heavy damage was done at Regensburg and Augsburg at a loss of thirty-three bombers by the Fifteenth and thirty-one by the Eighth Air Forces.

These were the last raids of BIG WEEK due to deteriorating weather.

The nature and success of the BIG WEEK campaign became clear only after the war ended. At the time, intelligence analyses tended to overestimate the damage done (especially to machine tools) and to assume a more serious impact on German productive capacity than was actually the case. Although 75 percent of the buildings were destroyed in plants that produced 90 percent of German fighters, it was tools rather than buildings that were crucial. Often, the most serious aspect of structural damage to plants was the difficulty it presented to the salvage and relocation of the machinery.

By 1943, German authorities had recognized the desirability of dispersal of aircraft and related plants. Beginning in October 1943, ball bearing plants in Schweinfurt relocated more than 25 percent of their machinery. The first raids of BIG WEEK led German authorities to order even greater dispersal, a process that was most convenient and successful in aircraft frame manufacture and final assembly. Plants operated successfully outdoors, often in wooded areas where they could not be spotted from the air. This dispersal, however, rendered the German aircraft industry highly vulnerable to concentrated attacks on transportation networks that the Allies later carried out.

Despite the BIG WEEK raids, the average monthly production of aircraft increased from 851 in the last half of 1943 to 1,581 in the first half of 1944. Of the 113,514 aircraft Germany manufactured during the war, 40,593 were produced in 1944. Yet without the damage and dislocation caused by the BIG WEEK bombings, these figures might have been even higher. Overall, the bombings accounted for a delay of approximately two months in production, which was somewhat offset by the unintended consequence of concentrated productive activity.

To the impact of bombing on the air defenses of the *Reich* must be added the destruction of German interceptors in the air. Claims of 600 *Luftwaffe* fighters destroyed in the air by Allied fighters and bombers seem from after-the-battle analyses to have been slightly understated, with a figure of 700 nearer the mark. This serious attrition in equipment was accompanied by an even more serious attrition in skilled fighter pilots.

After BIG WEEK, the *Luftwaffe* had to abandon all-out resistance to daylight bombing in favor of a strategy of selective attacks to conserve its remaining strength. Allied fighters increasingly were freed from escort duty to seek and destroy the

Luftwaffe, while bomber forces enjoyed a broader target menu. In the aftermath of BIG WEEK, it was clear that the *Luftwaffe* was in no position to seriously oppose the Normandy (q.v.) landings nor the concentrated attacks on German fuel supplies that began in June.

The cost of BIG WEEK was surprisingly low. Planners, preparing to accept losses as high as 20 percent, were relieved to find that losses peaked at less than 7 percent. More than 3,300 Eighth Air Force and 500 Fifteenth Air Force bomber sorties dropped 10,000 tons of bombs, with the Eighth Air Force losing 137 bombers and the Fifteenth Air Force losing eighty-nine. Only twenty-eight fighters were lost in 3,673 sorties. The total Allied aircrew toll was 2,600. In the coordinating nighttime raids, 2,351 RAF sorties dropped 9,198 tons and lost 157 bombers.

Joseph M. McCarthy

Additional Reading

Craven, Wesley F., and Cate, James L., *The Army Air Forces in World War II.* Vol. III: *From Argument to V-E Day, January 1944 to May 1945* (1951).
Rumpf, H., *The Bombing of Germany* (1963).
Verrier, Anthony, *The Bomber Offensive* (1969).
Webster, Charles, and Arthur Noble Frankland, *The Strategic Air Offensive against Germany, 1939–1945,* 4 vols. (1961).

Bir Hacheim

See GAZALA LINE *and* TOBRUK III

Bismarck (23–27 May 1941)

[See map 5 on page 1315]
On 18 May 1941, the bow of Nazi Germany's most powerful battleship, the *Bismarck,* sliced through the waters of the Baltic Sea north of German-occupied Poland. She was no stranger to these waters, as she had been training in the area, far beyond the prying eyes of the Royal Air Force (RAF) for almost nine months. The recently commissioned heavy cruiser *Prinz Eugen* was her companion on this sortie. This time, however, they both were under orders to break out into the North Atlantic to sever Britain's maritime lifeline.

Given the success already obtained by raiding operations conducted by other major German naval units, Grand Admiral Erich Raeder (q.v.) had reason to be optimistic about this sortie. He selected Admiral Günther Lütjens (q.v.), who recently led the battle cruisers *Scharnhorst* and *Gneisenau* on their Atlantic raid, to command the *Bismarck* group.

The original German plan anticipated a dual breakout by both the *Bismarck* group in the north, and the battle cruisers from the French port of Brest. Unfortunately, the German plan unraveled very quickly. First, the *Prinz Eugen* struck a mine in the Baltic, next the *Scharnhorst* experienced mechanical problems, and then the *Gneisenau* was damaged in an air raid. This forced Raeder and Lütjens to postpone the operation and debate their three alternatives. Should they delay their mission until all three ships were functional, postpone the sortie until the *Tirpitz* (the *Bismarck's* sister ship) was operational, or proceed once the *Prinz Eugen* was repaired? In the end, they chose the third option; although Lütjens had misgivings about sailing with this reduced force.

German setbacks were not confined to the availability of the ships intended for this raid. During the final rush to provision the *Bismarck,* a fuel hose ruptured, leaving her short 200 tons of fuel. That incident, however, was very minor in comparison to the fatal flaw in the German plan. The plan boldly assumed that the *Bismarck* group could sail through the Baltic Sea in daylight without being sighted. On 20 May, Swedish reconnaissance aircraft flew over the German ships. Later that day, the Swedish hybrid cruiser *Gotland* was spotted in the vicinity. These encounters led Lütjens to conclude that his mission was compromised, but his superiors dismissed his fears. By that evening, reports of the sightings reached the Royal Navy (RN).

As Lütjens' task force steamed up the coast of Norway, it was spotted twice by members of the Norwegian resistance. On 21 May, he anchored in Grimstad Fjord, near Bergen, and waited for weather conditions suitable for a breakout attempt. While his orders specified that the cruiser should refuel in Norway, he decided against topping off the battleship's tanks. During that brief sojourn they were photographed by an RAF Spitfire.

Unfortunately for Admiral John Tovey (q.v.), commander in chief of the RN's Home Fleet, this latest German threat materialized just when his forces were already stretched to the limit. In true British fashion, however, he managed to scrape together a reasonable force and planned to counter the *Bismarck.* He ordered two heavy cruisers, HMS *Norfolk* and HMS *Suffolk,* to patrol the Denmark Strait jointly. He reinforced the patrol line between Iceland and the Faroe Islands with three light cruisers. Finally, a task force composed of the aged battle cruiser HMS *Hood,* the recently completed

B

battleship HMS *Prince of Wales,* and ten destroyers was ordered to sea. The balance of his fleet, including the battleship HMS *King George V* and the carrier HMS *Victorious,* was placed on alert. Ships in the vicinity of the Home Fleet were ordered to reinforce the task force. He also advised all commands, including Force H, consisting of the battle cruiser HMS *Renown,* the carrier HMS *Ark Royal,* and a cruiser, of an imminent major German naval operation. Tovey then sat back and waited for Lütjens' next move.

Almost blissfully unaware that the RN was alerted to his position and intent, Lütjens made his next two major decisions. While he had little control over one, the actual timing of his breakout bid, the second was his alone. While the *Kriegsmarine's* operations staff recommended that he pass through the Iceland-Faroes gap, the final decision was left in his hands. Lütjens, however, preferred the route to the Atlantic through the Denmark Strait. On 22 May, he ordered his ships to sea, and their departure was confirmed by another RAF Spitfire later that evening. On the night of 23 May, the German ships entered the Denmark Strait. The HMS *Suffolk* and HMS *Norfolk* spotted them.

The HMS *Suffolk* had been recently equipped with the most modern radar set available to the RN, and that enabled her to thwart all of Lütjens' attempts to break contact. Lüetjens' efforts were further hampered by the restricted nature of the waterway. Nonetheless, his optimism about the mission was still unshaken, because according to German intelligence, the British Home Fleet was still in Scapa Flow. His complacency was rudely shattered on the morning of 24 May, when lookouts spotted two large warships bearing down on his force.

These two ships were the HMS *Hood* and the HMS *Prince of Wales.* Although the HMS *Hood* was equal to her German opponent in hitting power and speed, her armored protection was inferior. On the other hand, the HMS *Prince of Wales* was a very modern ship, and normally would have met the *Bismarck* on a relatively equal basis. Even as the British warship steamed into battle, however, civilian workmen on board were still making valiant efforts to ensure that her guns and other new equipment were functioning. If those disadvantages were not enough, the commander of the two British capital ships made three very costly errors.

In order to limit the possibility of *Bismarck's* shells striking the HMS *Hood* while she was most vulnerable, Admiral Lancelot Holland (q.v.) ordered a perpendicular approach. He in effect accepted the loss of nearly half of his fighting strength until the HMS *Hood* had passed beyond

this danger zone. Unfortunately, he was inadequately informed as to all of Lütjens' maneuvers. Furthermore, Holland ordered his ships to fire on the lead ship, believing it to be the *Bismarck,* but the German ships had switched positions during the night because of a malfunction in the *Bismarck's* forward radar set. Finally, Holland did not issue any battle instructions to his two ships.

The net result of all these factors was a slight edge for the Germans, of which they did not hesitate to take advantage. The *Prinz Eugen* found the range quickly, and her light shells started a fire on the *Hood's* quarterdeck. Shortly afterward, the *Bismarck* also found the range, straddling the *Hood* with her fourth and fifth salvoes, just as the British ship began turning in a futile attempt to bring her aft guns into action.

Suddenly, a large blue flame shot up from the center of the HMS *Hood* as she was cut in half by a tremendous explosion. While most naval historians believe that a shell from the *Bismarck* sunk the HMS *Hood,* others have argued that the *Prinz Eugen* scored the decisive hit. Of the *Hood's* complement of 1,421 sailors, only three survived. The Germans quickly concentrated their fire on the HMS *Prince of Wales.* In short order, she was hit by four 15-inch and three 8-inch shells. Since her main armament was suffering from repeated failures, the *Prince of Wales'* captain ordered a judicious withdrawal from the unequal confrontation.

Lütjens decided to let the disabled battleship leave the battle zone without interference because of the restrictive nature of his orders. He accepted battle because the two British ships were blocking his primary goal, entry into the Atlantic. Continuing the battle not only would have been a gross violation of his orders, but also would have risked exposing his ships to further damage. As well, he was now uncertain of the whereabouts of the British Home Fleet and wished to avoid being ambushed. He also may have been dismayed by the damage suffered by the *Bismarck.*

The *Bismarck* was hit by three 14-inch shells. One of these damaged her boats, but the other two hits were much more serious. The first created a large hole in the forecastle, which allowed 2,000 tons of seawater into her hull. The other hit rendered 1,000 tons of fuel oil inaccessible. Although Lütjens did not know the full extent of the damage until much later, he decided the *Bismarck* should go to France for repairs. Doing so meant that he would not have to run the gauntlet of the Denmark Strait again, and gave him lots of room with which to shake off the shadowing British

Some of the Bismarck's *115 survivors are pulled aboard the HMS* Dortshire, *27 May 1941. (IWM ZZZ 3130C)*

ships. He also decided that the undamaged *Prinz Eugen* should conduct an independent raid against the British supply lines.

On 24 May, Lütjens successfully achieved the latter objective. A few hours later, aircraft launched from the HMS *Victorious* made a desperate torpedo attack on the *Bismarck*. They obtained one hit, which resulted in negligible damage. The attack further undermined Lütjens' confidence in the intelligence reports he was receiving from Germany. Early the next morning, one of his many attempts to break contact with the persistent British cruisers was successful. Lütjens, however, was totally unaware of the success of the maneuver.

This failure ultimately sealed the *Bismarck's* fate. For some inexplicable reason, Lütjens broke radio silence six hours after his successful evasion and sent two lengthy messages to German-occupied France. These were intercepted by the British radio intelligence system, and Tovey was immediately given the *Bismarck's* bearings. Tovey lost some valuable time because the HMS *King George V* was not equipped with gnomonic (navigation or great-circle) charts. By the time that shortcoming was rectified, Tovey was 150 nautical miles behind his quarry.

The RN's luck improved dramatically on the night of 25–26 May. An RAF Catalina flying boat finally spotted the *Bismarck* and reported her position. On sighting this plane, the *Bismarck's* antiaircraft battery made a determined but futile effort to shoot it down. Less than two hours later, Force H, which had sailed from Gibraltar on 21 May, made the final and last desperate attempt to stop the *Bismarck* before she reached the safety of the *Luftwaffe's* air umbrella. On their second attack, aircraft from the HMS *Ark Royal* managed to score a torpedo hit on the *Bismarck's* stern. The explosion jammed her rudders at 12 degrees left, toward the onrushing battleships of the Home Fleet.

Throughout the night of 26 May, the *Bismarck* was kept under observation and harassed by a flotilla of British destroyers. At the same time, Tovey carefully marshalled his forces so that he could engage the *Bismarck* on the most advantageous terms. He was fully aware that the *Bismarck's* fighting power was not significantly diminished. Early on the morning of 27 May, both the battleships HMS *King George V* and the HMS *Rodney* engaged the unmaneuverable giant.

Although the *Bismarck* managed to find the range with her third salvo, some early hits on her fire control system limited the effectiveness of her batteries. Also, her inability to move away from the shellfire of her adversaries caused her to be hit by a comparatively high percentage of British shells. Within two hours, the *Bismarck's* upper works were thoroughly demolished, and her main battery was silenced. Her fully armored hull resisted the British shellfire, however, and she steadfastly refused to sink.

The Germans realized the *Bismarck* was now doomed, and orders were given to scuttle her. As the seacocks let the sea in, the cruiser HMS *Dorsetshire* closed in on the devastated wreck and scored three torpedo hits on her hull. To this day, debate rages as to whether or not these torpedos sunk her. A recent underwater exploration of the wreck of the Bismarck has lent some credibility to the German claim that scuttling was the main cause of her sinking. In any case, the *Bismarck,* as well as much of the German surface fleet, was successfully eliminated as a threat to Britain's maritime lifeline. Of her crew of more than 2,000, only 117 survived.

Peter K.H. Mispelkamp

Additional Reading

Ballard, Robert D., *The Discovery of the Bismarck* (1990).

Kennedy, Ludovic, *Pursuit: The Sinking of the Bismarck* (1974).

Muellenheim-Rechberg, Burkard, *Battleship Bismarck: A Survivor's Story* (1990).

Roberts, John, *The Battle-Cruiser Hood* (1982).

Bizerte and Tunis (6–7 May 1943)

The predawn hours of 6 May 1943 saw massive Allied movements along the front in Tunisia. The German *Afrika Korps* (q.v.) had conducted its last offensive one week earlier, pushing futilely against the Djebel Bou Aoukazu Pass. It was the last gasp of a desperate and poorly supplied command and resulted in only a minor adjustment to the front line. Still, the *Afrika Korps* and many of its Italian counterpart units stood ready for what all knew would be the final play in the North African campaign (q.v.).

No amount of determination and skill, however, can compensate for a lack of fuel and ammunition. When the Allied offensive began during the early morning hours of 6 May, it hit an Axis army that could neither move nor strike. The 6th and 7th Armoured Divisions of the British First Army drove quickly toward Tunis; the U.S. II Corps thrust the 1st and 9th Infantry Divisions toward Bizerte in two pincers; and the British Eighth Army pushed northward out of Enfidaville. Within twenty-four hours the two key cities fell.

Although isolated, the *Afrika Korps* veterans fought to the last round. The majority of the Axis forces, German and Italian, surrendered with little resistance. Short on water, food, fuel, and ammunition, all realized that theirs was a lost cause. They were left behind without hope of evacuation because Adolf Hitler and Benito Mussolini (qq.v.) both realized that the loss of North Africa meant the end of the Fascist regime in Italy. It was that political and strategic reality and not military practicality that led to the ill-fated Axis effort in the Tunisia campaign (q.v.). Of the nearly 300,000 Axis troops in Tunisia in late April 1943, only the *Luftwaffe*, the *Regia Aeronautica,* Axis naval personnel, and the wounded were successfully evacuated before the final week. Some 275,000 Axis troops were captured on 7 May. It was an ignominious end to a once proud force.

Carl O. Schuster

Additional Reading
Howe, George, *Northwest Africa: Seizing the Initiative* (1957).
Macksey, Kenneth J., *Afrika Korps* (1968).
Strawson, J.M., *The Battle for North Africa* (1965).

BODENPLATTE (BASEPLATE), Operation (1 January 1945)

Even before the start of the German Ardennes offensive (q.v.), the *Luftwaffe* decided to use all its available day fighters on a favorable day against the Allied fighter bases in Holland, Belgium, and northern France. The operation was supposed to be a low-level attack. The goal was to destroy as many Allied fighters as possible in the early morning, while they were still on the ground. The Germans hoped to eliminate the fighters that provided the strong escorts for Allied bombers, thus improving the *Luftwaffe*'s ability to defend Germany.

The weather in December 1944 made it impossible to schedule Operation BASEPLATE (*BODENPLATTE*) before 1 January 1945. Thus, in conjunction with the Ardennes offensive, the goal became also to deploy as many German fighter-bombers as possible in order to support the German Army. Major General Dietrich Peltz, commander of the II *Fliegerkorps,* was in charge of the planning and execution of the operation. The day fighters of the I *Fliegerkorps* were also placed under his command, giving him a strength of almost 850 aircraft. Three night-fighter wings would serve as pathfinders to the Allied leading positions.

The 16th *Flak* Division, over whose sector all the attack routes led, was informed about the large-scale operation, but it was not informed about the time of attack or the size of the German formations.

All units assigned to Operation *BODENPLATTE* formed on 20 December at air stations in western Germany. The pilots had enough time to get ready for their special mission. They had sketches and aerial photos of their targets, and they knew the special landmarks of their routes.

Launch time was scheduled for 0735 hours on 1 January 1945, but at the last minute, the time was pushed back to 0930 hours because of ground fog in the northern target area of the 3rd *Flieger-division*. Some units launched at the originally scheduled time, and thus, the attack was not completely synchronized. The most important targets, however, were attacked simultaneously. Those were the Allied air bases at Volkel, Gilze Rijen, Eindhoven, Antwerpen, St. Trond, Beauvechain, Le Culot, Metz, and several in the area of Brussels. The *Luftwaffe* succeeded completely in surprising the Allies. For four hours, the Allied air bases were repeatedly attacked. About 180 Allied planes were destroyed and 100 were damaged.

Luftwaffe losses were also considerable. Operation *BODENPLATTE* cost the Germans 277 planes and 232 pilots, including most of the group and wing commanders. Ironically, German *Flak* artillery played a big part in these losses, because it mistook the returning formations for the Allies and opened fire. German air defenders were insufficiently informed about the operation. They also did not expect the *Luftwaffe* to put up that many planes at one time.

The Allies were able to replace their lost planes within eight days. Thus, their superiority in the air was not reduced considerably. The German day fighters, however, were finished. They never recovered from the loss of planes and pilots and ceased to play any significant role in the air defense of Germany.

Ekkehart Guth

Additional Reading
Deichmann, Paul, *German Air Force in Support of the Army* (1968).
Girbig, Werner, *Start im Morgengrauen* (1973).

BOLERO, Operation (1942–1943)

BOLERO was the name given to the plan initiated by U.S. Army strategists to concentrate Allied forces in Great Britain in 1942–1943, in preparation for a cross-channel invasion in 1943, then code named ROUNDUP. Operation BOLERO was postponed in favor of Operation TORCH, the November 1942 Allied invasion of Vichy French northwest Africa (q.v.). Operation BOLERO finally was abandoned in 1943.

The reasons for its abandonment are still controversial, and expose essential differences in strategic thinking between Great Britain and the United States; differences that were a product of the two nations' distinct traditions, economies, and historical experiences. The role of President Franklin D. Roosevelt (q.v.) was decisive in the end, however, for it was he who finally ruled against Operation BOLERO and for Operation TORCH, against the advice of his military advisers.

In the early months of 1942, U.S. Army planners, concerned with the widespread dispersion of American forces and materiel to theaters ranging from the Middle East to the southwest Pacific, came up with the BOLERO plan. Operation BOLERO aimed at countering this dispersion by concentrating Allied forces in Great Britain, where many Allied troops were stationed already, prior to invading the Continent in 1943.

The originators of Operation BOLERO, including U.S. Army Chief of Staff General George C. Marshall and Major General Dwight D. Eisenhower (qq.v.) hoped in this way to defeat Germany quickly, and then to turn to deal with Japan. The plan, moreover, fitted in well with American traditions of mobilizing tremendous industrial and manpower resources for war in a short period, and then concentrating and using those forces for the rapid defeat of the enemy. Such an approach had proved its value in World War I.

British military and political leaders, although not averse to the BOLERO plan in principle, nonetheless had reservations. Britain had been fighting a peripheral war since the fall of France, using its strong navy to confine Axis power to the European mainland, and chipping away at that power with strategic bombing and support for resistance (q.v.) movements. That suited Britain's industrial economy, which was small-scale, as well as its manpower reserves, which were limited. British leaders were reluctant to abandon this strategy unless they could be assured of victory in a cross-channel invasion with low casualties.

It is often argued that in 1942–1943 the British were the better negotiators in the Western alliance, and that is why Operation TORCH was adopted and Operation BOLERO was dropped. That is not the case, however. Roosevelt, unwilling to take the political risk of postponing action

in the west until 1943, insisted on an offensive being carried out against Germany in 1942.

The only possible invasion in 1942 that fit into Operation BOLERO was a small-scale Allied landing on the Continent, conceived as a contingency invasion to help the Soviets if their defeat seemed imminent. That operation would be code named SLEDGEHAMMMER. The British determined quite rightly that Operation SLEDGEHAMMER would be suicidal, and refused to participate in it. That left Operation TORCH as the only practicable Allied offensive against Germany in 1942, and so it was adopted.

David Walker

Additional Reading
Dunn, Walter Scott, Jr., *Second Front Now— 1943* (1980).
Matloff, Maurice, and Edwin M. Snell, *Strategic Planning for Coalition Warfare, 1941–1942* (1953).

Brest (21 August–19 September 1944)

Brest is a major seaport and French naval base on the far tip of the Brittany peninsula. During World War II, the Germans used it as a U-boat base. After the Allied forces broke out at St. Lô (q.v.) in late July 1944, the U.S. VIII Corps, commanded by Major General Troy Middleton (q.v.), had the mission of turning west, clearing Brittany, and taking Brest.

Brest presented a formidable obstacle. Originally fortified by Vauban, the town was well protected on the landward side by steep hills and narrow valleys, intersected by many streams and small rivers. In the 19th century, Brest's defenses were strengthened by the addition of a ring of outlying forts. The Germans added modern artillery and interspersed pillboxes and strong points with interlocking fields of fire. The main element of the Brest garrison was the elite 2nd Parachute Division, commanded by Lieutenant General Hermann B. Ramcke, a veteran of Crete (q.v.).

The Allied attack got off to a good start on 21 August when Task Force B under Brigadier General James Van Fleet (q.v.) took Hill 154, overlooking the approach to Brest from the south. The rest of Middleton's divisions closed in on Brest from the north, with the 29th Infantry Division on the right, the 8th Infantry Division in the center, and the 2nd Infantry Division on the left. The attack then bogged down into a slow, grinding slugging match that moved from strong point to strong point. When weather permitted, Middleton called in air strikes, and the HMS *Warspite* shelled Brest from the sea.

On 8 September, the 2nd Infantry Division captured Hill 92, which commanded the approach to Brest from the northeast. The following day, the 29th Infantry Division took the strong point at Kergonant. VIII Corps had been part of General George S. Patton's (q.v.) Third Army. By 10 September, the main portion of Third Army was far to the east, on the other side of the Seine River. On that day, control of VIII Corps passed from Third Army to the newly activated Ninth Army of Lieutenant General William H. Simpson (q.v.). That same day, the 8th Infantry Division reached the Brest city walls.

On 12 September Ramcke refused an offer to surrender. Later that same day the 29th Infantry Division captured Fort Keranroux, an old French installation. On 16 September, the 29th took Fort Montbarey. The air strikes continued, meanwhile, virtually leveling the city. Most of the German defenders surrendered on 18 September, but Ramcke and his staff escaped across the harbor to the Crozon peninsula. He was captured the next day by the U.S. 13th Infantry Regiment.

Brest is one of the more controversial battles of World War II. In capturing the port, the VIII Corps took some 38,000 prisoners, and suffered over 9,800 casualties in the process. The logistical demands of the siege drew much-needed supplies away from the Allies' eastern drive toward Germany. When Brest fell, VIII Corps had over 25,000 tons of ammunition stockpiled. By 10 September, 12th Army Group commander General Omar Bradley (q.v.) gave Middleton's divisions supply priority over the divisions racing for the German border. In the three weeks leading up to the fall of Brest, the majority of missions flown by XIX Tactical Air Command were in support of VIII Corps.

The question remains then, was Brest worth the diversion of resources its capture required? In retrospect, the answer appears to be no. As a port, Brest was too far west, and the Allies were too short on overland transportation assets at the time to make full use of its capacity. Bradley later maintained it was necessary to capture Brest because the German 2nd Parachute Division was too large a threat to leave bottled up in the Allied rear area. But with no tanks, almost no organic transport, and cut off from the sea, it is difficult to see what kind of real threat Ramcke's troops could have presented.

David T. Zabecki

Additional Reading

Blumenson, Martin, *Breakout and Pursuit* (1961).
Weigley, Russell F., *Eisenhower's Lieutenants: The Campaigns of France and Germany, 1944–1945* (1981).

Britain, Air Campaign (13 August–12 October 1940)

[See map 8 on page 1318]

With the German occupation of Belgium and France in June of 1940, the British armed forces faced a new and menacing situation. The full military might of Germany was directed against Britain. In addition to threats of imminent invasion and disruption of sea traffic, the *Luftwaffe,* the world's largest air force, was within an hour's flight of London. The Royal Air Force (RAF) was the last and most important line of defense. It was clear, as Prime Minister Winston S. Churchill (q.v.) stated, that "the Battle of Britain is about to begin," and it would be fought in the skies over Britain.

Along with the German forces massing across the English Channel, important strategic and operational issues faced the RAF. Its command had little experience in planning for aerial combat, for the air battles of World War I had little, if any, relevance to the current threat facing Britain. In addition, it was widely believed that German bombers would decimate British cities with little difficulty.

The doctrine that bombers would always be able to get through air defenses, based on the experiences of World War I and the advances in aircraft technology, had become widely accepted. Only in 1937 was this theory challenged with the emergence of new fighter aircraft, particularly the Spitfire, which was faster, more formidable, and cheaper to produce than bombers. A reliance on fighters for air defense was advocated by Sir Hugh Dowding (q.v.), senior member of the Air Council and later chief of the RAF Fighter Command. In his view, the task of Fighter Command was to defend Britain. This could be done only by defeating German bombers in the air. The *Luftwaffe,* on the other hand, lacked both a similar vision and a coordinated plan for a full-scale air assault on Britain.

Another important concern was that Britain's primary air defense—the Royal Air Force supported by radar cover—required immediate attention and expansion. The air defense system was designed to cover the south and east of England, to defend against an enemy based in Germany, the

B

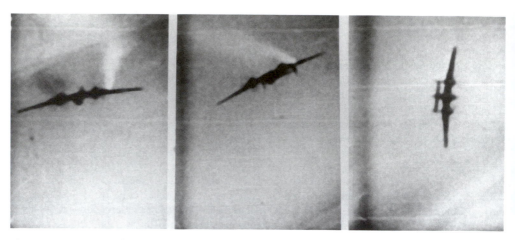

A gun camera sequence showing the destruction of a Bf-110 by a British fighter. (IWM C 2415)

northwest coast of France, Holland, or Belgium. It clearly was inadequate against an enemy entrenched along the entire north Atlantic coast of Europe. Air defenses needed to be extended to cover the north and west of Britain. Fortunately, programs for broadening such coverage were already approved, initiated, and now accelerated. Along with radar coverage and the forward observer posts, fighter squadrons were assigned to western and northern areas of the country.

A key element of Britain's air defense, the radar system, grew out of an informal collaboration of scientists, airmen, and government officials. By 1939, it consisted of a series of CHAIN HOME (q.v.) radar stations and the CHAIN HOME LOW sets, both of which tracked advancing planes. Of greater significance was the way information obtained from these stations was interpreted and used. Even by 1940, the echoes caused by aircraft on the cathode tubes were difficult to read, and judging elevation and the number of aircraft in a particular formation was even harder. Once German planes reached the coast of Britain, site of the radar stations, tracking these planes became the responsibility of the Observer Corps.

The reports from radar stations and observers were forwarded to the Filter Room at Fighter Command headquarters for evaluation. Next, the results of the evaluation went to the command Operations Room for the decision to sound the air-raid alarms and to contact the appropriate sectors for fighter response. The sector controller then ordered aircraft to be launched and guided them to the intercept. Once in the air, RAF pilots were guided solely by their controller, who was watching the plotting tables.

By the spring of 1940, more aircraft and trained crews were urgently needed, and on 14 May, the government created a separate Ministry of Aircraft Production (MAP). In this area efforts were already launched, and April and May reported a surge in aircraft production, from 860 in March to 1,081 a month later, and 1,279 in May. The new production ministry was headed by Lord Beaverbrook (q.v.). He recognized the deadly threat to Britain, and thus, he secured aircraft production as a priority over other munitions. He also encouraged the RAF to accept aircraft lacking some items. With the establishment of the MAP, production focused on five types of aircraft: the Wellington, Whitley V, and Blenheim bombers, and the Hurricane and Spitfire fighters. By mid-June a training aircraft was added to the priority list.

Britain was aided in its preparations for the inevitable German attack by decisions made by Adolf Hitler (q.v.). Instead of sending his forces against the island nation immediately after the fall of France (q.v.), Hitler waited until the *Luftwaffe* was fully deployed on French, Belgian, and Dutch airfields, and until Britain had a few weeks to contemplate its position. Hitler, whose primary ambitions lay in eastern Europe, believed he could come to terms with Britain. Churchill's rejection of Hitler's public peace offer in early July, while not entirely unexpected, did end any such hope. Hitler then issued a *Führer* Directive (q.v.) for the invasion, Operation SEA LION (q.v.).

According to German plans, the invasion could not come before mid-September 1940; but until that time the *Luftwaffe* would fly reconnaissance missions over Britain, probing air defenses and testing preparations. This would be followed by a major *Luftwaffe* offensive against the RAF six weeks in advance of the invasion. Depending on the degree of air superiority achieved over the following two weeks, Hitler would then decide if a full invasion was necessary. The Germans were confident of success, and General Josef Stapf told Hitler on 11 July that, "It will take between a fortnight and a month to smash the enemy air force."

The decision to postpone the air offensive was of the utmost importance, and between the British forces' evacuation from the continent at Dunkirk (q.v.) and the Battle of Britain two months had passed. This permitted the British to build up an essential reserve of fighter aircraft and manpower. By mid-August, the British frontline air squadrons contained 704 serviceable aircraft, almost double the number available after the evacuation at Dunkirk. While RAF fighter defenses were strengthened and extended, the number of squadrons was still well below that considered necessary by military planners. There also was an acute shortage of antiaircraft guns, which numbered only 2,000 in early August. As a result, gun density in some areas, including London and many aircraft factory sites, was reduced and weapons redeployed.

On the other side of the English Channel, the *Luftwaffe* was making its own preparations. Its three air fleets—*Luftflotte* Two based in Holland, Belgium and northeast France, *Luftflotte* Three in north and northwest France, and *Luftflotte* Five in Norway and Denmark—had a combined total of approximately 3,500 aircraft, including 1,000 long-range bombers and 1,000 fighters. The principal German aircraft were the Messerschmitt Bf-109, a fighter with a top speed of 350 mph, and the Heinkel He-111, the *Luftwaffe's* standard-level bomber, capable of carrying 7,200 pounds of bombs. Other German planes included the Junker Ju-87 (the *Stuka*) and Ju-88, Dorniers Do-17 and Do-217, and the Messerschmitt Bf-110, which served as long-range bomber escort. During the last week in July, final invasion plans were made, and the date of the attack was set for 10 August 1940.

As the date approached, the *Luftwaffe* intensified its preliminary raids and attacks, with the full all-out assault delayed because of weather until 13 August. Until the major air assault began, German flight operations established a regular pattern. Heavily escorted Ju-87s carried out five or six major raids each day involving hundreds of aircraft. Many targets were attacked more than once, including five radar stations that suffered damage. With many of the preliminary targets located along the coast, British fighters had little time to intercept, and the raids were quite successful. Still, the Supermarine Spitfires and Hawker Hurricanes performed well. Both were outstanding planes. The Hurricane, the first British interceptor to carry eight machine guns, was also the first British fighter to fly faster than 300 mph. The Hurricane was the most widely used fighter during the first two years of the war. The Supermarine Spitfire was the best British fighter of the war, with speeds of up to 360 mph and an altitude ceiling of 35,500 feet (*see* Fighter Aircraft, British).

On 13 August, *ADLERTAG* (EAGLE DAY), three waves of German bombers struck Britain, focusing on airfields in the south and southeast, as the *Luftwaffe* probed for weaknesses in British air defense capability. Radar tracked the German bombers, enabling RAF fighters to intercept many. Only a few bombs were dropped on seven RAF stations and none on three of the primary targets. Even though eight major air bases had been destroyed in the preliminary raids since early August, the ratio of aircraft losses was more than three to one in the British favor. Nevertheless, the German objective continued to be the reduction and elimination of British airpower, and it was working.

Luftwaffe tactics also shifted on 13 August when it commenced attacks on aircraft plants. The bombers came from *Kampfgruppe* 100, one of the few German bombing formations specializing in night attacks, and one that would lead many more attacks during the fall and winter. Over the next couple of days, however, action was surprisingly light.

On 15 August, the weather permitted multiple air attacks by all three *Luftwaffe* air fleets. The first wave of German bombers came in over the southeast; then, while British fighters challenged them, another fleet attacked in the northeast. Although radar picked up these formations, it did not provide accurate information necessary for determining the number of planes and their altitude. Despite repeated attacks from RAF fighters, most of the German He-111s successfully crossed the Channel.

An encouraging moment for the RAF came with their success against the bombers based in Norway and Denmark, whose losses were so severe that no further bombing raids came during the Battle of Britain from the northeast. Furthermore, these raids revealed the difficulty of *Luftwaffe* bombing operations by daylight when not escorted by Bf-109s. On the same day, the air attacks continued with five major assaults involving more than 1,700 German aircraft. The results had to be disappointing for the *Luftwaffe,* which lost seventy-six aircraft to thirty-four for the British. The defending forces believed, until after the war, that their successes were much greater.

Wherever the German air fleets appeared, they faced Hurricanes and Spitfires, and no serious gap in the air defenses. Finally, on 15 August, Hermann Göring (q.v.) issued directives that reiterated the goal of crushing the RAF and halted attacks on radar stations. The intense bombing raids continued over the next several days, with three major assaults coming on 16 August alone.

Although enjoying numerical superiority in aircraft, the *Luftwaffe* paid dearly for making repeated sorties. The German losses are all the more remarkable because the *Luftwaffe* was operating largely against targets near the coast, where warning time was too slim for the RAF to mass its squadrons. Still, the British tactics of splitting the German formations, with attacks both against the low-flying bombers and the high-flying fighters, proved successful and prompted the *Luftwaffe* to adopt much tighter formations. RAF pilots and aircraft were more than holding their own against the *Luftwaffe,* in spite of the exhausting pace and persistent attacks against RAF air bases.

Losses of British aircraft mounted, nonetheless. From 8 to 18 August, the RAF lost 183 aircraft (the *Luftwaffe* lost 367). With a production rate of 100 Spitfires and Hurricanes per month, the battle simply could not go on for long at that rate. In addition, casualties, aircraft repair, and the stress on the pilots took an increasing toll.

By 19 August, Göring stated that "we have reached the decisive period of the air war against England. The vital task is to turn all means at our disposal to the defeat of the enemy air force." The strategy remained the same—to shatter the RAF and thereby Britain's ability to defend itself. Over the next several days, weather conditions prevented the *Luftwaffe* from operating in strength, although raids persisted. The mass attacks resumed on 24 August and from that date until 6 September there was only a single day when the Germans sent less than 600 sorties against British targets.

While the strategy of the *Luftwaffe* continued to target the RAF, the tactics changed. Recognizing that attacks on coastal airfields and other targets had not seriously weakened RAF defenses, the Germans now focused their efforts on the southeast, against the RAF's Number 11 Group. The aim was to deeply penetrate British airspace and thereby draw greater numbers of fighters into combat. In addition, the seven master stations in that area, the control centers for the aircraft once they were in the air, became targets of unrelenting

Luftwaffe assaults in late August and early September. This was the most critical period of the battle.

With RAF defenses weakening, the German strategy shifted once again, this time on orders from Hitler. In part, this was the result of the success of British bombers, which hit targets in the *Reich* on a daily basis. The British targets were mostly airfields or factories, but also locations critical to the planned sea invasion. In mid-August British raids successfully blocked part of a canal leading from the Rhine to the invasion ports along the English Channel. It remained blocked for more than ten days, forcing a postponement of the planned invasion from 15 to 21 September. In addition, the RAF bombing of Berlin on 24–25 August, in retaliation for the bombing of London the previous day, shocked Hitler. He reacted angrily, and on 7 September, the *Luftwaffe* abandoned its air assaults on sector stations and began bombing London.

The London Blitz proved to be another mistake, for the raids strengthened British morale and determination and diverted the *Luftwaffe* from its prime objective, the destruction of British air defenses. During the Blitz, the *Luftwaffe*'s daylight raids contained large numbers of fighters guarding much fewer bombers, as the Germans anticipated strong fighter defense of London. The plan again was to draw as many RAF fighters into combat as possible. In addition, the *Luftwaffe* command was convinced that Fighter Command was down to its last 100 aircraft, and that their strategy would lead to the destruction of the remaining RAF fighter squadrons.

Another element of the German strategy was to bomb London heavily at night when air defenses were less effective. On the first evening of these attacks, 7–8 September, more than 250 *Luftwaffe* bombers dropped 300 tons of high explosives and 13,000 incendiaries. Over the next week, weather conditions slowed the German attacks. But even when the weather cleared, the expected death-blow to the RAF failed to materialize. The bombing raids on London did not cripple morale nor was the damage crippling the city or the fighters.

The *Luftwaffe*'s concentration on targets farther inland than the sector stations enabled the British to mass some RAF units, with Hurricane and Spitfire squadrons operating together whenever possible. The Hurricanes attacked the bombers while the Spitfires, flying at higher altitudes, intercepted the fighters. During the two weeks following the decision to attack London, the *Luftwaffe* lost 262 aircraft and the RAF lost 144, a marked contrast to the two weeks before 7 September when the British lost 277 defending the sector stations compared to the *Luftwaffe*'s 378.

British attacks on German preparations for the invasion also continued throughout September, with RAF bombers hitting a number of sites where barges were amassing. During a two-week period, 12 percent of the German invasion fleet was crippled and efforts to organize it seriously hampered. The results were important, on 11 September the invasion was postponed from 21 to 24 September. Admiral Erich Raeder (q.v.) expressed his pessimism, stating, "The present air situation does not provide the conditions for carrying out the operation, as the risk is still too great." Less than a week later, the *OKW War Diary* stated that, "The enemy air force is still by no means defeated; on the contrary it shows increasing activity. . . . The *Führer* therefore decides to postpone SEA LION indefinitely." By 23 September the British observed signs that the invasion forces were being reduced in number. Nevertheless, RAF bombing continued for another month.

By early October, the *Luftwaffe* began using its bombers only under the cover of darkness, sending fighters and fighter bombers against British targets by day. It had become clear that defeat of the RAF was not imminent, and on 12 October, Hitler postponed Operation SEA LION until the following spring. It never was launched, of course.

Thus the Battle of Britain came to an end. Through its victory, Britain put itself back in the war and strengthened American public opinion in its favor. More importantly, the German steamroller had been brought to a halt. Germany's strategic position, which had been on the rise until that point, leveled off and remained flat until it started its downhill slide after the German defeat at Stalingrad (q.v.). The Battle of Britain was one of the most strategically important battles of the war.

Robert G. Waite

Additional Reading

Bishop, Edward, *Their Finest Hour: The Story of the Battle of Britain 1940* (1968).
Collier, Basil, *The Battle of Britain* (1962).
Deighton, Len, *Fighter: The True Story of the Battle of Britain* (1977).
Hough, Richard and Denis Richards, *The Battle of Britain: The Greatest Air Battle of World War II* (1989).

Brody-Lwów (13–27 July 1944)

Between December 1943 and April 1944, the 1st, 2nd, 3rd, and 4th Ukrainian Fronts (army groups) pushed German Army Groups North Ukraine and South Ukraine almost all the way back into Poland. Around 17 April 1944, the 1st Ukrainian Front assumed a defensive posture along a line 270 miles to the west of Kovel, Tarnopol, and Kolomyya. On 23 June, Josef Stalin (q.v.) approved the plan for the 1st Ukrainian Front's new offensive operation.

The objective of what was called the Lwów-Sandomierz Operation was the encirclement and defeat of German forces in Galicia; the seizure of Lwów in the western Ukraine, and the Lublin region; and the establishment of a new line along the Vistula and San Rivers. This offensive was supposed to be carried out simultaneously with and in support of Operation BAGRATION, the Byelorussian offensive (q.v.).

For its part in the coordinated operation, the 1st Ukrainian Front, commanded by Marshal Ivan Konev (q.v.), was increased to its largest size in the three years of the war. As of 15 May, Konev had 1.2 million troops, 13,079 artillery pieces greater than 76mm, 1,056 rocket launchers, 2,200 tanks and self-propelled guns, and 3,000 aircraft. In the 1st Ukrainian Front's second operational echelon (near Tarnopol), was the Fifth Guards Army, under Colonel General A.A. Zhadov, plus two army corps in reserve.

German Army Group North Ukraine, commanded by Field Marshal Walther Model (q.v.), consisted of the Fourth *Panzer* Army, the Seventeenth Army (reconstituted after the Crimea), the First *Panzer* Army, and the Hungarian First Army. Army Group North Ukraine was covering the oil fields of Borislav-Drogobych, and the avenues of approach to Czechoslovakia, south Poland, and Silesia. Altogether, Army Group North Ukraine had 400,000 troops, 450 tanks, and 500 aircraft.

Operation BAGRATION started on 22 June. Within the first two weeks, German Army Group Center lost the equivalent of twenty-eight divisions. On 13 July, Konev launched his attack, preceded by heavy air strikes and artillery preparations. The Third Guards Tank Army made a slow start against the Fourth *Panzer* Army. On 14 July, the Soviet Thirteenth Army pushed a little deeper into the Fourth *Panzer* Army sector. That same day, the Thirty-eighth and Sixtieth Armies hit the First *Panzer* Army east of Lwów.

On 16 July, Konev committed his armor, sending his First Guards Tank Army against the Fourth *Panzer* Army in the north, and his Third Guards Tank Army against the First *Panzer* Army in the south. The Third Guards Tank Army swung north, and on 18 July, linked up with the Third

B

Guards Army, encircling the XIII *Korps* near Brody. Six divisions were caught in the trap, including the 14th *Waffen-SS Grenadier* Division (Galicia), composed mostly of ethnic Ukrainians. The Soviets committed more than 400 tanks and 150,000 troops to the reduction of the pocket. Of the 35,000 encircled troops, only 5,000 escaped, 10,000 were captured, and 20,000 died.

On the night of 18 July, the Fourth *Panzer* Army started falling back along its entire front. At that point, it reported having only twenty tanks and 154 self-propelled assault guns operational. On 20 July, the First Guards Tank Army reached Rava Russkaya, driving between the Fourth and First *Panzer* Armies. The Third Guards Tank Army started encircling Lwów from the north, while the Fourth Tank Army approached from the east.

Around Lwów, the First *Panzer* Army put up a stronger fight than expected, holding the city, and preventing Konev from launching his planned drive toward Stanisłzwów. Army Group North Ukraine no longer had any strategic reserves, however, and the three defensive lines around Lwów were far from complete.

On 21 July, the Third Guards Tank Army began to turn to Lwów from the north, and the Fourth Tank Army from the south. Attacking from Yavorov to the southwest, the Fourth Tank Army cut the German lines of communication to Przemyśl. Meanwhile, the Thirty-eighth and Sixtieth Armies were closing in on Lwów from the east.

On 22 July, units of the Fourth Tank Army conducted actions on the southeast avenues of approach to the city. Although individual detachments of the Polish Home Army (AK) (q.v.) took part in the fighting for Lwów, negotiations between representatives of the AK Tarnopol Department and the 1st Ukrainian Front never produced an agreement on a coordinated use of the AK 5th Division (*see* Army, Polish). Efforts to establish a corridor between the Bug and San Rivers for the purpose of bringing up AK forces to take Lwów were blocked by both the Red Army and the independence-oriented Ukrainian Insurgent Army (UPA) (*see* Resistance, Ukrainian).

On 24 July, the First *Panzer* Army still held Lwów, but the First Guards Tank and Third Guards Tank Armies were already fifty miles to the west, closing in on the San River. The *Stavka* (q.v.), however, forbade the 1st Ukrainian Front from driving on toward Kraków until the Germans were pushed out of Lwów. In the north, the Fourth *Panzer* Army was being pushed back toward Lublin. On 25 July, the Fourth Tank Army crossed the San.

The First *Panzer* Army finally had to abandon Lwów on 27 July. Along with the Hungarian First Army, it withdrew toward the Carpathians. The Fourth *Panzer* Army withdrew behind the Vistula. With the fall of Lwów, the Soviets now had control of all the Ukraine, including that portion of eastern Galicia that belonged to Poland prior to 1939. On 3 August 1944, the Ukraine People's Commissariat of Internal Affairs initiated the mass arrest of Polish Army officers, later sending them to Kiev.

V.I. Semenenko

Additional Reading

Erickson, John, *The Road to Berlin: Continuing the History of Stalin's War with Germany* (1983).

Koral, M.V., *Ukraina u druhij sritorij i Welykij Witchysnjanij Vijni: 1939–1945* (1994).

Manstein, Erich von, *Lost Victories* (1958).

Mellenthin, F.W. von, *Panzer Battles* (1956).

Ziemke, Earl F., *Stalingrad to Berlin: The German Defeat in the East* (1968).

Bruneval Raid (27–28 February 1942)

Operation BITING was a plan to raid an isolated German *Würzburg* radar site at Bruneval, France. The main force consisted of 120 parachutists commanded by Major John Frost (q.v.). Commandos (q.v.) from six LCA landing craft (q.v.) were to secure the beach for the main force to make its exit. An additional group of regular infantry was to wait offshore as a covering force. Radar expert Flight Sergeant C.W.H. Cox of the Royal Air Force accompanied the landing party. Sergeant Cox's orders were to learn as much as possible from the radar set and, if possible, dismantle it and bring it back to Britain.

The parachutists dropped on target, save one platoon that landed miles away and had to march back to the landing zone. The one sentry at the site was easily captured. The nearby German garrison reacted, however, and Sergeant Cox and Lieutenant D. Vernon of the Royal Engineers had to examine the radar set under fire. The assault force then withdrew to the beach for pickup.

The cliffs overlooking the beach were still in German hands, however, because the commando landing party was late. Following a 20-minute firefight with the Germans, the lost airborne platoon appeared and launched a surprise attack on the Germans. Simultaneously, the seaborne landing party came ashore and the combined British force drove off the Germans. The assault force was evacuated with only two killed, several wounded, and six missing. The Germans lost five killed, two wounded, and five missing—two of whom were captured, one of them a *Würzburg* radar technician. The Bruneval raid was a welcome boost to Allied morale in the dark days of 1942, and the Allies now had a part of Germany's radar secrets.

Tim Wilson

Additional Reading

Neillands, Robin, *By Sea and Land* (1987).
Saunders, Hillary St. G., *The Green Beret (The Story of the Commandos)* (1949).
Whitehouse, Arch, *Amphibious Operations* (1964).

Budapest (26 December 1944– 13 February 1945)

On 26 December 1944, after several futile attempts in previous months, troops of the Soviet 2nd and 3rd Ukrainian Fronts (army groups) completed the encirclement of Budapest. Trapped within the Hungarian capital were hundreds of thousands of civilians who would soon not only be bombed and shelled, but also lose their electricity, gas, and water services in most districts. The defense of the city was directed by *SS-Obergruppenführer* Karl Pfeffer-Wildenbruch, a man with considerable military experience as a Prussian gunnery and staff officer during World War I. His forces included the 8th and 22nd SS Cavalry Divisions as well as elements of the 13th Panzer Division, the 60th *Panzergrenadier* Division *"Feldherrnhalle,"* and the 271st *Volksgrenadier* Division. In addition, smaller units of the Hungarian Army participated in the battle with varying degrees of enthusiasm.

Almost as soon as Budapest was cut off, Adolf Hitler (q.v.) and his military advisers tried to organize a relief effort. The first attempt was made in early January by the IV *SS-Panzer Korps,* under SS-*Obergruppenführer* Herbert Gille. Launched from an area southeast of Komárno (about thirty miles west of Budapest), the attack soon bogged down in the Vertes Mountains. To make matters worse, Soviet units began an advance toward Komárno along the northern bank of the Danube, thereby exposing Gille's corps to attacks on its flank and rear.

The next major attempt to relieve Budapest got under way on 18 January. This time Gille's armored troops began their advance from the northern tip of Lake Balaton, drove straight toward the Danube, and then turned north toward Budapest. On the sixth day of the operation, 23 January, they got stuck at the Vali River, roughly fifteen miles short of their goal.

In the meantime, the Soviets had broken into Pest, the commercial and residential area of the city on the low eastern bank of the Danube. As they fought their way into the interior of Pest, many civilians fled across the river into Buda—soon to be followed by German and Hungarian Army units. Even before the evacuation was completed, all bridges across the Danube were blown up.

Now pressed together on the western bank in an area three miles wide and four miles long, Pfeffer-Wildenbruch's troops continued their resistance for several more weeks. On 10 February, Hitler conferred another high decoration on the SS-General (the Oakleaves to the Knight's Cross), but that gesture had little effect. Indeed, the very next day Pfeffer-Wildenbruch authorized his troops to break out of the city, toward the German lines to the west. Amazingly, about 700 members of the garrison eventually succeeded in reaching the German lines. Three divisional commanders, Major General Gerhard Schmidhuber (13th Panzer), SS-*Brigadeführer* Jochen Rumohr (8th SS), and SS-*Brigadeführer* August Zehender (22nd SS) did not survive the breakout attempt. As for Pfeffer-Wildenbruch, he went into Soviet captivity on 12 February, from which he would not return to Germany until the fall of 1955.

Among the survivors of the siege were approximately 124,000 Jews who had previously been consigned to a ghetto, had been in hiding, or had been placed under the protection of certain neutral legations. One of the most active in this regard was the Swedish legation, where Raoul Wallenberg (q.v.) in particular, used bribery, bluff, and deception to keep thousands of Jews out of German hands. Like many other persons in countries "liberated" by the Red Army, Wallenberg was arrested by the Soviet authorities and disappeared into the Gulag system.

Ulrich Trumpener

Additional Reading

Gosztony, Peter, *Endkampf an der Donau, 1944/ 45* (1969).
Ziemke, Earl F., *Stalingrad to Berlin: The German Defeat in the East* (1968).

Bulge, Battle of the

See ARDENNES OFFENSIVE

Byelorussia (22 June–July 1944)

After the German failure to retake Kursk (q.v.) in July 1943, the Red Army launched a fierce counteroffensive against Field Marshal Erich von Manstein's (q.v.) Army Group South, pushing it back against the Dnieper River (q.v.) between August and December. The Soviets also forced Field Marshal Günther von Kluge's (q.v.) Army Group Center from the Orel salient into the Hagen Line defensive sector east of the Byelorussian and northern Ukrainian borders in late August. The Soviets then concentrated on regaining the Ukraine, pressing into the border between Army Groups Center and South, and severely punishing the Second Army, the southernmost unit of Army Group Center in the northern Ukraine.

Von Kluge was forced to weaken his northern flank to bolster Army Group South, resulting in the Soviet recapture of Smolensk on 25 September. Von Kluge continued to withdraw westward into the Panther defensive line, which roughly followed the Sozh and Pronya Rivers, running approximately thirty miles east of the Dnieper, just inside Byelorussia's eastern border. These German positions east of the Dnieper between Vitebsk and Zhlobin, which protected the crucial rail lines from Nevel to Zhlobin, constituted the last natural barrier short of the Polish border. Marshal Konstantin Rokossovsky's (q.v.) Byelorussian Front (army group) drove a wedge between Army Groups Center and South, coinciding roughly with the Byelorussian-Ukrainian border.

Army Group Center, which settled into its Panther Line positions on 1 October 1943, remained the numerically strongest German force in the Soviet Union, with forty-two infantry and eight *Panzer* and *Panzergrenadier* divisions. It also had the longest front to hold and had lost considerable manpower over the summer to combat and to transfers, both to Army Groups South and North, and to the Italian and western fronts. Many of its divisions were de facto regiments.

Von Kluge's forces were organized into four armies. Aligned from north to south, they were the Third *Panzer* Army under General Georg-Hans Reinhardt (q.v.), the Fourth Army under General Gotthard Heinrici (q.v.), the Ninth Army under General Hans Jordan, and the Second Army under General Walther Weiss. The Germans faced four strong Soviet fronts. From north to south, they were the Kalinin Front under General Andrei Yeremenko (q.v.), the Western Front under General Vasily Sokolovsky (q.v.), the Byelorussian Front under Rokossovsky, and the 1st Ukrainian Front under General Nikolai Vatutin (q.v.).

The German Second Army, backed onto the Pripet marshes, constituted Army Group Center's most vulnerable point. Its right flank faced the Soviet wedge between it and Army Group South along the lower Pripet River, and its left flank held a bridgehead east of the Sozh River to protect the vital Byelorussian rail center of Gomel. The Germans vacated this bridgehead on 10 October to avoid encirclement, as the Byelorussian Front expanded bridgeheads around Gomel, threatening the boundary between Second and Ninth Army. Throughout November, Rokossovsky also expanded his bridgehead opposite Second Army's center, below the confluence of Dneiper and Sozh Rivers.

Coordinated attacks by the 1st Ukrainian and Byelorussian Fronts forced the Second and Ninth Armies to withdraw from Gomel. The Soviets drove a fifty-mile-wide wedge between the Second and Ninth Armies, penetrating deep into the Panther position. Rokossovsky also established a bridgehead in the northern sector of the Ninth Army at Propoysk.

The *Wehrmacht* lacked the strength to counterattack in November, withdrawing instead to a new defensive line roughly along the Dnieper River. With the front stabilized, the German Second and Ninth Armies counterattacked on 20 December to close the gap and reestablish a cohesive front. They only regained, however, part of the vital rail line east of Kobylschina.

During the same period, Fourth Army repelled four assaults at Orsha by the Western Front. The Third *Panzer* Army lost contact with Army Group North in November and was pressed back into an arc north of Vitebsk. With reinforcements, the Third *Panzer* Army withstood the Kalinin Front's six-week effort to cut off Vitebsk's rail lines to Polotsk and Orsha. Between October and December 1943, Army Group Center lost half of its position east of the Dnieper.

The *Stavka* (q.v.) concentrated on the southern and northern sectors of the line for the remainder of the winter, merely jockeying for position against Army Group Center. In January 1944, while Army Group South was being pushed back across the Ukraine (q.v.), the Byelorussian Front forced the Second Army back to the line of the Ipa River. Unseasonably mild weather, and the resulting soft ground, hampered the Soviet advance. Only minor gains were made against Army Group Center before the spring thaw made large-unit operations impossible. General Ernst Busch (q.v.), who assumed command of Army Group Center from von Kluge in October 1943, used this opportunity for successful anti-partisan campaigns in April and May, relieving pressure on his rear before the 1944 summer offensive began.

Both the Germans and the Soviets used the spring thaw to regroup and plan. In anticipation of the Allied landings in France, Adolf Hitler (q.v.) ordered most of von Busch's air support and tanks transferred to western Europe. Other Army Group Center units were transferred to Field Marshal Walther Model's (q.v.) Army Group North Ukraine (formerly Army Group South), where the main Soviet effort was anticipated.

The Soviets also regrouped and reinforced. Four fronts totaling sixteen armies and two cavalry-mechanized groups now faced Army Group Center. The 1st Baltic Front under General Ivan Bagramyan (q.v.) was in the wedge north of Vitebsk. Next came the 3rd Byelorussian Front under General Ivan Chernyakovsky (q.v.) south of Vitebsk. The 2nd Byelorussian front under General Matvei Zakharov was opposite Mogilev; and farthest south below Zhlobin was the 1st Byelorussian (formerly the Byelorussian) Front under Rokossovsky. Marshal Georgy Zhukov (q.v.) coordinated the planning and operations of the two fronts in the north, while Marshal Aleksandr Vasilevsky (q.v.) coordinated the two in the south.

Army Group Center's dispositions were the Third *Panzer* Army around Vitebsk, Fourth Army around Mogilev and Orsha, Ninth Army around Bobruysk, and Second Army along the Pripet River. Busch could field thirty-eight frontline and thirteen rear and reserve divisions, including four Hungarian. Air support was provided by the Sixth *Luftflotte,* but its 275 fighter/ground attack aircraft and 405 long-range bombers and reconnaissance aircraft were an inefficient mix for the task. Worse, most of the planes were not operational during the 1944 offensive, and those that were had little fuel.

The German Army high command (OKH) expected the Soviets to launch their summer offensive south of the Pripet marshes against Army Group North Ukraine, where they had gained the most ground during the preceding campaign. Von Busch, nonetheless, requested permission to withdraw Army Group Center ninety miles west to a more defensible position on the Berezina River. He was pessimistic about holding out if attacked in his current positions. His request was denied.

The *Stavka,* informed by the Western Allies of the target date for the Normandy Landings (q.v.), sent final directives to the front commanders on 31 May 1944. The main objectives of the summer offensive, Operation BAGRATION, would be the liberation of Byelorussia, followed by an advance to the Vistula and the East Prussian borders.

The Soviets attacked on the night of 22–23 June 1944, the third anniversary of Operation BARBAROSSA. Half of Bagramyan's forces screened the flank against Army Group North, while the rest thrust around the north of Vitebsk to link up with Cherniakhovsky, cutting off the city. By 25 June, Army Group Center committed all available reserves, including OKH reserves sent from Army Group North's sector. They failed, however, to delay the Soviet advance.

After failing to secure timely permission for a breakout by the five divisions trapped at Vitebsk, von Busch had little choice but to pass on to his subordinates Hitler's order for static defense throughout the sector. Vitebsk and Orsha fell on 27 June. Soviet armor thrust through the ensuing gap between the decimated Third *Panzer* and Fourth Armies and cut the Minsk-Moscow highway. On 27 June, the 2nd Byelorussian Front destroyed a force of 33,000 Germans trapped at Bobruisk. Another 37,000 Ninth Army troops remained cut off around the city. Ninth Army headquarters outside the pocket transferred its one remaining intact corps to the Second Army and attempted, with half of a *Panzer* division, to hold open an escape route for the Fourth Army, which started to withdraw against orders.

Rokossovsky, meanwhile, took Zhlobin on 26 June and pushed northwest, cutting the Warsaw-Minsk line of communications on 2 July. Cherniakhovsky drove on Minsk from the northeast, simultaneously threatening the road to Vilnius. Rolling down the Moscow-Minsk highway, the Fifth Guards Tank Army took Minsk on 3 July, and with it, 50,000 trapped *Wehrmacht* soldiers.

Army Group Center now faced total collapse. On 28 June, Hitler replaced von Busch with Model, who also retained command of Army Group North Ukraine to facilitate coordination and exchange of forces between the two groups. The Red Army steamroller voided Model's attempts to rally his forces as it steadily drove on. The 1st Byelorussian Front cleared the Pripet marshes and took Pinsk and Kovel on 5 July. The rail center at Baranovichi fell on 8 July, and on 13 July, Grodno in northwestern Byelorussia was taken. On 13 July, Bagramyan turned toward the Baltic to take Vilnius and Daugavpils, splitting Army Group North and cutting off the forces in East Prussia from those in the Baltic states.

The Soviet supporting offensive started on 14 July from south of the Pripet marshes by attacking Army Group North Ukraine. On the northern flank of this offensive, the 1st Ukrainian Front under General Ivan Konev (q.v.) drove northward over the Bug River to link up with the 1st Byelorussian Front south of Brest. This final German bastion in Byelorussia fell on 28 July 1944. Model managed to establish a defensive line in Poland, primarily because the Soviets had finally outrun their supply lines.

In thirty-six days, the Soviets advanced more than 200 miles, clearing Byelorussia, occupying part of northeastern Poland and much of Lithuania, and threatening East Prussia. They claimed to have killed 38,000 Germans, and captured 158,000 troops, 2,000 tanks, 10,000 guns, and 57,000 assorted vehicles. Army Group Center had been virtually destroyed.

Given Germany's multi-front war and its depletion of manpower compared with the Allies, the results of the Byelorussian campaign were perhaps inevitable. Mistakes made primarily by Hitler and the OKH staff facilitated Soviet victory. As so many times before, Hitler's stubborn refusal to permit mobile defense until German strong points were encircled or bypassed resulted in the death or capture of tens of thousands at Vitebsk, Bobruysk, and Minsk. Even as late as 1943, a timely withdrawal to shorter lines, as repeatedly advocated by the German field commanders, would have slowed or perhaps staved off Soviet progress.

The German forces in Russia also were severely weakened by transfers to Italy and western Europe. Miscalculation about Soviet intentions led to a further weakening of the sector subsequently attacked. The *Stavka* chose to concentrate on the flanks in late 1943 because they could not sustain a broad-front campaign, and Army Group Center offered the most effective resistance. In 1944, the Soviets chose Byelorussia as the target for two key reasons: it was the least westerly advanced sector, and the fronts north of the Pripet marshes had the most advantageous lines of communications. They could also be more easily reinforced prior to the attack without drawing too much attention. The addition of one complete army to each of the fronts went unnoticed by the Germans.

The Soviets counted on the Germans thinking that any attack would concentrate on the sector south of the marshes, where the greatest advances had been made the previous season. Thus, reinforcement of Army Group Center seemed unlikely. The wedges the Soviets held around Vitebsk and Zhlobin gave them just enough leverage for initiating a breakthrough.

Soviet operations were brilliantly executed. They exploited their air superiority to destroy the German field artillery, which was sited in open emplacements so they could be used in an antitank role. Tight concentrations of Soviet infantry and artillery attacked along relatively narrow sectors to breach the German lines. They exploited gaps with armor that drove straight through without attention to the flanks, bypassing German strongholds to be encircled and taken later by follow-on forces. A major factor in the speed of the Red Army advance was the massive materiel assistance from the United States, especially trucks that allowed Soviet infantry to keep pace with the armor, ensuring efficient combined-arms action.

Victory in Byelorussia brought the Red Army close to German soil. The Soviets directly threatened East Prussia, and had only Poland or Czechoslovakia to cross to reach the German heartland. They bore down on the German forces remaining in northern Russia as they continued their drive westward into east-central Europe and the Balkans.

Sidney Dean

Additional Reading

Adair, Paul, *Hitler's Greatest Defeat: The Collapse of Army Group Centre, July 1944* (1966).
Erickson, John, *The Road to Berlin* (1983).
Mellenthin, F.W. von, *Panzer Battles* (1956).
Seaton, Albert, *The Russo-German War, 1941–45* (1971).
Ziemke, Earl F., *Stalingrad to Berlin: The German Defeat in the East* (1968).

C

Caen (6 June–20 July 1944)

Caen, a bustling city in Normandy, was liberated by British and Canadian troops on 9 July 1944, although by then most of the city was in ruins from Allied bombing and shelling. Caen was one of the original D-Day objectives together with its airport at Carpiquet, a facility much coveted by the Second Tactical Air Force. Thirty-three days of hammerhead blows by the British Second Army were required to wrest it from the *Wehrmacht,* SS, and *Luftwaffe* divisions of *Panzer* Group West. The story of the fall of Caen is one of bitter battles, army versus air force recrimination, and serious errors in judgment as the civilian-soldiers who had reached command rank in the years leading up to the Normandy (q.v.) campaign learned their trade in the unmerciful schoolroom of war.

Original plans for the invasion, drawn up in early 1944, called for the British Second and U.S. First Armies to make a landing on the Normandy coast, with the British capturing a bridgehead that included Caen in order "to secure airfield sites and to protect the flank of the United States First Army while the latter capture Cherbourg." To this end, the British 6th Airborne Division would begin landing in the Caen area in the night preceding the cross-channel assault, with the British 3rd Infantry Division advancing from the beaches to the high ground of Bourguébus Ridge beyond the city. Such was not to be, however, as congestion on the beaches, skilled counterattacks by local German forces, and the intervention of the 21st *Panzer* Division prevented the Anglo-Canadian forces from executing the original plan. Also, and perhaps more importantly, as the British official history points out, "at times there was little evidence of the urgency which would have to characterize operations if they were to succeed fully." Troops were simply too tired and disorga-

nized to carry out what was, in retrospect, an overly ambitious operation.

What followed was reminiscent of World War I campaigns, as ill-equipped British and Canadian divisions—the Sherman tank and Bren gun were inferior to their German counterparts—attempted to batter their way to their objectives. Both sides faced serious difficulties. The British Second Army had to contend with the close bocage country (except around Caen itself), consisting of small fields and orchards as well as high hedges and sunken lanes. There the mobility of armored units was seriously hindered and their main armament's range was limited by the next bank and hedge. There could be no armored sweeps in such confined and defense-oriented country.

Panzer Group West, on the other hand, faced awesome Allied strength in the air. Fighter-bombers operated with complete air supremacy, which allowed them full mobility over the battlefield. The result was delay in getting reserves to the front, critical in the realm of armored formations that the German high command relied on to destroy the bridgehead.

A British attempt to outflank Caen by way of Villers-Bocage, from 11–14 June, was almost annihilated by the German *Panzers*. After that failure, air commanders such as Sir Arthur Tedder, deputy to Dwight D. Eisenhower, and Air Marshal Sir Arthur Coningham (qq.v.), commander of the Second Tactical Air Force, voiced their reservations over the army's sluggish advance and the fact that Carpiquet aerodrome was still in German hands. The only solution was for engineers to shoehorn the necessary airfields within the existing Allied perimeter.

The next attempt to take Caen was another flanking attack to the west of the city in Operation EPSOM, which saw the VIII Corps lead the assault with supporting operations by the XXX Corps. Delayed by a stormy Channel, which interfered with the necessary buildup of personnel and materiel, the offensive was launched on 25 June, although weather was still problematic and hampered air support. Lasting until 30 June, the grinding battle, against counterattacks by the II *SS Panzer Korps,* managed to gain some ground, but did not reach its main objective. Operation EPSOM, however, marked the beginning of the decline in German armored strength, which was used to plug holes in overstretched defensive positions.

Before Operation EPSOM turned part of the front into a gargantuan clash of armor and flesh, Field Marshal Gerd von Rundstedt (q.v.), German commander in chief West, proposed a counteroffensive to take place as soon as infantry divisions could release the *Panzer*s for a thrust to the sea. Until then it would be necessary to hold Caen to ensure lateral communications. After Operation EPSOM, General Bernard Montgomery (q.v.), Allied ground forces commander, decided to maintain pressure toward Caen. By doing this, he engaged eight *Panzer* divisions positioned between Caen and Caumont, thereby allowing the U.S. First Army to gather its forces for a major drive in the western part of the bridgehead.

On 1 July, Montgomery issued orders for the capture of Carpiquet airfield on 4 July, with a major attack on Caen planned for 8 July. The first task was assigned to the 8th Brigade of the Canadian 3rd Infantry Division, which had landed at JUNO Beach on D-Day. The operation would be difficult. Carpiquet, having been turned into a strong point to guard the western approaches to Caen, was garrisoned by the 26th *SS Panzergrenadier* Regiment of the 12th SS *(Hitlerjugend)* Division. The opposing formations had been at loggerheads for weeks, and fighting was fierce. The *Hitlerjugend* held on to their positions with grim determination, denying the airfield to the Canadians. In accordance with German defensive doctrine, the I *SS Panzer Korps* launched a counterattack to retake lost ground, but it was defeated by a Canadian defense heavily supported by artillery and Typhoon fighters from the RAF's Number 83 Group.

On 7 July, Montgomery wrote the chief of the Imperial General Staff, Field Marshal Sir Alan Brooke (q.v.), that he was satisfied with the way the British Second Army was drawing *Panzer* forces away from the Americans, but added that "We cannot be 100 percent happy on the eastern flank until we have got Caen." The main assault to capture the city, called Operation CHARNWOOD,

went in on 8 July, with I Corps on the left and VII Corps prepared to follow up on the right.

The German position near Caen had been strengthened greatly since D-Day. It consisted of a two- to three-mile-deep belt laced with antitank ditches, weapons pits, and minefields anchored in what had become nearly tank-proof villages. All this was supported by artillery and mortars positioned along the city's perimeter. Holding the area were the 16th *Luftwaffe* Division (with some tank support from the 21st *Panzer* Division), and the 12th *SS Panzer* Division (with some detachments from the 1st *SS Panzer* Division). The bulk of the 1st *SS Panzer* Division was in reserve.

Attacking were the British 3rd Infantry Division on the left, the British 59th Infantry Division in the center, and the Canadian 3rd Infantry Division on the right. Support came from the British 27th and Canadian 2nd Armoured Brigades. The total force was all of British I Corps. The 16-inch guns of the HMS *Rodney* and HMS *Roberts* along with smaller guns from various other ships, supplemented the field artillery barrage.

An important feature of the operation was the support given by the RAF's Bomber Command, which had engaged in similar operations a week before. Using heavy bombers to support a ground assault, however, was a technique still in its infancy, and the results of the bombing were ambiguous to say the least. In order to safeguard the attacking troops, a bombline of 6,000 yards was established ahead of the nearest soldiers, meaning that the bombs would fall on the Germans' rearward defenses, three miles behind the main defensive belt.

The plan may have had its weaknesses but it was well executed. On the evening of 7 July, 450 bombers required only an hour to carry out their mission. They were followed the next morning by fighter-bombers of the RAF's Second Tactical Air Force and the U.S. Ninth Air Force. Operational research carried out after the battle found that although the bombing had boosted Allied soldier morale, it had also clogged roads and streets with rubble that seriously delayed the advance. Pilots of the tactical air forces could, however, breathe a sigh of relief at the removal of Caen's substantial antiaircraft artillery network.

Fighting, as was typical of the Normandy campaign, was harsh and bloody. By nightfall on 8 July, patrols reached the outskirts of the city while the wings of the attack were some two miles apart. Field Marshal Erwin Rommel (q.v.), commander of Army Group B, chose to withdraw the heavy weapons of the LXXXVI, I *SS Panzer,* and II *SS Panzer Korps* during the night, leaving strong infantry and engineer units to hold on to Caen until attacked by obviously superior forces. With the Germans having effectively abandoned the city, British I Corps managed to push into Caen on 9 July, with little left to do by evening but the ubiquitous mopping-up operations. Total casualties incurred in capturing the city amounted to more than 6,500 within the three Anglo-Canadian divisions. Losses among the German formations are unknown, although estimated to have been severe.

By the time of its capture, Caen had lost much of its strategic value, as its evacuation by Rommel indicates. More important was the high ground to the south, Bourquébus Ridge, which required a set-piece offensive from 18–20 July, called Operation GOODWOOD. Although originally planned as a breakthrough battle involving the British I, VIII, and XII Corps as well as the Canadian II Corps, the operation in fact did no more than complete the capture of Caen by gaining the ground necessary to make the city secure from immediate German counterattacks or close observation. The cost was more than 5,500 casualties.

A mighty air attack succeeded in stunning the defenders but did not eliminate the antitank defenses that held up the assault. Further, the attempt to cram three armored divisions across the Orne bridges counted on the forward elements making excellent progress. Because of German antitank weapons, the expected progress was not made, and as a result, severe congestion brought the offensive to a grinding halt after winning only six miles of territory. Operation GOODWOOD, however, drew to the British front two more *Panzer* divisions the Germans could have better used attempting to blunt the American St. Lô (q.v.) breakout that occurred five days later.

By the end of the day on 20 July, the long, drawn-out battle for Caen effectively came to an end. With the *Luftwaffe* now a mere shadow of its former self, Field Marshal Günther von Kluge (q.v.), who succeeded von Rundstedt, could see no way to recapture the communications hub. He reported on 21 July that "My discussions with field commanders near Caen yesterday have convinced me that in our present position, there is no strategy possible that will counterbalance the annihilating effect of the enemy command of the air." Caen thus remained in Allied hands.

As with so many other aspects of the Normandy campaign, the slugging match that was the advance on Caen did not come under close scrutiny until long after the battle. Controversy has arisen over Montgomery's intentions in early 1944 and the manner in which the battle unfolded in

C

June and July. Although there is little doubt that he intended to use the Anglo-Canadian divisions around the city as a shield for the American buildup, he also obviously intended to capture the area on the first day of the landings. Not doing so led to bitter battles like Operations EPSOM and CHARNWOOD that sapped the strength of the British and Canadians (who suffered from serious infantry shortages at this stage in the war) while simultaneously whittling down German divisions and denying them the opportunity to stage an effective counteroffensive. The main reason Montgomery's plan could not be implemented according to his original concept was the loss of initiative and flexibility in the opening days of the campaign. The key factors delaying the advance were ground suitable for defensive operations and a skilled (as well as determined) German army, well able to take advantage of geography and topography.

William Rawling

Additional Reading

D'Este, Carlo, *Decision in Normandy: The Unwritten Story of Montgomery and the Allied Campaign* (1983).

Ellis, L.F., *Victory in the West*. Vol. I: *The Battle of Normandy* (1962).

McKee, Alexander, *Caen, Anvil of Victory* (1964).

Maule, Henry, *Caen: The Brutal Battle and Breakout from Normandy* (1976).

Sweet, John J.T., *Mounting the Threat: The Battle of Bourquebus Ridge, 18–23 July 1944* (1977).

Calabria (9 July 1940)

[See map 27 on page 1337]

The central Mediterranean was hotly contested during the early summer of 1940, as British and Italian fleets struggled to dominate vital supply lanes to North Africa. On 7 July 1940, the British fleet at Alexandria, under the command of Admiral Sir Andrew Cunningham (q.v.), put to sea to cover two convoys passing to Egypt from Malta. Simultaneously, an Italian fleet under the leadership of Admiral Inigo Campioni was returning to its home base of Taranto after successfully escorting troop ships to Libya.

Cunningham received word of the Italian naval movements and prepared his ships to intercept. To accomplish his task, he divided his fleet into three groups. The van, led by Vice Admiral John Tovey (q.v.), was composed of five light cruisers. The center section consisted of Cunningham's flagship, the battleship HMS *Warspite,* and its screen of destroyers. The trailing section contained the aging battleships HMS *Malaya* and HMS *Royal Sovereign,* the aircraft carrier HMS *Eagle,* and their attending destroyers.

The core of the Italian flotilla was the battleships *Conte di Cavour* and *Giulio Cesare.* Six heavy cruisers, twelve light cruisers, and twenty-four destroyers completed the task force. Campioni's fleet had fewer capital ships but greatly outnumbered the British in cruisers. It also represented a sizable portion of the Italian Navy.

On 8 July 1940, the pursuing British fleet defended itself against a poorly coordinated attack by Italian medium bombers off the coast of Crete. Italian S.M.79 bombers dropped more than fifty bombs, but only managed to inflict light damage on one cruiser, the HMS *Gloucester.* The following day, British scout planes spotted the Italian fleet and Cunningham ordered an attack by the Fairy Swordfish torpedo aircraft of the HMS *Eagle.* The aircraft returned without results, and Cunningham ordered his cruisers to increase speed and intercept the Italians, hoping to delay their retreat long enough for his battleships to engage with their surface guns.

At 1530 hours on 9 July, the cruisers of the British fleet began a running duel with their Italian counterparts. The battle was turning against the outnumbered British when HMS *Warspite* came up, driving the lighter Italian vessels to the safety of their own battleships. While the capital ships exchanged long-range salvos, the smaller ships reengaged. Three 6-inch shells hit the Italian cruiser *Bolzano,* jamming her rudder and causing significant damage. At 1557 hours, gunners aboard the HMS *Warspite* found the range of the *Giulio Cesare,* landing a 15-inch shell amidships at 26,000 yards. Recognizing the superiority of British fire control, the Italians disengaged, making speed for home waters covered by a smoke screen and a torpedo attack from the fleet destroyers.

Cunningham ordered an aggressive pursuit. At 1615 hours, HMS *Eagle* launched another unsuccessful air sortie against the Italian cruisers, while the British fleet steamed to within twenty-five miles of Punto Stilo on the Calabrian coast. The Italians responded by launching several attacks of their own, with land-based S.M.79s bombing their own fleet as well as the British. The HMS *Warspite* alone fought off twenty-two air attacks. Neither fleet received significant damage during the various naval and air engagements, and Cunningham ordered the pursuit terminated at 1730 hours.

While the action off Calabria yielded no material results, it did great damage to Italian morale. This battle aggravated the growing split between the Italian Navy and Air Force. Neither arm seemed capable of coordinated action. The action off Calabria also graphically illustrated the need for Italian naval aviation independent of the air force. Without proper air cover, the leaders of the Italian Navy became increasingly reluctant to commit their ships to battle.

Italian Foreign Minister Galeazzo Ciano (q.v.) summed up the contest by writing, "The battle was not a fight between British and Italians but a dispute between our sailors and our aviators." British spirits soared as a result of the battle. Cunningham took a numerically inferior fleet almost to the Straits of Messina with no damage. Subsequent naval actions displayed the growing temerity of the Italian Navy and guaranteed British control of the Mediterranean Sea.

Donald Frazier

Additional Reading
De Belot, Raymond, *The Struggle for the Mediterranean, 1939–1945* (1951).
Roskill, Stephen, *HMS* Warspite: *The Story of a Famous Battleship* (1974).

Cassino
See MONTE CASSINO

Caucasus (22 July 1942–February 1943)
[See map 9 on page 1319]
By mid-July 1942, the German summer offensive, Operation *BLAU* (BLUE), was well under way. The phased operations planned for the summer of 1942 were to encircle and destroy large elements of the Red Army west of the Don River between Voronezh and Millerovo and in a second giant pocket between Stalingrad and the Don bend. With the German flank anchored along the Don, and Soviet forces seriously depleted in these encirclements, the offensive would culminate in an invasion of the Caucasus. Indeed, the Caucasus region was the jewel of the German efforts that summer, as seizure of the oil fields in the region would cripple the Soviet war effort and enhance Germany's. This final phase of the offensive south of the Don into the Caucasus was known as Operation *EDELWEISS.*

Events transpired, however, to influence Adolf Hitler (q.v.) and the German high command to abandon the phased nature of the summer's operations and to strike simultaneously toward the

Don bend in the direction of Stalingrad and south into the Caucasus. This change in German planning, a clear violation of the time-honored military maxim of not dividing strategic efforts in divergent directions, was a result of Hitler's belief—shared by many of his field commanders—that the Red Army was on the verge of collapse. This assumption was not unreasonable, as the Soviet conduct of operations in the first weeks of the German offensive could only be described as disastrous.

Early in the offensive, on 28 June, Soviet resistance collapsed more rapidly than expected, on a scale not experienced in the previous year's fighting. This was, in part, due not only to poor Soviet combat performance, but also to Josef Stalin's (q.v.) new policy of avoiding large-scale encirclements, and to a panic-stricken Red Army that, once on the run, would not stop.

By late July, events in and around Rostov influenced the development of the campaign. Rostov, a major city on the lower Don and a key to any operations aimed at the Caucasus, was assaulted by the First *Panzer* and Seventeenth Armies beginning on 22 July. By the following day, elements of both armies had penetrated the city. On 24 July, the city was secured and within forty-eight hours, the Seventeenth Army had a five-mile-deep bridgehead on the south bank of the Don at Bataysk. So quickly did the Germans close on the Don that by 25 July, there were more than twenty German divisions within seventy kilometers of Rostov with little to do other than hold easily gained bridgeheads across the river.

At that point, Army Group A received *Führer* Directive 45 that formally initiated Operation *EDELWEISS*. Hitler and the German high command had come to the conclusion that the Red Army was on its last legs and that the offensive into the Caucasus did not have to wait until German forces had cleared the Don and taken Stalingrad. Army Group A was entrusted with the task of taking the Caucasus. To accomplish this, it had the First *Panzer* and Seventeenth Armies. These forces had special troops trained for alpine operations, including the Seventeenth Army's XLIX Mountain Corps. Army Group A later was augmented with elements of the Romanian Fourth Army and some divisions from the German Eleventh Army recently released from the Crimea (q.v.). Supporting Army Group A's flank to the east between the Manych River and Stalingrad was Army Group B's Fourth *Panzer* Army.

Hitler was so confident of success that even before Operation *EDELWEISS* got under way, several of the Eleventh Army's divisions were di-

verted to Leningrad (q.v.) and arrangements were made for the *Grossdeutschland* Division to be transferred to the west. Army Group A was directed to (1) encircle what remaining Soviet forces were south and southeast of Rostov; (2) clear the Black Sea coast to eliminate the Soviet Navy, capture the oil fields at Maykop, and occupy the passes in the western Caucasus; and (3) thrust south and east to close the Ossetian and Georgian military roads, capture the oil fields at Groznyy, and strike along the Caspian coast to Baku. At the end of July, the Germans had, altogether, ten infantry, three *Panzer*, and two motorized divisions, augmented by a half-dozen Romanian and Slovak divisions. Their mission was to subdue an area nearly the size of France.

Despite the seemingly meager forces Germany committed to Operation *EDELWEISS*, there was little the Soviets could do to oppose them. The Soviet situation could only be described as desperate with scattered, shattered remnants of previously defeated units widely separated south of the Don.

On 28 July, the Soviets reorganized their command structure, creating North Caucasus Front, commanded by Marshal Semyon Budenny (q.v.), from units of the broken Southern Front. The North Caucasus Front was to defend the Black Sea littoral and the west Caucasus. Local geography dictated that these forces were further subdivided into the Maritime Operational Group along the coast, and the Don Operational Group responsible for areas east of Krasnodar along the steppes and foothills north of the Caucasus. To defend the east Caucasus and the Caspian Sea, the Soviets had the Trans-Caucasus Front, which had served in a garrison role along the Turkish border.

On 28 July, Josef Stalin and the *Stavka* (qq.v.) issued another edict, the infamous Order No. 227, better known as "Not a step backward!—*Ni shagu nazad!*" This order was aimed at bolstering the deteriorating morale in the Red Army, evidenced by the quick collapse of the well-prepared defense at Rostov and the pell-mell retreat of units almost everywhere south of the Don bend. The sad state of Soviet morale and command and control is illustrated by a radio intercept made on 29 July by the First *Panzer* Army. It read: "We are going back. No reprisals (against the troops) work any more."

The last days of July and the first days of August were indeed characterized by little or no resistance to the German southern advance, whose main obstacles were logistical, delivering supplies and crossing the Manych. In several instances, the Germans kept the spearheads going with airlifts of fuel, and they began to press into service horse and camel caravans to supply the rapid advance. The rate of the German advance was impressive, with the First *Panzer* Army, under Field Marshal Ewald von Kleist (q.v.), advancing from the Don River east of Rostov, making forty miles a day in some cases. On 29 July, the 3rd *Panzer* Division of First *Panzer* Army crossed the Manych River after a daring and skillful assault across the still intact dam at Proletarsk. The First *Panzer* Army was in Vorshilovsk (Stavropol) on 3 August and in Armavir on 6 August. By 9 August, the first of the great Caucasus oil fields at Maykop fell to the 5th SS *Panzer* Division.

To the west, the infantry and mountain divisions of the Seventeenth Army made slower but nonetheless equally impressive gains. Marching across the open steppes in extremely hot weather, the Seventeenth Army's foot soldiers captured Krasnodar on 9 August. At that juncture, they began to fan out in a broad advance into the Caucasus mountains, with the objectives of the Black Sea ports of Novorossiysk, Tuapse, and Sukhumi.

Throughout the first two weeks of August, the Red Army avoided entrapment, continuing to fall back into the Caucasus. The Soviets were able to evacuate much of their industrial equipment in the Maykop fields to the south. Unfortunately for the Germans, the Soviets successfully demolished the oil wells, destroying them so completely that no significant production was reestablished until after the war. Budenny's North Caucasus Front, still weak and scattered, prepared to defend the Black Sea ports and stiffened its resistance to the German advance up the Caucasus passes.

Indeed, in the zones of the Seventeenth Army's advance, the progress of Operation *EDELWEISS* began to slacken, and by the end of August, it slowed to a crawl. After closing around Novorossiysk, the Seventeenth Army launched a six-division assault on the city on 28 August. The German forces fought their way forward through the mountains to the outskirts of Novorossiysk within a few miles of the sea. The Soviet defense held out until 6 September, when they evacuated the defending Soviet marine infantry by sea. The Soviets, however, continued to cling to the southern half of the bay.

To the east, the First *Panzer* Army, driving toward the oil fields at Groznyy, encountered problems as well. In eight days, the 3rd *Panzer* Division advanced eighty miles from Pyatigorsk to Mozdok on the north bank of the Terek River, capturing Mozdok on 24 August. Low on fuel, however, the First *Panzer* Army could not extend operations across the Terek. The fast flowing river was the last natural line before Groznyy and Makhachkala.

Unlike the Seventeenth Army's problems, which primarily were due to stiffening Soviet resistance and terrain, the First *Panzer* Army's efforts were hindered by logistics and declining strength caused by the diversion of forces to other areas. Despite resourceful measures to supply the forward columns, the First *Panzer* Army ran seriously short of fuel by late August. From that point on, the movement of any significant motorized formation was a major effort requiring careful planning and use of supplies, particularly fuel.

In the second week of August, the *Grossdeutschland* and 22nd *Panzer* Divisions were withdrawn to western Europe. By the end of August, the First *Panzer* Army suffered further reduction in artillery. Most importantly, perhaps, on 20 August, the *Luftwaffe* forces supporting Army Group A, were almost all diverted to the battle developing around Stalingrad. The degree of the First *Panzer* Army's problems became evident when, on 25 August, it had to give up a flanking movement on Groznyy by way of Ordzhonikidze because of insufficient resources, and to regroup for a frontal assault across the Terek via Mozdok.

For the Soviets, the situation was still quite desperate by late August, despite the general slowing of the German advance. The Soviet command was faced with the increasing problem of local populations collaborating with the German forces. This appears to have concerned the Soviets more in the Caucasus than perhaps anywhere else in the war. Local Cherkess, Chechens, and Dagestani proved to be valuable guides to the German forces. As the campaign progressed, the German mountain units employed platoons of local volunteers in the front lines and in counterguerrilla activities.

The Soviet leadership was so concerned over morale issues and the potential for local uprisings that Lavrenty Beria (q.v.), people's commissar of internal affairs, personally visited the region. For several weeks, he meddled in command arrangements and held the population in line thoroughly and ruthlessly with NKVD (q.v.) units in the area. Although the Soviets were still retreating almost everywhere, local forces were receiving reinforcements. Moreover, Soviet commanders were beginning to enjoy the advantages of shorter lines of communications and terrain, generally ideal for defense.

By the end of the first week in September, Hitler was clearly unhappy with the rate of progress. At the beginning of Operation *EDEL-WEISS,* the German high command expected to be in control of the Black Sea coast and on the Caspian Sea by the end of September. As the campaign progressed, however, the rate of progress slowed to a crawl, weather conditions became worse at higher elevations (the first snowfall began on 12 September), and local commanders started asking for more resources or permission to prepare for winter defenses. These factors made Hitler increasingly upset and concerned about the progress in the campaign for the Caucasus. On 10 September, after several disagreements with Field Marshal Wilhelm List, the commander of Army Group A, Hitler sacked him and assumed personal operational control over the army group.

Hitler's direct control did little to improve the situation. The First *Panzer* Army, having built up fuel and ammunition reserves, launched a local offensive on 18 September with the aim of widening the Mozdok bridgehead to the west. Soviet defenses collapsed completely, and within a few days, the 13th *Panzer* and 5th SS *Panzer* Divisions cleared out the entire Terek bend to Malgobek and Elkhotovo, where the advance stalled by the second week of October, thirty miles north of Ordzhonikidze.

Around Tuapse, the Seventeenth Army had considerably less success. Here the Germans hoped to break through to the sea and cut the Soviet Black Sea forces in two. Delayed by troop redeployments and logistical problems, the advance on Tuapse did not begin in earnest until 23 September and was repulsed with heavy losses within a few days. With the mountains and sea protecting their flanks, the Soviets were able to feed enough troops into the Tuapse area and halt the Germans.

By early October, local weather continued to deteriorate in the mountains and logistical problems still plagued the Germans. For these reasons, the Germans suspended all offensive operations in the Caucasus on 14 October, except on the Terek River and around Tuapse, where the Seventeenth Army made a renewed effort. The German infantry enjoyed some initial success. On 16 October, Shaumyan, ten miles east of Tuapse, fell to the Germans. From then on, however, the offensive stalled and the Germans called a halt to offensive operations on 4 November.

In the Terek bend, the First *Panzer* Army prepared for a resumption of limited offensive operations, reinforced with Special Purpose *Korps Felmy,* a division-size unit of Islamic Soviet prisoners of war. German objectives were to take Nalchik and to straighten the front lines, eliminating a Soviet salient threatening the First *Panzer* Army's positions inside the Terek bend.

The offensive began on 25 October, with the Romanian 2nd Mountain Division attacking toward Nalchik. The Romanians broke through the Soviet defenses within hours and made an unexpectedly rapid advance over the next two days. On the following day, the 13th and 23rd *Panzer* Divisions joined the offensive, striking west from positions inside the Terek bend. Again success exceeded all expectations. Nalchik fell on 27 October, and the *Panzer* divisions moved quickly up the Terek Valley. By the end of October, some 10,000 Soviet prisoners were taken, and von Kleist decided to add Ordzhonikidze to the objectives of this unexpectedly successful offensive.

On 2 November, the 13th *Panzer* Division was in Gizel, five miles west of Ordzhonikidze. The Soviets, however, were able to divert substantial reinforcements from surrounding areas, preventing the Germans from advancing farther. In fact, on 5 November, the 13th *Panzer* Division was almost encircled by counterattacking Soviet forces. German offensive operations ended on 9 November when they withdrew from Gizel to more defensible positions to the west.

After the battle for Nalchik and Ordzhonikidze, German offensive operations in the Caucasus ended, as weather conditions deteriorated rapidly. From that point on the situation in the Caucasus was determined by events elsewhere to the north. On 19 November, *Stavka* launched Operation URANUS, the winter counteroffensive at Stalingrad (q.v.). By the end of November, the German Sixth Army was encircled at Stalingrad and the strategic initiative on the eastern front passed to the Soviets. On 29 November, the Transcaucasus Front began its own offensive along the Terek. After a week of fighting, however, the German line held and the Soviets were repulsed. Nevertheless, Soviet success around Stalingrad and the Don bend placed Axis forces in the Caucasus in an ever more precarious position.

On 22 December, the First *Panzer* Army began an orderly withdrawal from its Terek positions to Pyatigorsk and the middle Kuma River. The German position in the Caucasus became increasingly desperate by the end of December, as the Soviet Fifth Shock and Fifty-first Armies, advancing south of Stalingrad, captured Kotelnikovo and Glubokiy, threatening Rostov and Army Group A's lines to the north. At the end of December, Hitler relented on the abandonment of the Caucasus, and Army Group A was ordered to withdraw.

Throughout the first week of January 1943,

C

Axis forces withdrew rapidly to the north, with the Soviets pursuing vigorously. Nonetheless, the Transcaucasus Front's pursuit was ineffective in disorganizing Army Group A's retreat. The Axis withdrawal continued throughout January. Some elements of the First *Panzer* Army withdrew north through Rostov, while the remainder of the First *Panzer* Army along with the Seventeenth Army withdrew to the *Gotenkopf,* a defensive bridgehead on the Taman Peninsula, which was anchored on Novorossiysk in the south and encompassed the lower sixty miles of the Kuban River.

By the first week of February, the strategic withdrawal to the Taman peninsula was completed. Hitler clung to the notion that from there, the Germans could renew an offensive to the Caucasus when the military balance changed later in 1943. In October 1943, however, the Seventeenth Army finally withdrew from the Caucasus across the straits of Kerch into the Crimea.

The Caucasus campaign proved, despite early spectacular successes by Axis forces, to be a failed gamble. Insufficient logistics support and combat forces throughout illustrated the risks inherent in pursuing multiple and geographically diverse objectives. In the early stages of Operation *EDEL-WEISS,* troops and materiel were bled off from Army Group A when an extra effort could well have proven decisive. Conversely, in December, when the Germans were mounting a desperate effort to relieve Stalingrad, many high quality *Panzer* and infantry units were tied down in the south. Although the Germans captured a significant portion of the Soviet oil production capacity, they were denied the Groznyy and Baku fields. The Germans never received a drop of oil for their efforts, as Soviet demolition, paratroop, and partisan activities thoroughly disrupted production.

Charles K. Dodd

Additional Reading

Carell, Paul, *Hitler Moves East, 1941–1943* (1965).

Erickson, John, *The Road to Stalingrad* (1975).

Ziemke, Earl, *Moscow to Stalingrad* (1987).

Celles (24–27 December 1944)

[See map 2 on page 1312]

At the start of the Ardennes offensive (q.v.), the XLVII *Panzer Korps* was given the mission of sending its 2nd *Panzer* Division and the 26th *Volksgrenadier* Division to the Meuse River. Moving in echelon, the divisions were supposed to avoid Bastogne, cross the river, and move into the area

south of Namur. The XLVII *Panzer Korps'* westward march ended on 24 December 1944 close to the town of Celles, about eight kilometers from the town of Dinant, on the Meuse.

In the course of its move west, the XLVII *Panzer Korps* had to leave the 26th *Volksgrenadier* Division behind for the fight for Bastogne (q.v.). With no accompanying support, the 2nd *Panzer* Division, commanded by Colonel Meinrad von Lauchert, broke through the Allied positions between Marche and Rochefort and prepared to cross the Meuse at Dinant. Together with the 116th *Panzer* Division to its north, and the *Panzer-Lehr* Division to its south, the 2nd *Panzer* Division became the spearhead of the Ardennes offensive. Of all the attacking German units, the 2nd *Panzer* Division moved the farthest. By 23 December, the 9th *Panzer* Division was supposed to be supporting the 2nd *Panzer* Division on its right flank, but the 9th *Panzer* Division never reached its assigned area.

On the night of 22–23 December, the 2nd *Panzer* Division's reconnaissance battalion led the division's movement west. The battalion was followed at a distance by the division's advanced guard, consisting of one *Panzergrenadier* regiment, elements of a *Panzer* unit, and a combat engineer company. As they moved, they continually encountered Allied attacks from the north. Elements of the advanced guard had to be used to establish flank security, which eroded their strength as they progressed.

The reconnaissance battalion reached the town of Foy-Notre Dame, five kilometers east of Dinant, on 23 December, and took the town after a short fight. Continuing on toward the Meuse, they reached Celles that evening. Anticipating mined roads ahead, the reconnaissance battalion established a defensive perimeter and spent the night there.

The following day, the U.S. 2nd Armored Division, commanded by Major General Ernest N. Harmon (q.v.), moved toward Celles from the north. On 25 December they cut off the 2nd *Panzer's* reconnaissance battalion and the resulting tank-on-tank fighting lasted all day. The main body of the 2nd *Panzer* Division immediately tried to establish contact with their forward unit in order to free them. They got stuck, however, southwest of Conneux, where they had to establish two defensive perimeters. Throughout the day, all contact was severed between the main body and the reconnaissance battalion, which soon started running out of fuel and ammunition.

On 24 December, the *Panzer-Lehr* Division was ordered to support the 2nd *Panzer* division

They succeeded in breaking through the American resistance at Rochefort and in clearing the way to the west. This success, however, came too late to help the 2nd *Panzer* Division, which was overcome with its own supply problems. Starting that same day, the Allied air forces intervened and seriously hindered the transportation of German fuel and ammunition. Elements of the 2nd *Panzer* Division were already stranded without fuel on the Hargimont-Buissonville road.

On 25 December, the 3rd battalion of the 2nd *Panzer* Division's divisional artillery regiment was caught by surprise and destroyed by Allied bombers while refueling. Other elements of the division were blocked and surrounded at Conneux. They were too far away to help the reconnaissance battalion in Celles, which was defeated that same day by the 2nd Armored Division.

On 26 December, the remainder of the 2nd *Panzer* Division, located in Marche, tried to relieve the group at Conneux. Despite American superiority, they got as close as 800 meters, but they did not have enough strength left to free the encircled forces. Their situation being hopeless, the encircled Germans were ordered to destroy all their equipment and try to reach Rochefort individually. During that night, 600 German soldiers managed to escape. On 27 December, the *Panzer-Lehr* Division established a bridgehead near Rochefort and collected the remnants of the 2nd *Panzer* Division. The XLVII *Panzer Korps* then went on the defensive.

The 2nd *Panzer* Division, spearhead of the Ardennes offensive, got as close as four kilometers to the Meuse River and Dinant. They were stopped by the 2nd Armored Division and almost completely destroyed. The battle between the two tank divisions with the same numerical designation lasted three days in the area of Conneux and Celles. The Germans lost 2,500 men killed and wounded, and 1,200 were taken prisoner. All the division's weapons, eighty-two tanks, eighty-three self-propelled and assault guns, the entire divisional artillery, and hundreds of vehicles of all kinds, were lost. The 2nd Armored Division suffered limited losses—seventeen soldiers killed, 227 wounded, and twenty-eight tanks knocked out. By the end of 1944, twenty-six of those tanks had been placed back in action. The American advantage in artillery and air support had proved decisive.

Ekkehart Guth

Additional Reading

Cole, Hugh M., *The Ardennes: Battle of the Bulge* (1965).

Dupuy, Trevor N., David L. Bongard, and Richard C. Anderson, Jr., *Hitler's Last Gamble: The Battle of the Bulge, December 1944–January 1945* (1995).

Eisenhower, John S.D., *The Bitter Woods* (1969).

Jung, H., *Die Ardennenoffensive 1944/45* (1971).

MacDonald, Charles B., *A Time for Trumpets: The Untold Story of the Battle of the Bulge* (1985).

Channel Dash (11–12 February 1942)

Operation CERBERUS, known as the Channel Dash, was the daring movement in February 1942 of three German warships from Brest Harbor up the English Channel to Wilhelmshaven. Following the destruction of the battleship *Bismarck* (q.v.), the heavy cruiser *Prinz Eugen* joined the battle cruisers *Scharnhorst* and *Gneisenau* in Brest. Acting as a "fleet-in-being," this concentration of German warships forced a much greater reaction by the British than the actual threat warranted.

Protecting these ships, however, proved a drain on German resources and Adolf Hitler (q.v.) was not pleased with their inactivity. In addition, he became convinced in late 1941 that the British would attempt to open a second front by reinvading Norway. To help ward off this threat, he ordered the new battleship *Tirpitz* to Norway and he pressured Admiral Erich Raeder (q.v.) to send the *Scharnhorst, Gneisenau,* and *Prinz Eugen* there as well. Faced with this pressure and with assurances from the *Luftwaffe* that air superiority could be maintained over the ships, Raeder agreed on 12 January 1942 to the movement. Because bringing the ships north via Iceland was deemed too dangerous, plans were laid to run the ships up through the English Channel to Wilhelmshaven, with further movement north to follow soon after.

As developed, the plan called for movement of the ships to begin at night on a day forecast for bad weather. Escorted by destroyers, E-boats, minesweepers, and constant overhead fighter patrols, the ships would pass through the narrowest part of the Channel in full daylight. The Germans hoped to surprise the British, who they correctly believed would expect a night passage. Because secrecy was of the utmost importance, obvious preparations were avoided. Despite the size and complexity of the operation, the Germans planned for complete radio silence. This was achieved to a remarkable extent, with even the normally gregarious German fighter pilots keeping quiet.

Despite all the German efforts at security, the British were warned several weeks in advance by agents in France to expect some sort of breakout attempt. Regular aircraft reconnaissance was scheduled and three layers of radar coverage were in operation. British preparations were based on the belief that any movement through the Channel would occur at night, with the German ships leaving Brest early in the afternoon.

Late in the evening of 11 February 1942, the German squadron put to sea under the command of Vice Admiral Otto Ciliax. Because of both equipment failure and operator error on the British side, the German warships sailed undiscovered or unreported for almost twelve hours until spotted mid-morning on 12 February by a British Spitfire pilot. Shortly after noon, British long-range guns at Dover opened fire, but their fire was slow and inaccurate. The German squadron sailed uninjured into the North Sea.

With low ceilings and poor visibility now shrouding the German ships, air attacks became extremely difficult. Despite these weather difficulties, overwhelming antiaircraft fire and fighter cover, a squadron of six Swordfish torpedo bombers made an attack in the early afternoon. All six were shot down with no damage to the German squadron. A destroyer attack three hours later also failed to do any damage, and attempts by bombers to hit the German ships continued until darkness without success. The Germans, however, did not complete their remarkable run unscathed. Both German battle cruisers struck mines. The *Scharnhorst* was holed twice and took on more than 1,000 tons of water before she docked at Wilhelmshaven.

The Channel Dash was both a physical and a morale blow to the British. They lost more than seventy aircraft in their attempts to destroy the German ships and there was an official inquiry into the failure. Newspaper coverage was indignant, saying the incident was equivalent to having the Spanish Armada sail through the English Channel unmolested. For the Germans, it was a minor victory that their propaganda machine attempted to raise to even greater proportions.

Despite German self-congratulations and British wailing, the movement was, in reality, a German retreat. German surface warships no longer would play any great part in the steadily intensifying Battle of the Atlantic (q.v.). Indeed, the concentration of German surface units in the north made Britain's naval problem simpler. British Home Fleet units stationed at Scapa Flow effectively prevented any German capital ships from breaking out and attacking the Atlantic convoys.

Budd A.R. Jones

Additional Reading
Potter, John D., *Fiasco: The Break-Out of the German Battleships* (1970).
Robertson, Terence, *Channel Dash: The Drama of Twenty-Four Hours of War* (1958).

Chir River (7–22 December 1942)

[See map 36 on page 1346]

In December 1942, the German Sixth Army was besieged in Stalingrad (q.v.). The commander of Army Group Don, Field Marshal Eric von Manstein (q.v.), planned to relieve the Sixth Army with General Hermann Hoth's (q.v.) Fourth *Panzer* Army, supported by the XLVIII *Panzer Korps*. On 7 December, before the XLVIII *Panzer Korps* could link up with the Fourth *Panzer* Army, elements of the Soviet Fifth Tank Army launched heavy attacks at various points along the Chir River. Two divisions of the corps were deployed along the west bank of the river, with the 7th *Luftwaffe* Field Division on the left, and the 336th Infantry Division on the right. To their rear, the 11th *Panzer* Division, commanded by Major General Hermann Balck (q.v.), formed the corps reserve.

By the end of 7 December, the Soviet I Tank Corps penetrated ten miles to the south, reaching State Farm 79. Balck, whose divisional command post was co-located with that of the 336th Division, attacked at dawn on 8 December, with one *Panzergrenadier* regiment conducting a holding attack against the Soviet front, and the 15th *Panzer* Regiment supported by another *Panzergrenadier* regiment delivering the decisive blow against the Soviet rear. By the end of the day, the I Tank Corps was thrown back across the Chir, minus fifty-three of its tanks. For the next three days, the 11th *Panzer* Division fought a series of running battles clearing out Soviet bridgeheads across the Chir.

Late on 11 December, the Soviets made two more major penetrations into the sector of the XLVIII *Panzer Korps*. After another night march the 11th *Panzer* Division attacked into the flank of one of the Soviet penetrations at Lissinski. After that threat was defeated, Balck moved his division fifteen miles to the northwest and attacked the Soviet bridgehead at Nizhna Kalinovski. At dawn on 13 December, the 11th *Panzer* Division was preparing to make its final attack when it was hit on the right flank by another strong Soviet assault. One of the German battalions was tempoarily surrounded, but Balck continued his assault on the bridgehead while he extracted his battalion. By the end of the day, the Soviets had been fought to a standstill, although the Nizhna Kalinovski bridgehead was not completely eliminated. By that point, the 11th *Panzer* Division had been marching by night and fighting by day for almost eight continuous days.

On 10 December, the Fourth *Panzer* Army started its attack to relieve the Sixth Army at Stalingrad. Despite being heavily engaged along the Chir, the XLVIII *Panzer Korps* was ordered to link up with and support the Fourth *Panzer* Army. In order to do so, the XLVIII *Panzer Korps* had to get across the Don River. On 15 December, the 11th *Panzer* Division started moving toward Nizhna Chirskaya, just below the confluence of the Chir and the Don. Balck's division was prepared to force a crossing of the Don on 17 December, but the Soviet high command struck first.

Ignoring the thrust of the Fourth *Panzer* Army, the Soviets struck a massive blow against the Italian Eighth Army, farther north along the Don. The Soviet drive threatened to take Rostov, at the mouth of the Don on the Azov Sea. Such a move would have cut off Field Marshal Ewald von Kleist's (q.v.) Army Group A in the Caucasus (q.v.). Von Manstein was forced to draw heavily from the Fourth *Panzer* Army to defend Rostov. That sealed the fate of the Sixth Army.

The new Soviet drive overlapped into the sector of the XLVIII *Panzer Korps,* overrunning units of the 336th Division. The assault crossing of the 11th *Panzer* Division was canceled, and once again Balck's troops were thrown into the breach as a fire brigade. The 11th *Panzer* Division attacked on 18 December at Nizhna Chirskaya. It then conducted another night march and attacked at dawn on 19 December at Nizhna Kalinovski. Balck's 15th *Panzer* Regiment, which was now down to about only twenty-five tanks, attacked two Soviet columns, destroying sixty-five Soviet tanks and suffering no losses of its own.

Bitter back and forth fighting continued along the Chir for the next two days. By 22 December, the series of defensive battles along the Chir were over, with the Germans the clear victors. That same day, however, the XLVIII *Panzer Korps* received orders to immediately move ninety miles to the west to form blocking positions in front of Rostov.

Despite their tactical success, the Germans were outmaneuvered by the Soviets at the operational level. Nonetheless, the operations of the 11th *Panzer* Division along the Chir River were

some of military history's most outstanding examples of maneuver warfare and mobile defense. Throughout the battle, the XLVIII *Panzer Korps'* two infantry divisions served as a shield and pivot, behind which the 11th *Panzer* Division formed the mobile counterattack force. This series of battles is still studied by students at the U.S. Army's Command and General Staff College.

David T. Zabecki

Additional Reading

Balck, Hermann, *Ordnung im Chaos: Erinnerungen 1983–1948* (1981).
Mellenthin, F.W. von, *Panzer Battles* (1956).

CLARION, Operation (22–23 February 1945)

Launched at 1300 hours on 22 February 1945, Operation CLARION sent all available Anglo-American airpower against German communications and transportation targets in an effort to shorten the war. Nearly 9,000 aircraft from bases in Britain, France, Holland, Belgium, and Italy participated in this operation, flying across Germany, seeking out and bombing all types of transportation targets—grade crossings, railway stations, trains, motor vehicles, barges, docks, and bridges. Most of these targets were located in small towns not previously attacked and only lightly defended, and the bombings came from lower altitudes than the usual raids on Germany. The objectives were to use the complete Allied air superiority to cripple Germany's transportation and communications systems, and to shatter public confidence prior to the final ground offensive against the *Reich.*

With several Allied armies ready in mid-February 1945 to resume the ground attack against German forces, Supreme Headquarters Allied Expeditionary Force (SHAEF) (q.v.) requested that the Allied air forces undertake Operation CLARION. A similar operation in the fall of 1944, termed HURRICANE, demonstrated to the German people the full impact of strategic bombing. Some Allied generals opposed the terror bombing of Operation HURRICANE, and likewise objected to Operation CLARION, believing that bombing transportation targets in small German towns would reinforce Nazi propaganda that labeled the Allies barbarians. Other generals objected to the efficacy of an operation that called for American and British bombers to cruise across virtually the entire *Reich,* bombing targets at will.

In January 1945, the Combined Strategic

Targets Committee singled out the use of aircraft over a widely diffused area as being a major flaw in the attacks on transportation. Some generals also objected to exposing Allied heavy bombers to ground fire by sending them in after minor targets at low altitudes of 10,000 feet or less. The decision was made, nevertheless, to launch Operation CLARION at the first available opportunity that would permit visual bombing.

Clear weather arrived on 22 February, and the bombing commenced. The Allied tactical air forces attacked targets in western and northwestern Germany, while the U.S. Fifteenth Air Force operated in a large area in southern Germany. RAF Bomber Command continued its attacks on the Ruhr, and The U.S. Eighth Air Force bombed towns in central and northern Germany. The Allied bombers met little resistance in the air, and the seventy fighters the *Luftwaffe* could put up offered no serious challenge to the American fighter escorts.

The results of Operation CLARION were immediately apparent, and the success prompted Allied planners to launch a second blanket assault the following day. The cities of Gelsenkirchen, Essen, and Berlin were again singled out for attack, as were eight major transportation targets in the south. The Allied bombers also finished off targets hit the previous day. Initial reports were good—the accuracy of the bombings was unexpectedly high, aircraft losses were very low, and hundreds of targets were hit or destroyed. Railway transport was effectively halted in many parts of Germany, and it appeared that the communications system was shattered.

Further assessment of the two-day operation was less reassuring, for there was no sign of a general breakdown or collapse of the transportation system. High priority military traffic continued to move, the morale of the German people had not been devastated, and the Joint Intelligence Committee concluded that the Operation CLARION had not greatly affected Germany's war capabilities.

Robert G. Waite

Additional Reading

Craven, Wesley Frank, and James Lea Cate (eds.), *Europe—Argument to V-E Day. January 1944 to May 1945* (1951).

Richards, Denis, and Hillary St. G. Sanders, *The Fight Is Won* (1954).

Colmar Pocket (December 1944–February 1945)

In the fall of 1944, the Allied 6th Army Group, under the command of General Jacob L. Devers (q.v.), was directed to continue the Allied push toward the Rhine River. Devers was ordered to attack the German forces in the Vosges Mountains of eastern France and then push into eastern Alsace. With the U.S. Seventh Army under General Alexander Patch and the French First Army under General Jean de Lattre de Tassigny (qq.v.), Devers began the attack on 14 November 1944. He ordered the Seventh Army to push north through the Saverne gap, while the French First Army was to push south toward the Belfort gap. Together they would try to surround the Vosges region and enter the Alsatian plain to the east.

On 19 November, the southern wing of the attack broke through the Belfort gap, reaching the outskirts of Mulhouse and the area of the upper Rhine. De Lattre's 3rd Combat Command was the first Allied unit to reach the Rhine River. After the capture of Belfort on 22 November, the French First Army swung north toward Colmar.

The U.S. Seventh Army pushed its way north and on 21 November forced its way through the Saverne Gap. Helped by the French success to the south, the Seventh Army pushed on toward Strasbourg. On 23 November, General Philipe Leclerc's (q.v.) French 2nd Armored Division—which had been transferred from the 12th to the 6th Army Group as part of the U.S. XV Corps in late September—entered Strasbourg. The success of the Seventh Army split the German front in half, leaving the German First Army to the north and the Nineteenth Army to the south. Devers then ordered the U.S. XV Corps to clear out northern Alsace and to link up with General George S. Patton's (q.v.) Third Army in front of the Saar region.

In early December, Devers ordered the U.S. VI Corps to also shift north to the Saar area. Devers and his intelligence staff were convinced that the German Nineteenth Army, which was still west of the Rhine around Colmar, was preparing to pull back over the river into Germany. Accordingly, he thought that the French First Army alone could clear the Colmar region east of the Vosges and west of the river. Devers reassured General Dwight D. Eisenhower (q.v.) that: "The German Nineteenth has ceased to exist as a tactical force." Ordered to clear out the Alsatian plain, the French First Army was reinforced by the French 2nd Armored Division and the U.S. 36th Infantry Division.

The German Nineteenth Army, however, was not preparing to pull back over the Rhine. On 23 November, Adolf Hitler (q.v.) had ordered

General Friedrich Wiese to hold fast in the Colmar region. Hitler also placed the Nineteenth Army under *Armeegruppe Oberrhein,* commanded by *Reichsführer-SS* Heinrich Himmler (q.v.). The Colmar pocket was not evacuated and the Germans built it up as a defensive sector.

Throughout December, the French First Army tried to smash the Colmar pocket. The French II Corps attacked in the north while the French I Corps assaulted the pocket from the south. The defenders, the German LXIII and LXIV Corps, assisted by the mountainous terrain and winter weather, did not give up much ground.

By the end of 1944, the Colmar pocket measured about sixty miles in length from just below Strasbourg in the north to Mulhouse in the south. Until the Colmar region was cleared, it was not advisable to allow the Seventh Army to support Patton in an attack against the Saar region. Once the pocket was cleared, the French First Army could then hold the front line along the Rhine River from the Swiss border to the Saar region, thereby freeing the Seventh Army to support the attack in the north.

On New Year's Eve 1944, the Germans launched Operation *NORDWIND* (q.v.) through the Low Vosges. The next day on 1 January 1945, Eisenhower ordered Devers to pull the entire 6th Army Group back to defensive positions in the High Vosges. The withdrawal, however, would mean abandoning Strasbourg, which the French were not willing to do. General Charles de Gaulle (q.v.) objected and ordered de Lattre to hold the city, which at the time was in the operational sector of the Seventh Army. The issue quickly elevated to a full-scale political confrontation involving British Prime Minister Winston S. Churchill and President Franklin D. Roosevelt (qq.v.). De Gaulle and Eisenhower met on 3 January, and Eisenhower finally agreed to holding Strasbourg and shifting the army boundaries to place the city in de Lattre's sector.

Operation *NORDWIND* (NORTH WIND) was fierce at first, but lost steam quickly. On 5 January the Germans attacked across the Rhine with one division, but they failed to reach Strasbourg. On 7 January they attempted to fight their way north out of the Colmar pocket, but were halted some thirteen miles south of Strasbourg. After several more days of heavy fighting, the Germans abandoned their attempt to achieve a breakthrough.

The renewed Allied attack to reduce the Colmar pocket began on 20 January in the south and on 23 January in the north. On 27 January, Hitler allowed the German forces in the pocket to withdraw. On 28 January, the U.S. XXI Corps was committed to the battle, giving de Lattre a total of twelve divisions. At the end of January, the Germans began their retreat across the Rhine, sustaining heavy casualties in the process.

By 9 February, the entire Colmar pocket was in Allied hands. In total, the 425,000 Allied troops involved in the battle suffered more than 18,000 casualties. Although 22,000 Germans were taken prisoner, more than 50,000 troops of the Nineteenth Army were able to withdraw back over the Rhine.

Ken Reynolds

Additional Reading

Clarke, Jeffrey J., and Robert Ross Smith, *Riviera to the Rhine* (1993).
Weigley, Russell F., *Eisenhower's Lieutenants: The Campaigns of France and Germany, 1944–1945* (1981).

Cologne Air Raid (30–31 May 1942)

By early spring 1942, RAF Bomber Command was on the verge of collapse because of the heavy operational demands placed on it. Truly large concentrations of aircraft—raids of over 1,000 or so—were thought by some to be unfeasible. It was, however, a well-accepted principle that only concentrated attacks on industrial and urban targets could do real damage. Bomber Command thus decided that a large-scale raid was needed on a sizeable German city to demonstrate that significant destruction of industrial targets from the air was possible, assuming enough aircraft were available to do the job.

On 26 May 1942, the operational order for Operation MILLENIUM was issued, with a window of five nights to make the raid. The success of the raid hinged on the wide use of the Gee radar-beam navigation system. This device had been in service for a while, but it never had been used on such a large scale. Aircraft from RAF Bomber Command made up a bulk of the force (about 500 aircraft), with aircraft and crews from Coastal Command (about 250), Army Co-operation Command, operational conversion units, testing units, and flying training commands making up the rest. For some crews, this was their first combat mission.

The German industrial complex at Cologne (Köln) was selected, not because it was easily accessible, but because the Rhine River bends recognizably there. Thus, if the Gee system were to fail, the target could be found easily by the pathfinders (q.v.).

On the night of 30 May 1942, 1,046 two-and four-engine bombers, protected by Fighter Command escorts and Coastal Command light bombers, flew toward Cologne. Of these, about 910 actually bombed their targets, releasing somewhat more than one million pounds of high explosive and two million pounds of incendiary bombs. Antiaircraft fire over the city was heaviest in the first few minutes, gradually diminishing to practically nothing. The bombers attacked in three separate waves for a total raid time of about two and a half hours.

The RAF lost forty-four aircraft (3.9 percent) from all its commands (including Fighter Command) on the mission—slightly higher than for most missions at that point in the war. Cologne was devastated, with the old city and the northern section receiving the most damage. A total of 469 Germans were killed, 5,000 were injured, and 45,000 were left homeless during the raid; 600 acres of the city were completely destroyed. Transportation came to a standstill. The German government forced refugees to sign declarations to the effect that they would not talk about the attack.

For the RAF, the Cologne raid was a watershed. It proved that massed attacks were effective and controllable. For the Germans it was a precursor of the end. Later, massed raids on Hamburg, Berlin (qq.v.), and dozens of other cities would dwarf the Cologne raid, but Cologne in late May 1942 proved that large-scale, concentrated night attacks were possible, and that they would pave the way to victory.

John D. Beatty

Additional Reading
Barker, Ralph, *The Thousand Plane Raid* (1966).
Harris, Sir Arthur, *Bomber Offensive* (1947).
Hastings, Max, *Bomber Command* (1979).

Commando Raids (1941–1942)

For two years after the fall of France, the Allies were on the defensive. Apart from the Royal Air Force (RAF), the Commandos (q.v.) were Britain's only means of offense. Throughout 1941 and 1942, they carried out a series of raids, mainly amphibious, designed to annoy and wear down the Germans and to raise morale in Britain and occupied Europe, as much as to inflict material damage.

Most of the raids were small scale, but four stand out: Lofoten (March 1941) the first major

raid; Vaagso (December 1941) for the degree of cooperation between the three services; Bruneval (q.v.) (February 1942) the first British use of airborne troops; and Saint Nazaire (q.v.) (March 1942) for strategic purpose and success.

The Lofoten Islands lie off the Norwegian coast near Narvik, 150 miles inside the Arctic Circle, and 800 miles from the Shetlands, the nearest point of Britain. On 4 March 1941, 500 troops of Number 3 and 4 Commandos, commanded by Brigadier Charles Haydon of the Irish Guards, landed escorted by five destroyers and two light cruisers. The force took the German garrison completely by surprise. Ships, factories, a power plant, and storage tanks containing a million gallons of valuable fish oil were destroyed. When the commandos returned home they brought with them 314 volunteers for the Norwegian forces-in-exile, 200 German prisoners, and a handful of Norwegian traitors. The commando's own casualties were negligible, but the Germans later took fierce reprisals on the Norwegian population.

On 26 December 1941, Number 3 Commando returned to Norway, this time to the island of Vaagso, further south. Assisted by detachments from Numbers 2, 4, and 6 Commandos, they completely destroyed the vital German oil installations there. This raid involved considerable risk to the ships involved. They were well within range of German airfields, and the narrow fjords, ice, and strong currents posed severe navigational problems. Despite this, accurate naval gunfire by the Royal Navy (RN) was a key factor in getting the commandos ashore safely. So too was the RAF's properly timed tactical air support.

The Vaagso raid increased Adolf Hitler's (q.v.) fears of a British invasion of Norway. In reaction, he ordered Admiral Karl Dönitz (q.v.) to station U-boats in Norway, and he also sent more German troops there. The German forces sitting in Norway were unable to influence the action in any of the major theaters of the war.

In late 1941, British agents in occupied France reported a chain of German air defense radars along the Channel coast. British intelligence obviously needed more technical details, and the commandos were tasked for the mission. The radar (q.v.) at Bruneval, near Le Havre, was selected. Although there was a beach nearby, the radar was on top of a 400-foot cliff, so a parachute drop was decided.

Assisted by snow and darkness, they dropped inland of the radar at midnight on 27 February 1942. While the bulk of the commandos kept German reinforcements away, others, accompanied by Royal Engineers and one RAF expert, captured the radar itself. They removed as much as they could carry, photographed and destroyed the rest, and kept one German operator alive for interrogation. The team was then recovered from the beach by the RN. The audacity of this raid was matched only by its success. The technical information gained, according to Prime Minister Winston S. Churchill (q.v.) was of immense help to the Allied air offensive.

The commandos' greatest and most famous success, aptly called "the greatest raid of all," was the attack on Saint Nazaire on the west coast of France. This was far more than a nuisance raid and had a clear strategic purpose in relation to the Battle of the Atlantic (q.v.). Convoys across the Atlantic were Britain's lifeline. Since 1940, the Germans had developed Saint Nazaire into a major U-boat base. Moreover, it was the only port on that coast capable of handling German capital ships, and its destruction would prevent the Germans from committing these ships to the battle, an act that could have been decisive.

The British force of three destroyers and a number of smaller craft carrying 268 commandos left southwest England on 26 March 1942. After bluffing their way past enemy coastal defenses in murky weather, they made their way up the Loire estuary before storming ashore in the middle of Saint Nazaire harbor at 0130 hours the next day.

The key to the operation was the HMS *Campbeltown* (formerly the USS *Buchanan),* which rammed the main lock gate at full speed and was then scuttled. The next day, delayed-action fuzes set off the five tons of high explosives hidden on board, putting the lock and dry dock out of action until after V-E Day, and killing 400 Germans in the process. Meanwhile, the commandos inflicted further damage: another lock, a torpedo store, and the pumping station were destroyed, and a merchantman sunk.

Casualties were heavy, 50 percent of the Royal Navy and 66 percent of the commando personnel involved, but the raid achieved its objectives completely. Three Victoria Crosses were awarded to participants in the raid.

Philip Green

Additional Reading
Neillands, Robin, *By Sea and Land* (1987).
Saunders, Hillary St.G., *The Green Beret (The Story of the Commandos)* (1949).
Whitehouse, Arch, *Amphibious Operations* (1964).

Convoy Battle in the North Channel (17–20 October 1940)

The devastation of Convoys SC-7 and HX-79 in October 1940 was typical of that suffered by Allied shipping at the time. Occurring at a time when the U-boats had intelligence, operational, and technical superiority, the convoy lost two-thirds of its ships in only four days. The Royal Navy (RN) was short of experience, radar (q.v.), and convoy escorts just as Admiral Karl Dönitz (q.v.) was gaining enough U-boats to initiate his wolf pack tactics. More importantly, Dönitz's code breakers were reading some of RN's convoy communications. He knew of the convoy's departure and likely route and positioned his U-boat patrol line accordingly to intercept.

Departing from Sydney, Cape Breton, on 5 October, this slow convoy of thirty-four merchant ships had only a single escort, the HMS *Scarborough* when it left port. SC-7 acquired two more escorts when the first German U-boat, the *U-48,* made contact on 17 October. Without waiting to make the required sighting report, the U-boat commander attacked immediately, sinking two ships within an hour. It was the beginning of what would mark the peak of the first German "Happy Time" in the Battle of the Atlantic (q.v.).

The paucity of escorts protecting the convoy was further compounded by poor tactics. The convoy commander dispatched one of the escorts to pick up survivors from the first torpedoed ship. It was a decision that cost him a third of his escort force, because the corvette never caught up with the convoy again. He made the same mistake with the next escort to arrive, leaving it behind to assist a damaged merchant ship. As it turned out, he dearly needed both escorts over the next three days. Once the *U-48* made its report that evening, Dönitz wasted no time reacting. Within hours, he assembled five more U-boats, including those commanded by famed U-boat aces Günther Prien, Otto Kretschmer (qq.v.), and Joachim Schepke. They made contact the next evening.

In an attack that began just after dark, the Germans sank more than fifteen Allied ships in less than six hours. The escorts proved completely ineffectual, abandoning their stations to rescue survivors at the expense of their primary mission, defending the convoy. The U-boats penetrated the convoy and attacked at will. By dawn, they had sunk seventeen ships and damaged two others. Kretschmer and two other U-boat captains expended all their torpedoes in the attack and turned for home. Prien and the others were not finished.

Spotting the forty-nine-ship convoy, HX-79,

Prien sent a sighting report and took station behind the convoy. Dönitz sent three more U-boats to assist. They intercepted the convoy during the evening of 19 October, sinking twelve ships and damaging another, despite the presence of a ten-ship escort group supported by a Dutch submarine. Once again, Allied tactics were at fault. The escorts attacked the Dutch submarine twice and wasted many depth charges on spurious contacts. Moreover, the absence of radar enabled the Germans to operate undetected on the surface throughout the night.

The German attacks on convoys SC-7 and HX-79 marked the two worst days for shipping losses in the entire war. U-boat effectiveness alarmed Britain's naval and political leaders. If the U-boats could devastate a convoy protected by eleven escorts, what hope did the Allies have? Fortunately, these attacks marked the high point of the German war on shipping. Dönitz lacked the numbers to sustain the wolf packs at sea. By the time Dönitz had the numbers, his technical and intelligence superiority began to wane. Britain was within months of breaking his codes and radar was beginning to appear on convoy escorts. Those developments and the introduction of escort carriers would turn the tide against Germany and ultimately cost it the Battle of the Atlantic.

Carl O. Schuster

Additional Reading
Hessler, Gunther, *The U-Boat War in the Atlantic* (1989).
Hough, Richard, *The Longest Battle* (1987).
Smith, Peter C., *Hold the Narrow Sea: Naval Warfare in the English Channel, 1939–1945* (1984).
Van der Vat, Dan, *The Atlantic Campaign* (1988).

Convoy Battle off Portugal (14–23 December 1941)

Convoy HG-76 was a convoy of thirty-two merchant ships escorted by thirteen destroyers and Britain's first escort carrier, HMS *Audacity*. Departing Gibraltar on 14 December 1941, it suffered nine days of German air and U-boat attack, losing two merchant ships, a corvette, and the escort carrier in the process. More importantly, the convoy's escorts sank five of the twelve U-boats deployed against it. It was the first convoy battle in which more U-boats than merchant ships were lost.

At the time, many Allied naval officers

thought the battle marked the turning point of the war, but they were to be sadly disappointed within a few months. The HG-76 victory was based on a combination of Allied code breaking and the brilliant training and employment of the escort group by the escort commander, Captain Frederic J. Walker (q.v.). Once implemented throughout the fleet, the tactics employed in the HG-76 defense provided the keys to Allied victory in the Battle of the Atlantic (q.v.).

The battle for HG-76 came at a time when both sides' intelligence services were serving their commanders well. The British code breakers were reading Germany's U-boat traffic and had an accurate and timely idea of where the U-boats were and where they were going. Admiral Karl Dönitz (q.v.) also knew the convoys' movements and intentions; his code breakers were reading the British convoy codes. It was that knowledge that enabled him to deploy his wolf pack against Convoy HG-76 in the first place. Meanwhile, Allied code breaking warned the convoy of the German intentions. As a result, the HMS *Audacity's* aircraft were able to locate and sink the first two U-boats that made contact. A four-day battle of attrition followed. Dönitz used FW-200 Kondor bombers and two waves of U-boats, but he was unable to stop or devastate the convoy.

Although HG-76 was not the decisive engagement that many had hoped, it did show the way to victory. Dönitz, suspicious about the security of his codes, had them and his encryption machines changed shortly thereafter. That change effectively blinded the British to his communications for most of 1942. Also, the introduction of the German FuMB radar warning device enabled the U-boats to dive before Allied air and naval units could get in position to attack.

Still, these tactics provided only temporary advantages. The Allies eventually cracked the new codes and produced centimetric radars that the Germans could not detect. With those developments and the introduction of growing numbers of convoy escorts and escort carriers, the pendulum swung decisively against the U-boats—this time for good. HG-76 had pointed the way.

Carl O. Schuster

Additional Reading
Hessler, Gunther, *The U-boat War in the Atlantic* (1989).
Hough, Richard, *The Longest Battle* (1986).
Van der Vat, Dan, *The Atlantic Campaign* (1988).

Convoy PQ-17 (1–9 July 1942)

[See map 5 on page 1315]

The safe passage of convoys carrying supplies to northern Russia from August 1941 until 1945, was one of the main commitments of the British Home Fleet. The first convoy sailed from the United Kingdom during August 1941, two months after the German invasion of the Soviet Union. It arrived safely and twelve more convoys completed the passage to Russia by the spring of 1942, with only the loss of one ship out of the 103 that sailed. It was during the spring of 1942 that the Germans decided to base heavy naval ships in Norway, including their new battleship, *Tirpitz,* to interdict the sea supply route to Russia.

The threat of surface, as well as U-boat attacks, posed a problem for the Allied command. In June 1942, Allied intelligence indicated that the German Navy was prepared to bring out heavy surface units to attack the next eastbound convoy as it passed east of Bear Island. The situation completely favored the German forces. Their ships operated close to the Norwegian coast and within range of shore-based aircraft. The Germans also provided a screen of U-boats in the channels between Spitsbergen and Norway. The British force, once committed to a convoy route, was soon out of range of shore-based air support, and the destroyers were generally too short of fuel to escort a damaged ship to a safe harbor.

In preparation for the sailing of Convoy PQ-17, the British Admiralty approved a plan whereby an attempt was made to divert enemy surface and air forces toward a dummy convoy formed at Scapa Flow. The dummy convoy was made up of ships of the 1st Minelaying Squadron and four colliers, and was escorted by two cruisers, HMS *Sirius* and HMS *Curacao,* five destroyers, and some trawlers. The dummy convoy sailed west of the Shetlands and then eastward hoping to attract the attention of German air reconnaissance. The only German air reconnaissance of Scapa Flow during the formation of the dummy convoy failed to observe the assembled ships. Having sailed, the convoy failed to attract German attention.

The eastbound PQ-17 sailed from Hval Fjord on 27 June 1942 and consisted of 34 merchant ships, an oiler for use by the escort, and three rescue ships. The escort consisted of six destroyers, four corvettes, three minesweepers, four trawlers, two antiaircraft ships, and two submarines. The route of the convoy to Archangel was considerably longer than that used by convoys sent to Russia in early 1942. The route went north of Bear Island with an evasive detour in the Barents Sea.

Convoy PQ-17 had problems from the start as part of it ran into drifting ice in thick weather in the Denmark Strait. Two merchant ships were damaged and had to return to base. The escort's oiler, the *Grey Ranger,* also was badly damaged and was replaced by the *Aldersdale.* PQ-17 was spotted by enemy aircraft and U-boats on 1 July and thereafter shadowed continuously, except for a few short intervals when fog prevented surveillance. The first air attack was made by nine German torpedo aircraft on 2 July and was unsuccessful with one German aircraft lost. The next series of air attacks on 4 July resulted in three ships sunk and four German aircraft shot down.

Two covering forces then moved into position to support PQ-17. One was the 1st Cruiser Squadron, consisting of four cruisers and three destroyers (two of which were American). The other was a "heavy force," led by the battleship HMS *Duke of York.* The battle group moved into a position northwest of Bear Island so as to give cover to Convoy PQ-17. Air reconnaissance of the Norwegian harbors showed that the *Tirpitz* and the heavy cruiser *Admiral Hipper* had left their base, but their exact locations were not known at that time.

The ice situation improved and the passage north of Bear Island widened. The Admiralty advised the senior officer of the escort that the convoy should pass "at least" fifty miles north of Bear Island. The senior officer, however, decided to keep to his original route. That decision was later overruled by the rear admiral commanding, 1st Cruiser Squadron, who ordered the escort and convoy to pass seventy miles north of Bear Island.

On 4 July, the Admiralty gave permission for the 1st Cruiser Squadron to proceed east, should the situation so demand, unless contrary orders were issued. The 1st Cruiser Squadron was to withdraw from escorting the convoy when it reached the position east of 25 degrees east, unless the Admiralty reported that the threat from the *Tirpitz* had diminished. At 1858 hours, the Admiralty signaled the rear admiral commanding, 1st Cruiser Squadron to remain with the convoy pending further instructions.

At 2111 hours, the Admiralty sent a "Most Immediate" signal ordering the 1st Cruiser Squadron to withdraw to the westward "at high speed," which was thought to prevent a major U-boat strike. At 2123 hours, the Admiralty sent an "Immediate" signal ordering the convoy to disperse and to proceed to Soviet ports, as there was a threat from surface ships, which did not materialize. At 2136 hours, another "Most Immediate" signal was received ordering the convoy to "scatter." It was later stated that the second signal was merely a correction to the earlier signal changing the term "disperse" to "scatter." Unfortunately, senior officers of both the 1st Cruiser Squadron and the escort interpreted the signal to mean that an attack by the *Tirpitz* was imminent, and the convoy was ordered to scatter, with the escort destroyers ordered to join the cruiser force and the remaining ships of the escort to proceed independently.

Although the *Tirpitz* and the *Admiral Hipper* left their base with six destroyers, they did not intercept the British naval force, nor the convoy, and so they returned to their base. At the time that the convoy was given the order to scatter, it had covered more than half its route with the loss of only three ships. Once the dispersal took place, the individual ships became spread over a wide area and were exposed to concentrated U-boat and air attacks. The German naval and air force commands took full advantage of the situation and kept up a continuous attack on the British merchant ships, which were then without an adequate escort cover. The merchant ships generally were armed only with antiaircraft guns mounted as supporting weapons. The main protection was supposed to come from the escort ships.

The thirty-four-ship convoy was devastated in very short order. Although widespread searches were made by a few Royal Air Force (RAF) Coastal Command aircraft and by minesweepers and corvettes, it was two weeks before the full extent of the disaster was known. Of the thirty-four ships that remained when the order for dispersal was given, twenty-one were sunk, including the oiler *Aldersdale* and one rescue ship. Only thirteen ships reached Archangel. The convoy was attacked by an unknown number of U-boats, six German bomber aircraft, and thirty-three torpedo aircraft.

Of all the convoys that sailed to northern Russia, the losses from Convoy PQ-17 were by far the highest. The total losses from all the convoys to Russia amounted to sixty-two ships out of 792 that sailed. The return trip losses were recorded as twenty-eight ships out of 739. The merchant navy's casualties were 829 officers and men. While providing protection to the Russian-bound convoys, the Royal Navy lost two cruisers, six destroyers, three sloops, two frigates, three corvettes, and three minesweepers, with the loss of 1,840 officers and men. The Soviet ambassador in London said in 1943, "The Russian convoys are a northern saga of heroism, bravery and endurance. This saga will live for ever."

Alan Harfield

Additional Reading

Irving, David, *The Destruction of PQ17* (1968).
Lund, Paul, and Harry Ludlam, *PQ17—Convoy to Hell: The Survivors' Story* (1968).

Convoy PQ-18 (12–20 September 1942)

After the debacle of Convoy PQ-17 (q.v.) in July 1942, British planners delayed their next Russia-bound convoy until September. In addition to being preoccupied with the Malta convoys (q.v.), the British also needed to assess the circumstances that had prompted the destruction of twenty-three Allied ships, two-thirds of PQ-17's original strength. At last, the availability of sufficient escort forces, along with pressure not to weaken Soviet Premier Josef Stalin (q.v.) at a critical juncture of the war, persuaded Britain to ready another convoy. German countermeasures loomed as threatening as ever, including a possible sortie of surface warships led by the battleship *Tirpitz*. To use Allied resources optimally, QP-14, a reverse convoy, would leave Archangel so that PQ-18's former escort could shepherd it through the zone of gravest danger.

Leaving Icelandic waters on 7 September, PQ-18 consisted of forty merchantmen, two fleet oilers, and a designated rescue ship. The Royal Navy (RN) committed seventy-six warships and three Royal Air Force (RAF) squadrons to cover the convoy throughout its voyage. Three destroyers, four corvettes, three minesweepers, four trawlers, two antiaircraft ships, and two submarines constituted PQ-18's permanent "through escort," along with two fleet oilers. Operating close by were the escort carrier HMS *Avenger* (with fifteen aircraft), the antiaircraft cruiser HMS *Scylla,* and seventeen additional destroyers. Other Allied units in the vicinity included two battleships, six cruisers, thirteen destroyers, and several auxiliaries. Submarines and reconnaissance aircraft monitored German ship movements off Norway.

Germany's forces in Norway were hardly weaker in September than in July, and certainly more experienced. Twelve submarines would scout and attack whenever conditions warranted. On 10 September, two days after aerial reconnaissance spotted PQ-18 northeast of Iceland, the pocket battleship *Admiral Scheer* (minus the *Tirpitz,* which remained behind), the cruisers *Admiral Hipper* and *Köln,* and five destroyers, sailed north from Narvik to Altenfjord ready for action against the convoy. Most menacing were some 225 *Luftwaffe* bombers, mainly Ju-88s and He-111s, which could carry bombs or torpedoes, as well as

The ammunition ship Mary Luckenback *explodes after being torpedoed during an air attack on Convoy PQ-18, 14 September 1942. (IWM A 12273)*

fighters and reconnaissance planes based at the Banak, Bardufoss, and Kirkenes airfields.

From Iceland, PQ-18's progress was generally to the northeast until it reached Spitzbergen. From there easterly courses would take it to approximately 40 degrees east before steering south to reach the White Sea, always keeping a distance of some 400 miles from Norway's North Cape. QP-14 would roughly parallel that route after its departure from Archangel on 13 September. On 17 September, it was joined by the HMS *Avenger* and her screen, while land-based aircraft covered PQ-18 for the remainder of her journey.

The struggle for PQ-18 began on 12 September with the loss of the *U-88* to the British destroyer HMS *Faulknor,* and lasted until 20 September when the *Luftwaffe* flew a last, futile mission against the convoy's survivors in the White Sea. While danger from aloft and below remained present throughout the period, 13 and 14 September witnessed the fiercest fighting as PQ-18 passed between Bear Island and Spitzbergen. Early on 13 September, a simultaneous attack by the *U-408* and the *U-589* claimed two ships out of the convoy's starboard column. Later that day, despite heavy antiaircraft fire and brave sorties by HMS *Avenger*'s outclassed fighters, massive strikes by *Luftwaffe* torpedo bombers sank eight more ships with minor losses to the Germans. An additional vessel was lost to *U-457*.

If, by 14 September, PQ-18 seemed destined to repeat PQ-17's fate, the worst was actually over. That day, the *Luftwaffe* renewed its attacks, but they came piecemeal with little coordination. Only one ship was lost while numerous German planes were shot down or badly damaged, and the destroyer HMS *Onslow* sank the *U-489*. Moreover, Germany's "fleet-in-being" concept continued to keep German surface warships safely but harmlessly in Norway's fjords. Despite daily air raids and

lurking U-boats, PQ-18 moved on. On 16 September, the Germans lost another submarine, the *U-457,* to the destroyer HMS *Impulsive.* As the convoy entered the White Sea on 18 September, German pilots claimed a last merchantman, largely because of unreliable Soviet air cover.

PQ-18's arrival in Archangel meant a bittersweet victory. The loss of thirteen merchant vessels seemed a high price to pay for the renewal of materiel shipments to the Soviets, particularly as U-boats raised the score by sinking two escorts and four merchantmen out of QP-14. On the other hand, Germany failed to close the route to Russia, losing some forty aircraft and three submarines in the process. Never again would the Arctic Sea be quite as deadly for the Allies as in that summer of 1942, and future convoys came through with only minor casualties.

Eric C. Rust

Additional Reading
Schofield, Brian B., *The Russian Convoys* (1964).
Smith, Peter C., *Arctic Victory: The Story of Convoy PQ-18* (1975).

Convoys HX-229 and SC-122 (14–20 March 1943)

March 1943 marked the climax in the battle for the North Atlantic, as dozens of German U-boats under the guidance of Grand Admiral Karl Dönitz (q.v.) inflicted heavy casualties on four large Britain-bound convoys (SC-121, HX-228, SC-122 and HX-299) in a series of concerted actions while sustaining relatively minor losses.

At the time, the Germans enjoyed several advantages over their opponents. German radio intelligence supplied accurate sailing dates for the convoys and their approximate routes. Dönitz assembled a record number of U-boats and formed them into wolf packs. Two supply submarines stood by to replenish U-boats with fuel, provisions, and additional torpedoes. Much of the action took place in the so-called Air Gap in the mid-Atlantic, a vast expanse of ocean beyond the surveillance radius of Allied planes based in Newfoundland, Iceland, Northern Ireland, and southwestern England.

The Allies encountered several handicaps as the engagement unfolded. On 10 March, the Germans introduced a new short-signal book. This rendered British ULTRA (q.v.) analysts incapable of effectively rerouting convoys away from known or suspected U-boat concentrations for nine days. Allied escort groups were relatively weak and multinational, some of them hastily detached from unmolested westbound convoys to help protect the larger and more valuable eastbound ones.

Several escort vessels had to leave the scene early because of fuel shortages or damage, while others lacked commanders experienced in antisubmarine warfare (ASW) (q.v.). Fierce spring storms kept merchantmen from maintaining assigned stations, thus producing many stragglers. The latter tended to fall easy prey to U-boats while trying to catch up with the main convoys, especially since air cover seldom protected vessels separated from their companions.

The dual battle for SC-122 and HX-229 followed in the wake of an earlier struggle when their predecessors, SC-121 and HX-228, ran into two wolf packs, *Gruppe Westmark* with seventeen U-boats and *Gruppe Neuland* with thirteen U-boats, respectively, after successfully eluding yet another German patrol line to the west, *Gruppe Raubgraf* with thirteen U-boats. Over a five-day period from 6 to 10 March, Convoy SC-121 lost twelve vessels (55,658 tons) sunk and one damaged, a quarter of its strength, in running attacks south of Iceland. Several hundred miles to the southwest, Convoy HX-228 encountered *Gruppe Neuland* on 10 to 12 March. Four merchantmen totaling 24,175 tons went down along with the British destroyer HMS *Harvester*. Two other Allied vessels were damaged. Two German U-boats, the *U-444* and *U-432*, also were sunk.

Encouraged by these results and using radio intelligence to his advantage, Dönitz quickly reorganized his patrol lines to catch SC-122 (fifty vessels, nine escorts, top speed 7 knots) and HX-229 (forty vessels, six escorts, top speed 9 knots), which left New York on 5 and 8 March, respectively. By 14 March, *Gruppe Raubgraf* redeployed south of Greenland, its boats scouting in a line abreast in a

southwesterly direction and expecting to make contact with the northeast-bound convoys at any moment. At the same time, U-boats previously engaged against SC-121 and HX-228, reformed some 400 miles to the east of *Gruppe Raubgraf* as *Gruppe Stürmer* (eighteen U-boats) and *Gruppe Dränger* (eleven U-boats), with both lines moving approximately west-southwest at 9 knots. *Gruppe Dränger* set up southeast of *Gruppe Stürmer* to guard against the possibility that one or both of the convoys might be diverted to more easterly courses and miss *Gruppe Raubgraf* and *Gruppe Stürmer* altogether.

Dönitz's caution was not misplaced. Both convoys steered temporarily to the east away from the suspected *Gruppe Raubgraf* pickets before again proceeding to the northeast after crossing each other's path with SC-122 in the lead by a few hours. Through this maneuver and a favorable following gale, SC-122 cleared *Gruppe Raubgraf* without being detected, while one U-boat briefly made contact with one of HX-229's rear escorts.

On the morning of 16 March, the Germans obtained a permanent fix on HX-229 when the *U-653*, homeward-bound with mechanical problems, happened to contact and report the convoy. This allowed *Gruppe Raubgraf* to abandon its patrol stations and move quickly southeast to catch up. At the same time, Dönitz instructed the northern section of *Gruppe Stürmer* to move south now that HX-229's position was known and SC-122 could not be far away. Actually, German radio intelligence confused the two convoys much of the time, primarily because a separate Convoy HX-229A operated farther west and out of danger; but this did little to affect the outcome of the battle.

By the morning of 17 March, HX-229 lost eight ships to *Gruppe Raubgraf*, with several *Gruppe Stürmer* U-boats closing in from the northeast. At the same time, SC-122 ran into the northern section of *Gruppe Stürmer* and suffered immediate disaster. The *U-338*, commanded by Lieutenant Commander Manfred Kinzel, in one of the war's more spectacular U-boat attacks and using only five torpedoes, sank three merchantmen and damaged a fourth, which the *U-665* eventually sunk.

That encounter made Dönitz realize his U-boats were at last in contact with both convoys. He therefore issued orders to bring up *Gruppe Dränger* against HX-229 and for the northern section of *Gruppe Stürmer* to engage SC-122. Indeed no fewer than thirty-seven U-boats were in contact with the convoys during the course of the action, although not all of them came within firing range.

During the remaining daylight hours of 17 March, Allied air patrols, flying at the limit of their operating radius, managed to prevent further losses, but as always, the nights belonged to the wolves. Before the convoys managed to shake off the last of the submarines and again enjoy solid air cover flown out of Northern Ireland on 20 March, fourteen additional vessels, many of them stragglers, went to the bottom, for a total of twenty-two Allied ships totaling 146,596 tons. The victims were of American, British, Panamanian, Dutch, and Norwegian registry and ranged in size from the Panamanian freighter *Granville* (4,071 tons) to the British whaling factory *Southern Princess* (12,156 tons).

The Germans lost only one boat, the *U-384*, as a result of the four-day action. A B-17 Flying Fortress from RAF Number 206 Squadron surprised her on the surface and bombed her on 19 March. There were no survivors.

The German success against SC-122 and HX-229, spectacular as it appeared to Dönitz, and seemingly devastating to the Allies, actually represented the last triumph for the German side before the tide of the Battle of the Atlantic (q.v.) broke and turned irrevocably in favor of the Western powers. The days of the wolf packs were numbered. Increasingly sophisticated antisubmarine measures from the air and at sea, along with superior Allied radar technology, sonar, (qq.v.) and ULTRA intelligence, forced Dönitz at first to abandon temporarily, and then later to scale back submarine activities in the North Atlantic by the end of May 1943, after a record loss of forty-one boats in that month alone.

Before long, the Bay of Biscay, home to Germany's U-boat bases in France, became a virtual submarine cemetery. In fact, two boats of *Gruppe Stürmer* went down before reaching their bases at Brest and Lorient. Moreover, the "Air Gap" was closed with the help of "hunter-killer" groups built around escort aircraft carriers. By spring 1943, few convoys came even close to the destruction that had devastated their predecessors on the North Atlantic run, while more and more submarines turned into ready-made "iron coffins."

Eric C. Rust

Additional Reading

Dönitz, Karl, *Memoirs: Ten Years and Twenty Days* (1959).
Middlebrook, Martin, *Convoy: The Battle for Convoys SC-122 and HX-229* (1976).
Rohwer, Jürgen, *The Critical Convoy Battles of March 1943* (1977).

Coventry Air Raid (14–15 November 1940)

[See map 8 on page 1318]

After weeks of continuous night bombing raids in the London area, the *Luftwaffe* changed its objective on the night of 14 November and bombed the city of Coventry. This attack, code named Operation MOONLIGHT SONATA, was partly in response to the British bombing of Munich. Coventry also contained many legitimate military production targets including armaments, munitions, and aircraft component factories.

Field Marshal Albert Kesselring (q.v.), commander of *Luftflotte* Two, sent thirteen Heinkel He-111s of *Kampfgruppe* 100 to mark the target. They used the new radio beam navigation aid named *X-Gerät* (X device) to guide them to the city. At 2015 hours, the bombers reached their destination and dropped at least 1,000 incendiary bombs. The ensuing fires were more than adequate to help the main German bomber force of 449 aircraft find its target. While approaching the British coastline from the Channel, a German pilot reported seeing a small pinpoint of white light and commented, "My crew and I speculated as to what it might be. As we drew closer it dawned on us: we were looking at the burning city of Coventry."

The second wave of attackers converged on the city from the Lincolnshire coast, Portland, and Dungeness. More than eight *Kampfgruppen* were involved in the attack, with each being assigned specific targets. Among these targets were the Standard Motor Company, the Alvis Aero Engine factory, and the Hill Street Gas Works. The bombers flew in widely dispersed formations at altitudes from 10,000 to 20,000 feet. This meant it was very difficult for defending night fighters to find their targets. The British fighters flew 119 sorties, but were unable to shoot down a single attacking plane.

The lightly opposed Germans were able to drop more than fifty tons of incendiaries, and 500 tons of high explosive bombs on Coventry, causing substantial damage and casualties. The city's railway lines and aircraft factories were especially hard hit. Many nonmilitary targets, including residential areas, were also destroyed. The bombs also damaged some of Coventry's most famous landmarks, such as St. Michael's Cathedral, Christ Church, and Ford's Hospital. Civilian casualties in dead and wounded exceeded 1,400. The people of Britain were outraged at what they believed was an attack on a nonmilitary target, but Coventry's industrial output had already led the Germans to call the city "the little Essen."

Recent reports have speculated the British knew of the upcoming raid on Coventry from ULTRA (q.v.) intercepts, but did not better prepare their defenses for fear of giving away the ULTRA secret to the Germans. While possible, this theory is not probable for explaining the Germans' success. Kesselring called this raid an exceptional fluke. He believed the convenient distance to the target from French bases, very good weather conditions, and the illuminating fires all contributed to the mission's success. Another factor was the success of the *X-Gerät* guidance system in directing the German bombers to their target. The British developed an effective jamming device for the earlier German *Knickebein* system but the *X-Gerät* operated at a higher frequency that was not disrupted by the jammers.

The British learned important lessons from the Coventry raid. They modified their jammers and introduced an effective airborne radar system, the AI Mark IV. This radar, installed on a British Beaufighter, gave the RAF its first truly effective night fighter.

Glenn Lamar

Additional Reading

Glitheroe, Graham, *Coventry under Fire: An Expression of the Great Raids on Coventry in 1940 and 1941* (1942).
Longmate, Norman, *Air Raid: The Bombing of Coventry, 1940* (1978).
Mason, Francis K., *Battle over Britain* (1969).
Pierce, Alfred, *Blitz on Britain* (1977).

Crete (20 May–1 June 1941)

[See map 10 on page 1320]
On 24 April 1941, Germany and its allies successfully concluded their campaign in Greece (q.v.). In the Mediterranean, however, the British still had almost complete freedom of movement, operating their convoy traffic from bases at Gibraltar, Malta, Crete, and Cyprus. This situation adversely affected the flow of supplies to the *Afrika Korps* (q.v.). Therefore, on 21 April, Adolf Hitler (q.v.) decided that following the occupation of Greece, the island of Crete would be taken as quickly as possible to give the Axis a base to operate against the Royal Navy (RN). The operation was code named *MERKUR* (MERCURY).

Crete, located only some 100 kilometers southeast of the tip of Greece, is more than 270 kilometers long, but only ten to sixty kilometers wide. The island is formed by an undersea mountain range, whose peaks rise as high as 2,500 meters above sea level. Only a small percent of the island's surface is flat land. In 1941, Crete had only three airstrips, located at Máleme in the west, Rethymnon in the center, and Iráklion farther to the east. Moreover, all three of those towns, the capital city, Khaniá, and the few relatively large ports were located on the northern side of the island, the side closest to Greece. Logically, the north side was where the Germans planned to launch their attack.

The task of taking the airfields fell to the Fourth *Luftflotte*. General Kurt Student's (q.v.) XI *Fliegerkorps* would provide 500 transport aircraft to lift his 7th Parachute Division, which would take the airfields by parachute and glider assault. They would be supported by 700 fighters and dive bombers from General Wolfram von Richthofen's (q.v.) VIII *Fliegerkorps*. Once the airfields and ports were secure, units of the 5th and 6th Mountain Divisions would land by plane and by ship. The German naval commander in Greece provided transport ships and naval security elements. Altogether, the Germans assembled 10,600 airborne troops and 14,000 mountain troops for the operation. About 5,000 of the mountain troops originally were scheduled to come in by air, the remainder in two separate ship convoys.

Creforce, the British Commonwealth forces on Crete, was under the command of New Zealand's Lieutenant General Sir Bernard Freyberg (q.v.). The Germans badly underestimated the Allied strength at only one division. Freyberg actually had about 31,000 troops, many of whom were part of the British force evacuated from Greece. They were organized into the New Zealand Division, the Australian 19th Brigade, and the strong British 14th Brigade. Freyberg also had 5,000 Greek troops from the island's garrison, and another 7,000 who had evacuated from Greece to the island along with their king and his government. In general, the defenders were well dug-in.

In the air, the *Luftwaffe* vastly outnumbered the small handful of Royal Air Force (RAF) fighters available. On the sea, the Royal Navy (RN) had overwhelming superiority; but German air superiority and the closeness of their air bases in Greece made daylight operations north of the island very hazardous for naval surface units. The air strikes in preparation for the assault started on 15 May. Two days later, Freyberg sent all his RAF planes to Cairo, rather than sacrifice them in a battle they had no hope of influencing. Meanwhile, the German airborne assault force assembled near Athens. The drops were organized into three phases because of the limited carrying capacity of the ten groups of Ju-52 transports.

The airborne landings started on the morning of 20 May. On the western end of the island, the paratroopers of the elite *Sturmregiment* jumped in to seize the airfield at Máleme, while elements of the regiment landed in gliders. Their mission was to eliminate the defender's air defenses and take the dominating terrain of Hill 107. Simultaneously, the 3rd Parachute Regiment jumped in to take Khaniá, nearby. Neither assault was completely successful, especially at Máleme, where the New Zealand 5th Brigade put up a stiff resistance.

On the rest of the island, the Germans were even less successful. On the afternoon of 20 May, the 2nd Parachute Regiment dropped in to take Rethymnon and the harbor at Scuda Bay. Takeoff delays in Greece resulted in a fragmented assault and high losses for the attackers. The 1st Parachute Regiment had similar problems at Iráklion. Some of the transports arriving late were shot down while in the process of releasing the paratroopers, many

of whom were killed or wounded while still in the air.

By dusk on 20 May, Operation *MERKUR* was off to a bad start. The attacks in the center and the east were beaten back. In the west, the Germans held only a tenuous position near Máleme, but the German leadership decided to press the attack there. During the night of 20 May, the Germans continued to push for control of Hill 107, which dominated the airfield. When its wire communications network was destroyed by German bombing, the New Zealand 22nd Battalion believed they were cut off and about to be overrun. Under cover of darkness, they withdrew from their positions on Hill 107. At the same time, paratroopers from the *Sturmregiment* moved in and occupied the former New Zealand positions. That would prove to be the turning point in the battle for Crete.

On the morning of 21 May, the German position improved, but it was still weak. With con-

A Ju-52 transport full of German paratroops crashes in flames near the Heraklion aerodrome on Crete, 20 May 1941. (IWM A 4155)

trol of the airfield, they were now able to bring in by air units from the 5th Mountain Division. That started to shift the balance in favor of the Germans, but their crisis was far from over. During the night of 21 May, the RN destroyed the first of the two reinforcement convoys, carrying 2,500 mountain troopers, air defense units, and light and medium equipment. Despite German air superiority, Admiral Sir Andrew Cunningham (q.v.), British naval commander in chief in the Mediterranean, ordered his ships to remain north of the island. The RN sustained heavy losses, but on the morning of 22 May, they also intercepted and dispersed the second German convoy. Most of that convoy was able to make it back to Greece.

Despite the interception of two reinforcement convoys, the mountain troops who came in by air shifted the balance in favor of the Germans. On the night of 21 May, the New Zealanders mounted an unsuccessful counterattack. On 22 May, Freyberg ordered a withdrawal from Máleme. By 26 May, the Commonwealth forces started to pull out of Khaniá. That same day, Freyberg decided to evacuate Crete and ordered all of his forces to move overland to Sfakia, a small harbor on the south side of the island. The evacuation, which lasted from 28–31 May, was hampered by limited port facilities and constant German air attacks. Meanwhile, on the night of 28 May, the RN evacuated 4,000 troops of the British 14th Brigade from Iráklion. Surrounded and cut off, the Australian 19th Brigade at Rethymnon surrendered on 30 May.

The Germans secured Crete on 1 June, but the cost was high. Casualties included 1,655 paratroopers killed, 2,046 wounded, 1,441 missing, and nearly 200 aircraft destroyed. The mountain troops fared better with 262 killed, 458 wounded, and 318 missing. These numbers do not include those killed at sea or in the air, which brought the total German losses for Operation *MERKUR* to 6,580. The high figure of missing in action, most of which were later assumed dead, resulted from guerrilla actions conducted inland by the people of Crete.

British losses were heavy too: 1,750 killed, 1,740 wounded, and 12,000 captured. Altogether, the British managed to evacuate 18,600, as many as 3,000 drowned when their ships were sunk by the *Luftwaffe*. The RN suffered 1,800 sailors killed and lost three cruisers and six destroyers. Seventeen other ships were heavily damaged, including a battleship and an aircraft carrier. There are no reliable figures for losses among the Greek soldiers or the civilian population of Crete.

The Nazi propaganda machine trumpeted

Crete as the glorious successor to the brilliant string of German victories since September 1939. Quite the contrary was true, however. Crete was the first major catastrophe for the *Wehrmacht*. The Germans badly underestimated the size of their enemy, and the Allies were able to estimate with fair accuracy the times and places of the landings. Perhaps the single greatest weakness of the German plan was its dispersed nature, attacking all three airfields rather than massing all combat power on one objective. Once on the ground, the paratroopers were forced to fight like conventional infantry until the arrival of the mountain troops. Airborne forces, which specialize in short-term operations, were not trained or equipped for that type of mission.

Despite these drawbacks and the high casualty rate of the airborne forces, the Germans did win. This happened for a number of reasons. German air superiority was a major factor, especially the disruption it inflicted on the British communications systems. The *Luftwaffe* extracted a heavy toll from the RN, and it constantly pounded Freyberg's troops as they withdrew to the south side of the island. Then there was the superb training of the German soldiers, and the German command system of decentralizing tactical execution down to the lowest possible level. Once the mountain troops entered the fight, they were able to operate over terrain the Allies considered impassable.

Despite Operation *MERKUR*'s tactical success, the Germans never again mounted a major airborne operation. Additionally, Operation *MERKUR* did not decisively alter the situation in the Mediterranean. Soon after the fall of Crete, German resources, particularly air units, were thrown into Operation BARBAROSSA, the attack on the Soviet Union (q.v.). Thus, with the shortage of German air units in the Mediterranean, they never had the opportunity to use "Aircraft Carrier Crete" against British naval superiority.

Ekkehart Guth

Additional Reading

Mühleisen, H.O., *Kreta 1941* (1968).
Pack, S.W.C., *The Battle for Crete* (1973).
Stewart, Ian McDougall, *The Struggle for Crete* (1964).
Vogel, D., "Das Eingreifen Deutschlands auf dem Balkan," in *Das Deutsche Reich und der Zweite Weltkrieg,* Vol. 3 (1984).

Crimea (September 1941–May 1944)

[See map 11 on page 1321]

The Crimean peninsula, which is roughly the size

of Belgium, completely dominates the northern part of the Black Sea. Its only connection with the Ukrainian mainland is the seven-kilometer-wide Perekop isthmus. The Crimea almost connects with the mainland again at its extreme eastward point near the town of Kerch. The distance between the two coastlines at that point is only about four kilometers. On the mainland side lies the town of Taman and the Kuban River delta, the gateway to the Caucasus.

The northern part of the Crimea is similar to the plains of southern Russia. The southern part of the peninsula contains the Jaila Mountains, with heights reaching over 4,500 feet. Before the war, the Crimea's population consisted of various ethnic groups. The majority were Russians and Ukrainians, but they lived together with Tatars, Jews, Gypsies, and about 50,000 ethnic Germans. The Germans, however, were transferred to more eastern parts of the Soviet Union as soon as the war started.

In September 1941, General Erich von Manstein's (q.v.) Eleventh Army had the almost impossible mission of occupying the Crimea, while simultaneously advancing toward the Don River. A shortage of German troops in the south and the wave of optimism that swept over the German high command following the earlier summer battles were the basis of these unrealistic orders. Von Manstein decided to make Crimea his first objective and delayed the advance toward Rostov on the Don. His reasoning was that a Soviet-held Crimea would constitute a threat against the right flank of Army Group South. The Soviets also had the capability of attacking the Romanian oil fields from air bases in Crimea, and Romanian oil was critical to the German war effort.

On 24 September 1941, LIV *Korps* made its first attempt to break through the Soviet defenses at Perekop. The defenders were well entrenched with an old fifteen-meter-deep Tatar ditch as the cardinal point of their defenses. Under heavy losses the Germans overcame this obstacle and advanced as far as Armyansk, half way down the narrow isthmus. There the attack stalled. Then a major Soviet attack on the mainland north of the Sea of Azov forced von Manstein to divert some of his forces to that threat. After that battle ended in a German victory, von Manstein had the freedom to focus the entire Eleventh Army on the Crimean objective. Before he could start, however, von Manstein had to give up some of his divisions, including his only motorized division, to other German units.

On 18 October, LIV *Korps* resumed its attack. The Soviets outnumbered the attackers and had air superiority. Casualties on both sides were staggering and the German divisions were nearly spent when they finally broke through the Soviet defenses on 25 October. Once they reached open country two days later, the Germans pursued the retreating Soviets as quickly as possible. The lack of any motorized forces, however, made it impossible for the Germans to reach Sevastopol before the Red Army. Von Manstein tried to take the city with a surprise raid, but it failed. Apart from the fortress city, the entire Crimea was in German hands by 16 November.

The Germans planned to conduct a set-piece siege, but the necessary artillery preparation could not start until 13 December. Poor traffic conditions on the peninsula and in the Ukraine made it difficult to transport the necessary heavy siege artillery to the front. The shortage of *Luftwaffe* units also made it necessary to reschedule the attack several times. By then, Eleventh Army was forced to give up yet another division because of a crisis at Rostov (q.v.).

The defenders of Sevastopol, commanded by Vice Admiral F.S. Oktyabrsky and his army deputy, General Ivan Petrov (q.v.), had completely reorganized their defenses with reinforcements shipped in via the Black Sea. On 4 December, Josef Stalin (q.v.) was told the situation was good inside the surrounded fortress. Meanwhile, a few weeks earlier, the Soviets had finalized their plans to conduct an assault landing at Kerch and attack into the rear of Eleventh Army. Unaware of these Soviet plans, von Manstein's forces started their attack on Sevastopol on 17 December. The main thrust was made by LIV *Korps* in the north toward Severnaya Bay. Control of this bay was necessary to cut off Sevastopol's ability to resupply from the sea.

The fortifications of Sevastopol included several defensive rings with a total depth of fifteen kilometers. Apart from numerous small strong points, trenches, and minefields, the defense was based on a chain of huge concrete forts armed with heavy guns. Thus, against stiff resistance the Germans advanced very slowly and suffered heavy losses. Eleven days after the start of the attack, the German 22nd Division finally reached Fort Stalin, which covered the bay. At that point, however, the German troops were nearly exhausted.

On 26 December, the Soviet Fifty-first Army landed at Kerch. In ferocious weather and without special equipment the men moved ashore and secured bridgehead positions around the town. The German XLII *Korps,* under Lieutenant General Hans von Sponeck, managed to contain the bridgehead with only one division, thus holding off the Soviet relief of Sevastopol.

Meanwhile, von Manstein wanted to continue the attack of the 22nd Division toward Sewernaja Bay. Three days later, however, soldiers of the Soviet Forty-fourth Army waded through neck-deep icy water to land at Feodosiya, just behind XLII *Korps'* lines. Von Sponeck was forced to give up his positions around Kerch. Without authorization from Eleventh Army headquarters, the 46th Division withdrew 120 kilometers to the west, leaving all its heavy equipment behind. This left von Manstein with no alternative but to pull one of his divisions from the Sevastopol attack and send it to the eastern end of the peninsula to halt the Soviet threat. By 31 December, a stalemate had set in.

At Kerch, the Soviets' first objective was to cut off the 46th Division, but the Germans managed to escape. On 2 January 1942, Red Army troops started an attack into the depth of the peninsula, but by then von Manstein had shifted enough of his forces to the east to halt the attack. The Soviets missed their chance to charge westward and cut the supply lines of Eleventh Army.

On 15 January 1942, German and Romanian troops started their own counterattack, and three days later they drove the Soviets out of Feodosiya. Upon entering the town, they found the corpses of their wounded comrades they had been forced to leave behind when the Forty-fourth Army landed. The Soviets had slaughtered them. The Germans then pushed as far as Parpach, the narrowest point of the Kerch sub-peninsula, where the lines stabilized until May 1942.

During the winter, meanwhile, the German high command considered the Eleventh Army as the theater reserve in case of a major Soviet breakthrough in the southern sector. In such an event, the Germans clearly would have to give up the Crimea. It was not until the dangerous Izyum salient north of the Sea of Azov stabilized that the position of von Manstein's forces in the Crimea was secured.

On 3 March 1942, a German high command directive specified the recapture of Kerch and the reduction of Sevastopol as prerequisites for the coming German summer offensive. The Eleventh Army still had its hands full defending itself from several powerful attacks launched by the newly-formed Crimea Front, under Lieutenant General D.T. Kozlov. A counterattack in late March by the newly arrived and inexperienced 22nd *Panzer* Division ended in disaster for the Germans. Then the Soviets made one last-ditch attempt between 9 and 11 April. After that failed, the offensive power of the Crimea Front was spent. The Germans then resumed the initiative.

After their last attack failed, the Soviets fortified the narrow neck of the Kerch sub-peninsula with strongpoints and a variety of obstacles. They had numerical superiority, with nineteen divisions and several independent brigades, but their defensive plans were unimaginative. The Forty-fourth and Fifty-first Armies deployed about two-thirds of their total forces on the northern part of the neck, where the front line formed a salient. General L. Z. Mekhlis, the Soviet local commander, expected the main effort of the German attack to be directed against this projection.

Von Manstein knew his only chance was to take the Soviets by surprise. He had only one *Panzer* and five infantry divisions at his disposal. On 8 May, he launched his main thrust against the southern part of the neck, with his XXX *Korps* penetrating the Soviet lines. Then the 22nd *Panzer* Division, supported by General Wolfram von Richthofen's (q.v.) VIII *Fliegerkorps,* passed through the breach and swung north on 11 May to encircle eight Soviet divisions.

The Soviet defense, handicapped by incompetent command, fell apart, and the remaining units fled eastward toward Kerch, where the Red Army tried to execute a beachhead evacuation. When von Manstein's units reached the city on 16 May, Soviet operations came to an abrupt end. The Eleventh Army took almost 170,000 prisoners. Von Manstein then regrouped his forces, and in the second battle for Sevastopol (q.v.), the Eleventh Army took the city. By 4 July 1942, the entire Crimea was in German hands.

Contrary to original plans, von Manstein's forces had not taken any significant part in the German summer campaign on the mainland. Only the XLII *Korps* and two Romanian divisions crossed the Strait of Kerch on 1 September and assisted the Seventeenth Army in the capture of the Taman peninsula in the Caucasus (q.v.). The bulk of the Eleventh Army was later transferred far north to the Leningrad (q.v.) sector.

The Germans had big plans for the Crimea, which included transforming it into a *Reich* territory settled by Germans and renamed *Gotenland.* The fact that the Soviets had deported the ethnic German population that was there already was a bit of a setback to these plans. Adolf Hitler (q.v.), however, considered moving in other German groups, like the German minority in Transnistria and even the South Tyroleans. During the short time the Germans actually held the peninsula they had no opportunity to implement these grandiose schemes. They occupied the Crimea just long enough for Otto Ohlendorf, chief of SS and police forces for the area, to kill the Jews and Gypsies or deport them to concentration camps. Regular *Wehrmacht* units also took part in these war crimes.

From an economic point of view, the Crimea was a disappointment. The Germans had to repair the infrastructure destroyed by the Soviets in the autumn of 1941, and they had to import huge quantities of food to prevent large-scale famine. Bad weather, poor harvests, and an unwise policy of fixed prices for agricultural products all slowed the economic recovery. It was not until 1943 that the Germans managed to stabilize the food situation in the Crimea. By that time, the Soviets had stopped the German advance on the mainland and were preparing to retake the peninsula.

At the beginning of October 1943, Hitler allowed General Erwin Jänecke's strong Seventeenth Army to withdraw from the Caucasus across the Straits of Kerch to the Crimea. This was already an overdue move. The Soviets were attacking the *Wehrmacht* fiercely all along the eastern front, and the Germans urgently needed some of their combat power that was tied down in the bridgehead as reinforcements for other parts of the front.

Once it withdrew from the Caucasus, the Germans kept the Seventeenth Army, with its five German and seven Romanian divisions, in the Crimea. Hitler insisted on holding the peninsula because of the political effect a German withdrawal might have on neutral Turkey and Germany's war-tested ally, Romania. From a strictly military point of view, the Seventeenth Army was wasted there.

Near the end of October, the Red Army once more assaulted across the Strait of Kerch and established bridgeheads on the Crimea. On 30 October, the supply lines of the Seventeenth Army were cut when other Soviet forces advancing from the mainland reached the Perekop peninsula. Jänecke's forces were capable of holding this northern entrance to Crimea, but now they had to defend on two fronts against a numerically stronger enemy. Soviet partisans (q.v.) on the peninsula also did their best to make the Crimea an uncomfortable place for the occupiers.

Surprisingly, things remained relatively quite in the Crimea until April 1944. The Germans used the time to strengthen their defenses and hoped to get authorization to evacuate early enough to stage an orderly withdrawal. On 8 April, the Soviets finally started their long expected offensive, with General Fedor Tolbukhin's (q.v.) 4th Ukrainian Front attacking from the mainland and General Andrei Yeremenko's (q.v.) Independent Coastal Army attacking from Kerch. By 11 April, the Soviets reached the railway junction at Dzhankoy, far behind the Perekop isthmus. This forced the Germans and Romanians to withdraw toward Sevastopol.

The fact that the inevitable retreat to Sevastopol was not authorized by Hitler until after it actually started is symptomatic of the breakdown in the German leadership during the final years of the war. Although it had to conduct a fighting withdrawal all the way, the Seventeenth Army reached Sevastopol in surprisingly good shape. As soon as it reached the fortress port it started evacuating its troops by sea, starting with the wounded and then the Romanian troops.

On 24 April, Hitler decided that Sevastopol had to be held, but the Sevastopol of 1944 was in no way comparable to the fortress of 1941–1942. Most of the fortifications were still in ruins and Jänecke had only five weak German divisions with little heavy equipment. Convinced that the course of action would lead to disaster, Jänecke continued to press for permission to evacuate. As a result, he was replaced with General Karl Allmendinger on 2 May.

After that things moved very quickly. The Soviets conducted a couple of probing attacks and then launched their final offensive on 5 May. The Second Guards Army attacked from the north via the Belbel Valley, and two days later, the Fifty-first Army and the Independent Coastal Army charged over the Sapun heights. This thrust almost resulted in a breakthrough. On 8 May, the Germans lost the old English cemetery, and like their Soviet predecessors two years earlier, had to retreat to the Chersones sub-peninsula.

On 9 May 1944, Hitler finally authorized the German evacuation; but by then the city and the harbor of Sevastopol were already in Soviet hands. Many of the defenders making their last stand at Chersones could not be picked up by the German Navy. The final fight ended on 13 May. The Germans once again lost a complete army-sized formation, but they had managed to evacuate almost 140,000 of the 190,000 troops they had in Crimea at the beginning of April.

Reiner Martin

Additional Reading
Erikson, John, *The Road to Berlin* (1977).
———, *The Road to Stalingrad* (1977).
Manstein, Erich von, *Lost Victories* (1958).

CROSSBOW, Operation (5 December 1943–29 March 1945)
Operation CROSSBOW was the code name for

the full complexus of Allied countermeasures to the German missile (*see* Missiles, Guided) weapons. As early as 1934, the German Army developed the prototype of a long-range rocket and by 1937 established with the *Luftwaffe* experimental station at Peenemünde on the Isle of Usedom in the Baltic.

By November 1939, the British learned about the project. The missile, a 13-ton, 46-foot long, liquid-fueled missile known as the V-2, could deliver a one-ton warhead up to 190 miles at a speed of over 3,600 miles per hour in a trajectory reaching more than fifty miles in altitude. Each one cost about $25,000 to produce. In 1941, the *Luftwaffe* initiated a competing program to develop a simpler and cheaper flying bomb, the V-1, which could deliver a 1,870-pound warhead up to 140 miles at a speed of 350 miles per hour. The V-1 cost only $500 to produce.

The launch of the first V-2 in June 1942 prompted greater efforts by British intelligence. In April 1943, Duncan Sandys, a member of the British War Cabinet and Prime Minister Winston S. Churchill's (q.v.) son-in-law, conducted a special review of intelligence that led the Allies to devote nearly 40 percent of all reconnaissance sorties from Britain to procuring information about these weapons via more than 1.25 million photographs. One of these photos, taken in May 1943, showed a V-1 and its launching ramp at Peenemünde (q.v.). Further reconnaissance of the site led to an attack by 597 RAF bombers on the night of 17–18 August that killed 732 persons, damaged some buildings, and forced the Germans to accelerate their planned dispersal of rocket production activities.

Other reconnaissance photos taken between May and September 1943 identified seven large sites in the Pas-de-Calais at Watten, Lottinghem, Wizernes, Mimoyecques, and Siracourt and on the Cherbourg peninsula at Martinvast and Sottevast. Attacks on these began with strikes by the U.S. Eighth Air Force against Watten on 27 and 30 August and 7 September. Continued attacks were carried out by the RAF's Second Tactical Air Force against Mimoyecques and Martinvast in November and December.

In addition to these large sites, aerial reconnaissance in Pas-de-Calais in October discovered oddly curved buildings that were christened "ski sites" because of their shapes. By 12 November 1943, twenty-one of these were identified, all aligned to bear on London. By 24 November, thirty-eight "ski sites" were in various stages of construction. Speculation that they were decoys or

were intended for massive interference with weather conditions or intended to inundate southern England with poison gas were considered, along with more accurate assessments of their purpose. In early December, the code name CROSS-BOW was given to all Allied operations against German long-range weapons production and use, from attacks on research stations to attacks on missiles in flight.

Intensified reconnaissance in the first two weeks of December 1943 revealed a chain of "ski sites," seventy-five in all. The majority were in the Pas-de-Calais aimed at London, with a cluster on the Cherbourg peninsula aimed at Bristol. Bombing of these sites by U.S. Ninth Air Force and RAF Second Tactical Air Force began on 5 December. A central military intelligence agency was set up for Operation CROSSBOW in the British Air Ministry and charged with planning attacks on the rocket sites. Attacks by the tactical air forces proved ineffective; 722 of the U.S. Eighth Air Force's heavy bombers escorted by 600 fighters dropped 1,700 tons of bombs on twenty-three of the "ski sites" on 24 December.

At this point, the world at large became aware via news reports of the existence of the German missile threat and Allied countermeasures. The British began to consider the nature of the threat posed to Operation OVERLORD by the missiles. The Americans created a committee to coordinate all relevant U.S. and British agencies in developing a solution to the problem.

Beginning on 25 January 1944, Brigadier General Grandison Gardner, commander of the Army Air Force Proving Ground Command at Elgin Field, Florida, built replicas of the "ski sites" and subjected them to various modes of attack. On 1 March, he submitted his conclusion that low-level attacks by fighters were far more effective than attacks from bombers at medium and high altitudes.

RAF Air Marshal Trafford Leigh-Mallory (q.v.), recalling the poor performance of the Second Tactical Air Force in December, was alarmed by the possibility of biological or chemical attacks on the British Isles or the cross-channel invasion forces. He insisted on the continued diversion of heavy bombers from the strategic bomber offensive—a diversion that continued to increase at the expense of D-Day preparations.

Constant repairs to the bombed sites and the discovery in March of new modified sites and simpler installations concealed in small buildings, led the British to expect 45,000 V-1s per month and V-2s once per hour, requiring the evacuation of London and several million hospital beds. On 18 April 1944, they demanded that Operation CROSSBOW bombings be given priority over all other air operations, except the bomber offensive.

General Dwight D. Eisenhower (q.v.) responded by giving Operation CROSSBOW priority over all other air operations. Despite continuous protest by Generals Carl Spaatz, Henry Arnold, and Lewis Brereton (qq.v.), operations against CROSSBOW sites in the spring of 1944 took the form of regular massive heavy bomber raids by the Eighth Air Force, supplemented by frequent, almost continuous, small-scale attacks by medium bombers of the Ninth Air Force and the RAF. In May 1944, this amounted to 4,600 tons of bombs dropped. An enormous tonnage of bombs was wasted on "ski sites" that the Germans only pretended to repair while putting their real efforts into the modified sites.

By 12 June, six days after the cross-channel invasion, eighty-three of ninety-six ski sites attacked were put out of commission for time durations lasting months. The cost was 36,200 tons of bombs in 25,150 sorties, and the loss of 771 airmen and 154 aircraft (610 men and seventy-nine aircraft were American). On 13 June, Operation CROSSBOW entered a new phase, as the first V-1s were unleashed on Britain, 300 in the first twenty-four hours.

Although some bomber and fighter raids were conducted against launching sites and manufacturing centers, Operation CROSSBOW now relied mainly on different methods. Radar-controlled aircraft guns and fighter planes shot down 6,844 of the 15,802 V-1s directed against Britain and Antwerp, while 232 of the missiles collided with barrage balloon cables.

The expanding Allied beachhead in France gradually overran the launch sites in Cherbourg and Pas-de-Calais, the last of them in September. Launches continued, however, from Holland as a new series of launching ranges were constructed there and used from 5 to 29 March 1945.

In all, 7,810 people were killed and 44,435 were injured by V-1s. Between 8 September 1944 and 27 March 1945, V-2s were launched against London, Antwerp, and Liège. Too fast for aerial interception, they killed 4,148 and injured 8,477.

Joseph M. McCarthy

Additional Reading

Craven, Wesley F., and Cate, James L. *The Army Air Forces in World War II.* Vol. III: *From Argument to V-E Day, January 1944 to May 1945* (1951).

Longmate, Norman, *The Bombers: The RAF Offensive against Germany, 1939–1945* (1983).

———, *The Doodlebugs: The Story of the Flying Bombs* (1981).

———, *Hitler's Rockets: The Story of the V-2s* (1985).

Czechoslovakia (March–May 1945)

In August 1944, German combat forces from Field Marshal Ferdinand Schörner's (q.v.) Army Group Center moved into Slovakia (q.v.) in an attempt to block the westward advance of the Red Army. The German move triggered a Slovak rising, which the Germans ruthlessly and efficiently put down. Most of the surviving insurgents were driven into the Tatra Mountains, where they later linked up with the advancing Soviets. On 14 October 1944, the Soviet 4th Ukrainian Front (army group), under General Ivan Petrov (q.v.), crossed into Slovakia from Hungary. Shortly after, Marshal Rodion Malinkovsky's (q.v.) 2nd Ukrainian Front crossed into southern Slovakia farther to the west. The Soviets advanced slowly, but steadily.

As a result of the Soviet approach, Germans from the *Reich* Protectorate of Bohemia and Moravia (q.v.) began to flee in large numbers. The Red Army continued its drive, bringing Bratislava under siege on 3 April 1945, and taking Brno on 26 April. By the end of April, the Germans held only parts of Moravia and most of Bohemia. Elements of General George S. Patton's (q.v.) U.S. Third Army were approaching the Czech border from the west, and units of Marshal Ivan Konev's (q.v.) 1st Ukrainian Front were poised to enter Czechoslovakia from Germany in the north.

Rumors about the capitulation of Germany were rampant and unrest mounted and spread into Bohemia. Strikes against the German occupiers were called in a number of cities, including Prague on 2 May. Revolutionary groups took control in various cities formerly held by the Germans.

The Czechs were concerned about the liberation of Prague, whether Soviet or American troops would get there first, and whether it would be declared an open city and thereby saved from destruction. Late in February 1945, the German occupiers were preparing to turn Prague into a fortress, with specific plans coming from army chief of staff General Heinz Guderian (q.v.). Bridges were to be destroyed, and the western part of the city heavily fortified. On 4 April 1945, Hans Frank (q.v.), the German *Reich* protector of Bohemia and Moravia, went to Adolf Hitler (q.v.)

with a plan for a separate peace with the Western powers. The measure would have saved lives, but it was rejected by Hitler.

Frank continued his efforts. On 1 May, after Hitler's suicide, Frank had the imprisoned leaders of the Czech resistance released in Prague. He hoped they would organize a government that would call for an American occupation. The protectorate government was on the verge of collapsing. By 5 May, Czech flags were replacing German flags at official locations, and on that day the Prague uprising began. A call to rebellion was broadcast over the radio and it quickly spread through Prague.

By evening, much of the city was under rebel control. The German occupation government collapsed. The retreating forces of Army Group Center withdrew to the west around Prague, mostly avoiding the city. On 6 May, however, a German radio broadcast announced: "Soldiers. Every resistance of the Czech population must be broken, even if you must use the harshest weapons." Units of the *Waffen-SS* (q.v.) responded and met stiff resistance in parts of the city.

The leaders of the resistance in Prague called for Allied troops to aid them and to occupy the city. On 6 May, the radio was broadcasting such calls in several languages for Soviet, American, and British troops. On 6 May also, elements of the U.S. Third Army liberated Pilsen, about fifty miles west of Prague. But then, to Patton's disgust, he was ordered to halt his advance and let the Red Army take Prague.

The capitulation of the Dönitz government on 7 May and Germany's unconditional surrender led Frank to begin discussions with the Czech resistance about the surrender of the German forces in Prague. On the morning of 8 May, leaders of the resistance called for the use of firearms only in self-defense. German forces agreed to lay down their arms in the early afternoon, but some units continued fighting. In the early morning hours of 9 May, units of Konev's Fourth Guards Tank Army entered Prague and reported, ". . . there are no American forces." The Red Army's Prague offensive officially ended on 11 May 1945, with the surrender of the last major German force.

John David Waite

Additional Reading

Brandes, Detlef, *Die Tschechen unter deutschem Protketorat*, Part II (1975).

Kennan, George F., *From Prague after Munich* (1968).

Minkus, Joseph A., *Slovakia: A Political History 1918–1950* (1963).

D

Dakar (23–25 September 1940)

On 23 September 1940, an Anglo-Free French force launched an assault against the Vichy French port of Dakar in French West Africa. The planning of Operation MENACE took place at a time when, following the fall of France, Great Britain faced the threat of imminent invasion, and the Allies desperately needed a victory. The operation against Dakar, however, had to be aborted after only two days of fighting because of strong and unexpected Vichy opposition.

Dakar was one of the most important naval bases in Africa, lying on the point closest to the Western Hemisphere. As a well-defended port, it was of considerable strategic importance in the Battle of the Atlantic (q.v.). Allied possession of Dakar would limit the number of Vichy naval and air bases available to the Germans, and thus reduce the number of submarines that could attack Allied convoys in the Atlantic. Continued Vichy control of Dakar, on the other hand, insured the expansion of German influence into the west coast of French Colonial Africa.

Following the fall of France, General Charles de Gaulle (q.v.) established Free French headquarters in London. His primary objective was to involve the Free French immediately in the Allied cause. He also realized that if the Free French could secure a territorial base at Dakar, they would no longer be seen as a movement-in-exile, but would be recognized instead as an independent and sovereign administration, established on national territory. The attack on Dakar, therefore, was an attack on the legitimacy of Vichy as the true government of France, and as such, was crucial to Free French prestige and morale.

The original plans for Operation MENACE called for a landing force to consist of Free French troops in what would be an all-French affair between the two regimes. The planners hoped the expedition would be able to land without serious opposition. As the plans developed, however, more and more British support was needed, and at a time when all British resources were being poured into the Battle of Britain (q.v.).

Before the Dakar expedition, the Free French secured control over substantial areas in both French Equatorial Africa and the territory of Chad, "without," as de Gaulle later stated in his memoirs, "a single drop of blood being shed." This encouraged both de Gaulle and British Prime Minister Winston S. Churchill (q.v.) to go ahead with the Dakar operation. Churchill even pictured the citizens of Dakar waking up one morning to the imposing sight of 100 ships before the city; the psychological effect of which might lead to bloodless victory. The reality, however, proved very different. Only twenty-three warships and eleven transports were used in the operation, and even these were rendered invisible to the local population by heavy offshore fog.

Operation MENACE was beset by problems from the start. The Allies were poorly informed about Dakar and underestimated the strength of the Vichy defenses, probably because the military information available dated back prior to World War I. The Allies even resorted to gathering additional intelligence from travel agencies in London. The naval force never was fully informed about either oceanic and tidal conditions or the shore defenses. Despite poor ship-to-ship communications and insufficient instruction and training for the landings, the invasion fleet set sail.

The invasion force consisted of 7,900 troops carried in eleven transport ships. Only 3,600 were Free French troops. The remainder were British troops who, for political reasons, were only to be committed as a last resort. The transports were escorted by the battleships HMS *Barham* and HMS *Resolution*, the carrier HMS *Ark Royal*, four cruisers, and sixteen destroyers. The force had to move at a slower pace than originally planned because of speed limitations on some of the troop transports. To make matters worse, the force left critical equipment behind in Britain, and a promised Polish brigade failed to materialize for embarkation in Liverpool.

A lack of discretion or any sense of operational security surrounded the whole operation. As post-operation analysis later indicated, many Free French officers openly discussed the operation in their London clubs and Liverpool pubs. The situation was compounded by an apparent communication breakdown between British naval authorities in Gibraltar and those in London, which allowed a Vichy cruiser squadron of six ships to leave Toulon and slip through the straits of Gibraltar into the Atlantic.

The Vichy cruiser squadron was heading for Cameroon and the Congo to wrest those colonies from Free French hands. Generally, it is believed that Vichy was unaware that Dakar was about to be attacked. The irony is that the cruiser squadron was intercepted by Admiral Sir Andrew Cunningham's (q.v.) Mediterranean Fleet, and forced to retreat to Dakar; precisely where the British did not want them. This action precluded any chance of a bloodless landing and an easy occupation.

On the first day of the operation, talks between de Gaulle and the Vichy representatives failed to produce any results. The Vichy warships then opened fire, and the Free French force attempted to land in Rufisque Bay. The assault was beaten off, and warships on both sides suffered some damage. On 24 September, the *Resolution* was hit by shellfire, and the next day it sustained serious damage from a torpedo. On 25 September, the *Barham* also took a hit from a 15-inch shell fired from the immobilized Vichy battleship *Richelieu*. At that point, Churchill ordered the operation called off.

De Gaulle's and Churchill's accounts of the expedition differ in terms of emphasis rather than circumstance. Churchill stressed the lack of secrecy surrounding the operation and placed emphasis on de Gaulle's insistence that the landings go ahead despite the fog that had diminished the psychological impact of the "Anglo-French Armada."

De Gaulle, on the other hand, emphasized that from the start he was opposed to launching a direct attack on Dakar, preferring instead to land troops nearby on Conakry. The troops would then march on Dakar from the land side under the pro-

tection of British warships. This alternative plan would have taken longer to execute and would have necessitated greater naval support, all at a time when Royal Navy ships were desperately needed elsewhere.

The failure of the Dakar expedition was a major setback for the Gaullist cause, and it delayed any immediate hopes of rallying West Africa and Algeria to the Free French. De Gaulle, in turn, was made a scapegoat for the failure by both the British press and Washington. Relations between de Gaulle and Churchill were never quite the same again, especially as a result of the hostility shown toward de Gaulle by President Franklin D. Roosevelt (q.v.) and the U.S. government. Roosevelt, believing de Gaulle a potential dictator, preferred maintaining close relations with the Vichy regime rather than working with the Free French. The immediate effect of the fiasco at Dakar was to dissuade people from joining the Free French cause.

Conversely, the Vichy government and press were able to rejoice over what they interpreted as a "great naval victory" and the "heroic stand" taken by Governor-General Pierre Boisson's troops. They gained political profit from an action which, in turn, impressed the Germans, who now realized that Vichy could be depended upon to defend Africa against the Free French. As a result, the Vichy regime was able to maintain considerable autonomy in both its colonial and naval affairs. Vichy naval leaders were particularly anti-British in the aftermath of the events at Mers el-Kebir (q.v.). The reaction of the Vichy authorities toward events at Dakar and Mers el-Kébir (q.v.) was linked. In May 1941, French Admiral Jean François Darlan (q.v.), angered by the Allied role in these two events, granted permission to the Germans to use French air bases in Syria for their operations against the British in Iraq.

Robert C. Hudson

Additional Reading

Aghion, Raoue, *Fighting French* (1943).

Burman, Ben L., *Miracle on the Congo: Report from the Free French Front* (1942).

Kersaudy, François, *De Gaulle and Churchill* (1981).

Denmark (9 April 1940)

On 9 April 1940, the Germans launched Operation *WESERÜBUNG*. The invasion of Norway (q.v.) began at 0130 hours. Four and a half hours later, at 0500 hours, Operation *WESERÜBUNG SUD*, the invasion of Denmark began. Germany cut off Denmark's communications to the outside world prior to the attack. Adolf Hitler (q.v.) abrogated a nonaggression treaty that he earlier had signed with Denmark.

The invasion of Denmark was a two-prong attack. In the first arm, troops were brought from the sea by transport into Copenhagen harbor and immediately seized the capital. The other attack arm invaded by ground from Germany, across Jutland. During the operation there were brief, token exchanges of fire, but nothing to seriously hamper the German time schedule. Casualties were exceptionally light for both sides, with Denmark losing only twelve killed.

The German minister to Denmark, Dr. Cecil von Renthe-Fink, presented an ultimatum to the Danish Foreign Ministry: Surrender now and retain your government with little interference from Germany, or have your capital bombed by units of the *Luftwaffe* already en route. The Danish government surrendered at 0720 hours. King Christian X (q.v.) and Premier Thorvald Stauning instructed all Danes to cooperate with the Germans. Denmark was occupied within twenty-four hours of the start of the invasion.

True to their word, the Germans allowed Denmark to keep its government until 1943. The main occupation force consisted of General Leonhard Kaupitsch's XXXI *Korps*, which had spearheaded the invasion. Denmark was unique among the countries occupied by Germany, as it was the only one to retain its government with little interference from Germany, at least for three years.

The invasion was a proverbial David versus Goliath battle; but in this case, David had no chance. Germany, with a population of 70 million and a well-honed military, invaded Denmark with 3.8 million people and a small, poorly trained, poorly equipped military. Denmark's military, in fact, had been significantly reduced by a pacifist government that felt its neutral status would protect it from outside aggression.

To preclude a complete takeover of the Danish Empire, Great Britain sent troops to occupy the Faroe Islands and Iceland, which then belonged to Denmark. This move enabled the Allies to establish strategic points in the North Atlantic for convoy protection. In the United States, Danish Ambassador Henrik Kauffman, angry at the German invasion and at Copenhagen's instant capitulation, placed Greenland at the disposal of the U.S. for construction of naval and air bases to protect convoys traversing the North Atlantic. He pinpointed German weather stations on Greenland for occupation by U.S. forces.

Kauffman also persuaded 90 percent of the Danish merchant fleet to side with the Allies, particularly Britain. These merchant sailors ultimately paid a high price. By the end of the war, 700 Danes had died and 60 percent of the Danish merchant fleet was sunk. Also, more than 1,000 Danish exiles had enlisted in the Royal Air Force and the British Army.

A Danish resistance (q.v.) movement was established with the help of the Special Operations Executive (SOE) (q.v.). It harassed the German occupiers, gave aid to SOE agents, committed acts of sabotage, and sheltered a majority of the Danish Jews. Miraculously, of the 8,000 Jews in Denmark, only fifty succumbed to the Nazi Holocaust (q.v.).

In late August 1943, as a result of increased acts of resistance, Germany ceased Denmark's control of its government and assumed executive control. In response, the Danish Navy scuttled its remaining ships. Nonetheless, Danish resistance continued until March 1945, when the Allies marched into Denmark. Germany finally surrendered the remainder of its force of more than 250,000 troops on 7 May 1945.

William H. Van Husen

Additional Reading

Esposito, Vincent L., *A Concise History of World War II* (1964).

Liddell Hart, Basil H., *History of the Second World War* (1970).

Palmer, P., *Denmark in Nazi Chains* (1942).

Dieppe Raid (19 August 1942)

In 1942, the Western Allies were determined to increase the intensity of raiding operations on the continent in the face of American pressure for Operation SLEDGEHAMMER (*see* BOLERO, Operation), the mounting Soviet cries for a second front, and the success of previous raids. Combined Operations, under Lord Louis Mountbatten (qq.v.), grasped the opportunity of a large-scale raid on a port to test newly developed tactics and amphibious equipment. Dieppe was the chosen port because its proximity to southern Britain allowed for maximum air support. The topography "imposed severe limitations on any plan of attack," but also offered accessible landing areas.

The German defenders, under Colonel General Kurt Hasse, took advantage of the topography, with artillery in well-sited and commanding positions. The German troops of the 571st Infantry Regiment around Dieppe were not first-rate, but reinforcements were available from the 10th

D

Panzer Division. Adolf Hitler (q.v.) also issued orders for "a state of permanent readiness," and the German high command surmised that a large-scale raid was a near certainty.

Planning for Operation RUTTER was well advanced by the end of April when General Bernard L. Montgomery (q.v.) offered the mission to the Canadians. General A.G.L. McNaughton (q.v.), commander of the Canadian First Army, was under pressure from the Canadian government and public to get the Canadians into action. He eagerly accepted the project, "subject to the plans of the raid being satisfactory." The Canadian 2nd Division was selected for the mission and Major General J.H. "Ham" Roberts was named military force commander. The naval force commander was the Royal Navy's Captain J. Hughes-Hallett, while Air Vice Marshal Trafford Leigh-Mallory (q.v.) was the air force commander.

The raid, originally scheduled for 7 July, was canceled because of poor weather conditions. Lord Mountbatten, without the approval of the chiefs of staff, succeeded in having the operation revised. Operation JUBILEE, as it was renamed, was set to go ahead on 18 August.

The plan of attack called for four preliminary flank landings and a frontal assault on the port across a frontage of approximately ten miles by a military force of close to 6,100. Canadians comprised 4,963, the British about 1,075, with fifty U.S. Army Rangers (q.v.). (Lieutenant Edwin Loustalot of the 1st Ranger Battalion became the first American killed in land fighting in Europe.) The naval force included 237 vessels, none mounting more than 4-inch guns. A total of seventy-four

squadrons of aircraft from a number of Allied countries were available for air support.

The attack went awry as the invading force neared the French coast. A brief gun battle with a German convoy at 0347 hours left the extreme eastern fringe of the flotilla dispersed and the German defenses along part of the coast alerted. British Number 3 Commando was unable to destroy the coastal battery at Berneval on the eastern flank of the landings, but neutralized it for two hours with accurate sniper fire. Number 4 Commando had greater success at the Varengeville Battery on the western flank, destroying six German guns before withdrawing.

On the inner eastern flank at Puys, the Royal Regiment of Canada was practically destroyed, suffering 94.5 percent casualties. Naval craft arrived late, and as the troops approached the beach they were met by a hail of gunfire that killed many before they left their landing craft. Those who made it ashore were decimated by heavy machine gun and mortar fire as they struggled through previously undetected barbed wire. The Royal Navy lost a number of craft as they vainly tried to evacuate the survivors. By 0835 hours, the survivors surrendered. Only two officers and sixty-five men, out of the 554 embarked, returned to Britain.

The landing at Pourville, on the inner western flank, occurred punctually at 0450 hours. The South Saskatchewan Regiment established itself ashore and the Queen's Own Cameron Highlanders of Canada successfully passed through. They met heavy resistance and were unable to achieve all of their objectives. Large numbers were evacuated but the losses were still heavy. The South Saskatch-

British tanks and landing craft burning on the beach at Dieppe after the failed raid on 19 August 1942. (IWM HU 1905)

ewan Regiment suffered casualties of nineteen officers and 320 other ranks out of 523 embarked, while the Camerons lost twenty-four officers and 322 men out of 503.

In their frontal assault, the Essex Scottish Regiment sustained heavy casualties in three futile attacks on the sea wall on the eastern section of the beach. Faulty communications with Roberts led to the commitment of the reserve battalion, *Les Fusiliers Mont-Royal*, and soon they too were pinned down on the beach. To the west, the Royal Hamilton Light Infantry and the Royal Marine A Commando penetrated into the town but became bogged down in vicious street fighting. Thirty Churchill tanks of the Calgary Regiment (Tank) were to have supported the drive into town, but they landed too late and were stuck on the beach.

By 0900 hours, with little chance of the situation improving, the order was given to withdraw. The last fighting was over by 1400 hours. The Allied casualty count was 3,367, including 1,946 captured and 907 fatalities. German losses were 314 killed and 294 wounded.

One of the greatest air battles of the war was fought over the beaches of Dieppe, with 730 Allied fighters involved. The British and Canadians lost ninety-eight aircraft. The Allies claimed ninety-one *Luftwaffe* aircraft, but the Germans reported their losses as only forty-eight. The RAF and RCAF did, however, prevent the *Luftwaffe* from harassing the evacuation.

No official blame was assessed for the dramatic failure of the raid and the responsibility was considered collective rather than individual. The most important lesson learned from the assault was the need for strong preliminary air and naval bombardment. Other conclusions drawn by the Allies included the need to develop specialized assault technology as well as the necessity of increasing the interservice training between attacking forces. The Allies also concluded that major seaports were too well protected to be taken. This realization led to the development of the artificial harbors (q.v.), used for the Normandy (q.v.) landings. The lessons learned from Dieppe were important for later amphibious landings, but the price was high.

Paul Dickson

Additional Reading

Atkins, Ronald, *Dieppe 1942: The Jubilee Disaster* (1980).

Robertson, Terence, *Dieppe: The Shame and the Glory* (1962).

Villa, Brian, *Unauthorized Action: Mountbatten and the Dieppe Raid* (1989).

DIVER, Operation (June 1944–March 1945)

With the launching of the German V-1 flying bombs against Britain in June 1944, a program called Operation DIVER was enacted to counter this serious threat. The plan called for attacks on the missile bases by bomber aircraft and for fighters to shoot the flying bombs out of the sky. Operation DIVER, which dealt with the V-1 flying bombs, was a part of the broader Operation CROSSBOW (q.v.), which dealt with both the V-1s and the V-2 guided missiles.

In late 1942, British intelligence received reports of German long-range missiles, secret weapons designed to target Britain from bases on the Continent. Accounts of the testing of these long-range rockets were reported in early 1943. Special reconnaissance flights were undertaken to secure photographic proof of the missiles, but the first reliable documentation of tests at Peenemünde came in July 1943. Air attacks on the research site and some of the factories producing the flying bombs failed to halt production and deployment.

The first attack by the missiles against Britain came on 13 June 1944 when one crossed the English Channel and hit a railway bridge in London. The flying bombs, code named "DIVER," were about twenty-five feet long, made of steel and a light metal alloy, and carried a warhead of more than 1,800 pounds of high explosive. By the end of the war, 9,251 were fired against Britain, and another 6,551 were fired against Antwerp.

Within three days of the first attack, 15 V-1s were reported by British defenses. Almost all had crossed the Channel and seventy-three landed in London. The initial projections of the damage caused by these attacks was staggering but the flight of the missiles proved to be very inaccurate.

Operation DIVER called for the use of fighter planes against the V-1s and for intensified bombing of the launch sites on the Continent. Fighters were to be the main line of defense, and planes from RAF Number 11 Group were ordered to fly at 12,000 feet along three patrol lines whenever an attack was underway. Within eight days after the first attack, Operation DIVER was in full swing with eleven fighter squadrons, two armed with Mosquitos, carrying out the patrols. Additional aircraft included Typhoons, Tempests Mark V, Mustangs Mark III, and Spitfires Marks XI, XII, and XIV.

Critical to the success of Operation DIVER was gaining accurate and timely information on the course and speed of the missiles. Once this information was gained from radar (q.v.) stations along the coast, it was relayed to the pilots who had to visually locate the flying bomb—no easy task. By the end of June 1944, two methods of interception emerged. The "close control" method was used by radar controllers on the coast who plotted the course and speed and relayed it to the pilots. They had about six minutes to intercept the missile over the Channel. The "running commentary" method was used over land, with the missile's course relayed to a number of fighters to intercept it.

Specific tactics for shooting the missile out of the sky also were developed. The best method was to fly ahead of it on a parallel course before firing a series of machine gun bursts to deflect and destroy it. Although these efforts of between 100 and 500 sorties each day met with some success, the number of missiles reaching London was much too high, and new tactics were developed. By mid-August, heavy antiaircraft guns were being used effectively against the V-1s.

Robert G. Waite

Additional Reading

Cooksley, Peter G., *Flying Bomb: The Story of Hitler's V-Weapons in World War II* (1979).

Irving David, *The Mare's Nest* (1964).

Richards, Denis and Hillary St.G. Saunders, *The Fight Is Won* (1954).

Dnieper River (25 August–23 December 1943)

Ten days into Operation *ZITADELLE* (CITADEL), the battle at Kursk (q.v.), Adolf Hitler (q.v.) canceled the operation to free troops from the east to meet the Allied invasion in Italy. Field Marshal Erich von Manstein's (q.v.) Army Group South was tasked with holding its gains and delaying the Soviet counteroffensive. The Fourth *Panzer* Army under General Hermann Hoth (q.v.) formed the left flank of Army Group South; Army Detachment Kempf held the sector containing Kharkov and Belgorod; the First *Panzer* Army held the Donets River line to the southeast of Kempf; and General Karl Hollidt's Sixth Army (newly formed after Stalingrad) was the army group's right anchor.

Soviet Premier Josef Stalin (q.v.) ordered the reinforced Voronezh and Steppe Fronts (army groups), under Generals Nikolai Vatutin and Ivan Konev (qq.v.), to take Kharkov. On 3 August 1943, the Soviets launched their assault northwest of Belgorod, opening a seven-mile-wide gap between the Fourth *Panzer* Army and Army Detachment Kempf. The Soviets took Belgorod on 5 August. That same day, the Bryansk Front captured Orel, 100 miles north of Kursk.

With reinforcements, von Manstein's northern sector had twenty-three divisions, including six *Panzer* divisions, facing eleven Soviet armies. The *Luftwaffe*, short of regular ammunition, dropped 4,000-pound antiship bombs on the massed Soviet armor. The first-day results were impressive, but the Soviets quickly learned to spread their tanks out. By 8 August, the gap between the Fourth *Panzer* Army and Detachment Kempf was thirty-five miles wide. Pressed by the Voronezh Front, Hoth stabilized his line around Akhtyrka, but the Soviets moved to encircle Kharkov. The Steppe Front bore down on the city from the northeast, while the Southwestern Front's Fifty-seventh Army cleared the west bank of the Donets River southeast of Kharkov. The Voronezh Front's First Tank Army, bypassing Kharkov to the north, swung southward. Von Manstein reacted by throwing his *SS Panzer* divisions up as a screen to the west of the city.

General Werner Kempf proposed an evacuation, but Hitler demanded Kharkov be held in all circumstances. Von Manstein replaced Kempf with General Otto Wöhler (q.v.) on 14 August, redesignating the unit the Eighth Army shortly thereafter. With his SS divisions tied down, von Manstein committed the Fourth *Panzer* Army to a counterattack. On 18 August, two German divisions broke out of their bridgehead at Akhtyrka, and on 20 August, they established contact with the 3rd *SS Panzer* Division, temporarily closing the main gap just as the Fourth *Panzer* Army's front between Akhtyrka and Sumy was torn open for ten miles.

With supplies and manpower decimated, Wöhler requested permission to abandon Kharkov, and von Manstein extracted grudging permission from Hitler. During the night of 21–22 August, the Germans abandoned Kharkov for the final time. Hoth was forced to withdraw south of Akhtyrka to the Vorskla River, stabilizing his position. By 27 August, the Fourth *Panzer* and Eighth armies held a solid arc between Sumy and Zmiyev.

Finally admitting the gravity of the situation in the south, Hitler ordered the start of construction of the Wotan-Panther Line. The idea was something like an "East Wall" version of the West Wall (q.v.), with the Wotan fortifications running along the Dnieper River to a point just north of Kiev, and then the Panther Line running north to Lake Peipus and the Gulf of Finland. By the end of September, 210,000 people were at work, many of them local civilians conscripted into construction battalions. Originally, Hitler had delayed authorizing construction of the line because he believed it would make his generals even more inclined to retreat. When he finally did authorize the construction, however, it already was too late.

Three days after the Soviets recaptured Kharkov, Marshal Konstantin Rokossovsky's (q.v.) Central Front attacked the Germans close to the boundary between Army Group South and Field Marshal Günther von Kluge's (q.v.) Army Group Center. In late August, the Southwestern and Southern Fronts struck Army Group South's southern flank, already weakened by the transfer of forces to the Kharkov area. The First *Panzer* Army held, taking heavy casualties. The Soviet Fifth Shock Army penetrated the Sixth Army's positions, opening a seven-mile-wide gap. On 31 August, von Manstein gave the First *Panzer* and Sixth Armies permission to withdraw to the Kalmius River.

On 3 September, von Manstein and von Kluge flew to Hitler's East Prussian headquarters in a desperate effort to convince him to turn the management of the war over to the military. They failed to convince him. On 8 September, the same day the Italian surrender was made public, Hitler made his last visit to the eastern front. Von Manstein had already asked Hitler seven times for permission to withdraw to the Dnieper. Hitler finally agreed in principle to a move to the Wotan Line. The new position would give von Manstein a 450-mile front to hold with thirty-seven infantry and seventeen *Panzer* divisions.

September was a race to the Dnieper between Army Group South and the Soviets. The Soviets committed 3.6 million troops and 4,400 tanks to the operation. They were aided by the increasing supply of American Lend-Lease (q.v.) trucks, which greatly enhanced their mobility.

Hitler gave the Germans orders to conduct a scorched-earth campaign as they withdrew, but most German units had all they could do just to survive. They fought by day and marched by night and only managed to reach the west bank of the Dnieper by abandoning large quantities of heavy equipment. On the extreme south flank, Hitler finally allowed the Seventeenth Army to withdraw from the Caucasus (q.v.) by crossing the Straits of Kerch to the Crimea (q.v.).

The German troops who reached the west bank of the Dnieper found few prepared positions or supplies waiting for them. If the Germans had started preparing the Wotan position earlier or had made the withdrawal earlier, there might have been a chance they could have held the Soviets at the river.

By the end of September, the Soviets reached the banks of the Dnieper from Smolensk, north of the Pripet marshes, to Zaporozhye, just north of the Crimea. They had at least twenty-three bridgeheads over the river. On 1 October, the Third Guards and Eighth Guards Armies attacked the First *Panzer* Army at its bridgehead east of the Dnieper. In two weeks of fighting, they forced the Germans across the river. In the south, the Southern Front pushed the Sixth Army back across the Dnieper, which left the Seventeenth Army cut off in the Crimea.

On 15 October, Konev's Steppe Front attacked out of its Dnieper bridgeheads toward Krivoy Rog, an important rail and iron ore center. The Soviets entered the city, fifty miles west of the Dnieper, on 25 October, only to be pushed out again by a counterattack from the XL *Panzer Korps*. On 20 October 1943, the Soviets introduced new front designations. Vatutin's Voronezh Front became the 1st Ukrainian Front; Konev's Steppe Front became the 2nd Ukrainian Front; General Rodion Malinovsky's (q.v.) Southwestern Front became the 3rd Ukrainian Front; and General Fedor Tolbukhin's (q.v.) Southern Front became the 4th Ukrainian Front.

Throughout October and November, the Soviets continued to gain bridgeheads across the Dnieper. In October, an attempt to widen a bridgehead at Bukrin with an airborne assault of 7,000 troops ended in disaster, with only 2,300 survivors. On 3 November, the 1st Ukrainian Front massed for an attack against the Fourth *Panzer* Army, liberating Kiev three days later.

The Soviets then advanced south of the Pripet marshes, reaching the Korosten-Zhitomir line by mid-November. A counterattack by the Fourth *Panzer* Army's *XLVIII Panzer Korps* drove the Soviets out of Zhitomir and back toward Kiev, but heavy rains and sheer exhaustion soon brought the German counterattack to a halt.

As November came to an end, the Soviets prepared for a major push to liberate the Ukraine (q.v.). With the battle for the Dnieper line and the loss of Kharkov, the Axis lost a valuable position that dominated the mineral resources and rich farmland of the Donets basin, as well as the natural defensive position of the Donets-Mius line. Despite von Manstein's continuing efforts to convince Hitler of the need for mobile defense, the Germans squandered their resources trying to hold the Donets and were unable to take advantage of the shortened front and the defensive features of the Dnieper. The Soviet manpower advantage, supplemented by recruitment from the newly liberated populations, permitted the Red Army to reach the Dnieper line with an intact offensive capacity.

D

An important factor in the rapid Soviet success in August 1943 was the Allied landing in Italy, which drew German forces from the eastern front, reducing Axis manpower and creating some disaffection and disorganization. Von Manstein made a fatal error by miscalculating the timetable for the anticipated Soviet offensive, expecting to have until September to prepare. Superior Soviet counterintelligence and deception measures led to this miscalculation, with the Soviets masking their preparations effectively by fleshing out standing units on the front with additional forces for the assault, rather than bringing up additional units.

The German withdrawal to the Dnieper did preserve valuable forces, which delayed the subsequent Soviet advance westward; but the withdrawal also set the stage for the final expulsion of the Axis forces from the Soviet Union. The German withdrawal initiated a fighting retreat that ran from the streets of Kharkov to the streets of Berlin.

Sidney Dean

Additional Reading

Carell, Paul, *Scorched Earth: The Russia-German War, 1943–1944 (1966).*

Manstein, Erich von, *Lost Victories* (1958).

Mellenthin, F.W. von, *Panzer Battles* (1956).

Ziemke, Earl F., *Stalingrad to Berlin: The German Defeat in the East* (1968).

Dodecanese Islands (10 September–30 November 1943)

[See map 10 on page 1320]

On 12 November 1943, Germany mounted a successful combined arms assault against the British garrison on Léros Island. That victory ended the Allied (primarily British) Dodecanese campaign. Lasting from 10 September to 30 November 1943, it was conducted with ad hoc forces and very little intelligence or logistical support. Like many other military campaigns that pursued objectives exceeding force capabilities, it ended in defeat. Although small compared to the other operations in Europe, the British failure in the Dodecanese had a political impact far beyond its military significance. Turkey remained neutral until March 1944, and Germany retained control of the Aegean until Soviet advances into Eastern Europe forced the Third *Reich* to evacuated its forces from Greece.

The roots of the Dodecanese campaign lay in Prime Minister Winston S. Churchill's (q.v.) long-held belief that Germany could be defeated by operations conducted against its "weak" southern flank. It was a belief based on the very accurate assessment, in both world wars, that Germany's southern allies were much weaker than Germany itself. In World War II, that belief was reinforced by his recognition of Soviet long-term aims in eastern Europe, thus focusing his attention on Italy's Dodecanese Islands in the Aegean Sea.

Given to Italy following the Italo-Ottoman War of 1911, the Dodecanese Islands dominated the Aegean and Turkey's coastal waters. As such, they were the perfect base for conducting operations against the Balkans or applying leverage against Turkey. The Italian surrender in September 1943, therefore, offered an unparalleled strategic opportunity at what appeared to be little cost.

Unfortunately for Churchill, the Germans recognized that as well, and quickly co-opted Italian control of their most significant islands. They took particular care to seize Rhodes, the dominant island of the group and one of only two with an airfield. By doing so, the Germans preempted Churchill's plan for taking the island. The Italian garrison simply surrendered to a much smaller German force. The Germans quickly reinforced, an action that eventually enabled them to win the campaign.

Recognizing the importance of Rhodes, Churchill viewed the 6,000-man German garrison as a mere inconvenience and directed his commanders to draw up immediate plans to seize it. His military chiefs pointed out that the British lacked the forces to conduct such operations without Allied support. Since neither the Americans nor the Soviets supported such a diversion of forces, Churchill had to pursue this strategy independently.

Promising aid and military assistance from forces he did not have, Churchill tried to entice the Turks into seizing the island for him. The Turks had little enthusiasm for undermining the German war effort and refused to provide air bases for British operations in the Aegean. Churchill remained undeterred and ordered the Middle Eastern Command in Cairo to carry on with what was available. That meant fighting the entire Dodecanese campaign with one brigade of the partially equipped Indian 10th Division, some independent special forces, and Royal Air Force (RAF) units.

By 14 September 1943, General Henry Maitland Wilson (q.v.), commander in chief of the Middle East Command, had dispatched special forces units to take the smaller islands: Léros, Sámos, and Kós. Of these, Kós was the most critical since it had the only other airfield in the Dodecanese chain. Without it, Wilson would have no air cover for his operations. He therefore improvised local transport to move one battalion to each of the islands and rushed an antiaircraft regiment to Kós. He also requested and received two Spitfire squadrons. Building up his defenses as fast as he could, he requested additional forces as he prepared to face what he knew was a difficult foe.

The Allied moves were detected by German intelligence. Adolf Hitler (q.v.) recognized the importance of the islands immediately and ordered them retaken at once. The first air strikes against Kós were conducted on 18 September. The RAF retaliated by attacking German airfields in Crete and around Athens. The effort, however, was not sustained. None of the major military commanders in the Mediterranean wanted the Dodecanese operation to interfere with the Italian campaign. As a result, the *Luftwaffe* was able to continue its attacks on Kós, going after the island's only airstrip. Wilson directed the clearing of additional runways and satellite fields, but the Germans attacked them nearly as quickly as they were built.

Ultimately, Wilson's most pressing problem was dealing with Churchill, who was eager to have the Dodecanese in British hands. Reminded that the forces assigned were inadequate, Churchill admonished Wilson for not realizing the benefits of using the Italian troops who were so conveniently scattered around the islands. Telling Wilson to be "innovative" in the use of his forces, he ordered the Middle East Command to seize Rhodes without delay. No additional forces were available and no landing craft could be spared for the operation. Wilson, meanwhile, found himself facing an increasingly aggressive enemy. The British were superior to the Germans in the area only in naval strength. Still, Wilson initiated planning for the assault on Rhodes, code named OCTOBER ACCOLADE. D-Day was scheduled for 20 October, but the Germans struck first.

By 28 September, the *Luftwaffe* disabled all the airfields on Kós and critically damaged the island's internal communications system. Also, several ships were sunk in the harbor and at nearby Léros, the primary British logistics staging base for the Dodecanese. Supplies to Kós now had to be delivered by parachute and the situation became critical.

ULTRA (q.v.) intercepts, agent reports, and aerial reconnaissance indicated the Germans were assembling an amphibious landing force at Naxos. Wilson immediately requested additional naval forces and two long-range fighter squadrons. He intended to send an additional battalion of troops and more antiaircraft guns. The Royal Navy (RN) complied, sending in seventeen destroyers on 1 October, but the requested air support was not assigned until 4 October. By then, Kós was in German hands.

Wilson's garrison on Kós consisted of a light infantry battalion, two antiaircraft regiments, and the original Italian garrison of 3,000 men. The German assault on Kós involved a combined airborne-amphibious assault. Air support was provided by medium and dive bombers based in Greece and on Rhodes, while the amphibious task group was escorted by two destroyers and four E-boats. Fortunately for the Germans, low fuel and German air supremacy forced nearby RN units to withdraw before they could intercept the amphibious force.

The German attack opened at dawn on 3 October with the airborne forces going after the airfield. The amphibious assault force was established ashore by 0900 hours. By late afternoon, the Germans began to drive the defenders into pockets. Cut off and unable to communicate with either its subordinate units or superior headquarters, the British garrison surrendered before midnight. The loss of Kós altered the strategic situation in the Aegean. Limassol Airfield in Cyprus (more than 200 miles away) was now the only operational Allied airfield in the region, and its aircraft were incapable of providing air cover over the Dodecanese Islands remaining in Allied hands.

The RAF Beaufighters could not stand up to the German Bf-109s and FW-190s, while the Spitfires lacked the range (even with drop tanks) to provide more than minimal air support. Allied command in the Mediterranean recommended abandoning the Dodecanese. They also acceded to Wilson's requests for air support, providing two squadrons of U.S. P-38s in the belief that it would facilitate the evacuation of the remaining islands. Churchill, however, would hear nothing of it. He not only wanted Kós retaken, but demanded that Wilson hold Léros at all costs and finalize plans for the assault on Rhodes.

With nearly a brigade scattered across nine island garrisons (Wilson had retaken six more islands in September), Middle East Command did not have sufficient forces to retake Kós, much less Rhodes. Wilson warned Churchill that Léros could not be held without a substantial increase in air and naval support. None was forthcoming but he reinforced the island garrison anyway, probably in the false hope that Churchill could provide him the support he required. The Germans, meanwhile, started their move against Léros.

First, the Germans moved two Ju-87 *Stuka* groups to Rhodes and began to attack British antiaircraft units and prepared positions. Although the *Stuka* was obsolete by this point in the war, it was still the most accurate bomber in the German inventory, and the absence of fighter opposition enabled the *Luftwaffe* to use it freely. They were joined in mid-September by two Ju-88 groups transferred from the Russian front. Heinkel He-111s and Ju-88s struck out from mainland airfields to attack British supply dumps, logistical facilities, and shipping in and around the island. The RN began to lose destroyers and transports almost immediately. By the end of October, the RN was all that stood between Léros and the Germans. As always, the Admiralty tried to do exactly that, and managed to delay the German assault for more than a month, albeit at heavy cost.

The uneven struggle between the RN and the *Luftwaffe* constituted the most critical element of this second phase of the Dodecanese campaign. The Germans hoped to follow up the Kós operation with an immediate assault on Léros, but the RN's intervention thwarted their plans. The Admiralty sent the 12th Cruiser Squadron and two fleet destroyers into the Aegean on 4 October. These reinforcements gave Middle East Command a force of four cruisers and ten destroyers. Additional submarines were also sent to the northern Aegean. The Admiralty hoped to conduct its operations under the cover of the U.S. P-38s, now operating out of Cyprus. Unfortunately, the planes were provided to support a four-day evacuation of the islands, and the RN's battle with the *Luftwaffe* lasted over a month.

The situation tipped in the *Luftwaffe*'s favor when the P-38s departed for Italy on 11 October. The Germans then resumed their efforts to reinforce the Léros invasion group, while the RN struggled to interdict German sea lines of communications, reduce the German landing force, and support the British island garrisons.

Over the next three weeks, the British sank an armed sloop, four landing craft, two minesweepers, a minelayer, and three merchant ships. At least two destroyers also shelled the German forces on Kós each night from 18 to 24 October, sinking at least one other landing craft and destroying equipment on shore. Mixed RN cruiser-destroyer task groups also patrolled in and among the islands. They managed to delay the German buildup, but were not able to prevent the Germans from capturing the small island of Levitha, fifteen miles west of Léros.

The German Navy supported the *Luftwaffe* effort, and its participation in the struggle tipped the balance against the RN. Grossly outnumbered by their British opponents and suffering from a fuel shortage, the Germans employed mines to restrict the RN's operations, laying more than 400 mines in Léros Channel and another 100 east of Kalimnos. These mines cost the British two submarines and three destroyers. Although these losses were not catastrophic, the presence of mines restricted RN operations around the islands after 28 October.

By 12 November, the British garrison on Léros numbered 2,500 troops. The German transport force was reduced by nearly a third. There were also nearly 2,700 Italian "combat troops" on the island, but neither the Germans nor the British expected much from them. The stage was set for the final battle of the Dodecanese campaign, the German assault on Léros.

The German attack began with a three-pronged assault against the main port of Léros. It was directed at seizing the port and the surrounding high ground. Resistance in the port area was very heavy and the Italian coastal batteries sank two German landing craft before the crews abandoned their guns. British resistance was so heavy on the first day that the supporting airborne landing was put off until the afternoon. By that time, the amphibious assault had captured the high ground north of the main bay and alongside the port of Léros.

When they did land, German paratroopers suffered heavy losses, with nearly eighty killed or wounded in the initial landing. The battle remained in doubt for three days while the two sides desparately fought over the two hills dominating the central part of the island. The RN sent in two destroyers to shell the German positions on the second night of the battle and the garrison was reinforced by another 400 men brought in from the nearby island of Sámos. It was all to no avail.

German airpower proved insurmountable, as the *Stuka*s silenced British artillery positions, attacked troop concentrations, and severely inhibited the garrison's daytime movements. The Germans, on the other hand, were able to reinforce their units and deploy reserves virtually unhindered. The British garrison's headquarters was encircled on the morning of 16 November. By late afternoon, the five-day battle for Léros was over. With it went any chance of a successful Allied campaign in the Aegean. Within a week, the RN evacuated British and Allied forces from the nearby island garrisons and the last Allied forces departed the Dodecanese on 28 November.

German operations against Kós and Léros were similar to the German invasion of Crete (q.v.)

in that they used air supremacy to limit the RN's ability to support their island garrisons. In contrast to Crete, however, the Germans were also able to conduct amphibious assaults in the face of British sea supremacy. Much of this was due to the effective employment of mines in the narrow channels of the Aegean.

More critically, however, was the truly effective interservice cooperation that characterized the German operations in the Aegean. The regional German command, Headquarters Southeast, enjoyed exceptional relations with its subordinate service components. In no other theater did the three German services cooperate so well. Amphibious groups were under naval command but consisted of army and *Luftwaffe* marine craft as well as naval. The landing forces themselves were organized into *Kampfgruppen* (battle groups) of army, *Luftwaffe*, and even naval ground forces under a single commander. Information was freely exchanged between the services, which greatly facilitated *Luftwaffe* operations.

The Allied campaign in the Dodecanese, on the other hand, shares many common features with the Dardanelles campaign of World War I. The objectives were based on a set of circumstances that changed before the operation was executed. The political leadership then remained oblivious to those changes and refused to alter its goals. Plans for the seizure of Rhodes, for example, were ordered even though the assault force had been significantly reduced, and the enemy heavily reinforced. This also led to the retention of Léros long after the loss of Kós made its defense untenable.

Unfortunately, the campaign's goals were based more on political desires than political or military realities. Churchill wanted Turkey to enter the war on the Allied side and use its sixty-five divisions to push the Germans out of Greece and Bulgaria. That was an illusion. Turkish leaders had no desire to participate in the war on either side but were most concerned about Soviet designs in the Balkans and Turkish Thrace. It had only been two years since Josef Stalin (q.v.) had tried to force Turkey to give the Soviet Union bases in the Dardanelles.

To the Turks, Germany offered the best hope for preventing the Soviets from dominating the Balkans. Moreover, Turkey has had a long-standing relationship with Germany dating back to 1845, and its leaders distrusted Churchill. The Turks, therefore, supported the German war effort while trying to avoid alienating the British. They also made overtures to the United States for aid and support.

An alternate explanation for Churchill's policies was that of a deception. Certainly, most of the German forces in the Aegean were there as the result of Allied Operation MINCEMEAT (q.v.). Although the Dodecanese campaign may have been conducted to give credence to Allied deception efforts in the Mediterranean, it should be noted that the Dodecanese campaign began well after the Sicily (q.v.) landings, and the Germans defended the Dodecanese with local forces drawn from the German garrisons in Greece, Yugoslavia, and Crete.

More significantly, Churchill's lobbying for additional forces suggests this was a serious effort and not part of any deception plan. The outcome in the Aegean would have been significantly different if Churchill had been able to convince the Americans to provide the required forces. The Americans looked upon the idea with suspicion, believing it to be yet another British attempt to delay the invasion of France. In that respect, they may have been right; the landing craft, naval, and air forces needed to conduct the campaign could only have come at the expense of either the Italian campaign or the buildup for Normandy (q.v.). Moreover, pushing beyond the Aegean would have required a huge commitment of forces and logistics.

At best, the Dodecanese campaign was a wasteful sideshow. Its successful conclusion would not have affected the postwar peace settlements or the war's outcome, unless it was followed by an immediate Western Allied offensive into the Balkans. Even that would have been a wasteful employment of forces. The Germans had to garrison those islands anyway, and a successful campaign would not have had an impact proportional to the effort required.

Carl O. Schuster

Additional Reading
Buckley, Christopher, *Five Ventures* (1977).
Holland, Jeffrey, *The Aegean Mission* (1988).

Donets River (3 February–18 March 1943)
German overextension during Operation *BLAU* (BLUE) resulted in a Soviet counteroffensive that began in November 1942. On 15 January 1943, a massive Soviet force struck the Hungarian Second Army south of Voronezh, opening a 175-mile-wide gap in the Axis lines. The Soviets then split their forces for a two-pronged drive to the Dnieper River: the northern arm taking Kursk and Belgorod north of Kharkov on 2 and 9 February; the southern arm taking Izyum on 5 February.

Field Marshal Erich von Manstein (q.v.) withdrew the right flank of his Army Group South to defensive positions on the Mius River (which empties into the Sea of Azov), shortening his line, as the Soviet Voronezh, Southwestern, and Southern Fronts (army groups) bore down. Adolf Hitler (q.v.) ordered General Hubert Lanz's Army Detachment, which had only three combat-ready divisions (including the newly arrived two-division SS Panzer Korps), to hold the key city of Kharkov under all circumstances.

On 13 February, the northern flank of the SS Panzer Korps was forced back to the Kharkov outskirts. On 14 February, the SS Panzer Korps commander, SS-Obergruppenführer Paul Hausser (q.v.), requested permission to withdraw from Kharkov in the face of impending encirclement and a popular uprising in the city. Pressured by Hitler, Lanz refused. Nonetheless, the SS forces evacuated Kharkov, contrary to direct orders, on 15–16 February.

On 20 February, Hitler replaced Lanz with General Werner Kempf. Army Detachment Kempf stabilized around Krasnograd as reinforcements arrived from the west. To the south, across the 110-mile gap between Detachment Kempf and the bulk of Army Group South, von Manstein positioned the reorganized Fourth Panzer Army under Colonel General Hermann Hoth (q.v.) and the First Panzer Army under Colonel General Eberhard von Mackensen (q.v.) for a counterattack. Meanwhile, the Soviet Sixth and First Guards Armies and Lieutenant General Markain Popov's (q.v.) five-corps-strong Armored Group flooded through the gap, driving for the railhead at Zaporozhye to cut off and destroy the German forces in the south—thought by Premier Josef Stalin (q.v.) to be in full retreat.

Von Manstein withdrew every Panzer division from the defensive line on the Mius River and placed them with the two assault armies, gambling that the remaining five corps under General Karl Hollidt could hold the Mius against the six attacking Soviet armies. The SS Panzer Korps, preserved through Hausser's initiative, was reassigned to the Fourth Panzer Army and advanced south from Krasnograd on 22 February to cut off the Soviet Sixth and First Guards Armies. The Fourth Panzer Army's XLVII Panzer Korps struck northward from northwest of Stalino. The First Panzer Army struck from northeast of Stalino, encircling and destroying Popov's Armored Group. General Wolfram von Richthofen's (q.v.) Fourth Luftflotte inflicted severe damage on the encircled Soviets.

By the first week of March, the Red Army had lost six tank corps and ten infantry divisions, suffering 23,000 dead, perhaps 100,000 wounded, and 615 tanks and 1,000 guns lost. The major Soviet units west of the Donets River were either destroyed or repelled, as the First Panzer Army retook the west bank of the Donets between Petrovskaya and Slavyansk. To the northwest, the Fourth Panzer Army closed the gap to Army Detachment Kempf. The SS Panzer Korps destroyed two Soviet tank corps and three infantry divisions south of Kharkov, then began a clockwise encirclement of the city on 7 March. On 11 March, the SS troops went in, retaking the city on 14 March.

With the fall of Kharkov, Soviet resistance west of the Donets collapsed. On 18 March, the Germans took Belgorod and the Donets River again constituted the front line. The Soviets began erecting defenses on the east bank of the river, expecting an immediate crossing to exploit their disarray. Von Manstein tried to persuade Hitler to allow an attack, but the Führer vacillated, finally electing to launch Operation ZITADELLE (CITADEL) at Kursk (q.v.) in July.

The reversal of fortunes in February and March 1943 can be attributed primarily to von Manstein's command abilities, coupled with his courage in demanding Hitler's permission to withdraw to the Mius. Within the period of a few weeks, von Manstein executed a disciplined withdrawal under pressure, launched a large-scale counterattack, eliminated the threat of encirclement, inflicted severe losses on the Soviets, and reestablished a solid defensive line in the south, halting the Soviet winter offensive—all the while outnumbered approximately eight to one.

Soviet mistakes helped the Germans. Misinterpreting von Manstein's withdrawal, they rushed forward across his front, exposing their flanks while overextending and spreading out their advance units. Stalin intended to annihilate the German southern sector by cutting off von Manstein's Army Group South as well as Field Marshal Ewald von Kleist's (q.v.) Army Group A. Success there could have led to a subsequent major Soviet drive with a high potential for victory farther north. That might have shortened the war on the eastern front, with far-reaching implications for Soviet territorial gains in Europe.

Sidney Dean

Additional Reading
Carell, Paul, Scorched Earth: The Russian-German War, 1943–1944 (1966).
Mellenthin, F.W. von, Panzer Battles (1956).
Ziemke, Earl F., Stalingrad to Berlin: The German Defeat in the East (1968).

DRAGOON, Operation

See FRANCE, SOUTHERN

Dresden Air Raids (13–14 February 1945)

[See map 20 on page 1330]

The Allied attack on Dresden, 13–14 February 1945, was the deadliest air raid in history. Over the course of fourteen hours and fifteen minutes, three separate attacks resulted in the deaths of approximately 135,000 men, women, and children. No strategic advantage was derived from the city's destruction.

The first assault occurred at 2215 hours on 13 February from 244 Royal Air Force (RAF) Lancaster bombers. High explosive bombs broke windows and roofs, making materials such as curtains and furniture accessible to the flames of the incendiary bombs that followed. In the resulting firestorms, temperatures within an eight-square-mile area reached over 1,000 degrees Fahrenheit, creating tornado-like ground winds. Many people were sucked into the center of the inferno; others were found nude, their clothes ripped off by the wind; others were found glued to streets of molten asphalt. The fires, visible on the ground from fifteen miles away, were a beacon for the next wave of bombers.

The second attack, also an RAF operation, came at 0130 hours on 14 February (ironically, Ash Wednesday) and involved 529 Lancasters, fully loaded with incendiaries. Most of the deaths on the ground were caused by suffocation and carbon monoxide poisoning as people huddled in their cellars, waiting for the fires from the first attack to be extinguished. While they waited, the fire consumed oxygen from the air. At 20,000 feet, the bomber crews were able to write their flight reports by the light of the fire below.

The third wave consisted of 1,350 American B-17 Flying Fortresses and B-24 Liberators. The 1st Air Division, with 450 B-17s, had as its target the Dresden railway station. Navigation errors caused some of the bombers to mistake Prague for Dresden, but 316 planes found Dresden; the remainder bombed the Czech capital. The bombings began at 1210 hours and ended at 1223. In eleven minutes, 771 tons of bombs fell on Dresden. The B-17s were escorted by 700 P-51 Mustangs, some of which were ordered to strafe "targets of opportunity." It is unclear why the Dresden-Klotzsche airfield was not a designated target, despite the presence of *Luftwaffe* fighter and transport planes. This lends support to the suppositions that civilians were the main targets at Dresden.

Many factors contributed to the Dresden

D

The ruins of Dresden in the summer of 1949, more than four years after the Allied bombing raids of February 1945. (IWM HU 3321)

tragedy. The first RAF attack was extraordinarily effective because the target area was marked with unusual precision. Slow-burning flares, dropped by an advance group of pathfinders, established a visual link with the ground and ensured subsequent attacks would be within a concentrated area. The mission also was successful because the bombers encountered no antiaircraft *Flak* and only minimal fighter opposition, which mystified the Allied aircrews.

There was no *Flak* because all the antiaircraft guns had been removed from Dresden one month prior to counter the Soviet offensive rolling in from the east. An Allied air attack on Dresden seemed unlikely since the city had no strategic importance. There were German fighter squadrons nearby that could have attacked the Allied bombers, but the fighters had recently received orders not to engage in defensive operations because fuel was in short supply as a result of Allied attacks on oil refineries.

Dresden, which was considered a safe city, was flooded with refugees fleeing the oncoming Soviets. Civil defense precautions adopted in other cities to mitigate the effects of possible firestorms were never implemented in Dresden. People felt safe. They were in a city of cultural rather than military significance.

Dresden, like Hiroshima and Nagasaki, is an example of the strategic Allied decision to weaken an enemy's will to fight by making war on civilians. Many historians today consider the Dresden attack an Allied war crime of major proportions.

Mary Anne Pagliasotti

Additional Reading
Copp, DeWitt S., *Forged in Fire* (1982).
Hastings, Max, *Bomber Command* (1979).
Irving, David, *The Destruction of Dresden* (1964).

DRUMBEAT, Operation (January–July 1942)

[See map 4 on page 1314]

For six months, from January to July 1942, less than a dozen German U-boats rampaged off America's East Coast, sinking nearly two million tons of shipping. The result for the United States was a naval disaster exceeding that of Pearl Harbor in its impact. Operating with virtual impunity, the U-boats often sank ships within sight of land and escaped unscathed. Some of their success can be blamed on America's general unpreparedness for war, but most can be traced to a combination of political interference by local authorities and the U.S. Atlantic Fleet

commander's outright refusal to implement coastal convoys for shipping protection.

The U.S. Navy's chief of naval operations (CNO), Admiral Ernest King (q.v.), preferred not to intervene in his fleet commanders' operations but as the disaster grew, he could wait no longer. Finally, in July 1942, he ordered the commander of the Atlantic Fleet, Admiral Royal Ingersoll (q.v.), to initiate coastal convoys. As a result, follow-on U-boats had a tougher time, sinking fewer ships and suffering heavier casualties in the process.

Planning for the attack on U.S. coastal shipping was initiated the day after Japan's attack on Pearl Harbor. Admiral Karl Dönitz (q.v.), commander of the German U-boat force, estimated correctly that war would be declared between the United States and Germany within days. He also accurately judged the unlikelihood of American defenses being ready for a U-boat incursion into their waters. Fortunately for the Allies, his proposal to commit a dozen U-boats to launch the first attack was turned down. Norway and the Mediterranean had a higher priority as areas of operations. Only five U-boats could be spared, all the longer-ranged Type IX's. Dönitz designated the operation *PAUKENSCHLAG* (DRUMBEAT).

The first of the U-boats departed their base in Brest, France, on 23 December 1941, arriving in American waters two weeks later. Interestingly, both American and British naval authorities were aware of their progress across the Atlantic. Germany's HYDRA U-boat codes had been broken by Allied cryptologists several months earlier. Viewing the U-boats' progress with alarm, King recalled twenty-five destroyers from convoy duty and Caribbean operations and assigned them to Admiral Adolphus Andrews, commander of the Eastern Sea Frontier. Unfortunately, the destroyers were employed as hunter-killer groups to attack submarine concentrations, rather than as convoy escorts. That would prove a costly decision.

The first attack on U.S. shipping took place off New York harbor on 14 January 1942. Over the next six months nearly 600 merchant ships were sunk. U-boats operating off the American East Coast called it their second "Happy Time." Until late May, U.S. coastal communities refused to enforce the blackout, leaving the merchant ships silhouetted against a bright background. Lighthouses and other navigational aids also continued operating. Meanwhile, coastal patrols, both naval and aerial, were limited in number and reach.

The most telling deficiency in America's coastal defenses was the lack of convoying, which left the U-boats to range freely, attacking unes corted merchant ships at their leisure. Even arming the merchant ships did little to deter the U-boats. Still, Ingersoll demurred on convoying because he believed he did not have adequate escort assets.

Operation DRUMBEAT was a bold initiative that devastated America's merchant marine at a time when the Allies could ill afford it. Fortunately, Adolf Hitler's (q.v.) concerns for Norway (q.v.) and the Mediterranean overrode Dönitz's arguments for the immediate use of more than a dozen U-boats, which could have constituted a serious blow against the United States. It was merely one of many strategic mistakes Hitler would make during the war.

Carl O. Schuster

Additional Reading

Gannon, Michael, *Operation Drumbeat* (1990).
Hessler, Gunther, *The U-Boat War in the Atlantic 1939–1945* (1989).
Hickam, Homer, *Torpedo Junction* (1989).

Dunkirk (22 May–4 June 1940)

In late May 1940, the rapidly advancing German Army forced the Allies into a small perimeter on the Channel coast of France. This perimeter eventually collapsed to the Dunkirk beachhead, from which 338,226 Allied soldiers were evacuated to Britain during Operation DYNAMO (q.v.). The rescue meant salvation for the British and an inexcusable missed opportunity for the Germans.

On the morning of 22 May, General Gerd von Rundstedt (q.v.) received instructions to swing Army Group A on a northerly axis in order to trap the retreating Allies. The left wing of the advance would be the XIX *Panzer Korps*, commanded by General Heinz Guderian (q.v.), Germany's foremost authority on tank warfare. His mission was to seize the channel ports before the Allies could escape. Guderian ordered his 2nd *Panzer* Division to Boulogne, the 10th *Panzer* Division to Calais, and the 1st *Panzer* Division to Dunkirk.

At 1050 hours on 23 May, General Friedrich Kirchner's 1st *Panzer* Division left Desvres, thirty-eight miles southwest of Dunkirk. By 2000 hours, its advance elements reached the Aa Canal, twelve miles from Dunkirk. By the following morning, the division had pushed to the outskirts of Bourbourg, ten miles short of their objective. At that point, most of the British forces were concentrated around Lille, about forty-three miles southeast of Dunkirk. It seemed certain the Germans would win the race to the coast. Field Marshal

John Gort (q.v.), commander in chief of the British Expeditionary Force (BEF), predicted that "a great part of the BEF and its equipment will eventually be lost even in the best of circumstances."

For the BEF, the "best of circumstances" materialized on the afternoon of 24 May when Adolf Hitler (q.v.) ordered the *Panzers* to halt along the Lens-Bethune-Aire-St.Omer-Gravelines line. That order shocked Guderian, who was rendered "utterly speechless." Hitler never fully explained the reasons for his action, and historians have offered a variety of speculations. With a personality as complex and twisted as Hitler's, there probably was not a simple explanation. Historian Basil Liddell Hart (q.v.) suggested Hitler's decision was based on three factors: (1) a desire to conserve the German tanks for future operations against France itself, (2) Hitler's own historical fear of marshy Flanders, and (3) General Hermann Göring's (q.v.) boasts for his *Luftwaffe*. Intertwined with these three military considerations Liddell Hart also suggested a political motive to spare Britain's dignity in order to facilitate peace negotiations.

On the morning of 24 May, Hitler visited von Rundstedt's headquarters at Charleville. In response to apprehensions of both *Panzer* group commander General Ewald von Kleist (q.v.), and Fourth Army commander General Günther von Kluge (q.v.), von Rundstedt pressed Hitler to slow down the pace of the German advance. Von Rundstedt's subordinates were becoming fearful of their thin, exposed flanks, the growing gap between the tanks and their support, and the lack of opportunities for maintenance. Commanders who were raised on the methodical advances of World War I were not prepared to accept the calculated risks of Guderian's new tactics, despite the potential for spectacular gains. World War I also left Hitler with a profound respect for the terrain of Flanders. The memory of the 1914 French "miracle of the Marne" haunted him. The wet marshland crisscrossed by numerous waterways favored the defense and certainly could not be considered tank country.

These factors encouraging caution were reinforced by Göring's bold claims for his *Luftwaffe*. Even before Hitler reached von Rundstedt's headquarters, Göring telephoned the *Führer* to expound upon the suitability of the *Luftwaffe* for destroying the retreating Allies. Additionally, Göring urged Hitler to pull back the lead *Panzer* elements in order to clear the target area for the bombers. Not only was Göring concerned with the glory of his air arm, but he also reminded Hitler that the final honors should go to the staunchly

National Socialist *Luftwaffe*, rather than the conservative and sometimes bothersome army generals. On 24 May, Guderian received the order that "Dunkirk is to be left to the *Luftwaffe*." The Royal Air Force (RAF), however, ultimately prevented the *Luftwaffe* from having a free hand in the sky.

The larger Allied defensive perimeter was formed by three critical defenses: the British position at Calais, the Belgian position along the Lys River, and the French at Lille. These three points formed a rapidly shrinking triangle, with Dunkirk inside; but the time gained at the outer defenses allowed the strengthening of the inner perimeter at Dunkirk.

Calais lay twenty-four miles west of Dunkirk. On 23 May, Brigadier Claude Nicholson arrived there with his British 30th Infantry Brigade to take charge of the port's defenses. Nicholson found an assortment of units there, including 800 French and a swarm of refugees. Prime Minister Winston S. Churchill (q.v.), nonetheless, had high hopes for the defense. By forcing the Germans to reduce Calais, the main British forces could gain time to withdraw to the coast. On 25 May, Churchill sent Nicholson a telegram saying, "every hour you continue to exist is of greatest help to the BEF."

Nicholson needed all the encouraging words he could get. That same afternoon the 10th *Panzer* Division demanded the unconditional surrender of Calais. Nicholson refused and the Germans attacked shortly after with aircraft and tanks. The bombing savaged many of the defending units. By 1100 hours on 26 May, the Germans entered Calais-Nord and began systematically to isolate the defenders. Later that afternoon German infantry surrounded the command post in the citadel and captured Nicholson.

Despite the surrender agreements, isolated pockets of British resistance continued to fight on into the night, but Calais effectively was in German hands. The defense was heroic, but of little practical value. Only one German division was engaged at Calais, while six other *Panzer* divisions were deployed along the Aa Canal line. Churchill's efforts to buy time now had to come from other sources.

With the defenses at Calais providing a shoulder in the west, the Belgian line along the Lys River formed the eastern flank of the Allied position. On 26 May, General Walther von Reichenau's (q.v.) Sixth Army bent the Belgian right flank, while the German Eighteenth Army pressed on the left. On the afternoon of 27 May, Belgian King Léopold III (q.v.) reported, "the moment is rapidly approaching when our troops will no longer be able to fight." Later that evening, Leopold began surrender talks. By 29 May, all Belgian resistance ended.

The collapse of the Belgian Army sealed the fate of the French First Army's strong point around Lille. As the most southern unit in the Allied pocket, the French already had the hardest time escaping the tightening German noose. The Belgian capitulation and the British withdrawal now made escape impossible. Six French divisions commanded by General C.S. Molinié were cut off and encircled. Molinié mounted a gallant defense of Lille and held off six German divisions for three valuable days. On 1 June, he had no choice but to surrender to the XXVIII Corps. Impressed by the First Army's determined stand, the Germans granted the French a surrender with full military honors.

In actuality, it was not the valiant efforts of the Allies, but Hitler's own decision to halt his *Panzers* that allowed the defenders the time necessary to organize the beachhead perimeter at Dunkirk. On 26 May, Churchill initiated Operation DYNAMO, the cross-channel evacuation. The next day, the French commander, General Marie Fagalde, and British General Ronald Adam, representing Gort, met in Cassel to discuss the defense of Dunkirk. They agreed to try to hold a thirty-mile stretch of the coast from Gravelines to Nieuport, Belgium. The inland perimeter would make maximum use of the canal network, with the British positioned east of Dunkirk and the French to the west. These initial defenses were manned by ad hoc units as they filtered into Dunkirk. The perimeter was organized just in time, because on 26 May, Hitler lifted his halt order for the *Panzers*.

By 29 May, Guderian advanced as far as Gravelines, halfway between Calais and Dunkirk, when he again was halted and forced to withdraw. Göring had already begun to make the *Luftwaffe* presence felt. On 27 May, "Bloody Monday," German aircraft hit the port with 30,000 incendiary and more than 15,000 high explosive bombs. The bombers also hit the town, killing some 1,000 civilians. The attacks reduced Dunkirk's embarkation facilities to only the east and west moles, but Operation DYNAMO continued. The worst of the bombing was over. The weather turned sour for the next day and a half, and Göring began to doubt he could finish the job.

On 29 May, conditions improved enough for the *Luftwaffe* to resume full-scale operations. Their target this time was the cluster of a dozen British ships along the eastern mole. Losses were heavy and Admiral of the Fleet Sir Dudley Pound (q.v.) withdrew the remaining destroyers from the opera-

A trawler crowded with troops turns toward England during the evacuation from Dunkirk, June 1940. (IWM HU 2108)

tion in order to prevent their loss. The absence of the destroyers hindered the evacuation, but hundreds of volunteer small vessels from Britain joined the armada and the operation continued.

The German high command did not seem to realize how truly desperate the Allied situation at Dunkirk was. German attention was rapidly turning south to Operation *ROT* (RED), the decisive campaign for France scheduled to jump off from the Somme in early June. Von Rundstedt already shifted his entire focus to the Somme. On 31 May, General Fedor von Bock (q.v.) also received orders reorganizing Army Group B for operations to the south. In an effort to centralize responsibility for what remained of the push to the Channel, General Georg von Kuchler's Eighteenth Army was given complete responsibility for the entire thirty-five-mile perimeter area.

Von Kuchler did not press the offense on his first day of command. Instead, he mustered his strength for a "systematic attack" on 1 June. This respite represented another gift of time for the Allies and another missed opportunity for the Germans. At 1100 hours on 1 June, von Kuchler launched his attack and quickly breached the canal just east of Bergues. The British reeled back, but again the Germans failed to exploit the advantage.

Von Kuchler established a line across the canal by dark and then decided to wait until daybreak to continue the operation. In the meantime, the British conducted an orderly withdrawal under cover of the remnants of the French defenders from Lille. Covered by the French, the remaining British units converged on Dunkirk all through the night of 1–2 June. British ships were waiting for them, and by 3 June, the evacuation of the BEF was complete; but the French forces who covered the British withdrawal were still in need of rescue. The last Operation DYNAMO troop carrier left Dunkirk at 0340 hours on 4 June. Although 123,000 French soldiers were saved (102,570 transported aboard British ships), many French felt the British had abandoned them at Dunkirk.

Dunkirk was a miracle. Well over 300,000 Allied soldiers were saved to fight another day, but Churchill soberly reminded his countrymen, "wars are not won by evacuations." Nonetheless, Britain was now able to protect itself from a possible cross-channel invasion. For Germany, Dunkirk was a missed opportunity to annihilate the British Army once and for all prior to launching the attack on the Soviet Union (q.v.). At the time of Dunkirk, Operation *ROT* and the final destruction of France were Hitler's first priority.

The *Luftwaffe* proved unable to live up to Göring's boasts. Their problem lay not in a lack of desire but in a lack of doctrine. German *Stuka* pilots were trained for ground support, not interdiction. As a result, German planes rarely strafed the packed beaches, and they never used fragmentation bombs or attacked deeper, vulnerable targets in Britain, such as Dover or Ramsgate. The *Luftwaffe* could not stop the evacuation, and the

*Panzer*s were not given a chance. Thus, Dunkirk ended as a missed opportunity for the Germans, a new lease on life for the British, and a death sentence for the French, who in two more weeks would be out of the war.

Kevin Dougherty

Additional Reading

Horne, Alistair, *To Lose a Battle: France 1940* (1969).
Jackson, Robert, *Dunkirk: The British Evacuation, 1940* (1976).
Lord, Walter, *The Miracle of Dunkirk* (1982).

DYNAMO, Operation (26 May–4 June 1940)
In May 1940, the fighting was not going well for the Allies in Europe. As early as 20 May, Prime Minister Winston S. Churchill (q.v.) suggested "as a precautionary measure the Admiralty should assemble a large number of small vessels in readiness to proceed to ports and inlets on the French coast." This initial guidance resulted in Operation DYNAMO and the evacuation of 338,226 Allied troops in what became known as the "Miracle of Dunkirk." Had the operation failed, the British Expeditionary Force (BEF) would have been destroyed and Britain would have been completely vulnerable to a cross-channel invasion.

The responsibility for planning Operation DYNAMO fell to Vice Admiral Sir Bertram Ramsay (q.v.). A volatile but extremely brilliant officer, Ramsay's headquarters was located in an old dynamo room of a power plant beneath Dover Castle. It was for that room that the operation was named. The original concept for the operation involved three phases. The first was an orderly withdrawal from the front lines of 2,000 troops a day beginning on 20 May. Next would be the emergency embarkation of base hospital units and staffs, approximately 15,000 soldiers, beginning on the night of 22 May. The final phase, if necessary, would be the evacuation of the main body of troops.

The bulk of the Operation DYNAMO fleet consisted of large-size vessels, to include fifty-six destroyers and torpedo boats, forty-five personnel carriers and ferries, and 268 minesweepers, trawlers, and assorted vessels. Of these, the HMS *Tynwald* carried the heaviest loads, bringing 7,500 men to safety in five trips.

The desperate nature of the situation and the necessity of transporting troops from the gently shoaling beaches to the deeper waters made all types of smaller craft a necessity as well. The ideal vessel was the broad beamed and shallow draft Dutch skoot, of which about fifty were available. The Admiralty, however, could not be choosy and requested information on all "self-propelled pleasure craft between 30 and 100 feet in length." Some 300 small craft responded and were assembled into what Ramsay proudly called the "Cockleshell Navy." Only a small handful of these volunteer crews were professional sailors, and their gallant exploits caught the popular imagination and became forever embedded in DYNAMO lore.

Ramsay gave the order for Operation DYNAMO to commence at 1857 hours on 26 May. HMS *Mona's Isle*, an armed landing vessel, was the first large troop carrier to arrive at Dunkirk (q.v.). It picked up 1,420 troops and, escorted by the destroyer HMS *Windsor*, it returned to Dover at noon on 27 May.

Luftwaffe activity also began in earnest on 27 May, and by the end of the day, the entire 115 acres of the port, as well as much of the town, was in ruins. After these massive attacks the only surviving embarkation facilities were the east and west moles, long wooden gangplanks extending 5,200 feet out into the water. These structures were not designed to be used by ships, but the Royal Navy had no other choice. Troops lined up on the moles in columns three abreast and waited their turn to board.

Captain W.G. Tennant was in charge of the troop loading at Dunkirk. The first two phases of Operation DYNAMO broke down in the wake of the tightening German noose. Many wounded still awaited evacuation. Tennant insisted that the wounded be loaded first, and in enforcing that policy several physically sound soldiers were shot while trying to buck the lines on the moles. Even without the problem of wounded, the loading was a slow, tedious process. It took a destroyer about seven hours to board 1,000 men.

By late in the day on 27 May, only 18,000 had been rescued. That night Tennant advised Ramsay that a faster method was needed. First, Tennant requested more vessels, specifically those which drew only two and a half feet of water. Next, he informed Ramsay that extensive bombing had made the port unusable and that all future embarkation would take place on the beaches east of Dunkirk.

The ships of the fleet had to cross the English Channel by using one of three routes identified by Ramsay's hydrographic officer, Commander Archibald Day. The shortest of these was Route Z, which, at thirty-nine miles in length took slightly over two hours to traverse. Route Z, however, ran parallel to the shore beginning well west of Dunkirk, and offered a very lucrative target to the *Luftwaffe*. As a result, it was considered too risky for daytime use. Route Y was the most northerly, relatively safe from German guns, free of mines, and easy to navigate, but its eighty-seven-mile course made it the slowest of the routes. Heavy use of Route Y would overburden Ramsay's timetable and limited assets.

The final alternative was Route X. At fifty-five miles it was feasible in terms of length. Being slightly northeast of Route Z, it approached the shore at more of a right angle, which provided a much less inviting target. Route X, however, was strewn with German contact mines, which floated dangerously with the tide. On 27 May, the destroyer HMS *Impulsive,* the minesweepers HMS *Skipjack* and HMS *Halcyon,* and the Trinity House pilot vessel *Patricia* set out to clear Route X. In so doing, they provided Ramsay with a relatively short and safe main route.

By this point, Operation DYNAMO was a race, pitting the British ability to sustain the evacuation against the German effort to bomb the operation into oblivion. Adolf Hitler's (q.v.) inexpli-cable decision temporarily to halt his tanks during the land battle allowed the British to hold their slight perimeter and keep the evacuation going. On 4 June at 0340 hours, the destroyer HMS *Shikari* left the waters off Dunkirk with the last of the beleaguered troops.

Operation DYNAMO was over and 338,226 British and French troops were saved, but the losses were high too. Only nine of the original force of destroyers, and nine of the original personnel carriers remained serviceable. The Royal Air Force lost 106 fighters in the struggle against the *Luftwaffe* in the skies over Dunkirk. Nearly all of the evacuated soldiers' heavy equipment had to be abandoned. Dunkirk was a miracle, despite all these losses. The British Expeditionary Force was still intact, and very shortly would be poised to defend Britain against a potential cross-channel invasion.

Kevin Dougherty

Additional Reading

Carse, Robert, *Dunkirk 1940* (1970).
Jackson, Robert, *Dunkirk: The British Evacuation, 1940* (1976).
Lord, Walter, *The Miracle of Dunkirk* (1982).

D

E

East Africa (19 January–27 November 1941)

By the beginning of 1941, the British were ready to strike at the Italians in East Africa. General Archibald Wavell's (q.v.) successful attack against Marshal Rodolfo Graziani's (q.v.) Italian forces in Egypt on 10 December 1940 allowed Wavell to shift forces, notably the Indian 4th Division, from Egypt to the Sudan to strengthen the attacking forces. Other units in the Sudan included the Indian 5th Division plus 4,500 troops of the native Sudan Defence Force. Neighboring Kenya contained 8,500 men in two East African brigades, which were reinforced by elements of two West African divisions, plus a steadily increasing number of South African units. Despite these additions, the British forces in the theater were still greatly outnumbered.

The Italian commander in chief in East Africa, the duke of Aosta (*see* Savoia, Amadeo di), had approximately 260,000 soldiers in his command. Close to 100,000 were Italian troops, the rest were Italian native colonial troops. The air forces of both sides were equipped with many obsolete biplanes, like the Italian Fiat CR.32 and CR.42 and the Royal Air Force (RAF) Gloster Gladiator.

The British attack had several major objectives. British Somaliland, overrun by the Italians in August 1940, and Ethiopia (q.v.), conquered in 1936, were both to be liberated. Campaign planners also targeted the Italian colonies of Eritrea and Italian Somaliland for conquest.

The British commander in the Sudan, Lieutenant General William Platt, launched the first attack on 19 January. His assorted Indian units quickly advanced into Eritrea, capturing Agordat and Barentu in the first week of February. The invasion soon ground to a halt, however, in front of the town of Keren. Perched on top of almost vertical cliffs, the Italian defenders controlled all approaches to the town. The duke of Aosta realized he had to stop the British attack at Keren or lose all of Eritrea. He sent his best unit, the elite Savoi Grenadiers Division, to stiffen the defenses. After seeing the positions his men would have to assault, Platt correctly predicted: "It is going to be a bloody battle. It will be won by the side that lasts the longest."

While the northern attack from Sudan stalled at Keren, the southern thrust from Kenya began. British Lieutenant General Alan Cunningham (q.v.) received steady reinforcements of South, West, and East African troops until he had 77,000 troops in what was named the East African Force. He launched a diversionary attack into southern Ethiopia and then ordered the invasion of Italian Somaliland on 10 February. The spearhead East Africa Brigade met surprisingly little resistance. Cunningham realized he had caught the Italians off balance and ordered an all out advance. On 19 February, the attackers crossed the Juba River and were less than a week away from Italian Somaliland's capital of Mogadishu.

That same day, the duke of Aosta issued a proclamation stating, "We will last somehow, at any cost." He was wrong. Italian East Africa was already penetrated in three places, Eritrea, Italian Somaliland, and western Ethiopia. This last attack, supervised by the British, was led by Ethiopian Emperor Haile Selassie (q.v.), exiled since 1936.

For some time a secret British force, code named Mission 101, was operating inside Ethiopia helping to arm the patriot forces that were carrying out guerrilla attacks against the occupying Italians. Men like Major Orde Wingate (q.v.) led Mission 101 as they prepared the way for Haile Selassie to reenter his country on 20 January 1941. Escorted by an Ethiopian and a Sudanese battalion, the emperor quickly gathered the support of the patriot forces operating in the west, and his column began to make slow progress toward Ethiopia's capital of Addis Ababa.

The southern attack under Cunningham made the fastest advance. Mogadishu fell on 25 February, and by 17 March, the eastern Ethiopian town of Jijiga was reached. The attacking forces averaged forty-six miles a day. The speed of this advance greatly demoralized the Italians, who pulled their troops out of British Somaliland for fear of being cut off from Ethiopia. Taking advantage of this, the British made an amphibious landing at Berbera, on the Gulf of Aden, and quickly reoccupied their colony.

Ethiopia was now open to attack from east and west. On 21 March, a Nigerian brigade successfully stormed an Italian stronghold in the mountains behind Jijiga. This opened the road to Ethiopia's second-largest city, Harar, which the attackers occupied on 27 March. Italian morale was completely shattered by this time and almost no resistance was put up as the British occupied Addis Ababa on 6 April. In an amazing campaign, the East Africa Force advanced 1,700 miles in eight weeks, suffering only 501 casualties.

Platt's force, meanwhile, was engaged in a bloody stalemate in front of Keren. Again and again the Italians met attack with counterattack and managed to hold their positions. Finally on 25 March, a force of heavy tanks broke through the Italian defenses. This victory, at the cost of almost 4,000 Indian casualties, sealed the fate of Eritrea and Italian East Africa. All that was left were mopping-up operations, in which the Ethiopian patriot forces played a significant role.

The British took Addis Ababa on 6 April, two days after the Italians withdrew. Haile Selassie reentered his capital on 8 May. The Duke of Aosta was surrounded at Amba Alagi and surrendered with 18,000 Italian troops on 19 May 1941. By that point the British had killed or captured 230,000 of the Italian East African Force. The last pocket of Italian resistance was a force of 21,000 at Gondar under General Gugliamo Nasi. The Italians finally surrendered on 27 November to a contingent of British colonial troops and a large number of Ethiopian patriot fighters.

The ease of the British victory has many explanations. Most of the attacking forces were composed of higher quality soldiers who were better led than their Italian counterparts, and British equipment was generally superior to that of the Italians. Ethiopian patriot forces also tied down large numbers of Italian troops. Probably the most important factor was the higher morale of British forces compared to their Italian counterparts, who seemed inclined either to surrender or desert.

Glenn Lamar

Additional Reading
Glover, Michael, *An Improvised War* (1987).
Great Britain, Ministry of Information, *The Abyssinian Campaigns: The Official Story of the Conquest of Italian East Africa* (1942).

Eastern Air War (June 1941–April 1945)

In the late 1930s, the Soviet Air Force had some of the most advanced combat aircraft in the world. The Polikarpov I-15 and I-153 biplane fighters were being replaced by Polikarpov I-16 monoplanes, with enclosed cockpits, cannon armament, and retractable undercarriages. The Tupolev Sb-2 and Ilyushin DB-3 were among the first mass-produced monoplane bombers in the world. After Soviet planes and pilots fought against elements of the German and Italian Air Forces during the Spanish civil war (q.v.), it became clear to Soviet air commanders that the I-16 and Sb-2 were becoming obsolete in comparison to their major *Luftwaffe* opponents, the Bf-109 fighter and the Ju-88 bomber.

Between the fear of Nazi espionage, and the fear engendered by Josef Stalin's purges (qq.v.) of the Soviet officer corps, the Soviet aircraft industry struggled to produce new types of fighter and bomber aircraft that could match or surpass the *Luftwaffe*'s. The new Soviet types were the Mikoyan-Gurevich MiG-3 fighter, the Yakovlev Yak-1 fighter, the Lavochkin LaGG-3 fighter, the Petlyakov Pe-2 fast twin-engine bomber, and the Ilyushin Il-2 *Shturmovik* heavily armored ground-attack aircraft. Soviet aircraft were designed for ease of construction and maintenance. They could operate on rough fields and in sub-zero temperatures, which sometimes grounded their *Luftwaffe* opponents.

Before large numbers of the new generation of Soviet aircraft could be introduced into operational units, the Germans struck. In June 1941, the *Luftwaffe* concentrated more than 2,700 aircraft (about 60 percent of total *Luftwaffe* strength) for the invasion of the Soviet Union. Many of these planes were transferred directly from occupied France. They were supported by 230 Romanian aircraft, and a small number of Hungarian aircraft. By way of comparison, the *Luftwaffe* committed 2,600 aircraft during the Battle of Britain (q.v.). Shortly after the invasion, the *Luftwaffe* was joined by the Finnish Air Force with 299 aircraft, some units of the Italian Air Force, and air units from Croatia and Spain.

The Soviet Air Force met the German invasion with obsolete aircraft types, mainly I-15s, I-153s, I-16s, Sb-2s, and twin-engine Yak-4 light bombers. Within days of the attack, more than 1,200 Soviet aircraft were destroyed by the *Luftwaffe,* mostly on the ground. The Soviet fighters that managed to get airborne used ineffective squadron formations. By comparison, the *Luftwaffe* used two-plane elements that had proved effective against Soviet aircraft in Spain.

Luftwaffe losses in Russia were heavier than expected, despite the inferior tactics and equipment of the Soviets. In the first three months of the invasion, the *Luftwaffe* lost 1,600 aircraft. German losses of aircrews during this period were also severe and proved difficult to replace. Again in comparison, the *Luftwaffe* lost more than 1,700 aircraft between 10 July and 21 October 1940 in the Battle of Britain.

The Soviet Air Force made enormous sacrifices and used desperate tactics, including air-to-air ramming, to slow the Germans. Also, the Soviet aircraft industry moved east, beyond the reach of the invaders. The *Luftwaffe,* lacking a long-range bomber force, could not attack Soviet aircraft factories east of the Ural Mountains.

By late 1942, the Soviet Army was holding precariously to a tiny strip of the west bank of the Volga River at Stalingrad (q.v.), drawing more and more of the German Sixth Army into a trap. The Soviet Air Force, with 600 Yak-1s, Lavochkin La-5Ns, Pe-2s, and DB-3s, helped to seal off the encirclement of the Axis forces.

In the course of the *Luftwaffe's* attempt to supply the surrounded Sixth Army, a large portion of instructors from *Luftwaffe* flight training schools were used to fly slow, lumbering transports through corridors of Soviet fighters and flak to icebound airfields at Gumrak and Pitomnik. Most did not survive, and *Luftwaffe* aircrew and training programs suffered. At the same time, *Luftwaffe* fuel reserves were seriously depleted. What fuel remained had to be used for combat operations; very little could be spared for training flights. This contributed to a serious decline in the quantity and quality of *Luftwaffe* aircrews.

During the battle of Kursk (q.v.) in the summer of 1943, use of the newly developed *Freya* radar enabled the *Luftwaffe* to inflict heavy losses on the Soviet Air Force, but *Luftwaffe* losses were even higher. More significantly, the *Wehrmacht* took heavy and irreplaceable tank losses, inflicted by Il-2s and Pe-2s, using tactics developed by Pe-

2 pilot I.S. Polbin. One such tactic, the "circle of death," subjected the German tanks to virtually continuous air attack against their most vulnerable points. Groups of La-5Ns, American-supplied Bell P-39 Aircobras, and Yak-9 fighters, flew above and ahead of the Pe-2 and Il-2 bombers, and took a heavy toll of Bf-109s and FW-190s. The Ju-87 *Stuka* dive bomber was particularly vulnerable to attacks by Soviet fighters. In all, the *Luftwaffe* lost about 900 aircraft during the heaviest week of the Kursk fighting, while the Soviets lost about 600.

The Soviet Air Force included combat units composed exclusively of women. Lily Litvak (q.v.), who eventually was killed in action, became a fighter ace. Other women pilots, flying Polikarpov U-2 single-engine biplanes, harassed German troops with night attacks. The *Wehrmacht* soldiers who survived these attacks called Soviet women pilots "The Night Witches."

Pressure on the Soviet Air Force was relieved somewhat when *Luftwaffe* fighters were withdrawn from the eastern front in order to counter British and American strategic bombing attacks on Germany in 1943–1944. During the Byelorussian (q.v.) offensive in June 1944, Soviet forces virtually destroyed the *Wehrmacht's* Army Group Center. Here, the *Luftwaffe* deployed about 2,600 aircraft on the eastern front against some 7,000 Soviet aircraft. *Luftwaffe* losses on the eastern front in 1943–1944 were particularly heavy at the Kuban bridgehead south of Rostov and at Yassy in eastern Romania. Although German aircraft production slightly outstripped Soviet production in 1944, *Luftwaffe* fuel supplies, which never fully recovered from the losses at Stalingrad and Kursk, continued to hamper eastern front air operations.

The Soviet Air Force concentrated 8,500 aircraft for the final assault on Berlin (q.v.). Il-2s and Pe-2s mounted devastatingly accurate attacks on Nazi strong points in the city, and at least one *Luftwaffe* jet fighter, an Me-262, was shot down by the Soviet Air Force in the closing days of the European war.

The number of *Luftwaffe* casualties on the eastern front—about half of the total *Luftwaffe* casualties throughout the war—does not in itself reveal the significant contribution to the defeat of the *Luftwaffe* made by the Soviet Air Force. The magnitude of the contribution becomes clear, however, when *Luftwaffe* losses in fuel and flight instructors on the eastern front are taken into account.

Dennis A. Bartels

Additional Reading

Jackson, Robert, *The Red Falcons: The Soviet Air Force in Action, 1919–1969* (1970).

Muller, Richard, *The German Air War in Russia* (1992).

Myles, Bruce, *Night Witches: The Untold Story of Soviet Women in Combat* (1981).

Wagner, Ray (trans.), *The Soviet Air Force in World War II: The Official History* (1974).

Eastern Naval War (June 1941–May 1945)

[See maps 12, 13, and 14 on pages 1322, 1323, and 1324]

Although not noted for major engagements between opposing fleets, the naval war on the eastern front was one of intensity and high casualties. The nature of the conflict varied with the fleet area, with submarine and amphibious operations being the only common activity found in all three fleet areas: the Arctic, Baltic, and Black Seas. The climate dominated two of the fleet areas, the Arctic and Baltic, where icing and wind conditions dictated the campaign seasons. Otherwise, the naval war between Germany and the Soviet Union was one of small units, small combatants, and mines, with the Germans having the upper hand in the last category until the very end of the war.

In the east, it was initiative and tactical proficiency more than technology and numbers that determined the outcome. In contrast to the western front, however, the eastern naval war was a sideshow to the main theater on land.

Despite having one of the largest submarine and naval air arms in the world, the Soviet Navy was ill-prepared for war and its performance in World War II reflected that unreadiness. It also suffered from having its fleet divided among three fleet areas: the Baltic and the Black Sea Fleets in their respective sea areas, and the Northern Fleet on the Soviet Arctic coast. Although the Soviet canal system enabled the navy to transfer units of up to destroyer size among the fleets, the fleets could provide almost no mutual support to each other. Therefore, with the exception of submarines, the fleets fought the war with the units they constructed in their own locations.

Although the *Kriegsmarine* (German Navy) was better prepared, it had few units to spare from its primary theater, the Battle of the Atlantic (q.v.). Admiral Erich Raeder (q.v.), therefore, dedicated little more than light units and convoy escorts to the Russian campaign, expecting the campaign to be over before any naval aspects could prove decisive. He also hoped to avoid reinforcing his Axis allies in the Baltic and Black Seas. Like Germany's other hopes in the Soviet Union, this one would be frustrated as well.

The naval war on the eastern front actually began on 21 June 1941, one day prior to the start of Operation BARBAROSSA. The German and Finnish Navies began minelaying in the Gulf of Finland. Detected by Soviet naval aerial reconnaissance, they faced little interference because Josef Stalin (q.v.) prohibited his fleet from "provoking" the Germans in any way. Thus, in the Baltic at least, the Soviets found themselves practically trapped in port before the war began.

The Soviet Baltic Fleet commander did place his units on alert, an action that enabled some units at least to escape from their forward bases near the Soviet-German frontier. On the whole, he could only lay mines and hurriedly evacuate his forces in the face of total German air supremacy and a rapid ground advance. The Baltic Fleet lost the bulk of its submarines and destroyers in the process, but successfully saved most of its personnel and thousands of soldiers in the process.

The situation was different in the Black Sea and Arctic Ocean. The Soviets had local superiority in numbers and the *Luftwaffe* was directed toward the ground campaign, leaving the Soviet Navy relatively free to operate. The Soviet Northern Fleet commander reacted aggressively, landing naval infantry on the Rybachiy peninsula and sending his destroyers and gunboats to attack the German Twentieth Mountain Army's coastal flank. He also ordered his submarines out to attack German shipping.

Although Soviet submarines never inflicted any significant damage on their German foes, they and the British submarines that joined them did dictate the pace and method of German logistical support to the Mountain Army in the Arctic since that region's road systems were so inadequate. German convoys essentially moved along the coast in short hops between minefield-protected fjords,

Initial German Naval Forces in the Baltic 21 June 1941

Type Ship	Number
Minelayers	10
Coastal Submarines	5
Motor Torpedo Boats	28
Magnetic Minesweepers	3
Ocean Minesweepers	20
Dual Subchasers/Minesweepers	30
Coastal Minesweepers	16
Command Ships for Inshore Minesweepers	2

with escort vessels often outnumbering the transports they protected. Moreover, the Northern Fleet conducted several amphibious landings in the German rear each year, tying down many German troops in coastal defenses who otherwise might have participated in the drive on Murmansk.

The Soviet Black Sea Fleet was even more aggressive, dispatching two flotilla leaders to attack Constanta, Romania, on 26 June 1941. One, the *Moskva*, was lost in a Romanian minefield. The fleet also carried out a series of raids on the Romanian coast and carried reinforcements to the Odessa garrison, which Stalin ordered be held at all costs. The siege of the city began with the approach of the Romanian Fourth Army in August 1941. For the next three months, the Black Sea Fleet ran the gauntlet of Axis air attacks to carry reinforcements and supplies into the besieged city, suffering heavy casualties in the process. There was little the small and vastly outnumbered Romanian Navy could do about it.

As the Romanian Army gained control over the harbor's entrance, a Soviet task force under Captain First Rank Sergei Gorshkov (q.v.) landed the 3rd Naval Infantry Regiment at the village of Grigoryevka shortly after midnight on 22 September 1941. Conducted in coordination with an airborne assault and an attack by the city's defenders, the landing took the Romanians completely by surprise and rolled them back nearly ten kilometers. The Romanian 13th Infantry Division was badly mauled in the process.

Romanian morale was so affected they lost the initiative for the remainder of the siege. Had the German advance on Crimea (q.v.) not rendered Odessa's defense redundant, the city probably never would have fallen. As it was, the Black Sea Fleet evacuated Odessa's entire garrison of more than 132,000 by 16 October, including key civilian technicians and leaders. Those troops were reorganized in Sevastopol where they tied down nearly ten Axis divisions until June 1942.

As at Odessa, the Black Sea Fleet supported the besieged garrison by carrying supplies and reinforcements into the city and evacuating the wounded and nonessential civilians. It also diverted Axis forces away from the city by landing a reinforced brigade at Feodosiya, on the southern Crimean coast. This two-pronged landing achieved local surprise and drew nearly two full divisions away from the German siege of Sevastopol (q.v.) before the landing force was crushed. More importantly, it highlighted the dangers of leaving the Soviet Navy unchallenged in the Black Sea. The landing so disrupted the German Eleventh Army

that it delayed the final assault on Sevastopol by six months. Meanwhile, the Romanian Navy limited itself to escorting convoys behind coastal minefields.

The fighting and operations of the opening months set the tone for the fighting in each fleet area for the remainder of the war. The Soviet Northern Fleet continued to conduct amphibious operations at will, providing little naval support to the Allied supply convoys sailing into Murmansk against tough German opposition. Its largest amphibious landing was conducted against German coastal positions on Cape Pikshuyev east of Petsamo on 28 April 1942. The landing of the 6,000-man 12th Naval Infantry Brigade and a *Spetsnaz* (q.v.) (Soviet special forces) detachment achieved tactical surprise and advanced eleven kilometers inland before encountering serious resistance. The force was later evacuated in the face of German counterattacks but the attack diverted German attention away from the main front. The losses among the naval infantrymen were so high, however, that the Northern Fleet did not conduct another similar-sized landing until 1944.

The Northern Fleet's submarines, meanwhile, continued their ineffectual attacks against the German coastal convoys. Escorting supply convoys carrying raw materials out of Siberia's northern coast and supplies back to those mining communities was a another primary mission of the Northern Fleet during the war. The Germans made several attempts to interdict this traffic, once sending the *Lützow* and several destroyers into the Kara Sea in an unsuccessful attempt to locate and destroy that traffic.

Fighting in the Baltic fell into a pattern of almost desperate Soviet attempts to break their submarines out to attack Germany's sea lines of communications with Sweden. More than half of Germany's high grade iron ore imports transited those waters. Recognizing the potential threat, the Finno-German naval command established a huge array of interlocking minefields and antisubmarine nets, supported by submarine and surface ship patrols to prevent the Soviets from breaking out of the Gulf of Finland.

For the Soviets, all their remaining surface ships, except for battleships and cruisers assigned to Leningrad's (q.v.) defense, were dedicated to supporting the submarines breaking through the barriers. The first of these operations was conducted on 12–19 June 1942. Two minesweeping flotillas units swept mines ahead of the first wave of eight submarines while several motor torpedo boat (MTB) squadrons attacked the Axis patrols. The submarines broke out in pairs and only one was lost to mines. The survivors operated off Sweden's east coast, sinking thirteen ships before withdrawing in July.

A second wave of seven submarines came out 11–21 August. They were supported by air and MTB forces as well as by minesweepers. One German minesweeper and one subchaser were sunk, while three Soviet submarines succumbed to mines and one was damaged. This second group sank five ships for a total of 10,000 gross registered tons (GRT). Although these losses may not seem severe, they induced the Swedish government to institute coastal convoys, while the Germans reinforced their minefields and patrols in the Gulf of Finland.

The third Soviet submarine wave came out 18–30 September. Despite greater air and naval support, seven of the submarines were lost on the outbound journey, with two severely damaged. The Soviets also lost more than eighteen surface units in the fighting to get the submarines past the first mine barrier. The last Soviet submarine returned in December just before the winter ice terminated operations in the northern Baltic. It would be April 1943 before operations could resume.

The Soviet Black Sea Fleet, meanwhile, continued to run supplies and troops into Sevastopol, while its submarines attacked the Axis coastal convoys off the Bulgarian and Romanian coasts. In contrast to the other fleets, its major surface combatants (except its one battleship) remained active. Its destroyers, and occasionally its cruisers, raided German ports and coastal convoys, but generally, neither the submarines nor the surface ships inflicted any serious damage. They were a nuisance, however, and the German high command wanted their activities, as well as the more effective amphibious operations, stopped.

Minefields took more Soviet submarines than Axis antisubmarine forces, but the German and Italian Navies were already dispatching reinforcements to the area, including a dozen submarines. Denied entry through the Turkish Straits, the Axis sent these units down the Danube River. The first German and Italian MTBs were enroute by April 1942. It was November before the German submarines (all Type II coastal variants) were on station. Undaunted, the MTBs quickly deployed to the Crimea and began engaging their Soviet counterparts in the Sea of Azov and off the Eastern Black Sea Coast—none of which prevented the Soviets from evacuating Sevastopol in June.

The last two years of the war were marked by a gradual shift in the balance of power in the east as Soviet airpower began to make its presence felt. German units in the Arctic came under increasingly intense and more frequent air attacks. German escort vessels were reinforced and their crews began to mount additional antiaircraft guns on their decks. More Soviet submarines were also available, but their tactics and effectiveness had yet to improve. Still, German casualties began to climb.

Soviet aircraft also became more aggressive over the Baltic but German antisubmarine warfare (ASW) efforts virtually terminated the Soviet submarine offensive that year. As before, the subs were supported by Soviet light forces and aircraft. Nonetheless, all three Soviet submarines of the first Soviet wave in April were either destroyed or damaged in the minefields. The next three waves of that summer fared no better, with none of the submarines breaking out into the Baltic. As a result, not one German ship was lost to Soviet forces in the Baltic, enabling the Germans to transport 10 million tons of iron ore and more than 250,000 troops undisturbed through those waters.

German losses to Soviet air attacks began to climb, however, with nearly a dozen units sunk or damaged that summer. The Baltic Fleet did manage to conduct some small-scale amphibious raids of company-size and smaller against several Baltic islands near Leningrad, but otherwise it was a year of futility and promise for the Soviet Baltic Fleet.

Fighting in the Black Sea, meanwhile, was characterized by both sides using submarines to attack the other's coastal convoys, which generally operated behind minefield-protected areas. Moreover, the size and numbers of ships in convoy were quite small, so targets were few and generally unimpressive from a tonnage perspective. Soviet airpower began to make itself increasingly felt, but not to the point that Axis naval forces felt constrained by its presence. The main focus of the Soviet naval effort and the naval fighting centered around three amphibious operations. Two were massive and dominated the naval operations of both sides for several months afterward.

The first operation involved a major amphibious assault on Novorossiysk. Supported by three days of advanced force operations, involving three cruisers, four destroyers, and several gunboats, the Soviets landed parts of three naval infantry brigades in the port area on 5 February 1943. Although the main landing force was destroyed in less than two days, a small diversionary force landed on the opposite bay and was reinforced in an effort to take the city from that direction. The Soviets landed an additional 17,000 troops over the next five days, and ultimately the Germans were unable to dislodge them. Soviet resupply efforts became the centerpiece for many naval engagements over the next seven months.

The German MTB force, supported by a company of the Brandenburg Division's (q.v.) *Kustenjägers* operated freely against Soviet coastal bases and shipping in the area, but they never were able to cut the Soviets off completely. The fighting continued throughout the summer of 1943. The Soviets tried to take the port again on 10 September, landing the 255th Naval Infantry Brigade directly in the port. This second assault was supported by twenty-five MTBs and 130 small vessels and landed nearly 9,000 troops in two waves. The initial assault was well-executed but the follow-on wave was botched, enabling the port's 240 defenders to contain the beachhead until reinforcements arrived. Lacking heavy weapons, the Soviet naval infantrymen suffered heavy losses but managed to hold the port facilities. The fighting did not ease until the Germans retreated from the area on 16 September.

The Soviets continued to land raiding parties along the Crimean coast and harass German coastal defenses. With Soviet air superiority protecting them, even the Soviet cruisers became more active, shelling German coastal positions and naval bases all along the Crimean coast. Soviet aggressiveness ended after German dive bombers sank three destroyers off the Crimean coast on 6 October. The Soviets made no further efforts to interfere with German coastal convoys near Novorossiysk, nor did they attempt to interdict the German evacuation from the Caucasus (q.v.).

The Soviets did conduct one last amphibious assault on 1 November, landing naval infantry units in two areas near Eltingen on the Kerch peninsula. Several sharp engagements were fought between Soviet supply convoys and German light units. Despite Soviet air supremacy, the Germans drove off all Soviet efforts to reinforce or supply the beachhead. The smaller force was destroyed, but the beachhead on the tip of the peninsula held. The Germans became increasingly concerned about the Black Sea Fleet's growing effectiveness.

These same concerns were facing German naval commanders in the Arctic as 1944 dawned. Soviet bombers became increasingly active, even attacking the *Tirpitz* in Alten Fjord on 11 February 1944. Soviet reconnaissance aircraft also established an almost permanent presence over German ports and fleet operating areas. Attacks on convoys, ports, and harbor facilities became more frequent. Moreover, the Soviets were beginning to employ combined MTB-submarine-air attack tactics. Still, German casualties climbed only slightly, with two British carrier raids inflicting more losses in a week than the Soviets did in the entire year.

The situation in the Baltic remained relatively unchanged. Soviet air attacks continued to escalate. The German antiaircraft cruiser *Niobe* and several minesweepers were sunk, but no submarines broke out into the Baltic until September, when the Germans evacuated Estonia and Finland surrendered. Freed of the Axis minefields and naval patrols, the Soviets began to retake islands in the Gulf of Finland in a series of small-scale amphibious operations. Minesweeping occupied the remainder of the fleet as the Soviets ignored the German evacuation of coastal garrisons until their home waters were cleared of mines.

In 1944, Axis forces in the Black Sea found themselves evacuating coastal bases and positions in the face of Soviet air and naval supremacy. The Soviet Army advanced steadily throughout the year. Nikolayev fell to the Soviets in March and even Odessa was threatened. Except for a small amphibious landing on the Kerch peninsula, however, the Black Sea Fleet remained fairly inactive.

The situation was similar for the Germans, who had lost their Italian allies the previous year and found themselves facing increasing opposition as they transported nearly 50,000 tons of supplies a month to the Crimea. They constantly patrolled the coast to prevent any additional amphibious landings.

The Germans evacuated Odessa in April 1944, leaving the Crimea an Axis island in a Soviet sea. The Crimea then was evacuated a month later, saving more than 130,000 troops from Soviet prisons. The only interference came from Soviet air attacks. In August, as Soviet forces reached the Romanian border, the Germans scuttled their submarines and withdrew their light surface units up the Danube. The naval war was over in the Black Sea.

In the Arctic, the Soviets supported the drive of a combined Finno-Soviet Army across Lapland (q.v.) by conducting several small scale amphibious landings and inserting agents and *Spetsnaz* teams along the Norwegian coast. The Soviets also began to assist Allied convoy escorts in the Barents Sea, but left all offensive action to its submarines and naval air arm. By then, Allied sea and air supremacy in the area had rendered all German naval activity a rather risky affair, so the few targets available were heavily protected. German losses to Soviet attacks remained fairly light.

Naval action in the Baltic, on the other hand,

came to be dominated by the massive German evacuation of Kurland (q.v.) and East Prussia. Fuel shortages severely restricted the number of escorts available to protect shipping just as the Soviet submarine force gained access to the open Baltic. Although they had no decisive effect on German shipping, the submarines did enjoy some spectacular successes. The first one came on 30 January 1945 when the Soviet submarine *S-13* sank the unescorted liner *Wilhelm Gustoff* northwest of the Bay of Danzig. Most of the ship's crew and 6,000 passengers died in the frosty Baltic waters. Ten days later, the German liner *General Steuben* succumbed to the same submarine in the same area. The final major sinking fell to *L-3* on 16-17 April when the transport *Goya* went down with more than 6,000 aboard (only 165 survived).

In total, Soviet submarines sank thirteen transports with an aggregate of 63,000 GRT between January and May 1945. Measured against that was the successful German evacuation of more than 2.3 million people and some 1.5 million tons of supplies and material in that same period. Mining by the Royal Air Force of the eastern Baltic and Oder Rivers sank another sixty-seven ships with an aggregate of some 138,000 GRT in those final months. The German evacuation continued to the war's final days, and in some cases beyond it by several weeks. It was an operation involving more than 500 ships and lasting nearly nine months. The Dunkirk (q.v.) evacuation pales in comparison.

The naval war in the east did not involve the major surface combatants of the opposing fleets, nor did any memorable engagements occur in that four-year struggle. Several factors do stand out, however. First and surprisingly, the German mine warfare force was far superior to its Soviet counterparts—so much so in fact, that the Soviets made the capture of German mine warfare personnel, files, and research facilities a high priority in the war's final days and into the immediate postwar period. Second, the Soviets' best naval personnel were siphoned off to the ground campaign, with a correspondingly deleterious effect on fleet proficiency. The Soviet submarine force, while determined, was not particularly effective.

Finally, despite much criticism to the contrary, it is apparent the Soviet Black Sea Fleet retained the initiative throughout the war. The Germans constantly had to divert forces either to protect their coastal flank or to repulse amphibious assault forces. It disrupted their timetables and inhibited their operations along the Black Sea coast and in the Caucasus. Nonetheless, at no time did any of the naval forces, either Axis or Soviet, exert a decisive influence on the situation ashore. They did, however, prevent the other navy from doing so. In that regard, perhaps both sides were successful.

Carl O. Schuster

Additional Reading
Achkasov, V.I., and N.B. Pavlovich, *Soviet Naval Operations in the Great Patriotic War* (1981).
Koburger, Charles W., Jr., *Steel Ships, Iron Crosses, and Refugees* (1989).
Ruge, Friedrich, *Der Seekrieg* (1957).
———, *The Soviets as Naval Opponents: 1941–1945* (1979).

Eben Emael (10–11 May 1940)

Eben Emael, the pivotal point in the Belgian defenses, was considered by many to be the most strongly fortified defensive position in the world. Some felt the fort was impregnable. Nearly all observers thought it was at least strong enough to hold off an attack until British and French reinforcements could arrive. These confident assumptions proved far short of reality when on 11 May 1940, the fort surrendered after less than thirty-six hours of resistance. The main attack was made by a force of less than eighty parachute engineers, using gliders and hollow charges to take the fort in a lightning quick stroke.

Eben Emael was a thoroughly modern fort, built between 1932 and 1935. It sat on the high ground at the angle between the Albert Canal and the Geer River. Sharply inclined 120-foot concrete embankments tied the fort into the natural water obstacle. All bridges over the canal were prepared for demolition. The commander of Eben Emael, Major Jean F.L. Jottrand, was responsible for the bridges at Canne and Petit Lanaye and the locks at Lanaye. Another commander at nearby Lanaken was responsible for the bridges at Vroenhoven and Veltwezelt.

The fort measured roughly 900 by 700 meters and contained two 120mm guns and sixteen 75mm guns housed in armored turrets and casemates. Troops could be billeted safely underground, but on 10 May, only 650 men were in garrison, well under the authorized strength of 1,200. In all, the fort was well-defended except for its exposed flat roof and its scarcity of air defense. These shortcomings proved its undoing.

In the fall of 1939, Adolf Hitler (q.v.) summoned General Kurt Student (q.v.), commander of 7th Parachute Division, to Berlin and gave him initial guidance for an attack on Eben Emael. The attackers would land by glider directly on the fort's roof and reduce its defenses with the newly developed and top secret *Hohlladung* (hollow charge). In addition to Eben Emael, Student was to capture the bridges at Canne, Vroenhoven, and Veltwezelt. This plan was code named Operation GRANITE.

Hitler personally selected Captain S.A. Koch to lead the mission. On 2 November, Koch's storm detachment was activated and encamped at Hildesheim. The group included a platoon of paratrooper engineers commanded by Lieutenant Rudolf Witzig. This force of two officers, seventy-three men, and eleven glider pilots would form the nucleus of GRANITE. Eventually, Koch's command grew to eleven officers and 427 men, all of whom were sworn to secrecy and given only the minimum essential information.

Koch had three missions: (1) capture the three bridges intact; (2) destroy the Eben Emael defenses; and (3) hold the bridges and fort until the arrival of ground troops. Witzig's platoon was primarily concerned with the capture of the fort. The Germans had very accurate intelligence of their objective based on espionage and reconnaissance. Models of Eben Emael were constructed for training, and Witzig was given a segment of the Beneš Line near Sumperk on which to practice the assault. The key to the operation was the destruction of the fort's artillery. Witzig's platoon repeatedly drilled on the swift emplacement of their explosives. German preparations and rehearsals were a case study in detail and thoroughness, and would pay big dividends during the mission.

At 0330 hours on 10 May, Witzig's Operation GRANITE force left Cologne aboard eleven large gliders, each carrying seven to eight men, towed by a Ju-52 transport. The gliders were piloted by highly skilled peacetime gliding competition veterans. They landed as planned right on the fort's roof, just five minutes before the German main attack force crossed the frontier. Two of the gliders, including the one carrying Witzig, had their tow ropes snap. Witzig landed not far from Cologne and had to be retrieved by another Ju-52.

When Witzig finally arrived at the objective, he found *Feldwebel* (Staff Sergeant) Helmut Wenzel had taken control of the situation and had secured all but the southeastern portion of the fort within fifteen minutes. The GRANITE force had not suffered at all by their lieutenant's late arrival. Wenzel later observed, "the officers had trained all of the men so well that the officers were expendable."

The gliders brought in two-and-one-half tons of explosives and under cover of smoke the well-rehearsed sappers set their powerful charges in gun barrels, ammunition caches, and exit passages. The surprised Belgians were trapped in their own fort.

The fate of Eben Emael now centered on Witzig's ability to keep the defenders underground until the lead elements of the Sixth Army could reach the scene. Likewise, the Belgians inside were trying to hold on until British and French reinforcements could arrive. Jottrand requested artillery fires from nearby Belgian forts at Pontisse and Neuchateau, but the Operation GRANITE force held on until 0600 hours the next morning when German ground troops started arriving. Their advance was facilitated by Koch's glider forces' capture of the Vroenhoven and Veltwezelt bridges before the Belgians could destroy them. The Belgians' fate was sealed and at 1230 hours, Fort Eben Emael surrendered.

Casualties in the attack were relatively light. The Belgians lost sixty dead and forty wounded, while the Germans suffered only six killed. The psychological impact of the fall of Eben Emael was devastating. The key to Belgium's defense surrendered almost without a fight, and King Léopold (q.v.) was forced to issue the order for a general withdrawal.

Additionally, Joseph Goebbels's (q.v.) propaganda machine had a field day with the effectiveness of the new hollow charges. Rumors quickly spread through the Allied camps of secret nerve gas, "fog pills," and "electromagnetic rays" to explain the fort's sudden surrender. The fall of Eben Emael marked the beginning of a desperate period for the Allies, and was a prelude to the near-disaster at Dunkirk (q.v.).

Kevin Dougherty

Additional Reading
Mrazek, James, *The Fall of Eben Emael: Prelude to Dunkirk* (1970).

El Alamein (23 October–5 November 1942)
[See map 15 on page 1325]
El Alamein was the culmination of a series of decisive battles in North Africa. The Allied victory in western Egypt ended years of see-saw fighting and helped lead to the defeat of all Axis forces in North Africa. Field Marshal Erwin Rommel's (q.v.) failure to break through the British defensive lines during the battles for Ruweisat Ridge (q.v.) in July and Alam el Halfa Ridge (q.v.) in September shifted the initiative to General Sir Bernard L. Montgomery's (q.v.) Eighth Army.

Already carefully preparing Britain's third major offensive in North Africa and resisting an impatient Prime Minister Winston S. Churchill's (q.v.) urging of earlier action, Montgomery set his attack for 23–24 October's full moon. Despite the Eighth Army's superior resources, intense fighting raged for twelve costly days, raising questions about Montgomery's operational plan. In the end, however, he won a great victory. As Churchill later noted, "Up to Alamein we survived. After Alamein we conquered."

The northern sector of the British line, from Tell el Eisa to Ruweisat Ridge, was held by Lieutenant General Sir Oliver Leese's (q.v.) XXX Corps, consisting of the Australian 9th, British 51st Highland, New Zealand 2nd, and South African 1st Divisions. Lieutenant General Sir Brian Horrocks's (q.v.) XIII Corps, which consisted of the 44th and 50th Infantry Divisions, the 7th Armoured Division, and the Free French Brigade, held the southern sector to the Himeimat Ridge area. Montgomery held the 1st and 10th Armoured Divisions of Lieutenant General Herbert Lumsden's X Corps behind XXX Corps for exploitation.

Montgomery chose an unexpected location and scheme of maneuver for Operation LIGHT-FOOT. Following an intense artillery preparation, Leese's infantry would attack the heavily defended northern sector of the line, opening two paths through the minefields for the armor. In the south, Horrocks's corps would conduct a secondary attack to fix the Axis forces in that sector. Once the paths in the north were open, Lumsden's X Corps would advance—the 1st Armoured Division between the Australians and the 51st Division, and the 10th Armoured Division through the New Zealanders—avoiding the minefields to engage enemy armor. Historians and analysts have questioned launching the main attack through the most strongly defended area, using infantry to precede armor, and confining tanks to corridors under enemy fire. The critics claimed the resources available justified a bolder plan. Certainly in men and materiel the Eighth Army held a great edge: Montgomery had some 195,000 troops, 1,029 tanks (including 300 U.S.-built Shermans), 2,311 guns, and 750 aircraft.

The careful defensive arrangements for the forty-mile front were completed by General Georg Stumme during Rommel's sick leave in Germany. They incorporated extensive minefields, formidable strong points, and troop deployments in depth. In place were almost 450,000 mines, more than 1,219 guns (including eighty powerful 88mm guns), nearly 489 tanks, and 50,000 German and 54,000 Italian troops. The Axis air forces had 675 planes. Backing the line were four armored divisions: the Italian *Ariete* and the 21st *Panzer* in the south, and the Italian *Littorio* and the 15th *Panzer*

E

Tracers etch the night sky during an Axis raid on forward British positions at El Alamein, 25 October 1942. (IWM E 18541)

in the north. The defenders thought an armored attack in the south would be the most likely British scheme of maneuver. Two motorized divisions, the Italian *Trieste* and the German 90th Light, stayed in reserve in the north. The German 164th Division and the Italian XX Corps held the main portions of the Axis line in the north, right in the Allied attack zone. With severe shortages of fuel and ammunition hampering all his units, however, Rommel had little confidence in his ability to stop an offensive.

The attack began at 2140 hours on 23 October, with more than 900 British guns pounding the breakthrough area. Initially there was little Axis response, because Stumme sought to conserve his ammunition. Later the next day Stumme died of a heart attack while visiting the front, and General Wilhelm von Thoma (q.v.) assumed command. That same day, Rommel received word to return from Germany.

None of the initial attacks went well. Efforts to open corridors near Kidney Ridge were costly and unsuccessful. With minefields deeper and denser than expected, the clearing process lagged, leaving the armor congested and vulnerable. By mid-day on 24 October, it was clear that Montgomery's plan was not working. Only the Australians gained ground against the Germans near the sea. The southern secondary attack also met stiff resistance. The Free French troops were forced back west of Himeimat Ridge, while 7th Armoured Division's attack stalled in minefields.

Despite renewed efforts, the offensive settled into a contest of attrition. Montgomery then tried to exploit the northern salient created by the Australians, but a British night attack on 28 October ran into a minefield and intense fire from the 90th Division. Six nights and five days of fighting produced many casualties but little progress. Concern grew in Cairo and London over the stalemate.

For the defenders, the situation had nevertheless grown steadily worse. With mounting tank losses and piecemeal counterattacks, Rommel already faced a crisis situation when he resumed command on 26 October. That same day he shifted all his armor northward and committed his reserves to a counterattack. When it failed, Rommel considered withdrawing to Fuka sixty miles west; but then he postponed the pullback, hoping firmness might make Montgomery abandon the offensive. On 29 October, Rommel had told his wife in one of his daily letters, "I haven't much hope left."

Montgomery, meanwhile, initiated a plan called Operation SUPERCHARGE. He attacked again in the original area and shifted northward

some infantry and armored units. The British also conducted amphibious feints along the coast in the Axis rear. After Operation SUPERCHARGE began at 0100 hours on 2 November, the fighting reached unprecedented intensity. The British advanced, losing almost 200 tanks. Rommel was left with only about thirty-five. On 3 November he ordered a slow pullback, but Adolf Hitler (q.v.) forbade the move, issuing a typical "victory or death" message. Rommel canceled the withdrawal with a deep sense of pessimism. That night the British breached his line.

By late afternoon on 4 November, a fifteen-mile gap near Tell el Aqqaqir let the British armored divisions advance. Soon they threatened to outflank the defenders. The Italian XX Corps was destroyed, the *Afrika Korps* on its left had been broken, and General von Thoma was captured. Rommel ordered a withdrawal at 1530 hours. The retreat stranded many Italian units, which lacked transport, but the German mechanized forces fared better. During 7–9 November, Rommel's force cleared the bottleneck area on the Egyptian-Libyan border. He abandoned eastern Libya and escaped Montgomery's intended attack at Mersa Brega on 14 December by withdrawing beyond El Agheila several hundred miles. Rommel would not make a strong stand until his forces reached the Mareth Line (q.v.) in Tunisia, 1,400 miles away.

Figures for Axis losses vary. Rommel claimed that the Germans and Italians lost 2,300 killed, 5,500 wounded, and 27,900 captured. The British claim to have killed 10,000, wounded 15,000, and captured 30,000. Rommel also lost almost all his tanks. Allied casualties totaled 4,600 dead, 9,300 wounded, and about 500 tanks disabled.

Credit for his victory has not prevented criticism of Montgomery's cautious approach and the high cost of his achievement. Certainly his later statement that everything went according to his plan is a misrepresentation of the facts. Montgomery also has been criticized for ineffective exploitation of the breakthrough at El Alamein. Operations to cut off and destroy the retreating Axis forces were too narrowly conceived and too cautiously executed. Instead of sending a well-supplied pursuit force through the desert to a distant objective, he kept all his armor near the coast, where it reached successive points too late to intercept Rommel's retreating main body. Lack of preparation and boldness, compounded by fuel shortages and an unwillingness to move at night, account for the pursuit's failure. Subsequent efforts to blame coastal rains obscure the issue.

Richard Wires

Additional Reading

Carver, Michael, *El Alamein* (1962).

Lucas, James S., *War in the Desert: The Eighth Army at El Alamein* (1982).

Messenger, Charles, *The Unknown Alamein* (1982).

Pitt, Barrie, *The Crucible of War: Year of Alamein, 1942* (1982).

El Guettar (17 March–8 April 1943)

On 20 March 1943, the 1st Ranger Battalion led the U.S. 1st Infantry Division's surprise attack against the Axis positions in front of El Guettar, Tunisia. The attack initiated the second phase of Operation WOP, the first American offensive against Axis troops since the disastrous defeat at Kasserine Pass (q.v.) three weeks earlier. Although not recognized at the time, the El Guettar battle marked the beginning of the end of the Tunisia campaign (q.v.), and the final emergence of the U.S. Army as an effective fighting force. It was here that the Americans successfully withstood their first German counterattack. El Guettar also demonstrated the success of Lieutenant General George S. Patton (q.v.) in resuscitating the defeated and demoralized U.S. II Corps.

Operation WOP had assigned very limited objectives to the II Corps because its performance in combat against the Axis troops had been disappointing up to that point. The Americans, therefore, were given the mission of tying down the Axis (primarily German) reserves by conducting spoiling attacks against key positions at Markassy and El Guettar. That would free General Sir Bernard L. Montgomery (q.v.) and his more experienced Eighth Army to assault the Mareth Line (q.v.). The planners of the operation hoped the Americans, as the weaker army, would draw German armored troops against them, which would put the Germans out of position to stop the "inevitable" British breakthrough. The Americans, therefore, were to follow a rigid plan of limited, phased attacks to avoid being caught spread out and ill-prepared as had happened at Kasserine Pass.

In that respect, the plan was a success. On 23 March, Colonel General Jürgen von Arnim (q.v.) launched the 10th *Panzer* Division against the American advance. Two U.S. infantry battalions were overrun, including their supporting artillery batteries; but an American antitank battalion sacrificed itself to stop the German vanguard. Von Arnim's advance then faltered in the face of intense American artillery fire. The tide of the battle shifted back and forth as *Luftwaffe* air support tipped the balance in favor of the Germans, only to lose the advantage again when the planes departed the battle area and American artillery came into play.

After five days of intense fighting, the Americans were able to resume their advance. Tactically they won, but the Axis forces were not yet defeated. Employing an aggressive defense centered around well-prepared positions, extensive minefields, and rapid counterattacks supported by the *Luftwaffe*, the Axis forces reduced the battle to a slugfest. The advantage slowly shifted to the Americans as the lack of supplies and replacements wore away at Axis morale and effectiveness. Still, the Americans made little progress until Allied airpower swept the *Luftwaffe* from the Tunisian skies at the start of April. German *Stukas* made their last appearance over North Africa on 3 April.

The pace of the American advance began to accelerate from that point on. The first Axis rear echelon troops began to withdraw on 6 April. By 8 April, the retreat became general, as von Armin successfully extricated his troops to new positions in eastern Tunisia. Advanced elements of II Corps linked up with the British Eighth Army twenty miles east of El Guettar on the evening of 8 April.

The II Corps fulfilled all of the objectives assigned to it under the original plan. It drew off Axis reserves that might otherwise have been committed against the Eighth Army's attack. Moreover, Operation WOP was conducted in full cooperation with the Eighth Army and other British forces. It was at the battle of El Guettar that the U.S. Army first demonstrated that it was ready for combat on the modern European battlefield. The U.S. 1st Infantry Division ("The Big Red One"), the 1st Ranger Battalion ("Darby's Rangers"), and Patton all established their reputations at El Guettar. Green troops, including those of units broken four weeks earlier, entered that battlefield, stood up to Germany's best, and came away as victorious veterans. Mistakes were made and many officers were replaced for incompetence, but the troops not only stood their ground, but also advanced, albeit at a cost. They would get better still as the war progressed.

Carl O. Schuster

Additional Reading

Bradley, Omar, *A Soldier's Story* (1951).

Farago, Ladislas, *Patton: Ordeal and Triumph* (1963).

Howe, George, *Northwest Africa: Seizing the Initiative* (1957).

E

Ethiopia (1935–1936)

The Italian invasion of Ethiopia (also known as Abyssinia) in 1935 and military actions in 1936 were part of the chain of events that preceded the European nations' entry into World War II. League of Nations (q.v.) diplomats failed to resolve the conflicts, abandoning Ethiopia through appeasement (q.v.). The inability of the League to present a strong collective force against Italy's invasion opened the door for other territorial acquisitions being rewarded with appeasement.

Italy and Ethiopia shared a historic relationship that presaged the 1935 invasion. In the late nineteenth century, two internal rivals, Emperor Johannes IV and Menelik II struggled to control Ethiopia. Italy supplied weapons to Menelik, and occupied Massawa in 1885. Two years later, Italian forces were defeated by Johannes's forces. When Menelik became emperor in 1889, he sought treaties with Italy for European recognition of his rule and for future support. Italy, however, sought Ethiopia as a protectorate, leading to confrontation and a second Italian defeat at Adowa in 1896.

The Italians, bitter about their loss, signed a 1906 treaty with Britain and France to protect each nation's interests and citizens in Ethiopia in case of any political chaos after the death of the ailing Emperor Menelik. After his death in 1913, Menelik's nephew ruled briefly, then was deposed in favor of his daughter, Empress Zauditu, under the regency of Haile Selassie (q.v.), who was interested in Westernizing and reforming Ethiopia.

After World War I, Italy claimed it should gain the African territory as compensation, because Britain and France received former German colonies in the Treaty of Versailles (q.v.). A secret treaty signed during the war promised Italy economic control of Ethiopia for possible use as a colony for Italian emigration. In return, Italy agreed to respect British and French interests in Africa.

In 1922, the Fascists gained control of Italy. Benito Mussolini (q.v.) began scheming to acquire Ethiopia, stockpiling weaponry and equipment for that purpose. In 1923, he assisted Ethiopia in obtaining membership in the League of Nations. Then he helped initiate internal improvements, like building railroads and improving the nation's agricultural base. In 1928, the two countries signed a treaty of friendship for economic cooperation, but this failed, causing Italian resentment.

In 1930, the empress died. Selassie became emperor, issuing a constitution. Mussolini continued to prepare for the conquest of Ethiopia and also showed interest gaining the territories of Libya, Eritrea, and Somalia. In January 1935, French prime minister Pierre Laval (q.v.) and Mussolini signed a secret agreement. Hoping to gain Italian support against Germany, France approved Italian actions in Ethiopia and agreed not to interfere. Mussolini worried primarily about British reaction to the takeover of Ethiopia, assuming that other European nations probably would not intervene.

Mussolini's ambitions caused some friction between Italy and Britain. At the Stresa Conference in April 1935, Italy hinted that war might be waged to acquire Ethiopia. The Italians claimed they could improve Ethiopia by ending slavery and modernizing the economy and society. Diplomat John Maffey wrote the Maffey Report, stating that British interests in Ethiopia would not be drastically affected by Italian domination. In Britain, war was not considered a solution to resolving the problem, with a peaceful solution supported in order to retain alliances. Anthony Eden (q.v.) traveled to Rome to talk with Mussolini, offering compensatory territory for the protection of British interests in Ethiopia.

A conference in August caused Italy to reject the British and French ideas for a protectorate over Ethiopia. In a show of military strength, the British transferred a naval force to the Mediterranean. At the same time, they sought a peaceful solution to preserve treaties already in effect, and considered economic sanctions the only viable form of force. That September, Ethiopia accepted and Italy rejected the League of Nations Committee of Five proposals for a peaceful compromise.

Mussolini secretly prepared and armed his troops and sought to prevent other powers from modernizing and equipping Ethiopian troops for full-scale war. He projected that the war might last two years. Many Italians did not want to fight Ethiopia, fearing possible losses as well as condemnation by their allies. Mussolini, himself unsure of military victory, hoped a quickly mobilized force using technologically superior weapons, like machine guns and airplanes, could subdue the Ethiopian forces.

On 3 October 1935, Italian troops invaded Ethiopia and crossed the Mareb River without declaring war. The Italians tried to depict the invasion as a preventative action against an Ethiopian threat to Italian interests. The League of Nations responded only with weak and unenforced economic sanctions. The initial Italian advance was limited to moving several miles into the interior and occupying Tigre. Both France and Britain sought diplomatic solutions. Mussolini secretly dispatched Ezio Garibaldi to London to press Italian claims on Tigre and a mandate over non-Amharic regions. In the Grandi-Vansittart negotiations, Britain, more concerned about German and Japanese threats, agreed to the Italian demands for control in Ethiopia.

When the war began, Selassie was aware that Ethiopia would be unable to defeat the Italian forces. He emphasized Ethiopian membership in the League of Nations, believing his country's newly acquired allies would defend Ethiopia. These allegiances, except for some arms shipments from Germany, faltered. Many nations, instead, sent aid to Italy.

In order to get help, Selassie encouraged the dissemination of atrocity stories and emphasized the vast differences in the technologies deployed. Italian weapons were state of the art, including tanks and motor vehicles. Ethopian arms were primitive, including spears and pack animals. Most Ethiopians had never seen airplanes before, and were overwhelmed by the weaponry and tactics the Italians employed. Medical evacuation was prevented by lack of transport, harsh terrain, and poor communications.

Military actions occurred in both the north and south of the country. In the north, Minister of Colonies Emilio de Bono led Italian troops into the interior and took Makale, but he refused to advance, as Mussolini ordered, to Amba Alagi. As a result, on 17 November, Pietro Badoglio (q.v.) replaced De Bono as commander in chief of Italian troops in East Africa. Under Badoglio the limited invasion became a full-scale war.

In December 1935, the Hoare-Laval Peace Plan was presented and initially seemed acceptable to both sides, but Sir Samuel Hoare's resignation and pressure from the media for hasty decisions resulted in diplomatic negotiations ending abruptly. In the field, no significant victories were attained by Italian forces. Attempting to divide the Italian troops, Ethiopian leaders launched an offensive and forced the Italians to retreat. Ethiopian forces under Ras Seyum reoccupied Abbi Addi, and another force, under Ras Mulugeta, moved toward Makale. The Italians, at that point, feared they had lost the initiative.

The Italians managed to regain the upper hand. On the southern front, they secured Gorahei. At Dolo, the force under Ras Desta was beaten by General Rodolfo Graziani (q.v.). In this engagement, the Italians used poison gas for the first time in the war. In the south, railroads also were destroyed to interdict supplies. At the battle of Tembien in late January 1936, the Italians used mustard gas. They were victorious at Wariew Pass and captured Neghelli in the south, cutting Kenyan supply routes and securing deep interior positions. At this point, the Italians realized that Ethiopian forces could not win.

The Italian counteroffensive in the north began in mid-February with overwhelming airpower and artillery. Badoglio defeated Ras Mulugeta at Amba Aradam, which crushed the Abyssinian forces physically and psychologically. At this point, Haile Selassie requested that Ethiopia become a British protectorate. The Ethiopians, led by Ras Kassa and Ras Seyum, also lost at the second battle of Tembien on 27 February 1936. At the battle of Shire two days later, the Italians attacked the force of Ras Imru. Selassie's troops suffered heavy casualties and many deserted.

During March and April, Italy attempted secret peace negotiations with Selassie, offering to recognize his dynasty and to assist economic improvements in Ethiopia in exchange for the land conquered by Italy in the nineteenth century. Selassie refused, realizing any sacrifices of territory would provide the Italians with the leverage needed to acquire all of Ethiopia. To exacerbate matters, the Italians bribed tribes in southern Ethiopia to fight against Selassie, who vainly attempted to counter-bribe these groups. On 3 March, Badoglio soundly beat Ras Imru, securing the northern front. Badoglio then moved toward the capital, occupying cities as he passed.

On 31 March, Selassie, who personally manned an antiaircraft gun against the Italians, lost at Mai Crew. The Italians had to defeat him to reach Addis Ababa. The retreating Ethiopian Army was crushed at Lake Ashangi. In mid-April, Italian troops took Dessie, effectively winning the war.

Ethiopia was the pre–World War II test site for chemical weapons. The Italian Air Force dropped 700 tons of mustard gas during the war, hoping to disable soldiers, supplies, and animal-based transport. Aerial spraying resulted in poison sticking to the ground and foliage, contaminating troops, peasants, and livestock. With minimal means of protection, people suffered abdominal and head injuries. Many were blinded and could not see to find their way to aid stations. Because of delays in treatment, skin wounds often festered into gangrene. The League of Nations collected reports and photos on the use of chemical weapons by Italy but did not intervene to stop their use. Approximately 15,000 Ethiopians were killed and 200,000 wounded in the war. Gas victims accounted for one-third of the war's casualties. In sharp contrast, the Italians suffered few casualties.

On 22 April 1936, the emperor and his family began their journey into exile, first to Jerusalem, then to Britain. On 2 May, they reached the capital at Addis Ababa, where they boarded a special train to Djibouti. The Ethiopian people felt betrayed at Selassie's departure and rampaged. A mob stormed the palace, seizing arms and plundering. The people shot off weapons and set fires, ruining European houses and buildings.

By 5 May, Italian troops reached the capital. Badoglio arrived that evening to assume command. On 7 May, Res Seyum surrendered to Badoglio, and two days later Ethiopia was annexed to the Italian Empire. The Italian king became emperor of Ethiopia. On 1 June, the imperial constitution, the *Legge Organica*, went into effect. Graziani was named viceroy of Ethiopia. At the same time, Selassie arrived in London to discuss the situation with the British government. The Italians had only conquered one-third of Ethiopia, and their implementation of rule over the entire population would prove ineffective.

On 28 July 1936, Ethiopian patriots attacked the capital. Their coup failed and the leaders were executed, but this proved an active opposition to Italian rule existed. Other attempts and subsequent executions occurred. The resistance movement subsided by December, only to be renewed in 1937 following mass executions of rebels and aristocratic leaders by the Italians. Italian attempts to mechanize agriculture and dominate the populace failed because of the cultural qualities and tenacity of the Ethiopians, who refused to submit to the Italians.

In 1940, the Italians used Ethiopia as a base to launch campaigns into the Sudan and British Somaliland. Winston S. Churchill (q.v.) encouraged Selassie to support an active resistance in Ethiopia. The British government demanded the emperor be restored and disseminated anti-Italian propaganda within Ethiopia to rally revolution against the Italian regime.

As a result of the British campaign in East Africa (q.v.), the British captured Addis Ababa on 4 April 1941. Selassie reentered the capital on 5 May, and the Italians in Ethiopia capitulated to the British on 19 May 1941. By June 1941, Selassie reconsolidated his power, revived the old constitution, and asked the Ethiopians to forgive Italy. Plans for postwar cooperation between the two countries were initiated. The peace treaty was signed in 1947, with diplomatic relations renewed in 1952. Four years later war reparations were determined.

Elizabeth D. Schafer

Additional Reading

Del Boca, Angelo, *The Ethiopian War 1935–1941* (1969).

Fuller, J.F.C., *The First of the League Wars: Its Lessons and Omens* (1936).

Mockler, Anthony, *Haile Selassie's War* (1984).

Sbacchis, Alberto, *Ethiopia under Mussolini: Fascism and the Colonial Experience* (1985).

F

Falaise-Argentan Pocket (3–21 August 1944)

Operation OVERLORD, the Normandy (q.v.) campaign, began with the amphibious and airborne landings of 6 June 1944 and ended when Allied forces reached the Seine River in the latter days of August. The last battle of that campaign was a pincer movement that trapped what was left of the German Fifth *Panzer* and Seventh armies near the town of Falaise.

The battle opened on 25 July when, following a month and a half of advances characterized by small gains and heavy casualties, the U.S. First Army broke out of the Normandy beachhead at St. Lô (q.v.) and began Operation COBRA, a spectacular three-day advance toward the south and east. The breach was enlarged in the two days that followed, preparing the way for further impressive advances the last two days of July.

By 3 August, it was evident that American forces were making important gains, and General George S. Patton (q.v.) was ordered to keep his newly-activated U.S. Third Army ready to exploit any further advantage. That same day, Adolf Hitler ordered a reluctant General Günther von Kluge, General Gerd von Rundstedt's (qq.v.) successor as commander in chief west, to launch a counterattack that opened on 7 August with elements of four *Panzer* divisions. A combination of determined American resistance on the ground, especially from the 2nd Battalion of the 120th Infantry Regiment at Hill 317, and well-executed air attacks, brought the German counterattack to a halt, with heavy casualties, near Mortain (q.v.). The result was a large German pocket, still open in the east, containing formations of the Fifth *Panzer* and Seventh armies.

In the north wing of the Allied advance, meanwhile, the Canadian First Army took over from the British Second Army on 7 August, but a series of offensives brought limited gains. Already, the Canadians had suffered one of their worst days of the war—second only to Dieppe in casualties—in the abortive Operation SPRING of 25 July. The battles that followed were little better.

Operation TOTALIZE, from 7 to 10 August, was initially successful but ground to a halt several miles short of its objective, the town of Falaise. The support of more than 1,000 aircraft from the Royal Air Force's (RAF) Bomber Command in the opening phase of the advance, the use of improvised armored personnel carriers to protect the infantry, and the fact that the Germans sent the bulk of their armor in the abortive counterattack toward Mortain, were insufficient to guarantee success. On the night of 12–13 August, 144 aircraft of Bomber Command attempted to block a German withdrawal by reducing Falaise to rubble. Operation TRACTABLE, from 14 to 16 August, barely reached the town's outskirts, and resistance there did not end until 18 August.

On the Allies' southern wing, the Americans on 8 August decided to turn the XV Corps to the north, toward Alençon and then Argentan. The Americans then carried out a series of swift maneuvers that brought them around the Fifth *Panzer* and Seventh armies and toward Falaise from the south. Though Patton ordered XV Corps to continue moving north slowly until it met up with the Canadians, that order was countermanded by the 12th Army Group commander General Omar N. Bradley (q.v.). This was Bradley's most controversial decision of the campaign.

American forces halted on 13 August when they reached the established boundary between the 12th and 21st Army Groups. On 14 August, Bradley ordered Patton to head for the Seine River in a "long hook" against German Army Group B's ultimate line of escape.

On 16 August, having replaced von Kluge with Field Marshal Walther Model (q.v.), Hitler finally acquiesced in a German withdrawal. As the gap between the two Allied armies narrowed, the Germans tried to extricate what equipment and personnel they could. By this time, the *Luftwaffe* was only a ghost of its former self. Even though pilots and ground crew put on a major effort, they were unable to stop the Allied air forces from turning the roads and tracks through the gap into corpse-strewn, equipment-littered killing zones.

The battle was another opportunity for the Allied air forces to take advantage of their awesome numerical superiority over the *Luftwaffe*. On 4 August, 21st Army Group commander General Bernard L. Montgomery (q.v.) issued a directive calling for an airborne drop to block the gap. The plan was later canceled as being far too hazardous. Instead, he decided to use the tactical air forces to interdict the German escape corridor.

The Allies owned the skies over the Falaise pocket. Air traffic control was a greater challenge than the *Luftwaffe,* although *Flak* took its toll. By the middle of August, Allied higher headquarters had to set aerial boundaries to avoid confusion. The U.S. IX Tactical Air Command was allocated the main task of attacking the German forces within the pocket, while the British Second Tactical Air Force hindered movement through the gap and intercepted supply echelons transporting materiel and reinforcements to the beleaguered German armies. Thousands of vehicles and artillery pieces were destroyed by Allied airpower.

The same day that Hitler agreed to a retreat, Montgomery and Bradley decided to use all the force at their disposal to close the gap and squash the pocket. Sometime during the evening of 19 August—while the tragic uprising in Warsaw (q.v.) was collapsing—soldiers of the Polish 1st Armored Division, exhausted and short of fuel, met troops of the U.S. 90th Infantry Division in Chambois, closing the gap. The encirclement was, however, by no means consolidated. German forces attempted to break out on 20 August, assaulting Canadian, American, and especially isolated Polish positions around St. Lambert. The 2nd *SS Panzer* Division also tried to reopen the gap from outside. Between 40 and 50 percent of those involved in the two-day attack, 20,000 German soldiers all told, managed to escape. The gap was finally closed in strength on 21 August, when battle groups of the Canadian 3rd and 4th Divisions joined up with the multinational force at St. Lambert and thrust on to Chambois.

German losses in the retreat are impossible to calculate with any accuracy. Those divisions of the 21st Army Group actually committed around the pocket reported the capture of 20,000 prisoners. The U.S. First Army recorded 9,000 prisoners on 21 August alone, about the same total as the Anglo-Canadian forces on that day. In all, about 50,000 German troops were taken prisoner, while another 10,000 were killed. Approximately 9,000 tanks, self-propelled guns, artillery pieces, and vehicles were destroyed or captured. The area was so strewn with the semi-decomposed bodies of men and animals that General Dwight D. Eisenhower (q.v.) exclaimed he had encountered "scenes that could be described only by Dante."

Because the Normandy campaign ended in success, there was little criticism at the time of the manner in which operations were planned and carried out. In the years that followed, participants and historians alike began to take a closer look at the battles of the summer of 1944, including Falaise.

Referring to the slow Canadian advance, that required fifteen days to move the thirty miles from Caen to Chambois, C.P. Stacey, official historian of the Canadian Army, admitted that, "Less raw formations would probably have obtained larger and earlier results." A more recent work by Professor John English speculates that, if the Canadian First Army had broken through on 7 August, its advance and subsequent reputation would have rivaled that of Patton's Third Army. Carlo D'Este suggests that Montgomery's failure to reinforce the Canadian First Army after its initial success in Operation TOTALIZE was his most serious error of the Normandy campaign. That higher command at the time was concerned about the lack of progress was evidenced by the replacement of the Canadian 4th Armoured Division's commander the very day the gap was closed.

Even though they had made spectacular advances in the weeks before the closing of the gap, the American armies, especially their leaders, are not immune from criticism either. The decision by Bradley to halt the XV Corps at Argentan while Canadian troops were still well north of Falaise became the subject of considerable polemic. Bradley later explained that he feared a head-on collision leading to a "calamitous battle between friends." He also suggested that XV Corps might have found itself in a precarious position, with flanks exposed, if it had gone any further. To complicate matters, Montgomery, the overall ground force commander under Eisenhower at the time, did not move the army group boundary, nor did Bradley request he do so. In any event, it would seem that in the near-chaotic conditions that almost always characterize a major advance, neither Eisenhower, Montgomery, nor Bradley felt the issue was of sufficient importance to press it.

After Falaise, the Allies quickly moved to the Seine, and then the Somme. They met little resistance from the Germans, whose main goal was to pull back to areas where they could regroup. The Germans had seen forty of their divisions destroyed since June, and were being pursued by four Allied field armies. It was the most crushing victory the Allies would experience in northwest Europe. Although it represented a substantial loss, more than 60,000 casualties, to the German Army, Falaise was no death knell. The *Wehrmacht* would demonstrate a remarkable recuperative ability, and the reconstituted Fifth *Panzer* and Seventh armies would reappear in the Ardennes (q.v.) offensive later that December.

William Rawling

Additional Reading
Blumenson, Martin, *The Battle of the Generals* (1995).
———, *Breakout and Pursuit* (1961).
D'Este, Carlo, *Decision in Normandy: The Unwritten Story of Montgomery and the Allied Campaign* (1983).
Weigley, Russell, F., *Eisenhower's Lieutenants: The Campaigns of France and Germany, 1944–1945* (1981).

FELIX, Operation (1940–1941)

Following the defeat of France in June 1940, Adolf Hitler (q.v.) had several options for continuing the war against the British Commonwealth. One was to strengthen his hand in the Mediterranean region by bringing Spain into the war on the Axis side and seizing the British base at Gibraltar. On 12 July 1940, the OKW (q.v.) therefore established a special group for the requisite planning.

On 22 July 1940, the head of the *Abwehr,* Admiral Wilhelm Canaris (qq.v.), and several other German officers traveled to Madrid where they talked to General Francisco Franco (q.v.) and his minister of war, General Juan Vigon. They then went to Algeciras where they stayed several days to reconnoiter the various approaches to Gibraltar. They returned to Germany with the conclusion that the Franco regime was reluctant to enter the war. We know now that Canaris was disloyal to Hitler and actually encouraged Franco not to enter the war on Germany's side, since an Allied victory was almost certain. Canaris's team determined, however, that the British stronghold might possibly be seized through an air-supported ground operation involving at least two infantry regiments, three engineer battalions, and a dozen artillery regiments.

In a conference with senior military leaders on 31 July, Hitler noted that the invasion of Great Britain, Operation *SEELÖWE* (SEA LION) (q.v.), might not be feasible in 1940. Also, the seizure of Gibraltar, by itself, was unlikely to have a major impact. Hitler also confirmed his intention to strike at the Soviet Union in 1941, thereby depriving Britain of a potential continental ally. Nevertheless, the idea of bringing Spain into the war continued to affect Hitler's thinking.

On 24 August, Hitler approved a general plan for seizing Gibraltar. Two months later, the *Führer* met Franco at Hendaye and proposed that Spain enter the war in January 1941. Gibraltar would be taken by special *Wehrmacht* units and then turned over to Spain. Franco, however, refused the bait, emphasizing Spain's need for large-scale economic and military assistance.

Despite these political problems, Germany's military leaders proceeded to prepare for a large-scale operation against Gibraltar. Code named Operation FELIX, their plan called for two German corps to enter Spain across the Pyrenees. One corps, under General Ludwig Kübler, was to traverse Spain and attack Gibraltar. The other, commanded by General Rudolf Schmidt, would secure its flanks. Air support would involve one fighter and two dive bomber wings. Overall direction of the operation would be assigned to Field Marshal Walther von Reichenau (q.v.).

To reconnoiter conditions in Spain, two German generals and a senior staff officer toured the country between 7 and 18 December, while Canaris once again conferred with Franco. Despite Franco's continuing resistance to Hitler's proposals, the German naval authorities and some army figures refused to give up. In the opening weeks of 1941, further efforts were made by both Berlin and Rome to lure the Spanish government into a more cooperative stance.

The Germans made no progress with Spain, and in mid-February, the OKW advised the naval high command that, for the time being, Operation FELIX was out, especially since the troops earmarked for it would soon be needed elsewhere. On Hitler's insistence, however, the OKW shortly thereafter developed a new plan for the capture of Gibraltar, one that might be implemented once the German invasion of the Soviet Union had been successfully executed. Code named FELIX-HEINRICH, the new plan was submitted to Colonel General Franz Halder (q.v.) on 10 March 1941. That plan too, was ultimately destined to gather dust in the archives.

Ulrich Trumpener

Additional Reading

Burdick, Charles, *Germany's Military Strategy and Spain in World War II* (1968).

Detwiler, Donald S., *Hitler, Franco, und Gibraltar* (1962).

Ruhl, Klaus-Jörg, *Spanien im Zweiten Weltkrieg: Franco, die Falange, und das Dritte Reich* (1975).

Finland (25 June 1941–4 September 1944)

[See map 16 on page 1326]

After the Finnish Winter War (q.v.) ended in March 1940, with substantial loss of Finnish territory, the country did not directly involve itself in the larger European conflict until June 1941. Yet the Finns were hardly unaware of the seriousness of their position in 1940, as the Soviets annexed the Baltic states (q.v.) and the Germans took over virtually all of Western Europe.

Consequently Finland was drawn—to some extent pushed itself—into the coming showdown between Germany and the Soviet Union. The Finns played a role in Adolf Hitler's (q.v.) eastern war between June 1941 and September 1944, when Finland made a separate peace with the Soviet Union. In Finland, this conflict was known as the "Continuation War," a follow-up to the Winter War.

Finland's participation in Hitler's attack on the Soviet Union resulted from a strange mixture of sentiments and speculations. On one hand, some politicians wanted revenge for the Soviets' victory in the Winter War. Some even talked about a "Greater Finland," taking the thoughts of revenge well beyond Finland's old 1939 boundaries. On the other hand, most Finnish leaders, including President Risto Ryti, saw the Soviet Union as a continuing threat to Finland's independence and security. The majority of Finns were inclined to look to Germany as the one power that could help the Finns win back their lost territories and act as a deterrent against the powerful neighbor to the east.

The Finns showed interest in a potential attack on the Soviet Union by entering into "informal" talks with the Germans in the fall of 1940. The first Finno-German military contacts were made in December 1940. At the end of January 1941, the chief of the Finnish General Staff, General Axel Heinrichs (q.v.), visited Germany. Although talks remained in early 1941 at the "hypothetical level" and no specific agreements were signed, there is little doubt the Finns knew about the upcoming German offensive.

The Finns allowed German troops transit rights through Finland. Between May and June 1941, Operation SILBERFUCHS (SILVER FOX) moved German forces into northern Finland in preparation for Operation BARBAROSSA. The Germans responded with material assistance to the Finns, including increased aid in the form of military equipment. In short, although there were no official or secret treaties between Finland and Germany before the launching of BARBAROSSA on 22 June 1941, Finnish participation was a foregone conclusion.

When the war broke out, the Finns insisted that their status was not one of an ally, but merely a "cobelligerent" of Germany, and that they were fighting a concurrent but separate war against the same enemy. Nevertheless, the Germans were part of the Finnish front in a very concrete way. The Finnish forces were organized into two armies, with Army Southeast in the south, and Army Karelia in the south-center. The northern part of Finland was held by the German XXXVI *Korps*, under General Eduard Deitl (q.v.). The opposing Soviet forces consisted of the First Army in the north, the Seventh Army in Karelia, and the Twenty-third Army in the Karelian isthmus.

On 25 June 1941, the Finns started an offensive back into eastern Karelia. On 1 July, the German XXXVI *Korps* and the Finnish III Corps launched Operation POLARFUCHS (POLAR FOX), driving toward Kandalaksha. Outnumbering the Soviet forces on the Karelian isthmus (230,000 Finns against 150,000 Soviets), Finland was able to retake the area lost in the Winter War, entering Viipuri on 29 August. The Finnish Army continued its advances until early December 1941 stopping about twenty miles north of Leningrad and controlling most of the area surrounding Lake Ladoga.

Despite German pleas, Marshal Carl Mannerheim (q.v.), leader of the Finnish forces, was unwilling to take part in an offensive against Leningrad (q.v.). Instead, he insisted on establishing favorable defensive positions along the Karelian isthmus. Two reasons explain this seemingly contradictory decision.

First, Mannerheim, a cautious and politically conscious commander, pointed out that German victory was far from a foregone conclusion. In case Germany lost, Mannerheim argued, Finland was better off without the moral responsibility of having participated in a full-scale assault on Leningrad. "The Russians will never forgive us," he said of a potential Finnish participation in a siege and leveling of Leningrad.

Even more important was the fact that the Finnish Army had been exhausted by their summer and fall offensives. An attack against Leningrad would have been too costly to the Finnish Army, Mannerheim calculated. By the end of 1941, the Finnish front stabilized for a two-year period, as Finns and Soviets dug their trenches along the Karelian isthmus.

Although insisting that it was fighting a separate war merely as a "cobelligerent" of Germany, Finland was pressured to join the Anti-Comintern Pact (q.v.) in November 1941. Partly because of this, and mostly due to Soviet pressure, the British declared war on Finland on 6 December 1941. Canada, Australia, New Zealand, and India followed the British lead. One important fact, however, separated the Finns from many other German Allies throughout the 1941–1944 Finno-Soviet conflict: the United States, which entered the war the day after the British declaration of war on Finland, never declared war on Finland. In fact, Washington waited until July 1944 to break off diplomatic relations with Helsinki.

To be sure, the static warfare on the Finnish front between 1941 and 1944 did not mean a complete halt in military operations. Between January and May 1942, for example, the Soviets launched a series of unsuccessful attacks against the Finnish lines. On the whole, however, the northeastern front was quiet, and the Soviets felt secure enough by late 1942 to move several divisions farther south. The static situation also enabled the Finns to send about 180,000 of their 630,000 troops home during 1942.

In early 1943, the battle of Stalingrad (q.v.) significantly changed the attitudes of many Finnish leaders. As Germany began to crumble, Ryti dropped the dreamers of a "Greater Finland" from a new Finnish government formed in March 1943, and a search for a separate peace began. The Americans and Swedes played the roles of mediators in this process, which stalled in 1943 for two reasons: the Finno-Soviet disagreement on borders, and the strong German grip on Finland. The Finns insisted the 1939 pre–Winter War borders should be the basis for negotiations. The Soviets held onto the demand for the 1940 borders. At the same time the Germans put considerable pressure on Finland by threatening to stop grain deliveries if Finland continued talks with the Americans.

Another mediating attempt by the U.S. in early 1944 led to tentative peace talks in Stockholm. Beginning in February 1944, the Finnish and Soviet ambassadors to Sweden tried to pave the way for possible peace. Again, the fear of Germany and explicit threats by German Foreign Minister Joachim von Ribbentrop (q.v.) led to a breakdown of negotiations in April.

The process that finally led to the Moscow Armistice of September 1944 began with the successful Allied landing at Normandy (q.v.) on 6 June. Soviet Premier Josef Stalin (q.v.), who had been demanding a second front throughout the war, saw that the Western pressure in France invited a full-scale Soviet assault on the eastern front. Before doing so, however, Stalin decided to take care of the "Finnish Problem."

On 10 June 1944, the Soviet Twenty-third Army went on the offensive in Karelia and quickly forced the Finnish Army onto the defensive. On 15 June the Finnish IV Corps withdrew to Viipuri, and three days later the Soviets once again pushed through the Finnish positions on the Mannerheim Line. Viipuri fell again on 20 June. On 28 June, meanwhile, a Soviet attack in the far north crossed the Murmansk rail line.

Afraid of a total collapse, Ryti looked to Germany for help. This time von Ribbentrop demanded the Finns sign an agreement in which they would promise to act in accord with the Germans until the end of the war. As a result, Ryti personally signed an agreement to that effect on 22 June. The Germans then sent enough material aid to help the Finns stop the Soviet advance in early July, at least temporarily.

The Ryti-Ribbentrop Pact did not, however, signify a complete Finno-German Alliance. Later, the Finns argued that the pact was a personal agreement between von Ribbentrop and Ryti, an agreement that did not constitute a formal treaty between two sovereign nations. That position was reinforced when Ryti resigned and was replaced by Mannerheim on 4 August.

One of Mannerheim's first moves as president was to declare that he was not bound by the Ryti-Ribbentrop Pact. He then began an earnest search for a separate peace with the Soviets. On 2 September 1944, in accordance with Soviet demands, Finland broke off diplomatic relations with Germany. A cease-fire went into effect on 4 September, and the Finnish peace delegation traveled to Moscow on 7 September, led by Juho K. Pasasikivi, who later succeeded Mannerheim as president.

F

On 19 September, Finland and the Soviet Union signed the Moscow Armistice. It was a costly peace for Finland. The boundaries of 1940 were restored. In addition, Petsamo, an area famous for its nickel mines, was ceded to the Soviets. They also obtained a fifty-year lease on the Porkkala peninsula, only twenty miles west of Helsinki. Finland agreed to pay $300 million in war reparations by 1950. Finally, Finland also had to drive the remaining German troops out of northern Finland. This proved far from an easy task, and would leave Finnish Lapland (q.v.) devastated.

Out of a population of a little over 4 million, Finland lost a combined total of approximately 86,000 in the Winter War, the Continuation War, and War in Lapland. Another 57,000 were permanently disabled. About 10 percent of prewar Finland was ceded to the Soviets. Some 420,000 refugees came from the ceded areas and required resettlement in other parts of Finland. And of course, the war reparations haunted the Finnish economy for several years after.

Despite the human, territorial, and economic costs, there were some positive legacies. Helsinki remained the only European capital involved in the war (aside from London and Moscow), that did not suffer foreign occupation. Also, despite its geographic location, Finland was not directly drawn into the postwar Soviet sphere of influence in Eastern Europe. Instead, Finland emerged from the war as one of the few European neutrals that was able to remain aloof from the Cold War—even though this Cold War neutrality was imposed on Finland by the Soviet Union.

Jussi Hanhimaki

Additional Reading

Lundin, Leonard, *Finland in the Second World War* (1957).

Nissen, Henrik S., *Scandinavia and the Second World War* (1983).

Ziemke, Earl F., *The German Northern Theater of Operations, 1940–1945* (1959).

FORTITUDE, Operation (1943–1944)

In 1944, the Allies were preparing for their most daring and decisive operation of World War II, Operation OVERLORD, the cross-channel attack on Adolf Hitler's (q.v.) *Festung Europa* (Fortress Europe). While history has shown that Operation OVERLORD was indeed dangerous and spelled the beginning of the end of the war, it was an operation with all the possibilities for disaster. It was clear that Hitler, indeed, intended to defend

France from invasion, and he sent Field Marshal Erwin Rommel (q.v.) to oversee the defenses of the northern French coastline.

General Dwight D. Eisenhower (q.v.) and his planning staff needed every advantage to see that Operation OVERLORD did not end in a crushing, bloody defeat on the Normandy beaches. To support Operation OVERLORD, Allied planners devised Operation FORTITUDE, a massive deception plan to mislead the Germans as to where the Allied amphibious and airborne assaults would come. Operation FORTITUDE was aimed at the Pas de Calais area, the closest point between France and Britain, offering the shortest route for the Allies into Germany's industrial heartland. Hitler and many of his generals firmly believed the Allies would assault Pas de Calais because it made military sense. Consequently, the *Führer* and his planners were more than ready to believe Operation FORTITUDE would be the main assault, regardless of any other operation. The stage was set for one of the most massive deception operations of the war.

The centerpiece of Operation FORTITUDE was the flamboyant and controversial Lieutenant General George S. Patton (q.v.), whom the Germans rated as probably the Allies' best tactical and operational commander. If Patton appeared to be in command of a force aimed at Pas de Calais, then it must be so. Lost on the Germans, however, was the fact that Patton was a general without command, a general still in disgrace.

Originally, Operation FORTITUDE was a part of an overall deception plan known as Operation BODYGUARD, which was a major plan to make the Germans look not only at the Pas de Calais area, but at Sweden and Norway as well as possible attack areas. While the Germans became increasingly concerned over Scandinavia, and indeed kept large numbers of troops there, Hitler and his advisers judged that Pas de Calais was where the Allies would attack.

Führer Directive Number 51, dated 3 November 1943, had the OKW (q.v.) more focused on the French channel coast for defenses, but there were those nagging doubts about other areas. Consequently, sufficient reinforcements were never sent to the Normandy area.

As all of the Allied deception plans were put in place, German intelligence reports began to talk about *"Armeegruppe Patton,"* and the OKW accepted these reports as proof that when the invasion came the main assault would be lead by Patton. Also, in Scotland, another fictitious army of twelve divisions under the command of Lieutenant General Andrew Thorne was fabricated. This British "Fourth Army" became another factor for German order of battle specialists to ponder. Fake radio messages and announcements of exercises involving both Patton's and Thorne's alleged massive commands were broadcast. For German intelligence the picture was one of two assaults, with Patton striking at Pas de Calais and Thorne striking at Norway. British MI-5 (q.v.) had a number of German agents who were now more than willing to work for the Allies to save themselves from the fate of captured spies, and their reports confirmed the view propagated by the Operation FORTITUDE planners.

There were camps set up with no soldiers, staffs from nonexistent divisions could be seen in British towns, and canvas and wood mock-ups of tanks and aircraft were constructed. German Field Marshal Gerd von Rundstedt (q.v.), one of the most experienced and steady German generals, firmly believed that Pas de Calais was the main objective of the cross-channel attack, and that if an assault came in the Normandy or Cherbourg area it would be a feint to draw needed troops from Pas de Calais.

What was at stake was keeping the powerful German Fifteenth Army tied down in Pas de Calais, while the decisive fighting raged in Normandy. Fifteenth Army controlled three corps and could deploy up to eighteen divisions. Operation FORTITUDE was aimed at making sure that Fifteenth Army did not move to reinforce German forces in Normandy.

When Operation OVERLORD began, German planners were certain that Normandy was a prelude for the major assault in Pas de Calais. OKW intelligence analysts continued to overestimate Allied strength by 50 percent, based on the successes of Operation FORTITUDE. They believed nearly fifty divisions under the "First U.S. Army Group" (FUSAG), commanded by the ruthless and hard-driving Patton, were poised to strike a blow at German defenses. It would have been the sensible thing to shift forces from Fifteenth Army to make up for the heavy casualties suffered by German defenders, but so great was the belief in Operation FORTITUDE that no forces moved.

Another German force remained idle in Norway. Operation FORTITUDE was achieving its major objective as German forces fighting in the hedgerows were being bled white. Hitler continued to deny permission to move any force, and even von Rundstedt continued to believe that an invasion was imminent throughout late June and early July. General Omar N. Bradley (q.v.), commander of U.S. ground forces for Operation OVERLORD, knew that the longer Operation FORTITUDE continued to deceive Hitler and the OKW, the better were his chances for tactical and operational success.

By the end of June, Allied intelligence detected the shift of the II SS *Panzer Korps* (9th and 10th SS *Panzer* Divisions) from the eastern front, while Fifteenth Army was still immobilized in Pas de Calais. Only one *Panzer* and two infantry divisions were detached from Fifteenth Army and moved into tactical assembly areas by late June, but there was no evidence that any other Fifteenth Army forces moved toward the Normandy area. The Germans preferred to shift the two SS *Panzer* divisions from the eastern front, rather than seriously weaken their defenses in Pas de Calais.

On 5 July, during a major reorganization of Allied forces, Operation FORTITUDE was reinforced by assigning all the mythical FUSAG units to Bradley's 12th Army Group, "except those specifically excepted," from the reorganization order. The impression was given to German intelligence that an attack on Pas de Calais by FUSAG was still planned, and that Patton would lead the daring assault. In reality, Patton was on his way to France to activate and take command of the U.S. Third Army.

As Patton's presence in France became known, it was announced that Lieutenant General Lesley J. McNair (q.v.) would assume operational command of FUSAG. McNair was killed in France on 15 July. His death was kept secret to avoid alerting the Germans that Operation FORTITUDE was indeed a very long and elaborate deception.

By early August, it was clear to German intelligence that Patton was in France and in command of American combat forces. By that time, it also was obvious that they had been deceived by Operation FORTITUDE, but by then it was too late to deploy the idle Fifteenth Army or any other forces. Normandy was secured and the Allies could not be turned back.

After World War II, the veil of secrecy was lifted on Operation FORTITUDE. One expert called it "perhaps the most complex and successful deception in the entire history of the war." Certainly the Germans were not aware of the magnitude of their blunder until August 1944. By that time, the Normandy foothold was firm, Patton was in the field, and Allied troops were relentlessly moving inland. By late August, Paris (q.v.) was liberated, and the Germans were in full retreat toward their own borders.

Three factors contributed to the success of Operation FORTITUDE: coordination, operational security, and the use of the well-known Patton. Operation FORTITUDE was coordinated up to the highest levels, and everyone understood that if it worked as planned, the chances for Operation OVERLORD's success increased. The operational security measures were extraordinary. There were very few indications that Operation FORTITUDE was not an actual plan of attack against Pas de Calais. The Germans, because of bogus radio traffic and reports of agents under British intelligence control, completed the picture of Operation FORTITUDE as an actual plan.

To use Patton as the commander of a nonexistent force, when Patton so wanted tactical and operational command in the field, had its risks. Patton was well-known for his tendency to talk too much at the worst times, but he maintained the fiction of FUSAG, and by doing so convinced the Germans that "America's best fighting general" would indeed lead the attack on Pas de Calais. Operation FORTITUDE stands as a masterpiece of deception, which worked for months and helped ensure Allied victory.

James J. Cooke

Additional Reading

Blumenson, Martin, *Breakout and Pursuit* (1961).
Brown, Anthony Cave, *Bodyguard of Lies* (1975).
Farago, Ladislas, *Patton: Ordeal and Triumph* (1963).
Howard, Michael, *British Intelligence in the Second World War.* Vol. V: *Strategic Deception* (1990).

France (10 May–21 June 1940)

[See map 17 on page 1327]

On 10 May 1940, Germany's *Fall GELB* (Case YELLOW) began to unfold as the war in Europe turned from *Sitzkrieg* to *Blitzkrieg*. A giant pincer movement of German armor swept into action from Dinant-Sedan to the North Sea. The main thrust, consisting principally of armor, pushed through the Ardennes Forest and smashed the French Meuse River line. The German *Panzer* forces exploited the breakthrough to trap masses of British and French troops in Belgium by cutting their supply lines to France. The offensive created havoc among Allied forces and reduced their defenses to shambles. How did it happen?

The Germans lacked the overwhelming superiority often credited to them. Their army was inferior in numbers to those of the Western Allies. The Germans attacked with 136 divisions, while the Allies—French, British, Belgian, and Dutch—fielded the equivalent of 156. Although German tank operations proved decisive, they had fewer and less powerful tanks than their opponents—about 2,800 against 4,000. Only in airpower were the Germans overwhelmingly superior, with more than 3,000 combat aircraft facing less than 2,000. Ironically, the fate of the Battle of France was decided in the Ardennes by a small portion of the massed German forces.

The German plan was to first take the Netherlands (q.v.), Belgium (q.v.), and Luxembourg. From these countries they would overrun France as well as secure air and naval bases for subsequent attacks on Britain. German leadership knew that a frontal assault on the Maginot Line (q.v.) would be costly. Their plan, superficially similar to the Schlieffen Plan (q.v.) of 1914, was to outflank these strong defensive forts by driving their mechanized forces across the Low Countries through Flanders in an arc toward Paris.

Allied officers, showing little imagination themselves, planned to defend as they had in 1914, by rushing the bulk of their forces into Belgium. These plans promised to result in the same "sterile and bloody" trench warfare reminiscent of World War I.

Doubts about the results of the attack led General Erich von Manstein (q.v.) to develop a change in the German plan, moving the center of gravity of the attack to the Meuse between Sedan and Dinant, allowing the *Panzer* forces to drive toward the lower Somme region, past Amiens and on to the sea. The French high command continued to believe that the main thrust would still be made through Holland and Belgium. Adolf Hitler (q.v.) quickly grasped the military significance of von Manstein's plan, which coincided with his own intuitions, and ordered it implemented.

This new plan, calling for a drive by tanks through the steep and wooded Ardennes, something not generally considered feasible, was surely one of the great master strokes of the entire war. It brought immediate and tragic consequences to the Allied cause. Historian A.J.P. Taylor has written that one can determine "with precise accuracy the moment when France was defeated." That moment was 1500 hours on 13 May 1940, "when the first German soldier crossed the Meuse."

Popular belief holds that the German plan succeeded because of French military defensive psychology. This is, at best, a partial truth. There were other reasons. Historian Louis Snyder writes, 'The myth of French military strength, notoriously exaggerated, was shattered by Hitler's fast-moving steel monsters. As it turned out the Germans were superior in . . . manpower, in leadership (and) in esprit de corps."

Surely, French overemphasis on defensive measures left the initiative to the Germans. The Maginot Line, running from the Swiss to the Belgian borders, which curiously aided the Germans more than the French, was the centerpiece of French defensive plans. At the outbreak of the war, 300,000 French soldiers marched into this defensive network and essentially played no part in deciding the outcome of the epic struggle.

From September 1939 until 10 May 1940, both sides, in a strange pseudo-war, avoided direct confrontations. French morale suffered during this "Phony War" (q.v.) and they even demobilized some of their forces. Misinterpreting the lessons of World War I, French military leaders held fast to the doctrine of the "continuous" front. Marshal Henri Philippe Pétain (q.v.) argued that adequate preparation could stop tanks, as the Soviets would prove later at Kursk (q.v.) in 1943. He also advocated the idea of the "return attack," which would avoid what he called a "premature" attack.

In 1940, the French Army simply was neither sufficiently well-equipped nor properly led to fight the defensive war expected of it. As events made clear, weak generalship was a critical factor. Top commanders were too old and too committed to past practices, while such young, dynamic leaders such as Charles de Gaulle, Alphonse Juin, Pierre Koenig, and Philippe Leclerc (qq.v.) had not yet fully emerged from the ranks. The government was weak and divided. Neither a Winston S. Churchill nor a Franklin D. Roosevelt (qq.v.) came forward.

Considering their own evident weakness, the British showed a strange mood of overconfidence as their troops arrived in France singing:

"We'll hang our washing on the Siegfried Line—if the Siegfried Line's still there!"

It was still there when they arrived, and when they left. It would be there when they returned four years later. Such braggadocio delighted Joseph Goebbels (q.v.). After the Dunkirk (q.v.) evacuation, German propaganda organs repeatedly played this song over the radio to the glee and derision of listening millions. To many Germans in those intoxicating days of 1940, war was still something glorious.

French opinion, always suspicious of British intentions, saw British dedication to a common victory as weak to nonexistent. "Perfidious Albion" was always willing to fight "to the last Frenchman." British trust of French capabilities and intentions was no better. Such attitudes did not make for an effective military alliance.

The early German success in the Low Countries was far less than decisive, but it drew Allied attention away from the Ardennes and trapped their best equipped and most mobile forces in Belgium, far from the critical Ardennes front. More than anything, it was the operational plans of General Maurice Gamelin (q.v.), the supreme commander of Allied land forces, that contributed to the German success. His operational strategy led his army straight into the trap that had been so carefully prepared for him. Military analyst Sir Basil Liddell Hart (q.v.) wrote, "By pushing into Belgium with their left shoulder forward, they played into the hands of their enemy." This maneuver was similar to the nearly disastrous Plan XVII of 1914. "I could have wept with joy," Hitler later exclaimed. "They have fallen into the trap."

Oddly, for all that was written about the debilitating effects of the French defensive strategy, it was their one offensive thrust of the war that doomed the entire French Army. Neither Gamelin nor his successors were able to rescue the French forces from their deadly predicament. Left facing General Heinz Guderian's (q.v.) Panzers at the critical point of attack in the Ardennes were three weak infantry divisions, consisting mostly of older men, ill-equipped and lacking adequate antitank weapons and air defenses.

General Ewald von Kleist (q.v.), commander of Panzergruppe Kleist, had the initial critical task of breaking through the Meuse Line and sweeping on to the North Sea. The Manstein plan required rapid movement through the rough Ardennes. Von Kleist positioned General Georg-Hans Reinhardt's (q.v.) XLI Panzer Korps on the northern flank, and Guderian's XIX Panzer Korps to the south. Following Guderian came General Gustav von Wietersheim's XIV Motorized Infantry Korps, with the foot soldiers of General Wilhelm List's (q.v.) Twelfth Army bringing up the rear. General Hermann Hoth's (q.v.) XV Panzer Korps, not directly under von Kleist, would cross the Meuse and cover his northern flank.

Guderian, a master of tank warfare, led the attack. Known as "der schnelle Heinz," he insisted on speed of operation. French military experts estimated it would take nine days for the Germans to reach the Meuse; Guderian said four, but he did it in two. French resistance was weak and poorly coordinated, although on 13 May *Panzer* attacks across the Meuse met furious resistance from machine gunners of the 42nd Colonial Demi-Brigade. All their courage, however, was no substitute for the lack of antitank guns. The German PzKpfw-IV tanks firing from the right bank blasted the French machine gun nests on the left bank.

German infantry crossed the Meuse on 13 May, and by 15 May, Guderian moved his tanks over in force and swept forward, ignoring all orders to halt. He drove his tanks almost unobstructed over French highways, often refueling at French service stations along the way. To the north, General Erwin Rommel's (q.v.) 7th *Panzer* Division crossed the Meuse by cable ferry and joined the battle. Guderian's right flank was well-protected, but the German high command worried about his left.

During the first four days of battle, *Panzergruppe Kleist* and the XV *Panzer Korps* destroyed eight divisions of the Second and Ninth Armies of General Gaston Billotte's (q.v.) 1st Army Group, and blasted a path for 2,200 German tanks and armored cars moving toward the Channel. This phase of the invasion, and the entire war, could have turned out much differently had the Germans found well-equipped French troops waiting for them on the left bank of the Meuse; but such was not the case.

Movement was rapid, with the German foot soldier making forty miles daily for nearly a week. Guderian's tanks forged far ahead, shooting up everything in their path. A French counterattack on 17 May was easily blunted. It did, however, throw a scare into the German high command, who remembered 1914, and feared another "Miracle of the Marne." German overconfidence that time contributed to a French victory, resulting in a stalemate and four years of bloody trench warfare.

One element in that 17 May counterattack was a tank unit led by an obscure brigadier general. Charles de Gaulle had been one of the French Army's earliest proponents of tank warfare. Taylor called the counterattack "an example of what the French could have done if their generals had been imbued with de Gaulle's offensive spirit." According to Liddel Hart, "The Battle of France is one of history's most striking examples of the decisive effect of a new idea, carried out by a dynamic executant."

By this time the French high command was in panic. In a telephone call early on 15 May, Premier Paul Reynaud (q.v.) told Churchill, "We are beaten: we have lost the battle." Churchill tried to reassure him by pointing out that Generals Gamelin and Georges (q.v.) were still confident. That evening, Gamelin, having lost his nerve broke down and stated, "It means the destruction of the French Army." The Germans were expected in Paris any day. Official papers were burned and Paris residents started fleeing the city.

On 19 May, sixty-eight-year-old Gamelin was sacked by Reynard in favor of seventy-three-year-old General Maxime Weygand (q.v.). The eighty-four-year-old Pétain of Verdun fame was recalled as ambassador to Spain to join the government. For better or worse, France would face what was, at best, an uncertain future with the command of its remaining forces in the hands of these aging veterans of earlier wars. Were they capable of coping with the rapidly deteriorating military situation? Weygand drew no-penetration lines on the map only to be informed that the rapidly moving Germans had already crossed them.

The Germans did not head for Paris as expected; Guderian moved instead toward the sea. He took Amiens and Abbeville on 20 May and reached the coast at Noyelles later that evening. On 21 May, the British Expeditionary Force (BEF) under Lord John Gort (q.v.), attacked with some resolve at Arras while trying to break through the German encirclement. A day later, a similar attack by French forces also failed. Two days after that, a French attack failed in the south. The Germans had by now established a strong defensive line across France. The Allied armies in Belgium were completely cut off and could be dealt with at will by the Germans.

For reasons never fully understood, the Germans then got cold feet. General Gerd von Rundstedt (q.v.), commander of Army Group A, feared that the French Army was still the fighting force of old and was nervous about the security of his left flank. He was fearful of losing too many of his prized tanks, soon to be needed for the second phase of the campaign through central France. Hitler, shared Von Rundstedt's fears. Marshal Hermann Göring (q.v.), resentful of the primary role played by the army commanders, asked that his *Luftwaffe* be allowed to finish off the beleaguered Allied troops that were starting to mass at Dunkirk. Some historians contend that Hitler did not want to embarrass the British who were, after all, "good Aryans." Possibly, all of these reasons played a role, but the historian must always beware of any single factor analysis. For whatever reason, Hitler halted his tanks for three days and permitted the "miracle of Dunkirk" to happen. Taylor holds that the Germans simply had not yet grasped "the full extent of their victory."

On 27 May, Lord Gort gave up any remaining hope of a French counterattack and decided to save his army. Initial expectations were that 10,000 troops could be saved. Fearing the worst, Churchill alerted the House of Commons that a disaster was in the making. The Dunkirk (q.v.) evacuation, however, exceeded all expectations. Göring's promise to finish the task with his *Luftwaffe* failed. British airpower inflicted heavy damage on German bombers, while protecting the 860 British vessels taking part in the evacuations. In all, 215,000 British and 123,000 French troops reached Britain safely. Through confusion over the evacuation procedures ordered by London, British forces were given priority over those of Allied countries, and 150,000 French troops were left behind.

In France, anti-British feelings, bad enough in the best of times, were enraged by this event. Had not retreat in the face of danger always been the British way out? Was it not so at Gallipoli in 1915, in Norway (q.v.) in June 1940, and now at Dunkirk? Because of such feelings, French participation in the evacuations was late and showed little enthusiasm. Ironically, some might even say bitterly, those 150,000 French soldiers remaining behind provided cover for the successful British evacuation. In Britain, the evacuation from Dunkirk was hailed as a great success, if not a victory. The British left behind large amounts of heavy equipment, but 200,000 of their soldiers would live to fight another day.

The battle for the rest of France began on 5 June. The French still had seventy divisions, including three British and two Polish divisions, plus the troops manning the Maginot Line. They established a continuous front following the "Weygand Line," running from the sea along the Somme River, the Crozat and Ailete Canals, and the Aisne River to Loguyon, just northeast of Verdun.

In his book *The Battle of France, 1940,* Colonel Adolph Goutard criticized the Weygand Plan for being "merely a return to the doctrine of the continuous front." Other critics have argued that his efforts to defend both the Maginot Line and Paris were not realistic. This is a spurious argument. After the loss of French industry in the north, retaining the industrial potential of Alsace and Lorraine (q.v.) was vital, and "*Paris sera Toujours Paris*" (a popular song title in 1940) could never be lightly sacrificed.

Considering the length of the front and the overall weakness of French forces, little hope could be held out for a successful defense against the pending German onslaught. Army Group A under von Rundstedt and Army Group B under General Fedor von Bock (q.v.) had a force of 143 divisions, seven more than on 10 May. With the outcome no longer in doubt, the second phase of the Battle of France was anticlimactic.

With superiority in numbers of men, quality of weapons, and with total command of the air, the

F

German soldiers parade along the Champs Eliseés and toward the Arc de Triomphe after the fall of Paris, 14 June 1940. (IWM PL 68706)

Wehrmacht moved south early on 5 June, starting from defensive lines established on the Somme. French defense forces often fought tenaciously but were unable to contain the German juggernaut. Von Bock wrote in his diary, "The French are defending themselves stubbornly." After 5 June, French troops gave a far better account of themselves than prior to that date, but efforts to halt the offensive at the Seine failed. The German Seventh Army forced a crossing east of Rouen on 8 June.

The German Fourth Army took Normandy and Brittany while others mopped up in the Champagne region and took the Maginot Line from the rear. The Second Army moved to the south of Lyons. The French Army no longer represented an organized force. The unequal struggle could no longer continue.

The crushing defeat of the French Army should not obscure French defensive efforts, often conducted with skill and daring. General Albrecht Schubert, commander of the XXIII *Korps,* wrote of his French foes: "The bearing and tactical skill of the enemy were totally different to [*sic*] those of earlier battles." Later he added, "The 14th Division fought on 9 and 10 June in a manner which recalls the attitude of the best French troops of 1914–1918 at Verdun." Similar acts of heroism occurred time and again, but were in vain in a war that was lost on 13 May, when Guderian's forces crossed the Meuse against inexcusably weak resistance.

The later, more tenacious French resistance can be attributed to Weygand who, despite his age, brought a new vigor and a grim determination to the struggle. One can only speculate what the difference might have been if the battle tactics and system of command he instituted had been in effect on 10 May. Before Weygand took command, for example, 135 Allied divisions caused 450 Germans killed or wounded per division. After Weygand took over, seventy-one Allied divisions more than tripled the number of casualties per division to 1,343. Put another way, the Germans suffered 61,200 casualties between 10 May and 3 June. Afterward, they suffered 93,300 inflicted by a greatly reduced force. The difference is noteworthy.

On 10 June, Italy declared war on an already beaten France to get in on the spoils of war. The outcome was little affected by this decision. Snyder writes, "The effect on France was negligible— Hitler had already won." The Germans entered Paris on 14 June. The French government had already moved to Tours and then to Bordeaux. An armistice was obtained with Hitler, the French Parliament voted itself out of existence, and inter-nal political power was conferred upon Pétain. France lost 92,000 killed, 250,000 wounded, and almost a half-million prisoners in a cause worthy of better results. Germany lost 28,000 soldiers killed, 111,000 wounded, and 18,000 missing.

On 21 June 1940, in Marshal Ferdinand Foch's old railroad car at Compiègne, where the Germans surrendered to the Allies in 1918, the German conquerors imposed cruel and bitter terms on their defeated foe. This was the most humiliating defeat in the history of France. No great power had ever fallen so far so fast. German forces would occupy more than half of France, including a 100 kilometer strip of the Atlantic coastline down to the Spanish border. A French rump state was allowed to exist south of the Loire River until November 1942, but the government could not be anti-German. For its duration, Pétain ruled over what became known as Vichy France (q.v.).

France, a very rich country, would now pay dearly for its military weakness. The German expenses incurred during the fighting and four years of military occupation were paid for many times over through occupation costs imposed. Taylor has written, "The Germans found in French storage depots enough oil both for the Battle of Britain and the first great campaign in Russia." He estimates that the occupation costs imposed would have kept an 18-million-man army in the field permanently.

The French people could now look forward to more than four years of harsh military occupation by a brutal enemy, flush with victory and determined to impose its values and order upon its defeated neighbor.

Paul J. Rose

Additional Reading
Beaufre, John, *1940: The Fall of France* (1967).
Goutard, Adolph, *The Battle of France 1940* (1958).
Horne, Alistair, *To Lose a Battle: France 1940* (1969).
Liddell Hart, Basil, *History of the Second World War* (1970).
Mendelssohn, P. de, *Design for Aggression: The Inside Story of Hitler's War Plans* (1946).
Taylor, A.J.P., *The Second World War* (1975).

France, Northern (6 June–September 1944)

[See map 18 on page 1328]
By June 1944, the majority of the German Army

was engaged on the Russian front, The remainder, some 45 percent, was scattered over various other fronts, largely as a result of the Italian campaign. For the defense of northern Europe there were some fifty divisions in northern France, Holland, and Belgium and in reserve in Germany. Only the *Panzer* and SS *Panzer* divisions, however, were fully up to strength in men and materiel. Field Marshal Gerd von Rundstedt (q.v.) was commander in chief west (*OB-West*). Under him was Field Marshal Erwin Rommel (q.v.), commander of Army Group B. Rommel's Seventh and Fifteenth Armies held a front from Holland to Brittany along the Atlantic coast with thirty-two infantry divisions and one *Panzer* division. Rommel also had operational control of another three *Panzer* divisions from von Rundstedt's strategic reserve of six *Panzer* and one *Panzergrenadier* divisions. The remaining divisions of the reserve could only be used on Adolph Hitler's (q.v.) personal authority.

There was a dichotomy in German defensive thinking to combat the expected Allied invasion. Those like Rommel favored defeating the assault on the beaches, with little depth and reserve, arguing (correctly, as events would soon prove) that Allied air supremacy would prevent the movement of German reserves. The Rundstedt school favored holding a "crust" on the coast backed by a large *Panzer* reserve in depth. Hitler's divided control of the *Panzers*, resulting in their piecemeal commitment, was a tactical compromise.

The Germans were convinced the Allies would assault across the shortest stretch of sea and land at the Pas de Calais. That area, therefore, was given priority in strength and reinforcement. This conviction, reinforced by a large and complex Allied deception plan (*see* FORTITUDE, Operation), was so strong that even six weeks after D-Day the Germans still refused to move divisions from Calais to Normandy.

An intensive bombing plan in the weeks preceding D-Day seriously damaged the French railway system, destroyed road bridges, and damaged German airfields. This interdiction hindered the movement of reserves and disrupted the German logistics chain from the Ruhr. Shortly after dawn on 6 June (D-Day), the Allies assaulted on a five-division front of fifty miles between Cherbourg and La Harve in Normandy; two U.S. divisions on the right and three British and Canadian on the left. Two U.S. and one British airborne divisions were dropped during the night 5–6 June to provide flank protection for the assault and (in the U.S. case) to secure some beach exits.

The weather was bad with a force-5 wind making rough seas. This caused some assaulting formations to miss their planned touch-down positions by as much as 1,000 yards, and on all beaches the high seas caused considerable losses to amphibious tanks and landing craft (q.v.). German resistance varied according to the density of the troops defending the beach, and while some formations had a relatively easy beach assault and were able to move quickly inland, others had a hard fight. U.S. V Corps was pinned down all day on OMAHA Beach, suffering heavy casualties. The assault was supported by heavy naval gunfire and bombing and ground attack from the air.

By nightfall on D-Day, the Allies established beachheads extending three miles inland on the right with U.S. VII Corps, and five miles inland on the British left. By dusk, V Corps managed to get off the beach and advance a mile inland. The beachheads, however, were not continuous.

Thanks to the convoluted German chain of command, the only attempted counterattack by armor on D-Day was from the 21st *Panzer* Division. It faltered with the tanks unable to get through the vital road center of Caen because of heavy bomb damage. Although established ashore, the Allies failed to reach their objectives planned for the end of D-Day by General Bernard L. Montgomery (q.v.), to whom General Dwight D. Eisenhower (q.v.) had delegated tactical ground command.

Montgomery had planned for the British-Canadian divisions to capture Caen and the high ground beyond it by the end of D-Day. The whole Allied landing area was supposed to be a continuous bridgehead. Then he planned to hold firm on the left, attracting the bulk of the German armor and reserves—since Caen guarded the best approach to the airfields around Paris—while U.S. forces swiftly secured the Brittany peninsula and the vital port of Cherbourg. The Allies would then pivot on Caen and execute a massive right hook to the Seine. In the event, however, by the end of D-Day, the British were three miles short of Caen and U.S. forces were meeting stubborn resistance in their attempt to link up. It took a further five days to establish all landing areas into one continuous bridgehead. In the British and Canadian sectors, a stubborn resistance stopped any movement toward Caen, and a counterattack by three *Panzer* divisions two days after D-Day nearly broke through to the coast.

The Allied forces found fighting in the compact, flat, high-hedgerow, and sunken-lane countryside of Normandy a hard, grinding task. Nonetheless, Montgomery's plan was working. The U.S.

F

front was facing, at this stage, no *Panzer* divisions, while three already had been drawn into the battle for Caen.

By 18 June, the situation in Normandy was rapidly turning into a stalemate. Adverse weather delayed the Allied buildup so that only twenty divisions now ashore faced eighteen German divisions, albeit most of them understrength. To retain the initiative, Montgomery ordered the U.S. First Army to drive west, seal off the Cotentin peninsula to isolate Cherbourg, and then capture it. At the same time, he ordered a fresh drive to take Caen (q.v.). Both the U.S. and British were to use new corps about to land. On that same day, Adolf Hitler (q.v.) launched his V-1 offensive (q.v.) on London from the Calais area.

Hitler remained convinced the main Allied assault was still to come in the Calais area, retaining large forces there to protect the V-1 sites and repulse the expected landings. On 19 June, an unprecedented gale blew until 22 June, delaying the arrival of the reinforcing corps and causing the postponement of both U.S. and British attacks. Damage to the artificial harbors (q.v.) was so bad that by the last day of the storm, the U.S. First Army was down to just a three-day stock of ammunition. The British harbor at Arromanches survived, but the American one at UTAH Beach was destroyed.

On 25 June, the postponed British attack to envelop Caen by a right hook was launched with enormous air and artillery support. It made slow progress, for the German Army fought desperately. The ferocity of the teenagers of the *Hitlerjugend* Division staggered the fresh British troops, most of whom had never been in battle before. Movement forward was impeded by three divisions being crammed into a two-mile-wide corridor with few roads. Every village became a horrendous bottleneck. By 29 June, the corridor was only six miles deep and that day a complete SS *Panzer Korps* arrived from the Russian front. Although the attack for Caen was halted, the plan for the British to engage and pin down German armor and reserves was working. Of the eight *Panzer* divisions now in Normandy, seven and a half were facing the British.

In the U.S. sector, Cherbourg was taken by the end of June. Delays in the buildup of men and materiel, the flooded terrain, and fanatical defense of a series of strong points, hampered U.S. operations, and postponed the planned U.S. breakout. Montgomery tried to break the deadlock with another all-out assault on Caen, coinciding with a fresh U.S. attempt to get through the German

defensive line. In early July, Hitler at last recognized that the Normandy landings were the main Allied effort and released infantry divisions from the Calais area.

On 8 July, preceded by a massed air raid intended to pulverize the German defenses, the British launched three divisions head-on at Caen with massed artillery, naval, and close air support. A total of 2,600 tons of bombs reduced Caen to rubble and caused many civilian casualties. The Germans suffered relatively few casualties, however, because most of their defensive positions were within the safety zone six kilometers from the Allied front line.

After bitter fighting, the assault, immobilized by the rubble, ground to a halt along the river line through the center of the city. U.S. operations also were slowed by German counterattacks. Thus by 9 July, the Allies were at their D-Day objective of Caen, but not in possession of it nor the real prize, the commanding heights beyond the city. The repeated British and Canadian assaults on Caen were drawing the bulk of the German *Panzers*, but the issue was still finely balanced. The arrival of fresh German divisions from Calais allowed the battered XLVII *Panzer Korps* to withdraw to rest and refit prior to a planned move west to mount a counteroffensive aimed at driving through the U.S. sector, splitting the Allies in two, and destroying them piecemeal.

This coincided with a crisis point on the British-Canadian front. In rough terms, two infantrymen were becoming casualties for every reinforcement available. At that rate of attrition the pool of reserves would be expended in fourteen days. The situation for armor was better; many tanks were lost but comparatively few crews. These two factors convinced Montgomery to launch Operation GOODWOOD, his much-maligned armored drive for the hills beyond Caen. Preceded again by the Allied strategic air forces—but with a fatal pause between the end of the air attack and the beginning of the ground assault—the drive petered out with vast losses in tanks. Too few infantry with the assaulting tanks, a mass of armor and vehicles in too confined a space, and an incredibly courageous and improvised defense by the Germans were the reasons for GOODWOOD's failure.

Failure or not, two German *Panzer Korps* remained in the Caen sector and the assault on U.S. forces did not take place. On 25 July, the U.S. First Army launched its breakout at St. Lô (q.v.). During the first two days it gained only two miles against strong resistance. Then the dogged persistence of the American infantry prevailed and breaches were made, loosening the U.S. armor. By 29 July, the Cherbourg peninsula was sealed off at its base and U.S. units turned South. The U.S. VII Corps reached Avranches on 31 July. At that time, the British front had advanced six miles and the whole Allied lodgement was still only a triangle with the corners at Caen, Avranches, and Cherbourg. Although holding strongly at Caen, the German line at the Avranches end was visibly cracking.

Montgomery decided to regroup and strike at the German center, the junction of British and U.S. forces at Caumont. From there the U.S. First Army would wheel left to the Seine, and the U.S. Third Army would wheel right to the west to take Brittany as a secure base. The U.S. VII Corps advanced southwest and two other U.S. corps attacked south, with their left flank on the west bank of the Drome River coinciding with the British attack with its right flank on the east bank. On 1 August, General George S. Patton's (q.v.) U.S. Third Army took control of VIII Corps and started its great drive west, clearing most of the Brittany peninsula in just five days. At that point the Allies had four field armies in France—the U.S. First and Third Armies under the 12th Army Group, and the British Second and Canadian First Armies under the 21st Army Group. Montgomery retained overall ground command.

German reinforcements, including two Panzer divisions, were rushed to Normandy in early August. Hitler denuded the Biscay, Mediterranean, and Calais sectors, finally recognizing that the decisive battle was in Normandy. Montgomery directed both the 12th and 21st Army Groups to strike south, east, and north to encircle the Germans in the Falaise area. The Germans, however, made one last counterattack. By Hitler's direct order, the concentrated strength of the remaining four Panzer divisions struck toward Avranches. They were held by the U.S. 30th Division near Mortain (q.v.) and hammered by the full weight of the Allied air forces. Apart from retaking Mortain, the German attack never hindered Patton.

On 13 August, U.S. forces moving north were within twenty-five miles of the Canadians, moving south to close the mouth of the trap. The remainder of the Allied forces, having encircled the Germans, were steadily reducing the perimeter. Desperate fighting by the Germans held the mouth open for the next five days. Great destruction, particularly in materiel, was meted out to the Germans trying to escape the net. Approximately 100,000 troops were trapped in the Falaise (q.v.) pocket, or "The Cauldron" as it became known.

There was, however, no capitulation. Although mopping up continued until the end of August, such was the tenacity of the battle-hardened German divisions, particularly the Panzers, that just under half escaped east across the Seine River.

The Allies were along the west bank of the Seine by the latter part of August. Paris (q.v.) was liberated on 25 August and the U.S. Seventh Army, which landed in southern France (q.v.) on 15 August, was advancing north to link up with Patton. On 1 September 1944, Eisenhower assumed direct command of all Allied ground forces in France, and Montgomery reverted to command of the 21st Army Group. Contrary to expectation, the Germans made no attempt to stand at the Seine, but withdrew to a line along the Albert Canal in Belgium, the River Meuse, and the Upper Moselle on the southwest German frontier.

Eisenhower gave orders for a broad advance by all armies to the Rhine River. Initially large distances were gained. In some cases, both U.S. and British forces advanced 250 miles in six days. Pockets of German resistance were still met, with the U.S. First Army capturing 25,000 prisoners in one action in the Forêt de Compiègne. The Canadian First Army met strong resistance from garrisons holding the Channel ports, while the British Second Army captured the vital port of Antwerp (q.v.) on 4 September. The Scheldt (q.v.) estuary connecting Antwerp to the sea took until 28 November to completely clear.

In mid-September, Montgomery devised a plan to seize crossings over rivers in Holland, culminating in a bridge over the Rhine at Arnhem (q.v.). Such a move would enable him to bypass the Siegfried Line (q.v.) and swing into the Ruhr, Germany's industrial heart, from the north. To carry out Operation MARKET-GARDEN, Eisenhower placed the Allied airborne corps of three divisions under Montgomery's command. Montgomery hoped that the British Second Army would advance to the Ruhr literally over a paratroop carpet holding the crossings. Mounted on 17 September, the plan was only two-thirds successful. The U.S. airborne divisions held their objectives, but the British airborne division, dropped at the farthest bridge, Arnhem, was unable to hold out for the nine days it took advancing troops to reach them.

By the end of October, the momentum of the Allied advance had slowed in the face of intense German defense and extremely overstretched lines of communication. There were now fifty-three Allied divisions along a line from Holland to Switzerland, connected to their main administrative bases—still at the Normandy beaches and Cherbourg—by a tenuous 500-mile supply line. Eisenhower's hopes of ending the war in 1944 were over. Hard up against the German West Wall (q.v.), a long and bitter winter campaign lay ahead.

B.K. Warner

Additional Reading

Bradley, Omar, *A Soldier's Story* (1951).
Eisenhower, Dwight, *Crusade in Europe* (1948).
Huston, James A., *Across the Face of France: Liberation and Recovery* (1963).
Montgomery, Bernard, *The Memoirs of Field-Marshal the Viscount Montgomery of Alamein* (1958).
Weigley, Russell F., *Eisenhower's Lieutenants: The Campaigns of France and Germany, 1944–45* (1981).

France, Southern (15 August–15 September 1944)

[See map 18 on page 1328]
At the Quebec Conference in August 1943, American military leaders presented a proposal for the invasion of southern France. The operation, code named ANVIL, was to take place at the same time as the planned landings in Normandy (q.v.) and would act as a supporting attack to Operation OVERLORD. At the Cairo Conference in November 1943, the Allied Combined Chiefs of Staff (q.v.) decided that the planning of Operation ANVIL should go ahead. The plan was then approved by President Franklin D. Roosevelt, Prime Minister Winston S. Churchill, and by Premier Josef Stalin (qq.v.) at the Teheran Conference (*see* Conferences, Allied).

The Americans forwarded three reasons for pursuing Operation ANVIL: (1) it would engage up to eleven German divisions and prevent them from interfering with the landings in Normandy; (2) it would draw German reserves from northern and central France to the south; and (3) it would liberate all of southern and central France.

By the spring of 1944, however, the whole operation was in doubt. The necessary men and materiel needed for an operation in southern France were unavailable as a result of the massive requirements for Operation OVERLORD, combined with the need to sustain the depleted Allied armies in northern Italy. On 21 March 1944, General Dwight D. Eisenhower (q.v.), Allied commander in chief in northwest Europe, decided that Operation ANVIL could not be carried out simultaneously with the landings in Normandy. ANVIL was delayed and the landing craft (q.v.) assembled for the assault were then transferred to Britain from the Mediterranean for use in Operation OVERLORD.

The transfer of the landing craft helped to fuel a bitter clash between the Americans and the British over the best strategy to defeat Germany. The debate about whether Operation ANVIL was necessary or not would continue until a week before it actually occurred.

Both British and American leaders agreed that the landings in Normandy were the first priority for the Allied war effort in the west. The key issue was how the Allied armies in Italy could best be used to help defeat Germany. Churchill and Field Marshal Sir Harold Alexander (q.v.), Allied commander in chief in Italy, felt that any landing in southern France that was not simultaneous with Operation OVERLORD would mean squandering Allied forces that could better be used elsewhere. They felt that any major effort in the Mediterranean region should support Alexander's forces in Italy.

On 7 June, Alexander proposed that he should attempt to follow up recent Allied victories by pushing into northern Italy. Thereafter, the Allied armies could turn east toward Vienna or west toward Turin, and then into France. This would require leaving all of the forces for Operation ANVIL in Italy at Alexander's disposal. Churchill also had his own plan for an amphibious operation against the Istrian peninsula at the head of the Adriatic Sea, where Allied forces could move through the Ljubljana gap into Austria and Hungary.

Eisenhower still believed that Operation ANVIL was essential to the success of Operation OVERLORD. Even a later landing in southern France would still force the Germans to keep forces away from Normandy, would assist the supply situation by capturing major French ports on the Mediterranean coast, and would allow more French soldiers to fight in their own country. Eisenhower had the full support of Roosevelt in the debate over Operation ANVIL. Since the Americans and the French bore the brunt of the proposed operation, it went ahead over the concerns of the British.

On 2 July, the operation's code name was changed from ANVIL to DRAGOON for security reasons. Scheduled for 15 August, the operation called for landings along a forty-five-mile stretch of the French Riviera coastline in the region of Provence. The initial assault wave would contain three experienced U.S. infantry divisions withdrawn from operations in Italy. Over the next few days, seven French divisions would land in support of the Americans. After gaining control of the landing zones, these forces would head for the naval base at Toulon, the port of Marseilles, and up the Rhône River valley leading north into central France.

Churchill made one last attempt to stop Operation DRAGOON when, on 4 August, he suggested that the Allies should make an amphibious assault on the Brittany peninsula to help the American forces near St. Lô (q.v.). Eisenhower opposed such a late change in plans and rejected Churchill's proposal.

The ground force for Operation DRAGOON was the U.S. Seventh Army, commanded by Lieutenant General Alexander Patch (q.v.). The Seventh Army consisted of the U.S. VI Corps, led by Major General Lucian Truscott, and French Army B, under General Jean de Lattre de Tassigny (qq.v.). Patch also had under his operational control the Provisional Airborne Task Force, the American-Canadian 1st Special Service Force (q.v.), and various French commando units. Operation DRAGOON's naval force, the Western Task Force of 835 warships and more than 1,300 smaller vessels and landing craft, was commanded by Vice Admiral H. Kent Hewitt (q.v.). The Mediterranean Allied Air Forces contributed more than 4,000 aircraft in support of the operation.

For two weeks prior to the invasion, Allied air forces attacked military targets along the Mediterranean coast from the Spanish border to Genoa. Special attention was paid to Marseilles, Toulon, and Genoa to prevent tipping off the Germans as to the actual location of the landings. On the morning of the invasion, forty-seven warships from five nations bombarded the landing beaches with 15,900 shells.

The activities of the Allied invasion fleet actually began on 9 August when the three American divisions were loaded into their transports in Naples. The fleet sailed from ports in Italy and North Africa and assembled west of Corsica. The convoy sailed north toward Genoa as a deception, but on the night of 14–15 August, it turned southwest toward France.

The German coastal defenses in Provence were weak in August of 1944. Central and southern France from the Atlantic to Italy was under the control of Army Group G, commanded by General Johannes Blaskowitz (q.v.). The Nineteenth Army, led by General Friedrich Wiese, was situated in southern France. In June, the Nineteenth Army

had fourteen divisions, but it lost four of them, including two of its three *Panzer* divisions, after the Allied landings in Normandy. On 2 August, Blaskowitz told the German Army high command, "The strength of the Nineteenth Army no longer guarantees a successful defense of the coast."

On 15 August, Wiese's forces amounted to one *Panzer* and seven infantry divisions to defend a stretch of coastline 400 miles long. Of his 59,000 troops, only two divisions, comprising the LXII *Korps,* were in the actual landing area. Another 170,000 German soldiers were located in southern France, but would require at least two days to reach the coast. Blaskowitz's air and naval defenses were also hopelessly understrength in comparison to the Allied naval and air forces.

On the morning of 15 August, three U.S. infantry divisions, the 3rd (Force Alpha), 45th (Force Delta), and 36th (Force Camel), landed along the coast from Cavalaire, twenty-five miles east of Toulon, to Saint-Raphaël, ten miles west of Cannes. The American forces made good progress as German resistance on the beaches was light. Establishing the beachheads cost 320 troops killed, most as a result of land and sea mines. By nightfall, more than 60,000 soldiers and 6,700 vehicles were ashore.

That same morning, other Allied landings and paratroop drops took place. The Anglo-American Provisional Airborne Task Force with 9,000 soldiers, commanded by Major General Robert Frederick (q.v.), dropped onto the rail and road center of Le Muy, thirteen miles inland. Two thousand Americans and Canadians of the 1st Special Service Force surprised the German coastal batteries on the islands of Port-Cros and Levant, south of the landing area. Other Allied special forces carried out their duties east and west of the main landings.

It soon became clear to the Americans that the German coastal forces were retreating. With little fear of a counterattack, the Allies reinforced their formations along the coast by bringing ashore the I and II Corps of French Army B from 16 to 18 August. On 17 August, German Army Group G received orders to pull all of its forces out of central and southern France. This included the Nineteenth Army in southern France and the First Army in southwestern France. Only those units defending port cities along the Atlantic and Mediterranean coasts were to remain in place. Blaskowitz's forces were ordered to join with Army Group B near Dijon in eastern France. The Nineteenth Army was ordered to retreat slowly up the Rhône River valley as a rear guard against the ad-

F

vancing Allied forces. This would allow the First Army time to withdraw from southwestern France.

On 19 August, Patch ordered French Army B to capture Toulon and Marseilles, while the U.S. VI Corps headed north and west toward Avignon and Grenoble. The Airborne Task Force was ordered to cover the VI Corps's right flank by securing a defensive line west of Cannes. The three U.S. divisions and a newly created armored unit, Task Force Butler, had to follow the Rhône River valley and the Grenoble corridor through the more mountainous terrain to the north.

The French II Corps was allotted the task of taking the well-fortified ports of Toulon and Marseilles. French units encircled the cities, isolating them from any possible reinforcements. Then the cities were successfully attacked from various directions. On 28 August, after ten days of fighting, Toulon and Marseilles fell—which was much more quickly than Allied planners had expected. The French suffered 4,000 casualties and took 37,000 Germans prisoner. The main ports of southern France, although severely damaged, were now in Allied hands and would be in operation by 4 September.

Between 21 and 28 August, the heaviest fighting of the campaign in southern France took place around the town of Montélimar. The Nineteenth Army was attempting to retreat along roadways on the east side of the Rhône River. The VI Corps was ordered to prevent the German forces from escaping to the north. Elements of the 36th Infantry Division and Task Force Butler blocked the highway north of Montélimar but were not strong enough to prevent five German divisions from breaking through. By spreading out to the west side of the Rhône and forcing their way through the gaps in the American roadblock, the German units were able to extricate themselves from the trap. The American units covering the roadblock were outnumbered and were low on ammunition and gasoline.

Crucial Allied air support was minimal because Montélimar was out of range for aircraft based in Corsica. As a result of the rapid Allied advance, there was insufficient time for engineers to build the required airstrips in southern France. When the gap was finally closed on 28 August, many of the Germans had already escaped north, although at the cost of 57,000 POWs and most of their equipment. Lieutenant General Jacob Devers (q.v.) later said: "At the end of the battle, for twenty miles south of Montélimar, both sides of the highway were littered with destroyed guns, trucks, automobiles, wagons, and armored vehicles bumper to bumper."

Elsewhere, the Anglo-American Airborne Task Force captured Cannes on 24 August and Nice on 30 August, securing the east flank of VI Corps from any possible German reinforcements from northern Italy. By 1 September, the entire French Mediterranean coast was under Allied control. After the battle around Montélimar, German forces stopped to fight only if their evacuation routes were threatened by Allied advances. Seeing this, Patch was forced to decide whether the Seventh Army should stop and regroup or press on at full speed with tired and depleted forces. He issued new orders on 29 August stating that the Seventh Army would continue northward at full speed in an attempt to cut off the retreating Germans. The VI Corps was to spearhead the attack through Lyons, the French II Corps was to advance west of the Rhône River on the left flank, and the French I Corps was to slip behind the VI Corps and head northeast toward the Swiss border.

What developed was an all-out race for the Belfort gap in eastern France. If the Germans reached this area, they could link up with Army Group B and create a defensive line along the Vosges Mountains in Alsace. If the Allies arrived at Belfort first, the Germans would be cut off from their only means of escape.

The French I Corps and U.S. VI Corps got to within thirty miles of Belfort by early September but were halted by German defense forces, especially the 11th *Panzer* Division under the brilliant leadership of Major General Wend von Wietersheim. The Seventh Army was unable to close the gap before the German forces passed into Alsace. The Nineteenth Army thereupon established a defensive line following its twenty-eight-day retreat covering more than 400 miles. The French and Americans stopped and regrouped their forces in front of the new German front line.

On the western flank, the French I Corps first linked up with General George S. Patton's (q.v.) U.S. Third Army on 11 September at Sombernon. Southwest France was now permanently cut off from the north. Since 17 August, the German First Army, commanded by General Kurt von der Chevallerie, had been evacuating southwestern France. The only forces left behind were the 86,000 troops manning the garrisons of the ports that Adolf Hitler (q.v.) had ordered to be defended to the last as "fortresses." Most of the port garrisons fell in August and September, but those in Lorient and Saint Nazaire were not attacked by the Allies and remained in place until the end of the war. During its withdrawal, the German First Army was harassed continually by the French Forces of the

Interior (q.v.). With the linkup of the U.S. Third and Seventh Armies, many German troops were trapped in the southwest and subsequently were gathered up by the French resistance.

At midnight on 14–15 September, Operation DRAGOON officially ended when the Seventh Army was transferred from the Mediterranean to the northwest European Theater of Operations. At that time, Devers's 6th Army Group came into existence as the right flank of the Allied front. French Army B became the French First Army. The new army group held two sectors of the front: the Alpine sector from the Mediterranean coast to the Swiss border facing Italy; and the main sector to the north, from Switzerland to Patton's Third Army.

DRAGOON was an operational success. It took only thirty days to reach its objective, instead of the ninety days the planners had expected. Total Allied casualties were slightly less than 14,000. Even though the Seventh Army was not able to destroy German Army Group G, it did capture 79,000 Germans. Southern France was liberated, and another Allied army group was brought into the fight on the western front.

Ken Reynolds

Additional Reading

Clarke, Jeffrey J., and Robert Ross Smith, *Riviera to the Rhine* (1993).

Weigley, Russell F., *Eisenhower's Lieutenants: The Campaigns of France and Germany, 1944–1945* (1981).

FRANTIC, Operation (June–September 1944)

AWPD/1, the U.S. Army Air Force's basic war plan, considered the possibility of operations from Soviet bases. In October 1943, the same month as the second disastrous raid on Schweinfurt (q.v.), Army Air Force chief General Henry H. Arnold (q.v.) succeeded in getting the inclusion of a proposal for shuttle bombing involving Soviet bases as one of the objectives of the new military mission in Moscow headed by Major General John R. Deane.

The Americans hoped to accomplish a number of things through this operation. First, Arnold and his subordinates wanted to stretch the *Luftwaffe* to the breaking point by forcing it to disperse its strength to cover three air "fronts." Second, American leaders in general wanted to show the Soviets that, in the absence of a "Second Front" in France, the Western Allies were waging war on Germany with everything at their disposal.

Third, Army Air Force generals wished to impress the Soviets with the contribution of strategic air forces to the joint effort against Germany.

Finally, and perhaps most importantly, the Americans were anxious to secure Soviet approval for the use of Siberian bases in the air war against Japan. If Operation FRANTIC, as the shuttle operation to Russia was called, was successful, this approval might be easier to secure and a precedent for such joint effort established.

Soviet reaction to the initial American proposal was cool at first although Foreign Minister Vyacheslav Molotov (q.v.) agreed "in principle" in October 1943 and Soviet Premier Josef Stalin (q.v.) gave his assent at the Teheran Conference in December. The Americans were quick to realize that this "agreement in principle" meant little and it was not until February 1944 that Stalin told U.S. Ambassador W. Averell Harriman (q.v.) that he "favored" the idea.

By March, the Americans secured the use of three bases in the Ukraine. Through March, April, and May work at Poltava, Mirgorod, and Piryatin progressed at a rapid rate. Located in the war-ravaged region between Kiev and Kharkov, the bases were rebuilt from the ground up. Soviet personnel, under American supervision, used a mix of U.S. and Soviet-supplied materials to extend the runways to accommodate heavy bombers, and built hangars, control towers, and other essential facilities.

American personnel began to arrive in March, though the Soviets limited the total U.S. ground establishment to 1,200. They agreed to provide laborers, kitchen personnel, guards, and the like, while the Americans brought in specialists, interpreters, and their own medical staff. Despite problems with group visas, the sometimes ponderous pace at which the Soviets operated, and wrangling over communications and target selection, the bases were essentially ready to receive aircraft by the end of May. To exercise control over the three bases, the U.S. Strategic Air Forces (USSTAF) established the Eastern Command under Major General Robert L. Walsh, who in turn reported to Deane.

With the Eighth Air Force absorbed in intensive operations against the Germans in northwest Europe in preparation for Operation OVER-LORD, USSTAF commander General Carl A. Spaatz (q.v.) chose the Fifteenth Air Force to conduct the first Operation FRANTIC mission. Code named FRANTIC JOE, this mission took place on 2 June 1944, with Lieutenant General Ira C. Eaker (q.v.) in the lead. The Americans wanted to leave nothing to chance so as to make a good im-

F

pression on the Soviets and distract the Germans during the final days before Operation OVERLORD. From this beginning, the Americans hoped eventually to operate three full bombardment groups from Soviet soil at the rate of 800 bomber sorties a month.

From a political and diplomatic standpoint, the mission of 2 June was a resounding success, despite initial U.S. and Soviet disagreement over the choice of targets. Eaker was enthusiastic about the operation and looked forward to a fruitful period of U.S./Soviet cooperation while exultant press releases played up the idea of Russo-American comradeship-in-arms.

The first Eighth Air Force mission of Operation FRANTIC, however, did not end on such a high note. On 21 June 1944, 114 B-17s and 70 P-51s struck at targets in the area of Berlin and went on to land at Eastern Command bases. A German reconnaissance aircraft trailed the task force to its bases, and that evening a force of 150 *Luftwaffe* bombers struck Poltava. The Germans destroyed forty-three B-17s and fifteen Mustangs while damaging twenty-six other bombers. Vast quantities of fuel and ammunition, so laboriously stockpiled during the preceding months, were also destroyed.

The Germans struck Mirgorod the following night, but the American aircraft there were dispersed earlier in the day. The Soviets, who assumed responsibility for air base defense, failed to bring down a single German raider. Hobbled, Eastern Command continued to work in a spirit of cooperation with the Soviets in order to salvage Operation FRANTIC.

With the accelerating success of the Soviet summer offensive, continuing lack of protection at Eastern Command bases, and further disagreements over target selection, Operation FRANTIC's role diminished rapidly. The Fifteenth Air Force flew several fighter-bomber missions to Eastern Command through July and into early August while Eighth Air Force bombers engaged in only three more shuttle missions on 6 August, 11 September, and 18 September. This latter mission did not involve bombing activity but was a politically charged supply-drop to Polish insurgents fighting the Germans in Warsaw (q.v.).

By this time, Operation FRANTIC bases were so far east of the Russo-German front that they served little purpose. All of Hitler's drastically reduced empire could be hit from bases in either Britain or Italy. Following the Warsaw mission, Eastern Command stood down as a mere 200 caretaker personnel remained through the winter at Poltava, while the other two bases reverted to So-

viet control as requested by Molotov in August. Thus, events conspired to keep Operation FRANTIC from ever developing into the hoped-for 800 monthly sorties.

Militarily, Operation FRANTIC had scant impact on the air war. Most of the sixteen targets actually hit could have been reached with far less expenditure of effort from either Britain or Italy. USSTAF intelligence concluded that at least a few aircraft were saved by using the Soviet bases.

The Soviets did not become easier to work with as a result of Operation FRANTIC. Though they once again agreed "in principle" to American units operating from Siberia at some point in the future, those operations failed to materialize. The Soviets also did not rethink their air doctrine to accommodate strategic operations, nor did they see their role in defeating Hitler as diminished by America's presence on the eastern front. Only at the lowest levels was true cooperation and friendship on a large scale evident. The Germans did not significantly reorient their defenses, and indeed they were given a great morale boost through their stunning victory at Poltava at a time when Germany's armed forces were everywhere in retreat.

Thus, in retrospect, it is evident that Operation FRANTIC failed to live up to American expectations as either a military operation or a diplomatic endeavor. Uneasy with an American presence on Soviet soil, Stalin may have tolerated Operation FRANTIC as a concession to the Americans for their Lend-Lease (q.v.) aid or to dispel German propaganda about the floundering "Grand Alliance." Whatever the Soviet motives, they immediately made it clear by late summer 1944 that Operation FRANTIC was of marginal value to them and then proceeded to move quickly to thwart plans for any expansion. It was an interesting experiment in Soviet-American cooperation. However, it failed to fulfill U.S. air objectives and became little more than a sideshow in the air war over Europe.

Mark Conversino

Additional Reading

Craven, Wesley F., and James L. Cate, *The Army Air Forces in World War II*. Vol. III: *Europe: Argument to V-E Day, January 1944–May 1945* (1948).

Deane, John R., *The Strange Alliance: The Story of Our Efforts at Wartime Cooperation with Russia* (1947).

Lukas, Richard C., *Eagles East: The Army Air Forces and the Soviet Union, 1941–1945* (1970).

Freiburg Air Raid (27 November 1944)

[See map 20 on page 1330]

The Black Forest city of Freiburg was no stranger to aerial bombardment. During World War I it was Germany's third most heavily bombed city—a fact due mostly to its closeness to the French border, just across the Rhine River from Alsace. A university town with virtually no heavy industry, Freiburg's sole strategic significance was its position astride the main rail line between Mannheim and Basel, Switzerland.

During World War II, Freiburg was bombed only twice. Ironically, the first attack was an accidental strike by the *Luftwaffe*. On 10 May 1940, the first day of the France (q.v.) campaign, a group of three He-111 bombers became separated from their main force on their way to attack the airfield at Dijon, France. Lost in heavy cloud cover, the He-111s mistook Freiburg for their secondary target and dropped sixty-nine bombs. Fifty-seven people died in the raid, but relatively little damage was done to the town. The real source of the attack immediately was covered up, with the Nazi government blaming "enemy aircraft." As a result, many people in Germany came to believe that it was the Allies who initiated the bombing of civilian targets in World War II. When the Allies finally did bomb Freiburg in November 1944, the results were far more deadly.

Planning for the Freiburg raid began with a 22 November message from SHAEF (q.v.) Headquarters to the U.S. Eighth Air Force and RAF Bomber Command requesting that all railway and highway bridges along the Rhine south of Karlsruhe be destroyed to support the offensive of the Allied 6th Army Group. Operation TIGER-FISH, as it was called, was carried out by Bomber Command's Number 1 Group. The operations order for the attack made a particular point of warning aircrews of the nearness to the target of Allied lines and the Swiss border.

In the late afternoon of 27 November the aircraft of Number 1 Group formed up in the skies over Reading, England, and at 1816 hours they crossed the French coast. At 1940 hours, just over Nancy, France, they made their final turn toward Freiburg. At the same time, six Mosquitoes broke off from the formation and headed toward the rail center at Mannheim, dropping "chaff" along the way in a spoof attack designed to draw attention from the main target.

The main bomber force was preceded by ten Mosquitoes and forty-nine Lancasters from Number 8 Pathfinder Group. The pathfinders started dropping their markers about 1955 hours. Five minutes later the lead planes of the main force arrived. The main force consisted of 285 Lancasters evenly divided into three waves. Each wave was allotted three minutes over the target. The first two waves carried high explosive bombs, the third wave carried incendiaries—a total of 1,725 tons of ordnance.

By 2018 hours the raid was over. Number 1 Group turned south shortly, then west, then northwest for the return flight to Britain. Beneath them Freiburg lay in flames. Ironically, the attack missed most of the rail targets, but much of the medieval inner city was destroyed. Twenty percent of the town's houses were destroyed, and 2,800 people died. Almost miraculously, the magnificent Gothic cathedral (dating from the year 1200) in the center of the town received only minor damage, while almost all the buildings surrounding it were flattened.

After World War II Freiburg rebuilt itself. Many of the medieval structures were restored or rebuilt. Some of the art nouveau architecture from the late nineteenth century, however, was not restored. Freiburg also became a major center for the study of military history. Currently it is the home of the German military archives. The German Army's Military History Research Office was also located in Freiburg until 1994, when it was moved to Potsdam and merged with a similar organization of the old East German government.

David T. Zabecki

Additional Reading

Ueberschär, Gerd R., *Freiburg im Luftkrieg 1939–1945* (1990).

G

Gazala Line (26 May–13 June 1942)

[See map 19 on page 1329]

Throughout the evening of 26 May 1942, thousands of tanks, armored cars, guns, and trucks rumbled across the stark and barren plateau of North Africa. Their path lit by brilliant moonlight, German and Italian mobile units under the command of General Erwin Rommel (q.v.) were once again on the march.

This onslaught was unleashed against the British Eighth Army, then entrenched in the Gazala Line. A front of immense minefields, the Gazala Line featured seven heavily fortified positions, which the British called "boxes." Vast supply depots, especially at Belhamed, were assembled close behind the front. Lieutenant General Neil Ritchie (q.v.) had under his command the equivalent of six infantry divisions and six brigades of armor.

Many different machines were found in the British array of 849 tanks, but the trump cards the British hoped to hold were 242 American-built Grant tanks, each armed with a high-velocity 37mm gun in the turret and a 75mm cannon in a side sponson mounting. Also coming rapidly into British hands were 122 new and lethal 6-pounder antitank guns.

Rommel's attack caught the British immersed in the process of absorbing and learning to handle their new equipment. Worst of all, British tanks, antitank batteries, and infantry failed to work together in mutual support in battle. A fundamental and thorough reorganization of the Eighth Army was in the final stages of planning. Rommel struck before these could be carried out. Moreover, Ritchie was confronted with corps commanders senior to him in years of service and experience in desert warfare. Such men were ill-disposed to receive directions from the man they viewed as merely a conduit from Field Marshal Sir Claude Auchinleck (q.v.), British Middle East commander in chief, in Cairo.

Did the British expect an Axis attack? Based upon information gleaned from ULTRA (q.v.) in the last half of April, Auchinleck warned Ritchie that Rommel would unleash a major offensive before the middle of June. But ULTRA did not indicate the main thrust of Rommel's advance. Both Auchinleck and Ritchie were convinced that Rommel would attack straight into the center of the British positions. They viewed the prospect of enemy operations against their southern flank as a feint to draw attention away from the center.

The main battle tanks equipping the German forces were 223 PzKpfw-IIIs, carrying the low-velocity 50mm gun, and forty PzKpfw-IVs with a short-barreled 75mm gun. Italian armor units drove into combat with 228 tanks that were well armed with a 47mm gun, but were very poorly armored and lacked ventilation and cooling for the crews. The Axis main strike force consisted of the German 15th *Panzer*, 21st *Panzer*, and 90th Light Infantry Divisions and the Italian *Ariete* Armored and *Trieste* Motorized Infantry Divisions.

German tanks worked hand in glove with artillery and antitank units in the *Panzer* division team. Amply supplied with armor-piercing and hollow charge ammunition, German artillery could effectively perform the tank-killing role. Forty-eight of the effective 88mm guns accompanied the *Afrika Korps* (q.v.) into battle. The excellent 50mm antitank gun was supplemented by 75mm high-velocity pieces and captured Soviet 76.2mm cannon, many of which were mounted on half-track and tank chassis and employed as tank hunters.

In the air war, Rommel enjoyed a considerable advantage. Some 500 German and Italian warplanes flew against almost 200 aircraft of the British Desert Air Force. The U.S.-built Curtiss P-40 could not match the formidable Bf-109F and the Macchi MC.202.

Rommel's plan of attack for Operation *VENEZIA* was to conduct a feint in the north coupled with a wide envelopment in the south, sweeping deep into the British rear. South African armored car units frequently reported the oncoming enemy, but Ritchie failed to assess the information correctly and continued to expect the main German attack against the British center positions.

Savage fighting erupted on 27 May as German tanks devastated two British armored brigades. To Rommel's amazement, however, two more British tank brigades unleashed a furious assault on his *Panzer*s. By nightfall, Rommel was on the brink of disaster. More than one-third of his tanks lay shattered, and the 15th *Panzer* Division was out of gas and ammunition deep in the British rear. The German supply columns were cut off from their combat units.

The British viewed Rommel's predicament with glee, but failed to take advantage of it. On 28 May, Italian armored units skillfully beat off two British tank units, and German light infantry and antitank guns drove off a third assault. On 29 May, Rommel personally led supply and fuel trucks through a minefield gap and steered them unerringly through a sandstorm to his waiting *Panzer*s. In the course of the day, scattered Axis armored divisions were once more effectively concentrated. British armor, committed piecemeal and belatedly, failed to prevent the consolidation of their foe.

Rommel then formed a defensive bridgehead east of the Gazala Line at its southern end. Antitank screens would hold off enemy counterthrusts. The two British "boxes" astride the Axis supply lines would then be assailed and destroyed.

In bitter fighting, Rommel personally led the attack against the stubborn Yorkshiremen defending the fortifications at Sidi Muftah. Their ammunition exhausted, the British were finally overrun on 31 May. This triumph proved crucial. Rommel's supply columns could now move safely through the cleared corridors in the minefields of the Gazala Line.

Finally, the British decided to attack the eastern front of the Axis salient with the Indian 9th and 10th Infantry Brigades plus the 22nd Armoured Brigade. The 32nd Army Tank Brigade was detailed to thrust against the northern flank of this wedge that became known as "The Cauldron."

Unfortunately, the control of the attack was entrusted to no single commander. Three officers each had a finger in the pie. Lieutenant General William H. Gott (q.v.) was the corps commander responsible for the 32nd Army Tank Brigade, while Major General Frank Messervy (q.v.) and Major General H.R. Briggs handled the assault on the eastern front of the wedge. When the Indian 10th Brigade opened the attack, Briggs was to exercise command. Then, as 22nd Armoured Brigade exploited the anticipated breach in the enemy's lines, control was supposed to pass to Messervy. Briggs would resume leadership again as the Indian 9th Brigade followed up the armored advance.

British infantry and armor also completely misunderstood their respective roles. Armor expected the infantry to clear out the Axis artillery and antitank guns. British tank crews were also under the impression that they were to deal with enemy armor only, that the protection of the infantry was to be no concern of theirs. The infantry, on the other hand, anticipated close support and cover from the armor.

At dawn on 6 June, the Indian infantry did wrest positions on Aslagh Ridge from the Italian infantry positioned there. When the 156 Grant, Crusader, and Stuart tanks surged forward they ran headlong into a tremendous hail of fire from concentrated German antitank guns. Sixty British tanks were soon cascading flames and smoke. Angry that the infantry failed to clear the way for them, the armor sheared off and wheeled north.

Clearly the British armor was committed too early in the battle, the consequence of divided and uncoordinated command. Seizing their opportunity, tanks from the *Ariete* and 15th *Panzer* Divisions counterattacked at noon and massacred the British and Indian infantry, who died or fell captive cursing their own armor.

To the north, the troops of the 21st *Panzer* Division were startled to see seventy Matilda and Valentine tanks lurching toward their positions on the Sidra Ridge. German antitank gunners leapt to their pieces for a perfect "target range shoot." The British tanks then blundered onto a minefield. German tanks sallied forth, took the British on the flank, pinned them against the minefield, and hammered them to pieces. Only twenty British tanks limped out of the debacle.

Early that afternoon, Rommel unleashed one of his most devastating counterthrusts. The 21st *Panzer* and *Ariete* Divisions knifed southeast toward Bir el Tamar. A task force of 88mm guns, led personally by Rommel, and the 15th *Panzer* Division thundered north from Bir el Harmat. That evening the Indian 10th Brigade, the support group of the 22nd Armoured Brigade, and four regiments of field artillery were encircled. In the carnage that followed the next day, these formations were annihilated.

The full weight of Axis forces now fell upon the stronghold of Bir Hacheim on the southern end of the Gazala Line. This "box" was defended by a Jewish battalion and a Free French Brigade. Fighting there was ferocious. French positions shuddered under the relentless pounding of *Luftwaffe* bombers. After five days, the French and Jewish survivors shot their way out and clambered aboard British trucks and ambulances.

The fortified British field positions, manned by tenacious defenders, had almost brought to grief the German mobile operation in the desert. The battles at Sidi Muftah and Bir Hacheim did cost Rommel the loss of more than one-third of his elite German infantry. The British now sought to secure their southern flank through a network of five defensive "boxes" from Alem Hamza to Acroma. Tactically, this defensive framework was formidable.

Rommel resumed his offensive. Twenty-seven PzKpfw-III Specials, armed with the high-velocity 50mm gun, now joined the array of German tanks. *Panzer* firepower was also buttressed by six PzKpfw-IV Specials, featuring the deadly long-barreled 75mm gun. During the afternoon of 11 June, the 21st *Panzer* and *Ariete* Divisions attacked directly north from the "Cauldron" wedge. The *Trieste*, 15th *Panzer*, and 90th Light Divisions swung northeast to circle the British flank.

How did Rommel's opponent react to his move? Ritchie wanted British armor to fight on the defensive under the cover of artillery and antitank guns in the "boxes," but Lieutenant General C.W. Norrie, British XXX Corps commander, ordered the 2nd and 4th Armoured Brigades to drive directly south and tackle the 15th *Panzer* Division head on. By this, he hoped to catch and destroy Rommel's scattered units one by one.

Messervy, however, wanted these armored brigades to concentrate at Bir el Gobi. There they would be in a position to thrust into the right flank of Rommel's entire advance. His two brigadiers, however, refused to carry out Messervy's orders. Messervy, en route to confer with Norrie and Ritchie, ran into the German 90th Light Division, and spent the rest of the day hiding in a dry well to elude capture.

Late in the morning of 12 June, the 15th *Panzer* Division went clanking forward to lure the British into the German trap. At noon, the 21st *Panzer* Division pounced on the rear and exposed

A British Matilda tank passes the "Knightsbridge" road junction shortly after the major tank battle there on 29 May 1942 during the battle of Gazala. (IWM E 12690)

flank of the British tanks with devastating effect. Norrie, meanwhile, instructed the 22nd Armoured Brigade, which lay to the north and smash through the 15th *Panzer* Division. The commander of the 22nd Armoured Brigade, Major General Herbert Lumsden, actually wanted to pull his armor back north to cover the position known as "Knightsbridge Box." Nonetheless, Lumsden did obey orders, and the 22nd Armoured Brigade stumbled right into Rommel's ambush. The *Trieste* Motorized Division and units from the 21st *Panzer* Division wreaked havoc among the British tanks.

The Germans regarded this "Battle of Knightsbridge" as the decisive culmination of the Gazala battles. The British lost 120 tanks and were forced to concede defeat. Rommel swiftly followed up his victory in the desert, attacking and seizing from the British the seaport and major supply base of Tobruk (*see* Tobruk III). With the fall of Tobruk on 21 June 1942, 5,000 tons of general provisions, 2,000 trucks of all types, and 2,000 tons of precious gasoline fell into Axis hands. Rommel subsequently invaded Egypt and drove all the way to the gates of Cairo and the Suez Canal.

The combined battles of Gazala and Tobruk cost the Allies 80,000 troops, including 45,000 prisoners (33,000 from Tobruk). The British also lost nearly 1,000 tanks and hundreds of guns. Ritchie was relieved of his command two days after the fall of Tobruk, and Auchinleck temporarily assumed personal command of the Eighth Army.

After the fall of Tobruk, the Eighth Army started its 250-mile withdrawal to Mersa Matrúh (q.v.).

Sherwood S. Cordier

Additional Reading

Agar-Hamilton, J.A.I., and L.C.F. Turner, *Crisis in the Desert, May–June 1942* (1952).

Barnett, Correlli, *The Desert Generals* (1961).

Heckmann, Wolf, *Rommel's War in Africa* (1981).

Mellenthin, F.W. von, *Panzer Battles* (1956).

German Surface Raiders (1940–1943)

Besides occasional forays by capital ships against Allied shipping, the *Kriegsmarine* (German Navy) in World War II relied almost exclusively on submarines and disguised commerce raiders, also known as auxiliary cruisers, to destroy Allied merchant vessels on the high seas. The raiders' efforts proved particularly impressive early in the war when the Allied convoy system covered only the North Atlantic and left vast expanses of the Central and South Atlantic, the Indian Ocean, and the Pacific vulnerable to commerce raiding by armed German merchantmen. Only when the full mobilization of Allied resources and their attendant superior technology began to overwhelm Germany's efforts at sea after 1942, did the era of the raiders reach its end—just as the halcyon days of the U-boats were over by the spring of 1943.

As in countless wars before, the advantages of commerce raiding in World War II went beyond the mere destruction of enemy ships, cargo, and personnel. While never designed to gain control of the seas for their own side, German auxiliary cruisers kept the Allies off guard, requiring them to divert warships, planes, and other resources from the principal theaters of action to peripheral waters. Moreover, raiders obtained valuable raw materials, vessels, and intelligence for the Germans, thus helping ease the blockade of Axis-controlled Europe. Psychologically, they struck terror into the hearts of Allied sailors because of the unpredictability and suddenness of their attacks. Lastly, they constituted an important link to Adolf Hitler's (q.v.) Japanese ally after overland connections were severed by 1941.

The raiders were led by men of much experience, imagination, cunning, and proven leadership qualities. In several cases they actually served in the merchant navy before the war. Some commanders, like Bernard Rogge (q.v.) *(Atlantis)*, Kurt Weyher *(Orion)*, Ernst-Felix Krüder *(Pinguin)*, and Otto Kähler *(Thor)*, earned not only the admiration of their own crews but the genuine respect of their enemy as well.

The German Navy originally planned to employ a total of twenty-six commerce raiders around the globe, but in actuality only nine saw service overseas between 1940 and 1943. Built in the 1930s as regular merchant vessels with a view toward quick conversion in case of war, they displaced generally between 3,300 and 8,800 tons, reached top speeds of 18 knots, and carried considerable concealed armament. Armament typically included six 150mm and various smaller caliber guns, four to six torpedo tubes, up to 380 mines, a pair of seaplanes for reconnaissance, and in some cases even a small LS-type PT-boat carried along in piggyback fashion. Crew sizes varied between 350 and 450 officers and men, some of whom eventually embarked as prize crews on captured vessels.

Raider tactics included assuming the outward appearance and behavior of genuine Allied or neutral vessels. This was accomplished through fake smokestacks, ventilators or other alterations to the ship's silhouette, through deceptive paint patterns or lettering on the hull, through misleading flags, rigging, or signals, and through assumed names and radio call signs. Some raiders masqueraded in several different disguises in the course of their missions. More than once, they fooled superior British warships that had approached for an inspection at short range.

Having gained the confidence of its intended victim, preferably a single vessel without naval escort or air cover, and having closed in for the kill, the raider would drop its disguises, display its armament, fire warning shots, and demand surrender. Sometimes the victims gave up without resistance or even sending an emergency signal. Sometimes, especially if armed, they returned fire and delayed and even avoided capture or destruction, while alerting shipping in the vicinity to the presence of the raider. For this purpose, ships used the internationally known and feared radio signal "RRR." In several cases regular duels were fought with damage and losses on both sides, while in other cases, the Allied vessel and crew fell into German hands with few complications.

The raiders would either destroy captured ships if they appeared of little value to the Axis powers, keep them as supply vessels for fuel and foodstuffs at remote rendezvous points, or dispatch them to friendly ports in France, East Africa, and Japan. The latter practice also relieved the burden of having to care for large numbers of prisoners who often included women and children and whose welfare was always of particular concern.

The raiders were virtually self-sufficient and enjoyed long endurance at sea as they replenished their stocks of fuel and food from the vessels they cornered. The *Pinguin* even employed one of her prizes as an auxiliary minelayer with considerable success along the South Australian coast in late 1940. Auxiliary cruisers were also able to resupply other German warships, including U-boats, in waters far from home.

To leave European waters safely and gain the open oceans turned out to be an especially challenging phase of the raider's assignment. The English Channel, the wide but busy passage between Scotland and Iceland, and the Denmark Strait between Iceland and Greenland, were the favored spots to break through the Allied blockade, weather permitting. The raider *Komet* even made a successful run through the Northeast Passage along the shores of the Soviet Union to enter the Pacific Ocean through the Bering Strait in 1940 before Germany's Operation BARBAROSSA eliminated that option the following year.

Once a raider reached its operational areas in the South Atlantic, the Indian Ocean, or the Pacific, it had relatively little to fear besides sudden encounters with superior enemy forces, mechanical breakdowns, and the dangers inherent in running the Allied blockade to reach home waters after a completed cruise. Radio traffic with the naval high command in Berlin was kept to a minimum to avoid giving away the vessel's position to the enemy. As a result, strategic coordination of raider activities was difficult to achieve. Most of the ships operated independently, even running the risk of being sunk by their own submarines in the Atlantic.

Several raiders spent more than one stint overseas. Only one survived the war unharmed while six were destroyed at sea by hostile action. The first and perhaps most notorious of these raiders, the *Atlantis* (q.v.), put to sea in late March 1940. The last raider to threaten Allied shipping, the *Michel*, was sunk by the U.S. submarine *Tarpon* in October 1943 in the Yellow Sea. The raiders were most active between 1940 and 1942. Together they destroyed 138 merchant vessels for a total of 871,447 tons, as well as the Australian light cruiser *Sydney* and the British auxiliary cruiser *Voltaire*. Several ships were damaged in their encounters with raiders but managed to make port. Considering these figures, which amount to approximately 7 percent of the tonnage sunk by German U-boats in World War II, and given the

considerable anguish and annoyance they caused for the Allies, the raiders' performance appears to have been worth the investment in scarce German resources.

The following brief summaries specify the achievements and fates of individual raiders in the chronological order of their deployment:

Atlantis (7,862 tons, a.k.a. *Schiff 16* or *Raider C*: Commanding Officer: Bernhard Rogge). Operations 1940–1941 in the Atlantic, Indian, and Pacific Oceans. Victims: twenty-two ships of 145,697 tons. Sunk 22 November 1941 by the British heavy cruiser *Devonshire* near Ascension Island.

Orion (7,021 tons, a.k.a. *Schiff 36* or *Raider A*: Commanding Officer: Kurt Weyher). Operations 1940–1942 in the Atlantic, Indian, and Pacific Oceans. Victims: eleven ships of 74,478 tons. Sunk 4 May 1945 in home waters through Allied aerial bombardment.

Widder (7,851 tons, a.k.a. *Schiff 21* or *Raider D*: Commanding Officer: Hellmuth von Ruckteschell). Operations 1940 in the Atlantic until returned home with engine trouble. Victims: ten ships of 58,644 tons; survived war.

Thor (3,862 tons, a.k.a. *Schiff 10* or *Raider E*: Commanding Officers: Otto Kähler, Günther Gumprich). Operations 1940–1942 in the Atlantic, Indian, and Pacific Oceans. Victims: twenty-two ships of 152,639 tons, plus HMS *Voltaire*. Wrecked 30 November 1942 by explosion in Yokohama, Japan.

Pinguin (7,766 tons, a.k.a. *Schiff 33* or *Raider F*: Commanding Officer: Ernst-Felix Krüder). Operations 1940–1941 in the Atlantic, Indian, and Pacific Oceans. Victims: thirty-two ships of 154,619 tons. Sunk 8 May 1941 by the British heavy cruiser HMS *Cornwall* near the Seychelles Islands.

Komet (3,287 tons, a.k.a. *Schiff 45* or *Raider B*: Commanding Officers: Robert Eyssen, Ulrich Brocksien). Operations 1940–1941 in the Pacific, Indian, and Atlantic Oceans. Victims: seven ships of 42,568 tons. Sunk 14 October 1942 by the British motor torpedo boat *MTB 136* in the English Channel.

Kormoran (8,736 tons, a.k.a. *Schiff 41* or *Raider G*: Commanding Officer: Theodor Detmers). Operations 1940–1941 in the Atlantic, Indian, and Pacific Oceans.

Victims: eleven ships of 68,274 tons, plus HMAS *Sydney*. Sunk 19 November 1941 off Australia by the *Sydney.*

Stier (4,778 tons, a.k.a. *Schiff 23* or *Raider J*: Commanding Officer: Horst Gerlach). Operations 1941–1942 in the Atlantic Ocean. Victims: four ships of 29,409 tons. Scuttled 27 September 1942 off Brazil after encounter with U.S. Liberty ship *Stephen Hopkins.*

Michel (4,740 tons, a.k.a. *Schiff 28* or *Raider H*: Commanding Officers: Hellmuth von Ruckteschell, Günther Gumprich). Operations 1942–1943 in the Atlantic, Indian, and Pacific Oceans. Victims: seventeen ships of 121,994 tons. Sunk 17 October 1943 by U.S. submarine *Tarpon* in the Yellow Sea.

Two additional German merchant vessels, *Coronet* (*Schiff 14* or *Raider K*) and *Schiff 5*, were converted for commerce raiding but saw no deployment. Both survived the war.

On several occasions between the fall of 1939 and the spring of 1941, the German naval high command released regular warships from duties in home waters and let them loose against merchant shipping in the Atlantic and Indian Oceans. The most notorious episode in this respect involved the pocket battleship *Admiral Graf Spee* whose spectacular end in Montevideo in December 1939, after the destruction of nine merchant vessels (50,089 tons), gave a welcome boost to Allied morale at a time when there was little to cheer about otherwise (*see* Platte River). At the same time, her sister ship, the *Deutschland* (later renamed *Lützow*) operated in the North and Central Atlantic with meager results (two ships of 6,962 tons).

Germany's third pocket battleship, the *Admiral Scheer*, was somewhat more successful in the South Atlantic and Indian Ocean in late 1940 and early 1941, capturing or sinking seventeen enemy ships (113,223 tons). Around the same time, the heavy cruiser *Admiral Hipper* turned in a respectable performance in the North Atlantic, accounting for ten Allied vessels of 42,060 tons. Even the battleships *Gneisenau* and *Scharnhorst* tried their luck in Atlantic waters in early 1941, bagging a total of twenty-two ships (115,622 tons). A similar prospect of easy prey led the *Bismarck* (q.v.) and her more fortunate consort, the heavy cruiser *Prinz Eugen,* into the North Atlantic in May 1941. Predictably, the *Bismarck* debacle ended such sorties of German capital ships once and for all.

Commerce raiding in World War II reflected the timeless precedents of bravery in combat, respect and even admiration for a clever opponent, as well as generosity and chivalry toward defenseless victims once the fight was over. With one controversial exception (Captain Hellmuth von Ruckteschell of *Widder* and *Michel* was sentenced in 1947 to ten years in prison for his attack methods and treatment of Allied sailors), no hint of war crimes or cruelty came to light to blot the record of commerce raiders and their crews. Indeed, in retrospect, both sides tend to assess this episode of the war at sea with an air of nostalgia. At the same time, there can be no question that large-scale commerce raiding is an experience unlikely to be repeated in the future. The Germans admitted this much after the sinking of the *Michel.* Today, global air and satellite surveillance alone would render commerce raiding by surface vessels a lethal and impractical undertaking.

Eric C. Rust

Additional Reading

Brennecke, Jochen, *Die deutschen Hilfskreuzer im Zweiten Weltkrieg* (1976).

Muggenthaler, August K., *German Raiders of World War II* (1977).

Germany Air Campaign (September 1939–April 1945)

[See map 20 on page 1330]

The air war over Germany began on 3 September 1939, only hours after the official outbreak of war, when a lone British Blenheim IV bomber conducted a reconnaissance of German shipping at Schilling Roads. From that modest beginning, it was more than two and one-half years before the RAF's Bomber Command staged its first really large bombing raid against Germany, the 1,000-plane raid against Cologne (q.v.) in May 1942. It was almost three years before the U.S. Eighth Air Force undertook its first operational mission from Britain against the Continent, a twelve-plane B-17 raid against rail yards at Rouen, France.

From the start of the war in 1939 to the launching of the Allied Combined Bomber Offensive against Germany in 1943 (Operation POINTBLANK), the British and Americans built almost from scratch the greatest air armada the world has ever seen. In doing so, they had to surmount enormous hurdles—inadequate aircraft for the mission, chronic shortages of equipment and trained personnel, and the conflicting strategies of the two allies, to name a few.

The Casablanca Conference in January 1943 proved to be the turning point. There the Allied leaders determined that Germany's defeat would assume the highest priority, and for this to occur it would be necessary to invade the continent of Europe. A combined bomber offensive was a crucial prerequisite to the land campaign. To prepare the Continent for the Allied invasion, American and British bombers were, in the words of the final directive, to engage in "the progressive destruction and dislocation of the German military, industrial, and economic system, and the undermining of the morale of the German people to the point where their capacity for armed resistance is fatally weakened."

A list of primary objectives for the bombing campaign was established, including (1) German submarine construction yards; (2) the German aircraft industry; (3) transportation facilities; (4) oil production and refining facilities; and (5) other targets in the German war industry. In actual practice these priorities proved relatively flexible, with commanders being given a fair degree of latitude to achieve them. Furthermore, the priorities were to change during the course of the war, as more pressing needs were identified.

The Casablanca Conference also attempted to resolve the long-standing disagreement between the British and Americans over the relative merits of nighttime area bombing, which was favored by the British, versus daylight "precision" bombing, favored by the Americans. The British, who had been flying at night against German targets since early in the war, contended it was safer. The American argument was that daylight bombing could hit precise targets, such as individual factories that could not even be seen, much less hit, at night. In answering the question of safety, Americans were convinced that even without long-range fighter escort their heavily armed B-17s and B-24s would still be able to bomb targets in Germany and return with an acceptable level of losses.

The upshot of this debate was that the U.S. Eighth Air Force and later the Fifteenth Air Force, both under the direction of General Carl "Tooey" Spaatz (q.v.), commander of the U.S. Army Air Forces in Europe, would proceed with day bombing, while British Bomber Command, under the leadership of Air Marshal Sir Arthur "Bomber" Harris (q.v.), would continue with night bombing.

In theory, the result would be around-the-clock bombing applying continuous pressure on the German population, war industries, and air defenses. The Americans would attack precision targets by day, such as individual factories. The British would attack area targets, such as cities, by night with an eye toward breaking German morale. The ultimate effect of this decision was to produce two distinctly different air wars over Germany between 1943 and 1945. The planned complementary nature of the two air campaigns proved rather elusive in practice, with each air force essentially pursuing its own objectives.

To combat the Allied air offensive, the Germans employed an extensive system of fighter aircraft and antiaircraft guns. To counter the threat posed by British bombers, the *Luftwaffe* formed their first night fighter unit in June 1940. Under the direction of General Josef Kammhuber (q.v.), a system of radars, fighters, and searchlights, known as the Kammhuber Line (q.v.), was created. Under this system, radars located and tracked enemy bombers. They then passed them off to the searchlights which, in turn, illuminated the target for patrolling night fighters. As the system became more refined, radar (q.v.) passed the enemy bombers directly to the waiting night fighters. By 1942, German night fighters began carrying their own radar sets to identify their targets with minimal or no assistance from ground-based radars.

The other major element in the German air defense system consisted of antiaircraft artillery *(Flak)* and searchlights working in tandem. Heavy *Flak* batteries were equipped with the exceptional 88mm gun, a weapon that saw continuous refinement throughout the war to improve its accuracy and ability to hit high altitude targets like the B-17, which could fly at over 30,000 feet. Efforts to develop even larger weapons were only marginally successful because *Luftwaffe* antiaircraft artillery units ranked considerably below the army and navy in the competition for scarce resources. As the war progressed, heavy *Flak* batteries gradually received radar sets sufficiently accurate for gun-laying. Thus, by the time the Combined Bomber Offensive began in 1943, these guns represented a significant threat to both day and night bombers.

Luftwaffe defense requirements represented an increasingly significant drain on scarce resources. The number of heavy *Flak* batteries increased from 791 in 1940 to 2,132 in 1943; and by the end of the war, *Flak* batteries employed the efforts of two million people. Despite the enormous investment of men and material, it has been estimated that an 88mm gun had to expend 16,000 rounds on average to bring down one bomber flying at high altitude.

Although the first American aircrews arrived in Britain in 1942, it was more than a year before they posed a serious threat to the Germans. This was a time of preparation, as aircrews learned the art of war and experimented with tactics to find out what worked and what did not. This was also a period of build-up for Eighth Air Force in Britain.

With significant air resources being diverted to support the Operation TORCH landings in Northwest Africa (q.v.), Eighth Air Force was still a mere shadow of the mighty force it would become by the end of the war. The resulting shortage of aircraft and trained crew members severely restricted the American effort against Germany. It was not until March 1943 that the Americans could consistently send a force of 100 bombers against the Germans. Two months later the buildup had proceeded so rapidly that a force of almost 300 bombers could be sent against enemy targets.

By the spring of 1943, Britain had been at war with Germany for three and one-half years, and their air commanders and bomber crews had several years' experience staging major operations over the Continent. This time period saw one of Bomber Command's most ambitious operations to date, the air campaign against the Ruhr (q.v.). Harris's objective was quite simply the destruction of the main cities of the Ruhr, Germany's industrial heart.

The four-month offensive began with a 442-bomber raid on Essen on the night of 5–6 March. By the time it ended in early July, the campaign had produced encouraging results with many of the Ruhr's major cities suffering substantial damage. In addition to the widespread destruction they inflicted, the British also were encouraged by significantly improved bombing accuracy. In 1941, Bomber Command did well to get one-fifth of its bombs within five miles of the target. By 1943, this improved to two-thirds of the bombs within three miles. This success, however, came at a heavy cost in lost bombers and aircrews. During forty-three major raids, the Germans managed to shoot down 872 bombers and damage another 2,126.

Although not apparent at the time, by 1943 the Germans essentially had lost the air war over Germany. During the early years of the war in 1940–1941, a time of rapid buildup in Allied war production, the German aircraft industry virtually stood still. So quick were Germany's victories over Poland and France (qq.v.) that there appeared to be no need for increased production. In contrast, the Americans and British produced 400 percent more fighters than the Germans in the last quarter of 1941. Low aircraft production rates, heavy attrition, and Allied attacks on the German aircraft industry began to seal the *Luftwaffe*'s fate, just at

the time the Allied bomber offensive began to pick up momentum.

Stunned by their heavy losses in the Ruhr air campaign, the British first started to employ "window," long strips of aluminum-coated paper, to blind the German radar network in a series of devastating raids against Hamburg (q.v.) in late July 1943. Under Operation GOMORRAH, the RAF launched a total of 3,000 sorties on 24, 27, and 29 July, and one in early August. With the city's defenses confused by "window," Bomber Command achieved one of its greatest successes at a surprisingly small cost. The fire-storm that developed from the raid of 27 July killed 42,000 people. In all, these raids destroyed or damaged one-third of Hamburg's apartments and one-half of its houses. For Harris, it confirmed that his area bombing campaign was headed in the right direction. What he did not know at the time was that the conditions that made the Hamburg firestorm possible rarely occurred. The success at Hamburg led directly down the dead-end street that was to be the Berlin air offensive (q.v.) of the winter of 1943–1944.

The first raid in the campaign against Berlin was carried out on the night of 18 November 1943 by a force of 444 Mosquitoes and Lancasters. From then until early March, Bomber Command launched sixteen major raids against the city. Based on the results at Hamburg, Harris was convinced that the RAF could destroy Berlin, too. Although the destruction was indeed great—2,000 acres were leveled and 1.5 million people left homeless—Berlin's wide avenues and open spaces vastly reduced the likelihood of a Hamburg-type firestorm. Berlin's air defenses were extremely well developed. The city was beyond the range of Oboe, a radio navigational guide, thus, forcing the bombers to rely on the less accurate H2S radar system.

Over the Berlin air offensive's four-month course, Bomber Command's losses gradually rose above the "acceptable" 5 percent level, peaking at more than 9 percent for the final mission on the night of 23–24 March 1944. At that attrition rate, even many of the most experienced bomber crews were being shot down. Harris admitted that the campaign, in his words, "did not appear to be an overwhelming success." Considering the vast resources employed in the effort, and the fact that Bomber Command failed to bring Berlin to its knees, many historians have deemed the campaign a failure.

As for the American effort, the last six months of 1943 produced several major setbacks that deeply undermined the initial premise that unescorted bombers could hit their targets in Germany successfully and return with acceptable loss rates. On 17 August 1943, Eighth Air Force sent 376 B-17s against the ball bearing plant at Schweinfurt and the Messerschmitt factory at Regensburg (q.v.), in what was the largest raid and deepest penetration into German territory to that point. Sixty of the unescorted bombers were shot down, a disastrous loss rate of 16 percent.

An additional series of missions in October culminated in the infamous Schweinfurt (q.v.) raid of 14 October. Dispatched in two groups, the force of 291 bombers met continuous waves of German fighters. Sixty of the bombers, slightly more than one in five, fell before the German air defense. Although the raid caused significant damage and accelerated the dispersal of the bearing industry, it also demonstrated that Eighth Air Force had at least temporarily lost air superiority in its struggle with the *Luftwaffe*. It was also apparent that air superiority would not be regained until adequate numbers of long-range escort fighters became available.

Eighth Air Force initially relied on the P-47 Thunderbolt as an escort fighter, but the buildup of fighter units was extremely slow. By early June 1943, Eighth Air Force had only three groups of P-47s, fewer than 225 aircraft to face 600 *Luftwaffe* fighters. To make matters worse, the P-47s could fly no more than 175 miles before having to return to their bases. This effectively restricted them to escorting the bombers on raids to France and the Low Countries.

The critical breakthrough was the development of drop tanks, which extended the fighters' range. The first drop tanks, made of resinated paper, did not become available in sizeable numbers until July 1943, and only allowed the P-47s to escort the bombers as far as the German border. Also, the tanks could not be pressurized for high altitude flight. The solution came in the fall of 1943 with the introduction of metal pressurized drop tanks, which had sufficient capacity to take escort fighters well into Germany.

The escort problem was solved once and for all with the introduction of the P-51 Mustang. Perhaps the best fighter aircraft employed by any side in World War II, Mustangs first became available for combat operations in December 1943. After they were equipped with drop tanks in March 1944, they could escort the bombers anywhere in Germany, and were more than a match for the *Luftwaffe*'s Bf-109s and FW-190s.

Although the emergence of long-range escort fighters was crucial to the success of the American daylight bomber offensive, American strategists recognized that escort fighters alone were insufficient, particularly if air superiority was to be achieved before Operation OVERLORD, the Allied invasion of the Continent planned for late spring 1944.

Beginning 20 February 1944, under Operation ARGUMENT, more than 3,300 bombers from Eighth Air Force in Britain and 500 bombers from newly formed Fifteenth Air Force in Italy launched a coordinated series of raids against German aircraft factories, particularly those producing fighter aircraft and their components. The raids continued for five more days with bombers dropping 10,000 tons, an amount equal to the total dropped by Eighth Air Force in its first year of operation.

The results of BIG WEEK (q.v.), as the operation became known, were somewhat mixed. While it is true that more than half the German aircraft plants were destroyed, it is also true that Operation ARGUMENT galvanized the German aircraft industry into an intense program of dispersal and rebuilding, so that by May 1944 German fighter production reached a new monthly high of 2,200 aircraft. Where the *Luftwaffe* suffered the greatest damage was in air-to-air combat with American bombers and their escorting fighters. A total of 225 German airmen were killed during BIG WEEK, approximately one-tenth of the *Luftwaffe*'s interceptor pilots. Many were veteran pilots who could not be replaced. In contrast, the 226 bombers and aircrews lost by the Eighth and Fifteenth Air Forces, while not insignificant, were quickly replaced.

Just as the Allied bomber offensive was beginning to reach full stride in the spring of 1944, it hit a snag. The bombers were diverted from strategic targets in Germany to tactical targets in France in support of Operation OVERLORD.

At the Tehran Conference the Allied Combined Chiefs of Staff decided that all available airpower in Britain would support the upcoming Normandy (q.v.) invasion, but there was a significant difference of opinion over how best to achieve this. In greatly simplified terms, the British favored attacks on the transportation system in France, particularly the rail network, as the best way to prevent the Germans from reinforcing their troops in the invasion area. The American plan, pushed by Spaatz, favored an intensive campaign against the German petroleum industry. Although supreme Allied commander General Dwight D. Eisenhower (q.v.) came down on the side of the transportation plan, he did permit some attacks against the oil industry.

Despite his own conviction that any shift from targets in Germany would lead to a resurgence of German morale, Harris threw the weight of Bomber Command's efforts against the railways of northern France. In March 1944, Bomber Command devoted 70 percent of its effort to German targets. By May, 75 percent of the effort was against French targets. Eighth Air Force applied substantial pressure against transportation targets. In the long run, however, its continued assaults on German aircraft industry and attacks on synthetic fuel plants, beginning in May, proved more important.

Two major raids by the Eighth Air Force against German synthetic oil plants on 12 and 28 May, combined with raids by Fifteenth Air Force against Ploesti (q.v.), caused a 50 percent drop in oil production. The results of the oil campaign were striking. German petroleum stocks fell from 927,000 tons in March to 472,000 tons in June. Aviation fuel stocks dropped from 180,000 tons in April to 10,000 tons in August. It was estimated that the American air campaign destroyed 98 percent of Germany's aviation fuel production capacity by that point. So successful was the campaign that U.S. strategic bombers devoted much of their efforts to petroleum targets for the remainder of the war. By the fall of 1944, the *Luftwaffe*—short on fuel, trained pilots, and aircraft—was no longer in a position to influence the outcome of the war.

Although it was becoming increasingly apparent by the fall of 1944 that the bombing of oil targets was crippling the German war machine, Harris remained unconvinced. Air Marshal Charles Portal (q.v.), chief of RAF air staff, found Harris extremely reluctant to shift his efforts to the oil targets. Harris stubbornly persisted in the belief that destroying German civilian morale through the area bombing of cities remained the best way to win the war. As late as January 1945, Bomber Command was still devoting the largest share of its effort to leveling German cities, with only 20 percent of its sorties against oil production facilities.

On the night of 13–14 February 1945, Bomber Command launched what to this day remains one of the most controversial (perhaps heinous) Allied attacks of the war, the infamous Dresden (q.v.) raid. At that stage of the war, Dresden was one of Germany's few relatively intact large cities. It was also packed with refugees fleeing the advancing Soviet Army. The raid on Dresden was supposed to create great confusion and hamper the movement of troops and supplies to the front. The city was totally unprepared for the howling, tornado-like firestorm created by the British bombs. The next day, the Americans attacked the city with an additional 400 bombers. Estimates of German dead ranged from 35,000 to 135,000.

Shortly after the Dresden raid came Operation CLARION (q.v.) on 22–23 February, a long-standing plan to strike simultaneously at transportation targets over most of Germany. This massive operation used tactical aircraft against targets in western and northwestern Germany: Fifteenth Air Force in southern Germany, Eighth Air Force in middle and north central Germany, and RAF Bomber Command against the Ruhr. Although the raids initially appeared quite successful, subsequent assessments revealed the effects to be largely temporary.

For the remainder of the war, Allied strategic bombers roamed at will across what was left of the *Reich*, continuing to attack oil production facilities and the transportation and communications network. Bombers also devoted efforts to stamp out the *Luftwaffe*'s embryonic jet aircraft force, and when necessary, to assist ground forces in a tactical role, such as the crossing of the Rhine in March 1945.

The prewar apostles of airpower were convinced that airpower alone could win wars. While there is no doubt that Allied airpower played a crucial role in the war's final outcome, it was merely one component of a successful war machine. The Allied air offensive succeeded in virtually destroying the German *Luftwaffe* and gaining air superiority by the summer of 1944. It was this air superiority that made possible the invasion of the Continent and permitted the heavy bombers to lay waste to German cities and industries.

The campaign against the oil industry was especially successful. By April 1945, oil production was only 5 percent of what it had been before the bombing campaign began, despite an all-out German effort to keep it going. Ultimately, the attacks on the transportation network also proved successful. By the spring of 1945, traffic on Germany's rail network, which was one of Europe's best before the war, was at a virtual standstill.

All of this success came at a terrible cost. In 1944 alone, Eighth Air Force lost 2,400 bombers. RAF Bomber Command lost more than 8,000 bombers, and 55,000 crewmen died during the war. Only one of every four aircrews to join an operational Bomber Command unit survived the war without being killed, seriously injured, or captured.

The cost to the German civilian population was even more staggering. More than 600,000 died in bombing attacks and an additional 800,000 received serious injuries. The Allied bomber offensive also destroyed an estimated three million dwellings. Despite this incredible loss, there is no evidence that these bombings ever succeeded in breaking German morale.

James C. Ruehrmund, Jr.

Additional Reading

Craven, Wesley Frank, and James Lea Cate, eds., *The Army Air Forces in World War II*, 7 vols. (1948–1954).

Harris, Sir Arthur, *Bomber Offensive* (1947).

Hastings, Max, *Bomber Command* (1979).

Messenger, Charles, *"Bomber" Harris and the Strategic Bombing Offensive, 1939–1945* (1984).

Middlebrook, Martin, and Chris Everitt, *Bomber Command Diaries: An Operational Reference Book, 1939–45* (1995).

Murray, Williamson, *Strategy for Defeat: The Luftwaffe, 1933–1945* (1982).

Webster, Charles, and Arthur Noble Frankland, *The Strategic Air Offensive against Germany, 1939–1945*, 4 vols. (1961).

Germany, East (January–May 1945)

[See map 21 on page 1331]

By the end of 1944, the eastern front had frozen along a line running from Memel on the Baltic through central Poland into Slovakia and Hungary. So far, only a small segment of the *Reich*—the region east of Gumbinnen and Goldap in East Prussia—had fallen into Soviet hands, but it was clear that further Soviet thrusts were imminent. Moreover, with several large air armies at their disposal and with a superiority of about seven-to-one in both infantry and artillery, the Soviet fronts (army groups) deployed between the Baltic and the Carpathian Mountains had very good prospects indeed.

On 12 January 1945, the 1st Ukrainian Front, commanded by Marshall Ivan Konev (q.v.), opened a major offensive from its large Baranow bridgehead in southern Poland. Two days later, Marshal Georgy Zhukov's (q.v.) 1st Byelorussian Front struck at the Germans from its two smaller Vistula bridgeheads in central Poland. Within a few days, infantry and armored columns of both Soviet fronts had ground their way through the German lines and rapidly advanced toward the west. Konev's tanks reached the Oder River in Silesia at several places by 22–23 January and seized most of the upper Silesian industrial region within the next six days. By the end of January, Zhukov's armies, farther north, reached and in some places even crossed the central portions of the Oder River in eastern Brandenburg, thus placing them in striking distance of Berlin, 60 miles to the west.

With supplies running low and its northern flank open to possible counterattacks out of Pomerania, Zhukov's front temporarily halted its offensive. Increased strafing by the *Luftwaffe*, a thaw early in February, and the existence of several German strongholds behind his lines (especially at Posen), further impeded Zhukov's operations. In Silesia, on the other hand, Konev's armies were able to resume their advance in the second week of February and to reach the banks of the Neisse River. At the same time, the Silesian capital of Breslau (now Wrocław), was cut off and soon subjected to a destructive siege. The German garrison, commanded by Major General Hans von Ahlfen until 9 March and Lieutenant General Hermann Niehoff thereafter, held out until 6 May.

On 13 January, one day after Konev struck in southern Poland, the 3rd Byelorussian Front, under General Ivan Chernyakovsky (q.v.), opened a separate offensive into East Prussia. The next day, Marshal Konstantin Rokossovsky's (q.v.) 2nd Byelorussian Front joined the operation by striking at the German armies deployed in that province and the adjacent West Prussian region. The advance of the two Soviet fronts ran into bitter resistance from the Third *Panzer* Army and the Fourth and Second Armies. Though all three German armies were badly mauled, a number of German divisions clung to Königsberg (now Kaliningrad) and portions of the East Prussian coast until April.

German defensive operations in East Prussia and West Prussia, as well as those eventually conducted in Pomerania, were greatly facilitated by the assistance received from the cruisers, destroyers, and a multitude of other vessels of the German Navy. Aside from supporting the German ground forces with their guns, these ships provided the means for resupplying isolated units, for evacuating large numbers of refugees, and for shifting army and SS troops to and from the eastern front. Indeed, from the beginning of 1945 to the very last days of the war, the German fleet in the Baltic and merchant vessels protected by that fleet moved literally hundreds of thousands of civilians and soldiers, most of them taken to relative "safety" in the west—Schleswig-Holstein and Denmark.

While a large portion of East and West Prussia fell into Soviet hands by the end of January, Soviet pressure on the Germans defending Pomerania peaked only in the following month.

After fending off a German counterattack in Stargard in mid-February, the Red Army launched its East Pomeranian offensive on 24 February. Within two weeks, Soviet troops crushed or routed most of the German divisions facing them, allowing the 2nd Byelorussian Front to sweep both westward to the lower reaches of the Oder River and eastward toward the Danzig bight. After several weeks of fierce fighting, remnants of the German Second Army withdrew from Danzig (now Gdansk) on 28 March. A small number of German divisions, commanded by Lieutenant General Dietrich von Saucken, held onto the flooded Vistula delta and adjacent coastal strips until VE Day.

About half of the German population in the provinces conquered by the Red Army between January and March escaped to the west before it was too late. Most of the other civilians were overrun (and sometimes killed) by Soviet troops during their flight to the west, or even before they had a chance to leave their homes. Most of the Germans in the latter two categories were subjected by Soviet soldiers to plunder, rape, and incendiarism for extended periods of time. There is some evidence that these excesses, in turn, often played havoc with the discipline and effectiveness of the Red Army.

The defeats suffered by the *Wehrmacht* during the opening months of 1945 caused Adolf Hitler (q.v.) to institute numerous changes in the upper echelons of his eastern forces. Within a few days after the onset of Konev's offensive, the commander of Army Group A, Colonel General Josef Harpe (q.v.), was dismissed. In his place, Hitler appointed one of his favorite generals, Ferdinand Schörner (q.v.), who would direct the army group (renamed Army Group Center on 26 January) with an iron fist until the bitter end.

Also on 26 January, Hitler fired the army group commander in the northern sector of the front, Colonel General Georg-Hans Reinhardt (q.v.), and replaced him by the Austrian-born General Lothar Rendulic (q.v.). In between these two army groups, Hitler, two days earlier, created a new senior command, Army Group Vistula, with *Reichsführer-SS* Heinrich Himmler (q.v.) at its head. This outlandish decision was made worse by the simultaneous appointment of *SS-Brigadeführer* Heinz Lammerding as the army group's chief of staff. Lammerding, a highly decorated fighting soldier, had only limited experience in advanced staff work.

Hitler's wrath also led to several changes among army commanders on the eastern front. Particularly affected was the Fourth Army in East

Prussia, where General Friedrich Hossbach (q.v.) was fired on 30 January, as was his successor, General Friedrich-Wilhelm Müller on 10 April. Moreover, catastrophic setbacks on the eastern front also led to growing friction between Hitler and the chief of the army general staff, Colonel General Heinz Guderian (q.v.). After a particularly violent clash, the latter was sent on "sick leave" and replaced on 28 March by General Hans Krebs (q.v.).

While both Breslau and Königsberg were gradually being turned into rubble by bitter fighting, another major city in eastern Germany, Dresden (q.v.), was devastated by a series of air attacks, with the Royal Air Force dropping 1,478 tons of high explosives and 1,182 tons of incendiary bombs during the night of 13–14 February. The U.S. Army Air Force followed up the next day with another 771 tons of bombs. Since Dresden was crammed with 250,000 refugees from the Silesian battle zone, the death toll was never firmly established, but it most likely was between 40,000 and 50,000. Thereafter, many other cities and towns in eastern and central Germany were bombed or strafed by British and American planes. It was only during the last three weeks of the war that the Soviet Air Force took over more and more of those functions in the eastern half of the *Reich*.

By mid-March, the Red Army was holding a line roughly following the course of the Oder and Neisse Rivers, and it was obvious that another major offensive, toward Berlin and into Saxony and western Pomerania, was likely to be launched in the near future. Frantic efforts were made to bolster the German defenses, but with general chaos spreading through the German economy, and particularly its transportation system, these efforts were not very effective.

On 16 April, Zhukov and Konev's fronts opened their last great offensive, the Berlin (q.v.) offensive, with massive artillery bombardments of the German lines. Although the capable new commander (since 22 March) of Army Group Vistula, Colonel General Gotthard Heinrici (q.v.), did his best to block the Soviet advance, tank columns of both Soviet army groups managed to break through within a few days, with Zhukov's forces racing toward the German capital from the east and northeast, while Konev's armor approached the city from the southeast, and eventually even from the south.

The two German armies defending the Neisse and central Oder line, General Fritz-Hubert Gräser's Fourth *Panzer* Army and General Theodor Busse's Ninth Army, were both badly mauled.

Moreover, remnants of Busse's divisions eventually found themselves surrounded in southeastern Brandenburg and had to form a defensive cauldron. After many costly encounters with the enemy, Busse and 30,000 of his men reached the Elbe River in early May and surrendered to the Americans. Their escape to the west was greatly assisted toward the end by the newly created German Twelfth Army, commanded by General Walter Wenck, which had originally been formed to defend the Elbe line against the Western Allies.

By 25 April, the Soviet ring around Berlin had closed, and after seven days of bitter fighting the city was formally surrendered by General Helmuth Weidling. Hitler committed suicide in his bunker on 30 April, and his example was soon followed by many others in the besieged government quarters in central Berlin, among them Joseph Goebbels (q.v.) and Krebs.

Four days after Konev and Zhukov struck at the Germans, the 2nd Byelorussian Front began its offensive along the northern reaches of the Oder River. Faced by the Third *Panzer* Army under General Hasso-Eccard von Manteuffel (q.v.), Rokossovsky's troops initially encountered fierce resistance, but by 25 April, they acquired sufficient momentum to advance rapidly toward the west. The port city of Stettin (now Szczecin) was taken on 26 April, Prenzlau two days later, and the Mecklenburg port of Rostock on 2 May. Despite assistance from the so-called Twenty-first Army (actually a headquarters with only a handful of troops), von Manteuffel had to give more ground and by 7 May, Soviet troops occupied all of Mecklenburg and held a line running from Wismar on the Baltic to the Elbe north of Wittenberge.

By the time the German capitulation came into effect, one minute after midnight on 8–9 May, large segments of Saxony and all of Thuringia, which were allotted to the Soviet Union as part of its postwar occupation zone, were effectually under American military control and would remain so until the beginning of July.

Farther to the east, in the German territories lying beyond the Oder and western Neisse Rivers, Polish authorities were beginning to take administrative control—except in the northern half of East Prussia (including the city of Königsberg), which would soon be annexed by the Soviet Union. The eastern provinces of the *Reich*—24.3 percent of its 1937 territory—were thus separated from Germany. Most of the Germans still living in those provinces were expelled within the next twelve months. The "Oder-Neisse Line" has

remained in effect ever since, and today forms the officially reorganized border between the reunited Federal Republic of Germany and its Polish neighbor.

Ulrich Trumpener

Additional Reading
Duffy, Christopher, *Red Storm on the Reich: The Soviet March on Germany 1945* (1991).
Erickson, John, *The Road to Berlin: Continuing the History of Stalin's War with Germany* (1983).
Toland, John, *The Last 100 Days* (1965).
Ziemke, Earl F., *Stalingrad to Berlin: The German Defeat in the East* (1968).

Germany, West (January–May 1945)
[See map 21 on page 1331]
By the beginning of 1945, the Western Allies had landed seventy-three divisions in northwestern Europe—forty-nine American, twelve British, and eight French. In addition, one Polish and three Canadian divisions were deployed at the northern end of the western front. Two additional Canadian divisions came later from Italy.

After spectacular successes during the summer of 1944, General Dwight D. Eisenhower's (q.v.) forces had ground to a halt at or near Germany's western borders, and only one German city of any significance, Aachen (q.v.), had so far been taken. Moreover, as a result of Adolf Hitler's Ardennes offensive (qq.v.) in late December 1944, the Western Allies were, at least temporarily, in an unbalanced position.

Nevertheless, with a superiority of roughly ten to one in tanks, more than three to one in aircraft, and at least two and one half to one in artillery and troops, the prospects of Eisenhower's forces were very good indeed. Moreover, continued massive air strikes by the Royal Air Force (RAF) and the U.S. Army Air Force (USAAF) against a broad range of military and civilian targets inside the *Reich* made it obvious to an increasing number of Germans that, despite occasional German "successes" at the front, the war was going very badly for them and total defeat was a distinct possibility. This impression was reinforced by a gradual breakdown of the German transportation system, particularly its rail network, and the resultant supply problems that both the *Wehrmacht* and the civilian population were beginning to experience in many regions of Germany.

While January and early February 1945 saw successful Allied offensive action both in the

Ardennes and in Alsace, the decisive thrust of Eisenhower's armies into the interior of Germany would only begin in mid-March. That thrust was preceded and made possible by a costly British-Canadian offensive in the north from 8 February to 10 March, which gained some ground between the Meuse and the Rhine Rivers (*see* Reichswald) and by a big American push toward the Rhine in the middle sections of the front that got under way on 23 February.

Helped initially by the capture of a usable bridge at Remagen (q.v.) on 7 March, the U.S. First, Third, and Seventh Armies in the second half of the month secured and quickly enlarged several bridgeheads on the right bank of the Rhine. Farther north, Field Marshal Bernard L. Montgomery's (q.v.) 21st Army Group, on 23–24 March, likewise crossed the Rhine on a broad front and rapidly advanced into the largely flat terrain of northwestern Germany.

These Allied thrusts, first to the Rhine and then across it, played havoc with the German army groups that Adolf Hitler (q.v.) had entrusted with the defense of his western provinces. In the north, Army Group H, under Colonel General Johannes Blaskowitz (q.v.), found itself split into several fragments, with some of its divisions retreating into the southeastern sections of the Netherlands. Several of Army Group H's divisions also got caught in the Ruhr pocket (q.v.). Created around 1 April by the encirclement of most of Field Marshal Walther Model's (q.v.) Army Group B between the Rhine, the Lippe, and the Sieg Rivers, that pocket progressively shrank under American pressure. By 17 April, most of the German troops within the pocket had surrendered. Model himself hid out for an additional four days and then committed suicide.

The third German Army group on the western front, Army Group G, was commanded by the experienced SS General Paul Hausser (q.v.). Deployed from the German Palatinate to the Swiss border, Hausser's divisions in late March and the opening days of April were unable to block the advances of American and French troops across the Upper Rhine and their subsequent thrusts toward Karlsruhe, Heilbronn, and Würzburg.

Faced with catastrophic setbacks along the western front, Hitler ordered drastic action against "defeatists" and anyone retreating without prior authorization. A "Flying Special Tribunal, West," headed by Lieutenant General Dr. Rudolf Hübner (a former dentist), imposed numerous death sentences on both officers and enlisted personnel of the *Wehrmacht* during the final months of the war.

Beginning in mid-February, a number of German senior commanders on the western front were fired, usually but not always on Hitler's personal orders. The commander of the Seventh Army, General Erich Brandenberger (q.v.), was replaced on 20 February by General Hans Felber; who in turn was forced to hand over command to General Hans von Obstfelder five weeks later on 26 March. On 15 February, the commander of the Nineteenth Army, Siegfried Rasp, was removed and General Hermann Foertsch was appointed in his place. On 10 March, Field Marshal Gerd von Rundstedt (q.v.), once again and for the last time, lost his position as the German commander in chief, west. He was succeeded by Field Marshal Albert Kesselring (q.v.), who had hitherto been in charge of the Italian theater of war. The last major change came on 12 April, when Hausser lost command of Army Group G and was succeeded by General Friedrich Schulz, a relatively young man who had spent most of the war on the Russian front. In addition to these turnovers, the *Wehrmacht* lost the seasoned commander of the First Parachute Army, General Alfred Schlemm, who was seriously wounded on 21 March and eventually replaced by General Günther Blumentritt.

As conditions in Germany became more and more chaotic, Hitler "created" several new field armies—at least on paper and in his own mind. Late in January, for instance, an Eleventh Army (with only a handful of actual troops) was formed in Pomerania for use against the Red Army. Eventually, however, the Eleventh Army staff, under General Walter Lucht, was moved to the Harz Mountain region for action against the Western Allies. Early in April, as American units were racing eastward, a new Twelfth Army was hastily assembled on the western side of the Elbe River. Made up of several new divisions and commanded by General Walther Wenck, this force fought quite effectively against American spearheads in the Magdeburg-Dessau region. Then it was partially redeployed against the Soviets in the area lying southwest of Berlin. Although Wenck's troops failed to "relieve" the German capital, as Hitler expected of them, they did help remnants of the German Ninth Army during their retreat from the Oder front to American-held territory on the western bank of the Elbe in early May.

In April two more phantom armies were added to the German order of battle. One, calling itself the Twenty-first Army and headed by General Kurt von Tippelskirch, made a brief appearance in Mecklenburg and surrendered near Ludwigslust on 3 May. The other, the Twenty-fourth Army, was supposed to cover Germany's border with Switzerland. Commanded by General Hans Schmidt, this "army" seems to have consisted of at most two understrength divisions and was formed primarily to confuse the Allies. Suffice to add that even during its brief sojourn in the Austrian Alps, both the Allies and certain senior commanders on the German side were not quite sure of the exact status and position of Schmidt's force.

While many Allied air strikes in 1945 were directed with great effectiveness at important industrial and transportation targets in the western half of the *Reich*, the "area bombing" of German cities and towns by RAF Bomber Command continued until mid-April. Particularly devastating were night attacks on Worms (in the Rhine Valley), Pforzheim (on the northern edge of the Black Forest), Würzburg (in Franconia), and Paderborn (in Westphalia). In Würzburg, 89 percent of the city's developed area was destroyed and 4,000 inhabitants died in one night. In Pforzheim, one attack wiped out 83 percent of the town and more than 17,000 civilians died in the ensuing firestorm. The towns of Kleve and Wesel, near the Dutch border, were effectively pulverized by repeated air attacks between 7 February and 23 March. With 97 percent of their developed areas destroyed, they were possibly the most devastated urban sites in all of western Germany.

Once they crossed the Rhine River, American, British Commonwealth, and French troops in some regions advanced very quickly, encountering little or no resistance as they progressed toward the east. In other areas, especially around Aschaffenburg, Heilbronn, Kassel, and Nuremberg, American units ran into bitter resistance and were blocked for several days on end. Nevertheless, the Allied sweep through the western half of the *Reich* achieved growing momentum. Münster (in Westphalia) fell on 3 April; Karlsruhe and Kassel fell on 4 April; Würzburg and Eisenach on 5 April; Göttingen on 8 April; and Essen and Hannover on 10 April. On 12 April, the U.S. Ninth Army crossed the Elbe River, and reached the Mulde River on 13 April. By 18 April, Magdeburg was captured, and by 20 April, Leipzig was in American hands. At about the same time, the British Second Army reached the Elbe near Lauenburg, but it then paused for nine days before pushing across the river and on to the Baltic Coast.

With large portions of Germany being overrun by both the Red Army in the east and Eisenhower's forces in the west, Hitler on 20 April divided the regions still under German control into two administrative spheres. The northern reaches of the *Reich* (the *Nordraum*), were placed under the command of Grand Admiral Karl Dönitz (q.v.), while the *Südraum* was entrusted to Field Marshal Kesselring. A few days later, the OKW (q.v.) split into two regional command posts, the northern headquarters moving from Mecklenburg to Schleswig-Holstein and the southern section winding up in the Bavarian Alps.

On 22 April, French units entered Stuttgart shortly before and much to the disgust of the Americans. The next day, the city of Ulm, on the Danube, fell into Allied hands. On 25 April, units of the U.S. 69th Division met Red Army troops in eastern Saxony, near Torgau on the Elbe (*see* Elbe River Meeting), thus cutting the last territorial connection between German forces in the north and those in the *Südraum*. Three days later, American troops captured Augsburg. The Bavarian capital of Munich fell on 30 April.

Designated by Hitler as his successor, Dönitz on 2 May moved his command post to Flensburg, close to the Danish border. He subsequently formed a provisional government that excluded the most notorious Nazis, but kept some members of the old *Reich* cabinet, like Lutz Graf von Schwerin-Krosigk. On 4 May, Dönitz authorized Admiral Hans-Georg von Friedeburg (q.v.) and General Eberhard Kinzel to sign the surrender of all German forces in the Netherlands, northwestern Germany, and Denmark. Accepted by Montgomery at his command post near Lüneburg, the surrender was slated to come into effect at 0800 hours the following day. In addition, Blaskowitz, the commander of Army Group H in the Netherlands, concluded a separate agreement with Lieutenant General Charles Foulkes (q.v.) of the Canadian I Corps at a battered hotel in Wageningen on 5 May.

While Dönitz tried to delay a general German surrender in order to give fleeing German soldiers and civilians in the eastern stretches of the *Reich* more time to get away from the Soviets, partial surrenders to the Western Allies continued in several areas. The most important of these involved the surrender of Army Group G to General Jacob Devers (q.v.) at Haar, near Munich, and of the Nineteenth Army to the U.S. VI Corps at Innsbruck—both signed on 5 May.

By 6 May, Eisenhower had become well aware of Dönitz's delaying tactics and made it known to the Germans that they must surrender on all fronts. Faced with this pressure, Dönitz authorized Colonel General Alfred Jodl (q.v.) to sign a general surrender document. He did so at SHAEF headquarters in Reims at 0241 hours on 7 May. A more formal surrender was subsequently signed in

Berlin by Field Marshal Wilhelm Keitel (q.v.) shortly before midnight on 8 May.

The condition of western Germany at the close of hostilities can be described by only one word—chaos. Most urban areas were badly damaged by Allied bombing or ground combat. The transportation system was in shambles and food was scarce in all but a few isolated rural areas.

While it was difficult enough for the Western powers to take over governmental responsibility in their respective occupational zones, they also had to deal with millions of German refugees from the east, millions of captured *Wehrmacht* personnel, and millions of liberated foreign laborers, former POWs, and former concentration camp inmates. By and large, they dealt with these problems quite effectively in the months after VE Day. Some of their measures, such as the forced repatriation of many people to the Soviet Union or to Soviet-controlled eastern and southeastern Europe, have been subjected to harsh criticism. A recent controversy over the fate of many German soldiers in American and French custody during the spring and summer of 1945 has likewise led to a general consensus in the Western world that the Allies did not always live up to the high moral and humanitarian standards they had set for themselves.

Contrary to Allied fears, there was practically no sabotage or resistance from Nazi fanatics once hostilities had ended. While a good many prominent Nazis went into hiding by VE Day, almost all of them were interested only in their own survival (usually involving an escape to "safer" countries, be they on the Iberian peninsula, in South America, or in the Middle East). The situation in the western half of Germany was further stabilized by the "automatic arrest" of certain categories of Nazi Party and state functionaries, many of whom would be kept behind barbed wire for extended periods of time.

The precarious existence of the German central government in the northern portion of Schleswig-Holstein ended abruptly on 23 May, when Dönitz and most of his associates were arrested by British troops. From that moment on, the fate of the western half of Germany lay exclusively in the hands of the principal occupying powers, that is, the Americans, the British, and the French.

In early July, the victors, in consonance with certain wartime agreements, carried out some major adjustments with regard to territorial authority. Large parts of Saxony and all of Thuringia, overrun by U.S. troops in April 1945 and since administered by them, were now turned over to

the Soviets. In a similar manner, the Red Army evacuated the western half of Berlin so that the Americans, the British, and the French could each assume control of certain districts in the former German capital. Except for insignificant "adjustments" in some spots, these new "zonal" boundaries in Germany and the new "sector" boundaries inside of Berlin were destined to remain in place for the next forty-five years.

Ulrich Trumpener

Additional Reading

Dollinger, Hans (ed.), *Die Letzten Hundert Tage: Das Ende des Zweiten Weltkrieges in Europa und Asien* (1965).

McDonald, Charles B., *The Last Offensive* (1973).

Steinert, Marlis G., *23 Days: The Final Collapse of Nazi Germany* (1969).

Toland, John, *The Last 100 Days* (1965).

Weigley, Russell F., *Eisenhower's Lieutenants: The Campaign of France and Germany, 1944–1945* (1981).

Gleiwitz Raid (31 August 1939)

World War II opened with stories in German newspapers of Polish "attacks" on German territory. A small Silesian town, Gleiwitz, was the center of such actions. On 1 September, Adolf Hitler (q.v.) told the *Wehrmacht*, "I have no choice but to meet force with force," and he sent it into Poland for revenge.

What he did not tell the troops was that members of his own SS (q.v.) were the "invaders." Their mission had been to secure a propaganda coup that would influence both home and neutral audiences. While few were fooled, the "Gleiwitz Raid" provides a good example of Nazi tactics.

Reinhard Heydrich (q.v.) masterminded this operation. His high drama and attention to quirky details gave, in the words of James Lucas, an impression that he "had seen too many spy films." Operation HIMMLER was the code name for these over-complicated plans, with the SD's (q.v.) Alfred Naujocks as leader.

In essence, three attacks were directed against the municipality. The most important involved capturing its small radio station and then broadcasting an inflammatory anti-German message in Polish. To make the charade more convincing, a group of condemned criminals from the Sachsenhausen concentration camp were dressed in Polish uniforms secured from Admiral Wilhelm Canaris of the *Abwehr* (qq.v.). The prisoners, code named

G

CANNED GOODS, were to be given lethal injections, shot, and left behind as "casualties."

Everything went as planned, indeed the whole operation seemed rather mundane. As Naujocks puts it, "We seized the radio station, broadcast a speech of three or four minutes . . . fired some pistol shots and left." Blanketed by the much more powerful signal from Radio Breslau, few if any heard the message. Still, the CANNED GOODS were available for reporters on 1 September, and Hitler had a fig leaf of respectability for starting World War II. Hitler stated that when the Germans had won, no one would ask whether they had told the truth or not.

John Dunn

Additional Reading

Höhne, Heinz, *The Order of the Death's Head: The Story of Hitler's SS* (1970).
Schellenberg, Walter, *Hitler's Secret Service* (1956).

Gothic Line (August–December 1944)

[See map 22 on page 1332]

Even before the Allied invasion of Sicily (q.v.), the German high command (OKW) began considering how the war in Italy should be fought. The OKW and Field Marshal Erwin Rommel (qq.v.), who up to that point had the most experience against the Western Allies, favored abandoning Italy south of a line running from Pisa on the west coast to Rimini on the Adriatic. This would enable Germany to concentrate on defending the areas of the industrial north. Adolf Hitler and Field Marshal Albert Kesselring (qq.v.), German commander in chief in the southwest, wanted to defend the entire country, trading time for space and wearing the Allies down. The concept involved a slow and deliberate withdrawal up the boot of Italy, through a series of strongly fortified defensive lines.

In November 1943, the Germans began occupying the Gustav Line (q.v.), which ran between Gaeta, south of Rome, and the mouth of the Sangro River. The defense of middle Italy rested with the Tenth Army, commanded by General Heinrich Vietinghoff-Scheel (q.v.). He had ten combat-ready divisions, but the Allies had an overwhelming advantage in air superiority. On 18 May, the Allies finally broke through the Gustav Line after a series of successive battles around Monte Cassino (q.v.). The Tenth Army started to withdraw north, but on 23 May, the Allies also broke out of the Anzio (q.v.) beachhead. Instead of trying to cut off Tenth Army, the Allied force at Anzio drove for

Rome. As a result, Tenth Army was able to withdraw north, relatively unmolested.

Kesselring also commanded Army Group C, which consisted of Tenth and Fourteenth Armies, and Army *Liguria*. The Tenth Army was the strongest, with the LXXVI and XIV *Panzer Korps*, the LI Mountain *Korps*, and Group *Hoppe*. The Fourteenth Army, under General Joachim Lemelsen, had only the I Parachute *Korps*, but it included *Panzergrenadier* and infantry divisions. Army *Liguria* was reorganized as Army *von Zangen* at the end of July 1944. Commanded by Italian General Rodolfo Graziani (q.v.), it included LXXV *Korps*, *Korps Liebe*, and various Italian units of dubious reliability.

The new German main defensive position north of Rome was called the Gothic Line, which ran roughly from La Spezia on the west coast to Pesaro on the Adriatic. Forward of this position, the Germans established a series of lesser blocking positions; the Trasimine Line, about 135 kilometers north of Rome, and the Arno Line, which ran from Pisa to Florence to the Adriatic. The Arno Line was about thirty kilometers south of the Gothic Line. The Germans held the Allies at the Trasimine Line for almost two weeks in mid-June, and then continued the withdrawal to the Arno Line.

The Germans knew they could not hold the Arno Line for very long, but the delay bought more time to complete the defenses of the Gothic Line. It was an impressive position, with minefields, barbed wire, and carefully sited artillery and machine gun positions built into the rock and reinforced with concrete. The Germans planned to hold this line until autumn, at which point the September rains and then the November snows would stall the Allies for the rest of the winter. The Tenth Army manned the eastern sector of the line, Fourteenth Army the middle sector, and Army *Liguria* the extreme western end. In total, the Germans had twenty-two divisions in the combat zone by the end of July. They had approximately 800,000 troops of all sorts in Italy, 300,000 of them frontline combat troops.

In June 1944, the Allied 15th Army Group in Italy was commanded by British General Sir Harold Alexander (q.v.). The east side of the Allied line was held by the U.S. Fifth Army, commanded by Lieutenant General Mark Clark (q.v.). Fifth Army consisted of II and VI Corps, and the French Expeditionary Corps. Elements of IV Corps formed the army reserve. To the west of Fifth Army, the British Eighth Army was commanded by General Sir Oliver Leese (q.v.). Eighth

Army consisted of the X and XIII Corps, with the Canadian I Corps in reserve. On the extreme eastern flank of the Allied line, the Polish II Corps and British V Corps came directly under Alexander. The Allies at that point had twenty-five divisions in the combat zone.

The German primary objective since the landings in southern Italy had been to keep the Allies out of the Po River Valley (q.v.) and upper Italy. Securing the Po Valley plain was a top priority because the Germans desperately needed the armament industries in Milan and Turin to compensate for the heavy destruction to German industry from Allied strategic air attacks. The agricultural capacity of the Po Valley (rice, wheat, fruits) also was becoming increasingly important as the Germans continued to lose agricultural regions in eastern Europe.

Construction of the Gothic Line started in August 1943. The Germans assumed the Allies would launch a main attack along the Adriatic coast, because the Apennine Mountains were less steep there than in the middle or in the west of the Italian peninsula. Accordingly, the Germans built their best positions in the eastern sector of the line, between Monte Gridolfo and Pesaro. The line ran along the south of the Apennines, from Viareggio on the Tyrrhenian Sea, to Pesaro on the Adriatic.

As impressive an obstacle as the Apennines may have first appeared, the Gothic Line contained some significant weaknesses. The line was constructed by *Organisation Todt* (q.v.), essentially a civilian enterprise. Those responsible for carrying out the construction often did so with little regard for the advice of the combat-experienced military. The result was numerous tactical flaws that weakened the overall position. The main fighting line, for example, ran exclusively along the front slope of the mountains, which easily came under Allied observation during daylight. The outpost positions were placed only 300 to 400 meters in front of the mountain passes, making an echeloned defense impossible. Finally, fighting positions were emplaced in soft ground, mutual fire support of the positions often was impossible, barbed wire obstacles were too low, and the tank ditches were not wide or deep enough.

Despite these shortcomings, the Gothic Line was still a formidable obstacle. The heaviest concentrations of defensive positions were clustered around the terrain's natural choke-points, the mountain passes. The Futa Pass, which was only two kilometers wide, had a total of three fortified primary positions, twenty-six secondary positions, and 138 tertiary field fortifications. The less heavily defended Il Giogo Pass was covered by fifty-six field fortifications, backed by another fifteen one kilometer to the rear.

The Gothic Line was a defense system consisting of four parallel lines: an outpost line, a secondary line, the main line (called the Green Line), and a back-up line (called the second Green Line). The first two lines were only meant to delay the attacker and force him to deploy. The Green Line was the main line of resistance, with the second Green Line serving as the last possibility to keep the Allies from entering the Po Valley plain. The Gothic Line's key weakness, however, was the lack of heavy weapons and manpower, both in critically short supply as Germany entered the last year of the war.

After capturing Rome, the Allies did not vigorously pursue the Germans as they withdrew north, preferring to rely on their materiel superiority as a means of conserving the lives of their troops. There also was some strategic confusion within the Allied coalition. Prime Minister Winston Churchill (q.v.) had long advocated a plan of moving up the Adriatic side of Italy and into the Balkans in order to link up with the Soviet Army as far east as possible. He already saw the postwar political structure very clearly and he wanted to protect the British sphere of interest in the Near East.

President Franklin D. Roosevelt (q.v.) and the U.S. Joint Chiefs of Staff opposed any such move. They wanted to defeat Germany from the west as fast as possible, in order to free American units for the fight against Japan. The American plan finally carried, which meant that in late July, 15th Army Group had to give up four French and two U.S. divisions for the invasion of southern France (q.v.). This left the Germans with a two-division superiority in the battles for the Gothic Line.

The slow fighting withdrawal from the Arno to the Gothic Line caused high losses in men and materiel on both sides. The overall operational plan of 15th Army Group called for the British to move north along the Adriatic coast. On 25 August, the Eighth Army started its attacks along the German forward positions. The British crossed the Arno Line after hard fighting. They drove deep into sectors of the Gothic Line, but they could not break through. Heavy fighting, especially around Gemmano, lasted into September. By early September, the Eighth Army overran the German positions between Pesaro on the coast and Foglia, about twenty-five kilometers inland. Airpower and the Allies' massive materiel superiority again were the keys to the British success.

G

The U.S. Fifth Army, meanwhile, started its attack in early September, which now forced the Germans to fight along the whole line from Tuscany to the Adriatic Sea. The Americans moved toward Lucca and Pistoria, starting their attack from Florence, which the Germans gave up without a fight. When the Fourteenth Army had to weaken the center of German defensive line in order to send reinforcements to the Adriatic sector, the Americans took advantage and crossed the Arno Line, moving north almost without fighting. They took Pisa and undefended Pistoria, and then halted to reorganize for the coming fight for the mountain passes.

On 10 September 1944, the Fifth Army started its attempt to break through the Gothic Line near the middle of the Italian peninsula. This was the area from which the Fourteenth Army had just shifted three divisions to the east in order to bolster the Tenth Army's position along the Adriatic coast. The result was a gap in the Fourteenth Army's lines, and a front that was stretched too thin. The American primary axis of attack ran along Highway 65, from Florence to Bologna, and then into the Po Valley. That route, however, ran through the Futa Pass (903 meters), the most heavily defended pass in the Gothic Line. The Americans decided, instead, to detour through the Il Giogo Pass, a few miles to the east.

U.S. II Corps spearheaded the attack, supported by Allied airpower and massive artillery. The Fifth Army continued to apply pressure all along the German line from the west coast to the boundary with the British Eighth Army. It was not an easy fight. The narrowness of the pass severely restricted the ability of the attackers to mass. Although three divisions attacked, no more that 1,000 Allied troops could maintain contact with the defenders at any one time.

Eventually the Germans were forced to succumb to the constant pressure. On 17 September, the Americans took the hills on both sides of Il Giogo Pass and the Germans withdrew to the north. The situation at the Futa Pass became untenable. Threatened on their flank, the Germans were forced to pull back there as well. The Americans broke through the Gothic Line along a fifty-kilometer stretch. The first wave quickly turned east toward Imola, in a move to relieve pressure on the British Eighth Army and box in the German Tenth Army. A second American wave headed north for Bologna, where the Allies hoped to reach the Po Valley as early as possible.

The German Fourteenth Army was overwhelmed by the American attack with its massive use of airpower. The Fourteenth Army was powerless to stop the Allied thrust toward the flank of Tenth Army. At that point, Army Group C decided the main Gothic Line was no longer tenable. On 24 September, it ordered the withdrawal to the second Green Line, about fifteen kilometers north. The second Green Line was a much inferior position, however, and the German units continued to sustain high losses, especially from Allied airpower.

Over on the Adriatic coast, the British continued their attacks, passing Cattolica and closing on the second Green Line. They broke through it on 17 September and continued to move north, toward the Rimini Line, a hastily constructed line that ran from south of Rimini to the Republic of San Marino. The fighting continued to cause high losses on both sides. The British V Corps entered San Marino on 20 September.

The Tenth Army withdrew to the Rimini Line on 18 September. With the help of extra divisions transferred over from the Fourteenth Army, they were able to hold off the British temporarily. When the British attacked on a broad front, they used battlefield searchlights on a large scale. This tactic not only blinded the German defenders, but had a psychological impact, impressing the German soldiers with the Allies' superior resources.

Heavy Allied air attacks continued during the following days. The uninterrupted and systematic attacks pounded German artillery positions, armored vehicles, and every German firing position they could locate. The fight for Rimini was one of the heaviest and most costly between the British and the Germans. On 21 September, the Germans took advantage of the heavy rains to break contact and withdraw from Rimini. The Tenth Army abandoned the Rimini Line and the remainder of its positions along the Gothic Line as well. Eleven German divisions were destroyed during the fighting, with 16,000 men killed. British losses were almost as high at 14,000.

At the beginning of October, the Americans made a new push east of Highway 65. They broke through the second Green Line in some places and prepared to continue the attack toward Bologna. The German Fourteenth Army and elements of the Tenth Army were ordered to stop the breakthrough at all costs in a desperate attempt to stabilize the front before winter set in. During October, the main fighting continued south of Bologna. After 21 October, the strength of Fifth Army's attacks slackened. The fighting dragged on at a lower level, without either side gaining much advantage.

On the west coast, the German defenders sat exposed in front of the British, without fixed positions. Heavy autumn rains turned the numerous river plains along the east coast into one large swampy area, unsuitable for armored vehicles. From the Apennine Mountain range, thirteen rivers ran down toward the Adriatic, all generally perpendicular to the British direction of attack. All the rivers had high dikes, a complicated system of deep irrigation channels, and they now had high water. From the end of September to early December, the defenders made skillful use of terrain conditions in what became know as the "Battle of the Rivers." By the end of 1944, the Eighth Army still had not crossed the last six rivers. The British got to thirty kilometers from Bologna. On the Adriatic coast, they reached Lake Comacchio.

The bad weather the Germans had hoped for finally set in. The Allies had to suspend major operations before achieving their breakthrough to Bologna. In the end, the Germans were able to achieve their strategic objective for the winter of 1944–1945. The Gothic Line itself had been a disappointment, but the fighting skill of the German soldiers tipped the balance. The Allies did not resume major offensive operations until April 1945.

Ekkehart Guth

Additional Reading

Fisher, Ernest F., Jr., *Cassino to the Alps* (1977).
Graham, Dominick, and Shelford Bidwell, *Tug of War: The Battle for Italy 1943–1945* (1986).
Kesselring, Albert, *A Soldier's Record* (1954).
Senger und Etterlin, Frido von, *Neither Fear nor Hope* (1964).
Westphal, Siegfried, *Der Feldzug in Italien* (1954).

Gran Sasso Raid (12 September 1943)

Shortly after 1400 hours on 12 September 1943, eight gliders landed in the central grounds of the Campo Imperiale Hotel on Gran Sasso in the Abruzzi mountains, west of Rome. Within moments, approximately seventy German paratroopers and SS commandos, debarked and spread out across the hotel grounds, with *Waffen-SS* Captain Otto Skorzeny (q.v.) in the lead. A master of unconventional warfare, Skorzeny had only one objective—to rescue Benito Mussolini (q.v.), Italy's deposed Fascist dictator. The attack's very audacity paralyzed the compound's Italian guards. They surrendered quickly. A few minutes later, a light Fieseler *Storch* aircraft flew in and took the former Italian dictator and Skorzeny to a nearby airfield

for further transport to Berlin. It was a masterful stroke that embarrassed the Allies and bolstered Axis morale. The entire raid took less than twenty minutes.

Planning for the operation began within days of Mussolini's overthrow on 25 July 1943. Realizing the Germans might rescue Mussolini and attempt to rally Fascist support to keep Italy in the war, the government of General Pietro Badoglio (q.v.) took strong measures to hide and secure Mussolini. They moved him several times over the next few months and posted a guard force of nearly a battalion around the facilities in which he was held.

Given the mission of rescuing Mussolini, Skorzeny discovered that his primary challenge was in locating *Il Duce*. On at least one occasion, the Italians successfully spirited the former dictator away just as Skorzeny was moving in. Finally, on 7 September, German signals intelligence intercepted a report indicating Mussolini was being held somewhere in the Abruzzi mountains. The exact location was confirmed by a ruse in which a German doctor attempted to establish a hospital at the hotel on Gran Sasso mountain. With Mussolini located, Skorzeny prepared for the raid.

His plan called for twelve DFS-230 gliders carrying a total of 120 troops (including Italian General Ferdinando Spoleti) to conduct a vertical assault, regain custody of Mussolini, and hold the hotel until a battalion of paratroopers could reach and secure the mountain's base. Skorzeny then expected to lower *Il Duce* via the cable car that connected the hotel to the valley below. Spoleti was "volunteered" for the mission because he had once commanded some of the troops at the hotel. Skorzeny rightfully believed the troops would hesitate to fire on their old commander.

Only eight of the gliders successfully made the landing. Once Skorzeny had Mussolini in custody, communications problems forced him to change his plans. Instead, he flew the former dictator directly out from the hotel grounds. The Fieseler *Storch* was renowned for its short takeoff and landing capability. It was a daring and risky move, but its success ensured that the raid and Skorzeny would never be forgotten.

The Gran Sasso raid was a major political and propaganda success. Mussolini's daring "escape" rallied the Fascist faithful in Northern Italy. It also earned Skorzeny an Iron Cross and promotion to major. More importantly, it launched him on his career as "Hitler's Commando." By war's end, Skorzeny was in charge of all German special forces.

Carl O. Schuster

Additional Reading
Infield, Glenn B., *Skorzeny: Hitler's Commando* (1981).
Lucas, James, *Kommando* (1985).
Skorzeny, Otto, *Skorzeny's Secret Missions* (1951).

Granville Raid (8–9 March 1945)

Germany's last attack in France took place on 8 March, 1945. Oddly enough, it was launched from British territory, the occupied island of Jersey. Involving some 600 men, the Granville raid was launched by the commander of the German garrisons in the Channel Islands, Admiral Friedrich Huffmeier. His intentions were to inflict whatever damage he could on the Allies and if possible, capture vitally needed supplies, primarily food, for his nearly starving garrison.

Although the raiding force failed to seize the supplies, it captured a coastal freighter and some sixty-seven prisoners, sank one Allied patrol craft, severely damaged three small freighters, and inflicted some damage on the small Allied logistics base at Granville. It was a remarkable feat given that the Allies had total naval, air, and ground supremacy in the area. Although just a small footnote in the history of a world war, the Granville raid demonstrates what a well-trained, determined force can do against a complacent enemy.

Carl O. Schuster

Additional Reading
Cruikshank, Charles, *The German Occupation of the Channel Islands* (1975).
Hooke, William, *Channel Islands* (1953).
Wood, Alan and Mary, *Islands in Danger* (1965).

Greece (28 October 1940–29 April 1941)

[See map 6 on page 1316]

When Germany invaded on 6 April 1941, Greece already had been at war with Italy for six months. In April 1939, Italian forces attacked Albania (q.v.) and followed this up on 28 October 1940 with an attempted invasion of Greece through Albania. So successful was the Greek Army that in six months of hard winter fighting in the mountains, they not only kept the Italians out of Greece, but also pushed them back into Albania in several places. When Albania was attacked by Italy, Neville Chamberlain (q.v.), who was then British prime minister, guaranteed support to Greece in the event of Axis aggression.

In November 1940, Britain honored that pledge by sending five Royal Air Force (RAF) squadrons from Egypt under Air Vice Marshal J.H. D'Albiac. The force consisted of three squadrons of obsolete Blenheims and two of obsolete Gladiators. Further support was provided by the Royal Navy (RN), with a force entering the Adriatic in December to bombard the Albanian port of Valona.

Subsequent events in Greece must be seen against the wider diplomatic and military picture in the eastern Mediterranean and the Balkans in 1940 and 1941. British successes against Italy by land (in Ethiopia [q.v.] and Cyrenaica) and on the sea (at Taranto and Cape Matapan [qq.v.]) put them in a strong position. They even had ground forces to spare after the conquest of Cyrenaica (northeast Libya).

Winston S. Churchill and Foreign Secretary Anthony Eden (qq.v.) hoped to build up a Balkan bloc to prevent any German move southward. But with Hungary and Romania having thrown in their lot with the Axis (from January 1941 there were 80,000 German troops in Romania), there was little chance of this. Adolf Hitler (q.v.) needed the Balkans, including Greece, to secure the right flank of his forthcoming invasion of the Soviet Union and to threaten the British position in Egypt. Yugoslavia was a small and virtually defenseless country, and its attitude, if threatened, was unknown.

Greece was ambivalent on whether to accept British help against the German threat. Not much was offered and premature acceptance might provoke rather than deter a German attack. Nor was Greece a truly united country. The seizure of power by Ioamis Metaxas (q.v.) in 1936 had left a deep Left-Right split. This event would have dramatic repercussions following the liberation of Greece in 1944. Six hundred officers, who had been dismissed for holding Republican views, were not even allowed to rejoin the Army after Italy invaded.

Greece's gallant defense against the Italians was eating up all its military strength, and there would be little left to face the might of Germany. Britain was still undecided. What forces it could send would probably have little effect on the outcome and could well be put to better use elsewhere. But what impression would America and other neutrals gain of Britain's resolve if it stood back and watched Greece go under?

In January 1941, Metaxas died, and on 23 February, his successor, Alexandros Koryzis, accepted the British offer. The Greeks wanted nine divisions, but all that could be promised was 100,000 men, less than half their request. The British force included 17,000 Australians and

16,000 New Zealanders, and was known as the Imperial Expeditionary Force. Early in March, Lieutenant General Sir Henry Maitland Wilson (q.v.) arrived in Athens to begin planning the British part in Greece's defense. This was complicated by two closely related factors. First, the main Greek defense, the Metaxas Line, was built in the northeast to counter an invasion from Bulgaria, Greece's ancient enemy. Second, nobody knew what Yugoslavia would do, and any German invasion through southern Yugoslavia would immediately outflank the Greek defenses.

In any event, the Anglo-Greek forces were geographically split and uncoordinated. The bulk of the Greek force that could be spared from the Albanian front manned the Metaxas Line. Four British divisions and three weak Greek divisions manned the Aliákmon Line, named for the river that flows eastward from the Albanian border to its mouth near Mount Olympus.

On 6 April, the Germans invaded Yugoslavia and Greece simultaneously. The attack on Greece was commanded by General Wilhelm List (q.v.), who had thirteen divisions and 200 tanks under his Twelfth Army. The attack, Operation MARITA, was launched initially from Bulgaria, and later through southern Yugoslavia. The Luftwaffe had 780 aircraft in the area, and their Italian allies had another 300. Against this force the RAF (with some naval reinforcements) had only eighty.

The campaign was brief—a triumph for the Germans, a disaster for the British and Greeks. On 9 April, the Greek Army on the Metaxas Line was forced to capitulate, and Salonika, the country's second city, fell. On 21 April, another Greek force, 140,000 strong, laid down their arms in Epiris. That was suspicious, especially since its commander, General Georgios Tsolakoglou, was appointed prime minister by the occupying Germans. Koryzis committed suicide in shame of a defeat for which he was not responsible. Thus with Greece disintegrating, the British decided to evacuate the Imperial Expeditionary Force, also known as "W Force." Only 58,000 of the promised 100,000 troops had arrived by this time.

The contribution of the British consisted mainly of a series of rear guard actions in the mountain passes of northern and central Greece, notably at Vevi on the Yugoslav border, the area around Mt. Olympus and Thermopylae. D'Albiac's airmen, outnumbered ten to one, fought with great gallantry, but they soon ceased to be an effective force, and the army was left without air cover. The bulk of the ground fighting fell upon the Australian and New Zealand infantry. They performed with the same courage and endurance as their ANZAC fathers had shown at Gallipoli a generation earlier and a mere 250 miles away.

The evacuation, started on 24 April, was completed in five days, mostly from beaches and small ports on the Peloponnesian peninsula. After German paratroopers captured the bridge over the Corinth Canal, the Thebes rear guard of 7,000 men were lifted from beaches near Athens. The Germans entered the city on 27 April. In the end, some 50,000 troops, or about eighty percent of the British force, were evacuated from Greece, but all equipment except personal weapons was destroyed. The successful completion of the evacuation was a feather in the cap of the RN, operating under difficult circumstances. But as Churchill noted after Dunkirk (q.v.), "evacuations do not win wars." Although the RN controlled the eastern Mediterranean, the skies around Greece were now dominated by the newly arrived Luftwaffe. Consequently, the British evacuation ships had to arrive on station an hour after sunset, and be clear of land by 0300 hours to ensure they would not be caught in the daylight.

German losses in the Greek campaign were 1,500 killed (including 200 valuable pilots) and 3,700 wounded. The Italians and the Greeks each suffered about 30,000 casualties, and 270,000 Greeks were captured. Of the 900 Commonwealth troops killed and 1,500 wounded, 600 and 900, respectively, were either Australians or New Zealanders. British equipment losses included seventy-two planes, 100 tanks, 400 guns, and 8,000 vehicles. The RN lost two warships and four transports, plus twenty-one smaller vessels. In compensation, one cruiser, six destroyers, and four submarines of the Greek Navy escaped to fight under British command.

Despite the help Britain was able to send, Greece was overwhelmed by a superior enemy. It must not be forgotten that for six months Greece's gallant and ill-equipped army kept the Italians at bay. Not one Italian soldier was on Greek soil when Greece surrendered to Germany. Another feature, commented on by many British soldiers, was the warmth and friendliness shown them by the Greek people as they departed, even though they were abandoning them to Nazi occupation.

Historians have long argued whether it was right to send British help to Greece. With hindsight, it is argued that had this force been kept in North Africa, it might have captured all of Libya before General Erwin Rommel (q.v.) and German reinforcements could arrive. As it was, Rommel was able to drive the weakened British back into

Egypt, and it was not until El Alamein (q.v.) in October 1942 that the Axis threat to the Suez Canal was finally removed and Britain's position in the Middle East solidified.

Militarily the Greece expedition was a disaster, "a gamble without hope," as one author described it. The decision was made on moral and political grounds. The British ambassador thought that if no help were sent, "We shall be pilloried by the Greeks and the world in general." Anthony Eden wrote: "No doubt our prestige will suffer if we are ignominiously ejected, but . . . to have fought and suffered in Greece would be less damaging to us than to have left Greece to her fate."

Philip Green

Additional Reading

Papagos, General Alexandros, *The German Attack on Greece* (1946).

Smith, E.D., *Victory of a Sort—The British in Greece 1941–46* (1988).

Greece (1 October 1944–12 February 1945)

Events in Greece in 1944 and 1945 must be seen as part of a longer story, reaching forward to the Cold War and back to the bitter prewar divisions between Monarchists, Republicans, and Communists. The trauma of defeat and foreign occupation in 1941 exacerbated rather than healed these divisions, with the result that the tale of Axis occupation is as much one of Greek against Greek as of Greek against Italian and German.

The left versus right civil war, fought in three distinct phases, lasted from 1943 to 1949, and cost 150,000 Greek lives. In the second phase (1944–45), British troops sent to liberate Greece were forced to intervene on the side of the established government against the Communist insurrection. The story of Greece in these years is remarkably similar to that of neighboring Yugoslavia except, significantly, the Greek Communists did not produce a leader of Tito's (q.v.) caliber.

Immediately after the Axis occupation in April 1941, two resistance forces emerged. The National Popular Liberation Army (ELAS) was set up clandestinely by the Communist Party, while the smaller force, the EDES, was politically Republican. The former group was led by the "Red Colonel," Euripides Bakirtzis, and the Moscow-trained secretary general of the Greek Communist Party, Georgios Siantos. The latter force was led by two regular officers, Napoleon Zervas and Dimitrios Psaros. The British SOE (q.v.) supported both

groups, sending logistic help and a liaison team headed by Brigadier E.C.W. Myers and Colonel D.M. Woodhouse. The two resistance movements cooperated only once, when under British control they combined to destroy the Corgopotamus Viaduct and sever the major railway line in Greece.

By the winter of 1943–1944, the two resistance movements were at each other's throats. When the Italians surrendered in September 1943, they left the bulk of their weapons and equipment in Greece to the ELAS. They used the weapons to fight their political opponents, the EDES, rather than the Germans. The EDES was defeated, and its leader, Psaros, killed. In March 1944, the political wing of the triumphant ELAS, the EAM, set up government on Greek soil in opposition to the legitimate Royalist one in exile under British protection.

Two conferences were held in 1944 in an attempt to avoid further conflict in Greece. One in Lebanon was chaired by the legitimate prime minister, Georgios Papandreou (q.v.), and the other in Caserta, Italy, was chaired by Lieutenant General Sir Henry Maitland Wilson (q.v.), British commander in the Middle East. The rival resistance leaders attended both. It was agreed that when liberation came the resistance movements would subordinate their political activities to the legitimate Greek government, and place their military wings under British command.

Liberation came fairly peacefully in 1944. On 1 October, British commando (q.v.) units landed at Póros. Two days later Allied forces landed near Pátrai on the Peloponnesian peninsula. The Germans, as a result of heavy defeats in the Soviet Union, decided to withdraw their forces to defend Germany. As they left, the German commander in Greece, Field Marshal Maximilian von Weichs (q.v.), was instructed to "foster the strife between the two groups after our departure as much as possible." Hot on the Germans' heels came the British, assuming the Caserta agreement would work. They brought more administrative units designed for relief work among the starving civilian population than fighting troops.

Relations between the British, under Lieutenant General Ronald Scobie, and the Communist ELAS were strained from the start. In December, they turned into open hostilities. The immediate cause came when police opened fire on a peaceful left-wing demonstration in Athens. There is evidence the incident was stage-managed by the Communists. Ioannis Ioannides, organizing secretary of the Greek Politburo, admitted that the "ELAS was to clash with the British if political maneuvers failed." ELAS units were in position to attack British positions even before the Athens demonstration.

Apparently, the Communists saw their opportunity to take over the country by force while the government forces were virtually nonexistent and the British weak and thinly spread. They received no physical or moral support from Soviet Premier Josef Stalin (q.v.), who regarded Greece as outside his sphere of influence. Moreover, he had no wish to antagonize his Western Allies at this stage.

The British policy was to provide small but secure bases from which the Greek government could operate. They concentrated their meager forces in Athens, Salonika, Patras, and Volos. Almost all the fighting took place in Athens, where at one stage the British were reduced to holding a square mile of the city, the airport, and the adjacent port of Piraeus.

After Churchill and Field Marshal Sir Harold Alexander (q.v.) visited Athens on Christmas Day 1944, reinforcements were sent from Italy. The British then went on the offensive, and by mid-January, the defeated ELAS asked for a truce, but not before eliminating all traces of the Republican EDES resistance under Zervas.

On 12 February 1945, the Agreement of Varkiza formally ended this second stage of the Greek civil war. The ELAS agreed to hand in their arms, to hold free elections supervised by an Allied commission, and a plebiscite to decide whether King George II (q.v.) would return from exile. Meanwhile, Archbishop Damaskinos, a man respected for his uncompromising attitude toward the German occupation, would act as regent.

The British deployed 75,000 troops (including Indian) to Greece, mainly from Italy, where they were sorely needed to fight the Germans. Casualties included 237 killed and 2,100 wounded. The RAF sent eight squadrons and flew some 1,600 missions. For the men involved, sorting out a bloodthirsty squabble between "allies" in the middle of a major war, the situation was, to say the least, perplexing. Their task was not made easier by carping criticism in some British and American newspapers, and by some Labour Party members in the British Parliament. Lord Hunt, then a brigade commander (and later to lead the 1953 British conquest of Mount Everest) wrote:; "I have never, before or since, been subjected to greater stress."

The Greek viewpoint was best summed up by George Kartalis, an EDES leader: "Why so much hate? Why all this evil? The war will surely end and the Allies will win. But what will become of Greece?"

Sadly for Greece, after free elections were held and the king had returned following the plebiscite, there was a third stage of the civil war to come, from late 1946 to July 1949. Fought with only limited British logistic and training support for the government forces, this stage ended only when Tito closed his border to the Greek Communist rebels following his break with Moscow.

This unhappy saga, with its mixture of resistance to Axis occupation and Communist rebellion against an established government, spans both World War II and the Cold War that followed. It is evidence too, of another key fact of twentieth-century history. The British inability to maintain adequate support for the Greek government in the third phase, and their request to the United States to take over this burden, marked a significant step in Britain's retreat from world power status.

Philip Green

Additional Reading
Mazowerz, Mark, *Inside Hitler's Greece: The Experience of Occupation, 1941–1944* (1993).

Papastratis, Procopis, *British Policy toward Greece during the Second World War* (1984).

Smith, E.D., *Victory of a Sort—The British in Greece 1941–46* (1988).

Woodhouse, C.M., *Struggle for Greece* (1976).

Guernica Air Raid (26 April 1937)

The growing military power of Nazi Germany was demonstrated to the world on 26 April 1937 when waves of Heinkel and Junker bombers from Germany's *Kondor Legion* (q.v.) carried out a three-hour precision air raid against the ancient and traditional Basque capital city of Guernica, leaving it almost completely in ruins. Heinkel fighter aircraft escorting the bombers strafed civilians who fled into the open countryside to escape the bombs. Civilian dead numbered 1,654 with 889 wounded.

As the defenseless city was of no military or strategic importance to either the Republican or the Insurgent armies of the Spanish civil war (q.v.), this attack was perceived by the world as a wanton act of terrorism ordered by a vindictive General Francisco Franco (q.v.), leader of the Insurgent (also called the National list) forces. He considered the Basques traitors and used the raid as a means of destroying Basque autonomy and support for the Republican government. Franco denied the purpose of the raid and questioned the extent of the damage to the city.

Adolf Hitler (q.v.) simply dismissed the allegations of German involvement. At that time, it was even argued that the "Communists" had burned the city. Hermann Göring (q.v.), commander of the *Luftwaffe*, admitted in 1946 at his trial before the International Military Tribunal at Nuremberg (q.v.), that Germany had in fact used the Spanish civil war and Germany's support for Franco as a means of testing combat readiness of its new weapons.

Hitler's Germany and Benito Mussolini's (q.v.) Italy became the chief benefactors of Franco's insurgency against a left-leaning popular front government of the Spanish Republic in Madrid. Hitler supplied a large number of "volunteers" to Franco's army. In the summer of 1936, Hitler sent aircraft to transport the Army of Africa from Morocco to the Spanish mainland. Italian fighter aircraft also flew in support of this operation. Additional units of the *Luftwaffe*, including the *Kondor Legion,* were later sent to Spain.

The popular front government was supported by the Basque minority in northern Spain. In exchange for this support, Madrid promised home rule for the Basque province. When Franco declared himself the head of the Spanish state in October 1936, the first Basque provincial government under José Antonio Aquirre was established a week later. In November 1936, Franco's insurgents began their siege of Madrid, forcing the Republican government to flee to Valencia. Franco also ordered the bombing of other Spanish cities remaining loyal to the Republican cause.

The bombing of Guernica immediately became the symbol of the brutality of the Spanish civil war and the ruthlessness of Franco's Fascist insurgency supported by Germany and Italy. A week after the attack, the Spanish artist, Pablo Picasso, who had condemned the reactionary attack on popular Spanish democracy and whom the Republican government had appointed as director of the Prado Museum in Madrid, began his famous and complex mural depicting the bombing of Guernica. In it he clearly illustrated his abhorrence of Franco's Fascists and their tactics. The world would discover and visualize these horrors when the mural was displayed at the Spanish Pavilion at the International Exhibition in Paris later that summer.

Steven B. Rogers

Additional Reading

Blunt, Anthony, *Picasso's Guernica* (1969).
Jackson, Gabriel, *The Spanish Republic and the Civil War, 1931–1939* (1965).
Salas Larrazabal, Jesus, *Guernica* (1987).
Thomas, Gordon, and Max Morgan Witts, *Guernica: The Crucible of World War II* (1975).

Gustav Line (October 1943–May 1944)

[See map 1 on page 1311]

On 29 September 1943, General Dwight D. Eisenhower and Italian Marshal Pietro Badoglio (qq.v.) signed the armistice that ended Italy's participation in the war on the Axis side. Two days later the Allies captured Naples. Eisenhower and British General Sir Harold Alexander (q.v.) confidently and publicly predicted that Rome would be in their hands by the end of October. Alexander set Civitavecchia, forty miles beyond Rome, as the next objective for General Mark Clark's (q.v.) U.S. Fifth Army. That they had to wait another seven months, until 4 June 1944, before Rome was captured is a measure of the determination and efficiency of German resistance in the winter of 1943–1944, combined with the strength of their defensive position, the Gustav Line.

Also called the Winter Line, the Gustav Line ran from the Tyrrenhian coast in the west to the Adriatic in the east, following the rivers Gargliano, Rapido, and Sangro. The inherent defensive advantages afforded by rivers and mountains were greatly improved by manmade positions, with concrete bunkers, machine gun pits blasted out of rock, barbed wire, and massive minefields. The line was particularly strong in the key western sector, where Monte Cassino (1,700 feet) completely dominated the Liri Valley and Route 6 from Naples to Rome—the Allies' main axis of advance. A quotation from Clark's autobiography vividly illustrates the strength of this obstacle:

> "A whole book could be devoted to the vast job the German Todt Organization had done in converting the mountains behind the enemy's river defense line into the bastion of reinforced steel and concrete."

Another quotation, from an order signed personally by Adolf Hitler, makes clear the importance he attached to the position:

> "The Gustav Line must be held at all costs for the sake of the political consequences which would follow a completely successful defense. The *Führer* expects a struggle for every meter."

The line was defended by the German Tenth Army, commanded by General Heinrich von

Vietinghoff-Scheel (q.v.). The LXXVI *Panzer Korps* held the eastern side, and the XIV *Panzer Korps* held the western flank. The Allies in Italy were under the supreme command of Alexander and his 15th Army Group. Alexander had General Sir Bernard L. Montgomery's (q.v.) Eighth Army (V and XIII Corps) in the east, and Clark's Fifth Army (U.S. VI and British X Corps) on the western flank. In December 1943, Montgomery returned to Britain in preparation for Operation OVERLORD, and General Sir Oliver Leese (q.v.), previously commander of XIII Corps, assumed command of the Eighth Army.

In January 1944, the French Expeditionary Force under General Alphonse Juin (q.v.) joined the Fifth Army in corps strength. Both the British and French Corps of Fifth Army were, in fact, imperial formations: the former had Canadian, Indian (including Gurkha units) and New Zealand divisions; the latter's four divisions included one Algerian and one Moroccan division. There also was a Polish division in the British Eighth Army.

The Allies outnumbered the Germans—peak strengths in the theater were twenty-eight and twenty-three divisions, respectively—and Allied divisions usually had more troops. The Allies also enjoyed virtual command of the sea and air and superior logistical support. The German commander in chief, Field Marshal Albert Kesselring (q.v.), was not too alarmed by the possibility of sea power being used to turn his flank. On 1 November 1943, he issued a directive to von Vietinghoff to ignore this danger and to concentrate on delaying the Allies as far south as possible to gain time for the further strengthening of the Gustav Line. The German advantages were terrain and severe winter weather, both of which strongly favored the defense. To these must be added the courage and skill of the German soldiers.

On the Adriatic side, the Eighth Army made slow but steady progress. British commandos (q.v.) captured Termoli on 2 October, and the 78th Division quickly crossed the River Biforno to link up with them. Advancing along the coast and helped by naval gunfire support, the same division crossed the Trigno on 22 October, captured Vasto on 5 November, and was up to the River Sangro (q.v.) by 8 November. On a parallel axis fifteen miles inland, the Indian 8th Division took Montefalone, Palmoli, Casalanguido, and Perano in the space of three weeks. By 11 November, it too had reached the Sangro, about ten miles from the river's mouth.

On 20 November, five British battalions established a bridgehead on the northern bank in torrential rain. Their Bailey bridges were washed away and they were cut off, but the Germans had insufficient reserves to take advantage. It was not until a week later, when an armored brigade succeeded in getting 100 tanks across, that the bridgehead was secure and the advance could continue. On 27 December, three days after Montgomery handed command over to Leese, the Canadian 1st Division captured Ortona and its excellent harbor after a week of bitter street fighting and intensive naval and air bombardment.

It was the western sector, however, through which passed the route to Rome, that was the more important. Events there were dominated by two places: the abbey of Monte Cassino (q.v.) and the town of the same name, lying at the mountain's base and forming the key point in the whole Gustav Line; and Anzio (q.v.), where the Allies attempted to use their sea power to outflank the German defenses.

In this sector of the Italian front, the events of the winter of 1943–1944 are best studied in three phases: (1) the advance to the Gustav Line in the last three months of 1943; (2) the three assaults on Cassino and Monte Cassino in the first three months of 1944 (all unsuccessful), and the first mounted simultaneously with the landing at Anzio; and (3) the successful attack between Cassino and the sea that breached the Gustav Line, linked up with Anzio, and led finally to the capture of Rome.

In the first phase, it took the Fifth Army three months of hard fighting to advance the average of twenty-five miles from the Volturno (q.v.) to the Gargliano and Rapido Rivers. Before the Americans could start their attack on the Gustav Line, which lay behind these last two rivers, they had to first break two outlying defensive lines. The first was the Barbara Line, which ran from Mondregone on the coast through Presenzano to the Matese Mountains. The second was the Bernhard (or Reinhard) Line, which formed a bow in front of the main Gustav Line from Sant' Ambrogio to Presenzano to Castel di Sangro, and included the three formidable mountains of Difensa, Maggiore, and Camino. Though not so strong as the Gustav Line, these two subsidiary lines were, nonetheless, formidable obstacles.

The terrain was not conducive to fluid maneuver, and the Allied advance consisted of a series of old-fashioned infantry attacks at battalion, brigade, and divisional level. All the attacks were made on well prepared defensive positions, on steep hills or fortified villages, and often in appalling weather. Under such conditions, the infantry relied heavily on artillery support. In one instance, an infantry brigade attack on Monte Cassino in

G

Aerial view of the ruined town of Cassino, Italy, after several weeks of intense fighting between Allied and Axis forces, March 1944. (IWM C 4244)

December was supported by the artillery of two corps, with 1,300 tons of ammunition falling on four targets within seventy-five minutes.

In early November, British patrols reached the Gargliano, but it was not until the end of the year that the U.S. Fifth Army had completely closed in along the Gustav Line, from the mouth of the Gargliano in the west, to Castel di Sangro in the middle of the Italian peninsula. At that point, the assault on the Gustav Line itself could start.

The primary purpose of this assault was to force a crossing of the Gargliano and Rapido Rivers, and in this the Allies had an early success. On 17 January, X Corps launched an attack by three divisions, the 5th, 46th, and 56th. By the end of the next day, the 5th and 56th Divisions were completely across the Gargliano near its mouth. They established a firm bridgehead threatening the town of Minturno. The attack was supported by a massive naval bombardment, as well as by organic artillery.

Although the 46th Division was unsuccessful in its attempt to capture Sant' Ambrigio at the confluence of the Liri, Rapido, and Gargliano, the overall British progress forced von Vietinghoff to shift a division from the Adriatic sector. Despite a strong German counterattack on 24 January, which temporarily recaptured Castelforte and

Monte Rotondo, the bridgehead on the north bank remained firmly in Allied hands in the months ahead, and it was slowly expanded.

Further inland, the first five weeks of 1944 were occupied in attempts by American and French divisions to cross the Rapido (q.v.) and to capture Monte Cassino and the town. On 21 January, five companies of the U.S. 36th Division crossed the river, only for their bridgehead to be eliminated by German paratroopers during the night. Five days later, the 36th Infantry Division tried again, and this time established a firm bridgehead just north of Cassino from which attacks on the town and mountain could be launched. Despite fighting with great courage, the attackers were unable to overcome a combination of terrain, winter weather, and tenacious defenders, and on 11 February, the assault was called off.

Though Allied efforts on the Rapido and around Cassino made little gain, they distracted German attention and drew reserves from Anzio, where Major General John Lucas's (q.v.) VI Corps landed on 22 January. It is interesting to note how confident the Allies still were at this point about a swift advance to Rome. On the same day as the Anzio landing, they dropped two million leaflets on Rome announcing its imminent liberation.

On 3 February, Alexander ordered the formation of a new corps from Eighth Army units to be assigned to Fifth Army. The New Zealand Corps, composed of the New Zealand 2nd and Indian 4th Divisions, was commanded by Lieutenant General Sir Bernard Freyberg (q.v.). It was this corps that made the second attack on Monte Cassino, after the controversial Allied air attack on the ancient monastery that crowned the mountain. The Indians got within a few hundred yards of the top of the mountain, and the New Zealanders got into the outskirts of the town, all to no avail. After four days, this attack, too, was called off.

Preparations were made immediately for another attack, again by Freyberg's corps, this time with the town of Cassino as the main objective. Delayed by bad weather, the attack finally was launched on 15 March. It was preceded by a bombardment of 1,000 tons of bombs and 1,200 tons of shells. Churchill quoted Alexander as saying: "it seemed to me inconceivable that any troops should be left alive after eight hours of such terrific hammering." The defenders, however, were very much alive, and determined to fight. Both Freyberg's two divisions and their opponents, the German 1st Parachute Division, were among the best infantry soldiers in the world. For four days, they fought to a draw among the rubble and ruins of Cassino. Although Freyberg was convinced that he would succeed with another attack, Alexander, on 23 March, suspended further frontal attacks on the Gustav Line until the weather improved.

The Allies, meanwhile, launched Operation STRANGLE, a massive air interdiction campaign aimed at disrupting the German lines of communication, particularly the three main railway lines from northern Italy. While the Allies were failing to capture Cassino, there was stalemate at Anzio too, where 150,000 troops were crammed into a bridgehead five miles by ten. To quote Churchill again: "instead of hurling a wild cat onto the shore all we got was a stranded whale and Suvla Bay over again."

Alexander took advantage of the enforced lull to rest his men and to regroup his divisions, moving the bulk of his forces over from the Adriatic sector. Operation STRANGLE began to have its effect too. Although the Germans were able to maintain themselves during the lull, they were not able to build up reserve stocks. Thus, when the Allied offensive renewed in May, the Germans had insufficient resources for a prolonged effort.

The final, and successful, attack was launched on 11 May, on a twenty-mile front between the sea and the Liri River. It was preceded by yet another massive artillery bombardment of some 2,000 guns, with the Allied air forces joining in at daylight. Von Vietinghoff was taken completely by surprise; twelve hours earlier, he had reported to Kesselring that all was quiet, and he had gone to Rastenberg to receive a decoration from Hitler. The Allied deception plan had worked perfectly. While twenty-three German divisions were more or less evenly spread along the line, the Allies had only three of their twenty-eight in the Adriatic sector. In the primary sector of the attack, the Allies mustered a three to one superiority. Furthermore, by not knowing where and when the attack would fall, von Vietinghoff scattered his reserves and positioned them too far back.

The fighting was fierce, but the Gustav Line was finally breached in many places by this great assault. On 18 May, the British 4th Division captured the town of Cassino, and on the same day, the 12th Podolski Regiment hoisted the Polish flag over the ruins of the Benedictine monastery atop Monte Cassino. It is noteworthy that the monastery was not captured by actual fighting. After repulsing two Polish attacks the previous day, the defenders withdrew at night when breaches of other parts of the line made their own position untenable. It is also significant that when Monte Cassino finally fell, it was to attacks from the north, as officers with experience in mountain warfare, such as Juin and Frank Tuker (Indian 4th Division) had always predicted.

On 24 May, Hitler authorized Kesselring to abandon the Gustav Line. Meanwhile, the Allies were also at last breaking out of Anzio. On 25 May, units of II Corps made contact with VI Corps, which was advancing northward along the Tyrrenhian coast. The German withdrawal was skillfully conducted, with the mountainous terrain affording them a series of strong rear guard positions that prevented the Allies from making full use of their copious armor. The Germans were aided, too, by Clark's decision to press on northward from the Anzio beachhead at full speed to capture Rome, which he did on 4 June. Had he moved east from Anzio, the bulk of the German forces retreating from the Gustav Line would have been trapped.

For the last half-century, military historians have debated the rights and wrongs of three key issues of this winter campaign. Should and could Lucas have advanced further inland immediately after his unopposed landing at Anzio? Was the bombing and destruction of the Monte Cassino monastery necessary? Would Clark have inflicted more damage on the Germans if he had ignored the glittering prize of Rome and struck eastward to cut off the retreating Tenth Army? These are all fascinating topics that throw much light on the problems and responsibilities of high command in modern war. What should always be remembered is that at regimental, company, and platoon level, the Gustav Line campaign involved some of the hardest infantry fighting between the Western Allies and Germany in World War II.

Philip Green

Additional Reading
Clark, Mark, *Calculated Risk* (1951).

D'Este, Carlo, *Fatal Decision: Anzio and the Battle for Rome* (1991).

Graham, Dominick, and Shelford Bidwell, *Tug of War: The Battle for Italy, 1943–1945* (1986).

Jackson, W.G.F., *The Battle for Italy* (1967).

Majdalany, Fred, *Cassino, Portrait of a Battle* (1957).

Trevelyan, Raleigh, *Rome '44* (1981).

H

Habbaniya (2–19 May 1941)

In the spring of 1941, the brief but intense fighting at Habbaniya in central Iraq became the focus of a larger struggle to protect Britain's Iraqi oil sources and strategic position throughout the Middle East. Severe British military defeats in North Africa and Greece (qq.v.) had emboldened some Iraqi nationalists. The crisis began on 1–3 April when a former prime minister, Rashid Ali al-Gailani, seized power in Baghdad with help from a disgruntled army faction. Perhaps only a figurehead for his anti-British military backers, Rashid Ali appeared to be pro-Axis, causing the alarmed British to take immediate countermeasures.

The terms of a 1930 treaty not only gave Britain two air bases, Habbaniya and Shu'ayba near Basra, but also the right to move British troops across Iraq. That provision was now invoked. In March 1941, London transferred protection of Iraq to India Command. On 18–19 April, a brigade of the Indian 10th Division landed at Basra and a half-battalion of British infantry soon followed. Orally and then on 27 April in writing, Rashid Ali demanded the British forces proceed to Palestine before further units entered Iraq; but Britain's ambassador asserted his nation's rights. Evacuation of British dependents via Habbaniya and Basra began; other Britons and Americans took refuge in their respective embassies in Baghdad.

The Royal Air Force (RAF) base at Habbaniya was home to Number 4 Flying Training School and a principal staging base for flights to India. A fenced compound with a seven-mile perimeter and designed for comfort, the base was not defendable against Iraqi ground attack. Enemy control of a nearby desert plateau also placed the entire base within easy gunfire range. Among the roughly 2,250 troops available (The King's Own Royal Regiment arrived from India in late April) were many technical and support personnel. The complement had only thirty or so trained pilots to fly some eighty varied and mostly obsolete planes, and the British could count on only two old howitzers and about eighteen armored cars. Further complicating the situation were many civilian dependents and evacuees.

Overnight on 29–30 April, an Iraqi force of 9,000 deployed on high ground around Habbaniya but took no action. Fighting began on 2 May after the Iraqis ignored Air Vice Marshal H.G. Smart's demand to withdraw. At dawn, his motley assortment of aircraft bombed the Iraqi positions. Iraq then retaliated with air attacks and continuous artillery fire, but the Iraqi gunners' failure to hit the essential water tower and power plant showed an unexpected lack of determination as well as skill.

The British, meanwhile, conducted night raids on Iraqi lines. Such actions continued for three days. On 2 May, London transferred Iraq back to Mideast Command and Prime Minister Winston S. Churchill (q.v.) ordered troops sent from Palestine. After vain protest from the already hard-pressed Middle East commander in chief, General Sir Archibald Wavell (q.v.), Major General J.G.W. Clark led a relief force of motorized troops, artillery units, supply trucks, and desert fighters on the 500-mile trek to central Iraq. By the time it arrived, however, Habbaniya's defenders had already forced an Iraqi withdrawal.

Air actions proved decisive. Iraq could field about fifty good planes, including Italian fighters and American bombers. Refittings gave the British sixty effective aircraft, plus some Blenheims flown in; but losses among the old aircraft were heavy. Still, the makeshift air force flew more than 1,500 sorties, dropped about 100 tons of bombs, and fired 250,000 rounds at Iraqi positions and vital supply convoys. Airborne evacuation of non-combatants proceeded whenever possible.

Habbaniya's vigorous defense led the worried Iraqis to withdraw before dawn on 6 May. The British continued ground and air attacks as the Iraqis retreated toward Baghdad, fifty miles to the east. Iraqi troops, nevertheless, mounted a stiff but vain counterattack near Fallujah to keep possession of a key bridge spanning the Euphrates River. Arrival of the Palestine relief force on 18 May allowed further advances. With British units converging on Baghdad, resistance soon collapsed.

Rashid Ali and other Iraqi leaders fled abroad. Their regime lacked specific plans, clear support from the divided army, and military aid from foreign sympathizers. Only a few German and Italian planes, with maintenance crews, had landed at Mosul in northern Iraq. While *Luftwaffe* planes saw some action, their role was minimal, and RAF units soon eliminated their threat. British troops entered Baghdad on 31 May and Mosul on 4 June.

The British victory restored the regent to power, and Iraq joined the Allies in early 1943. Britain's continued military presence, however, fed a slowly growing Iraqi nationalism. Lebanon and Syria (q.v.) were also wrested from Vichy France by British and Free French forces in June–July 1941. As a result, the immediate challenge to Allied supremacy in the far eastern Mediterranean and Middle East had ended.

Richard Wires

Additional Reading

Guedalla, Philip, *Middle East, 1940–1942: A Study in Air Power* (1944).
Longrigg, Stephen H., *Iraq, 1900 to 1950* (1953).
Warner, Geoffrey, *Iraq and Syria, 1941* (1979).

HAIFISCH (SHARK), Operation (April–August 1941)

Operation *HAIFISCH* (SHARK) was one of the central elements in the elaborate German deception plan designed to divert Soviet attention from the massive military buildup prior to the 22 June 1941 launching of Operation BARBAROSSA, the invasion of the Soviet Union. Starting on 31 July 1940, those deception efforts involved several complementing and overlapping measures. The actual military preparations, Operation *AUFBAU OST* (BUILDUP EAST), started that day under the cover story that they were preparations for Germany's previously postponed Operation SEA LION (q.v.), the invasion of Britain. The plausible arguments to support this cover story included the explanation that the large German troop concentrations in the east were rehearsals being conducted beyond the range of British bombers and reconnaissance aircraft. On 15 February 1941, the Germans added a twist to the deception by leaking suggestions to the Soviets that BARBAROSSA itself was a deception designed to divert British attention from SEA LION.

On 24 April, General Walther von Brauchitsch (q.v.), commander in chief of the German Army, issued the orders for *HAIFISCH*. The plan called for units of the German Army to occupy the French coastline and use it for a staging ground for the invasion of Britain. According to an army memorandum describing Operation *HAIFISCH*, "The purpose of this operation is to exploit previous experience and utilize new combat and transportation methods to eliminate the English Motherland as the basis for the continuation of the war against Germany." The entire operation was to be completed by early August.

Under Operation *HAIFISCH*, the German military command prepared detailed plans for the invasion, a combined operation of the army, navy, and air force, and identified the equipment and manpower required for the surprise landing on the English Channel coast. The *Luftwaffe* was to secure a landing zone, after which the main German assault would be launched directly along the mouth of the Thames River. The number of troops, vehicles, ships, weaponry were all listed in detail by the planners of Operation *HAIFISCH*.

In conjunction with *HAIFISCH*, the German high command planned supporting diversionary operations from Norway and Denmark against the British coast, and from Brittany against southwestern England. These auxiliary operations were given the code names *HARPUNE NORD* (HARPOON NORTH) and *HARPUNE SUD* (HARPOON SOUTH).

Simultaneously with the issuing of the *HAIFISCH* order, classified telegrams were sent to the German military attaches in Moscow, Berne, Tokyo, and six other countries. The bogus telegrams, which the Germans planned would fall into Soviet hands, indicated that some eight German divisions would soon be withdrawn from the area of the Soviet border. Even *Reich* Propaganda Minister Joseph Goebbels (q.v.) participated in the deception. By June 1941, Goebbels already was privy to the actual plan for BARBAROSSA. In a signed article in the 13 June edition of the Nazi

Party newspaper, *Völkischer Beobachter,* Goebbels hinted the long-awaited cross-channel invasion was imminent. As soon as the issue was out long enough for the foreign press to get copies, the German police made a big show of rounding the paper up. In order to complete the masquerade, Goebbels then went into a short period of simulated disgrace.

Incredible as it seems, the Soviets seem to have bought the whole story. On 20 March 1941, General Filip I. Golikov (q.v.), the head of Soviet military intelligence, wrote: "Rumors and documents implying that war with the Soviet Union is inevitable this spring must be regarded as false reports emanating from the British, and possibly even the German intelligence services." Josef Stalin (q.v.) personally believed that all indications of a coming German invasion were British dirty tricks, aimed at provoking war between Germany and the Soviet Union to forestall SEA LION. Successful as the deception measures were, the Germans continued to follow through after the start of the invasion, only canceling *HAIFISCH* and the *HARPUNE* operations on 7 August 1941.

Robert G. Waite

Additional Reading
Höhne, Heinz, *Canaris: Hitler's Master Spy* (1979).
Oberkommando des Kriegesmarine, "12 April 1941–31 August 1941," National Archives, Record Unit PG32444, Microfilm T1022, roll 1762.
Whaley, Barton, *Codeword BARBAROSSA* (1973).

Hamburg Air Raids (24–30 July 1943)

[See map 20 on page 1330]

Known as Operation GOMORRAH, the bombing of Hamburg involved a week-long series of five air raids, 24–30 July, 1943. During these operations, the Allied bomber commands flew more than 3,000 sorties and dropped more than 9,000 tons of bombs, half of which were incendiaries. The impact of these raids on Hamburg was absolutely devastating. More than a third of the houses and most of the commercial buildings were destroyed, more than 42,000 people died with nearly as many injured, and nearly one million people fled the city.

A British Lancaster bomber, seen from another Lancaster above, silhouetted against flares, smoke, and anti-aircraft fire, during the July 1943 attacks on Hamburg. (IWM C 3371)

The attacks against Hamburg resulted from agreements reached at a meeting of Allied leaders on 10 June 1943 at the Casablanca Conference. They agreed upon a strategy of a "Combined Bomber Offensive" (q.v.) against Germany. The U.S. Eighth Air Force would conduct daylight raids and RAF Bomber Command would attack by night. The targets were to be the key population centers of Germany. In early July, planning for Operation GOMORRAH began, and after ten days of preparation, British Bomber Command issued orders that "the old Hanseatic city of Hamburg is to be leveled."

The third-largest city in the German *Reich* (after Berlin and Vienna), Hamburg was also continental Europe's leading seaport and commercial center. Before the war, it accounted for more than half of Germany's total volume of foreign trade. The ship building industry located there also was the most important in all of Germany and northern Europe. Hamburg was clearly a target of great significance.

On 24 July 1943, the day of the first air attack, the head of Bomber Command, Air Marshal Sir Arthur Harris (q.v.), stated that the battle for Hamburg could not be won in a single night, and that at least 10,000 tons of bombs would be needed to devastate the city. Operational strategy called for British pathfinder aircraft to arrive over the city just before midnight. At that time, they would drop yellow target indicators and flares as a means of providing the bombers with clear and accurate aiming points.

The main attack force—347 Lancaster bombers, 246 Halifax bombers, 125 Stirling bombers, and 73 Wellington bombers—would reach Hamburg at midnight and begin unloading their cargo of bombs. Of these 792 planes, 740 arrived at the target on time. According to plans, the RAF was to conduct a series of area raids, or saturation bombing, while U.S. Eighth Air Force was to conduct precision raids on the harbor area and industrial sites.

To disrupt ground defense radars, the planes dropped tens of thousands of pieces of the so-called "window," long, narrow aluminum strips. The saturation bombing continued for more than two hours with devastating results. Firestorms consumed Hamburg's downtown and outlying areas and 1,400 people were killed. Only twelve Allied aircraft were shot down, a number considerably less than anticipated, a result attributed to the effectiveness of "window."

Raids continued over the next several days and nights. On the morning of 25 July, 122 American B-17s bombed the city, and another fifty-four B-17s attacked the following day. During the night of 28 July, 739 planes of the original force of 786 dropped 2,312 tons of bombs. In the last raids under Operation GOMORRAH, a fleet of 726 aircraft arrived over Hamburg shortly before midnight on the night of 29 July. The bombs and incendiary devices fell over an area of sixteen square kilometers, destroying additional buildings.

In order to reach the goal of 10,000 tons of bombs, another raid came on 3 August, when 425 planes dropped 939 tons of bombs. At the conclusion of Operation GOMORRAH, Harris informed Prime Minister Winston S. Churchill (q.v.) that "Hamburg has disappeared from the map."

Although the destruction of Hamburg was near complete, the U.S. Strategic Bombing Survey later concluded that, "neither the area raids directed against entire sections of the city, nor the precision attacks on specific industrial targets, were as effective in disrupting the enemy's ability to wage war as the destruction of transportation facilities in general throughout the industrial regions of the country." The battle of Hamburg, however, was fought for different reasons. The objective had been the city's systematic destruction.

Robert G. Waite

Additional Reading

Brunswig, Hans, *Feuersturm uber Hamburg: Die Luftangriffe auf Hamburg im zweiten Weltkrieg und Ihre Folgen* (1978).

Craven, Wesley Frank, and James Lea Cate (eds.), *Europe—Torch to Pointblank, August 1942 to December 1943* (1949).

Musgrove, Gordon, *Operation Gomorrah: The Hamburg Firestorm Raids* (1981).

Webster, Charles, and Arthur Noble Frankland, *The Strategic Air Offensive against Germany, 1939–1945, Endeavour* (1961).

Hammelburg Raid (26–27 March 1945)

On 25 March 1945, troops from General George S. Patton's (q.v.) U.S. Third Army crossed the Main River near Mainz, Germany. Twenty-four hours later, Patton dispatched a reinforced company-sized mechanized task force to liberate the American prisoners in German prisoner-of-war camp Oflag XIIIb at Hammelburg, near Schweinfurt. The unit formed for the mission was drawn from one of General Patton's most capable units, Lieutenant Colonel Creighton Abrams's (q.v.) Combat Command B of the 4th Armored Division. Designated Task Force Baum, after its commander Captain Abraham J. Baum, the force consisted of sixteen tanks, twenty-seven half-tracks, three 105mm self-propelled howitzers, and 294 troops.

Task Force Baum fought its way sixty miles behind German lines and liberated the camp by the early evening hours of 26 March. Once in possession of the camp, however, the task force lacked both the vehicles to transport more than a handful of the American POWs and the combat power to hold the camp until Allied reinforcements arrived. Undaunted, Captain Baum led his troops and about 250 POWs on a desperate drive back to American lines. They never made it. Task Force Baum was destroyed before sunrise the next day. All of its troops were either killed or captured.

The inadequacy of the force and the mystery surrounding its actual mission makes Task Force Baum's raid on the Hammelburg POW camp one of General Patton's most controversial operations in World War II. Many, including Abrams, believed Patton launched the raid solely to rescue his son-in-law, Lieutenant Colonel (later General) John K. Waters, who was a prisoner in the camp. In the process of taking the camp, Waters was seriously wounded. His life was saved by a Serbian POW doctor in the camp, but Waters had to be left behind when Task Force Baum made its attempt to return to American lines.

There are several factors that support the Waters-rescue theory. The day before the raid, Patton wrote his wife that their son-in-law would soon be in American hands. Patton also assigned to the force one of his aides, Major Alexander Stiller, for the sole purpose of identifying Waters. Task Force Baum lacked the vehicles and supplies to transport more than a handful of prisoners—yet the camp was known to hold at least 1,200 American POWs and possibly another 3,000 Allied POWs. Moreover, the camp lay in the adjacent U.S. Seventh Army's area of responsibility. No effort was made even to inform that unit of the operation, much less coordinate or arrange support for it.

The raid, nonetheless, stands as a heroic effort. Task Force Baum defeated superior German forces to reach the camp, gave the assembled prisoners an honest assessment of their chances for rescue, and attempted to bring as many back as possible. Although Captain Baum ultimately failed in his assigned mission, his efforts facilitated Patton's drive into Germany by drawing several thousand German troops away from the Third Army's main axis of advance.

Waters and Baum were finally rescued when the U.S. 14th Armored Division liberated Hammelburg on 5 April. Patton sent his personal physician to the camp to care for Waters, who immediately was evacuated by air to Frankfurt. Patton's aide, Stiller, was finally rescued on 1 May, when American forces liberated a POW camp at Moosburg.

Patton later claimed that he had launched the Hammelburg raid as a diversionary feint and that he had not known that Waters was there. The incident threatened to become the major scandal of Patton's career, but it quickly was overshadowed by the death of U.S. President Franklin D. Roosevelt (q.v.).

Carl O. Schuster

Additional Reading
Baron, Richard, *RAID! The Untold Story of Patton's Secret Mission* (1981).
D'Este, Carlo, *Patton: A Genius for War* (1995).

Herrlisheim (8–19 January 1945)
The fight for the small French town of Herrlisheim was one of the series of bitter battles that collectively came to be known as Operation *NORDWIND* (q.v.), the final German offensive in Alsace. It also was one of the worst maulings ever suffered by an American armored division. On 5 January, the XIV *SS Korps* attacked east across the Rhine River with the 553rd *Volksgrenadier* Division and established a bridgehead in the vicinity of Gambsheim, north of Strasbourg. The following day, a task force from the U.S. 79th Infantry Division attempted to clear the Gambsheim area but was driven back.

With the U.S. VI Corps under pressure from three sides, the 6th Army Group was forced to commit its final reserve, the newly arrived and inexperienced 12th Armored Division. The Germans, meanwhile, were rapidly reinforcing their units on the French side of the Rhine. Allied intelligence estimated the Gambsheim bridgehead was held by only 500 to 800 infantrymen and disorganized *Volkssturm* (q.v.) with little armor support. By the time the Americans attacked, the bridgehead, now centered on Herrlisheim, was held by major elements of the 10th SS *Panzer* Division.

On 8 January, the 12th Armored Division's Combat Command B (CCB) attempted to push into Herrlisheim from the town of Rohrwiller, to the north. Unable to cross the many small canals and water obstacles, CCB's tanks could not follow and support the infantry. As a result, CCB's infantry took heavy casualties trying to move across the flat and open ground of the Rhine plain. On 9

January, the 56th Armored Infantry Battalion forced its way into Herrlisheim, only to be cut off. By the time the 56th fought its way back out of the town on 10 January, it had been reduced to an effective strength of only 150 men.

On 16 January the 12th Armored Division attacked Herrlisheim again, this time with both combat commands. CCB resumed its attack from Rohrwiller, while Combat Command A (CCA) attacked from the south. To reach Herrlisheim, CCA had to cross a flat open plain bounded by Herrlisheim in the north, the town of Offendorff in the east, and the Steinwald woods in the south. The Germans held both towns and the woods with tanks and antitank guns. The open space in between was a perfect tank killing ground.

The attack went badly from the start. The 43rd Tank Battalion reached the southern edge of Herrlisheim, but was driven back with a loss of twelve tanks. The following day the division resumed the attack, and by mid-morning on 17 January the 43rd Tank Battalion and the 17th Armored Infantry Battalion forced their way into Herrlisheim. Shortly after, all radio contact was lost with the 43rd Tank Battalion, and that unit was never heard from again. The 17th Armored Infantry Battalion was quickly cut off in the town as well, and fierce building-to-building fighting continued for the rest of the day and into the night.

In the early morning hours of 18 January, fewer than 150 survivors of the 17th Armored Infantry Battalion managed to escape from Herrlisheim. Later that morning, Allied aerial reconnaissance spotted fourteen burned-out Sherman tanks just on the southern outskirts of the town. The 43rd Tank Battalion had been ambushed in the town and then forced back out into the open fields to face German antitank guns and the Panther tanks of the 10th SS *Panzer* Division. An entire American tank battalion had been wiped out. During the battle the battalion commander, Lieutenant Colonel Nicholas Novosel, was wounded seventeen times. He and some 300 of his men were captured.

On 19 January, units of the 12th Armored Division started to pull back toward the west. The 10th SS *Panzer* Division made several determined attempts to break out of the bridgehead, but ultimately they were held in check by Allied air attacks. Late on 19 January, the 12th Armored Division was relieved in position by two regiments of the 36th Infantry Division. The 12th Armored Division went into corps reserve, having lost 70 combat vehicles and 1,200 casualties in its attempt to take Herrlisheim.

David T. Zabecki

Additional Reading

Clarke, Jeffrey J., and Robert Ross Smith, *Riviera to the Rhine* (1993).

Phibbs, Brendan, *The Other Side of Time: A Combat Surgeon in World War II* (1987).

Pommois, Lise M., *Winter Storm: War in Northern Alsace, November 1944–March 1945* (1991).

Hungary (September 1944–March 1945)

[See map 32 on page 1342]

With Romania's defection from the Axis camp and the simultaneous collapse of German Army Group South Ukraine in August 1944, Hungary suddenly found itself threatened not only from the northeast (where the Soviet 4th Ukrainian Front was advancing toward the Carpathian and Beskide Mountains), but now also from the southeast.

The Hungarian cabinet, headed since 30 August by army General Géza Lakatos, included several ministers whose loyalty to the Axis cause seemed assured. On 7 September, a secret Crown Council decided and notified the German high command that unless the *Wehrmacht* offered massive assistance at once, Hungary would feel free to drop out of the war. Two days later, the commander of Army Group South Ukraine, Colonel General Johannes Friessner (q.v.), talked to the regent of Hungary, Admiral Miklós Horthy (q.v.) and to Lakatos and concluded (correctly) that they were pessimistic and likely to take Hungary out of the Axis camp. On 11 September, Horthy told the cabinet that he wanted to conclude an armistice with the Allies, but most of the ministers refused to back him.

At about the same time, the Hungarian Third Army was formed under General Jozsef Heszlenyi to help defend the southern borders of the country. Already deployed in the southeast was the Hungarian Second Army, under General Lajos Veress, which, together with the German Sixth Army, combined into an army (effective 17 September) group headed by General Maximilian Fretter-Pico. Both in Transylvania and the Banat, understrength German and Hungarian divisions could not prevent the slow but steady advance of the 2nd Ukrainian Front (army group), commanded by General Rodion Malinovsky (q.v.).

On 19 September, the Soviet troops reached Timosoara. Two days later they occupied Arad, but a subsequent Soviet thrust toward Oradea was temporarily blocked. In the north, units of the 4th Ukrainian Front, under General Ivan Petrov (q.v.), seized the strategic Dukla Pass in the

Beskide Mountains, thereby gaining access to northern Slovakia. On that same day, 6 October, Malinovsky's forces attacked on a broad front. By 9 October, some Soviet units had reached the Debrecen region. Even though German counterattacks subsequently pinched off and destroyed some of those units, anxiety in Budapest reached new heights.

With the knowledge of Prime Minister Lakatos, Horthy had secretly established contact with Moscow and by 11 October knew the Soviet terms for an armistice. Those terms included the immediate evacuation of all territory Hungary had acquired since 1937, much of it with German help. Four days after his representatives in Moscow accepted the terms, Horthy issued a public announcement, via Radio Budapest, that the war was lost and that Hungary had asked for a cease-fire.

With the Hungarian officer corps deeply divided on this issue and the Lakatos cabinet resigning in protest, the Germans had no difficulty in blocking Hungary's exit from the war. *Waffen-SS* (q.v.) units in and near Budapest had already taken various precautions, including the arrest of Horthy's son. On 16 October, the Germans stormed the royal palace and "persuaded" the elderly regent to accept "asylum" in Germany. In his last official act, Horthy appointed Ferenc Szálasi, leader of the fascistic Arrow-Cross Party, as his successor. For the next five months, this fanatic presided over the gradual collapse of his country.

The political changes in Budapest were followed by increasing divisions in the Hungarian Army. Some officers, including the commander of the First Army in the north, General Bela Miklós, and the chief of the general staff, Janos Vörös (q.v.), defected to the Soviets, as did many soldiers. Moreover, many of the soldiers who remained on duty were dispirited. In December 1944, Miklós formed a provisional government at Debrecen (by then in Soviet-occupied territory) and subsequently declared war on Germany.

Malinovsky's armies, meanwhile, fought their way toward the Tisza River. Between 10 and 29 October, the Germans and Soviets fought a massive tank battle near Debrecen. The Germans withdrew, but then counterattacked, cutting off and almost destroying three Soviet corps. By 29 October, the Soviets reached a line running from Mohács northeast toward the Carpathians, putting them in some places within fifty miles of Budapest. During the next ten days, they pushed on and reached the entire length of the Danube between Mohács and the southern outskirts of Budapest. Despite Malinovsky's urgings, his troops failed to capture the city on the run. Indeed, the German and Hungarian defenders of Budapest (q.v.) were to hold out for a long time, even after the Red Army closed a ring of steel around the city on 26 December.

In the second half of November, Malinovsky's front began receiving additional support from Marshal Fedor Tolbukhin's (q.v.) 3rd Ukrainian Front. By 5 December, some Soviet units reached the northern end of Lake Balaton, and gained ground in many regions during the ensuing weeks. On 22 December, Adolf Hitler (q.v.) dismissed Friessner and appointed General Otto Wöhler (q.v.) in his place. (Army Group South Ukraine, appropriately, had long since been renamed Army Group South). Once the Soviets completed their encirclement of Budapest, Hitler ruled the city had to be held at all cost. It held until 13 February, resulting in enormous destruction to the city.

By the beginning of 1945, Hitler became increasingly preoccupied with the Hungarian theater of war, especially since the oil fields south of Lake Balaton were vital to Germany's crumbling war effort. Indeed, in mid-Janaury, Hitler ordered the transfer of the Sixth *Panzer* Army, headed by SS-*Oberstgruppenführer* Sepp Dietrich (q.v.), from western Europe to the Danubian basin. The transfer, involving the 1st, 2nd, and 12th SS *Panzer* Divisions, among others, was hampered by transportation problems; but by late February, Dietrich had much of his army ready for an offensive into Hungary.

Called *FRÜHLINGSERWACHEN* (AWAKENING OF SPRING), the operation was launched on 6 March, but it soon bogged down in the mud and mire. On 16 March, the Red Army began its own offensive all across Hungary. Almost everywhere, the exhausted German and Hungarian units were crushed or pushed aside. By the end of March, Soviet armor was reaching Hungary's border with Austria, thus completing the conquest of Germany's last ally. Approximately one million Hungarians, civilians and soldiers, had left their country by that time, many of them never to return.

Ulrich Trumpener

Additional Reading

Fenyo, Mario D., *Hitler, Horthy, and Hungary: German-Hungarian Relations 1941–1944* (1972).

Gosztony, Peter, *Endkampf an der Donau, 1944–45* (1969).

Ziemke, Earl F., *Stalingrad to Berlin: The German Defeat in the East* (1968).

Hürtgen Forest (12 September– 16 December 1944)

[See map 34 on page 1344]

By August 1944, Allied forces had broken out of the hedgerows of Normandy, Paris had been liberated, and the German Army was fleeing, apparently in disarray, back to the *Reich*. Many soldiers believed that with just a little push, the war with Germany would be over by Christmas. At Supreme Headquarters, Allied Expeditionary Forces (SHAEF) (q.v.), there was less optimism because they saw the German resistance stiffening at the Siegfried Line, Adolf Hitler's (q.v.) defensive line on the western border of Germany.

The Siegfried Line, or West Wall (q.v.), was a series of prepared positions that would be very costly to assault. General Dwight D. Eisenhower (q.v.) hoped to accomplish his mission of defeating Germany with a minimum of casualties, but looming ahead of the rapidly advancing Allies was the Siegfried Line, and part of that defensive system was the dark, forbidding *Hürtgenwald*—the Hürtgen Forest.

Trying to avoid a direct assault on the Siegfried Line and the Hürtgen Forest, Eisenhower weighed his situation. First, it was painfully apparent by September 1944, that supplies were becoming very short and his two dynamic and demanding subordinates, Lieutenant General George S. Patton and General Bernard L. Montgomery (qq.v.), were in direct competition for supplies and the ear of their commander. Montgomery was able to convince Eisenhower to attempt a combination land and airborne assault toward Arnhem (q.v.), called Operation MARKET-GARDEN. One of the reasons Eisenhower allowed Montgomery to make his attempt to defeat the Germans in Holland was the specter of the *Hürtgenwald* and the Siegfried Line. Montgomery's "dagger thrust" into Holland, however, was a dismal failure, and new plans had to be considered at SHAEF.

By the beginning of September 1944, Lieutenant General Courtney H. Hodges's (q.v.) U.S. First Army had breached the Siegfried Line in two places, the more significant of which was at the city of Aachen (q.v.). Hodges's quarter-of-a-million-man army comprised three U.S. Corps, the VII, V, and VIII, deployed from north to south facing into the *Hürtgenwald*. The Hürtgen Forest covered more than 200 square miles of dense woods, deep ravines, and high ridges. It also hid many Siegfried Line pillboxes, fortifications, and minefields. The *Hürtgenwald* actually was a number of major forests, but Germans and Americans alike simply called it all the Hürtgen Forest. Major General

James M. Gavin (q.v.) compared the fight in the woods to a World War I battle when he said that the conflict was like Paschendaele. That battle, too, had been a slaughter-pen.

To Hodges's infantrymen, contained in eight veteran, hard-fighting combat divisions, the *Hürtgenwald* promised to be a dismal fight. Infantry without proper support from artillery, armor, and air would have a difficult time in any terrain. The *Hürtgenwald*'s road network was very poor, and the fall rains turned the few trails through the woods into knee-deep, muddy quagmires. Not only would the advance be slow, but also the resupply of ammunition, food, and equipment would be almost nil. To make matters worse, those combat infantry veterans knew that to be wounded in such a situation meant long hours of travel to aid stations, mainly by walking or being carried on a hand-litter—if even that was possible in such circumstances. Artillery was fired so that the shells would burst in the tree tops, and deadly splinters of wood and steel would rain down on the lightly protected foot soldiers, Germans and Americans alike. It was indeed a poor place to fight an infantry battle, where aerial observation was severely restricted, and where combat service support would be, for all purposes, nonexistent.

Mesmerized by the rapidity of the advance across France, Hodges allowed his corps commanders to start their move against the German positions on 12 September 1944. The defending German forces in the forest, however, were veteran units. And unknown to Hodges or to higher headquarters, many of those combat units had their staffs intact and were being quickly bolstered by reinforcements from the *Reich*.

The Allies made a critical error by underestimating the resilience of the German war machine. Simply put, the Americans had morale and momentum, but the equation was balanced out by the Germans having the element of surprise and a desperation born of having now to defend their homeland. The great German military theoritician, Carl von Clausewitz, argued a century before that in combat a determined defense was actually the strongest method of waging war. While the offense promised more of a decision, a well-prepared defender could very well balance out the odds. That was to be proven true in *Hürtgenwald* in the fall of 1944.

To complicate matters for Allied planners, the Roer River cut through the Hürtgen Forest at the halfway point. It was not the river so much that bothered Allied operations and intelligence officers; it was the existence of a number of sizable dams which, if destroyed, could flood the area. If Hodges's troops crossed the Roer and the Germans opened the dams and flooded the plains, the attackers could very well be trapped. Initially, the dams were not an Allied objective, nor was the small town of Schmidt (q.v.), which controlled the routes to the dams. Neither Hodges nor his corps commanders seemed to see the value in taking the town or the dams. It was a costly oversight.

The battle for the Hürtgen Forest began on 12 September 1944, and ended in the Americans breaking off the fight on 16 December, when the Germans launched their Ardennes (q.v.) offensive. American divisions literally were chewed up in the deep, oppressive woods, and the combat infantrymen fought in appalling conditions that recalled the misery of World War I. Six U.S. combat infantry divisions—the 1st, 4th, 8th, 9th, 28th, and 104th—fought and were unsuccessful. In addition, vast numbers of other combat, combat support, and combat service support units were engaged during the three-month series of battles.

More than 33,000 American troops were either killed, wounded, captured, or felled by the diseases caused by long periods of exposure. Trench foot, pneumonia, and simple combat fatigue claimed their share. The U.S. lost more than 25 percent of all troops engaged; quite high for American casualties in World War II. Despite the fact that German records were lost in the last days of the war, it is most probable that their casualty rates were even higher.

The Hürtgen Forest campaign also produced a postwar bitterness, especially on the part of the U.S. 28th "Keystone" Division (Pennsylvania National Guard). The veterans felt that their operations, from 2–16 November, were poorly planned and represented the thinking at the headquarters of Hodges and V Corps Commander Lieutenant General Leonard Gerow (q.v.) that the Germans were indeed beaten, and that combat in this area, which offered so little in roads for support and resupply, would be against half-hearted defenders.

The IX Tactical Air Command (TAC) was tasked to support U.S. operations in the Hürtgen Forest, but as the battle continued into late October and early November, rains and then snow set in, making flying a near impossibility. Many senior American generals who had fought in World War I compared the *Hürtgenwald* to combat in the Meuse-Argonne offensive in the rainy fall of 1918. It was difficult for aircraft to fly in the bad weather, and the terrain was hard to see. The constant pounding of artillery from both sides made the landscape difficult to follow from the air. Simply, through no fault of their own, the much vaunted American air arm did not function well in support of combat operations. Ground commanders had perhaps expected too much from the IX TAC.

By mid-November, combat in the mud, snow, cold, and chewed-up terrain began to produce serious effects for the Americans. Physical problems had always been present in the cold and damp of the forest, but by November, unit commanders began to show severe signs of strain, and many had to be relieved from their commands, from company level up. Individual replacements sent to the bloodied units were very quickly killed or wounded in higher percentages than in other units committed outside of the *Hürtgenwald*. To put this into perspective, the 4th Infantry Division went into combat on 16 November, and by the last week of the month, they had lost 6,000 troops—4,000 in battle and an alarming 2,000 to trench foot, pneumonia, and combat fatigue. The *Hürtgenwald* literally was consuming U.S. combat divisions at an alarming rate.

By the middle of November, Allied intelligence finally realized that the Germans had pulled themselves together, but they never did fully comprehend the German order of battle. Attacks from the air, mainly carried out by the Royal Air Force against the Roer dams, merited very little. All in all, the Hürtgen Forest operation was a dismal failure.

The surprise German Ardennes offensive, starting on 16 December, ended the Hürtgen Forest operation. For all of the reasons cited above, the offensive thrust into the dark woods was a battle which, as Gavin later stated, "should not have been fought." Based on a poor intelligence picture of the enemy and the terrain, the U.S. believed in a quick victory of the type experienced in July and August. The error resulted in a campaign that failed and produced very heavy losses of life and blood.

James J. Cooke

Additional Reading
Currey, Cecil B., *Follow Me and Die* (1984).
MacDonald, Charles B., *The Battle of the Hürtgen Forest* (1963).
Whiting, Charles, *The Battle of the Hürtgen Forest: The Untold Story of a Disastrous Campaign* (1989).

HUSKEY, Operation
See SICILY

I

Iceland (10 May 1940–1945)

A Danish colony before World War II, Iceland's strategic position astride the Atlantic Ocean's northern gateway made its position a critical concern after Denmark's surrender to Germany in April 1940. Located just outside bomber range of the North American land mass, Iceland was ideally positioned to decisively influence the Battle of the Atlantic (q.v.). Whoever possessed the island could base air and naval forces to dominate the sea and the skies of the western and central Atlantic, through which virtually all of Britain's vital sea commerce had to transit. In effect, Iceland was a potential knife at Britain's seaborne jugular vein.

Even Britain's normally lethargic Prime Minister Neville Chamberlain (q.v.) recognized the gravity of the strategic situation. On 10 May 1940, he deployed a Royal Marine Coastal Defense Battalion to the island. That small unit was the foundation of what became a 22,000-man garrison by August 1940. Iceland's importance is best demonstrated by the fact that the British deployed a full division to the island at a time when Britain itself was threatened by invasion (*see* SEA LION, Operation). The British garrison, designated Alabaster Force, expanded throughout the summer of 1940 and eventually included the 49th West Riding Division, augmented by Royal Navy coast watchers and some eight coastal defense batteries.

Adolf Hitler (q.v.) also considered seizing the island, ordering the preparation of a plan for Operation *IKARUS* (q.v.). The plan was prepared in late April 1940, but it remained stillborn in the face of Allied maritime supremacy.

In April 1941, the United States assumed responsibility for the defense of Iceland—a responsibility it maintained throughout the war and all through the period of the Cold War that followed. In July 1941, the U.S. Marine Corps 1st Marine Expeditionary Brigade deployed to the island. One month later they were joined by a squadron of U.S. Army Air Forces P-40Es. U.S. Army troops replaced the marines that August, and brought in an entire air wing of fighters and bombers to defend the island's airspace. This was a good four months before America was officially at war.

At the start of 1942, U.S. Navy patrol planes and antisubmarine warfare units started operating from Iceland out into the North Atlantic. These patrols continued well into the 1990s. Iceland's strategic importance to the Atlantic sea lanes continues, and its security remains a cornerstone of NATO defensive strategy to this day.

Carl O. Schuster

Additional Reading
Morison, Samuel Eliot, *History of U.S. Naval Operations in World War II* (1947–1962).
Roskill, Stephan, *The War at Sea* (1954–1958).

IKARUS, Operation (June 1940)

Recognizing Iceland's strategic position astride the British sea lanes in the North Atlantic, Adolf Hitler (q.v.) ordered the *Kriegsmarine* to develop a plan for the conquest of that island. The operation was designated *IKARUS*, but logistical realties and the Royal Navy's total supremacy at sea precluded the plan ever progressing beyond the planning stages. The *Kriegsmarine's* feasibility study called for the landing of approximately 5,000 motorized troops drawn from the 2nd Mountain Division, reinforced by amphibious engineers, artillery, coastal defense units, and ground-based air defense units.

Fortunately for the Allies, Britain deployed ground forces to the island almost immediately upon Denmark's surrender to German forces in April 1940. By the time German planning was completed in late June of that year, Britain had a garrison of nearly 12,000 troops on the island (*see* Iceland). Given all the obstacles facing any German landing—including British sea supremacy, lack of German airpower over the island, and the presence of a reinforced British garrison—success would have been difficult to achieve. Even if the landing had succeeded, the force easily could have been isolated by Allied naval forces.

Carl O. Schuster

Additional Reading

Schenck, Peter, *Operation Sea Lion* (1990).

Schuster, Carl O., "Operation Icarus," *Command Magazine* (5 June 1993).

Italy, Southern (July–October 1943)

[See map 22 on page 1332]

After their forces secured control over North Africa (q.v.), the Allied leaders and strategic planners began to focus on the next move against German-occupied Europe. At the Casablanca Conference (*see* Conferences, Allied), they decided to invade Sicily, thereby securing shipping routes through the Mediterranean, and possibly forcing Italy into surrender. The British emphasized the Mediterranean strategy, while the Americans believed engaging Nazi forces in northwest Europe was the path to victory. In fact, the initial 1943 decision on Italy was to invade Sicily only.

Italy was vulnerable in the spring and summer of 1943. Benito Mussolini's (q.v.) regime faced serious problems, unrest, and dissatisfaction. There was a growing sense that Mussolini was being manipulated by Adolf Hitler (q.v.) and that the country was at the mercy of the Nazis. As Mussolini requested the return of Italian troops from the eastern front to defend their homeland, Hitler responded by sending in more German soldiers. Under the leadership of Field Marshal Albert Kesselring (q.v.), German troops were dispersed throughout Sicily and along the Italian peninsula.

The Allies invaded Sicily (q.v.) on 10 July 1943. By 17 August they were in control of the entire island. The events in Sicily led Italian military leaders to recognize the overall gravity of their situation by late July. They became determined to oust Mussolini in order to avoid fighting on the mainland that would lead to widespread destruction and loss of life. The removal of Mussolini from power went smoothly and more easily than expected. On 24 July, King Victor Emmanuel III (q.v.) demanded his resignation and promptly arrested him. Mussolini's successor, Pietro Badoglio (q.v.), announced that Italy would remain in the war, but he also initiated secret negotiations with the Allies.

Unknown to the Italians, the German military leaders had decided that if the Allies invaded the mainland, their troops would fall back northward. In light of Allied air and amphibious superiority, they believed that Italy could not be held. The plan was for Kesselring to conduct a fighting withdrawal from southern Italy, destroying bridges and other strategic assets along the way, and retreat to the north, around Florence.

Among the Allied leaders, only Prime Minister Winston S. Churchill (q.v.) pressed for an invasion of the southern Italian mainland. He believed that such a move would enable the Allies to threaten an invasion of the Balkans and that possession of the airfields around Foggia would enable Allied bombers to reach the Romanian oil fields. Furthermore, he believed that the Germans would not fight in southern Italy, and that Rome might even be taken without a battle. With Mussolini gone, it was an attractive possibility.

The Italian leaders wanted the Allies to land fifteen divisions in the north, thereby conquering the nation quickly. The Allies proposed landing south of Rome, which the Italians feared would lead to widespread fighting and destruction. On 3 September 1943, the Italian government signed a secret armistice with the Allies. On the same day, British and Canadian troops of the Eighth Army initiated Operation BAYTOWN, crossing the Straits of Messina and landing on the "toe" of the mainland.

Meanwhile, the Allied Fifth Army, which consisted of U.S. VI Corps and British X Corps, prepared for the 9 September launch of Operation AVALANCHE, a landing at Salerno (q.v.), south of Naples. On that same day, the British also would execute Operation SLAPSTICK, by landing the British 1st Airborne Division by sea at the port of Taranto, in the "heel" of the Italian boot.

It was time to strike decisively, but the Allies lacked sufficient reserves and the preparations were inadequate. There was, furthermore, no Allied master plan for operations in the Mediterranean after the Sicily campaign. When the Italian armistice was announced, the Allied troops expected no resistance. What they encountered were determined German forces.

Kesselring ordered his units to continue falling back as the British Eighth Army advanced through Calabria. The German units at Salerno were to hold their positions to support the withdrawal from the south. The Fifth Army landed at Salerno, and despite heavy resistance established a firm beachhead. A counterattack came on 12 September, as German forces rushed south from Rome to join with those moving up from Calabria; but Allied troops fought back and by 15 September were moving inland.

General Dwight D. Eisenhower (q.v.) next ordered Allied ground forces commander General Harold Alexander (q.v.) to move on Rome. While most German military leaders wanted to retreat north, Kesselring persuaded Hitler that he could hold the territory south of Rome. Kesselring's forces began building successive defensive positions across the peninsula. The Allied forces would have to fight for every mile.

As the Fifth Army advanced north from Salerno, they linked up with the Eighth Army coming up from Calabria. The Eighth Army moved along the Adriatic coast side of the peninsula, while the Fifth Army moved up the Tyrrhenian coast. Because of the rugged Apennine Mountains running down the center of Italy, it was effectively impossible for the Allies to outflank the German forces. The Italian coast had only relatively few spots suitable for amphibious operations. Furthermore, the Allies lacked the capability to supply both arms of the advance and to establish new beachheads. This was due in part to the intensification of fighting in the Pacific and preparations for the invasion of France, which meant fewer resources for the Italian campaign.

Along the Adriatic coast, the Eighth Army fought its way north toward the town of Pescara, an important junction of the few good roads leading through the mountains. But the German forces held fast in the south, stalling the advance. Continuous assaults and efforts to reach Pescara lasted until early 1944. Along the Tyrrhenian coast, the Fifth Army faced a similar situation. Naples was taken on 1 October, and the Allied troops pushed toward Rome, 100 miles to the north.

For the first forty miles, the mountains came right down to the sea. This proved to be ideal defensive terrain for the Germans, who constructed a series of defensive positions: the Volturno Line, the Barbara Line, the Reinhard Line, and the Gustav Line (q.v.). Also called the Winter Line, the Gustav Line was the strongest of the four. Its key point was the town of Cassino, above which lay the Benedictine abbey, Monte Cassino. In company and battalion-size actions, Allied troops pushed forward, battling hard for every mile of territory.

The Allies managed to break through the forward lines by around Christmas and reached the Gustav Line in mid-January. The fighting there continued for another five months, with the battle for Monte Cassino (q.v.) lasting from 1 February to 18 May 1944. In an attempt to outflank the Gustav Line, the Allies conducted Operation SHINGLE, an amphibious landing at Anzio (q.v.) on 22 January 1944. That operation came perilously close to failure.

The stiff German resistance in southern Italy surprised the Allies, who had expected a rapid advance northward. Because the invasion of the mainland had been carried out only over his opposition, Alexander did not receive additional troops or supplies. In fact, he repeatedly was expected to advance, but he did not have the required manpower. The divisions among the Allied leaders, the lack of clear objectives, the terrain, all lead to horrible and costly fighting and heavy losses in Italy in 1943 and 1944.

Thomas F. Hale
Robert G. Waite

Additional Reading
Fisher, Ernest F., *Cassino to the Alps* (1977).
Graham, Dominick, and Shelford Bidwell, *Tug of War: The Battle for Italy 1943–1945* (1986).
Jackson, W.G.F., *The Battle for Italy* (1967).
Nicholson, G.W.L., *The Canadians in Italy* (1956).

K

Kasserine Pass (14–22 February 1943)

[See map 23 on page 1333]

Facing the closing jaws of two Allied armies as he retreated into Tunisia (q.v.), Field Marshal Erwin Rommel (q.v.) looked for ways of striking back, defeating one Allied army before the two could link up. General Sir Bernard L. Montgomery's (q.v.) cautious advance across Libya gave Rommel a window of opportunity to seize the initiative, but he had to act fast.

For his target, Rommel chose the inexperienced Americans, whose enthusiastic but scattered advance across Algeria made them vulnerable to piecemeal engagement and defeat in detail. Unfortunately, Rommel did not command all the Axis forces in Tunisia. He commanded only the *Panzerarmee Afrika* in southern Tunisia, while Colonel General Jürgen von Arnim (q.v.) commanded the Fifth *Panzerarmee* in the north. Rommel, therefore, sought the support of the German theater commander, Field Marshal Albert Kesselring (q.v.), the *OB Süd* (Commander in Chief, South). Kesselring, a brilliant commander in his own right, had no great love for Rommel. The result was a compromise plan which in the end, despite its flaws, led to one of the most devastating defeats suffered by the U.S. Army in World War II. Fortunately for the Allies, Kasserine Pass was not the decisive defeat it could have been. Nonetheless, Kasserine Pass devastated American morale and confirmed British leaders' worst fears about American combat effectiveness.

The stage was set when von Arnim's 21st *Panzer* Division took the vital Faid Pass from its French garrison. That left the U.S. II Corps positioned between the Faid and Maknassy Passes, the latter held by the Italian *Cenauro* Armored Division. The Americans were arrayed forward of Kasserine Pass as General Dwight D. Eisenhower (q.v.) was preparing to attack the east coast port of

Sfax in the hope of severing Rommel's supply lines. Unfortunately, the II Corps commander, Major General Lloyd Fredendall (q.v.) deployed his forces poorly. Few II Corps units were in mutually supporting positions and many were exhausted after the rapid race across Algeria. Logistics and command and control arrangements were inadequate and most combat units were poorly trained, especially above the battalion level.

Both Rommel and von Arnim saw the opportunity. Their only disagreements were on how best to hit the Americans and who would be in charge of the attack. Kesselring forced an agreement on 9 February 1943, stating that von Arnim's forces would lead off the offensive with the 10th *Panzer* Division driving on Sidi Bou Zid, beginning 12 February. Rommel, despite being the senior commander, would follow two days later with a much smaller drive on Gafsa. In contrast to the situation to the east of Tunisia, the *Luftwaffe* had air superiority over Tunisia and eastern Algeria. Only rain and the poor road system inhibited German preparations.

Rain delayed von Arnim's attack two days, but his opening assault enjoyed massive air support and caught the Americans almost completely by surprise. ULTRA (q.v.) intelligence led the Allies to believe von Arnim's attack would be a feint to draw forces away from Rommel, who they all believed would lead the main attack. Eisenhower, in fact, visited Sidi Bou Zid just hours before the attack on 14 February.

Within the first few hours of the battle, Combat Command A (CCA) of the U.S. 1st Armored Division was all but destroyed. The Americans fled the battlefield toward Sbeitla, the next township to the northwest, leaving more than forty tanks, nearly sixty half-tracks, and the guns of five artillery batteries behind. The division's Combat Command C (CCC) launched an immediate counter-attack, only to be destroyed by the combined firepower of the 21st and 10th *Panzer* Divisions. The Americans abandoned another brigade's worth of equipment and the U.S. retreat became a rout.

Rommel awoke on 16 February to discover that Gafsa, his initial objective, had been abandoned. He saw an immediate opportunity to drive on, seize the Kasserine Pass, and bag all of II Corps between the pincers of his force and von Arnim's. Unlike Rommel, however, von Arnim was not a daring commander. He preferred a more deliberate approach and delayed his attack on Sbeitla until 17 February. Rommel asked Kesselring for von Arnim's two *Panzer* divisions to make a drive on the main American supply dump at Tebessa. Rommel had visions of rolling up the entire Allied line in Tunisia. Kesselring tentatively approved and notified both Rommel and von Arnim. It was at this point, however, that the Axis's divided command and the animosity between Rommel and von Arnim combined to serve the American interests.

Although ordered to turn his *Panzer* divisions over to Rommel, von Arnim noticed that his orders said "command" of the divisions was to go to Rommel. As far as von Arnim was concerned, that did not necessarily mean the entire division had to go. Von Arnim thus kept the tank battalions, including the new Tiger tanks and much of the artillery, sending only the divisional headquarters and remaining elements to Rommel. That robbed Rommel of much of the divisions' combat firepower. Moreover, the ensuing dispute with von Arnim delayed the offensive for forty-eight hours, as Rommel appealed again to Kesselring and the Italian *Commando Supremo,* which still nominally directed strategy in North Africa. Kesselring's response struck a strange compromise, giving the two divisions to Rommel but limiting his objective to El Kef.

Rommel's drive on Kasserine Pass met resistance almost immediately. The Americans had used the delay to occupy the high ground dominating the pass. More significantly, von Arnim did not dispatch the divisions immediately, using them instead to continue his own northern thrust until the last moment. The result was that the divisions had to withdraw to Sbeitla before they could move against Kasserine Pass. Subsequently, the 21st *Panzer* Division made the initial attack alone, as the 10th *Panzer* Division slowly made its way through Sbeitla. The 10th *Panzer* Division, in fact, stopped to rest there during the early hours of the new offensive and did not begin to move forward until Rommel found its commander and ordered

him to move. Even so, Rommel discovered that von Arnim had withheld two battalions and the Tiger tanks. Lacking the overwhelming firepower Rommel had planned on, his drive faced some tough going before a massive barrage by the new *Nebelwerfers* (multiple rocket launchers) broke the American resistance on 20 February. Rommel was able to enter the pass that afternoon as the Americans literally abandoned their positions and fled to the northwest.

As the battle reached its decisive point and the American lines stood open for a classic "Rommel Drive" into the rear, Rommel uncharacteristically dawdled in the pass, examining the battlefield. Without his personal leadership and drive, the 10th *Panzer* Division's momentum slowed. They never took Thala, the next town north, whose defenses consisted of only a French light infantry battalion. Beyond that, nothing stood between the Germans and El Kef.

The Americans, meanwhile, were destroying equipment and supply dumps, evacuating airfields, and abandoning their positions all up and down the line. The old Rommel would have exploited the situation to drive on to Algeria, which would have inflicted an almost permanent blow to American morale. But the 10th *Panzer* Division's commander, Colonel Fritz von Broich, was no Rommel, and the Rommel on this battlefield was not the dynamic leader of the past. The German advance halted, not because of Allied resistance, but from sheer lack of initiative.

The Allies did not suffer from the divided command structure that crippled Rommel's efforts. General Sir Harold Alexander (q.v.), commander of Allied ground forces in Tunisia under Eisenhower, recognized the threat and Rommel's intent almost immediately. He ordered all retreats to stop and sent the British 1st Armoured Division—which was still reequipping with U.S.-built Sherman tanks—to drive southward and intercept Rommel's advance along the Thala-Sbiba line. The leading elements of two of the division's brigades were entering those villages by the time Rommel got the 10th *Panzer* Division moving forward on 21 February. Informed of Alexander's "no retreat" order and the movement of Allied armored forces, Rommel canceled the offensive on 22 February and refused to be swayed otherwise. Rommel felt the momentum had been lost and he began to fear that Montgomery might break through the Mareth Line (q.v.) while he was attacking the Americans. Not even Kesselring could make Rommel resume the advance.

Although Rommel failed to inflict the truly

decisive defeat he had hoped for, the battle of Kasserine Pass severely battered the Americans. More than 200 U.S. tanks were destroyed and nearly 4,000 American troops were captured. Allied faith in American troops was shaken as well. British commanders now openly spoke of them as "Our Italians."

Eisenhower reacted to the debacle immediately, bringing in new leaders at virtually every level of command. Most importantly, he appointed Major General George S. Patton (q.v.) as the new commander of II Corps on 24 February. It was a fortuitous choice. A dynamic and forceful leader and an intense disciplinarian, Patton instilled the II Corps with a fighting spirit and tactical cohesion that would serve it well for the rest of the war. The results of his efforts were demonstrated four weeks later at El Guettar (q.v.).

In the final analysis, the Allied leaders in North Africa were fortunate that the Axis chain of command was divided and that the antipathy between Rommel and von Arnim precluded their cooperating effectively to destroy the scattered American forces at Kasserine Pass.

Carl O. Schuster

Additional Reading
Blumenson, Martin, *Rommel's Last Victory* (1965).
Cortesi, Lawrence, *Rommel's Last Stand* (1984).
Howe, George, *Northwest Africa: Seizing the Initiative* (1957).
Irving, David, *The Trail of the Fox* (1977).
Macksey, Kenneth J., *Afrika Korps* (1968).

Keyes Raid (17–18 November 1941)
In the autumn of 1941, the British Eighth Army, encamped on the Egyptian-Libyan border, was striving to relieve the encircled British garrison at Tobruk (*see* Tobruk II), which was being supplied by sea. Their main opposition, the German *Afrika Korps,* was led by General Erwin Rommel (qq.v.). Even by this point in the war, Rommel had acquired the status of a legend, and beating or removing him became almost an obsession with the British high command.

After much planning and discussion, the British decided to attempt to either capture or assassinate Rommel in a commando raid on his rear headquarters at Beda Littoria, Libya. Geoffrey Keyes (q.v.), who at the age of twenty-four was the youngest lieutenant colonel in the British Army, volunteered to lead the raid. His superior, Colonel Robert Laycock (q.v.), considered the measure

"desperate in the extreme" with little chance of anyone getting out alive. Prior to the raid on Rommel, Keyes had led several successful commando raids in the Middle East and had received the *Croix de Guerre* from the French *Chasseurs Alpin* for his services in the Narvik (q.v.) campaign in Norway in 1940.

Keyes' commando unit landed by boat behind German lines. Rough seas swamped several of the boats, with the result that only thirty-eight of his fifty-five commandos got ashore. To reach Rommel's headquarters they had to march 125 miles through the Libyan desert. They arrived after dark on 17 November, and Keyes personally led the assault into the darkened building. Rommel was not there. The British, however, achieved complete surprise, and the Germans managed to fire only one shot—the one that hit Keyes just above the heart, killing him instantly.

The raid failed because of faulty intelligence. Rommel never lived at the rear headquarters, but rather in his own villa in Beda Littoria. On the night of the raid he was at another house near Gambud. On learning of the raid, the sensitive and gallant Rommel sent his personal chaplain to conduct funeral services for Keyes and the four Germans killed in the raid. Rommel had a solid wooden cross bearing Keyes' name and rank placed over the grave. After the war the cross was removed to the Keyes family's local church in Tingewick, Buckinghamshire. Keyes was awarded the Victoria Cross posthumously for leading the raid.

Although the raid failed to achieve its purpose, it did much to lift British morale at a time when they had little to cheer about. Winston S. Churchill (q.v.), in an effort to console Keyes' father, Admiral of the Fleet Sir Roger Keyes (q.v.), told him, "I would rather have Geoffrey alive than Rommel dead."

Paul J. Rose

Additional Reading
Keyes, Elizabeth, *Geoffrey Keyes V.C. of the Rommel Raid* (1956).
Liddel Hart, Basil (ed)., *The Rommel Papers* (1953).
Young, Desmond, *Rommel* (1950).

Kharkov (12–27 May 1942)
The city of Kharkov in the Ukraine was taken by the *Wehrmacht*'s Army Group South on 24 October 1941 as part of the drive on the Donets River, following the Soviet defeat around Kiev (q.v.) in September. Kharkov's position as a major transport

hub and heavy industry center made it a strategic target. Its geographic location also predestined Kharkov as a jumping-off point for further German offensives.

The German advance received setbacks during the winter of 1941–1942. On 19 January 1942, the Red Army struck at Army Group South, concentrating on the area south of Kharkov, between the German Sixth and Seventeenth Armies. The Soviets achieved little result, except for creating a bulge between the two armies west of Izyum.

On 23 February, a lull set in along the entire German-Soviet front while both sides prepared upcoming operations. In April, in accordance with planning for the upcoming Operation *BLAU* (BLUE), Army Group South split into Army Groups A and B. Army Group A, under Field Marshal Wilhelm List (q.v.), was to strike into the Caucasus, while Army Group B, under Field Marshal Fedor von Bock (q.v.), covered this thrust with an offensive along the Don River to Stalingrad. The boundary between the new groups lay south of Kharkov. General Erich von Manstein's (q.v.) Eleventh Army opened a preliminary offensive in Crimea (q.v.) on 8 May.

Meanwhile, Marshal Semen Timoshenko (q.v.), the commander of the Southwestern Front (army group), massed forces at Izyum and at St. Salchow-Volchansk, southeast and northeast of Kharkov, respectively, in preparation for a pincer attack to retake the city and then drive to the Dnieper River, some 100 miles to the west. The battle for Kharkov fell into three phases: the Soviet attack from 12 to 16 May; the German counterattack from 17 to 22 May; and the final destruction of Soviet forces from 23 to 27 May.

On 12 May, after a massive artillery preparation, Timoshenko launched the assault with twenty-three to twenty-four infantry divisions, three to five armored divisions, and twelve cavalry divisions, plus an additional seven to nine armored brigades and a motorized brigade. The main thrust with the bulk of the armor and cavalry was in the southeast. On 13 May, the high-pressure assault broke through the initial German defenses and reached Kharkov, forcing the remaining intact German perimeter units to withdraw to the city to avoid being cut off. Soviet cavalry units then branched off from the southern pincer to move westward against Krasnograd on 16 May. By that point, however, *Luftwaffe* air strikes redirected from the Crimea had done much to blunt the Soviet drive.

The Germans and their allies launched the counterattack on 17 May with a northward stroke at the rear of the southernmost Soviet elements. The thrust was spearheaded by the First *Panzer* Army, driving from Slovyansk-Alexandrovka, followed by the Seventeenth and Sixth Armies attacking from the west and northwest. Within twenty-four hours, Axis armor thrust forty kilometers through the Soviet rear, driving to the Donets River. Timoshenko ceased offensive operations on 21 May in the face of encirclement, but he reacted too slowly. On 22 May, the Germans sealed the "cauldron," trapping three Soviet armies west of Izyum. On that same day, Soviet forces northeast of Kharkov withdrew over the Donets River to their pre-offensive positions, harassed by smaller-scale Axis attacks.

Starting 23 May, the Axis forces systematically tightened the ring. Repeated Soviet attempts to break out and run for the Donets failed. Relief efforts by armor-supported infantry divisions from east of the Donets could not break into the ring from the outside. As the circle tightened, the Red Army positions increasingly assumed the role of a shooting range for the *Wehrmacht*. The *Luftwaffe* took the opportunity to battle-test their new 30mm Mk-101 cannon mounted on the Henschel Hs-129. The cannon's tungsten-core shells accounted for a major portion of Soviet tank losses at Kharkov.

On 26 May, the Germans split the cauldron. By 27 May, the demoralized, disorganized Soviets were defeated, with only pockets of resistance remaining to be mopped up over the next few days. The Red Army lost twenty infantry divisions, seven cavalry divisions, and fourteen armored brigades. The *Wehrmacht* took 240,000 prisoners, 2,026 guns, and 1,249 tanks. The commanders of the Soviet Sixth and Fifty-seventh Armies numbered among the dead. The *Wehrmacht* lost no time in exploiting the victory, resuming offensive operations according to plan, capturing the areas around Volchansk and Izyum-Kupyansk in June in preparation for Operation *BLAU,* which began on 28 June.

The impact of this battle for Kharkov was far-reaching. The Soviet attack was intended as the first in a series of preliminary offensives that were to build up to a general offensive. Success there would have paved the way for Soviet thrusts along the entire front. Even if the Soviets could have achieved a local victory in the southwest, it would have affected the German ability to launch Operation *BLAU,* for which Kharkov was a vital base. It also would have opened a path for cutting the German lines of communication in the southern sector.

The German victory bolstered *Wehrmacht* morale after the setbacks of the 1941–1942 winter operations and the failure to take Moscow (q.v.). Germany then retained the initiative for summer operations. The destruction of three armies weakened Soviet forces in the region by 30 percent, facilitating the subsequent German drive. The operation also depleted Soviet supplies, and created a bulge for the Axis forces to exploit, easing their drive into the Don-Donets corridor.

Several factors contributed to the outcome of the battle. The Red Army had dispersed its forces along the entire front from Leningrad to south of Kharkov in expectation of launching a wide-front offensive. That weakened the Soviet striking power. Expecting a renewed German offensive against Moscow, the Soviets placed the greater part of their reserves in the central sector, too far away to support Timoshenko when he needed assistance. The Izyum bridgehead was not established in sufficient force to make it a stable platform for offensive operations against a well-prepared enemy.

The Germans, planning to launch Operation *BLAU* in late June, were in a high state of readiness when the Soviet attack came. The 17 May counterattack by the First *Panzer* Army occurred quickly because such a thrust was already planned, as part of Operation FRIDERICUS, to destroy the Soviet salient at Izyum in preparation for Operation *BLAU*.

The May 1942 battle of Kharkov demonstrated effective cooperation between the Germans and their allies. In addition to German forces, von Bock had a Romanian Corps and Italian, Hungarian, and Slovak units in defensive positions south of Kharkov. A Croatian regiment earned a special citation for its part in the defense of Kharkov from the northeastern pincer. These Axis forces subsequently pressed eastward with the Germans.

Sidney Dean

Additional Reading

Anders, Wladyslaw, *Hitler's Defeat in Russia* (1953).

Mellenthin, F.W. von, *Panzer Battles* (1956).

Ziemke, Earl F., *Stalingrad to Berlin: The German Defeat in the East* (1968).

Kiev (10–26 September 1941)

In July 1941, a bitter struggle erupted between Adolf Hitler (q.v.) and some of his generals, led by army chief of staff Franz Halder (q.v.). Even at this early stage of the war, it was obvious to the generals that all of the German army groups would not be able to accomplish their assigned missions under Operation BARBAROSSA. Army Groups South and North needed reinforcements, particularly more armored divisions, in order to capture the Ukraine and to link up with the Finns at Leningrad (q.v.).

Hitler favored using Army Group Center's *Panzer* units for these tasks, thereby postponing the attack on Moscow (q.v.). For him the Soviet capital was not a primary objective. His priorities were (1) the natural resources in southern Russia; (2) the Crimea; and (3) the link-up with the Finns at Leningrad. The generals, on the other hand, wanted to continue the advance on Moscow. They argued that the capital was not only the political center of the country, but also one of the major industrial sites and a transportation nexus. The capture of Moscow also would be a severe blow to Soviet morale that might even lead to the breakup of the Soviet Union itself.

The conflict within the German top leadership stalled German field operations until 21 August 1941. On that day, Hitler finally ordered a major encirclement operation aimed at destroying the Soviet forces in the northern Ukraine. For that operation, Army Group Center had to support Army Group South by sending a substantial part of its *Panzer* divisions to the south. Moscow for the moment was off the immediate agenda.

The operational situation at the end of August actually was favorable to Hitler's plan. After reaching the Smolensk area, the right flank of Field Marshal Fedor von Bock's (q.v.) Army Group Center was no longer protected by the Pripet marshes, and his forces had expanded steadily southward to secure this flank. Throughout August, General Heinz Guderian's (q.v.) Second *Panzer* Group and General Maximillian von Weichs's (q.v.) Second Army attacked Admiral Nikolai Kuznetsov's (q.v.) weakened Twenty-first Army near Gomel. In the process, the Germans advanced half the distance between Smolensk and Kiev. Army Group South, meanwhile, advanced into the southern Ukraine toward the Dnieper River. The Soviet bridgeheads on the western bank were reduced, and by the end of August, General Karl von Stülpnagel's (q.v.) Seventeenth Army and General Ewald von Kleist's (q.v.) First *Panzer* Group were able to establish their own bridgeheads at Kremenchug and Dnepropetrovsk.

At that point the Soviets still held the Ukrainian capital of Kiev. The main German force was 200 kilometers to the east. On 5 August, Soviet Premier Josef Stalin (q.v.) ordered the defense of the Dnieper River line at all costs and the *Stavka* (q.v.) sent three additional armies to reinforce the Dnieper bend. These units were subordinated to General Mikhail Kirponos's Southwestern Front, responsible for the defense of the river line. Between Kirponos and the *Stavka* in Moscow was yet another level of command, the Southwestern Theater (TVD) under Marshal Seymon Budenny (q.v.). This command structure proved to be cumbersome once the fighting actually started.

The German attack started on 25 August. Guderian's XLVII *Panzer Korps* and XXIV *Panzer Korps* struck southward from Gomel and Starodub. They got off to a good start by capturing a bridge over the Desna River before the Soviets could destroy it. After that, however, things started to get difficult for the Germans. Heavy Soviet resistance forced Guderian to commit a third unit, the XLVI *Panzer Korps.* Even then it took the Germans nearly a week to fight their way out from the Desna bridgehead. On Guderian's right, the Second Army supported the *Panzers* by attacking Cernigov.

In Army Group South, the Germans needed more time to prepare for the offensive. Bridgeheads were enlarged and the First *Panzer* Group was withdrawn from the Dnepropetrovsk area in order to launch its attack from the more westerly Dnieper crossing at Kremenchug. Thus, von Kleist was unable to commit his tank forces until 12 September. By that time, the Soviets started to realize the danger of their situation, but the German operation also was gaining momentum.

Guderian's forces crossed the Seym River on 9 September and raced south across the vast plain of the northern Ukraine, toward the rendezvous point with the First *Panzer* Group. That point was roughly 200 kilometers east of Kiev. On 13 September, the leading elements made initial contact, and by 15 September, a thin line was established around the Southwestern Front. Four days earlier, Kirponos had requested permission to withdraw his troops from what would become the Kiev Pocket. That request was personally rejected by Stalin, who also replaced Budenny with Marshal Semen Timoshenko (q.v.) as commander of the Southwestern TVD.

The Soviet high command ordered the immediate destruction of the German armored spearheads. Marshal Boris Saposnikov (q.v.), the chief of staff in Moscow, reminded Kirponos of the fate that had befallen General Dimitry Pavlov (q.v.), the former commander of the Western Front, who was executed over the disaster at Minsk (q.v.). Nonetheless, on 16 September Timoshenko decided to order a withdrawal on his own. All his reserves were exhausted during the fight at the Desna or were trapped in the pocket. For him it was obvious that Stalin's orders were nothing but wishful thinking. Kirponos, however, dared not execute the order immediately and wasted an additional two days asking Moscow for permission that never came. When he finally decided to follow Timoshenko's order on 18 September, it was too late. An orderly withdrawal was no longer possible. The units of the Southwestern Front disintegrated and most of its soldiers were captured.

The final act of the battle of Kiev was played out by the *Luftwaffe.* The II *Fliegerkorps* in the north and V *Fliegerkorps* in the south supported the operation by attacking the Soviet lines of communications and by screening the eastern front line of the pocket during the first days after Guderian's and von Kleist's troops linked up. Although their capabilities were reduced by a shortage of planes and supplies, the importance of the *Luftwaffe's* contribution was recognized even by the ground commanders.

Between 16 and 26 September, the Red Army units in the great Kiev cauldron (originally about 200 kilometers across) were torn apart by the infantry divisions of the German Second and Sixth Armies. The Germans also formed a tight ring around Kiev before capturing the city on 19 September. After occupying Kiev, the Germans were forced to fight huge fires caused by Soviet remotely controlled bombs. These fires caused some German casualties, which provided the pretext for Paul Blobel's *SS Sonderkommando 4a* of *Einsatzgruppe* C (*see Einsatzgruppen*) to annihilate Kiev's Jews. Almost 34,000 people were killed by this unit in the valley of Babi Yar (q.v.). This carnage was carried out with the active support of German regular army units deployed in Kiev.

According to the records of Army Group South, the Germans took 665,000 prisoners during the battle and captured 3,500 guns and 900 tanks. The Soviet Twenty-first and Fifth Armies were destroyed, along with major portions of the Fortieth and Thirty-seventh Armies. The Southwestern Front effectively ceased to exist. Kirponos was killed while trying to make his way to the east, and many other Soviet generals were taken prisoner. General Andrei Vlasov (q.v.) managed to escape. His Thirty-seventh Army defended Kiev long and skillfully. Ironically, later in the war, Vlasov would change sides and fight for Hitler.

After the battle, the Soviets had to use the last of their reserves to reestablish a new line of resistance in front of Army Group South. Luckily for them, the German forces in the Ukraine were also very weak after Kiev. But Hitler decided to launch another offensive before winter—this time against Moscow. Army Group South had to give up ten divisions for this operation and lost the combat power necessary to exploit the weak Soviet position in the southern sector for a rapid advance toward the Caucasus (q.v.).

Kiev was one of the most impressive German victories of the war. From the tactical point of view, Hitler was right when he ordered the operation. Halder, however, also was right when he argued in August that the *Wehrmacht* was only able to complete one large-scale operation before winter. When Hitler tried to take both Moscow and the Ukraine, he failed. The 1941–1942 battle for Moscow was the first major setback for the Germans. Most likely Hitler would have been better off to follow the advice of his generals. The real problem of Germany's war in the Soviet Union was the discrepancy between the objectives of its leadership and the *Reich*'s resources in men and materiel.

Reiner Martin

Additional Reading

Erikson, John, *Stalin's War with Germany,* 2 vols. (1983).
Guderian, Heinz, *Panzer Leader* (1952).
Seaton, Albert, *The Battle for Moscow* (1971).
———, *The Russo-German War 1941–45* (1971).
Ziemke, Earl F., and Magna E. Bauer, *Moscow to Stalingrad, Decision in the East* (1987).

Kurland (July 1944–May 1945)

[See map 32 on page 1342]

At the beginning of July 1944, Germany's Army Group North was still firmly entrenched in the Panther Line, to which it had withdrawn in February following the retreat from Leningrad (q.v.). This defensive line ran from the Gulf of Finland down the Narva River, along the western shore of Lake Peipus, and further south over Pskov and Polotsk. The Soviets launched an offensive on 10 July and pushed the army group back but could not achieve a breakthrough. The Soviet summer offensive against Army Group Center in Byelorussia (q.v.), however, created a huge gap on Army Group North's southern flank. On 30 July, Soviet troops reached the Gulf of Riga near Tuckum, severing Army Group North's land contact with the rest of the German line.

Although a German counterattack reestablished the land link on 20 August, Adolf Hitler (q.v.) refused to withdraw the army group from its exposed position in the Baltic states. In mid-September, following Finland's surrender and again under attack, General Ferdinand Schörner (q.v.), the Army Group North commander since 23 July, ordered the evacuation of Estonia and a retreat to prepared positions around Riga. Unable to crack the German defenses surrounding the Latvian capital, the Soviets shifted their forces and on 5 October launched an attack toward Memel. On 10 October, the Soviets reached the Baltic coast north of Memel and again isolated the army group.

Schörner quickly retreated from the Riga area and established a front in Kurland, a broad peninsula in northwest Latvia. On 20 October, Hitler ordered Army Group North (renamed Army Group Kurland in January 1945) to go over to the defensive in Kurland, where it remained until Germany's surrender in May 1945.

During the army group's seven-month isolation in Latvia, the Soviets launched six offensives, known as the six Kurland battles, in an attempt to destroy the German Sixteenth and Eighteenth Armies and to capture the port of Libau, through which the army group received its supplies. With their backs to the sea, the Germans gave up little ground in these battles, aided by weather, difficult terrain, surprisingly good morale, and a relatively large number of troops, tanks, and artillery for the length of the front.

Ignoring army chief of staff General Heinz Guderian's (q.v.) repeated demands for the evacuation of the army group to assist in the defense of Germany itself, Hitler withdrew only about a dozen divisions from Kurland. Despite the German Navy's ever-increasing obligations to support the land front in eastern Germany and evacuate civilian refugees, it managed to maintain Army Group Kurland's supply line to the end. On 8 May 1945, German naval vessels evacuated more than 25,000 troops from Kurland, but later that day approximately twenty divisions with more than 200,000 men surrendered.

Several possible reasons explain Hitler's decision to leave 300,000 seasoned troops in Kurland at a time when enemy armies had entered German territory from both east and west. One theory is that he believed the army group tied down a disproportionate number of Soviet divisions, which otherwise would appear at more vulnerable sectors of the eastern front. Although Schörner's forces engaged a large number of Soviet units (about 150 divisions) until the end of 1944, the Soviets had withdrawn nearly half those divisions by mid-January 1945.

Another theory is that Hitler, confident he

would score a major victory in the Ardennes offensive (q.v.), intended to use the German position in Latvia as a springboard for an offensive against the Soviets after he had driven the British and American forces from the Continent. Yet if this was the main reason, he probably would have evacuated the bridgehead after the attack in the Ardennes failed. Still another possible reason is that he believed the retention of a position in the Baltic states deterred Sweden from declaring war on Germany. Although the Nazis feared the Swedes might enter the war, it is difficult to imagine the hard-pressed divisions in Kurland posing a real threat to Sweden.

The most likely reason for Kurland's defense is that Hitler accepted Grand Admiral Karl Dönitz's (q.v.) argument that the navy required the Baltic to test new types of submarines and train U-boat crews. For military and geographic reasons, submarine training was possible only in the eastern and central Baltic. These new U-boats, the Types XXI and XXIII, were technologically superior to existing submarines, and with these new weapons Dönitz planned to turn the tide in the Battle of the Atlantic (q.v.). The war ended, however, before more than a handful of these U-boats were operational. Dönitz's unsuccessful attempt to seize the island of Gogland from Finnish forces, and his insistence on the defense of the Baltic islands Dagö and Oesel provide additional evidence for this theory.

Howard D. Grier

Additional Reading

Erikson, John, *Stalin's War with Germany,* 2 vols. (1983).

Seaton, Albert, *The Russo-German War 1941–45* (1971).

Ziemke, Earl F., *Stalingrad to Berlin: The German Defeat in the East* (1968).

Kursk (5–17 July 1943)

[See map 24 on page 1334]

In February and March 1943, Field Marshal Erich von Manstein (q.v.), commander of German Army Group South, conducted a skillful counteroffensive that brought the Soviet winter campaign to a standstill. As a result, the Germans found themselves in more or less the same positions they held in 1942, prior to the start of their attack toward Stalingrad and the Caucasus (qq.v.). They shortened their front line at Demyansk and Rshew and began to assemble a strategic reserve of armored divisions in preparation for Adolf Hitler's (q.v.)

next move. Hard-pressed now on all sides, the *Führer* wanted to mount another summer offensive in the east and regain the initiative in at least one of the European theaters of war.

The failure of the 1942 campaign in the Soviet Union had a severe affect on Germany's political position in the world. After the loss of Stalingrad, Finland was looking for an opportunity to cut its connections with the *Reich*. In Romania anti-German movements were gaining momentum, and war-tired Italy pressed for peace between the Germans and the Soviets. It was obvious to Hitler that Benito Mussolini's (q.v.) troops were unable and unwilling to defend even their own country against the Allied attack that was expected soon.

The Allied powers, meanwhile, increased their pressure on the neutral states and the attitude of these countries toward Germany stiffened remarkably in the first half of 1943. Hitler tried to counter these developments by offering German weapons to the neutrals and his allies, although these deliveries weakened the efforts to reinforce the *Wehrmacht*. Nevertheless, he probably was correct in assuming that only a significant German victory could restore the international image of powerful *Reich*.

As surprising as it appears now in retrospect, the Soviets had been trying to negotiate an armistice with Germany since November 1942. (They even renewed their offers after Kursk.) They were afraid of burning their country out in the war against Hitler, which would leave them in a position of relative inferiority compared with Great Britain and the United States in the postwar period. Hitler never showed any real interest in the Soviet peace overtures, probably because of a mixture of mistrust and ideological blindness.

On 13 March 1943, Hitler gave the order for a combined operation of Army Groups Center and South near Kursk. After consulting with the commanders of the armies and army groups involved, he issued Operations Order Number 6 for Operation *ZITADELLE* (CITADEL) on 15 April 1943. Its objective was the reduction of the Kursk salient, a huge bulge situated between the two army groups, measuring 180 kilometers north to south and 100 kilometers in depth.

The plan was a repetition of the battles of encirclement conducted by the *Wehrmacht* so often during the war, and therefore, quite obvious to the Soviets. Two strong attacking forces were to break through the north and south flanks of the salient, link up near the city of Kursk, and encircle the large Soviet force consisting of about 40 percent of the Red Army's infantry and 80 percent of its armor. By so weakening their enemy, the Germans hoped to prevent a future Soviet offensive and bring the eastern front to a standstill. This would have allowed them then to move troops to western and southern Europe, giving them a strong enough force in those areas to repel any Allied invasion. Moreover, the shortened front line after Operation *ZITADELLE* would be easier to defend.

It was critical that the Germans start Operation *ZITADELLE* as early as possible, because the Soviets expected an attack in this area and were improving their defenses daily. Originally, the attack was scheduled for 3 May, but Hitler delayed it because he considered the attacking units' equipment inadequate. The new date, 12 June, was delayed once again; this time because of bad weather conditions and the threat of an Allied landing in Italy.

On 18 June, Hitler held a meeting at his headquarters in Rastenburg, East Prussia. He ordered 5 July as the final date for the attack. By that time, however, the Army high command (OKH) was already convinced that the chances for success had become very dim. The OKH advocated canceling *ZITADELLE,* and instead suggested waiting for a Soviet offensive and using newly re-equipped *Panzer* divisions as a counterattack force. Hitler once again ignored the advice of his generals and insisted on his scheme. Even Hitler considered it a gamble, but seduced by his unexpected successes in the past, he convinced himself that Operation *ZITADELLE* would be a victory that would "shine out to the world like a beacon."

By postponing Operation *ZITADELLE* over and over again, the Germans threw away the advantage of surprise. On the other hand, they had time to build up extremely strong forces, including nineteen *Panzer* divisions with more than 2,500 tanks and assault guns, and 1,800 aircraft. Among these armored units were nearly all of Germany's Tiger and Panther tanks and Ferdinands, the new heavy and super-heavy tanks and assault guns on which Hitler pinned so much faith. The troops had a long period to rest and prepare for the battle. Large-scale operations against Soviet partisans (q.v.) in the rear of Army Group Center were conducted to ensure the reliability of supply lines, but the success of these operations may not have contributed much to the overall results.

The *Wehrmacht* also did its best to deceive the Soviets as to the German intentions. Mock troop movements in southern Ukraine were staged in order to give the impression of a coming attack in this area. The Red Army was not deceived. The Soviets knew from ULTRA (q.v.) intercepts provided by the British exactly what the German plans were.

After two years of fighting, the Red Army was now close to gaining the upper hand. Industrial production increased remarkably and the Red Army was receiving large quantities of supplies from its Western allies. The Soviets used the time between March and July 1943 very effectively. They were well aware that the Kursk salient was nothing short of an invitation for another German encirclement operation. Consequently, they constructed superb defenses. The main belt of defense had a depth of five to six kilometers. Two more defensive belts were located ten to twelve and thirty to forty kilometers behind the first. The total length of the trenches in the northern half of the salient ran 5,000 kilometers, dug by a civilian labor force of 300,000.

The two Soviet Fronts in the salient, Marshal Konstantin Rokossovsky's (q.v.) Central Front in the north and General Nikolai Vatutin's (q.v.) Voronezh Front in the south, had a total of 20,000 guns and rocket launchers, including large artillery divisions from the *Stavka's* (q.v.) strategic reserve. The Soviets also laid close to a million mines.

East of Kursk, the Red Army assembled a group of reserve units, the Steppe Front, which included five armies supported by one air army. These troops, commanded by Marshal Ivan Konev (q.v.), could be used either as reinforcements or as the core of a counterattack force. According to Soviet sources, the three fronts had a combined strength of about 3,600 tanks and 3,100 aircraft. In retrospect it appears clear the *Wehrmacht* picked the worst possible place to launch its attack.

In the north, the main German attack was carried out by Army Group Center's Ninth Army, Commanded by General Walther Model (q.v.). It attacked from the area of the major German logistics base just south of Orel. North to south Model's force consisted of the XXIII *Korps,* XLI *Panzer Korps,* XLVII *Panzer Korps,* XLVI *Panzer Korps,* and XX *Korps.* This force had a total of eight infantry divisions, six *Panzer* divisions, and one *Panzergrenadier* (mechanized infantry) division. The Ninth Army's reserve was Group von Esebeck, with three more *Panzer* divisions. The entire force was supported by the Sixth *Luftflotte.*

Facing Model's main thrust was the Central Front, with Thirteenth Army in the center, Forty-eighth Army on the right, and Seventieth Army on the left. The Sixteenth Air Army supported Central Front.

At 0330 hours on 5 July 1943 the battle

started. Using remote-control mini-tanks, the Germans cleared the minefields. Initially, they faced only light Soviet resistance. By the end of the first day, Model was relatively satisfied with the results. His troops had penetrated the Soviet first defensive belt. The XLVII *Panzer Korps,* heavily supported by the *Luftwaffe,* made especially good progress. Unfortunately, the Sixth *Luftflotte* was not strong enough to support all of Model's corps at the same time. Even so, it claimed to have shot down 162 Soviet aircraft on that first day.

During the night of 5 July and the following day, resistance stiffened remarkably. Soviet artillery and aircraft hammered the Ninth Army, and units of the Soviet Second Tank Army moved northward to start the counterattacks. The overall pace of the German attack slowed down. It soon became obvious that Rokossovsky was trying to prevent at any cost the Germans from breaking through and resuming mobile warfare.

During the third day, 7 July, the attackers made almost no progress at all and their losses started to mount—10,000 casualties during the first two days of the attack. Moreover, the Ninth Army was starting to run out of tank gun ammunition. More unsuccessful efforts followed on 8 July, and this time the Germans had to defend their own positions against Soviet counterattacks. After that, Model decided to hold up for a day to give his troops time to rest and resupply.

The second phase of the attack in the north was fought from 10 to 12 July, and centered around the Olchowatka and Teploje Heights. Control of these hills was a prerequisite for a German breakthrough. The Soviets knew this very well and used the XVII Guards Corps, the 1st Guards Artillery Division, and dug-in tanks for their defense. Two well-prepared German attempts to carry the ridge failed. Army Group Center promised the Ninth Army an additional infantry and *Panzer* division to help break the deadlock.

On the morning of 12 July, General Markain Popov's (q.v.) Bryansk Front and the left flank armies of General Vasili Sokolovsky's (q.v.) Western Front opened Operation KUTUZOV, a three-pronged offensive against the north flank of the Orel salient, the reverse bulge in the line north of Kursk. The Second *Panzer* Army of General Rudolf Schmidt was holding almost 300 kilometers of front in that sector with only fourteen divisions. The Soviet thrust initially forced the Army Group Center commander, Field Marshal Günther von Kluge (q.v.), to divert the two divisions intended for the Ninth Army. By the end of the day, he had to pull two more divisions from

Model. The Ninth Army's attack effectively was over.

In the south, the main effort of von Manstein's attack was delivered by Colonel General Hermann Hoth's (q.v.) Fourth *Panzer* Army, with its LII *Korps* on the left flank, XLVIII *Panzer Korps* in the center, and the II SS *Panzer Korps* on the right. Supporting Hoth on his right was the Eighth Army (also called Group Kempf), with the III *Panzer Korps* on the left and *Korps Raus* in the center. General Werner Kempf's XLII *Korps* on his right did not take part in the operation. Altogether, Army Group South had seven infantry, six *Panzer,* and five *Panzergrenadier* divisions committed to Operation *ZITADELLE.* The XXIV *Panzer Korps* formed the army group reserve, and the Fourth *Luftflotte* provided the air support.

On the Soviet side, Vatutin's Voronezh Front faced the sector of the German attack with three armies in the first echelon: the Fortieth Army on the right, Sixth Guards Army in the center, and Seventh Guards Army on the left. His reserve consisted of the First Tank Army and the Sixty-ninth Army. The Second Air Army provided the air support for the Voronezh Front.

At the unusual time of 1500 hours on 4 July, the first units of Army Group South began their preliminary attacks. Despite unfavorable weather conditions, which included heavy rainfall, Hoth's armored divisions advanced more or less on schedule for the first two days of the attack. Soviet resistance in the south was relatively light, and the *Luftwaffe* managed to establish air superiority over the battlefield—although the Fourth *Luftflotte* was not strong enough to support all the advancing units simultaneously.

The III *Panzer Korps* of Group Kempf was less fortunate. Against stiff resistance its 6th *Panzer* Division failed to advance along the Donets River, thereby causing a gap between the III *Panzer Korps* and the II SS *Panzer Korps,* which weakened the momentum of the whole attack. *Korps Raus* also made poor progress and was tied down securing Kempf's ever-extending right flank against the Seventh Guards Army. The Soviets, meanwhile, managed to withdraw most of their troops and equipment from their first defensive lines.

Some of the new German weapons did not quite meet Hitler's expectations. By the evening of 5 July, only forty of the 200 new PzKpfw-V (Panther) tanks were still operational. Most suffered mechanical breakdowns.

The Soviets held off launching a counterattack during the first days of the attack because the Germans were too strong. Vatutin instead decided to dig in some of the tanks of his First Tank Army in order to stiffen his defenses even more. In the days that followed, the Fourth *Panzer* Army continued its advance northward. It faced mounting resistance and beat back numerous counterattacks from the Voronezh Front's tactical and operational reserves. On 11 July, Hoth's *Panzer* forces inflicted particularly heavy losses on the Soviets, but the defenses held.

On 12 July, in another attempt to break through the Soviet lines, the II SS *Panzer Korps* attacked northeast toward the village of Prochorowka. At the same time, the Steppe Front committed the Fifth Guards Army and the Fifth Guards Tank Army to a counterattack from the same area. The result was the largest tank engagement ever fought to that time. About 1,300 armored vehicles were involved. Neither the Soviets nor the Germans achieved a clear tactical victory, and the losses on both sides were staggering.

By 12 July, with Model's Ninth Army already halted in the north, the original *ZITADELLE* plan was dead. Army Group South now concentrated on closing the gap in its own salient between the Fourth *Panzer* Army and Group Kempf. They accomplished this on 15 July, and two days later, the Fourth *Panzer* Army planned to conduct a smaller scale encirclement code named ROLLAND. Von Manstein and Hoth hoped to destroy the opposing Soviet forces and come out of the whole thing with at least a tactical success, but these plans were canceled when Hitler decided to withdraw the II SS *Panzer Korps* from the eastern front. Seven days earlier, the Allies had landed in Sicily.

During the Allied invasion of Sicily (q.v.), the Italian Army virtually folded and German forces on the island were too weak to stop the attack. On 12 July, Hitler informed von Kluge and von Manstein of his decision to break off the Kursk operation in order to send reinforcements to Italy. Von Manstein argued that nearly all the Soviet reserves had been committed and that the Germans were on the verge of achieving a tactical success. He urged Hitler to continue the fighting for a couple more days to take advantage of the favorable situation. Hitler approved at first, but then quickly changed his mind again.

The Soviets regained the initiative immediately. From 12 July, the Western Front and Bryansk Front conducted continuous attacks against Army Group Center north of Orel. On 17 July, Red Army forces in southern Ukraine also launched an offensive that Army Group South was hard pressed to contain.

The battle of Kursk was a severe defeat for Germany. According to von Manstein, the Germans lost 20,000 soldiers dead and wounded. According to Soviet accounts, the Germans lost closer to 70,000. Red Army's casualties were, no doubt, more than that. These numbers, still the subject of debate, tell only one side of the story. More important for the future course of the war was the *Wehrmacht*'s inability to weaken the Soviets and stabilize the eastern front.

The Germans wasted most of their armored reserves in a battle whose chances for success were very dim from the outset. Even Model and Kempf had their doubts about the operation, but they did not openly oppose Hitler. By the time Hitler decided to halt the Kursk operation, the chances for a German victory in Italy had also passed. From that point on, the *Reich* had to fight on several fronts simultaneously. The Germans had failed to win the war as long as the Soviet Union was the only active front. Now they had to fight on more than one front. After Kursk, the *Wehrmacht* rapidly lost ground against the ever-increasing power of the Red Army.

Reiner Martin

Additional Reading

Caidin, Martin, *The Tigers Are Burning* (1974).
Guderian, Heinz, *Panzer Leader* (1952).
Jukes, Geoffrey, *Kursk, The Clash of Armor* (1968).
Manstein, Erich von, *Lost Victories* (1958).
Mellenthin, F.W. von, *Panzer Battles* (1956).
Parotkin, Ivan, *The Battle of Kursk* (1974).
Ziemke, Earl F., *Stalingrad to Berlin: The German Defeat in the East* (1968).

L

Lapland (20 September 1944–24 April 1945)

[See map 16 on page 1326]

Lapland, which extends from northern Norway all the way to the northeastern parts of the Soviet Union, did not become a battleground in World War II until the fall of 1944. Between 20 September 1944 and 24 April 1945, however, the Finns and Germans fought a war that devastated most of Finnish Lapland. The Soviets and Norwegians, meanwhile, fought against the German troops in Nordkalotten, an area on the northernmost tip of Scandinavia.

The Finnish War of Lapland began as a result of the Moscow Armistice, signed 19 September 1944. As part of that agreement the Finns vowed to drive the still-remaining 220,000 troops of the German Twentieth Mountain Army out of northern Finland. In order to remove the possibility that the Soviets might accuse the Finns of not acting according to the terms of the armistice, Marshal Carl Mannerheim (q.v.), president of Finland, ordered the Finnish troops on the offensive immediately. The next day, 20 September 1944, the War of Lapland between the Finns and their former cobelligerents, the Germans, began. On 3 October, Adolf Hitler (q.v.) approved Operation *NORD-LICHT* (NORTHERN LIGHTS), the withdrawal of the Twentieth Mountain Army into Norway.

The Soviets, meanwhile, attacked Petsamo, a part of Finnish Lapland that was ceded to the Soviet Union under the Moscow Armistice. The struggle over that area, strategically important for its nickel mines, was short. The Soviets took Petsamo in October 1944, and the Germans retreated into Norway. The Soviets did not stop, however, and crossed the Norwegian border on 18 October 1944. As they entered into Norwegian

territory, the Red Army caused an immediate conflict of interests among the Allies.

Norway was supposed to be in the British "sphere of influence," because the Norwegian government had taken refuge in Britain and trained the few thousand Norwegian soldiers that returned to fight the Germans in northern Norway in 1944. The first Allied troops to enter Norway, however, were the Soviets, a fact causing considerable uneasiness among the Western Allies and Norwegians. In the end, the Soviets did not invade Norway in full force. Soviet-Norwegian cooperation was remarkably smooth, and the Soviets made no claims on Norwegian territory.

The war in Finnish Lapland was devastating. The Germans, who already were withdrawing before the Finns attacked, used scorched earth tactics as they moved toward Norway. The city of Rovaniemi, for example, was virtually destroyed and had to be completely rebuilt after the war. The war in Lapland also caused another tragic problem. As the Germans retreated and destroyed most of the areas they passed through, thousands of people were left homeless.

In Finnish Lapland alone approximately 50,000 people lost their homes and required evacuation. As the cold Nordic winter approached, these people's lives were in deep jeopardy. Rescue came from the neutral Swedish government, which had the necessary resources to provide shelter and food for the refugees. Thus, by the end of 1944 most of the refuges from Finnish Lapland, and a few thousand from Norwegian Lapland, were saved.

Although the war of Lapland lasted until the end of April 1945, most of Finnish Lapland was free of the Germans by Christmas 1944. Only the very northwestern tip of Finland, the Kilpisjarv area, remained in German hands until 24 April

1945. On that day, the remaining Germans crossed into Norway and Finland's part in World War II was over. The Germans left behind an empty landscape, barren of people and animals, and full of burned houses, blown-up bridges, and demolished roads.

The events in northern Scandinavia between the fall of 1944 and the spring of 1945 left one other important legacy. Due to the border changes in Nordskalotten, especially the acquisition of Petsamo by the Soviets, the USSR and Norway became the northernmost point where East and West, NATO and the Warsaw Pact, shared a frontier during the Cold War.

Jussi Hanhimaki

Additional Reading

Nissen, Henrik S. (ed.), *Scandinavia and the Second World War* (1983).

Polvinen, Tuomo, *Between East and West: Finland in International Politics, 1944–1947* (1986).

Ziemke, Earl F., *The German Northern Theater of Operations, 1940–1945* (1959).

Leningrad (8 September 1941–27 January 1944)

[See map 25 on page 1335]

Following the German invasion of the Soviet Union on 22 June 1941, the German Sixteenth and Eighteenth Armies and the Fourth *Panzer* Group swept through the Baltic States. By early August, Army Group North had established a front stretching almost 150 miles from Kingisepp and Narva, on the Estonian frontier near the Gulf of Finland in the north, to Novgorod, at the northern end of Lake Ilmen, directly to the south. Leningrad, the objective of Army Group North, was situated only seventy miles behind the Narva-Luga sector of the front. The Germans were well-equipped and morale was high after their quick advance through the Baltic states.

Given Leningrad's strategic importance, the Soviet *Stavka* (q.v.) established this front as a separate and independent operational theater and deployed six rifle divisions, a militia division, and one mountain brigade along the Luga River between Narva and Novgorod. With the exception of some coastal defense artillery near Kingisepp, however, the Soviets had almost no armor or artillery deployed against the superior German forces.

Consolidating its own forces along the Luga front, Army Group North, under the command of Field Marshal Wilhelm Ritter von Leeb (q.v.), launched a massive offensive on 8 August 1941. It appeared at first that the Red Army would not be able to maintain its defensive positions, but its forces refused to retreat toward Leningrad, and they managed to keep the Germans in check for three days. By 12 August, realizing that it would not be possible to hold for much longer, Soviet cavalry forces deployed at the southern end of Lake Ilmen with orders to attack the weak right flank of the Sixteenth Army near Staraya Russa.

German countermeasures over the next few days took the pressure off the Soviet defenses along the central sector of the Luga front, but the relief was only temporary. The entire Soviet defense along the front collapsed by mid-August and the Germans captured Narva, Kingisepp, and Novgorod. Elements of the Sixteenth Army also broke through the Soviet southern flank and captured Chudovo, cutting the vital railroad link between Leningrad and Moscow.

Once Army Group North established its bridgeheads along the Luga, there was little that stood between it and Leningrad. The citizens of Leningrad met the challenge and stood unified to meet the German threat. Civilian and paramilitary organizations worked around the clock beside regular Red Army units to fortify the city's defenses. Local Communist Party officials established "destruction battalions" consisting of party and NKVD (q.v.) personnel to assist in the defense of the city.

During the latter half of August, party and military officials, including Premier Josef Stalin (q.v.) disagreed on the best and most efficient way to defend Leningrad. As a result, the Germans continued to advance on the city as the Soviet military position steadily deteriorated. Army Group North, however, was experiencing its own logistical problems in the wake of the Soviet retreat from the Luga front. Even as it forced the Red Army to retreat toward Leningrad, the German Army high command (OKH) was having difficulty coordinating offensive efforts with its Finnish allies. With their own forces stretched to the limit, the Germans hoped the Finnish Army would apply pressure on Leningrad from its frontal line across the Karelian isthmus, ten miles north of the city.

Field Marshal Carl Mannerheim's (q.v.) hesitation to commit his forces to an attack on Leningrad was a result of Finland's 1918 treaty with the Soviet Union—it promised not to use the Karelian isthmus for an attack on the city. Additionally, he opposed Germany's plans to raze the city and exterminate its population through terror and starvation. Hitler had instructed his field commanders not to accept any Soviet offer to surrender. The Finns, despite their desire for a military victory over the Soviet Union to secure their own borders, refused to attack Leningrad from the north. Instead, the Germans sealed off the city from the south, and subjected it to murderous artillery bombardments and air raids.

The German siege of Leningrad coincided with Army Group Center's offensive against Moscow (q.v.). Adolf Hitler (q.v.) issued *Führer* Directive 35 on 6 September 1941. Known as Operation *TAIFUN* (TYPHOON), it called for the transfer of the Fourth *Panzer* Group and various *Luftwaffe* units from Army Group North to Army Group Center to support an attack on the Soviet capital once Leningrad had been encircled. Hitler believed the siege of Leningrad could be accomplished with six or seven infantry divisions and supporting artillery. In fact, he greatly underestimated the Soviet resolve to defend Leningrad, whose perimeter was never completely sealed. Throughout the siege, Soviet military reinforcements and supplies were able to move in and out of Leningrad across Lake Ladoga from the north and through the rather porous southern perimeter.

Even before the city was encircled, German armored units launched a frontal attack on Leningrad. They were soon mired down in the extensive antitank ditches surrounding the city. Soviet military and civilian defenders used effective mortar fire, supported by naval artillery, to slow down the German attack, but by 10 September, a German armored column reached the Dudergof Heights, the last major Soviet defensive position located only six miles from the center of Leningrad. Yet after four days of direct frontal assault, the Germans had still not captured the city.

The OKH, quickly realizing that the depletion of valuable German manpower and supplies at Leningrad endangered the chances for success in its offensive against Moscow, finally issued the order that Leningrad should not be taken, but only encircled. Hitler, believing that victory at Leningrad was at hand, issued his own directive that none of Army Group North's armor and *Luftwaffe* units would be redeployed to Army Group Center until Leningrad fell. The Germans continued to advance on the city, further depleting their strength. The Soviet defenders persevered, and on 17 September, the first and only German frontal assault on Leningrad was finally halted. The Fourth *Panzer* Group and several *Luftwaffe* units were then transferred to Army Group Center.

The siege of Leningrad continued for more than two years. The Germans hoped that deprivation and starvation would accomplish what tanks and planes could not. Their primary goal was to ensure that food and military supplies did not reach the city, and Army Group North's Eighteenth Army conducted a number of smaller military operations in the hope of completely sealing off the city. During the latter half of September 1941, the Germans captured Shlisselburg, located where the Neva River flows into Lake Ladoga.

In mid-October, von Leeb sent a German expeditionary force from Chudovo toward Tikhvin with the intention of linking up with the Finnish Army deployed on the Svir River east of Lake Ladoga, thereby cutting the Soviet railroad to the southern shore of the lake. This move effectively would have cut off the last possible supply route for the besieged inhabitants of Leningrad. The Germans, however, failed to accomplish this goal by the end of October, when the troops became bogged down in the mud of the autumn rainy season. The rail terminus at Tikhvin was not captured until 8 November, and the Germans hoped Leningrad was finally isolated. The Soviets, however, bypassed Tikhvin by running trucks across frozen Lake Ladoga.

Army Group North's reserves were expanded in the effort to take Tikhvin. Now, having accomplished the encirclement of Leningrad, von Leeb was faced with another obstacle. The Germans never intended for the war against the Soviet Union to last until the onset of winter. But the major military objectives had not been reached, and Hitler had to continue the war into 1942. Each of the three German army group commanders was assigned a "minimum boundary," where his forces should be before completing the 1941 phase of Operation BARBAROSSA. If reached, each army group would be in a good position to continue its offensive in the spring of 1942. Army Group North was ordered to reach the Svir River, thereby linking up with the Finnish Army and its supply line. Von Leeb found it necessary to move his forces another thirty miles to the east by the end of December 1941. The only way Army Group North could accomplish this objective was to first destroy Red Army units isolated in a pocket west of Leningrad.

With food and other supplies almost completely exhausted in Leningrad by the end of December 1941, thousands of Soviet civilians perished from exposure and starvation. When the Soviets finally forced the Germans to abandon Tikhvin in December, the Finnish Army along the Svir River remained hesitant to advance any further against the Soviets. The winter supply lines across frozen Lake Ladoga were reopened, and Leningrad's future, although extremely grim, was no longer completely hopeless. The city's two million inhabitants, and the remnants of the Soviet Twenty-third and Fourty-second Armies, continued to hold out against the German siege.

During the first week of January 1942, the *Stavka* took advantage of the German inability to completely isolate Leningrad and the weaknesses in the German lines to launch a new winter counteroffensive. Three Soviet armies—two new ones brought up from reserves and a third refitted army from the Moscow sector—joined the two armies that had forced the Germans out of Tikhvin, and advanced on a broad front running from Lake Ladoga to Lake Ilmen westward toward the Luga River. By breaking through the German lines on this new front, the Red Army would not have to advance far before it threatened the German supply lines to the Leningrad sector, thereby relieving the pressure on the city.

German military leaders anticipated a major offensive would probably occur south of Lake Ilmen, and they held the Red Army at bay for five days. By 13 January, the Soviets penetrated the German lines north of the lake despite their erratic efforts, but they did not advance very far. Hitler made it clear to his field commanders that Army Group North was not to retreat. Operating in subzero temperatures in an area of vast peat bogs and swamps covered in deep snow, the *Wehrmacht* and the Red Army battled each other with neither side finding any clear advantage. Even though the Red Army had penetrated the German lines between Lake Ladoga and Lake Ilmen, the German troops surrounding Leningrad were still seventy miles away to the north and west and in no clear danger of attack from the rear. The Soviets would have to cut the Chudovo-Leningrad rail line if there was any hope of relieving the besieged city.

By the end of February 1942, the situation in Leningrad was becoming more precarious for the city's inhabitants; exposure to sub-zero temperatures and hunger continued to take their toll. Nevertheless, the Germans, fearing they might become trapped in the mud and flooding of the approaching spring thaw, made no attempt to leave their positions and advance farther into the city. Hitler was eager for his commanders to take the initiative and bring the siege to a quick and successful conclusion, while turning back the Soviet counteroffensive between Lake Ladoga and Lake Ilmen before the spring thaw. Throughout March and April 1942, units from the *Wehrmacht*

and the Red Army fought it out along the wide front that had been stationary for almost seven months.

In April, Stalin ordered his troops in Leningrad and on the northern sector of the front (now reinforced with new units and replacements) to take the offensive. The siege of Leningrad was to be broken at all costs. Spring and the melting ice permitted ferries to transport more supplies across Lake Ladoga than could be moved across the ice. A pipeline and electric cable laid in the lake also permitted fuel and electricity to reach the city.

By June 1942, as most of the women, children, and elderly were evacuated, an additional quarter-million Soviet troops arrived to reinforce the city's defenses and to prepare for the lifting of the German siege. German units tried unsuccessfully to interdict Soviet traffic across the lake. The Germans believed that should the Soviets completely evacuate Leningrad, the city would lose its strategic significance, and more importantly, permit the redeployment of valuable Soviet troops to the central and southern sectors of the Russian front.

Even as the weather conditions improved, Army Group North maintained it positions around the city while waiting for the ground to dry enough to permit armored units to move freely. Once this occurred, Army Group North was to finish off Leningrad and then link up with the Finnish Army on the Karelian isthmus. The summer months were wet, however, and the Germans held to their positions. Once again, they were unable to link up with the Finns on the Svir River, and Mannerheim refused to move against Leningrad from the north.

In late August 1942, the Soviets finally made their move, attempting to break the German bottleneck along the Neva River, east of the city. This offensive, while appearing to threaten the German stranglehold on Leningrad, became hopelessly stalled by late September. Although it prevented the Germans from conducting operations that would have allowed them to link up with their Finnish allies on the Karelian isthmus, the Soviets were unable to lift the siege. By the middle of October, Army Group North was able to turn its attention once again to the Soviet defensive perimeter. The arrival of another winter meant several more months of cold, deprivation, and the possibility of a final German attack.

That attack never came. The winter of 1942 was not as severe as the previous one. With the fuel and electricity reaching the city along with other supplies moving across the ice of Lake Ladoga, the

L

Soviet defenders were able to hold their own against a static German perimeter. German commanders also feared that the Red Army might make another attempt to break through their stronghold along the Neva. Stalin once again took the initiative, ordering an attack on the German bottleneck on 12 January 1943. By the end of the first week, Soviet troops had retaken Shlisselberg and opened a new corridor south of Lake Ladoga to Leningrad.

German fortunes in the north were further diminished in February 1943 with the surrender of the German Sixth Army at Stalingrad (q.v.) and Finland's plans to sue for a separate peace with the Soviet Union. In order to counter the new Soviet offensive east of the city, the Germans consolidated their remaining troops around the Leningrad perimeter. The Soviet advance stalled again, and by April, the Red Army had failed to take pressure off the defenders of Leningrad. With the return of spring mud and flooding, both the *Wehrmacht* and the Red Army had time to regroup.

Hitler and his generals recognized the importance of finally defeating the Soviets at Leningrad. Once the ground dried in early summer, troops deployed elsewhere along the front could be moved into position for a final attack on the city. With the capture of Leningrad, Army Group North would be able to join forces with the Finns to defend the Karelian isthmus from further Soviet incursions. Finland would not have to sue for peace, and German control of the Baltic Sea and its vital supply lines would be secured. Yet new Soviet offensives along the Dnieper River, in the south, and at the Nevel, in the north, prevented additional German troops from moving into position at Leningrad or coming to the aid of their Finnish allies.

By August and September 1943, German military interest in Leningrad began to wane. The unstable situation farther south along the front had far-reaching implications for the overall German war effort in the east. While assuming responsibility for areas of the front once held by Army Group Center, Army Group North began making plans for a possible retreat to defensible positions in the vicinity of the Narva River, Lake Peipus, and Lake Pskov, more than 100 miles to the southwest of Leningrad. By December 1943, the OKH, thinking that yet another Soviet offensive in the vicinity of Leningrad would be limited to the scale of the earlier ones, considered Army Group North capable of meeting this challenge during the German strategic withdrawal. OKH began transferring some of Army Group North's best units to Army Group Center.

The new Soviet offensive came on 14 January 1944, striking Army Group North at its weakest points east and south of Leningrad. Soviet gains, however, were modest. The Germans, thinking the Soviets had committed all of their available troops, remained certain that they had enough manpower and weapons to halt the Soviet attack. After five days, however, the tide turned against the Germans, with the Red Army threatening to isolate several important German positions. Hitler would have to give the order to retreat to a line running along the Chudovo-Leningrad railroad, to save the threatened units.

As the Soviets continued their advance at the end of January 1944, Army Group North began its planned large-scale retreat to the Luga River, arguing that it would only be able to defend that line if it had enough troops left to man the defensive positions there. With Army Group North in full retreat to the Estonian border, the 890-day siege of Leningrad was over. On 27 January 1944, General Leonid Govorov (q.v.), commander of the Leningrad Front, announced the complete lifting of the blockade. The official death toll for the siege was 632,000, although the actual total probably was closer to one million. The Germans hit the city with more than 150,000 artillery rounds, and 100,000 incendiary and 4,600 high explosive bombs.

Steven B. Rogers

Additional Reading

Clark, Alan, *Barbarossa: The Russian-German Conflict, 1941–1945* (1965).
Fadeev, Alexander A., *Leningrad in the Days of the Blockade* (1971).
Salisbury, Harrison E., *The 900 Days: The Siege of Leningrad* (1969).
Werth, Alexander, *Russia at War, 1941–1945* (1964).
Wykes, Alan, *The Siege of Leningrad* (1968).
Ziemke, Earl F., *Stalingrad to Berlin: The German Defeat in the East* (1968).
Ziemke, Earl F., and Magna E. Bauer, *Moscow to Stalingrad: Decision in the East* (1988).

Lorraine (1 September–16 December 1944)

At the beginning of September 1944, the U.S. Third Army under Lieutenant General George S. Patton (q.v.) began sixteen weeks of operations against German forces defending the territory between the Moselle and the Sarre Rivers in eastern France and western Germany. These operations, lasting until mid-December, were unofficially known as the Lorraine Campaign.

The troops under Patton's command entered the Lorraine with high spirits, an optimistic outlook, and a contagious feeling that the final victory of World War II was near. They had just completed one of the most successful operations in modern military history, the swift pursuit of German forces across northern France. Operating well in advance of the Operation OVERLORD timetable, Patton's troops had suffered only light losses. American forces had cleared the Argonne Forest and Verdun regions, scenes of bloody fighting during World War I, in a matter of days without encountering the expected German resistance.

The Third Army mission of driving through Lorraine was an important part of the strategy of a broad advance devised by General Dwight D. Eisenhower (q.v.), the supreme Allied commander, who on 1 September assumed direct operational command of ground Allied forces in northern France. The Third Army was to drive on the axis of Metz-Saarbrücken-Frankfurt as a subsidiary effort to the main Allied drive north of the Ardennes on the Maubeuge-Liege axis being conducted by the 21st Army Group and the U.S. First Army. Eventually, the Third Army was to form the lower pincer of a massive envelopment, with the dual goals of neutralizing the industry of the Saar basin and ultimately aiding in conquering the Ruhr, the industrial heart of Germany.

The primary Third Army forces involved in the Lorraine campaign consisted of two corps, the XII, commanded by Major General Manton S. Eddy (q.v.) and the XX Corps, commanded by Major General Walton H. Walker (q.v.). Eddy's corps had the 4th Armored Division, 80th Infantry Division, and 35th Infantry Division. Walker's corps had the 7th Armored Division, 5th Infantry Division, and 90th Infantry Division. XV Corps, commanded by Major General Wade H. Haislip had originally been assigned to Third Army, but had operated for some time with the U.S. First Army. XV Corps was scheduled to rejoin Third Army during the latter part of September to take a brief but important part in the campaign. In the air, Third Army was supported by the XIX Tactical Air Command (TAC) under Brigadier General Otto P. Weyland. In September 1944, the Third Army, on paper, consisted of approximately 314,814 officers and men with 669 medium tanks. Actual combat personnel numbered fewer.

Facing the Third Army in Lorraine was a tattered but still formidable German force under the overall command of Field Marshal Gerd von Rundstedt (q.v.), the commander in chief, west. *(OB-West)* Directly subordinate to von Rundstedt was the commander of Army Group B, Field Marshal Walther Model (q.v.). In the Lorraine area Army Group B had the German First Army, under *General der Panzertruppen* Otto von Knobelsdorff. The battle-hardened First Army consisted of elements of the 3rd and 15th *Panzergrenadier* Divisions, the 17th SS *Panzergrenadier* Division, the 48th Division, the 553rd and 559th *Volksgrenadier* Divisions, the 106th *Panzer* Brigade, and the recently formed 462nd Division.

Sharing the southern portion of the front facing the U.S. Third Army in Lorraine was Army Group G, commanded by *Generaloberst* Johannes Blaskowitz (q.v.). Army Group G's primary fighting force was General Friedrich Wiese's Nineteenth Army. It consisted of the remnants of seven retreating and exhausted divisions, including the 11th *Panzer* Division, the 16th Division, the 159th Reserve Division, and the 21st *Panzer* Division.

The U.S. Third Army arrived in the Lorraine region in late August, but further advance was stalled and soon halted because of logistical and supply problems—especially a shortage of transportation and gasoline. Another reason for the halt was a shift of some U.S. forces from the U.S. First Army, on the Third Army's northern flank, to positions farther north for the purposes of aiding the 21st Army Group in trapping retreating German units in the vicinity of Mons, Belgium. This was done at the behest of Field Marshal Bernard L. Montgomery (q.v.), despite strong protests from Patton. These troop redeployments, plus the need to refit, rest, and replenish, prompted Eisenhower to order Patton to keep his units relatively static.

Within a week, however, on 4 September, Patton received operational instructions from the supreme commander ordering the U.S. Third Army to attack in the Moselle region, to occupy the sector of the Siegfried Line covering the Saar, and then to seize Frankfurt-am-Main. The Third Army commander in turn issued an operational directive to his corps commanders outlining two objectives: (1) attack and seize a bridgehead east of the Moselle and (2) continue east to seize a bridgehead across the Rhine. In view of the Allied successes in the recent fighting in France, these objectives did not seem overly optimistic in early September 1944.

The logistical situation in the U.S. Third Army area had improved to such a degree by 4–5 September that Patton ordered Eddy's XII Corps and Walker's XX Corps to begin their attacks. The initial efforts to cross the Moselle north of Nancy by units of the XII Corps' 80th Infantry Division were repulsed by fierce German counterattacks and stalwart rear-guard actions on 4–5 September near Pont-a-Mousson, as were similar attacks near Toul two days later. Although the Germans could not hope to permanently stop the stronger American forces, the XII Corps advance in this sector came to a halt by 10 September. Stalled in the North, the 4th Armored Division and the 35th Infantry Division proceeded to attack south of Nancy and established bridgeheads across the Moselle on 11–12 September. Drawing on these successes, the 80th Infantry Division again attacked in the north and crossed the Moselle around midnight 11 September. The 80th Infantry Division encountered fierce German counterattacks on its bridgeheads during the next two days, but maintained its positions with reinforcement from the 4th Armored Division, which soon broke free and began a fiercely resisted advance toward Arracourt.

During the next three days, the XII Corps drove toward Nancy in two columns north and south of the city against stiffening enemy resistance over rough terrain that favored the German defenders. Due to these advantages favoring the enemy, the XII Corps plan called for encircling Nancy (q.v.) from the north and south rather than risking a costly frontal assault. After requesting and receiving air attacks conducted by B-26 bombers of the IX Bomber Command to soften German resistance in the Forêt de Haye and heights outside of Nancy, American units entered the city as the bulk of the German force withdrew on 15 September.

Immediately afterward, the XII Corps, which formed the center of the Third Army line, was ordered to attack toward the northeast with the 4th Armored Division in a zone that would have it cross the Rhine near Darmstadt. There it was supposed to establish a bridgehead on the eastern bank. In route the XII Corps was to crack the German West Wall (q.v.) defenses between Sarreguemines and Saarbrücken. If a large enough hole was created by the 4th Armored Division spearhead, the 35th and 80th Infantry Divisions, followed by reinforcements from the 6th Armored Division, were to pour through the gap and head for the Rhine.

Soon after the American advance began on 18 September, however, it was met by an unexpected German counterattack conducted by the recently formed Fifth *Panzer* Army under General Hasso von Manteuffel (q.v.). The American drive ground to a halt on 26 September near the Seille River.

As the XII Corps was advancing toward the

Moselle River and Nancy on 4–5 September, the XX Corps in the north began its movement to the east. Its ambitious goals included crossing the Moselle and Sarre Rivers, taking Metz, and advancing onward to the Rhine at Mainz, and then to Frankfurt. The XX Corps used the 7th Armored Division to spearhead its 6 September drive to the Rhine against an estimated four and a half German divisions to its front. The Germans were favored in their defense by the rugged, wooded, and hilly terrain of the region and the many permanent fortifications around Metz.

The U.S. forces immediately encountered stiff German resistance as they left their Meuse River assembly areas. By 7–8 September the 7th Armored Division and the 4th Infantry Division's 11th Infantry Regiment had succeeded in forcing the Moselle and establishing a bridgehead under heavy German fire east of Dornot. Two days later the 10th Infantry Regiment began crossing the Moselle near Arnaville. After establishing a bridgehead there, the Americans repelled repeated German counterattacks with the aid of close air support provided by the XIX TAC.

Once the larger bridgehead was established, the XX Corps commander ordered a withdrawal from the precarious position held by the 7th Armored Division and 11th Infantry Regiment at Dornot. Bridges were completed over the Moselle near Arnaville by 12 September and XX Corps units crossed, continuing the drive for Metz. The increasingly rugged terrain, however, did not favor the tactics of the XX Corps' armored units. Walker therefore decided to have his forces skirt the Metz defenses and encircle the city.

Following bloody clashes at Sillegny and Pournoy, the two most bitterly fought battles of the Lorraine campaign, the XX Corps drive toward Metz stalled at the Seille River on 24 September. Unexpectedly stiff German resistance, increasingly poor weather that prevented air support, and continuing supply and gasoline shortages, brought the entire U.S. Third Army advance to a halt by the end of September.

During the opening phases of the offensive in Lorraine, the U.S. Third Army's 450-mile-long southern flank, which extended back to Brittany, was protected by the XV Corps. Haislip's command consisted of the 79th Infantry Division and the French 2nd Armored Division, commanded by Major General Philippe Leclerc (q.v.). During the Third Army advance in Lorraine, the mission of the XV Corps was to cover the weakly held Third Army southern flank. The 79th Infantry Division became involved in many minor skirmishes with

German forces during the advance from Andelot to Charmes between 11–12 September. The French 2nd Armored Division clashed with the Germans at Dompaire and Damas on 13 September. After obtaining close air support in the Dompaire and Damas areas, the French forced the Germans to withdraw.

In addition to protecting the Third Army flank, the XV Corps also was ordered to prepare to secure its own bridgehead across the Rhine near Mannheim if the opportunity arose. If not, XV Corps would cross the Rhine on the bridgeheads established by either the XII or XX Corps. On 17 September, both divisions of XV Corps reached the Moselle.

On 18 September, the 21st *Panzer* and *Panzer Lehr* Divisions and the 111th and 113th *Panzer* Brigades of the German Fifth *Panzer* Army began a counteroffensive against the U.S. XII Corps near Luneville, with the objective of destroying the Moselle bridgeheads at Pont-a-Mousson. XV Corps helped stem this drive by attacking the German flank. Following a 19–22 September tank battle between the 4th Armored Division and the 113th *Panzer* Brigade near Arracourt and Lezey, the XV Corps began pushing the Germans back, linking up with the XII Corps at Luneville on 20 September.

The German drive began to slow and in desperation, Adolf Hitler (q.v.) replaced Blaskowitz with *General der Panzertruppen* Hermann Balck (q.v.) on 22 September. During the next week the U.S. XV Corps continued its advance to the La Vezouse River and engaged armored units of the 11th *Panzer* Division near Moyenvic and Vic-sur-Seille. While the Fifth *Panzer* Army counteroffensive met with some initial success and did push units of the XV Corps back, a stubborn defense by XII Corps' 4th Armored Division combined with air support from the XIX TAC halted the German drive.

The final German push on 29 September was obviously weaker than those of previous days. Clearly, the back of the Fifth *Panzer* Army had been broken. Following a final American tank sweep on 30 September, the Lorraine campaign in the XV Corps sector ended. Except for some fierce fighting in early October along the thirty-mile XII Corps front, and several unsuccessful attempts by the U.S. 5th Infantry Division to capture Fort Driant outside Metz, the U.S. Third Army front fell into a month-long lull.

The October lull, like that of late August, was caused by a lack of transportation, supplies, and gasoline in the south. Those resources were being directed north to support Allied offensive activity in Belgium, where an all-out drive was underway to secure the port of Antwerp (q.v.). The Lorraine operations again were assigned a low priority, and the U.S. Third Army was forced to abandon its immediate plans to cross the Seille River and continue the drive for Metz and the Rhine.

SHAEF (q.v.), meanwhile, developed plans for resuming the main Allied offensive in the north, with the U.S. Third Army continuing its supporting advance toward the Rhine and Frankfurt from Lorraine beginning around 8 November. Patton ordered the XII Corps to resume its general eastward advance with infantry followed by armored units, while the XX Corps was to launch an attack north and south of Metz (q.v.) with the goal of creating a "Metz pocket." By the time of the proposed jump-off date, the Third Army had six infantry and three armored divisions, plus supporting troops, totaling almost a quarter of a million men.

The Germans too were content to avoid full-scale combat operations in October. Like the Americans, they suffered from a lack of supplies, combat exhaustion, and the diversion of troops to the north, especially to Aachen (q.v.). The Germans spent considerable time during the month shifting troops and finding replacements before the next phase of the American drive expected to hit the German First Army. By early November the troop redeployments were completed. Army Group G strength stood at 140 tanks and 136,161 officers and men, although actual combat strength was nearer to 92,094. Stocks of ammunition and other supplies were still chronically short and dangerously low.

To compensate for the lack of men and materiel, the Germans planned to conduct an elastic defense in depth, screened by a lightly held line in front of the main line of defense. When the American attack began, the forward troops were supposed to fall back to the main line of defense, causing the initial American softening-up effort to fall on empty territory. Behind the main line of defense the Germans created an intermediate position consisting of antitank ditches, vehicle obstacles, and mines. If both the main and intermediate positions fell, the fortifications of the West Wall offered a final line of resistance before the Rhine.

When the XII Corps resumed the offensive on 8 November, it quickly became apparent that the terrain and weather had so altered the tactical situation that a rapid campaign would not be possible. The ground east of the Moselle was dotted

L

with forests and hills, interspersed with marshes, lakes, and the western approaches to the Vosages Mountains.

As planned, the XII Corps assault began with units of the 26th, 35th, and 80th Infantry Divisions moving forward after a massive air and artillery bombardment. The Americans encountered little initial resistance as they crossed the Seille River and advanced through Chateau-Salins and Morville toward Koeckling Ridge. There they were halted until 14–15 November by stiffening German resistance. Other XII Corps units encountered heavy fighting at Guébling, Fresnes, Morhange, and in the Forêt de Gremecey, but managed to cross the Nied River and reach the area around Faulquemont by 16 November.

In the XX Corps area, American infantry and armor units rapidly advanced on Metz. They crossed the Moselle on 9 November and outflanked several of the German-held forts around the city. In the face of increased German resistance they began the planned envelopment movement on 15 November. As American pressure on the nearly encircled city increased, the Germans began to withdraw and eventually surrendered on 21 November. German units in some of the outlying Metz forts continued to resist until as late as 13 December before surrendering.

After the fall of Metz, U.S. XX Corps continued its village by village advance toward the Sarre River. They started on 19 November amid increasingly poor weather that hampered air and armored operations, and against determined, but obviously weakening, German resistance. XX Corps units cleared the area west of the Sarre River by the last day of November and created a bridgehead at Saarlautern on 3 December.

Both XII and XX Corps participated in operations to breach the West Wall (which the Americans called the Siegfried Line) between 1 and 18 December. Units of the 95th Infantry Division captured the first bunkers of the defensive system near Saarlautern on 3 December. The sector of the wall that XX Corps faced was the strongest in the system. Efforts to breach the line required heavy bunker-to-bunker fighting against what now nearly constituted fanatical opposition.

The U.S. Third Army's operations against the West Wall were still underway without a decision in sight when the Germans launched the Ardennes offensive (q.v.). Faced with a new and unexpected threat to the Allied armies in the west, Patton was ordered to divert units from his attacks in Lorraine for action in the north. By 19 December active offensive operations in the Lorraine area ended, as the Third Army turned north to help contain and then reduce the "Bulge."

German losses in the sixteen weeks of the Lorraine campaign were much higher than those they inflicted on the Americans. Although the exact numbers of Germans killed and wounded are not known, at least 75,000 Germans were taken prisoner. German materiel losses also exceeded those of the U.S. Third Army, which itself lost 105 light tanks, 298 medium tanks, 1,080 vehicles, and thirty-four artillery pieces. Third Army casualties totaled 6,657 officers and men killed in action, 36,406 wounded, and 12,119 missing. American non-battle casualties caused by fatigue, exposure, and disease exceeded 42,000.

During the Lorraine campaign, the U.S. Third Army liberated more than 5,000 square miles of German-held territory and caused the loss to the Germans of three crucial defensive positions on the Moselle, Nied, and Sarre Rivers. Although operations ended before the Third Army could breach the West Wall, the American operations had dramatically reduced both the size and freedom of movement of the German forces in Lorraine. Strategically, the campaign caused the loss to the German war economy of the military production of the Lorraine and Saar basin and forced the OKW (q.v.) to redeploy scarce forces away from the defense of Aachen, the Ruhr, and the pending Ardennes offensive.

Clayton D. Laurie

Additional Reading

Balck, Hermann, *Ordnung im Chaos: Erinnerungen 1893–1948* (1981).
Cole, Hugh M., *The Lorraine Campaign* (1950).
Weigley, Russell F., *Eisenhower's Lieutenants: The Campaigns of France and Germany, 1944–1945* (1981).

Low Countries (April–May 1945)

[See map 26 on page 1336]

In the autumn of 1944, the Allies abandoned any planning for major operations in the Low Countries and henceforth concentrated their main offensive efforts further south along the Rhine. The failure of Operation MARKET-GARDEN (q.v.), the German military recovery in northwest Europe, adverse weather conditions, an awkwardly extended front, and the long delay in opening the vital supply port of Antwerp (q.v.) combined to force this decision on them.

Allied operations in the Low Countries were executed mainly by the Canadian First Army of the

21st Army Group, in flanking support of the British Second Army's drive into northern Germany. In the winter of 1944–1945, the First Army's front stretched 225 kilometers, from Walcheren in the west, along the river lines of the Lower Maas, Waal, and Nederrijn (Lower Rhine), to Cuijk in the east. Defending the area was German Army Group H composed of the Twenty-fifth Army in the western Netherlands and the First Parachute Army in the northeast.

While in winter quarters, the 21st Army Group controlled the Nijmegen salient. It was an "island" of flooded lowlands bounded by the Nederrijn and Waal Rivers south of Arnhem, created by Operation MARKET-GARDEN and containing the only Allied-held bridgehead across the main course of the Rhine. Throughout the winter, the Allies maintained aggressive patrolling in this sector. Although some sharp local encounters took place, such as the reduction of the German bridgehead at Venlo on the west bank of the Maas in early December, or the stiff (and perhaps unnecessary) action fought at Kapelsche Veer along the lower Maas from 26 to 30 January, the front remained essentially static until the spring.

On 9 March 1945, Field Marshal Bernard L. Montgomery (q.v.), in preparing follow-on plans to the Rhineland campaign (q.v.) begun on 7 February, outlined the upcoming tasks of the Canadian First Army: (1) attack the Ijssel defenses from the east (rear); (2) capture Zutphen and Deventer, and advance to the North Sea (thereby preventing German forces in the Netherlands from interfering with British Second Army's thrust toward Hamburg and Bremen); (3) cross the Ijssel and take Apeldoorn; and (4) advance north and west to the Ijsselmeer, achieving a link with forces operating northward beyond the Nijmegen salient and Arnhem. These orders were confirmed on 28 March, once the success of the Allied breakthrough on the Rhine became known. It was clear that any campaign in the Low Countries would be secondary to the main Allied efforts along the Rhine and later, in northern Germany.

On 1 April, the Canadian I Corps, recently transferred from Italy, replaced the British II Corps in the Canadian First Army's order of battle. This army's seven divisions henceforth included five Canadian (two armored), one British, and one Polish (armored).

The Low Countries campaign proper was launched on 2 April as an important northern corollary to Operation PLUNDER, the British Second Army's major Rhine crossing between Rees and Emmerich, begun on 23 March. The Canadian II Corps crossed the Rhine at Emmerich into the Allied bridgehead and struck north and northeast on the left of the Second Army's XXX Corps. Elements of I Corps crossed the Ijssel south of Deventer while others advanced on the flooded Nijmegen "island." Throughout the campaign, the Germans mounted a static defense based on the numerous water lines and much flooded terrain. Despite some incidence of fierce fighting, especially in northeast Holland, it was clear that German resistance in the Netherlands was crumbling. Nevertheless, ultimate Allied success in the sector depended to a large degree on the superb work of the engineer and service corps units of the Canadian and British armies, which built dozens of bridges, maintained roads, and provided outstanding logistic and communication support under extremely unfavorable topographical and climatic conditions.

The Twente Canal was crossed on the night of 2–3 April, while Zutphen and Deventer, well-protected by a maze of waterways, were captured following difficult engagements on 8 and 10 April, respectively. The Canadian 2nd and 3rd Divisions, with right flank support provided by the Polish 1st Armored and Canadian 4th Armoured Divisions, thrust toward the Kuesten Canal, crossed it on 17–19 April after a fierce struggle, and advanced 160 kilometers to the North Sea during the next two weeks. In the midst of this drive, 696 French Special Air Service paratroopers launched Operation AMHERST, an airborne drop behind German lines on the night of 7–8 April in the general triangle Groningen-Coevorden-Meppel. The French force facilitated the advance of the Canadian II Corps into northeastern Netherlands by capturing key bridges, crossroads, and communication centers, and by disrupting and confusing the Germans. Groningen was captured on 16 April after a bitter four-day struggle with Dutch SS troops.

On the Canadian I Corps front, the British 49th (West Riding) Division, supported by Canadian armor, secured the lightly defended Nijmegen "island" by 3 April. Arnhem was assaulted on 12 April and cleared two days later. To the north, Apeldoorn was captured by the Canadian 1st Division on 17 April following several days of sharp encounters on the city's outskirts. The 1st Division then immediately struck northwest to Harderwijk on the Ijsselmeer, cutting Holland in two and trapping the remnants of the depleted Twenty-fifth Army in so-called *Festung-Holland.* The 1st division also advanced east to Barneveld and Voorthuizen where it joined with the Canadian 5th Armoured Division advancing from Arnhem.

On 12 April, Montgomery countermanded earlier plans to clear the Germans from the western Netherlands (excepting the route north from Arnhem) as operations there would require logistic support urgently needed by the British Second Army. Accordingly, the Canadian I Corps was ordered to clear western Holland only from the Ijssel west to the Grebbe Line, a series of German field fortifications based on the Grebbe River fifteen to twenty kilometers east of Utrecht and running through Amersfoort. Offensive operations were suspended on the Grebbe Line on 19 April. The Canadian 1st and British 49th Divisions were detailed to guard this rear flank of 21st Army Group's drive into northern Germany.

Fighting in the northeast Netherlands did not cease with the adjournment of hostilities in the western part of the country. With the Canadian 5th Armoured Division sent to bolster the Canadian II Corps on 21 April, a difficult battle ensued between 23 April and 2 May for the Delfzijl pocket at the Dutch-German frontier on the Ems River estuary. The tenacious defense mounted over sodden and exposed ground by the composite German force was reminiscent of the struggle for the Scheldt (q.v.) estuary the previous autumn. For the remainder of the war, and on a front eventually stretching 175 kilometers from the Ijsselmeer to Oldenburg, the main role of the Canadian II Corps (especially the Canadian 4th Armoured Division) was to protect the Second Army's left flank by advancing across the boggy, difficult battlefield of the North German Plain between the Ems and Weser Rivers. That task was complicated by the spirited resistance offered throughout by the vastly understrength German II Parachute *Korps*.

The final two weeks of the war in the western Netherlands were concerned with the humanitarian and political issues of providing relief for the starving population there. An advance beyond the Grebbe Line would have resulted in the Germans flooding the lowlands, thereby worsening an already desperate situation in which nearly five million people (including refugees) were at risk—especially in the major centers of Amsterdam, Rotterdam, and The Hague.

Arthur Seyss-Inquart (q.v.), the notorious *Reichskommissar* for the Netherlands, was willing to allow the Allies to provision the Dutch population in exchange for a truce in the western Netherlands. Pending a meeting of representatives from both sides, the 21st Army Group drew up extensive plans for secure air, land, and sea routes to supply the stricken area with 2,000 tons of food daily, as well as fuel and medical supplies. On 28 April, the first discussions were held and military operations were officially suspended. As the German negotiators did not have authority to conclude any final arrangements, a further meeting took place on 30 April, this time between Seyss-Inquart and Lieutenant General Walter Bedell Smith, chief of staff to General Dwight D. Eisenhower (qq.v.). Smith's attempts at gaining the German capitulation in the area, as opposed to a truce, were rejected.

Allied supply and medical teams immediately began entering German-held territory, although airdrops by the Royal Air Force's Bomber Command actually began on 29 April. With the assistance of the U.S. Eighth Air Force, by 8 May more than 11 million individual rations were dropped into the worst affected areas. As a result of the Canadian First Army's efforts in liberating the Netherlands and in providing humanitarian assistance, a strong bond developed between the two nations that has been maintained to the present day.

On 4 May 1945, all German forces along the 21st Army Group's front surrendered unconditionally, with the formal cease-fire coming into effect at 0800 hours the next morning. In the final month of the war, 126,500 Germans were captured in the western Netherlands (including 118,000 who held out behind the Grebbe Line until the end), with an additional 30,000 surrendering in the northeast. German combat deaths numbered in the thousands, while the Canadians alone sustained 6,300 casualties over the same period, including 1,482 fatalities.

Serge M. Durflinger

Additional Reading
Stacey, C.P., *The Victory Campaign* (1960).
Vogel, R., and T. Copp, *Maple Leaf Route: Victory* (1987).

M

Maginot Line (10 May–27 June 1940)

[See map 17 on page 1327]

Since earliest times fighting people have improved their military defenses, either to better protect their homeland or to secure their bases while attacking their neighbors. The purpose was to create obstacles between the homeland and a feared enemy. One man behind fixed barriers, the belief goes, is worth several on the attack.

In analyzing this defensive psychology, some adages come to mind. "Wars are not won by remaining in a fixed position," or "The attacker has the advantage since he can choose the time and place of attack and can then concentrate his forces at this point." Or as Carl von Clausewitz has written, while "we occupy . . . an unassailable position we . . . oblige our enemy to look for the solution in some other way."

These adages applied with compelling logic in 1940 to the Maginot Line (henceforth called the "Line"), built by France after World War I to defend against the traditional German enemy. The Line was a series of forts running from the Swiss to the Belgian borders. After suffering more than five million casualties in World War I, France, a country of forty million people with a declining birth rate, sought to improve its defenses against its aggressive neighbor of seventy million.

Many myths surround the Line. One was that an impregnable "wall of steel and concrete" had been built from the Swiss border to the English Channel. In fact, for diplomatic and economic reasons, the Line protected the Franco-German but not the Franco-Belgian border, and was far from impregnable anywhere. Another myth is that the Line failed since it did not prevent the invasion of France. The Line, an "inanimate object of concrete and steel," is not at fault for the way it was used, nor that the Germans went around rather than through it. It was never tested under the conditions for which it was designed, nor was maximum use ever made of its capabilities.

The Line was designed to protect the Franco-German border from Longuyon east of the Ardennes to the Rhine River at Lauterbourg. Belgium, a weak and unreliable ally, was expected to help defend the Belgian border to the sea. From Lauterbourg to the Swiss border, weak forts on the left bank of the Rhine were the main defensive barrier. Three fortified regions (FR) were planned. The Metz FR and Lauter FR were constructed, but a third FR between the Vosges and Swiss border, to prevent passage through the Belfort gap, was never completed.

The role of the Line in the 1940 campaign was marginal, but its use must be seen within the context of the German invasion. By 1 September 1939, it was on a war footing. Families were moved out and "interval troops" were moved in between the strongpoints. Except for the abbreviated "Saar offensive," the Allies did nothing between the German invasion of Poland (q.v.), starting on 1 September 1939, and the invasion of France (q.v.) on 10 May 1940. Seventy-three French divisions waited out the Polish campaign opposite a skeleton force of nineteen weak German divisions. Great care was taken not to provoke the enemy. German aircraft flew over the Line at will, while forces in the Line whiled away the time.

On 10 May, General Fedor von Bock (q.v.), commander of German Army Group B, rushed into Belgium "flapping his matador's cloak" (a colorful simile coined by Liddell Hart) to convince the French high command that the main blow would be struck there. Meanwhile, General Wilhelm von Leeb's (q.v.) Army Group C exerted a constant pressure on the Line itself.

From 10–17 May, little action took place

along the Line. On the first day of the fighting, a French light cavalry division moved out and encountered General Heinz Guderian's (q.v.) armored forces moving across rough terrain through Luxembourg toward the Meuse. The division withdrew and did not bother to disrupt the Germans.

On 11 May. German activity was noted only in the air. The troops manning the Line suffered their first losses when a trunk rail line was bombed. On 12 May, German pressure increased all along the Line. Some fighting took place along the Longwy salient, where French troops pulled back. On 13 May, Guderian's troops crossed the Meuse west of the northern end of the Line against fiercely resisting but weak infantry troops that were easily silenced by *Stuka* dive-bombing attacks and artillery.

German probing attacks on 14 May extended the breach in the west to thirty-nine miles. In the east, German 280mm railway guns fired on Hockwald and Schoenenberg. Along the Rhine, both sides remained inactive. By 17 May, jittery French officials, thinking Guderian was heading for Paris, withdrew some interval troops from the Line to protect the capital. This process continued in stages until the end of the fighting, denuding the Line of badly needed support. The German capture of La Ferte, a weak and somewhat isolated fort on the extreme western tip of the Line, demonstrated the fallacy of this policy.

While the main attack continued in the west, the Germans probed for other weak spots in the Line that could be expected to tie down the French troops. Line forts fired steadily, inflicted casualties on the enemy, and suffered few in return. The morale of the troops manning the Line was high, sustained by optimistic radio reports that indicated they were winning the war. On 20 May, pleased with the breakthrough on the Meuse, Adolf Hitler (q.v.) called off a planned direct assault on the Line, apparently to avoid needless casualties. During the rest of the first phase of the Battle of France, relative calm prevailed along the Line.

The French government left Paris on 10 June, the day Italy declared war on France. By 12 June, General André Prételat, French commander of the Metz FR, was authorized to withdraw from the Line and move south to help defend Lyons. All forts were instructed to demolish their "vital working parts." With heavy hearts the troops burned records and prepared to move south; but it was too late. The lines of retreat were blocked by Guderian's sweep toward the Swiss border.

On 14 June, the German Army moved into Paris and the section of the Line between Saaralbe and St. Avold was attacked by General Erwin Witzleben's (q.v.) First Army. The forts at Teting, Witring, and Bambesch fought until the full weight of German artillery overwhelmed them. French morale was high and resistance was stiff. On 15 June, four German divisions crossed the Rhine at Rheinau, Neuf Breisach, and Marckolsheim. Weak bunkers on the left bank were reduced by *Stuka* and artillery fire. Anthony Kemp writes that at this time, many German commanders were "determined to bag a fort and earn a medal."

Radio broadcasts declaring the end of the war and telling the Maginot Line soldiers to surrender were resisted until representatives from General Maxime Weygand (q.v.) arrived on 27 June, five days after the armistice, to make the order official.

Historian Anthony Kemp maintains that had the Line been wisely used it "could have changed the course of history" on at least two occasions. One was to use it as a secure base for a "vigorous offensive" into Germany during the Polish Campaign in 1939. The second was between 10 and 12 May 1940 to support a "strong counterattack" against the vulnerable flanks of the German columns moving through the rough Ardennes, thereby upsetting the enemy's timetable. French commanders, however, were not prone to take advantage of such opportunities.

Paul J. Rose

Additional Reading

Horne, Alistair, *To Lose a Battle: France 1940* (1969).

Kemp, Anthony, *The Maginot Line: Myth and Reality* (1982).

Osgood, Samuel, *The Fall of France, 1940: Causes and Responsibilities* (1966).

Wiliams, John, *The Ides of May: The Defeat of France, May–June 1940* (1968).

Malmédy Massacre (17 December 1944)

During the first phase of the Ardennes offensive (q.v.), the I SS *Panzer Korps* of the Sixth *Panzer* Army had the mission of breaking through the Allied front lines in the Monschau-Losheim sector and advancing without consideration for its flanks across the Meuse River to Antwerp. The corps consisted of the 1st and 2nd SS *Panzer* Divisions, the 12th and 277th *Volksgrenadier* Divisions, and the 7th Parachute Division. The 1st SS *Panzer* Division formed the left wing of the corps. Its spearhead, *Kampfgruppe* Peiper, commanded by SS-*Obersturmbannführer* Joachim Peiper (q.v.), broke through toward the west between Malmédy and St. Vith on 17 December.

That afternoon, a few kilometers south of Malmédy, close to the town of Baugnez, a tragedy occurred that later became known as the "Malmédy massacre." Seventy-one American soldiers were shot by German soldiers of the 1st SS *Panzer* Division in a field close to the crossroads of Butgenbach, Malmédy, and Ligneuville. Most of the reports about this incident—which was prosecuted by a U.S. military court after the war—were, and still are, contradictory.

The established facts are that on 17 December, at 1300 hours at the crossroads in Baugnez, the advance element of *Kampfgruppe* Peiper ran into a small group of trucks and jeeps belonging to Battery B of the U.S. 285th Field Artillery Observation Battalion. Twenty U.S. soldiers were killed in the ensuing fight. The others, about 125, surrendered and were gathered in a field behind a restaurant at the crossroads, together with other U.S. soldiers who had escaped and were recaptured. There were also some prisoners that *Kampfgruppe* Peiper had brought along.

Peiper's unit, which did not want to be delayed by prisoners, left them behind with two tanks and some infantrymen as guards. Peiper marched on with his advance element toward Ligneuville. The exact sequence of events that followed is still in doubt and was never satisfactorily explained during the trial after the war. What did happen might have been the sort of error that occurs so often in war, especially when one side believes it is facing armed opponents.

At about 1400 hours, an armed group of U.S. soldiers who previously had escaped from the Germans took the risk of moving toward the crossroads. At about same time, the main body of *Kampfgruppe* Peiper arrived. Another fight erupted, and most of the Americans involved were killed. Hearing the shooting, the guards in the field shot at the captured Americans because they believed the latter were trying to take advantage of the situation to escape. Brutal actions by the Germans against the wounded in the field followed, and also against prisoners who were captured again after having escaped. Photos of the incident, however, prove that some of the American soldiers killed were, in fact, armed at the time.

For propaganda reasons, the U.S. Army magnified the scope of the incident and even added in a high number of killed civilians. There were, in fact, civilians killed near Malmédy, but they were the victims of American bombing attacks. The American soldiers' magazine, *Yank*, published the exaggerated version of events in its 14 January 1945 issue. That in turn sparked numerous unauthorized and illegal revenge actions by American troops against German prisoners.

At the conclusion of the war, in May 1945, Peiper and seventy-three members of the 1st SS *Panzer* Division—many chosen arbitrarily—were brought before a U.S. military court. The accused were charged with the deliberate and unprovoked execution of the U.S. prisoners in the field. The accused were pressed for confessions. Peiper and forty-two of his unit were sentenced to death; twenty-two were sentenced to life imprisonment; and eight were sentenced to ten to twenty years.

Rather than a proper legal proceeding, the trial was more an example of "victor's justice." Contradictory information about numbers, differing interpretations of the incident, different versions of the times, and the unacceptable methods of questioning the suspects gave the American defense team ample grounds for an appeal. As a result, the death sentences later were changed to long prison terms.

Ekkehart Guth

Additional Reading
Bauserman, John M., *The Malmédy Massacre* (1994).
Berthold, W., *Malmedy, Das Recht des Siegers* (1979).
Cole, Hugh M., *The Ardennes: Battle of the Bulge* (1965).

Malta Air Campaign (June 1940–June 1943)

[See map 27 on page 1337]

With war anticipated in the Mediterranean area, the British Committee of Imperial Defence decided that Malta should be reinforced both with men and with armament. The implementation of the plan, however, was slow and by June 1940 there were only thirty-four heavy antiaircraft guns, eight Bofors guns, and twenty-four searchlights stationed on the island. Britain's neglect of Malta's defenses was paid in the deaths of Maltese and British citizens during what became known as the siege of Malta.

At the war's outbreak in 1939, it was established that, due to the nearness of the Italian airfields, four fighter squadrons would be required to protect the island from air attack. By March 1940, however, the island's only air defense was four Gloster Sea Gladiator biplanes. The first Italian air raid came on Tuesday 11 June 1940 and was quickly followed by six more before the day's end, leaving eleven Maltese civilians dead and 130 injured. It was the first in a two-year series of blows the island would suffer during the "siege."

Britain mounted several convoy operations to supply the island with food, fuel and other critical supplies (*see* Malta Convoys). In fact, these convoy operations often became the central feature naval operations in the Mediterranean campaign (q.v.). Certainly, the island could not have survived without them. Conversely, Britain's strategy in the Mediterranean could not have survived without Malta.

Recognizing the air threat to the island, Britain periodically reinforced the island's air cover over the next two years by flying in aircraft from a number of aircraft carriers, including the HMS *Ark Royal,* HMS *Furious,* and HMS *Eagle.* A total of twenty-five operations were mounted, with 764 aircraft ferried, of which 718 arrived safely in Malta. The aircraft were mainly Hurricane and Spitfire fighters, although in July 1941, seven Swordfish aircraft reached the island from HMS *Ark Royal.* Nonetheless, the bombings continued.

The island suffered more than 3,205 air raids between June 1940 and December 1942. Property damage and the loss of both civilian and military lives was extensive. The island's antiaircraft defenses fought back vigorously, destroying a confirmed 236 Axis aircraft between June 1940 and October 1942, with a further 165 damaged. At the height of the battle of Malta, Lieutenant General Sir William Dobbie, the acting governor and commander in chief, received a message dated 15 April 1942 from His Majesty King George VI (q.v.), which read:

> To honour her brave people I award the George Cross to the Island Fortress of Malta to bear witness to a heroism and devotion that will long be famous in history.

The presentation was not held until 13 September 1942. The prestigious award was highly appreciated by the Maltese and without doubt helped to boost the morale of the people and defenders at a most critical time in the siege.

Field Marshal the Viscount John Gort (q.v.) arrived on Malta on 7 May 1942 to take over from General Dobbie who, due to ill health, had to be relieved from his arduous command. Lord Gort arrived by Sutherland flying boat from Gibraltar while an air raid was in progress. A bomb fell near the house in which Sir William and Lady Dobbie were waiting together with a number of other officials. As soon as the oath of office was administered, Dobbie and his party departed on the same aircraft that brought Lord Gort.

At the time Lord Gort took over, Malta was facing an acute shortage of all essential supplies. Fighter cover had diminished and it was anticipated that, as soon as the island was a helpless target for the Axis air forces, the enemy would attempt an invasion. It was during this time frame that convoy operations VIGOROUS, HARPOON, and PEDESTAL (q.v.) were mounted to get supplies into the island. Fighters were also flown in to strengthen the island's air defenses.

As no British aircraft carrier was immediately available to bring fighter aircraft to a point where they could be ferried in, Prime Minister Winston S. Churchill (q.v.) requested assistance from the United States. President Franklin Roosevelt (q.v.) agreed and the USS *Wasp* was dispatched with forty-seven replacement Spitfires to a launch point 600 miles from Malta. Only one failed to reach the island.

In addition to the civilian casualties from enemy bombing, the Maltese people suffered from outbreaks of typhoid in July 1942, and polio the following November. The polio outbreak crippled 415 people and killed seventeen. These outbreaks greatly concerned the medical authorities on the island as, like all other stores, medical supplies were continually in short supply.

At the close of 1942, the air raids gradually diminished. In 1943, the number shrank to 127, and in 1944, to just eight. The final Axis air raid took place on 28 August 1944. The event that probably gave the biggest boost to the morale of the civilian population of Malta, which endured concentrated air attacks and shortages of food during the two-year siege, was the arrival of British King George VI on 20 June 1943. The king wrote in his diary concerning the events of that day: "On Sunday at 8:15am I was on the bridge (of the HMS *Aurora)* as we came in to the Grand Harbour. A lovely sunny morning. A wonderful sight. Every bastion and every view point lined with people who cheered as entered. It was a very moving moment for me. I had made up my mind that I would take a risk and get to Malta and I had got there and by sea." The king sailed through a hostile sea, with enemy air bases only sixty miles away, to show his support for the citizens and defenders of Malta.

During the course of the siege, eighty-three British civil awards were made to Maltese civilians and forty-one military decorations were made to Maltese servicemen who served in the Royal Malta

Artillery and the King's Own Malta Regiment, for their gallantry and work during island's defense.

Alan Harfield

Additional Reading

Bradford, Ernle, *Siege: Malta 1940–1943* (1985).

Brennan, Paul, et al., *Spitfires over Malta* (1943).

Norman, Kathleen, *For Gallantry: Malta's Story* (1956).

Vella, Philip, *Malta: Blitzed but Not Beaten* (1985).

Malta Convoy PEDESTAL (10–15 August 1942)

[See map 27 on page 1337]

Malta's supply situation became desperate following the successive failure of two convoys to beat the Axis blockade in June 1942. Moreover, the Germans and Italians were reinforcing their air forces on Sardinia and Sicily and their surface craft and submarines were becoming more active in the waters around the island. Despite these problems, the Allied leadership decided to make another attempt to resupply Malta by convoy, code named Operation PEDESTAL. Involving ships from as far away as Great Britain, PEDESTAL proved a turning point in the siege of Malta (q.v.).

The operation began on the night of 10 August 1942, when fourteen fast merchant ships, including the American tanker *Ohio* manned with a British crew, and a heavy escort of warships from the British Home Fleet, entered the Mediterranean. The convoy, officially known as WS-21S, was commanded by retired Royal Navy (RN) Commander A.G. Venables, who embarked on the vessel *Port Chalmers*. The RN escort consisted of three aircraft carriers, the HMS *Eagle,* HMS *Victorious,* and HMS *Indomitable;* two battleships, the HMS *Nelson* and HMS *Rodney;* seven cruisers; thirty-two destroyers; eight submarines; and numerous other small vessels including minesweepers and corvettes.

The main escort withdrew when the convoy reached the Sicilian Narrows, and returned to its normal duties in the Atlantic. Its departure left only four cruisers and twelve destroyers to accompany the supply ships to Malta. The Axis mustered a force of eighteen Italian and two German submarines to attack the convoy. They were supported by nineteen motor torpedo boats (MTBs) and 850 aircraft. In order to assure the destruction of the vital convoy, the Axis ordered an additional surface force of six cruisers and eleven destroyers to intercept it.

M

The crippled tanker Ohio *limps into Malta's Grand Harbor, supported by the destroyers HMS* Penn *(left) and HMS* Ledbury *(right), 22 August 1942. (IWM GM 1505)*

HMS *Eagle* became the first Allied casualty when it was torpedoed on 11 August by the U-boat *U-73*, sinking in only eight minutes. The convoy and its escort ships were subjected to continued attack from the surface, subsurface, and air over the next three days. The casualty list rose considerably. The *Deucalion* was damaged by torpedo bombers and then sank; the HMS *Indomitable* was damaged; and the destroyer HMS *Foresight* was sunk. The cruisers HMS *Nigeria* and HMS *Cairo* and the tanker *Ohio* were all hit by torpedoes.

Still, the convoy continued its slow progress toward Malta. Then, the vessels *Empire Hope* and *Clan Ferguson* were lost; bombers hit the cruiser HMS *Kenya;* and the merchant ship *Brisbane Star* was hit and the *Ohio* was hit again. A combined air and U-boat attack sank two American supply ships, the *Almeria Lykes* and the *Santa Elisa,* and two British ships, the *Wairangi* and the *Glenorchy.* The cruiser HMS *Manchester* went down after an E-boat attack, and a tanker carrying aviation fuel, the *Waimarama,* was hit by bombs and burst into flame. Some survivors from the burning vessel jumped into the sea and were rescued by Lieutenant Commander Roger Hill, who took his destroyer, HMS *Ledbury,* through the flaming sea to pick up the men in the water.

Fortunately for the convoy, the Italian Naval squadron was withdrawn just as it was about to mount its attack, due to lack of air cover from the Italian Air Force. Aerial attacks continued on the now decimated Allied convoy, with many ships, including the *Ohio,* being hit repeatedly. The merchant ship *Dorset* sank almost within sight of Malta. Despite it all, they made it. On 13 August, the *Port Chalmers, Rochester Castle,* and *Melbourne Star* entered Malta's Grand Harbour to cheering crowds; the *Brisbane Star* arrived the next day.

The *Ohio,* meanwhile, which was carrying vital fuel, oil, and kerosene, was lying crippled some miles off Malta. Singled out by Axis aircraft, she was torpedoed and set on fire, her boilers were out of action, and her engines had failed. She was abandoned and twice reboarded, but her British crew refused to give up the ship, and the RN mounted a rescue operation to save it. The destroyers HMS *Bramham* and HMS *Penn* were secured alongside and towed the ship while the HMS *Ledbury* steered the group toward port. The Axis made another attempt to sink the stragglers, but were driven off by gunfire from the destroyers. The *Ohio* entered Grand Harbour early on the morning of 15 August with her decks almost awash.

Five supply vessels reached Malta with desperately needed stores—a fact that gave a major boost to the morale of Malta's besieged population. Operation PEDESTAL paid a high price in loss of lives, both merchant and Royal Navy, and of ships. In the end, however, it was worth it because the supplies delivered enabled Malta to carry on to victory.

Alan Harfield

Additional Reading

Bradford, Ernle, *Siege: Malta 1940–1943* (1985).

Smith, Peter, *Pedestal: The Malta Convoy of August 1942* (1970).

Malta Relief Convoys (August 1940–December 1942)

[See map 27 on page 1337]

Malta effectively became a besieged island with Italy's entry into the war and with the German land forces' advance along the coast of North Africa (q.v.). With the sky controlled by German and Italian Air Forces, the only means of resupply was by sea. During the vital siege years of 1940 to 1942, a number of convoys were formed and attempted to bring supplies of ammunition, food, and aircraft fuel to Malta (q.v.).

The first of the convoys departed from Alexandria, Egypt, in August 1940 under the code name Operation HATS. Three ships, the *Cornwall,* the *Volo,* and the Royal Fleet Auxiliary *Plumleaf* were escorted by a force of two aircraft carriers, a battle cruiser, three cruisers, and sixteen destroyers. The convoy was attacked on 31 August and the *Cornwall* was damaged, but 40,000 tons of stores reached their destination.

Another convoy set sail from Gibraltar in January 1941. It was followed by a number of smaller convoys sailing from Alexandria between February and May. During this period, a total of thirteen supply ships reached the port capital of Valletta, usually under cover of the British fleet. The supply ships brought a total of 100,000 tons of stores, kept the garrison and civilians fed, the few aircraft flying, and the submarines refueled.

As the Axis tightened their control over the sea and sky around Malta, a disparate stopgap measure was initiated using larger British submarines as supply vessels. Each boat brought to the island much needed reinforcements, mail, medical stores, and aviation fuel. Between June and December 1941, sixteen trips were made by the submarines.

Surface ships continued to play a part in the resupply. During the second half of 1941, two convoys from Gibraltar set sail under the code names of Operation SUBSTANCE (July 1941) and Operation HALBERD (September 1941). The cruiser HMS *Manchester* and the destroyer HMS *Firedrake* were damaged and the cargo ship *Sydney Star* was torpedoed in the first convoy, but 65,000 tons of stores were delivered. The second convoy, consisting of nine cargo ships, was escorted by an aircraft carrier, three battleships, five cruisers, and eighteen destroyers. The convoy was attacked on 27 September and the battleship HMS *Nelson* was damaged and the cargo ship *Imperial Star* sunk, but 85,000 tons of stores reached their destination.

In January 1942, three convoys were dispatched from Alexandria under the operational titles of ME-2, ME-3, and ME-4. On 12 February, convoy ME-5, consisting of three fast freighters, the *Clan Chattan, Clan Campbell,* and *Rowallan Castle,* all veterans of the Malta run, departed Alexandria escorted by the cruiser HMS *Carlisle* and eight destroyers. The convoy came under air attack by Ju-88 bombers, and the *Clan Campbell* was damaged and diverted to Tobruk. The escort was reinforced on the following day by two cruisers and another eight destroyers. Additional air attacks followed and the *Clan Chattan* was hit in the hold starting a fire causing ammunition to explode. The crew was taken off by destroyers and the ship was then sunk. The remaining cargo ship, the *Rowallan Castle,* was damaged and taken in tow by HMS *Zulu.* The air attacks continued without respite and on the orders of the fleet commander, the *Rowallan Castle* was sunk. Convoy ME-5 had ceased to exist.

Convoy MW-10 was mounted in March 1942 and proved costly in both ships and men. Four cargo ships, the *Breconshire, Clan Campbell* (now repaired), *Pampas,* and *Talabot* set out with five cruisers and seventeen destroyers. The convoy came under almost continual attack from the air, but the *Talabot* and *Pampas* reached Valletta's Grand Harbour unharmed—except for two bomb hits on the *Pampas,* both of which failed to explode. The *Breconshire* was hit and disabled eight miles from the harbor, and as the sea was rough, she could not be taken in tow.

The *Clan Campbell* was sunk by a bomb about twenty miles from Malta. The destroyer HMS *Legion* was badly damaged and had to be beached. She was later taken into Grand Harbour where she was bombed again and sunk on 26 March. The HMS *Southwold* was lost on 24 March and another cruiser and two other destroyers were damaged. Grand Harbour was then attacked by 326 bombers of the German and Italian Air Forces. The anchored merchant ships were easy targets. The *Pampas* and *Talabot* were sunk on 26 March and the *Breconshire,* which had been brought into Marsaxlokk Bay, was sunk the following day.

The Malta resupply problem was now becoming acute. Not only were supplies of food, ammunition, and fuel short, but because of the heavy losses of merchant ships the actual means of sending supplies was becoming critical.

The next convoy to run the blockhead was dispatched from Gibraltar in June 1942, code named Operation HARPOON. The convoy consisted of six cargo ships, the *Trolius, Burdwan, Chant, Orari, Tanimbar,* and the *Kentucky,* escorted by twenty-nine naval vessels, including two aircraft carriers. Opposite Sardinia, the *Tanimbar* was damaged during air attacks. After the main element of the escort force returned to Gibraltar, the convoy was attacked on 15 June by an Italian naval squadron, and in subsequent air attacks lost two destroyers and the cargo ships *Burdwan, Chant,* and *Kentucky.* Despite heavy losses, 25,000 tons of supplies reached Malta.

At the time the Operation HARPOON convoy was heading toward Malta from Gibraltar, a second convoy, code named Operation VIGOROUS, was dispatched from Alexandria. That convoy met with heavy naval and air opposition. After a cruiser and five destroyers were sunk and three cruisers damaged, the remaining ships returned to Alexandria. The next major convoy to Malta was mounted in August 1942 under the code name Operation PEDESTAL (q.v.). It turned into one of the epic convoy battles of the war.

The final convoys of 1942 were dispatched from Alexandria in November and December. The first, code named Operation STONEHENGE, consisted of four cargo vessels, the *Denbighshire, Bamtam, Robin Locksley,* and the *Morcamoon,* with an escort of five cruisers and seventeen destroyers. It arrived at Malta without loss and only one cruiser, HMS *Arethusa,* damaged, delivering 35,000 tons of stores. The second convoy, code named Operation PORTCULLIS, also consisted of four cargo vessels escorted by one cruiser, eighteen destroyers, and a minesweeper. It arrived at Grand Harbour without a single loss and delivered 55,000 tons of much needed supplies.

After 1942 the strategic situation in the Mediterranean shifted in favor of the Allies and the stranglehold on Malta finally eased. During the course of the Mediterranean campaign (q.v.), Malta, because of its location, was one of the most strategically important pieces of ground. If Malta had fallen, the British would have lost control of the central Mediterranean, and most likely would have been defeated in North Africa. The Axis failure to invade Malta early in the war was a strategic error of tremendous importance.

Alan Harfield

Additional Reading
Bradford, Ernle, *Siege: Malta 1940–1943* (1985).
Macintyre, Donald, *The Battle for the Mediterranean* (1964).
Vella, Phillip, *Malta: Blitzed but Not Beaten* (1985).

Mannerheim Line (6 December 1939–15 February 1940)

[See map 16 on page 1326]

When the Winter War (q.v.) between Finland and the Soviet Union erupted on 30 November 1939, there was only one serious fortification along the entire 800-mile Russo-Finnish border. The ninety-mile-long Mannerheim Line, named after Marshal Carl Mannerheim (q.v.), stretched along the Karelian isthmus from the Gulf of Finland to Lake Ladoga. Although far inferior to its French model, the Maginot Line (q.v.), the Mannerheim Line proved a far more serious obstacle than General Kirill Meretskov (q.v.), commander of the Soviet Seventh Army, had expected.

After their initial retreat from the border in early December 1939, the Finnish forces dug in at the Mannerheim Line on 6 December. Ten days later, after regrouping his forces, Meretskov started his first major offensive. The Finns, however, were well prepared for the attack. Remaining silent during the Soviet artillery preparation, the Finnish guns opened fire and successfully stalled the advancing Soviet infantry. The next day, the same scenario was repeated, causing the Red Army to cease its efforts until 25 December. This time the fighting continued for two days, but even this third Soviet attack failed, and the Mannerheim Line stood intact at the end of December.

Between 8 December and 11 January, two Soviet divisions were annihilated trying to break through the Mannerheim Line. Finnish losses for the same period totaled only about 900 killed and 1,170 wounded. Given the simultaneous Finnish victory at Suomussalmi (q.v.), the Red Army's credibility in the world's eyes seemed threatened. Soviet Premier Josef Stalin (q.v.) thus demanded a new offensive, this time based on a careful analysis of the strengths and weaknesses of the Mannerheim Line. On 7 January General Semen

Timoshenko (q.v.) assumed command of the Soviet operations in Finland, and the forces opposite the Mannerheim Line were reorganized into the Seventh and Thirteenth Armies, with a total of fourteen infantry divisions, six tank brigades, and supporting specialist units.

On 15 January 1940, the Soviet artillery began massive preparations against the Finnish fortifications. Two weeks later, the Soviets began the assault on the line. The Finns were overwhelmed, with their 3rd Division bearing most of the weight of the attack. On 11 February, the Soviet 123rd Division broke through the Finnish lines near Summa. The Finnish 5th Division counterattacked unsuccessfully the next day. On 15 February, Mannerheim ordered his troops to retreat to an intermediate position, approximately twenty miles behind the original line. The Soviets broke through the secondary positions on 19 February and took Viipuri on 11 March.

The fall of the Mannerheim Line proved an important turning point in the Winter War. From then on, the Finnish forces were in constant retreat, unable to hold back the Soviet advance. The Moscow Peace Treaty of 12 March 1940 was, therefore, a welcome relief for the exhausted Finnish Army, and saved it from total annihilation. Yet the myth of the Mannerheim Line became one of the central themes exploited by those Finnish leaders who wished to seek revenge against the Soviets. An unfortunate consequence of this agitation was the disastrous Finnish-Soviet War of 1941–1944 (q.v.).

Jussi Hanhimaki

Additional Reading
Engle, Eloise, and Lauri Paananen, *The Winter War: The Russo-Finnish Conflict, 1939–1940* (1973).
Nevakivi, Jukka, *The Appeal That Was Never Made: The Allies, Scandinavia, and the Finnish Winter War, 1939–1940* (1976).

Mareth Line (20–28 March 1943)

After their long, phased withdrawal from Egypt and Libya during the last eight days of 1942 and the opening six weeks of 1943, the remnants of Field Marshal Erwin Rommel's (q.v.) *Panzerarmee Afrika* established new defensive positions in southeastern Tunisia. By mid-March, all Axis forces in that region were officially reorganized into the Italian First Army. It was Commanded by General Giovanni Messe, a veteran of Operation BARBAROSSA, who was assisted by Italian chief of staff Brigadier General Giuseppe Mancinelli and German Colonel Fritz Bayerlein (q.v.).

By this time, a major portion of Messe's Army (General Taddeo Orlando's XX Corps, General Paolo Berardi's XXI Corps, and Lieutenant General Hans Cramer's *Afrika Korps*) was deployed in and around the Mareth Line, a series of French-built fortifications seventy-five miles northwest of Tunisia's border with Libya. About twenty-two miles long, the Mareth Line stretched from the coast on the Gulf of Gabès to the Matmata Hills. Beyond those hills lay a strip of desert extending northward to Tebaga Gap.

Facing Messe's forces was General Sir Bernard L. Montgomery's (q.v.) Eighth Army. In addition, Messe had to worry about Major General George S. Patton's (q.v.) U.S. II Corps, which hovered along the northwestern edges of the Italian First Army's rear area. Indeed, Patton launched a diversionary attack toward Maknassy a few days before Montgomery struck at the Mareth Line, and thereby drew some of Messe's reserves away from the Mareth-Gabès area.

For his own attack, Montgomery had 160,000 troops, 740 tanks, and more than 1,700 guns (including 1,000 antitank guns). This gave him an advantage over Messe's forces of more than two to one in men and guns and close to five to one in tanks. Moreover, Allied fighters and bombers had almost complete control of the skies and subjected the Italian First Army to bombings on a scale unseen in Africa.

After taking out some of the advance posts, the British XXX Corps, commanded by Lieutenant General Sir Oliver Leese (q.v.), launched a frontal assault on the coastal sector of the Mareth Line during the night of 20–21 March 1943. After penetrating into positions of the *Giovanni Fascisti* Division, Leese's troops were thrown back on 22 March by elements of Major General Willibald Borowietz's 15th *Panzer* Division.

In the meantime, a large armored column, the New Zealand Corps under Lieutenant General Sir Bernard Freyberg (q.v.), completed its advance toward the Tebaga gap on the western side of the Matmata Hills. Faced initially by General Alberto Mannerini's *Raggruppamento Sahariano* (eight battalions plus fourteen batteries of artillery), Freyberg's troops were able to overpower some of the Italian units during the night of 21 March. Fully aware of these developments on his right flank, Messe rushed several German and Italian units into the breach and eventually placed Major General Kurt von Liebenstein of the 164th Light Division in command of the Tebaga gap sector.

As Axis strength steadily increased, Montgomery sent Lieutenant General Sir Brian Horrocks (q.v.) with the X Corps headquarters and the 1st Armoured Division to reinforce Freyberg's men in the Tebaga area. Aided by massive air strikes, Freyberg's and Horrocks's combined forces successfully broke through the Tebaga gap and reached the vicinity of El Hamma on the afternoon and evening of 26 March. For two days, they were held by an antitank screen and a counterattack into their flank by elements of 15th *Panzer* Division.

The delay was sufficient to permit Messe to withdraw his Italian divisions from the Mareth Line. Although about 5,000 Italians and more than 1,000 Germans were captured, the bulk of the Italian First Army safely made it back to new positions at Wadi Akarit, where it had over a week's time to prepare for Montgomery's next onslaught.

The Mareth Line operation is regarded by some historians as a fairly impressive display of Montgomery's leadership. Others have characterized his offensive as rather unimaginative both in its conception and its execution, pointing out that the frontal attack in the coastal sector was quite costly and the flanking move behind the Matmata Hills was not carried out with enough vigor. What can be said with some assurance is that the survival of most of Messe's Army delayed the inevitable Allied victory in North Africa by several weeks.

Ulrich Trumpener

Additional Reading

Ellis, John, *Brute Force: Allied Strategy and Tactics in the Second World War* (1990).

Messe, Giovanni, *La Mia Armata in Tunisia* (1960).

Messenger, Charles, *The Tunisian Campaign* (1982).

Theil, Edmund, *Rommels Verheizte Armee* (1979).

MARKET-GARDEN, Operation

See ARNHEM

Matapan (28–29 March 1941)

[See map 27 on page 1337]

Throughout March 1941, convoys transporting men and equipment of the Imperial Expeditionary Force to Greece (q.v.) from British bases in Egypt steamed back and forth across the eastern Mediterranean. Although they had superior air and naval forces in the theater, neither the Germans nor the Italians initially made a determined attempt to stop the flow of supplies. That changed at the end of the month when the Italians were persuaded by their allies to intervene with their fleet. The activity preceding this operation did not escape the British, who, on 25 March, learned from ULTRA (q.v.) intelligence that a major Axis operation was being mounted.

Surmising that the convoy lanes between Egypt and Greece were the target, the British naval commander in chief in the Mediterranean, Admiral Sir Andrew Cunningham (q.v.), canceled one convoy and ordered another back to Egypt. He also dispatched a force of three light cruisers and four destroyers under the command of Vice Admiral H.D. Pridham-Wippell to patrol south of Crete.

Hard news of Axis intentions came on the afternoon of 27 March when the Royal Air Force (RAF) sighted three Italian cruisers heading southeast toward Crete. This was the advance group consisting of the battleship *Vittorio Veneto,* six heavy cruisers, two light cruisers, and thirteen destroyers, and commanded by Admiral Angelo Iachino (q.v.). Unaware of the exact composition of the enemy fleet, Cunningham put to sea that night with the battleships HMS *Warspite,* HMS *Barham,* and HMS *Valiant,* the carrier HMS *Formidable,* and nine destroyers.

The battle off Cape Matapan opened at 0745 hours on 28 March 1941 when Pridham-Wippell sighted three enemy heavy cruisers from the north. Recognizing that his light cruisers were outgunned by his opponent's 203mm guns, he decided to lure the enemy toward Cunningham's main force, 100 miles southeast.

After pursuing for an hour, the Italians broke away northwestward. Pridham-Wippell followed to maintain contact, unaware that he was being drawn onto the guns of the *Vittorio Veneto.* That startling revelation became apparent at 1058 hours when the battleship was spotted coming from the north followed shortly thereafter by 380mm shell salvoes plunging close alongside. Trapped in a pincer with the cruisers he was pursuing on his port bow and the battleship on his starboard. Pridham-Wippell extricated his force by laying smoke and turning away southward.

Iachino chased the British cruisers but was unable to score any hits. Eighty miles to the east, Cunningham ordered the HMS *Formidable* to launch an air strike to help the beleaguered cruisers. Although the six British Albacore torpedo bombers that attacked scored no hits, Iachino was concerned enough by the possible presence of an aircraft carrier to turned for home.

Cunningham's only hope of catching the faster Italian ships lay with the HMS *Formidable's* airmen. They did not let their admiral down. A mid-afternoon strike by three Albacores and two Swordfish put a torpedo into the *Vittorio Veneto's* stern, while an evening attack by six Albacores and four Swordfish crippled the heavy cruiser *Pola.* Both warships were stopped as a result of the damage, but the battleship was quickly repaired and her speed restored to fifteen knots. Efforts to repair *Pola* were unsuccessful, and as night fell, Iachino, hampered by poor aerial reconnaissance, and therefore unaware that British battleships were in the area, ordered two cruisers and four destroyers to stand by the heavy cruiser.

At that point, Cunningham's renowned steely resolve became the decisive factor. Advised by his staff that it was too risky to commit his capital ships to a confused night action, the British admiral nevertheless chose to use his battleships to follow up a destroyer attack. Cunningham's confidence was well-founded. As commander of the Mediterranean Fleet's destroyers in the mid-1930s, he had played a leading role in increasing night fighting efficiency throughout the fleet. The Italian navy, on the other hand, devoted little time to night training during the interwar years and lagged well behind the British in that respect. The lack of radar (q.v.) in Italian ships also became a significant factor.

At 2040 hours, Cunningham's boldness was rewarded when Pridham-Wippell reported that radar had detected a warship stopped five miles to the west. Cunningham's force, twenty miles to the east, headed toward the contact and an hour later, the HMS *Valiant's* radar detected a ship lying motionless nine miles ahead on the port bow. Hopes ran high that it was the *Vittorio Veneto.* Handling his battleships like destroyers, Cunningham made the unprecedented maneuver of turning his battle line toward an enemy of unknown strength at night. As they approached, lookouts sighted yet another group of ships, the two cruisers and four destroyers sent to assist the *Pola.*

The battle of Matapan now reached its dramatic conclusion. Undetected by the enemy, Cunningham's battleships (the *Formidable* was detached) maneuvered to within 3,500 yards before opening fire. At that point-blank range, the British gunners, guided onto their targets by searchlights, hit with devastating accuracy, and within four and a half minutes the heavy cruisers *Fiume* and *Zara,* and the destroyer *Alfieri* were mortally damaged by the deluge of 15-inch shells. The three surviving Italian destroyers moved to counterattack and Cunningham finally turned away to eastward. As the main battle line withdrew with the HMS *Formidable,* they left behind a confused melee in which four British destroyers sank one of their Italian counterparts without loss. The two remaining Italian destroyers escaped.

While this battle raged, Iachino's main force made good its escape. Pridham-Wippell's cruisers and two flotillas of destroyers from Cunningham's main force, commanded by Captain P. Mack, were dispatched to find and attack the *Vittorio Veneto* but failed to make contact. At around 2300 hours, as the action to the eastward was reaching its climax, they received an ambiguous signal from Cunningham ordering all ships not engaging the enemy to withdraw northeastward.

Not realizing the order was not intended for them, Pridham-Wippell and Mack broke off the search. On their way to rejoin Cunningham's main body, Mack's destroyers encountered the damaged *Pola* and *Zara*. The *Zara* was sunk immediately by torpedoes, while the *Pola* was similarly dispatched after the destroyer HMS *Jervis* went alongside to take off survivors.

Pridham-Wippell and Mack rejoined Cunningham in the early morning of 29 March and after a brief search for the *Vittorio Veneto,* headed for Alexandria. German reconnaissance aircraft spotted the British ships late that morning and an attack was mounted later in the afternoon. Several bombs burst close to the HMS *Formidable* but all British ships escaped unscathed and the force reached Alexandria on the evening of 30 March. Although Cunningham was disappointed that the *Vittorio Veneto* had eluded him, the battle of Matapan was unquestionably a British victory. The Mediterranean Fleet had suffered no losses. The Italians, however, lost the heavy cruisers *Fiume, Pola,* and *Zara* as well as the destroyers *Alfieri* and *Carducci*. The triumph at Matapan confirmed the Royal Navy's ascendancy over the Italians and blunted their will to conduct offensive operations in the Aegean and eastern Mediterranean. The Italian fleet never again operated east of the Gulf of Sirte, which allowed British supplies to continue to flow unencumbered into Greece. Later, when the Greece and Crete (q.v.) campaigns ended in disaster, Cunningham's ships were able to evacuate Allied soldiers without the threat of interference from the Italian Navy. The Royal Navy, however, suffered heavily at the hands of the *Luftwaffe* during the evacuation of Crete.

Michael Whitby

Additional Reading

Barnett, Correlli, *Engage the Enemy More Closely: The Royal Navy in the Second World War* (1991).

Pack, S.W.C., *Night Action Off Cape Matapan* (1972).

Mediterranean Campaign (1940–1944)

[See map 27 on page 1337]

The four-year naval battle for the Mediterranean began with Italy's entry into the war as a German ally on 10 June 1940. The resulting campaign was one wholly concerned with the application of sea power to support operations ashore. The naval operations in the Mediterranean ran the gamut from sea denial to sea control to power projection. It was very much a war of swinging fortunes and fluctuating momentum, but throughout it all, control of the sea determined success, while loss of control led to failure. The Axis failure in this campaign ultimately drove Field Marshal Erwin Rommel (q.v.) out of Africa and Italy out of the war. Allied success brought the first Allied troops back into Western Europe.

Theoretically, Italy gained naval superiority in the Mediterranean when the French surrendered to the Germans in June 1940. Italy had the second largest submarine fleet in the world (more than 100 boats), as well as four modernized battleships, two new ones, and a third in construction. More importantly, the Italian Navy had the potential support of one of the world's reputedly strongest air forces. Italy's ships were fast and powerfully armed. Perhaps more importantly, Italy's strategic location dominating the sea lanes of the central Mediterranean gave it a potential choke hold on Allied maritime commerce.

Only the British base on Malta, located midway between Sicily and Italy's African possession of Libya, occupied a similar position vis-à-vis Italy's sea lanes. The first three years of the campaign, in fact, revolved around Britain's effort to retain that island. It was from Malta that the bulk of Britain's sea denial operations were launched against Italy's sea lanes. Given the small size and aged units of the British Mediterranean Fleet, Malta's defense and Britain's hold on the Mediterranean initially appeared tenuous indeed. Fortunately for the British, events proved otherwise.

Controlling the Mediterranean was critical to the British Empire, for it was through the Mediterranean that oil and other vital materials flowed from its eastern possessions to Britain. It also was the most efficient route for shipping supplies and material for the defense of those possessions. Traveling around Africa tripled the transit time, effectively quintupling the amount of shipping required to achieve the same tonnage. Britain did not have any merchant shipping to waste. The Mediterranean had to be held at all costs.

Although outnumbered and encumbered with much slower units, the Royal Navy (RN) enjoyed several advantages over its Italian opponents. It had a more aggressive and professional leadership. Italy's admirals adhered to the "fleet-in-being" strategy, where preservation of units took precedence over all other considerations. The RN's sailors also were superior in technical ability to those of the Italian Navy, which relied on conscripts to man its ships.

The Italians also suffered from flawed tactics, equipment, and doctrine. Doctrinally, they had no procedures for joint air-navy operations, no specific antisubmarine doctrine, and no air defense tactics. Each ship's captain was supposed to use his own initiative. Sonar (q.v.) was not introduced until late 1942. More significantly, the Italians did not train or prepare for night combat. Their surface ships had no radar (q.v.) or nightfighting equipment. Italian surface and antiaircraft gunnery was poor throughout the war. They had no aircraft carriers and commissioned none during the war. Their submarines lacked night periscopes and were not trained in conducting either day or night surface attacks. Italian conning towers and silhouettes were too large. Submarine fire control equipment was nonexistent, and the captains computed their own firing solutions. Italian submarines were large, unwieldy, and slow to dive. Finally, the Italian Navy suffered from fuel shortages throughout the war. Available fuel dictated the size and duration of every naval operation.

That was the situation when Admiral Andrew Cunningham (q.v.) first engaged the Italians on 9 July 1940. This first engagement set the pattern for most of the campaign. Both British and Italian task groups were steaming in support of convoys—the Italians were en route to Libya, the British to Malta. Both had a fair idea of the other's movements, if not intentions. The Italian Air Force made an appearance, conducting an unsuccessful high altitude bombing attack on the British task group. Both convoys reached their destinations unscathed, but the actions of the escorts following their respective convoy deliveries highlights the differences between the two fleets.

The Italian task group tried to evade contact and run for home, while the smaller British force moved to intercept. The resulting battle of Calabria (q.v.) was inconclusive. The Italian battleship *Cesare* suffered some minor damage before escaping. The Italian Air Force returned to the scene, bombing its own fleet this time, with no better results than it had achieved against the British. Although not a decisive engagement, it gave the British more confidence. Cunningham then dispatched his cruisers and destroyers on sweeps to interdict Italian shipping in the Ionian and Aegean Seas.

Nonetheless, Cunningham was worried. The Italian Fleet represented a significant force and it was growing. Moreover, the Italian Air Force might do better next time. The British Admiralty recognized this as well, and formed Force H in Gibraltar to operate in the western Mediterranean and eastern Atlantic. That freed Cunningham to concentrate on the central and eastern Mediterranean. Unfortunately, Force H's first duty was the distasteful attack on the Vichy French Fleet at Mers el-Kébir (q.v.). This incident soured Britain's relations with its former ally, but the British considered it necessary to prevent the surrender of the French fleet to the Axis. Cunningham achieved the same result by negotiating the disarming of French ships in Alexandria, Egypt.

In September 1940, Cunningham received reinforcements, the most significant of which was the armored aircraft carrier HMS *Illustrious*. Arriving just as the Italians started their offensives against Egypt and Greece, HMS *Illustrious*'s Fulmar fighters and Swordfish torpedo bombers gave Cunningham the aerial striking power he so desperately needed. He wasted no time in using it. On 11 November 1940, the carrier's aircraft struck the Italian fleet at its main base in Taranto (q.v.), sinking three battleships and damaging another. Several cruisers and destroyers were also damaged and the nearby seaplane base was destroyed. The Italian battleship force was cut to two, and only two of the sunken battleships ever returned to service. As a result, the RN suddenly had naval superiority in the Mediterranean.

A second attack in January 1941, this time by RAF bombers based in Malta, severely damaged another Italian battleship and forced Italy's remaining operational battleship to flee to Genoa, where it would have no impact on the naval situation around Malta. These air strikes convinced Benito Mussolini (q.v.) and the Italian Navy to order the construction of aircraft carriers, but it was too late.

Cunningham used his newfound superiority to strike at Italian sea lanes, bases, and forces in Africa, but the swing of fortune in Britain's favor was not to last. The *Luftwaffe*'s X *Fliegerkorps* (X Air Corps) deployed to the Mediterranean in January and took station in Sicily. Arriving as the British Eighth Army was driving the Italians out of Cyrenaica, Adolf Hitler (q.v.) dispatched these highly trained and well equipped combat veterans to redress the strategic balance along his southern flank. Their arrival preceded by one month the initial deployment of what would become the *Afrika Korps* (q.v.).

The Germans announced their presence during one of Britain's efforts to resupply Malta (q.v.). Catching the convoy and its escorts west of Malta on the afternoon of 10 January 1941, the Germans launched wave after wave of *Stuka* dive bombers and Ju-88s. Although the convoy reached Malta, the HMS *Illustrious* and a light cruiser were critically damaged, and another cruiser was sunk. Two weeks of intensive daily bombing of Malta then followed. Virtually every air, ground, and naval facility on the island was hit. The Germans recognized the importance of Malta, but fortunately for Britain, the Germans had little stomach for invading it. Hitler relieved the pressure on Malta in February when he deployed half of X *Fliegerkorps* to North Africa to support the *Afrika Korps.*

It was about that time that Mussolini prevailed upon the Italian fleet commander, Admiral Angelo Iachino (q.v.), to take some action to regain the initiative. He took the fleet out from Naples on 26 March 1941 and conduct a sweep against British shipping in the eastern Mediterranean. Warned by Italian code breakers that the British thought the Italian force consisted of only four ships, he steamed eastward toward Alexandria. X *Fliegerkorps* was supposed to provide air reconnaissance and strike support, but somehow it never arrived in time. The result was one of the greatest naval defeats in modern times, the battle of Cape Matapan (q.v.). The Italians lost three heavy cruisers and four destroyers in a short night engagement. The British force suffered no combat losses at all, and Iachino fled back to Italy with the Italian's last remaining battleship.

Despite the dispersion of its forces throughout the Mediterranean, the *Luftwaffe* continued to make its presence felt. As a result, the RN could no longer risk carriers in the central Mediterranean, and the British attacks on the Libyan coast became prohibitively expensive. The *Luftwaffe's* most visible contribution to the campaign came in May 1941, when Hitler launched the invasion of Crete (q.v.). Best known for the German airborne assault of that strategic eastern island, the battle for Crete actually was a costly naval campaign as well. Cunningham's decision to remain and support the British Army throughout the campaign, including the evacuation, proved very expensive. Britain lost more warships in that

single operation than in any other during World War II.

Meanwhile, the aerial siege of Malta continued, albeit at a slower pace. Once the battle for Crete ended in June, Axis air forces resumed daily raids, driving the island's residents underground. Malta remained defiant despite the adversity. Malta's two motor torpedo boat flotillas made nightly forays against Italy's coastal shipping while the British 14th Destroyer Flotilla conducted antishipping sweeps north of Libya.

The British 10th Submarine Flotilla operated further afield, attacking Italian shipping and troop convoys as far away as the Dodecanese Islands. Its primary targets, however, were the Italian transports supplying Rommel's *Afrika Korps.* The British submarines gained in effectiveness as Axis air strikes against Malta receded. The RN was assisted in its operations by RAF Coastal Command and Fleet Air Arm torpedo planes stationed on Malta. These forces decimated Rommel's supply lines. His *Panzer*s thus found their fuel rationed just as they were achieving their greatest tactical successes.

Malta gained another element of importance in April 1941, one that went beyond its strategic position. The British began to decrypt *Luftwaffe* and *Afrika Korps* radio traffic. Within a few months, they went on to decrypt German and Italian naval communications as well. From Malta, decrypted messages were transmitted to Alexandria, Cairo, and London for use by Allied commanders. By June 1941, Malta was monitoring Axis radio traffic throughout the Middle East and the Balkans, for subsequent transmission and decryption in London. Malta thus became more than a thorn in Rommel's side; it was Britain's eyes into the Axis mind. Reading Rommel's orders, thoughts, status reports, and (more significantly from a naval perspective) his maritime convoy routes and schedules gave Allied commanders unequaled insight into Axis operations and intentions.

Although the Italian signals intelligence service could decrypt some of the RAF's lower-level codes, the Axis never achieved a similar intelligence success. The Germans did briefly have some success against the RN's heavy warship broadcasts in 1942 and 1943, but they lacked the forces to exploit the advantage.

In late summer 1941, Hitler ordered six U-boats into the Mediterranean. He added four more boats two months later. Arriving in September 1941, the first group of U-boats sank more ships during their first six weeks than Italy's subs sank in the entire campaign. Despite their successes in the Mediterranean, however, the U-boats would have made a more significant contribution to the German war effort if they had remained in the Atlantic. Their presence did nothing to deter or degrade the devastating attacks of the Malta Striking Forces (air, surface, submarine) against Rommel's supply lines. In November 1941, less than 40 percent of Rommel's supply ships successfully delivered their cargos. As a result, he had little with which to resist the British offensive to relieve Tobruk (*see* Tobruk III).

Rommel's supply situation became desperate and he appealed to Hitler for reinforcements. Hitler responded by redeploying the Second *Luftflotte* (Air Fleet) from Russia to Sicily in December 1941. Its orders were to combine with the X *Fliegerkorps* and dominate the central Mediterranean, suppress Malta, and interdict British seaborne supply lines into Malta and Tobruk. Its arrival coincided with the Italian 10th Light Flotilla's (q.v.) successful sinking of the battleships HMS *Queen Elizabeth* and HMS *Valiant* in Alexandria Harbor (q.v.). Both ships were put out of action for months.

Meanwhile, the combined air attacks on Malta so destroyed the island's facilities that its submarines and destroyers had to withdraw. More significantly, the Italians delivered for the first time in eight months an unscathed and massive supply convoy to Rommel. Resupplied and replenished, he struck back again, driving the British Eighth Army out of Benghazi. The *Luftwaffe* also prevented Malta from being supplied. It was the beginning of the worst days of the siege. The islanders and their defenders were put on half rations.

Cunningham ordered the island resupplied at all costs. Its loss would determine the outcome of the entire campaign, possibly the war. Admiral Phillip Vian (q.v.) was chosen to command the operation, which consisted of five fast transports escorted by four light cruisers and sixteen destroyers. On 22 March 1942, Iachino moved in for the kill. The Italian Air Force arrived first on the scene but accomplished nothing. The follow-on Luftwaffe attack was equally ineffective. Iachino arrived next, hoping that the presence of the Italian battleship *Vittorio Veneto* and three cruisers would give him the superior firepower for victory. Instead, he suffered another defeat at the second battle of Sirte (q.v.). Iachino did succeed, however, in delaying the convoy so it did not arrive at Malta that night. It arrived in the morning, followed by the *Luftwaffe* shortly thereafter. In the resulting air raid, only 5,000 of the 26,000 tons of supplies were salvaged.

The tug of war for Malta continued throughout the summer of 1942. While Rommel drove across Africa, his supplies arrived steadily, indeed, almost without interruption. Mussolini and Field Marshal Albert Kesselring (q.v.) planned to seize Malta and prepared a joint airborne-amphibious task force for that purpose. Rommel, however, was able to convince Hitler that such an invasion was unnecessary. Egypt, he argued, would fall without it. All he needed was the planes to support his army. It was a major strategic mistake.

Although the aerial and naval siege of Malta continued, there were not enough aircraft to support both Rommel and the suppression of Malta. In August, Malta received desperately needed fuel and supplies from the Operation PEDESTAL (q.v.) convoys. Sixty Spitfire fighters and antiaircraft ammunition also arrived.

Axis aircraft losses began to climb. Their twin-engine bombers were particularly vulnerable to the Spitfires, and eventually were withdrawn from the attacks. As a result, the Malta Striking Forces returned in October 1942. Rommel's supply lines began to suffer accordingly. Losses among his supply convoys rose above 60 percent. The *Afrika Korps* lacked the fuel to move its supplies, much less its combat forces. The British El Alamein (q.v.) offensive in October caught most of Rommel's air support on the ground, due to lack of fuel. His tanks also had their mobility reduced by fuel shortages.

Neither the German nor the Italian Navy was in a position to deter, much less destroy, the Allied Operation TORCH landings in Northwest Africa (q.v.) the next month. Germany rushed more reinforcements into North Africa to halt the Allied advance, but by November 1942, no Axis convoy could cross the Mediterranean safely. By March 1943, convoy losses exceeded 70 percent. The German victory at Kasserine Pass (q.v.) did little to alter the overall situation. No army can fight without supplies. The Axis army in North Africa (now pinned into Tunisia's northeast corner) surrendered on 12 May 1943.

The surrender of Axis forces in North Africa effectively ended the contest between the Axis and Allied navies. Although German U-boats and light craft would continue to be a problem in the central and eastern Mediterranean, they were more of a nuisance than a serious impediment to Allied operations. The only exceptions were in the Dodecanese and Aegean areas.

The Italian Navy was essentially out of the fight and would suffer its next combat losses in the run to surrender in September 1943. It was the *Luftwaffe* and not any Italian forces that posed the greatest threat to Allied naval forces supporting the landings in Sicily (q.v.) and Italy. Allied naval supremacy tied down thousands of troops in the German rear awaiting amphibious assaults, even though the shortage of landing craft actually precluded the Allies from fully exploiting their naval supremacy.

Ironically, German naval authorities proved more innovative than either their Italian comrades or their Allied opponents. In July, the Germans were able to evacuate Sicily—almost without loss—in the face of overwhelming Allied air and naval supremacy. The Germans then went on to seize many Italian ships, particularly light craft, for use in the Aegean. There, imaginative local German commanders employed them not only to supply island garrisons in the Aegean, but also to conduct successful joint airborne-amphibious landings to recapture the Dodecanese Islands (q.v.). In doing so, they thwarted Prime Minister Winston S. Churchill's (q.v.) plans to bring Turkey into the war as an Allied country.

The Germans also were able to deliver supplies to their armies in Italy via Italian coastal waters, despite the Allies' overwhelming naval supremacy. The Germans employed naval special forces, including the *Brandenburgers* and *Kleinkampfverbände* (qq.v.), against the Anzio (q.v.) landing and against Allied coastal traffic. These operations, however, did nothing to inhibit Allied naval operations.

The Mediterranean Campaign cost the Axis 2.1 million tons of shipping and the Allies 1.7 million tons. The campaign was one of rapidly shifting momentum. Like the cavalry battles of old, the introduction of fresh forces often altered the balance and tide of battle. With that shift went the fortunes of war on both land and sea. For the Axis, it was their lack of initiative and daring that caused them to squander their opportunities. The victory in Crete was not exploited by further landings. More importantly, Malta was never taken. It was that failure that ultimately cost them the campaign and possibly the war.

For the Allies, primarily the British, it was a brilliantly fought campaign in which few opportunities were missed and many were created by sheer initiative and determination. The risks were great and the potential payoff unknown. For Great Britain, success in the Mediterranean offered the opportunity for eventual victory, while defeat there meant the possible loss of the war. Only the Atlantic Campaign (q.v.) had a greater importance. That they won is a testament to the fighting spirit and skills of the Royal Navy.

Carl O. Schuster

Additional Reading

Ansel, Walter, *Hitler and the Middle Sea* (1972).
Bradford, Ernle, *Siege: Malta, 1940–1943* (1985).
Hough, Richard, *The Longest Battle* (1986).
Macintyre, Donald, *The Battle for the Mediterranean* (1964).

M

Mersa Matrúh (26–29 June 1942)

Mersa Matrúh, an Egyptian village located at about 100 kilometers from the border between Libya and Egypt, was the site of a series of engagements that began on 26 June 1942 between the British Eighth Army and Field Marshal Erwin Rommel's *Panzerarmee Afrika*.

Immediately following the 21 June seizure of Tobruk (*see* Tobruk III), General Ugo Cavallero and Field Marshals Albert Kesselring and Erwin Rommel (qq.v.) met in Derna to decide the next course of action for the Axis. Kesselring wanted to suspend ground operations in North Africa to concentrate the full force of the *Luftwaffe* against the island fortress of Malta (q.v.). With Malta out of the way, Kesselring argued, the Axis lines of communication between Italy and North Africa would be secure, and then the drive into Egypt could resume. Kesselring's subordinate, Rommel, wanted to continue the pursuit of the British, with Alexandria as the final objective. Kesselring decided to go for Malta, and he had the full backing of the Italian and German military staffs. Rommel, however, went over Kesselring's head and appealed directly to Adolf Hitler (q.v.). The German dictator sided with his then-favorite general.

By 23 June, the Eighth Army had completed its retreat, and took up positions Mersa Matrúh in a defensive line about twenty kilometers long and four kilometers deep. The British position was strong on the flanks and weak in the center. In the north the British X Corps under Lieutenant General Sir William Holmes had the Indian 10th Division in Mersa Matrúh, supported by the 50th Infantry Division to its south.

In the south, the XIII Corps under Lieutenant General Sir William Gott (q.v.) had the New Zealand 2nd Division and the British 1st Armoured Division on the extreme southern flank. Between the two corps there was a gap of about fifteen kilometers, covered only by a thin minefield and some smaller units. Farther in the Eighth Army's rear, the Indian 5th Division was close to Sidi Haneish. Elements of the British 7th Armoured Division and the Indian 29th Brigade were in a more forward positions in the Bir Qa'im area.

Rommel's forces consisted of the *Afrika Korps* (the 15th and 21st *Panzer* Divisions and the 90th Light Division), the Italian *Trieste, Brescia,* and *Trento* Divisions, and the Italian XX Armored Corps (*Ariete* and *Littorio* Armored Divisions). On 23 June, lead elements of the *Afrika Korps* (q.v.) crossed into Egypt. Both sides were severely depleted from the recent fighting at the Gazala Line (q.v.), but the Axis forces were weaker. The entire *Afrika Korps* only had forty-four operational tanks at that point. The British 1st Armoured Division had 159 tanks, sixty of which were U.S.-made Grants.

Rommel's plan was to drive off the 1st Armoured division with the *Afrika Korps'* two *Panzer* divisions, and then cut off and encircle Marsa Matrúh. On 26 June, Rommel began his attack from the march, with very little advance reconnaissance. The Mersa Matrúh positions came under heavy artillery fire from the *Brescia* and *Trento* Divisions, while the 90th Light and the *Littorio* Divisions tried to complete the encirclement from the south. In the meantime, the 21st *Panzer* Division also penetrated the center.

On 27 June, the 21st *Panzer* Division moved across the front of the New Zealand 2nd Division with little opposition. Later that day, the 21st *Panzer* Division, separated from the 15th *Panzer* Division, came under heavy attack by the British from both the east and the west. Rommel, meanwhile, took the 90th Light Division around the southern flank of British X Corps, and cut the coastal road about thirty kilometers east of Mersa Matrúh. The 21st *Panzer* Division, however, was still cut off, and 15th *Panzer* Division and Italian XX Armored Corps were too weak to break through the 1st Armoured Division to rescue it. Rommel was still confident and ordered the 21st *Panzer* Division to stand fast.

Late in the day on 27 June, Gott, worried that his New Zealand 2nd Division was about to be cut off, ordered the withdrawal of XIII Corps. Because of a breakdown in British communications, X Corps did not learn until 0430 hours on 28 June that XIII Corps was in full retreat, and their southern flank was open. Later that day, the 90th Light Division and the *Littorio* Division completed the encirclement of Mersa Matrúh. The British withdrawal in the south relieved the pressure on the 21st *Panzer* Division, which turned to pursue the British and overran elements of the Indian 29th Brigade.

During the night of 28 June, groups of the Indian 10th Division tried a breakout of the Mersa Matrúh position at the head of Wadi Nagamish,

but they were driven back by the *Littorio* Armored Division. Other Indian troops took advantage of large gaps that existed in the Axis lines, and succeeded in escaping from encirclement. Also taking advantage of the darkness, other British units were able to break contact and fall back toward the positions of the Indian 5th Division along the coast toward El Daba. The *Afrika Korps* and the *Littorio* Armored Division pursued, while all other Axis units concentrated on eliminating the Mersa Matrúh pocket and mopping up the occupied territory.

The concentric attack developed slowly because of the minefields and strong fire from the British artillery. On the morning of 29 June, the garrison of Mersa Matrúh was overwhelmed. At 0930 hours, the Italian 7th *Bersaglieri* Regiment entered the conquered stronghold, taking 6,000 Allied prisoners. About the same time, the 21st *Panzer* Division intercepted a retreating British column to the east, capturing another 1,600.

Mersa Matrúh hit the Eighth Army hard. The 50th Infantry and Indian 10th Divisions were so shattered that they made little contribution to the early stages of the subsequent fights around El Alamein. On the other hand, the victory led the Axis to believe that Egypt was within easy reach, and that it would be very easy to bounce the British out of their defensive positions. As the subsequent battles at Ruweisat Ridge, Alam el Halfa, and El Alamein (qq.v.) were to show, it was an unwarranted assumption.

Francesco Fatutta

Additional Reading

Agar-Hamilton, John A.I., and Leonard Turner, *Crisis in the Desert: May–July 1942* (1952).
Barnett, Correlli, *The Desert Generals* (1961).
Heckmann, Wolf, *Rommel's War in Africa* (1981).
Maughan, Barton, *Tobruk and El Alamein* (1966).
Mellenthin, F.W. von, *Panzer Battles* (1956).
Pitt, Barrie, *The Crucible of War: Year of Alamein, 1942* (1982).

Mers el-Kébir (3 July 1940)

"This was a hateful decision, the most unnatural and painful in which I have ever been concerned." This was how, with hindsight, Prime Minister Winston S. Churchill (q.v.) described one of the lowest moments in Anglo-French relations during World War II. Churchill was referring to the naval action of 3 July 1940, when, for the first time in 125 years, ships of the Royal Navy opened fire on French warships at the naval base of Mers el-Kébir, near Oran on the North African coast.

The attack at Mers el-Kébir took place only days after the French surrender to Germany. The attack was part of Operation CATAPULT, a naval action that involved the simultaneous seizure, control, disablement, or destruction of all the accessible vessels of the French fleets at Plymouth, Portsmouth, Dakar, and Mers el-Kébir.

Before attacking the French fleet, Admiral James Somerville (q.v.) radioed Admiral Marcel Gensoul an ultimatum. Somerville offered the French Admiral several options: (1) join the British Navy in combat against the Axis powers; (2) sail to a British port; (3) sail to the Antilles; (4) put in at an American port; or (5) scuttle his ships where they were. Should Gensoul go to Britain or the United States, he and his crews would be offered repatriation to France and his ships would be returned after the war. If he rejected this offer, his ships would be sunk. He was given six hours to decide. In his radio message to the French Admiralty, he mentioned only the option to scuttle his ships.

The attack started at 1754 hours, when salvos from Somerville's Force H, which consisted of the battleships HMS *Valiant* and HMS *Resolution* and the battle cruiser HMS *Hood,* opened fire on five ships of the French Atlantic Fleet, commanded by Gensoul. The bombardment lasted for some ten minutes and resulted in the deaths of 1,297 French sailors. Of the four French battleships at Mers el-Kébir, the *Bretagne* was blown up, the *Dunkerque* ran aground, and the *Provence* was beached. The *Strasbourg* escaped, and although attacked by torpedo aircraft from the HMS *Ark Royal,* it managed to reach the French naval base at Toulon. Ironically, Somerville's flagship, the HMS *Hood,* which led the attack, had only a few days previously been on joint patrol with the *Dunkerque.* That the British attacked their recent allies can be understood only in the light of the conditions at the time. Churchill was afraid that the French Navy, the fourth largest in the world in total tonnage, would pass into German hands, despite the fact that in Article 8 of the recently signed Franco-German armistice of 22 June 1940, the German government had solemnly declared they had no intention of using French warships for their purposes during the war. Churchill did not trust Adolf Hitler (q.v.). In his postwar memoirs, Churchill noted that the addition of the French ships to those of Germany, Italy, and Japan, "confronted Great Britain with mortal dangers."

Churchill believed his fears were justified. Just

hours before the attack at Mers el-Kébir, all French vessels stationed in the British ports of Portsmouth and Plymouth were taken under British control by surprise and without any resistance, demonstrating how easily the Germans could have taken possession of any French warships in German-controlled ports. This self-justification, however, did not take into account that allied French naval personnel in British ports probably would have been less vigilant than in German-controlled ports. It also did not take into account the plan by Admiral Jean François Darlan (q.v.) for all ships to be mined for scuttling should the Germans attempt to take them over. This is precisely what happened when the Germans occupied the French naval base at Toulon (q.v.) on 27 November 1942.

Whatever the rights and wrongs of the issue, less than generous attitudes toward the British rankle to this day among veteran French sailors whenever the name Mers el-Kébir is mentioned.

Robert C. Hudson

Additional Reading
Boutron, Jean, *Mers el-Kébir* (1980).
Pilmmer, Charlotte and Denis, *Matter of Expediency* (1978).

Metz (27 September–13 December 1944)

Having pushed the German Army 500 miles across northern France in less than a month, General George S. Patton's (q.v.) U.S. Third Army was poised for the final plunge to the Rhine River. At the beginning of September 1944, Allied intelligence officers promised that nothing stood in his way except for a few shattered remnants of German formations and the thinly held Siegfried Line. That estimate, however, failed to take three factors into account: (1) the German ability to recover when given even the slightest chance; (2) the degradation of the Allies' fighting power in poor weather; and (3) the fortress of Metz.

Metz sits astride one of the classic invasion routes between Germany and France. The fortress had been in the possession of both countries at various times over the centuries, so its defenses faced both directions. The strongest faced west. These consisted of a ring of casemated forts approximately ten kilometers from the city built by the Germans between 1870 and 1912. They were now garrisoned by the 14,000-strong 462nd *Volksgrenadier* Division.

On 10 September, the Allied 12th Army Group commander, General Omar N. Bradley (q.v.), ordered the Third Army to advance toward

Mainz and Mannheim. With only the sketchiest knowledge of the fortifications, Patton ordered the XX Corps under General Walton Walker (q.v.) to take Metz. The XX Corps started to attack the outer defenses of the city on 27 September. The brunt of the fighting fell on 5th Infantry Division. The Americans attacked from the march with poorly synchronized artillery and engineer support, directly into the German strength. Even after being reinforced by a combat command of 7th Armored Division, the 5th Infantry Division had nothing but casualties to show for a week of frontal assaults.

The 5th Infantry Division tried again south of the city, crossing the Moselle near Dornot, but the tiny bridgehead could not be sustained and was evacuated after two days under pressure from the 17th SS *Panzergrenadier* Division. Three days later, a second attack, supported by thirteen battalions of artillery plus close air support, won a permanent bridgehead farther south at Arnaville. Counterattacks from 17th SS and 3rd *Panzergrenadier* Divisions were beaten back. The 7th Armored Division passed through the 5th Infantry Division, but the intended exploitation was stalemated in the rough terrain east of the bridgehead. By mid-September, the XX Corps called off any further attacks and sought to consolidate its position.

In the second half of September, the Allies' overall operational priority shifted away from pursuit into Germany and toward the ill-fated Operation MARKET-GARDEN (q.v.). Thus by the end of the month, Patton could add logistical problems to terrain and the enemy on his list of frustrations. He did, however, put the "October lull" that followed Operation MARKET-GARDEN to good use by refitting and resupplying his troops, gathering intelligence on the Germans, and preparing to tackle the fortress once again. The 90th Infantry Division provided the one bright spot that month by securing a bridgehead for future operations across the Moselle north of Metz.

Not all news that month was good for the XX Corps. From 3 to 15 October, the 5th Infantry Division failed again to subdue Metz's forts through direct attacks. During that period, one infantry battalion reinforced by tank destroyers and twenty-three battalions of artillery took on the strongest and newest of the forts, Fort Driant. The assaulting infantry suffered 50 percent casualties before the attack was called off. Patton, however, could not ignore Metz. In fact, he had to completely abandon his "let the flanks take care of themselves" philosophy, lest the fortress become an obstacle to his main effort, which was the XII Corps attack

toward the Saar River. By the end of October, Patton began planning once again to subdue Metz.

The Third Army was large and well equipped for the November general offensive. In addition to six infantry and three armored divisions, its nondivisional units included twenty-two antiaircraft artillery battalions, five tank battalions, fourteen tank destroyer battalions, thirty-eight field artillery battalions, and fifteen combat engineer battalions.

To start Patton's offensive, the XX Corps—now reinforced with the 95th Infantry and 10th Armored Divisions—attacked on 9 November. The 95th Infantry Division took over the 90th Infantry Division's positions and launched a demonstration at Maizieres-les-Metz, distracting General Hermann Balck's (q.v.) defenders. Walker seized the opportunity and slipped the 90th Infantry Division and 10th Armored Division farther north. He then launched the 90th Infantry Division over the Moselle at Königsmacker without a telltale artillery preparation. With surprise complete, the 90th Infantry Division secured its bridgehead.

Heavier than normal rains had turned the river into a torrent, making it impossible for the engineers to keep their bridges intact. Five days later, the Moselle subsided enough to allow the 10th Armored Division to cross. Simultaneously, the 5th Infantry Division expanded its Arnaville bridgehead, threatening Metz from the south. Finally, the Third Army was making some tangible progress.

The infantry divisions of XX Corps now closed in on Metz; the 90th Infantry Division from the north, the 95th Infantry Division from the west and northwest, and the 5th Infantry Division from the south and southeast. Over the next two days, the Americans proved they had learned from their previous mistakes. German forts, which previously would have consumed U.S. strength in frontal assaults, were bypassed and eliminated afterward with demolitions. The first of Walker's troops entered Metz on 17 November.

Sensing the inevitable, Balck refused to throw any more of his scarce units into the meat grinder. In fact, he in effect disobeyed Adolf Hitler (q.v.) by withdrawing the remainder of his forces through the gap that existed in the American lines to the east until 19 November, leaving the Metz garrison to its fate. On that day, the 5th Infantry and 90th Infantry Divisions linked up east of the city, completing the encirclement. The 10th Armored Division, meanwhile, continued on to the Saar River

Patton entered Metz on 25 November. Some Germans, however, obeyed Hitler's "hold to the last man" order. Indeed, the XX Corps needed almost an entire month to subdue the outlying fortresses. After three months of fighting, the last fort, Jeanne d'Arc, finally fell on 13 December. The cost in American resources, especially time, had been great. With its lines of communication to the west now secure, Third Army turned east to its next objective, the Siegfried Line (q.v.).

Robert Kirchubel

Additional Reading

Balck, Hermann, *Ordnung im Chaos: Erinnerungen 1893–1948* (1981).

Cole, Hugh M., *The Lorraine Campaign* (1950).

Weigley, Russell F., *Eisenhower's Lieutenants: The Campaigns of France and Germany, 1944–1945* (1981).

MINCEMEAT, Operation (Spring 1943)

When World War II began, all sides saw the need for the use of deception as a part of military operations. Deception, however, is only worthwhile if it is integrated with the overall tactical, operational, or strategic planning. Any deception operation must complement other operations, and cannot stand alone.

Commanders, at whatever level the deception is employed, must be fully aware of the plan and approve it as part of the operation. Deception plans, especially at the strategic level, are usually complex, require in-depth planning, vigorous security measures, and careful execution. There is always a danger that a well-carried-out plan that was not approved and coordinated could very well backfire and cause confusion for those the plan was put in place to assist. Contrary to the popular view, the deception plans are not the product of eccentric and brilliant planners locked away from the mainstream of military operation planners. Isolation is a key to disaster.

One of the best planned, coordinated, and executed deception plans of World War II was Operation MINCEMEAT, or as it is more popularly known, "The Man Who Never Was." While Allied planners were putting the finishing touches on Operation TORCH, the invasion of Northwest Africa (q.v.) in 1942, officials decided to formulate plans for the next stage in the liberation of Europe, the invasion of Sicily. The Sicily (q.v.) operation would be the first step in the invasion of Italy.

Few Allied officers believed the invasion of Sicily would be easy, because the Germans and Italians would bitterly contest this first operation against Europe proper. Since the invasion would be a combined airborne/amphibious operation, there was great potential for disaster. The Germans had to be convinced that the Allies were not planning to land in Sicily, so they would not reinforce the large German and Italian garrisons there. Gaining time to get troops and equipment ashore and for the paratroops to secure drop zones and then move on to other objectives would be critical. Stiff resistance or an early counterattack could spell defeat.

The plan known as Operation MINCEMEAT rose out of this operational requirement. Lieutenant Commander Ewen Montagu (q.v.) was head of Section 17M of Royal Naval Intelligence, the department of the Admiralty in London that was directly concerned with strategic deception. Montagu had known since late September that the Spanish were passing information and classified materials to German *Abwehr* (q.v.) agents in Spain. Taking advantage of this knowledge, he proposed a daring and complex plan which, if successful, would give the German planners in Berlin a vast quantity of highly believable, but patently false information about the Allies' next move after the conclusion of the North African (q.v.) campaign.

Montagu's objective was to deceive the Germans regarding the actual landings in Sicily. To implement the plan, he and his staff decide to obtain a body, place misleading documents on the corpse, put it in waters off the Spanish coast, and then rely on the pro-German Spanish authorities to turn those documents over to German intelligence.

Operation MINCEMEAT was very complex, but once Montagu received permission to implement the plan, he began to assemble a group of experts, including Sir Bernard Spilsbury, one of Britain's leading pathologists, and the coroner of London, Bentley Purchase. Pledged to absolute secrecy, Spilsbury and Purchase assisted Montagu in obtaining the body of a young man who had recently (within hours) died of pneumonia. Pneumonia produced the exact same results as drowning, and Spilsbury was convinced that after several hours in the water, Spanish pathologists would be unable to tell the difference in cause of death.

Obtaining the body was difficult enough. Manufacturing an identity and creating proper documentation with real signatures was another problem. The cadaver was named Captain (brevet major) William Martin (q.v.), Royal Marines, and he was made a member of the staff of Lord Louis Mountbatten's Combined Operations (qq.v.) Headquarters. A major on such a staff would have access to highly classified material, and it would not be unreasonable to assume that a junior field grade officer would be used as courier for such materials.

While Martin's past life was carefully constructed (certainly *Abwehr* operatives would check on him in Britain), letters were drafted for Mountbatten's signature and for that of Sir Archibald Nye (q.v.), vice chief of the Imperial General Staff. These letters would spell out British intentions to make an assault on Greece (falsely code named HUSKY) and an assault on Sardinia (code named BRIMSTONE). The letters were written with numerous references to a landing in Sicily as only a deception to cover an actual assault on Sardinia. These letters appeared official, highly classified, and bore authentic signatures that would confuse German experts. The actual code name for the Sicily invasion was used in the letters to make the Germans think that any future intercepted references to HUSKY meant Greece.

Major Martin, now with a life story and highly sensitive documents, set sail on the British submarine *Seraph*. The body was packed in dry ice. Before dawn on 30 April 1943, the submarine commander took the body from the container and placed it in the currents off Huelva, Spain. Five hours later Martin washed up on shore, where the Spanish took possession of the cadaver. Immediately the *Abwehr* was alerted and copies of the documents were made. In a few days, Admiral Wilhelm Canaris (q.v.), chief of the *Abwehr,* and Adolf Hitler (q.v.) were examining these highly classified documents. The plan worked well so far, as no operative discovered that Major Martin really did not exist.

Hitler was already convinced that the British would make a try at some action in the Balkans, and the *Führer* decided that Operations HUSKY and BRIMSTONE were indeed legitimate operations. He began to reinforce the Balkans at the expense of Sicily and Italy. In Sicily, German Field Marshal Albert Kesselring (q.v.) commanded 300,000 Axis troops, some of doubtful quality. The most critical time for the amphibious and airborne assault on Sicily would be the first two to three days, while the beachheads were being established and the paratroops were moving from their drop zones. It was critical that the Germans counterattack immediately, but the deception plan worked. Troops earmarked for Sicily and southern Italy went elsewhere to counter a nonexistent Allied invasion.

Documents taken from Major Martin convinced the Germans that Greece was the likely place for the next invasion. Carefully placed hints and rumors in London and elsewhere tricked German agents into believing that they had corroboration for the freak venture. Hitler left two German divisions in Sicily but did not reinforce them. Coastal defenses in the north and west of Sicily, away from the actual landing sites, were strengthened. The *Führer* refused to be swayed from his conviction that Greece was the next Allied target. The invasion began on 10 July 1943. It took two weeks for the Germans to realize they had been tricked. By that time it was too late. The Allies were in Sicily to stay and to prepare for the next operation, the invasion of Italy proper.

Montagu, who was responsible for Operation MINCEMEAT, was awarded the Military OBE in 1944, and Major Martin, the "Man Who Never Was," was laid to rest with military honors in a quiet cemetery in Huelva, Spain. To this day, no one really knows who is interred under the tombstone that bears Martin's name.

Operation MINCEMEAT was a classic deception operation. It was a complex plan that supported the main Allied strategic and operational objectives. It was integrated into the entire plan for the invasion of Sicily, and it was understood by all of the commanders who needed to know. Operation MINCEMEAT was a prime example of successful deception planning and implementation forming an integral part of an overall strategic concept.

James J. Cooke

Additional Reading

Howard, Michael, *British Intelligence in the Second World War.* Vol. 5: *Strategic Deception* (1990).

Montagu, Ewen, *Beyond Top Secret Ultra* (1978).

——, *The Man Who Never Was* (1953).

Minsk (27 June–9 July 1941)

Hitler's *Führer* Directive 21, *Fall* BARBAROSSA, required an especially strong concentration of armored and motorized units with Army Group Center in order to enable it to destroy the Soviet forces in Byelorussia. The Germans considered the destruction of these troops as the prerequisite for the follow-on attacks against Leningrad and Moscow (qq.v.). Consequently, operation plans issued by German Army headquarters (OKH) in January 1941 allocated two of the four available *Panzer* groups to Army Group Center.

On the eve of the attack, Army Group Center, commanded by Field Marshal Fedor von Bock (q.v.), consisted of three field armies and the two *Panzer* groups. The southern wing of the army group was held by General Günther von Kluge's (q.v.) Fourth Army, with twenty-one infantry divisions, and General Heinz Guderian's (q.v.) Second *Panzer* Group, with one cavalry, five *Panzer,* and three *Panzergrenadier* divisions. That wing conducted its attack just north of the Pripet marshes, the boundary between Army Groups Center and South.

In the northern wing of Army Group Center, General Adolf Strauss's Ninth Army, with twelve infantry divisions, and General Hermann Hoth's (q.v.) Third *Panzer* Group, with four *Panzer* and four *Panzergrenadier* divisions, attacked out of the Suwalki bend in East Prussia. General Maximilliam von Weichs's (q.v.) Second Army was held in OKH general reserve, behind von Bock's second echelon. The entire effort in the center was supported by General Albert Kesselring's (q.v.) Second *Luftflotte.* With a strength of approximately 1,000 aircraft, it was the largest of the German air fleets deployed in the east.

The Soviets had strong forces in the sector opposing Army Group Center. General Dimitry Pavlov's (q.v.) Soviet Western Front consisted of four armies. Three of those armies, the Third, Fourth, and Tenth, were positioned in the Białystok salient, which protruded far west of the border at Suwalki and Brest-Litovsk. It proved to be a trap for the bulk of Pavlov's troops. The Soviet Thirteenth Army was located farther to the east near Minsk. All Soviet armies had motorized corps. Additional corps were held in frontal level reserve. In combat strength the attackers and the defenders were about evenly matched. In materiel the Soviets even had a slight numerical advantage.

Initially, Hoth's attack hit the Soviet Eleventh Army, a Northwestern Front unit. The real German purpose, however, was to penetrate into the rear of Western Front and link up with the southern wing of Army Group Center. During the first days of the war, the progress of Hoth's northern Third *Panzer* Group suffered from the very difficult and sandy terrain. Only a few roads suitable for vehicles passed through the vast forests east of Suwalki. Forest fires, Soviet resistance, and traffic jams led to the slow advance of XXXIX *Korps* and VII *Panzer Korps.* It was not until midday on 23 June that the Germans reached the bridges over the river Nemen, fifty kilometers from the border.

The Soviets tried to launch counterattacks against the advancing Germans north of Białystok. The 7th *Panzer* Division was hit by the Soviet 5th Tank Division, which crossed the Nemen on 23 June. On 24 June, parts of the Soviet II Mechanized Corps, under General Ivan Boldin, deputy commander of the Western Front, attacked infantry units of the German Ninth Army south of Grodno. Both attacks were beaten off easily. The Soviets were unable to launch coordinated attacks at that time because of a lack of communications combined with the destructive effects of *Luftwaffe* attacks against their troop columns. After crossing the Nemen, Hoth's troops gained momentum. On 24 June, the 7th *Panzer* Division captured Wilna, and four days later Hoth's and Guderian's forces linked up near Minsk, cutting off the supply lines to the Western Front.

South of Białystok, the Germans crossed the Bug River and captured the old fortress of Brest. The Soviets, caught by surprise, failed to destroy the bridges, which permitted the rapid advance of Guderian's Second *Panzer* Group toward Slonim and Minsk. In Brest, however, the attackers received a foretaste of the fanatic resistance that later became commonplace in Russia. Parts of two rifle divisions and a force of NKVD (q.v.) troops defended the citadel of Brest for more than a week, causing heavy German casualties.

Guderian's armored units, XXIV *Panzer Korps,* XLVI *Panzer Korps,* and XLVII *Panzer Korps,* bypassed Brest and attacked the Soviet Fourth Army, driving its shattered remnants eastward into the Pripet marshes. Operating on much better terrain than Hoth's units, Guderian's tanks reached Kobrin, sixty kilometers from the line of departure, on the first day of the war. On 24 June, Slonim fell. On 27 June, the Soviets were forced to give up Bobruysk, about 350 kilometers away from where Guderian's tanks had started.

When his units were attacked on the left flank by Soviet troops trying to escape eastward, Guderian ordered the XLVI and XLVII *Panzer Korps* to swing north and link up with Hoth's forces. Guderian preferred to advance as far as Smolensk, thereby closing the armored pincers 300 kilometers farther to the east. Hoth and von Bock favored this option, too, and some of the OKH staff were willing to consider it. The Germans at that time held the clear superiority in mobile warfare. Making a bold thrust to Smolensk and preventing the Soviets from building new defenses along the Dnieper and Dvina Rivers were what the field commanders wanted to do.

Adolf Hitler (q.v.), however, favored a more shallow envelopment. He was particularly concerned about overextending the flanks of the *Panzer* groups, and warned about what he saw as a dangerous gap forming between armored spearheads and the comparatively slow-moving infantry. In the end, Hoth and Guderian were ordered to meet at Minsk, but they were given permission to send some of their troops eastward to establish bridgeheads on the eastern bank of the Dnieper and Dvina. Army chief of staff General Franz Halder (q.v.) issued the order for the Minsk option, but he personally hoped the *Panzer* commanders would ignore the order and send the larger part of their forces deep into the east. After the battle, Hitler criticized both Hoth and Guderian for having used too many of their troops for the chase to the rivers. From that point mistrust between the top levels of the German leadership and some of the field commanders grew, and direct interference by Hitler into field operations steadily increased.

For the Soviets, a coordinated defense was nearly impossible. Western Front headquarters was getting very little intelligence and it lost most of its communications equipment on the first day of the war. Soviet troop morale was mixed at best. Some units, like the defenders of Brest, fought to the last. Elsewhere, the larger part of three infantry divisions simply deserted to the Germans. Pavlov, probably because of his lack of intelligence, made the Soviet situation worse with two critical tactical errors. On 24 June, he ordered his reserves forward from the Minsk area in order to attack the German troops near Grodno. By doing this he stripped Minsk of its defenders and brought even more Soviet troops into what later became a huge pocket. The next day, with the direct route between Białystok and Minsk already cut by the XLVII *Panzer Korps,* Pavlov delayed the withdrawal of the Soviet Third and Tenth Armies.

On 27 June, the Soviet Thirteenth Army, which had just arrived near Minsk, was hit by a coordinated attack from divisions of both Guderian's and Hoth's *Panzer* groups. When the Germans closed the pocket near the Byelorussian capital, most of Thirteenth Army's units were trapped. Only the XLV Rifle Corps escaped to the east. At the same time, infantry units of the German Fourth and Ninth Armies linked up 100 kilometers east of Białystok, splitting the envelopment into a westerly pocket near Białystok and an easterly one in the Novogrudok area. The *Stavka* (q.v.) learned about this double envelopment on 30 June from German radio intercepts. Pavlov and most of his staff were recalled to Moscow, court-martialed, and executed.

Within the two pockets the fighting raged for another few days. German infantry units clearing the area suffered an unexpectedly high number of casualties, and armored divisions lost several days screening the encirclements against Soviet troops trying to escape. By 3 July, the Białystok pocket was virtually cleared, but not until 9 July was the fighting in the Novogrudok area completed. Nevertheless, a considerable number of Soviets managed to escape through the German lines. Others just vanished into the forests and formed partisan (q.v.) groups in the German rear.

The battle of Minsk was a clear success for the *Wehrmacht.* According to German sources, the Red Army lost 323,898 prisoners, 1,809 guns, and 3,332 tanks. That was approximately as many tanks as the Germans had when they started the war against the Soviet Union. The defenders were taken completely by surprise, even though the Soviet political leadership in Moscow had received many indicators of an impending attack prior to 22 June.

One of the keys to the battle was German air superiority. From the first day, Kesselring's air fleet virtually cleared the skies of the Soviet Air Force. Another factor was the superior tactical leadership of the battle-tested German Army. The battle of Minsk, however, did indicate a few serious problems on the German side. The western Soviet terrain had proved less suited for mobile warfare than the rest of Europe, and the infrastructure of the Soviet Union (even in its more westerly areas) was completely inadequate. The attackers also recognized the difficulties that arose from the differing march speeds of infantry and armored units. Finally, the German Army would also have to face growing interference by Hitler in combat operations. Relations between the *Führer* and the field commanders took a nose dive, leading to troops frequently receiving contradicting orders.

Josef Stalin (q.v.), whose own incompetence helped to make the disaster even worse, tried to shift the blame by executing not only Pavlov, but also General A.A. Korobkov, the Fourth Army commander, and General I.S. Kosobutsky, the XL. Rifle Corps commander. Both had managed to escape from the Minsk pocket.

On 1 July, well before the end of the battle, Halder ordered Army Group Center's two *Panzer* groups to resume their eastward attacks by 3 July. Their new objective was Smolensk (q.v.).

Reiner Martin

Additional Reading

Erikson, John, *Stalin's War with Germany,* 2 vols. (1983).
Seaton, Albert, *The Russo-German War 1941–45* (1971).
Ziemke, Earl F., and Magna E. Bauer, *Moscow to Stalingrad: Decision in the East* (1987).

Monte Cassino (1 February–18 May 1944)

[See map 1 on page 1311]

In the winter of 1943, General Sir Harold Alexander's (q.v.) 15th Army Group resumed its march on Rome. It soon encountered the formidable German defenses, the Winter Line or Gustav Line (q.v.). A hundred miles south of Rome and ten miles deep, this German defensive belt ran from the mouth of the Garigliano River on the Gulf of Gaeta, along its tributary, the Rapido, to the Adriatic Sea north of the Sangro River. The line was held by the German Tenth Army, commanded by General Heinrich von Vietinghoff-Scheel (q.v.). Although General Mark Clark's (q.v.) Fifth Army attacked it and registered some progress, resistance was tenacious, and terrain difficulties, constant rain or snow, and a morass of mud produced a stalemate by year's end.

Given Field Marshal Albert Kesselring's (q.v.) location of the defensive zone, it was inevitable that Cassino, a town of 25,000, and Monte Cassino would be its hub. Cassino was astride Route 6, the principal road from Naples to Rome (eighty miles to the north) through the Liri Valley. Von Vietinghoff said that it was impossible to exclude the high ground of Monte Cassino.

Defense of the immediate Cassino area fell to the XIV *Panzer Korps* commanded by General Frido von Senger und Etterlin (q.v.), an outstanding commander. Monte Cassino itself was held by the tough, elite German 1st Parachute Division, commanded by General Richard Heidenrich.

Dominating Cassino town was Monte Cassino. At the top of this 1,700-foot tall peak, the last bastion of the Apennine Mountains, was the great monastery founded by St. Benedict in the year 529. Regarded as the mother of all Christian monasteries, it was destroyed many times over the centuries but repeatedly rebuilt. A powerful structure, its walls were fifteen feet thick. During the early Middle Ages, the monastery preserved much of the West's written archives. Itself a work of art, it also housed countless artistic treasures, some sent there expressly for wartime safekeeping.

Allied troops stalled in the freezing mud of the valley below Monte Cassino became obsessed by the abbey. Easily observed by the Germans from the heights, the Allies were absolutely certain their enemy was using the monastery as an observation post. Soldiers reported seeing a telescope there and a German tank on its approaches. An Italian civilian said there were machine guns and some German soldiers in the building. On 13 February, General Ira C. Eaker, head of the Mediterranean Allied Air Forces, flew with General Jacob Devers

(qq.v.) several hundred feet above the monastery. They reported both a radio mast and troops moving in and out of the building.

The Germans were definitely entrenched farther down the slopes below the monastery, but they denied their troops were using the building. The German ambassador to the Vatican, Baron Ernst von Weizsäcker (q.v.), even issued a statement saying that there were no troop concentrations of any size "within its immediate vicinity." After the bombing, Kesselring declared the charge that German troops were in the monastery "a baseless invention." Von Senger also denied it. Documentary proof of orders by Kesselring and von Senger supports their claims. Nevertheless, it also must be pointed out that by enclosing the monastery hill within their defensive perimeter, the Germans exposed the building to inevitable attack.

In any case, the Germans were able to call down highly accurate artillery fire on Allied troops in the valley. One Royal Artillery lieutenant who arrived at Cassino in early February noted in his diary: "One trained gunnery officer with binoculars could control nearly the whole battlefield by directing shell and mortar fire within a matter of seconds." There was hardly an Allied soldier who did not believe the Germans were in the monastery.

In February 1944, troops of the U.S. 34th and 36th Infantry Divisions of the Fifth Army attacked at Cassino. They managed to entrench themselves precariously in positions on high ground northeast of the monastery that took seven hours to reach by mule. Their assault, known as the first battle of Cassino, was repulsed by 11 February. When relieved by the Indian 4th Division, the two U.S. divisions were down to just 20 percent of effective strength. The task of breaking the German line then fell to the New Zealand Corps, commanded by Lieutenant General Sir Bernard C. Freyberg (q.v.). He insisted on a preliminary aerial bombardment of the monastery.

In mid-February, there were perhaps 800 people in the monastery seeking refuge. Five monks also remained. Conditions were desperate; food and water were in short supply and typhoid had broken out. On 14 February, the Allies dropped leaflets warning that the monastery would be bombed. It ended with: "Our warning is urgent: leave the Monastery. Abandon it at once." There is some disagreement about why there was no immediate departure. The monks said that fighting precluded it and that the Germans agreed that everyone would leave early on the morning of 16 February; but some survivors subsequently

M

Rear view of the ruined Monte Cassino Monastery after it finally fell to Polish troops. Photo taken 19 May 1944. (IWM NA 15141)

reported the Germans prevented them from leaving. Certainly the time between the leaflet drop and the bombing was very short. This was because the Allies did not want to give the Germans time to move out equipment presumed to be in the monastery.

Just before 0930 hours on 15 February 1944, the first wave of 144 B-17 Flying Fortresses converged on the monastery. It was the first time that heavy bombers were used in such close support of infantry. They were followed later in the day by eighty-six B-26 Marauder medium bombers. The planes dropped more than 450 tons of explosives on the monastery. Their bombs killed about 300 people and destroyed the basilica, frescoes of Luca Giordano, seventeenth-century choir stalls, the baroque organ, and the high altar. The destruction was not complete; somehow the tombs of St. Benedict and his sister, St. Scolastica, survived.

Fortunately, the loss was not as great as it might have been. In October 1943, Colonel Julius Schlegel of the Hermann Göring *Panzer* Division had persuaded Abbot Diamare to let the abbey's treasures be removed. These included the reliquary of St. Benedict and the famous library, as well as priceless bronze statues from Rome and Pompeii sent there for safekeeping. Soldiers of the Hermann Göring *Panzer* Division took the art work to German headquarters at Spoleto. Later, it was sent to the Vatican. In the process, however, the Germans diverted eighteen cases of bronzes and jewelry to Germany as a present for Göring. Schlegel also, on his own initiative, persuaded Diamare to allow the evacuation of most of the monks and civilian refugees then at the monastery.

The bombing of Monte Cassino stunned the Roman Catholic world and provided a propaganda windfall for the Germans. It was indeed ironic that the Allies had destroyed an emblem of the very civilization they were fighting to save. Kesselring announced: "United States soldiery, devoid of all culture, have, in powerless rage, senselessly destroyed one of Italy's most treasured edifices and have murdered Italian civilian refugees—men, women, and children—with their bombs and artillery fire. Thus it has been proved that Anglo-Saxon and Bolshevik warfare has only one aim: to destroy the venerable proofs of European culture."

Was the bombing a mistake? Clark argued against it, but in the end he gave the order. Well after the event he wrote, "I say the bombing . . . was a mistake, and I say it with full knowledge of the controversy that has raged round this episode." Clark said there was no evidence the Germans were using the monastery as an observation post, but that he was told that Alexander had decided the monastery should be bombed if Freyberg demanded it.

Freyberg considered the monastery bombing a military necessity, and Clark, as army commander, had no choice but to give the authorization. Clark said: "I was never able to discover on what he [Freyberg] based his opinion." His critics later charged that Clark, a Roman Catholic, wanted to avoid responsibility by shifting the blame. After all, it was Clark who argued for a frontal assault. In contrast to Clark, Alexander never sought to avoid responsibility for the decision.

The amphibious landing at Anzio (q.v.) was another factor. The situation on the beachhead was precipitous, and success on the Gustav Line would preclude it from becoming another Gallipoli. This was ironic because Anzio was conceived as a means of breaking the deadlock to the south.

Knowing that his troops would soon replace the Americans before Cassino, Major General Frank Tuker, commander of the Indian 4th Infantry Division attached to the New Zealanders and an expert on mountain warfare, conferred with French General Alphonse Juin (q.v.), considered by many the top Allied tactical commander in Italy. They agreed the best way to exert pressure on the German defenders was to flank Cassino well to the north, followed by a river crossing to the south. Both strongly opposed a frontal assault but agreed that if this had to be done it should be preceded by a massive air bombardment.

Unfortunately, Tuker was ill when the decision for the bombing was made. If he had not been away from his command, he might have talked Clark out of the direct attack that forced the bombing. Bombing the monastery failed to turn the battle in favor of the Allies. If anything, it was a defensive bonanza for the Germans. As soon as the attack was over, they occupied the rubble, although almost immediately they were subjected to another bombing attack by fifty-nine fighter bombers dropping another twenty-three tons of bombs.

The destruction of the monastery made no difference to the outcome of the second battle of Cassino (15–19 February). It had, in fact, been hurried before a major German counterattack could occur at Anzio (it took place on 16 February) and because rain was imminent. It happened so soon after the replacement of the American divisions that the New Zealanders had no time to make a proper reconnaissance. In fact, the main infantry attack did not occur until three days after the bombing. The 2nd Gurkhas reached a ridge 300 yards from the rear walls of the monastery, but their position was helpless and they were withdrawn on the morning of 19 February. New Zealanders, who attacked from south of Cassino town, managed to reach the railroad station before they, too, were driven back across the Rapido by intense German fire.

A massive Allied bombing of Cassino made no difference in what is known as the third battle of Cassino (15–25 March). This Allied air raid was followed by a heavy artillery barrage. New Zealand troops then entered the town's ruins, but poor communication, caused in part by sheets of rain, stalled their drive.

It was essential to the Allies that the battle around Cassino be won before the Normandy (q.v.) invasion. Eaker's Mediterranean Allied Air Forces undertook an interdiction campaign (Operation STRANGLE) to cut supplies to the German forces south of Rome, while a masterful Allied deception feigning an amphibious attack north of Rome led Kesselring to weaken the Gustav Line. As a result, by May 1944, Allied troops there enjoyed a three to one advantage in men. They employed 2,000 guns in an assault that began on 11 May. In Operation DIADEM, British, Canadian, French, Polish, and U.S. units smashed through a twenty-mile zone between Cassino and the sea. The Poles occupied the monastery on 18 May, shortly after the Germans abandoned it. At the same time, the Allies broke out from the beachhead at Anzio on 23 May.

Kesselring regrouped north of Rome and declared it an open city. Alexander ordered VI Corps from the Anzio beachhead to cut off Tenth Army's retreat, but Clark wanted Rome and thought the plan a ruse by Alexander to let the British Eighth Army take Rome first. After the Anzio breakout, Clark changed the direction of the thrust from Anzio so that Americans might liberate the Eternal City. This decision, which dumbfounded his subordinates, allowed the German Tenth Army to escape from the Gustav Line to what became the Gothic Line (q.v.) in the north. The fighting in Italy would continue. In the fighting for Cassino the Allies suffered 4,100 dead and 16,000 wounded.

The bombing of Monte Cassino monastery

was the most controversial Allied decision of the Italian campaign. Recriminations concerning it continue to this day. It has been called everything from a tragic mistake to a war crime. The monastery was rebuilt after the war and was reconsecrated by Pope Paul VI in 1964.

Spencer C. Tucker

Additional Reading

Böhmler, Rudolf, *Monte Cassino* (1964).

D'Este, Carlo, *Fatal Decision: Anzio and the Battle for Rome* (1991).

Graham, Dominick, and Shelford Bidwell, *Tug of War: The Battle for Italy: 1943–45* (1986).

Hapgood, David, and David Richardson, *Monte Cassino* (1984).

Majdalany, Fred, *Cassino, Portrait of a Battle* (1957).

Senger und Etterlin, Frido von, *Neither Fear nor Hope* (1960).

Trevelyan, Raleigh, *Rome '44* (1982).

Mortain (7–11 August 1944)

After the Allies broke out at St. Lô (q.v.), they started pushing the German Army back to the Seine River. Adolf Hitler (q.v.) was determined to reverse this situation. On 2 August 1944, he ordered Field Marshal Günther von Kluge (q.v.), commander of German Army Group B, to mount a strong armored counterattack to take Avranches on the coast. Hitler wanted von Kluge to use eight of the nine *Panzer* divisions in the Vire-Mortain area.

The *Führer* expected this armored force would drive to the sea and isolate General George S. Patton's (q.v.) newly activated U.S. Third Army in the Brittany peninsula. Hitler's grandiose scheme, however, created an operational dilemma for German military commanders in the west. If the attack failed, the resulting chaos and overextension of forces would make it virtually impossible for the German forces to withdraw across the Seine River in any semblance of order.

Von Kluge was ordered to mount the attack immediately. Because he thought it would take too long to assemble and prepare all eight *Panzer* divisions, he planned an attack with only four. Three would create the penetration, and the fourth would pass through the gap and take Avranches. Hitler learned of the plans for the reduced attack one day before the scheduled jump-off. He objected that the force was not strong enough to accomplish the mission he had given von Kluge. Grudgingly, however, Hitler allowed the attack to continue.

The attack began without artillery preparation shortly after midnight on 7 August. The operation was under the control of Lieutenant General Hans von Funck's XLVII *Panzer Korps,* with the 116th *Panzer* Division on the right, the 2nd *Panzer* Division in the center, and the 2nd SS *Panzer* Division on the left. The 1st SS *Panzer* Division followed, prepared to exploit the breakthrough. The total attack force actually numbered about 200 tanks. The attack struck at the boundary between U.S. VII Corps and XV Corps, which also was the boundary between the First and Third Armies. The brunt of the assault fell on the 30th Infantry Division.

The 2nd SS *Panzer* Division quickly took Mortain and then started moving toward Avranches. The *Panzers* ran into trouble, however, when they tried to go around the high ground outside the city. Hill 317 was held by 30th Infantry Division's 2nd Battalion, 120th Infantry Regiment. The Germans overran the battalion command post and captured the command group, but the main body of the battalion held out on the hill. From that position they had an almost perfect field of observation.

Captain Reynold C. Erichson assumed command of the battalion. For five days they held Hill 317, calling in air strikes and artillery fire on the Germans. The 2nd SS *Panzer* Division repeatedly tried to sweep the Americans off the hill. At first the Allies tried to resupply the battalion by air, but ground fire from the Germans was too intense to allow pilots to get low enough to make the drops. Then American artillery units took projectiles designed to deliver propaganda leaflets, replaced the leaflets with bandages and morphine, and fired the medical supplies into the battalion's position over the heads of the Germans. By the time the battle was over, half of the battalion's 600 soldiers were killed or wounded, but Allied control of Hill 317 had seriously hurt the Germans.

The other arms of the German attack experienced trouble as well. Allied top leadership had expected some sort of attack, learning of it through ULTRA (q.v.) intercepts. The commander of the 12th Army Group, General Omar N. Bradley (q.v.), positioned his forces in depth to deal with such an attack. Over the course of the next several days, Bradley fed elements of 4th Infantry, 2nd Armored, 3rd Armored, and 35th Infantry Divisions into the battle. The top Allied commanders, in fact, hoped to draw out the battle. The German *Panzer* units tied down at Mortain would be unable to interfere with Allied efforts to encircle the German Seventh Army by closing the pincers of a large-scale double envelopment near Falaise (q.v.).

By the evening of 7 August, Allied airpower managed to knock out forty of the seventy German tanks that penetrated the American lines. Von Kluge wanted to withdraw his forces, but Hitler, characteristically, insisted on continuing the attack. At first, a renewed offensive was scheduled for 9 August. That date slipped when the Germans began to realize what was happening to them around Falaise.

On 11 August, von Kluge met with the Seventh Army commander, SS General Paul Hausser (q.v.). Together they decided that they had no alternative but to withdraw the *Panzers* from the Mortain area to oppose the Allied thrust toward Falaise. Hitler finally agreed, and the *Panzers* withdrew on the night of 11 August—too late already to help large segments of Seventh Army.

What if von Kluge had used all eight *Panzer* divisions? The Germans just might have made it to Avranches. Even if the twelve U.S. divisions south of the Avranches bottleneck had been cut off, however, the Allies had plans to resupply them by air with 2,000 tons per day. Allied air superiority would guarantee the supplies got through. Once the Germans reached Avranches, there would have been very little they could have accomplished there. American armor and artillery support in the area were so strong that it would have been only a matter of time before the *Panzers* themselves were cut off.

In the end, the Mortain attack was just another in a long line of Hitler's half-baked military schemes that did more than anything else to assure German defeat.

David T. Zabecki

Additional Reading

Blumenson, Martin, *Breakout and Pursuit* (1961).

Featherston, Alwyn, *Saving the Breakout: The 30th Division's Heroic Stand at Mortain, August 7–12, 1944* (1944).

Mason, David, *Breakout: Drive to the Seine* (1968).

Weigley, Russell F., *Eisenhower's Lieutenants: The Campaigns of France and Germany, 1944–45* (1981).

Moscow (2 October 1941–February 1942)
[See map 35 on page 1345]
The battle for Moscow actually was a series of separate engagements that took place over several months across a front 250 miles wide and 180 miles deep. These widely separated actions pitted sixty-nine divisions of German Army Group Center against fifteen ill-equipped Soviet armies (500,000 troops). As Operation *TAIFUN* (TYPHOON) rolled eastward starting on 2 October 1941, Soviet authorities became increasingly alarmed. On 10 October, the Soviet government formally announced its decision to defend the city against the Germans.

Aside from its psychological and historical significance as the Soviet capital, Moscow was an obvious target for other reasons. As a minor industrial city, Moscow was home to numerous armament plants and it also was the hub of the Soviet rail network east of the Ural Mountains. In the developing battle for Moscow, each side had advantages. The Germans had the initiative and numerical superiority. The Soviets had the advantages of dense forests (which impeded mechanized movement) in front of Moscow, ever-decreasing hours of daylight for the Germans to maneuver, and shorter supply lines. The German advance also was impeded by an extremely primitive Soviet communications infrastructure.

On the right of Army Group Center, General Heinz Guderian's (q.v.) Second *Panzer* Group took Orel on 8 October, and Chern on 24 October. The Second *Panzer* Group and General Maximilian von Weichs's (q.v.) Second Army also trapped and destroyed three Soviet armies at Bryansk between 6 and 20 October. In the center, General Hermann Hoth's (q.v.) Third *Panzer* Group and General Erich Hoepner's (q.v.) Fourth *Panzer* Group encircled Vyazma, killing or capturing 600,000 Soviet troops (*see* Vyazma-Bryansk). The Third *Panzer* Group took Kalinin on 15 October. With General Günther von Kluge's (q.v.) Fourth Army only forty miles from Moscow, it seemed certain that Army Group Center would be able to conquer the capital easily.

By 28 October, however, most of the German attacks toward Moscow ground to a halt in the soft and muddy ground. With the onset of winter weather and the hardening of the ground, Operation *TAIFUN* resumed on 15 November. Only six Soviet armies stood between Army Group Center and its objective, but the farther the German forces advanced, the more costly Operation *TAIFUN* became. The German *Panzers* had unexpectedly met their match in the Soviet T-34, with its sloped armor, powerful main gun, high speed, and wide tracks for increased mobility in mud and snow.

Meanwhile, the southern advance of Guder-

M

ian's Second *Panzer* Group stalled before Tula and Kashira. That left Hoepner's Fourth *Panzer* Group and von Kluge's Fourth Army to make a frontal assault on the capital. By 2 December a battalion of the 2nd *Panzer* Division was able to push patrols into Khimki, less than twenty miles from the Kremlin. Several field commanders recommended holding in place for the winter, but Field Marshal Fedor von Bock (q.v.), commander of Army Group Center, responded that per Adolf Hitler's (q.v.) directive, the offensive would continue. Finally, on 5 December, in the face of increasingly stout Soviet resistance, Hitler halted the offensive and ordered Army Group Center into defensive positions for the winter. To that point, Operation *TAIFUN* had advanced less than 100 miles, had incurred 250,000 casualties, and had depleted Army Group Center's tank strength by two-thirds.

Based on information provided to Josef Stalin (q.v.) by his agent in Tokyo, Richard Sorge (q.v.), that Japan was preparing for war against the United States rather than the Soviet Union, the Soviet leader ordered the deployment west of thirty well-equipped, winter-trained Siberian divisions. By early December, General Georgy Zhukov (q.v.) had 578,000 troops defending the capital. His plan was simple and straightforward—cut off the German salients north and south of Moscow and then encircle and destroy Army Group Center.

On 5–6 December 1941, the Soviets counterattacked along a 600-mile front, running from 100 miles south of Leningrad to Kursk, 250 miles south of Moscow. Although the Soviet forces were unable to achieve their objectives and decisively defeat Army Group Center, Moscow, and probably the entire Soviet Union, was saved. Furthermore, by the end of December, Soviet forces had recaptured much of the territory lost since October. Enraged by the perceived failure of his subordinates, Hitler replaced nearly forty army, corps, and division commanders during a five-day period. Guderian was relieved of his command on 26 December, and Hoepner was relieved on 8 January. Germany thus was condemned to enter 1942 with an unfinished two-front war.

On 5 January, Stalin, shunning the cautious advice of Zhukov to concentrate only on Army Group Center, ordered a renewal of the Soviet offensive along a 1,000-mile front, from Lake Lagoda in the north to the Black Sea in the south. Stalin planned to trap major elements of Army Group Center, which controlled the key road and rail network around Vyazma, in a pincer movement. Zhukov's Western Front, spearheaded by Lieutenant General Mikhail Yefremov's Thirty-third Army, drove due west to Vyazma. The Twenty-second, Thirty-ninth, and Twenty-ninth Armies of General Ivan Konev's (q.v.) Kalinin Front attacked from the north in an effort to trap the Fourth *Panzer* Army (the *Panzer* Groups were redesignated *Panzer* Armies) and the Ninth Army in a pocket.

Although momentum favored the Soviet counterattack, their forces were severely depleted from the fall campaigns. In contrast, the German troops had withdrawn to a series of well-supplied and well-fortified towns—Demyansk, Rzhev, Vyazma, Bryansk, Orel, and Kursk. Soviet forces nearly encircled the German II *Korps* at Demyansk. Kept alive by means of an airlift, the II *Korps* was not relieved until the last week of April 1942.

By 27 January 1942, the Soviet Twenty-ninth Army nearly reached the Minsk-Smolensk-Moscow road, trapping General Walther Model's (q.v.) Ninth Army. Model counterattacked, however, killing 27,000 Soviet soldiers. In early February, Yefremov's forces reached the outskirts of Vyazma. An attempt to close the pocket with a parachute assault of 7,000 Soviet troops in mid-month was a disastrous failure and the Soviet offensive stalled. Soviet troops started to suffer from shortages of food, ammunition, and warm clothes. German forces, meanwhile, created a 300-mile-long solid defensive line, from Rzhev in the north to Vyazma, Bryansk, and Orel in the south. In late March, Yefremov attempted once more to break through the German lines. Yefremov failed to retake Vyazma, and he and his forces were surrounded. Severely wounded and facing imminent capture, Yefremov shot himself.

Although the first Soviet counteroffensive of the war proved abortive, the fighting around Moscow cost the Germans 500,000 dead and wounded, with 1,300 tanks, 2,500 guns, and 15,000 vehicles either destroyed or captured. Soviet losses probably were twice as high, but Moscow was saved, and 11,000 Soviet towns and villages were liberated. Soviet forces pushed the front ninety to 180 miles westward, and the German assault prompted the creation of Soviet partisan (q.v.) forces that continued to snipe away at the *Wehrmacht's* rear areas throughout the war. Perhaps most significantly, Soviet forces stalled the German advance, and dealt a severe blow to the myth of German invincibility.

David A. Foy

Additional Reading

Erickson, John, *The Road to Stalingrad* (1975).

Jukes, Geoffrey, *The Defense of Moscow* (1970).

Piekalkiewicz, Janusz, *Moscow 1941: The Frozen Offensive* (1985).

Seaton, Albert, *The Battle for Moscow, 1941–42* (1971).

Turney, Alfred, *Disaster at Moscow* (1971).

Ziemke, Earl, F. and Magna E. Bauer, *Moscow to Stalingrad, Decision in the East* (1987).

M

N

Nancy (5–29 September 1944)

In the late summer of 1944, the American drive across France ground to a halt because of shortages of supplies and especially gasoline. Lieutenant General George S. Patton's (q.v.) U.S. Third Army stopped shortly after crossing the Meuse River on 31 August. After a delay of several days, fuel supplies increased to the point where the Third Army could start moving again. On 4 September, Patton ordered Major General Manton Eddy's (q.v.) XII Corps to seize the city of Nancy and prepare for an exploitation to the Rhine River.

On 5 September, Eddy's 80th Infantry Division attempted to cross the Moselle River at Dieulouard, north of Nancy. The attack was repulsed by the 3rd *Panzergrenadier* Division. Eddy then decided to take the city from the south with his 35th Infantry Division and 4th Armored Division. Major General John S. Wood (q.v.), commander of the 4th Armored Division, objected to the plan because the southern approach would require his unit to cross not only the Moselle, but six other tributaries and canals. Wood pointed out that even though the Germans might be stronger in the north, the Moselle was the only water barrier on that approach.

Based on Wood's objections, Eddy modified the corps plan of attack. He still had the 35th Infantry Division and the 4th Armored Division's Combat Command B (CCB) making the main effort from the south, but the 80th Infantry Division also would make another attempt from the north. The 4th Armored Division's Combat Command A (CCA), commanded by Colonel Bruce C. Clarke (q.v.), would be held in corps reserve to exploit success on either wing.

The XII Corps crossed the Moselle against stiff opposition on 11 September. The 35th Infantry Division and 4th Armored Division's CCB made slow progress against elements of 553rd *Volksgrenadier* and 15th *Panzergrenadier* Divisions. It took CCB three days to work its way to the Marne-Rhine Canal, where it had to wait another two days because of insufficient bridging equipment. By that time, Wood had already committed his CCA to the north of Nancy.

Late on 12 September, CCA reached the bridgehead at Dieulouard that the 80th Infantry Division had established that day. That night, the bridgehead was counterattacked by units of the 3rd *Panzergrenadier* Division. Elements of CCA crossed the bridge and broke up the attack. The next day, Clarke decided to send the main body of CCA across the Dieulouard bridgehead, despite the heavy German presence on the opposite bank. The lead unit across was the 37th Tank Battalion, commanded by Lieutenant Colonel Crieghton Abrams (q.v.).

Rather than defending the bridgehead, CCA drove deep into the German rear. By 1700 hours on 13 September, CCA reached the outskirts of Château-Salins, some twenty miles from their starting point. In the process, CCA destroyed twelve German tanks and eighty-five other vehicles, and captured 354 prisoners. CCA's losses were twelve dead and sixteen wounded. The following day, CCA bypassed the town of Château-Salins and continued to drive deep into the German rear, cutting their lines of communications to Nancy.

Late on 14 September, CCA reached Arracourt, fifteen miles east of Nancy and just across the Marne-Rhine Canal from CCB. During the day's advance, CCA destroyed another twenty-six German armored vehicles and 136 other vehicles, and captured 400 more prisoners. CCA's losses for the day were thirty-three casualties and two tanks. Late that evening, reconnaissance patrols of CCA and CCB established contact with each other, completing the double envelopment of Nancy.

Starting on the morning of 15 September, CCA started a four-day campaign of destruction behind the German lines. CCB crossed the Marne-Rhine Canal the next day. The series of raids and ambushes around Arracourt cost the Germans another 1,000 prisoners and 240 vehicles destroyed. With its communications cut, the 553rd *Volksgrenadier* Division withdrew from Nancy. Against little opposition, the 35th Infantry Division occupied the city on 15 September.

The Germans, meanwhile, were increasing the pressure on the 80th Infantry Division's bridgehead at Dieulouard. The Fifth *Panzer* Army, commanded by General Hasso von Manteuffel (q.v.), also was massing to attack into the XII Corps' right flank. At 0800 hours on 19 September, the 113th *Panzer* Brigade hit CCA at Arracourt. The fighting that started in the morning fog lasted all day. By the time it was over, the Germans had lost fifty tanks.

Between 20 and 25 September, CCA was subjected to a string of piecemeal attacks from the 111th *Panzer* Brigade and the 11th *Panzer* Division. On 24 September, the 559th *Volksgrenadier* Division attacked CCB near Château-Salins. The Germans almost overran the American positions until they were driven off by fighter bombers from XIX Tactical Air Command. The following day, the U.S. Third Army was ordered to suspend its offensive operations. The 35th Infantry Division and the 4th Armored Division pulled back slightly on 26 September and formed defensive positions. The Germans continued to attack for three more days, until clearing weather brought more Allied aircraft overhead.

The armored actions fought around Arracourt, east of Nancy, amounted to one of the largest tank battles fought on the western front. When it was over, the Fifth *Panzer* Army had fewer than twenty-five operational tanks. The 4th Armored Division destroyed 281 German tanks, killed 3,000 German soldiers, and captured another 3,000. In the process, the 4th Armored Division suffered only 626 total casualties.

David T. Zabecki

Additional Reading
Cole, Hugh M., *The Lorraine Campaign* (1950).
Weigley, Russell F., *Eisenhower's Lieutenants: The Campaigns of France and Germany, 1944–1945* (1981).

Narvik (9 April–9 June 1940)

[See map 30 on page 1340]

For two months in 1940, the world's attention focused on the small Norwegian town of Narvik. Strategically, its loss ended the Allies' last hope of retaining a foothold in Norway. There were tactical implications as well. It was at Narvik, more than anywhere else, that airpower's dominance in modern warfare was first demonstrated convincingly. The Allies had supremacy on land and sea. The Germans had it only in the air. That was enough.

Narvik was the most distant objective in Germany's Operation *WESERÜBUNG* (WESSER EXERCISE), the invasions of Norway and Denmark (qq.v.) that began on 8 April 1940. Narvik's strategic importance lay in it being the only winter transshipment point for Swedish iron ore en route to Germany. More than one-third of Germany's iron ore imports passed through that port, and its seizure was entrusted to a force of ten destroyers carrying 2,000 mountain troops under Colonel Eduard Dietl (q.v.).

Protected by a diversion conducted by the battle cruisers *Scharnhorst* and *Gneisenau,* and also by heavy storms that precluded Allied aerial reconnaissance, the German force entered Narvik Fjord unmolested on 9 April. In the process, the destroyers sank two Norwegian coastal defense ships, the *Eidsvold* and *Norge.* By afternoon, the town and the fjord were in German hands.

Everything had not all gone Germany's way, however. The Royal Navy (RN) intercepted the invaders' ammunition ship and one of their two oilers, thus forcing the Germans to fight with limited ammunition and fuel. The Germans brought in the converted whaler, *Jan Willem,* from their naval base in Russia, but it could only refuel two ships at a time, and those very slowly.

The British reaction was swift. At dawn on 10 April, the 2nd Destroyer Flotilla struck, sinking two German destroyers and damaging another. The British raiding force intercepted and sank another German ammunition ship as they departed the fjord. Both the German and British flotilla commanders died in the engagement, with the latter, Captain Bernard Warburton-Lee, earning the Victoria Cross for the action.

The RN returned to Narvik on 13 April. This time the battleship HMS *Warspite* supported the destroyers, and its intervention was decisive. Despite receiving warning of the attack via intercepted and decrypted RN signals, the Germans were overwhelmed. Their torpedos proved unreliable and the *Luftwaffe* had no combat aircraft within operating range. All the remaining German destroyers were sunk in a four-hour engagement. British losses were light.

The British naval victory set the stage for the land campaign that followed. On 14 April, the 24th Guards Brigade, including Polish and French units, landed thirty nautical miles northwest of Narvik. Unfortunately, the British army commander, General P.J. Macksey, and the naval commander, Admiral Lord Cork, had different instructions from their respective ministries and highly divergent views of how to proceed. The former was specifically prohibited from landing against opposition, while the latter was instructed to "act boldly" in recovering the town. The result was deadlock. Cork shelled Narvik almost daily. Macksey refused to assault directly, instead moving slowly to encircle the town. As a result, the battle became a race between the Allies' powerful but slow-moving ground forces and the combined German Army and *Luftwaffe* forces from central Norway.

It was a race the British and French made no serious effort to win. They always outnumbered Dietl's command on the ground, but never fully exploited their naval and initial air supremacy to full advantage. By the second week in May, the *Luftwaffe* moved into range, and every day brought its planes and additional German ground forces ever closer. By 20 May, the *Luftwaffe* became the dominant force in the area, sinking ferries, attacking Allied columns, troops, and ships wherever it encountered them. Allied air reinforcement arrived piecemeal and was quickly destroyed.

Germany's successful invasion of Belgium and Flanders (q.v.), which started on 10 May, effectively ended the Narvik campaign. The British cabinet ordered the evacuation of Narvik on 27 May. Ironically, it was that order which compelled the Allied commander, now General Claude Auchinleck (q.v.) to assault the town rather than abandon his Norwegian allies. Outnumbered eight to one by the British and French forces, Dietl gave ground. By 1 June, he and his men were pinned against the Swedish border, facing internment. Adolf Hitler (q.v.) was desperate to save them, parachuting supplies and ordering a risky amphibious landing nearby (which never took place). Dietl, however, was saved by the Allied evacuation, which took place from 5–9 June 1940.

Narvik was an example of a sound Allied idea, poorly implemented. Germany's naval deficiencies, particularly its poor torpedoes, reduced the possibility of victory in the face of the RN's aggressiveness. Had the RN's victories in the fjords been followed by an immediate assault on Narvik and aerial reinforcement, the Allies might have gained

the port. As it was, Germany was able to import Swedish iron ore through Narvik into the war's final months.

Carl O. Schuster

Additional Reading
Macintyre, Donald, *Narvik* (1971).
Ziemke, Earl F., *The German Northern Theater of Operations, 1940–1945* (1959).

Netherlands (10–15 May 1940)
[See map 17 on page 1327]
On 10 May 1940, the Germans launched their attack in the west. In accordance with their *Fall GELB* (Case YELLOW) plan, General Gerd von Rundstedt's (q.v.) Army Group A (forty-five divisions) made the main attack through the Ardennes toward Sedan, France. To von Rundstedt's north, General Fedor von Bock's (q.v.) Army Group B (thirty divisions) conducted a supporting attack designed to draw the bulk of the Allied forces into Belgium and Flanders (q.v.), where they could be enveloped and defeated by von Rundstedt. The northernmost wing of von Bock's attack was General Georg von Kuchler's Eighteenth Army, which swept into the Netherlands and knocked it out of the war in just five days.

The Dutch Army consisted of four army corps of two divisions each and fourteen regiments of artillery. The Dutch Army Air Service had less than a dozen squadrons of planes and a few antiaircraft guns. At the helm of this modest force was General Henri Winkelman (q.v.). Dutch defense was based on an east-to-west echelon of positions of increasing strength.

The forward position ran along the line of the Ijssel and Meuse Rivers, and was manned by minor frontier and coastal forces. Behind it lay the Peel-Raam Line, defended by the Dutch III Corps. The innermost position was the Grebbe Line, the core of "Fortress Holland," occupied by strong frontier battalions and the II and IV Corps. The south flank of this position was protected by several river estuaries, which the Dutch planned to flood in order to stem the German advance. The area behind the Grebbe Line was the only territory the Dutch planned to defend to retain, and they would only have to hold it long enough for help to arrive from General Henri Giraud's (q.v.) French Seventh Army.

The Germans, for their part, were relying on help from German sympathizers inside Holland, the *Bau-und-Lehrkompanie Brandenburg*, or the *Brandenburger*s (q.v.), led by Captain Theodor von

Hippel. When the invasion came, the *Brandenburgers* (commandos under the control of the *Abwehr*) conducted largely unsuccessful operations against the bridges at Maastricht and Arnhem, but they were able to seize the one at Gennep. Three Dutch fifth columnists masquerading as policemen marched a group of "captured" German POWs, all carrying weapons, to the bridge, which they easily seized from the surprised defenders.

When the attack came, the Germans countered Dutch plans to destroy the key bridges and flood the low-lying areas by striking rapidly in the rear with airborne forces. Early on 10 May, the paratroopers landed near Moerdijk, Rotterdam, The Hague, and other key locations. Their instructions were to seize intact the critical bridges over the Meuse and Waal Rivers, and hold them until the lead elements of Kuchler's Eighteenth Army could arrive and cross.

The mission to take The Hague fell to General Hans von Sponeck's 22nd Infantry Division. Intent on meeting with Queen Wilhelmina (q.v.) and obtaining her submission and cooperation, von Sponeck wore his full-dress uniform. His plan was to seize the airfields at Valkenburg, Ypenburg, and Ockenburg, and then close in on the capital. Sponeck initially was able to capture the airfields, but the Dutch I Corps counterattacked and regained the ground. By late evening, the Dutch had taken approximately 1,000 German prisoners, and Sponeck himself was among the wounded. For the time being, the attack on The Hague was a failure.

General Kurt Student's (q.v.) 7th Parachute Division had greater success. After it captured the bridges at Moerdijk and Rotterdam, the 9th *Panzer* Division raced forward and crossed. By the afternoon of 12 May, lead German elements reached the Moerdijk bridge, northwest of Breda. By the time the French Seventh Army arrived, it was too late.

At 0700 hours on 10 May, the French initiated their Dyle Plan with the Breda Varient (*see* Belgium and Flanders). Giraud's Seventh Army started its 125-mile march, but when they reached Breda they found that the Dutch had already withdrawn northward to cover Rotterdam, and the 9th *Panzer* Division was already in firm possession of the area. Stunned by this development, Giraud began falling back toward Antwerp. In the process he was savagely bombed and strafed by the *Luftwaffe*. On the afternoon of 12 May, Giraud received instructions to regroup his forces west of the Escaut River.

The 9th *Panzer* Division's arrival at Moerdijk cut the Netherlands in two and rendered Giraud powerless. Furthermore, the Belgian Army to the south abandoned the Albert Canal Line and left the Seventh Army's southern flank exposed. In the northern part of the Netherlands, the main German forces penetrated the Ijessel-Meuse and Peel-Raam Lines in succession, and the Dutch had no choice but to fall back into Fortress Holland.

By this time, the Dutch Air Force was reduced to just one air-worthy bomber, but even that last hope was shot down on 13 May. The *Luftwaffe*, in control from the beginning, was now completely unopposed. Waterways and harbors were mined from the air, bombing attacks on The Hague and other cities were redoubled, and Giraud's mechanized columns were continually harassed. To escape this punishment from the air, Giraud withdrew to a tiny corner of Holland running from Bergen op Zoom to the Turnhout Canal in Belgium.

Behind the strongly fortified Grebbe Line lay the major Dutch cities of Rotterdam, Utrecht, and Amsterdam. On 13 May, the Germans launched a coordinated attack from the south and east against Fortress Holland. By 1800 hours that same day, the 9th *Panzer* Division passed through Dordrecht and linked up with the airborne troops south of Rotterdam. The *Luftwaffe* stepped up its efforts, but for the time being at least, the Grebbe Line held. By the morning of 14 May, the Dutch still held the dike across the Zuider Zee to the province of Friesland in the north, and a line from Muiden on the Zee to Corinchem.

Despite the defiant stand on 13 May, it was obvious that the end was near. Queen Wilhelmina, the royal family, and most of the government boarded British ships and escaped to London to establish a government-in-exile. From London, Queen Wilhelmina continued to command the vast Dutch colonial empire for the duration of the war.

The queen escaped just in time. On 14 May, the Germans demanded the surrender of the Netherlands. At the same time, the *Luftwaffe* was instructed to deliver even more devastating attacks. The most notorious strike was against Rotterdam (q.v.), where almost 900 civilians died and two square miles of the city were destroyed. The attack compelled General Winkelman to surrender in order to prevent further destruction. At 1115 hours on 15 May, the capitulation document was signed. Dutch resistance had lasted only five days. Adolf Hitler (q.v.) placed the conquered country under the administration of Arthur Seyss-Inquart (q.v.), a rabid Nazi.

Casualties in the Netherlands campaign were

relatively light on both sides. Germany's *Blitzkrieg* (q.v.) tactics and the vertical envelopments had gobbled up the country before any protracted battles could develop. The capture of Holland denied the Allies the use of its airfields and ports, and provided Germany with both forward bases and an early warning position. More importantly, the attack caused the Allies to commit Giraud's Seventh Army right where the Germans wanted it.

Kevin Dougherty

Additional Reading

Baldwin, Hanson, *The Crucial Years* (1976).

Horne, Alistair, *To Lose a Battle: France 1940* (1969).

Jacobsen, H.A., and J. Rohwer, *Decisive Battles of World War II: The German View* (1965).

Steenbeek, Wilhelmina, *Rotterdam: Invasion of Holland* (1973).

NORDWIND, Operation (31 December 1944–25 January 1945)

When Germany launched its Ardennes offensive (q.v.) on 16 December 1944, the Allies responded by disengaging forces north and south of the zone of attack and rushing those units into the threatened area. On 19 December, General Dwight Eisenhower (q.v.) decided to suspend all offensive operations of Lieutenant General Jacob Devers' (q.v.) 6th Army Group in Alsace. Devers was ordered to extend his forces to the north to assume part of the frontage of Lieutenant General George S. Patton's (q.v.) U.S. Third Army.

The 6th Army Group's new area of responsibility ran from Saarbrücken in the north to the Belfort gap and the Swiss border in the south. The southern sector of the line was held by General Jean de Lattre de Tassigny's (q.v.) French First Army, facing east along the Rhine River. The French II Corps was north of Colmar, and the French I Corps was south of the city. The northern sector of the army group line was held by Lieutenant General Alexander Patch's (q.v.) U.S. Seventh Army. Patch's forces were deployed in almost a right angle. The U.S. XV Corps faced mostly north, holding the Sarre River valley and the sector between Saarbrücken and Bitche, France. The U.S. VI Corps held the sector from Bitche to Lauterbourg—at the point where the Franco-German border leaves the Rhine and turns west—and then another 42 miles south along the Rhine to Strasbourg.

The German forces facing the 6th Army Group were handicapped by a split and illogical command structure. On 10 December Hitler had created Army Group *Oberrhein,* placing it under the command of *Reichsführer-SS* Heinrich Himmler (q.v.). Himmler had no experience as a military commander, but he had long been pressuring Hitler for a field command. Army Group *Oberrhein* was totally independent of Colonel General Johannes Blaskowitz's (q.v.) Army Group G—and even independent of Field Marshal Gerd von Rundstedt (q.v.) as *OB-West.* Army Group *Oberrhein* controlled the German Nineteenth Army in the Colmar Pocket (q.v.), and the XIV SS *Korps* east of the Rhine. Army Group G's First Army held the German line from Lauterbourg to the west.

With a front line of 126 miles and an initial force of only eight divisions to hold it, the Seventh Army was spread thin. Since there was little of strategic value in the low plain between the Vosges Mountains and the Rhine River, Eisenhower believed that the 6th Army Group could fall back, if necessary, as long as they were able to hold the key passes through the Vosges Mountains. Devers, under constant pressure to make more of his forces available to support the Allied counterattacks in the Ardennes sector, planned a series of three successive fall-back lines. The first position ran roughly along the trace of the old Maginot Line (q.v.), and the final position was the eastern edge of the Vosges.

The German offensive in the Ardennes was going badly, but Adolf Hitler (q.v.) recognized that the Allies had become significantly weaker in the south. Thus, he decided to launch a new offensive to exploit the Allied weakness and to seize the initiative on the battlefield. The Germans hastily planned Operation *NORDWIND* (NORTH WIND) between 21 and 27 December.

NORDWIND's primary attack force was *SS-Obergruppenführer* Max Simon's XIII SS *Korps,* consisting of the 17th SS *Panzergrenadier* and 36th *Volksgrenadier* Divisions. The XIII SS *Korps* was to attack the U.S. XV Corps down the Sarre River valley. The secondary attack would come in the Bitche area, with General Erich Petersen's XC *Korps* on the right, and Lieutenant General Gustav Höhne's LXXXIX *Korps* on the left. Each corps had two *Volksgrenadier* divisions. In reserve, and under the control of Army Group G, was Lieutenant General Karl Decker's XXXIX *Panzer Korps,* consisting of the 21st *Panzer* and 25th *Panzergrenadier* Divisions. The objective of both the primary and secondary attack was the Saverne gap, the key link between the High Vosges and Low.

The German plan also called for a supporting effort from Himmler's Army Group *Oberrhein* that was to establish a small bridgehead over the Rhine north of Strasbourg. Then Himmler's Nineteenth Army was to attack northward out of the Colmar Pocket to link up with both the bridgehead and Army Group G's forces at the Saverne gap. If the plan succeeded, five American divisions would be trapped in the Low Vosges.

After the overwhelming intelligence failure in the Ardennes, Allied commanders were much more cautious. Devers and Patch anticipated the new German offensive, and they prepared for it. Using the Low Vosges as the dividing line between his two corps, Patch concentrated his strength in Major General Wade H. Haislip's XV Corps, west of the Vosges. XV Corps had the 103rd, 44th, and 100th Infantry Divisions on line, with the 12th Armored Division in reserve. East of the Vosges, Major General Edward H. Brooks's VI Corps had the 45th and 79th Infantry Divisions between Bitche and Lauterbourg, and the 36th Infantry Division along the Rhine. The 14th Armored Division was in reserve.

The center between the two U.S. corps was very thinly held by a three-battalion mechanized task force. Just before the start of the battle, Patch also deployed along the Rhine elements three green and newly arriving divisions. The infantry regiments of the 42nd, 63rd, and 70th Infantry Divisions were committed without their supporting artillery or engineers, which had not yet arrived in the Seventh Army's area of operations.

NORDWIND kicked off in the final few hours of 31 December 1944. The following day, Eisenhower ordered Devers to pull his forces directly back to the eastern edge of the High Vosges. That, however, would mean temporarily abandoning Strasbourg, which the French were not willing to accept. Brigadier General Charles de Gaulle (q.v.), the head of the provisional French government, protested immediately and sent General Alphonse Juin (q.v.) to Eisenhower's headquarters.

Juin told Eisenhower's chief of staff, Lieutenant General Walter Bedell Smith (q.v.), that de Gaulle had ordered de Lattre to ignore Eisenhower's order and defend the city—which actually was in the U.S. Seventh Army's sector of responsibility. Smith told Juin that a failure to comply with Eisenhower's orders would result in the French forces being cut off from American supplies. Juin fired back that the French would no longer permit the Allies to use the French railroads, and might even withdraw from Eisenhower's command.

De Gaulle also appealed directly to U.S. President Franklin D. Roosevelt and British Prime Minister Winston Churchill (qq.v.). Roosevelt declined to intervene, but Churchill flew to Versailles on 3 January for a meeting with Eisenhower and de Gaulle. In order to keep the coalition together, Eisenhower changed his orders. Devers was permitted to conduct a slow fighting withdrawal, and the army boundaries were shifted north to put Strasbourg in de Lattre's area of responsibility.

Almost from the start, *NORDWIND* failed to live up to the expectations of either side. Despite some local bitter fighting, the U.S. XV Corps stopped the XIII SS *Korps* cold. The two-corps attack from the Bitche area made somewhat better progress, but by the end of 2 January it, too, had almost ground to a halt. This undoubtedly had a bearing on Eisenhower's 3 January decision to reverse his orders. The attack against VI Corps threatened to regain momentum when the Germans committed the 6th SS Mountain Division, but the Americans continued to feed more infantry into the threatened area. On 4 January, the German High Command terminated *NORDWIND* proper, but a series of follow-up attacks continued for three more weeks.

On 5 January, Army Group *Oberrhein* launched the 553rd *Volksgrenadier* Division across the Rhine and established a bridgehead near Drusenheim-Gambsheim. Newly committed and inexperienced U.S. units were immediately pushed back. The Germans advanced to within seven miles of Strasbourg before they were stopped by the commitment of part of the 6th Army Group's reserve. On 7 January, the Nineteenth Army launched Operation *SONNENWENDE* (WINTER SOLSTICE), attacking north out of the Colmar Pocket. The French stopped that attack thirteen miles south of Strasbourg. *SONNENWENDE* formally ended on 13 January.

On 6 January Blaskowitz finally obtained permission from Hitler to commit the *Panzer* units that had been held in reserve. The following day, the Germans launched a major attack near Lauterbourg, with both armored divisions of the XXXIX *Panzer Korps* and the 245th *Volksgrenadier* Division in support. On 9 January Decker's *Panzers* broke through the center of VI Corps and drove the Americans back to the Haguenau forest. Brooks was forced to commit his reserve, the 14th Armored Division. By 15 January the fighting centered on the towns of Rittershoffen and Hatten, both just north of the Haguenau forest and about a mile apart. That bitter but indecisive fighting continued until 20 January.

On 16 January, the XXXIX *Panzer Korps* launched another drive from Lauterbourg, south to the west bank of the Rhine, linking up with the German forces in the Gambsheim bridgehead. In the fierce fighting that followed, the newly committed U.S. 12th Armored Division took a severe beating. Its 43rd Tank Battalion was cut off and destroyed near the town of Herrlisheim (q.v.). Despite a number of local gains, however, the Germans simply did not have the reserve forces nor the logistics support to exploit any successes.

On the night of 24–25 January, in a snowstorm, the Germans launched their final attacks against the U.S. VI Corps positions along the Moder River near Haguenau. The following day Patch's forces began to counterattack along the Seventh Army's line. The German high command halted all offensive operations in Alsace, and began shifting their better forces to the eastern front to face the Soviets. By the end of the month Hitler replaced Blaskowitz with *SS-Oberstgruppenführer* Paul Hausser (q.v.).

Although Operation *NORDWIND* itself lasted from 31 December to 4 January, the entire series of German offensives in Alsace is often collectively referred to as *NORDWIND,* and sometimes as the New Year's Eve offensive. The Seventh Army's casualties for January 1945 numbered about 14,000; the Germans lost some 23,000. Given their strategic position at that point in the war, all the Germans realistically could have hoped for was a delaying action. They did not even get much of that for their efforts. The division of responsibility and apparent lack of coordination between Army Group G and Army Group *Oberrhein* only made the German task that much more difficult.

David T. Zabecki

Additional Reading
Bonn, Keith E., *When the Odds Were Even: The Vosges Mountain Campaign, October 1944– January 1945* (1994).
Clarke, Jeffrey J., and Robert Ross Smith, *Riviera to the Rhine* (1993).
Luck, Hans von, *Panzer Commander* (1989).
MacDonald, Charles B., *The Mighty Endeavor: American Armed Forces in the European Theater in World War II* (1969).

Normandy Campaign (6 June–21 August 1944)
[See map 28 on page 1338]
As World War II moved into 1944, the German

Reich faced the problem of opposing an almost certain Allied landing in western Europe with diminishing resources in both men and materiel. The Allies wanted to force a decision in the west as well as to establish a front in northwestern France to relieve pressure on the Soviets in the east. In November 1943, the Germans started to reverse their previous trend of weakening the defenses in western Europe in favor of other locations and they started to rebuild in the west. The German OKW (q.v.) believed the war would become hopeless if the Allies were able to establish their new front in the west.

The German strategic objective was to prevent an Allied landing by reinforcing the existing defensive structures, and, failing that, to push the Allies back into the sea after a landing. The Atlantic Wall (q.v.), a chain of fortifications stretching from Norway to the Spanish border, was to be the backbone of the German defenses. The plans called for an average of fifteen to twenty bunkers for each kilometer of coastline, tied in with major fortifications at all harbors. The plan, however, was too ambitious. By the time the landings actually came, only the coast of the Pas de Calais was fortified to the point it was almost unassailable. The remainder of the coast had only a thin string of linear positions, without sufficient depth for a successful defense.

Shortly before the end of 1943, Adolf Hitler (q.v.) appointed Field Marshal Erwin Rommel (q.v.) commander of Army Group B in the West. Rommel and his staff were then ordered to review the German defensive capabilities along the coasts of Denmark, Flanders, the Channel, Normandy, and Brittany. He found the defenses to be too weak, and he initially ordered improvement measures using the troops and resources already in position. His immediate measures, however, failed to address the key problem—an invader who could penetrate the coastal defenses to a depth of one kilometer would have a clear path.

There were two basic opinions on the German defense. Rommel believed that it was necessary to prevent the invasion force from establishing itself on the beachhead. Once the Allies got ashore and were able to start building air bases, their superior airpower would become the decisive factor. Thus, Rommel advocated a very strong defense at the coast, coupled with reserves held close to the coast that could be committed to an immediate counterattack. The weak point in Rommel's reasoning was that it required an almost immediate decision as to the location of the main attack.

Field Marshal Gerd von Rundstedt (q.v.), the *Oberbefehlshaber-West* (commander in chief west, or *OB-West*) had a slightly different point of view. He agreed that it would be best to destroy any amphibious invasion while it was still in the water, but failing that, he believed a strong mobile reserve should be held at sufficient depth to deal with any enemy penetration.

Hitler at first agreed with Rommel. Then after von Rundstedt objected, Hitler decided that no single commander in the west should retain control of all the available reserves. By May 1944, Army Group B was given a reserve force of three *Panzer* divisions, while another three *Panzer* divisions plus a *Panzergrenadier* division were held in OKW reserve.

The Germans did not know the exact time and place of the Allied landings, which made their own preparations more difficult. Based on the assumption that the attack would come in the Pas de Calais area, the Channel coast and the Fifteenth Army were given the top priority for the buildup. The best units and the strongest fortifications of the *Atlantikwall* were located there. The main landing was expected in that area because it was the shortest path to the German industrial region of the Ruhr. Despite the important harbor of Cherbourg, the Germans generally considered a landing on the Normandy coast unlikely for operational reasons.

With their reconnaissance assets almost completely gone by this point in the war, the Germans assumed the Allies would have the benefit of tactical surprise. Nonetheless, the Germans believed their preparations would be effective and they could hold the enemy along the coast. A well-established warning system made it possible for the positional units to be alerted rapidly. Early warning was expected from Allied telecommunications with the French resistance groups, against whom the Germans planned countermeasures. If an attack did come in Normandy, the main defensive problem would be one of moving up reserves in time to cut off any beachhead and pushing the enemy back into the sea.

When the Allied assault did come, Normandy became the scene of the largest series of landing operations in history. More than two million troops on both sides fought for a decision in a few weeks' time and in a confined space. In the north, Normandy is almost surrounded by the English Channel, and in the south by the Atlantic. West of the Cotentin peninsula are numerous small islands—Guernsey, Jersey, and Alderney—which were also in German hands.

The Allies chose five sectors of the Normandy coastline for their landings. Four, code named OMAHA, GOLD, JUNO, and SWORD, were between the mouths of the Orne and Vire Rivers. The fifth beach, UTAH, was west of the Vire on the Cotentin peninsula. This western sector is a fifteen-kilometer strip on the east coast of the peninsula between St. Martin-de-Varreville and La Madeleine. It is flat with a rising sand beach. East of the mouth of the Vire, between Grand-Camp-les-Bains and Vierville-sur-Mer, is a thirty-meter-high cliff, Pointe du Hoc. It is almost vertical and looks out over the whole bay. This steep coastline runs for thirty kilometers to Arromanches, with only four valleys running inland. From Arromanches to the mouth of the Orne, the coast is flat and has large sandy beaches. Thus, sixty kilometers out of the entire landing line of ninety kilometers were ideal for amphibious landing. The strongest German positions along the line were in the OMAHA sector, with Pointe du Hoc on the left fortified with a casemated battery of 155mm guns.

The coastal terrain and the Normandy landscape played a decisive role in the Allied landings and the German defense. Normandy, especially the Calvados coast and the area south of it, is one of the most beautiful countrysides in France. Numerous fields fenced in by *bocages* (hedgerows) are typical of the area. From a tactical standpoint, each *bocage* is a limited area, easy to defend. Several fields can make up a defensive position echeloned in depth. The *bocages* constituted a major obstacle for the Allies, particularly in their ability to move with tanks. In addition to the *bocages,* the terrain in western Normandy consists of numerous swamps within a network of small rivers, ditches, and dams.

Most of the key Allied commanders were well-known to the Germans. The supreme Allied commander was General Dwight D. Eisenhower (q.v.). The Allied ground forces commander for the initial phase of the landings was General Bernard L. Montgomery (q.v.). The principal American ground commander, General Omar N. Bradley (q.v.), commanded the U.S. First Army, while General Sir Miles Dempsey (q.v.) commanded the British Second Army. Admiral Sir Bertram Ramsay (q.v.) commanded Allied naval forces, and Air Marshal Sir Trafford Leigh-Mallory (q.v.) commanded the Allied Expeditionary Air Forces.

The Allied landing forces were well-trained and prepared. The entire operation was code named OVERLORD, and the first phase of the invasion involved a force of 155,705 troops, and

N

almost 50,000 vehicles, including 1,000 tanks. The U.S. 4th Infantry Division landed on the westernmost UTAH Beach. The U.S. 1st Infantry Division and elements of 29th Infantry Division landed on OMAHA Beach. On the first day of the operation, called D-Day, U.S. forces landed 57,500 troops. The British 50th Infantry Division landed on GOLD Beach, in the center. Next came the Canadian 3rd Infantry Division on JUNO Beach, and on the east flank, the British 3rd Infantry Division landed on SWORD Beach. The British landed 53,815 troops on D-Day, and the Canadians landed 21,400. Finally, a special group of three U.S. ranger (q.v.) companies was assigned to take the German battery at Pointe du Hoc.

Several hours before the amphibious landings, the Allies dropped three airborne divisions on the flanks of the landing sites to seal off the area and secure key inland bridges. The 15,000 paratroopers of the U.S. 82nd and 101st Airborne Divisions landed on the extreme west flank, in the vicinity of Saint Mère-Église. The 7,990 British paratroopers of 6th Airborne Division landed northeast of Caen.

Allied air and naval forces played a key role. The combined Allied air forces committed 31,000 aircrew and 11,590 planes, including 3,500 transport gliders. The Allied navies committed 195,701 sailors and 6,900 units—warships, landing ships, and transports—to the crossing of the Channel. The naval phase of the Allied operation was code named NEPTUNE. The Germans expected the large numbers, characteristic of the Western Allies. In retrospect, the amount of materiel and the number of troops seemed to guarantee the invasion beforehand.

Hitler's intention to fight the adversary along the coast and from the *Atlantikwall* positions resulted from materiel shortages and the lack of mobility of German defensive units. The twenty-two "home divisions" of the *Atlantikwall* generally were not combat-experienced and did not have the organic mobility assets to shift to mobile warfare, if necessary. Many of these units were manned with old men, boys, and other troops unfit for frontline combat. There were, however, some seasoned units along the coast. The *Wehrmacht*'s *Panzer* divisions, *Waffen-SS* (q.v.) units, and parachute divisions were well equipped and generally up to strength.

OB-West had a total of sixty divisions at his disposal, which was significantly more than the Allies could put ashore in the early stages. The German defenders, however, were painfully aware of the Allies' key advantage: the attacker could

mass his assault on one weak point of the coastal defenses. The Germans, on the other hand, had to secure and defend a line 4,000 kilometers long.

By the summer of 1944, the Germans had put all available men and materiel—considering the situation on all fronts—in readiness for the Allied invasion. Although the *Atlantikwall* had its weak spots, it also had strengths with a total garrison of almost two million troops. In the period just prior to 6 June, German forces in Normandy alone included five infantry divisions, one airborne division, and one *Panzer* division, all under Seventh Army of Rommel's Army Group B. These units were not all up to full strength, but the positions they occupied were much better suited for defensive than for offensive operations.

Eisenhower had one other clear advantage over von Rundstedt. While the Allied commander in chief directly commanded all the ground, naval, and air forces at his disposal, *OB-West* did not have direct command over the German Naval and *Luftwaffe* units. At this stage of the war, however, the *Kriegsmarine* was completely incapable of offering any resistance to the Allied fleet. Because of heavy seas on the night of 5 June, the few German picket boats in the Seine Bay had orders to remain in harbor. Also, there was not much left of the *Luftwaffe,* which in the early campaigns of World War II was so critical to the success of German ground operations. The *Luftwaffe*'s Third *Luftflotte* had only 319 operational aircraft on 6 June. The Allied air forces enjoyed a 20 to 1 superiority in aircraft.

The commanders in charge of the defense were some of Germany's best. Von Rundstedt had led troops west to the Meuse River in France and east to the mouth of the Don. Rommel, the legendary commander of the *Afrika Korps* (q.v.), was the most experienced commander in fighting the Western Allies. German commanders who later became involved in the fight included Field Marshal Günther von Kluge (q.v.), whom Hitler valued because of his successes in the east with his well-planned defensive methods, and Field Marshal Walther Model (q.v.), known for his reckless use of groggy troops to restabilize the German line in the east after the breakdown of Army Group Center in Russia.

There were few direct indicators that pointed to a major landing in Normandy. For months, German leadership had read Allied telecommunications that continually mentioned the coming invasion; thus the defenders were somewhat desensitized to the subject. There were many false alarms as well. As a result, German units were not at a

American troops carrying full equipment wade onto a Normandy beachhead during the Allied landings on 6 June 1944. Hundreds of others move toward the beach in landing craft. (IWM EA 25636)

particularly high state of alert when the landings started. When the Allied landing fleet did finally appear off the Calvados coast, the attackers had achieved tactical surprise.

The three airborne divisions started their parachute drops at midnight on 5 June, followed by glider landings of the heavier equipment starting about 0400 hours. The drops around Caen were very successful, but the Germans did manage to disrupt the drops on the Cotentin peninsula to some degree. At 0630 hours, the amphibious landings started. The Germans put up a grim and determined resistance. In the British sector, the small and understrength German 716th Infantry Division fought especially well. On OMAHA Beach, the 352nd Infantry Division inflicted severe casualties on the U.S. 1st Infantry Division. The German troops fought bravely, but in the end they were no match for the overwhelming Allied firepower. Cruisers and battleships offshore pounded the coastline, while Royal Air Force (RAF) and U.S. Army Air Force (USAAF) aircraft struck farther inland, into the German operational rear. On D-Day alone, the Allies flew 14,000 sorties, compared to the *Luftwaffe*'s 500.

When the landings started, the 21st *Panzer* Division was the only armored unit under von Rundstedt's direct control. It spent the first part of D-Day engaging British airborne forces around Caen. Von Rundstedt repeatedly requested the release of the other *Panzer* units from the OKW reserve so he could mount a counterattack. Later in the day, the 21st *Panzer* Division was sent to help 716th Infantry Division, but only reached the coast around 1600 hours. The 21st *Panzer* Division started to counterattack, but the assault was broken up by the fire from three British battleships. Faced with a lack of supplies and further threats to the German flank, the 21st *Panzer* Division pulled back and dug in.

At 1530 hours, Hitler finally released the 12th SS *Panzer,* 17th SS *Panzergrenadier,* and the *Panzer-Lehr* Divisions, but it was too late for them to influence the D-Day fighting. The 12th SS *Panzer* Division had to move almost 150 kilometers and did not reach the coast until the next morning. As the *Panzer-Lehr* Division moved up, it was hit repeatedly by Allied air strikes, and only reached the combat zone on 9 June.

All the Allied positions held. By the end of D-Day, they had the equivalent of eleven divisions on the ground in France. Although they could not be dislodged from the beaches, the Allies did generally fail to reach their D-Day objectives. The beachheads were not linked. Instead of a uniform depth of ten to fifteen kilometers, the maximum depth of OMAHA Beach was no more than 2.5 kilometers. In fact, the fighting at OMAHA Beach still could go either way. The British had not taken Caen, and the fight for Pointe du Hoc had lasted longer than planned. Still, the Atlantic Wall had been breached.

All German counterattacks during the next several days failed. The British took Bayeux on 8 June and then linked up with the Americans. Almost the entire coast between the mouths of the Orne and the Vire was in Allied hands. On the east flank, the Germans contained the British and continued to hold Caen. By 11 June, the Allies finally succeeded in connecting all their beachheads, which now formed a line 100 kilometers long and ten to fifteen kilometers deep.

Hitler, meanwhile, continued to insist on an active defense, including his usual demand for an unconditional holding of the line. Convinced that the Normandy landings were a feint for the main attack that would come later, he ordered the reinforcement of the Fifteenth Army in the Pas de Calais on 9 June. By 8 June, however, von Rundstedt and Rommel were convinced that Normandy was the main attack. The Allies were already so successful there it seemed totally foolish not to reinforce that success.

The Allies continued landing men and materiel through the artificial harbor (q.v.) they constructed especially for the invasion. After 11 June, there was little the defenders could do to hinder them. The Germans could only shift their limited resources very slowly because of the constant threat of Allied airpower, which continued to strike the road networks in the German rear. By 15 June, the Seventh Army, commanded by SS General Paul Hausser (q.v.), had fifteen divisions in Normandy, but the U.S. First and British Second Armies had a total of twenty. At that point, approximately 200,000 German soldiers were facing 300,000 Allied troops.

From 17 to 22 June, a strong storm in the Channel disrupted the Allied landing operations. Von Rundstedt and Rommel, however, had already come to realize that Germany would lose the fight for the beachheads. They planned to engage the Allies in a tank battle farther in from the beaches, out of Allied naval gunfire range. *Panzer* units were moved into the Normandy sector, but only slowly and on a small scale. At a meeting in France on 17 June, Hitler continued to insist that the main assault would come in the Pas de Calais.

Hitler still was clinging to that belief at a 29 June meeting held in Germany with von Rundstedt, Rommel, and the OKW senior staff. Hitler, therefore, continued to forbid his field commanders from using the available reserves in the west to conduct a mobile defense. Later, during a telephone conversation, OKW chief of staff Field Marshal Wilhelm Keitel (q.v.) asked von Rundstedt what he thought should be done about the German situation. The *OB-West* reportedly replied, "End the war, you fools!"

On 27 June, the U.S. VII Corps under General James L. Collins (q.v.) captured the port of Cherbourg. The remainder of the Cotentin peninsula fell by 1 July. The Germans, however, had sabotaged Cherbourg so effectively that it took until August before large supply ships could use the docks. In the British sector, the defenders were holding on fairly well, thanks to the German penchant for investing lower-level tactical commanders with as much local authority as possible. At the end of June, the British Second Army resumed the drive for Caen, but that attack eventually stalled.

On 2 July, Hitler sent an officer to von Rundstedt's headquarters to award the field marshal the Oak Leaves to the Knight's Cross, and to tell him he was relieved. The next day, von Kluge became *OB-West,* charged with defeating the 929,000 troops the Allies now had in France.

Hitler tied von Kluge's hands too, and forced him to fight a static battle of attrition. The bulk of the Fifteenth Army was still held in place in the Pas de Calais. On 8 July, the British started a major push for Caen (q.v.). Despite Hitler's orders to hold, von Kluge was forced back and the British took most of the city the following day. After that, the German right flank stabilized somewhat, but the bulk of the German *Panzer* forces had been drawn into the British sector, creating opportunities for the Americans on the west flank.

With Cherbourg and the Cotentin peninsula in Allied hands, Bradley was able to concentrate all of his U.S. First Army in the drive toward St. Lô. The German Seventh Army put up stiff resistance, and the Americans only took the town on 18 July. One day earlier, Rommel's staff car was attacked near St. Lô by RAF fighters. Critically injured in the resulting wreck, he was evacuated back to Germany, never to return to the fighting. Von Kluge assumed direct command of Army Group B, while still remaining *OB-West.*

On 18 July, the British also launched Operation GOODWOOD to the south of Caen. The attack stalled by 21 July, hampered by bad weather and high casualties. Montgomery later maintained that the primary objective of Operation GOOD-WOOD had been to tie down as much German armor as possible in order to facilitate an American breakout. Many historians, however, believe (as Eisenhower himself did at the time) that

GOODWOOD was supposed to have been the eastern arm of a twin breakout.

On 24 July, the Allies declared an end to Operation OVERLORD. Although forty-eight days had passed since the start of the landings, the Allies were only at roughly their D+5 objectives. On the other hand, they had the equivalent of thirty-four divisions ashore. The following day the Americans launched Operation COBRA, the breakout at St. Lô (q.v.). Following a massive carpet bombing by Allied air, the main penetration was made by VII Corps, which had increased in strength to six divisions. Facing them were the German 5th Parachute Division, the battle-weary *Panzer-Lehr* Division, and the 352nd Infantry Division.

The American breakthrough came on 27 July. That same day Hitler finally authorized the release of some of the units in the Pas de Calais. On 30 July, U.S. forces took Avranches. Two days later, the U.S. Third Army was activated under General George S. Patton (q.v.). General Courtney Hodges (q.v.) assumed command of the U.S. First Army, while Bradley activated the headquarters of the 12th Army Group. On 3 August, units of Patton's VIII Corps poured through the Avranches gap and turned west into Brittany to seize the port of Brest (q.v.).

Hitler continually demanded a large-scale counterattack, using at least eight of the nine *Panzer* divisions available to *OB-West*. On 7 August, XLVII *Panzer Korps* attacked toward Avranches, but only with four *Panzer* divisions, all that von Kluge could muster in the time and space available. Heavy fighting took place around Mortain (q.v.), but the German counterattack halted a few days later fifteen kilometers short of Avranches. The *Panzers* were then forced to withdraw because much of the American force in Brittany had turned back toward the west, and General Henry Crerar's (q.v.) Canadian First Army was attacking toward Falaise (q.v.).

On 9 August, the U.S. XV Corps drove toward Argentan, while the Canadian II Corps closed in on Falaise, a little less than thirty kilometers to the northwest. With the major portion of the Seventh Army and elements of the Fifth *Panzer* Army in danger of being encircled, von Kluge again asked Hitler for permission to maneuver. As usual, Hitler insisted on rigidly holding position.

By 17 August, both Allied corps reached their objectives. Fourteen divisions and almost 100,000 German troops were nearly surrounded, but the small gap between Falaise and Argentan remained open. Hitler blamed von Kluge, whom he also suspected of involvement in the plot that resulted in the 20 July bomb blast at Hitler's headquarters. Von Kluge was relieved and replaced by Model. The next day, on his way back to Germany, von Kluge committed suicide.

Model tried to extract his forces from the Falaise pocket, but the gap was closing fast. Abandoning equipment, vehicles, and horses, about 40,000 troops managed to escape. After the Allies closed the gap on the evening of 18 August, they took almost 50,000 prisoners in the pocket. Another 10,000 German troops were killed during the operation. The Germans made several attempts to reopen the pocket from the outside, but failed. As late as 21 August, handfuls of German troops managed to infiltrate their way out of the pocket.

The fall of Falaise and the loss of the Seventh Army units in the pocket spelled the end of the battle for Normandy. Starting with the initial landings, the fighting fell into four major phases: (1) the landings and the struggle for the coastal area (6–14 June); (2) the breakout from the beachheads and the occupation of the Cotentin peninsula (14 June–16 July); (3) the breakthroughs at St. Lô. and Avranches (17–30 July); and (4) the encirclement of the Seventh Army at Falaise (31 July–21 August).

During each phase of the campaign, the *Wehrmacht* was overcome by a combination of Allied equipment, firepower, and overwhelming air superiority. The German situation was made that much worse by Hitler's refusal to let his field commanders maneuver. The two major elements of combat power are fire and maneuver. Hitler severely restricted the *Wehrmacht*'s use of the second, and the Allies had overwhelming superiority in the first.

At the end of June, the German high command estimated that 95 percent of the German casualties to that point were inflicted by Allied artillery and airpower. On 6 June alone, Allied air strikes and naval shore bombardment caused somewhere between 4,000 and 9,000 German casualties. Some units, like the 352nd Infantry Division, the 716th Infantry Division, and the 3rd Parachute Division were under constant attack almost the entire month of June. By mid-July, the 3rd Parachute Division had a 65 percent casualty rate; the 352nd Infantry Division had only 180 survivors; and the 716th Infantry Division had been destroyed completely.

Losses on both sides were heavy. It is difficult to convey the scale of the carnage by citing mere statistics. By 12 July, the Germans lost 65,865 troops, dead, wounded, and captured. They lost

N

another 21,000 when Cherbourg fell and the 709th Infantry Division was captured. By the end of July, German losses reached 127,247. By 13 August, the Germans lost 158,980 troops; but Allied losses were close to 170,000. By the time the last German soldiers crossed over to the east bank of the Seine River in late August, German losses totaled about 250,000 troops and thirty-nine divisions.

Thousands of the soldiers—German, American, British, and Canadian—who fought in the Normandy campaign are still there in the region's many military cemeteries.

Ekkehart Guth

Additional Reading
Ambrose, Stephen H., *D-Day June 6, 1944: The Climactic Battle of World War II* (1994).
Bennett, Ralph, *Ultra in the West: The Normandy Campaign 1944–45* (1979).
Essame, Hubert, *Normandy Bridgehead* (1970).
Guth, Ekkehart, *"Deutsche Strategie im Westen," Normandie 44*, F. Bedarida (ed.) (1984).
Harrison, Gordon A., *Cross-Channel Attack* (1951).
Hastings, Max, *Overlord: D-Day and the Battle for Normandy* (1984).
Keegan, John, *Six Armies in Normandy* (1982).
Ose, D., *Entscheidung im Westen 1944* (1984).
Ryan, Cornelius, *The Longest Day: June 6, 1944* (1959).
Spidel, Hans, *Invasion 1944: Rommel and the Normandy Campaign* (1968).
Thompson, R.W., *D-Day: Spearhead of Invasion* (1968).
Wegmüller, Hans, *Die Abwehr der Invasion* (1986).

Norsk Hydro Raids (16–28 February 1943)

The fall of Norway (q.v.) in May 1940, provided the Germans with a source for "heavy" water (water with an additional oxygen atom in the molecule), a compound considered vital to the development of nuclear weapons. The Norsk hydroelectric plant at Vemork was the world's single largest supplier of this substance, and German scientists ordered a tenfold increase in production.

Using information gathered by Norwegian agents, British Combined Operations (q.v.) decided to destroy the stockpiles of heavy water. It planned to land a team of glider-borne saboteurs near the plant and then assault the buildings, using plastic explosives to rupture the facility's massive holding tanks. On 18 October 1942, a four-man team, code named Operation SWALLOW,

commanded by Lieutenant Jens Poulsson, parachuted into Norway and prepared for the coming operation. On 19 November, two Horsa gliders carrying thirty-four trained raiders, code named Operation FRESHMAN, met disaster when one aircraft crashed into a mountain and the other landed at sea. Survivors were captured, interrogated, tortured, and divulged the nature of their mission before being shot. Hearing of the debacle, the Operation SWALLOW team sought refuge in the mountains and awaited orders.

The British Special Operations Executive (q.v.) organized a second attempt, code named Operation GUNNERSLIDE, which was launched on 16 February 1943. A nine-man team of Norwegian expatriates, commanded by Lieutenant Joachim Ronneberg, made a parachute landing and linked up with the Operation SWALLOW team. After leaving a four-man radio detachment in the mountains, the raiders proceeded to Vemork.

The unit divided on reaching the vicinity of the Norsk hydroelectric plant. A four-man demolition squad, organized into two teams, was ordered to destroy the heavy water stockpiles. The remaining five men, armed with automatic weapons, were to supply covering fire. After scaling a cliff and fording the freezing Mans River, the GUNNERSLIDE operatives eluded German sentries and without opposition, penetrated the plant around midnight 27 February. Team members detonated high-explosive charges, destroying hundreds of gallons of heavy water and causing extensive damage to storage tanks and pipelines. The raiders then successfully withdrew, the entire mission succeeding without a shot fired.

General Nikolaus von Falkenhorst (q.v.), the German commander in the area, conceded that the raid was "the best coup I have ever seen." British intelligence officers estimated that the successful operation against the Norsk hydroelectric plant retarded German heavy water production by two years, causing a serious setback to their atomic weapons program.

Donald Frazier

Additional Reading
Hankelid, Knut, *Skis against the Atom* (1954).
Kurzman, Dan, *Blood and Water* (1997).

North Africa Campaign (September 1940–May 1943)

[See map 29 on page 1339]
The campaign for North Africa was a struggle for control of the Suez Canal and access to Mideast oil.

With the increased mechanization of modern armies, oil had become a critical strategic material. Britain, in particular, depended on access to the oil from the Mideast. The Suez Canal also provided Britain a lifeline to its overseas dominions. That lifeline ran through the Mediterranean, and thus the North African campaign and the Mediterranean campaign (q.v.) were in a very real sense extensions of each other.

The maneuvering for North Africa began as early as October 1935, when Italy invaded Ethiopia (q.v.). As a result of that move, Egypt became very wary of Italy's imperialistic aspirations, since Rome also controlled next-door Libya. The Egyptians, therefore, granted Britain permission to station relatively large forces on their territory. Britain and France also agreed to divide the responsibility for maintaining naval control of the Mediterranean, with the main British base located at Alexandria, Egypt.

Italy was the wild card in the Mediterranean. If it remained neutral, British access to the vital sea lanes would be almost assured. If Italy sided with Germany, the powerful Italian Navy had the potential to shut down the Mediterranean from its main base at Taranto, supported by Italian Air Force bases on Sicily and Sardinia. Italy remained neutral when Germany invaded Poland (q.v.) in September 1939. When Germany invaded France (q.v.) in June 1940, however, Benito Mussolini (q.v.) could not resist the opportunity to partake in the spoils. Italy declared war on France and Britain on 10 June 1940, six days after the evacuation at Dunkirk (q.v.). Britain and Italy were now at war in the Mediterranean.

On paper, at least, Italy enjoyed a considerable advantage over Britain in the theater of operations. In June 1939, Admiral Sir Andrew Cunningham's (q.v.) Mediterranean Fleet had only forty-five combat ships, against the Italian Navy's 183. The French surrender on 25 June 1940 placed the entire burden for the Mediterranean sea lanes on the Royal Navy (RN).

The Royal Air Force (RAF) was in a slightly better position, with 205 aircraft against the 313 of the Italian Air Force. On the ground, Marshal Rudolofo Graziani (q.v.) had some 250,000 troops in Libya, while General Sir Archibald Wavell (q.v.), British commander in chief of the Middle East, had 100,000 to defend Egypt, as well as Sudan and Palestine. The British ground forces, however, were better organized, trained, equipped, and led.

The British and Italian armies faced each other across the Libyan-Egyptian border, in an area known as the Western Desert. It is an inhospitable region with no growth and virtually no water. From Marsa Matrúh in western Egypt, to El Aghelia on the east side of Libya's Gulf of Sidra, only one major road connected the region's few towns and villages. A sandy coastal strip of varying width runs along the southern shore of the Mediterranean. Inland, a sharp escarpment rises to the 500-foot-high Libyan plateau. There are only a few passes where wheeled or even tracked vehicles can ascend the escarpment. Once on the plateau, however, military vehicles have good cross-country mobility across the limestone ground covered by a thin layer of sand. The commander of the 21st *Panzer* Division, Major General Johann von Ravenstein, described the area as a tactician's paradise and a logistician's hell.

On 13 September 1940, Graziani reluctantly moved into Egypt, almost a month after he had been ordered to do so by Mussolini. Some six Italian divisions moved east, bypassing a small British covering force, and halting at Sidi Barrani, just short of the British main positions at Mersa Matrúh. Graziani apparently had no intention of going any deeper into Egypt. The Italian control the airfield at Sidi Barrani, however, seriously reduced the operational reach of the British, and posed a threat to the Royal Navy. With the Battle of Britain (q.v.) in full swing and England facing possible German invasion from Operation SEA LION (q.v.), the British were in no immediate position to counter the Italian thrust.

By October 1940 the threat from SEA LION had passed, and the British began to reinforce Wavell. Through December, an additional 126,000 Commonwealth troops arrived in Egypt from Britain, Australia, New Zealand, and India. On 11 November the RN seriously reduced Italian naval superiority by conducting a surprise air attack against Taranto (q.v.). On 9 December, the Western Desert Force (later the British Eighth Army), under General Sir Richard O'Connor (q.v.), attacked at Sidi Barrani (q.v.).

The British pushed the Italian Tenth Army out of Egypt, scoring another major victory on 3 January 1941 at Bardia (q.v.), just inside Libya. Driving into Cyrenaica (eastern Libya), the British took Tobruk (*see* Tobruk I) on 22 January. O'Connor continued to pursue the Italians, trapping them at Beda Fomm (q.v.) on 7 February 1941. The Italian Tenth Army collapsed. In a period of two months a British force of about two divisions advanced 500 miles, destroyed ten Italian divisions, and captured 130,000 prisoners, 380 tanks, and 845 guns. In the process, the British suffered about 555 dead and 1,400 wounded.

Immediately following on the high point of the British successes in North Africa, Prime Minister Winston S. Churchill (q.v.) decided on 22 February to commit British troops against the Axis in Greece (q.v.). Most of those forces came out of Cyrenaica, which left Wavell only five brigades in Libya. Only a few weeks earlier, however, Adolf Hitler (q.v.) had decided to shore up the Italians in North Africa by sending German forces. On 8 January, the *Luftwaffe*'s X *Fliegerkorps* arrived in Sicily from Norway and immediately started attacking Allied shipping destined for the Libyan port of Benghazi. That forced the British forward units in Libya to resupply through the port of Tobruk, more than 450 miles away.

Two German divisions and two additional Italian divisions crossed from Italy into Libya. On 12 February, Lieutenant General Erwin Rommel (q.v.) assumed command of the German units that later were named the *Deutsches Afrika Korps* (q.v.). Rommel lost no time in regaining the initiative. He probed El Agheila on 24 March, and when he found the British defenses were only a thin shell, he launched a general offensive despite Hitler's orders to maintain a general defensive posture.

Rommel drove rapidly to the east, bringing Tobruk (*see* Tobruk II) under siege on 10 April. Unable to take the port on the run, he left a siege force of mostly Italian units, and continued his drive for the Egyptian border. The Tobruk garrison, which would hold out for 240 days, continued to be a thorn in the Axis's side.

On 14 April, Rommel's main force reached Sollum on the Egyptian border and they occupied the key terrain of the Halfaya Pass. The German high command, meanwhile, was concerned about the speed of Rommel's advance and his failure to take Tobruk. They sent General Friedrich Paulus (q.v.) to North Africa to assess the situation. Paulus's report back to Berlin described Rommel's weak overall position and his critical shortages of fuel and ammunition. The report also reached Churchill via ULTRA (q.v.).

Churchill concluded the Germans were ready to collapse with one strong push. Meanwhile, a British resupply convoy, code named TIGER, was enroute to North Africa carrying 295 tanks and forty-three Hurricane fighter aircraft. Churchill started pressuring Wavell to mount an immediate counteroffensive. Despite heavy air attacks, the TIGER convoy arrived on 12 May, after losing one transport carrying fifty-seven tanks.

Prior to launching his counterattack, Wavell wanted to gain control of the Halfaya Pass. On 15 May he launched Operation BREVITY, under the command of Brigadier William Gott (q.v.), to secure the pass and Fort Capuzzo beyond. Rommel skillfully parried the British thrust and the British withdrew from Fort Capuzzo the next day. By 27 May the Germans recaptured the Halfaya Pass. Unable to advance any farther because of supply problems, they dug in and fortified their positions with 88mm antiaircraft guns.

Under continuing pressure from Churchill, Wavell launched his major attack on 15 June. Operation BATTLEAXE started with a frontal attack on the Sollum-Halfaya Pass (q.v.) axis. Skillfully using the 88mm antiaircraft guns in an antitank role, the Germans blunted the British attack, and then Rommel counterattacked. BATTLEAXE was over by 17 June, with Wavell losing ninety-one of his new tanks. Churchill relieved Wavell on 21 June and replaced him with General Sir Claude Auchinleck (q.v.) the following month. General Sir Alan Cunningham (q.v.) was given command of the newly renamed Eighth Army.

Auchinleck resisted Churchill's constant pressure for an immediate British counterattack. When Hitler launched Operation BARBAROSSA against the Soviet Union (q.v.) on 22 June, Rommel's force in North Africa slipped even lower than it had been on the German priority scale for logistical sustainment. Most of the *Luftwaffe* units in the Mediterranean were sent to Russia, which gave the British a freer hand in attacking Rommel's supply convoys on the sea and from the air. Rommel continued to grow weaker. By November he had 414 tanks, 320 aircraft, and nine divisions (three German), four of which were tied down at Tobruk. The British had some 700 tanks, 1,000 aircraft, and eight divisions.

Operation CRUSADER opened on 18 November with British XIII Corps advancing on the Halfaya Pass, and XXX Corps attempting to sweep around Rommel's southern flank to reach the besieged garrison at Tobruk. The XXX Corps reached Sidi Rezegh (q.v.), twenty miles southeast of Tobruk. After a series of furious tank battles on 22 and 23 November, Rommel drove deep into the British rear with two *Panzer* divisions. He attempted to relieve the Axis forces at Halfaya, and at the same time cut off the Eighth Army.

With his tank losses mounting, Cunningham wanted to halt the attack. Auchinleck immediately relieved him and replaced him with Major General Neil Ritchie (q.v.). The British continued to press on, and on 29 November they broke through to Tobruk. By 8 December Rommel finally was overcome by attrition and began to withdraw. In order to avoid encirclement in the Benghazi bulge,

Rommel retreated back across Cyrenaica, reaching El Agheila on 6 January 1942. CRUSADER was a clear victory for the British, but they were unable to exploit it because of a lack of reinforcements.

As Rommel withdrew to the east, the RAF continued to attack his supply convoys in the Mediterranean. Axis losses in November 1941 reached 62 percent. Hitler reacted by shifting the Second *Luftflotte* from Russia to Sicily and by ordering the German Navy to send ten U-boats into the Mediterranean. In December, Rommel's resupply situation improved significantly. Meanwhile, the Japanese attack on Pearl Harbor caused the British to reroute forces from North Africa to India and Singapore. By mid-January Rommel, who now had shorter supply lines, was ready to resume the offensive.

On 21 January 1942, Rommel launched his second offensive, and quickly drove the British back about 300 miles. Rommel recaptured Benghazi on 29 January and continued east, reaching Gazala on 4 February. There he halted along the Eighth Army's defensive line between Gazala and Bir Hacheim. Then, for nearly four months, both sides sat on either side of the Gazala Line, building up strength.

On 26 May, Rommel launched Operation *VENEZIA,* his attack against the Gazala Line (q.v.). Both sides were roughly equal in strength, but Ritchie had his armored units widely separated, while Rommel kept his concentrated. Using his armor, Rommel swept around the Free French Brigade at Bir Hacheim, on the southern end of the line, and turned north, cutting across the Allied rear. A secondary attack in the north pinned down the Allied forces there.

By 28 May, the Axis armored forces behind the Allied lines were in trouble. Rommel had lost more than one-third of his tanks, and the remainder were running short of fuel and ammunition. On 29 May the Italian Trieste Division managed to clear a path through the center of the Gazala Line. That opening became a lifeline to Rommel's armor. On 30 May, Rommel consolidated his remaining armor in a defensive position that came to be called the "Cauldron."

On 5–6 June, Rommel successfully beat off Ritchie's series of piecemeal counterattacks. On 10–11 June the Free French finally were driven out of Bir Hacheim, and on 11 June, Rommel's armor broke out of the Cauldron. The Eighth Army started falling back to the Egyptian border again. On 15 June German tanks reached the coast, and Rommel turned his attention to Tobruk. This time he would not make the same mistake of leaving a British fortified position in his rear area.

Tobruk fell on 21 June (*see* Tobruk III), and in the process the Axis forces captured two and a half million gallons of much-needed fuel, as well as 2,000 wheeled vehicles. The fall of Tobruk, however, had unforeseen consequences for the Axis. Churchill learned of the news during a meeting with Franklin D. Roosevelt (q.v.). The American president immediately offered the British help. The resulting 300 Sherman tanks and 100 self-propelled guns would later play a pivotal role at El Alamein.

The British withdrew to defensive positions at Mersa Matrúh, about 100 miles inside Egypt. Rommel pursued. Auchinleck relieved Ritchie and personally assumed command of the Eighth Army. Rommel, with only sixty tanks, attacked at Mersa Matrúh (q.v.) on 26 June, and routed four British divisions in three days of fighting. The British continued to withdraw to the vicinity of El Alamein, another 120 miles to the east.

Less than 100 miles from Alexandria, Auchinleck was determined to hold near El Alamein. Under constant pressure from Rommel, he improvised a fluid defensive line based on Ruweisat Ridge (q.v.), a few miles south of the El Alamein defensive perimeter. Rommel attacked on 1 July, attempting to bypass El Alamein. For three weeks Auchinleck skillfully battled Rommel to a standstill. Auchinleck launched a major counterattack on 21–22 July, but gained no ground. (The battle of Ruweisat Ridge sometimes is called El Alamein I.) Exhausted, both sides paused to regroup.

Despite the fact that Auchinleck had halted Rommel's advance, Churchill relieved him in early August and replaced him with General Sir Harold Alexander (q.v.) as commander in chief of the Middle East, and Lieutenant General Sir Bernard L. Montgomery (q.v.) as commander of the Eighth Army. Although Churchill desperately wanted a clear victory for political and morale purposes, neither of his new commanders was inclined to go over to the offensive without first massing an overwhelming advantage.

On 30 August 1942, Rommel launched what he believed would be the final attack in his drive to the Nile. The British, however, had made extensive preparations around El Alamein, based on a plan devised by Auchinleck and adopted by Montgomery. The British commander also had the advantage of knowing Rommel's intentions through ULTRA intercepts. Rommel intended to sweep south of Ruweisat Ridge, cut off El Alamein, and take it from the rear. In preparation, the British laid extensive minefields and heavily fortified Alam el

Halfa Ridge, southeast of El Alamein. By 3 September, the Axis attack, short of fuel, petered out. Montgomery counterattacked immediately, but called it off as soon as the Axis forces were pushed back. Both sides again hunkered down to build up their strength. The battle of Alam el Halfa (q.v.) was the turning point of the war in North Africa.

Montgomery used the time to rest and train his troops, integrate the new American tanks he had received, and carefully plan his set-piece counterattack. Rommel, meanwhile, became ill and returned to Germany on sick leave. When Montgomery finally launched the attack, his forces and equipment were three times greater than his opponents'.

The battle of El Alamein (q.v.) started on 23 October with a massive artillery preparation fired by 900 guns. Rommel immediately returned from Germany to assume command of the battle. The Allies tried for five days to break through the Axis positions, sustaining 10,000 casualties in the process. On 30–31 October, Montgomery renewed the attack, with strong support from the RAF. Critically short on fuel and ammunition, Rommel started to disengage on 3 November. At first, Hitler insisted on his usual standfast orders. On 4 November he grudgingly gave Rommel permission to withdraw, and the 1,400-mile pursuit to Tunisia began.

For the next three months, Montgomery followed more than pursued Rommel across the northern coast of North Africa. Despite constant urgings from his German and Italian superiors who wanted him to save Libya, Rommel was more interested in preserving his force to fight another day. He paused at El Agheila between 23 November and 18 December, and again at Buerat and Wadi Zemzem, from 26 December to 16 January 1943. Rommel reached Tripoli on 23 January, and the Tunisian border at the end of January. By the time he got there, however, another Allied force was waiting for him in Tunisia (q.v.).

On 8 November 1942, just four days after Rommel started his long withdrawal, the British and Americans executed Operation TORCH, the Northwest African landings (q.v.). In a coordinated series of landings, the Western Task Force, under Major General George S. Patton (q.v.), landed on the Atlantic coast near Casablanca; the Central Task Force, under Major General Lloyd Fredendall (q.v.), landed just inside the Mediterranean around Oran, and the Eastern Task Force, under Major General Charles Ryder, landed near Algiers. Although all the landing sites were in Vichy French territory, the ultimate objective of the landings was the port and airfield complex of Bizerte and Tunis in Tunisia. Command of those facilities would allow the Allies to bomb Sicily, protect the Malta convoys (q.v.), and strike at Rommel's supply lines.

While the Allies established themselves ashore and attempted to come to terms with the Vichy French, the Germans reacted swiftly, sending troops from Sicily to Tunisia on 9 November. Hitler also gave the order for the German military in occupied France to take control of Vichy France. The French fleet at Toulon (q.v.), however, scuttled itself before the Germans could seize it.

From the moment the Allies landed, the campaign in Northwest Africa and the race for Tunis was a logistical battle. The side that could mass forces the fastest would win. For the Germans, control of the Tunis complex was critical to prevent Rommel from being trapped between Montgomery in the east, and the newly formed British First Army in the west. On 28 November the Allies reached Tebourba, only twelve miles from Tunis, but a well-conducted Axis counterattack drove them back twenty miles in seven days.

The Germans won the initial race for Tunis because they had the shorter supply lines, and their aircraft, operating from closer bases, had much longer loiter times over the contested area. In January 1943 the winter rains and resulting mud brought mechanized operations to a halt in northern Tunisia. Waiting for better weather in the spring, the Allies continued to build up their forces. The British First Army, under Lieutenant General Sir Kenneth Anderson (q.v.), was organized into three corps, the V British, the II U.S., and the XIX French. The Axis forces in northern Tunisia now consisted of General Jürgen von Arnim's (q.v.) Fifth *Panzer* Army.

Once Rommel's *Panzerarmee Afrika* crossed into southern Tunisia it occupied positions in the old French fortifications of the Mareth Line. Rommel's ten divisions were well below half strength, with only 78,000 troops and 129 tanks. Before he had to face the rapidly closing Montgomery, Rommel intended to eliminate the threat of the Allied First Army in his rear. On 14 February the Germans launched the first leg of a two-pronged offensive, with von Arnim's forces attacking that day through the Faid Pass for Sidi Bou Zid. The following day, Rommel in the south attacked toward Gafsa. The bulk of Rommel's forces, however, remained in the Mareth Line. By 18 February the Kasserine Pass (q.v.) was in Axis hands, and U.S. ground forces had suffered their first major defeat of the war.

Rommel tried to advance north toward Thala

through the Kasserine Pass on 19 February, but the support he expected to receive from von Arnim did not materialize. After several days of slow advances he reached Thala on 21 February but could advance no farther. Hampered by a divided German command structure and rapidly massing Allied reinforcements, the attack stalled. The Allies pushed forward and recaptured Kasserine Pass on 25 February. Rommel returned to the Mareth Line to prepare to face Montgomery.

When the Eighth Army reached Tunisia the Allies modified their command structure to conform with decisions made at the Casablanca Conference (*see* Conferences, Allied). General Dwight D. Eisenhower (q.v.) became the supreme commander of all Allied forces in the Mediterranean west of Tripoli. Alexander became Eisenhower's deputy, and at the same time commander of the 18th Army Group, which controlled the First and Eighth Armies, and the separate U.S. II Corps. General Mark Clark (q.v.) took command of the Fifth Army, which was covering Spanish Morocco. Air Marshal Sir Arthur Tedder (q.v.) assumed command of the Allied air forces, and Admiral Cunningham retained command of the naval forces.

On 24 February the Germans, too, realigned their command structures. Rommel became the commander of *Armeegruppe Afrika,* which included the *Afrika Korps,* von Arnim's Fifth *Panzer* Army, and the Italian First Army under Field Marshal Giovanni Messe. The Axis forces finally had a unified command structure in Tunisia, but Rommel probably was not the best choice. By that point in the war he had become frustrated and dispirited, the cumulative effects of the long seesaw campaign. To make matters worse, von Arnim, who detested Rommel, continued to do, for the most part, whatever he pleased.

The Axis position in North Africa was hopeless; the final outcome clearly in the hands of the logisticians. As the Allies consolidated their control over the North African coast, the pressure on Malta eased, which in turn enabled the Allies to further restrict the Axis supply convoys. Without coordinating with Rommel, von Arnim on 26 February launched Operation *OCHSENKOPF (OXHEAD),* a drive toward Beja. By 3 March that offensive stalled, at the cost of seventy-one precious tanks.

Montgomery's forces crossed into Tunisia on 4 February. They reached Medenine on the 16th and established defensive positions. Hoping to catch the British off-balance, Rommel attacked south from the Mareth Line on 6 March. Warned by ULTRA, Montgomery was waiting. The Germans ran into skillfully prepared antitank defenses

and lost fifty-two tanks in very short order. Right after the failure of the Medenine attack, Rommel returned to Germany a sick man, and von Arnim assumed overall Axis command.

After the American debacle at Kasserine Pass, command of the U.S. II Corps passed to Patton. He wanted to mount an attack to drive to the coast, but Alexander would authorize only limited attacks designed to draw German forces away from the Mareth positions. Alexander at that point simply did not trust American units. In fact, many among the British forces disparagingly referred to their American allies as "Our Italians." Patton's limited attack between 17 and 25 March was successful, however, tying down the 10th *Panzer* Division near El Guettar (q.v.).

On 20 March, Montgomery attempted a night frontal penetration of the Mareth Line (q.v.). The attack failed by 22 March. The next day he shifted the weight of the main attack around the southwestern flank of the line, through the Matmata Hills. By 26 March his forces broke through the Tebaga gap. The Italian First Army and the remainder of the *Afrika Korps* were forced back. Under continuous pressure from the Eighth Army on one side, and U.S. II Corps on the other, the Axis forces withdrew to Enfidaville.

By 7 April, the Allied First and Eighth Armies linked up, squeezing the Axis into an ever-tighter pocket. On the east coast, the Eighth Army took Gabes on 6 April, Sfax on 10 April, Sousse on 12 April, and Enfidaville on 21 April. In the north, the U.S. II Corps, now under Major General Omar N. Bradley (q.v.), took Mateur on 3 May and Bizerte on 7 May. Montgomery's 7th Armoured Division also captured Tunis on 7 May. The remaining Axis forces in Tunisia were now caught in two pockets, one between Bizerte and Tunis, and the other on isolated Cap Bon.

The Axis surrendered on 13 May 1943. Their losses in Tunisia alone totaled 40,000 dead or wounded, 267,000 prisoners, 250 tanks, 2,330 aircraft, and 232 ships. British and American casualties were 33,000 and 18,558, respectively. For the entire North African campaign, the British suffered 220,000 casualties. Total Axis losses came to 620,000, which included the loss of three field armies. The losses were huge for what amounted to, at best, a secondary theater for both the Axis and the Allies. In the end, logistics and sea power were the determining factors in the campaign.

David T. Zabecki

Additional Reading
Barnett, Corelli, *The Desert Generals* (1982).

Greene, Jack, and Alessandro Massignani, *Rommel's North Africa Campaign: September 1940–November 1942* (1994).

Howe, George, *Northwest Africa: Seizing the Initiative in the West* (1957).

Liddell Hart, Basil H. (ed.), *The Rommel Papers* (1953).

Mellenthin, Friedrich Wilhelm von, *Panzer Battles* (1956).

Pitt, Barrie, *The Crucible of War: Western Desert 1941* (1980).

———, *The Crucible of War: The Year of Alamein 1942* (1982).

North Cape (26 December 1943)

During his conference with Adolf Hitler (q.v.) on 19–20 December 1943, Admiral Karl Dönitz (q.v.) informed the German dictator that the battle cruiser *Scharnhorst* and some destroyers would attack the next convoy sighted on the Murmansk run. Dönitz did not have long to wait. On the morning of 22 December 1943, a *Luftwaffe* pilot on a meteorological mission reported a convoy in the vicinity of the Faroe Islands. Since the last two arctic convoys had arrived untouched, Vice Admiral Sir Bruce Fraser (q.v.), commander of the British Home Fleet, assumed that Dönitz would probably use the *Scharnhorst* against the next convoy, JW-55B. Shortly after the convoy was sighted, a stream of ULTRA (q.v.) intercepts indicated the degree of German interest in the convoy and their intent to attack it with their surface fleet. Shortly after, ULTRA confirmed that the *Scharnhorst* and five destroyers had deployed.

The Royal Navy (RN) prepared its plans to fight JW-55B through every possible peril with great diligence. The Distant Covering Force, commanded by Fraser, comprised the battleship HMS *Duke of York,* the light cruiser HMS *Jamaica,* and several destroyers. Between the convoy's escort and Fraser's task force was a cruiser squadron under Rear Admiral Robert Burnett. His command comprised the heavy cruiser HMS *Norfolk,* and the light cruisers HMS *Sheffield* and HMS *Belfast.* The last line of defense was the convoy's escort of nine destroyers, which Fraser cautiously reinforced after receiving the ULTRA report.

The German naval command in the Arctic was caught fully unprepared by Dönitz's decision to go on the offensive. The commander of the battle fleet had recently gone on leave, and command of the German arctic surface fleet fell on the shoulders of the area destroyer commander, Rear Admiral Eric Bey. Apart from the *Scharnhorst,* the only other ships available were five big Z.23-class destroyers under Captain Rolf Johannesson.

Bey was severely handicapped by more than his lack of big-ship command experience. The speed with which his superiors rediscovered their offensive spirit found him very short in experienced manpower. His command staff was pulled together on an ad hoc basis and worked under the assumption that no major operations were in the offing. Furthermore, some key positions were simply not filled, and by far the most crucial of these was this complete lack of a *B-Dienst* staff. These specialists were specifically trained in deciphering and identifying the sources of Allied radio transmissions. In addition, the German sortie was heavily compromised by their ignorance of UL-TRA and their complete lack of faith in their own radar equipment.

Bey's search for JW-55B throughout the morning of 26 December was hampered by severe Arctic conditions. At 0820 hours, he made a minor course adjustment that Johannesson failed to follow. This left the *Scharnhorst* sailing alone and directly toward JW-55B. At 0926 hours, the *Scharnhorst* was suddenly illuminated by the bright pink glow of an RN star shell. Burnett's cruisers sighted the *Scharnhorst* and opened fire. The HMS *Norfolk* was the only ship in range, and she released six rapid broadsides before Burnett decided to break off the engagement. Bey, however, decided to ignore Burnett's challenge and continued his search for the convoy itself. The HMS *Norfolk* managed to score two hits. One was a dud, but the other destroyed the *Scharnhorst's* forward radar set. After this brief engagement, Bey made a half-hearted attempt to rejoin his destroyers. Unfortunately, Johannesson showed no inclination to investigate the pink glow of the star shells south of his position. The German destroyers were never a factor in the further events of the day.

Although Burnett was subjected to some criticism by Fraser for failing to maintain contact with the *Scharnhorst,* the cruiser commander was certain that he would encounter the *Scharnhorst* again. He did so at 1220 hours, again catching Bey off-guard. This time, however, Bey fought back. The *Scharnhorst* scored two hits on the *Norfolk,* one of which eliminated one of her main turrets. After this brief exchange of gunfire, Burnett contented himself with shadowing the *Scharnhorst.*

Had Bey been a little more aggressive, he still might have been able to find the convoy. Instead, he began to seriously consider aborting the mission. Around 1300 hours, Bey finally concluded that enough was enough, and decided to return to

Alten Fjord by the quickest route. That decision was his last, and perhaps most fatal error. Had Bey steered directly into an approaching storm front, the *Scharnhorst* might have been able to evade her pursuers. It appears, however, that Bey was completely unaware of the approaching HMS *Duke of York,* and his shore-based assets failed to advise him of her approach.

Shortly after 1600 hours, the British battleship's radar made its first fix on the *Scharnhorst* at a range of about twenty-three miles. Fraser decided to close the range further before engaging. At 1645 hours, Fraser reached his optimum tactical position and ordered a salvo of four star shells to illuminate the target. When they burst, the *Scharnhorst* was observed steaming serenely with her turrets still trained fore and aft. The British battlewagon's first three salvoes were all close to the mark, scoring at least one hit.

Shortly afterward, the *Scharnhorst* recovered from her initial surprise and opened fire. She also changed course to the east, but did so on an erratic course, allowing her B turret to support her sole aft turret. Apparently, her A turret was already eliminated by HMS *Duke of York's* first salvoes. The *Scharnhorst's* fire was relatively accurate, with two 280mm shells tearing away part of her adversary's radar and telecommunications array. The temporary damage to HMS *Duke of York's* radar momentarily deprived Fraser of much-needed targeting information. More disconcerting was that the German vessel was taking full advantage of her superior speed and rapidly pulling away from him, despite being hit by at least two more shells.

For a brief moment, Fraser was clearly disillusioned and feared that the *Scharnhorst* had once again escaped. Then the British destroyers reported that the range gap was once again narrowing, and the HMS *Duke of York* managed to find the range quickly. At 1820 hours, one of her 14-inch shells scored a crucial hit on the *Scharnhorst's* starboard-side machinery. Despite a very quick and effective damage crew response, she had now lost her edge in speed. This allowed two pursuing groups of British destroyers to get within torpedo range. Despite being showered by shrapnel, they obtained a minimum of three torpedo hits on the *Scharnhorst,* further slowing her down.

At about 1900 hours, Fraser closed in for the kill. As the range narrowed, the British shells demolished the *Scharnhorst's* upper works and armament, but even at close range, there was little chance that they would penetrate her main armored deck. Fraser realized this, and once the *Scharnhorst* was battered into relative submission,

he ordered the HMS *Jamaica* to finish her off with torpedoes. The HMS *Belfast* and four destroyers joined the melee, and they combined to hit the hapless German ship eleven times.

At 1948 hours, the *Scharnhorst* finally rolled over and sank. Only thirty-six of her crew of almost 2,000 were fished out of the frigid arctic waters by the British destroyers. In all, she was hit by thirteen of HMS *Duke of York's* 14-inch shells, and at least fourteen torpedoes, not to mention dozens of hits from 4.5- to 8-inch shells. British casualties and damages were extremely light.

The battle of the North Cape was the last big ship battle to occur in Europe. With the loss of the *Scharnhorst,* the *Kriegsmarine* was now clearly on the defensive. Only the *Tirpitz* was to remain a threat to the convoys on the Murmansk run. This battle, unlike any others of World War II, revealed the degree to which the German surface fleet was incapable of successfully challenging the Royal Navy for control of the seas. While Bey's handling of his forces was at best erratic and confused, his errors were aided and abetted by his superiors' actions and lethargy. All in all, the *Scharnhorst's* last operation was poorly considered, planned, and executed.

Today, the HMS *Belfast* is a floating museum under the administration of the Imperial War Museum. It is anchored in the River Thames, directly across from the Tower of London.

Peter K.H. Mispelkamp

Additional Reading

Bekker, C.D., *Defeat at Sea: The Struggle and Eventual Defeat of the German Navy, 1939–1945* (1950).

Taylor, John E.S.R., *Northern Escort* (1945).

Northwest Africa Landings (8–14 November 1942)

[See map 29 on page 1339]

The Allied invasion of French Northwest Africa, Operation TORCH, began on 8 November 1942. Vichy French forces capitulated three days later. The largest amphibious operation to date, Operation TORCH involved landings in nine sectors around the port cities of Casablanca, Oran, and Algiers by an assault force of roughly 107,000 troops. In conjunction with British forces already in the Middle East, the operation's aim was the expulsion of German forces from North Africa and control of the entire southern Mediterranean shore. The Allies ultimately achieved this when Axis forces in Tunisia surrendered on 13 May 1943.

Following Germany's defeat of France and the creation of Marshal Henri Philippe Pétain's Vichy government (qq.v.) in June 1940, French Northwest Africa held great importance for both Great Britain and the United States. The German-French Armistice Treaty barred German use of the French fleet or French colonial ports. Yet Berlin's word meant little to London or Washington. Great Britain, at war with Germany and Italy, viewed Axis control of Northwest Africa as a threat to its naval bases at Gibraltar and Freetown and to its lines of communications to the Middle Eastern theater. For the United States, still at peace, Axis influence in Northwest Africa meant direct peril for the Western Hemisphere.

Until mid-1942, Anglo-American efforts to keep Northwest Africa in friendly hands were limited. London's attempt to create a counter French government in North Africa, its support of the Free French General Charles de Gaulle (q.v.), and its attacks on Mers el-Kébir and Dakar (qq.v.) only antagonized the Vichy regime. The United States, still weak militarily, maintained diplomatic relations with Vichy France in an effort to strengthen Pétain's resolve against German demands.

In December 1940, President Franklin D. Roosevelt (q.v.) sent counselor Robert D. Murphy to make contact with General Maxime Weygand (q.v.), Vichy's delegate-general for French Africa. In March 1941, Murphy and Weygand concluded an economic accord whereby the United States provided material aid for French North Africa in return for augmented consular representation there, the prime function of which was political observation.

Anglo-American staff talks began in Washington in early 1941. They affirmed the "Atlantic First" principle for a possible joint war against Germany and Japan. They also noted the importance of the Mediterranean and North Africa for the European theater, acknowledging for the first time the possibility of a Northwest African operation. In August 1941, at the Placentia Bay Conference (see Conferences, Allied), British Prime Minister Winston S. Churchill (q.v.) again raised the prospect of French Northwest Africa's invasion with Roosevelt. Roosevelt, concerned about a German move there, was favorably inclined.

More detailed Allied operational discussion began once America entered the war in December 1941. Roosevelt, Churchill, and their respective chiefs of staff convened in Washington that month for the Arcadia Conference. Churchill and the British chiefs, favoring a peripheral strategy for victory in Europe, suggested the closure of a ring around Germany from Archangel through Turkey, along the northern Mediterranean coast, to the western European seaboard. This ring would blockade the Axis powers, open the Mediterranean to Allied shipping, and allow a return to the Continent.

For 1942, Churchill proposed Operation SUPER-GYMNAST, the Allied occupation of the Atlantic and Mediterranean coasts of French Northwest Africa, and the subsequent capture of the Mediterranean's southern shore. Roosevelt noted that a German defeat in Africa, though not militarily decisive, could have negative repercussions for Adolf Hitler (q.v.) within Germany. Preliminary studies for Operation SUPER-GYMNAST emerged at Arcadia. Details remained vague, but the Allies decided in principle on Northwest Africa as their first major objective.

General George C. Marshall (q.v.), U.S. Army chief of staff, preferred a different strategy. Marshall objected to the expense and delay of peripheral actions like Operation SUPER-GYMNAST and advocated a direct assault on German-controlled Europe. He called for the methodical buildup of Allied forces in Great Britain (Operation BOLERO) followed by a cross-channel invasion of occupied France for the spring of 1943 (Operation ROUNDUP). This approach would benefit from the use of Britain as a base while providing the best chance to ease pressure on the Soviet Union, which was enduring the main German onslaught.

Operation SLEDGEHAMMER, an emergency measure for the case of a Soviet near-collapse, envisioned a small cross-channel attack in 1942 to create a bridgehead for the larger Operation ROUNDUP in 1943. Marshall presented his scheme to Roosevelt in March 1942. The president approved the draft plans, and in April, Marshall and presidential adviser Harry Hopkins (q.v.) journeyed to London to gain British support.

London was unconvinced. The Allies, argued the British chiefs of staff, had neither the troops nor the landing craft (q.v.) for a cross-channel attack in 1942. The British were likewise skeptical regarding 1943. In June, the British War Cabinet concurred that unless Germany were previously disabled, an unlikely eventuality, Marshall's scheme would bring disaster. Churchill sent Vice Admiral Lord Louis Mountbatten (q.v.) to Washington to convince Roosevelt. The admiral was persuasive, yet the president insisted on bringing American troops into action against Germany in 1942. Such action would provide a domestic political boost while assuaging Soviet calls for a second front. Operation SUPER-GYMNAST was the best alternative.

Marshall, realizing that the North African endeavor would draw valuable forces from the Pacific, while eliminating the continental attack for 1942 and probably for 1943 as well, made a final effort. He suggested that Roosevelt warn London that Washington would concentrate its forces in the Pacific should the cross-channel invasion not occur as suggested. Roosevelt rejected this approach. On 24 July 1942 in a conference including Marshall and Hopkins in London, the formal decision to proceed with Operation SUPER-GYMNAST occurred. Operation TORCH became the new code name. As a formality, Operation TORCH remained officially contingent on the impossibility of Operation ROUNDUP for 1943. Roosevelt, meanwhile, named 30 October 1942 as the deadline for TORCH.

The Allies agreed on Operation TORCH only in outline form. Detailed planning began in mid-August. Here new problems emerged. The question of landing sites triggered the so-called Transatlantic Essay Contest, from late August to early September 1942. The joint Anglo-American planners expected an Axis reaction within two weeks and agreed that the Allies should land as close to Tunisia as possible to capture its key ports before the Axis could do so. Bône, Algiers, and Oran thus appeared essential initial targets. Casablanca was also desirable as a supply port. Due to maritime commitments in other theaters, however, the Allies lacked resources for four landings.

Marshall deemed Casablanca imperative, arguing that without immediate control of Casablanca, a German move into Northwest Africa via Spain could trap Allied troops within the Mediterranean. He wished to omit the Algiers and Bône landings, and advance more methodically toward Tunisia. Churchill and the British chiefs of staff disagreed. Allied troops, argued London, had to close quickly on Tunisia, for German control of Tunisia could turn Operation TORCH into a catastrophe. Control of Algeria east of Oran was essential. Casablanca was superfluous, for Spain would likely not join the Axis.

Compromise came in early September. Casablanca, Oran, and Algiers would be the initial targets, and Allied forces would be divided into respective Western, Central, and Eastern Task Forces. The troops would land at several points around the well-defended port cities and take the cities by land. Maritime support for the landings remained difficult due to heavy obligations in other theaters. This problem moved the target date back to 8 November, and it found resolution only when Roosevelt and Churchill personally induced their respective naval commanders to cooperate more fully. The Allies would share naval support, with the United States responsible for the Atlantic and Britain responsible for the Mediterranean. The U.S. Army Air Force would support the Casablanca and Oran landings, while the Royal Air Force would support the Algiers landing.

Issues of command were comparatively simple. The Allies believed that American com-

American troops land on the beaches at Surcouf, 20 miles east of Algiers, Operation TORCH, 9 November 1942. (IWM NA 30)

mand would avoid another British-French confrontation while bringing Vichy's officials in North Africa to the Allied side. Thus, there was no dissent with the appointment of Lieutenant General Dwight D. Eisenhower (q.v.), American commanding general for the European Theater of Operations, as commander in chief for Operation TORCH.

The Western, Central, and Eastern Task Forces fell under the respective American commands of Major General George Patton, Major General Lloyd Fredendall (qq.v.), and Major General Charles W. Ryder. Patton's and Fredendall's forces were exclusively American. The Western Task Force, consisting of 35,000 troops in thirty-nine ships, sailed directly from the United States. The Center Task Force, consisting of 39,000 troops in forty-seven ships, sailed from Great Britain via Gibraltar. Ryder's 33,000-man Eastern Task Force was a mixed Allied force. It too sailed from Britain via Gibraltar, in thirty-four ships.

Following the capture of the ports, the troops under Patton and Fredendall were to form the U.S. Fifth Army, then occupy French Morocco while guarding against a possible counterattack from Spanish Morocco. Ryder's troops would become the British First Army, pass to the command of British Lieutenant General Kenneth Anderson (q.v.), and press toward Tunisia (q.v.).

The most puzzling problem involved the stance of France's armed forces in Northwest Africa, which stood under the command of a Vichy government unlikely to sanction an Allied incursion. The Axis permitted the French to maintain 120,000 troops in North Africa, as well as certain naval and air units. Though much of the French equipment was poor, the French fighting spirit, particularly in the navy, was not lacking. The Allies searched for a major French figure who could lend legitimacy to the Allied presence in Northwest Africa. De Gaulle lacked full Allied confidence and Vichy's commanders viewed him as a traitor.

The Allies thus chose General Henri Giraud (q.v.), who had escaped from German captivity in April 1942 and was living in unoccupied France. Untainted by Vichy or de Gaulle, Giraud's voice would hopefully find echo in North Africa. In June 1942, Giraud agreed to cooperate with the Allies, and chose Major General Charles Mast, a corps commander in Algeria, as his deputy on the scene.

Mast's network of conspirators in North Africa agreed to aid the Allied invasion by seizing key installations and by arresting noncooperative officers. In a secret meeting near Algiers on 23 October with Murphy and Eisenhower's deputy, Major General Mark W. Clark (q.v.), Mast revealed the locations of French troops and batteries, port capacities, and other military information.

In return for French cooperation, Murphy gave Washington's word to restore French imperial sovereignty and to reequip French troops to fight the common Axis enemy. Yet relations between Washington and the French conspirators lacked complete openness. Murphy never revealed the exact landing sites and did not inform Mast of Operation TORCH's timing until 5 November. Giraud, meanwhile, insisted on holding supreme command of the operation and only acceded with reluctance to Eisenhower's leadership.

Hitler and the German supreme command were concerned about Allied designs in Northwest Africa ever since Britain's raid on Dakar in September 1940. Before Germany's June 1941 attack on the Soviet Union (q.v.), Berlin worked to set up bases in the Northwest African region for a future war with the United States, and Hitler meant to return to this project after the expected victory in the east. As 1942 progressed, Berlin received numerous reports that the Allies would attempt a landing in the area. Yet to the German leadership, Northwest Africa was but a single possible Allied target, and not even the most likely. Moreover, neither Hitler nor Italian dictator Benito Mussolini (q.v.) trusted the French enough to allow rearmament in North Africa sufficient to meet a large-scale landing.

In late October 1942, Berlin became aware of the Allied shipping concentration at Gibraltar for the Algerian landings. German analysts believed, however, that the buildup aimed to reinforce Britain's base at Malta. Italy's supreme command worried more over a landing in French Africa, but Rome's concerns found little echo in Berlin. As the convoys left Gibraltar for Algeria on 5 November, German analysis remained unchanged. As the Allied landings began on the morning of 8 November, there was no Axis interference. Berlin learned of the landings from British news reporting.

Vichy's resistance to the landings was partially effective. Mast's conspirators surfaced prematurely and were arrested. All three Allied forces met hostile fire from the North African shore, particularly from French naval batteries. Resistance was sporadic at Algiers and Oran, but quite determined in French Morocco. In Vichy, Pétain met Roosevelt's explanatory telegram with scorn. "We have been attacked," protested the marshal, "and we shall defend ourselves." Giraud's voice failed to halt the resistance, for as Eisenhower later explained, "The name of Marshal Pétain is still something to conjure with in North Africa."

Yet the name of Admiral Jean François Darlan (q.v.), commander in chief of the French armed forces, who was in Algiers visiting his ill son, held heavy authority as well. Darlan was a confidant of Pétain as well as an exponent of collaboration with Berlin. Yet on the afternoon of 8 November, he surrendered Algiers as Ryder's troops reached the outskirts of the city. On 9 November, Clark arrived in Algiers to negotiate a general cease-fire. Following heated negotiations, Darlan ordered the cease-fire on the morning of 10 November. In addition, he agreed to assist the Allied effort and to attempt to bring the French fleet from Toulon to Africa.

At Oran, American troops had already induced surrender. French Morocco complied with Darlan's cease-fire order on 11 November, thus sparing Casablanca an assault. On 14 November, the colonies of French West Africa broke with Vichy and joined Algeria and Morocco on the Allied side. Already on 12 November, Anderson's First Army easily captured Bône, and was en route to Tunisia.

Speed was necessary, for the German reaction to Operation TORCH was swift. On 9 November, following a Berlin ultimatum, the *Wehrmacht* began to create a bridgehead in northern Tunisia intending to push the Allies from French North Africa. French forces in Tunisia did not resist the German landings. On the morning of 11 November, German troops occupied the free zone of France, likewise without resistance. Following these actions, Hitler officially repudiated the Armistice Treaty of 1940. Yet Germany failed to capture the French fleet at Toulon (q.v.), which was scuttled rather than being allowed to fall into foreign hands.

Operation TORCH was primarily successful. The landings in Northwest Africa met with triumph, and the Allies gained a firm foothold from which they could launch attacks on the European continent. The Allied casualty figure of 1,469 was far below that predicted by planners in the event of determined French resistance. Yet the Allies made several miscalculations.

First, they underestimated the political consequences of the negotiations with Darlan, who on 13 November became the high commissioner for North Africa. The arrangement with Darlan was a necessary expedient if the Allies were to pacify their flank and press quickly toward Tunisia. Still, the public outcry over the "Darlan Deal" did not subside in London or Washington until Darlan's assassination by a French nationalist on 24 December and Giraud's subsequent accession as high commissioner.

Second, the Allies overestimated the difficulties involved in capturing the eastern Algerian ports and underestimated the speed with which Germany would react. They thus lost the race for Tunis, and would not capture it until the spring of 1943.

Norman J. W. Goda

Additional Reading

Barnett, Correlli, *The Desert Generals* (1982).
———, *Hitler's Generals* (1989).
Howe, George F., *Northwest Africa: Seizing the Initiative* (1957).
Liddell Hart, Basil H., *The Rommel Papers* (1953).

Norway (9 April–9 June 1940)

[See map 30 on page 1340]

When German military units invaded Norway in the early hours of 9 April 1940, Norway's long-term strategic policy of rigorous neutrality was shattered. The assault also meant that the uneasy quiet in Europe, the so-called Phony War (q.v.) following the Nazi devastation of Poland (q.v.) the previous fall, was coming to an end with the German armed forces seizing the initiative and the momentum in the conflict. As a military operation, the German occupation of Norway was a complete success and provided important strategic gains. Well planned and skillfully executed in the face of superior British sea power, the operation demonstrated the capabilities of the German armed forces.

During the 1930s, it became apparent that the efforts of the League of Nations (q.v.) to maintain peace were not effective, and Norway's political and military leaders strengthened their commitment to strict neutrality. In addition, Norway's strategic location on the North Sea meant that it faced possible attacks from the Soviet Union or Germany; but Norwegian military planners believed that Britain's control of the seas would help deter such an assault.

After war broke out in September 1939, Norway's strategic position gained additional importance for the British. First Lord of the Admiralty Winston S. Churchill (q.v.) had already proposed on 19 September 1939 that action be taken to prevent the transport of Swedish ore from Narvik in northern Norway to Germany. He called for a blockade of the Norwegian coast, proposing that a minefield be laid across Norwegian territorial waters to force German transport ships into the open sea, past waiting British warships. At that time, however, the issue was not of great urgency and the proposal was shelved until late November. The mining issue was again delayed until 12 January 1940, when the British cabinet decided no action would be taken against Narvik.

In February 1940, the War Cabinet revived plans for an occupation of Norway to be carried out by the middle of March, before the ice in the North Sea thawed and before Germany could resume the transport of iron ore. Code named Operation AVONMOUTH, it called for a joint British and French occupation of Narvik and then all of Norway. A British combat force was assembled, but the end of the Finnish Winter War (q.v.) in mid-March forced the abandonment of these plans. This was only a temporary delay, however. On 29 March 1940, the British War Cabinet decided to strike as soon as "the Germans set foot on Norwegian soil, or there is clear evidence that they intend to do so."

Among Germany's naval planners, the logic of an invasion and occupation of Norway grew out of lessons learned in World War I. At that time, Germany's ocean fleet proved to be largely ineffectual as an offensive weapon. Submarines, on the contrary, proved their worth, and with the growing threat of war with Britain in the late 1930s, German naval strategists looked to establishing submarine bases at Norwegian ports, locations closer to the North Atlantic.

Both Admiral Rolf Carls, naval commander in the Baltic, and Grand Admiral Erich Raeder (q.v.), supreme commander of the German Navy, looked favorably upon the plan that came up for serious discussions in early October 1939. It was decided that a German base ought to be established at either Narvik or Trondheim, ice-free ports accessible by rail and situated outside of the narrow passage between Norway and the British Shetland Islands. While German naval planners believed that Germany, acting in concert with the Soviet Union, could pressure Norway into permitting the establishment of a submarine base, chief of the general staff General Franz Halder (q.v.) opposed the plan. At a 10 October 1939 meeting, Adolf Hitler (q.v.) showed little interest in it, and the plan was shelved.

Raeder persisted and in late November 1939 the plan was again discussed at a meeting of the German naval war staff. Raeder identified the British threat, arguing that Britain might occupy Norway in response to a German invasion of the Netherlands. Furthermore, a German preemptive attack on Norway would strike hard at Britain's economy, which enjoyed a flourishing trade with the Scandinavian nations. Raeder gained support from Vidkun Quisling (q.v.), a Norwegian Army officer and former minister of defense, who came to Berlin for meetings in December 1939. Quisling told high German officials of an alleged secret agreement between Britain and Norway that would permit the establishment of a British base on Norwegian soil in case of war.

The German Naval High Command (OKM) Staff met on 12 December 1939 to discuss the conversations with Quisling, details of which were reported to Hitler. On 14 December, Hitler finally approved a proposal by Raeder to develop plans for the occupation of Norway. Completed by the end of the month, Operations Plan *STUDIE-NORD* (STUDY NORTH) provided a summary of the main military and political issues relating to Norway.

Although preoccupied with the planning for the western campaign, Hitler demonstrated a growing interest in Norway, largely as a result of the rumors and speculation in the newspapers that Allied forces would intervene in Finland. On 10 January 1940, Hitler released Operations Plan *STUDIE-NORD* to the various high commands of the armed services for their review. At that time, only the navy showed an interest, largely because of its commitment to keep British forces out of Norway and from controlling German shipping and sea routes. Hitler's interest in Norway was heightened by the postponement of offensive actions in the west which, he believed, might give the Allies time to intervene in the North Sea or Baltic regions.

On 27 January 1940, Hitler granted General Welhelm Keitel (q.v.) permission to prepare plans for Operation *WESERÜBUNG,* the invasion of Norway. By the end of February, planning had advanced far enough to determine that Operation *WESERÜBUNG* would be separate in timing and the allocation of resources from the planned invasion of Western Europe. The "Directive for *FALL WESERÜBUNG,*" the occupation of Norway and Denmark, was issued by Hitler on 1 March 1940. It established the general requirements for the operation and authorized the armed forces to commence operational planning. The strategic objectives of *WESERÜBUNG* were based on the need to preempt British action in the Scandinavian region, to secure iron ore exports from Sweden, and to improve the position of Germany's navy and *Luftwaffe* against British forces.

The operational orders for the invasion of Norway were actually prepared following a high-level military conference on 5 March 1940. The orders called for the simultaneous landing of troops at seven different locations along the coast.

The first wave would consist of three divisions, followed by the second wave of two divisions, and finally the last wave of a single division.

Secrecy was of the utmost importance for the success of Operation *WESERÜBUNG*, as German cargo ships and virtually the entire German Navy would be involved. The element of surprise would safeguard the naval force during the invasion, while the *Luftwaffe*, which was to play an important role in the operation, provided the air superiority for the safe return of the German fleet. The Germans believed their naval weaknesses would be compensated by air superiority. The *Luftwaffe* mustered 220 bombers, more than 100 fighter and reconnaissance planes, and 400 to 500 transport planes for its role in *WESERÜBUNG*.

German plans (as well as British and French plans) for the occupation of Norway under the cover of the Soviet-Finnish War were interrupted by the Soviet-Finnish peace treaty on 12 March 1940. Hitler now had to look for other justifications to invade Norway, and he ordered a heightened watch of British intentions in the North Sea. The German Navy war command concluded that Britain would continue to focus on this region and would move to interfere with German shipping there, while possibly looking for a pretext to occupy Norway. The German military planners concluded that "sooner or later Germany will have to decide to launch Operation *WESERÜBUNG*. Therefore, it is useful to carry it out as soon as possible, at the latest by 15 April, because after that date the nights will be too short." Operation *WESERÜBUNG* was now a question of timing, not of pretext.

A top-level German military conference on 2 April 1940 was attended by Hitler, General Keitel, chief of the OKW, Field Marshal Hermann Göring (q.v.), commander of the *Luftwaffe,* Grand Admiral Erich Raeder, commander of the navy, and General Nikolaus von Falkenhorst (q.v.), the leader of Operation *WESERÜBUNG*. When von Falkenhorst reported that the weather and ice conditions were now suitable for the invasion, Hitler issued the order that it was to begin at 0515 hours on 9 April 1940.

Secrecy remained essential to the successful occupation of Norway and Denmark. German troop and ship movements at the end of March and early April gave rise to numerous rumors and speculation. Norwegian officials received some indication on 5 April 1940 that their country might be the target, but the reports were vague and the government felt confident that Germany would not invade without provocation, such as

British moves into Norwegian waters. Early on 8 April, British ships laid a minefield near Narvik and two brigades and one battalion of troops were prepared for action in case of a German move, but the German armed forces were already seizing the moment.

On 6 and 7 April, news of a major breakout of German vessels was reported in London. Nevertheless, British and French military officials remained preoccupied with the Narvik minefield and the possibility of a German threat against the Atlantic shipping routes. Warnings of an imminent German invasion were not given to the Norwegian government until late on 8 April 1940.

Once the invasion was launched, it was decisive and completely surprised Norway's government. In nearly simultaneous actions, six German battle groups seized all of Norway's major ports, Oslo, Narvik, Trondheim, Bergen, Stavanger, and Kristianland. Oslo was captured by a force of only 1,500 paratroopers, but not before the defenders managed to sink the cruiser *Blücher.*

Even with some advance warning, the Norwegian cabinet did not issue an order for an immediate and general mobilization, thereby insuring an inadequate and hastily improvised armed resistance. The government refused the Nazi ultimatum to surrender, and resistance gave the government and King Haakon VII (q.v.) enough time to flee to central Norway. The king also rejected the German demand that the government resign and that it be replaced by a government led by Quisling.

The Allies struck back immediately, sinking the cruiser *Karlsruhe* on 9 April, and the cruiser *Königsberg* the next day. Between 14 and 19 April an Anglo-French force counter-invaded at Andalsnes, Namos, and Narvik. By 2 May, the Allies were forced to evacuate their troops, except around Narvik (q.v.).

General Otto Ruge (q.v.) took command of the Norwegian forces. His plans depended upon quick and forceful assistance from the Allies, aid that should have come before superior German forces were able to crush the Norwegian defenders. After three weeks of fighting, southern Norway conceded to the German invaders. In the north, around Narvik, Norwegian and Allied forces maintained pressure on the German troops, but were gradually pushed back.

The resistance of the Norwegian government appears to have surprised the Nazi political and military leaders, who expected a quick capitulation and the acceptance of German terms of surrender. The German minister in Oslo, Dr. Curt Bräuer, became responsible for hastily organizing the negotiations with the Norwegians. With no clear directions, he approached the few representatives of the Norwegian Ministry of Foreign Affairs in Oslo with the same terms, but they were soon rejected.

On 9 April, Quisling returned to Norway and in a radio broadcast proclaimed a new government with himself as prime minister. Although this was not part of the original German plans, Norwegians believed it revealed Nazi intentions and rejected Quisling. In the meantime, Hitler grew impatient and angry at the Norwegians for rejecting his offers.

On 24 April, Hitler appointed Josef Terboven (q.v.) *Reich* commissioner for the occupied Norwegian territory, a position he held until the end of the war. Terboven's tasks were to further Germany's war efforts and to organize an occupation government that included Quisling as the minister-president.

Events outside of Norway eventually sealed the country's fate, as the rapid success of the German armed forces in France (q.v.) prompted the Allies to decide on 24 May 1940, that Norway was to be evacuated. Allied evacuation came on 8 June, and the Norwegian command signed an armistice with the Germans the following day. During the evacuation, the aircraft carrier HMS *Glorious* was sunk, and the German battle cruisers *Scharnhorst* and *Gneisenau* were heavily damaged.

Compared to other military operations, the number of casualties on both sides during the April 1940 invasion and occupation of Norway remained relatively low. Germany had 1,317 men killed. The British lost 1,896 men on the ground and more than 2,500 at sea, while Norwegian losses amounted to 1,335. The most significant losses were ships. The British lost one aircraft carrier, two cruisers, nine destroyers, and six submarines. The German Navy suffered far more heavily, losing three cruisers, ten destroyers, eight submarines, eleven transports, and eleven other ships.

Although the campaign was relatively small in scope and size, it did have significant consequences. Along with boosting the reputation of Germany's military forces, particularly among the neutral states of Europe, it gave Germany naval and air bases flanking and threatening the British Isles. With its daring move against Norway, German armed forces gained the initiative in the war. The German Navy, on the other hand, suffered losses to its surface fleet it could ill afford.

Robert G. Waite

Additional Reading

Ambrosius, H.H., et al., *Unser Kampf in Norwegen* (1940).

Andenaes, Johs, O. Riste, and M. Skodvin, *Norway and the Second World War* (1966).

Ash, Bernard, *Norway 1940* (1964).

Curtis, Monica (ed.), *Norway and the War: September 1939–December 1940* (Documents on International Affairs) (1941).

Derry, T.K., *The Campaign in Norway* (1952).

Hubatsch, Walter, *Weserübung: Die deutsche Besetzung von Dänemark und Norwegen 1940*, 2nd ed. (1960).

Ziemke, Earl F., *The German Northern Theater of Operations, 1940–1945* (1959).

Nuremberg Air Raid (30–31 March 1944)

[See map 20 on page 1330]

On the night of 30–31 March 1944, Bomber Command launched a raid on the German city of Nuremberg. It was the costliest night attack of the war for the Royal Air Force (RAF). Of the 795 bombers launched, ninety-five never returned from Germany, twelve others were completely destroyed, and an additional fifty-eight were heavily damaged—some to the point that they were scrapped. The loss in aircraft amounted to 12 percent. At the time, many in Britain compared the Nuremberg raid to the disastrous charge of the Light Brigade at Balaklava, during the Crimean War. A total of 545 British airmen died in that single raid, a 21 percent personnel loss. It was a dismal night for the RAF.

The 1,500-mile round trip from Britain to Nuremberg took eight hours. It was conducted in bright moonlight. From Aachen, on Germany's western border, all the way to the target, the RAF bombers were under continuous attack from German night fighters. The defenders even dropped flares from above to illuminate the bombers. The Germans lost only nineteen airmen in the process, a very favorable twenty-eight to one exchange ratio. Damage on the ground was minimal. About 130 civilians died, and 256 buildings were damaged. Thousands were left homeless, but the German war industry was hardly scratched.

The RAF losses over Nuremberg culminated a trend starting back in January of that year. For a bombing mission to be successful, the Allies figured their loss percentage had to be less than 4 percent. That January, the overall rate had been near 7 percent. Throughout February and March, the losses continued to mount. On 19–20 February at Leipzig, Bomber Command lost 9.6 percent, and over Berlin (q.v.) on 24–25 March, they lost 9 percent. In a period stretching from November 1943 to the Nuremberg raid in March 1944, more than 5 percent of Bomber Command's planes never returned. That amounted to 1,047 aircraft lost, with another 1,682 heavily damaged, most to the point of never flying again.

The Nuremberg disaster was a turning point for the RAF. Reluctantly, Bomber Command shifted to the operational concepts of POINT-BLANK, the Combined Bomber Offensive (*see* Strategic Bombing and Germany Air Campaign). POINTBLANK was a plan proposed by U.S. Army Air Force (USAAF) General Ira Eaker (q.v.) at the Casablanca Conference in January 1943 (*see* Conferences, Allied). Under this plan, RAF and USAAF bombers would concentrate on targeting factories for submarines, fighters, bombers, ball bearings, and synthetic rubber. Eaker's goal was to reduce those commodities by 89 percent, 43 percent, 65 percent, 76 percent, and 50 percent, respectively, by 1 April 1944. The aim was to weaken Germany's warmaking capability to the point it would be unable to resist the coming Allied invasion.

POINTBLANK concentrated on sustained "precision" bombings on select industry, as opposed to sporadic area bombings on urban centers—the strategic terror bombing of cities. In addition to industrial centers, POINTBLANK concentrated on military and economic centers to cripple Germany's capacity for war. Air Marshal Sir Arthur Harris (q.v.) resisted this policy and continued his own policy of strategically bombing cities. To appease the Americans, his bombers would target areas around German aircraft factories and oil refineries, going to great pains to show the bomb damage of these factories to the Allies. After Nuremberg, however, Harris came to realize that defeating Germany by turning its cities into ashes would not work with the resources he had at hand.

On 14 April 1944, the leaders of the Combined Bomber Offensive, Eaker and Harris, began taking their operational directions from supreme Allied commander General Dwight D. Eisenhower (q.v.). Bomber Command's operations were shifted to tactical missions in support of the upcoming Operation OVERLORD.

Harris went to his grave convinced that if he had had the necessary resources and a free hand outside the controls of the supreme Allied commander, his theory of bombing Germany to oblivion would have assured victory. The bombing of cities, he believed, would have destroyed the morale of the German people, who would do whatever was necessary to stop the carnage. What Harris failed to recognize was that when Germany was bombing British cities, the British resolve to continue the war intensified. Many historians argue that the strategic bombing of urban centers, in fact, solidified German resolve and made it difficult for Germany to negotiate any form of surrender with the Allies.

William H. Van Husen

Additional Reading

Hastings, Max, *Bomber Command* (1979).
Middlebrook, Martin, *The Nuremberg Raid 30–31 March 1944* (1986).
Terraine, John, *A Time for Courage* (1985).
Webster, Sir Charles, and Arthur Noble Frankland, *The Strategic Air Offensive against Germany, 1939–1945,* Vol. 3 (1961).

Oran
[See map 27 on page 1337]
See MERS EL-KÉBIR

OVERLORD, Operation
See NORMANDY CAMPAIGN

P

Paris, Liberation of (19–26 August 1944)

On 6 June 1944, Allied forces landed at Normandy (q.v.). After several costly battles they finally forced a breakout from Normandy near the end of July. The main objectives for General Dwight D. Eisenhower (q.v.) were the destruction of German armed forces, moving as rapidly as possible toward Germany and bringing the war to an end. His was a military mission, but there were also critical political considerations.

One of the most pressing was the question of whether Paris would be liberated or bypassed by the Allied armies. In a strictly military sense, the actual physical liberation of the French capital could be a detriment to the military operations. The allocation of troops, the drain on food and fuel supplies to assist the city, and the possibility of heavy casualties caused by fighting in a restricted urban terrain mitigated against liberation. The feeling on Eisenhower's staff was that a bypassed Paris would soon see the cut-off German garrison surrender on its own.

Despite cogent military arguments for not committing valuable resources to liberate the city, political considerations began to overshadow the situation. French resistance leaders loyal to General Charles de Gaulle (q.v.) warned their leader that if the Allies did not soon enter the city there could very well be a Communist-lead uprising that could threaten eventual Gaullist control of the French government.

The Communist resistance, well organized and well lead, was openly hostile to the Gaullist groups who continually counseled caution in dealing with the occupying powers. It was feared that an uprising would motivate the Germans to destroy the city in the process of restoring order. The Allies, when Paris was finally taken, might then find a pile of rubble with the Communists in political control.

What neither the Communists nor the Gaullists knew was that General Dietrich von Choltitz (q.v.), the new Paris commander, had orders from Adolf Hitler (q.v.) to destroy the city before allowing it to fall to the Allies. Politically then, the race for Paris was also a race to preserve the city from destruction and to save the city for de Gaulle and the non-Communist forces of the resistance.

Eisenhower had issued orders to General Pierre Joseph Koenig (q.v.), commander of the French Forces of the Interior (FFI) (q.v.), that no insurrection against the hated Nazis was to take place; but events were taking charge of the situation. Von Choltitz, the hero of Sevastopol (q.v.) in Russia and known for his unwavering dedication to duty, was personally told by the *Führer* to begin preparations for the destruction of the city. Von Choltitz, however, harbored grave doubts about the *Führer's* mental condition and the order to destroy Paris. Unknown to either Eisenhower or von Choltitz, de Gaulle had secretly informed Koenig that Paris would indeed be liberated regardless of Eisenhower's warning.

On 19 August, the Gaullists moved first by occupying the Paris Prefecture of Police. While the Gaullists were raising the French Tricolor over the building, the Communists were putting up posters calling for insurrection. Von Choltitz deployed infantry, backed by armor, around the city, and the fighting intensified. Late in the afternoon, three German tanks began firing at the Prefecture of Police. The Germans, however, did not awe the Parisians, who fought back with old weapons and homemade bombs. Von Choltitz received reports that a number of his tanks had been burned by homemade gasoline bombs and his casualties were mounting. While blood was flowing in Paris, both Hitler and the Americans received word that the city was in a state of insurrection. Hitler was more determined than ever to lay waste to the city. Eisenhower had to decide if indeed he could scrap his plans and assist the city. There was no such hesitation for de Gaulle, who was just as determined that the city would be liberated in his name.

By 20 August, von Choltitz was faced with a moral dilemma. The German commander had plans for the mining and destruction of public monuments, bridges, power, and water plants in Paris. The great museums and the Eiffel Tower would suffer the same fate as an electrical power station. Even von Choltitz, who had a reputation as a fierce soldier, knew that such wanton destruction would be viewed as an unforgivable crime against humanity. These plans also deepened his doubts about the German leadership and their grasp on reality. Sweden's consul general, Raoul Nordling, pleaded with the German commander to save the city, and the diplomat tried to effect a momentary cease-fire within the city. The Communist commander, Henri Tanguy (alias Colonel Rol), refused to accept a cease-fire and violence once again began to increase.

On 21 August, against orders from his Allied superiors, Major General Philippe Leclerc (q.v.), commander of the French 2nd Armored Division, began to move his division toward Paris. Within the resistance in Paris there was dissension among the Gaullist and Communist leadership. Rather than split the anti-Nazi resistance, they decided that the fight against the Germans would continue. On 21 August, von Choltitz, now convinced that Paris should be spared, sent Nordling to ask the Allies for assistance. He continued to ignore orders to begin the destruction of Paris. While Nordling was on his mission to urge the Allies into Paris, Leclerc learned that Eisenhower had agreed to send the French 2nd Armored Division into Paris. The situation was growing more critical by the hour. On 23 August, the fighting in Paris was severe, and Nordling reached Lieutenant General Omar N. Bradley (q.v.), who was impressed with the information that the Swedish diplomat imparted. Von Choltitz would hold off destruction hoping that the Allies would arrive quickly. Bradley alerted the U.S. 4th Infantry Division to move into Paris before the German commander changed his mind.

The decision to move troops into Paris was a difficult one for Eisenhower, who wanted to avoid a commitment of forces to the liberation of the city. Political events beyond his military control, however, motivated the order to go in. No one had anticipated the outbreak of the insurrection or the intense political motivations of the Gaullists or the Communists.

Of great concern was the threat that von Choltitz might very well begin the destruction of this city that housed vast architectural and artistic treasures. If the Allies failed to heed the calls from Paris and the city was leveled, what would be the long-range implications for relations with France? Did the Allies really want de Gaulle to emerge as the hero of the liberation? All of these questions had to be factored into the decision to alert and send the 4th Infantry Division to assist the French 2nd Armored Division in Paris.

By dawn of 24 August, the 2nd Armored Division had reached Rambouillet, only twenty miles from the French capital, while almost every section of Paris was fighting the Germans. Von Choltitz was also under mounting pressure from the *Führer*'s headquarters to reduce Paris to a heap of ruins. Early in the day, de Gaulle arrived at the Chateau of Rambouillet, where he received continual information from Paris. With anticipation growing, Leclerc split his forces upon entering Paris. One column entered through the Port de Sevres; a second column entered through the Porte de Vanves. The main force passed through the Port de Orleans. By 2130 hours, his tanks were in front of the *Hotel de Ville* (city hall) in the center of Paris. The bells of Notre Dame Cathedral announced that the French forces of liberation had entered Paris.

On 25 August, the French and the Americans of 4th Infantry Division cleaned out pockets of German resistance and collected prisoners, who were only too glad to be taken by soldiers rather than the populace of the city. That morning, von Choltitz received frantic calls from Hitler's headquarters asking about the extent of destruction in the city, but the German commander of Paris was preparing to surrender to the Allies. In fact, late that afternoon, von Choltitz and his staff surrendered to French officers, while at the same time, Leclerc entered the Prefecture of Police where the insurrection had begun. In Paris, some Germans who were aware of the surrender laid down their arms, while others who had not been reached continued to fight, with rising casualties.

De Gaulle arrived in Paris on the evening of 25 August, and went to the War Ministry to receive members of the Gaullist resistance. From the War Ministry, he proceeded to the *Hotel de Ville* where he addressed the wildly cheering Parisians. On 26 August, in triumph, de Gaulle, followed by the resistance, paraded from the *Arc de Triomphe* to Notre Dame Cathedral to celebrate the libera-

American troops march through the Arc de Triomphe and down the Champs Elyseés after the liberation of Paris, August 1944. (IWM OWIL 36114)

tion of the capital. Despite some sniper fire, the parade and the mass were completed and Paris was declared officially liberated.

Even a half-century after the liberation, it is difficult to assess the Allied and German casualties. The Allies committed only two divisions in taking the city. The low number of troops involved was due to the speed required to get into the city, the crumbling will of the German defenders, and the decision of von Choltitz not to destroy the city as he had been ordered.

The cost to the Allied supply system, already taxed by rapid combat, was high. On the other hand, having to care for a city in ruins with all bridges and essential services destroyed would have been almost impossible. The taking of Paris was a psychological victory for the Allies. It was a major capital, and Paris had been a prize for Hitler in 1940. In 1944, however, the liberation of Paris was a clear indication that Fortress Europe (q.v.) was crumbling, and that the end of the Third *Reich* itself was in sight.

James J. Cooke

Additional Reading

Aron, Robert, *France Reborn* (1964).
Collins, Larry, and Dominique Lapierre, *Is Paris Burning?* (1965).

Schoenbrun, David, *The Soldiers of the Night: The Story of the French Resistance* (1980).

PASTORIUS, Operation (12–27 June 1942)

During World War II, German intelligence organized and attempted only one major sabotage operation against the United States. This mission, code named Operation *PASTORIUS,* took place in June 1942 when eight German agents were sent to the United States with instructions to cripple American aircraft production. To accomplish this, the saboteurs planned to blow up the aluminum manufacturing plants located in Philadelphia, Pennsylvania; Massena, New York; East St. Louis, Illinois; and Alcoa, Tennessee. According to German engineers, the destruction of these factories would seriously curtail aircraft production for at least ten months. A second aim of the mission was to establish a fifth column among German-Americans.

The agents, divided into two four-man teams, were transported to the United States by U-boats to selected sites off New York and Florida. Once ashore, they intended to make their way to the big cities and blend in with the general population. After waiting three to four weeks, the saboteurs planned to carry out their mission.

The first four-man team landed near Amagansett, a small community on the southern shoreline of Long Island, on the night of 12 June 1942 and immediately ran into trouble. Coast Guardsman John C. Cullen spotted the agents as they landed and questioned them. They told him they were fishermen from Southampton whose boat had run aground. Cullen suspected that something was amiss, but being unarmed did not want to arouse their suspicions. When one of the agents offered him $300 to forget the whole matter, Cullen took the money and quickly disappeared. Cullen immediately reported the incident to his superiors, who notified Coast Guard headquarters in New York City. The next day the FBI was called in to investigate. The agents, meanwhile, made their way to the railway station and boarded a train for New York. There they checked into two hotels and remained out of sight.

Five days later a second U-boat deposited the other four agents on a secluded beach south of Ponte Verda, Florida, totally undetected. Like their counterparts in New York, the saboteurs brought with them large quantities of explosives, civilian clothing, forged identity papers, and almost $100,000 in American currency. After changing clothes and burying the explosives, the four men took a bus to Jacksonville, Florida, where they spent the night. The next day the group split up, with two of the men traveling to New York to join the agents already there. The other two headed to Chicago.

The German agents never had an opportunity to carry out their mission. The leader of the operation, George J. Dasch, developed second thoughts about the whole affair. He was a German national but had lived in the United States from 1922 to 1939. Furthermore, he had married an American and had developed a strong affection for the United States. Convinced that the operation could not succeed, Dasch decided to surrender to the FBI and turn state's evidence before the situation got out of control. Dasch called the FBI office in New York on 14 June 1942 and told them his story, but the agent who answered the phone did not take his allegations seriously.

When he could not get the authorities in New York to believe him, Dasch decided to go to FBI headquarters in Washington, D.C. There he insisted on being taken to FBI Director J. Edgar Hoover (q.v.), but instead saw two of his assistants. Dasch informed them of the details of the operation, but he could tell that they did not believe him. Only after he gave them the name of another German agent did the two men believe his story.

Once the FBI had the details of the mission it did not take them very long to apprehend all of the German agents. By 27 June 1942, the last of the saboteurs were captured. Dramatic accounts of the thwarted German operation appeared in all of the newspapers and several other publications, declaring that the FBI had once again saved the nation. It would be years before the public learned what had really transpired. In July 1942, a secret military trial was held where all of the defendants were found guilty of espionage and sentenced to death. Dasch and Ernst Burger, another saboteur who testified for the prosecution, had their sentences commuted to life imprisonment. The other six were executed.

Michael G. Mahon

Additional Reading

Dasch, George J., *Eight Spies against America* (1959).

Hoyt, Edwin P., *U-Boats Offshore: When Hitler Struck America* (1978).

Peenemünde Air Raid (18 August 1943)

[See map 20 on page 1330]

Shortly after 0100 hours on 18 August 1943, the first of more than 200 British bombers arrived over the German rocket research center at Peenemünde, on the Baltic coast. For the next fifty minutes, they dropped nearly 2,000 tons of bombs on the center's housing area, experimentation facility, and production works. Timed to follow the American daylight raids on Regensburg and Schweinfurt (qq.v.), and in coordination with a diversionary night raid against Berlin, the Peenemünde raiders escaped effective German engagement until they were almost over the target. The results were devastating. More than 600 workers and nearly 200 scientists and technicians were killed, including Dr. Walter Thiel, the rocket propulsion expert who was developing the engines for Germany's liquid fuel rockets. Although not as destructive as planned, the raid delayed development of the V-2 missile by at least several months.

The 18 August raid was the first of several launched against the secret German research center. As such, it was the culmination of one of the most intense Allied intelligence efforts of the war. Although British intelligence had received many reports and indicators of a German "secret weapons research facility" since 1938, there was little substantiated evidence to confirm its existence or location. In fact, Winston S. Churchill's science adviser, Dr. Frederick Lindemann (qq.v.), seriously doubted Germany's ability to build a rocket that could threaten Britain.

Lindemann dismissed as a fabrication the Oslo Report, which provided the first real information on Peenemünde and its rocket systems. Nonetheless, the growing number and increasingly detailed reports, including ULTRA intercepts, indicated that some kind of new long-range weapon system was being tested in the Baltic.

By March 1943, the indications had become so strong—including a bugged conversation between two captured German generals—that Churchill appointed a special team to investigate the evidence and determine conclusively if indeed the Germans were working on long-range rockets. Headed by the prime minister's son-in-law, Duncan Sandys, the team correlated all the reports coming from neutral and occupied countries, as well as signal intercepts and photographic evidence. Finally, on 23 June 1943, Dr. R.V. Jones was able to prove that the weapon photographed on a trailer at Peenemünde was a large rocket and not a new torpedo. Six days later Churchill ordered the research center destroyed as soon as possible. The Royal Air Force's Bomber Command was given the task and every available heavy bomber was assigned.

The raid marked several firsts for both sides. It was the RAF's first night precision raid. It was the first one to be led by a master bomber (q.v.) using the special Oboe and H2S radar bombing systems and new, more accurate bombing techniques. All previous night raids had been directed at the center of a city, but Peenemünde's small size precluded a mass bombing approach.

Accuracy was of paramount importance. Each wave over Peenemünde had an aim point centered on a specific facility or area, with subsequent waves being assigned "down range" aim points that would be illuminated by the damage and fire caused by the previous wave's bombs. It was largely successful, with miss distances being reduced from the normal five to ten miles to less than 600 meters.

Despite the technological bombing improvements, the center's small size enabled it to escape a crippling blow. Most of the subsequent bombing waves missed their targets and many critical facilities, including the liquid oxygen generator and the rocket engine test stands, were left unscathed.

For the Germans, the raid took place on the first night they employed modified "Wild Boar" tactics against night bombers. Instead of deploying radar-equipped night fighters against the bomber stream under tight air control with day fighters operating over the target, the German fighters flew essentially on their own initiative. The German air intercept controllers provided a running commentary of the bombers' positions, movements, and likely targets to the fighters, which then maneuvered to intercept the bomber stream. Engagements occurred whenever the fighters located a bomber, either visually or by radar (q.v.) for the night fighters, or visually in the target area's air defense force searchlights for the day fighters. The result was a general melee over the target area.

The new tactics met with mixed success. Allied bomber losses increased temporarily, but most engagements took place after they had dropped their bombs. Fortunately for the Peenemünde bombers, the diversionary raid against Berlin drew off the bulk of the 400 fighters available that night. Nonetheless, the raiding force lost forty-one bombers to the night fighters and three more to antiaircraft fire. The Germans lost twelve fighters, mostly single-engine day fighters.

The Americans conducted three later raids against Peenemünde, all in daylight and under fighter escort. Although they inflicted greater damage than the first raid, the impact was not as great because the Germans dispersed their research facilities and scientists throughout Germany after the August 1943 attack. Peenemünde still served as the final test site for live firings and rocket motor development.

There is no doubt the German rocket program was hindered by the August 1943 raid. Although the extent of the delay cannot be judged, the resulting dispersal of the research teams hindered effective collaboration between those working on the V-2 and those working on the air defense rocket systems. It also precluded the Germans' exploiting the efficiencies that were previously gained by having all their rocket and missile researchers in one facility. Given Adolf Hitler's (q.v.) emphasis on the so-called revenge weapons at the expense of other rocket systems, the Peenemünde raids essentially inflicted a death sentence on the German air defense missile program.

Carl O. Schuster

Additional Reading
Babington-Smith, Constance, *Evidence in Camera* (1958).
Hinsley, F.H., et al., *British Intelligence in the Second World War*, Vol. 3, Part 1 (1984).
Jones, R.V., *Most Secret War* (1978).
Middlebrook, Martin, *The Peenemünde Raid 1943* (1982).

Platte River (13–17 December 1939)

In August 1939, Grand Admiral Erich Raeder (q.v.) began to prepare contingency plans in case Britain and France, contrary to Adolf Hitler's (q.v.) expectations, did decide to go to war over Poland. The commander in chief of the *Kriegsmarine* fervently hoped that Hitler's now-famous intuition would prove right, because he knew the German fleet was woefully inadequate to the task of combating both of these powers.

During that fateful month, twenty German U-boats were secretly ordered to waiting positions around the British Isles. Furthermore, two of Germany's armored ships, the *Deutschland* and the *Admiral Graf Spee,* were also ordered to sail to isolated areas of the North and South Atlantic Oceans. They each were assigned a supply ship, which carried enough fuel, munitions, and other supplies to keep the two raiders at sea indefinitely. On 1 September 1939, German troops invaded Poland (q.v.). Two days later, Britain and France declared war on Germany.

On that fateful day, *Kapitän zur See* Hans Langsdorff (q.v.), commander of the *Graf Spee,* opened his sealed orders in a remote area of the South Atlantic. These orders instructed him to commence attacks on Allied shipping upon authorization from Berlin. He was ordered, however, to avoid engaging warships.

On 26 September, the *Kriegsmarine* finally obtained Hitler's reluctant approval to initiate commerce raiding against Britain. Langsdorff found his first victim four days later, initiating his personal cat-and-mouse game with the Royal Navy. At one point, as many as eight Allied task forces were searching for him in the South Atlantic and Indian Oceans. Langsdorff's successful attack on the diminutive motor tanker *Africa Shell* was noteworthy because its master confidently predicted that British cruisers would be the cause of the *Graf Spee's* demise.

Throughout October and November, Langsdorff ran up his tally of victims, while replenishing from his supply ship, the tanker *Altmark,* on an irregular basis. At these meetings, he regularly transferred prisoners to the supply ship. During this period, Langsdorff used a variety of subterfuges to mislead his intended prey. By far the most elaborate was the construction of a fake turret in a "B" turret position, and painting the sloped edges of the *Graf Spee's* distinct battle tower matte black. This gave the ship the appearance of a forward tripod mast, and made the *Graf Spee* look like a French cruiser. Langsdorff, however, soon decided to eliminate the dummy turret because it interfered too much with his real forward turret.

As his return to Germany loomed closer, Langsdorff started to agitate for a full release from his operational restrictions against engaging Allied warships, but these appeals fell on deaf ears. On 24 November, he decided unilaterally to break the restrictions. While en route to his last area of operations, Langsdorff's tactics became bolder, allowing some victims to send distress signals. These reports were carefully studied by Commodore Henry Harwood, the commander of the Royal Navy's South American Squadron, which comprised the heavy cruiser HMS *Exeter,* and the light cruisers HMS *Ajax* and HMNZS *Achilles.* Harwood deduced that the *Graf Spee* would probably strike next in the area around the River Platte, near Montevideo, Uruguay. The *Graf Spee* dispatched her last victim on 7 December, but only after her boarding crew found documents indicating that the River Platte was a major focal point for Allied shipping.

By this time, Langsdorff had sunk or captured more than 50,000 tons of Allied shipping. The crew of his last victim, the SS *Streonshalh,* was to be transferred to the *Altmark* at a later date, but fate intervened in the form of Commodore Harwood's squadron. Having lost the use of his reconnaissance aircraft on 11 December, Langsdorff had to rely on lookouts. On the evening of 12 December, they spotted masts, which Langsdorff concluded belonged to a convoy. He increased speed to attack this prize, while ignoring the counsel of his senior officers against seeking combat.

When Harwood's lookouts spotted the smoke emitted by the *Graf Spee's* diesels, the HMS *Exeter* was detached to investigate. At 0616 hours, 13 December, she spotted the German warship, and within ten minutes all four British ships opened fire. The German raider scored three early hits on HMS *Exeter,* forcing the other two ships to close in an attempt to draw the *Graf Spee's* fire. The HMS *Exeter* made a desperate torpedo attack, and then briefly left the battle area. At 0700, she made a valiant attempt to reenter the fray, but was quickly disabled and limped away.

Langsdorff had little time to relish this limited success because his attention was now clearly focused on avoiding torpedo attacks from the light cruisers. After another exchange of gunfire, both commanders decided to end the engagement. While Harwood shadowed the German ship, Langsdorff wrestled with the problems of evading the cruisers and repairing his damage. The *Graf Spee* received sixteen hits, all but two from the

6-inch guns of the light cruisers. Two hits were of particular concern. One punched a big hole in her forecastle, and the other destroyed her fuel and oil filtration systems. These hits limited her ability to return to Germany, and Langsdorff decided to enter the neutral port of Montevideo for repairs. In all, the *Graf Spee* had suffered thirty-six fatalities among her crew, with another fifty-three injured; but none of the sixty-two Allied prisoners were among the casualties.

On the British side, the HMS *Exeter* was hardest hit, receiving eight hits from 280mm shells. Her captain had no choice but to quit the battle scene, leaving the two light cruisers to shadow the German raider. The HMS *Ajax* was struck by two of the *Graf Spee's* big shells, eliminating both of the light cruiser's forward turrets. The HMNZS *Achilles* suffered no damage. The two light cruisers' casualties were eleven killed and five wounded. Like Langsdorff, Harwood's remaining ships were critically short of ammunition.

On her arrival in Montevideo, the *Graf Spee* became the pawn of a major diplomatic struggle. Although the Uruguayan government estimated that she needed fourteen days of repairs in order to be seaworthy, it granted four. At first, the British ambassador protested, maintaining that she should only receive forty-eight hours. Once he was informed of Harwood's situation, he quickly changed gears. The British forced the *Graf Spee* to remain in port for another twenty-four hours by ordering a British merchantman to sail just before the *Graf Spee* was scheduled to leave. Despite this tactic, by 15 December, only one Allied warship, the heavy cruiser HMS *Cumberland,* arrived to reinforce Harwood.

As Langsdorff struggled to gain more time for repairs, he became increasingly aware of his rapidly deteriorating situation. The longer he stayed in port, the more ships the British would be able to concentrate against him. After taking stock of his ammunition, Langsdorff concluded that he could not realistically expect to defeat Harwood, and that his only option was to scuttle his ship. He transferred the bulk of his crew to a German merchantman, the *Tacoma,* which followed the *Graf Spee* out on the morning of 17 December. After the scuttling charges were set, the demolition party joined their shipmates on the *Tacoma.* On 20 December, Langsdorff committed suicide in Argentina. Both the *Tacoma* and the bulk of the *Graf Spee's* crew were interned there.

The battle of the River Platte was very detrimental to the *Kriegsmarine's* conduct of the war at sea. As a result, restrictions on German ship com-

manders' freedom of action were increased because Hitler's paranoid fear of losing major warships determined policy. The battle also marked the first use of radar (q.v.) in naval combat, by the *Graf Spee.*

On 16 February 1940, the *Altmark* (q.v.) was intercepted in Norwegian waters by the British destroyer HMS *Cossack.* The British commander was operating under orders from Winston Churchill (q.v.) to ignore Norwegian neutrality and board the *Altmark* to free the *Graf Spee's* prisoners.

Peter K.H. Mispelkamp

Additional Reading

Bekker, C.D., *Defeat at Sea: The Struggle and Eventual Defeat of the German Navy, 1939–1945* (1950).

Bennett, Geoffrey, *Battle of the River Platte* (1972).

Pope, Dudley, *The Battle of the River Platte* (1956).

Powell, Michael, *Death in the South Atlantic: The Last Voyage of the Graf Spee* (1957).

Ploeşti Air Raid (1 August 1943)

On 1 August 1943, U.S. bomber units executed a large-scale minimum-altitude attack on the Ploeşti oil refineries in Romania. In the Ploeşti area were twelve large oil refineries with an estimated annual capacity of nine million tons. According to U.S. estimates, these refineries produced 86 percent of the refined petroleum products of Romania, and had 96 percent of its cracking capacity.

Ten of the refineries were located in the city itself, one was very close to Ploeşti, and the last was twenty miles to the north in Campina. The oil fields of Ploeşti were one of the main sources of energy for the German military machine in the war against the Soviet Union. According to Allied estimates, 60 percent of Germany's crude oil came from the Ploeşti fields.

The targets in Ploeşti were: Astra Romana (15 percent of the Romanian total production): Romano Americana (11 percent); Concordia Vega (13 percent); Phoenix Unirea (6 percent); Dacia Romana (3 percent); Phoenix Orion (4 percent); Columbia Aquila (3 percent); Standart Petrol Block (5 percent); Redeventa (2 percent); and Xenia Redeventa (3 percent). In Campina, the Steaua Romana refinery produced 13 percent of total Romanian oil production, and the Creditul Minier refinery at Brazi produced another 5 percent. The refineries Astra Romana, Romano-Americana, Concordia Vega, Standart Petrol Block, and Steaua Romana were considered the priority targets because of their larger capacities and important cracking units. A target linked to Astra Romana was the Constanta pumping station at Ploeşti, a terminal for many Ploeşti refineries that pumped oil to the Constanta port on the Black Sea.

Even before the beginning of Axis hostilities against the Soviet Union in June 1941, the German military mission in Romania was assigned as its main task the protection of Romanian oil fields and installations. The defenses in the Ploeşti area were strong. Protective walls were built around the refineries and the storage tanks were camouflaged. The blackout discipline of the town was considered good. Strong antiaircraft defenses surrounded Ploeşti, and the city also had inner antiaircraft defenses. The air bases at Bucharest thirty miles to the south, and the aerodromes in the immediate area could put up a strong defensive force. The Romanian Air Force totaled about 6,000 men and 600 aircraft. Besides operations on the eastern front, its main mission was the protection of the oil production zone.

During the summer of 1941 and the fall of 1942, the Soviets bombed the Ploeşti fields without serious result. The U.S. Army Air Force also had attacked Ploeşti ineffectively. As part of Operation TIDAL WAVE, the 1 August 1943 attack was planned by the staff of Major General Lewis Brereton (q.v.), commander of U.S. Ninth Air Force, who decided to launch the attack from bases in Libya. The units assigned to the mission were the 44th, 93rd, 98th, and 376th Bombardment Groups (BG), which were assigned the targets in Ploeşti, and the 398th BG sent against the targets in Campina. Each B-24 bomber was armed with 1,000- and 500-pound demolition bombs, with incendiary bombs mixed in. The attack this time was planned for minimum altitude, 100 to 300 feet.

After flying more than 1,100 sorties during the first three weeks of July 1943, the five combat groups were withdrawn from combat and trained near Benghazi, Libya, where they attacked reproductions of the Ploeşti targets. On 1 August 1943, 177 aircraft carrying 1,726 crew members under the command of Brigadier General Uzal G. Ent headed toward the Ploeşti area, across the island of Corfu, the mountains of Yugoslavia, and the Danube River.

At Ploeşti, the 398th BG, led by Colonel Jack Wood, left the formation and headed toward Campina. Despite the fact that this combat unit was less experienced and had difficulties finding the target, its losses were smaller and its objective was completely destroyed. By mistake, the 376th

BG, followed by the 93rd BG, flew too close to Bucharest, and when Ploeşti was finally reached they encountered heavy fire from the ground defenses. The 93rd BG, under the command of Lieutenant Colonel George S. Brown (q.v.), turned east and then, despite being attacked by enemy fighters, bombed the Astra Romana, Orion, and Columbia Aquila refineries, targets assigned to the 98th and 44th Bombardment Groups. During the attack, eleven bombers were lost.

The 98th and 44th Bombardment Groups, commanded by Colonels John R. Kane and Leon W. Johnson, respectively, arrived at their assigned targets immediately after the 93rd BG's bombing run. Under very difficult conditions resulting from the alerted defenses, smoke, and ground explosions, they managed to hit their targets. These two groups were also attacked from the air. They claimed forty-six enemy fighters destroyed, but lost thirty-three bombers.

Trying to avoid the fire of the ground defenses, the 376th BG turned east and then north. It still met very strong antiaircraft fire. With the exception of six planes led by Major Norman C. Appold, which bombed the assigned target of the Concordia Vega refinery, the 376th only managed to bomb targets of opportunity.

The five U.S. bombardment groups did not return to their bases as a unified force. Only the 98th BG and the 44th BG remained together. Ninety-two planes reached Benghazi; nineteen landed in Malta, Sicily, or Cyprus; seven landed in Turkey; and another three crashed at sea. A total of 532 U.S. airmen were lost (prisoners or dead), and fifty-four planes were destroyed. Five participants in the air raid on Ploeşti were awarded the Medal of Honor for heroism.

Despite accurate bombing under very difficult conditions, which caused heavy damage, the results of the Ploeşti raid were less than expected. It was estimated that 40 percent of the refining and cracking capacity was destroyed for four to six months. After the 1 August raid, the Astra Romana refinery was quickly repaired. The Romano Americana refinery escaped the low-level raid, but was heavily bombed on 10 August 1944. The production facilities of Columbia Aquila were completely destroyed, but the tank farm remained almost intact. The Steaua Romana refinery was very heavily damaged.

Several air raids on Ploeşti followed, but the refineries did not stop functioning. The Germans lost the Romanian oil only in August 1944, when, after a successful coup d'état, Romania left the Axis.

Radu Ioanid

Additional Reading

Dugan, James, *Ploesti: The Great Air-Ground Battle of 1 August 1943* (1962).

Newby, Leroy W., *Target Ploesti* (1983).

Sweetman, John, *Ploesti: Oil Strike* (1974).

Wolff, Leon, *Low-Level Mission* (1957).

Poland (1 September–6 October 1939)

[See map 31 on page 1341]

"We in Poland do not recognize the concept of peace at any price. There is only one thing in the life of men, nations and states that is without price, and that is honor." With this verbal slap in the face, Poland's foreign minister, Józef Beck (q.v.), indicated his country's willingness to pick up the gauntlet of German aggression.

Adolf Hitler's (q.v.) response came a few months later with the invasion that started World War II. After a month of bitter fighting, pitting Germany's *Fall WEISS* (Case WHITE against the Polish Plan *ZACHOD* (Plan WEST), the *Führer* gained an impressive victory. This struggle, far more crucial than often realized, greatly impacted the war. Firstly, it eliminated any chance for the original Allied team of Britain, France, and the Eastern European countries to contain the Third *Reich* by themselves. More importantly, powerful precedents for the postwar world order were established by Soviet participation in the new Allied coalition that emerged.

Although Nazi racial antipathy for the Slavs played a part, the root cause for conflict was territorial. The Versailles Treaty's (q.v.) award of former Prussian lands, particularly the Polish Corridor (q.v.) to Danzig, rankled many Germans. As Gustav Stresemann (q.v.) put it in 1925: "No German government from the nationalists to the Communists would ever recognize this frontier." Indeed, neither nation was completely satisfied with the 1919 border settlements. Each charged the other with mistreatment of minorities, and both used the status of Danzig (q.v.) as a symbol of this struggle.

A prewar balance of power kept the contest at the saber-rattling and propaganda level. France, in 1921, and Britain, in 1939, both pledged to maintain Polish independence. While presenting a considerable challenge, this combination was not sufficient by itself to halt the Third *Reich*. Hitler was willing to throw the dice of war, save for one unknown, the Soviet Union.

The USSR was the great European enigma, the key to peace or war. Its power could upset the plans of either side, and thus was courted by all. In an ominous preview of the campaign, London, Paris, and Warsaw sent weak and inconsistent signals to Moscow. Berlin, on the contrary, produced a package that sold very well and netted the 23 August 1939 Molotov-Ribbentrop Non-aggression Pact (q.v.). With its "secret additional protocol," the Soviet Union became a Nazi ally. Y-Day, the start of *Fall WEISS,* followed within a week.

"Close your hearts to pity. Proceed brutally . . . the stronger is the right." With these instructions, Hitler unleashed his *Wehrmacht* to invade Poland, initiating World War II's first campaign. Two major task groupings were formed for the attack: Army Group North, 630,000 men under Fedor von Bock (q.v.), and Army Group South, 886,000 men under Gerd von Rundstedt (q.v.). They fielded a total of seventy divisions and 1,500 aircraft, the *Wehrmacht*'s entire strike force. Their overall commander, General Walther von Brauchitsch (q.v.), ordered them to:

> forestall an orderly mobilization and concentration of the Polish Army, and to destroy its mass which is expected west of the Vistula-Narew line, by concentric attacks from Silesia on one side and Pomerania-Prussia on the other.

Such a strategy of encirclement, or *Kesselschlacht,* was not new—its proven track record went back to Hannibal's victory at Cannae in 216 B.C. Enhancing the chances for success were Germany's significant, albeit untried, air and mechanized forces. Also, the Poles would be outnumbered in every category save courage. Despite these advantages, *Fall WEISS* was not a sure thing. There was a strategic Achilles' heel.

Massing such overwhelming superiority came at the price of leaving western Germany weakly guarded. It was, in the words of General Ludwig Beck (q.v.), "a dance on a powder keg to which an ignited fuse had already been attached." If France and Britain launched their own attacks, vital Rhine industries could be lost. The Anglo-French combination could throw ninety-eight divisions and 3,500 aircraft against a very incomplete fortress system, the West Wall (q.v.), with its thirty divisions and 1,000 planes. In addition, the Germans did not have the fuel and munitions for a lengthy struggle. With this in mind, Hitler demanded "sudden, heavy blows and . . . rapid successes." Anything less could spell disaster.

Plan *ZACHOD* was based on this German dilemma. Poland's military was well aware of its limitations, but also saw a possibility to thwart

Hitler's aggression. Marshal Edward Śmigły-Rydz (q.v.), the Polish commander in chief, declared:

> my plan of operations is based on the hypothesis of a German attack against Poland with the majority of their forces. . . . Its aim is to prevent destruction of our army before the start of our allies' offensive in the west.

The Poles were organized into seven field armies and four reserve groups. They opted for a fighting withdrawal, reserving the possibility of counterattack after significant Nazi forces were drawn back to the Rhine to face the British and French. Many critics have argued that their initial dispositions were faulty, given their meager forces. To oppose Hitler's mechanized forces the Poles had a paper army of two million men, but general mobilization did not begin until too late. Forces ready on the first day consisted of 600,000 troops in thirty infantry divisions, eleven cavalry divisions, one mechanized and one motorized brigade. Against the overwhelming strength of the *Luftwaffe,* the Poles could muster 450 planes, many of doubtful quality.

Plan ZACHOD certainly spread these units thinly, but there was no other viable option. Forward deployments were necessary to protect Polish mobilization centers. They also served to prevent a German fait accompli in the disputed territories, where a bloodless victory might induce yet another Munich-style sell-out by Britain and France. Finally, one can not over stress that Śmigły-Rydz and his generals counted on serious Anglo-French efforts against western Germany. By treaty, military convention, and simple logic, they had every right to plan for such.

Hitler, on the other hand, guessed that indecision and weakness were still the hallmarks of London and Paris. Calling British Prime Minister Neville Chamberlain and French Prime Minister Édouard Daladier (qq.v.) "a couple of tea-swilling old women," he predicted a peaceful western front. This calculated risk caused some dissent within the German high command, but the *Führer's* perfect track record to that point made debate impossible.

In Poland, meanwhile, appeasement (q.v.) claimed its final victim. While the speed and force of Germany's 1 September *Blitzkrieg* produced tactical surprise, the Poles knew an attack was imminent. Call-ups of selected reservists commenced in March 1939. On 27 August, Śmigły-Rydz ordered a general mobilization. This brought immediate complaints from the ambassadors of

Britain and France. After all, "it could provoke Hitler." The marshal then agreed to delay mobilization until 31 August. General Pavlo Shandruk described the results, "order and countermanding order produced simply disorder." As a result of this confusion, together with early *Luftwaffe* strikes, the Polish Army never reached a complete state of readiness.

The invaders, on the other hand, were at full strength. In numbers, the *Wehrmacht* possessed tremendous technological advantages. Those of firepower, and above all mobility, were most significant. This was very evident on 1 September when Germany unleashed a ring of fire along Poland's frontiers. The well-orchestrated attack combined sharp blows from sea, air, and land. The earliest fighting started at 0445 hours when marines from the battleship *Schleswig-Holstein* attempted to storm a small Polish fort in Danzig, the Westerplate (q.v.). Overconfidence resulted in a sharp rebuff. Indeed, despite massive superiority, Nazi forces lost a week and 300 casualties before capturing what they ruefully dubbed "little Verdun."

An equally tenacious defense of Gdynia and the Hel peninsula frustrated German efforts to make use of Danzig. Coast defense batteries and, by Polish standards, an unusually heavy concentration of antiaircraft guns, allowed Admiral Józef Unrug's (q.v.) meager collection of naval infantry, reservists, and civilian volunteers to withstand repeated assaults. The Germans did not secure complete control until 2 October.

Other victories, however, more than compensated the Germans for those setbacks. All along the front, *Luftwaffe* planes delivered well-coordinated assaults on communication centers and troop concentrations. Although they did not completely destroy the Polish Air Force on the ground, the Polish planes that remained were so vastly outnumbered that defensive air operations had little impact on the campaign.

Wehrmacht ground forces often played the aerial trump card to overcome Polish defenses. Often, however, the superior speed of the mechanized units allowed them to bypass Polish positions, followed up with devastating flank and rear attacks. General Heinz Guderian's (q.v.) advance across the Polish Corridor provides a good example. Despite a defense enhanced by gullies, ravines, and small woods, he was able to smash his *Panzer* and motorized divisions into East Prussia by 3 September. By next day, most of the fighting there was over. The Germans suffered 880 casualties; the Poles lost two divisions. On receipt of this news, Śmigły-

Rydz gloomily predicted that it was but the first of many "bad experiences."

Even nature seemed to conspire against the Poles. Western Poland's rather flat geography is cut by many rivers. Full, they made good barriers and defensive lines. In September 1939, little rain and a hot summer drained away much of their value. Major Franciszek Skibinski noted that the San was low enough for "a hen to cross with ease."

Y-Day's heaviest fighting was along the southeastern frontiers. There was the key to Poland's entire defense plan—Army Kraków. With five divisions and a belt of Silesian fortifications, it was the pivot on which the other armies would gradually withdraw to the east. Hit by an overwhelming combination that included four *Panzer* and four light divisions, Army Kraków's commander, General Antoni Szylling (q.v.), was hard-pressed to maintain his positions.

Despite conducting a highly successful ambush of the 4th *Panzer* Division at Mokra, Army Łódź just to the north also suffered from German hammering. General Juliusz Rommel, the commander of Army Łódź, ran into the same problem as Szylling—too few reserves. This shortage became critical during the 4–5 September battle of Piotrków, where German mechanized units drove a wedge between the two armies and secured vital road links to Warsaw. That, together with Polish defeats in Pomerania and along the Prussian frontier, marked the end to the first phase of the Polish campaign.

By the evening of 5 September, Poland's armies were in retreat. "The entire front has collapsed," said Śmigły-Rydz, "and there is no alternative but to withdraw immediately beyond the Vistula, if this is still possible." Just as Poland's marshal sensed doom, frontline German commanders like Guderian smelled victory and convinced the German high command to expand its operational scheme to include sweeps beyond the Vistula River.

Those actions initiated a most unbalanced race. Because of the Piotrków breakthrough, German units were closer to Śmigły-Rydz's new defense line than his own forces—and being mechanized, the German units were faster. The Poles, on the other hand, were handicapped by poor communications and a road net clogged with fleeing civilians. They also suffered greatly from *Luftwaffe* attacks. General Tadeusz Kutrzeba (q.v.) called the air strikes, "hell come to earth," while another veteran recalled that "everything on both sides of the road seemed to be burning." Such attacks could be avoided, but only at the cost of hiding troop concentrations by day and marching at night. Such tactics often worked, but lack of sleep greatly reduced the fighting stamina of the Polish soldiers.

The Polish problems were compounded by the retreat of the high command from Warsaw to Brześć (Brest) on 7 September. As the latter location had only the most rudimentary communications assets, the move effectively cut off Śmigły-Rydz and his advisers from direct contact with the fighting. The severance became permanent and

Surviving members of the Polish 15th Division after surrendering to the German 76th Infantry Regiment, Andrzejewa, Poland, 13 September 1939. (IWM MH 18249)

adversely affected all remaining operations. Uncoordinated and piecemeal attacks became more numerous and information on German actions less accurate. Although the Polish disintegration had begun, the separated and uncoordinated commands still managed to strike back.

An overconfident 4th *Panzer* Division was rebuffed in its attempt to storm Warsaw on 8 September. This failure required the *Wehrmacht* to return on 15 September and conduct a regular siege lasting until the end of the month. A more serious effort was Kutrzeba's Bzura River offensive of 9–16 September. This, the major Polish counterattack of the campaign, resulted from Army Poznań being bypassed by German units. The German high command lost track of it and believed its three divisions were already part of the Warsaw garrison. Thus, General Kutrzeba's assault began with the advantage of tactical surprise. Reinforced to nine divisions and two cavalry brigades, his goals were to recapture the cities of Łęczyca and Piątek, and draw *Wehrmacht* forces away from Warsaw.

Two German divisions were routed on the first day of the counterattack, but by the third day, reinforcements checked the advance, and the Poles had to abandon the initiative. Pounded by round-the-clock air attacks and significantly outnumbered, Kutrzeba strove to escape eastward in the hope of reaching Warsaw. While scattered Polish units broke through, most were destroyed. The Bzura River offensive clearly demonstrated the tremendous firepower and mobility of German forces. Despite initial surprise and superior numbers, the Poles were unable to exploit their early gains. In the end, they were encircled and lost more than 100,000 casualties. As General Kurt Meyer (q.v.) noted, "the Poles attack with enormous tenacity, proving over and over that they really know how to die."

Courage and élan were not sufficient to change the course of the campaign. Poland's only salvation was strong Anglo-French actions against the West Wall. This action was promised no later than 16 September, and with such in mind, Śmigły-Rydz attempted to preserve what remained of his army by creating northern and southern front commands. By 11 September, however, the former was severely punished by Guderian's advance on Brześć. Once again, Polish infantrymen were outmaneuvered by *Panzer*s and crushed by superior numbers.

Disaster in the north produced a "last stand" scenario with directions for all surviving Poles to make for the "Romanian bridgehead." This involved a withdrawal to Poland's southeast corner, where a benevolently neutral Romania could provide supplies and secure flanks. There the remnants of Poland's armed forces would fight on until the promised Western offensive.

While 250,000 troops still engaged the Germans, getting them all to the southeast was impossible. Many were eliminated en route in what journalist Franciszek Czarnomski described as "a march not like that of an army, but more like the flight of some biblical people, driven onward by the wrath of heaven, and dissolving in the wilderness." Most never made the "bridgehead." By 15 September, resistance mainly centered around besieged positions like Warsaw, Lwów, Hel, and Brześć. Some Polish mobile forces still remained, but a complete breakdown of communications allowed for no coordination of their actions.

Poland's fate for long years to come was sealed by the events of the following two days. On 16 September, France failed to provide the promised offensive "with the main body of her forces." On the next day, veteran fence-sitter Josef Stalin (q.v.) launched the Red Army into eastern Poland. These twin blows spelled the end of any chance at continued resistance. Śmigły-Rydz now issued his last order directing all Polish soldiers to make for neutral countries. It was hoped that once interned, some would filter through and form the nucleus of a reborn Free Polish command in France or Britain.

While almost 100,000 troops made it to Hungary, Romania, or the Baltic states, the majority were rounded up by German and Soviet forces. Fighting continued into October, with the last major battle fought near Kock. Here a collection of *uhlan*s (Polish lancers), airmen, sailors of the Pinsk Flotilla, and regular infantrymen battled German motorized troops for three days. Finally, on 6 October, General Franciszek Kleeberg (q.v.) surrendered the last operational unit of the Polish Army.

The campaign costs were high for both sides. German losses numbered 48,000 casualties, 560 aircraft, and 670 tanks. Poland suffered 200,000 military casualties and maybe half again as many civilian casualties. Another 787,000 troops were prisoners of war in Germany or the Soviet Union. One might conclude that such a poor showing supports an overall negative assessment of the Polish military. Such a conclusion, however, would be premature. Śmigły-Rydz made some poor decisions and the Plan *ZACHOD* deployments stretched army resources beyond proper bounds, but these were not the root causes for Poland's 1939 disaster.

Before addressing that question, it might prove useful to compare the fighting with other early World War II campaigns. German losses in Poland accounted for half of the total they suffered in all other battles until the invasion of the Soviet Union (q.v.). Also, the *Wehrmacht* forces consumed eight months of fuel, ammunition, and vehicle production in a little more than one month of operations against Poland. Thus, partially mobilized, vastly outnumbered, and hit by enemies from all sides, the Poles resisted for thirty-six days and inflicted serious damage to the German war machine. Britain, France, Belgium, and the Netherlands fought Germany for thirty-nine days in 1940, and caused fewer losses. When one considers that these nations, in the words of General Norwid-Neugebauer, "had ample time for a leisurely mobilization," superior naval forces, and near parity in ground and air units, the Polish campaign obtains more significance in perspective.

Poland was the *Wehrmacht*'s greatest challenge up to Operation BARBAROSSA, and its victory demonstrated high degrees of technical competence and professionalism. One must also credit Hitler for his diplomatic and geopolitical insights. Yet without denigrating such obvious qualities, none of them represent the major cause for Poland's defeat. The lackluster leadership of Britain and France were the main reason. Presented with the opportunity of forcing Hitler to fight a two-front war, they opted otherwise. This, then, was the fatal flaw in Plan *ZACHOD*.

The Polish military expected to take heavy, even near fatal, blows. At the same time, it anticipated that western Germany would be hit with equal force. The capture or destruction of key Rhineland industries was very possible. Indeed, German generals like Wilhelm Keitel, Alfred Jodl, Gerd von Rundstedt, and Erhard Milch (qq.v.) all agreed that a strong Allied assault would have forced massive troop transfers from the east. Instead, while the Poles reeled under German hammer blows, France launched a few reconnaissance patrols, and the British argued over the legality of bombing private property. As can be imagined, this "Phony War" (q.v.) allowed Hitler to allocate maximum resources to the destruction of Poland. When that work was accomplished, he was able to shift his power westward to be used in *Fall GELB* (Case YELLOW), the invasion of France (q.v.).

The Anglo-French failure relieved Germany of the danger of a two-front war; one that probably would have ended in its collapse. Now the Europeans had to call in outside forces to defeat Germany. By doing so, they lost their predominant position in world affairs.

John Dunn

Additional Reading

Bethell, Nicholas, *The War Hitler Won: The Fall of Poland, September 1939* (1973)

Garlinski, Jozek, *Poland in the Second World War* (1985).

Kennedy, Richard M., *The German Campaign in Poland* (1956).

Zaloga, Steven, and Victor Madej, *The Polish Campaign 1939* (1985).

Poland-East Prussia (July 1944–April 1945)

[See map 32 on page 1342]

In early 1945, the Red Army reached the frontiers of the Third *Reich*. The previous six months had seen the near total destruction of German forces in the east, as well as the collapse of most of the Axis puppets in Eastern Europe. In June 1944, the Soviet *Stavka* (q.v.) had massed eleven fronts (army groups) stretching from the Baltic states in the north to the Black Sea in the south. The 1st Baltic Front, 1st, 2nd, and 3rd Byelorussian Fronts, and the 1st and 4th Ukrainian Fronts all played significant roles in the expulsion of Axis forces from Poland. The troops that breached the German line and destroyed Army Group Center were an impressive force totaling 166 infantry divisions, nine rifle brigades, 31,000 artillery pieces, 5,200 tanks and self-propelled guns, and 6,000 aircraft.

By late June 1944, the Red Army had on average a four to one superiority over the Axis forces. In sharp contrast to earlier campaigns, the quality of equipment and proficiency of its users were far superior to the near-helpless Red Army of 1941. In the first five days of Operation BAGRATION, the offensive in Byelorussia (q.v.), the 1st and 3rd Byelorussian Fronts penetrated sixty-eight miles on a 125-mile front. The Germans were incapable of stopping the massive juggernaut, though they did inflict serious losses and temporary delays. German resistance crystallized briefly in isolated pockets, notably near Minsk. By 3 July, however, Minsk fell and Army Group Center virtually disintegrated.

After the Germans were pushed out of Byelorussia, Josef Stalin (q.v.) issued a new series of orders through the *Stavka*. The new plan intended to exploit the westward progress, continue the liberation of Poland and the Baltics, and drive on to Berlin. The 1st Baltic Front was given the mission of seizing Daugavpils and Kaunas, in Lithuania, while the 3rd Byelorussian Front was to occupy a line from Vilnius to Lida and force bridgeheads over the Neman River. To the south, the 2nd Byelorussian Front would seize the Novogrudok-Neman-Białystok line, while the 1st Byelorussian Front would move toward Baranovichi and the old fortress of Brest and establish footholds across the Bug River. The Soviet Army was, by this time, well supplied with trucks and other mechanized vehicles, while the Germans were becoming hamstrung with shortages of every kind. On 20 July 1944, the 1st Byelorussian Front crossed the Bug River in three places. Lublin fell the same day, and the Soviets reached the banks of the Vistula River on 25 July. Warsaw was in sight. Brest was encircled and fell after one day of resistance.

To the north and south, the other fronts reached their objectives against varying degrees of resistance. Small pockets isolated in the Baltic states remained cut off until their surrender in May 1945. General Josef Harpe's (q.v.) Army Group A—as Army Group North Ukraine had been redesignated—could do little more than hold on where possible, even if only temporarily. Adolf Hitler's (q.v.) impractical "no retreat" orders rendered realistic resistance impossible as early as 1943. By 1944, the folly of this doctrine was rapidly destroying what little mobile formations the Germans had left. To make matters worse, Hitler's ill-advised plan to counterattack the Western Allies in the Ardennes (q.v.) drew even more German troops and equipment from the already hard-pressed east.

Any delays and casualties inflicted on the Red Army, by this point, were caused by the ability and tenacity of the German soldier, rather than the efficiency of the German high command. The Soviets, on the other hand, finally were reaping the benefits of a long, painful learning experience. Under unified and coherent leadership, the Red Army had men like Marshal Georgy Zhukov, General Ivan Konev, General Ivan Chernyakovsky, and General Konstantin Rokossovsky (qq.v.) commanding veteran troops who had learned much in three years of war. Although the German troops were tough veterans, they were war-weary and at the end of their logistical tethers. Any strategic ability on the part of their commanders was more than negated by Hitler's fantasies.

At the end of July 1944, the *Stavka* altered the orders given to the fronts. Now the 1st and 2nd Byelorussian Fronts pressed on to the Narew River and Warsaw. The 2nd Byelorussian Front was to attack toward Ostrołęka and Łomża, and the 1st Byelorussian Front toward the Warsaw suburb of Praga, seizing several bridgeheads across the Vistula and Narew Rivers. These operations were carried out with minimal difficulty. In August, the 2nd Byelorussian Front reached the Ostrołęka-Łomża axis. By this time the offensive began to run out of steam. Stalin's final objective of Berlin was not yet realistic at this point, and the immense progress made by the Red Army left it exhausted after nearly two months of fighting. Supplies were in abundance, but they had to be brought forward and issued to the spearhead units.

By August, the Soviets closed on the Vistula River. The Germans were not in good shape. The equivalent of twenty-eight German divisions numbering 350,000 troops had been destroyed, and those left were mere shadows of their former selves. Hitler, however, persisted with his "no retreat" orders, and his commanders obeyed. Not only were the German forces in the Baltic cut off, but several other formations were encircled and eventually destroyed in their attempts to hold untenable positions.

On 29 August, Stalin issued a contentious order: all fronts were ordered to dig in on a line from Jelgava to Jusefuv, generally along the Vistula/ Narew river line. The 1st and 2nd Byelorussian Fronts continued limited attacks to clear Praga and strengthen the Narew bridgeheads, but no real attempt was made to cross the Vistula and relieve the Warsaw resistance fighters. This led to one of the more controversial episodes of World War II.

General Tadeusz Bór-Komorowski (q.v.) of the Polish Home Army (AK) (q.v.) ordered a general uprising beginning 1 August. Although initially successful in Warsaw, the Germans quickly reacted and began a step-by-step elimination of the Home Army. The Soviets made half-hearted attempts to help, mainly in the form of airdropped supplies; but after their own offensive, they were too weak to make a sustained relief attempt. Stalin also considered the Poles to be "adventurists" and "irresponsible." The fact that the Home Army represented the non-Communist resistance was not lost on him either. Historians have argued whether or not this was a deliberate attempt to exterminate a free Poland. German Army chief of staff General Heinz Guderian (q.v.) was of the impression that the Soviet halt was a result of exhaustion and heavy German resistance. The Germans took sixty days to wipe out the Home Army, and with it most of Warsaw (*see* Warsaw Rising). In the process, the Germans suffered some 10,000 casualties, a figure that attests to the stout stand of the Poles.

The *Stavka,* meanwhile, was not idle. In late

fall 1944, plans were under way for the eviction of all remaining German forces in Poland. The planned Vistula-Oder offensive clearly outlined the mission of the Soviet fronts in accomplishing the goal of liberating the remainder of Poland and the final destruction of the Third *Reich*. The 1st, 2nd, and 3rd Byelorussian Fronts, under Zhukov, Rokossovsky, and Chernyakovsky, respectively, and the 1st Ukrainian Front under Konev, rested on the Narew and Vistula line. The 4th Ukrainian Front, under General Ivan Petrov (q.v.), lined the San River in southern Poland and Galicia, while General Rodion Malinovsky's (q.v.) 2nd Ukrainian Front and General Fedor Tolbuhkin's (q.v.) 3rd Ukrainian Front faced Hungary and the Balkans.

Stalin's orders were clear and simple. The destruction of Army Group A was the major objective, with the drawing off of German reserves from western Europe as a secondary objective—in response to Western Allied requests resulting from the Ardennes offensive.

Zhukov's 1st Byelorussian Front was ordered to take Poznan and destroy any forces it cut off in the Warsaw/Radom area. To accomplish this mission, Zhokov's Forty-seventh Army was supported by the left flank of the 2nd Byelorussian Front, which would encircle Warsaw from the north and west, thus cutting off the German Warsaw garrison. The 2nd Byelorussian Front had orders to press on to Marienburg and isolate Modlin in an effort to prevent any Germans from escaping.

Konev's 1st Ukrainian Front provided the main thrust of the offensive, with five combined arms armies, two tank armies, and four tank/ mechanized corps pushing on the Piotrków-Radomsko-Częstochowa-Miechówice axis and continuing on to Breslau. Before this force could attack, they had to break out of the Sandomierz bridgehead. Three armies and six artillery divisions were to break the German line, and two combined arms armies in the second echelon would exploit to Szydlowiec-Ostrowiec and push on as far as possible. Farther to the south, the 4th Ukrainian Front had orders to occupy Kraków, with the rest of the front moving on to Czechoslovakia.

Well rested and resupplied, the 1st Ukrainian Front and 1st Byelorussian Front together had 163 divisions, 32,143 artillery pieces, 6,460 tanks and self-propelled guns, and 4,772 aircraft. Total ground strength was 2,200,000 troops. Overall, the Red Army had a six to one advantage over the German defenders. The Soviet losses from the 1944 summer offensive had been replaced.

The second half of the offensive to liberate Poland started on 12 January 1945. Radom was immediately invested and fell on 16 January. On 13 January, Nowy Miasto fell to the First Guards Tank Army under General Mikhail Katukov. On 17 January, Zhukov's 1st Byelorussian Front, along with the Soviet-controlled Polish First Army, liberated the remains of Warsaw. Over the the next four to six days, the 1st Byelorussian and 1st Ukrainian Fronts forced a 310-mile wide gap in the German lines and penetrated sixty to 100 miles. Harpe was incapable of doing more than delaying the inevitable, but he did this with obstinacy.

By the end of January, Konev's forces cleared the Tomaszów Mazowiecki-Częstochowa region of southern Poland. A line running from Bydgoszcz to Poznán was under Soviet control by 4 February 1945, negating an important part of Hitler's "fortress" line.

The German defense unraveled quickly. Between 19 and 25 January, Konev's forces took Kraków and surrounded Poznán, another key part of Germany's "fortress" line. On 22 January, Konev's engineers threw several bridges across the Oder River and formed shallow bridgeheads. The battle, however, was far from over. Many pockets of resistance remained, and the speed of the advance had disorganized the Red Army. Zhukov also reached the Oder and bridged it, but a ninety-mile gap had opened between Zhukov and Rokossovsky. That needed to be closed before any farther advances could be made.

On 28 January, the 1st Byelorussian Front entered German Pomerania. Despite the last-ditch counterattacks launched by Germany's newly formed Army Group Vistula—commanded for some strange reason by Heinrich Himmler (q.v.)— Rokossovsky's 2nd Byelorussian Front continued to advance, taking Bischofsburg at the end of January. Lansberg and Barenstein fell in early February. German forces elsewhere were unable to assist in the defense of East Prussia. Königsberg became cut off when Zhukov's and Rokossovky's troops reached the Frisches Haff on the Baltic Sea. On 8 April, the 3rd Byelorussian Front broke through the defenses of Königsberg, and the city fell the next day.

Konev's 1st Ukrainian Front, although at the Oder River, needed to clean up pockets of German resistance in the Polish southwestern region around Katowice and Oppeln. Once again, by mid-February, the Soviet offensive had outrun its supplies and fuel. Although Zhukov and Konev made several attempts to exploit the Oder crossings and continue the attack to Berlin, the German forces in Pomerania (some forty understrength divisions) and fatigue and overextension of the Soviet forces dictated a halt.

P

The gap between Zhukov and Rokossovsky took three weeks to close. Moreover, the Red Army had taken heavy casualties. Some Soviet divisions were operating at only 50 percent strength and Zhukov's two tank armies had only 740 tanks between them. The situation was much the same elsewhere along the Soviet front. Most of the spearhead units were showing the strain of nearly six months of hard campaigning. The Soviets always could replace their losses, but not immediately.

The Germans, by contrast, were nearly finished. Army Group A, consisting of the Fourth *Panzer* Army, the Seventeenth Army, and Army Heinrici (formerly the First *Panzer* Army), was a formidable force on paper, but actual strength amounted to little more than a glorified corps. No replacements or supplies were forthcoming, except some elderly *Volkssturm* and young Hitler Youth (qq.v.) troops of questionable military value.

Hitler's persistently unsound strategy sealed the fate of the Third *Reich*. He steadfastly refused to evacuate the cut-off forces in the Baltic and East Prussia, maintaining they were necessary to protect U-boat facilities and ports. No reinforcements would be possible from these forlorn posts, whose time was limited. Any other strategic reserves were thrown away in the Ardennes offensive. Most German commanders, with the exception of Hitler and his coterie, knew the end was only a matter of time.

After the war, many German and Soviet commanders indicated that they thought the Soviet attack was halted too early and could have driven on to Berlin. Zhukov, however, rightly stated: "To exaggerate the capabilities of one's troops and to underrate the strength and ability of the enemy are equally dangerous." The Germans were beaten and battered, but were still able to inflict casualties when the Soviets were careless or impulsive. History had clearly taught Zhukov and his front commanders that much. Critical supply and bridging units, as well as aviation assets, still lagged far behind in the Soviet rear. A foolhardy and premature attack on the Oder-Neisse line could have been a military disaster for the Soviets.

Tim Wilson

Additional Reading

Erikson, John, *Stalin's War with Germany,* 2 vols. (1983).

Seaton, Albert, *The Russo-German War 1941–45* (1971).

Ziemke, Earl F., *Stalingrad to Berlin: The German Defeat in the East* (1968).

Po Valley (April–May 1945)

[See map 22 on page 1332]

After three months of largely stationary warfare in the mountains of northern Italy, the 15th Army Group, commanded by General Mark Clark (q.v.), launched a spring offensive on 9 April 1945. That afternoon, the artillery of Lieutenant General Richard L. McCreery's (q.v.) British Eighth Army and more than 800 Allied heavy bombers began pounding the positions of General Traugott Herr's German Tenth Army. Herr was holding a line from the Adriatic coast in the Lake Comacchio area to the vicinity of Bologna. During the next two days, British, Polish, New Zealand, and Indian troops broke into and through German positions in several places, and thereby unhinged Herr's defenses.

On 14 April, after a much needed break in the weather, the U.S. Fifth Army (which included a Brazilian and a South African division), commanded by Lieutenant General Lucian K. Truscott (q.v.), struck in the region between the Ligurian coast and Bologna. While some divisions of General Joachim Lemelsen's Fourteenth Army held onto their positions for several days, large sections of the German front rapidly disintegrated. By 20 April, the commander in chief of German Army Group C, Colonel General Heinrich von Vietinghoff-Scheel (q.v.), ordered his forces to withdraw toward the Po River.

Aided by Allied air forces, battle groups of both the Eighth and Fifth Armies rapidly advanced northward, cutting off the retreating Germans in several areas. With all permanent bridges across the Po River out of commission since the autumn of 1944, most German troops reached the south bank of the river and were forced to abandon their vehicles and heavy equipment before making their way across the water in small boats or by swimming. Although in some places pontoon bridges were available, they were under almost constant air attack and only occasionally useable.

The partial disintegration of von Vietinghoff's army group was reflected in the capture of several German generals, including the commander of the LXXVI *Panzer Korps*, Lieutenant General Gerhard von Schwerin. Two divisional commanders also were killed in action: Major General Hellmuth Pfeiffer near Finale on 22 April, and Major General Walter Jost near Villadosa on 24 April.

On the evening of 24 April, the Fifth Army controlled the south bank of the Po River along a front extending sixty miles from west of Parma to Felonica, northeast of Ferrara. Moreover, several Fifth Army units bounded across the Po River and were racing north toward the Alps. In the Eighth

Army sector farther east, progress was equally swift. By 25 April, several Eighth Army divisions moved rapidly toward the Alps and toward the eastern reaches of Venetia. Encountering only sporadic resistance, American units reached Verona on 26 April and Milan two days later. On 29 April, the British 56th Infantry Division entered Venice. Three days later, the New Zealand 2nd Division arrived at Trieste, where it accepted the surrender of German forces that previously had engaged Marshal Tito's (q.v.) Yugoslav forces.

While remnants of German Army Group C withdrew into the Alps under constant pressure from Allied troops and a variety of Italian partisan units, negotiations for an armistice in the Italian theater were in high gear. For some time, von Vietinghoff and the senior SS general in Italy, SS-*Oberstgruppenführer* Karl Wolff (q.v.), were in touch with various Allied representatives to establish conditions of surrender for German forces south of the Alps.

On 29 April, the senior intelligence officer of Army Group C, Lieutenant Colonel Viktor von Schweinitz (a great grandson of the nineteenth-century U.S. diplomat John Jay) and an SS officer representing Wolff, SS-*Sturmbannführer* Eugen Wenner, signed a formal surrender document at Allied headquarters in Caserta. The German capitulation in the Italian theater went into effect on 2 May 1945. Field Marshal Albert Kesselring (q.v.), the recently appointed commander in chief of German forces in the southern half of Axis-controlled territory, initially opposed the deal and removed both Wolff and von Vietinghoff from their posts.

After much friction and confusion within the German ranks, and following confirmation of Hitler's death, Kesselring relented and the cease-fire went into effect at 1400 hours (Italian time) on 2 May. Two days later, a German corps commander, General Frido von Senger und Etterlin (q.v.), met General Clark in Florence and arranged the actual surrender of Army Group C and various *Luftwaffe* and naval units operating in the Italian theater. In the weeks to follow, approximately 250,000 German POWs were sent to compounds in northern and central Italy.

The triumph of the 15th Army Group did not come easily, but in many ways, the defeat of the Germans was a foregone conclusion. Despite the vast superiority in the quality of German weapons, tanks, and vehicles, the Allies enjoyed complete control of the skies over northern Italy. As a result, not even the best German divisions in the theater were able to exploit their tactical skills. The logistic support of German fighting units, before and during April 1945, was dramatically curtailed by repeated Allied air strikes on railways and roads linking Germany with Italy. Adolf Hitler's (q.v.) insistence that Army Group C stay and fight south of the Po River made the German situation in Italy even more precarious. Once the Allied flood started in mid-April, German defeat was inevitable.

Ulrich Trumpener

Additional Reading

Fisher, Ernest F., Jr., *The Mediterranean Theater of Operations: Cassino to the Alps* (1977).

Graham, Dominick, and Shelford Bidwell, *Tug of War: The Battle for Italy, 1943–1945* (1986).

Haupt, Werner, *Kriegsschauplatz Italien, 1943–1945* (1977).

Kesselring, Albert, *Kesselring: A Soldier's Record* (1953).

Linklater, Eric, *The Campaign in Italy* (1951).

Senger und Etterlin, Frido von, *Krieg in Europa* (1960).

R

Rapido River (20–22 January 1944)

[See map 1 on page 1311]

On 20 January 1944, the U.S. 36th Infantry Division (ID) began a forty-eight-hour battle to establish bridgeheads on the west bank of the Rapido River. Their objective was to draw enemy reserves that could be used against the Anzio (q.v.) landings scheduled for 22 January, and to facilitate operations against the German strong point at Monte Cassino (q.v.).

Rough terrain and skillful German defense had stalled the 15th Army Group for more than two months following its successful advance from the Volturno River (q.v.). Costly battles for minor gains demonstrated the futility of an overland advance to Rome and fueled the debate for an amphibious assault to unhinge the German defenses. Prior to the decision to invade at Anzio, Lieutenant General Mark W. Clark (q.v.), the U.S. Fifth Army commander, had already started to launch local attacks to move his front line closer to the proposed beachhead.

Most critical to Clark's overland advance was the Liri Valley. Armored formations could operate there and drive a wedge toward Anzio in the German lines. Clark planned for British X Corps and the French Expeditionary Corps to seize the flanks of the Liri Valley prior to U.S. II Corps' advance in the center. Neither flank attack made much progress, and II Corps' small gains managed only to force the Germans to evacuate a hilltop position in X Corps' zone.

American units considered crossing the Rapido as early as November, but commanders of both the 3rd and 36th IDs discounted any possibility of success unless Allied forces held the flanking high ground. Echoing his subordinates, Major General Geoffrey Keyes proposed that his U.S. II Corps not cross the Rapido, but attack with X Corps along the Garigliano River, and then advance north into the Liri Valley. After Allied planners shelved that idea, Keyes requested that the British 46th Division, on his left, attack forty-eight hours prior to his own forces to seize German observation posts overlooking the river. Unfortunately, the British delayed their operation at the last minute, and even failed to make the commanding ridge an objective.

Keyes and Major General Fred L. Walker, commander of the 36th ID, recognized that American forces would be attacking at a disadvantage against 15th *Panzergrenadier* Division, but neither general requested the crossing be postponed. Both knew that Clark considered the Rapido operation essential to the Anzio landing, and they knew he would not consider a delay.

Many obstacles confronted Walker's division. Although the Rapido measured only twenty-five to fifty feet wide and nine to twelve feet deep, it flowed swiftly and had nearly vertical banks. Moreover, winter rains had turned the approach routes to the river into mud, and the flat terrain offered almost no cover or concealment from German troops (considered the best in XIV *Panzer Korps*) who overlooked the Rapido. In addition, Walker had to leave one of his three infantry regiments in reserve because another corps unit might be needed at Anzio.

Keyes attempted to alleviate the shortage of infantry by attaching to Walker's command twelve artillery battalions, the 34th ID's tanks and tank destroyers, and the tanks and guns of Combat Command B, 1st Armored Division. In addition, Walker received the 19th Engineer Regiment, along with elements of 16th Armored Engineer Battalion. The engineers provided more than 300 assault boats and eight footbridges for the assault regiments.

Getting the equipment to the river, however, proved a problem. Because of the mud, even light trucks could not approach the river. Since the Germans controlled the Rapido by fire during daylight, the attacking forces had to carry all crossing equipment to the river in addition to their own combat loads. In addition, the divisional engineers lacked the manpower to support two simultaneous regimental assaults. As a remedy, each regiment received a battalion from 19th Engineer Regiment. The lack of habitual association between these units, however, complicated rehearsals and planning, and the close coordination essential for a river crossing never developed. Walker exacerbated problems by replacing one of his assault regiments with another after rehearsals had already started. The last-minute arrival of 500 individual replacements for both infantry regiments further complicated team-building.

Walker planned for a sixteen-battalion preparatory artillery barrage to precede the 2000 hours crossings on 20 January. Once the regiments crossed the river, artillery fires would shift to a creeping barrage 150 to 200 yards in front of the infantry. After the engineers finished building infantry footbridges, they would then erect heavier bridges for tank units.

A heavy fog helped conceal 141st and 143rd Infantry Regiments as they moved forward from their assembly areas, but enemy fire destroyed some boats, and others were lost when the German artillery's counter-barrage began. By H-Hour, the engineers had lost more than 25 percent of their equipment, and half of 141st Infantry's boats were damaged beyond use. Cloth tape marking the paths to the river fared no better. Some units lost their way in the dark after German fire destroyed the tape. Others went astray because preceding units had trampled the white tape into the mud.

The 1st Battalion, 141st Infantry completed its crossing by 0400 hours on 21 January. Then German fire and lack of bridges forced 141st Infantry's follow-on battalion to return to its assembly area. The 1st Battalion was forced to dig into its shallow bridgehead, unable to retreat or advance.

To the south, 143rd Infantry Regiment attempted to cross at two sites. Both assault battalions attacked in a column of companies. Only the 1st Battalion got across the river, but it returned to the east bank when no reinforcements followed. The 3rd Battalion wandered into a minefield and later lost most of its boats.

The attack surprised the Germans, but they considered the assault to be only a reconnaissance in force, and they committed no reinforcements to the defense. With an unclear picture of the situation, Clark ordered Keyes to send tanks across the Rapido. Despite Walker's protests, Keyes directed him to renew the attack and to build the forty-ton bridges needed for the tanks to cross.

Walker ordered his regiments to attack at 1400 hours, but boat shortages and confusion at the crossing sites stalled any assault until 1600 hours. Screened by smoke, the 143rd Infantry Regiment managed to cross all three battalions, but the heavy bridging equipment from II Corps did not arrive until 0400 hours on 22 January. Even under noncombat conditions, this equipment required at least six hours to erect. Unable to reinforce his units with tanks, the 143rd's commander ordered his units to withdraw later that day.

The 141st Infantry Regiment finally crossed its 2nd and 3rd Battalions during the night of 21 January, but neither unit located any survivors from the 1st Battalion. Attempts to erect a Bailey bridge failed, and the strong current and enemy fire soon destroyed all but one footbridge. Walker and the regimental commander failed to comprehend the deteriorating situation of the two battalions, and eventually every company commander and all the battalion staff officers but one were dead or wounded. Effective resistance ceased after German fire destroyed the last footbridge, and only a few handfuls of U.S. soldiers managed to recross the Rapido.

Keyes ordered Walker to ready 142nd Infantry Regiment for yet another assault, but then he relented. One infantry battalion had ceased to exist, and the five other battalions lost more than half their authorized manpower. The 36th ID suffered 1,681 casualties in forty-eight hours and failed to achieve any of its objectives. The Germans suffered few casualties and realized the scope of the attack only after interrogating the more than 500 American prisoners they captured.

Clark later adamantly defended his decision to attack. Both the U.S. Senate and House of Representatives conducted inconclusive hearings on the Rapido River crossings in 1946.

Roger Kaplan

Additional Reading
Blumenson, Martin, *Bloody River* (1970).
———, *Salerno to Cassino* (1969).
Smith, Lee C., *A River Swift and Deadly* (1989).

Regensburg Air Raid (17 August 1943)
[See map 20 on page 1330]
The U.S. Eighth Air Force attack on the twin tar-

gets of Regensburg and Schweinfurt on 17 August 1943 marked the first anniversary of the operational debut of the American strategic bombing force over Europe. The raid also marked the deepest penetration of Germany and the largest force dispatched to that time, 376 B-17s. It also was the costliest. The U.S. Army Air Force lost sixty planes—thirty-six of which were over Regensburg. The air assault on Regensburg was, however, successful, with every important building at the Messerschmitt fighter plane complex damaged.

Operation JUGGLER, the August bombing raid against the Regensburg Messerschmitt complexes, was to include the precision bombing of the airplane factory at Wiener Neustadt, a site just outside of Vienna. These two locations produced almost half of all German single-engine fighters. Operation JUGGLER originated as an effort to coordinate the strategic operations of the Eighth Air Force, flying out of Britain, and the Ninth Air Force, based in North Africa. Planners believed that a simultaneous assault on Regensburg and Wiener Neustadt would catch the German forces off guard and would deal German fighter plane production a decisive blow.

Allied planners in Britain also called for the simultaneous assault on the Messerschmitt complex and the ball bearing industry in Schweinfurt. Because of the distance to Regensburg, the planes of the 4th Bomb Wing were equipped with long-range tanks, and after bombing Regensburg they were to continue on an unprecedented flight to bases in North Africa. On 16 August, favorable weather forecasts for both the bombing raids and the flight to Africa finally arrived. The decision was made to launch the air assault the next day.

The force attacking Regensburg departed three hours before the planes for Schweinfurt. This allowed the fighter escorts to return to Britain, refuel, and escort the bombers heading to the ball bearing plants at Schweinfurt. At that point in the war, Allied fighters did not have sufficient range to escort the bombers all the way to Regensburg, and could barely reach Schweinfurt. Both forces encountered almost continuous fighter opposition from the *Luftwaffe* all the way to the targets. Of the 376 B-17s participating in both raids, thirty-six were lost over Schweinfurt and another twenty-four were lost over Regensburg—a brutal 16 percent loss rate. The U.S. bombers managed to shoot down twenty-five *Luftwaffe* fighters in the process.

The air raid on Regensburg did, in large measure, accomplish its objectives. The planes blanketed the entire area with high explosives and incendiary bombs, damaging every important

building at the Messerschmitt site and destroying some completed fighters sitting outside. But the test of flying B-17s on to North Africa, a strategy aimed at taking advantage of the better weather in the Mediterranean region and causing confusion among the German defensive forces, proved unsatisfactory. The required maintenance crews were simply not available for duty in North Africa, and landing at fields so far from their home base was a serious strain on the flight crews.

Operation JUGGLER was an important initial step in strategic air planning, called POINT-BLANK, which was to provide Allied air superiority before launching an invasion of France. Along with seriously disrupting German industry, it was designed to severely impact fighter production. Yet in spite of the raid on the factories at Regensburg and Wiener-Neustadt, German fighter strength continued to increase at an alarming pace. In light of this, the Eighth Air Force and American planners gradually turned away from the original plan of precision attacks deep inside Germany. Control of the air over Germany was still some time off.

Robert G. Waite

Additional Reading
Craven, Wesley Frank and James Lea Cate (eds.), *Europe—Torch to Pointblank, August 1942 to December 1943* (1949).
Jablonski, Edward, *Double Strike: The Epic Air Raids on Regensburg/Schweinfurt* (1974).
Webster, Charles, and Arthur Noble Frankland, *The Strategic Air Offensive against Germany, 1939–1945. Endeavour* (1961).

Reichswald (8 February–10 March 1945)

The Battle of the *Reichswald* was the opening phase of Operation VERITABLE, the February 1945 Canadian offensive in the Rhineland. The offensive pushed east across the Dutch-German border capturing Kleve, then south between the Rhine and Maas Rivers. The thrust was supposed to meet the U.S. Ninth Army attacking northeast, cutting off German units and defenses in the process. The ultimate objective of Operation VERITABLE was the bridgeheads across the lower Rhine.

The defenders were General Alfred Schlemm's First Parachute Army, part of Colonel General Johannes Blaskowitz's (q.v.) Army Group H. The German objective was to prevent the Allies from breaking through and reaching the Rhine.

British Lieutenant General Sir Brian Horrocks (q.v.) and his XXX Corps led the offensive. Brilliant staff work by the XXX Corps mustered 170,000 men with equipment in the forests south of Nijmegen, the Netherlands. The Canadian II Corps and the British 79th Armoured Division later joined, bringing the Allied force to a total of 200,000 troops and 35,000 vehicles. Several XXX Corps divisions came under the operational control of the Canadian II Corps during the operation.

The Allies' overwhelming superiority in men and equipment was to a great degree offset by terrain and weather. There were only two main roads along the principal axis of attack. The thick Reichswald Forest, eight miles deep and five miles wide, restricted vehicular movement and the use of armor. The Germans developed a defense-in-depth behind the West Wall (q.v.), with two fortified towns, Kleve and Goch, on relatively high ground dominating their approaches. One week prior to the offensive, a thaw turned the ground to mud. The Germans also opened the floodgates on the Maas, overflowing the river. The first phase of the operation, planned for completion in three or four days, lasted more than two weeks.

Any German reinforcement to the area would have to come through the historic town of Kleve—birthplace of British King Henry VIII's fourth wife, Anne. Reluctantly, Horrocks opted for the destruction of the town by the Royal Air Force (RAF) Bomber Command on 8 February 1945.

The set-piece offensive began on 8 February, with a five-hour opening barrage from more than 1,000 artillery pieces. XXX Corps then proceeded across the flooded valley and into the *Reichswald* Forest. From north to south, the Canadian 3rd, Canadian 2nd, 15th Scottish, 53rd Welsh, and 51st Highland Divisions advanced, supported by two tank brigades. Two armored and two infantry divisions followed in the second and third echelons.

The German forward defensive unit, the mostly unfit 84th Infantry Division under Major General Martin Fiebeg, was virtually destroyed the first day. After the opening barrage, Schlemm began to advance his II Parachute *Korps'* 6th and 7th Parachute Divisions, under Major General Eugen Meindl. On 9 February, the Germans counterattacked, but they merely slowed the rate of the Allied advance at a terrible cost to II Parachute *Korps*.

On 10 February, the 43rd Wessex Division reinforced the Allied attack, but it became snarled in traffic and mud. The 43rd Wessex Division captured Kleve on 11 February and advanced 8,000 yards to the escarpment dominating heavily fortified Goch. Savage combat ensued from 18 to 21 February. Goch eventually was captured by the 15th Scottish and 51st Highland Divisions.

Flooding of the Roer dams in the south, meanwhile, held up the U.S. Ninth Army. Slow Allied progress gave the *Wehrmacht* time to shift Lieutenant General Smilo von Lüttwitz's XLVII *Panzer Korps'* veteran but battle-weary 15th *Panzergrenadier* and 116th *Panzer* Divisions. With ninety tanks, von Lüttwitz attacked the 53rd Welsh Division in the *Reichswald*. The Germans were repelled. By 17 February, the 53rd Welsh Division cleared the remainder of the *Reichswald*.

On 19 February, the *Panzer-Lehr* Division counterattacked unsuccessfully in the Moyland Wood vicinity. The attack achieved initial surprise but was beaten back by the Fort Garry Horse and the Queen's Own Cameron Highlander Regiments. The *Panzer-Lehr* reeled back with heavy losses. In the following days, the commander of Canadian II Corps, Major General Guy Simonds (q.v.), used all his available artillery assets to clear the Moyland Wood.

The Allies took Goch and its environs by the morning of 22 February. That broke the German defensive anchor, and the exploitation phase of Operation VERITABLE began on 26 February. It was, however, no exploitation at all, as remnants of the II Parachute and the XLVII *Panzer Korps* fought frantically for each piece of ground west of the Rhine. On the left, the Canadian II Corps had the towns of Kalkar, Uedem, and Xanten as objectives From 25 February to March, the Canadian II Corps spent much blood in capturing the German Schlieffen Position and in trying to penetrate the "Hochwald gap." On the right, the XXX Corps aimed at Geldern, where it was to link up with the U.S. Ninth Army.

Lieutenant General William Simpson's (q.v.) Ninth Army offensive, Operation GRENADE, began on 23 February. The battle of attrition in the *Reichswald* drew the quality German reserves away from Ninth Army's Roer River crossing sites. Operation GRENADE succeeded well beyond expectations on the first day. The forces of Operations VERITABLE and GRENADE linked up at Geldern on 3 March.

The German OKW (q.v.) ordered a withdrawal across the Rhine on 6 March, and on 10 March, the battle of the *Reichswald* came to an end. Total British and Canadian casualties were 15,634, of which two-thirds came from XXX Corps. Most Canadian losses were sustained by the 2nd and 3rd Divisions. German losses were wildly estimated to be as low as 22,000 to as high as 75,000. At least 16,500 German prisoners were taken. Eleven German divisions were either destroyed or heavily damaged. Operation VERITABLE was a delayed and costly success.

Samuel J. Doss

Additional Reading
Elstob, Peter, *Battle of the Reichswald* (1970).
Horrocks, Brian, *Corps Commander* (1977).
MacDonald, Charles B., *The Last Offensive* (1973).

Remagen Bridge (7–17 March 1945)

As the Allied armies approached the Rhine River in early March 1945, SHAEF (q.v.), not expecting to capture a bridge intact, planned for American troops to pause along the river while Field Marshal Bernard L. Montgomery's (q.v.) 21st Army Group pushed across between Düsseldorf and the Dutch border. Then, using the favorable north German terrain, Montgomery's forces would capture the Ruhr, Germany's main coal and industrial region.

American commanders, most notably Generals Omar N. Bradley and George S. Patton (qq.v.), disliked their secondary role, and argued that their troops should cross the Rhine as soon as possible in order to keep the *Wehrmacht* off balance. Capture of a Rhine bridge would have greatly strengthened the American case, and on several occasions U.S. troops narrowly missed seizing bridges. One of the last remaining bridges stood at Remagen, twenty kilometers upstream from Bonn. Because of the poor road network and the rough terrain on both banks, it was one of the least desirable crossings.

At noon on 7 March 1945, Task Force Engemann—which consisted of the U.S. 14th Tank and 27th Armored Infantry Battalions of Combat Command B (CCB), 9th Armored Division—reached Remagen to discover that the town's Ludendorff Railway Bridge was still standing. Although under orders to move south to block the German Seventh Army's retreat, CCB's commander, Brigadier General William Hoge, allowed the task force to try to capture the bridge. Lieutenant Colonel Leonard Engemann's troops encountered little resistance from Remagen's confused defenders: a platoon of convalescents under town commander Captain Willi Bratge, a few poorly trained and inadequately armed *Volkssturm* (q.v.) men, and at the bridge, Captain Karl Friesenhahn's group of superannuated engineers. None of the German officers at the scene had received recent orders, intelligence, or clarification of the shifting situation. The engineers did have the bridge wired for demolition, but with German troops streaming eastward over the bridge—a situation that prompted many of Remagen's demoralized defenders, particularly the *Volkssturm,* to join the flight—Friesenhahn wanted to delay destroying the bridge until the last possible moment.

At 1600 hours, alerted by Bratge that American tanks and infantrymen were in Remagen, Friesenhahn set off a charge that cratered the approach leading onto the bridge. He could not, however, detonate the main charge, because a lucky round from a U.S. tank had severed the electrical cables between the charge and the power source. While U.S. infantrymen, led by Sergeant Alex Drabik (q.v.) and Lieutenant Karl Timmerman, charging forward onto the bridge, one of Friesenhahn's sergeants ignited the backup charge, a low-quality industrial explosive that wrenched but failed to destroy the thirty-year-old structure. In a matter of minutes, Timmerman's troops reached the east bank and secured the bridge.

The Germans reacted quickly, launching counterattacks with long-range artillery, airplanes, and even V-2 missiles and frogmen in a vain effort to destroy both the railway and the supplementary pontoon bridges the Americans quickly established at Remagen. On 17 March, the Ludendorff Bridge, weakened by explosions, near misses, and a week of continual overuse, collapsed into the Rhine, killing twenty-eight U.S. engineers and injuring ninety-three.

The events at Remagen were undoubtedly among the most dramatic in World War II, yet their strategic impact was limited. The capture of the Ludendorff Bridge and the establishment of an Allied bridgehead on the east bank of the Rhine further demoralized the Germans and forced them to expend their meager reserves there rather than against Montgomery's northern crossing or elsewhere. It also restored American pride and gave Bradley's armies a base from which to launch, in late March, the southern pincer that formed the Ruhr Pocket (q.v.). As events would show, however, the Germans were too weak to defend the Rhine adequately, and the capture of the Remagen Bridge, though heroic, did not shorten the war appreciably.

David K. Yelton

Additional Reading
Hechler, Ken, *The Bridge at Remagen* (1957).
MacDonald, Charles B., *The Last Offensive* (1973).

Rhineland (February–March 1945)

SHAEF (q.v.) launched the Allied Rhineland offensives, Operations VERITABLE, GRENADE, LUMBERJACK, and UNDERTONE, in pursuit of three main goals. The primary objective was to drive the *Wehrmacht* out of the area north of the Mosel River in preparation for the main Allied thrust into Germany—Field Marshal Bernard L. Montgomery's (q.v.) crossing of the Rhine north of the Ruhr. Secondly, SHAEF wanted to conquer the Rhineland south of the Mosel in order to protect Montgomery's right flank and to gain a secure staging area for American troops to launch a secondary drive into Germany via the Frankfurt-Kassel corridor. The final objective for these offensives was to inflict as much damage as possible on the German western armies.

The German defensive strategy, based on holding the line of the West Wall (q.v.) and Roer River, played directly to the third Allied objective. Adolf Hitler (q.v.) wanted to hold that line because it would provide a secure buffer for the Rhine River and the Ruhr region. The Rhine was an important transportation route for Ruhr coal, especially given the German rail net's virtual collapse under Allied bombings, and the Ruhr was Germany's main industrial area. Most importantly, Hitler hoped to stalemate the war by forcing the Allies to pay dearly for every foot of German territory. Eventually, he expected his supposedly inferior and weak-willed Western adversaries would beg him for peace if they were forced to pay a high cost in human lives. This strategy, though consistent with National Socialism's warped ideological notions, was not well tailored to the reality of the German military situation in early 1945.

On 7 February 1945, the Canadian First Army, supported by the British XXX Corps and three Canadian divisions transferred from Italy launched Operation VERITABLE (*see Reichswald*) with the aim of seizing the area between the German-Dutch border and the Rhine northwest of the line Venlo-Rheinberg as a prelude to Montgomery's crossing. Weather and terrain posed a greater challenge to the British and Canadian forces than did the Germans during the initial phase of Operation VERITABLE, as much of the area was under water because of heavy rains and German destruction of flood control installations. What was not inundated quickly turned into a sea of mud, which led to congestion on the few good roads and delayed the Anglo-Canadian offensive.

On 9 and 10 February, the Germans reinforced the weak infantry divisions opposing Operation VERITABLE with elements of the 7th Parachute, 15th *Panzergrenadier,* and 116th *Panzer* Divisions. These troops, further reinforced on 19 February by the elements of the *Panzer-Lehr* Division, took up positions in the *Reichswald,* a densely forested patch of relatively high ground, and the towns of Kleve and Goch, which bordered this area to the north and south, respectively.

These reserves, which formerly had supported the Roer River sector, enabled the Germans to put up a stiff fight, particularly in the *Reichswald* and at the towns of Moyland, Kalkar, and Goch. They were gradually worn down, however, and forced to retreat. On 22 February, poor road and weather conditions hampered exploitation of an Allied breakthrough at Moyland and again allowed the *Wehrmacht* to recover. The Germans formed a new a perimeter centered on Wesel's intact Rhine bridge. The Wesel bridgehead's German defenders held off both the Anglo-Canadians in the north around Xanten, and the Americans in the south until 10 March, when the last German defenders crossed the bridge, destroying it in their wake.

With this, Operation VERITABLE met its strategic objective of clearing the staging area for Montgomery's planned push across the Rhine. Success came at a relatively high price, as the British and Canadians suffered 15,634 casualties, nearly double the rate suffered by the Americans in any of the supporting offensives. German losses, however, were higher, with at least 22,000 killed and wounded and another 16,500 captured. By drawing the best German reserves into battle and decimating them, Operation VERITABLE helped ensure the success of Operation GRENADE.

Operation GRENADE was executed by the U.S. Ninth Army, supported by one corps from the U.S. First Army. Its objective was to secure the southern flank of Montgomery's Rhine crossing from potential German counterattack by clearing the area between the Roer River and the Rhine between Venlo and Rheinberg in the north and Düren and Cologne in the south. The Urftalsperre and Schwammenauel Dams on the Roer River posed the main threat to Operation GRENADE. By destroying the dams, the Germans could literally flood any attempt to cross the Roer.

The U.S. First Army launched a limited offensive on 31 January to seize the dams and forestall this possibility. Although American troops took the dams on 9 February, the Germans damaged the Schwammenauel Dam's flood gates, thereby keeping the Roer Valley inundated for two weeks. That not only expanded the Roer's width in some areas to more than 300 meters (from a normal thirty), but it also increased the current dramatically, up to fifteen kilometers per hour near Düren. In response, the Ninth Army commander, Lieutenant General William H. Simpson (q.v.), delayed Operation GRENADE from 10 until 23 February, by which time he hoped the flooding would subside.

For the crossings, the Ninth Army and the supporting VII Corps from the U.S. First Army mustered fourteen divisions, totaling 380,000 troops, 2,000 guns, 375 aircraft, and 1,400 tanks. The German defenders, weakened by the transfer of reserves to meet both Operation VERITABLE and the limited offensive of Lieutenant General George S. Patton's (q.v.) U.S. Third Army toward Trier and Bitburg, could assemble no more than 54,000 troops and 180 tanks. Clearly, Operation GRENADE's success depended more on concentration of force than surprise and subtlety.

A six-hour preparatory bombardment preceded the 23 February assault crossing, which was hindered more by the Roer's swift current and a shortage of boats than by German resistance. The VII Corps, crossing near Düren where the Roer current was swiftest, faced the greatest problems and the strongest opposition, but it managed to establish itself firmly on the east bank. Elsewhere, German resistance was occasionally bitter, but thoroughly uncoordinated. By 25 February, the Ninth Army unleashed its armor in a northeasterly thrust to exploit the breakthrough, while the VII Corps secured Operation GRENADE's flank along the Erft River. German reserves, consisting of elements of the 3rd *Panzergrenadier* and 9th *Panzer* Divisions, were simply too weak to slow the Americans. The *Wehrmacht* could only take comfort in the fact that the bridges at Neuss, Oberkassel, Krefeld-Uerdingen, and Rheinberg were demolished before U.S. troops could capture them.

American commanders had hoped to trap the German defenders of the Roermond salient between the pincers of Operations GRENADE and VERITABLE. On 3 March, the Ninth Army units linked up with British troops of Operation VERITABLE, but Roermond's defenders successfully withdrew into the Wesel bridgehead. Although it failed to encircle large pockets of German troops, Operation GRENADE achieved its objective of clearing the right flank of Montgomery's staging area and inflicted about 36,000 casualties on the *Wehrmacht,* at a cost of only 7,300 U.S. casualties.

The primary goal of Operation LUMBERJACK was to preempt any German counterattack against the Ninth Army's flank as it wheeled north-

eastward during Operation GRENADE. The objective of LUMBERJACK was to secure the area between the Düren-Cologne line and the Mosel, and in so doing, to inflict maximum damage on the German forces. The entire U.S. First Army was to push to the Rhine, seizing Cologne in the process. The First Army was then to turn southeastward to meet Patton's Third Army, which would be moving through the Eifel Mountains and down the Mosel Valley, near the town of Brohl, thereby trapping much of the German Seventh Army in the Eifel.

The First Army began Operation LUMBERJACK on 1 March as it pushed over the Erft River against only isolated pockets of opposition in the prepared defenses along the river. German resistance collapsed rapidly and by 7 March, Cologne was in American hands. As the First Army pushed south, its primary objective became the Ahr River valley, the main line of retreat for the Seventh Army's LXVI and LXVII *Korps*. While driving toward the Ahr, the U.S. 9th Armored Division's Combat Command B seized an unexpected bonus, the Ludendorff Railway Bridge at Remagen (q.v.), twenty kilometers upstream from Bonn. Although that eventually diverted the First Army away from its objective of encircling the Eifel region, elements of that unit did link up with the Third Army near Brohl on 10 March.

The Third Army's push encountered initially stiff resistance along the West Wall and the Prüm and Kyll Rivers, but on 4 March, the 5th Infantry Division breached the German lines near Bitburg. Through that breach, the 4th Armored Division, one of Patton's favorite units, launched a drive that carried them the forty-four miles to the Rhine in less than five days, inflicting 5,700 casualties on the Germans at a cost of only 100 American casualties. The 4th Armored Division, however, narrowly missed capturing a bridge over the Rhine at Urmitz—between Neuwied and Koblenz. Other Third Army units made steady, if less impressive gains of their own, hampered more by the poor road network and the weather than by the sporadic German resistance.

When Operation LUMBERJACK came to a close on 10 March, the Allies had achieved their objectives of clearing the Rhineland north of the Mosel and mauling four corps of the German Fifteenth and Seventh Armies. Furthermore, they also had gained a bridge over the Rhine, although not in a terribly desirable location.

Operation UNDERTONE, the final stage of clearing the Rhineland, aimed at removing German forces from the Saar and Palatinate, a rough triangle bounded by the Mosel River on the northwest, the Rhine River to the east, and the French border in the south. Operation UNDERTONE consisted of a U.S. Seventh Army frontal assault on the West Wall in the Saarland, supported by a Third Army thrust across the Mosel and Saar Rivers. Patton, in order to take advantage of the disorganization of the Germans in the aftermath of Operation LUMBERJACK, launched his offensive early on 13 March. The *Wehrmacht* fought hard in the Trier-Merzig area and at Koblenz, but elsewhere along the Mosel the Germans could do little to stop Patton. Although the veteran 6th SS Mountain Division put up extremely fierce local resistance, by 20 March, Third Army units reached the Rhine at Mainz, Worms, and Ludwigshafen.

On 15 March, the U.S. Seventh Army attacked the German First Army, holding the strongest portion of the West Wall. At first the Americans advanced slowly. By 20 March, Seventh Army units breached the center of the German line, and this, coupled with Patton's threat to their rear, forced the Germans to withdraw. The French First and U.S. Seventh Army efforts to push down the Rhine and encircle the retreating Germans failed because of determined German resistance. By 24 March, however, the Germans had been thrown back over the Rhine.

Operation UNDERTONE was a complete success both in seizing territory and in the damage it inflicted upon the *Wehrmacht*. Although some German troops conducted a skillful withdrawal over the Rhine, the Allied armies inflicted an estimated 200,000 casualties on the *Wehrmacht* in the Saar-Palatinate, while losing approximately 20,000 troops.

The Rhineland campaign was a clear strategic victory for the Allies. Not only did they meet their geographic objective of clearing the Rhine's left bank in preparation for Montgomery's crossing, they also severely battered the German western armies. The Germans lost more than a quarter of a million troops in the defense of the Rhineland, at a time when their ranks could not be refilled. The success of the Rhineland campaigns, coupled with the subsequent crossing of the Rhine, broke the back of organized German resistance on the western front and marked the beginning of the final chapter in the defeat of Nazi Germany.

David K. Yelton

Additional Reading

Allen, Peter, *One More River to Cross: The Rhine Crossings of 1945* (1980).

MacDonald, Charles B., *The Last Offensive* (1973).

McKee, Alexander, *The Race for the Rhine Bridges, 1940, 1944, 1945* (1971).

Stock, James W., *Rhine Crossing* (1973).

Thompson, R.W., *The Battle for the Rhineland* (1958).

Whitaker, W. Denis, and Shelagh Whitaker, *Rhineland: The Battle to End the War* (1989).

Roslavl (1–8 August 1941)

After the German victory at Smolensk (q.v.), Adolf Hitler (q.v.) and his generals hesitated over continuing the advance to Moscow, or shifting the emphasis to the Ukraine. One of the major proponents of the Moscow option was Colonel General Heinz Guderian (q.v.), commander of the Second *Panzer* Group. Before he even knew Hitler's decision, Guderian proposed another supporting operation at a conference held at Army Group Center headquarters in Borisov on 27 July 1941.

Guderian wanted permission immediately to eliminate a large concentration of Soviet troops at Roslavl, located on the right flank of the Second *Panzer* Group. The Soviet troops there were the ragged stragglers of some twenty-one Soviet divisions. Roslavl also was an important road center that would give the Germans control of the transportation network to the southwest of Moscow. The plan was approved by Field Marshal Fedor von Bock (q.v.), commander in chief of Army Group Center.

In order to carry out his plan, Guderian requested additional augmentation. Army Group Center attached the VII *Korps* to the Second *Panzer* Group for the operation. *Armeegruppe Guderian,* as the temporary formation was called, had a total of fourteen divisions, organized into the VII and IX *Korps* and the XXIV and XLVII *Panzer Korps.* The commander of the IX *Korps* was *General der Infantrie* Hermann Geyer, who made a name for himself during World War I as one of General Erich Ludendorff's (q.v.) most trusted staff officers. Ironically, Geyer had been Guderian's superior twice during the interwar years.

The attack started on 1 August with VII *Korps* and XXIV *Panzer Korps* leading off. While Guderian was near the front with his 3rd *Panzer* Division, they were subjected to an inadvertent air attack by *Luftwaffe* aircraft. One bomb landed only a few feet in front of Guderian's command car. On 2 August, the remainder of Guderian's units joined the attack to complete the encirclement.

On 4 August, Guderian returned to Army Group Center headquarters for his first conference with Hitler since the start of the Russian campaign. Hitler still had not made up his mind between Moscow or the Ukraine, but on returning to his own headquarters, Guderian ordered preparations for an attack against Moscow (q.v.).

On 5 August, Guderian was back out in the field directing operations around Roslavl. Although there were several small breakouts in various places, the Soviet troops inside the pocket were being progressively pinned against the swamps and the front of the town. By 8 August, the battle for Roslavl was over. The Germans captured 38,000 prisoners, 200 tanks, and an equal number of artillery pieces.

The road to Moscow from the southwest was now clear. On 12 August, however, Hitler issued *Führer* Directive 342, ordering Army Group North to continue its push toward Leningrad (q.v.), and Army Group South to move into the Crimea (q.v.) and the Donets basin. Army Group Center was ordered to halt temporarily and support the efforts on both of its flanks. As a result, the German thrust for Moscow lost its momentum.

David T. Zabecki

Additional Reading

Guderian, Heinz, *Panzer Leader* (1952).
Seaton, Albert, *The Russo-German War 1941–45* (1971).
Ziemke, Earl F., and Magna E. Bauer, *Moscow to Stalingrad: Decision in the East* (1987).

Rostov (20–30 November 1941)

After the Germans secured the Ukraine in September 1941, Army Group South, under Field Marshal Gerd von Rundstedt (q.v.), continued moving to the east and south. In front of them lay the strategic city of Rostov, on the Sea of Azov, at the mouth of the Don River. Rostov not only controlled access to the Don and its tributaries, but it also was the gateway to the Caucasus Mountains and the oil-rich territory to the south.

The German drive was spearheaded by General Ewald von Kleist's (q.v.) First *Panzer* Army. Opposing them, Marshal Semen Timoshenko (q.v.) recently had doubled the strength of the Southern Front (army group) by deploying the Thirty-seventh Army and the Fifty-sixth Independent Army. On 17 October, the Soviets hit von Kleist's force fifty miles north of Rostov. Timoshenko was hoping to create a diversion away from the Caucasus, but the results of his attack

were not good. While the XIV *Panzer Korps* held its ground against the Soviets, the III *Panzer Korps* broke contact and turned southeast toward Rostov.

On 21 November, the 1st SS *Panzer* Division took the city, but the III *Panzer Korps* came under immediate pressure from the south across the frozen river, and from the north out of the open steppes. Realizing he had overextended himself, von Kleist withdrew from Rostov on 22 November, and ordered the III *Panzer Korps* to take up defensive positions behind the Mius River, forty-five miles to the west. The following day, von Kleist had to revoke that order. Although von Rundstedt approved of von Kleist's withdrawal, Field Marshal Walther von Brauchitsch (q.v.), commander in chief of the German Army, insisted that Rostov be held.

The loss of Rostov notwithstanding, the *Stavka* still insisted on a major counterattack against the First *Panzer* Army. On 24 November, General N.T. Cherevichenko's Southern Front got that mission. On 28 November, he counterattacked at Rostov with a total of twenty-one divisions from the Thirty-seventh and Ninth Armies. At that point, two divisions of the III *Panzer Korps*, the 13th *Panzer* and 1st SS *Panzer* Divisions, were worn out, short of supplies, and more than two-thirds below their normal strength. Later that same day, von Kleist ordered the corps commander, General Eberhard von Mackensen (q.v.), to give up the city.

On 30 November, von Kleist once again ordered his forces to fall behind the Mius River. Although tactically it was the right move, a forty-five-mile German retreat was more than Adolf Hitler (q.v.) could tolerate. He insisted that von Brauchitsch get von Rundstedt to delay von Kleist's order. Von Rundstedt refused and offered his resignation. On 1 December, Hitler appointed Field Marshal Walther von Reichenau (q.v.) to replace von Rundstedt, insisting the Germans establish a line somewhere east of the Mius River. Von Reichenau, however, was unable to overcome the tide of events, and the withdrawal was completed that same night.

On the morning of 2 December, Hitler left his headquarters at the *Wolfsschanze*, in East Prussia, and flew to von Kleist's headquarters at Mariupol on the Sea of Azov. At Mariupol, Hitler met with and harangued von Kleist, von Reichenau and Josef Dietrich (q.v.), commander of the SS 1st *Panzer* Division. The visit was very unusual; Hitler seldom ventured that close to the front. It also was pointless, because there was nothing the Germans could do at that point to reverse the situation around Rostov.

Von Rundstedt's departure was a foreshadowing of things to come. By the first week in December, von Brauchitsch asked to be relieved for reasons of health. The next week, Field Marshal Fedor von Bock, commander of Army Group Center, did the same thing. In middle January, Field Marshal Wilhelm von Leeb (q.v.), commander of Army Group North, resigned in another disagreement with Hitler. Thus all four of the German Army's top commanders were gone within a span of six weeks. Hitler did not replace von Brauchitsch, taking the opportunity to make himself the direct commander in chief of the German Army.

David T. Zabecki

Additional Reading

Carell, Paul, *Hitler Moves East, 1941–1943* (1965).
Erickson, John, *The Road to Stalingrad* (1975).
Ziemke, Earl F., and Magna E. Bauer, *Moscow to Stalingrad: Decision in the East* (1968).

Rotterdam (10–15 May 1940)

Rotterdam, located at the mouths of the Rhine and Meuse Rivers, is the water gate to the North Sea and the industrial heartland of northern Europe. The city's Waal Harbor encompasses 741 acres, and is the largest dredged harbor in the world. The city's key location and its excellent harbor made it one of the world's three busiest seaports at the outbreak of World War II, and the decisive key to "Fortress Holland."

The strategic features of the city and its port made Rotterdam one of the targets for General Kurt Student's (q.v.) 7th Parachute Division. On 10 May 1940, German paratroopers landed and established a bridgehead across the river just south of the city. The mission of the airborne troops was to hold the bridgehead until the arrival of General Georg von Kuchler's Eighteenth Army. Student's troops accomplished this task without difficulty, and by 1800 hours on 13 May, the 9th *Panzer* Division had passed through Dordrecht and penetrated into the south of Rotterdam. Still, the Dutch Army was able to mount a temporary defense, and demolition parties managed to destroy oil reserves to prevent their capture by the Germans. By evening, an exasperated von Kuchler ordered his forces to "break resistance at Rotterdam with all means."

The redoubled efforts were successful, and by the next morning, negotiations for a cease-fire began between Dutch and German representatives. There were also reports that British paratroopers had reinforced "Fortress Holland." The reports were false, but the Germans were taking no chances. They issued an ultimatum to the Dutch that unless Rotterdam surrendered, it would be destroyed.

Negotiations started again, but the *Luftwaffe* already had been called in to break the Dutch resistance. Poor communications prevented the XXXIX *Panzer Korps* commander, General Rudolf Schmidt, from aborting the air attack. At 1400 hours, sixty He-111 bombers hit the old center of the city. The attack lasted just twenty minutes, but it was completely unopposed as the Dutch Air Force had been annihilated.

The attack destroyed 25,000 houses and left 78,000 people homeless. The 28,000-ton liner *Statendam,* one of the largest ships in the Dutch passenger fleet, was also crippled. In the terror of the moment, the Dutch foreign minister fixed the casualty toll at 30,000. In fact, just under 900 people were killed, but the exaggerated report helped add to the Allied alarm at the apparently invincible fury of the German offensive.

The bombing struck terror in the hearts of the Dutch. Determined to spare Utrecht from Rotterdam's fate, General Henri Winkelman (q.v.) surrendered the Dutch forces at 0930 hours on 15 May. The German war machine had conquered Holland in just five days.

The bombing of Rotterdam was one of the many unnecessary cruelties of the war. It also helped harden the Allies to Adolf Hitler's (q.v.) ruthless methods. When later in the war the Germans protested the wanton destruction of Allied air attacks, they callously were told to "Remember Rotterdam."

Kevin Dougherty

Additional Reading

Baldwin, Hanson, *The Crucial Years* (1976).
Jacobsen, H.A., and J. Rohwer, *Decisive Battles of World War II: The German View* (1965).
Steenbeek, Wilhelmina, *Rotterdam: Invasion of Holland* (1973).

Ruhr Air Campaign (March–June 1943)

By March 1943, Air Chief Marshal Sir Arthur Harris (q.v.) believed RAF Bomber Command was ready to initiate his "city-busting" strategy. He amassed the operational strength, technology, and tactics to launch what he considered the "true" strategic bombing campaign against Germany. Opposed to morale bombing and having no faith in precision bombing, Harris intended to "reduce production in the industries of the Ruhr at least as much by the indirect effect of damage to services, housing, and amenities, as by any direct damage to the factories or railways themselves."

Although Bomber Command would strike against several targets outside the Ruhr, including Berlin, Munich, Stuttgart, and Nuremberg, the primary focus for the next four months would be Essen (five strikes), Dortmund (two), Cologne (four), Bochum (three), Duisburg (five), and Düsseldorf (two). Despite the heaviest defenses in Germany, the Ruhr cities were reachable in darkness during the short nights of Spring and within range of Bomber Command's new blind-bombing device, Oboe, the perfect test for Harris's new force.

Key to the campaign would be the nature of Bomber Command in 1943. By March, Harris's force had expanded to 600 bombers (primarily four-engine Stirlings, Halifaxes, and Lancasters), supported by high-flying, high-speed Mosquitoes. Missions dropping 2,000 tons of bombs became commonplace. On 11–12 June, Bomber Command sent 783 aircraft to Düsseldorf and 72 to Münster. Equipped with Oboe and H2S and guided by pathfinders (q.v.) of Number 8 Group, Bomber Command could attack German cities while blinded by clouds and industrial haze.

Oboe relied on a pair of ground stations in Britain transmitting radio pulses to pathfinder aircraft, which amplified the pulses and transmitted them back to the ground stations for determining range. Limited to line-of-sight operation, Oboe could only be used within 270 miles of the transmitters. H2S eliminated this restriction because the Pathfinders carried the radar sets with them. A system of radar map-reading, H2S generally lacked the accuracy of Oboe. Pathfinder aircraft used these blind-bombing capabilities to augment visual aiming with flares. RAF Mosquitoes dropped red target indicators, reinforced by pathfinder green indicators aimed at the red markers. When clouds or smoke blocked the view of the ground, Pathfinders dropped sky markers, though their tendency to drift made them a poor substitute for the more accurate ground markers.

The main force followed in a bomber stream generally lasting thirty to forty minutes, spreading high explosive and incendiary bombs around the red and green markers. The targets were the city centers, chosen because they were easiest to locate and the most flammable. They were the perfect target for a force that considered bombs dropped within three miles of the aiming point acceptable

accuracy. Attacking individual industries would have been less economical and required a larger force. For Harris, industrial destruction was "regarded as a bonus."

Arrayed against Bomber Command were two German defensive organizations. Lieutenant General Josef Kammhuber's (q.v.) XII *Fliegerkorps* controlled more than 500 Bf-110 and Ju-88 night fighters. In the *Himmelbett* (Four-poster Bed) system, Freya search radars located British aircraft while individual controllers vectored the night fighters into the general area of the bombers through the *Benito* ground-control procedure. Operating much like Oboe, the German fighters received radio transmissions from the ground and retransmitted them. Ground stations used the signals to determine range and direction. Once within range, night fighters used their *Lichtenstein* radar to close on RAF aircraft hiding in the darkness of the night skies. During the Ruhr campaign, Kammhuber's *Himmelbett* system could control no more than thirty-six night fighters over the Ruhr at a time, and the RAF learned to jam the *Benito* transmissions.

Colonel General Hubert Weise's Air Command Center *(Luftwaffenbefehlshaber Mitte)* controlled the *Flak* artillery defending German cities, manned by more than one-half million men. In mid-1943, the primary German antiaircraft gun was the famous 88mm *Flak* 41, capable of firing twenty rounds per minute up to 35,000 feet. Directed visually by searchlight or electronically by *Würzburg* aiming radar, Weise organized the Ruhr's 200 batteries of six to eight guns each into *Grossbatterien* of two to three batteries each. Collectively, they could fill the Ruhr skies with more than 200 tons of shells per minute. Smoke screens and target indicator decoys augmented the *Luftwaffe* defenses. Night fighters presented the greatest lethal threat to RAF bombers, while *Flak* was the greatest cause of damage. Oboe, H2S, and the skill of RAF pathfinders made passive defenses ineffective.

The first target of the Ruhr campaign was Essen (5–6 March 1943), home to the huge Krupp armaments factory. A thick industrial haze had previously protected Essen from British attacks, but Oboe peeled away this obstacle to the pathfinders. The main force pressed the attack in a surrealistic atmosphere historian Max Hastings described as "a dazzling web of lights, the flicker of flak, the curling, twisting pattern of tracer, the glow of fires and incendiaries in all the colours of the rainbow." No visual identification of the target was possible, but 153 aircraft dropped their bombs within three miles of the Krupp works. The center of the city was virtually devastated and the loss of German lives (nearly 500) was the greatest for any Bomber Command strike to that time.

German Propaganda Minister Joseph Goebbels (q.v.) called the damage at Essen "ghastly." It would be the only time Harris would aim at a specific industry during the Ruhr Campaign. Three nights later, beyond Oboe range, H2S-guided bombers made a scattered and less-effective attack on the center of Nuremberg, revealing the limitations of the technology.

The most successful effort of the campaign was the 29–30 May attack on Wuppertal. Despite the widespread use of decoy markers by the defenders, 611 bombers destroyed 90 percent of the Barmen district with the first of the great urban firestorms, killing more than 3,000 people and destroying 34,000 housing units, five of six key industries, and 1,000 acres of developed area. It was the most destructive raid of the war to that time.

The least effective raid was the 16–17 April attack on Pilsen, Czechoslovakia. Although not actually part of the Ruhr, Pilsen contained industries closely linked to those of the Ruhr, and therefore it was included in the campaign. Pilsen, however, was beyond the range of Oboe. Pathfinder Force misidentified the target and only six bombers dropped their loads within three miles of the target, at a cost of thirty-six bombers and crews. Inmates at an asylum seven miles away experienced the horrors of a steady rain of more than a thousand tons of death and destruction. A month later, 170 bombers returned in an attempt to destroy Pilsen's large Skoda arms factory, losing nine bombers and failing to hit the target.

Failure meant repeat missions and additional casualties until the target was destroyed. Bomber Command losses rose as the nights grew shorter in late spring and early summer and as German defenses rose to the challenge. Casualty rates of up to 20 percent of the attacking force were not unusual. It was a battle fought one night at a time, with no quarter given, nor taken.

The Ruhr campaign involved forty-three major attacks by more than 18,000 bomber sorties, dropping 34,000 tons of bombs on the cities of the Ruhr. Bomber Command lost 872 aircraft. Despite these losses, Bomber Command ended the effort 150 aircraft stronger than when it began, ready to concentrate on the next target on the road to Berlin—Hamburg (q.v.). New technology and tactics opened all of Germany to night bombing, though defenses, weather, and operational limitations ensured success only against area, not precision, targets.

If the objective was the selective destruction of German industries, the Ruhr campaign was a failure. Bombs fell on open areas or lightly populated suburbs near the location of most industries. Overall damage was nowhere near as high. Harris's city-busting strategy caused unprecedented damage to German cities, but its contribution to the war effort remains the subject of controversy even today.

The Ruhr campaign's impact on German industry and morale was unmeasurable, but clearly it did not destroy either one. The RAF's greatest success was the forced diversion of enemy resources and forces away from other purposes and fronts to defend German cities from the British onslaught. According to the official history of the British bomber offensive, the Ruhr campaign made Bomber Command "into an effective bludgeon," but with only the "potential of a rapier." The Ruhr campaign created the Bomber Command that would inflict ever-increasing destruction on German cities for the following fifteen months.

Stephen L. McFarland

Additional Reading

Harris, Arthur, *Bomber Offensive* (1947).
Hastings, Max, *Bomber Command* (1989).
McFarland, Stephen L., *America's Pursuit of Precision Bombing* (1995).
McFarland, Stephen L. and Wesley P. Newton, *To Command the Sky: The Battle for Air Superiority over Germany, 1942–1944* (1991).
Webster, Charles, and Arthur Noble Frankland, *The Strategic Air Offensive against Germany, 1939–1945. Endeavour* (1961).

Ruhr Dams Air Raid (16–17 May 1943)

The principal German dams, keystones of the industrial Ruhr's power, coke, and steel industries, were priority targets for the Royal Air Force (RAF) from the outbreak of war. Not until 1943, however, did the means of attacking them become available when Dr. Barnes Wallis (q.v.), designer of the Wellington bomber, invented a new bomb powerful enough to destroy dam walls and yet small enough to be carried in Lancaster bombers.

Wallis's bomb packed 6,000 pounds of explosive in a five- by four-foot cylinder. When dropped with induced back spin, it would skim over water, like a pebble over a pond, hit the dam wall, sink, and detonate at a preset depth. The shock wave of

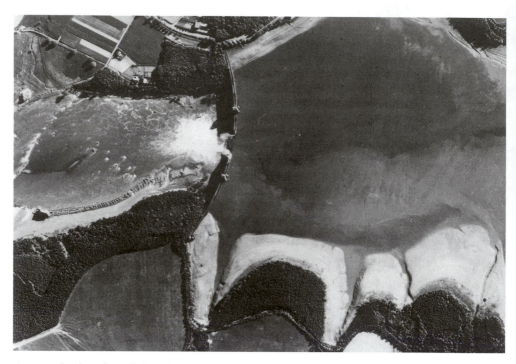

A post-strike photo shows the breach in the Möhne Dam caused by the RAF's No. 617 Squadron during the raid on 16 May 1943. (IWM CH 9687)

the explosion at that depth would be enough to destroy the biggest of the targets, the Möhne Dam, a concrete wall 800 feet long, 150 feet high, and 140 feet thick at its base.

The flying skills required to place the bomb exactly for successful detonation were formidable. Aircraft had to fly straight and level precisely sixty feet above the dam surface to an exact distance from the wall. To reach such standards, Number 617 Squadron was newly formed from experienced crews who had already completed a tour of thirty missions. A young, highly decorated officer, Guy Gibson (q.v.), commanded. After intensive practice in low flying, navigation, and dummy attacks on a disused dam, eighteen aircraft took off on the night of 16–17 May, the night chosen for the attack as the dams were full. Moonlit conditions gave such good visibility for German night fighters that all other RAF operations were canceled.

Two aircraft were lost on the way to the dams, the remainder flew so low that they had to pull up to avoid power lines. The targets were heavily defended, with some antiaircraft guns even mounted on the dam walls. The Möhne Dam was attacked first. Spotlights mounted on each aircraft gave the pilots their exact height over the water, but also provided antiaircraft gunners with an excellent aiming mark. The aircraft had to attack individually, so each in turn as it made its bombing run was subjected to the concentrated fire of all antiaircraft defenses.

Having completed his run, Gibson continued to fly his aircraft within range of the defenses, attempting to draw fire away from the attacking aircraft. Four bombs were needed to breach the Möhne Dam; the Eder Dam was breached with two; and the third target, the Sorpe Dam, was hit by one bomb and damaged. Of the bombing force, eight aircraft were lost, two badly damaged and fifty-three out of 133 airmen killed. Although the reservoirs were emptied, agricultural havoc caused in their areas, and hundreds of civilians drowned, both dams were repaired in six months and only 10 percent of coke production was lost.

Postwar research showed that only the destruction of all the dams in the valley would have seriously affected German industry. At that stage of the war, however, the effect of the raids on British morale was incalculable, and 617 Squadron became world renowned as the "Dambusters."

B.K. Warner

Additional Reading
Gibson, Guy, *Enemy Coast Ahead* (1946).
Brickhill, Paul, *The Dambusters* (1951).

Ruhr Pocket (1–18 April 1945)

[See map 21 on page 1331]

The Ruhr *Kessel* (Ruhr Pocket) came into existence on 1 April 1945, when units of Lieutenant General Courtney H. Hodge's (q.v.) U.S. First Army linked up in the Lippstadt area, west of Paderborn, with units of Lieutenant General William Simpson's (q.v.) U.S. Ninth Army. An American ring was thereby formed around Field Marshal Walther Model's (q.v.) Army Group B, as well as two corps belonging to the adjacent Army Group H. Initially, the Ruhr pocket was approximately 120 kilometers long and ninety kilometers wide. On three sides the German defenses were anchored on the Lippe, Rhine, and Sieg Rivers (in the north, west, and south, respectively), while the eastern end of the pocket ran along the edges of the Rothaar Mountains.

Caught within the pocket were the remnants of eighteen German divisions, seven corps commands, and the headquarters of the Fifth *Panzer* Army of Colonel General Josef Harpe (q.v.) and the Fifteenth Army of General Gustav-Adolf von Zangen. In addition, a *Flak Korps,* commanded by Lieutenant General Heinrich von Rantzau, was deployed in the region with hundreds of the versatile 88mm antiaircraft guns at their disposal. Although the hills of the Sauerland and the densely populated Ruhr Valley with its numerous industrial and mining centers, offered some advantages to the Germans, their resistance to American attackers was half-hearted in many areas. By 11 April, the Germans had abandoned Essen (the home of the Krupp company) and Bochum.

During the opening phases of the battle, thirteen American divisions were deployed around the Ruhr Pocket, with Major General John B. Anderson's XVI Corps in the north, elements of Major General Raymond S. McLain's (q.v.) XIX Corps advancing from the northeast, and Major General James A. Van Fleet's (q.v.) III Corps from the southeast. The southern edge of the pocket was entrusted to Major General Matthew B. Ridgway's (q.v.) XVIII Airborne Corps, while three divisions from Lieutenant General Leonard T. Gerow's (q.v.) Fifteenth Army were to keep the Germans busy along the Rhine River.

With progress slower than expected, four additional U.S. divisions were thrown into the battle, and the armored divisions were exhorted to be more aggressive. On 14 April, the commander of the 13th Armored Division, Major General John B. Wogan, was seriously wounded at a roadblock while trying to get a northward thrust underway. By the evening of the same day, infantry units of 8th Armored Division reached the Ruhr River southeast of Essen, thus establishing contact with 79th Infantry Division of XVI Corps, which previously had advanced to the river from the north. The Ruhr Pocket was thus split into two smaller pockets, and German resistance almost everywhere began to crumble.

During the next three days, most of the *Wehrmacht* units in the area surrendered or tried to go into hiding. Model retreated with some of his staff officers to a wooded region near Duisburg. On 21 April, he shot himself. Harpe tried to make his way to German-held Dutch territory, but was captured almost immediately by soldiers of the 17th Airborne Division. His chief of staff, Major General Friedrich-Wilhelm von Mellenthin (q.v.), and several other staff officers from the Fifth *Panzer* Army were somewhat more skillful and eluded capture until 3 May. The only senior officer who successfully went into hiding (until 1946) was Lieutenant Colonel Roger Michael, Army Group B's chief intelligence expert—having a British mother, he spoke English perfectly. The total number of POWs taken in the Ruhr *Kessel* exceeded 317,000, including thirty general officers. Most of the German troops were only too happy to be out of the war.

Ever since 1945 there has been some debate about the wisdom of Generals Dwight D. Eisenhower and Omar N. Bradley (qq.v.) to divert so much American strength (eighteen divisions, finally) for the reduction of the Ruhr Pocket. Given the Ruhr area's well-deserved reputation as Germany's most important industrial region, it is understandable that the two generals opted for that strategy.

Ulrich Trumpener

Additional Reading

Kessler, Leo, *The Battle of the Ruhr Pocket, April 1945* (1990).

MacDonald, Charles B., *The Last Offensive* (1973).

Weigley, Russell F., *Eisenhower's Lieutenants: The Campaigns of France and Germany, 1944–45* (1981).

Whiting, Charles, *The Battle of the Ruhr Pocket* (1970).

Russo-Polish War (1919–1921)

Considered a sideshow by contemporary Western analysts, the Russo-Polish War was of singular importance to eastern Europe. It not only influenced the interwar balance of power, but it also impacted directly on the military and diplomatic strategies of World War II. The armies of both nations were shaped by this contest, and while Poland's victory allowed for gains of territory and prestige, the parallel Soviet defeat engendered fear and a desire for revenge.

The war was part of a general pattern that resulted from a simultaneous collapse of the German, Austrian, Ottoman, and Russian Empires in 1918. A power vacuum was created that drew a wide variety of rival ethnic and political factions into conflict. The most significant of these struggles was between Bolshevik Soviet Union and newly independent Poland.

While some experts argue that the Russo-Polish War was avoidable, doing so required considerable levels of faith and good will, rare commodities in the diplomatic market of those days. How could the Bolsheviks be sure that Poland's warlord, Józef Piłsudski (q.v.), was not part of a "capitalist cabal" striving for Soviet destruction? The Soviet Union's Communist Party founders were in the midst of a civil war that featured a vast array of enemies, many supported by France. As the latter was also a supporter of the Poles, such suspicion can be viewed as reasonable.

How could the Poles trust Vladimir Lenin to break with Russian tradition and peacefully allow Polish independence? Over 100 years of domination, interspersed with revolt and repression, made trust very illusive. It was a zero-sum game: any Polish gain was a Soviet loss, and vice versa. To the Poles, these elements of mutual suspicion, nationalism, and divergent political systems combined with territorial disputes to make war highly probable.

The intensity and scope of this conflict, much greater than all the other border wars of 1918–1921, was due mainly to the aspirations of Piłsudski. As de facto ruler of Poland in 1918–1919, he shaped his nation's military-diplomatic strategies in an effort to create a Polish-dominated confederation of anti-Soviet states. Success for this plan required an independent Ukraine, which in all probability would mean the end of the Bolshevik revolution. Claiming that "Poland will be great, or she will not exist," Piłsudski opted for an aggressive posture that soon collided with Lenin's desire for pro-Communist states in Eastern Europe and Germany.

First blood went to the Russians with their successful 5 January 1919 assault on Wilno. By February, they crossed the Szczara River and captured Pinsk. As both sides discovered in the Russo-Polish War, rapid victory was often followed by rapid defeat. Piłsudski personally directed a Polish counterattack that recaptured Wilno on Easter Sunday, 20 April 1919.

These operations were rather typical of the entire campaign. Noted military historian Marjan Kukiel described it as "a war of movement" in which "swiftness of movement, suddenness of concentration, the tactics of surprise—were the dominant factors." Two reasons for these significant differences from the tactics of recent World War I were the theater's large size and the small armies involved. Neither side ever mustered more than 300,000 troops, which varied in quality. They ranged from well-armed elite formations like the Bolsheviks' Lettish Rifle Regiment or Piłsudski's Legion, to shanghaied conscripts and peasants armed with scythes. To be sure, armored cars, tanks, aircraft, radio sets and other "high tech" weaponry of the period were employed. Most weapons were captured or cast-off surplus commodities, with unreliable sources for spare parts. In many cases the variety of military hardware represented a quartermaster's nightmare. One Polish division had Japanese rifles and nonmatching German-made ammunition. Even when supplies meshed, there often were insufficient quantities for long battles. One interesting and rather successful weapon was the armored train. Carrying artillery, machine guns, and up to 300 infantrymen, these trains were the true mobile strike forces of the campaign.

Also different from World War I experiences were the long supply lines. All forces made use of the region's sparse railway network. Just as important, however, were the thousands of farm wagons and peasant carts conscripted into military service. Reliance on long supply lines vastly reduced an army's movement, and also presented wonderful targets for cavalry or air raids. Daring commanders abandoned these unreliable supply lines and lived off captured supplies.

In reviewing the command systems of both sides one finds tremendous variety. They featured a mix of professional and amateur talent jumbled with a large number of prima donnas. Whereas the Russians had a shortage of politically reliable senior officers, the Poles were overloaded with generals. Piłsudski complained that this in turn caused an excess of staffs and orderlies, to the point that some divisions saw a third of their strength frittered away in rear area administrative detachments. Also, as Poland was not a state before 1918, its soldiers had been trained in either Germany, France, Russia, or Austria, which guaranteed confusion even under the best of circumstances.

The war often saw mediocre leaders trying to

fight with World War I tactics, not realizing they possessed different tools and rather limited resources. Indeed, the great debacles of the campaign were often the result of attempts at cordon defenses with small numbers of infantry and artillery. Such tactics were invitations to the likes of Piłsudski, Marshal Mikhail Tukhachevsky, or Marshal Semyon Budenny (qq.v.). These leaders created new strategies that allowed for optimal use of their military assets. They realized that the keys to success were not trench lines, or ponderous artillery barrages. Concentration of force, quick jabs, and use of the sparse but all-important railway lines were their alternatives. Success in the Russo-Polish War went to the side that could smash through the thinly held enemy screen and capture rail junctions and supply centers.

A perfect example of such tactics can be seen in the 5 March 1919 Polish invasion of the Ukraine. Six weeks into the campaign, after the capture of the key rail center of Kalinkovichi, Piłsudski was able to pour a motley collection of Poles, Ukrainians, Ruthenians, and Tartars deep into enemy territory. Soviet General Alexander Yegorov's Army of the Southwest was scattered. Although Poland's motorized assault and capture of Zhitomir on 28 April is worthy of note, most of the fighting was done by foot soldiers, some marching up to sixty-five kilometers in one day. On 8 May, Kiev fell and the Poles halted to regroup. Although casualties were light, only 450 in total, 200,000 Polish troops were stretched along a 1,000-kilometer front.

Like many generals later in World War II, Piłsudski outran his supply lines. In addition, the Ukrainian response to his proposed independence and national army was lukewarm. Now it was Russia's turn for an offensive, which began on 18 May at Elizavetsgrad. The *KonArmiya* (Cavalry Army), a 16,000-man elite Soviet strike force, smashed into Poland's worn out infantrymen. Directed by Budenny, and moving at the then incredible speed of 120 kilometers a day, the Russian forces seemed to be everywhere, and soon threatened to encircle Kiev. At the same time, revitalized Bolshevik infantry units were pressing a counterattack. General Edward Śmigły-Rydz (q.v.), the Polish local commander, saw retreat as his only viable option. Thus ended the Ukrainian campaign, or as one veteran put it, "we ran all the way to Kiev, and we ran all the way back." Poland's failure to engage the Soviets in concert with the anti-Bolshevik White Russians was a huge error.

While the cavalry razzia continued, a much more dangerous Russian offensive began in the north. This sector, quiet since the fighting for Wilno, erupted into the decisive campaign of the war. Directed by Tukhachevsky, 160,000 Soviet troops assaulted General Stanisław Szeptycki's First, Fourth, and Seventh Armies. Although Piłsudski was able to transfer some reserves to bolster this front, Budenny's massive assault completely disrupted the flow of reinforcements. By early July, twenty-three Soviet divisions faced thirteen Polish divisions. On 2 July, Tukhachevsky issued his orders of the day, which included the exhortation, "To the West! Our time has come. To Wilno, Minsk, and Warsaw—march."

The July offensive smashed through Polish lines and caused a near rout of the entire front. The Russians seemed to be, in the words of Piłsudski, "advancing like a monstrous storm cloud which nothing can hinder." Minsk fell on 11 July and Wilno on 14 July. Only the huge Pripet marshes prevented a link-up of Tukhachevsky with Budenny and Yegerov.

The Red Army's twin successes came at the worst possible moment for the Poles. In addition to the obviously grave military repercussions, they complicated the European-wide boundary settlements being discussed at Spa, Belgium. Here, on 10 July, Prime Minister Władyslaw Grabski agreed to accept the Curzon Line (q.v.), a British-devised border between Poland and Russia. The Curzon Line was very unfavorable to Polish interests, but the pressing need for Western support brought Polish acceptance. This proposal was then telegraphed to Moscow as part of a general armistice package.

Soviet reactions were completely different. With cavalry screens only 170 kilometers from Warsaw, Lenin labeled the deal a "swindle," and convinced the Politburo to reject any peace plans and instead "probe Europe with the bayonets of the Red Army." This set the stage for the decisive battle of the campaign, what the Poles would later call the "Miracle of the Vistula."

Elements of geography, luck, and genius play important roles at this stage. First, one must note the significance of the Pripet marshes in east-west movement. Large military units could not travel there. This resulted in the creation of two separate Russian armies with two different goals and the most tenuous of communications links. Tukhachevsky's forces continued moving toward Warsaw, but Budenny's Cossack units pulled Yegorov toward the city of Lwów. Poor direction from Moscow, combined with an attitude that the war was almost won, allowed for this dispersal of strength. The best Polish troops, concentrated around Warsaw, were now presented with a chance to hit the army of their choice.

Both Soviet groupings were facing the same problems Piłsudski had in the Ukraine. Rapid advances outran supply lines, while desertions and casualties eroded the Soviets' numerical advantage. The Poles, on the other hand, were retreating into their own supply centers, a superior rail network, and newly raised reinforcements. By August 1920, both sides had about 200,000 men in the Warsaw sector.

Polish forces were ready to counterattack, but uncertain as to how and where. Everyone had a plan, including General Maxime Weygand (q.v.) who was sent by France to save the day. Piłsudski, needing munitions much more than advice, disregarded the French plan for a stabilized front followed by a slow buildup and then a renewed offensive. Instead, influenced by his studies of Napoleon and Ignacy Pradzynski, who planned the defense against the Russian assault on Warsaw in 1831, Piłsudski opted for striking the Soviets while moving and off balance. His target was the "Mozyr Group" that weakly guarded Tukhachevsky's southern flank. Warsaw was to serve as bait and distraction for the other Bolshevik forces.

Polish concentrations began on 6 August and centered along the Vistula and Wieprz Rivers near Deblin. Urgent appeals from the capital, now under attack, caused offensive action to begin on 16 August 1920. Instant success was the result, with Polish divisions advancing thirty kilometers by day's end. Piłsudski could not believe his plans were working this well. "I thought that I was dreaming or in a world of fairyland," he later wrote; but by 18 August, he realized that his "dream" was Tukhachevsky's nightmare.

Hit from the rear as they attacked the Warsaw defenses, Soviet forces disintegrated into a mob of columns rapidly fleeing eastward. They left behind 1,000 machine guns, 231 artillery pieces, and 140,000 casualties. Using reinforcements and escapees from Warsaw, Tukhachevsky attempted a stand on the Niemen River in September. Piłsudski's response was a holding action along the front, followed by flank attacks. Success again went to the Poles, who by 25 September drove off their Soviet opponents. The next day, in the battle of the Szczara, they captured 160 guns and 50,000 prisoners.

News from the south was almost as spectacular. Between 30 August and 2 September 1920, in the hills between Zamość and Komarow, General Władysław Sikorski (q.v.) conducted a series of ambush battles that resulted in the rout of the KonArmiya. Deprived of his elite strike force, Yegorov directed a retreat for the Army of the Southwest. Polish and Ukrainian forces followed in close pursuit. The largest mechanized operation of the war took place at this time when a composite motorized regiment captured the key rail junction of Kovel on 13 September. By month's end, Sikorski had elements of his army patrolling the Zbruch River.

At this point, both nations were ready for serious peace negotiations. Despite repeated victories, Poland was bankrupt and involved with other border disputes in the west. The Soviets were just as drained and still facing dangerous opposition from "White" and "Green" anti-Bolshevik factions. This combination allowed for an armistice on 18 October 1920, followed by the Treaty of Riga. While far short of Piłsudski's goals, the latter gave the Poles extensive lands east of the Curzon Line. Most importantly, the treaty provided them with key north-south railway lines and control of geographical features well suited for defense against future Soviet aggression.

These "losses" embittered some Soviets, among them the former Komissar of the Southwest Army, Josef Stalin (q.v.). The Soviets still viewed Poland as a bridgehead of international capitalism, and a potential future enemy. Indeed, one gets the impression that the very cold peace of 1921–1939 was always viewed as temporary by the Soviets.

In Poland, the situation was somewhat similar. Piłsudski, who dominated the government from 1926 to 1935, directed a strategy of Oczy na Wschod (Eyes East). This stressed the possibility of renewed hostilities where Poland would fight without significant allies. As such, a great deal of Polish strategic and tactical planning was aimed at defending its eastern borders. Critics have argued that these actions reduced efforts to plan for a war against Germany.

Another result was that studies of the war played an important role in shaping Polish and Soviet military doctrine. Despite his 1920 defeats, Tukhachevsky became the Red Army's leading theorist. His support for mechanization and a professional officer corps can partially be traced to the experiences of the march to Warsaw. Piłsudski, arguing that "mass strategy . . . gave no definite results in the World War," presented in its place an "Open Air Strategy." This called for a fluid deployment offering the commander several operational prospects. Above all else, it stressed the need for mobility.

In conclusion, the Russo-Polish War shaped military thinking, diplomatic relations, and the frontiers for interwar Eastern Europe. Kukiel best sums up this campaign with his observation that "the fate of the Communist revolution was pronounced for long years to come by the decisive battle of Warsaw."

John Dunn

Additional Reading
Davies, Norman, *White Eagle, Red Star* (1972).
Piłsudski, Józef, *Year 1920* (1972).

Ruweisat Ridge (1–22 July 1942)

The battle for Ruweisat Ridge, the first of the series of battles at El Alamein, is sometimes called "first Alamein." During this battle the British stopped the Axis drive to the Suez Canal and set the stage for the battles of Alam el Halfa and El Alamein (qq.v.) that were to follow. Of all the El Alamein battles, British Military Historian Sir Basil Liddell Hart called Ruweisat Ridge "the most crucial."

Following the British defeat at the Gazala Line (q.v.) and the fall of Tobruk (*see* Tobruk III), the British Eighth Army withdrew to defensive positions at Mersa Matrúh, about 100 miles inside Egypt. Field Marshal Erwin Rommel (q.v.) and his *Panzerarmee Afrika* pursued. On 25 June 1942, the British commander in chief in the Middle East, General Sir Claude Auchinleck (q.v.), relieved General Neil Ritchie (q.v.) and personally assumed command of the Eighth Army. Rommel, with only sixty tanks, attacked at Mersa Matrúh (q.v.) the next day, and routed four British divisions in three days of fighting. The British continued to withdraw to the vicinity of El Alamein, another 120 miles to the east.

Both sides were spent. Rommel had only about fifty-five tanks and Auchinleck's remaining effective forces consisted of only two infantry divisions and a disorganized armored division. Less than 100 miles from Alexandria, Auchinleck was determined to hold. The place where he chose to make his stand consisted of a line running from the Egyptian coastal village of El Alamein, south to the salt marches of the Qattara Depression. Under constant pressure from Rommel, Auchinleck improvised a fluid defensive line based on the Ruweisat Ridge, which ran east and west about ten miles south of El Alamein, and Bab el Qattara, a few miles south of Ruweisat. Auchinleck's intention was to channel Rommel's attack into paths that the British could easily counterattack.

Attempting to bypass El Alamein, Rommel attacked on 1 July with his *Panzer*s in the center supported by a secondary attack in the north near the coast. The German 90th Light Division was stopped by intense artillery fire and counterattacked at Alam el Onsol by the 4th Armoured Brigade. On 2 July and again on 4 July the 15th and 21st *Panzer* Divisions attacked around both sides of Ruweisat Ridge. They were driven back by the 1st Armoured Division, the 22nd Armoured Brigade, and the South African 1st Brigade. On 3 July, an attack in the south by the Italian *Ariete* Division was checked by the New Zealand 2nd Division. Rommel had to give up any ideas of a quick victory.

On 10 July, Auchinleck committed the newly arrived Australian 9th Division against the Italian *Sabratha* Division in the north. The Allied drive toward Tell el Eisa forced Rommel to commit his remaining reserves. On 13 and 14 July, attacks by the 15th and 21st *Panzer* Divisions were turned back with heavy losses. On 14 July, Auchinleck counterattacked at Ruweisat Ridge. The following day Rommel took Point 63, at the extreme western end of the ridge, but suffered heavy losses in the process.

Informed through ULTRA (q.v.) intercepts of Rommel's critical supply situation, Auchinleck attacked again at Ruweisat Ridge on 21 July. At that point the Eighth Army had about 300 tanks, and the Germans and Italians had about fifty each. Despite some initial success, the Axis forces held the British back and prevented them from recapturing Point 63. Fierce fighting continued through 22 July, resulting in the decimation of the 23rd Armoured Brigade. After that, everything ground to a standstill and the battle petered out with both sides exhausted. Each side suffered about 13,000 casualties in the three weeks of fighting.

The battle for Ruweisat Ridge was a tactical draw, but operationally it was a decisive victory for the Allies. Rommel was robbed of his last chance to take Cairo. With his forces depleted and at the end of a long and tenuous supply line, Rommel could not hope to rebuild his forces as quickly as the British, who were sitting virtually on top of their major base of operations. Rommel tried to attack one more time, at the end of August at Alam el Halfa Ridge to the southwest of El Alamein. The British held him there too, with General Sir Bernard L. Montgomery (q.v.) executing a plan developed by Auchinleck. Then in late October, Montgomery himself went on the offensive at El Alamein.

Despite Auchinleck's great accomplishment in stopping Rommel, Prime Minister Winston S. Churchill (q.v.) relieved him in early August. General Sir Harold Alexander (q.v.) became the new commander in chief in the middle east and Montgomery assumed command of the Eighth Army.

David T. Zabecki

Additional Reading

Agar-Hamilton, John A.I., and Leonard Turner, *Crisis in the Desert: May–July 1942* (1952).

Barnett, Correlli, *The Desert Generals* (1961).

Pitt, Barrie, *The Crucible of War: Year of Alamein, 1942* (1982).

S

Saint Lô Breakout (25–31 July 1944)

[See map 28 on page 1338]

After the initial success of the Allied invasion of Normandy (q.v.), a growing discrepancy between the progress inland predicted by the planners and the actual movement of troops on the ground became painfully apparent. Various options to include an amphibious assault outside of the Normandy beachhead and a large-scale airborne operation were considered but found to be impractical. Finally, General Omar N. Bradley (q.v.) developed a plan for the U.S. First Army to break the stalemate. This plan, which became Operation COBRA, coordinated a heavy air bombardment with an overwhelming ground attack. It also sealed the fate of Germany.

Operation COBRA was preceded by British Operation GOODWOOD on 18 July 1944 (*see* Caen). Whether Operation GOODWOOD was initially designed with the primary objective of aiding Operation COBRA by causing the Germans to commit their mobile reserve and the secondary intention of achieving a breakthrough, or vice versa, is still subject to debate. Unfortunately, it was also the cause of controversy and misunderstanding throughout the rest of the war.

Either way, the plan for Operation GOODWOOD was very similar to Operation COBRA, a heavy air strike followed immediately by the ground attack. In the eyes of General Bernard L. Montgomery (q.v.) the GOODWOOD attack was a success. By 20 July, the British VIII Corps had advanced six miles, secured Caen, and doubled the size of the Orne bridgehead. This, however, was far from the decisive breakthrough envisioned by General Dwight D. Eisenhower (q.v.) and other Allied commanders.

The overall concept for Operation COBRA was to break out of the Normandy peninsula, gain control of Brittany, and then swing wide to the east. The British and Canadian armies on the Allied left flank would attack to the south and east in order to screen the location of the main effort. The U.S. First Army would pivot on its left flank and swing south with its right flank to secure the peninsula. The U.S. VIII Corps would then turn west into Brittany toward Rennes and St. Malo (q.v.). They would be followed on the extreme right flank by the U.S. Third Army, which would assume command of the operation on order.

U.S. VII Corps, commanded by Major General J. Lawton Collins (q.v.), was the main effort of the First Army. In contrast to the usual American preference for broad-front assaults, the VII Corps would attack on a narrow front some 7,000 yards across the St. Lô-Périers Road. The attack would be closely coordinated with heavy artillery and aerial carpet bombing. In support of VII Corps, the U.S. V, VIII, and XIX Corps would initially pressure the Germans to prevent their withdrawal, and later increase the pressure to exploit the advantage.

Collins organized the Operation COBRA attack into two phases. After the carpet bombing, the 9th, 4th, and 30th Infantry Divisions would attack abreast to create a penetration near Marigny and open a gap for later exploitation. The exploitation phase consisted of the 2nd and 3rd Armored Divisions and 1st Infantry Division passing through the gap. Both armored divisions were configured under an older table or organization, which gave them twice the number of tank battalions of a normal armored division. The 1st Infantry Division, reinforced with armor, would turn southwest toward Coutances to cut off the Germans against the VII Corps line. Armor elements would block reinforcements and isolate bypassed German units, which could be destroyed in detail later.

The German LXXXIV *Korps,* commanded by General Dietrich von Choltitz (q.v.), held the positions along the St. Lô-Lessay Road with many units but relatively few troops. The majority of LXXXIV *Korps* had seen heavy fighting and its divisions were at a significantly reduced strength. The corps reserve consisted of the battle-weary 353rd Division located south of Périers.

Field Marshal Günther von Kluge (q.v.), commander in chief west, had great difficulty in massing a strategic reserve. What he had was a piecemeal collection of reserves incapable of being concentrated in a timely manner. He succeeded in bringing forward four infantry divisions between 10 and 22 July to replace five *Panzer* divisions, which he planned to use as a mobile reserve. Operation GOODWOOD, however, had forced the recommitment of this armor and nullified von Kluge's efforts.

Directly opposing the VII Corps between the Taute and the Vire Rivers lay the once elite *Panzer-Lehr* Division, commanded by General Fritz Bayerlein (q.v.). The division was seriously understrength and could muster only about 3,200 combat-effective troops to block VII Corps. The division's front extended three miles along the St. Lô-Périers Road, with small outposts north of the road and the main defense to the south in a series of strong points. On the west flank, an attached regiment from the 5th Parachute Division blocked the road to Marigny. In the east, 450 combat troops of the much depleted *Kampfgruppe Heinz* of the 275th Division established strong points near Hebecrevon. Behind the main defenses, Bayerlein kept several companies of infantry and a few tanks in reserve.

On 19 July, Bradley met with Air Chief Marshal Trafford Leigh-Mallory (q.v.) to discuss the COBRA air support plan. The conference failed to result in a firm agreement, but Bradley left satisfied that bomb size would be limited to 100 pounds in order to reduce the counter mobility effects of the craters, and that the bombing run would be parallel to the line of troops to reduce the risk of friendly casualties from short drops. The air force representatives apparently arrived at a different conclusion.

On 24 July, elements of the U.S. Eighth Air Force departed Britain in accordance with the original plan. After they were in the air, Leigh-Mallory decided to postpone the operation because of bad weather. It was too late to recall many of the bombers, and more than 300 dropped their ordnance before they could be notified to abort the mission. The bombers also approached perpendicular to the line of troops. Tragically, many bombs landed 2,000 yards north of the St. Lô-Périers Road, causing twenty-five deaths and 131 injuries to the 30th Infantry Division. In addition to the friendly casualties, the bombing caused serious confusion over whether or not Operation COBRA had been delayed. Not knowing for sure, Collins ordered a compromise measure resulting in the 9th, 4th, and 30th Infantry Divisions conducting a limited attack to the St. Lô-Périers Road. By the end of the afternoon, VII Corps had regained the original defense line from which it had withdrawn prior to the bombing.

The bungled bombing raid cost Bradley the element of surprise. Additionally, he had to contend with the possibility of a repeat of the short drops and more friendly casualties, but if he insisted on a change in the bombing route, Operation COBRA would be delayed for several days. Prospects of good weather on 25 July were improving and pressure for an Allied breakthrough was high. Accordingly, Bradley set the new time for Operation COBRA at 1100 hours on 25 July.

Several adjustments were made for the second bombardment. All targets north of the St. Lô-Périers Road were switched from the air to the artillery. A special reconnaissance aircraft would gather exact atmospheric data and determine if there was adequate visibility for the mission. Finally, the bombers would come in as low as safety allowed and would bomb visually, if possible; but the approach would still be perpendicular to the line of troops.

At 0940 hours on 25 July, 1,900 heavy bombers, 400 medium bombers, and 550 fighter-bombers from the Eighth Air Force and the Allied Expeditionary Air Force began saturating an area south of the St. Lô-Périers Road 2,500 yards deep and 7,000 yards wide. They dropped more than 5,000 tons of bombs. Bayerlein described the attack as being "like a conveyor belt" of destruction that left his front line as cratered as the moon. He reported at least 70 percent of his force was initially taken out of action either as direct casualties or as victims of shock and daze. Three of his battalion command posts were destroyed and Bayerlein's communications network was in a shambles.

Despite the extra precautions, thirty-five heavy bombers and twenty-four medium bombers dropped their ordnance on American positions. The result was 111 killed and 490 wounded. Among the dead was General Lesley J. McNair (q.v.), the former commander of U.S. Army Ground Forces, who was in the forward area to observe the effects of the bombing. The demoralizing effects of this second short drop swept through the U.S. ranks. In the 30th Infantry Division alone 164 cases of combat exhaustion were attributed to the disaster. Nearly 900 American casualties resulted from the two short bombing incidents, and Eisenhower resolved never again to use heavy bombers in a tactical support role.

Despite the initial disorganization and discouragement caused by the short bombing, VII Corps launched its attack as scheduled at 1100 hours. The three infantry divisions attacked along a six-mile front with heavy artillery support. To their surprise the massive bombardment had dazed but not destroyed the German defenders. Well-positioned automatic weapons that survived the air attack slowed the American advance. Nonetheless, the Americans made steady progress. By evening, the VII Corps had advanced a total of two miles and crossed the St. Lô-Périers Road. This penetration, however, was short of Marigny and St. Gilles, which had been established as one of the prerequisites for initiating the exploitation phase.

Collins now had to weigh the advantages to be gained by refusing the Germans any time to regroup, against the advantages of waiting and having all initial objectives secured. He boldly concluded, "We had broken through the principal defenses of the Germans. I felt that the added punch of the armored divisions would be sufficient to make a clean break-away." During the afternoon of 25 July, Collins decided to launch the exploitation phase the next day.

Once von Choltitz learned the Americans had crossed the St. Lô-Périers Road, he committed a reinforced regiment from the LXXXIV *Korps* reserve. This element of the 353rd Division secured la Chapelle-en-Juger in order to block the American penetration. General Paul Hausser (q.v.) also committed part of the Seventh Army's reserve to the same location for the same purpose. Thus, the Germans effectively controlled the vital road network in the center of the American attack zone.

The disruption in communications, however, left the German high command ignorant of the loss of Hebecrevon and the subsequent open road to St. Gilles. This left the Germans very vulnerable along the west bank of the Vire River. The German line was further weakened by von Kluge's insistence that all available personnel be positioned on the front, rather than in depth. This configuration robbed the Germans of the flexibility to react to a penetration by repositioning a blocking force from the rear.

Collins's plan to deepen the penetration involved one armored column taking Marigny and another seizing St. Giles. General Clarence Huebner (q.v.), the commander of the U.S. 1st Infantry Division plus the attached Combat Command B (CCB) from the 3rd Armored Division, was responsible for clearing the road to Marigny. In his way stood the German 353rd Division and two companies of the 2nd SS *Panzer* Division. The German defense was tied into the thick hedgerows that bordered the open fields. Many of the American Sherman tanks had been fitted with sets of steel tusks, called the "Rhino," to batter through these obstacles. These devices helped overcome the hedgerows, but the tough defenders still prevented the capture of Marigny and its critical road network until the morning of 27 July.

General Maurice Rose's Combat Command A (CCA) of the 2nd Armored Division, with the attached 22nd Infantry Regiment, had better success in its mission to take St. Gilles. Rose passed through the 30th Infantry Division's zone and overcame scattered resistance to reach the objective by mid-afternoon on 26 July. With this achieved, the exploitation phase of Operation COBRA began. The German line was now definitely penetrated. The VII Corps had achieved its breakthrough.

Rose continued down the St. Gilles-Canisy Road in order to capture the high ground five miles past St. Gilles. In his path stood only scattered remnants of the *Panzer-Lehr* Division. Rose advanced easily, slowed only by bomb craters. By the morning of 27 July, he captured St. Samson-de-Bonfosse and le Mensil-Hermann. CCA's Operation COBRA mission was complete.

In contrast to Rose's success, Huebner was still unable to secure Marigny, but VIII Corps had begun to move. Despite not having a secure pivot point at Marigny, the 1st Infantry Division had to continue its thrust westward to Coutances in order to block the rear of the Germans facing north against VIII Corps. On 27 July, Huebner made an attempt to capture the three hills that formed a ridgeline along the St. Lô-Coutances Road, but he was unsuccessful. That evening, Bradley called on VIII Corps to assist Huebner in capturing his remaining two objectives, Monthuchon and the high ground north of Coutances. By this time, however, the bulk of the Germans had escaped. In three days, the 1st Infantry Division captured only 565 prisoners. VII Corps' main effort to this point was something of a disappointment.

According to the initial plan, the main battle was to have been fought in a triangle formed by St. Lô, Lessay, and Coutances. By failing to capture Coutances, the 1st Infantry Division allowed a large number of Germans to escape before the trap could be closed. Consequently the fighting now shifted to the area south of the St. Lô-Coutances Road. In order to facilitate this change, Collins detached CCB from the 1st Infantry Division and returned it to the 3rd Armored Division. He augmented the 4th Infantry Division with the 1st Infantry Division's 26th Infantry Regiment and placed the rest of the 1st Infantry Division in reserve. Then on 30 July, he ordered the 4th Infantry Division and the 3rd Armored Division to attack south toward Villedieu-les-Poêles.

After these changes, Collins quickly became disappointed with the operation, feeling that the 3rd Armored Division was showing excessive caution. To remedy the situation, he divided the division into its two combat commands, placing CCA under operational control of the 1st Infantry Division and CCB under the 4th Infantry Division. In this configuration VII Corps attacked with the infantry abreast and the armor spearheading. The new task organization breathed fresh life into the attack. By 1 August, VII Corps advanced more than thirty miles due south of the St. Lô-Périers Road. In switching his direction, Collins engineered an extraordinary gain that outflanked the German left.

According to the original plan, General George S. Patton's (q.v.) Third Army was to become activated and assume command of the operation as the forces neared Brittany. VIII Corps, scheduled to come under Third Army control, was to link the post-COBRA exploitations with the entrance into Brittany. To smooth the transition, Bradley made Patton his deputy and gave him responsibility for supervising the VIII Corps.

Patton had much to gain from this arrangement. The quicker he got VIII Corps to the threshold of Brittany, the quicker he would be able to activate his Third Army. Patton used the VIII Corps' infantry to clear the area of obstacles and then attacked with the 4th Infantry Division and the 6th Armored Division on 28 July. By the end of the day, VIII Corps controlled Coutances. The next objective was Avranches, which marked the end of the Cotentin and the beginning of the Brittany peninsula. Avranches proved a more difficult objective to capture, but after a series of attacks and counterattacks, VIII Corps was firmly in control of the last natural defensive line before Brittany on 31 July.

Von Kluge described the situation as a "madhouse." Historian Max Hastings called Operation COBRA "the supreme American military achievement in the Normandy campaign." The Germans may have escaped the initial COBRA thrusts, but they fell victim to its later developments. The Germans failed to react to the situations created by Operation COBRA, while the Americans remained flexible and adjusted their exploitation efforts to reinforce success. The result was the breakthrough at St. Lô and the breakout into Brittany. The German fate was sealed.

If the American breakthrough had failed, the German Army in reserve in the Pas de Calais probably would have attacked the Caen bridgehead. If this had happened, the Allies may have been able to continue to land troops, but they could not have supplied them, nor would they have had any room to maneuver. Thus if Operation COBRA had failed, the Allies might have lost the initiative gained by Operation OVERLORD.

Kevin Dougherty

Additional Reading
Blumenson, Martin, *Breakout and Pursuit* (1961).

Eisenhower, Dwight D., *Crusade in Europe* (1948).

Hastings, Max, *Overlord: D-Day, June 6, 1944* (1984).

Johns, Glover S., Jr., *The Clay Pigeons of St. Lô* (1958).

Weigley, Russell F., *Eisenhower's Lieutenants: The Campaigns of France and Germany, 1944–1945* (1981).

Saint-Malo (5 August–2 September 1944)
Following the Allied breakout at St. Lô (q.v.), the U.S. VIII Corps turned west to clear Brittany. Their main objective was the major port of Brest (q.v.), at the far western end of the peninsula. At first, there was some indecision about whether to bypass or to take Saint-Malo, a medium-sized port on the north shore, just at the base of the peninsula. Lieutenant General Omar Bradley (q.v.), the 12th Army Group commander, had ordered Saint-Malo taken immediately. Lieutenant General George Patton (q.v.), the Third Army commander, wanted to bypass it and go straight for Brest. The corps commander, Major General Troy Middleton (q.v.), felt the port with its strong German garrison would represent too large a threat to his rear area. Bradley finally ordered Saint-Malo taken.

Saint-Malo sits on the east bank of the Rance River at the point of its juncture with the sea. The oldest part of the town is formed by a large eighteenth-century citadel that guards the entrance to the harbor. Although the massive citadel walls formed an impressive defensive bastion—even by

modern standards—the fortress had only a half-dozen light field guns. On the opposite bank of the Rance estuary sits the town of Dinard, which was also heavily garrisoned by the Germans. About four thousand meters off shore, the Germans also held the heavily fortified island of Cézembre. Both Dinard and Cézembre were well armed with artillery, and all three positions could provide mutual fire support.

The mission of capturing Saint-Malo fell to the U.S. 83rd Infantry Division, commanded by Major General Robert C. Macon. Believing Saint-Malo would fall quickly, the Americans attacked on 5 August with the 83rd Division's 330th Infantry Regiment and Brigadier General Herbert L. Earnest's Task Force A. When that attack stalled, Task Force A was redirected to Brest (its original mission) and the remaining regiments of the 83rd Division moved up to continue the attack.

The 83rd was reinforced with the 121st Infantry Regiment from the 79th Infantry Division. On 6 August, the attack resumed down both banks of the Rance. The 121st and 331st Infantry Regiments moved along the west bank against Dinard; the 330th and 331st Infantry Regiments attacked Saint-Malo itself along the west bank.

Under the command of Colonel Rudolf Bacherer, the German forces in Dinard put up a stiff resistance. When the Americans finally took Dinard on 14 August, they captured some four thousand prisoners, including Bacherer. Saint-Malo and its citadel, however, proved an even tougher nut to crack.

After carefully moving through the modern sections of Saint-Malo and reducing the various German strong points, the Americans finally ran up against the citadel. The citadel was virtually impervious to infantry attack. For days the Americans pounded it with heavy field artillery and medium bombers of the IX Bomber Command. The shelling seemed to have no effect, and the German commander, Colonel Andreas von Aulock, steadfastly refused to surrender. On 17 August the Americans planned another air strike that would include one of the first tactical uses of napalm. Forty minutes before the scheduled strike, von Aulock raised a white flag and announced his intention to surrender. The air strike was diverted to Cézembre island.

The Americans now had Saint-Malo itself, but Cézembre still controlled the deep water channel to the port and the approaches to the lesser ports of Granville (q.v.) and Cancale. With a garrison of only about 300, Cézembre managed to hold out for two more weeks, despite heavy air strikes and shelling from the HMS *Warspite*. The 330th Infantry Regiment was alerted for an amphibious assault. They were already in their landing craft when the Cézembre garrison finally surrendered on 2 September.

The battle for Saint-Malo was a tactical success. The 83rd Infantry Division sustained relatively modest casualties and bagged more than ten thousand prisoners. On the operational level, however, it contributed very little. Prior to and during the siege, the Germans destroyed the port so thoroughly as to place it beyond all hope of immediate repair and use.

David T. Zabecki

Additional Reading
Blumenson, Martin, *Breakout and Pursuit* (1961).

Saint Nazaire Raid (28 March 1942)

[See map 5 on page 1315]
During World War II, the Biscay port of Saint Nazaire contained one of the few dock facilities large enough to accommodate the German pocket battleship *Tirpitz*, sister ship to the *Bismarck*. The 85,000-ton dry dock and repair facilities (known as the *Normandie* dock for its planned use by the ocean liner *Normandie*), was the only one on the French coast that could hold ships as large as the *Tirpitz*. Admiral Sir Roger Keyes (q.v.), commander of Combined Operations prior to Lord Louis Mountbatten (q.v.), planned to deny the use of the Saint Nazaire port facilities to the Germans. Destruction of the dock would force the *Tirpitz* to operate from Norway, where it would be far more difficult for her to reach the Atlantic convoys bound for Britain. Thus Operation CHARIOT was born.

The centerpiece of Operation CHARIOT was an unorthodox method to destroy the dock with the HMS *Campbeltown*, an obsolete ex-U.S. destroyer (USS *Buchanan*). The ship was to be packed with four tons of timed amonal explosives and sailed right up onto the dock caisson. The crew would then evacuate and be picked up by accompanying motor launches. When the HMS *Campbeltown* exploded it would totally wreck the dock. The plan was devised by Captain J. Hughes-Hallet, chief naval planner at Combined Operations.

The raid was executed by a composite naval and commando (q.v.) force, under the command of Lieutenant Colonel A.C. Newman and Commander R.E.D. Ryder. In the early morning hours of 28 March 1942, the commandos, traveling in

the motor launches, and the HMS *Campbeltown* arrived at Saint Nazaire, flying the German ensign and flashing German recognition signals. Initially fooled, the Germans opened fire on the flotilla at 0130 hours. The launches and the HMS *Campbeltown* weathered the intensive barrage. Most of the commando launches landed successfully, and they began the systematic destruction of the dock facilities. At 0134 hours, the HMS *Campbeltown* rammed the dock and stuck fast. The commandos and crew made their way into the dock area, destroying anything of military value they found. The fire was intense. German reinforcements arrived and several commando launches were unable to land as a result of the fire. As the commando force withdrew, many were left behind and had to surrender.

At 1030 hours, the HMS *Campbeltown* exploded and totally destroyed the *Normandie* dock, killing scores of German observers and souvenir hunters, who assumed the British had only tried to ram the dock. The Germans were unable to repair the dock and it remained useless to them for the duration of the war.

Operation CHARIOT was a successful but costly operation. Of the 611 British participants, 169 were killed, 200 were wounded and captured, while five escaped to reach Spain. The Germans lost around 400, most of whom died when the HMS *Campbeltown* exploded. The consequences of the raid were far-reaching. The *Tirpitz* was never able to use Saint Nazaire as a repair and supply port. That hampered the German ability to further interfere with the Atlantic convoys at a time when the U-boat campaign was inflicting grievous losses on Allied shipping. For the French, it was an important boost to morale—"You were the first to give us hope."

Tim Wilson

Additional Reading

Chant-Sempill, Stuart, *St. Nazaire Commando* (1985).
Mason, Daivd, *Raid on St. Nazaire* (1970).
Neillands, Robin, *By Sea and Land* (1987).
Saunders, Hillary St.G., *The Green Beret (The Story of the Commandos)* (1949).

Saint Vith (16–22 December 1944)

[See map 2 on page 1312]

In the opening phases of the Ardennes offensive (q.v.), the German LXVI *Korps* of General Hasso von Manteuffel's (q.v.) Fifth *Panzer* Army had the mission of capturing St. Vith. In the process of doing so, the LXVI *Korps'* 18th and 62nd *Volksgrenadier* Divisions were supposed to cut off the U.S. 106th Infantry Division in the Schnee Eifel and destroy it. The final capture of the town would then be accomplished by the Fifth *Panzer* Army's two *Panzer Korps*.

The possession of St. Vith was important for the Germans. The town sat at one of the major crossroads through the Ardennes, and astride a major east-west rail line. Thus, the city was supposed to serve as a major transit point for the Fifth *Panzer* Army. Possession of that key node on the road network to Antwerp would also help *SS-Oberstgruppenführer* Josef Dietrich's (q.v.) Sixth *Panzer* Army, which formed the right wing and main effort of the Ardennes offensive.

The attacking elements for the German divisions were organized into small *Stosstrupp*s and storm companies. The soldiers of these *Volksgrenadier* divisions, however, were not experienced fighters. For the most part, they were members of the navy and air force, without infantry training. The green U.S. 106th Infantry Division had similar problems. Two of their infantry regiments, the 422th and 423rd, had landed in Normandy only two weeks earlier. They were supposed to be placed in a "quiet sector" to let them get used to combat operations.

At 0400 hours on 16 December 1944, the *Stosstrupp*s of the 18th and 62nd *Volksgrenadier* Divisions started to infiltrate the American positions. The 18th *Volksgrenadier* Division was able to accomplish its missions, but the 62nd *Volksgrenadier* Division failed on 16 and 17 December. Both units sustained heavy losses in the forest fighting. The delays caused the German operations schedule to slip, which in turn caused coordination problems between the two *Panzer Korps*.

To expedite the capture of St. Vith, the LXVI *Korps* was augmented by the well-equipped *Führer-Begleit-Brigade* (Hitler's Escort Brigade). With their help, the attack was resumed on the afternoon of 19 December. That effort stalled too, because of traffic chaos on the few narrow and steep roads, which were also being used by units not involved in the St. Vith attack.

On 16 December, Major General Troy Middleton (q.v.), commander of the U.S. VIII Corps, ordered the 7th Armored Division to move from its reserve position close to Heerlen, the Netherlands, toward Bastogne. Middleton then changed his mind and turned the division toward St. Vith to support the 106th Infantry Division. The 7th Armored Division had to move about 100 kilometers over icy and crowded roads. Elements

of the division's Combat Command B (CCB), commanded by Brigadier General Bruce C. Clarke (q.v.), reached St. Vith late on 17 December.

On 20 December, the LXVI *Korps* finally managed to get control of its units in time and space. Working together, the 62nd *Volksgrenadier* Division and the Escort Brigade started to make major inroads into the American positions. The 106th Infantry Division was completely encircled, and the LXVI *Korps* captured over 8,000 American prisoners, along with their weapons, ammunition, food, vehicles, and supplies. Those troops of the 106th Infantry Division who avoided capture made their way to St. Vith and joined the 7th Armored Division.

After its arrival, the 7th Armored Division was faced with constant attacks from the Germans, who were searching for a weak point to break through. Meanwhile, the holdup at St. Vith was starting to cause serious problems for the Sixth *Panzer* Army, whose supply trains were stuck east of the city in the Eifel. Dietrich, therefore, sent the II SS *Panzer Korps* south to take St. Vith. The American defense was overcome by the combined pressure of the LXVI *Korps* and the II SS *Panzer Korps*.

Faced with the overwhelming superiority of the Germans, Clarke moved the American forces out of the city shortly before midnight on 21 December. The heavy frost settling in that night turned muddy paths into solid roads, which helped the retreat. St. Vith was occupied that night by the 18th *Volksgrenadier* Division. The Americans, however, conducted such a skilled delaying withdrawal that the Germans made little additional headway that day.

The fight for St. Vith delayed the advance of the right wing of the Fifth *Panzer* Army and the left wing of the Sixth *Panzer* Army for so long that it was a major factor in the Germans losing the race to the Meuse River. The entire time schedule of the Ardennes offensive was disrupted, and that destroyed the surprise factor upon which the whole operation was based. The 7th Armored Division also was fortunate in that it operated almost exactly on the boundary between the two German *Panzer* Armies, which caused coordination problems for the Germans.

The fighting delay of the American units as they slowly withdrew from St. Vith was a success. Holding St. Vith for as long as they did delayed the Germans, but it was not the only reason for the failure of the Ardennes offensive and the race to the Meuse. Other significant factors included the difficult terrain, the winter weather, the lack of fuel,

and Allied air superiority—particularly after the weather cleared on 24 December.

Ekkehart Guth

Additional Reading

Cole, Hugh M., *The Ardennes: Battle of the Bulge* (1965).

Dupuy, R. Ernst, *St. Vith: Lion in the Way* (1949).

Dupuy, Trevor N., David L. Bongard, and Richard C. Anderson, Jr., *Hitler's Last Gamble: The Battle of the Bulge, December 1944–January 1945* (1995).

Eisenhower, John S.D., *The Bitter Woods* (1969).

Jung, H., *Die Ardennenoffensive 1944/45* (1971).

MacDonald, Charles B., *A Time for Trumpets: The Untold Story of the Battle of the Bulge* (1985).

Salerno (9–18 September 1943)

[See map 22 on page 1332]

On 9 September 1943, the Allied Fifth Army launched an amphibious assault on Salerno as part of an operation to gain a foothold in southern Italy. The German defenders mounted a powerful counterattack that nearly split the army in two. A desperate race followed in which both sides frantically rushed in reinforcements. After nine days of fighting, the Germans withdrew north toward the Gustav Line, leaving the Allies in control of the beachhead.

Salerno was one of three courses of action considered for Operation AVALANCHE. The other two possible landing sites were the Gulf of Gaeta or a direct assault on the Bay of Naples. The deciding factor was that Salerno lay within supporting range of Allied fighter planes based in Sicily. Thus on 16 August, General Dwight D. Eisenhower instructed General Bernard L. Montgomery (qq.v.) to launch a supporting assault across the Straits of Messina between 1–4 September, Operation BAYTOWN.

General Mark Clark (q.v.) would follow by landing at Salerno on 9 September with Fifth Army, consisting of Major General Ernest Dawley's U.S. VI Corps and Major General Richard McCreery's (q.v.) British X Corps. Clark planned to have X Corps land to the north and VI Corps to the south, with the Sele River as the corps boundary. The main attack force was to be proceeded by three U.S. ranger (q.v.) battalions and two British commandos (q.v.), which would secure the northern flank and establish blocking positions on the two roads

leading south from Naples. Only the U.S. 36th Infantry Division would land in the initial assault wave of VI Corps. Two regimental combat teams of the U.S. 45th Infantry Division were to serve as a floating reserve; and the British 7th Armoured Division would follow into X Corps sector after D+4 for the advance on Naples.

Both corps were to push forward and establish a perimeter along the arc of hills that overlooked the beaches. X Corps was to seize the port of Salerno and the Montecorvino airfield, which Clark hoped to have operational by D+1. Then X Corps was to break out to the north and seize Naples by 21 September when the first major follow-on convoy was to arrive offshore.

The all-important air plan was based on three principles that were becoming standard for Allied operations. First, Allied airpower would neutralize the *Luftwaffe* and drive it back from its forward airfields. Next, vulnerable transportation networks would be bombed to cut the Germans' ability to reinforce. Finally, Allied fighters would cover the beachhead until the army could break out, disperse its shipping, and reduce its vulnerability to *Luftwaffe* attack. Close air support would be provided only after these three primary tasks were accomplished.

McCreery also planned detailed close naval gunfire support for X Corps' assault. Clark, however, planned to rely purely on surprise and did not want to give the Germans any warning with preparatory fires. Clark wanted naval gunfire used on an as-needed basis. When the Allies lost the element of surprise during the landings, the wisdom of McCreery's precautions became readily apparent.

A key factor in the Salerno equation was the timing of Italy's defection from its alliance with Germany. Both Eisenhower and 15th Army Group Commander General Sir Harold Alexander (q.v.) believed that Operation AVALANCHE could succeed only if it coincided with the confusion of a sudden Italian surrender. After delicate negotiations, including a clandestine delegation headed by Brigadier General Maxwell Taylor (q.v.), the Italian government agreed to announce the armistice as the Operation AVALANCHE force approached Salerno.

The Germans, however, were not caught off guard. At 2000 hours on 8 September, the German defenders received word of the Italian defection and immediately began implementing Operation *ACHSE* (AXIS) (q.v.), the planned disarmament of the Italian forces. For the most part the Italians willingly threw down their weapons. They gave the Allies no real support and the disarmament was completed just prior to the landings of the rangers and commandos.

Field Marshal Albert Kesselring (q.v.), commander of German forces in the Mediterranean, assigned General Heinrich von Vietinghoff-Scheel (q.v.) and the Tenth Army to defend southern Italy. Von Vietinghoff made each of the potential Allied landing sites the responsibility of one of his corps commanders, who were to cooperate with the Italian troops in the area as much as possible. General Traugott Herr's LXXVI *Panzer Korps* was responsible for the area south of the Salerno-Bari line. Because this terrain in the "toe" region of Italy was easily defended, Herr was given just three weak divisions.

To the north, General Hans-Valentine Hube's XIV *Panzer Korps* defended the Naples area. Because Hube felt a landing at Salerno could be blocked quickly, he initially deployed his two divisions in and north of Naples, leaving Salerno itself to the Italians. By the end of August, however, Hube reconsidered the situation and moved the 16th *Panzer* Division onto the high ground overlooking Salerno. Rather than try to stretch his defense across the entire thirty miles of Salerno beach, Hube deployed his units in strongpoints, with mobile patrols to cover the gaps. He assigned the Italian 222nd Coastal Division to what he considered the low risk sectors of the beach.

As early as 29 August, the Germans began to suspect an amphibious assault. Five heavily guarded Allied aircraft carriers were spotted departing Gibraltar heading east. These observations, tied with reports of Allied landing ships in Sicily, caused the Germans to go to an increased state of readiness. On 8 September, the Germans received reports of Allied shipping twenty-five miles south of Capri. The XIV *Panzer Korps* went to full alert. The Allies not only failed to receive the expected support from the Italians, they also lost the critical element of surprise.

As planned, the British Eighth Army crossed the Straits of Messina on 3 September and started working its way north through the Calabria region. Six days later, Clark's forces hit the beaches at Salerno. At 0200 hours, the Germans, using recently seized Italian coastal batteries in X Corps' landing sector, opened fire on the ships carrying the rangers and commandos. McCreery immediately ordered full fire support, and British naval gunners successfully suppressed the enemy. The rangers and commandos landed against light opposition and secured their objectives. The British 46th Division landed clear of the German strongpoints, but the British 56th Division met heavy

resistance. Again, naval gunfire was the key to a successful landing. The British divisions, however, were not able to make much progress once on the shore. By the end of D-Day, 46th Division had not secured the port, and 56th Division had not secured the airfield.

In the U.S. VI Corps sector, Clark stuck to his plan to land without fire support in the hope of achieving surprise. The Americans landed quietly, but soon were taking effective enemy fire from well-concealed positions. Von Vietinghoff quickly assessed the situation and concluded that another major invasion farther to the north was unlikely. He therefore instructed XIV *Panzer Korps* to make a "ruthless concentration of all forces at Salerno" and drive the Allies back into the sea.

General Hermann Balck (q.v.), acting corps commander in Hube's absence, felt he did not have the necessary strength across his large sector to execute von Vietinghoff's order with the vigor with which it had been given. Balck insisted on keeping a large portion of his corps prepared for another landing, and left the 16th *Panzer* Division to contain Salerno. The 16th *Panzer* Division launched numerous piecemeal tank attacks, which generally were too small to have any effect. *Luftwaffe* activity was enough to harass the landing force, but British Spitfires were able to intercept and turn back several air attacks. The landings continued to progress. At 2045 hours, Clark reported to Alexander that the entire 36th Infantry Division was ashore.

From most indications at the end of D-Day the landings had been a success. The Allies secured the beachhead and took relatively few casualties for an opposed landing. Their key problem was the failure of X Corps to establish its flank on the Sele River. A gap, therefore, existed between the two Allied corps. On Kesselring's part, there was great relief that Rome was not the Allies' immediate objective. He quickly set out to clear his lines of communications through Rome and provide support to von Vietinghoff. The latter could easily hold the British Eighth Army in the south with a relatively small force, while concentrating the rest of his divisions at Salerno. He still controlled the ring of high ground outside the beachhead and could bring observed artillery fire onto the unloading operations.

Both sides had reasons to feel confident. The deciding factor would boil down to who could reinforce the fastest. For the Allies, Clark had already decided to send ashore the U.S. 179th Infantry Regiment from his floating reserve. Eisenhower also offered Clark the use of 82nd Airborne Division and additional landing craft capable of moving 1,800 troops.

American troops evacuate one of the first casualties from the Salerno landings, 9 September 1943. (IWM NA 6623)

The Germans were making similar preparations. Herr was ordered to break contact with Eighth Army and move the bulk of his LXXVI *Panzer Korps* toward Salerno. Balck's XIV *Panzer Korps* received instructions to leave the Gulf of Gaeta open and send 15th *Panzergrenadier* and Hermann Göring *Panzer* Divisions south to block the approaches to Naples. Adolf Hitler (q.v.) felt his Tenth Army was doomed and refused the authority to release one division from Rome and two from General Erwin Rommel's (q.v.) command in northern Italy. Kesselring, however, remained confident. Even without this additional support von Vietinghoff would have six experienced, mobile divisions around Salerno before Clark could have four ashore.

For the next three days, both sides busied themselves with the receipt of reinforcements, the repositioning of troops, and a variety of probing attacks, initiated for the most part by the Allies. On the morning of 13 September, von Vietinghoff discovered the gap between the two Allied corps. He interpreted this as an indication that the Allies intended to withdraw, and he moved quickly to prevent their escape. By dusk, the Germans gained control of the Persano crossing over the Sele River and pushed a sizable force through the Sele-Calore corridor into the U.S. sector. This drive forced Clark to relocate his headquarters to the British sector, where the threat was not as great. German artillery, meanwhile, rained down on the port and forced operations to cease at 1500 hours. The harbor remained closed for almost two weeks. The situation started to grow critical enough for Clark to direct his staff to begin planning an evacuation.

The Fifth Army reached this crisis state because it could not build up its beachhead by water as fast as the Germans could reinforce by land. The landing craft shortage, always a problem for the Allies, became the critical factor. By carefully juggling landing craft, Alexander was able to begin moving the U.S. 3rd Infantry Division to Salerno; but even that measure was not enough. The only remaining possibility for rapid reinforcement was the U.S. 82nd Airborne Division. Starting at 2230 hours on 13 September, 1,300 paratroopers jumped into a drop zone five miles north of Agropoli, behind the Allied lines. By 0300 hours, the regimental commander, Colonel Rueben Tucker, reported to the VI Corps command post, and his unit was attached to 36th Infantry Division. The reinforcements were small in number, but provided a significant boost to Allied morale.

The Germans too had been reinforced by a regimental-sized element of the 26th *Panzer* Division. Von Vietinghoff urged Balck and Herr to attack with all their resources, but the opportunity to split the Allies had passed already. In both the X and VI Corps sectors the beachhead held, and Allied reinforcements were streaming in. The British 7th Armored Division came ashore and reported to X Corps. The U.S. 180th Infantry Regiment landed and formed the reserve of Fifth Army near Monte Soprano. Finally, 2,100 more 82nd Airborne Division paratroopers landed just south of Paestum. On the night of 14 September, Eisenhower reported, "I have every confidence that we will come out all right."

Despite all indications to the contrary, von Vietinghoff clung to his belief that the Allies were evacuating the beachhead. At that point, Kesselring intervened, ordering the Tenth Army to withdraw to the vicinity of Rome. Before withdrawing, Kesselring instructed von Vietinghoff to make one final effort to push the Allies back into the sea, and sent one regiment from 1st Parachute Division to help.

On 16 September, von Vietinghoff launched his final attack, but that only confirmed that the beachhead would hold. Additionally, he received word that the advance guard of the British Eighth Army moving up from the south had made contact with the German blocking forces near Lagonero. Von Vietinghoff then requested permission from Kesselring to begin a general withdrawal no later than the night of 18 September. The Allies did not pursue, and the battle of Salerno was over.

On 20 September, the advance elements of Eighth Army made contact with X Corps. Their arrival would have been cause for rejoicing a few days earlier, but now it carried no particular significance. The Fifth Army had fought and won at Salerno on its own. In the process, the Allies suffered 9,000 casualties. Clark later called Salerno "a near disaster" and this close brush with defeat would profoundly affect his planning for the Anzio (q.v.) landings. For the time being, however, the Fifth Army had secured a lodgment in southern Italy and on 1 October, they entered Naples unopposed.

Allied planners learned some valuable lessons from Salerno. The value of naval gunfire was once again demonstrated, but problems still existed with the ability to observe and adjust it. Fighter cover and close air support would have to be more responsive in future operations, which meant a greater role for naval aviation. Clark was unable to field an army-level reserve until late in the battle,

which pointed to the necessity for such a force to block counterattacks and exploit successes.

Finally, there were the command problems. The British-American coalition suffered from the routine difficulties of any international operation, but Clark's most pressing concern was Dawley. Clark was particularly disturbed by his seeming indifference to the threat to his left flank, and he believed Dawley did not work well under pressure. On 20 September, Dawley was relieved and Major General John Lucas (q.v.) assumed command of VI Corps. On the German side, Tenth Army saved itself from what Hitler felt was sure annihilation. Kesselring and Clark began preparations for their next meeting, which would come four months later at Anzio.

Kevin Dougherty

Additional Reading

Blumenson, Martin, *Salerno to Cassino* (1969).
Graham, Dominick, and Shelford Bidwell, *Tug of War: The Battle for Italy, 1943–1945* (1986).
Jackson, W.G.F., *The Battle for Italy* (1967).

Sangro River (23–30 November 1943)

The British Eighth Army defeated elements of LXXVI *Panzer Korps* in a series of limited but heavily supported attacks between 23–30 November 1943. The attacks permitted General Bernard L. Montgomery's (q.v.) Eighth Army to cross and advance three miles beyond the Sangro River into the Bernhard Line.

Following a 400-mile advance from Calabria, the Eighth Army's right flank began closing on the Sangro River in early November. Montgomery was ordered to seize the Pescara-Avezzano road twenty miles to the north. The mountain approaches to Avezzano prevented the British XIII Corps, on the left, from launching any major attack. Poor roads leading to the New Zealand Division, in the center, prohibited assaults there as well. Only the coastal corridor leading to Pescara, in the V Corps' zone, permitted sustained, large-scale operations. Accordingly, Montgomery planned to attack there across a narrow front, while the New Zealand Division conducted a supporting attack on V Corps' left flank.

Montgomery's troops had to contend with both the Sangro River and the German 65th Infantry Division. The Sangro's gravel and boulder-strewn bed measured 300–400 meters wide, and the river flowed along several, normally knee-deep, channels. Autumn rains, however, could swell the

depth fourfold and magnify the current, making bridges essential for any attack. The Germans destroyed the four bridges spanning the Sangro and mined the banks to deter the Royal Engineers.

The German 65th Infantry Division presented less of a challenge. Judged the worst division in the German Tenth Army, the 65th consisted of untested, young troops formed the previous year. Although strong in antitank guns, the 65th Infantry Division had only seven artillery batteries and had to stretch its 6,500 soldiers across a front wider than that of the opposing V Corps. The closest reserves, elements of 90th *Panzergrenadier* Division, were located twelve miles from the German main defensive line, and tank units were another five miles north.

Montgomery attempted to divert German attention from the coast by ordering XIII Corps to maintain heavy pressure on the narrow valleys leading to Avezzano. Despite heavy rains and deep mud, XIII Corps steadily approached the upper Sangro. Deception operations also included fake radio traffic to convince the Germans that the Indian 8th Division would reinforce Montgomery's left instead of his right. In addition, Allied naval units tied down enemy reserves near Pescara, twenty-five miles north of the Sangro, reinforcing German fears of an amphibious assault.

Lieutenant General Sir Charles W. Allfrey's V Corps reached the lower Sangro on 9 November, and the 78th Division began unopposed night patrols the following day. Rather than contest the river itself, the Germans decided to defend along the Li Colli ridge, a forty-foot-high escarpment that paralleled the Sangro 2,000 meters to the north. A lateral road enhanced German mobility, and farm houses and olive groves added to the German defensive works.

British engineers crossed the Sangro River to prepare fording sites and to remove mines. Increasing rainfall, however, swelled the river and made fording operations almost impossible. Instead, the 78th Division seized and slowly expanded two bridgeheads near Fossacesia. By 22 November, six infantry battalions and elements of two armored regiments crossed the Sangro, but both the Germans and the British lacked the forces to dislodge the other.

Meanwhile, Montgomery took direct control of his center by placing the New Zealand Division, reinforced with the Indian 19th Infantry Brigade, under Eighth Army command. The remainder of the Indian 8th Division sidestepped past the New Zealanders, along poor roads and trails, to join V Corps. Montgomery's reinforced division attacked

S

the center of the German line for almost a week and forded the Sangro on 23 November. Despite this assault, as well as sorties in XIII Corps' sector, the Germans expected the Eighth Army to launch its main attack against the 65th Infantry Division.

Montgomery hoped to attack on the night of 19 November, but strong rains caused him to postpone the operation. He believed that no crossing could succeed without forty-eight hours of dry weather preceding it. He later declared that the operation required a week of fair weather. Engineer units scurried to prepare fording sites, but the surging Sangro River made the emplacement of bridges a necessity. Renewed rains disrupted British efforts to construct four bridges, as the river swelled to a width of 1,000 feet.

Concerns over weather caused Montgomery to modify his battle plan. He instructed Allfrey to reorganize the bridgehead into two divisional sectors with the Indian 8th Division on the left and the 78th Division on the right. The Indians would attack in two stages beginning 26 November to seize Santa Maria, a village on the Li Colli ridge. Two days later, the 78th Division would attack through Santa Maria to seize Fossacesia to the northeast. If weather permitted, tanks would exploit any breaks in the German line.

Weather delayed the attack until 27 November, but the Indians seized their intermediate objectives in the morning and captured Mozzagrogna, a village several hundred meters southwest of Santa Maria. The Indian 17th Infantry Brigade, however, retreated when it misinterpreted a German sixteen-tank assault as the vanguard of a major counterattack. Rather than retake the town, Allfrey used the day to bring up the 4th Armoured Brigade's 124 tanks and to let the battleground dry out.

Backed by corps artillery, the Indians attacked early on 29 November and recaptured Mozzagrogna. By mid-morning, nine artillery battalions blasted the German positions around Santa Maria, allowing two infantry battalions from the 78th Division to seize the town easily. Allfrey, however, failed to exploit these limited advances. Instead, he waited until nightfall to continue the drive toward Fossacesia. Indian troops opened a path for tanks to attack northeast from Santa Maria, and a brigade-size force of British tanks and infantry advanced up the ridge toward the Adriatic Sea.

The limited but violent British attacks almost destroyed the two-battalion 145th *Grenadier* Regiment, and nearly halved the 361st *Panzergrenadier* Regiment. The V Corps penetrated the Bernhard Line, and elements of two New Zealand brigades crossed the Sangro farther to the west. Only a large, well-staged counterattack could restore the German line, but LXXVI *Panzer Korps* did not expect the 4th Parachute Regiment and the 90th *Panzergrenadier* Division to be in position until 3 December. German reserves could do little but hold a defensive line parallel to Li Colli ridge, while engineers prepared positions just above the Moro River, five miles to the north.

Despite his superiority in infantry, tanks, and artillery, Montgomery broke off the attack on 1 December. His artillery had almost exhausted its ammunition, and several bridges showed signs of weakening. He also wanted to replace the 78th Division with the fresher Canadian 1st Division. Worsening weather also concerned him. Renewed rains swelled the Sangro River, and by 4 December, only one span remained in the V Corps' sector.

Caution also checked Montgomery's advance to the west. Although the Germans feared that renewed New Zealand Division attacks would again enable the Eighth Army to break the Bernhard Line, Montgomery and the division commander, Lieutenant General Sir Bernard Freyberg (q.v.), preferred to consolidate their positions instead of exploiting the opening. When the New Zealanders attacked one week later, the German reinforcements easily rebuffed them.

Montgomery's victory at the Sangro River permitted the Eighth Army to resume its northward advance, but his tactics promised only small, measured gains at great cost in time and materiel. The British gained only six miles in three weeks and relied on unsustainable high artillery expenditures to propel their attacks—145,770 rounds on 27–30 November or approximately one German death per 1,000 rounds fired. Measured advance also did not minimize casualties; British killed and wounded greatly exceeded German losses—2,547 Commonwealth troops versus 1,133 Germans during November. More significantly, Montgomery's army failed to exploit its successes, even though two-thirds of the available infantry battalions remained uncommitted. Despite several opportunities, the Eighth Army failed to rupture the German defenses, and its operational pauses enabled the Germans to reconstitute their lines and force yet another series of set-piece battles.

Roger Kaplan

Additional Reading

Graham, Dominick, and Bidwell Shelford, *Tug of War: The Battle for Italy, 1943–1945* (1986).

Jackson, W.G.F., *The Battle for Italy* (1967).

Molony, C.J.C., *The Campaign in Sicily, 1943, and the Campaign in Italy 3rd September 1943 to 31st March 1944* (1973).

Montgomery of Alamein, Field Marshal The Viscount, *El Alamein to the River Sangro* (1948).

San Pietro (12–18 December 1943)

San Pietro is a small town located at the entrance to the Liri Valley, from where the southern road to Rome winds its way. The terrain of the area is extremely mountainous and rugged. From October through December 1943, it was the operational focus of the U.S. Fifth Army's II Corps and several battalions of the German 5th Mountain Division.

Situated between Mt. Lungo and Mt. Sammucro and at the head of the Via Casilina (Highway 6 to Rome), San Pietro found itself in the path of both the retreating German forces and the advancing Allied armies. To the Germans, it represented the last place to slow, if not stop, the Allied push toward Rome before winter set in.

San Pietro offered the perfect tactical conditions to halt a much superior force. Given ample time, the Germans constructed a formidable series of defensive obstacles. They planted the terraced mountain fields and roads with a deadly crop of antipersonnel and antitank mines. Because of these massive defenses, many Americans came to call the place "Death Valley."

At the beginning of December, the Fifth Army began its advance. Units of the 36th Infantry Division's 143rd Infantry Regiment were ordered to take the village. The area was defended by four German battalions located in the mountains around the town, with an additional battalion holding the town itself. The 1st Battalion of the 143rd Infantry Regiment and the 3rd Ranger Battalion were given the task of capturing Mt. Sammucro. The 143rd Infantry Regiment's 2nd and 3rd Battalions were to take the town itself, and other units of the Fifth Army were directed to take Mt. Lungo. Because of the rugged terrain, supply operations were extremely difficult, forcing the attacking American infantry to carry enough food and ammunition for several days on their backs.

Mt. Sammucro was taken with little difficulty, mostly because of the surprise achieved by the attackers. The rangers, however, ran into very stiff resistance on an adjacent ridge. It was there the German forces were ordered to hold their positions at any cost. After several unsuccessful attacks, the 143rd's 1st Battalion (reinforced by a battalion of the U.S. 504th Parachute Infantry Regiment)

moved along the ridge and succeeded in capturing the German positions.

On 14 December, the 143rd's 2nd and 3rd Battalions moved in to take the town, which was defended by a deadly network of pillboxes supported by mortar fire. With clear skies, the *Luftwaffe* bombed and strafed the attackers as they moved forward. Additional units of the U.S. 141st and 142nd Infantry Regiments were called in for support, as well as virtually every Fifth Army artillery piece within range.

By the following day, the 141st was able to advance, but the 2nd and 3rd Battalions of the 143rd were pinned down by heavy machine gun and mortar fire. Tanks were called in, but with the pinpoint accuracy of the German artillery, they too failed to advance. As night fell some units were forced to withdraw by flanking fire from German positions.

On 16 December, the 142nd was able to take Mt. Lungo. Throughout that day much of the bloodiest fighting occurred as the Germans launched numerous counterattacks to cover their withdrawal from the town. At the time, however, the Americans could only guess at the motives for the vicious German resistance. When American patrols finally entered San Pietro on 18 December 1943, they found it deserted.

After the dust settled and the troops collapsed with exhaustion, the true cost of the battle was felt. It was said that 1st Battalion of the 143rd Infantry Regiment lost a man for every yard of ground taken, and at the conclusion of the battle, the regiment required 1,100 replacements.

The battle of San Pietro became the subject of a famous American wartime propaganda film. Directed by John Houston and constructed from official U.S. Army combat footage, the film was intended to spur on the civilian support of the war effort. But after audiences at the original screenings reacted with revulsion to the many scenes of bloody American casualties, the film was withdrawn and heavily cut.

Rob Nadeau

Additional Reading

Fisher, Ernest F., *Cassino to the Alps* (1977).

Scapa Flow (13 October 1939)

[See map 5 on page 1315]

Shortly before midnight on 13 October 1939, a German U-boat, commanded by Lieutenant Commander Günther Prien (q.v.), entered the supposedly impregnable British naval base at Scapa

Flow and sank the British battleship HMS *Royal Oak* one hour later. Some 833 British sailors died in the attack. It was a daring feat conducted on the surface in the middle of Britain's most important naval base, home port to the Home Fleet, the nation's main battle fleet. No other naval disaster in the European theater so devastated British morale. It made the U-boat's commander an instant hero in the *Reich*.

Planning for the operation began on 3 September 1939. Then Commodore Karl Dönitz (q.v.), commander of the U-boat arm, had considered the operation from the war's beginning. Located between several islands within the Orkney Islands, Scapa Flow was also the British Home Fleet's main operating base during World War I, and two U-boats were lost trying to penetrate its defenses in that conflict. Surrounded by rocky reefs in waters swept by high winds and treacherous currents, Scapa Flow was protected by minefields and antisubmarine nets. All but one of the channels leading into the base was blocked by sunken merchant ships (so-called block ships) and entry through the remaining channel was controlled via nets.

Dönitz combed *Luftwaffe* aerial photographs taken both just before and just after the war's start, looking for a weak point in the base's seemingly impenetrable defenses. Prewar merchant ship and U-boat patrol reports, particularly that of the *U-16*, just returned from the Orkneys on 11 September, were scrutinized for the latest information on tides, currents, lighting, and defenses. Finally on 26 September, the *Luftwaffe* provided detailed aerial photography of all the defenses in and around the Scapa Flow area. It was this set of photographs that revealed a small channel, only fifteen meters wide, leading into the harbor. The coastline in the area appeared uninhabited and the waters unpatrolled.

Dönitz felt a surfaced U-boat could penetrate the base by navigating through the seven-meter-deep channel on the surface at night. Mid-October offered the best possible combination of night visibility, tides, and currents for the attempt. All that remained was the selection of the right boat and its commander.

On 30 September, the choice settled on Prien and his Type VII boat, the *U-47*. Known for his aggressiveness and skilled seamanship, Prien was a natural choice. He already was one of Germany's leading U-boat aces, having sunk more than 40,000 tons of shipping, including nearly 10,000 tons on his last patrol. Recognizing the danger, Dönitz handed all the relevant materials over to Prien on 4 October and asked him to consider the operation. Prien had the right to refuse. He studied the charts, photos, and navigational documents overnight. He accepted the mission the next day.

The *U-47* departed Wilhelmshaven on 8 October and made a direct transit to the Orkneys, arriving off Lamb Head just before midnight on 13 October. There, illuminated under the Northern Lights, Prien carefully guided the *U-47* through the narrow channel. He hoped to use his boat's battery power for the transit, but the force of the currents nearly drove him ashore. He had to use the U-boat's engines to maintain maneuverability. He came within meters of running aground on several occasions and actually grounded briefly on an uncharted rock before he entered the main harbor just before 0100 hours. The Northern Lights diminished rapidly as he made a quick survey of the harbor. Disappointed at finding the bulk of the fleet gone, Prien settled on attacking what he believed to be two battleships (HMS *Royal Oak* and the battle cruiser HMS *Repulse*) anchored near the shore.

Only one of his first three torpedoes detonated. Fortunately for Prien, the British thought it was an internal explosion. No alert was sounded while Prien desperately turned his submarine around to fire his rear torpedo tube. Again there was no result. With surprising patience and courage, Prien remained in the center of the harbor for the twenty minutes it took his crew to reload their torpedo tubes. This time all three torpedoes struck and detonated against the HMS *Royal Oak*'s hull. The aging battleship went down in minutes, taking most of her crew with her.

Then, with the harbor lights coming on and its defenses swarming around him, Prien guided his craft back out the channel against a current that nearly equaled his submarine's maximum surface speed of twelve knots. Hugging the coast to avoid searchlights, he was nearly caught by a patrolling destroyer, but somehow, his luck held until he had cleared the narrow channel. By dawn, *U-47* was clear of the chaotic harbor and submerged. Prien returned to a hero's welcome in Wilhelmshaven two days later.

Prien's attack on Scapa Flow stunned the Royal Navy. Although the post-attack board of inquiry settled on the absence of block ships and net defenses on the channel Prien had used, many British felt at the time, and some continue to believe today, that he could not have navigated that channel without assistance from ashore. Spurious reports of car headlights and men on the channel shore continued to be reported long afterward.

The reality is that the defenders were probably less than fully alert when Prien entered the harbor. After all, who would have thought an underpowered submarine could navigate such a narrow and shallow channel at night without navigational aids—particularly one swept by powerful swirling currents and high winds.

Prien's mission required him to exercise exceptional daring and judgment. The margins for error were very small and he needed a lot of luck. The Royal Navy should have been very relieved indeed that *U-47* was saddled with horribly defective torpedoes—only four functioned of the seven fired. Otherwise, HMS *Repulse* might have been lost as well. Nonetheless, the raid was a remarkable feat that stands out today as one of the greatest naval operations in history.

Carl O. Schuster

Additional Reading

Dönitz, Karl, *Memoirs: Ten Years and Twenty Days* (1959).
Porten, von der, Edward, *The German Navy in World War Two* (1969).
Prien, Günther, *U-Boat Commander* (1969).

Scheldt (2 October–8 November 1944)

[See map 26 on page 1336]

The Scheldt campaign was fought by the Canadian First Army to clear both banks of the forty-five-mile-long Scheldt estuary in the Netherlands, thereby opening a channel to Antwerp (q.v.), a major port capable of discharging more than 40,000 tons of supplies daily, and desperately needed to resupply the stalled Allied drive on Germany. The campaign was characterized by wet weather, vicious fighting, and fierce German resistance over a wretched terrain of flooded, muddy lowlands crisscrossed by well-defended dikes and canals. The use of armor and the mass movement or concentration of troops was impossible.

On 2 October, the Canadian 2nd Infantry Division advanced from the Antwerp area with the goal of capturing and isolating the narrow causeway linking Zuid (South) Beveland to the mainland fifteen miles north. Their right flank was protected by the Canadian 4th Armoured Division of the British I Corps, which struck northwest on Bergen op Zoom. The revitalized German forces in the area included the elite and heavily armed 6th Parachute Regiment. By 8 October, German resistance slowed the advance and inflicted heavy casualties on the Canadians. Fierce fighting continued for more than a week in and around the village

of Woensdrecht, which commanded the bottleneck entrance to the isthmus. The town was not captured until 16–17 October, following blistering Allied artillery and air attacks.

The advance on Zuid Beveland was delayed by the need to eliminate German resistance north and east of the isthmus up to the River Maas. This task was carried out by the British I Corps of the Canadian First Army, supported on the right by the British Second Army. On 24 October, the attack on Zuid Beveland commenced in the face of tenacious opposition and arduous terrain. The Beveland Canal, running north to south and splitting Zuid Beveland in two, was reached two days later. To outflank this obstacle, a successful amphibious assault was launched across the Scheldt from Terneuzen by a brigade of the British 52nd Lowland Division. The two forces linked up on 29 October and advanced steadily until 31 October, when all remaining German forces were evacuated to Walcheren across a heavily defended narrow causeway.

While these actions were in progress, the Canadian 3rd Infantry Division crossed the 150-foot wide Leopold Canal and invested the Breskens pocket on the south bank of the Scheldt. The canal, on the south and west, and the Braakman inlet, on the east, provided formidable defensive positions for the 14,000 high-caliber troops of the German 64th Division. Moreover, as a good deal of the pocket was flooded by the Germans, the few suitable points of attack were well covered.

On 6 October, preceded by a heavy artillery bombardment from 327 guns and supported by twenty-seven Wasp flamethrowing vehicles showering fire on the German defenders entrenched on the opposite bank, elements of the Canadian 7th Infantry Brigade transported in assault boats won the narrowest of bridgeheads across the Leopold despite fierce German resistance. The appalling ground conditions over which the Canadians had to attack impeded their advance almost as significantly as did German counterattacks. Only after five days of bitter combat were the Canadians able to enlarge their bridgehead.

The second phase of the operation, dislodging the Germans from the Breskens pocket, began on 9 October with a surprise dawn amphibious assault across the Braakman inlet from Terneuzen by troops of the Canadian 9th Infantry Brigade. They were ferried across in ninety-six Buffalo tracked amphibious landing vehicles, each capable of transporting thirty men. A strong bridgehead was won behind the main German defensive network along the Leopold Canal. By 14 October, the

entire 3rd Infantry Division had penetrated the bastion of the Breskens pocket.

The Germans continued a fighting withdrawal away from the developing Canadian pincers until their last positions of stubborn resistance along the North Sea coast were finally overrun on 2 November. The Canadians took 12,800 prisoners in the process. German artillery support from the many Atlantic Wall (q.v.) coastal batteries in the pocket and on Walcheren Island inflicted heavy losses on the Canadians, while adverse weather conditions often denied effective close air support to the Canadian attacks.

The final stage of the campaign was the invasion of strongly fortified Walcheren Island, commanding the mouth of the Scheldt estuary. On 30 October, 243 Lancaster bombers destroyed the Westkapelle dike and flooded most of the island, thereby inundating several German gun emplacements, destroying supplies, hampering troop movements, and isolating the German garrison to only a few locations. From 31 October to 2 November, the 2nd Infantry Division was severely mauled in its attempts to force the causeway leading from Beveland. An attack by a brigade of the 52nd Lowland Division across the mud flats from Zuid Beveland met with success on 3 November. That force then moved inland at a persistent pace.

The main Allied attack was launched on 1 November against Westkapelle, on the extreme west of the island, by Royal Marines and Dutch commandos from Number 4 Special Service Brigade under Canadian command. German coastal artillery, which was not affected much by the preliminary naval and air bombardments, engaged at short range the twenty-seven Allied assault craft covering the landing. Nine were sunk and eleven damaged, resulting in 300 British casualties. Heavy fighting ensued before the Royal Marines were able to break out from their bridgehead. Also on 1 November, Number 4 Commando and a brigade from the Lowland Division landed at Flushing and overcame the resistance in that area by 4 November. All German resistance on Walcheren ceased four days later. The British took 8,000 prisoners.

Minesweeping of the Scheldt estuary began on 4 November with 100 ships engaged. Some 267 mines were swept before the channel opened to shipping. The first Allied ship docked at Antwerp on 28 November 1944, eighty-five days after its capture. At the end of the campaign, the Canadian First Army cleared the enemy from territory up to the Maas, suffered 12,873 casualties, and captured more than 41,000 prisoners.

Serge M. Durflinger

Additional Reading
Thompson, R.W., *The Eighty-Five Days: The Story of the Battle of the Scheldt* (1957).
Whitaker, W. Denis, and Shelagh Whitaker, *Tug of War: The Canadian Victory That Opened Antwerp* (1984).

Schmidt (6 October–8 November 1944)

[See map 34 on page 1344]

The battle for the small German town of Schmidt was the centerpiece of the bitter and protracted struggle for the dense and dark Hürtgen Forest (q.v.). Although American units first moved into the Hürtgen Forest on 12 September 1944, both sides initially failed to appreciate the importance of Schmidt—the key to the network of roads that led to a series of important dams on the Roer River. By opening or destroying the dams, the Germans could flood the open plains that extended east of the Hürtgen Forest to the Rhine and trap or halt the advancing Americans.

On 6 October, the 9th Infantry Division of U.S. VII Corps attacked toward Schmidt with the 39th and 60th Infantry Regiments. After five days of heavy fighting in the bunker- and pillbox-studded woods, both regiments had advanced only a kilometer and a half. On 12 October German Regiment Wegelein launched a fierce counterattack into the exposed left flank of the 60th Infantry. By 16 October, the 9th Infantry Division had suffered 4,500 casualties and had only about three kilometers of ground to show for it.

First Army commander Lieutenant General Courtney Hodges (q.v.) reacted by shifting corps boundaries to give U.S. V Corps responsibility for Schmidt. The V Corps commander, Major General Leonard T. Gerow (q.v.), ordered a new attack on the town by the 28th Infantry Division, a Pennsylvania National Guard outfit commanded by Major General Norman Cota (q.v.). Gerow reinforced the attack by giving Cota three additional engineer battalions and a towed antitank battalion—in addition to the standard attachments from the corps of a tank battalion and a self-propelled tank destroyer battalion. Gerow also placed eight battalions of V and VII Corps artillery in direct support of the division.

The 28th Infantry Division opened its operation on 2 November, with the 112th Infantry Regiment making the main attack from a ridge line at the edge of the town of Vossenack, across the Kall River gorge, to the towns of Kommerscheidt and Schmidt on the opposite ridge line. The 109th Infantry Regiment attacked on the left, down the

Vossenack Ridge; and the 110th Infantry Regiment attacked on the right. Contrary to standard military wisdom, all three regiments proceeded on divergent axes.

That same day, the senior leadership of German Army Group B was conducting a map training exercise based on a theoretical American attack toward Schmidt. When the word came of an actual attack, Field Marshal Walter Model (q.v.) immediately ordered elements of the 116th *Panzer* Division into the area.

By 3 November, the 1st and 3rd battalions of the 112th Infantry Regiment had moved from Vossenack, across the deep and heavily wooded Kall River gorge, and up onto the opposite ridge to take both Kommerscheidt and Schmidt. With no supporting tanks or antitank weapons, the two infantry battalions set up a thin and tenuous defensive perimeter.

The only way into Schmidt for the Americans at that point was along a steep and narrow forest trail that ran down one side of the Kall gorge and up the other. On 4 November, 1st Lieutenant Raymond Fleig somehow managed to get three Sherman tanks down the trail and up into Kommerscheidt. Meanwhile, a German *Panzer* regiment of some 25 tanks counterattacked at Schmidt and drove the surviving Americans back along the ridge into Kommerscheidt. The Germans attacked Kommerscheidt later that day; but reinforced with Fleig's tanks, the Americans held on. Their only line of support remained the Kall Trail.

On 5 November the Germans renewed the attack on Kommerscheidt. By noon that day, nine more American tanks and nine tank destroyers had managed to negotiate the Kall Trail. The 1st Battalion, 112th Infantry, continued to hold. The following day, the reconnaissance battalion of the 116th *Panzer* Division attacked through the gorge to cut the Kall Trail. The attacks continued against Kommerscheidt, and by noon the Americans had only six tanks and three tank destroyers operational. Cota committed many of his engineer units as infantry to the fight in the Kall gorge.

On 7 November, Cota ordered a new attack to retake Schmidt, but the Germans attacked Kommerscheidt with some fifteen tanks and two battalions of infantry. In the late afternoon, most of the Americans had been forced out of Kommerscheidt and into the thick woods on the eastern side of the Kall gorge. Cota then asked Gerow for permission to withdraw all his forces west of the Kall River. Reluctantly, First Army commander Hodges finally agreed, and the withdrawal started the next day.

In the battle for Schmidt, the 112th Infantry Regiment suffered 167 killed, 232 captured, 431 missing (most later declared dead), 719 wounded, and 544 nonbattle casualties from frostbite and trenchfoot. The 28th Infantry Division and its attached units suffered a total of 6,200 casualties—one of the heaviest losses suffered by an American division in Europe during a single battle.

David T. Zabecki

Additional Reading
MacDonald, Charles B., *The Battle of the Huertgen Forest* (1963).
———, *The Siegfried Line Campaign* (1963).
MacDonald, Charles B., and Sidney T. Mathews, *Three Battles: Aranville, Altuzzo, and Schmidt* (1952).

Schweinfurt Air Raid (14 October 1943)

[See map 20 on page 1330]

Launched on 14 October 1943, the major air assault on Schweinfurt was part of the new Allied strategy to destroy the munitions plants and war production centers in Germany, and thereby gain control of the sky. After limited successes in the air war over Germany in 1942 and the first half of 1943, the U.S. Army Air Force (USAAF) in the summer of 1943 launched an all-out assault on German cities, regardless of losses. By early fall, American air groups were striking points deep in southern Germany.

Schweinfurt, located in south-central Germany and a center of the critical ball bearing manufacturing industry, offered an important strategic target. Germany's major producers of ball bearings, the industrial plants of Kugelfischer, VKF, Fichtel & Sachs, and Deutsche Star Kugelhalter, were concentrated there.

The first raid on Schweinfurt came on 17 August 1943. A force of 183 B-17s dropped 430 tons of high explosives. The damage inflicted on the productive capacity of the ball bearing plants was disappointing and the loss of Allied planes serious. Having outranged their escort, the bombers were subject to fierce German fighter attacks on their return flight to bases in Britain; thirty-six aircraft were shot down.

Preparations for the destruction of the Schweinfurt ball bearing industrial plants began on the afternoon of 13 October 1943. Led by Lieutenant General Frederick L. Anderson, discussions focused on the need for a second decisive and devastating assault. If successful, the air raid would

also strengthen the American strategy of daylight raids, destroy German attack planes, and eliminate a key element of Germany's wartime production.

The raid on Schweinfurt proceeded as planned with three bomber divisions—Air Task Forces 1, 2, and 3—proceeding by different routes. The 320 planes in the final assault began dropping their bombs at 1439 hours on 14 October and the last plane completed its run sixteen minutes later.

The damage done to the ball bearing plants appeared to be considerable, with production capability initially cut by an estimated 75 percent. At VKF, the administration building and a number of manufacturing structures were damaged and left in flames; its assembly and manufacturing facilities almost completely destroyed. Several dozen employees were wounded. The destruction at Kugelfischer also appeared extensive, particularly at the generator and manufacturing plants buildings. The Fichtel & Sachs plant sustained 101 direct hits from American bombs, causing heavy damage to the administration building, warehouse, and various manufacturing structures. The warehouse at Deutsche Star Kugelhalter was also destroyed and a number of buildings damaged. Most of the bombs hit their targets during the raid, and relatively few bombs fell in the city itself.

USAAF leaders were initially convinced that Schweinfurt's industrial capacity had been decimated. While the estimates of destruction proved far too optimistic, postwar testimony of Albert Speer (q.v.), German minister of munitions, and other industrial leaders showed that German concern was deep-seated.

On the return flight to their bases in Britain, the three air task forces followed roughly the same route over northern France. German fighter planes from the 7th *Fliegerdivision* immediately pursued the returning bomber force, concentrating on the planes of Air Task Force 3. The German fighters shot down sixty B-17s, five more planes crashed in Britain, and fifteen were damaged beyond repair. Of the 291 planes used in the raid, eighty went out of service. The German defenders, however, lost 288 planes. The damage to the Allied air fleet meant that another raid against this crucial war industry had to wait for weeks.

Of the sixteen air raids on Schweinfurt during the war, the 14 October attack was the most important. It caused the most damage, the greatest interference with production, and, in fact, led to a reorganization of the German ball bearing industry. With ball bearing manufacturing concentrated in only a few locations, additional raids might well have devastated the industry.

The Eighth Air Force did not hit Schweinfurt for another four months. The 14 October mission demonstrated the high cost of penetrating the *Reich* by daylight without fighter escorts. Too many bombers were lost, and it was clear that long-range fighter escorts were essential.

Robert G. Waite

Additional Reading

Cadin, Martin, *Black Thursday: The Raid on Schweinfurt* (1960).
Coffey, Thomas M., *Decision over Schweinfurt: The U.S. Eighth Air Force Battle for Daylight Bombing* (1977).
Jablonski, Edward, *Double Strike: The Epic Air Raids on Regensburg/Schweinfurt* (1974).

SEA LION, Operation (Summer 1940)

Operation SEA LION (SEELÖWE), the aborted German plan to invade Britain in late summer 1940, is one of the best illustrations of Adolf Hitler's (q.v.) lack of long-range planning. Prior to the outbreak of the war, neither he nor the German high command seriously considered a landing in Great Britain. In May 1939, both determined that there was no need to invade; instead, Germany would rely upon an air and submarine blockade of Britain in the event of war. In mid-October 1939, after the Poland (q.v.) campaign, Grand Admiral Erich Raeder (q.v.) ordered plans to secure bases on the North Sea from which Germany could launch air and naval attacks against Britain. Those plans were initiated with the invasions of Denmark and Norway (qq.v.) on 9 April 1940.

Prior to the summer of 1940, official German military policy toward Britain was little different from that of World War I. That changed with France's sudden and dramatic collapse. Although the *Oberkommando der Kriegsmarine* (Naval High Command or OKM) and the *Oberkommando des Heeres* (Army High Command or OKH) began separate preliminary studies in late 1939 for a possible invasion of the British Isles, these were still in the developmental stages. The exception was the decision to invade southern Holland so that the Dutch estuaries could be used as a staging area for a possible invasion fleet.

Hitler was convinced that Great Britain would sue for peace once its French ally was eliminated. On 21 May 1940, he nevertheless authorized Raeder to begin preliminary preparations for an invasion. From the outset, the *Kriegsmarine* made it clear that any invasion would require

German air supremacy to prevent the Royal Air Force (RAF) and Royal Navy (RN) from interfering with the assembly and passage of German transport vessels.

With preconditions for success firmly stipulated, the *Kriegsmarine* proceeded rapidly with preparations. Since it had largely ignored amphibious warfare before the war, it had no landing craft. Moreover, the *Kriegsmarine* had limited the efforts of the German Army's *Wasser-Pionieren* (water engineers) to obtain any before the war. As a result, amphibious assault ships had to be improvised from available resources. In June 1940, the OKM began to inventory all available ships in both Germany and German-occupied areas. The OKM's Merchant Shipping Division requisitioned approximately 2,000 Rhine River barges as well as tugboats and other light seagoing craft. All these vessels had to be installed with ramps, and because many barges had no engines, more than 250 tugboats and 1,300 motor boats were acquired to pull them across the Channel.

By 14 June, only forty-five seaworthy barges were available for deployment and the *Kriegsmarine* estimated another fourteen weeks would be required before all landing craft were assembled and properly equipped. Meanwhile, the OKH developed schemes for special invasion craft. One, dubbed the "War Crocodile," was an amphibious ferro-concrete vessel ninety feet long, twenty feet wide, twelve feet high, and capable of carrying 200 men. More successful were amphibious and submersible tanks equipped with periscopes and air intakes (*see* Tanks, Special).

On 2 July, Hitler ordered the three service branches to coordinate their planning, and on 16 July, he issued *Führer* Directive 16, approving the army's plan, Operation SEA LION, for a surprise landing along a broad front between Ramsgate and Lyme Bay. Although OKH's plan was approved, the OKM raised sharp objections. On 17 July, Raeder declared that the *Kriegsmarine* simply did not possess the strength to carry out the army's plan. It had to convert vessels for landing troops on beaches, clear the landing area of mines, and lay mines along both flanks of the crossing to prevent the Royal Navy from interfering. Raeder informed Hitler that the *Kriegsmarine* could not complete these tasks before the end of August and that, in the best of circumstances, it would not be ready to execute Operation SEA LION until 15 September.

The gravest difference between the OKH and OKM centered on the extent of the landing front. The army demanded a broad front between Ramsgate and Lyme Bay, while the navy argued that its limited resources allowed for only a narrow front between Folkestone and Beachy Head. The army was not alone in its dispute with the navy. The *Luftwaffe* also disagreed with the OKM over the number of aircraft assigned to the supporting deception plan. When Hitler accepted the OKM's limited plan on 27 August, the OKH argued that a landing should take place only as a coup de grace once Britain had already been defeated from the air.

From the outset Operation SEA LION hinged on the successful conclusion of the Battle of Britain (q.v.). Both the OKH and OKM agreed that the *Luftwaffe* must have absolute command of the air before any invasion could go forward. On 1 August, Hitler issued *Führer* Directive 17, for the combined air and sea campaign against Britain. The air war, however, quickly developed a life of its own.

Overestimating the damage done to the RAF and to British industry, Hitler came to see the strategic bombing offensive as an end in itself. The *Luftwaffe* was ordered to concentrate on bombing industry and London. This decision gave the British fighter defenses time to recover and allowed the RAF to escalate its attacks on the Channel ports where the German Navy had assembled transport vessels for Operation SEA LION.

By 17 September, it was clear that the *Luftwaffe* had failed to establish air supremacy, forcing Hitler to postpone Operation SEA LION until further notice. On 12 October SEA LION was deferred until the spring of 1941. It never took place, of course, and on 13 February 1942 SEA LION was finally formally canceled.

After the initial postponement of SEA LION, Hitler turned his attention to the Soviet Union. As early as 31 July, Hitler had declared, "If Russia is smashed, Britain's last hope will be shattered." Operation SEA LION thus was shelved in favor of Operation BARBAROSSA, which Hitler hoped would indirectly force Britain to come to terms with Germany. It was a major mistake that led Germany into the very two-front war that Hitler had blamed for Germany's defeat in 1918.

Justin D. Murphy

Additional Reading
Ansel, Walter, *Hitler Confronts England* (1960).
Fleming, Peter, *Operation Sea Lion* (1956).
Schenk, Peter, *Operation Sea Lion* (1989).
Wheatley, Ronald, *Operation Sea Lion: German Plans for the Invasion of England, 1939–1942* (1958).

Sevastopol (7 June–4 July 1942)

[See map 11 on page 1321]

Sevastopol, the huge harbor and fortress on the Crimea, was one of the first objectives in the German summer offensive of 1942. Like the reduction of the Izyum Salient and the clearing of the Kerch sub-peninsula, the Germans considered the capture of Sevastopol a prerequisite for Operation *BLAU*.

The objective held both strategic and operational importance for the German war effort. With Crimea completely in German hands, Adolf Hitler (q.v.) hoped to draw neutral Turkey into an alliance against the Soviet Union. Also, without the use of air bases on the peninsula, the Soviet Air Force was unable to strike the Romanian oil fields at Ploeşti. The oil from there was critical to the German war machine. From an operational point of view, a German-controlled Crimea would ease the supply problems of Army Group South by blocking the Soviet Navy from the major portion of the Black Sea.

The Soviets, in anticipation of an attack, transformed Sevastopol into one of the strongest fortresses in the world. To the north of the port, the defenders established three defensive belts between the Belbek Valley and the Sewernaja Bay, the city's harbor. In addition to many small strongpoints, trenches, and minefields, the northern sector was fortified with huge concrete bunkers armed with artillery up to 305mm. East of the city the spurs of the Jaila Mountains, covered with thick scrub, offered superb natural obstacles. The terrain south of the city was very mountainous, and the Soviets built their machine gun emplacements right into the rocks. Behind the eastern and southern sectors, the Soviets prepared a second defensive belt, which started at the end of the bay, followed the steep Sapun heights, and ran southward to Fort Maxim Gorky on the coast. Two more defensive rings around the actual town, and the separately fortified Chersones sub-peninsula in the west completed Sevastopol's formidable defenses.

In combat strength the opponents were about evenly matched. The overall command of Sevastopol rested with Vice Admiral F.S. Oktyabrsky. His major combat force was Lieutenant General I.E. Petrov's (q.v.) Coastal Army, which had been evacuated from Odessa the previous October. It had seven rifle divisions, a dismounted cavalry division, and three naval infantry brigades, for a total of about 106,000 troops.

General Erich von Manstein's (q.v.) Eleventh Army, with its three-division XLII *Korps* committed to the Kerch sub-peninsula in the east, could concentrate eight German and two Romanian divisions against Sevastopol. Neither side had any significant numbers of tanks, although von Manstein had some assault gun units. Both sides had ample artillery. The Soviets had about 600 guns, and the Germans had about 700, including the monstrous 800mm "Dora," the largest gun ever constructed (*see* Artillery, Railway). In the air, General Wolfram von Richthofen's (q.v.) VIII *Fliegerkorps* had overwhelming superiority.

After four days of artillery and aerial bombardment, the first phase of the German attack started on the morning of 7 June 1942. The main effort was made in the north by the LXIV *Korps*. The well-prepared defenses and stiff resistance of the Soviets made the German progress painfully slow. It was not until 13 June that the 22nd Division captured Fort Stalin. The Romanian Mountain Corps in the center spent most of the first phase covering the LXIV *Korps'* left flank. In the south, the XXX *Korps* started its attack on 11 June and after stiff opposition, broke through the Soviets' first line.

Von Manstein regrouped his forces and started the second phase of the attack on 17 June. To the Soviets' surprise, the XXX *Korps* turned westward and reduced Fort Maxim Gorky I, the strongest fort in the north. By 19 June, they reached the bay. Meanwhile the XXX *Korps* attacked along the major road in the south leading into the city. By 26 June, the Eleventh Army controlled most of Sevastopol's outer defenses, except for the Sapun heights; but after nineteen days of fighting, the German troops were near exhaustion.

Time was starting to run out for von Manstein. The German Army high command threatened to pull the VIII *Fliegerkorps* from Crimea if von Manstein did not accomplish his objective within a few days. Without *Luftwaffe* support, von Manstein knew that victory would be impossible. Thus he decided to take a risk. On 28 June, he sent the 22nd and 24th Divisions across the bay in assault boats to outflank the Sapun heights. The operation was a complete success, and the XXX *Korps* captured the heights three days later.

The Soviet defense crumbled. Remnants of the Coastal Army withdrew west to the Chersones sub-peninsula, where the fighting ended on 4 July. Oktyabrsky and Petrov left Sevastopol on one of the last planes out. During the battles, thousands of Soviet civilians and wounded soldiers had taken shelter in the large caves under the overhanging cliffs along Sewernaja Bay. When the Germans tried to clear the caves, some of them were blown up by the Soviet commissars in charge, burying attackers, defenders, and civilians.

The Germans captured 90,000 prisoners and 460 guns at Sevastopol. In exchange, they suffered 24,000 casualties. Soon after Sevastopol fell, Hitler transferred the bulk of the Eleventh Army north to the Leningrad (q.v.) sector. Later that year, the Germans would sorely miss this strong and experienced field army in the south.

Reiner Martin

Additional Reading
Manstein, Erich von, *Lost Victories* (1958).
Ziemke, Earl F., and Magna E. Bauer, *Moscow to Stalingrad: Decision in the East* (1987).

Sicily (10 July–17 August 1943)

[See map 33 on page 1343]
On 10 July 1943, American and British forces launched Operation HUSKY, the invasion of Sicily. It was the first major opposed amphibious operation since Gallipoli, and its seven-division initial assault echelon made it modern history's largest amphibious assault. The Allies met weaker resistance than they expected, and caused the German and Italian forces to evacuate the island after little more than a month of fighting.

The Americans and British had discussed two basic courses of strategic action at the Casablanca Conference in January 1943 (*see* Conferences, Allied). The alternatives were to avoid land combat with Axis powers or to invade Sardinia, Sicily, Italy, Greece, or the Dodecanese Islands. While General George C. Marshall (q.v.) expressed his satisfaction with the idea of avoiding combat in order to prepare for Operation ROUNDUP (as the projected cross-channel invasion of northwestern Europe was then called), the Allied heads of state rejected his proposal. The British favored action in the Balkans, but the Americans feared such a step would delay the cross-channel invasion. Few felt the Allies were strong enough to invade Italy directly, so the options narrowed to Sardinia and Sicily.

Sicily had several advantages. Its capture would make the Mediterranean safe for shipping, would engage and destroy more German divisions, would capture more and better airfields within bombing range of southern Italy, and might cause the Italian government to seek peace. A Sicily operation also would satisfy the Americans because it would save shipping, use troops already in the theater of operations, and provide a logical conclusion to the Mediterranean campaign (q.v.). The British agreed to Sicily because of the shipping consideration, and the possibility of eliminating Italy from the war. The Sicily option was compatible with the British objective weakening the Axis as best they could at the time.

The defenses of Sicily were tenuous. General Alfredo Guzzoni commanded the Italian Sixth Army, consisting of eight coastal divisions, four mobile divisions, and two German divisions—about 275,000 troops in all. The German units included the reliable 15th *Panzergrenadier* Division and the Hermann Göring *Panzer* Division. The training and staffing of the Italian divisions, however, was poor. Two battalions, in fact, were commanded by second lieutenants who retired in 1918 and only recently were recalled to active service. The Italian units were dispersed along the coast and offered an incoherent resistance at best.

The average density of forces in Sicily was forty-one men per mile. Field Marshal Albert Kesselring (q.v.), German commander in chief south, noted, "the defense forces at our disposal were quite inadequate for even minimum demands." Faced with this situation, Benito Mussolini's (q.v.) guidance to the Italian chiefs of staff on 14 June admitted that the Italian forces were no longer capable of taking the initiative, and that a fierce counterattack was the only course of action in case of invasion. In suggesting that the Italian Army could even counterattack, Mussolini was at odds with his army chief, General Vittorio Ambrosio (q.v.).

Recognizing his lack of armored forces, Ambrosio favored what he called a "modern technique" of breaking up the landing on the beach, or even better, crushing the enemy while he was still at sea. According to his analysis, "It is all the more necessary to stop the attack on the beach before it can secure a foothold as, not having enough armor, we shall not be able to halt a well equipped adversary once he has landed and started to make his way inland." Kesselring agreed that the only hope was immediate counterattacks while the Allies were still trying to establish a beachhead. Thus, the four mobile divisions were dispersed as local reserves, instead of being concentrated as a central counterattack force.

At the Casablanca Conference, the Combined Chiefs of Staff (q.v.) selected General Dwight D. Eisenhower (q.v.) as the supreme commander for Operation HUSKY. Admiral Sir Andrew Cunningham would command the naval forces, and Air Chief Marshall Sir Arthur Tedder (qq.v.) would command the air forces. General Sir Harold Alexander (q.v.) would command the ground force, Fifteenth Army Group, consisting of Lieutenant General George S. Patton's Seventh Army

and General Sir Bernard L. Montgomery's (qq.v.) Eighth Army.

Eisenhower's staff immediately began to plan Operation HUSKY. Unfortunately, all the operation's principal commanders were currently fighting in Tunisia (q.v.) and could not participate in the planning. The planners considered control of the sea, control of the air, and the quick seizure of port facilities to be critical to success. Because of the supremacy of the Royal Navy (RN) in the Mediterranean, the first requirement posed no problem. Air superiority also posed little problem, with 3,700 Allied aircraft facing 1,400 of the Axis. Allied fighters, however, would be operating at extended range, so seizure of Sicily's thirty airfields was important. The staff planners estimated that sustaining the operation would require a daily port capacity of 6,000 tons. Thus, the seizure of port facilities was critical.

To accomplish the seizure of airfields and port facilities the planners proposed two simultaneous assaults on the island, one in the west and one on the southeast. When Montgomery learned of the plan he objected. Writing to Alexander on 24 April, he pointed out that all the planning was based on the assumption of light resistance. Montgomery insisted the Allies should plan on fierce resistance from the Germans at the least. He wanted his own force strengthened by another division. He also recommended eliminating the proposed landings in the Gela-Licata area, which would give him a stronger and more unified landing. That would preclude seizing some of the airfields, but he did not believe he could hold what initially was required under the original plan anyway.

Both Tedder and Cunningham disagreed with Montgomery. Even though Alexander recognized the validity of air and naval arguments, he nonetheless accepted Montgomery's plan "from a purely military point of view." The modified plan called for landings on either side of Cape Passero, with the British on the east side, and the Americans on the west side. That plan enabled Montgomery and Patton to provide mutual support in case either ran into trouble. Patton's first objectives would be Scoglitti, Gela, and Licata. That allowed Montgomery to shift his left flank objective from the Gela area to the center of Cape Passero. Montgomery's attack up the eastern coast would be the Allies' main effort, with Patton covering the left flank and rear.

On 9 July, an armada of 2,590 vessels rendezvoused in the central Mediterranean. The total assault force consisted of 160,000 troops, 600 tanks, 1,800 guns, and 14,000 vehicles. Admiral Sir Bertram Ramsay (q.v.) was in command of the landings. At 0245 hours on 10 July, the ships reached their debarkation points without incident, but the landings suffered from problems typical of a nighttime operation conducted in high winds and sea swell. Ships lowered the landing craft too far out at sea. Boat waves formed late and many boats missed their assigned beaches, became stuck on sandbars, or capsized in the surf.

Nonetheless, the landings were successful, largely because there was almost no resistance from the Italian coastal divisions. Montgomery, for example, occupied the harbors at Syracuse and Augusta without a shot being fired. Kesselring, observing that "one disappointment followed another," wondered whether the Italians were guilty of "cowardice or treachery?"

Both Montgomery and Patton elected to precede their landings with airborne assaults. The U.S. 82nd Airborne Division's 505th Parachute Infantry Regiment and the Airlanding Brigade of the British 1st Airborne Division attacked fifteen minutes before the beach landings, but problems with the air force caused neither to be very effective. Only one-eighth of the 226 planeloads of 505th paratroopers landed on their assigned drop zones, and only twelve of the 137 British gliders landed near their objectives.

At 0600 hours on 11 July, Guzzoni launched a coordinated counterattack with the *Livorno* and Herman Göring *Panzer* Divisions. By noon, German tanks were within 2,000 meters of the beach and firing on unloading parties. Determined Allied resistance and massive naval gunfire forced Axis units to withdraw after losing one-third of their tanks. That night Patton ordered the remainder of the 82nd Airborne Division to deploy from its staging area near Tunis and drop onto the beaches to reinforce the Seventh Army.

As the 144 transport aircraft made their approach in the dark, they passed over the Allied fleet, which less than an hour earlier had been attacked by the *Luftwaffe*. Allied antiaircraft guns on both ship and shore mistakenly opened fire on their own planes. Some of the transports turned back. Of those that continued on, six were shot down before dropping their paratroopers. Seventeen others were shot down on the return trip, and thirty-seven were badly damaged. It was one of the Allies' worst friendly fire incidents of the war.

On 12 July, Guzzoni began a slow, systematic withdrawal to the San Stefano Line. His ultimate intention was to evacuate Sicily after delaying the Allies as much as possible. Still reeling from losses

in Stalingrad (q.v.) and Tunisia, Adolf Hitler (q.v.) did not issue his usual hold-at-all-costs order.

Montgomery's attack up Sicily's eastern coast progressed more slowly than Alexander had hoped. On 17 July, Patton offered a plan for his Seventh Army to overrun western Sicily and capture the port of Palermo. Alexander approved and by 22 July, Patton entered Palermo. The following day, he captured the western tip of Sicily. From there, the Seventh Army launched its own drive for Messina across the northern end of the island.

On 26 July, the King Victor Emmanuel III (q.v.), responding to the war-weariness of his people, placed Mussolini under arrest. With this unstable political situation in his rear, Kesselring ordered the evacuation of Sicily. The withdrawal was a masterpiece on the order of Dunkirk (q.v.). The Germans delayed first on the San Stefano Line, then the San Fratello Line, and then the Tortorici Line. Along the north coast of the island, Patton's forces systematically outflanked the Axis defenses with a series of amphibious "end runs." On 11 August, the Germans started the actual crossing from Sicily to Italy across the Straits of Messina.

The Allies did little to hinder them. Eisenhower assumed the bulk of the crossings would take place at night, and deployed his air forces accordingly. Actually, most of the crossings took place during the day under heavy air defense cover. By 17 August, the Germans had successfully evacuated 39,569 German troops, some 62,000 Italians, 9,605 vehicles, forty-seven tanks, ninety-four guns, 1,100 tons of ammunition, and 970 tons of fuel. Despite the evacuations, the Sicily campaign cost the Axis about 31,000 casualties, plus 7,000 Germans and 140,000 Italians captured. Allied losses were about 7,000 killed and 15,000 wounded.

The key lessons from Sicily were those involving the defense against amphibious assaults. Kesselring concluded that naval gunfire made a linear defense useless. "Positions in depth," he wrote, "were an indispensable complement to coastal fortifications." Even more importantly, he recognized the need to hit the attacker when he was most vulnerable, while still at sea and unloading. In order to accomplish this, "local reserves must be so strong and so close that they could immediately equalize their own repulses." These were the same considerations that would face Field Marshal Erwin Rommel (q.v.) a year later on the French coast.

Kevin Dougherty

Additional Reading

D'Este, Carlo, *The Battle for Sicily, 1943* (1991).

Garland, Albert N., and Howard McGraw Smith, *Sicily and the Surrender of Italy* (1965).
Jackson, W.F.G., *The Battle for Italy* (1967).
Kesselring, Albert, *Kesselring: A Soldier's Record* (1954).
Morison, Samuel Eliot, *Sicily-Salerno-Anzio* (1964).

SICKLE, Operation (1942)

SICKLE was the code name for the buildup of U.S. air forces in Britain during 1942. It took place at the same time as Operation BOLERO (q.v.), the buildup of U.S. ground forces in Britain in preparation for either Operations ROUNDUP or SLEDGEHAMMER, the cross-channel attack. Neither of those operations took place and the ultimate cross-channel invasion was Operation OVERLORD on 6 June 1944.

In meetings between the United States and Great Britain from January to March 1941, a plan for overall mutual strategy in the event that the U.S. entered the war was negotiated. These plans were known as ABC-1 and were released on 27 March, the same day the U.S. Congress appropriated $7 billion for Lend-Lease (q.v.).

The ABC-1 plans were general in nature and had to be further refined for operational use. On 29 March, the ABC-2 Report was released, calling for the increase in aircraft production necessary in order to have enough planes to increase the size of the U.S. Army Air Corps to fifty-four air groups. In the event of the fall of Great Britain, an increase to 100 air groups would be required. Additional aircraft production was also required to supply aircraft requested by other nations under Lend-Lease. The ABC-2 Report was revised several times to show a required high of 270 air groups by December 1943.

In April 1941, the joint U.S. Army-Navy Board finalized a plan code named RAINBOW 5, one of five war plans generic in nature, detailing actions to be taken against potential enemies. RAINBOW 5 detailed a war scenario in Europe that came closest to the strategy agreed upon by the U.S. and Britain in the ABC-1 plan. Part of the RAINBOW 5 strategy included a section on strategic bombing (q.v.). This laid the groundwork for the Air War Plans Division of the newly renamed U.S. Army Air Forces (USAAF) to develop its own war plan. President Franklin D. Roosevelt (q.v.) called for an estimate from the War Department of "overall production requirements required to defeat our potential enemies." The War Department submit-

ted its plan with an annex from the Air War Plans Division (AWPD). The annex was AWPD Document Number 1.

AWPD/1 outlined the four major missions of the U.S. Army Air Force (USAAF): (1) "to conduct a sustained and unremitting air offensive against Germany and Italy"; (2) "to provide close and direct air support of the surface forces"; (3) strategic defense against Japan; and (4) the defense of the Western Hemisphere. AWPD/1 also called for basing fifty-two U.S. air groups in Great Britain (Task Force BR) and in Northern Ireland (Task Force MAGNET).

The AWPD/1 plan was formally adopted by Roosevelt and Prime Minister Winston S. Churchill (q.v.) during the Arcadia Conference on 13 January 1942 (see Conferences, Allied). The agreement was that "the movement of U.S. Army Air Forces to the United Kingdom should proceed as soon as forces and shipping become available." Major General Carl Spaatz (q.v.), commanding general of Air Force Combat Command, was chosen to supervise the buildup and subsequently to command USAAF in Britain. The U.S. Eighth Air Force was activated in January 1942, with Brigadier General Ira Eaker (q.v.) as head of the VIII Bomber Command.

Soon after the Arcadia Conference, the combined U.S. and British staff planners developed a set of war plans for potential operations in the European theater. In addition to Operations BOLERO and SICKLE, Operation ROUNDUP was an invasion of France planned for Spring 1943. Operation SLEDGEHAMMER was an emergency landing in France should the Soviet Union be on the brink of surrender, or in case the German Army displayed signs of weakness that would make the success of an early invasion likely. Although modified somewhat due to changes not anticipated at inception, AWPD/1 was largely the guideline used in the buildup of the U.S. air forces in Britain.

By June 1944, there were 127 U.S. airfields in Britain, 75 dedicated to bombers. There also were 10,343 U.S. aircraft in the European Theater of Operations, with the USAAF totaling 109 air groups in theater.

Randy MacDonald

Additional Reading

Freeman, Roger A., *The Mighty Eighth: Units, Men, and Machines: A History of the U.S. Eighth Army Air Force* (1970).
Steele, Richard W., *The First Offensive Plan* (1973).

Sidi Barrani (9–12 December 1940)

Sidi Barrani was Britain's first major land victory of the war and it initiated the 1940–1943 struggle for North Africa (q.v.). Libyan forces were so crushed along the Egyptian border that they abandoned all Cyrenaica (eastern Libya). Without full exploitation, however, Britain's victory was soon reversed.

Shortly after Italy entered the war in June 1940, Benito Mussolini (q.v.) ordered an attack on Egypt without delay. The cautious Italian Tenth Army commander, Marshal Rodolfo Graziani (q.v.), delayed, believing his nearly 300,000 troops were inadequately trained, poorly equipped, and often low in morale. On 19 August, Mussolini again demanded action. Finally, on 13 September, more than six Italian divisions crossed the border; but after fifty miles they halted unexpectedly near Sidi Barrani.

For several months, Graziani stockpiled supplies, constructed fortified camps south into the desert, and prepared for his next advance into Egypt. His hesitancy reflected exaggerated estimates of British strength. He was confident about his defensive arrangements; but the distances between the Italian strongpoints prevented mutual support, the gaps were poorly patrolled, the reserves remained too far back, and supply shortages left minefield and artillery coverage incomplete.

In late October 1940, British Mideast commander in chief General Archibald Wavell (q.v.) ordered action by General Richard O'Connor's (q.v.) Western Desert Force (which later became the Eighth Army). O'Connor's forces consisted of the 7th Armoured Division ("The Desert Rats"), the Indian 4th Division, and the 7th Royal Tank Regiment, armed with Matilda tanks. Intended as a large-scale raid, O'Connor planned an armored strike through the desert flank behind the Italians, accompanied by a coastal attack. With 30,000 troops and 275 tanks of various models, he faced 80,000 Italian troops and 120 light tanks.

Operation COMPASS began late on 7 December. Advancing from Mersa Matrúh, the main attack force moved thirty miles that night, and forty miles the following night, arriving undetected at concentration point "Piccadilly." Attacking early on 9 December in an unguarded area, the Indian 4th Division moved northwest to take the strong Nibeiwa-Tummar positions from the Libyan 2nd Division, then it headed north to Sidi Barrani. The 7th Armoured Division went west behind the Rabia-Sofafi position of the Italian *Cirene* Division, before swinging north to Buqbuq.

On 10 December, both drives reached the coast. Meanwhile, "Selby Force" attacked the

Hundreds of Italian prisoners being marched away after being captured at Sidi Barrani. Photograph taken on 16 December 1940. (IWM E 1378)

Maktila positions of the Libyan 1st Division and Sidi Barrani, aided by Royal Navy gunfire support. By 12 December, the Italians were driven from Egypt having lost 39,000 prisoners and about 400 guns. The British suffered only 600 casualties.

Just inside Libya, the retreating Italians crowded into the coastal fortress of Bardia. The British high command, however, hampered O'Connor's ability to exploit the situation by pulling the Indian 4th Division back into Egypt for further deployment to Sudan. The move took place right after the fall of Sidi Barrani, weeks before the replacement force, the Australian 6th Division, arrived from Palestine. As British military historian Sir Basil Liddel Hart (q.v.) noted: "Thus on 11 December, the third day of the battle, the routed Italians were running westwards in panic while half the victor's force was marching eastwards—back to back! It was a strange spectacle, that entailed a fateful delay."

After the unnecessary three-week delay, O'Connor pursued the Italians into Libya and attacked at Bardia (q.v.) on 3 January 1941.

Richard Wires

Additional Reading

Carver, Michael, *Dilemmas of the Desert War: A New Look at the Libyan Campaign, 1940–1942* (1986).

Jackson, W.G.F., *The North African Campaign, 1940–1943* (1975).

Liddell Hart, Basil, *History of the Second World War* (1970).

Moorehead, Alan, *The March to Tunis: The North African War, 1940–1943* (1965).

Sidi Rezegh (18 November–7 December 1941)

Sidi Rezegh was the key battle in Britain's Operation CRUSADER to regain supremacy in North Africa. For more than two weeks, fighting at the escarpment and airfield southeast of Tobruk raged intensely with repeated tank clashes and shifting control of key terrain. Despite the Axis forces' initial success, the British managed to prevail in the end. They failed, however, to achieve the destruction of General Erwin Rommel's (q.v.) Axis forces but they did lift his eight-month siege of Tobruk (*see* Tobruk II).

The British were numerically superior. General Alan Cunningham's (q.v.) Eighth Army had 118,000 troops and 580 tanks, against 100,000 Axis troops and 400 tanks of various models in eight Italian and three German divisions. For the seventy-mile advance from Egypt to Tobruk, Cunningham split his troops and tanks between two corps. Lieutenant General C.W.N. Norrie's XXX Corps, which consisted of the 7th Armoured Division, the 4th and 22nd Armoured Brigades, and the 1st and 2nd South African Divisions, was to advance through the desert from Maddalena to reach Gabr Saleh, where the British expected Rommel to rush his armor into defeat. XXX Corps would then drive westward to Sidi Rezegh, where forces breaking out from Tobruk would make contact.

Lieutenant General A.R. Godwin-Austen's XIII Corps, consisting of the New Zealand Division, the Indian 4th Division, and the 1st Army Tank Brigade, was to advance in the north, outflanking and isolating Axis border posts and then move west toward the Tobruk enclave. Concern over the twenty-mile gap between the two corps, which widened as XXX Corps moved westward, led to an even greater dispersal of the tank units into smaller formations. Loose control of the armored units further undermined their effectiveness.

Rommel upset British plans because he had plans of his own to attack Tobruk on 21 November. Under Rommel, General Ludwig Crüwell now headed the restructured *Afrika Korps* (q.v.), which consisted of the 15th and 21st *Panzer* Divisions, and new *Afrika* Division. Rommel still had formidable advantages over the British. His armor and his 88mm antitank guns had greater firepower, his units' composition allowed greater independence and flexibility, and his *Panzers* sat between Britain's two separate corps. Especially important was Rommel's ability to throw his tanks against the small individual elements of Cunningham's badly fragmented armor. With the German *Panzers* positioned around Gambut in the north, Italy's mobile forces held the desert near Bir el Gobi, while the Italian XXI Corps waited to attack Tobruk.

XXX Corps' three-pronged desert attack on 18 November had the advantage of surprise, and on 19 November, lead tanks of the 7th Armoured Brigade reached the airfield at Sidi Rezegh, twelve miles from the perimeter at Tobruk. The 7th Armoured Brigade was alone, however, because both of the flank columns ran into problems. The 4th Armoured Brigade on the right was severely mauled by the 21st *Panzer* Division, and 22nd Armoured Brigade on the left encountered the *Ariete* Division's punishing gunfire at Bir el Gobi. After losing a quarter of its tanks, the 22nd Armoured Brigade then raced to help the 4th Armoured Brigade, instead of advancing to the airfield. During 20–21 November, the 7th Armoured Brigade nonetheless gained ground from the Axis units at Sidi Rezegh.

Meanwhile, the troops of the Tobruk garrison attacked the Italians encircling them. The *Afrika* Division (later renamed the 90th Light Division) stopped them with guns emplaced on high ground. Rommel shifted his *Panzer* divisions to Sidi Rezegh. The subsequent fighting left the British with enormous tank losses. Only the belated arrival of the weakened 22nd and 4th Armoured Brigades on 21–22 November and Axis refueling problems provided relief. On mid-day of 22 No-

vember, the 21st *Panzer* Division overran the Sidi Rezegh airfield in the face of uncoordinated British defenses. The day's fighting left the British with fewer than fifty operating tanks. Exacerbating their troubles, at dusk the 15th *Panzer* Division captured the 4th Armoured Brigade's headquarters, together with many of its tanks.

On 23 November, Rommel struck with all his armor and motorized units—the Italians from the south, the Germans from the east—producing fierce but confusing fighting as the hard-pressed British struggled to hold their positions. By afternoon, the British positions were ringed and penetrated. Evening found both sides exhausted. The British lost more tanks and 3,000 prisoners, the Germans lost nearly half their remaining 160 tanks. Some historians have criticized the Axis' costly attack when they had no tank reserves. The results of 23 November, however, were a sweeping Axis success; but the veterans of the *Afrika Korps* referred to that day as *Totensonntag* (the Sunday of the Dead).

Then the situation slowly started changing. Believing XXX Corps' armor fatally crippled, Rommel on 24 November led his two *Panzer* divisions east toward Egypt, gambling on paralyzing the British rear areas. During the move, known as Rommel's "dash to the wire," he missed the opportunity to wipe out the remnants of XXX Corps and he failed to rout his opponents.

In the absence of the Axis armor between 24–29 November, the British units recovered somewhat. During the earlier period of confused fighting, Cunningham wanted to withdraw. The British commander in chief in the Middle East, General Claude Auchinleck (q.v.) relieved Cunningham late on 23 November and replaced him with Major General Neil Ritchie (q.v.). On 2 December, Rommel's armor returned westward to try to stop the XIII Corp's New Zealand Division advancing near the coast after linking up with Tobruk. XIII Corps thus eventually accomplished XXX Corps' mission.

The intense fighting around Sidi Rezegh continued into early December, showing clearly that Rommel's forces remained a formidable threat. Not until 8 December did the battle's last phase end when Rommel abandoned his investment of Tobruk. The British took Gazala on 17 December, Benghazi on 25 December, and El Agheila on 6 January. Operation CRUSADER cost the Allies 18,500 casualties, and the Axis 24,500, plus another 36,000 captured. Rommel was pushed back, but the British had insufficient reserves to exploit their success. Thus, only a few weeks later,

Rommel launched his second major drive to the east.

Richard Wires

Additional Reading

Agar-Hamilton, John A.I., and Leonard C.F. Turner (eds.), *The Sidi Rezegh Battles, 1941* (1957).

Crisp, Robert, *Brazen Chariots* (1960).

Lucas, James S., *Panzer Army Africa* (1978).

Siegfried Line Campaign (September 1944–February 1945)

[See map 34 on page 1344]

Meant as an answer to France's Maginot Line (q.v.), the West Wall (q.v.)—which the Allies called the Siegfried Line—was principally constructed between 1936 and 1938. The line consumed one-third of the total German cement production and the work of 500,000 men in 1938, but its value had eroded considerably by 1944. The 37mm antitank guns of the earlier period were obsolete by the time the Allies approached, and the guns needed to stop modern tanks did not fit into the small bunkers. Despite its weakened potential, however, the Siegfried Line was an obstacle that scared Allied planners.

The Siegfried Line was strongest around Aachen (q.v.), and this is precisely where the Americans first chose to breach the line. The U.S. 3rd Armored Division led the attack on 13 September 1944, covered by the 1st Infantry Division on the left and the 9th Infantry Division on the right. Initially, Major General J. Lawton Collins's (q.v.) VII Corps made good progress against the fresh 12th Infantry and the weak 116th *Panzer* Divisions guarding the city; but by 17 September, the 12th Infantry Division had fought the VII Corps to a standstill. That same day marked the beginning of Operation MARKET-GARDEN (*see* Arnhem). Allied attention shifted north, the opportunity at the Siegfried Line passed, and the Americans could not exploit their temporary advantage. The Germans used the ensuing pause to reorganize and strengthen their positions.

After the failure of MARKET-GARDEN, Lieutenant General Courtney Hodges's (q.v.) U.S. First Army returned to the control of General Omar N. Bradley's (q.v.) 12th Army Group. The Allies' offensive hopes rested on Hodges as he now prepared to attack the Siegfried Line and continue toward Düsseldorf, the industrial heart of the Ruhr. Hodges gave Major General Charles H. Corlett's XIX Corps the mission of taking Aachen.

Heavy rains delayed the start of the assault, and from the American's perspective weather would hamper the entire operation. Thorough preparations and rehearsals paid off, however, and Corlett initially made good progress, despite the German Seventh Army's reinforcing efforts and counterattacks. The defenders were fighting for the first major city in Germany threatened by the Allies. The Americans therefore experienced a new, tougher type of fighting. Although the XIX Corps and VII Corps completed the encirclement of Aachen on 16 October and captured the city on 21 October, it took the Americans nine days to advance the last five kilometers. Such a slow pace was unacceptable. Additionally, the 30th Infantry Division had suffered 3,100 casualties, mostly riflemen. Bradley relieved Corlett of his command.

If any portion of the Siegfried Line was suited more for defense and less for offense than the Aachen area, it was in the Hürtgen Forest (q.v.). There, just southeast of Aachen and guarded by two bands of the Siegfried Line, the U.S. 9th Infantry Division attacked on 6 October. Without air support and against defenders much better served by the terrain and roads, the 9th Infantry Division required ten days to go three kilometers. That token advance cost the division 4,500 casualties.

Hodges reacted by shifting unit boundaries. On 2 November, the 28th Infantry Division (Pennsylvania National Guard) attacked toward the town of Schmidt (q.v.), at the center of the Hürtgen Forest. The town was secured the next day, but on 4 November, the 116th *Panzer* Division, supported by the German 89th Infantry Division, recaptured it. The battle for the Kall River Valley, and specifically for its centerpiece, Schmidt, raged until 8 November. On that day General Dwight D. Eisenhower (q.v.), Bradley, and Hodges met and decided to pull the 28th Infantry Division out of the valley, but not before the division had lost 6,200 troops.

The 12th Army Group, meanwhile, readied Operation QUEEN, a concerted effort to pierce the Siegfried Line and reach the Rhine River at Cologne. Arrayed to the north, the Ninth and First Armies would move on 5 November with ten divisions massed along a thirty-eight-kilometer front. Bradley, however, wanted to wait until General Bernard L. Montgomery's (q.v.) 21st Army Group returned control of two U.S. divisions. That, plus poor flying weather, delayed the attack until 16 November. The 12th Army Group's plan called for Lieutenant General George S. Patton's (q.v.) Third Army to begin a supporting attack farther south on 10 November. Anxious for action

somewhere, Bradley asked Patton to move up the date of his own attack. The Third Army's commander gladly obliged.

True to his word, Patton started his offensive on 9 November. He boasted that he would cover the sixty-five kilometers to the Siegfried Line in two days, but he failed to account for the stout resistance of the Metz (q.v.) garrison. It was two weeks before the Third Army's advance elements even closed on the German frontier and the Saar River. The first of Patton's divisions to break free of Metz, the 10th Armored Division, also was the first to reach the Siegfried Line. Northwest of Saarlautern, the 10th Armored Division ran into a combination of antitank ditches, pillboxes, and concrete "dragon's teeth" just beyond the river. The unit came to a complete halt. By 26 November, Major General Manton Eddy (q.v.) called off the assault in acknowledgment of the tremendous infantry casualties sustained by his U.S. XII Corps.

Southeast of Saarlautern, the 95th Infantry Division fought its way across the Saar River on 2 December. With the terrain and forts of Lorraine behind it, the Third Army now stood ready to enter the heart of the *Reich*. But the heavy combat of the previous three months put Patton's personnel status at 11,000 understrength. Hardest hit were the infantry units. Although U.S. intelligence optimistically noted the waning German strength, at that same time, Adolf Hitler (q.v.) was gathering all available forces for his Ardennes offensive (q.v.).

The Battle of the Bulge interrupted the assault on the Siegfried Line for over a month. In January 1945, when the Allies resumed their drive east, they decided to concentrate north of the Ruhr with Montgomery's 21st Army Group, leaving Bradley in a supporting role. The 12th Army Group was to attack where the Siegfried Line passed through the Eifel Mountains, in terrain much more difficult than the Allies had just experienced in the Ardennes. Bradley initially planned to launch Major General Matthew B. Ridgway's (q.v.) XVIII Airborne Corps on 28 January, followed the next day by the VIII Corps, and then the V Corps on 30 January. He held the VII Corps in reserve.

It took Ridgway's two lead divisions, the 1st Infantry Division and the 82nd Airborne Division, four days to reach the Siegfried Line. When they reached the line, however, they found it virtually undefended. The Ardennes offensive had consumed much of the remaining German strength; what survived was needed elsewhere. On the left, the V Corps made even better progress, easily moving through the fortifications, splitting the boundary between the Fifth *Panzer* Army and the

Fifteenth Army, and occupying positions behind the Roer River dams.

At that point, Montgomery declared he was finally ready to cross the Rhine by 8 February. The 12th Army Group continued limited attacks in support of Montgomery, but its own offensive toward the Eifel Mountains was officially called off. Although the 12th Army Group had penetrated the northern portion of the Siegfried Line and the German defenses were in disarray, the overall plan denied Bradley a decisive exploitation.

Bradley gave Patton permission to continue his "probing attacks." As usual, the Third Army commander gave these instructions a liberal interpretation, and on 4 February, he ordered the VIII Corps onto Prüm and the XII Corps to take Bitburg. Initially light resistance gave way to a tougher defense on 5 February. Poor flying weather during the next two days even permitted the Germans to launch limited counterattacks. They were unable to exploit the situation, however, and by 6 February, Patton felt confident enough to commit his reserve, the 11th Armored Division. By the day's end, the VIII Corps had torn an eighteen-kilometer gap in the Siegfried Line.

Immediate counterattacks were at the heart of the German defensive doctrine, and on the very next day, the veteran 2nd *Panzer* Division hit the VIII Corps. The issue hung in the balance for two days. The Germans committed reinforcements and adjusted their own unit boundaries. Ultimately, however, they did not have the strength to do more than delay the Americans.

To the south, Eddy's XII Corps had to contend with a swollen Sauer River and stubborn Siegfried Line defenses. The XII Corps created a series of small and unconnected bridgeheads across the Sauer on 9 February. By 12 February, Eddy consolidated these into a considerable threat to the southern wing of the Siegfried Line. Two weeks later, the 5th Infantry Division conducted a night crossing of the Prüm River and captured Bitburg on 26 February. Now the Germans were levered out of the northern Siegfried Line, and Patton noticed the first cracks in German cohesion and discipline.

The opening phases of the Siegfried Line campaign were inconclusive. Shifting Allied priorities, specifically concerning Operation MARKET-GARDEN, provided the Germans with much needed breathing space. Likewise, American commanders consistently attacked the strongest sectors of the line, usually with predictable results. Both decisions played directly into the defenders' hands. Ultimately, Hitler's reckless squandering of Ger-

many's meager operational reserves during the Ardennes offensive eliminated any staying power left in the Siegfried Line. In the later phases of the campaign, once they recovered from the Ardennes, the Allies quickly put the Siegfried Line behind them.

Robert Kirchubel

Additional Reading

Homze, Edward L., *Foreign Labor in Nazi Germany* (1967).

MacDonald, Charles B., *The Siegfried Line Campaign* (1963).

MacDonald, Charles B., and Sidney Mathews, *Three Battles: Arnaville, Altuzzo, and Schmidt* (1952).

Weigley, Russell F., *Eisenhower's Lieutenants: The Campaigns of France and Germany, 1944–1945* (1981).

Sirte I (17 December 1941)

[See map 27 on page 1337]

As with so many of World War II's Mediterranean naval engagements, the first battle of Sirte centered around the efforts of the antagonists to deliver a vital supply convoy to their respective forces engaged ashore. In this instance, the Italian convoy was en route to North Africa. Their disastrous convoy losses of the previous two months gave this particular four-ship fuel convoy a vital importance for the Axis forces there. The same held true for the Royal Navy (RN), which was trying to deliver a single tanker, the SS *Breconshire,* to Malta, whose fuel situation was becoming critical.

Each side believed the other was tying to intercept its convoy, and they approached the battle from that perspective. As a result, both combat forces fought until the approaching darkness posed the risk of the other breaking off to attack the convoy. At that point, both forces withdrew. Since neither convoy was engaged, both sides interpreted the results of the battle as a victory.

The Italian force was larger. Their convoy was escorted by eight destroyers, which in turn were supported by a task force composed of elements of the Italian main battlefleet—four battleships, five heavy cruisers, and fourteen destroyers. All available Italian and German aircraft were also ordered in support. The Royal Navy force consisted of the *Breconshire*'s escort of seven destroyers, the antiaircraft cruiser HMS *Carlisle,* and two light cruisers. Both convoys departed port on 16 December; the Italians from Naples, and the British from Alexandria.

For once, the Axis had the intelligence advantage. Italian radio intercepts indicated that a British task force of three cruisers had departed Alexandria, and German reconnaissance aircraft tracked the force's westward progress. The *Luftwaffe,* pilots, however, misidentified the *Breconshire* as a battleship. The British only knew that the Italian battleships had departed Taranto. Neither side knew the other was escorting a convoy and, therefore, interpreted the movements of the other ships as an attempt to intercept. In addition to having superior force, the Italians were supported by the Italian Air Force, which started on mid-day 17 December to harass the British task group with high-level bombing and low-level torpedo plane attacks.

The Italian force was commanded by Admiral Angelo Iachino (q.v.), the commander of the Italian Navy. His British opponent was Rear Admiral Phillip Vian (q.v.), commander of Force B. The German U-boat threat and a lack of escorts prevented the commander of the British Mediterranean Fleet, Admiral Sir Andrew Cunningham (q.v.), from sending his available battleships in support.

Cunningham ordered Vian to dispatch the *Breconshire* to Malta and move north to engage the Italians. At the same time, he ordered Force K, a task group of two cruisers and four destroyers, to move out from Malta and escort the *Breconshire* into port. Italian cryptologists, meanwhile, decrypted a British submarine signal that reported the Italian convoy's movements to Cunningham's headquarters in Alexandria. Iachino, therefore, interpreted Vian's movements as a threat to his own convoy. Iachino detached his battleships to intercept Vian.

Force K rendezvoused with Vian on the morning of 17 December. Vian then moved north to engage the Italian task group, hoping to catch them just after sundown. His movements were delayed by the almost constant air attacks that plagued him throughout the day. Moreover, he received no information on the Italians' movements, while they had an almost running commentary on his. Luckily, Vian sustained virtually no damage from the Axis air attacks, but the constant harassment and lack of information on the Italian movements prevented him from detaching the *Breconshire* before nightfall. The Italians, on the other hand, saw only their own aircraft in the skies as they steamed southward. They therefore were able to maneuver their own convoy out of Vian's reach.

The two forces sighted each other at 1745 hours, just as the last Italian air attack of the day

was ending. Vian immediately ordered Force K and the *Breconshire* to the southwest, and then charged toward the Italians at flank speed. The Italian battleship *Littorio* opened fire eight minutes later, at a range of seventeen nautical miles. The Italian cruisers joined in five minutes after that.

Vian opened fire as his cruisers came in range. He ordered his destroyers in close to launch torpedoes, covering their movements with a smoke screen. Both sides exchanged fire without effect as the sun quickly slipped below the horizon. Iachino ordered his ships to cease-fire at 1804 hours and ordered his force to break away to the north. The danger to his own convoy was past and his ships were ill-equipped for a night engagement. Vian did not pursue because his primary mission, the protection of the *Breconshire,* precluded him from chasing the Italians too far. The engagement lasted only eleven minutes, and neither side suffered any damage in the process.

The first battle of Sirte seems inconsequential in the greater scheme of the Mediterranean campaign (q.v.). No significant losses or strategic results were suffered or achieved. The battle is noteworthy, however, for what it demonstrated. Given proper intelligence and air support, the Italians proved capable of aggressive action, but they were inhibited by their inability to engage in night combat. The RN's natural aggressiveness also was demonstrated. Both sides claimed victory, but the Italians could have and should have achieved more. Both their airpower and their gunnery were ineffective. In that respect, the first battle of Sirte stands as a microcosm of the Italian naval effort in the Mediterranean.

Carl O. Schuster

Additional Reading

Bragadin, Marc Antonio, *The Italian Navy in World War II* (1957).

Macintyre, Donald, *The Battle for the Mediterranean* (1964).

Pack, S.W.C., *The Battle of Sirte* (1975).

Sirte II (22 March 1942)

[See map 27 on page 1337]

The second battle of Sirte, on 22 March 1942 in the central Mediterranean, featured a classic convoy defense by Royal Navy (RN) warships against an Italian surface force. The victory gave a much needed boost to British morale but demonstrated the vulnerability of Malta's lifeline.

March 1942 found Malta (q.v.) in desperate need of supplies. During the previous winter, only

a few ships fought their way through the Axis air and naval forces that dominated the Mediterranean. Indeed, in February the last convoy to attempt passage was forced back to Alexandria, Egypt, after enemy aircraft caused the loss of two of four merchantmen. The Royal Navy's commander in chief in the Mediterranean, Admiral Sir Andrew Cunningham (q.v.), was determined to make the next attempt succeed.

On the morning of 20 March, a naval supply ship and three merchantmen departed Alexandria for Malta with an escort of one antiaircraft cruiser and six destroyers. Over the next two days, the escort was reinforced by the cruisers HMS *Cleopatra,* HMS *Dido,* HMS *Euryalus,* HMS *Penelope,* and ten destroyers. This strong, well-trained escort, virtually all the RN warships in the eastern Mediterranean, was commanded by Rear Admiral Philip Vian of *Altmark* (q.v.) fame.

The Army and Royal Air Force (RAF) also contributed. Fighters provided air cover for the first two days, and in an attempt to divert attention from the convoy, the British Eighth Army staged feints against *Luftwaffe* airfields in North Africa. Despite these measures, German aircraft detected the convoy on the evening of 21 March. Early the next morning, a British submarine patrolling off Taranto reported Italian warships heading south. These were the battleship *Littorio* and three destroyers, which were soon joined by three cruisers and four more destroyers. Admiral Angelo Iachino (q.v.) commanded the force. The convoy came under air attack early on 22 March. Approximately 150 German and Italian high-level and torpedo bombers attacked throughout the day, but effective antiaircraft defense and skillful evasive action prevented any hits.

Meanwhile, Iachino's force closed steadily, and at 1427 hours, his cruisers were sighted north of the convoy. Vian immediately implemented the tactics he had devised for such a confrontation. Five destroyers remained with the convoy while the cruisers and remaining destroyers laid smoke and headed toward the enemy. These tactics were aided by a strong southeast wind that held the smokescreens in place.

When British warships emerged from their smokescreen, the Italian cruisers turned away to northwest in an attempt to lure them into *Littorio*'s 380mm main guns. Vian was not fooled and turned back to the convoy before the battleship was sighted. The Italians regrouped, headed south, and sighted the convoy at 1630 hours. Iachino was determined to bar the route to Malta, or at least to force the convoy to make a longer southerly pas-

sage to expose it to further air attack the following morning. He altered course to the west and then southwest. Vian reacted by ordering the convoy southward and implementing the same tactics he used earlier. Sporadic fighting ensued over the next two and a half hours as both admirals sought to achieve their objectives.

The first engagement was typical of what followed. The HMS *Cleopatra* and HMS *Euryalus* exchanged fire with two Italian cruisers but turned back into the smoke when the *Littorio* joined the fray. The HMS *Dido,* HMS *Penelope,* and four destroyers then emerged from different points to continue the action. Several such engagements took place, but each time the Italians attempted to break through to the convoy, British warships blocked the way.

Unwilling to expose his warships to torpedoes, Iachino turned away. Dense smoke and increasingly high seas impaired shooting throughout the action, and although both sides scored hits, no significant damage resulted. Finally, at 1800 hours, Iachino achieved a good position to threaten the convoy, but torpedo attacks by the destroyers HMS *Jervis,* HMS *Kipling,* HMS *Kingston,* and HMS *Legion,* supported by Vian's cruisers, drove the Italians off for the last time. The second battle of Sirte was over.

Sirte II proved a hollow victory for the British. Vian's cruisers headed back to Alexandria the night of the battle and the convoy dispersed for the final run to Malta. German bombers renewed their attacks the next morning and sank two merchantmen within sight of their destination. The remaining two were destroyed in harbor, and only 5,000 of the 25,000 tons of supplies carried by the convoy were unloaded. In return, the Italians lost two destroyers that foundered during the voyage back to base. Although British morale received a shot in the arm, it was several more months before Malta was supplied on a regular basis.

Michael Whitby

Additional Reading

Bragadin, M.A., *The Italian Navy in World War Two* (1957).

Vian, Philip, *Action This Day* (1960).

Smolensk (4 July–6 August 1941)

[See map 35 on page 1345]

Before the battle of Minsk (q.v.) had come to an end, German Army Group Center started the second phase of its attack along the Minsk-Moscow axis. This thrust was directed against the key city of Smolensk, located 300 kilometers west of the Soviet capital and 600 kilometers east of the 1939 German-Soviet border. On 3 July, the Second *Panzer* Group of General Heinz Guderian (q.v.) and the Third *Panzer* Group of General Hermann Hoth (q.v.) were placed under the command of General Guenther von Kluge's (q.v.) newly formed Fourth *Panzer* Army. That force was supposed to break through the Soviet lines. The Soviet defenses were expected to be rather thin after their crushing defeat at Minsk. The Second *Panzer* Group was supposed to advance east along the Minsk-Moscow highway, with the Third *Panzer* Group moving along a parallel axis, farther to the north. In the area near Smolensk, the armored pincers would once again come together, forming a new pocket.

During these operations, the infantry units of Army Group Center, General Maximillian von Weichs's (q.v.) Second Army and General Adolf Strauss's Ninth Army, were still busy clearing the Minsk pocket, but they also had to capture the area between the Dvina and Dnieper Rivers. This area was known as the Orsa-Vitebsk land bridge. For this task, they were given seven infantry divisions as reinforcements from the reserves of the army high command (OKH).

General Semen Timoshenko (q.v.), commander of the Soviet Western Front (army group), had seven armies available to stop the German advance. In the first echelon, the Twenty-Second Army was in the north, flanked by Twentieth Army, Thirteenth Army, and Twenty-First Army in the south. Timoshenko's Fourth Army was in bad shape and in the process of retreating from Berezina. The Nineteenth and Sixteenth Armies were still moving up to the front and were not yet in position. Timoshenko's forces also suffered from a shortage of tanks and artillery.

When the operation started, the *Luftwaffe* still had clear air superiority, but initial *Panzer* thrusts lacked some of the momentum of earlier attacks. Several armored units were still engaged in cordoning the Minsk pocket, and this time the *Panzer* groups had to worry more about their flank security. Since Army Groups North and South were unable to keep pace with Field Marshal Fedor von Bock's (q.v.) Army Group Center, the farther he advanced the longer his exposed flanks grew. Moreover, Guderian's right flank was no longer naturally screened by the Pripet marshes. There also were tensions between *Panzer* group commanders and their new superior, von Kluge. With some justification, they regarded him as a watchdog sent by the German high command to keep them under control. The *Panzer* groups therefore advanced

more carefully on extended frontages, rather than attacking along narrow corridors. As Hoth put it, "More like the fingers of an outspread hand rather than a clenched fist."

Heavy rains turned the roads into rivers of mud, and determined Soviet resistance brought the left flank of Guderian's attack to a halt. After regrouping his forces, he resumed the attack farther to the south. On 10 and 11 July, his tanks crossed the Dnieper River near Orsha and Novy Bykhov and encircled elements of Thirteenth Army east of Mogilev. The XLVI *Panzer Korps* advanced to the Elnya heights, which the Germans saw as a potential staging point for the follow-on offensive toward Moscow.

To the north, Hoth centered his attack on Vitebsk, capturing the city on 9 July. Then he deployed the LVII *Panzer Korps* to the north near Velikiye Luki, while the XXXIX *Panzer Korps* continued the attack eastward. It passed Smolensk and on 16 July cut the Minsk-Moscow highway at Yartsevo. The most important supply line of the Soviet troops in the Smolensk area was cut and three field armies were almost completely encircled.

For more than a week the pocket remained open because of the gap between Smolensk and Yartsevo. The *Luftwaffe* tried to screen the gap but was only partially successful. An airborne operation would have been ideal for such a mission, but the Germans no longer considered making airborne assaults after suffering heavy losses in the battle of Crete (q.v.). According to German estimates, 100,000 Soviets escaped through the gap. Their retreat was accelerated by pressure from German infantry units advancing over the Orsha-Vitebsk land bridge—a serious tactical error on the German side.

The Soviets tried desperately to stop the German *Panzer* columns. Despite some local successes, like the recapture of Rogachev on 13 July, their efforts remained fruitless. Counterattacking units were too weak and most of their equipment was outdated. When the Germans finally closed the pocket, they faced fanatic and dogged resistance from the Soviet troops inside.

After the first phase of the battle, the *Stavka* (q.v.) formed five army groups by using new units and remnants of destroyed formations. The new fronts were ordered to attack German armored divisions and encircle them, thereby relieving pressure on the trapped Soviet troops near Smolensk. The Soviets had no success, but fierce breakout attempts kept German units busy well into August.

By the time the fight was over on 6 August, the Germans nearly doubled the number of prisoners taken by Army Group Center. The Red Army lost 3,200 tanks and nearly the same number of guns. Four Soviet field armies, the Thirteenth, Sixteenth, Nineteenth, and Twentieth, were completely or partially destroyed. In the central sector, the Germans had reached their objectives for the first phase of the Russian campaign and confidence ran high. The Germans, however, did suffer some heavy losses in men and equipment. Armored units in particular sustained heavy losses and were now well below their authorized strengths. They badly needed a rest. Even gasoline was starting to run short because of the *Wehrmacht*'s overextended supply lines.

After the battle of Smolensk, Army Group Center halted its advance for several weeks. According to the Soviet point of view, this was the result of their own defensive efforts around Smolensk. There may be some validity to this, but the main reason for the halt was a bitter struggle that had erupted within the German leadership over what the next primary objective should be—Moscow, Leningrad, or Kiev? The Soviets used this time well by restructuring their command and control system and reorganizing their forces into smaller units that were easier to handle. They also built up new and strong defenses in the area between Moscow and Smolensk.

Reiner Martin

Additional Reading

Erikson, John, *Stalin's War with Germany*, 2 vols. (1983).

Seaton, Albert, *The Russo-German War 1941–45* (1971).

Ziemke, Earl F., and Magna E. Bauer, *Moscow to Stalingrad: Decision in the East* (1987).

Sollum-Halfaya Pass (15–17 June 1941)
When Lieutenant General Erwin Rommel (q.v.) landed in Tripoli on 12 February 1941, his instructions from Adolf Hitler (q.v.) were to concentrate his newly arrived forces and use them as a backbone to stiffen the demoralized Italians. Hitler did not contemplate any offensive by the new *Afrika Korps* (q.v.) until the end of April. Even British Intelligence agreed with this assessment. Rommel, however, had his own ideas.

On 31 March, Rommel launched his first offensive against the British, who still had not recovered from the withdrawal of some of their best units, shipped off to fight in Greece. In Rommel's own words: "On the 31st of March our attack

moved forward against the British positions at Mersa el Brega, and a fierce engagement took place in the early hours of the morning with British reconnaissance troops." By 3 April, Rommel recaptured Benghazi, Libya. On 6 April, he scored a great coup when his forces captured General Richard O'Connor (q.v.), who typically had gone to the front to see the action for himself.

Rather than fight for Cyrenaica (the eastern province of Libya nearest the frontier of Egypt), British Middle East commander in chief General Sir Archibald Wavell (q.v.), decided to evacuate the hard-won territory, as he tried to trade space for time to meet Rommel's threat. On 9 April, the Australian garrison at Tobruk, under General Sir Leslie Morshead (q.v.) was ordered to hold out against the Germans no matter the cost (*see* Tobruk II). In Winston S. Churchill's (q.v.) words, Tobruk had to be held "to the death without thought of retirement."

Rommel quickly grasped the British situation: "the British apparently intended to avoid, in any circumstances, fighting a decisive action; so . . . I decided to stay on the heels of the retreating enemy and make a bid to seize the whole of Cyrenaica at one stroke." On 28 April, the *Afrika Korps* and its Italian allies, including the veteran *Ariete* Division, stood on the frontiers of British Egypt, only one month after Rommel had delivered his opening blow at Mersa el Brega.

The Imperial Expeditionary Force in Greece (q.v.), meanwhile, started evacuating that country on 29 April. With the *Afrika Korps* poised to push through the British defenses on the Egyptian border, Churchill announced the main objective was now "a victory in the Western Desert to destroy Rommel." Throughout the month of May, under increasing pressure from Churchill, Wavell tried desperately to formulate a counterattack to parry Rommel's impending assault into Egypt. Adding to Wavell's worries, ULTRA (q.v.) intelligence indicated that Rommel was in the process of being reinforced by the 15th *Panzer* Division.

On 15 May, Wavell ordered Operation BREVITY, commanded by Brigadier William Gott (q.v.), in an attempt to knock the Germans and Italians off balance. Using the 2nd Royal Tank Regiment, the Guards Brigade, and 4th Armoured Brigade as his main striking force, Gott hit along the frontier in a line running from Sollum to Halfaya Pass. Although the British scored early successes against the Italians at Halfaya Pass, Rommel quickly struck back. Faced with a strong attack by the *Afrika Korps' Panzers*, Gott executed a withdrawal that left only the Halfaya Pass in

British hands. On 27 May, Rommel launched a successful three-pronged attack on the Halfaya Pass. Gott was forced to retire, losing 160 tanks.

Gott's losses were a critical blow to Wavell's scheduled major offensive to drive the Germans back. The plan for the subsequent Operation BATTLEAXE called for the main blow to be delivered in the same Bardia-Sollum-Halfaya-Capuzzo area that was still littered by the burned-out British tanks destroyed during Operation BREVITY. As planned by Brigadier John Harding and General Beresford Peirse of XIII Corps, the main blow of Operation BATTLEAXE was to be delivered by 7th Armoured Division and the Indian 4th Division (newly returned to North Africa).

Unfortunately, the "Desert Rats" of 7th Armoured Division never fully recovered from the hasty retreat through Cyrenaica. In Wavell's haste to answer Churchill's call for an offensive, the reconstitution of the 7th Armoured Division was haphazard and piecemeal. Even the division commander, Major General Sir Michael Creagh, voiced concern over the unit's condition for a major attack. The division would only have five days to train before the start of Operation BATTLEAXE.

Rommel, meanwhile, sensing what was to come, prepared a masterful defense by forming a veritable line of iron with dug-in tanks and antitank guns. One of the most significant German weapons was the 88mm antiaircraft gun, which during Operation BATTLEAXE would make one of its first appearances as a tank-killer.

On 14 June, Rommel's intelligence system picked up the single code word "Peter," and concluded that the British were about to attack. The British had preceded Operation BREVITY with a single code signal as well, "Fritz." On the morning of 15 June, after an ominous radio silence that alerted the Germans even more, the British commenced the attack at 0400 hours.

When the British blow fell, Rommel held the main forward positions of Sollum, Halfaya, and Capuzzo with infantry units. He held his main strike force, the newly arrived 15th *Panzer* Division, in reserve. As soon as the British attack started, Rommel ordered the German 5th Light Division to move up from Tobruk. By mid-morning, all three German strongpoints were under concerted attack by the Indian 4th and 7th Armoured Divisions plus two additional tank regiments. Simultaneously, the 7th Armoured Brigade, part of 7th Armoured Division, pushed toward Bardia. By the day's end, Capuzzo had fallen.

German tanks advance through the desert shortly before the battle of Sollum, June 1941. (IWM MH 5588)

Although the Axis defenses at Capuzzo collapsed, events were not developing as well for Operation BATTLEAXE at other points along the line. At Halfaya Pass, which the British attacked from both ends, the tank assault ground to a halt. The British Matilda tanks, although highly effective against the Italians, were simply no match for the well-positioned German 88mm guns. The Matildas broke apart, as if torn open by giant can openers. The 22nd Guards Brigade and the 4th Armoured Brigade, fresh from their success at Capuzzo, were stopped short before Sollum by stiff German resistance, especially at the southernmost outpost of the Sollum defenses, Strongpoint 208, manned by the elite Oasis Company.

On 16 June, Rommel, seeing the British attacks stalled at Sollum and Halfaya, launched his counterattack. The 15th *Panzer* Division roared south on both flanks of Capuzzo. In what appeared to be the main counterattack, German tanks engaged 4th Armoured Brigade in fierce tank-on-tank combat. The German 5th Light Division, meanwhile, delivered the main punch of Rommel's two-pronged attack. Driving through the desert, the 5th Light Division rapidly shifted direction and aimed for the Halfaya Pass. Engaging the 7th Armoured Brigade west of Sidi Omar, the 5th Light Division slowly pushed the British tanks back.

That was all Rommel needed. As he later wrote, "this was the turning point of the battle. I immediately ordered the 15th *Panzer* Division to disengage all its mobile forces as quickly as possible and leaving only the essential minimum to hold the position north of Capuzzo, to go forward on the northern flank of the victorious 5th Light Division towards Sidi Suleiman. The decisive moment had come."

On the morning of 17 June, in the early hours of the North African dawn, the German blow fell on the British at Halfaya. By 0600 hours, the Germans were at Sidi Suleiman, and by 1600 hours, they reached Halfaya. Rommel had struck hard and fast. When the 5th Light and 15th *Panzer* Divisions reached the Halfaya Pass, they turned and advanced side by side. The German operation took the British completely by surprise. The 5th Light Division swept around to the flank and rear of 7th Armoured Division.

Creagh felt he could not strike back without the added weight of the 4th Armoured Brigade. General Frank Messervy (q.v.), commander of the Indian 4th Division, also felt he needed the 4th Armoured Brigade tanks to hold back movement of the 15th *Panzer* Division to his south. Thus, Messervy concluded that the Indian 4th Division would have to withdraw, since he was virtually isolated by Rommel's attack. With the Indian Division retiring, 7th Armoured Division and the rest of the British tank forces had to withdraw as well, since no tank formation can operate long without infantry support.

The British withdrawal on 17 June marked the effective end of Operation BATTLEAXE. Since the start of the battle on 15 June, the British lost ninety-one tanks, almost half their armored strength, and 1,000 casualties. The *Afrika Korps* lost only twelve tanks with fifty damaged. Churchill wrote in his diary, "on the 17th everything went wrong." The failure of Operation BATTLEAXE marked the end of General Wavell's command in the Middle East. Churchill cabled him, "I have come to the conclusion that public interest will best be served by appointment of General Auchinleck to relieve you in command of Armies of Middle East."

Wavell was replaced by General Sir Claude Auchinleck (q.v.) in July, and General Sir Alan Cunningham (q.v.) assumed command of the Western Desert Force, which was redesignated the British Eighth Army.

John F. Murphy

Additional Reading
Barnett, Correlli, *The Desert Generals* (1964).
Barnett, Correlli (ed.), *Hitler's Generals* (1989).
Fraser, David, *Knight's Cross: A Life of Field Marshal Erwin Rommel* (1992).
Liddell Hart, Basil H. (ed.), *The Rommel Papers* (1953).

Soviet Oil Fields (1940)

At the start of World War II, both Germany and the Western Allies focused their attentions on the Soviet oil fields in the Caucasus. Although Germany and the Soviet Union were not at war until June 1941, Adolf Hitler (q.v.) wanted the Caucasus oil fields left intact for future German capture and exploitation. The Allies too realized the importance of the Caucasus oil fields to the German war effort, noting that the Soviet Union was providing nearly 800,000 tons of oil to Germany by the end of 1939.

In 1940, France and Great Britain drew up plans to bomb the Soviet oil fields and refineries in the Transcaucasus. The French were the more aggressive, pushing for strikes throughout the early months of 1940. Stationing bombers in Syria, the French awaited targeting intelligence from the British, who employed high altitude reconnaissance aircraft operating out of Syria and Iraq. Prime Minister Neville Chamberlain (q.v.) demurred, believing a strike on the oil fields might bring the Soviet Union actively into the war as a German ally. Ultimately, the fall of France in June 1940 ended the planning. The Germans captured a set of the plans and shared them with Josef Stalin (q.v.), much to the world's embarrassment. More importantly, the incident reinforced the Soviets' already considerable distrust of Western Allied intentions.

Prime Minister Winston S. Churchill (q.v.) resurrected the plan in the summer of 1942, as German Army Group A drove ever deeper into the Caucasus (q.v.). Fortunately, the German defeat at Stalingrad (q.v.) precluded the planned strike from being executed. Such an attack might have prompted Stalin to seek accommodation with Hitler. Stalin, nonetheless, was well-informed of Churchill's planning through Soviet spies within British intelligence. It will never be known to what extent the planned strike on the Soviet oil fields affected Stalin's attitude toward his erstwhile allies. It certainly did not enhance Churchill's credibility with the Soviet dictator during or after the war.

Carl O. Schuster

Additional Reading
Piekaliewicz, Janusz, *Air War 1939–1945* (1985).
Schuster, Carl O., "Allied Plans to Strike Stalin's Oil Fields," *Strategy and Tactics* (January 1988).

Soviet Union Campaign (22 June 1941– September 1944)

[See map 35 on page 1345]

On 21 July 1940, Adolf Hitler (q.v.) ordered the German Army to develop preliminary plans for a campaign against the Soviet Union. After he made his own changes, the blueprint for the German attack was issued in *Führer* Directive 21, *Fall* BARBAROSSA, dated 18 December 1940.

Hitler wanted *Lebensraum* (q.v.) in Eastern Europe. Moreover, he wanted to destroy Bolshevism and the Jewish "race," the targeted mortal enemies of National Socialism (q.v.). The plan to attack the Soviet Union also had a long-term strategic goal. Hitler was surprised that Great Britain was unwilling to terminate hostilities after the 1940 fall of France (q.v.). The United Kingdom continued to oppose German supremacy in continental Europe. Hitler finally backed down from invading Great Britain directly, but he hoped to convince the British that their resistance was fruitless by destroying the Soviet Union, Britain's last potential ally in Europe. He also calculated that Germany, possessing all the resources of Europe, would be able to cope with all potential future enemies, including the United States.

The war against the Soviet Union was a classical war of aggression. Any talk of a Soviet preemptive strike is groundless. Between the summer of 1940 and the start of the war, Germany did not feel threatened by the Soviet Union in any way. The concentrations of Soviet troops near the borders of the newly expanded *Reich* were not seen as indicators of an impending attack. Immediately after the war against the Soviets, Hitler planned to annex huge territories, including the Baltic states (q.v.), the remaining parts of prewar Poland, and the Crimea. The mass of Soviet territory in Europe was to be divided into smaller states controlled completely by the *Reich*—in Hitler's words, "a

German India." A substantial reduction of the Slavic population, meaning nothing less than systematic mass murder, was part of the far-reaching German plans for the areas to be occupied. Enough room would be made for organized settlers, belonging to the "superior races."

The realization of these plans was only conceivable because sections of Germany's elite shared at least some of Hitler's visions. Elements of the military, the bureaucracy, the economy, and even the churches had a certain affection toward these fascist dreams, and helped to fulfill them.

Germany's state of military preparedness contrasted sharply with these far-reaching plans, but the leadership was very optimistic about the prospect of success. In a couple of weeks, the *Wehrmacht* planned to destroy the Red Army and reach the Archangel-Gorky line, the initially planned limit of the advance. This overwhelming optimism led Hitler to accept the risks of a possible two-front war. He expected the Soviet Union to be destroyed before Great Britain could recover.

Fully convinced of a quick success, German tanks and vehicles had only enough fuel for a two-month operation. Ammunition was available for only a half year. As late as 22 June 1941, 40 percent of the German infantry and 25 percent of the *Panzer* divisions were not fully ready for battle. Many of those units had captured French or Czech equipment or were below their authorized strength. The Germans did not anticipate high casualties and had no real plans to replace men or equipment.

The German task was eased to some degree by the Soviets themselves. In the great purges (q.v.) of the 1930s, most of the Red Army's top leadership perished. The Red Army needed these men desperately when, in 1941, it was still in a state of rebuilding. Many new and modern weapons were about to be introduced, but they were not yet available in sufficient quantities. Thus, the Red Army was not prepared for battle in 1941, and Josef Stalin (q.v.) was doing his best to avoid war. The Kremlin had received many indications of German intentions. In March 1941, the U.S. State Department informed the Soviet ambassador in Washington that it had "authentic" information regarding a plan for a German attack in the near future. Stalin's own spies, particularly Richard Sorge (q.v.), provided massive and creditable evidence of the pending invasion. The British also warned the Soviets.

Stalin still did not order any countermeasures. He assumed the British wanted to draw him into the war, mistrusted many of the indicators, and was trying not to provoke the Germans. He was convinced that Hitler would not start to fight on two fronts simultaneously. Finally, Stalin underestimated the *Wehrmacht* and placed too much faith in the strength of the Red Army.

The original German plan called for the invasion to be made by three army groups, each supported by an air fleet. Attacking from East Prussia, Army Group North, commanded by Field Marshal Wilhelm von Leeb (q.v.), was given the task of occupying the Baltic states and capturing Leningrad. In the north, the Finns also joined the attack to recapture areas lost to the Soviets during the 1939–1940 Winter War (q.v.). The objective of German and Finnish troops in the area was the interdiction of the Murmansk railway.

To the south was Army Group Center, commanded by Field Marshal Fedor von Bock (q.v.). It was the strongest of the attacking arms, the only one that had two *Panzer* groups (later renamed *Panzer* armies). Each of the flank army groups had only one *Panzer* group, which limited their ability to conduct large-scale encircling operations. The task of Army Group Center was to destroy the Soviet forces in eastern Poland and Byelorussia and advance into the area around Smolensk.

Army Group South, commanded by Field Marshal Gerd von Rundstedt (q.v.), attacked from southern Poland and Romania into the Ukraine. The Romanian Army also took part in these operations. The border between Army Groups South and Center was the vast and nearly unpassable Pripet marshes.

Altogether German strength was about 3.2 million men, 3,500 tanks and assault guns, and slightly more than 2,000 combat aircraft. The campaign was supervised primarily by German Army headquarters (OKH), with Field Marshal Walther von Brauchitsch (q.v.) as commander in chief, and Colonel General Franz Halder (q.v.) as chief of staff. Quite often Hitler personally interfered with the operations and did so more as the war continued.

The Red Army also was organized into army groups, which they called fronts. Northwestern Front opposed Army Group North; Western Front faced Army Group Center; and Southwestern Front together with Southern Front defended the Ukraine. Northern Front covered the Finnish theater of operations. Right after the start of the war the Soviet high command, *Stavka* (q.v.) was reorganized. Although Stalin held unlimited power, he actually practiced a policy of delegation in the decision making process. In May 1941, the Germans estimated the Red Army's tank strength at 10,000 and

the number of first-line aircraft at 4,000. Although outnumbering the Germans, the Soviet equipment was considered qualitatively inferior. In general, this was correct during the early stages of the war.

The Germans and their allies were very successful in the first weeks following the initial attack on 22 June 1941. Army Group North cleared the Baltic states, which at first welcomed the Germans as liberators. By the second half of August, German tanks cut the Moscow-Leningrad railway. Other units approached the outskirts of Leningrad (q.v.), starting the siege that lasted 900 days. The main geographic objectives in the north were achieved, but Army Group North was unable to destroy the opposing Soviet forces completely. Despite heavy losses, the Northwestern Front was far from being annihilated. The Finns, too, reached the pre-1939 frontier and at that point they stopped. They did not consider their fight a war of aggression.

After four weeks, the armored pincers of Army Group Center reached Smolensk. They were already two-thirds of the way to Moscow and had destroyed substantial parts of Marshal Semen Timoshenko's (q.v.) Western Front in the battles of Minsk and Smolensk (qq.v.). By using newly raised units, however, the Red Army managed to establish a new line of resistance. The Western Front was even able to counterattack the forward German positions near Smolensk.

The advance of Army Group South was a disappointment for the OKH. Facing an enemy roughly twice its own strength, it made slow progress during the first weeks of the campaign. Its left wing, especially, hung far behind the right wing of Army Group Center, and a dangerous gap formed between the two army groups, demanding countermeasures.

Despite impressive territorial gains and enormous Soviet losses, the German concept of *Blitzkrieg* (q.v.) failed essentially. After six weeks of fighting, the Red Army still was not destroyed and the invaders faced a mounting resistance all along the front. Moreover, German casualties were well above levels the *Wehrmacht* had expected. As matters stood in late 1941, the Germans had the capability to conduct only one more big operation before winter. The generals, especially Halder, wanted to capture Moscow. Hitler favored the economically important Ukraine. He made the worst possible decision and ordered both operations; first the Ukraine and then Moscow. The battle of encirclement conducted in the Ukraine by Army Groups South and Center ended with an impressive German victory (*see* Kiev). The follow-up campaign against Moscow (q.v.), carried out by a reinforced Army Group Center, began on 2 October. After initial success, it was halted—first by mud from the autumn rains, then by the winter, and finally by Soviet reinforcements massed near the city's gates.

By December 1941, Army Groups North and South experienced their first setbacks. The attempt to close off the encirclement of Leningrad ended in disaster. The Germans wanted to link up with the Finns east of Lake Ladoga. They managed to capture Tichwin on 8 November but soon had to withdraw after suffering heavy losses. The attack on Murmansk and the attempts to cut the railway line failed as well. Logistics, weather problems, determined resistance, and operational failures all conspired against German success.

Meanwhile, Army Group South, weakened by the diversion of some of its units to the Moscow attack, reached the rivers Donec and Mius in November. On the shores of the Sea of Azov, it fought and won another battle of encirclement. Finally, on 21 November 1941, the Germans captured Rostov (q.v.) on the Don, gateway to the Caucasus. Two weeks later, however, they had to retreat because of continued Soviet attacks. Meanwhile, in the Crimea (q.v.), the German Eleventh Army failed in its first attempt to capture the fortress of Sevastopol (q.v.).

With worn-out divisions and lacking reserves and winter equipment, the *Wehrmacht* now had to face a Soviet winter counteroffensive. The Red Army was wise enough to assemble strong strategic reserves during the summer. These reserves were now used to conduct counterattacks all along the front. On 6 December, the first blow fell on Army Group Center. The Soviets first planned to reduce German positions threatening Moscow, then they intended to encircle and destroy Army Group Center.

By the beginning of January 1942, the Soviet counteroffensives had extended the length of the entire front from Murmansk to the Crimea. As a result of this first major Soviet offensive action, the Red Army regained huge tracts of territory, especially in the sector of Army Group Center. They did not, however, manage to destroy the major German formations. Like the *Wehrmacht* a few months earlier, the Red Army attacked everywhere at once and the *Stavka* could not turn the tactical successes into operational victory.

On 19 December 1941, Hitler removed von Brauchitsch from his post as commander in chief and assumed direct personal command of the German Army. German troops were ordered to resist fanatically and to use *Igel* (Hedgehog) tactics

in order to stem the Soviet tide. The *Wehrmacht* weathered the immediate crisis fairly well, but its total strength was sapped almost beyond complete recovery. Since the outbreak of the war, the Germans suffered 1.1 million casualties. These losses could not be replaced, qualitatively or quantitatively. By May 1942, the *Wehrmacht*'s 225 divisions were 740,000 troops below their authorized strength; the *Luftwaffe* was 45 percent under strength; and the number of tanks was about the same as in June 1941. On the other hand, the Soviets greatly increased their military capability. Even Hitler could not deny the fact that in 1942 his troops were no longer capable of attacking all along the front at the same time.

In his *Führer* Directive 41 of 5 April 1942, Hitler ordered a new summer offensive concentrated in the southern sector. In a three-phase encirclement operation, the troops were to advance along the Don toward Stalingrad. Afterward, the Germans intended to occupy the area south of the Don, famous for its oil fields, and pass the Caucasus mountains toward the Turkish and Iranian borders. In May and June, the Germans conducted a number of successful preliminary operations in the Crimea and near Izyum. These victories caused Hitler to decide to weaken his forces for the summer offensive, Operation *BLAU* (blue). He thus shifted the Eleventh Army to Leningrad. It arrived just in time to counter a Soviet attack, but the Eleventh Army was too weak to conduct offensive operations on its own.

The German summer offensive began on 22 June 1942. They broke through the Soviet lines initially, but the pockets they formed were mostly empty. The Red Army had learned to withdraw in time, avoiding the horrific losses of 1941. On 23 July, Hitler issued *Führer* Directive 45, which was more an operational order than a real directive. This directive guaranteed the German failure by abandoning the original attack plan and ordering an attack everywhere at once. The German forces in the original operational sector of Operation *BLAU* were reorganized into two army groups. Army Group A was ordered to take the Caucasus (q.v.), and Army Group B was sent toward Stalingrad (q.v.).

The German front became extremely overextended and logistical problems hampered all operations severely. By November 1942, Army Group A penetrated deep into the Caucasus, but it did not have sufficient strength to reach its final objective. Sixth Army, the centerpiece of Army Group B, squandered its combat power in the street fighting at Stalingrad. At the same time, a numerically superior Red Army prepared to conduct its first major encirclement against the invaders.

Operation *BLAU* was the last German strategic offensive in the Soviet Union. From there on the Soviet Army held the initiative on the battlefield. How did this come to pass? From the beginning, the Soviet Union fought a total war. The entire resources of the country were mobilized for the war effort. That policy, together with good organization and the far-sighted eastward evacua-

Soviet light tanks and ski infantry attack during the Soviet Winter Offensive of 1942–1943. (IWM RUS 1656)

tion of industries, led to an enormous increase in Soviet industrial production. In deference to the political mood at home, the Germans did not shift to a total war footing until 1943, and they did not reach their maximum armament output until 1944. By then, it was too late.

The Soviet Union also received large quantities of American and British materiel, particularly, means of transportation and food. Those supplies allowed the Soviets to concentrate on the production of weapons. Some of the newer designs, like the famous T-34 tank, were often superior to their German counterparts. Stalin also threw away the ideological ballast. The Soviets were now told to fight for "Mother Russia," rather than for Communism or world revolution. Reverting to nationalism, the Kremlin even gained the support of the Orthodox Church.

The cruel and barbaric German occupation policy also stiffened the Soviet will to resist. During the early months of the war, many Soviet soldiers deserted, often willing to support the Germans. Ukrainians and Lithuanians initially welcomed the invaders as liberators; but faced with forced labor, the systematic extermination of certain groups like the Jews and Gypsies, and the high death rate of Soviet POWs, Stalin's regime soon came to be regarded as the lesser of the two evils. Few German officials seemed to recognize this problem, resulting in economic losses for Germany and a strengthening of the Soviet partisan (q.v.) movement.

Stalin and his commanders greatly improved their operational abilities during the course of the war. In 1941, grave errors brought the Soviet Union to the edge of destruction; but in 1942, the strategy of flexible defense saved many troops. The later Soviet operations usually were characterized by sound military planning.

On the German side, operational thinking became more and more dominated by Hitler's political and economic thinking, thereby sacrificing military rationality to an increasing degree. The objective of Operation BARBAROSSA was the destruction of the Soviet Union. The objective of Operation *BLAU* was to capture its natural resources, primarily oil, which Germany needed for its own military machine. The *Wehrmacht*'s operations were subordinated to these aims, which were increasingly beyond the bounds of their capabilities. After Halder was replaced by General Kurt Zeitzler (q.v.) as army chief of staff in September 1942, this tendency increased. Retreats frequently were delayed too long, and troops were sacrificed for unattainable economic and political goals.

German operations also suffered from seriously underestimating the Red Army's fighting strength. This tendency had its roots in Nazi ideology and plagued the Germans throughout the war. The coordination between Germany and its allies, especially Finland and Japan, was also bad. Japanese neutrality in the case of the Soviet Union, for example, enabled Stalin to use many Asian-based Soviet troops against Germany. On the other hand, the threat of a possible Allied attack in western or northern Europe tied down many German troops there. The "little second front" in Africa and later in Italy sapped the German armies in the east as well. When the *Luftwaffe* had to start defending the home air space against Allied bombing, this caused a serious reduction in the fire support available for the army in the field. One and a half years after the start of the war, all hope of a German victory was dead. Yet Hitler refused to consider any Soviet peace overtures. The longest leg of the war was yet to come.

On 19 November 1942, the Soviets began Operation URANUS, the counterattack against the Germans at Stalingrad. Penetrating mainly through the weak sectors held by Germany's Romanian and Italian allies, Soviet spearheads encircled the German Sixth Army within three days. Hitler immediately rejected any suggestion of a breakout and withdrawal. All attempts to relieve the Sixth Army failed. Despite its hopeless situation, the Sixth Army continued to fight on until 2 February 1943.

Meanwhile, Army Group A in the Caucasus began a belated withdrawal. Thanks to Soviet slowness to react, the German troops escaped via Rostov and the Kuban delta, where a bridgehead to the Crimea held until September. In the northern sector of the war, the Soviets were somewhat less successful. At Leningrad, however, they did manage to break through and link up with the besieged city in January 1943.

As the Soviet counterattacks in the south continued, the Red Army approached the Donets River (q.v.), and once more, the entire German southern sector was threatened by encirclement. The situation remained tenuous until a German counterattack with a small force of armored divisions stabilized the front. By that point, the Red Army had overextended its own supply lines and the Soviet troops were exhausted. This last significant German victory restored the front line of the winter of 1942–1943, with only the Kursk salient remaining in Soviet hands.

Both the *Wehrmacht* and the Red Army needed to recover from the winter fighting, and

the front remained relatively quiet until July 1943. The Germans withdrew from Demjansk and Rshev, thereby shortening their lines and consolidating their reserves. They also managed to strengthen their *Panzer* forces somewhat. The Soviets used the time to reconstitute their units and to plan the resumption of their next offensive.

Germany threw away the biggest part of its strategic reserve at the battle of Kursk (q.v.) in July 1943. Due to determined Soviet resistance, combined with the Allied invasion in Italy, Hitler aborted the offensive on 12 July, seven days after it started. The Soviets, meanwhile, began another series of offensives, forcing the Germans to abandon all areas east of the Dnieper River. The unavoidable retreat, however, was delayed too long, and the planned "final" defensive line along the broad Dnieper River (q.v.) was just so much wishful thinking. When German forces arrived at the line they found the Soviets had already established several bridgeheads over the river.

By October and November 1943, these bridgeheads were substantially widened, and Army Groups South and Center lost contact with each other after the Soviets broke through in the Pripet marsh area. The Crimea was still in German hands, but cut off from the mainland. The Soviets attempted another breakthrough near Newel, between Army Groups Center and North, but the Germans held.

Between December 1943 and April 1944, the Red Army cleared the rest of the Ukraine (q.v.). Suffering heavy casualties, the Germans were driven back into Romania, Hungary, and southern Poland, where the line stabilized briefly. In May 1944, the Crimea finally fell, costing the Germans another field army. Three months earlier, the Soviets lifted the siege of Leningrad, forcing the remnants of Army Group North to retreat behind Lake Peipus.

The backbone of the *Wehrmacht* was finally broken by Operation BAGRATION, the huge 1944 summer offensive the Red Army conducted against Army Groups Center and South (renamed Army Group North Ukraine). Hitler's hedgehog tactics turned defeat into catastrophe, costing the Germans far more troops than they lost at Stalingrad. Byelorussia (q.v.) was lost and the Red Army reached the borders of the *Reich*.

In the far north, Finland sued for peace on 25 August 1944 after the Soviet offensive in Karelia. Under Soviet pressure the German troops in northern Finland had to withdraw into Norway, a retreat that resulted in German-Finnish hostilities. The last major offensive on Soviet territory was conducted against Army Group North in September 1944. After they were pushed out of Soviet territory, some of the northern German units returned to Germany; others remained in Kurland (q.v.) until the end of the war.

From a military point of view, Germany's defeat had become inevitable long before its last troops were forced out of Soviet territory. Although exact information on Soviet strength during the war is still in question, the Red Army's superiority became absolutely overwhelming by the second half of 1943. Better use of German combat resources might have slowed down the Soviet advance but would not have stopped it.

Stalingrad was not necessarily the single turning point of World War II in Europe, but after that battle the chances of a German victory in the east, which had been steadily declining since July 1941, shrunk to zero. Total victory had become unattainable much earlier still, particularly from the point when the United States entered the war.

The results of the bloody war in the east are horrifying. According to recently published Soviet statistics, about 27 million inhabitants of the Soviet Union lost their lives, including 8.5 million soldiers. The Germans lost approximately three million troops, but these numbers tell only part of the story. Other victims included German civilians, on whom the Red Army took revenge as they entered Germany; Soviet POWs who died in German captivity; and the millions of people who fled or were expelled during and after the war. Soviet POWs returning home after the war often were treated as traitors and exiled to work camps.

Victory over Germany paved the way for the Soviet Union to emerge as one of the world's two superpowers. From 1943 on, Soviet influence within the anti-Hitler coalition grew steadily. The Russo-German War ranks as one of the most important factors in the rise of the bipolar international system that came to characterize the era of the Cold War. That system dominated world politics up until the beginning of the 1990s.

Reiner Martin

Additional Reading

Erikson, John, *Stalin's War with Germany*, 2 vols. (1983).

Keegan, John, *Barbarossa: Invasion of Russia, 1941* (1970).

Seaton, Albert, *The Russo-German War 1941–45* (1971).

———, *Stalin as a Military Commander* (1976).

Whaley, Barton, *Codeword Barbarossa* (1973).

Ziemke, Earl F., *Stalingrad to Berlin: The German Defeat in the East* (1968).

Ziemke, Earl F., and Magna E. Bauer, *Moscow to Stalingrad: Decision in the East* (1987).

Spanish Civil War (1936–1939)

What began as a revolt of the country's generals against the democratic government in the summer of 1936 turned into a prolonged, bitter civil war that lasted until the spring of 1939. It also became the issue that split Europe politically and ideologically most sharply in the prewar years. The Spanish civil war was a bloody conflict lasting three years, destroying cities, and costing more than 500,000 lives. For Europe, it was a proxy war between Fascism (q.v.) and its opponents, a battle between the Right and the Left, where each side tested its weapons, its ideologies, and its resolve. It was a dress rehearsal for World War II at the expense of the Spanish people.

A nation of deep and proud traditions, Spain in the mid-1930s was divided socially and politically by a number of conflicting contenders for power. The Second Republic, established in 1930, was socially very heterogeneous, with an entrenched aristocracy and a deeply conservative Catholic hierarchy commanding considerable authority. The country's army was still hurting from losses to the United States in 1898 and to Moroccan tribesmen in 1921. Within Spain there was a long tradition of political influence peddling, and its intellectuals were still brooding over the country's steady decline since the sixteenth Century. In rural areas, poverty was widespread, and in urban centers, there existed an impoverished but small working class.

These differences became more acute during the Second Republic and they went far in shaping its political life. The prime minister from 1931 to 1933, Manuel Azana, moved against what he viewed as the two greatest threats to democracy—the Catholic Church and professional military officers. He also introduced land reform that split up some of the largest rural estates. While a conservative coalition governed from 1934 to 1936, its policies intensified Spain's social and political divisions through a declared "state of alarm" that permitted it to suspend civil liberties and imprison thousands.

Each government of the Second Republic was guided by its own social and economic hatreds. When Azana returned to government in February 1936 as the head of a popular front government, his legislative program called for renewed land reform and school construction, greater autonomy for the municipalities, autonomy for the Basque provinces, and the reemployment of all workers fired for political or union activity since 1933. However, growing civil disorder, general strikes, anticlerical violence, and rural chaos sparked by squatters seizing land, further alarmed the reactionary and monarchist officers whose planning for a military rising to save the nation intensified. Active preparations for a coup, in fact, began in March 1936.

The dissident generals, led by Francisco Franco and Emilo Mola (qq.v.), launched their rebellion in Spanish Morocco on 17 July 1936. Franco immediately went on the radio to explain the motives of the military rising, announcing that anarchy and revolutionary strikes were destroying the nation; that regionalism was devastating national unity; that enemies of public order had maligned the armed forces; and that the constitution had effectively been suspended. His announcement and actions caught the government in Madrid by surprise. On 17 July, local uprisings took place in a number of Spanish communities. The most crucial events of the first few days took place in Madrid and Barcelona, Spain's two largest cities, where Insurgent military troops were thwarted by local forces loyal to the republican government. Within several days, it became clear to Franco and Mola that their objectives could only be met by military conquest of the entire nation.

With assistance from Benito Mussolini's (q.v.) Italy, the major force of the Insurgent Army was transported to Spain from Morocco in July 1936, and it advanced rapidly through the southern countryside toward Madrid. Mussolini and Adolf Hitler (q.v.) provided transport and military forces with the expectation that this assistance would lead to a quick victory. By November, Italy and Germany were sending large amounts of military aid to Franco's troops and waging a clandestine submarine war at sea.

Within Spain, the Insurgent forces, also known as the Nationalists, could count on the Catholic Church hierarchy, the army, and on broad support among the middle and upper classes in rural agricultural areas. The popular front government and its supporters, known as the Loyalist or Republican forces, did gain the support of the air force and navy and also had mass support in industrial communities, on the east coast, and in the capital.

Aid for the Loyalists came from foreign volunteers (including many prominent intellectuals) and from the Soviet Union and Mexico. While

S

France supported the Loyalists, it did not intervene directly and chose to sponsor a nonintervention agreement among all the European states, hoping that this would deter Italy and Germany. While the Insurgent forces could feed themselves and launch massive military campaigns, the Loyalists, supported by a majority of the population, were able to produce more goods, but had to improvise their military actions. From the beginning, the conflict had the makings of a stalemate, a protracted and bitter fight.

During the first year of the civil war, the focus was on Madrid, as Franco's Insurgents hoped for a quick victory and mounted a formidable military campaign against the government. From mid-August to late September 1936, four military columns of Insurgent troops fought their way northward to Madrid. The fighting was savage, with the battles for the towns of Badajoz and Toledo especially heavy and bloody. At the same time, the Insurgent forces in the north gained control of the region bordering France.

In October 1936, columns moving on Madrid from the southwest met stiffening resistance from the Loyalist militia forces. On 20 October, Franco issued a general order for the capture of Madrid, and the Insurgent generals hoped their reputation for terror would paralyze the will of Madrid's Loyalist defenders. The fighting around the capital continued for more than ten days and captured the attention of the world. By 18 November, the Insurgent offensive was exhausted and the assault on Madrid was suspended.

As the Insurgent forces marched on Spain's capital in October 1936, the popular front government attempted to negotiate with the generals, who simply refused to talk. The government was then overthrown by public pressure in Madrid. In fact, the Loyalist militia in Madrid held out throughout this political and military turmoil, and the capital did not fall. With Madrid holding firm, the conflict broadened. In areas loyal to the republic, committee and militia rule took over local administration. In some communities, the most extreme social revolutionaries seized control and launched their own reign of terror against the church and the rich, the pillars of the old order, and others perceived as supporters of the Insurgents.

The first three months of the civil war in Loyalist-held areas was a period of the greatest terror. In a number of communities, revolutionary tribunals handed out death sentences, and random terrorist acts took an additional toll of human life. Church properties were frequently targeted, and

these actions sparked the resentment of the middle class. The social and economic divisions of Spanish society widened further. In territory controlled by the Insurgent forces, no such revolution took place, since the military and its conservative allies were accustomed to obeying authority. Still, as military authority was established, the arrest, torture, and execution of strikers or those suspected of having Loyalist or leftist connections became widespread.

When Madrid failed to capitulate to the Insurgent forces, the Insurgents turned to Germany and Italy for additional aid. In November 1936, Nazi Germany sent the *Luftwaffe*'s *Kondor Legion* (q.v.), manned by about 6,000 troops, along with some artillery and tanks. Hitler, however, was cautious and he remained concerned about being drawn into a protracted war outside the sphere of essential German interests. Nazi Germany provided only enough support to keep the war going and world attention away from German rearmament. Mussolini's commitment was greater; between December 1936 and April 1937, Italy sent 100,000 troops to Spain to aid the Insurgents. At the same time, the Anglo-French Non-Intervention Commission kept foreign aid from reaching the Loyalist forces.

Representatives of the Loyalist government presented evidence of Fascist interference to the League of Nations (q.v.), but little was done to stem the flow of outside military aid to the Insurgents. The seeming inability of democratic nations to support Spain's legal government further convinced many contemporaries, who viewed the conflict as a battle of competing ideologies and an example of ruthless power politics, of the inherent weakness of the democratic powers.

Neither side in the conflict was united in purpose. Factions within the Loyalists and Insurgent forces battled among themselves almost as much as against their opponents. The Loyalists organized an anti-Fascist front of various left-wing parties with widely differing agendas. The Syndicalist and anarchist militants, especially the Syndicalist workers in Catalonia, supported what they termed "revolutionary improvisation." The more moderate Loyalist supporters, including the Socialists and Communists, adopted the view that a disciplined regular army and a central government was essential to military victory over the Insurgent forces.

In the first year of the conflict, extreme militants among the Loyalist forces gained control, inaugurating a piecemeal program of collectivization as they sought to carry out social revolution.

The Republican government moved to halt these efforts and was aided by the Communists. In October 1936, the agricultural minister ended the agrarian experimentation, as collectivization and worker control were replaced by centrally controlled nationalization and economic planning. In November 1936, a coalition government of radical factions was organized under Largo Caballero, but it fell in May 1937. The new government, led by Socialist Juan Negrin, did not fare much better in holding together disparate radical forces. In addition, the central government in Madrid had to contend with the growing separatist movements in Catalonia and the Basque region.

The political differences among the Insurgents was less pronounced as the generals quickly asserted their dominance over their diverse supporters. Among the various Insurgent factions, the Traditionalists (or Carlists) wanted to reestablish the monarchy; the Falange was committed to fascist social reorganization; and the generals sought to establish a stable regime. Led by Franco, leader of the Spanish Army in Morocco, the military faction successfully merged the rival factions and held them together.

With Madrid still under Loyalist control, the capital remained the principal military front until March 1937 while each side moved to reorganize its armed forces. At the same time, a separate war was being fought in the northern coastal provinces of Spain. Basque nationalists announced their loyalty to the government and military pressure against them increased. The northern campaign was the most important area of German operations, and the *Kondor Legion* operated virtually unchallenged. On 26 April 1938, a market day, its aviators bombed the regional center of Guernica (q.v.). A town without defenses, Guernica was destroyed and its inhabitants machine-gunned by the German fighter planes. Other Basque towns suffered a similar fate as the Insurgents, with their Nazi aid, moved to obliterate Basque autonomy.

The fighting also continued in other regions of northern Spain. By mid-April 1938, Insurgent forces reached the sea, cutting off Barcelona and the province of Catalonia from the other Loyalist-held areas. In July, Loyalist forces launched an assault in this area but they were finally driven back later in the fall. It became clear to all parties that the conflict would be settled only by foreign assistance or intervention.

The leader of the republic, Prime Minister Negrin, hoped to achieve a compromise peace in September 1938, but other international events sealed the fate of the Spanish republic. The Munich Agreement (q.v.), under which British Prime Minister Neville Chamberlain (q.v.), acceded to Hitler's demands on Czechoslovakia and dealt a deathblow to the diplomatic hopes of the Spanish republic. New aid to the Insurgents came from Italy and Germany, and Franco's forces once again went on the offensive, capturing new territory.

By the end of 1938, the Loyalist government retreated to an area in Catalonia, close to the French border, and in February 1939, Negrin sought to end the conflict on a non-reprisal basis. With an Insurgent victory quickly approaching, half a million Spaniards crossed the border into France seeking refuge from the Insurgent forces. By the end of February, Loyalist generals recognized that further military resistance was futile. On 27 February 1939, France and Britain announced their recognition of a Nationalist government supported by the Insurgent forces. In late March, the last of the Loyalist forces surrendered, and on 1 April 1939, the conflict ended with the complete victory of Franco and his Insurgent forces.

The great issue of the interwar years, the Spanish civil war was fought with brutality and a passionate intensity by each side. Among intellectuals and the political Left in Europe, the efforts of the popular front government were seen as a heroic attempt to halt the spread of Fascism. Some 40,000 volunteers came to the aid of the Loyalists, including the Abraham Lincoln Brigade from the United States, the International Brigade, British writer George Orwell, American writer Ernest Hemingway, and French intellectual André Malraux (q.v.). This conflict drew Europe's intellectuals actively into the great issues of the day as no other twentieth-century conflict had.

With the Insurgent victory, however, momentum in Europe shifted from the democratic powers to the Fascists. In many ways, this bloody conflict served as a rehearsal and an essential prelude to World War II. The violence of the Spanish civil war was soon to be repeated. The war served as a crucial diversion to Hitler's conquests in central Europe. The failure of the Western powers' policies toward Spain revealed the weaknesses of appeasement (q.v.). The inability of the League of Nations to control intervention in the conflict meant the end to the hope of universal collective security, and Soviet intervention in support of the Loyalists further isolated it within Europe.

Robert G. Waite

Additional Reading
Frank, Willard C., Jr., "The Spanish Civil War and the Coming of the Second World

War," *International Review of History* (August 1987), pp. 368–409.

Fraser, Ronald, *Blood of Spain: An Oral History of the Spanish Civil War* (1979).

Jackson, Gabriel, *The Spanish Republic and the Civil War, 1936–1939* (1965).

Rolfe, Edwin, *The Lincoln Battalion: The Story of the Americans Who Fought in Spain in the International Brigades* (1939).

Thomas, Hugh, *The Spanish Civil War* (1961).

Ugarte, Michael, *Shifting Ground: Spanish Civil War Exile Literature* (1989).

Spitzbergen Raid (7 September 1943)

[See map 5 on page 1315]

A Norwegian island located several hundred miles above the Arctic Circle, Spitzbergen gained a strategic importance in World War II that it retains to this day. In Adolf Hitler's (q.v.) eyes, its importance lie in its coal mines and its location flanking the Allied convoy routes to the Soviet Union. For the Allies and Germany's Hermann Göring (q.v.), however, its coal mines and position vis-à-vis convoy routes were secondary to its importance to their meteorological services.

It is in the Arctic that Europe's weather is born, and Spitzbergen was the largest and most centrally located of the Arctic islands from which the Arctic weather can be observed. Such direct observations were critical to accurate weather forecasting in those pre-satellite days. This made Spitzbergen a key objective in the Weather War (q.v.), fought between the Germans and Western Allies in World War II. Both sides deployed weather stations to the island and it was the site of the only engagement in which the German battleship *Tirpitz* fired its main battery in combat.

The Allies were the first to seize the island, one year after the German conquest of Norway. Code named Operation GAUNTLET, an Allied naval task force led by Admiral Sir Phillip Vian (q.v.) arrived at the island on 25 August 1941 and evacuated its 3,200 inhabitants. Vian also destroyed the island's infrastructure, blocked its coal mines, burned its coal stocks, and demolished the radio, weather, and power stations before withdrawing. The operation took seven days.

The Germans reacted quickly, landing a *Luftwaffe* meteorological team on the island's northwestern face. They cleared a runway in the snow and landed supplies so the team could winter over. The team's presence enabled the Germans to make accurate weather forecasts in support of

Admiral Karl Dönitz's (q.v.) U-boats in the Atlantic campaign (q.v.).

The Allies returned in May 1942, landing a company of Free Norwegian ski troops to capture the German weather team. German bombers, however, destroyed most of the Allied equipment in a surprise air raid. The Royal Navy (RN) then landed a full battalion of reinforcements in July and made an unsuccessful attempt to round up the German weather teams. Allied troops were withdrawn in October, leaving only a weather team and a small detachment of Free Norwegians to garrison the island over that winter.

Hitler's interest returned to the island in mid-1943, and he ordered the German Navy to retake and hold the island. Thus was born Operation ZITRONELLA, the northernmost amphibious raid of the war. Supported by the battleship *Tirpitz*, the battle cruiser *Scharnhorst*, and nine destroyers, a battalion from the German 329th Infantry Regiment landed at three locations near the island's main facilities on 7 September 1943. Under cover of overwhelming naval gunfire support, they easily overran the small Norwegian garrison of 140 men, destroyed the weather station, and captured most of the Norwegians' files, equipment, and supplies in the process. The only German casualties came from "friendly fire" when the *Tirpitz* fired on its troops by mistake.

Although ordered to hold the island, Dönitz knew its defense was impossible in the face of Allied naval supremacy. He had the troops withdrawn after completing their mission. The operation took just four hours.

Operation ZITRONELLA was the German Navy's last major fleet operation of the war outside the Baltic Sea. It was also the last successful operation conducted by the *Scharnhorst*, which was sunk on its very next sortie (25 December 1943). The Allies returned to Spitzbergen and reestablished the weather station on 8 September 1943, the day after the raid. No additional major military operations were conducted on the island, although the Germans proved surprisingly adept at landing and maintaining weather parties on the island's remote northern interior. One of those weather teams became the last German unit to surrender to the Western Allies in September 1945.

Carl O. Schuster

Additional Reading

Farnes, Olaf, *War in the Arctic* (1991).

Liversidge, Douglas, *The Third Front* (1960).

Piekalkiewicz, Janusz, *Secret Agents, Spies, and Saboteurs* (1973).

Stalingrad (23 August 1942–2 February 1943)

[See map 36 on page 1346]

The battle of Stalingrad was a decisive turning point for the Soviet Union in its monumental struggle against the forces of Nazi Germany. In the summer of 1942, Adolf Hitler (q.v.) turned his attention toward the oil-rich lands of the Caucasus in southwestern Russia. The German war effort was hampered by a constant shortage of fuel for the thirsty forces of the mechanized *Wehrmacht*. Not only would Operation *BLAU* (BLUE), as the southern offensive became known, enable the Germans to solve their own oil supply problems, but also capturing the region would deprive the Soviets of the oil they needed.

On 28 June 1942, the Germans began their two-pronged offensive, with one arm heading eastward toward the territory between the Don and the Volga Rivers, and the other arm driving southeastward into the Caucasus. As Army Group South, under Field Marshal Fedor von Bock (q.v.), moved down the corridor created by the Donets and Don Rivers, von Bock feared the Soviets might attack the German flank from Voronezh. General Hermann Hoth's (q.v.) Fourth *Panzer* Army received orders to capture the city, leaving the Sixth Army, commanded by General Friedrich Paulus (q.v.), to travel the corridor alone without tank support and to cross the great bend of the Don River near Stalingrad.

Hoth's forces became enmeshed in the fighting at Voronezh (q.v.), wasting both time and tanks needed to assist Paulus's infantry. Hitler worried that the Fourth *Panzer* Army might get bogged down and felt compelled to control the situation more closely. As the result of Hitler's successes early in the war, the *Führer* increasingly believed that Germany's victories stemmed from his own invincibility and military genius. In mid-July, he began to tamper with the organization, leadership, and battle plan of Operation *BLAU*.

First, he dismissed von Bock, replacing him with Field Marshal Maximilian von Weichs (q.v.). Then he split Army Group South into Army Groups A and B. Von Weichs retained command of the northern Army Group B. Field Marshal Wilhelm List (q.v.), commanding Army Group A, headed for the Caucasus (q.v.). Hitler also transferred his eastern front headquarters from Rastenburg to Vinnitsa in the Ukraine, along with his entourage. Hitler further amended the plan on 13 July, requiring Paulus to capture Stalingrad, thereby making the city a major objective. Paulus was to hold the city and prevent a flanking maneuver by the Red Army against Army Group A. On 17 July, Hitler again amended the plan by shifting the Fourth *Panzer* Army to Army Group A to support its crossing of the Don.

Stalingrad, standing on the western banks of the Volga River, was one of the most important industrial cities for the Soviet Union's war effort, as well as a transportation and communications center for the region. Its 500,000 inhabitants produced a quarter of the Soviet Union's tanks and vehicles. The city also became something of a fixation for both Hitler and Soviet Premier Josef Stalin (q.v.) because of the symbolic importance and propaganda value attached to its name.

As the Germans began proceeding toward the Volga, the Soviets abandoned their earlier strategy of holding positions at all costs. Now instead, Red Army units started deliberately and gradually melting away before the oncoming *Wehrmacht,* drawing it deeper into Soviet territory and into a potential trap. The Soviets, in fact, intended to make their stand at Stalingrad. Stalin sent units and materiel to reinforce his namesake, converting it into a bastion of resistance and preparing it for the full weight of the German assault.

A month after Operation *BLAU* commenced, Stalin issued an order to be read to every Soviet soldier defending the city. It proclaimed, "Not one step backward!" Soviet forces in the city numbered 300,000; the Germans mustered 230,000 troops for the attack.

On 29 July, Hitler, frustrated with the Sixth Army's slow progress, once again diverted Hoth's Fourth *Panzer* Army, this time northwestward toward Stalingrad's exposed southern side. By sending the Fourth *Panzer* Army and its logistics train to support Army Group A, Hitler had deprived the Sixth Army of fuel and the ability to move forward quickly to cross the Don and lunge for Stalingrad. With fuel gauges resting on empty, the Sixth Army was forced to halt for eighteen days before getting across the Don River. After Hoth's *Panzers* got into position south of the city, the Sixth Army refueled and prepared for the pincer attack on the north side to finally seize Stalingrad.

Advance units of Paulus's forces broke through to the Volga in the northern suburbs of the city on 23 August. That evening, General Wolfram von Richthofen's (q.v.) VIII *Fliegerkorps*, with 600 *Luftwaffe* bombers, began three days of air raids against the city that burned almost all the wooden structures, killing 40,000 and wounding 150,000 civilians. During the first two weeks of September, the Germans launched two thrusts in the southern sector of Stalingrad to reach the western bank of

the Volga. As a result, Hoth's *Panzer* forces finally cleared a path to the river's shore. The two Soviet armies inside the city, the Sixty-second and Sixty-fourth, seemed trapped with their backs against the river.

Throughout September, the Sixth Army and portions of the Fourth *Panzer* Army worked their way into the downtown area. By early October, street fighting began in earnest with the two opponents contesting every foot of ground. The rubble-choked streets of Stalingrad proved to be a haven for its defenders. Here, General Vasily Chuikov (q.v.), commander of the Sixty-second Army, developed the guerrilla tactics that sucked the strength and resources out of Paulus's forces.

Chuikov employed close combat tactics, utilizing every street, building, room, basement, sewer, and tunnel as a fighting position. By controlling a number of locations, he created a series of isolated strongpoints and commanding positions from which to harass the German troops. Chuikov encouraged his men to fight as if "there was no land beyond the Volga," although from across the river supplies, ammunition, and replacements were ferried in to keep the defenders fighting.

Buildings provided good vantage points for Soviet snipers, which they used extensively and to great effect. The Red Army established a training school for snipers in the Lazur Chemical Works, run by a deer hunter from the Urals. In a period of ten days he shot forty Germans. In response, the Germans brought in their own master sniper and the two men stalked each other for four days. The Russian, Vasily Zaitsev, placed himself in an ideal location with the sun at his back and got a comrade to raise his helmet and do a little acting. The German fired, "saw" the man fall back, and heard him scream. As he raised his head above the sheet metal he was hiding behind to check his handiwork, Zaitsev killed him.

Shifting the battle to the streets hampered German attempts to capture Stalingrad quickly and made the use of tanks nearly impossible. The German Army at this point possessed little experience with the exhausting and demoralizing nature of hand-to-hand combat and city fighting. In addition, once the German infantry penetrated the streets and buildings, support from the *Luftwaffe* became impossible for fear of bombing their own troops.

The Soviets proved extremely tenacious street fighters, and the Germans discovered how difficult it was to root them out of their defensive positions. The brutal fighting, costing 20,000 German casualties per week, continued throughout October and the early part of November, as another frigid Russian winter approached. By mid-November 1942, the exhausted Germans made one last push to wipe out the three remaining Soviet pockets within Stalingrad, but they simply lacked the wherewithal to complete the job.

In the meantime, the *Stavka* (q.v.) put together a plan for a wide encirclement of the Sixth Army by breaking through the German flanks and cutting off their communications lines and escape routes. Marshal Georgy Zhukov, together with General Aleksandr Vasilevsky (qq.v.), outlined the plan for Stalin in mid-September. Code named Operation URANUS, it called for an attack against the weakest points in the German line, their northern and southern flanks. Hitler had shored up these areas with troops from his Italian, Romanian, and Hungarian allies. These forces lacked quality equipment, training, combat experience, and Nationalist Socialist fanaticism. The German military forces viewed their Axis allies with a certain disdain. Employing such lackluster units in the all-important task of protecting the Sixth Army's vulnerable flanks left the Germans in a precarious position.

The Soviets tried quietly to build up their troop strength opposite the German salients, massing two full fronts (army groups)—more than one million troops and 900 tanks. Led by Zhukov, the Soviets jumped off on 19 November. The Don Front, under Marshal Konstantin Rokossovsky (q.v.), and the Southwestern Front, commanded by General Nikolai Vatutin (q.v.), struck first at the German northern flank. They decimated the Romanian Third Army. The following day, the Stalingrad Front, under General Andrei Yeremenko (q.v.), exploded into action on the German southern flank. That attack forced the retreat of the Fourth *Panzer* Army and overran part of the Romanian Fourth Army.

The attack came as a great surprise to Paulus and his troops, who within five days found themselves trapped inside the Stalingrad pocket, cut off from supplies and reinforcements. Despite the speed with which the Red Army closed the neck of the bag, the Germans put up a skillful and concerted fight. For the immediate future, the Soviets ignored the pocket holding Paulus's forces and concentrated their efforts on putting the greatest possible distance between their cornered prey and the nearest German force capable of freeing them.

In late November, Paulus asked Hitler for permission to break out, while his forces still had a chance of success. Hitler responded by assum-

ing direct command of the Sixth Army and ordering Paulus to hold fast and create "Fortress Stalingrad." He also gave Field Marshal Erich von Manstein (q.v.) the task of breaking in with the newly established Army Group Don, which consisted of what remained of the Third and Fourth Romanian Armies, the snared Sixth Army, and Hoth's Fourth *Panzer* Army. His forces already exhausted and under-powered, von Manstein struck on 12 December.

At first Operation *WINTERGEWITTER* (WINTERSTORM) made good headway. The German relief effort forced the Red Army to rush in reinforcements to block Hoth's spearhead. The Soviets also counterattacked along the Chir River (q.v.) to smash the Italian Eighth Army, and along the Don River to the southwest of Stalingrad imperiling von Manstein's own troops. Eleven days after Operation *WINTERGEWITTER* began, the advance slowed to within thirty miles of Stalingrad. Von Manstein urged Paulus to escape, believing it was the Sixth Army's last chance, but Paulus refused to go against Hitler's direct orders to maintain "Fortress Stalingrad." The Sixth Army was trapped.

Meanwhile, *Luftwaffe* chief Hermann Göring (q.v.) promised that his pilots could supply the German troops imprisoned within the city with 500 tons of food and equipment each day. In order to bring in that quantity of ammunition, fuel, and food would require more than 200 sorties per day by Ju-52 transport planes. Paulus estimated his needs at 700 tons daily. But the greatest single day's delivery was only 180 tons, and the daily average a mere seventy tons. Between the Red Air Force and the weather, the airlift proved a disaster. The German wounded suffered in unheated buildings or on windswept runways, sometimes waiting all day to be evacuated by *Luftwaffe* planes. Göring's vaunted *Luftwaffe* lost 500 planes in its attempt to provide relief and supplies to the men caught in the Soviet trap.

The Soviets now turned their attention back to the destruction of the Sixth Army, which suffered tremendously from disease, battle casualties, and frostbite, but continued to hang on grimly. On Christmas Day 1942, 1,280 German soldiers died of frostbite, starvation, typhus, and dysentery. Paulus suffered from a case of dysentery during most of the battle and an increasingly strong tic on the right side of his face. On 8 January, the Soviets offered the Sixth Army an ultimatum: capitulate or be annihilated. Paulus refused, according to Hitler's orders. After several more weeks of brutal but hopeless fighting, the German troops, now out of ammunition, reduced to eating raw horseflesh,

S

Wrapped in anything they can find to protect themselves from the bitter Russian winter, German POWs are marched through the streets of Stalingrad. (IWM NYP 68082)

and losing control of the last airfield, started surrendering on 31 January 1943.

The day before, the Nazis had celebrated the tenth anniversary of Hitler's coming to power with special speeches by Göring and Joseph Goebbels (q.v.). The festivities were interrupted by a British daylight air raid on Berlin timed to coincide with the event. Paulus repeatedly had asked for permission to surrender the remainder of his troops, but Hitler demanded that the Sixth Army fight to the last man.

To stiffen Paulus's resolve, Hitler promoted him to the rank of Field Marshal, knowing that no German field marshal had ever been captured alive. Ironically, on the same day he received word of the promotion, Paulus and his southern forces surrendered to the Sixty-fourth Army commander General Mikhail Shumilov (q.v.) in the basement of the downtown department store that served as his temporary headquarters. Hitler believed that Paulus would do the "honorable" thing and commit suicide. The news of his surrender infuriated Hitler, as did Paulus's unwillingness to take his own life.

On 2 February 1943, the German XI *Korps* and its commander, General Karl Strecker, who had been holding out, finally gave up their futile gesture of defiance and surrendered.

The defeat of the Sixth Army represented a particularly crushing blow for Nazi Germany. Nearly a quarter of a million Germans died during the battle for Stalingrad; 100,000 alone after the encirclement. Another 94,000 German soldiers and officers marched into a captivity—only 6,000 of whom would survive the war. The once invincible *Wehrmacht* never really recovered from the losses incurred at Stalingrad.

More significantly, German morale suffered a devastating shock. Nazi propaganda had led the German people to believe that they were winning the Stalingrad battle. It was a terrible shock to discover they had lost it. German women came to fear and dread the name of the city that devoured their husbands, sons, and fathers. The terrible effect of Stalingrad on Germany's morale allowed the first serious doubts to corrupt the German people's faith in their ultimate victory. Indeed, the outcome of the battle of Stalingrad, according to historian William Craig, represented "a mind-paralyzing calamity to a nation that believed it was the master race."

Prior to the Soviet victory at Stalingrad, the Germans tentatively held the upper hand in the war; but the liquidation of 330,000 Axis troops proved instrumental in weakening Germany's dominant position in eastern Europe. After January 1943, the Germans were unable to muster another major offensive on the eastern front. The Soviets then turned their "Red tide" against the Germans, steadily driving them off the soil of Mother Russia.

For the Soviet Union, the victory over their hated enemy created the sense of confidence and hope it needed to prosecute the war to its ultimate and successful conclusion. The shift from a defensive to an offensive posture during the battle gave the Soviets the opportunity to demonstrate their patriotism and loyalty, as well as proving the strength and tenacity of the Soviet "steamroller."

The battle had been won, but at a terrible price. The city of Stalingrad lay in ruins and a great many of its inhabitants perished during the fighting. The Red Army suffered an estimated 750,000 casualties to secure its first major victory over the Nazis, although official figures were never released. Stalingrad signaled the beginning of the end for the Third *Reich*. The absolute failure of the elite German troops to accomplish their objective, coupled with the immense loss of life and the humiliation of the defeat, was one more in a long string of indicators—that started with the Battle of Britain (q.v.)—that the Germans might eventually lose the war.

Susanne Tepe Gaskins

Additional Reading
Chuikov, Vasily, *The Battle for Stalingrad* (1964).
Clark, Alan, *Barbarossa: The Russian-German Conflict, 1941–1945* (1985).
Craig, William, *Enemy at the Gates: The Battle of Stalingrad* (1973).
Erickson, John, *The Road to Berlin* (1983).
———, *The Road to Stalingrad* (1975).
Jukes, Geoffrey, *Stalingrad, The Turning Point* (1968).
Schröter, Heinz, *Stalingrad* (1958).
Seaton, Albert, *The Russo-German War, 1941–1945* (1971).
Wieder, Joachim, and Heinrich von Einsiedel, *Stalingrad: Memories and Reassessment* (1995).

Suomussalmi (11 December 1939–6 January 1940)

[See map 16 on page 1326]

The battle of Suomussalmi was the greatest Finnish victory in the Finnish Winter War of 1939–1940 (q.v.), and remains one of the best examples of the Finns' *Motti* tactics. The Soviet 163rd Division began its advance across the northeastern

Finnish border in early December 1939, attmpting to cut Finland in two. The Finnish 9th Brigade, led by Colonel Hjalmar Siilasvuo, cut the Soviets off from their supply lines on 11 December.

Accepting help from their 44th Division, the Soviets did not try to retreat, but attempted to hold back Siilasvuo's troops. Help for the Soviets, however, was long in coming. When the Finnish forces received significant reinforcements on 22 December, they were able to break the 163rd Division into smaller units. The Finns then surrounded and destroyed these *Mottis* one by one, virtually annihilating most of the 163rd Division.

On 2 January 1940, Siilasvuo turned his troops against the Soviet 44th Division. The results were largely the same; the invaders were broken into small units and destroyed one by one. Humiliated, remnants of the 163rd and 44th Divisions tried to flee back across the border, but most of the survivors fell victim to the savagely cold winter or were shot down by Finnish ski patrols. The Finns had, for a while at least, stopped the advance of a vastly superior enemy.

A great triumph for the Finns, Suomussalmi could not affect the eventual course of the war. Although the success resulted in a suspension of Soviet operations in northeastern Finland until February 1940, Soviet troop strength and firepower were eventually too much for the Finns.

When the full-scale Soviet assault began, Finland was forced to the brink of collapse within a month. Yet Suomussalmi, along with the success of the Mannerheim Line (q.v.), secured a brief breathing spell for the Finns in early 1940. More significantly, it revealed the relative weakness of the Red Army, not only to the Finns and the Soviets, but to the rest of the world. The Soviet eagerness to engage in peace talks during February 1940, can be attributed partially to the fact that the Red Army's reputation could not withstand another Suomussalmi. Suomussalmi played an important role in the survival of Finland during the Winter War.

Jussi Hanhimaki

Additional Reading

Engle, Eloise, and Lauri Paananen, *The Winter War: The Russo-Finnish Conflict, 1939–1940* (1973).

Nevakivi, Jukka, *The Appeal That Was Never Made: The Allies, Scandinavia, and the Finnish Winter War, 1939–1940* (1976).

Syria (8 June–11 July 1941)

Following the Armistice of Compiègne on 22 June 1940, the civilian and military authorities in the French mandates of Syria and Lebanon (known as the Levant) remained loyal to the newly established government at Vichy. From late December 1940, an experienced senior general of the French Army, Henri Dentz (q.v.), presided over both Levant states as "high commissioner," with headquarters at Beirut.

By May 1941, the Army of the Levant, commanded by General Raoul de Verdilhac, consisted of two mechanized regiments, four battalions of the French Foreign Legion (q.v.), a mixed colonial regiment (made up of Frenchmen and Senegalese), ten battalions of North African troops (Algerians, Tunisians, and Moroccans), three battalions of Senegalese, and a number of locally recruited units, the *Troupes Speciales*. French airpower in the Levant consisted of sixty fighter planes and thirty bombers. The coastal waters were patrolled by a handful of small vessels.

Since August 1940, Axis supervision of the French administration in the Levant was handled primarily by an Italian "armistice commission" under General Fedele de Giorgis. In January 1941, a German diplomat, Werner Otto von Hentig, likewise began to keep an eye on the situation in Syria and Lebanon. He was replaced in May 1941 by Rudolf von Rahn, a highly energetic junior diplomat who established an impressive record as a political and military troubleshooter both there and eighteen months later in Tunisia (q.v.).

When, in April 1941, a group of Iraqi nationalists under Rashid 'Ali al-Gaylani seized power in Baghdad and proceeded to challenge the British military presence in their country (*see* Habbaniya) the Germans induced the Vichy authorities to deliver French military equipment to the Iraqi rebels and to allow German war planes to stop over in Syria on their way to Iraq. Largely in response to these developments, and in consonance with a policy statement made in 1940 that Britain would not tolerate hostile forces to occupy or use the Levant states, the British government came to the conclusion that military action would have to be taken in the area.

The British expected such action would be supported by General Charles de Gaulle's (q.v.) Free French movement. They also hoped that Turkey, likewise, would give some military assistance. But for several weeks the British commander in chief Middle East, General Sir Archibald Wavell (q.v.), felt he simply did not have enough forces to take any action. As a result, the invasion of the French mandates was postponed until 8 June, although raids by Royal Air Force (RAF) planes

against some airports in Syria had been initiated several weeks earlier.

The Allied invasion force initially was composed of eighteen infantry battalions (nine Australian, six Free French, two Indian, and the British Royal Fusiliers), plus a number of mounted, mechanized, and artillery units. Overall direction of the invasion was in the hands of General Sir Henry Maitland Wilson (q.v.), commander in Palestine and Transjordan. Naval support along the Lebanese coast was provided by Vice Admiral E.L.S. King's 15th Cruiser Squadron, while an assortment of RAF squadrons under Air Commodore L.O. Brown was expected to deal with the Vichy Air Force and to support the ground operations.

Code named Operation EXPORTER, the invasion plan called for one Australian brigade to advance from Palestine toward Beirut along the coastal road, with amphibious support from a battalion of the Special Service Brigade. Another Australian brigade was to thrust northward in to the Litani River valley and beyond, while a third column, made up of the Indian 5th Brigade and Free French troops, would move from the Deraa area toward Kuneitra and Damascus.

When the invasion began in the early hours of 8 June, the Vichy Army of the Levant put up far more resistance than some Allied planners had expected. Attempts by the Free French to bring Vichy troops over to their side failed almost everywhere. Leaflets informing the people of Syria and Lebanon that General Georges Catroux, de Gaulle's representative in the Middle East, had come to put an end to the mandate and to give them liberty and independence likewise had little discernable effect. By 13 June, Allied advances in several sectors had ground to a halt. In some places, like Ezraa, Kuneitra, and Merjayun, Dentz's troops launched successful counterattacks. Moreover, German bombers based in the Dodecanese Islands scored hits on several of the British ships providing fire support along the Lebanese coast. In turn, a Vichy French destroyer trying to reach Lebanon from the west was sunk by British torpedo planes off Cyprus.

On 15 June, Australian troops took Sidon, twenty-five miles south of Beirut. Six days later, after fierce fighting, Indian and Free French troops, supported by a company of Australian machine gunners, entered Damascus. At about the same time, Anglo-Indian mounted troops made their way into northern Syria from Iraq, but they were soon blocked by Vichy forces near Palmyra. Effectively supported from the air, Vichy defenders, including two companies of the Foreign Legion, held on to the oasis for almost two weeks.

The final 23 June–11 July phase of the Syrian campaign was characterized by a significant increase in Allied strength on the ground, in the air, at sea, and growing exhaustion of the Vichy troops. By early July, three brigades of the newly arrived Indian 10th Division were advancing from northern Iraq into the northern third of Syria, thereby threatening the flank and rear of Dentz's forces. In the coastal sector, the bulk of the Australian 7th Division, command by Major General A.S. Allen, gradually dislodged the French defenders in the Damour River area and closed in on Beirut, while other Allied units pushed westward from Damascus toward the coast.

Faced with a steadily deteriorating military situation, Dentz secured permission from the Vichy government on 7 July to open negotiations for a cease-fire. Making use of the American consul-general in Beirut, the French high commissioner notified the British accordingly, and on 9 July, received their terms. Although the Vichy government objected to several items, it authorized Dentz on 11 July to proceed with a purely military agreement. The armistice came into effect on all fronts shortly after midnight. Several hours later, a Vichy delegation headed by de Verdilhac crossed the Australian lines and were taken to Acre, Palestine.

In the ensuing negotiations, the Allies were represented by Wilson and Catroux, although the latter was barred from signing the final document. De Verdilhac's delegation eventually agreed to a modified surrender document that included several clauses that were offensive to the Free French. Among the objectionable clauses was a provision giving Dentz's troops a choice between repatriation to Vichy France or joining de Gaulle's Free French Forces. After the Vichy government was given a chance to study the agreement, the document was formally signed on 14 July.

Much to the chagrin of the Free French movement, only about one-third of the civilian officials in Syria and Lebanon and fewer than 6,000 of Dentz's soldiers opted to throw their lot with de Gaulle. The others, more than 20,000 officers and men, chose repatriation. They were transported to Marseilles in eight convoys between 7 August and mid-September. Many were eventually transferred to garrisons in French North Africa. Dentz was made a grand officer of the *Légion d'Honneur,* but contrary to German wishes, the Vichy authorities did not offer him another major command.

The conquest of Syria and Lebanon cost the British Empire and Commonwealth 3,300 casualties, including prisoners taken by Dentz's forces. The Free French lost approximately 1,300 men, and their Vichy opponents about 6,000. Eight hundred Frenchmen were buried side by side in a Damascus cemetery, all of them, Free French and Vichy alike, resting under one sign: *Morts pour la France* (Died for France).

After considerable friction between British representatives and de Gaulle's delegate-general in the Levant states, General Catroux, the latter officially proclaimed Syria's independence in September 1941. Two months later, Lebanon received a similar assurance, but in reality the people of both states continued under foreign control for several more years.

Ulrich Trumpener

Additional Reading

Mockler, Anthony, *Our Enemies the French: Being an Account of the War Fought between the French and the British, Syria 1941* (1976).

Warner, Geoffrey, *Iraq and Syria, 1941* (1974).

S

T

Taranto (11 November 1940)

[See map 37 on page 1347]

During the first year of World War II, naval aircraft achieved rather questionable results, leaving doubt in some military minds as to their ability to hit and sink enemy vessels. One of the few opportunities for naval aviation to prove itself came during the Norway (q.v.) campaign, when dive bombers based on the Orkney Islands managed to sink the German light cruiser *Königsberg* in Bergen harbor. In those early years, the Royal Navy's (RN) best attack aircraft was the ten-year-old Fairey Swordfish, a slow and somewhat matronly torpedo-carrying biplane. Despite its age, it was an efficient, reliable, and sturdy weapon. Its characteristics were best suited for night operations. It was these aircraft that would prove finally in an actual combat operations the power of attack from the air.

Ever since the Italian invasion of Ethiopia (q.v.) in 1935, the Royal Navy had planned for the possibility of attacking the harbor of Taranto, the main operational base of the Italian Navy. Right from the start, some of the planning included the use of carrier-borne aircraft. This was further supported by the fact that from 1930 on, British aircraft carriers had the ability to conduct night landings. Thus, what became known as Operation JUDGEMENT was conceived in Alexandria, Egypt, by Admiral Sir Andrew Cunningham (q.v.) and Rear Admiral A.L. St. G. Lyster, commander of the HMS *Illustrious,* and was not an entirely new idea.

The Cunningham-Lyster plan called for an attack to be made by two carriers, the HMS *Eagle* and the newest carrier in the Royal Navy, the HMS *Illustrious.* The originally scheduled date was 21 October 1940, the 135th anniversary of the battle of Trafalgar; but more importantly, it was the date of a full moon. The thirty Swordfish aircraft of the two ships started training together in preparation, but a few days before the scheduled attack, a fire on the HMS *Illustrious* destroyed several planes. Then it was discovered that the HMS *Eagle* had sustained more serious damage than previously thought from recent near misses by Italian bombers. The HMS *Eagle* needed to be docked for immediate repairs.

When the next full moon came around, the HMS *Illustrious,* reinforced by five aircraft from the HMS *Eagle,* had to carry out the attack alone. Twenty-one planes took part in the operation, eleven armed with torpedoes, the rest carrying bombs and flares. All were fitted with additional fuel tanks to increase their range.

At dusk on 11 November, the HMS *Illustrious* and her escorts were in the Ionian Sea, 170 nautical miles from Taranto. The Italians were unaware of this fact, despite several indicators that should have warned them. In Taranto, all six of the Italian Navy's battleships were moored in the outer bay of the harbor, the Mar Grande. They were screened by 4,200 meters of torpedo nets, far short of the 12,800 meters the Italian Navy estimated they needed. The big ships were also defended by twelve 4-inch guns, 200 smaller guns, plus many barrage balloons.

On board the *HMS Illustrious,* the attack aircraft started launching at 2030 hours. After ten minutes, the first wave of ten aircraft was on its way to Taranto, followed an hour later by the remaining eleven. The first Swordfish reached Taranto at about 2300 hours with complete surprise. The attack technique consisted of the planes gliding in very close with their engines cut off and delivering their torpedos a few hundreds meters from their designated targets. That made it easier to avoid the antiaircraft fire, which was the only real threat to the attackers.

With the aid of the full moon, their own flares, and the Italians' antiaircraft tracers, the Swordfish were easily able to find their targets, which were sitting ducks. The first hit was scored on the battleship *Conte di Cavour* at 2314 hours, and two other torpedos struck the battleship *Littorio.* The second attack wave arrived at 2350 hours. A third torpedo hit the *Littorio* and one hit the battleship *Duilio.* Of eleven torpedos launched, five hit their targets.

By 0122 hours, it was all over. The only battleship that sank was the *Cavour,* but in shallow water. Several hours later the *Littorio* and the *Duilio* were driven ashore by tugs in order to facilitate quicker salvage operations. Their repairs lasted four and six months, respectively. The *Cavour* was refloated and rebuilt, but never recommissioned. The Italians lost fifty-one sailors. The British lost only two planes, and one of the aircrews was rescued by the Italians. Thus with a single blow and at a very small expense, the British Fleet Air Arm deprived Italy of its naval superiority in the Mediterranean.

The results of the Taranto raid had a profound strategic impact on the remainder of the war in the Mediterranean. It had even broader strategic implications as well. Taranto became a lesson for the Japanese, who slightly more than a year later were to do something very similar but on a larger scale to the U.S. Pacific Fleet at Pearl Harbor.

Francesco Fatutta

Additional Reading
Cunningham, Sir Andrew, *A Sailor's Odyssey* (1951).
Schofield, B., *The Taranto Night* (1974).
Smithers, A.J., *Taranto 1940* (1995).

TIGER, Exercise (26 April 1944)
As a prelude to the Normandy (q.v.) Landings, Supreme Headquarters, Allied Expeditionary Forces (SHAEF) (q.v.) ordered rehearsals of several aspects of the amphibious assault. One of these practice assaults, Exercise TIGER, began on the morning of 26 April 1944 at Slapton Sands, an invasion training beach between Dartmouth and Plymouth on the southern coast of Britain. Slapton Sands had water behind it and high ground commanding the beach. There, army engineers constructed replicas of the German fortifications at Normandy's UTAH Beach. Members of the U.S. 4th Infantry Division (American Assault Force U), scheduled to land at UTAH Beach, took part in the exercise.

General Dwight D. Eisenhower (q.v.) and his party boarded observation craft at 0600 hours to watch the maneuver scheduled to begin an hour and a half later. At 0700 hours, naval bombardment of beach fortifications began. H-Hour was then postponed and the 0730 landing did not take place, causing a backup of landing ships, tank (LSTs) and their cargo of duplex drive (DDs) amphibious tanks.

While the LSTs milled around offshore, aircraft fired rockets onto the beach, blowing up barbed wire, tank ditches, and prepared positions. Next, the DDs made their way to the beach. One sank in the choppy waters. Because the landing craft, vehicles and personnel (LCVPs) were launched from eight miles out, the remainder of the DDs arrived on the beach at the same time as the first wave of infantry. Once on shore, the tanks were held up while engineers coordinated the demolition of obstacles with hand-emplaced explosives. That delay pointed out vulnerabilities and other problems for the actual assault.

That night, as the second and third waves of Exercise TIGER moved toward the beach, nine German E-boats from Cherbourg attacked the LSTs. The LSTs were unable to conduct evasive maneuvers and there were no destroyer escorts. The E-boats sank LSTs *507* and *531* and seriously damaged LST *289,* killing ninety-seven sailors and 441 soldiers. The attack destroyed the entire LST reserve for Operation OVERLORD.

Because the topographical features of Slapton Sands were similar to OMAHA and UTAH Beaches, SHAEF feared the Germans had gathered valuable intelligence. Two officers familiar with the OVERLORD assault plan were among the missing and rumors suggested that they were captured. Divers finally found their bodies, ending that portion of the security scare. SHAEF imposed strict censorship on the entire incident to avoid alerting the Germans to its importance.

Eisenhower and his party were disappointed by the exercise. The H-Hour delay, the confusion in the movement of the LCTs and the LCVPs, the launch of the infantry craft from eight miles out, the poorly coordinated engineer actions, and the disastrous attack by German E-Boats all made Exercise TIGER fall far short of SHAEF's expectations. The failures were treated as lessons learned, however. Only a few days later, the Allies corrected most of the mistakes during Exercise FABIUS, conducted between 2 and 6 May. One month later the Allies launched Operation OVERLORD.

Robert F. Pace

Additional Reading
Butcher, Harry C., *My Three Years with Eisenhower: The Personal Diary of Captain Harry C. Butcher, USNR; Naval Aide to General Eisenhower, 1942 to 1945* (1946).
Eisenhower, John S.D., *Allies: Pearl Harbor to D-Day* (1982).
Lewis, Nigel, *Exercise Tiger: The Dramatic True Story of a Hidden Tragedy of World War II* (1990).

Tobruk I (6–22 January 1941)

The Libyan port of Tobruk was one of the centerpieces of the bitter struggle for North Africa in 1941 and 1942. The British first took Tobruk during the exploitation phase of Operation COMPASS, launched on 9 December 1940 to drive the Italians out of Egypt. Major General Richard O'Connor's (q.v.) Western Desert Force soundly defeated the Italians inside Egypt at Sidi Barrani (q.v.) on 11 December. The Italians fled back into Libya, but O'Connor was not able to pursue immediately. Just when Sidi Barrani fell, he lost one of his two divisions. The Indian 4th Division was withdrawn for redeployment to Sudan three weeks before the arrival of its replacement, the Australian 6th Division.

After the unnecessary delay, O'Connor crossed into Libya and captured the coastal fortress of Bardia (q.v.) on 5 January. Continuing the drive with the British 7th Armoured Division (the "Desert Rats") and the Australian 6th Division, the Western Desert Force brought Tobruk under siege on 6 January. Tobruk, which was some seventy miles inside Libya, was defended by 32,000 Italian troops, 220 guns, and seventy tanks under the command of General Petassi Manella. By 9 January the encirclement of Tobruk was complete.

On 21 January the Australian 6th Division began the attack on Tobruk. After a heavy artillery preparation, the southeast corner of the defenses collapsed. Later that day Fort Palastrino fell and General Manella was captured. The remainder of the garrison surrendered on 22 January, after destroying some of the port facilities. The British, however, were able to put the port back in operation very quickly.

About 27,000 Italians surrendered at Tobruk. The Allies sustained some 500 casualties in the siege. O'Connor continued his drive to the west, taking Derna on 30 January, Benghazi on 7 February, and winning a major victory at Beda Fomm (q.v.) on 6 February.

David T. Zabecki

Additional Reading
Carver, Michael, *Tobruk* (1964).
Heckstall-Smith, Anthony, *Tobruk: The Story of a Siege* (1959).
Pitt, Barrie, *The Crucible of War: Western Desert, 1941* (1980).

Tobruk II (10 April–10 December 1941)

[See map 19 on page 1329]

The Libyan port of Tobruk was one of the centerpieces in the see-saw struggle for North Africa in 1941. By holding out for 240 days, the besieged British garrison preserved a presence in Libya and prevented an invasion of Egypt by posing a constant threat to the Axis armies' rear areas. Twice the Axis tried to reduce the fortress; twice the British mounted futile attempts to relieve it. Tobruk became a symbol of defiance for embattled Britain.

In mid-February 1941, British forces occupied all of Cyrenaica (eastern Libya) following their victory at Sidi Barrani (q.v.) in December 1940. Allied troop transfers to Greece and East Africa, however, left the British thinly spread and ill-prepared. Major General Richard O'Connor (q.v.) and his experienced desert units were withdrawn and replaced by Major General Philip Neame and the understrength and inexperienced 2nd Armoured Division, Australian 9th Division, and an Indian Brigade.

British Middle East commander in chief General Sir Archibald Wavell (q.v.), discounted the immediate threat when Lieutenant General Erwin Rommel (q.v.) and his lead German units arrived in Libya in mid-February. Wavell told London on 2 March that an attack was unlikely before summer; but Prime Minister Winston S. Churchill (q.v.) warned that the Germans might strike before attaining full strength. Churchill also urged holding the narrow El Agheila bottleneck. When the Axis attack came, however, Wavell ordered a fighting withdrawal, which allowed the German armor to reach Cyrenaica's open country. The consequence was disastrous for the Allies.

Adolf Hitler (q.v.) had told Rommel that the loss of Libya "must be prevented under all circumstances." Knowing that all of his forces would not arrive until April–May, Rommel rushed arriving units into forward positions, emplacing dummy tanks to fool the British and to forestall the preemptive attack he expected them to launch. When none came by mid-March, Rommel began testing his opponent's defenses. German air superiority meanwhile, helped conceal his weakness from the

British. By late March, Rommel's probes had reoccupied El Agheila and beyond.

Disregarding orders to await his full complement, Rommel launched a full-scale attack on 2 April with the fifty tanks of the 15th *Panzer* Division, backed by two of the new Italian divisions. The result was a rout. On 6 April a German patrol captured Generals Neame and O'Connor—the latter having been sent back to the forward area to advise Neame. Despite driving across open desert reversing O'Connor's earlier route, Rommel failed to trap any major British forces. Failing to take Tobruk on the run, he bypassed the fortified port and continued to drive toward the east. Rommel soon controlled all of Cyrenaica except the coastal enclave at Tobruk. In under two weeks, he recaptured the gains Britain had won during its two-month advance.

Wavell's doubts about holding Tobruk gave way under pressure from Churchill, who considered it "unthinkable" to abandon the fortress. Thus Wavell complied while also planning Egypt's defenses. Tobruk's 36,000-man garrison was formed around Major General Leslie Morshead's (q.v.) Australian 9th Division. During the siege, supplies and reinforcements came in by sea, including the 18th Infantry Brigade of the Australian 7th Division and units of the 1st and 7th Royal Tank Regiments.

Tobruk had been strongly fortified by Italy. Double thirty-mile perimeter lines, anchored by numerous fortified points, lay nine miles inland from the harbor. The Italian-built concrete artillery emplacements, largely impervious to German guns, and old antitank ditches were hastily improved. The British mined the area and assembled a force of about fifty tanks. Morshead declared, "There'll be no Dunkirk here. . . . No surrender and no retreat."

Rommel moved quickly to reduce Tobruk. After some probing attacks on 11 April, he ordered elements of the 5th Light Division to attack on 14 April along the middle southern perimeter. The weakly held line broke, but Rommel's armor was stopped by strong artillery fire, costing him nearly half his tanks. An Italian assault on 16–17 April also collapsed, with the Australians taking almost 1,000 prisoners. Intense air action made Tobruk costly for both sides.

Rommel attacked again on 30 April with non-tank units of the 15th *Panzer* Division. Striking at night in the southwest, the German infantry opened a mile-long breach early on 1 May; but then the exploiting tanks ran into mines. A second wave of tanks and infantry made a three-mile lateral advance to the southeast; but they were halted by British artillery sited behind the minefields. British tanks counterattacked and Rommel's Italian support troops hastily withdrew.

After losing half of his seventy tanks, Rommel abandoned the attack. Morshead's counterattack on 3 May also failed to recover the lost ground. The German high command, meanwhile, had sent General Friedrich Paulus (q.v.) to check on Rommel. After first cautioning Rommel, then agreeing to the 30 April attack, Paulus forbade further assaults. Given the German preparation for the invasion of the Soviet Union (q.v.), Rommel's superiors were more interested in restraining him.

Wavell's pleas for more tanks led Churchill to strip home units and send a convoy, code named TIGER, through the risky Mediterranean. The 238 tanks he received on 12 May let Wavell reequip four regiments. Even though the British Matilda tanks were vulnerable to German antitank guns, Wavell attacked twice from Egypt. During Operation BREVITY, launched on 15 May, the British took the Halfaya Pass then Fort Capuzzo. Rommel regained the pass on 27 May, emplacing four 88mm guns there.

On 15 June, the British launched Operation BATTLEAXE to relieve Tobruk and crush Rommel's forces. Wavell's failure to concentrate his armor, however, was a major weakness in the British plan. Commanding XIII Corps, Lieutenant General Noel Beresford-Peirse launched a frontal assault against the Halfaya Pass with 25,000 troops. On his right wing, many of the Matilda tanks were destroyed by the German 88s at Halfaya, which the British came to call "Hellfire Pass." The XIII Corps' center encountered the 15th *Panzer* Division massing on its front, and the 7th Armoured Division on the corps' left wing was turned by the 5th *Panzer* Regiment. On 16 June, a strong counterattack forced a British withdrawal.

Operation BATTLEAXE was the biggest armored struggle thus far in North Africa; but in three days, the British gained nothing, suffered almost 1,000 casualties, and lost ninety-one tanks to Rommel's dozen. Churchill relieved Wavell of his command on 21 June and replaced him with General Sir Claude Auchinleck (q.v.). General Alan Cunningham (q.v.) was placed in command of the Eighth Army. Having prevented two major relief attempts, Rommel maintained pressure on Tobruk. The stalemate continued for months with each side intent on breaking the deadlock.

After eight months of siege, Britain finally relieved Tobruk with Operation CRUSADER, launched on 18 November 1941. From the outset,

British Matilda tanks move forward near Tobruk, 12 September 1941. (IWM E 5559)

Cunningham's operational plans were flawed and Rommel's reactions were unexpected. The resulting prolonged and unnecessarily costly fighting produced neither the total destruction of the Axis forces, nor the permanent control of the region that was the operation's goal.

For the seventy-mile advance from Egypt to Tobruk, Cunningham split his troops and about 580 tanks between two corps. Lieutenant General C.W.N. Norrie's XXX Corps, which consisted of the 7th Armoured Division, the 4th and 22nd Armoured Brigades, and the 1st and 2nd South African Divisions, was to advance through the desert from Maddalena to reach Gabr Saleh, where the British expected Rommel to rush his armor into defeat. XXX Corps would then drive westward to Sidi Rezegh, where forces breaking out from Tobruk would make contact.

Lieutenant General A.R. Godwin-Austen's XIII Corps, consisting of the New Zealand Division, the Indian 4th Division, and the 1st Army Tank Brigade, was to advance in the north, outflanking and isolating Axis border posts and then move west toward the Tobruk enclave. Concern over the twenty-mile gap between the two corps, which widened as XXX Corps moved westward, led to an even greater dispersal of the tank units into smaller formations. Loose control of the armored units further undermined their effectiveness.

Rommel upset British plans because he had plans of his own to attack Tobruk on 21 November. Under Rommel, General Ludwig Crüwell now headed the restructured *Afrika Korps* (q.v.), which consisted of the 15th and 21st (ex-5th Light) *Panzer* Divisions, and the new 90th Light Division. Rommel still had formidable advantages over the British. His armor and his 88mm antitank guns had greater firepower, his units' composition allowed greater independence and flexibility, and his *Panzers* lay between Britain's two separate corps. Especially important was Rommel's ability to throw his more than 400 tanks against the small individual elements of Cunningham's badly fragmented armor. With the German *Panzers* positioned around Gambut in the north, Italy's mobile forces held the desert near Bir el Gobi, while the Italian XXI Corps waited to attack Tobruk.

Little in XXX Corps' three-pronged attack toward Sidi Rezegh went well. The 22nd Armoured Brigade on the left suffered heavy tank losses at Bir el Gobi, the 4th Armoured Brigade on the right was mauled by German forces, and the 7th Armoured Brigade in center found itself alone when it reached Sidi Rezegh (q.v.). Initially unsure of the attack's scope and aims, Rommel surmised its intent by 20 November, moving his armored force west for a showdown. At Sidi Rezegh airfield, his *Panzers* faced Allied units still divided and weakened by Axis air strikes and artillery fire from the 90th Light Division. The 7th Armoured Brigade's early gains disappeared during 21–23

November. Rommel's ability to deal piecemeal with the opposing tank units underscored the mistakes in British planning.

Late on 23 November, the strain of losing 300 tanks made Cunningham propose withdrawing from Sidi Rezegh. Auchinleck arrived at Cunningham's headquarters that night, took charge, and ordered Cunningham to attack "relentlessly." The next day, Auchinleck told his troops that Rommel was desperate: "We will not be distracted and he will be destroyed." Two days later, he replaced Cunningham with General Neil Ritchie (q.v.), but maintained close personal control over the Eighth Army.

The distraction Auchinleck mentioned was Rommel's next surprise. Convinced the British faced defeat, Rommel gambled on a decisive thrust to Egypt, personally leading almost all his armor, some eighty tanks. On 24 November, the *Panzers* and the Italian *Ariete* Armored Division reached the Sidi Omar area. En route Rommel just missed discovering two big British desert depots. Yet his plan to relieve isolated border fortresses and cut off the expected British retreat met stiff resistance and failed. Radio failures left Rommel uninformed and out of touch with the situation. The British did not panic or retreat, and the XIII Corps was threatening Rommel's own rear. Rommel had to return west.

The four-day absence of Rommel's armor from the main battle proved to be the turning point. The British got a much-needed respite. Upon his return, Rommel faced a new crisis in the Sidi Rezegh area. Remnants of the XXX Corps had regrouped, the forces in Tobruk were attacking outward, and the XIII Corps units had arrived. Although Axis forces still held the border positions, Auchinleck pressed XIII Corps' advance to Tobruk, profiting from the absence of Rommel's armor.

Throughout the offensive, the Tobruk garrison fought hard to connect with British forces attempting its relief. Major General Ronald Scobie of the 70th Division had additional Polish infantry and about 100 tanks of the 32nd Army Tank Brigade. Encircling Tobruk were four understrength Italian divisions and the German 90th Light Division. On 20–21 November, Tobruk's garrison won ground in heavy fighting during the attempt to link up with British forces at Sidi Rezegh. The arrival of a German unit, however, prevented the linkage. On 26 November, having learned the New Zealand Division would attack Sidi Rezegh early that day, Scobie struck out again. The delayed New Zealanders, advancing via Belhamed, later established a tenuous link with the Tobruk garrison in the El Duda sector. Fierce Axis counterattacks on 26 and 27 November twice broke the connection. The return of the German *Panzer* divisions further intensified the fighting.

After repeated clashes, the Allied corridor held and Tobruk was relieved on 29 November. Operation CRUSADER ended on 10 December. It succeeded in relieving Tobruk, but it had failed to crush the Axis forces. Rommel's subsequent careful withdrawal from eastern Libya proceeded amid Italian protests and considerable hesitation by the British. By January Rommel's remaining armor and troops were safely back at El Agheila. The Axis units pocketed near the Egyptian border surrendered by mid-January.

The criticisms of Operation CRUSADER are justified. The planning was poor and British strength was misused. Only timely intervention by Auchinleck and the failed gamble of Rommel's "dash to the wire" saved the British operation. British casualties came to 18,000. Rommel's loss of more than 30,000 men and 340 tanks lulled the British into a false sense of security, however. Within weeks, Rommel attacked again.

Richard Wires

Additional Reading

Barnett, Correlli, *The Desert Generals* (1982).
Carell, Paul, *The Foxes of the Desert* (1961).
Carver, Michael, *Dilemmas of the Desert War: A New Look at the Libyan Campaign, 1940–1942* (1986).
———, *Tobruk* (1964).
Harrison, Frank, *Tobruk; The Great Siege Reassessed* (1996).
Heckmann, Wolf, *Rommel's War in Africa* (1981).
Heckstall-Smith, Anthony, *Tobruk: The Story of a Siege* (1959).
Pitt, Barrie, *The Crucible of War: Western Desert, 1941* (1980).

Tobruk III (20–21 June 1942)
[See map 19 on page 1329]
Tobruk had great symbolic as well as military importance in 1942. Britain's costly relief of the port/fortress on 29 November 1941 after an eight-month Axis siege (*see* Tobruk II) failed to prevent General Erwin Rommel (q.v.) from withdrawing the bulk of his forces westward to safety around El Agheila. From there, on 21 January, his strengthened and resupplied units attacked General Neil Ritchie's (q.v.) thinly spread Eighth Army in the hope of taking Tobruk and again reaching Egypt.

At this point in the war, the British had been weakened by troop exhaustion, poor deployment of units, and troop withdrawals to meet new threats in Asia. While the 7th Armoured and the Indian 4th Divisions were reequipping and the newly arrived and still weak 1st Armoured Division was widely dispersed in forward areas, the weakened Rommel struck at the British without his superiors' permission. The unexpected 21 January attack sent Italian units along the coast while German tanks battered the British advanced positions. Initial success and a large and much-needed capture of Allied materiel prompted Rommel to continue his drive against the confused Allies. Rommel took Benghazi in late January, and by 4 February, his forces reached the hastily prepared Gazala Line, forty miles from Tobruk. Then, for the next four months, relative calm prevailed.

Each side prepared for an attack; but Prime Minister Winston S. Churchill's (q.v.) repeated insistence that his Middle East commander in chief, General Sir Claude Auchinleck (q.v.), clear North Africa immediately was unrealistic, given British resources. Auchinleck delayed action until June. Rommel planned his attack for May. Despite receiving Italian reinforcements and more aircraft, he worried about Britain's continuing buildup, fearing also that an Axis action against Malta might drain his own forces. In late May, Rommel's strength approached Britain's; 113,000 troops to Britain's 125,000, 570 to 940 tanks, and 500 to 700 planes. Authorized only to take Tobruk, and to proceed to the Egyptian border if successful, Rommel envisioned much greater gains.

Britain's defensive line stretched from Gazala on the coast, south through the desert forty-five miles to a strongpoint at Bir Hacheim. Special "boxes" defendable in all directions were connected by deep minefields extending well behind the British line. Ritchie deployed XIII Corps, consisting of the South African 1st Division and the 50th Division, in the north. XXX Corps was in the south, with the Free French holding Bir Hacheim. He kept his armor behind the line in support: the 1st and 32nd Tank Brigades in the north; the 1st Armoured Division near the Knightsbridge track junction; and 7th Armored Division south behind Bir Hacheim. Other units held desert outposts southeast of the line. The area around Tobruk was defended by the South African 2nd Division and the Indian 9th Brigade. Most military analysts believe Ritchie's scattered armor deployments reduced his effectiveness for counterattacking.

Rommel launched Operation VENEZIA on 26 May. That afternoon, Italian and German units under General Ludwig Crüwell attacked the Gazala Line (q.v.). That evening, Rommel led his armor south around Bir Hacheim and then north into the British rear; but the attack ran into problems. Axis frontal assaults failed to dislodge the British, Free French troops stopped Italian tanks at Bir Hacheim, and German armor suffered heavy losses against XXX Corps. In tank battles around El Adem south of Tobruk and the Knightsbridge track junction, well behind Britain's defense line, powerful German 88mm guns decimated the British armor. Each side lost about 370 tanks, but Rommel could not immediately replace his losses.

With the Allied main line holding and his armor stalled, Rommel shifted his approach by 29 May, attacking the line's center and southern points in force. When Axis forces finally breached the center of the line, they did not fan out, but protected the gap itself against repeated British assaults. Intense fighting in the bulge that came to be known as "The Cauldron" cost both sides heavy casualties. French tenacity in holding Bir Hacheim, meanwhile, also frustrated Rommel. Because Allied patrols raiding his supply route weakened the *Panzer* divisions farther north, Rommel bolstered the Italians, but the defenders held firm against repeated heavy air and armor attacks.

After more than two weeks of fierce conflict, French General Pierre Koenig (q.v.) was forced to withdraw his garrison from Bir Hacheim during the night of 10–11 June. With his supply lines now open and secure, Rommel broke out of the Cauldron on 11 June. On 12 June he struck at Knightsbridge, inflicting further huge tank losses on the Allies. By 13 June, it was clear the Axis had won the Gazala battle and Ritchie began withdrawing toward the Egyptian border.

Rommel reached the Tobruk perimeter on 18 June. Pushing his armor well east of Tobruk while other units surrounded it, he gave the impression of again bypassing the trapped British garrison, as he had done during his first offensive. But early on 20 June, he attacked the perimeter, this time from the southeast. The combined ground and air assaults showed his determination not to leave an enemy fortified position in his rear area this time.

Three armored divisions made a coordinated assault, and by 1600 hours they were in control of the airfield. Three hours after that, the 21st *Panzer* Division reached the harbor. Major General H.B. Klopper, commander of the South African 2nd Division, put up a determined resistance. While waiting for help from Ritchie that never came, the defenders destroyed as much of the port facilities

and war materiel as they could. The last of the defenders finally surrendered on the evening of 21 June. Despite their efforts, the Axis forces captured two and a half million gallons of much-needed fuel, plus about 5,000 tons of general supplies and 2,000 wheeled vehicles. That materiel was a great help to Rommel in his further eastward drive. About 33,000 Allied soldiers were taken prisoner; but units of the Coldstream Guards, who refused to surrender, managed to escape to the east.

By 28 June, Rommel had a forward line at Mersa Matrúh in western Egypt. Control of the battle areas enabled him to recover and repair many of his tanks. For his sweeping victories at Gazala and Tobruk, Adolf Hitler (q.v.) promoted Rommel to field marshal. Hitler then persuaded Benito Mussolini (q.v.) to give Suez priority over Malta (q.v.). Rommel thus won permission to continue his drive to the Nile.

In blaming Ritchie for losing Tobruk, historians have cited his slowness in reacting to situations and his costly piecemeal assaults. Auchinleck relieved him on 25 June and assumed personal command of the Eighth Army. After a small fight at Mersa Matrúh (q.v.), Auchinleck withdrew farther into Egypt and prepared to make a stand in the vicinity of El Alamein. The stage was being set for the great battles to follow.

Richard Wires

Additional Reading

Agar-Hamilton, John A.I., and Leonard Turner, *Crisis in the Desert: May–July 1942* (1952).
Barnett, Correlli, *The Desert Generals* (1982).
Carver, Michael, *Dilemmas of the Desert War: A New Look at the Libyan Campaign, 1940–1942* (1986).
———, *Tobruk* (1964).
Pitt, Barrie, *The Crucible of War: Year of Alamein, 1942* (1982).

TORCH, Operation

See NORTHWEST AFRICA LANDINGS

Toulon (27 November 1942)

[See map 27 on page 1337]
At dawn on 27 November 1942, German *Panzers* forced their way into the French naval base at Toulon, on the French Mediterranean coast. Adolf Hitler (q.v.) had given the orders for the German forces in occupied France to take over Vichy France. SS General Paul Hauser's (q.v.) II SS *Panzer Korps* had the mission of seizing the French

High Seas Fleet by a *coup de main*. Hitler intended to add the French warships to his own meager fleet, and perhaps use the seizure as leverage to energize his lethargic Italian allies.

The French Navy anticipated the German move, however, and they were prepared for it. The fleet's deputy commander, Admiral Jean de Laborde, ordered the ships scuttled just as the Germans broke into the base. Although the Germans had a long established plan for the operation, it fell apart in the execution. The 4,500 German naval personnel who were supposed to actually take control of the French ships did not arrive on time for two reasons: first, the German Navy had a general distaste for the operation, and second, Hitler wanted his vaunted SS to be able to take the lion's share of the credit.

Within thirty minutes, virtually the entire French fleet was on the harbor bottom. It was, however, a closely run thing, with some of the demolition charges detonating as the Germans approached the ships' gangways. By the time it was over, one battleship, two battle cruisers, seven cruisers, thirty destroyers, eighteen minor surface combatants, a seaplane tender, and twenty-eight submarines sank into the mud. Four submarines escaped into the open ocean. Hitler's dreams of naval power in the Mediterranean went down with the French fleet.

Carl O. Schuster

Additional Reading

Piekalkiewicz, Janusz, *Sea War: 1939–1945* (1987).
Roskill, Stephen W., *The War at Sea 1939–1945: The Period of Balance* (1956).
Tute, Warren, *The Reluctant Enemies* (1990).

Tunis

See BIZERTE AND TUNIS

Tunisia (12 November 1942–9 May 1943)

[See map 23 on page 1333]
The Tunisian campaign was the final act in the dramatic North Africa campaign (q.v.). It was the natural result of two factors—the Allied landings in Northwest Africa (q.v.) and Tunisia's geographic position dominating the Axis lines of logistics to North Africa. The former placed significant Allied forces in position to seize Tunisia, while the latter made it imperative for the Germans that the Vichy French protectorate stay out of Allied hands. Both sides realized Tunisia's strategic importance. With

Axis sea convoys already under attack from Malta-based Allied forces, the addition of Allied power in Tunisia would place the Axis logistics train in an ever-constricting vice. Allied possession of Tunisia, on the other hand, would make the Axis position in North Africa untenable. With that in mind, both sides raced to seize the country against a backdrop of political maneuvering almost Byzantine in nature. The result was a six-month-long campaign that both determined the fate of Axis forces in North Africa, and set the stage for Benito Mussolini's (q.v.) downfall six months later.

Given the shorter distances between their operating bases and the objective (150 km versus 800 km), the Allied forces had the advantage. Field Marshal Erwin Rommel's (q.v.) defeat at El Alamein (q.v.) in October 1942 led Adolf Hitler (q.v.) to rush reinforcements into Libya. These reinforcements, however, were not applied against the British forces steadily advancing from Egypt; rather they were dispatched to Tunisia under the command of General Walter Nehring. At that point, only a German parachute regiment, an airborne engineer battalion, a reconnaissance company, and some naval infantry were present in Tunisia—all with the agreement of the Vichy French authorities. Elements of an Italian infantry division were just entering the country. As Rommel was being pushed back across the northern rim of North Africa, Hitler ordered him to stand fast near Derna, Libya, and directed Nehring to assist the Vichy French in the defense of Tunisia. Expecting the French forces to resist the Allied advance from the west and Rommel to hold the British coming from the east, Hitler gave Nehring an independent command, the XC *Korps*. It made sense at the time because Rommel's and Nehring's commands were separated by nearly 2,000 kilometers. Fortunately for the Allies, both of Hitler's assumptions proved false, and the Axis forces had a divided command structure in Tunisia until it was too late.

Nehring arrived in Tunis on 16 November. His original instructions were to avoid confrontation with French forces, which impeded his efforts to establish a defensive perimeter on Tunisia's western frontier. Realizing the changing strategic winds, the commander of the French division in Tunisia, General Georges Barre, employed passive resistance to delay the Axis forces without provoking an open breach with Germany. By 17 November, the Axis had approximately 3,000 troops in Tunisia as opposed to 17,000 French, and advance elements of the Anglo-American armies from Operation TORCH were rapidly approaching from the west.

For the Allies, the advance across Algeria was delayed by similar considerations. Local French commanders, particularly Admiral Jean François Darlan (q.v.), were reluctant to cooperate because of their oaths to Marshal Henri Philippe Pétain (q.v.) in Vichy. The result was a series of political discussions, while Allied forces advanced cautiously across Algeria facing passive resistance from Vichy troops. Neither side wanted to initiate hostilities. Meanwhile, two Allied columns marching on Tunisia, "Hartforce" and "Bladeforce," crossed the border on 16 November. Hartforce, consisting primarily of the British 11th Infantry Brigade, took the coast road, while Bladeforce, drawn from the American 1st Armored Division, reached the border inland near Beja, the location of Barre's headquarters.

Both forces ran into German troops on 20 November, encountering stiff resistance despite having superior numbers. In a pattern that would be repeated often in Tunisia, the *Luftwaffe* provided excellent support, while the Allied air forces were noteworthy primarily in their absence. Bladeforce, nonetheless, broke through the Axis defenses and penetrated to within forty-five kilometers of Tunis on 25 November. It was halted only by the desperate ground fire of some *Luftwaffe* air defense batteries and a German reconnaissance company. British commando and airborne landings at Depienne on 29 November were also quickly pushed back.

Despite some initial local successes, the Axis situation was critical. Only one tank battalion and some additional infantry had arrived since 17 November, and the French troops were becoming increasingly hostile. Also, additional Allied troops were flowing eastward, using the French rail system in Algeria. Nehring believed the Allies were winning the race and reported his concerns to Field Marshal Albert Kesselring (q.v.), commander in chief of German forces in the central Mediterranean *(OB Süd)*. The result was a rapid and massive dispatch of reinforcements to Tunisia by air. It was this "air bridge" that tipped the balance in favor of the Axis.

By 27 November, Nehring had the bulk of the 10th *Panzer* Division in Tunisia and nearly 26,000 troops. He initiated a series of limited counterattacks on 1 December. Directed against the more spread out American forces, these attacks gradually forced Bladeforce back to Mebjez El Bah, while the reinforced German Airborne Engineer Battalion fought a delaying action against Hartforce west of Mateur. Rain, poor roads, and *Luftwaffe* raids delayed Allied supplies and reinforce-

ments. In reaction, the Allies halted their advance and began digging in on 28 November.

Another significant factor in the battle for Tunisia was the 23–27 November German occupation of Vichy France, which settled the question of Tunisia's French garrison. Two battalions of German troops disarmed the 12,000-strong French garrison in Bizerte, which surrendered quietly on 7 December. Barre's troops in the remainder of Tunisia had already gone over to the Allies. On 8 December, Nehring turned command in Tunisia over to Colonel General Jürgen von Arnim (q.v.). The XC *Korps* was reorganized and became the Fifth *Panzerarmee.* The buildup phase of the Tunisian campaign was over.

The situation in Tunisia remained fairly stable for the rest of 1942, with the British First Army and the American II Corps standing roughly along the western Tunisian frontier. Thus it remained until Rommel entered Tunisia from the southeast on 13 February 1943, having escaped General Sir Bernard L. Montgomery's (q.v.) efforts to trap him in Libya. Although a shell of its former self, Rommel's *Panzerarmee Afrika* remained a potent foe. Rommel placed the bulk of his forces along the Mareth Line to hold Montgomery while he planned his future operations.

Fortunately for the Allies, the Axis command structure remained divided. Complicating matters, von Arnim disliked Rommel intensely. Seeing how thinly stretched Allied forces were in Tunisia, Rommel wanted to drive the Americans out before Montgomery could mount an assault on the Mareth Line. Von Arnim wanted a more limited offensive to expand the Axis bridgehead in Tunisia. Thus he extended only marginal cooperation to Rommel. The result was the 14–22 February battle of Kasserine Pass (q.v.), which decimated the U.S. II Corps, but had no lasting impact on Allied fortunes in Tunisia. A coordinated offensive could have devastated the Allied forces, but von Arnim refused to synchronize his actions with Rommel.

On 24 February, Hitler finally unified the Axis command in Tunisia by making Rommel the commander of Army Group *Afrika,* which included von Arnim's Fifth *Panzerarmee* and the Italian First Army of Marshal Giovanni Messe. The changes came too late, however. Rommel left Africa for the last time on 9 March, leaving von Arnim in overall command. Kasserine Pass was the last Axis victory in North Africa.

By early March, the Allies had streamlined their chain of command and revitalized the U.S. II Corps, now under Lieutenant General George S. Patton (q.v.). General Sir Harold Alexander (q.v.), commander of the Allied 18th Army Group, was placed in overall command of Allied forces in Tunisia. On 20 March, he launched a limited offensive to reduce the Axis perimeter. Montgomery's Eighth Army led the main effort, assaulting the Mareth Line (q.v.), while Patton's II Corps attacked at El Guettar (q.v.). The *Luftwaffe* made its presence felt initially, but the Allies gained air superiority over Tunisia by 6 April. That had an immediate effect on Allied fortunes, forcing Axis troops back to Enfadaville.

Allied air and naval forces then stepped up their attacks on Axis shipping and transport aircraft supplying Tunisia. Armed with ULTRA (q.v.) intelligence and vastly superior air and naval forces, the Allied commanders eviscerated the Axis air and sea bridges to Tunisia. By late March, Axis fuel supplies fell below minimum requirements and no new tanks arrived after 1 April. Von Arnim would have to fight the final battles with the equipment he had on hand.

Alexander, meanwhile, rearranged his forces, placing the Americans on the northern coast and the British First Army, with the French XIX Crops in the center, while the Eighth Army retained its position on the Allied southern flank. He launched a second offensive on 22 April. Once again, Montgomery led the main effort, with U.S. II Corps in a supporting role. Axis resistance was heavy and von Arnim employed his declining armored forces well, using sharp counterattacks to contain British breakthroughs. Nonetheless, by 1 May the Axis forces had been pushed back into a pocket eighty by thirty kilometers. Despite the inevitability of defeat, Hitler refused to evacuate. Von Arnim was told to resist to the "last round."

The final Allied offensive came on 6 May. Lacking fuel and ammunition, most Axis units surrendered quickly. Bizerte and Tunis (q.v.) fell on 7 and 8 May, respectively. Within twenty-four hours, the last real vestiges of Axis resistance ended. The last Axis forces on Cape Bon surrendered on 12 May. More than 275,000 Axis troops marched into captivity and the North Africa campaign was finally over.

The Tunisian campaign was typical of the war in North Africa. Logistics were the key to victory in North Africa and Tunisia reflected that. When the Axis forces had the supplies and equipment, they seized the initiative, keeping the Allies off balance, constrained only by the availability of logistics support to exploit their victories. In Tunisia, the Axis made maximum use of their shorter logistics lines to gain and hold the key terrain early in the campaign. But their divided command

structure and the personal animosity between the principal commanders precluded the full exploitation of tactical opportunities. For their part, the Allies made their share of mistakes; but having materiel supremacy over their opponents they achieved ultimate victory despite these errors.

Carl O. Schuster

Additional Reading

Howe, George F., *Northwest Africa: Seizing the Initiative in the West* (1956).

Jones, Vincent, *Operation Torch* (1972).

Macksey, K.J., *Afrika Korps* (1968).

U

Ukraine (November 1943–July 1944)

[See map 32 on page 1342]

Between August and November 1943, the 1st, 2nd, 3rd, and 4th Ukrainian Fronts (army groups) progressively pushed German Army Group South from the Donets River (q.v.) back to and across the Dnieper River (q.v.). On 6 November, General Nikolai Vatutin's (q.v.) 1st Ukrainian Front liberated the Ukrainian capital city of Kiev. By 1 December, the Soviets were across the Dnieper in most places, forcing the Germans out of their only partially prepared Wotan defensive positions. Now, 70 percent of the Red Army's tank units, more than half of its combat aircraft, and 40 percent of its artillery were poised to drive the Germans from the remainder of the Ukraine.

The Soviets enjoyed an especially large numerical advantage in fighter aircraft. With more than half of the *Luftwaffe*'s fighter force tied down defending the skies over Germany from British and American bombers, the Soviets had a four to one superiority over the German Fourth *Luftflotte* which supported Army Group South. In late 1943, the Soviets had 350 aviation regiments, totaling 10,200 aircraft; in comparison, the *Luftwaffe* had less than 3,000 planes.

On 11 November 1943, *Wehrmacht* units from the Fastov region counterattacked in the general direction of Kiev, taking Zhitomir on 20 November. Prolonged back and forth fighting continued until 24 December, when the left wing of the 1st Ukrainian Front mounted a major assault against Army Group South's First and Fourth *Panzer* Armies. Attempts by General Hermann Balck's (q.v.) XLVIII *Panzer Korps* to contain the Soviet offensive met with only temporary success. On 31 December, the Red Army occupied Zhitomir again.

The Soviet First Tank Army reached as far as Zhmerinka and crossed the upper Bug River, but having suffered heavy casualties, it had to withdraw. The pressure on the Fourth *Panzer* Army was great. Field Marshal Erich von Manstein (q.v.), fearing that Army Group South would be cut off, requested permission to abandon the Dnieper bend and pull the Seventeenth Army from the Crimea (q.v.). Typically, Adolf Hitler (q.v.) refused.

On 5 January 1944, Marshal Ivan Konev's (q.v.) 2nd Ukrainian Front attacked southwest from the Cherkassy area. By 28 January, they trapped the German XI and XLII *Korps* in a pocket near Korsun. Konev used his Twenty-seventh Army and Fourth Guards Tank Army to form the inner ring of the encirclement. The Sixth Tank Army and Fifth Guards Tank Army formed an outer ring to prevent any attempts to relieve the pocket from the outside. Some 70,000 to 80,000 German troops were in the ring twenty miles in diameter.

The Germans tried to keep the Korsun pocket resupplied by air, losing forty-four Ju-52 transports to Soviet fire in a five-day period. Von Manstein tried to break the blockade with armored assaults, but failed. On 9 February, General Wilhelm Stemmermann, commander of the XI *Korps,* refused a Soviet surrender ultimatum. By 15 February, the diameter of the Korsun pocket was reduced to about ten miles. That same day, Hitler finally gave permission for a breakout. On the night of 17 February, the encircled Germans started breaking out in the direction of Lysyanka, ten miles to the southeast, where the III *Panzer Korps* was located. Some 38,000 Germans escaped by abandoning their heavy equipment and their wounded. Almost 20,000 German soldiers died in the Korsun pocket, and 17,000 were captured, including 1,500 wounded.

On 27 January 1944, the left wing of the 1st Ukrainian Front began the Rovno-Lutsk operation, splitting the boundary between Army Groups Center and South. Two Soviet cavalry (horse) corps passed through forests and marshes around the left flank of the Fourth *Panzer* Army to capture Rovno on 2 February. Soviet forces then severed the key communications line between Kovel and Rovno, and on 11 February, captured the major railway junction at Shepetovka.

On the southern flank, General Fedor Tolbukhin's (q.v.) 4th Ukrainian Front took Nikopol on the east bend of the Dnieper on 7 February. Despite poor weather and knee-deep mud, the 4th Ukrainian Front turned south into the Crimea. General Ivan Malinovsky's (q.v.) 3rd Ukrainian Front took Krivoy Rog on 22 February. The Nikopol-Krivoy Rog region contained rich iron and manganese mines.

In February 1944, the tenth session of the Supreme Soviet of the Soviet Union made the decision to create "national armies," and appoint people's defense and foreign affairs commissariats in all republics. On 11 March, V.F. Gerasimenko was appointed people's commissar of defense of the Ukraine, although this post was not introduced in the other republics. This can be explained by the serious straining of national and political tensions in the Ukraine as the Red Army entered its western regions. Initially, the people's foreign affairs commissar for the Ukraine was A.E. Korneichuk, but on 13 July, D.Z. Manuilsky, a crony of Josef Stalin (q.v.), assumed that post.

In early March, Vatutin was fatally wounded by partisans of the Ukrainian Insurgent Army (UPA). Marshal Georgy Zhukov (q.v.) personally assumed command of the 1st Ukrainian Front. On 4 March, Zhukov launched the Soviet's 1944 spring offensive, striking southwest from Shepetovka toward the junction of the First and Fourth *Panzer* Armies. The next day, the 2nd Ukrainian Front attacked southwest toward Uman; and on 6 March, 3rd Ukrainian Front joined the offensive. The timing of the attacks surprised the Germans, who expected the Soviets to wait for better campaigning weather. With fresh supplies of U.S. Lend-Lease (q.v.) trucks, the Soviets were beginning to acquire a mobility they had never had before.

Zhukov's forces reached Tarnopol on 9 March, outflanking German positions along the Bug River. Konev's forces reached the Bug on 12 March. On 21 March, the 1st Ukrainian Front's First Tank Army attacked south from Tarnopol, reaching the Dniester River a week later. The drive penetrated deep into the rear of the First *Panzer* Army. The 2nd Ukrainian Front drove a wedge between the First *Panzer* Army and the Eighth Army, reaching the Prut River on the Romanian border by 26 March. When Konev's Sixth Tank Army linked up with Zhukov's First Tank Army, the encirclement of the First *Panzer* Army was complete. In the south, the 3rd Ukrainian Front pushed the Sixth Army back across the mouths of the Dnieper and then the Bug, sealing off the Crimea.

On 25 March, von Manstein flew to Berchtesgaden to convince Hitler to allow the First *Panzer* Army to break out of its encirclement. Hitler grudgingly agreed, but then on 30 March he relieved von Manstein, replacing him with Field Marshal Walther Model (q.v.). Both of the army groups in the south were also renamed, with Army Group South becoming Army Group North Ukraine and Army Group A becoming Army Group South Ukraine.

To everyone's surprise, First *Panzer* Army managed to break out in early April and escaped in fairly good order. Model then launched a counteroffensive along the Dniester, taking the railway center at Delatyn. For the next several months the sector in front of Army Group North Ukraine remained fairly stable.

With the 2nd Ukrainian Front up against the Romanian border, Konev turned south for a combined drive with the 3rd Ukrainian Front on the Black Sea port of Odessa. When the Sixth Army abandoned Odessa on 10 April, Hitler relieved Marshal Ewald von Kleist (q.v.), commander of Army Group South Ukraine, and replaced him with General Ferdinand Schörner.

Meanwhile, General Erwin Jänecke's Seventeenth Army (which contained seven Romanian divisions) still was bottled up in the Crimea. Jänecke's 230,000 troops were incapable of holding the Crimea once the Soviets cut it off, but those troops could have been very useful to the Germans on the Ukraine mainland. On 8 April, the Second Guards and Fifty-first Armies of the 4th Ukrainian Front attacked the Crimean peninsula from the north, while the Independent Coastal Army came across the Kerch Strait from the Caucasus. By 17 April, the Soviets had pushed the Seventeenth Army back to Sevastopol, taking 37,000 prisoners in the process. Hitler gave the order to evacuate—too late, as usual. When Sevastopol surrendered on 9 May 1944, another 30,000 Axis troops fell into Soviet hands.

Once Odessa and then the Crimea fell, the sector in front of Army Group South Ukraine also

stabilized. The Soviets now were in control of almost all of the Ukraine, including its most important industrial and agricultural areas. The Soviets by then were already shifting forces for Operation BAGRATION, their major offensive in Byelorussia (q.v.). The last part of the Ukraine finally passed into Soviet hands with the battle for Brody-Lwów (q.v.) in July.

During the period of Nazi occupation of the Ukraine, 264 villages were razed. Seven million Ukrainians lost their lives in military fighting and in more than 200 concentration camps, forced labor camps, and Jewish ghettos.

V.I. Semenenko

Additional Reading

Erickson, John, *The Road to Berlin: Continuing the History of Stalin's War with Germany* (1983).

Koral, M.V., *Ukraina u druhij sritorij i Welykij Witchysnjanij Vijni: 1939–1945* (1994).

Manstein, Erich von, *Lost Victories* (1958).

Mellenthin, F.W. von, *Panzer Battles* (1956).

Ziemke, Earl F., *Stalingrad to Berlin: The German Defeat in the East* (1968).

USSR

See Soviet Union

U

V-1/V-2 Offensive (June 1944–April 1945)

In the early hours of 13 June 1944, a special *Luftwaffe* unit deployed in northern France. *Flak-Regiment* 155(W), commanded by Colonel Max Wachtel, launched ten Fieseler 103 flying bombs toward London. Six of these devices, later known as *Vergeltungswaffe* (Reprisal Weapon) Number One, or V-1 for short, crashed almost immediately or disappeared without a trace. The other four reached southern England, where one, coming down on Bethnal Green, killed six people and seriously injured another nine. Two and a half days later, on the evening of 15 June, Wachtel's men launched a second attack against Britain, this time on a much larger scale. From then until late March 1945, more than 22,000 V-1s were sent off against various targets in Britain and on the Continent, with Belgian cities, in particular, becoming favorite targets.

Originally developed under the code name *Flakzielgerät 76* (FZG-76), the V-1 flying bomb was twenty-five feet long, had a wingspan of sixteen feet, and weighed more than two tons. Powered by a pulse jet, it was designed to carry a one-ton warhead on a preset course for approximately 140 miles (which was later improved to 250 miles). Producing a lot of noise and going at an average speed of about 350 mph, the V-1s were quite vulnerable to interception by Allied fighter planes, as well as to antiaircraft fire from the ground. Moreover, the "Buzz Bombs," as the Allies called them, were never very reliable in terms of staying on course, and many came down in places quite remote from their intended targets.

The Allies responded to the V-1 offensive with Operation DIVER (q.v.), which included numerous air attacks on suspected launching sites, supply depots, and other relevant targets. They were unable, however, to stop an ever-increasing number of the bombs from coming across the Channel. When the German armies in France were routed in late August 1944, the V-1 launches from the ground were temporarily choked off, but a small number of air-launched missiles continued to hit British targets. More importantly, by 8 September, the Germans were able to launch their second "reprisal weapon," the V-2.

Developed by an Army team headed by Colonel Walter Dornberger and Dr. Wernher von Braun (qq.v.), the V-2 was a liquid-fuel guided missile, forty-six feet long, and weighing approximately thirteen tons. Its effective range was about 190 miles, during which the rocket (with a one-ton warhead in its nose) rose to an altitude of fifty to sixty miles. Coming down at supersonic speed, the V-2 was invulnerable to interception, thus making it a far more formidable challenge to the Allies than the Buzz Bomb. Despite numerous bombings and strafings carried out by the Royal Air Force (RAF) and the U.S. Army Air Force (USAAF) against suspected launch sites (especially in the Netherlands and northwestern Germany), storage facilities, and production plants, V-2 bombardments of British and continental targets continued throughout the fall and winter of 1944–1945.

It was only in late March 1945 that the combined V-1 and V-2 campaign finally fizzled out. According to the best available sources, a total of more than 3,150 V-2 rockets were launched against the Allies before April 1945, with more than 1,600 aimed at Belgian targets (especially Antwerp), more than 1,400 at Britain, and the remainder coming down in France, Holland, and Germany. Although no precise figures are available, it is clear that the V-1/V-2 offensive caused extensive material damage and killed thousands of people. One of the most costly missile strikes oc-

curred on 16 December 1944, when a cinema in Antwerp was hit, killing almost 300 soldiers and injuring 194 others.

During the opening phases of the V-weapons offensive, an aging artillery general, Erich Heinemann, was officially in charge of the whole operation, while Lieutenant General Richard Metz supervised the various launch groups in the field. Gradually, however, many of their functions were taken over by SS General Heinz Kammler, an engineering expert with boundless energy and drive.

After the cessation of missile launches in April 1945, most of the launch crews were assembled in a special division which, under the command of Colonel Gerlach von Gaudecker, surrendered to U.S. forces on 1 May.

While the V-weapons were never a serious threat to the Allied cause, most experts are agreed that British and American countermeasures against both the Buzz Bombs and the missiles absorbed a large number of Allied resources, particularly in terms of sorties by RAF and USAAF bombers and fighter planes. These sorties began in earnest in 1943, highlighted by the famous British attack on the Peenemünde (q.v.) proving grounds on the Baltic Sea coast during the night of 17–18 August, and continued at irregular intervals thereafter right down to March 1945. From December 1943 until 12 June 1944, the Allies directed more than 25,000 sorties against suspected V-weapons installations, dropping more than 36,000 tons of bombs and losing 154 aircraft in the process.

Once the V-1 appeared over Britain, the Allies intensified their efforts, dropping 23,000 tons of bombs on various Operation CROSSBOW (q.v.) targets during the second half of June 1944. After further massive air strikes in July and August, Allied countermeasures were scaled back somewhat, but it is clear that from then until April 1945, Operation CROSSBOW continued to absorb a sizeable amount of Allied airpower. It is known, for instance, that during this period, German V-1 sites and production facilities were bombarded by 1,000 sorties from heavy bombers and more than 10,000 sorties from fighters and fighter-bombers.

Ulrich Trumpener

Additional Reading

Collier, Basil, *The Battle of the V-Weapons, 1944–45* (1964).

Garlinski, Jozef, *Hitler's Last Weapons: The Underground War against the V-1 and V-2* (1978).

VARSITY, Operation (24 March 1945)

Operation VARSITY, the last airborne operation of the war in Europe, was the airborne component of Operation PLUNDER, the crossing of the Rhine River by Field Marshal Sir Bernard L. Montgomery's (q.v.) 21st Army Group. In March 1945, Montgomery carefully marshalled his forces of close to one million troops along the lower Rhine, opposite the German industrial region of the Ruhr. The 21st Army Group forces designated to make the crossing of the Rhine included the nine divisions of the British Second Army, and the twelve divisions of the U.S. Ninth Army. Opposing the Allies, German Army Group H had about 85,000 worn and demoralized troops, and a total of only thirty-five tanks.

Montgomery decided that there would be no repeat of the disaster that befell the British 6th Airborne Division at Arnhem (q.v.) during Operation MARKET-GARDEN. This time, the airborne forces would drop within supporting artillery range of the main assault force. That also meant that the ground force would have to be on the east side of the river when the airborne troops went in. Therefore, contrary to previous Allied practice in World War II, the airborne assault would take place after the start of the surface assault.

The VARSITY phase of the operation was conducted by Lieutenant General Lewis H. Brereton's (q.v.) First Allied Airborne Army. The combat force was Major General Matthew B. Ridgway's (q.v.) XVIII Airborne Corps, which consisted of the U.S. 17th Airborne Division, under Major General William M. Miley, and the British 6th Airborne Division, under Major General E.L. Bols.

At 2100 hours on 23 March 1945, Operation PLUNDER started, with the 21st Army Group crossing the Rhine between Emmerich and Wesel. Operation VARSITY went in the next morning at 1000 hours. The 6th Airborne Division took off earlier that morning from bases in Britain. The 17th Airborne Division took off from fields in France. Both forces rendezvoused in the air over Belgium, and proceeded to the drop area over Wesel.

The total airborne force consisted of 21,680 troops carried by 1,696 transports and 1,348 gliders. They were escorted by 889 fighters, while another 2,153 fighters flew cover over the target area and provided a defensive screen to the east. Behind the airborne force came 240 B-24 bombers, which had been rigged to drop supplies and equipment. The force went in with a total of 109

V

tons of ammunition, 696 vehicles, and 113 artillery pieces.

By 1230 hours, all the troops had jumped and all the gliders had landed. Things did not go well, however. The Germans anticipated an airborne assault, correctly estimated the general area where it would occur, and massed all of Army Group H's mobile antiaircraft pieces accordingly. The airborne force lost forty-four transports, fifty gliders, and fifteen resupply bombers. The parachute drops were widely scattered and off target. The gliders, for the most part, landed accurately. Nonetheless, the airborne soldiers consolidated where they could and moved out to take their objectives. By nightfall, almost all the first day's objectives were seized. In the process, the two divisions virtually eliminated the German 84th Division. The 17th Airborne Division took 2,000 prisoners, and the 6th Airborne Division took 1,500.

Operation VARSITY was a success, but an expensive one. Casualties that day among the airborne divisions were much higher than for the ground divisions. On 24 March, the 17th Airborne Division alone reported 159 killed, 522 wounded, and 840 missing (although about 600 of the latter eventually showed up). By comparison, the U.S. 30th and 79th Infantry Divisions taking part in the ground assault had combined losses of 41 killed, 450 wounded, and 7 missing.

The operational effectiveness of Operation VARSITY is also open to question. By dropping close enough to the ground force to receive artillery support and achieve a quick linkup, the airborne assault really did not contribute any additional depth to the operation. Given the Allies' overwhelming strength compared to the Germans, the two airborne divisions probably did not accomplish much more than what the ground units could have without them.

David T. Zabecki

Additional Reading

MacDonald, Charles B., *The Last Offensive* (1973).

Stock, James W., *Rhine Crossing* (1973).

Weigley, Russell F., *Eisenhower's Lieutenants: The Campaigns of France and Germany, 1944–45* (1981).

Vienna (5–14 April 1945)

By April 1945, Vienna was of little or no strategic importance to the outcome of World War II. Soviet troops had already advanced to within 100 miles of Berlin (q.v.) and the end of the war was in sight. For this reason, the battle for Vienna is often passed over altogether, or given slight treatment in general accounts of the war. The battle was, however, decisive for Austrian perceptions of the war, their relationship to National Socialism, and East-West relations.

Vienna, the capital of the old Austro-Hungarian Empire before World War I, was the city where Adolf Hitler (q.v.) had tried his fortunes as a young painter between 1907 and 1913. In the closing days of World War II, he did not spare the Austrian metropolis from destruction. Instead, he ordered the city, under the military command of Lieutenant General Rudolf von Bünau, used in the last line of defense against the advancing Soviet troops of General Fedor Tolbukhin's (q.v.) 3rd Ukrainian Front. It was a tragic, desperate decision that condemned the city to needless suffering.

Tolbukhin's troops, acting apparently on information supplied by Austrian anti-Nazi opposition groups within the German Army, advanced on the city from the south, by way of Baden and the Vienna Woods. By 6 April, Red Army tanks occupied key positions north and northwest of the city without encountering major opposition from the Germans. The city was in turmoil. Distrust ruled on all sides. Von Bünau and his officers openly worried whether any Austrian units could be trusted, and the conspirators, some of whom were arrested and hanged, played a dangerous game of trying to assist an enemy army. In addition, slave laborers, whom the Nazis had brought to Vienna from all over Eastern Europe, and some residents of the city took up arms in open revolt against the Germans. Chaos ruled the streets.

As the situation deteriorated for the German troops, von Bünau was forced ultimately to give up his military sanctuary in the inner part of the city and to withdraw his forces across the Danube Canal to the north and east of the center of Vienna. The retreating Germans blew up all but one of the bridges that crossed the canal. In the ensuing artillery barrages, large strips of territory bounding the canal were heavily damaged, including the famous Viennese amusement park, the Prater.

The sporadic fighting lasted until 14 April when virtually all the German troops were withdrawn from the city or captured. The Soviet victors moved quickly to put in place a civilian government staffed by Austrians. The Soviets brought Karl Renner, former Austrian chancellor, back to Vienna to head up the new government. The Soviet occupation of the city caused friction with the civilian population. Some Soviet troops engaged in

looting and rape, which inspired deep-seated resentment among the Viennese. For a time, the local population was given over to mob rule until civil order was restored.

For Austrians, and the Viennese in particular, the battle for Vienna came to represent their ambivalent attitude toward the war itself. One could point both to collaboration with and resistance to Nazi rule. One recognized that the Soviets had liberated the city, but also imposed their own sometimes harsh rule. Vienna would remain an area of conflict between East and West until 1955 and the evacuation of Soviet and other Allied troops from the city.

William D. Bowman

Additional Reading
Croy, Otto R., *Wein 1945: Ein Tagebuch in Wort und Bild* (1975).
Ziemke, Earl F., *Stalingrad to Berlin: The German Defeat in the East* (1968).

Volturno River (12–15 October 1943)
On 13 October 1943, Lieutenant General Mark Clark's (q.v.) Fifth Army began a two-day battle to cross the Volturno River and to facilitate an Allied advance north to a line stretching west from Civitavecchia to San Benedetto del Trente on the Adriatic. Clark's Army, consisting of the U.S. VI and British X Corps, reached the Volturno on 6 October, less than a month after invading the Italian mainland at Salerno (q.v.). X Corps arrayed its one armored and two infantry divisions across the twenty-mile coastal zone on the Allied left, while VI Corps' three infantry divisions held a thirty-five-mile front extending into the Apennine Mountains. Opposing them was General Hans-Valentine Hube's XIV *Panzer Korps,* consisting of two *Panzer* and two *Panzergrenadier* divisions.

Although Fifth Army outnumbered the Germans in both personnel and equipment and benefited greatly from Allied air superiority, Clark's command faced several disadvantages. The terrain clearly favored the Germans. The rugged mountains on Hube's left required fewer defenders and prevented VI Corps from concentrating its firepower. To the west, high ground north of the Volturno permitted the Germans to dominate the crossing sites. Moreover, Hube's force, veterans of both Italy and Russia, possessed more battle experience than their British and American opponents.

Nonetheless, Allied command expected little resistance. Despite the growing German commitment in southern Italy, both General Dwight D. Eisenhower, commander of the Mediterranean theater, and General Sir Harold R. Alexander (qq.v.), the commander of the 15th Army Group in Italy, believed that Allied forces could advance beyond Rome before winter began. Alexander's initial objectives for Clark, the high ground south of the Rapido and Garigliano Rivers, sixteen to thirty-four miles beyond Fifth Army's northernmost units, reflected that optimism. Allied success clearly depended on crossing the Volturno quickly and with few losses. German intentions, however, were just as critical.

Neither Hube nor his superior, Tenth Army commander General Heinrich von Vietinghoff-Scheel (q.v.), intended anything but a delaying action along the Volturno. Both knew, however, that determined resistance was essential if the German main defensive belt to their rear, the so-called Winter Line, was to be completed. Consequently, the XIV *Panzer Korps* placed all its divisions in the line.

Clark hoped to begin his attack before the Germans could consolidate their positions astride the Volturno, but autumn rains and the skeletal road network prevented his two corps from conducting simultaneous assaults. Clark finally opted for an attack along the entire Fifth Army front to begin on the night of 12 October. He reasoned that such an assault would force Hube to disperse his units, thus permitting multiple Allied crossings.

Slightly after midnight on 13 October, the Fifth Army front erupted in flame and explosions. On Clark's right, the 45th Infantry Division attacked westward along the Calore River toward Monte Acero, a key hill overlooking the German left flank. While elements of two regimental combat teams (RCT) assaulted the hill from the south and the east, units from the division's third RCT swung around the village of San Salvatore to attack Monte Acero from the west. The Americans possessed the hill by nightfall and sent patrols west to the Volturno the following day.

Simultaneously, the U.S. 3rd Infantry Division on the left and 34th Infantry Division in the center of VI Corps began their assaults. While two battalions each attacked on the 3rd Infantry Division's flanks, three more crossed in the division's center near a hairpin loop in the Volturno. Firing too high, the Germans failed to stop the assault, and by 0800 hours, 7th Infantry Regiment had advanced more than a mile. Daylight permitted American tanks and tank destroyers to dominate the crossing site and U.S. armor soon moved north of the river. Flanking attacks also succeeded, as quick-moving units and effective supporting fires

combined to overwhelm the surprised German units. U.S. Engineers erected an eight-ton bridge on 13 October, but a thirty-ton bridge capable of supporting tanks had to wait until the next day.

Unlike its sister division, the 34th Infantry Division's zone of attack lacked any low terrain except the Volturno's riverbanks. Supporting fires from eight artillery battalions assisted the assaulting units cross the river, but the Germans managed to contest every inch of ground. Fighting continued through the night and by the next afternoon, the division had forced the 3rd *Panzergrenadier* Division from the river.

While VI Corps pressed the Germans back, British X Corps met with varying success, even though only one German division opposed it. Few roads ran through X Corps' zone, and recent rains had created additional water obstacles. The German defenders, moreover, enjoyed flat, treeless fields of fire to their front. Like its American counterpart, X Corps attacked with three divisions abreast: the 46th Infantry Division making the main assault on the left, the 7th Armoured Division in the center, and the 56th Infantry Division on the right.

The attack along the German extreme right succeeded brilliantly. While two tank squadrons conducted an amphibious landing on Hube's seaward flank, the 46th Infantry Division's assault battalions crossed the Volturno. Naval gunfire devastated the German positions within range, and by nightfall, British units had penetrated three miles despite repeated German counterattacks. The division made smaller advances on 14 October as it focused on crossing more of its units and expanding the bridgehead.

Attacks in the British center and right achieved little success. In the center, the 7th Armoured Division conducted assaults on 12 October to divert attention from the other two divisions. Assault forces twice tried to establish a bridgehead but succeeded only on the third attempt early on 13 October. Occupying a narrow river bend exposed to fire from the north and east, the British slowly built up their foothold and advanced 1,000 yards north the next day.

To the east, the 56th Infantry Division failed to establish a bridgehead. The one good crossing site in the division's zone offered the Germans excellent observation and fields of fire. The 56th Infantry Division attempted a feint crossing near its boundary with the U.S. 3rd Infantry Division, but German fires forced the British to withdraw before daylight. Lead elements at the main crossing site met heavy opposition as well, with the Germans sinking several assault boats and repulsing the attackers. The 56th Infantry Division's commander later decided that an assault crossing was not possible, prompting Clark to shift the X Corps boundary east to give the 56th Infantry Division one of the American bridges across the Volturno. British troops crossed the river on 14 October and began preparations to exploit their position on the 15th *Panzergrenadier* Division's flank.

Hube recognized the futility of further resistance and requested permission to withdraw. Since German plans required a delaying action only until 15 October, von Vietinghoff agreed to let XIV *Panzer Korps* disengage that day. Fifth Army won the first battle in its march toward Rome, but at a price. Allied casualties exceeded German losses, and Hube's forces remained intact.

Roger Kaplan

Additional Reading

Blumenson, Martin, *Salerno to Cassino* (1969).
Fifth U.S. Army Historical Section, *From the Volturno to the Winter Line* (1945).
Molony, C.J.C., *The Campaign in Sicily, 1943 and the Campaign in Italy, 3rd September 1943 to 31st March 1944* (1973).

Voronezh (28 June–13 July 1942)

In the early summer of 1942, Adolf Hitler (q.v.) and the German army high command prepared to resume offensive operations against the Soviets aimed at capturing the lower Don River and the Caucasus (q.v.). Despite the disappointments and heavy losses of the fall and winter of 1941–1942, the Germans believed another summer offensive aggressively executed could irreparably cripple the Red Army and deprive the Soviet Union of the economic resources of the Caucasus. Voronezh, a city of 300,000 and an important industrial and transportation center on the Don River, became the focus of the first phase of this offensive. The outcome of that battle had a significant impact on the course of the German summer offensive of 1942.

For the 1942 summer offensive—Operation *BLAU* (BLUE)—the Germans envisioned a sweep along a front of approximately 350 miles running from Taganrog in the south to Kursk in the north. The plan called for a general advance to the Don River from Voronezh in the north to Stalingrad on the Volga River just east to the Don bend. With their left flank anchored along the Don and Soviet land and river transport interdicted at the Volga, the Germans would be free to advance south into the northern Caucasus.

The breadth and depth of the operation, combined with the wear and tear the German Army had sustained in the previous year's fighting, necessitated a phased offensive in which German armor and air forces could be concentrated for a succession of decisive engagements. Operation *BLAU* envisioned quick and relatively tight encirclements in a better use of forces and time than the huge sweeping "Cannaes" of Operation BARBAROSSA.

Operation *BLAU* was carried out by Army Group South, commanded by Field Marshal Fedor von Bock (q.v.). (On 7 July, Army Group South was split into Army Group A and Army Group B under von Bock and Field Marshal Wilhelm List [q.v.], respectively; General Maximilian von Weichs [q.v.] replaced von Bock on 13 July.) To execute the first phase, combined Axis forces advanced to the Don River between Voronezh and Korotoyak. They included the German Second and Sixth Armies, the Fourth *Panzer* Army, and the Hungarian Second Army. Three German *Panzer Korps*, the XXIV and XLVIII of the Fourth *Panzer* Army, and the XL of Sixth Army, spearheaded the advance. While sources vary, it appears the Germans had available some 1,000 tanks for the first phase of Operation *BLAU.*

Soviet forces opposing the axis armies around Voronezh included the Bryansk Front, under General Filip Golikov (q.v.), and the Southwestern Front under General Semen Timoshenko (q.v.). The two fronts together had ten field armies. These forces, rebuilding from the disastrous spring fighting at Kharkov (q.v.), enjoyed a slight numerical superiority in infantry and armor. In addition to these frontline troops, the *Stavka* (q.v.), anticipating a renewed effort to take Moscow by means of an indirect approach via Tula or Voronezh, held four reserve armies behind the Don River between Voronezh and Moscow. Included in these forces were six tank corps with 1,600 tanks.

Operation *BLAU* was planned to start in late June. Before the offensive began, however, its security was compromised. On the afternoon of 19 June, Major Joachim Reichel, chief of operations of the 23rd *Panzer* Division, XL *Panzer Korps,* disappeared in an army observation plane. Reichel carried the operational orders of XL *Panzer Korps* and the outlines of the first phase of the operation. This important intelligence was recovered by Soviet troops and sent immediately to the *Stavka.* Although Soviet aerial reconnaissance confirmed the German offensive preparations, Josef Stalin (q.v.) disbelieved the evidence and ordered plans for a local offensive aimed at taking Orel.

The German offensive began on the morning of 28 June with the Second Army and the Fourth *Panzer* Army jumping off toward the Don River and enjoying all the advantages of surprise. The XXIV and XLVIII *Panzer Korps* quickly broke through the Soviet lines. By that evening, the 24th *Panzer* Division had advanced thirty miles, crossing the Tim and Kschen Rivers and overrunning the Soviet Fortieth Army's headquarters.

Stalin and the *Stavka* were gravely concerned over the rapid German advance and the threat to Moscow should the Germans take Voronezh. They ordered an immediate counterattack with local forces and released several powerful tank corps from the reserves around Voronezh. By 30 June, seven Soviet tank corps converged on Voronezh for the counterattack. Colonel General Yakov N. Fedorenko, chief of Soviet tank forces, was sent to direct operations. Five Soviet tank corps, the I, IV, XVII, XVIII, and XXIV, were launched against the lead elements of the Fourth *Panzer* Army.

Despite the preponderance of Soviet armor and its qualitative superiority—they had some 800 T-34s and heavy KV tanks—the Soviet efforts failed. Soviet attacks were poorly supported logistically, uncoordinated, and committed piecemeal. Over the next four days, superior German tactics, experienced crews and commanders, and coordinated air support inflicted heavy losses on the Soviets. Stalin, aware that Soviet armor had local superiority, harangued his commanders on the spot (particularly Golikov) and attempted to intervene in local troop dispositions. It was all to no avail. There was little the Soviets could do as the situation at Voronezh deteriorated. Soviet commanders lost contact with their armored forces as the rapid German advance, coupled with the highly effective *Luftwaffe,* decimated the Soviet command and control system.

Events to the south placed Soviet units in Voronezh in an even more precarious position. On 30 June, the German Sixth Army began its attack around Volchansk. Spearheaded by the XL *Panzer Korps,* the Sixth Army advanced rapidly eastward, then north in an attempt to trap Soviet forces in front of Voronezh and along the Oskol River to the south. By 1 July, the Sixth Army essentially had smashed much of Southwest Front along the Oskol River. Stalin and the *Stavka,* in a direct departure from their tactics the year before, ordered units in the rapidly developing pocket to withdraw immediately to the Don River. The withdrawal became a disorganized rout as Soviet units raced to reach the Don, and the road to Voronezh opened for German forces—a situation recognized by German and Soviet commanders alike.

V

At that juncture in the offensive, the German army high command needed to make some decisions. It was now apparent that the neat, tight encirclements originally envisioned were not going to occur. Hitler, in particular, was insistent on trapping and destroying as much of the Red Army as possible. In view of the recent withdrawal of Soviet units to the east, Hitler wanted an immediate turn south to ensure the encirclement of Red Army units along the Donets River as part of the second phase of Operation *BLAU.*

Ironically, Hitler wanted to avoid "heavy fighting" for Voronezh, a city of dubious military value, while the Red Army escaped to fight a later day. Von Bock, however, believed that Voronezh could be taken easily. Hitler, at a special conference in Poltava on 3 July, attempted to resolve the issue by giving rather ambiguous orders, essentially allowing von Bock to ignore Voronezh if capturing the city would involve heavy fighting.

Events soon transpired that indicated to the Germans that Voronezh would indeed be an easy city to capture. By the evening of 4 July, the 24th *Panzer* and *Grossdeutschland* Divisions captured two intact bridges over the Don River just west of Voronezh. By 6 July, both the XLVIII and the XXIV *Panzer Korps* crossed the Don at Voronezh and the 24th *Panzer* and *Grossdeutschland* Divisions advanced into the city against moderate resistance. Influenced by von Bock's optimism that the city could be taken easily, Hitler on 6 July formally ordered the capture of the city. Hitler also was becoming more concerned over the commitment of armor to Voronezh, and he ordered supporting units of the Sixth Army (notably the XL *Panzer Korps*), to drive south along the west bank of the Don River to encircle retreating Soviet units in the Donets area.

On 7 July, Stalin ordered the formation of a new front, the Voronezh Front, under General Nikolai Vatutin (q.v.). At the same time, the concentration of Soviet units in the area and the commitment of reserves began to have an impact on the fight for the city. Inside the city, fighting intensified as Red Army troops poured in. Despite making few gains on that day, German radio announced the capture of Voronezh. Fierce fighting for Voronezh, however, continued until 13 July—mainly in the university quarter and in the woods north of town. Heavy fighting died down after the second week of July as many German units withdrew to the south. Significantly, the north-south railway and main road through Voronezh remained under control of the Red Army, thus depriving the Germans of the one real military value

to Voronezh's capture—the interdiction of Soviet supply lines along the east bank of the Don. Most of Voronezh remained in German hands until the spring of 1943 when the Soviets liberated the city.

The fighting around Voronezh, while lasting more than two weeks, had important implications beyond denying the capture of the entire city by the Germans. Although the Germans took most of their geographic objectives in the first phase of Operation *BLAU,* and conditions necessary to continue were met, the damage inflicted on the Red Army was relatively slight—except for heavy tank losses. The Fourth *Panzer* and Sixth Armies took a total of only 73,000 prisoners, but destroyed 1,200 tanks by 8 July. Moreover, the misapplication of available forces by Hitler and von Bock resulted in the commitment with relatively little military reward of two valuable *Panzer Korps* during the crucial second week of July. Finally, the conduct of operations during the battle of Voronezh had a significant impact on command and control for both sides.

The careers of both Golikov and von Bock suffered as a result of their performance. Hitler lost further confidence in his "old school" Prussian generals. Stalin and the *Stavka,* with the experience of a rout rather than an orderly retreat from Voronezh and Rostov, instituted a series of measures to stiffen discipline and improve the Red Army's performance in the months to come.

Charles K. Dodd

Additional Reading
Carell, Paul, *Hitler Moves East, 1941–1943* (1965).
Erickson, John, *The Road to Stalingrad* (1975).
Ziemke, Earl F., *Moscow to Stalingrad* (1968).

Vyazma-Bryansk (6–20 October 1941)
As German forces encircled Leningrad (q.v.) in the fall of 1941, Adolf Hitler (q.v.) turned his attention to Army Group Center and its continuing drive on Moscow. His *Führer* Directive 35 of 6 September 1941, which resumed this assault, ordered the beginning of Operation *TAIFUN* (TYPHOON). An initial objective of Operation *TAIFUN* was to capture fortified cities and towns surrounding Moscow that served as Soviet communication centers. Although the Soviets had assembled a massive force of fifteen armies (eighty divisions) to protect Moscow, the figures were misleading. Average Soviet unit strengths dropped sharply since the summer, so that the 800,000 troops defending the various approaches to the

capital comprised the equivalent of no more than twenty-five full-strength divisions. Furthermore, the Soviet forces had only 770 tanks and 364 aircraft. In contrast, the German forces consisted of fourteen *Panzer* divisions, nine *Panzergrenadier* divisions, and forty-four infantry divisions, grouped into five armies.

Field Marshal Fedor von Bock (q.v.), commander of Army Group Center, planned to knock out the strategic towns of Vyazma (approximately 150 miles west of Moscow) and Bryansk (approximately 220 miles southwest of Moscow) quickly and simultaneously with a massive armor assault prior to attacking Moscow itself. The leading units in the German assault were General Heinz Guderian's (q.v.) Second *Panzer* Group, General Hermann Hoth's (q.v.) Third *Panzer* Group, General Erich Hoepner's (q.v.) Fourth *Panzer* Group, and General Maximillian von Weich's (q.v.) Second Army. Soviet forces in the Vyazma-Bryansk area were subordinate to the Bryansk Front, commanded by General Andrei Yeremenko (q.v.), and the Western Front under General Ivan Konev (q.v.).

On 30 September 1941, Guderian turned his Second *Panzer* Group to the northeast and began an advance that covered fifty miles the first day and 100 miles over the next three days. On 8 October, his forces took Orel, approximately 130 miles in the Soviet rear. On 6 October, his leading units emerged from the forest into Bryansk. Simultaneously, von Weich's force attacked from the west, trapping and destroying the Third, Thirteenth,

and Fifteenth Armies. Only a few Soviet troops escaped, including a wounded Yeremenko. To the north, meanwhile, Hoepner's and Hoth's *Panzer* groups penetrated the Soviet lines surrounding Vyazma, trapping the Western Front's Nineteenth, Twentieth, Twenty-fourth, and Thirty-second Armies. Surviving Soviet forces at Vyazma surrendered on 14 October and at Bryansk on 20 October.

As a result of the Vyazma-Bryansk fiasco, Soviet forces suffered one of their heaviest defeats of the year, and the road to Moscow lay essentially open. Russian prisoners numbered 663,000, and 1,242 tanks and 5,412 guns fell into German hands. Other effects of the disaster were even more far-reaching. As news of the defeats reached Moscow, citizens panicked and fled, making a mockery of the authorities' 10 October decision to defend Moscow at all costs. Civil disorder and flight became so widespread in Moscow that martial law was proclaimed on 19 October. Konev was blamed for the debacle and he was replaced by General Georgy Zhukov (q.v.), who was given the unenviable task of defending Moscow (q.v.).

David A. Foy

Additional Reading

Erickson, John, *The Road to Stalingrad* (1975).
Seaton, Albert, *The Battle for Moscow, 1941–42* (1971).
Ziemke, Earl F., and Magna E. Bauer, *Moscow to Stalingrad, Decision in the East* (1987).

V

Warsaw (8–27 September 1939)

[See map 31 on page 1341]

"I wanted Warsaw to be great. Today Warsaw, defending the honor of Poland, is at the pinnacle of her greatness." Thus did Lord Mayor Stefan Starzyński (q.v.) describe his city's defense during the Polish campaign of 1939. Lengthy and terribly destructive, it was one of the key siege operations of World War II. Indeed, the battle represented a significant challenge to German forces and their *Fall WEISS* (Case WHITE) plan for the conquest of Poland (q.v.).

Warsaw was where the pincers of Germany's Army Groups North and South were to meet, and it was there that the Poles decided to sacrifice their capital in a major defensive action. As Warsaw was the hub of the national communications network, its capture was imperative for a German victory. In addition, political, diplomatic, and psychological factors spurred the *Wehrmacht* to seize the city.

With a population of 1.3 million, Warsaw was Poland's largest city. It contained more than 25,000 buildings over an area of 103.5 million cubic meters. Except for the struggle along the Baltic, Warsaw was the first place in the September campaign that the German attackers faced defenders under heavy cover. The tactics of *Blitzkrieg* (q.v.) were not adaptable to street fighting—a fact the *Wehrmacht* learned the hard way.

Despite the obvious value of holding Warsaw, Poland's leaders were at first somewhat ambivalent toward the capital's defense. Early radio messages told men of military age to leave the city. By 5 September, there was a general evacuation of government ministries. The next day, Marshal Edward Śmigły-Rydz (q.v.) and the military's supreme headquarters evacuated 125 miles eastward to Brześć (Brest).

Firm action finally took place on 8 Septem-

ber with the establishment of a city defense committee. Chaired by Starzyński and comprising both civil and military members, its Order Number 1 proclaimed that the capital would be defended. Detailed plans followed at a rapid pace and Warsaw was organized for a protracted siege. All public transportation was commandeered for the military and food was rationed. The populace was militarized and formed into labor battalions and a citizen's guard. Starzyński maintained civic morale via frequent appearances and radio speeches.

General Juliusz Rommel, the commander of Army Warzawa, was in overall command. The actual defense of the city was in the hands of General Walerian Czuma (q.v.) His 120,000 soldiers worked with civilians to create street barricades and defense positions. Chaim Kaplan, an eyewitness, gave a grim description:

> The streets are sown with trenches and barricades. Machine guns have been placed on the roofs of houses and there is a barricade in the doorway of my apartment. . . . If fighting breaks out in the street no stone will remain upon another.

Every city block was converted into a minifortress, and as fighting destroyed these, the rubble could still be used for cover and ambush attacks. Augmenting Warsaw's defenses was a ring of old Russian-constructed fortresses. Modlin, the largest, was just outside the city limits and contained a 25,000-man garrison. Artillery and antitank rifles were carefully deployed at street junctions. Because of the heavy cover, these positions were difficult to detect, and could engage attacking armor at ranges guaranteed to produce kills. Machine guns, similarly employed, caused considerable trouble for attacking infantry. The "Molotov Cocktail," often

attached to a hand-grenade, produced a fire bomb that could be used against almost any type of target.

Defense against the *Luftwaffe* was not quite so simple. Warsaw had the Pursuit Brigade of the Polish Air Force, with fifty-four fighters. Although they had some success during the first few days of German aerial attacks, lack of spare parts and advancing *Panzers* caused the unit's withdrawal on 8 September. This left antiaircraft artillery as the sole defense against air attack. Although strong by Polish standards, the capital's forty guns were spread thin. The 40mm Bofors guns were organized into a mobile column, while the larger 75mm pieces were emplaced near the city's bridges on the Vistula River. As most districts relied on machine guns for defense, German planes faced only sporadic opposition.

Warsaw's defenders were seriously hampered by *Luftwaffe* attacks. Although engine noise provided some early warning, most defenders could only conduct passive resistance from air-raid shelters. While historians agree that in the end, it was massed artillery fire that produced the greatest destruction in Warsaw, the air assaults contributed the important element of disruption to the Nazi victory. Bombing and strafing attacks were so effective that major Polish counterattacks were restricted to nighttime.

Inadequate supplies also created difficulties for the defenders. Artillery units were ordered to conserve munitions from the beginning, and despite this, they consumed half their stocks by 16 September. Hospitals were poorly organized, and there was a shortage of medical supplies, and even bandages. Food, however, created the greatest problem. By 14 September, there was enough for only two more weeks—assuming none was lost in the fighting. By 24 September, many defenders were hungry and drinking water was hard to obtain.

Despite these handicaps, morale among Warsaw's defenders remained high. This was largely due to the inspiring leadership of Starzyński and to the fact that Warsaw had successfully withstood the Red Army advance in 1920. For whatever reasons, the capital was prepared to live up to its motto: *Contemnit Procellus* (Defying the Storms).

German air attacks hit the city first and caused heavy casualties. On 8 September, elements of 4th *Panzer* Division joined the attack and received a bloody nose in the suburb of Ochota. There a five-hour battle resulted in the loss of sixty German armored vehicles, followed by a successful Polish counterattack. These losses convinced the *Wehrmacht* that a direct assault would be too costly, and a siege more effective and efficient. At about the same time, the Poles' Bzura River offensive also drew off German strength.

Artillery bombardment of the city began on the same day. As heavy guns were needed to reduce the fortress at Modlin, shelling of the city proper was rather light at first. This escalated, along with limited infantry attacks as the German desire to avoid casualties was modified by the political need to capture Warsaw before Soviet forces entered the conflict.

Heavy fighting resumed on 15 September when German Third Army units smashed their way into the Praga district. By 18 September, Modlin was cut off from the city and the Bzura offensive to the southwest was over. Five days later, thirteen German divisions and more than 1,000 guns began the assault on the city that reached its crescendo on 25 September—"Black Monday." The main attacks were aimed at the Wola, Ochota, and Mokotów districts. The waterworks, Warsaw's Achilles' heel, was a special artillery target.

Despite tenacious efforts, the Poles were in very bad shape. Supplies were low, casualties heavy, and water sources gone. On 26 September, two of the city's three defensive lines fell to the Germans. The next day, capitulation papers were signed for Warsaw and Modlin. The terms of the agreement gave the defenders three days to organize a total surrender. Though some soldiers used this time to escape, more than 140,000 surrendered at the deadline.

The costs of the Warsaw siege were heavy. Polish dead included 2,000 military and 60,000 civilians. Damage inflicted on real estate was estimated at $570 million, with more than 12 percent of the city completely demolished, including irreplaceable art works and historic sites. Despite this, the siege ended in a defiant note as witnessed by the surrender speech given to troops at Krasiński Square:

Soldiers of Warsaw! Our misfortune is temporary. Victory is on our side. *Poland is not yet lost as long as we live.* And this which has been taken by force, we will take back by force. . . . Remember that we will leave the world, but the fame and memory of your deeds will live forever.

John Dunn

Additional Reading
Bielecki, Tadeusz, and Leszek Szymanski, *Warsaw Aflame* (1973).

Korwin-Rhodes, Marta, *The Mask of Warriors* (1973).

Polonius, Alexander [Franciszek Bauer-Czarnomski], *I Saw the Siege of Warsaw* (1941).

Warsaw Rising (1 August–2 October 1944)

The rising in Warsaw of the Polish Home Army (*Armia Krajowa* or AK) (q.v.) on 1 August 1944 was the act that Poland's underground resistance and leaders in exile had worked for since their country was invaded by the Germans in September 1939. The initial leadership, Stefan Rowecki and Władysław Sikorski (qq.v.), had devised a three-stage strategy, beginning with sabotage raids, gradually escalating to local revolts, and then finally culminating in a national insurrection to be known as *Powstanie* (Rising). The strategic plan did not progress beyond the first stage due to the harsh reprisals enacted by the Germans, but the idea of a coordinated military action remained. It was intended to assist the advancing liberating forces of the Allies, although it was also meant to restore national pride and provide Poland with a vital say in its postwar fate.

It was fateful for Operation *BURZA* (TEMPEST), as the action came to be known, that the Western powers were not the forces closing in on Poland, but the Soviet Red Army. Under Josef Stalin's (q.v.) direction, political considerations were very much in the forefront and any group seeking to secure Poland's independence, a non-Communist one especially, was suspicious in his eyes.

The Poles appreciated the difficulties of working with the Soviets, and a powerful group within the AK (principally its intelligence men) tried to have the Rising abandoned, or at least postponed, until circumstances were more propitious. General Tadeusz Bór-Komorowski (q.v.), who had replaced Rowecki as commander of the Home Army after the latter's arrest by the *Gestapo* (q.v.) in 1943, wished to proceed as originally planned, albeit in a reduced form centered on Warsaw. The divisions within and the limited capabilities of its leadership were major problems for the AK. Bór-Komorowski was not as able as Rowecki, and the loss of Sikorski in an air crash was a serious blow to the Polish leadership.

The first Soviet forces entered Poland in early 1944. AK units came out into the open to assist them, but the situation was tense and quickly degenerated into gun battles with NKVD (q.v.) agents keen to eliminate the AK or force them into General Zygmunt Berling's (q.v.) Soviet-controlled Polish First Army. These incidents made the AK wary of operating on any scale, especially in rural areas. To compound their problems, the AK was very short of arms and equipment. The Allies did make airdrops—about 500 in all, 200 during the Rising—but they were not enough.

Timing was crucial if the Rising was to have a chance of succeeding. With the belief that Soviet units would soon be in the city, the AK neglected to accord the still considerable amounts of German manpower in Warsaw the respect they deserved. During the Soviet advance, however, General Konstantin Rokossovsky (q.v.) held back his forces in order to build them up for the push needed to break the unexpectedly firm German stand. This lull along the front, often attributed to cynical machinations by Stalin, gave the Germans the breathing space needed to deal with the Poles. The AK's seizure of most of Warsaw was, in fact, a major military misjudgment.

Bór-Komorowski became infected with the same sense of urgency and desperation coming over most patriotic Poles who viewed the growth of communist groups with alarm. He had 40,000 men and women in the city awaiting his call to arms. Two of his leading subordinates, Generals Tadeusz Pełczyński and Leopold Okulicki (q.v.), demanded action before the Soviets could cross the Vistula River. Attempts at working peaceably with the Soviets had failed, most recently in Wilno that July, and the AK's hopes now centered on Warsaw.

A plan was approved with the optimistic belief that a civil administration could be set up within twelve hours of liberating the city. Bór-Komorowski's operational commander for Warsaw was Colonel Antoni Chruściel. He felt the AK could maintain an offensive for several days, capture weaponry, and then defend their gains for at least two weeks. That would be enough time for the Soviets to come to the rescue and for the Poles to have asserted themselves as the rightful masters of their capital city.

Chruściel believed this despite the fact that three battle-hardened *Panzer* divisions (3rd SS, Hermann Göring, and 5th SS) had recently arrived in the city, thereby combining with the two *Panzer* divisions already there and consolidating in the western suburb of Praga. This development also indicated that the Germans were not going to retreat, but intended to fight hard for the city. This should have warned the Poles, but only a few sensed the danger. The British were offering no help, which General Kazimierz Sosnkowski (q.v.), the Polish military chief in London, considered a crucial prerequisite for success.

Colonel Iranek-Osmecki, Bór-Komorowski's intelligence chief, was one of those who spoke out against the Rising, but his objections were overridden and a plan was detailed. It included a synchronized seizure of key objectives; the city center, the two main railway stations (Central and Gdansk), and the bridges over the Vistula. AK units began assembling at prearranged points. They were not alone, for the Communist Peoples' Army and many unaligned civilians also took part.

Adolf Hitler (q.v.) placed German combat units in Warsaw under Lieutenant General Reiner Stahel, who had specific instructions for dealing with any outbreaks of trouble. The German defenses were not as disorganized as the Poles anticipated; quite the opposite, given the strength of the SS divisions.

To compound their many problems, the AK lost the initiative, having their hand forced by the Germans' sudden call for 100,000 Polish "volunteers" to serve at the front. Fearing the depletion of their manpower, the AK decided to act. Conflicting reports were reaching them and Bór-Komorowski believed those that said the Soviets were already in the suburbs. At 1700 hours on 1 August 1944, the AK's elite *Kedyw* Battalion attacked the Kammlet tobacco factory and the Warsaw Rising was underway.

AK forces wore red-and-white arm bands and carried small arms and homemade grenades called *filipinkas*. The factory and power station near the river were both secured and radio communications were set up. The AK also seized and held the city center, the Old Town, and most of the west bank of the Vistula to the south. In Praga on the east bank, at the airfields, and at the bridges, the AK's attacks with light weapons against fixed defenses failed. The latter was a particularly serious blow to the Poles' prospects, but morale was still good, and by nightfall they had run up their national flag atop Warsaw's highest building. After a couple of days, the AK held most of the city.

A prime AK objective was Stahel's headquarters in the Palais Bruhl at the Saxon Gardens, in the city center. Chruściel set up his own headquarters in the Victoria Hotel overlooking the objective, but his troops struggled trying to encircle Stahel's HQ. The fighting was brutal and building-to-building. Weaponry was improvised from water pipes and rubber tubing. The AK pleaded for Allied airdrops.

There were 11,000 German troops actually in the city (including *Wehrmacht,* SS, police, and *Luftwaffe*) besides the *Panzer* divisions available nearby. While three of the tank units held off the Soviets from attacking Praga, the Hermann Göring *Panzer* Division fought its way back into the city, its primary objective being the relief of Stahel's HQ.

The fear of humiliation a German defeat would entail led Hitler to intervene by placing *SS-Reichsführer* Heinrich Himmler (q.v.) in charge of suppressing the Rising. This was an ominous development for the people of Warsaw because Himmler was determined to show how ruthless he could be in carrying out the *Führer's* orders. Himmler organized a force of 6,500 troops commanded by anti-partisan specialist *SS-Obergruppenführer* Erich von dem Bach-Zelewski. The force consisted of a regiment of German criminals under Oskar Dirlewanger, several thousand Soviet POWs led by Mieczysław Kamiński (a unit that contained many Ukrainians and Azerbaijanis who had long-standing ethnic animosities against the Poles), and some sixteen companies of police under *SS-Gruppenführer* Heinz Reinefarth.

By holding the bridges, the Germans had control of the commanding points, which enabled them to isolate the AK groups and destroy them. After their initial setbacks, the Germans soon retook Wola and Ochota in the west of the city. They then proceeded to follow a careful strategy, using fresh forces pouring in to drive wedges from Wola to the Kierbiedz Bridge via Warsaw's two main arteries. This split the AK into three separate pockets: Mokotów and Czerniaków in the south; Powiśle facing the river and the city center, with the Old Town a little to the north; and the northernmost suburb of Żolibroz fringing on the German-controlled Citadel. The Germans then smashed these three strongholds street-by-street, using their extensive firepower, including armored trains, dive bombers, dynamite, and arson. Meanwhile, the AK was hampered by communications problems in their attempts to form a coordinated defense against these assaults.

Now divided, the AK forces set up separate commands for those areas under Colonels Kamiński, Pfeiffer, and Ziemski, respectively. The latter's Group North also controlled the Kampinos Forest on Warsaw's outskirts. By 6 August, AK units in the area of the Citadel and on the east bank of the river were smashed. The battle for the Saxon Gardens continued to rage, with the 1,600-strong *Kedyw* Battalion fiercely resisting Reinfarth's force. Superior German strength, however, eventually prevailed, and on 7 August, the Germans seized the entire area. Dirlewanger and Kamiński lost control of their men, and the German troops murdered indiscriminately, shooting prisoners and

After the Polish resistance ends, General Tadeusz Bór-Komorowski surrenders to SS Gruppenführer Erich von dem Bach-Zelewski. (IWM MH 4489)

wounded, and razing buildings. The AK responded in kind to any Germans unfortunate enough to be captured.

The *Kedyw* Battalion now retreated to concentrate in the northwest, where they still held the power station. The Old Town too was now under considerable pressure, the Germans having the capacity to attack it from three sides. By 11 August, it was in danger of falling. A special AK assault unit tried to get through to relieve them, but failed. Meanwhile, a tense and vicious close-quarters battle was raging in the city's sewers, as the Germans tried to halt the AK's use of the system for moving troops and messages around.

Airdrops were made by the Western Allies, but these were not enough. As the AK shrank into smaller areas, it became more difficult to avoid the dropped materiel falling into the hands of the Germans. By 15 August, the AK was surrounded in the Old Town and the Germans were closing in with Goliath remote-controlled mini-tanks laden with high explosives. Still the Poles there resisted, and the Germans had to call for more troops. A chance to surrender was rejected, and the AK fought on even harder, despite Bach-Zalewski's threat to destroy the entire city.

On 19 August, the AK massed in the north-ern pocket of Zoliborz and attacked southward, attempting to seize the Gdańsk Station, which would relieve the Old Town. They failed, tried again two days later, and then lost control of the Towarowa Yards to the Germans, whose grip was getting tighter all the time. With the Old Town set to fall, Bór-Komorowski fled the area just before the Germans took it. On 1 September, the remaining Poles forced their way into the Saxon Gardens. Some 2,000 escaped to the city center and 1,000 fled to Zoliborz via the sewers. The Germans found 30,000 corpses in the streets when they went in and proceeded to burn alive those who were wounded.

The Germans now held great swaths of Warsaw. They concentrated on taking the city center and clearing the riverbanks between the bridges. The AK in the center held out, but a German attack on the Powiśle power station was successful. Once dislodged from there, no AK bridgehead existed for the Soviets to cross directly and relieve the city center.

On 7 September, the Germans entered the area in force, using Polish women as human shields. This left just four small areas under AK control: the city center, Zoliborz, Czerniaków, and Mokotów. A few days later, a Soviet/Polish First Army offensive was

renewed and the AK hurriedly tried to reinforce Czerniaków for use as a bridgehead.

The Soviets now increased their supplies to the Poles, making drops to beleaguered Zoliborz. Meanwhile, two battalions of Berling's Polish Communists crossed the Vistula. One managed to establish a small bridgehead near Zoliborz. The other made it into Czerniakow, where they linked up with a depleted AK force of 400 on 15 September. They were, however, pinned down by heavy German attacks.

Berling tried to place a third unit on the west bank to assault the German rear, but the situation continued to deteriorate. All his remaining troops were evacuated on 24 September. The Germans now controlled all the positions along the Vistula. The next AK position to fall was Mokotów, stormed from two sides. Some Poles tried to escape through the sewers as before, but the Germans were now wise to that tactic and gassed them. The AK had, by now, also been forced from Czerniaków, but they grimly held on to their other two areas. The end, however, was nigh, and Bór-Komorowski knew it. The same day he asked for terms, and on 2 October, the Poles surrendered.

The AK fought for sixty-three days and 15,000 of its soldiers were dead. Some 150,000 civilians died, as well as 10,000 Germans. It was a heroic sacrifice, the tragedy of which the final AK radio broadcast managed to capture:

> Immortal is the nation that can muster such universal heroism. For those who have died have conquered, and those who live will fight on, will conquer, and again bear witness that Poland lives when the Poles live.

Chris Westhorp

Additional Reading

Ciechcinowski, Jan, *Warsaw Rising* (1974).
Deschner, Gunther, *Warsaw Rising* (1972).
Korbonski, Stefan, *Fighting Warsaw: The Story Behind the Polish Underground State, 1939–1945* (1956).
Orpen, Neil, *Airlift to Warsaw: The Rising of 1944 Betrayed* (1984).
Zawodny, J.K., *Nothing but Honour: The Story of the Warsaw Uprising, 1944* (1978).

Weather War (1942–1945)

Airpower's growing importance and its sensitivity to weather made weather forecasting an increasingly critical aspect of military operations. Virtually every major military operation of the war was predicated on anticipated weather conditions. Having bombers arrive over a target "socked in" by fog or thunderstorms was every bit as disruptive to one's operational plans as having them hit the wrong target. Knowing in advance when the enemy's aircraft, or your own, would be grounded by fog might provide the key to victory or enable the prevention of a tactical reverse. For amphibious operations (q.v.) in particular, the weather forecast determined if there even were to be an operation.

This need for accurate weather forecasting led to one of World War II's most interesting but obscure campaigns. All of it took place above the Arctic Circle, because it is in the polar regions that Europe's weather is born. Although not a war of major campaigns and large numbers of troops, ships, or planes, the "Weather War" had an impact on the fighting in the Atlantic and European theaters.

Fought across an area stretching from Greenland to Spitzbergen (q.v.) to Novaya Zemlya, it was a war of small units composed of both scientists and soldiers and individual ships fighting the elements every bit as much as each other. Greenland, for example, formed an army of twenty-six men, the smallest to participate in World War II, to engage German weather parties on its coast in cooperation with U.S. Coast Guard vessels patrolling offshore (*see* Army, Greenland). Stealth, audacity, and innovation were the hallmarks of that struggle and losses were proportionally high. Often the protagonists had to halt the fighting and work together to survive against the greater enemy, the Arctic weather.

Despite the almost minuscule size of the forces involved, the outcome of this struggle impacted on such critical operations as the German Channel Dash, the Allied strategic bombing campaign, the German Ardennes offensive, and the Normandy landings (qq.v.). As with so many other campaigns, it was one that Germany lost. In the end, the Germans had to turn to technology to obtain their weather data. Ironically, it was a German weather team that became, on 9 September 1945, the last Axis force to surrender to the Western Allies.

Carl O. Schuster

Additional Reading

Hessler, Gunther, *U-Boat War in the Atlantic 1939–1945* (1990).
Howarth, David, *The Sledge Patrol* (1957).
Hummelchen, G., and J. Rohwer, *Chronology of the War at Sea: 1939–1945* (1972).

Liversidge, Douglas, *The Third Front* (1960).

Willoughby, Malcolm, *The U.S. Coast Guard in World War II* (1989).

West Wall

See Siegfried Line

Westerplatte (1–7 September 1939)

Danzig (q.v.), already symbolic of interwar tensions, was also the scene of World War II's first battles. These fights featured bitter, albeit small-scale combat, centered about Poland's concessions within the free city. The largest of these, the military depot at Westerplatte, maintained a heroic defense against vastly superior German forces, thereby gaining among Poles a stature similar to the Alamo for Americans.

WYKONAĆ PEKING (INITIATE PEKING) was the coded warning to Polish naval forces that war with Germany was imminent. Sent out on 30 August 1939, it allowed some warning to the motley collection of soldiers, sailors, and civilians who took up arms to defend three positions inside Danzig. The first two, a railway station and a post office, were overrun in the early hours of 1 September.

Westerplatte was a different story. Its commander, Major Henryk Sucharski, deployed his 182-man garrison in well-concealed reinforced shelters and machine gun bunkers. Despite covering fire from the 280mm guns on the German battleship *Schleswig-Holstein,* German naval infantry units were repulsed in their first effort to obtain a quick victory.

Reinforcements arrived from SA, SS (qq.v.), and *Wehrmacht* units, in all, 3,500 German troops. Ground, air, and sea bombardment continued round the clock. In addition to causing casualties, this massive firepower cleared away the natural cover, destroyed supplies, and severed communications.

Finally, on 7 September, under cover of a smokescreen, German forces were able to capture what they now grimly referred to as *kleines Verdun* (little Verdun). Victory was purchased with more than 300 casualties, but it allowed Adolf Hitler (q.v.) to claim that the first of many "Germanic" cities had returned to the *Reich.*

John Dunn

Additional Reading

Kosiarz, Edward, *Poles on the Seas, 1939–1946* (1969).

Pruszynski, Ksawery, *Poland Fights Back: From Westerplatte to Monte Cassino* (1945).

Winter War, Finnish (30 November 1939–12 March 1940)

[See map 16 on page 1326]

The Molotov-Ribbentrop Pact (q.v.) of 1939 included a secret protocol in which Finland and the Baltic states (q.v.) were placed in the Soviet sphere of influence. Accordingly, after the Germans and the Soviets divided Poland in September 1939, Moscow started expanding its new "security zone." In late September and early October, the Soviet Union forced Estonia, Latvia, and Lithuania to sign mutual assistance pacts and to allow Soviet bases in their territories.

Soon thereafter, Moscow started pressuring Finland. The Finno-Soviet negotiations of October–November 1939, however, did not lead to the results Moscow wanted. Instead of accepting the relatively modest Soviet demands for territorial concessions in the Karelian isthmus, the Finnish government discounted the importance Josef Stalin (q.v.) placed on the close proximity of the Finnish border to Leningrad (approximately thirty miles). Thus, after several weeks of hard bargaining with their eastern neighbor, the Finns still held on to their uncompromising position, and the negotiations in Moscow ended on 13 November without a treaty.

On 26 November 1939, Soviet Foreign Commissar Vyacheslav Molotov (q.v.) handed the Finnish ambassador a protest note claiming that Finnish artillery had fired over the frontier and killed several Soviet soldiers (the so-called Mainila Shots). Four days later, the Red Army crossed Finland's eastern frontier, officially pronouncing Finland the aggressor. The Finnish Winter War had begun.

At the start, Finland was defended by an army of only 150,000 troops organized into nine divisions. The Soviets attacked initially with twenty-six divisions organized into four armies. The Soviet Seventh Army, the strongest with twelve divisions, attacked the five Finnish divisions on the Karelian isthmus. The Eighth Army advanced around the north side of Lake Ladoga. The Ninth Army attacked from Russian Karelia toward the northern end of the Gulf of Bothnia. The Fourteenth Army in the far north attacked from the area of Murmansk. As the war progressed, the Soviets committed more troops and equipment to the fight. On 7 January 1940, General Semen Timoshenko (q.v.) assumed command of the Soviet operations.

The result of the ensuing conflict seemed clear from the outset. With a population less than five million, Finland faced a major power with a population of more than 190 million. To worsen the situation, Stalin cut off any chance for a negotiated settlement by establishing a Finnish puppet government. The so-called Terijoki Government was led by Otto V. Kuusinen, a Finnish Communist who emigrated to the Soviet Union in 1918 and became a prominent figure in the Comintern (q.v.).

The attack on Finland combined with Moscow's refusal to recognize the legitimate Finnish government, led to the expulsion of the Soviet Union from the League of Nations (q.v.). Aside from that, the only help Finland received from abroad included sympathetic world opinion, token forces of volunteers, and more significantly, limited shipments of arms.

Against incredible odds the Finnish Army held its main defensive positions on the Karelian isthmus for two months, creating the near-legendary reputation of the skiing Finnish Army. Because the Soviet forces were poorly organized and the Finns were fighting on familiar terrain, the Mannerheim Line (q.v.) held the numerically superior Red Army.

Moreover, on their northeastern frontier the Finns inflicted substantial losses on the Soviets by using their *Motti* tactics; i.e., breaking up the invading divisions into small fragments, encircling these *Motti*s, and destroying them one by one. The most significant success these tactics came in a series of battles at Suomussalmi (q.v.) between December 1939 and January 1940, when Finns annihilated the main part of the Soviet 163rd and 44th Divisions.

These successful operations were largely responsible for the Soviet decision to agree to negotiate with the legal Finnish government in January 1940. At the same time, Great Britain and France were considering sending an expeditionary force to help the Finns in their struggle. Since the Soviet demands during the peace negotiations, beginning in early February, were far more harsh than what the Finns had expected, the growing Allied interest in Finland provided something of an option for the Finnish government.

For several reasons, Finland eventually turned down the Allied offer of assistance and opted for a negotiated settlement with Moscow. First, although worried about the growing Allied interest, the Soviets launched a major offensive on 6 February 1940 and finally forced a retreat of the Finnish Army by 17 February. Second, the amount of assistance tentatively offered by the Western powers amounted to only 22,000 men, and those troops could not be assured of reaching Finland before late March 1940. Taking into account the Soviet advances in February, the aid promised would have been too little, too late. Finally, on 24 February, the Swedish government refused to allow the passage of any foreign troops through its territory, closing the only route that a potential Allied expeditionary force could have taken to reach Finland. Thus, the only feasible alternative for the Finns was to reach a settlement with Moscow.

Ironically, one factor that prolonged the conclusion of the peace treaty was the earlier Finnish success in the war. The rampant celebration of Finland's success during December and January made it hard for the Finnish government to reconcile public opinion to the harsh peace terms that Moscow was pushing. The Soviet advance on the Karelian isthmus continued in early March, however, leading the commander in chief of the Finnish forces, Marshal Carl Mannerheim (q.v.), to press his government into accepting the peace terms. As Mannerheim put it in a meeting among Finnish government leaders, members of parliament, and the military leadership on 8 March 1940: "continued hostilities can lead only to a weakening of the [Finnish] position and to further losses of ground." With some hesitation, the Finnish government decided to accept the peace terms and the Treaty of Moscow was signed on 12 March 1940.

The peace treaty included large territorial concessions. Finland was obliged to cede to the Soviet Union all of the Karelian isthmus, several islands in the eastern part of the Gulf of Finland, most of Finnish Karelia, and parts of northeastern Finland. Furthermore, the Hanko peninsula, the southernmost part of Finland located seventy miles southwest of Helsinki, was leased to the Soviet Union for thirty years. As a result, Finland had to deal with the resettlement of approximately 400,000 refugees from the formerly Finnish areas of Karelia. Yet, because of its partially successful and definitely stubborn resistance, Finland escaped the fate of the Baltic states, which were annexed by the Soviet Union in June 1940.

At no time in the Winter War did the Finns have more than 200,000 soldiers under arms. The Soviets eventually committed 1.2 million troops, 1,500 tanks, and 3,000 aircraft. The Finns suffered 23,000 dead and 45,000 wounded. Soviet losses were at least 70,000 dead and 200,000 wounded, and may have been much higher. At the time, many Western observers concluded that the large dispar-

ity in losses and the apparent poor performance of the Red Army were a direct result of Stalin's earlier purges (q.v.) of the military leadership.

Most members of the Finnish government opted for the peace treaty out of military necessity. Some political leaders, however, did not accept that view, pointing to the possibility of Allied aid. They labeled the peace as a "sell-out." That belief became increasingly popular in Finland during 1940 and 1941, and created a general willingness among the population to seek revenge. That attitude, combined with the memories of an admittedly heroic and relatively successful resistance, led to a national feeling that overwhelmingly supported Finland joining forces as a cobelligerent of Germany against the Soviets in the summer of 1941.

Jussi Hanhimaki

Additional Reading

Chew, Allen F., *The White Death: The Epic of the Soviet-Finnish Winter War* (1971).

Condon, Richard W., *The Winter War: Russia against Finland* (1972).

Engle, Eloise, and Lauri Paananen, *The Winter War: The Russo-Finnish Conflict, 1939–1940* (1973).

Nevakivi, Jukka, *The Appeal That Was Never Made: The Allies, Scandinavia, and the Finnish Winter War, 1939–1940* (1976).

Tanner, Väinö, *The Winter War: Finland against Russia, 1939–1940* (1957).

WUNDERLAND (WONDERLAND) I and II, Operations (Summers 1942 and 1943)

Germany conducted three operations against the Soviet Union's Arctic sea lanes, or "northern sea route," during World War II. Conducted during the late summer and early fall months of 1942 to 1944, these operations were intended to interdict the increasingly important Soviet shipping through those waters. Although the operations had little strategic impact on the war, they led to Germany's deepest penetration of Soviet territory and resulted in the war's easternmost Russo-German military engagements.

The first two operations were designated *WUNDERLAND* I and II. The were conducted in the summers of 1942 and 1943, respectively. Originally, they were planned for pocket battleships (*Admiral Scheer* in *WUNDERLAND I* and *Lützow* in *WUNDERLAND II*), but in the event only the *Admiral Scheer* entered Soviet Arctic waters. As a result, *WUNDERLAND II* and the subsequent 1944 operation were conducted by U-boats alone, supported by aerial reconnaissance.

The German Navy first began to target the northern sea route in the late spring of 1942 as a result of Adolf Hitler's (q.v.) direction that the navy do all it could to support the war effort on the eastern front. Both Admirals Erich Raeder and Karl Dönitz (qq.v.) knew that Soviet commerce transited those waters. Moreover, German intelligence reported that transportation was one of the Soviet Union's most serious strategic concerns in 1942. The redistribution of Soviet industry and raw materials placed an additional strain on an already overstretched rail and river network.

On the land, the German spring offensive of 1942 promised to exacerbate the already serious transportation problem. Transporting critical, low-volume raw materials and supplies to the Western theater via the Arctic sea lanes offered a partial solution for the Soviets. The Ob River and the Soviet Arctic waters offered relatively safe transportation during the spring and summer when the military rail load was at its peak. Timber, tin, industrial diamonds, and tungsten went north via river to Port Dickson and other Arctic ports, where they then went to Murmansk, Archangel, or down the Ob River. From there the materials went by river and canal to the factories east of Moscow or Gorky. Critical raw materials from the Far East also came in via the northern sea route.

As German forces closed in on the Caucasus (q.v.)—the Soviet Union's other source of critical raw materials—the northern sea route became even more important. Planning to interdict that route began in June 1942. The Soviet Arctic waters were not totally unknown to the Germans. The Auxiliary Cruiser *Komet* made a transit of those waters in 1940 en route to the Pacific. The Germans learned from that cruise that the former whaling port of Port Dickson was the central shipping point for the Soviet Arctic convoys. The largest Soviet Arctic port east of Archangel, it was the last stopping off point to link up with icebreakers before entering the Vikitsky Straits, which marked the Kara Sea's eastern boundary. Radio reconnaissance indicated that the ships sailed independently from mid-July until the first ice came in late August. From that point, ships were organized into convoys, which were led by icebreakers. Ships coming from Asian Russia had to be led through the Vikitsky Strait by icebreakers because the Laptev Sea formed ice sooner than the Kara. The Germans could not determine specific ice conditions on the Kara Sea because the Soviets encrypted their weather and ice reports.

Admiral Hermann Böhm, the German naval commander in Norway, ordered *WUNDERLAND I* to begin in July 1942, after the destruction of Allied Convoy PQ-17 (q.v.). Initially, a weather party from the *U-435* landed on Spitzbergen Island to measure and track the Arctic conditions. Remaining on the island for about eight days, the team sent its observations to the *Luftwaffe* weather service, which then provided weather predictions to the surface force commander, Captain Wilhelm Meendsen-Bohlken, aboard the *Admiral Scheer*. Two U-boats, meanwhile, reported on ice conditions in the Kara Sea. Because of Soviet coastal defenses and minefields, all German units had to pass north of Novaya Zemlya, within 250 nautical miles of the North Pole.

Following four days of weather reports, the *Admiral Scheer* departed Narvik, Norway, and steamed toward Cape Zhelaniya. This marked the initiation of the second, more active phase of the operation. Although the Soviets were aware of the U-boat activities, they did not divine their purpose, since most of the units had been involved in the attack on PQ-17. As a result, the Soviets misjudged the *Scheer's* intentions as it steamed past Cape Zhelaniya on 19 August. Believing the *Scheer* would attack the weather station and seaplane base there, the local Soviet Air Force headquarters and the border patrol posts made no reports to Soviet naval authorities for almost twenty-four hours.

By then the *Scheer* was already in the central Kara Sea. Its seaplane already had located a convoy entering the waterway via the Vikitsky Strait, and the *Scheer* moved to intercept. Fortunately for the Soviets, fog, mists, and drifting ice prevented the German captain from searching aggressively. The same factors prevented him from intercepting another convoy the seaplane spotted on 23 August. Finally, on 25 August, the *Scheer* encountered the icebreaker *Alexandr Sibiryakov* near Belucha Island. The ancient icebreaker was, of course, no match for the pocket battleship, and was sunk after forty-five minutes of futile resistance—but not before providing the Soviet Northern Fleet with an accurate report on the German force.

The Northern Sea Route Directorate desperately rerouted convoys to avoid the surface raider, and requested air support from Northern Fleet headquarters. The fleet commander, Admiral Arseni Golovko, denied the request, incredibly citing "German air supremacy" as the reason. Instead, Golovko deployed submarines off Cape Zhelaniya and requested a squadron of destroyers from the Soviet Pacific Fleet.

Soviet tracking of the *Scheer* ended with the sinking of the icebreaker. Panic-stricken and highly inaccurate reporting followed from nearby NKVD (q.v.) observation posts. Attempts the following day to locate the *Scheer* by aerial reconnaissance failed. The roving fog and mists protected the *Scheer* as much as they did the Soviet convoys the Germans were hunting.

The *Scheer* was supported by the *U-601*, which was patrolling just west of Vikitsky Strait. Reporting any ships it could not intercept, the U-boat also plotted Soviet reporting stations and defenses in the area. As a hunter, however, it enjoyed little success, sinking only a coastal freighter east of Port Dickson before withdrawing to Cape Zhelaniya on 28 August.

Captain Meendsen-Bohlken, meanwhile, decided to attack Port Dickson in the hope of catching a convoy forming. A Soviet naval observation post identified the *Scheer* as it approached the port shortly after midnight on 26–27 August. Visibility was less than three nautical miles as the ship entered the alerted harbor. The port's coastal defenses were supplemented by the armed icebreaker *Dezhnev*, two steamships, and some recently delivered 152mm guns, which were en route to a nearby coastal defense site.

Poor visibility limited the range of the engagement to less than two nautical miles. The *Scheer* concentrated on the *Dezhnev* and the steamships during the first exchange of fire, which lasted twenty-three minutes. The icebreaker was hit and forced to ground itself in the harbor's soft mud. Believing the *Dezhnev* and the steamships fatally damaged, the *Scheer* then shelled some nearby port facilities before returning to finish off the main port itself. During the second attack, which lasted thirty minutes, the Germans inflicted some additional damage to the three Soviet ships and set the port's fueling areas on fire. The *Admiral Scheer* then departed Port Dickson and left the Kara Sea at high speed to avoid being trapped by the now growing ice floes. Despite the damage, the Soviets had the port fully operational three days later.

Minelaying marked the third and final phase of *WUNDERLAND I*. The minelayer *Ulm*, which was supposed to mine Cape Zhelaniya after the *Scheer's* departure, encountered three American destroyers on 26 August, and was sunk after a brief gun battle. Subsequently, the cruiser *Hipper* planted the minefield on 3 September, five days behind schedule. Two U-boats also successfully laid minefields in the Matochkin and Yugor Straits, effectively restricting entry to the Kara Sea from the west.

As a result of *WUNDERLAND I,* the Ger-

mans believed the Soviets had lost three patrol boats, a weather station, and four steamers, and had suffered extensive damage to their primary Arctic port. Several convoys also were held up on the Pacific side of the Vikitsky Strait until the *Scheer*'s departure from the Kara Sea was confirmed. Admiral Böhm, however, felt the Germans could accomplish much more with a second attempt, particularly since the air over the Kara Sea was almost devoid of Soviet aircraft.

WUNDERLAND II began on 1 August 1943, when the *U-255* established a forward operation base for a BV-138 seaplane in northwestern Novaya Zemlya. The seaplane conducted a week-long aerial reconnaissance of the Kara Sea, flying out as far as the Vikitsky Straits. The *WUNDERLAND II* plan called for the seaplane to guide four U-boats and the *Lützow* into the Kara Sea to destroy Soviet shipping. During two separate sorties, however, the seaplane failed to locate any shipping. As a result, the *Lützow*'s participation was canceled and the three U-boats were sent alone to penetrate the Vikitsky Strait into the Laptev Sea. There, they sank two steamers, the *Petrovsky* and the *Dikson*. Later, the *U-711* shelled a Soviet communications relay station in Asian Russia and put sailors ashore to reconnoiter Wardroper Island. No other German forces ever set foot so deeply into Soviet territory, except as prisoners of war. Another group of U-boats, meanwhile, laid mines east of the Yugor Straits, off the Ob Estuary and Port Dickson. These units later withdrew and were replaced by the *U-703,* the *U-601,* and the *U-960.*

On 30 September, the three U-boats intercepted Soviet Convoy VA-18, a four-ship convoy bringing supplies from Vladivostok. VA-18 was escorted by a minelayer and three small minesweepers. Despite having the advantages of surprise and overwhelming firepower, the U-boats only managed to sink two of the freighters and one minesweeper.

The *WUNDERLAND* operations ended when the German U-boats withdrew on 4 October 1943. In 1944, German U-boats again attacked the northern sea route, but achieved only limited suc-

cess. Patrolling in the Vikitsky Straits the summer and early fall, four U-boats intercepted two convoys but sank only four ships. On 24 September, three U-boats formed a combined raiding party that successfully destroyed the communications station on Sterligova and took some prisoners. Although all the U-boats returned to Narvik by 4 October 1944, the Soviet Northern Fleet continued its U-boat alert until well into November, deploying escort and patrol forces into the waters on both sides of the Vikitsky Straits, and claiming the destruction of ten nonexistent U-boats in the process.

The German operations in the Kara Sea had no significant impact on Soviet industrial production. Soviet shipping was disrupted only briefly. Some Soviet naval forces were diverted away from those attacking the German sea lanes in Norway. That, perhaps, was the most the Germans could have hoped for. The convoys transiting the Kara Sea were small and few in number, which limited the opportunities for interception and made it easy for the ships to escape. Given these factors and the fog, ice, and uncertain water depths, only a radar-equipped task force supported by light units and aerial reconnaissance could have achieved much in the short operational time available each season (thirty to forty-five days). The German Navy's limited appreciation for radar (q.v.) and its lack of long-range destroyers placed such a force beyond its capability. Nonetheless, these operations highlighted the difference between the naval operations in the Arctic and those conducted in the other seas of the eastern front, and marked the deepest penetration of the Soviet Union in World War II.

Carl O. Schuster

Additional Reading

Golovko, Arseni, *With the Fleet* (1979).

Hummelchen, G., and J. Rohwer, *Chronology of the War at Sea, 1939–1945* (1972).

Rugge, Friedrich, *Der Seekrieg 1939–1945* (1954).

Showell, Jak P., *The German Navy in World War II* (1979).

Y

Yugoslavian National Liberation (April 1941–April 1945)

Prince Paul, regent of Yugoslavia, hesitated to follow the example of Romania and Bulgaria and join the Tripartite Pact. Impressed by the rapid fall of France and hopeful that Germany might support Yugoslavia's acquisition of Salonika, he signed the pact on 25 March 1941. Two days later the Yugoslav Army overthrew Paul's government in the name of young King Peter (q.v.). Though the new government proclaimed its neutrality, this was not sufficient for Adolf Hitler (q.v.). The Germans attacked and Yugoslavia fought and fell alone.

Operation "25" started on 6 April 1941. The Second German Army, commanded by General Maximillian von Weichs (q.v.) and the First *Panzer* Group, commanded by General Ewald von Kleist (q.v.), attacked northern and southern Yugoslavia from Austria and Bulgaria, respectively. In the north, they were assisted by the Hungarian Third Army and the Italian Second Army. General Wilhelm List's (q.v.) Twelfth Army also moved into southern Yugoslavia from Bulgaria, but it was really part of the force attacking Greece (q.v.). The partially mobilized Yugoslav Army tried to attack Italian forces in Albania, but made little real progress. Belgrade (q.v.) fell on 13 April and the Yugoslav Army capitulated four days later.

Defeated Yugoslavia was partitioned. An expanded Croatia (q.v.) was handed over to its homegrown anti-Serbian Fascists, the *Ustaša* (q.v.), led by Ante Pavelić (q.v.). A puppet government, headed by Milan Nedić, was set up in German-occupied and administered Serbia. Italy took control of Bosnia, Montenegro, and Dalmatia, and joined Germany in the dismemberment of Slovenia. Macedonia was assigned to Bulgaria and the Hungarians took a section of territory adjacent to their border.

King Peter fled and a government-in-exile was set up in London. Colonel Draža Mihailović (q.v.) represented that government within Yugoslavia. He commanded a segment of the Royal Yugoslav Army which had refused to surrender and withdrew into a forest area near Doboj in Serbia. He was appointed both commander in chief and minister of war by the government-in-exile, but he failed to become the leader of a vital national liberation movement. As a champion of Serbian dominance within the country, Mihailović alienated the other nationalities resentful of Serbian arrogance. In addition, he was reluctant to expose his forces to decimation and to risk reprisals against civilians by engaging in large-scale operations against the Germans.

Mihailović's forces, the *Četniks* (q.v.), were ready to engage in limited operations but wanted no part in a national rising. Like Mihailović, they wanted to re-create a regular army and conserve it until defeat of the Germans by the Allies. They saw their army as a counterpoint to the Communist-led Yugoslav partisans (q.v.). When the time came, the *Četniks* would challenge the partisans and save Yugoslavia from Communism. During their wait, fearful of the growing strength of the partisan movement, the *Četniks* chose to collaborate with the Germans to crush the Communist menace.

Tito's (q.v.) partisans, meanwhile, quickly demonstrated their intention to engage in determined resistance against the occupiers and their Yugoslav minions. Despite the hindrance of the Nazi-Soviet Nonaggression Pact, Tito, whose independence was stimulated by Josef Stalin's purges (qq.v.) and his personal experiences during two protracted stays in Moscow, began immediately after the German invasion to prepare for resistance. At the end of April, despite the recognition by the Soviet Union of German dominance in Yugosla-

via, Tito issued instructions for the Communists to prepare their cells for action by gathering intelligence and arms.

Tito moved from Zagreb to Belgrade in May, and he was prepared to issue his call to action when the Germans invaded the Soviet Union (q.v.) on 22 June 1941. On 4 July, the Politburo of the Yugoslav Communist Party was rechristened the General Staff of the National Liberation Movement. The party, which had been illegal since 29 November 1920, had 12,000 members and a 17,000-member youth organization. Underground regional organizations were developed to include a clandestine radio station. Although Tito was lightly armed, he had the services of 300 experienced veterans of the Spanish civil war (q.v.). In addition to party members, there were many nonparty contacts and sympathizers willing to join in the struggle against the Fascist occupiers and their Yugoslav collaborators. The atrocities of Pavelić's Ustaša, in particular, won thousands of supporters for Tito in Croatia and Bosnia.

Tito was determined not merely to engage in small and dispersed guerrilla operations but to organize an army which, although it would avoid pitched battles, would be able to conduct an extensive guerrilla campaign and tie down a maximum number of German troops. The occupiers, he reckoned, would not be able to garrison the entire country. His guerrilla army would be able to occupy remote areas and to organize them as liberated territories. If the Axis forces staged major operations against these strongholds, they would be abandoned with fighting retreats.

In July 1941, a partisan-led revolt in Montenegro reduced Italian control to a few garrison towns. In August, the Germans experienced a widespread uprising in Serbia. By autumn 1941, headquarters, including an arms factory and a printing press, was established at Užice in Serbia. Mihailović was directed by the Yugoslav government-in-exile to assume command over the Communist-led forces. Cooperation between the partisans and the Četniks soon collapsed, however. They possessed conflicting objectives. The partisans desired to use the struggle against the Fascist occupiers of Yugoslavia as an opportunity to revolutionize the country and ultimately to transform it into a federated socialist state.

The Četniks, who wanted to reestablish the Serbian-dominated monarchy, saw the partisans as their long-term enemies. The Četniks, despite appeals for action from the British (who provided them with supplies and gold), preferred to reach an accommodation with the Germans and pre-

serve their forces for the ultimate conflict that would come after the Allied defeat of Germany.

Although Stalin had instructed him to cooperate with the non-Communist forces, Tito refused to subordinate his partisans to Mihailović. In the midst of a German campaign to pacify Yugoslavia, Mihailović's Četniks attacked Užice on 1 November. They were beaten off, but from that time on the partisans were forced to contend with the armed hostility of the Četniks as well as the occupation forces and the Ustaša. The Četniks subsequently received arms from the Italians, who encouraged Mihailović's anti-Communist campaign. The internecine struggle was a boon to the Germans, who were aware of the potential danger posed by the Communist-led partisan movement. They seized the opportunity to drive both the partisans and Četniks from Serbia.

Hard-pressed by the Germans and the Italians, the partisans were forced to suspend operations and seek refuge in the mountains of Bosnia and Montenegro. Conditions were dismal and the Soviets, anxious not to offend their Western allies, and faced with a perhaps insuperable logistical problem, did not respond to the desperate pleas for aid. There were a number of defections, but due to the leadership of Tito, backed up by the veterans of the Spanish civil war and former officers of the Yugoslav Army, the partisan movement survived and was developed into a well-organized army of five brigades.

During the summer of 1942, Tito, pressed by the Germans, moved his main force in the partisans' 115-day, 200-mile "long march" from Montenegro and eastern Bosnia to the mountainous region of northwestern Bosnia. There, without any external recognition or support, Tito established control over a large area around Bihać.

In November 1942, an assembly convened at Bihać and established the Anti-Fascist Council for the National Liberation of Yugoslavia (AVNOJ), which foreshadowed the partisan claim to be the government of Yugoslavia. Under the direction of Tito, AVNOJ functioned as the government of the areas controlled by the partisans. It assumed civil administration, kept order, set prices, and instituted revolutionary social changes.

By 1943, Tito had almost 150,000 partisan fighters organized into twenty-eight brigades. The very survival of this force was put in question by Operation WEISS (WHITE), launched by the Germans on 20 January. Fearing an Allied attack through the Balkans, Hitler ordered a merciless anti-partisan campaign. The main partisan force, numbering about 20,000, was attacked by a com-

bined force of Germans, Italians, Bulgarians, *Četniks,* and *Ustaša.* Outnumbered six to one, the partisans lost a fourth of their fighters and half of their equipment. The partisans staged a desperate withdrawal across the Neretva River, and choosing the weakest point of their encircling foes, destroyed the Italian *Murge* Division on Mount Prenj. They then pursued the *Četniks* into Montenegro and liquidated them as an effective fighting force.

German General Alexander von Löhr (q.v.) did not allow the partisans time to recuperate. In coordination with the Italians and Bulgarians, he launched Operation *SCHWARTZ* (BLACK). The partisans were again able to break through the encircling force. The occupiers massed 117,000 troops, but 19,000 partisans escaped through the narrow gorge of the River Sutjeska into the wilds of Bosnia's Zelengora Mountains. Tito lost all of his wounded, which the partisans always attempted to evacuate with their army, and 30 percent of his fighters; but his movement survived.

The fortunes of the partisans changed in the autumn of 1943. Italy surrendered in September, and large amounts of Italian arms and supplies fell into the partisans' hands. They were able to take advantage of the Italian capitulation by moving into the former Italian satellite state of Croatia and occupying the coast of Dalmatia. At the same time, the British decided to provide supplies and air cover for the partisans. Although the British temporarily continued to provide support to Mihailović, this was eventually terminated due to his reticence to act against the Germans. In June 1944, the British withdrew their recognition of Mihailović and the government-in-exile was forced to dismiss him as minister of war.

The upswing in partisan fortunes produced a flood of new recruits, and the movement soon boasted 300,000 fighters. On 29 November 1943, at Jajce in Bosnia, the Council for the Liberation of Yugoslavia formally asserted its claim to be the provisional government of Yugoslavia and conscription was imposed on all males in liberated territory. Tito was proclaimed marshal of Yugoslavia and premier of the new government. After the Teheran Conference in December *(see* Conferences, Allied) British aid increased. The British supplied arms and evacuated wounded partisans to hospitals in Italy. A Soviet military mission was sent to Tito's headquarters in February 1944, and some Soviet materiel support started flowing in during the last stages of the war. The absence of earlier Soviet support, however, intensified the independence of Tito and his national Communist

movement. The greatest service provided by the Soviets was their 1944 advance on Belgrade.

The partisans were unable by themselves to dislodge the Germans from Serbia. In fact, in the spring of 1944, the Germans invaded Bosnia and forced the evacuation of Jajce. In an airborne attack, code named *RÖSSELSPRUNG* (KNIGHT'S MOVE), Tito's headquarters at Drvar was raided on 25 May (his birthday), and he almost was captured. He subsequently established his headquarters on the Adriatic island of Vis, where British ground, air, and sea forces provided protection.

By the time the Soviets and partisans entered Belgrade on 20 October 1944, the partisans had established their control over much of Yugoslavia. Stalin agreed to recognize Tito as the commander of Yugoslav forces and to relegate the occupation of the country to him. Tito continued to clear Germans from his territory, but his prime concern was to occupy Istria and Trieste to bolster Yugoslav claims to these territories held by Italy before the war. On 30 April 1945, Tito's Fourth Army occupied Trieste two days before the arrival of Allied troops. He later was forced to evacuate the city.

At the end of the war, Tito had 800,000 men and women under arms. Their task now was not only to defend Yugoslavia against its external enemies but also to buttress Tito against those internal forces opposed to his desire to transform Yugoslavia into a united and socialist state. He single-mindedly pursued this goal, although there were some tactical delays along the way. On 16 June 1944, Tito signed an agreement with Ivan Subasić, representative to King Peter, to provide for a regency council to represent the king. The three regents, a Serb, a Croat, and a Slovene, were not Communists, but Tito, who exercised the real authority in the country, approved of them. The AVNOJ, according to the agreement, was to serve as the legislature until the election of a constituent assembly. The agreement was approved at Yalta in February 1945 and imposed upon the king.

In March, Tito formed a government that included Subasić as foreign minister, and other representatives of the government-in-exile; but Tito was premier. Before elections were held, Subasić resigned in September over the disenfranchisement of "collaborators," a term the Communists interpreted broadly. Non-Communist parties boycotted the November election. According to Tito, his list won 96 percent of the vote. On 29 November 1945, the constituent assembly formally announced the transformation of Yugoslavia into a

people's republic. In 1946, Mihailović was found guilty of collaborating with the Germans and shot.

Bernard A. Cook

Additional Reading

Adamic, Louis, *The Eagle and the Roots* (1952).

Deroc, Milan, *British Special Operations Explored: Yugoslavia in Turmoil 1941–1943 and the British Response* (1988).

Milazzo, Matteo J., *The Cetnik Movement and the Yugoslav Resistance* (1975).

Roberts, Walter R., *Tito, Mihailović, and the Allies, 1941–1945* (1973).

Appendixes

Appendix A

Chronology of World War II in Europe

No historical event, even one as large as World War II, stands in isolation. In addition to establishing a time line for the key events of the war from 1939 to 1945, this chronology also outlines the major events leading up to the war and the major events resulting directly from it. The chronology starts, therefore, with the collapse of the German empire at the close of World War I and ends with the departure of the last American soldier from Berlin in 1994.

1918

NOVEMBER
9   The kaiser abdicates and a republic is declared in Berlin.
11   The armistice ends the fighting of World War I.

1919

JANUARY
5   Russo-Polish War starts.
    The German Workers' Party is founded.
12   German troops crush the Sparticast Rebellion.
18   The Peace Conference at Versailles begins.

FEBRUARY
9   The Constitutional Assembly in Weimar elects Ebert the president of
    Germany.
22   Communists in Munich declare a soviet republic in Bavaria.

APRIL
28   The Covenant of the League of Nations is adopted.

MAY
7   The peace treaty is presented to the German delegation at Versailles.

JUNE
21   The German High Seas Fleet scuttles its ships in Scapa Flow.
28   The peace treaty ending World War I is signed at Versailles.

JULY
1   Mussolini publishes the *Fascist Manifesto*.

SEPTEMBER
12   Hitler attends his first meeting of the German Workers' Party.
16   Hitler joins the German Workers' Party.

1920

JANUARY
1   The Treaty of Versailles becomes effective, officially ending World War I.

4   Allied governments present the "Black List" of accused German war criminals to the German Foreign Ministry, requesting extradition to try them in Allied military tribunals. The list includes the names of all German generals and admirals, as well as many junior officers and noncommissioned officers who were national war heroes.

11   The Council of the League of Nations meets for the first time.

23   The Allies accept a compromise: a German civil court in Leipzig will try the "criminals." Only 113 are tried; most are acquitted.

MARCH

11   The German Workers' Party changes its name to the National Socialist German Workers' Party (NSDAP).

13–17   Kapp-Lüttwiz *Putsch* in Berlin.

APRIL

1   Hitler leaves the German army to devote all his efforts to the NSDAP.

OCTOBER

18   The Russo-Polish War ends.

1921

MAY

6   The Russo-German Commercial Agreement is signed, establishing military-industrial cooperation.

JULY

21   U.S. bombers under General Billy Mitchell sink the former German battleship *Ostfriesland* in a dramatic demonstration of air power.

NOVEMBER

7   Mussolini declares himself *Duce* of the Fascist Party.

11   The U.S. signs a separate peace treaty with Germany.

DECEMBER

10   Britain renounces the Anglo-Japanese Alliance of 1902.

1922

FEBRUARY

6   The Washington Naval Treaty is signed.

APRIL

16   Germany and the Soviet Union sign the Treaty of Rapallo.

JUNE

24   German Foreign Minister Rathenau is murdered by right-wing extremists.

OCTOBER

24   Mussolini and the Fascists march on Rome.

29   King Victor Emmanuel III invites Mussolini to form a government.

1923

JANUARY

10   German general strike paralyzes the coal mines and factories in the Ruhr.
The last U.S. occupation forces leave Germany.

11   French and Belgian forces occupy the Ruhr.
The first indications of spiraling inflation hit Germany.

19   The Allied Control Commission seizes control of the coal mines and factories in the Ruhr.

22   Radical German nationalists begin random attacks and acts of sabotage against Franco-Belgian forces. Many of those captured are shot on the spot.

JULY

1　Inflation reaches 100 percent per week in Germany. The mark falls to 160,000 to the U.S. dollar.

NOVEMBER

8　Hitler's Beer Hall *Putsch* in Munich fails.

1924

JANUARY

1　*Sportflug, G.m.b.H.* (Sportflying Incorporated) is formed in Germany to train pilots secretly.

21　Lenin dies, setting off an internal power struggle that Stalin eventually wins.

FEBRUARY

26　Hitler, Ludendorff, and Röhm go on trial for the Beer Hall *Putsch*.

APRIL

1　Hitler is sentenced to five years in Landsbreg Prison.

MAY

4　The Nazis win 6.5 percent of the vote in German elections.

SEPTEMBER

8　The Allied Control Commission begins inspections for illegal arms in Germany.

DECEMBER

7　The Nazis win 3.0 percent of the vote in German elections.

20　Hitler is released from prison after serving only eight months.

1925

APRIL

25　Von Hindenburg is elected president of Germany.

MAY

28　The first group of German aircraft and aviators depart from Stettin to establish a Russo-German flight training and test center at Lipetsk in the Soviet Union.

JULY

18　Hitler's book, *Mein Kampf,* is published.

31　The Ruhr occupation ends.

DECEMBER

1　Germany, France, Britain, Italy, and Belgium sign the Treaty of Locarno.

1926

MAY

12　Piłsudski establishes a military government in Poland.

21　The Paris Air Agreement is signed.

OCTOBER

9　Von Seeckt resigns as head of the German military.

DECEMBER

1　Hitler appoints Goebbels Nazi Party *Gauleiter* of Berlin.

1927

FEBRUARY

28　The Allied Control Commission is dissolved.

1928

MAY

20　The Nazis win 2.6 percent of the vote in German elections.

AUGUST

27　The Kellogg-Briand Pact is signed.

1929

FEBRUARY

11   Mussolini and the Vatican sign the Latern Treaty.

1930

APRIL

21   The first London Naval Treaty is signed.

JUNE

30   The last French occupation troops leave the Rhineland.

SEPTEMBER

14   The Nazis win 18.3 percent of the vote in German elections.

1932

JANUARY

31   The Finnish-Soviet Nonaggression Pact is signed.

FEBRUARY

25   Hitler becomes a German citizen.

APRIL

10   Von Hindenburg is reelected president of Germany.

13   German Chancellor Brüning bans the Nazi SA.

JUNE

2   Von Pappen is named German chancellor.

JULY

31   The Nazis win 37.4 percent of the vote in German elections.

NOVEMBER

6   The Nazis win 33.1 percent of the vote in German elections.

8   Roosevelt is elected U.S. president.

17   Von Pappen resigns as German chancellor.

DECEMBER

2   Schleicher becomes German chancellor.

5   Einstein is granted a U.S. visa.

1933

JANUARY

28   Schleicher resigns as German chancellor.

30   Hitler becomes chancellor of Germany.

FEBRUARY

27   *Reichstag* fire.

28   German president von Hindenburg signs an emergency decree suspending constitutional guarantees of free speech, free press, and privacy.

MARCH

5   The Nazis win 43.9 percent of the vote in German elections.

21   At a meeting of the new *Reichstag,* Göring assures a Nazi majority by excluding the Communists from their seats.

23   The Enabling Act gives Hitler dictatorial powers.

27   Japan withdraws from the League of Nations.

MAY

10   The Nazis start large-scale book burning.

JULY

8   Germany and the Vatican sign a concordat.

SEPTEMBER

2   The Soviet-Italian Nonaggression Pact is signed.

14 Germany announces its intention to withdraw from the League of Nations.

NOVEMBER
12 The Nazis win virtually 100 percent of the vote in sham German elections.
16 The United States recognizes the Soviet Union.

1934

JANUARY
26 The German-Polish ten-year Nonaggression Pact is signed.

JUNE
14–15 Hitler and Mussolini meet for the first time in Venice.
30 Hitler launches the "Night of the Long Knives" to suppress his own SA.

JULY
25 Austrian chancellor Dollfuss is assassinated.

AUGUST
2 German president Hindenburg dies, and Hitler assumes presidential powers and the title of *Führer*. Hitler also becomes commander in chief of the armed forces, and all German soldiers are required to take a loyalty oath to him personally.
19 A German plebiscite gives an 88 percent approval rating to Hitler's new status.

OCTOBER
1 Hitler secretly orders the creation of a German air force and the expansion of the army and navy.

DECEMBER
5 Fighting breaks out between Italian and Ethiopian troops.
29 Japan announces its intention to terminate adherence to the Washington and London naval treaties, effective in two years.
30 Mussolini issues secret orders for the conquest of Ethiopia.

1935

JANUARY
13 Voters in a plebiscite in the Saar vote overwhelmingly to return to Germany.

MARCH
11 Germany makes public the existence of the *Luftwaffe*.
16 Germany introduces military conscription in violation of the Versailles treaty.

MAY
12 Polish dictator Piłsudski dies.

JUNE
7 Laval becomes premier of France.
18 The Anglo-German Naval Agreement is signed.
28 Germany commissions its first U-boat since 1918.

AUGUST
31 The first U.S. Neutrality Act is signed.

SEPTEMBER
15 The German *Reichstag* adopts the Nuremberg Laws.

OCTOBER
3 Italy invades Ethiopia.

DECEMBER
23 The Italians start using mustard gas in Ethiopia.

1936

FEBRUARY
1 The second U.S. Neutrality Act is signed.
10 Himmler and the *Gestapo* assume absolute control over German internal security.

MARCH

7   Germany remilitarizes the Rhineland.

25   The second London Naval Treaty is signed.

APRIL

13   Metaxas becomes the prime minister of Greece.

MAY

5   Italian forces enter Addis Ababa.

JUNE

18   Britain, Canada, and Australia abandon League of Nations' sanctions against Italy.

JULY

4   The Council of the League of Nations votes to end sanctions against Italy.

17   The Spanish Civil War starts.

25   Hitler agrees to Franco's request for airlift support.

OCTOBER

25   The Rome-Berlin Axis Pact is signed.

29   Soviet advisors and equipment begin operating in Spain.

NOVEMBER

3   Roosevelt is elected to a second term.

6   The *Kondor Legion* arrives in Spain.

18   Germany and Italy recognize the Franco government.

25   Germany and Japan sign the Anti-Comintern Pact.

DECEMBER

11   George VI accedes to the British throne.

31   Japan repudiates the Washington and London naval treaties.

1937

APRIL

26   German planes destroy Guernica.

MAY

1   The third U.S. Neutrality Act is signed.

28   Chamberlain becomes British prime minister.

JUNE

11   Eight high-ranking Soviet generals are executed for treason.

SEPTEMBER

7   Hitler makes his *Lebensraum* speech and declares the Treaty of Versailles dead.

NOVEMBER

5   Hitler holds the "Hossbach Meeting" at the *Reich* Chancellery.

6   Italy joins Germany and Japan in the Anti-Comintern Pact.

DECEMBER

11   Italy withdraws from the League of Nations.

1938

FEBRUARY

4   After sacking Blomberg and Fritsch, and thirteen other generals, Hitler assumes direct control of the German military, creating the OKW.

MARCH

12   Austrian chancellor Seyss-Inquart announces the *Anschluss*.

13   The German army moves into Austria.

A Nazi government in Vienna declares Austria a province of the German *Reich*.

APRIL

10   An Austrian plebiscite approves the *Anschluss* by 99.73 percent.

Daladier becomes the French premier.

MAY

29   Hitler orders completion of the West Wall.

JULY

11–13   British troops are sent to Palestine to quell an Arab uprising.

AUGUST

3   Italy enacts anti-Semitic laws.

SEPTEMBER

15   Chamberlain meets with Hitler at Berchtesgaden over the Sudeten Czech crisis.
22   Chamberlain meets with Hitler at Godesberg.
29–30   Munich Conference and Agreement.

OCTOBER

1   German forces begin the occupation of the Sudetenland.
2   Poland occupies the Teschen section of Czechoslovakia.

NOVEMBER

7   Herschel Grynszpan assassinates Ernst vom Rath in Paris.
9–10   *Kristalnacht.*

1939

JANUARY

26   Barcelona falls to Spanish Nationalists.
29   Hitler approves Plan Z.

FEBRUARY

27   Britain and France recognize the Franco government.

MARCH

13   Slovakia declares independence from Czechoslovakia.
15   The German army occupies Bohemia and Moravia.
17   Chamberlain abandons the policy of appeasement.
19   Germany annexes Memel.
27   Franco's government joins the Anti-Comintern Pact.
28   Madrid surrenders to Franco, effectively ending the Spanish Civil War.
31   France and Britain guarantee the territorial integrity of Poland.

APRIL

1   The U.S. recognizes the Franco government.
7–10   Italy invades Albania.
13   France and Britain guarantee the territorial integrity of Greece and Romania.
15   Italy annexes Albania.
28   Hitler repudiates the German-Polish Nonaggression Pact.

MAY

22   Germany and Italy establish a formal military alliance, the "Pact of Steel."
31   Germany and Denmark sign a ten-year nonaggression pact.

JULY

26   The U.S. revokes its 1911 commercial treaty with Japan.
31   The Nazi-controlled Danzig Senate demands that Polish customs officials leave the free city.

AUGUST

2   Einstein writes a letter to Roosevelt suggesting the possibilities for developing an atomic bomb.
23   The Molotov-Ribbentrop Pact is signed.
    Albert Förster, the Nazi Party *Gauleiter* of Danzig, becomes the city's head of state.
25   The Anglo-Polish Alliance Treaty is signed.
27   A German He-178 makes history's first flight powered by a jet engine.
31   Nazi SS troops conduct the Gleiwitz Raid.

20	German forces reach the English Channel.
26	Operation DYNAMO: British forces start the Dunkirk evacuation.
28	The Belgian army surrenders.

JUNE

4	British forces complete the Dunkirk evacuation.
	Churchill gives his "We shall fight on the beaches" speech.
5	German forces launch the attack into France proper.
9	Norway surrenders and British forces evacuate Narvik.
	German forces reach the Seine.
10	Italy declares war on France and Britain.
14	German forces enter Paris.
	German forces breach the Maginot Line south of Saarbrücken.
15	Soviet forces invade Lithuania.
17	Churchill gives his "Finest Hour" speech.
	Soviet forces invade Latvia and Estonia.
18	De Gaulle broadcasts from London his first message to the French people.
22	France surrenders to Germany.
28	Britain recognizes De Gaulle's Free French government.
30	German forces occupy Guernsey.
	Stalin establishes the State Defense Committee (GKO).

JULY

1	The French government moves to Vichy.
3	The British navy fires on French ships at Mers-el-Kébir.
9	Battle off Calabria.
	Pétain is given dictatorial powers in France.
16	The Germans start preparations for Operation SEA LION.
19	Roosevelt signs an appropriations bill to create a two-ocean navy.
23	Leval is named Pétain's vice president.

AUGUST

3	Italian forces invade British Somaliland.
6	The Soviet Union annexes the Baltic states.
13	Operation *ADLERTAG:* the Battle of Britain starts.
20	Churchill says of the RAF, "Never . . . was so much owed by so many to so few."
21	Trotsky is assassinated in Mexico City.
25–26	The RAF conducts its first air raid on Berlin.
27	The U.S. Congress authorizes the federalization of the National Guard.

SEPTEMBER

3	The U.S. and Britain announce the Destroyers-Bases Deal.
7	Start of the London Blitz.
9	U.S. destroyers begin operating with the Royal Navy in the North Atlantic.
13	Italian forces invade Egypt.
15	Turning point of the Battle of Britain.
16	Italian forces occupy Sidi Barrani.
	The U.S. Selective Service bill becomes law.
23–25	Battle of Dakar.
27	Germany, Italy, and Japan sign the Tripartite Pact.
29	Germany annexes Luxembourg.

OCTOBER

7	German forces enter Romania.
12	Hitler postpones SEA LION.
17–20	Convoy battle in the North Channel.
28	Italy invades Greece from Albania.
31	British forces land on Crete.

3   British forces start arriving in Greece.
5   Roosevelt is elected to a third term.
11   Taranto air raid.
14–15   Coventry air raid.
17   After prevailing in the Battle of Britain, Dowding and Park are dismissed.
23   Romania joins the Axis.
24   Slovakia joins the Axis.
26   German occupation forces establish the Warsaw Ghetto.
30   Germany annexes Alsace and Lorraine.

DECEMBER

9–12   Battle of Sidi Barrani.
13   Leval is dismissed by Pétain and arrested.
29   Roosevelt gives his "Arsenal of Democracy" speech.
29–30   Much of London is gutted in a series of firebomb raids.

1941

JANUARY

3–5   Battle of Bardia.
6   Roosevelt gives his "Four Freedoms" speech.
6–22   First battle of Tobruk.
19   British forces open an offensive in Italian East Africa.

FEBRUARY

5–7   Battle of Beda Fomm.
10   Darlan is named vice premier of the Vichy government.
12   Rommel arrives in Tripoli.

MARCH

2   German forces enter Bulgaria.
4   Lofton Islands raid.
7–27   British forces are withdrawn from North Africa and sent to Greece.
11   Roosevelt signs the Lend-Lease bill.
24   Rommel launches his first offensive.
28–29   Battle off Cape Matapan.

APRIL

2–3   German forces move across Hungary toward Yugoslavia.
4   Italian forces abandon Addis Ababa.
6   German forces invade Yugoslavia and Greece.
9   Rommel's forces capture Bardia.
10   The siege of Tobruk begins.
     Destroyer USS *Niblack* fires the first American shot of the war by dropping depth charges on a U-boat.
11   Hungarian forces invade Yugoslavia.
12   German forces capture Belgrade.
17   Yugoslavia surrenders.
18   Admiral King orders U.S. ships in the Atlantic to attack any Axis ship within twenty-five miles of the Western Hemisphere.
23   Greece surrenders.
     The "America First" Committee holds its first rally in New York.
25   Rommel's forces take the Halfaya Pass.
28   Rommel's forces capture Sollum.
28–29   British forces evacuate Greece for Crete.

MAY

2–19   Battle of Habbaniya.

4 Hitler's "Thousand-Year *Reich*" speech.
5 Haile Selassie returns to the Ethiopian throne.
7 Stalin assumes the premiership of the Soviet Union.
10 Rudolf Hess parachutes into Scotland.
13 Bormann is named to succeed Hess as Nazi Party chancellor.
15 British forces launch Operation BREVITY.
  Britain's first jet aircraft, the Gloster Pioneer, makes its first flight.
20 German airborne forces land on Crete.
24 The *Bismarck* sinks the HMS *Hood*.
27 The Royal Navy sinks the *Bismarck*.
31 British forces evacuate Crete.

JUNE
4 Former kaiser Wilhelm II dies in Doorn, Holland.
6 Keitel issues the Commissar Order.
8 British and Free French forces invade Syria.
  German troops arrive in Finland in preparation for the attack on the Soviet Union.
15 British forces launch Operation BATTLEAXE.
15–17 Battle of Sollum-Halfaya Pass.
22 Operation *BARBAROSSA:* German forces invade the Soviet Union.
25 Finland declares war on the Soviet Union.
27 Hungary declares war on the Soviet Union.
30 German forces take Lwów.

JULY
1 Auchenleck succeeds Wavell as British commander in chief, Middle East.
3 Stalin orders a scorched earth policy.
5 Tito announces a Communist resistance movement in Yugoslavia.
7 U.S. Marines relieve British forces in Iceland.
9 German forces capture 300,000 Soviet troops near Minsk.
10 Stalin assumes the role of commander in chief of the Red Army.
12 Britain and the Soviet Union sign a mutual assistance treaty.
17 Rosenberg is appointed *Reich* minister for the eastern territories.
19 The U.S. Navy is ordered to escort ships to and from Iceland.
27 German forces complete the encirclement of Smolensk.

AUGUST
1–8 Battle of Roslavl.
9–12 Placentia Bay Conference.
25 British and Soviet forces invade Iran.

SEPTEMBER
4 USS *Greer* incident.
8 German forces start the siege of Leningrad.
11 The U.S. Navy is given "shoot on sight" orders.
16 German forces trap almost 700,000 Soviet troops in the Kiev pocket.
19 German forces take Kiev.
23 De Gaulle establishes *Comité National Français*.
24 The Germans isolate all Soviet forces in the Crimea.
27 The first U.S. Liberty Ship, the S.S. *Patrick Henry,* is launched.
28–30 Babi Yar massacre.

OCTOBER
2 Operation *TAIFUN:* Start of the German drive on Moscow.
6–16 Battles of Vyazma and Bryansk.
10 Zhukov is named commander of all forces defending Moscow.
11 PQ-1, the first arctic convoy reaches Archangel.
15 German forces reach the Don River.

16   Richard Sorge is arrested in Japan.

16–17   USS *Kearney* incident.

23   The Lend-Lease Act is extended to the Soviet Union.

24   German forces take Kharkov.

25   German forces break through the Soviet lines in the Crimea.

31   The USS *Reuben James* is sunk by a U-boat.

NOVEMBER

15   German forces resume Operation *TAIFUN* after it bogged down in mid-October.

17–18   Keyes raid to assassinate Rommel.

18   British forces launch Operation CRUSADER and the battle of Sidi-Rezegh.
Brooke replaces Dill as chief of the Imperial General Staff.

20–22   German forces take Rostov.

22   The German raider *Atlantis* is sunk.

27   New Zealand forces make the initial link-up with the besieged Tobruk garrison.
Italian forces surrender in East Africa.

DECEMBER

1   After suffering a heart attack, von Rundstedt is retired as commander of Army Group South.

6   Soviet forces counterattack in front of Moscow.

7   Japanese forces attack Pearl Harbor.
Hitler issues the *Nacht und Nebel* decree.

8   America, Britain, Australia, Canada, New Zealand, and South Africa declare war on Japan.

10   British forces lift the siege of Tobruk.

11   Germany and Italy declare war on the United States.

12   Romania and Hungary declare war on the U.S.

13   Bulgaria declares war on the U.S.

14–23   Convoy battle off Portugal.

17   First battle off Sirte.

18–19   Alexandria raid.

19   Hitler relieves von Brauchitsch as chief of the German army and assumes personal command.

22   The ARCADIA Conference opens in Washington.

26   Soviet forces land on the Kerch Peninsula.

1942

JANUARY

1   Twenty-six nations sign the Declaration of the United Nations.

17   British forces recapture Sollum and the Halfaya Pass.

14   German U-boats start attacking shipping off the U.S. East Coast.

20   The Nazi leadership outlines the "Final Solution" at the Wannsee Conference.

21   Rommel launches his second offensive.

26   The first contingent of U.S. troops to reach Europe arrives in Northern Ireland.

FEBRUARY

1   Quisling is appointed minister-president of Norway.

6   Britain and the U.S. establish the Combined Chiefs of Staff.

9   Speer succeeds Todt as German armaments minister.

11–12   Channel Dash.

19   Eisenhower becomes chief of the War Plans Division of the U.S. General Staff.

22   Harris is appointed head of RAF Bomber Command.

25   More than 110,000 American citizens of Japanese descent are ordered into internment camps.

27–28   Bruneval Raid.

MARCH

9   Admiral King becomes U.S. chief of naval operations.

10   Von Rundstedt is brought back from retirement as commander in chief, West.

18   Mountbatten is named chief of Combined Operations.

22   Second battle off Sirte.

28   Saint Nazaire raid.

APRIL

1   The first Arctic convoy, PQ-13, reaches Murmansk.

14   Laval becomes the premier of Vichy France.

26   Hitler assumes total power in Germany.

27   Roosevelt places the American economy on a total war footing.

MAY

8   German forces in the Crimea start preparatory attacks for a major drive into the Caucasus.

12   Lead elements of the U.S. Eighth Air Force arrive in Britain.

12–27   Battle of Kharkov.

22   Mexico declares war on the Axis.

26   Start of the battle of Gazala-Bir Hacheim.

27   Heydrich is mortally wounded by partisans near Prague.

30–31   The RAF conducts a 1,000-plane raid on Cologne.

JUNE

5   The U.S. declares war on Bulgaria, Hungary, and Romania.

7   The siege of Sevastopol starts.

9–10   Nazi troops destroy Lidiče in retaliation for the assassination of Heydrich.

11   Rommel's forces attack out of "The Cauldron."

13   British units abandon Gazala.
       The British Guards Brigade is forced to abandon the "Knightsbridge" defensive position.

13–16   British forces lose 230 armored vehicles in fighting against Rommel's forces.

21   Rommel's forces capture Tobruk.

23   Rommel's forces cross into Egypt.

25   Eisenhower is appointed commander of U.S. ground forces in Europe.

26–29   Rommel's forces capture Mersa Matrúh.

27   The FBI announces the arrest of eight German saboteurs, landed by submarine a week earlier.

28   German forces launch their summer offensive in Russia.

JULY

1–9   Battle of Convoy PQ-17.

1–22   Battles of Ruweisat Ridge.

4   German forces take Sevastopol and all of the Crimea.
       U.S. bombers fly their first mission in Europe.

7   German forces take Voronezh.

25   German forces take Rostov.

29   German forces enter the Caucasus.

AUGUST

8   Roosevelt and Churchill select Eisenhower to command Operation TORCH.

10–15   Malta convoy PEDESTAL.

13   Montgomery assumes command of the Eighth Army.

15   Alexander succeeds Auchinleck as British commander in chief, Middle East.

19   Dieppe Raid.

21   German forces cross the Don River.

22   Brazil declares war on Germany and Italy.

| 23 | German forces reach Stalingrad. |
| 30 | The battle of Alam el Halfa starts. |

SEPTEMBER

5	The battle of Alam el Halfa ends.
12	The British transport *Laconia* is sunk by a German U-boat.
	American pilots in three RAF Eagle Squadrons are transferred to U.S. command.
12–20	Battle of Convoy PQ-18.
13–17	The first Moscow Conference.
17	Dönitz issues the Laconia Order.
	The MANHATTAN Project starts.
24	Hitler dismisses Halder as chief of staff of the German army.

OCTOBER

| 18 | Jodl issues the Commando Order. |
| 23 | British forces launch their attack at El Alamein. |

NOVEMBER

5	Rommel's forces start retreating from El Alamein.
8–14	Operation TORCH: Anglo-American forces land in Northwest Africa.
9	German forces invade Tunisia from Italy.
11	All French resistance in North Africa ends.
	German forces occupy the remainder of France.
12	British forces retake Tobruk for the last time.
18	Laval is given total authority in Vichy France.
19	Soviet forces counterattack at Stalingrad.
23	The German Sixth Army is encircled at Stalingrad.
24	Von Manstein assumes command of Army Group Don.
27	The French fleet scuttles itself at Toulon.

DECEMBER

1	Darlan assumes leadership of the Imperial Council of France.
2	American scientists in Chicago achieve the first nuclear chain reaction.
7–22	Battles along the Chir River.
12	Manstein launches a drive to relieve the Sixth Army at Stalingrad.
24	Darlan is assassinated in Algiers.
28	Hitler approves the withdrawal of Army Group A from the Caucasus.
30–31	Battle of Barents Sea.

1943

JANUARY

12–18	Soviet forces open a narrow land corridor to Leningrad.
14–23	Operation SYMBOL: The Casablanca Conference.
14–27	Soviet forces attack across the Don.
15	British forces start the drive on Tripoli.
18	Armed resistance starts in the Warsaw Ghetto.
23	British forces take Tripoli.
25	Soviet forces retake Voronezh.
27	U.S. bombers conduct the first all-American raid on Germany.
28	Germany finally shifts its economy to a wartime footing.
30	The RAF conducts its first daylight raid on Berlin.
	Kaltenbrunner is appointed to succeed Heydrich as head of the RSHA.
	Vichy France forms the *Milice* to combat the Resistance.
	Dönitz replaces Raeder as commander in chief of the German navy.
31	Paulus surrenders at Stalingrad.

FEBRUARY

| 1 | German forces complete the withdrawal from the Caucasus to the Taman Peninsula. |

3	Start of the battles along the Donets River line.
5	Mussolini dismisses Ciano as foreign minister.
6	Soviet forces cross the Donets River.
12	British forces enter Tunisia.
14	Soviet forces retake Rostow.
	Soviet forces retake Kharkov.
14–22	Battle of Kasserine Pass.
16–28	Norsk Hydro raids.
22	German forces counterattack in the Donets area.

MARCH

5	RAF bombers use the Oboe system for the first time in a raid on Essen that marked the start of the Ruhr air campaign.
	Britain's first jet fighter, the Gloster Meteor, flies for the first time.
6	Patton replaces Fredendall as U.S. II Corps commander.
9	Rommel leaves North Africa on sick leave.
14	German forces recapture Kharkov.
14–20	Battle of convoys HX-229 and SC-122.
17–25	Battle of El Guettar.
20–28	British forces break through the Mareth Line.
20–31	Following a series of savage convoy battles, the introduction of new antisubmarine tactics brings about the turning point in the Battle of the Atlantic.

APRIL

12	Germany announces the discovery of mass graves of Polish officers in the Katyń Forest.
19	Start of the Warsaw Ghetto uprising.
22	Start of final Allied offensive in North Africa.

MAY

6–7	The Allies capture Bizerte and Tunis.
12–13	Axis forces surrender in Tunisia.
12–25	Operation TRIDENT Conference in Washington.
16	The Warsaw Ghetto falls.
16–17	Ruhr Dams air raid.
22	Dönitz orders all U-boats in the North Atlantic to break off operations.
27	British special operations troops drop into Yugoslavia to assist Tito's partisans.

JUNE

| 3 | De Gaulle and Giraud assume the co-presidency of the Committee of National Liberation. |
| 10 | The Allies issue the directive for Operation POINTBLANK. |

JULY

4	Sikorski is killed in an air crash near Gibraltar.
5–17	Operation *ZITADEL:* The Battle of Kursk.
10	Operation HUSKY: The Allies invade Sicily.
12	Soviet forces start their counteroffensive at Kursk.
22	Allied forces take Palermo.
24	Allied bombers use "window" to confuse German radar for the first time.
24–30	Hamburg air raids.
25	Mussolini is overthrown and arrested. Badoglio forms a new Italian government.

AUGUST

1	Ploești air raid.
11	German forces in Sicily start their evacuation across the Messina Strait.
14–24	Operation QUADRANT Conference in Quebec.
17	Allied forces enter Messina and complete the capture of Sicily.
	Regensburg and Schweinfurt air raids.

17–18	Peenemünde air raid.
23	Soviet forces reoccupy Kharkov for the second time.
24–28	German occupation forces put down an uprising in Denmark.

SEPTEMBER

1	Dönitz sends U-boats back into the North Atlantic.
3	Operation BAYTOWN: The British Eighth Army lands in Italy at Calabria.
7	Spitzbergen raid.
8	The Italian surrender is announced.
9	Operation AVALANCHE: The U.S. Fifth Army lands in Italy at Salerno.
	A German bomber sinks the Italian battleship *Roma*.
	German forces occupy Rome.
12	Skorzeny rescues Mussolini at Gran Sasso.
14	British forces occupy the islands of Kos and Leros in the Dodecanese.
	German forces start withdrawing to the Dnieper River line.
15	Mussolini establishes the puppet Italian Social Republic.
17	German forces start withdrawing to the Gustav Line.
19	Finland signs an armistice with the Allies.
22	Alten Fjord raid.
25	Soviet forces retake Smolensk and Rosavl.
27	P-47s with extended-range belly tanks start escorting U.S. bombers over Europe.

OCTOBER

1	Allied forces take Naples.
	Soviet forces cross the Dnieper River.
3	German forces take Kos island.
4	Cunningham becomes Britain's first sea lord.
9	Soviet forces reoccupy the Taman Peninsula.
12–15	Battle of Volturno River.
13	Italy declares war on Germany.
14–15	Schweinfurt air raid.
31	German forces are cut off in the Crimea.

NOVEMBER

3	Soviet forces break out of their Dnieper bridgeheads.
6	Soviet forces retake Kiev.
9	Giraud resigns from the French Committee of National Liberation, and De Gaulle becomes president.
16	German forces recapture Leros island.
22–26	Operation SEXTANT: The Cairo Conference.
23–30	Battle of the Sangro River.
28	Operation EUREKA: The Teheran Conference starts.

DECEMBER

1	Teheran Conference ends.
2	Bari air raid.
5	Allies start Operation CROSSBOW.
12–18	Battle of San Pietro.
13	P-51s start escorting U.S. bombers on raids over Europe.
24	Eisenhower is appointed supreme commander, Allied Expeditionary Force for Operation OVERLORD.
26	Battle off North Cape.

1944

JANUARY

4	German school children are mobilized for war service.
19	Soviet Forces enter Estonia.
20–22	Battle of the Rapido River.

| 22 | The Allies land at Anzio. |
| 27 | Soviet forces lift the siege of Leningrad. |

FEBRUARY

11	German defenders repulse the first Allied assault on Monte Cassino.
15	Allied air forces bomb Monte Cassino.
20–27	Allied air forces launch the BIG WEEK air raids.
23	Truscott replaces Lucas in command of the U.S. VI Corps at Anzio.
29	Vatutin is ambushed and killed by Ukrainian nationalist rebels.

MARCH

6	U.S. bombers attack Berlin for the first time.
15	Allied air forces bomb Monte Cassino for second time.
15–25	German defenders repulse attacks on Monte Cassino by New Zealand and Indian units.
19	Soviet forces enter northern Romania.
	German forces occupy Hungary.
24	Ardeatine Caves massacre.
27	German forces occupy Romania.
30	Hitler dismisses von Mannstein and von Kleist.
30–31	Nuremberg air raid.

APRIL

4	De Gaulle assumes command of all Free French forces.
10	Soviet forces retake Odessa.
12	German forces in the Crimea withdraw to Sevastopol.
26	Exercise TIGER.

MAY

7–9	Soviet forces retake Sevastopol.
12	The last German troops evacuate the Crimea.
16	The Allies penetrate the last of the Gustav Line defenses.
18	Polish forces take Monte Cassino.
23–25	The Allies breakout from Anzio beachhead.
25	Clark abandons efforts to cut off the German Tenth Army and shifts the axis of his attack toward Rome.

JUNE

1	German forces start conducting a fighting withdrawal from the Gustav Line to the Gothic Line.
4	The Allies enter Rome.
5	Three Allied airborne divisions take off for France.
6	Operation OVERLORD: The Allies land at Normandy.
8	British and U.S. forces link up at Normandy.
10	SS troops destroy Oradour-sur-Glâne.
	U.S. forces link up UTAH and OMAHA Beaches.
10–13	Soviet forces attack into Finland.
12	Allies link all Normandy beachheads.
13	The first V-1 lands in Britain.
18	Soviet forces breach the Mannerheim Line.
22	Operation BAGRATION: Soviet forces start the Byelorussian offensive.
	Roosevelt signs the "GI Bill of Rights" into law.
22–27	U.S. forces capture the port of Cherbourg.
25–30	Operation EPSOM: British forces attempt to take Caen.

JULY

1	The Bretton Woods International Monetary Conference opens.
3	Soviet forces recapture Minsk.
	Hitler once again relieves von Rundstedt, appointing von Kluge commander in chief, West.

8–9	Operation CHARNWOOD: British and Canadian forces take Caen.
13–27	Battles of Brody and Lwów.
17	Rommel is wounded in Normandy.
18–20	Operation GOODWOOD: British and Canadian forces fail to take the high ground south of Caen.
20	Stauffenburg attempts to kill Hitler.
	Soviet forces cross the Bug River into Poland.
21	Zeitler resigns as chief of staff of the German army and is replaced by Guderian.
23	Soviet forces retake Pskov, the last major town in the prewar Soviet Union.
25–31	Operation COBRA: U.S. forces break-out at St. Lô.
28	Soviet forces capture Brest-Litovsk.
29	The first jet in combat, the Me-262, enters action.

AUGUST

1	Start of the Warsaw Rising.
3	Soviet forces cross the Vistula River.
3–21	Battle of Falaise-Argentan.
4	Anne Frank and her family are captured by the *Gestapo*.
	South African forces enter Florence.
6	British forces reach the Arno River.
7–11	German forces counterattack at Mortain.
8	Eight German officers, implicated in the July plot to assassinate Hitler, are executed.
15	Operation DRAGOON: The Allies land in southern France.
17	Model replaces Kluge as German commander in chief, West.
	German forces in St. Malo surrender.
20	U.S. forces cross the Seine.
20–23	Soviet forces occupy Romania.
21	The Dumbarton Oaks International Peace and Security Conference opens in Washington.
25	Free French forces enter Paris.
	Romania declares war on Germany.
26	Soviet forces in Romania reach the Danube.
28	French and American forces liberate Marseilles.
30	Soviet forces take Ploeşti.
	British forces launch their offensive against the Gothic Line.
31	Soviet forces occupy Bucharest.

SEPTEMBER

1	Eisenhower formally establishes his headquarters in France and assumes direct control of all Allied ground forces.
2	British forces break through the eastern end of the Gothic Line.
	Allied forces enter Belgium.
3	British forces liberate Brussels.
4	British forces enter Antwerp.
	Finland ceases fire on all fronts.
5	Von Rundstedt is reinstated as German commander in chief, West.
	The Soviet Union declares war on Bulgaria.
6	Soviet forces in Romania enter Yugoslavia.
8	Bulgaria declares war on Germany.
	The first V-2 missiles land in Britain.
11	U.S. forces cross from Luxembourg into Germany near Aachen and start probing the Siegfried Line.
	Soviet forces enter Hungary.
12	U.S. forces enter the Hürtgen Forest.
12–16	Operation OCTAGON: the Second Quebec Conference.

13 U.S. forces reach the outskirts of Aachen.
15 U.S. forces take Nancy.
   The Operation DRAGOON invasion force moving from Southern France comes under Eisenhower's overall command.
16 Soviet forces enter Sofia.
17–26 Operation MARKET-GARDEN: Allied airborne forces land between Arnhem and Eindhoven.
18 U.S. forces take Brest.
21 Canadian forces enter Rimini.
22 Eisenhower orders Patton's Third Army to halt because of supply shortages.
25 Germany forms the *Volksstrum*.
27 American forces start their attack on Metz.

OCTOBER

1 British commando units land in Greece.
   Canadian forces cross the Antwerp-Turnhout Canal.
2 The Warsaw insurgents surrender.
   The Allies start an offensive to clear the Scheldt estuary.
3 Hitler approves the withdrawal of German forces from Finnish Lapland.
6 Soviet forces enter Czechoslovakia from Hungary.
6–16 U.S. forces mount the first attack on Schmidt.
9–17 The second Moscow Conference.
12 British airborne forces land at Athens airfield.
13 The first V-1s and V-2s land on Antwerp.
14 Rommel is forced to commit suicide.
   Allied forces and Greek partisans liberate Athens.
18 Soviet forces cross the Norwegian border.
20 Soviet forces enter Belgrade.
21 U.S. forces capture Aachen.
28 Soviet-Bulgarian armistice.
31 Aarhus air raid.

NOVEMBER

2–8 U.S. forces mount the second attack on Schmidt.
7 Roosevelt is elected to a fourth term.
8 Canadian forces clear the Scheldt estuary.
12 The RAF sinks the *Tirpitz*.
18 U.S. forces again advance into the Hürtgen Forest.
22 U.S. forces capture Metz.
23 French forces liberate Strasbourg.
27 Freiburg air raid.
28 The Allies open the port of Antwerp.
   Soviet forces cross the Danube.

DECEMBER

3 The British Home Guard is demobilized.
7 French forces attack German units trapped in the Colmar pocket.
16 German forces launch the Ardennes offensive.
16–22 Battle of Saint Vith.
17 Malmédy Massacre.
20 German forces surround Bastogne.
24–27 Battle of Celles.
26 Soviet forces encircle Budapest.
   Patton's Third Army relieves Bastogne.
31 Hungary declares war on Germany.
   German forces in Alsace launch Operation *NORDWIND*.

1945

JANUARY

1 The German Air Force launches Operation *BODENPLATTE*.
7 German forces break out of the Colmar pocket.
8–19 Battle for Herrlisheim.
12 Soviet forces start the Vistula-Oder offensive.
17 German forces start withdrawing from the Ardennes.
Soviet forces take Warsaw.
18 The Soviet-installed Lublin Committee declares itself the government of Poland.
19 Soviet forces take Kraków.
25 The Germans start large-scale evacuations across the Baltic.
27 Soviet forces liberate Auschwitz.
28 The Allies eliminate the Bulge, restoring the line of 16 December.
Soviet forces enter German Pomerania.

FEBRUARY

1 Soviet forces establish a small bridgehead over the Oder River and come to a halt.
2 Churchill and Roosevelt meet at Malta prior to the Yalta Conference.
3 French and American forces liberate Colmar.
4–9 Operation ARGONAUT: The Yalta Conference.
7 U.S. forces finally take Schmidt.
8 British and Canadian forces move into the *Reichswald*.
9 Allied forces eliminate the Colmar pocket.
British and Canadian forces penetrate the Siegfried Line and reach the Rhine.
11 Soviet forces break out from the Oder bridgehead.
12 German women between the ages of 16 and 60 are declared eligible for *Volkssturm* service.
The Greek civil war comes to a temporary end.
13 Soviet forces take Budapest.
13–14 Allied air forces conduct incendiary air raids on Dresden.
18 Chernyakhovsky dies of wounds received in East Prussia.
22–23 Allied air forces launch Operation CLARION.
26 Egypt and Syria declare war on Germany and Japan.

MARCH

1 Saudi Arabia and Turkey declare war on Germany and Japan.
3 Finland declares war on Germany effective 15 September 1944.
5 U.S. forces enter Cologne.
6–10 German forces launch the Lake Balaton counterattack in Hungary.
7 U.S. forces cross the Rhine at Remagen.
8–9 German forces conduct the Granville raid.
10 Von Rundstedt is replaced by Kesselring as German commander in chief, West.
12 Anne Frank dies of typhus in Bergen-Belsen.
19 Hitler orders a scorched earth policy for Germany.
20 U.S. forces take Saarbrücken and Zweibrücken.
24 Operation VARSITY: Allied airborne forces land across the Rhine near Wesel.
26–27 Hammelberg Raid.
27 The last V-2 lands in Britain.
U.S. forces capture Frankfurt.
28 Eisenhower orders all Western Allied forces to halt at the Elbe River.
Hitler dismisses Guderian as German army chief of staff.

APRIL

1 Allied forces close the Ruhr Pocket.
5–14 Soviet forces take Vienna.
9 Allied forces start their spring offensive in Italy.
RAF bombers sink the *Admiral Scheer* and *Hipper* at Kiel.

1766 APPENDIX A

12	Roosevelt dies in office and is succeeded by Truman.
13	Allied forces liberate the Bergen-Belsen and Buchenwald concentration camps.
14	U.S. forces split the Ruhr Pocket.
15	Canadian forces liberate Arnhem.
	The Provisional Austrian government nullifies the *Anschluss* and declares the Republic of Austria.
16	Soviet forces start the final assault on Berlin.
	Allied air forces cease strategic operations against Germany.
17–20	U.S. forces capture Nuremberg.
18	U.S. forces enter Czechoslovakia.
20	German forces withdraw to the Po River.
	The remaining German forces in France surrender.
21	Model commits suicide.
22	U.S. forces cross the Danube.
23	Allied forces establish bridgeheads over the Po River.
	Hitler assumes personal command of the defense of Berlin.
25	U.S. and Soviet forces meet at the Elbe River.
26	U.S. forces enter Austria.
26	Pétain is arrested by the Free French.
28	Mussolini is executed by Italian partisans.
29	German forces in Italy surrender.
29	U.S. forces liberate the Dachau concentration camp.
	Battle of Convoy RA-66, the last convoy battle of the war.
	Hitler designates Dönitz his successor as president and Bormann his successor as chancellor.
30	Hitler and Goebbels commit suicide.

MAY

1	Dönitz establishes the "Flensburg Government."
2	Soviet forces complete the capture of Berlin.
3	British forces occupy Hamburg.
4	The U.S. Fifth and Seventh armies link up at the Brenner Pass.
5	German representatives arrive at SHAEF to discuss surrender.
6	U.S. forces take Pilzen, Czechoslovakia, and are ordered to halt their advance.
7	Jodl signs the German surrender at Reims.
8	V-E Day.
	British and Norwegian troops land in Norway.
9	Keitel signs Germany's unconditional surrender in Berlin.
	Soviet forces enter Prague.
11	German Army Group Center surrenders to the Soviets.
23	Himmler commits suicide after being captured.
	Allied forces arrest Dönitz and members of the Flensburg Government.

JUNE

| 5 | The four Allied commanders in chief meet in Berlin and sign the Four Power Declaration on the Assumption of Supreme Authority in Germany. |
| 26 | The United Nations charter is signed. |

JULY

5	Churchill fails to gain reelection as British prime minister.
	The Polish communist government is recognized by Britain and the U.S.
16	The United States successfully tests the first atomic bomb at Alamagordo, New Mexico.
17	Operation TERMINAL: The Potsdam Conference opens.
26	Atlee forms a new British government.
31	Laval surrenders to U.S. forces in Austria.

2   The Potsdam Conference ends.

6   U.S. air forces drop an atomic bomb on Hiroshima.

8   The Soviet Union declares war on Japan.

9   U.S. air forces drop an atomic bomb on Nagasaki.

14 Japan accepts the Allied surrender terms.

15 Pétain is sentenced to death, but De Gaulle commutes his sentence to life in prison.

30 The Allied Control Council begins functioning in Germany.

SEPTEMBER

2   Japanese representatives sign the instrument of surrender on the USS *Missouri.*

OCTOBER

2   Eisenhower relieves Patton as military governor of Bavaria.

15 Laval is executed for treason.

20 The Allied Council recognizes the provisional Austrian government.

24 The U.N. charter comes into force.

    Quisling is executed for treason.

NOVEMBER

15 Austria holds democratic elections.

20 The Allies convene the International Military Tribunal at Nuremberg.

30 The Allied Control Council establishes three air corridors between Berlin and the British and American zones.

DECEMBER

21 Patton dies of injuries received in a car accident on 9 December.

1946

MARCH

5   Churchill delivers his "Iron Curtain" speech at Westminster College in Fulton, Missouri.

APRIL

19 The League of Nations passes out of existence.

OCTOBER

16 Keitel, Jodl, Ribbentrop, and other Nuremberg defendants are executed. Göring commits suicide in his jail cell a few hours earlier.

DECEMBER

12 The "Doctors' Trial," the first of the twelve American Military Tribunals opens in Nuremberg.

1947

JUNE

1   Kennan's "X" article appears in *Foreign Affairs.*

1948

MARCH

21 The Soviets walk out of the Allied Control Council meeting in Berlin, starting the chain of events leading to the Berlin Blockade.

31 The U.S. Congress passes the Marshall Plan.

    The Soviets start controlling Western rail traffic into Berlin.

JUNE

2   The three Western occupation zones in Germany unite.

23 The Soviets blockade Berlin.

24 The Berlin Airlift starts.

1949

APRIL

4   NATO is established.

11   The "Ministries Trial," the last of the twelve American Military Tribunals, closes in Nuremberg.

MAY
12   The Soviets lift the Berlin Blockade.

23   The Federal Republic of Germany is established, and a four-power agreement formally ends the Berlin Blockade.

OCTOBER
7   The German Democratic Republic is established.

31   The Berlin Airlift ends.

1951

JULY
23   Pétain dies in prison.

OCTOBER
24   The U.S. Congress officially ends the war with Germany.

1953

MARCH
5   Stalin dies in office.

1954

OCTOBER
23   The Allied occupation ends in West Germany.

1955

MAY
5   The Federal Republic of Germany becomes an independent and sovereign state and joins NATO.

14   The Warsaw Pact is established.

15   The Allied occupation ends in Austria.

SEPTEMBER
26   Raeder is released from Spandau Prison.

OCTOBER
23   Voters in a plebiscite in the Saar region vote overwhelmingly to rejoin Germany.

1956

OCTOBER
1   Dönitz is released from Spandau Prison.

1957

JANUARY
1   The Saar region is reunited with Germany.

1961

AUGUST
13   East Germany starts to erect the Berlin Wall.

1962

MAY
1   Eichmann is executed in Israel.

1966

OCTOBER
1   Speer is released from Spandau Prison.

1970

DECEMBER
7   Poland and West Germany sign a treaty recognizing the Oder-Neisse Line as the boundary between the two countries.

1972

NOVEMBER

9 A four-power agreement supports the application of the two German states for United Nations membership.

DECEMBER

21 The two Germanies normalize relations.

1975

AUGUST

1 The final act of the Helsinki Conference on European Security and Cooperation formalizes the long-delayed peace settlement in central Europe.

1987

AUGUST

17 Rudolf Hess, the last prisoner in Spandau Prison, commits suicide at the age of ninety-three.

1989

NOVEMBER

9 The East German government opens the Berlin Wall.

1990

MARCH

11 Lithuania declares independence.

SEPTEMBER

12 The 2+4 Treaty provides the framework for the reunification of Germany.

OCTOBER

3 Germany reunifies.

1991

JULY

1 The Warsaw Pact disbands.

AUGUST

20 Estonia declares independence.
21 Latvia declares independence.

SEPTEMBER

6 Russia recognizes the independence of the Baltic states.

1993

SEPTEMBER

18 The last Russian forces leave Poland.

1994

AUGUST

31 The last Russian forces leave Berlin.

SEPTEMBER

8 The last U.S. forces leave Berlin.

Appendix B

Tables of Comparative Ranks

Military organizations are hierarchical structures, and a soldier's, sailor's, or airman's responsibility and authority are usually—although not always—reflected in the rank held. The following tables of comparative ranks provide a rough equivalency guide across the different services and the major nations involved in World War II in Europe. One of the tables also includes the major Nazi organizations, which were organized along military lines.

The rank structures and even the rank insignia of World War II have changed little since 1945. Officer ranks in most of the world's armies are virtually the same, while the enlisted ranks have undergone only moderate changes. Those of the modern German Army, the *Bundeswehr,* are perhaps the most different from those of the wartime *Wehrmacht.* Despite the changes, today's soldiers in most of the world's major armies would have very little difficulty recognizing the World War II ranks of their respective organizations. The converse is also true.

A word of caution is necessary in using these tables. It is virtually impossible to construct a comprehensive and completely accurate table of comparative ranks. There are many reasons for this. Firstly, organizations sometimes change their rank structures and titles, and in some armies they were changed more than once during the course of the war. These tables attempt to show the most representative structure.

Another reason is that the same rank title does not necessarily mean the same thing from one country to the next. As an example, in the British services the various ranks of warrant officer represent the highest of the enlisted grades, the most senior noncommissioned officers (NCOs). American warrant officers (not included in these tables) are a category of specialist officers who occupy a middle ground, above the highest NCOs, but below the lowest ranking commissioned officers. The confusion between British and American meanings of warrant officers causes misunderstandings within NATO to this day.

Finally, in some countries there was not a perfect correlation even among the ranks of their different services. This was particularly true of British and German enlisted ranks. The British Army, for example, had three warrant officer ranks, while the Royal Navy and Royal Air Force had only one, and the Royal Canadian Air Force had two. Within the American military, the rank structures generally line up, although laymen are sometimes confused by the fact that a U.S. Navy captain is the same rank as a U.S. Army colonel, but an army captain is the same rank as a navy lieutenant. The important thing is that the navy captain and the army colonel both wear the same rank insignia on their collars—an eagle holding arrows and olive branches in its talons. (On the U.S. Navy dress uniform, however, the captain wears the same four sleeve stripes worn by captains in many of the world's navies.)

These tables use only the most simplified and basic versions of the ranks. In the German Army, for example, the rank title for a general (the specific rank between lieutenant general and colonel general) was

a function of that officer's branch of service. Hence, the exact rank title could be general of infantry, general of artillery, general of pioneer troops, etc. The British Army had an especially rich and complex system of rank titles for NCOs. Corporals and lance corporals in the Royal Artillery were (and still are) called bombardiers and lance bombardiers. Sergeant major was a position title, rather than a rank, but in units of the royal household cavalry it was called corporal-major. Many regiments had their own peculiar variations of rank insignia. The rank structure and insignia scheme for the bandsmen of the various British regiments—the trumpet majors, pipe majors, drum majors, band lance bombardiers, and the kettle drummers of the household cavalry—were probably the most complex of all.

These tables, then, are only rough approximations at best. The entire issue of comparative ranks confirms one of the most important observations of Carl von Clausewitz: "Everything in war is simple, but the simplest thing is difficult."

Table of Comparative Officer Ranks

US Army / Air Force	U.S. Navy	British Army	Royal Navy	Royal Air Force	Soviet Army / Air Force	French Army	Italian Army	Polish Army	German Army / Air Force	German Navy	Waffen-SS (Germany)
No Equivalent	No Equivalent	No Equivalent	No Equivalent	No Equivalent	Marshal of Soviet Union	No Equivalent	First Marshal of the Empire	No Equivalent	**Reichsmarschall** *Reich* Marshal (Note 2)	No Equivalent	No Equivalent
General of the Army	Fleet Admiral	Field Marshal	Admiral of the Fleet	Marshal of the RAF	Chief Marshal	Marshal of France	Marshal of Italy	Marshal of Poland	**Generalfeldmarschall** Field Marshal	**Grossadmiral** Grand Admiral	**Reichsführer-SS** *Reichs* Leader SS
No Equivalent	No Equivalent	No Equivalent	No Equivalent	No Equivalent	Marshal	No Equivalent	No Equivalent	No Equivalent	No Equivalent	No Equivalent	No Equivalent
General	Admiral	General	Admiral	Air Chief Marshal	Army General	General of Army	General of Army	General of Army	**Generaloberst** Colonel General	**Generaladmiral** General Admiral	**Oberstgruppenführer** Colonel Group Leader
Lieutenant General	Vice Admiral	Lieutenant General	Vice Admiral	Air Marshal	Colonel General	General of Corps	General of Corps	No Equivalent	**General der Infantrie** (Note 3)	**Admiral** Admiral	**Obergruppenführer** Senior Group Leader
Major General	Rear Admiral	Major General	Rear Admiral	Air Vice Marshal	Lieutenant General	General of Division	General of Division	General of Division	**Generalleutnant** Lieutenant General	**Vizeadmiral** Vice Admiral	**Gruppenführer** Group Leader
Brigadier General	Commodore (Note 1)	Brigadier	Commodore First Class	Air Commodore	Major General	General of Brigade	General of Brigade	General of Brigade	**Generalmajor** Major General	**Konteradmiral** Rear Admiral	**Brigadeführer** Brigade Leader
No Equivalent	No Equivalent	No Equivalent	Commodore Second Class	No Equivalent	No Equivalent	No Equivalent	No Equivalent	No Equivalent	No Equivalent	**Kommodore** Commodore	**Oberführer** Senior Leader
Colonel	Captain	Colonel	Captain	Group Captain	Colonel General	Colonel	Colonel	Colonel	**Oberst** Colonel	**Kapitän zur See** Captain	**Standartenführer** Standard Leader

(continued on next page)

Table of Comparative Officer Ranks (continued)

US Army / Air Force	US Navy	British Army	Royal Navy	Royal Air Force	Soviet Army / Air Force	French Army	Italian Army	Polish Army	German Army / Air Force	German Navy	Waffen-SS (Germany)
Lieutenant Colonel	Commander	Lieutenant Colonel	Commander	Wing Commander	Lieutenant Colonel	Lieutenant Colonel	Lieutenant Colonel	Lieutenant Colonel	**Oberstleutnant** Lieutenant Colonel	**Fregattenkapitän** Frigate Captain	**Obersturmbannführer** Senior Storm Battalion Leader
Major	Lieutenant Commander	Major	Lieutenant Commander	Squadron Leader	Major	Chief of Battalion	Major	Major	**Major** Major	**Korvettenkapitän** Corvette Captain	**Sturmbannführer** Storm Battalion Leader
Captain	Lieutenant	Captain	Lieutenant	Flight Lieutenant	Captain	Captain	Captain	Captain	**Hauptmann** Captain (Note 5)	**Kapitänleutnant** Captain Lieutenant	**Hauptsturmführer** Chief Storm Leader
No Equivalent	No Equivalent	No Equivalent	No Equivalent	No Equivalent	Senior Lieutenant	No Equivalent	First Lieutenant	No Equivalent	No Equivalent	No Equivalent	No Equivalent
First Lieutenant	Lieutenant Junior Grade	Lieutenant	Sub-Lieutenant	Flying Officer	Lieutenant	Lieutenant	Lieutenant	Lieutenant	**Oberleutnant** Senior Lieutenant	**Oberleutnant zur See** Senior Lieutenant	**Obersturmführer** Senior Storm Leader
Second Lieutenant	Ensign	Second Lieutenant	Commissioned Warrant Officer (Note 4)	Pilot Officer	Junior Lieutenant	Second Lieutenant	Second Lieutenant	Sub-Lieutenant	**Leutnant** Lieutenant	**Leutnant zur See** Lieutenant	**Untersturmführer** Junior Storm Leader

Notes:

1. The rank of commodore was reestablished by the U.S. Navy in April 1943.

2. The rank of *Reichsmarschall* existed only in the German Air Force in World War II. Hermann Göring was the only officer to hold that rank.

3. General of the Infantry, General of the Artillery, etc.

4. The Royal Navy had two grades of warrant officer: one was the lowest commissioned rank; the other was the highest enlisted rank.

5. In cavalry units, *Rittmeister*, literally "Riding Master."

Table of Comparative Enlisted Ranks

U.S. Army / Air Force	U.S. Navy	British Army	Royal Navy	Royal Air Force
First Sergeant Master Sergeant (Note 1)	Chief Petty Officer	Warrant Officer First Class (Note 3)	Warrant Officer	Warrant Officer First Class
Technical Sergeant	Petty Officer First Class	Warrant Officer Second Class (Note 3)	Chief Petty Officer	Warrant Officer Second Class (Note 7)
No Equivalent	No Equivalent	Warrant Officer Third Class (Note 3)	No Equivalent	No Equivalent
Staff Sergeant (Note 2)	Petty Officer Second Class	Staff Sergeant	Petty Officer	Flight Sergeant
Sergeant (Note 2)	Petty Officer Third Class	Sergeant	Leading Seaman (Note 6)	Sergeant
Corporal (Note 2)	Seaman First Class	Corporal	Leading Seaman (Note 6)	Corporal
No Equivalent	No Equivalent	Lance Corporal (Note 4)	Able Seaman	Senior Aircraftman
Private First Class	Seaman Second Class	No Equivalent	No Equivalent	Leading Aircraftman
Private	Apprentice Seaman	Private (Note 5)	Ordinary Seaman	Aircraftman Second Class

(continued on next page)

Table of Comparative Enlisted Ranks *(continued)*

U.S. Army / Air Force	Soviet Army / Air Force	German Army	German Navy
First Sergeant Master Sergeant	**Starshina** Sergeant Major	**Stabsfeldwebel** Staff Sergeant	**Stabsoberfeldwebel** Staff Senior Sergeant
Technical Sergeant	**Starshiy Serzhant** Senior Sergeant	**Oberfeldwebel** Senior Sergeant	**Oberfeldwebel** Senior Sergeant
No Equivalent	No Equivalent	No Equivalent	**Stabsfeldwebel** Staff Sergeant
Staff Sergeant (Note 2)	**Serzhant** Sergeant	**Feldwebel** Sergeant	**Feldwebel** Sergeant
No Equivalent	No Equivalent	**Unterfeldwebel** Junior Sergeant	**Obermaat** Senior Mate
Sergeant (Note 2)	**Mladshiy Serzhant** Junior Sergeant	**Unteroffizier** Noncommissioned Officer	**Maat** Mate
No Equivalent	No Equivalent	No Equivalent	**Matrosenoberstabsgefreiter** Seaman Senior Staff Corporal
Corporal (Note 2)	**Yefretor** Corporal	**Stabsgefreiter** Staff Corporal	**Matrosenstabsgefreiter** Seaman Staff Corporal
No Equivalent	No Equivalent	**Obergefreiter** Senior Corporal	**Matrosenhauptgefreiter** Seaman Chief Corporal
Private First Class	No Equivalent	**Gefreiter** Lance Corporal	**Matrosenobergefreiter** Seaman Senior Corporal
No Equivalent	No Equivalent	**Oberschütze** Senior Rifleman	**Matrosengefreiter** Seaman Lance Corporal
Private	**Krasnoarmeyets** Private	**Schütze** Rifleman	**Matrose** Seaman

Notes:

1. In the U.S. Army, the first sergeant is the senior NCO at company level, the same grade as a master sergeant. The senior NCO at battalion level and above held the grade of master sergeant and the job title of sergeant major. The actual rank of sergeant major was not introduced into the U.S. Army until the late 1950s.

2. The U.S. Army also had three ranks for technicians. These ranks were the same pay grades as staff sergeant, sergeant, and corporal, and they were designated technicians grade 3, grade 4, and grade 5, respectively. The rank of technical sergeant, which was in pay grade 2, was not one of the technician ranks.

3. Warrant officers in the British Army are the highest ranking NCOs. At company level and above, their job title is often sergeant major.

4. Corporals in the Royal Artillery are called bombardiers and lance bombardiers.

5. Privates in the Royal Artillery are called gunners; in the Royal Engineers they are called sappers; and in the cavalry, they are called troopers.

6. The Royal Navy rank of leading seaman equated to both corporal and sergeant in the British Army. There were degrees of seniority and responsibility within the one rank.

7. The rank of warrant officer second class existed only in the Royal Canadian Air Force.

Table of Comparative Ranks
German Organizations*

German Army/Air Force (Note 1)	Waffen-SS	SA	NSDAP (Note 2)
Reichsmarschal Reich Marshal	**No** Equivalent	**No** Equivalent	**No** Equivalent
Generalfeldmarschal Field Marshal	**Reichsführer-SS** Reich Leader-SS	**Stabchef der SA** Staff Chief	**No** Equivalent
Generaloberst Colonel General	**Oberstgruppenführer** Colonel Group Leader	**No** Equivalent	**Reichsleiter** (Note 3)
General der Infantrie (Note 4)	**Obergruppenführer** Senior Group Leader	**Obergruppenführer** Senior Group Leader	**Gauleiter** District Leader
Generalleutnant Lieutenant General	**Gruppenführer** Group Leader	**Gruppenführer** Group Leader	**Hauptbefehlsleiter** Chief Command Leader
Generalmajor Major General	**Brigadeführer** Brigade Leader	**Brigadeführer** Brigade Leader	**Hauptdienstleiter** Chief Service Leader
No Equivalent	**Oberführer** Senior Leader	**Oberführer** Senior Leader	**Hauptbereichsleiter** Chief Area Leader
Oberst Colonel	**Standartenführer** Standard Leader	**Standartenführer** Standard Leader	**Hauptabschnittsleiter** Chief Section Leader
Oberstleutnant Lieutenant Colonel	**Obersturmbannführer** Senior Storm Battalion Leader	**Obersturmbannführer** Senior Storm Battalion Leader	**Hauptgemeinschaftsleiter** Chief Community Leader
Major Major	**Sturmbannführer** Storm Battalion Leader	**Sturmbannführer** Storm Battalion Leader	**Gemeinschaftsleiter** Community Leader
Hauptmann (Note 5) Captain	**Hauptsturmführer** Chief Storm Leader	**Hauptsturmführer** Chief Storm Leader	**Haupteinsatzleiter** Chief Mission Leader
Oberleutnant Senior Lieutenant	**Obersturmführer** Senior Storm Leader	**Obersturmführer** Senior Storm Leader	**Obereinsatzleiter** Senior Mission Leader
Leutnant Lieutenant	**Untersturmführer** Junior Storm Leader	**Sturmführer** Storm Leader	**Einsatzleiter** Mission Leader

(continued on next page)

Table of Comparative Ranks *(continued)*
German Organizations

German Army/Air Force	Waffen-SS	SA	NSDAP (Note 2)
Stabsfeldwebel Staff Sergent	**Sturmscharführer** Storm Platoon Leader	**Hauptruppführer** Chief Troop Leader	**Hauptbereitschaftsleiter** Chief Readiness Leader
Oberfeldwebel Senior Sergeant	**Hauptscharführer** Chief Platoon Leader	**Obertruppführer** Senior Troop Leader	**Oberbereitschaftsleiter** Senior Readiness Leader
Feldwebel Sergeant	**Oberscharführer** Senior Platoon Leader	**Truppführer** Troop leader	**Bereitschaftsleiter** Readiness Leader
Unterfeldwebel Junior Sergeant	**Scharführer** Platoon Leader	**Oberscharführer** Senior Platoon Leader	No Equivalent
Unteroffizier Noncommissioned Officer	**Unterführer** Junior Platoon Leader	**Scharführer** Platoon Leader	No Equivalent
Stabsgefreiter Staff Corporal	No Equivalent	No Equivalent	**Hauptarbeitsleiter** Chief Work Leader
Obergefreiter Senior Corporal	No Equivalent	No Equivalent	**Oberarbeitsleiter** Senior Work Leader
Gefreiter Lance Corporal	**Rottenführer** Squad Leader	**Rottenführer** Squad Leader	**Arbeitsleiter** Work Leader
Oberschütze Senior Rifleman	**Sturmmann** Storm Trooper	**Obersturmmann** Senior Storm Trooper	**Oberhelfer** Senior Helper
Schütze Rifleman	**SS-Mann** SS Trooper	**Sturmmann** Storm Trooper	**Helfer** Helper

Notes:

* This table lists the German title in **bold** letters, with the rough English translation of the title directly underneath. In many instances, the translated title will not make "sense" in the English translation, as English and American organizations often do not have equivalent titles.

1. The German police used the same officer rank titles as the army, up to **Generaloberst,** the highest police rank.

2. This list represents only a selection of the many rank titles of the National Socialist German Workers' Party (Nazi Party).

3. **Reichsleiter.** The German noun "Führer" means leader in the sense of a guide, while the noun "Leiter" means leader in the managerial sense, although a Leiter is more than just a manager. In English, a Führer would be a leader who guides the organization (that he is leading), while a Leiter would be more of an administrative leader.

4. General of the Infantry, General of the Artillery, etc.

5. In cavalry units, **Rittmeister,** literally "Riding Master."

Appendix C

Glossary of Acronyms, Abbreviations, and Foreign and Military Terms

Ia German staff section, operations

Ia/Art German staff section, operations—artillery subsection

Ia/Mess German staff section, operations—maps and survey subsection

Ib German staff section, supply

Ic German staff section, intelligence

Id German staff section, training

IIa German staff section, personnel (officers)

IIb German staff section, personnel (enlisted)

III German staff section, judge advocate

IVa German staff section, administration

IVb German staff section, medical

IVc German staff section, veterinary

IVd German staff section, chaplain

V German staff section, motor transport

VI German staff section, Nazi Party affairs

VII German staff section, civil affairs and military government

AA antiaircraft

AAA antiaircraft artillery

Abn Airborne

Abt *Abteilung* (branch)

Abwehr German military intelligence

ACC Allied Control Commission

ACV auxiliary aircraft carrier [U.S.]

AD armored division

AEAF Allied Expeditionary Air Forces

AEF Allied Expeditionary Forces

AF air force

AFHQ Allied Forces Headquarters

AFV armored fighting vehicle

AGF Allied Ground Forces

AGRA Army Group Royal Artillery

AIF Australian Imperial Force

AK *Armeekorps* (army corps) [German]

AK *Armia Krajowa* (Polish Home Army)

AMCs armed merchant cruisers

AMF Australian Military Force

AMG Allied Military Government

AMGOT Allied Military Government of Occupied Territories

Amt Office

ANC Army Nurse Corps [U.S.]

ANZAC Australian and New Zealand Army Corps

AOA American Ordnance Association

AOC air officer commanding [British]

AOK *Armee-Oberkommando* (the staff of a German numbered army)

APC armored personnel carrier

APDS armor-piercing discarding sabot

Arfu *Artillerieführer* (artillery leader)

Arko *Artillerie-Kommandeur* (artillery commander)

Armd armored

Armeegruppe German army group

Arty artillery

ARV armored recovery vehicle

ASDIC early British term for sonar, from Allied Submarine Detection Investigation Committee

ASF Army Service Force [U.S.]

ASW antisubmarine warfare

AT antitank

ATA Air Transport Auxiliary [British]

ATC Air Transport Command [U.S.]

ATS Auxiliary Territorial Service [British]

Ausf. *Ausführung* (model)

Auto automatic

AVG auxiliary aircraft vessel [U.S.]

AVRE armoured vehicle Royal Engineers

B- U.S. bomber model aircraft designation, e.g., B-17

BAR Browning automatic rifle [U.S.]

BARV beach armored recovery vehicle

Bazooka handheld antitank rocket launcher [U.S.]

BB- battleship designation [U.S.]

BBC British Broadcasting Corporation

BCATP British Commonwealth Air Training Plan

BCRA *Bureau Central de Renseignements et d'Action* (Central Intelligence and Operations Bureau)

B-Dienst German naval intercept service

BDJ *Bund Deutsches Jungvolk* (German Youth Association)

BDM *Bund Deutscher Mädel* (Association of German Maidens)

Bde brigade

BEF British Expeditionary Force

BEW Board of Economic Warfare [U.S.]

Bf- *Bayerische Flugzeugwerke*, designation of the early Messerschmitt fighter designs, the Bf-109 and Bf-110. In 1938 the company's the name changed to Messerschmidt AG, and all subsequent designs were designated Me-.

bhp brake horsepower

Big Four the United States, Great Britain, the Soviet Union, and China

Big Three the United States, Great Britain, and the Soviet Union

Blitz a term the British adopted to refer to the German aerial campaign against Britain

Blitzkrieg mobile warfare (literally, lightning war)

Bn battalion

BND *Bundesnachrichtendienst* (German Federal Intelligence Service)

BOAC British Overseas Airways Corporation

box trail The rearward extension of the carriage of an artillery piece by which the piece is anchored to the ground in its firing position and which remains in a fixed position for both transport and firing of the piece. It generally is less stable than a split trail (q.v.). Because of this, a box trail often is employed with a firing platform under the center of the carriage. This system offers a greater arc of traverse than a split trail.

BP Bletchley Park

Br British

Brig brigadier [British]

BSC British Security Coordination

C- U.S. cargo aircraft model designation, e.g., C-47

CA- heavy cruiser designation [U.S.]

CAM catapult merchant ship

Can Canadian

CAP Civil Air Patrol [U.S.]

CAPF Canadian Army Pacific Force

CAS Chief of Air Staff [British]

CATF Combined Airlift Task Force

Cav cavalry

CB Companion of the Order of the Bath [British]

CB counter-battery artillery fire

CB- battle cruiser designation [U.S.]

CBE Commander Order of the British Empire [British]

CBO combined bomber offensive

CCA Combat Command A, of a U.S. armored division

CCB Combat Command B, of a U.S. armored division

CCG Control Commission for Germany

CCR Combat Command Reserve, of a U.S. armored division

CCS Combined Chiefs of Staff [U.S. and British]

CDL canal defense light

CDU Christian Democratic Union [German]

CG commanding general

CGS Chief of the General Staff [British]

CI counterintelligence

CIA Central Intelligence Agency

CIC Counterintelligence Corps [U.S.]

CIGS Chief of the Imperial General Staff [British]

CinC commander in chief

CINCAF Commander in Chief, Allied Forces

CINCMED Commander in Chief, Mediterranean

CIP Counterintelligence Police

cl class of ship

CL- light cruiser designation [U.S.]

CLNAI National Liberation Committee of Upper Italy

cm centimeter

CMHQ Canadian military headquarters

CNF *Comité National Français*

CNO Chief of Naval Operations [U.S.]

CNR *Conseil National de la Résistance* (National Council of the Resistance)

Co company

CO commanding officer

CofS chief of staff

COHQ Combined Operations Headquarters [British]

COI coordinator of information

Comando Supremo Italian armed forces high command

COMINCH Commander in Chief, U.S. Navy

COMINT communications intelligence

Commo communications

COMNAVEU Commander U.S. Naval Forces, Europe

comps compilers

COMMZ communications zone—the rear echelon areas behind the fighting forces

COSSAC Chief of Staff to the Supreme Allied Commander

Counter-battery artillery fire specifically directed against the enemy's artillery or heavy weapons

CP command post

CV- aircraft carrier designation [U.S.]

CVE- aircraft carrier, escort designation [U.S.]

CVO Commander, Royal Victorian Order [British]

CW chemical warfare

CW continuous wave

D+# days elapsed since D-Day

DAF Desert Air Force [British]

DAK *Deutsches Afrika-Korps* (German Africa Corps)

DD duplex drive amphibious tank

DD- destroyer designation [U.S.]

D-Day day on which an operation commences

DE- destroyer escort designation [U.S.]

DEMS defensively equipped merchant ship

Dept department

DF direction finder/finding

DFC Distinguished Flying Cross [U.S. and British]

Div division

DLMs light mechanized divisions [French]

DMS- destroyer minesweeper designation [U.S.]

DNI director of naval intelligence

Dogface slang term for an American infantryman

DP dual purpose

Drôle de Guerre the phony war

DSC Distinguished Service Cross [U.S. and British]

DSO Distinguished Service Order [British]

DUKW two-and-one-half-ton amphibious truck, known as the "duck"

EAC European Advisory Commission

EAM Ethnikon Apeleftherotikon Metopon (Greek National Liberation Front)

E-boat *Eilboot* (fast boat), a small, fast German attack boat armed with torpedoes

EC European Community

ECM electronic countermeasures

EDES Ethnikos Dimokratikos Ellinikos Syndesmos (National Republican Greek League)

E+E escape and evasion

Einsatzgruppen operational groups of SS troops in the occupied territories

EK *Eisernes Kreuz* (Iron Cross)

ELAS Ethnikos Laikos Apeleftherotikos Stratos (Greek National Popular Liberation Army)

ELINT electronic intelligence gathering

Engr engineer

EOD explosive ordnance disposal teams

Ersatzheer German replacement army

ETO European Theater of Operations

EW electronic warfare

FA field artillery [U.S.]

Fallschirmjäger paratrooper

FANY Field Auxiliary Nursing Yeomanry [British]

FBI Federal Bureau of Investigation [U.S.]

FCA HQ First Canadian Army Headquarters

FDP Free Democratic Party [German]

FDR Franklin Delano Roosevelt

Feldheer German field army

FFI *Forces Françaises de l'Intérieur* (French Forces of the Interior)

FHO *Fremde heere ost* (Foreign Armies East)— a German intelligence organization specializing in the Soviet Union

FHQu *Führerhauptquartier* (Hitler's headquarters)

Flak *Flugzeugabwehrkanone* (antiaircraft guns), term widely adopted by the Allies to refer to the fire from antiaircraft guns

FM field manual [U.S.]

FM frequency modulation radio

FNFL *Forces Navales Françaises Libres* (Free French Naval Forces)

fps feet per second

FR fortified region

Freikorps (Free Corps)—private militia groups during the period of the Weimar Republic

Front Soviet army group

FUSAG 1st U.S. Army Group—a ghost unit created by the Allies for the FORTITUDE deception operation

FW- Focke-Wulf, German aircraft manufacturer designation, e.g., FW-190

FWD forward headquarters

G-1 U.S. administrative staff section (divisional level or higher)

G-2 U.S. intelligence staff section (divisional level or higher)

G-3 U.S. operations and training staff section (divisional level or higher)

G-4 U.S. logistics staff section (divisional level or higher)

G-5 U.S. civil affairs staff section (divisional level or higher)

GAU *Glavnoye Artilleriyskoye Upravleniye* (Main Artillery Directorate) [Soviet]

Gauleiter Nazi Party regional leader

GC George Cross [British]

GCI ground controlled intercept

Gd guards

geh. *geheim* (secret)

GenStdH *Generalstab des Heeres* (General Staff of the Army)

Geschwader *Luftwaffe* wing

Gestapo *Geheimstaatspolizei* (Secret State Police)

GHQ general headquarters

GI government issue, slang term referring to the American soldier

GKdo *Generalkommando* (German corps-type headquarters)

GKO State Defense Committee [Soviet]

GMC gun motor carriage

GNP gross national product

GO general order

GOC general officer commanding [British]

grt gross register tons

GRU *Glavnoe Razvedyvate'noe Upravlenie* (Main Intelligence Directorate of the General Staff) [Soviet Army]

H–Dienst Harbor Service

He- Heinkel, German aircraft manufacturer designation, e.g., He-111

HE high explosive

HEAT high explosive antitank

Hedgehog antitank obstacle made of three crossed angle irons. Also, a naval antisubmarine weapon

Heeresgruppe army group

HF high frequency

HF/DF high frequency direction finding

H-Hour the time on D-Day when an operation commences

Hiwi Hilfswillige—Russian and Polish prisoners volunteering for service with the German forces

HJ *Hitlerjugend* (Hitler Youth)

HMAS His Majesty's Australian Ship

HMCS His Majesty's Canadian Ship

HMNZS His Majesty's New Zealand Ship

HMS His Majesty's Ship

hp horsepower

HQ headquarters

HSSPF *Höhere SS-und Polizeiführer* (senior SS and police commanders)

Hull-down a defensive fighting position for an armored vehicle in which the main portion of the vehicle's hull is protected by a depression in the earth or by a revetment specifically dug for that purpose. A tank in a hull-down position, for example, will have only its turret and main gun exposed, presenting a much smaller target. Hull-down is also known as hull defilade.

HUMINT human intelligence

HVAR high-velocity aircraft rocket

Hvy heavy

HWE Home War Establishment [Canadian]

ICBM intercontinental ballistic missile

ICC Inter-Allied Control Council

ID infantry division

i.G. *im Generalstab* (in the General Staff), a designation that followed the rank title of all German General Staff officers, for example, *Oberst i.G.*

IG inspector general [U.S.]

Il- Ilyushin, Soviet aircraft manufacturer designation, e.g., Il-2

ILR *Infantrie-Lehrregiment,* the German Infantry School training regiment

IMT International Military Tribunal

Ind Indian

Inf infantry

Info information

Intel intelligence

Intsum intelligence summary

It Italian

IWM Imperial War Museum, London

Jabo the German slang term for a fighter-bomber, from *Jagdbomber*

Jäger German light infantry

JCS Joint Chiefs of Staff [U.S.]

Jeep a corruption of GP (general purpose) quarter-ton truck

JG *Jagdgeschwader* (fighter wing)

JIC Joint Intelligence Committee

JS *Jagdstaffel* (fighter squadron)

JSM Joint Staff Mission [British]

Ju- Junkers, German aircraft manufacturer designation, e.g., Ju-52

JV *Jagdverband* (fighter formation)

Kampfgruppe German task force

KBE Knight Commander of the Order of the British Empire

KCB Knight Commander of the Order of the Bath [British]

KG *Kampfgeschwader* (bomber wing)

KGB *Komitet Gossudarstvennoi Bezopastnosti* (Soviet Committee for State Security)

KHz kilohertz (1,000 cycles per second)

KIA killed in action

KKV *Kleinkampfverbände* (small fighting units)—German special forces units

Km kilometer

KM *Kriegsmarine* (German navy)

KONR Committee for the Liberation of the Peoples of Russia

K rations U.S. Army field rations

Kreisleiter Nazi Party district leader

Kripo *Kriminalpolizei* (criminal police)

KTB *Kriegstagebuch* (war diary)

kts knots

KZ *Konzentrationslager* (concentration camp)

LAF Lithuanian Activist Front

LAH *Leibstandarte Adolf Hitler* (Hitler's bodyguard unit)

Landser slang term for the German common soldier

Lay precision aligning an artillery piece to a base direction. Aiming the gun at all targets is then accomplished by shifting from that base direction

LCA landing craft, assault

LCI landing craft, infantry

LCM landing craft, mechanized

LCS London Controlling Section

LCT landing craft, tank

LCVP landing craft, vehicle and personnel

LF low frequency

LOCs lines of communications, i.e., supply routes

LOCUS landing craft obstacle clearance units [British]

LRDG Long-range Desert Group [British]

LSD landing ship, dock

LSH landing ship, headquarters

LSI landing ship, infantry

LST landing ship, tank

Lt light

Luftflotte air fleet (*Luftwaffe* numbered air force)

Luftflotte-Reich German Home Air Command

LVF *Légion des Volontaires Français* (French volunteer legion of the *Waffen*-SS)

LVT landing vehicle, tracked

Lw *Luftwaffe* (German Air Force)

M- U.S. model number designation, e.g., M-1 rifle, M-4 tank

MAAF Mediterranean Allied Air Force

MACs merchant aircraft carriers

MAD magnetic anomaly detection

MAP Ministry of Air Production [British]

Maquisards troops of the *Maquis*, the French resistance

MBE Member of the Order of the British Empire [British]

MC Military Cross [British]

MCWR Marine Corps Women's Reserve

Me- Messerschmidtt, German aircraft manufacturer designation, e.g., Me-262

MEK *Marine-Einsatz-Kommando* (naval replacement command)

MG *Maschinengewehr* (machine gun)

MGB motor gun boat

MHz megahertz (1,000,000 cycles per second)

MI military intelligence

MIA missing in action

MiG- Mikoyan and Gurevich, Soviet aircraft manufacturer designation, e.g., MiG-3

MI-1 Military Intelligence 1, British intelligence administration

MI-2 Military Intelligence 2, British intelligence for East Europe and Asia

MI-3 Military Intelligence 3, British intelligence for West Europe and the Americas

MI-4 Military Intelligence 4, British intelligence map support

MI-5 Military Intelligence 5, the British Security Service

MI-6 Military Intelligence 6, the British Secret Intelligence Service

MI-7 Military Intelligence 7, British press intelligence

MI-8 Military Intelligence 8, British signals intelligence

MI-9 Military Intelligence 9, British intelligence support for Allied prisoners and escape and evasion

MI-10 Military Intelligence 10, British intelligence technical support

MI-11 Military Intelligence 11, British field security police

MI-12 Military Intelligence 12, British postal security

MI-14 Military Intelligence 14, British intelligence for Germany

MI-15 Military Intelligence 15, British intelligence photo reconnaissance

MI-16 Military Intelligence 16, British intelligence for science

MI-17 Military Intelligence 17, British intelligence coordination

MI-19 Military Intelligence 19, British intelligence for enemy POWs and refugees from Europe

MILORG Military Organization—the armed Norwegian resistance group

Mk- Mark, British model number designation

mm millimeter

MNBDO Mobile Naval Base Defense Organization

MP *Maschinenpistole* (submachine gun)

MP Member of Parliament

MP military police

mph miles per hour

MT motor transport

MTB motor torpedo boat

MTO Mediterranean Theater of Operations

MUR *Mouvements Unis de la Résistance* (United Resistance Movement)

NAAF North African Air Force

NATO North Atlantic Treaty Organization

NBS Norden bombsight

NCO noncommissioned officer

Nebelwerfer multiple-barrel rocket launcher mounted on wheels and fired electrically

NKVD *Narodnyy Kommissariat Vnutrenniakh Del* (Soviet People's Commissariat for Internal Affairs), predecessor to the KGB

nm nautical miles

NRMA National Resources Mobilization Act [Canada]

NSDAP *Nationalsozialistische Deutsche Arbeiterpartei* (National Socialist German Workers' Party), the Nazi Party

Null-Tag (Zero Day), also *0–tag*, the German equivalent of D-Day

NZ New Zealand

OB *Oberbefehlshaber* (commander in chief)

OBE Officer of the Order of the British Empire

OC Office of Censorship [U.S.]

OCS officer candidate school [U.S.]

ODESSA *Organisation der ehemaligen SS-Angehörigen* (Organization of Former SS Members)

OECD Organization for Economic Cooperation and Development

OEEC Organization for European Economic Cooperation

OFEC Office for Economic Coordination

Oflag *Offizierslager* (officer prisoner of war camp)

OG operational group

OGBM *Otdelny Gvardeskiy Batal'on Minerov* (separate guard battalion)

OKH *Oberkommando des Heeres* (German Army high command)

OKL *Oberkommando der Luftwaffe* (German Air Force high command)

OKM *Oberkommando der Kriegsmarine* (German Navy High Command)

OKW *Oberkommando der Wehrmacht* (High Command of the German Armed Forces)

Op operation

OP observation post

opord operations order

ORA *Organisation de Résistance de l'Armée*

ORG Operational Research Group

Orpo *Ordnungspolizie* (Order Police)

OSS Office of Strategic Services [U.S.]

OT *Organisation Todt* (German construction engineering organization)

OWI Office of War Information [U.S.]

OWM Office of War Mobilization [U.S.]

P- U.S. fighter (pursuit) aircraft model designation, e.g., P-51

PAF Polish Air Force

Pak *Panzerabwehrkanone* (antitank gun)

Panzerfaust (Panzer Fist)—single-shot, shaped charge antitank weapon

Panzergrenadier German mechanized infantry

Panzerschreck (*Panzer* Terror)—a shoulder-fired antitank rocket launcher, copied after the U.S. bazooka

PCNL Polish Committee of National Liberation

pdr pounder (British projectile weight/gun-size measurement, e.g., 2–pdr, 6–pdr)

Pfc private first class [U.S.]

PFF Pathfinder Force

PHOTINT photographic intelligence

PIAT projector, infantry, antitank [British]

PLUTO pipeline under the ocean

PM prime minister [British]

PNF *Partito Nazionale Fascista* (Fascist National Party)

Pol Polish

POW prisoner of war (also PW)

PPA Polish People's Army

PUC Presidential Unit Citation [U.S.]

PWE Political Warfare Executive [British]

Pz *Panzer* (armor)

PzDv *Panzer* division

PzGr *Panzergrenadier* (mechanized infantry)

PzKpfw *Panzerkampfwagen* (armored fighting vehicle)

QM quartermaster (supply)

q.v. *quod vide* (which see)

RA *Regia Aeronautica* (Italian Air Force)

RA Royal Artillery

RAAF Royal Australian Air Force

RAC Royal Armoured Corps

RAD *Reichsarbeitsdienst* (German Labor Service)

RAF Royal Air Force

RAN Royal Australian Navy

RCAF Royal Canadian Air Force

RCM radar countermeasures

RCN Royal Canadian Navy

RCT regimental combat team

RDF radio direction finding

RE Royal Engineers

recce reconnaissance

Regt regiment

REI *Régiment Étranger d'Infanterie* (infantry regiment of the Foreign Legion)

Reichsheer the German Army of the Third *Reich*

Reichsleiter Nazi Party national level leader

Reichswehr the German armed forces of the Weimar Republic

RFSS *Reichsführer-SS* (*Reich* Leader of the SS)

RKFDV *Reichskommissar für die Festigung des deutschen Volkstums* (*Reich* Commissioner for the Strengthening of Germanism)

RM *Regia Marina* (the Italian Navy)

RM Royal Marines

RMVE *Régiment de Marche de Volontaires Étrangers*

RN Royal Navy

RNVR Royal Navy Volunteer Reserve

RNZAF Royal New Zealand Air Force

ROA *Russkaia Osvoboditel'naia Armiia* (Russian Liberation Army)

RPC remote power control

RSHA *Reichssicherheits-Hauptamt* (*Reich* Main Security Office

RSI *Republica Sociale Italiana*

RTR Royal Tank Regiment

RTTY radio teletype

RuSHA *Rasse- und Siedlungshauptamt* (Race and Resettlement Office)

S-1 personnel staff section (U.S. regimental level or lower)

S-2 intelligence staff section (U.S. regimental level or lower)

S-3 operations staff section (U.S. regimental level or lower)

S-4 supply staff section (U.S. regimental level or lower)

SA *Sturmabteilungen* (storm battalions)

SACEUR Supreme Allied Commander, Europe

SACMED Supreme Allied Commander, Mediterranean

SAM surface-to-air missile

SAS Special Air Service [British]

SBG small box girder bridge

SBS Special Boat Section [British]

SCAEF Supreme Commander, Allied Expeditionary Force

SCAO senior civil affairs officer

SCR Signal Corps Radio [U.S.]

SD *Sicherheitsdienst* (Security Service)

SdKfz *Sonderkraftfahrzeug* (Special Motor Vehicle)—special combat vehicles that included armored cars and half-tracks

SFHQ Special Forces Headquarters

SHAEF Supreme Headquarters Allied Expeditionary Force

SIGINT signal intelligence

Sipo *Sicherheitspolizei* (Security Police)

SIS Secret Intelligence Service, also known as MI-6

Sitrep situation report

Sitzkrieg British slang term for the "Phony War"

Smersh *Smert' Shpionam* (Death to Spies)— Soviet military counterintelligence

SMLE short magazine Lee-Enfield—standard British service rifle

SOE Special Operations Executive [British]

SOF special operations force

SOL *Service d'Ordre Légionnaire*

SOP standing operating procedure

SOS Service of Supply [U.S.]

SP self-propelled

SPARS U.S. Coast Guard Auxiliary (from the motto *Semper Paratus*)

SPD Social Democratic Party [German]

Spetsnaz *Spetsialnoye Nazhacheniya*, Soviet special forces

SPFs special purpose forces

split trail the rearward extension of the carriage of an artillery piece by which the piece is anchored to the ground in its firing position and which can be closed to transport the piece, or opened to form a fork to emplace the piece. It generally is more stable than a box trail (q.v.), but it limits the gun's angle of traverse.

SPOC special operations center

Sq squadron

SS *Schutzstaffel* (Protective Bodies)

SS- submarine designation [U.S.]

SSS Selective Service System [U.S.]

SSTV *SS-Totenkopfverbände* (SS-Death's Head Formations)— concentration camp guard units

SSVT *SS-Verfügungstruppe* (SS-Reserves)

Stabschef chief of staff

Stalag *Mannschafts-Stammlager* (Enlisted Men's Prisoner of War Camp)

STAVKA Soviet high command

STO *Service de Travail Obligatoire* (Mandatory Labor Service)

STOL short takeoff and landing

StuG *Sturmgeschütz,* assault gun

Stuka *Sturzkampfflugzeug* (dive bomber), specifically, the Ju-87

super charge a special propellant charge designed to achieve greater than the originally designed range from an artillery piece

SWS special wireless section

TA Territorial Army [British]

TA traffic analysis

Tac tactical

TAF tactical air force

TBS talk between ships

TD tank destroyer

Teller Mine a German antitank mine, the general diameter and shape of a dinner plate, hence its nickname, from the German word for a plate

TF task force

TG task group

TM technical manual [U.S.]

T/O&E table of organization and equipment [U.S.]

Tommy slang term for the British soldier

TOT time on target—a method of timing artillery so that fire from several points of origin falls on the target simultaneously. The purpose is to maximize the effects of surprise.

U-Boat *Unterwasserboot* (German submarine)

UDT underwater demolition team [U.S.]

UHF ultrahigh frequency

U.K. United Kingdom

U.N. United Nations

UPA Ukrainian Insurgent Army

USA United States Army

USAAF United States Army Air Forces

USAR U.S. Army Reserve

USCG United States Coast Guard

USCGC United States Coast Guard Cutter

USN United States Navy

USNR United States Naval Reserve

USNS United States Naval Ship

USO United Service Organization [U.S.]

USS United States Ship

USSTAF United States Strategic Air Forces

UXB unexploded bomb

V- *Vergeltungswaffen* (reprisal weapons), German missiles

VC Victoria Cross [British]

V-E Victory in Europe

VHF very high frequency

V-J Victory over Japan (end of World War II)

Volksdeutsche ethnic Germans residing in border areas of countries adjacent to Germany

Volksgrenadier hastily assembled and poorly trained German divisions raised at the end of the war

Volkssturm people's militia

VT variable time—artillery proximity fuze

VVS *Voenno-Vozhdusnis Sili* (Soviet Air Force)

WAAC Women's Auxiliary Army Corps [U.S.]

WAAF Women's Auxiliary Air Force [U.S.]

WAC Women's Army Corps [U.S.]

Waffen-SS Armed SS

WAFS Women's Auxiliary Ferrying Service [U.S.]

WASPS Women's Air Force Service Pilots [U.S.]

WASU West African Student Union

WAVES Women Accepted for Voluntary Emergency Service

Wehrmacht the German armed forces

WFst *Wehrmachtführungsstab* (German armed forces operations staff)

WIA wounded in action

WLA Women's Land Army [British]

WMC War Manpower Commission [U.S.]

WP white phosphorous

WPB War Production Board [U.S.]

WPD War Plans Division [U.S.]

WRNS Women's Royal Naval Service

WSA War Shipping Administration [U.S.]

WVS Women's Voluntary Service [British]

XO executive officer

Yak- Yakovlev, Soviet aircraft manufacturer designation, e.g. Yak-7

ŻOB *Żobydska Organizacja Bojowa* (Jewish Fighting Organization) in the Warsaw Ghetto

Appendix D

Allied and Axis Code Names

All sides in World War II used code names for people, places, organizations, and operations. The Allies alone assigned more than 10,000. The following list contains approximately 650 of the most important code names, arranged according to the Allied (except Soviet), Allied (for persons and groups), Soviet, and Axis (German) names. For additional code names, see Christopher Chant's *Encyclopedia of Code Names of World War II* (1986).

Allied (except Soviet) Operational Code Names

Code Name	Date	Remarks
ABC-1	January–March 1941	U.S.-British military staff Conferences in Washington, D.C. The "Europe first" strategy if the U.S. entered the war.
ABIGAIL	16 December 1940	British area bombing of Mannheim, Germany.
ACCOLADE	1941	Proposed attack on the Dodecanese Islands in the Aegean Sea.
ACROBAT	1941	Proposed advance into Tripolitania, Libya by Commonwealth forces.
ALSOS	1943–1945	Special intelligence operation that sought information on German nuclear fission.
AMHERST	7–8 April 1945	Airborne drop by French SAS paratroopers in the northern Netherlands.
ANKLET	December 1941	Royal Navy operation to cut German communications in northern Norway.
ANVIL	1943	Early name for Operation DRAGOON.
APHRODITE	Summer 1944	U.S. attacks on German V-weapon sites using remotely controlled bombers.
APOSTLE	10 May 1945	The return of Allied forces to Norway following the German surrender.
ARCADIA	December 1941–January 1942	U.S.-British Washington Conference.
ARCHERY	December 1941	Royal Navy raid against Stadlandet, Norway.
ARENA	1945	Allied plan to capture the Ruhr industrial region by airborne assault.

Allied (except Soviet) Operational Code Names

Code Name	Date	Remarks
ARGONAUT	January–February 1945	Code name for the Malta and Yalta Conferences.
ARGUMENT	20–27 February 1944	U.S. bombing of aircraft production facilities in central Germany.
ARIEL	June 1940	Evacuation of British troops from French ports.
ATHLETIC	October 1944	Royal Navy carrier-based air strikes at Bodo and Lodingen, Norway.
AVALANCHE	9 September 1943	U.S. amphibious invasion of Italy at Salerno.
AVONMOUTH	March 1940	Proposed Anglo-French occupation of Norway.
BACKBONE	November 1942	British plans for operations in Spanish Morocco.
BARCLAY	1943	Deception plan designed to induce the Axis to reinforce their forces in southern France and the Balkans.
BARITONE	August 1942	British reinforcement of Malta.
BARRACUDA	1943	Planned sea and airborne assault on Naples.
BATTLEAXE I	November 1941	British offensive against German and Italian forces in North Africa.
BATTLEAXE II	15 June 1942	Continuation of BATTLEAXE I.
BAYTOWN	3 September 1943	British amphibious invasion of Calabria, Italy, across the Straits of Messina.
BENEFICIARY	June–July 1944	Plan to break out of the Normandy beachhead by a combined airborne-amphibious attack at St. Malo.
BEGONIA	September 1944	Royal Navy minelaying operations in Aaramsund, Norway.
BELLOWS	August 1942	British reinforcement of Malta—part of Operation PEDESTAL.
BERLIN	25–26 September 1944	Escape of British and Polish paratroopers encircled at Arnhem, Netherlands.
BERTRAM	26 September–23 October 1942	British deception efforts for the El Alamien attack.
BETA	1945	British plans for reopening English Channel ports closed by mining and wreckage.
BIBENDUM	6 June 1944	French resistance operations impeding German *Panzer* units moving into Normandy during Operation OVERLORD.
BIG WEEK	20–27 February 1944	Unofficial code name for Operation ARGUMENT.

Allied (except Soviet) Operational Code Names

Code Name	Date	Remarks
BIGOT	1944	Classification of special intelligence in support of OVERLORD.
BINGO	November 1944	USAAF attacks against electrical power transformers in German-held areas of Italy.
BITING	27–28 February 1942	Commando raid on the German radar site at Bruneval, near Le Havre, France.
BLACKCOCK	14 November 1944	Commonwealth offensive in the Roermond-Velno region of the Netherlands.
BLOCKBUSTER	8 February–10 March 1945	Canadian offensive in the Rhineland.
BLUECOAT	29 July 1944	British Second Army attack south from Chaumont, France.
BLUES	June 1944	Royal Navy carrier-based air strikes on southern Norway.
BODYGUARD	1943–1944	Allied deception plan for the invasion of Europe.
BOLERO	1942–1944	Allied build up of troops and materiel in preparation for a cross-channel attack.
BONIFACE	1944–1945	Code name to denote ULTRA intelligence. The enemy was supposed to think that it was a reference to an agent.
BONUS	1942	Early code name for Operation IRONCLAD.
BRADDOCK II	1944	The air dropping of small incendiary devices to European workers for use in sabotage efforts.
BRASSARD	17 June 1944	French amphibious invasion of Elba Island.
BRAWN	6 May 1944	Abortive operation to attack the battleship *Tirpitz* in Alten Fjord, Norway.
BREAST PLATE	1943	Proposed British amphibious assault on Sousse, Tunisia, from Malta.
BREVITY	15 May 1941	Commonwealth offensive in the Western Desert of Egypt.
BRIMSTONE	1943	Planned Allied invasion of Sardinia.
BUFFALO	23 May 1944	Plans for a U.S. breakout from the Anzio beachhead.
BUICK	1 August 1944	USAAF airdrops to the French Maquis.
BUNGHOLE	February 1944	U.S.-British operations to parachute U.S. specialists into the Balkans to assist guerrillas.
BUTTRESS	September 1943	Planned amphibious assault on the toe of Italy at Reggio by Commonwealth forces from North Africa.

Allied (except Soviet) Operational Code Names

Code Name	Date	Remarks
BURZA	1 August 1944	"TEMPEST," code word for the uprising of the Polish Home Army.
CADILLAC	14 July 1944	USAAF airdrop to the French Maquis.
CAESAR	June 1940	Early code name for Operation CROMWELL.
CALENDAR	April 1942	British reinforcement of Malta.
CALIPH	1944	Proposed Allied landings in the Bordeaux region of France.
CALLBOY	October 1941	British reinforcement of Malta.
CAPRI	1943	Proposed attack against Medenine, Tunisia.
CARBONADO	1945	Revised plans for Operation BETA.
CARPETBAGGER	4 January–September 1944	Airdrops in support of partisan operations in western Europe.
CATAPULT	3 July 1940	Destruction of the French fleet by the Royal Navy at Mers el-Kébir.
CATHERINE	Late 1939	A proposed British naval offensive in the Baltic Sea.
CENT	10 July 1943	Code name for the Scoglitti area beaches during the invasion of Sicily.
CHAIN HOME	1936–1945	British radar defense network on the eastern and southern coasts of Great Britain.
CHARIOT	28 March 1942	British commando raid on the port of Saint-Nazaire, France.
CHARNWOOD	8 July 1944	British offensive near Caen, Normandy.
CHASTISE	May 1943	RAF attacks on German dams.
CHATTANOOGA CHOO-CHOO	1944–1945	Air strikes on rails and rail-related targets in France and Germany.
CHEADLES	Late 1940	RAF nuisance raids against *Luftwaffe* airfields in France.
CHILI	February–March 1945	Series of low-level RAF raids in the Baltic.
CHOKER I	Spring 1945	A proposed Allied airborne operation against the Siegfried Line in the vicinity of Saarbrücken.
CHOKER II	Spring 1945	A proposed Allied airborne crossing of the Rhine in the vicinity of Frankfurt.
CIRCUS	1941–1942	RAF raids on European coastal areas.
CLARION	22–23 February 1945	Air attacks on communications in central Germany.
CLAYMORE	4 March 1941	British Commando raid on Norway's Lofoten Islands.
CLIPPER	18 November 1944	British XXX Corps offensive at Geilenkirchen, Germany.

Allied (except Soviet) Operational Code Names

Code Name	Date	Remarks
COBRA	25–31 July 1944	U.S. breakout from Normandy beachhead after Operation OVERLORD.
COCKADE	1943	Allied diversionary operations to pin down German forces in the west.
COMET	September 1944	British Second Army plan to seize the river crossings near Arnhem, Netherlands.
COMPASS	7 December 1941	Counteroffensive against Italian forces in Egypt.
CORDITE	Early 1941	Proposed British invasion of the island of Rhodes in the Aegean Sea.
CORKSCREW	11 June 1943	U.S. amphibious landing at Pantelleria Island (located between Sicily and Tunisia).
CORNCAKE	June 1943	British operation to embark agents from the Norwegian coast.
CRICKET	30 January–2 February 1945	Code name for the Malta Conference.
CROMWELL	1940	Alarm signal for a German invasion of Britain.
CROSSBOW	December 1943–March 1944	Air attacks on German V-weapon sites.
CROSSWORD	2 May 1944	Covert operation leading to the German surrender in Italy.
CRUSADER	18 November 1941	Commonwealth offensive against German and Italian forces in the Western Desert of Egypt.
CRUX III	January 1944	British transfer of agents and supplies to Norway.
CYCLE	June 1940	Evacuation of British and French troops from Le Havre, France.
DAGGER	1944–1945	Planned U.S. Ninth Army operation to clear the Germans from the west bank of the Roer River after the destruction of the dams.
DEADLIGHT	Post–1945	Scuttling of German U-boats after the end of the war.
DEMON	24 April–1 May 1941	The British evacuation of Greece.
DIADEM	11 May 1944	The final Allied assault on the Gustav Line.
DIME	10 July 1943	Code name for the Gela area beaches during the invasion of Sicily.
DIVER	June 1944–March 1945	Defensive measures against V-1 rockets.
DOUBLE-CROSS	1940–1945	Control of German agents in Great Britain.
DOVE	15 August 1944	U.S. airborne and glider portion of Operation DRAGOON.
DRAGOON	15 August 1944	Joint U.S.-British amphibious invasion of southern France.

Allied (except Soviet) Operational Code Names

Code Name	Date	Remarks
DUCK	April 1940	Royal Navy destroyers bombarding German airfield at Stavanger, Norway.
DUNLOP	April 1941	British reinforcement of Malta.
DYNAMO	26 May–4 June 1940	Evacuation of Allied forces from Dunkirk, France.
ECLIPSE	1944	A proposed operation in the case of a rapid internal collapse of Nazi Germany. The plan included an airborne assault on Berlin.
ENCORE	February 1945	Limited objective operation by IV Corps against Monte Belvedere, Italy.
EPSOM	18 July 1944	British offensive west of Caen, France.
EUREKA	26 November–2 December 1943	Code name for the Teheran Conference.
EXCESS	January 1941	Major Royal Navy convoy to resupply Malta.
EXPLOIT	1944	U.S. Army deception plan for the Rhine River crossing.
EXPORTER	June 1941	British occupation of Syria.
FABIUS	May 1944	Amphibious landing exercise in preparation for Operation OVERLORD.
FANFARE	1943–1945	Code name for all Allied operations in the Mediterranean theater.
FIREBRAND	15 June– 4 October 1943	Planned U.S. invasion of the Italian island of Corsica.
FLASH	1943	Failed attempt to assassinate Adolf Hitler in coordination with the German underground.
FLASHLAMP	24 June 1944	RAF operation to attack German coastal gun batteries at the start of Operation OVERLORD.
FLASHPOINT	March 1945	U.S. Ninth Army assault crossing of Rhine River, part of Operation PLUNDER.
FLAX	5 April–13 May 1943	Allied air interdiction of German and Italian sea traffic in the Straits of Sicily prior to Operation HUSKY.
FOREMOST	September 1941	British transfer of money and supplies to the French resistance.
FORTITUDE	1943–1944	Allied deception plan for OVERLORD:
—NORTH		—in the Scandanavian countries.
—SOUTH		—in the Channel coast areas of France and Belgium.
FOURTH TERM	8 February 1945	Limited objective operation by IV Corps in the Serchio Valley, Italy.
FOXLEY	June 1944	Planned British SOE operation to assassinate Hitler.

Allied (except Soviet) Operational Code Names

Code Name	Date	Remarks
FRANKTON	12 December 1942	Royal Navy landing of commandos to destroy German shipping at Bordeaux and Bassens, France.
FRANTIC	June–September 1944	Allied shuttle bombing of Germany using bases in Soviet-held territory for long-range missions.
FRANTIC JOE	2 June 1944	The first bombing mission under FRANTIC.
FREEDOM	Fall 1944	Allied rescue of 300 POWs from Bulgaria, through Turkey and Egypt, into Italy.
FRESHMAN	19 November 1942	Failed British airborne operation to destroy the heavy water plant in Norway.
FRY	4–5 April 1945	British and Italian occupation of the islands in Lake Comacchio, Italy.
FULL HOUSE	6 June 1944	Allied air attacks behind the beaches in support of Operation OVERLORD.
GAFF	1944	Allied operation for the assassination of German Field Marshal Erwin Rommel.
GANGWAY	1943	Plan for an unopposed landing at Naples.
GARDEN	17–26 September 1944	Allied ground portion of Operation MARKET-GARDEN, to seize the Rhine bridges.
GAUNTLET	25 August 1941	British seizure of Spitzbergen Island.
GIANT I	1943	Plan for an air landing and drop along the Volturno River.
GIANT II	1944	Plan for an airdrop near Rome.
GLIMMER	6 June 1944	Deception operation off the coast of Boulogne-sur-Mer, France.
GOBLET	1943	Proposed Allied amphibious landing at Cotrone, Italy.
GOLD	June 1944	Code name for Asnelles beach at Normandy.
GOLDFLAKE	9 February 1945	Movement of the Canadian I Corps from the Italian to the European theater.
GOMORRAH	24–30 July 1943	U.S. and British aerial destruction of Hamburg, Germany, using incendiary bombs.
GOODWOOD	18–20 July 1944	British offensive to capture the high ground south of Caen, France.
GRAPEFRUIT	9 April 1945	Proposed offensive in northern Italy.
GRAPESHOT	April 1945	The final Allied Offensive in Italy.
GRASP	July 1940	British seizure of French ships in Britain, Gibraltar, Malta, and Singapore.

Allied (except Soviet) Operational Code Names

Code Name	Date	Remarks
GRENADE	23 February–10 March 1945	U.S. and Canadian ground offensive in the Rhineland in support of Operation VERITABLE.
GUIDANCE	April 1944	Royal Navy midget submarine attack on a German floating dry dock in Bergen, Norway.
GUNNERSLIDE	16–28 February 1943	British and Norwegian operation to destroy the heavy water plant in Vemork, Norway.
GYMNAST	1942	Early name for Operation TORCH; also called Operation SUPER-GYMNAST.
HALBERD	September 1941	Royal Navy convoy to resupply Malta.
HALCYON	1 June 1944	Y-Day, when Allied forces would be ready for D-Day.
HALPRO	12 June 1942	U.S. air strike against Ploeşti oil fields.
HAMMER	April 1940	Proposed British capture of Trondheim, Norway.
HANDS-UP	1944	Proposed assault at Vannes, France.
HARDIHOOD	1943–1944	Assistance to Turkey to induce it to enter the war on the side of the Allies.
HARLEQUIN	September 1943	Loading exercise associated with COCKADE.
HARPOON	June 1942	Royal Navy convoy to resupply Malta from Gibraltar.
HATS	August–September 1940	Royal Navy convoy to resupply Malta.
HECKLE	14 September 1944	Royal Navy midget submarine attack on a German floating dry dock at Bergen, Norway.
HERCULES	Early 1944	British plans for amphibious invasion of the island of Rhodes.
HURRICANE	14 October 1944	RAF bombing of Duisburg.
HURRY	August 1940	British reinforcement of Malta.
HUSKY	10 July 1944	Allied amphibious invasion of Sicily.
HYDRA	18 August 1943	The RAF air raid against German missile research facilities at Peenemünde.
IMPERATOR	1942	Proposed large-scale British commando raid on the French Channel coast.
IMPLEMENT	May 1944	Royal Navy submarine attacks against ore carriers off the coast of Spain.
INDEPENDENCE	December 1944	Plan for French First Army to attack German garrisons on the French coast.
INDIGO	1942	Plans for the U.S. occupation of Iceland
INFATUATE	October 1944	Allied assault on Walcheren, Netherlands.
INFLUX	1940	Proposed British invasion of Sicily.
INSECT	January 1942	British reinforcement of Malta.

Allied (except Soviet) Operational Code Names

Code Name	Date	Remarks
IRONCLAD	5 May 1942	British assault on island of Madagascar.
JAEL	1943	Early code name for BODYGUARD.
JERICHO	18 February 1944	RAF bombing of German prison in Amiens, France, permitting mass escape of POWs.
JOSS	10 July 1943	Code name for the Licata area beaches during the invasion of Sicily.
JUBILANT	1945	Proposed airborne operation to rescue Allied POWs in Germany.
JUBILEE	19 August 1942	Large-scale Commonwealth raid on Dieppe, France.
JUDGEMENT	11 November 1940	Royal Navy attack on Italian naval base at Taranto.
JUGGLER	17 August 1943	U.S. Eighth Air Force bombing of Regensburg.
JUNO	June 1944	Code name for Courseulles beach at Normandy.
JUPITER	1942	Planned British invasion of Norway.
KAPUT	April 1945	U.S. Ninth Army operations along the Elbe.
KEELHAUL	1946–1947	The forced repatriation by the Western Allies of Soviet citizens after the war, in compliance with the Yalta agreements.
KITBAG	27 December 1941	Royal Navy raid on German bases in Norway.
L.B.	May 1942	British reinforcement of Malta.
LEVER	5 April 1944	U.S. offensive across Reno River, Italy.
LIGHTFOOT	23 October 1942	British attack at El Alamein.
LINNET I	September 1944	Planned airborne drop at Tournai, Belgium.
LINNET II	September 1944	Planned airborne drop at Aachen, Germany.
LITTLE VITTLES	1948–1949	Airdrops of candy to children in Berlin; performed concurrently with Operation VITTLES.
LOCOMOTIVE	September 1943	Royal Navy submarine operation carrying Norwegians and supplies to Spitzbergen.
LUCKY STRIKE	June 1944	Plan for the 21st Army Group to capture the Seine ports as an alternative to the proposed earlier capture of Brittany.
LUDLUM	15 March 1944	The Allied bombing of Monte Casino abbey.
LUMBERJACK	1 March 1945	U.S. ground offensive in the Eifel region of Germany.

Allied (except Soviet) Operational Code Names

Code Name	Date	Remarks
LUSTRE	Spring 1941	Troop convoy operations from Alexandria, Egypt, to Greece.
MAGNET	14 January 1942	Movement of U.S. V Corps into Northern Ireland.
MALLORY MAJOR	12–15 July 1944	U.S. air interdiction of Pô River bridges to cut off German reinforcements in Italy.
MANDIBLES	1940	Proposed British operation against German forces in the Dodecanese Islands.
MANHATTAN	1942–1945	Allied atomic energy program.
MANHOLE	February 1944	RAF operation to infiltrate a Soviet advisor team into Yugoslavia by glider.
MANNA	23 September 1944	British Special Boat Squadron insertion into southern Greece.
MARIE	1940–1941	Proposed Anglo-Free French operation against the port of Djibouti, Ethiopia.
MARKET	17–26 September 1944	British, Polish, and U.S. airborne and glider portion of Operation MARKET-GARDEN.
MAURICE	April 1940	British assault in central Norway.
MENACE	23–25 September 1940	French attempt to seize Dakar, Senegal.
M.G.I.	March 1942	Royal Navy convoy to resupply Malta.
MILLENNIUM	30–31 May 1942	First 1,000-bomber raid on Cologne, Germany.
MINCEMEAT	Spring 1943	Allied deception plan for Operation HUSKY.
MINERVA	6 November 1942	Embarkation of General Henri Giraud from southern France.
MONTAGNARD	1943	Build up of French Resistance forces near Vercours, France.
MULBERRIES	1944	Artificial harbors used during Operation OVERLORD.
MUSKET	1943	Proposed Allied amphibious invasion of Taranto, Italy.
MUSKETOON	September 1942	British commando operation to destroy a power station in Norway.
MUSTANG	1943	Planned overland seizure of Naples after initial landings at Calabria.
NEPTUNE	6 June 1944	The assault phase, to include the naval portion of Operation OVERLORD.
NESTEGG	9 May 1945	Allied reoccupation of the Channel Islands.
NOAH'S ARK	Fall 1944	Allied air-supported guerrilla operations in the Balkans and Greece.
NUNTON	March 1944	Allied cover and deception plan in Italy.

Allied (except Soviet) Operational Code Names

Code Name	Date	Remarks
OCTAGON	September 1944	Code name for the second Quebec Conference.
OCTOBER ACCOLADE	October 1943	Proposed British operation to seize island of Rhodes.
OLIVE	25 August 1944	Allied attack on the German Gothic Line in northern Italy.
OMAHA	June 1944	U.S. V Corps invasion beach on the Calvados coast of Normandy.
OVERCAST	July 1945	Relocation of German scientists and engineers to the U.S. after the war.
OVERLORD	6 June 1944	Allied invasion of Normandy, France.
OYSTER	1942	RAF daylight attack on the Phillips factory in Eindhoven, Netherlands.
PANTHER	17 January 1944	British X Corps ground offensive across the Garigiano River, Italy.
PAPER CLIP	April–May 1945	American operation to seek enemy technical experts.
PEDESTAL	3–15 August 1942	Royal Navy convoy to resupply Malta.
PENITENT	1943	Proposed Allied operations on the Dalmatian coast of Yugoslavia.
PERPETUAL	November 1941	British reinforcement of Malta.
PERPETUAL	8 November 1942	Allied Eastern Task Force landing at Bejaia, Algeria.
PICKET	March 1942	British reinforcement of Malta.
PILGRIM	1942	U.S. plans to seize the Spanish Canaries and other Atlantic Ocean islands.
PINPOINT	July 1942	British reinforcement of Malta.
PIRATE	1943	British and Canadian exercise by Force J in preparation for Operation NEPTUNE.
PLOUGH	1942	Proposed Allied commando operations in Norway.
PLUNDER	23 March 1945	British 21st Army Group offensive across the Rhine River.
PLUTO	1944	Undersea oil supply to Operation OVERLORD.
POINTBLANK	10 June 1943– 16 April 1945	The Combined Bomber Offensive against Germany.
PORTCULLIS	December 1942	Royal Navy convoy to resupply Malta from Alexandria, Egypt.
PRINCIPAL	January 1943	British attacks against Italian ships at Palermo, Sicily.
PUGILIST-GALLOP	Spring 1943	Proposed Allied final attack on the Mareth Line in Tunisia.
PUMA	1942	Projected invasion of the Canary Islands.

Allied (except Soviet) Operational Code Names

Code Name	Date	Remarks
QUADRANT	August 1943	Code name for first Quebec Conference.
QUEEN	16–24 November 1944	U.S. 12th Army Group offensive between the Wurm and Roer rivers in Germany.
QUICKSILVER	1943–1944	Deception operations in concert with Operation OVERLORD.
R4	April 1940	British plan to occupy Norwegian ports in the event of a German invasion.
RAILWAY	June 1941	British reinforcement of Malta.
RAINBOW	1939–1941	Series of U.S. contingency plans (ORANGE, YELLOW, GREEN, and BLUE) in the case of war with the Axis.
RANKIN	1940–1944	A series of Allied plans for the immediate occupation of Europe in the event of a sudden German collapse.
RATTLE	1943	Combined operations meeting to discuss plans for Operation OVERLORD.
RATWEEK	1944	Allied plans to interdict German troops withdrawing from Yugoslavia.
RED STOCKING	1942–1945	Allied overflights to intercept agent signals.
RESERVIST	8 November 1942	Landing and seizure of strategic points at Oran, Algeria, to prevent sabotage.
RETRIBUTION	April–June 1943	Operations to keep German and Italian forces from escaping to Italy after their defeat in Northwest Africa.
REUNION	August 1944	Evacuation of more than 1,000 U.S. fliers from Romania and 300 from Bulgaria after Romania's withdrawal from the Axis.
RHUBARB	Mid–1941	RAF attacks against the German-held coast of France.
ROAST	1 April 1945	Allied operations to clear Comacchio Spit, Italy.
ROCKET	June 1941	British reinforcement of Malta.
ROMEO	15 August 1944	French commando raid on Cap Negre, France; part of Operation DRAGOON.
ROOFTREE	November 1942	Joint army-navy plan for participation in Operation TORCH.
ROSE	9 April 1945	Allied ground offensive to reduce the Ruhr pocket in Germany.
ROSEBUD	June 1944	Deception operation after D-Day invasion; also called Operation FORTITUDE SOUTH II.
ROUNDHAMMER	1943	An early cross-channel invasion plan, falling between SLEDGEHAMMER and ROUND-UP.

Allied (except Soviet) Operational Code Names

Code Name	Date	Remarks
ROUND-UP	1941–1943	Proposed Allied plans for a cross-channel invasion of northwestern Europe.
ROYAL FLUSH	June 1944	USAAF air strikes against German trains, supply points, and airfields behind the Normandy invasion areas.
RUGBY	15 August 1944	Allied airdrop portion of DRAGOON.
RUPERT	10 April 1940	Allied expedition to Narvik, Norway.
RUTTER	July 1942	Early code name for Operation JUBILEE.
SALIENT	June 1942	British reinforcement of Malta.
SATIN	December 1942	Proposed Allied amphibious landing at Sfax, Tunisia.
SATURN	1944	Proposed Allied plans for the occupation of Turkey.
SCIPIO	6 April 1942	British Eighth Army attack at Wadi Akarit.
SCORCHER	May–June 1941	British occupation of Crete.
SEAGULL	September 1942	British operation to destroy German mines off Sulitjelma, Norway.
SEXTANT	1943 November	Code name for the Cairo Conference.
SHINGLE	22 January 1944	Allied amphibious landing at Anzio, Italy.
SHRAPNEL	1940–1941	British plan to occupy the Cape Verde Islands.
SICKLE	1942	Movement of U.S. air forces to Britain.
SITKA	1944	Allied expedition to Port Cros near Levant Island, France.
SKYSCRAPER	Spring 1943	Combined commanders plans for the cross-channel invasion.
SLAPSTICK	9 September 1943	British airborne landing at Taranto, Italy, in support of Operations AVALANCHE and BAYTOWN.
SLEDGEHAMMER	Fall 1942	Proposed limited cross-channel invasion of northwestern Europe.
SOAPSUDS	1943	Early code name for Operation TIDAL WAVE.
SOURCE	12 September 1943	British midget submarine attack on the German battleship *Tirpitz* at Alten Fjord, Norway.
SPLICE	May 1941	British reinforcement of Malta.
SPOTTER	May 1942	British reinforcement of Malta.
SPRING	25 July 1944	Canadian First Army operation near Caen, France—a follow-up to Operation GOODWOOD.
SPRINGBOARD	1942	Proposed U.S. seizure of Madeira Islands, Portugal.

Allied (except Soviet) Operational Code Names

Code Name	Date	Remarks
STARKEY	1943	Allied deception operations against the Pas-de-Calais section of France.
STATESMAN	1943	Early code name for Operation TIDAL WAVE.
STATUS	September 1941	British reinforcement of Malta.
STONEHENGE	November 1942	Royal Navy convoy to resupply Malta from Alexandria, Egypt.
STRANGLE	15 March–10 May 1944	Allied air interdiction in central Italy.
STUD	June 1944	USAAF air strikes against German trains, supply points, and other targets behind the Normandy invasion areas.
STYLE	June 1942	British reinforcement of Malta.
SUBSTANCE	July 1941	Royal Navy convoy to resupply Malta from Gibraltar.
SUNRISE	April 1945	Negotiations for surrender of German forces in Italy to the Allies.
SUPERCHARGE	2 November 1942	Follow-up to Operation LIGHTFOOT in Egypt.
SUPER-GYMNAST	1942	*See* GYMNAST.
SUSSEX	9 April–31 August 1944	The parachute insertion of intelligence teams into France to support the Allied OVERLORD landings.
SWALLOW	18 October 1942	The parachute insertion of Norwegian commandos to prepare for the raid on the Norsk Hydro heavy water facility.
SWAMP	June 1944	RAF attacks on German U-boats in defense of Operation OVERLORD.
SWORD	June 1944	Code name for Dourves beach at Normandy.
SWORDHILT	August 1944	Planned airborne-amphibious assault to seize the area east of Brest, France.
SYMBOL	January 1942	Code name for the Casablanca Conference.
TALISMAN	1945	Early name for Operation ECLIPSE.
TAXABLE	June 1944	Deception operation for supposed Anglo-American fleet near Le Havre, France.
TERMINAL	8 November 1942	Operations in Algiers harbor.
TERMINAL	July–August 1945	Code name for the Potsdam Conference.
THRUSTER	1942	Proposed Allied invasion of the Azores.
THUNDERBOLT	8 November 1944	U.S. ground offensive toward Metz, France.
THUNDERCLAP	1945	RAF plan to destroy German morale, which culminated in the 13–14 February attack on Dresden.

Allied (except Soviet) Operational Code Names

Code Name	Date	Remarks
THWART	July 1940	Submarine landing of British agents in Norway.
TIDAL WAVE	1 August 1943	U.S air attack on the Ploeşti, Romania, oilfields, from bases in North Africa.
TIGER	May 1941	British convoy to deliver fighter aircraft from Gibraltar to Alexandria, Egypt, using merchant ships.
TIGER	26 April 1944	U.S. VII Corps rehearsal for Operation OVERLORD.
TIGERFISH	27 November 1944	RAF Bomber Command raid against Freiburg, Germany
TINDALL	1943	Allied deception operations in Norway.
TOKEN	March 1945	Rehearsal for Allied airborne assault across the Rhine River.
TOLSTOY	October 1944	Code name for the second Moscow Conference.
TOPFLIGHT	June 1944	Signal for the release of press information on the OVERLORD landings.
TORCH	8 November 1942	Allied amphibious landings in Morocco and Algeria.
TORTURE	June 1944	See Operation BIBENDUM.
TOTAL GERMANY	3 September 1939	Signal to Royal Navy forces that a state of war existed between Britain and Germany.
TOTALIZE	7–10 August 1944	Canadian ground offensive toward Falaise, France.
TRACER	June 1941	British reinforcement of Malta.
TRACTABLE	14–16 August 1944	Second Allied attack toward Falaise, France.
TRANSFIGURE	August 1944	Allied plans for an airborne drop west of the Seine River, France.
TREACLE	August 1941	Royal Navy insertion of the Polish Carpathian Brigade into Tobruk to relieve the Australian 18th Infantry Brigade.
TRIDENT	May 1943	Code name for the Washington Conference.
TROJAN HORSE	1943	Deception operation, part of Operation MINCEMEAT.
TUBE ALLOYS	1942–1945	British participation in the atomic bomb project.
TUNGSTEN	April 1944	Royal Navy carrier-based air attacks against the battleship *Tirpitz* in Norway.
UNDERTONE	15 March 1945	U.S. Seventh Army offensive in the Saar-Palatinate region of Germany.
UPSILON	November 1942	Landing supplies for British coast watchers on the Norwegian coast.

Allied (except Soviet) Operational Code Names

Code Name	Date	Remarks
UTAH	June 1944	Code name for the beach at Normandy used by the U.S. VII Corps on D-Day.
VARSITY	24 March 1945	Allied airborne operation across the Rhine River in support of Operation PLUNDER.
VENERABLE	14 April 1945	French operation to open the port of Bordeaux.
VENETTA	1944	Deception operation in southern France.
VENUS	September 1943	British submarine resupply on the coast of Norway.
VERITABLE	7 February 1945	Canadian offensive on northwest Germany between the Maas and Rhine rivers.
VERT	6 June 1944	"GREEN," French operation to sabotage German rail and ground communications lines in support of Operation OVERLORD.
VIGOROUS	June 1942	Royal Navy convoy to resupply Malta from Alexandria, Egypt.
VIOLET	6 June 1944	French operation to sabotage telephone lines in support of Operation OVERLORD.
VITTLES	26 June 1948–31 October 1949	The Berlin Airlift.
VULCAN	6–9 May 1943	Final Allied ground offensive in Tunisia against German forces on Cap Bon.
WADHAM	1943	Proposed Allied landings on the Cotentin Peninsula in France.
WEBFOOT	January 1943	Allied rehearsal for Operation SHINGLE.
WHIPCORD	November 1941	Aborted British plan for the invasion of Sicily.
WHITE	November 1940	British reinforcement of Malta.
WILFRED	April 1940	Royal Navy operations to support mining and troop landings in Norway.
WINCH	April 1941	British reinforcement of Malta.
WINDOW	July 1943	British name for chaff, tinfoil strips dropped by aircraft to jam German radars.
WOP	17 March 1943	Opening attack by the U.S. II Corps against Gafsa, Tunisia.
WORKSHOP	1940–1941	Proposed British plan to capture the Italian island of Pantelleria.
WYKONAĆ PEKING	30 Aug 1939	"INITIATE PEKING," code word warning the Polish Navy of imminent war.
ZACHOD	September 1939	"WEST," Polish plans to defend against a German attack.

Allied (except Soviet) Operational Code Names

Code Name	Date	Remarks
ZEBRA	25 June 1944	USAAF airdrop of supplies to the French Maquis.
ZEPPELIN	Spring 1943	Deception plan in preparation for Operation HUSKY.

Allied Code Names for Persons and Groups

Code Name	Person or Group
ADMIRAL Q	U.S. President Franklin D. Roosevelt.
AGENT	British Prime Minister Winston S. Churchill.
ALI BABA	The Soviets.
BRAID	U.S. General George C. Marshall.
BRISSEX	British intelligence agents dropped into Normandy in June 1944.
CAMEL	U.S. 36th Infantry Division in southern France, 1944.
CARGO	U.S. President Franklin D. Roosevelt.
CASANOVA	U.S. 95th Infantry Division in France, 1944.
CELESTES	Chinese Premier Chaing Kai-shek (for the Cairo Conference).
COLLONDON	U.S. Secretary of State Edward R. Stettinius.
COLONEL WARDEN	British Prime Minister Winston S. Churchill.
COMPOST	British Foreign Secretary Anthony Eden.
DELTA	U.S. 45th Infantry Division in southern France, 1944.
DESTINY	The U.S. army.
DUCKPIN	U.S. General Dwight D. Eisenhower.
DUNKER	Soviet Foreign Minister Vyacheslav Molotov.
EAGLE	U.S. General Mark W. Clark.
EAGLE TAC	U.S. General Omar N. Bradley's headquarters.
ECUADOR	The Greeks.
FORMER NAVAL PERSON	British Prime Minister Winston S. Churchill.
GLYPTIC	Soviet Premier Josef Stalin.
GOLLIWOG	The Free French.
HANGMAN	Clandestine British SOE organization in Norway.
ICEBLINK	U.S. Secretary of State James F. Byrnes.
IVAN	Soviet Premier Josef Stalin.
KILTING	U.S. President Harry S Truman.
KINGPIN	French General Henri Giraud.
LAUNDRESS	The Vichy French.
LONDON	U.S. VIII Corps near Wesel, Germany.
LOOK	U.S. General Dwight D. Eisenhower.
LUCKY	U.S. Third Army.
MOSSBANK	Vichy French Foreign Minister Pierre Laval.

Allied Code Names for Persons and Groups

Code Name	Person or Group
PARIS	U.S. XVIII Corps west of Erle, Germany.
PETER	Soviet Foreign Minister Vyacheslav Molotov.
PINETREE	The headquarters of the VIII Bomber Command, at High Wycombe, England.
PRINCESS	Underground intelligence network in Denmark.
SHARPENER	U.S. General Dwight D. Eisenhower's advanced command post at Portsmouth, England, May 1944.
SHELLBURST	Forward headquarters of SHAEF at Tournieres, France, August 1944.
SINBAD	U.S. Secretary of State Cordell Hull.
SKYE	Bogus American unit in Scotland; part of Operation FORTITUDE NORTH.
TELEGRAPH	U.S. General Walter Bedell Smith.
WIDEWING	SHAEF headquarters at Bushy Park, near London.
VICTOR	British Prime Minister Winston S. Churchill.

Soviet Operational Code Names

Code Name	Date	Remarks
BAGRATION	22 June 1944	Offensive against German Army Group Center. Named after a nineteenth-century Russian general.
MALYY SATURN	16 December 1942	"LITTLE SATURN," code name for reduced version of Operation SATURN.
MARS	25 November 1942	Offensive against the German Ninth Army in the Rzhev salient.
KOLTSO	January 1943	"RING," final operation for the destruction of German forces encircled near Stalingrad.
KUTUZOV	12 July 1943	Counteroffensive against the Orel salient during the battle of Kursk.
RUMYANTSEV	August 1943	Second stage of the battle of Kursk.
SATURN	December 1942	Proposed creation of a second ring at Stalingrad using forces of the Southwest Front and the Voronezh Front.
SINYAVINO	19 August–30 September 1942	Relief operation for Leningrad.
STAR	2 February–3 March 1943	Offensive by the Voronezh Front and the south wing of the Bryansk Front against German Army Group B to liberate the Kharkov industrial area.
URANUS	19 November 1942	Encirclement of German forces at Stalingrad.

Axis Code Names

Code Name	Date	Remarks
AB-AKTION	1939–1942	*Ausserordenlusche Befriedungsaktion,* "Extraordinary Pacification Action," liquidation of Polish intelligentsia.
ACHSE	1943	"AXIS," plans for capture or destruction of Italian forces and occupation of Italy in event of government collapse or military surrender. Partially implemented in September 1943. Also known earlier as operations *ALARICH* and *KONSTANTIN.*
ADLERHORST	1940–1944	"EAGLE'S NEST," Hitler's Bavarian headquarters.
ADLERTAG	13 August 1940	"EAGLE DAY," *Luftwaffe* offensive against RAF bases in Britain.
AIDA	21 January–26 May 1942	With Italy, offensive operations against the British Eighth Army in Libya and Egypt.
ALARICH	1943	Early name for Operation *ACHSE.*
ALPENVEILCHEN	11 January 1941	"ALPINE VIOLETTES," proposed plan to reinforce Italian forces in Albania.
ALTONA	22 June 1941	Cancellation code word for Operation *BARBAROSSA.*
AMERIKA	September 1939	Hitler's command train during the Polish campaign.
ANGRIFFSTAG	10 May 1940	"ATTACK DAY," offensive in the west; also called *A-Tag,* "A-Day.*"
ANTON	11 November 1942	Part of ATTILA, occupation of Vichy France after Allied Operation TORCH landings and French surrender.
ASTER	Spring 1945	Withdrawal of German troops from the Baltic states.
ATTILA	11 November 1942	Plan for occupation of Vichy France.
AUFBAU OST	9 August–22 June 1941	"BUILD-UP EAST," preparations for Operation BARBAROSSA.
AUGSBURG	Late 1939	Delay in the western offensive.
AUSLADUNG	February 1943	"UNLOADING," efforts to extend the Tunis bridgehead. Part of Operation *OCHSENKOPF.*
BAEDECKER RAIDS	1942–1943	Bomber raids on historic British towns. Also called "Cathedral Raids." Named after Karl Baedecker, ninetenth-century author of travel guides.
BARBAROSSA	22 June 1941	"RED BEARD," invasion of the Soviet Union.
BEOWULF	September–October 1941	Occupation of the Baltic islands.
BERNHARD	1942–1945	Counterfeiting of British five-pound notes.

Axis Code Names

Code Name	Date	Remarks
BETTELSTAB	Summer 1942	"BEGGAR'S STAFF," proposed operations against the Oranienbaum pocket in the Soviet Union.
BIRKE	3 October 1944	"BIRCH," withdrawal of the German Twentieth Army from northern Russia and Finland into Norway.
BIRKHAHN	1945	"BLACK COCK," evacuation of German troops from Norway.
BLAU	Spring 1941	"BLUE," proposed plans for invasion of Caucasus region before BARBAROSSA.
BLAU	June 1942	Offensive of the northern wing of Army Group South toward Voronezh.
BLAUFUCHS	June 1941	"BLUE FOX," transferring XXXVI Infantry Korps from Germany to Norway and Finland in preparation for Operation BARBAROSSA.
BLÜCHER	August 1942	Assault against the Kerch Strait in the Crimea.
BLUME	1943–1944	"FLOWER," code name used for alert of the Allied invasion of Western Europe.
BODENPLATTE	1 January 1945	"BASE PLATE," *Luftwaffe* attacks on Allied airfields in the Low Countries and northern France.
BRAUNSCHWEIG	July 1942	"BRUNSWICK," Army Group South offensive toward Stalingrad and the Caucasus.
BRÜCKENSCHLAG	1942	"BRIDGING," proposed offensive to close the Toropets bulge in the Soviet Union.
BÜFFEL-BEWEGUNG	1943	"BUFFALO STAMPEDE," Army Group Center offensive in central Russia.
CERBERUS	11–12 February 1942	Breakout of the battleships *Gneisenau* and *Scharnhorst* from Brest, France, and the "Channel Dash" to the North Sea.
CHRISTOPHERUS	January 1942	Appropriation of civilian vehicles for operations in the Soviet Union.
CLAUSEWITZ	June 1942	Operation *BLAU,* Phase II.
CLAUSEWITZ	April 1942	The German defense of central Berlin.
COTTBUS	3–23 June 1943	Counter-partisan offensive in Polotsk-Borisov-Lemel region of Byelorussia.
DAMPFHAMMER	June 1942	"STEAM HAMMER," Operation *BLAU,* Phase III.
DANZIG	Late 1939	Order to proceed with the offensive in the west.
DERFFLINGER	Mid–1942	Planned Ninth Army drive from Rzhev to Ostashkov in the Soviet Union.

Axis Code Names

Code Name	Date	Remarks
DONNERKIEL	21 March–2 May 1943	"THUNDER KEEL," antipartisan offensive in the Velizh-Vitebsk region of Byelorussia.
DONNERSCHLAG	December 1942	"THUNDERBOLT," planned breakout of the Sixth Army from Stalingrad.
DORTMUND	22 June 1941	Go-ahead code word for Operation *BARBAROSSA*.
DREIECK UND VIERECK	16–30 September 1942	"TRIANGLE AND QUADRANGLE," antipartisan offensive in Bryansk region of Russia.
EDELWEISS	31 July 1942	German advance into the Caucasus.
EICHE	12 September 1943	"OAK," Skorzeny's rescue of Mussolini at Gran Sasso.
EILBOTE	18 January 1943	"EXPRESS COURIER," operation to capture the Kebir River dam and drive the French off the Eastern Dorsal in Tunisia.
EINHORN	1944	"UNICORN," *See GEMSBOCK*.
EISENHAMMER	Spring 1944	"IRON HAMMER," attacks on Allied shipping.
ELBE	Late 1939	Early code name for *AUGSBURG*.
ELEFANT	January 1942	"ELEPHANT," appropriation of civilian trucks for operations in the Soviet Union.
ENDLÖSUNG	20 January 1942	"FINAL SOLUTION," the plan to exterminate the Jews of Europe.
ENGLANDSPIEL	March 1942	"ENGLAND GAME," a highly successful *Abwehr* operation to turn SOE operations in the Netherlands.
ERNTEFEST	November 1943	"HARVEST FESTIVAL," the liquidation of the Jews in the Majdanek, Poniatowa, and Trawniki concentration camps.
FALL BLAU	1938–1939	"Case BLUE," plans for the *Luftwaffe* offensive against Britain.
FALL GELB	1939	"Case YELLOW," plan for the invasion of France, Belgium, and the Netherlands.
FALL GRÜN	1938	"Case GREEN," proposed attack on Czechoslovakia.
FALL GRÜN	1940	"Case GREEN," planned invasion of Ireland.
FALL ROT	June 1940	"Case RED," second half of the Battle of France; also called simply *ROT*.
FALL WEISS	1 September 1939	"Case WHITE," the invasion of Poland.
FELIX	Late 1940	Proposed plans to capture Gibraltar.
FELIX-HEINRICH	Late 1941	Proposed plans to capture Gibraltar after Operation BARBAROSSA.

Axis Code Names

Code Name	Date	Remarks
FELSENNEST	10 May–6 June 1940	"AERIE," Hitler's field headquarters on the western front.
FEUERWEHR	1944	"FIRE BRIGADE," antipartisan/anti-guerrilla operations in northern Greece.
FEUERZAUBER	1942	"FIRE MAGIC," early name for Operation *NORDLICHT*.
FISCHFANG	16 February 1943	"FISH TRAP," German counterattack against the Allied Beachhead at Anzio.
FISCHREIHER	July–November 1942	"HERON," attack on Stalingrad by Army Group B.
FREISCHÜTZ	21–30 May 1943	"FREE MARKSMAN," antipartisan operation in the Bryansk region of Russia.
FRIDERICUS	19 May 1942	General offensive toward the Dneiper River in the Soviet Union.
FRITZ	1941	Early name for Operation *BARBAROSSA*.
FRÜHLINGS-ERWACHEN	6 March 1945	"AWAKENING OF SPRING," Army Group South offensive south of Budapest, Hungary.
FRÜHLINGS-FEST	April 1943	"SPRING FESTIVAL," antipartisan operation in the Ushachi region of Byelorussia.
FRÜHLINGS-WIND	14 February 1943	"SPRING WIND," Fifth Panzer Army attack on Sidi-bou-Zid, Tunisia.
FÜNFUNDZWANZIG	6 April 1941	"25," taken from *Führer* Directive 25; the invasion of Yugoslavia.
GEMSBOCK	6–14 June 1944	Antipartisan/antiguerrilla offensive in Yugoslavia and Albania.
GEORG	Fall 1942	Eighteenth Army in Operation *NORDLICHT*.
GÖTZ VON BERLICHINGEN	April 1942	*Luftwaffe* air strikes against Soviet naval forces at Leningrad.
GERTRUD	1942	Proposed plan to invade Turkey in event of Turkish alliance with Allies.
GISELA	1942	Proposed plan for the occupation of Spain and Portugal.
GNEISENAU	1944	German position line on the Crimea flanking Simferopol.
GOTENKOPF	1943	"GOTH'S HEAD," bridgehead on the Taman Peninsula, eastern side of the Kerch Strait in the Soviet Union.
GRANIT	10–11 May 1940	"GRANITE," glider assault on Fort Eben Emael, Belgium.
GREIF	16 December 1944	"GRIFFEN," diversionary operations supporting *WACHT AM RHEIN*.

Axis Code Names

Code Name	Date	Remarks
GRÜN	1937	"GREEN," plans to concentrate German land forces in case of a general European war.
HABICHT	March 1943	"HAWK," proposed crossing of the Donets River in the Chuguyev-Kupyansk region of the Soviet Union.
HAGEN	July 1943	Fortification line constructed across the base of the Orel salient.
HAIFISCH	April–August 1941	"SHARK," deception plan for *BARBAROSSA.*
HANNOVER	24 May 1942	Operation against the Soviet pocket west of Vyazma.
HARPUNE	Fall 1940–July 1941	"HARPOON," cover operations for *BARBAROSSA.*
HARPUNE NORD	1941	"HARPOON NORTH," diversionary operations in Norway and Denmark.
HARPUNE SÜD	1941	"HARPOON SOUTH," diversionary operations along the Brittany coast of France.
HARTMUT	April 1940	Submarine operations in support of Operation *WESERÜBUNG.*
HEINRICH	November 1943	Antipartisan operation west of Nevel in the Soviet Union.
HERBST-GEWITTER	Late 1943	"AUTUMN THUNDERSTORM," antipartisan operations on Yugoslavia's Dalmatian coast and Korcula Island.
HERBSTNEBEL	20 April 1945	"AUTUMN MIST," evacuation of the Po River plain in Italy. Also an early code name for the Ardennes Offensive.
HERBSTREISE	Fall 1940	"AUTUMN JOURNEY," planned deception landings in support of Operation *SEELÖWE.*
HERKULES	1942	"HERCULES," plans for the invasion of Malta.
HEU-AKTION	June 1944	"HAY ACTION," Rosenberg's forced relocation of workers from the east to Germany.
HIMMLER	31 August 1939	"Polish" attack on Germany faked by the SS as an excuse for German invasion of Poland.
HORRIDO	Early 1944	Antipartisan offensive in Northern Greece and Albania.
HUNDESOHN	8 September 1944	"SON OF A BITCH," German occupation of Bulgarian-occupied territory after Bulgaria's declaration of war on Germany.
IKARUS	June 1940	Proposed invasion of Iceland.

Axis Code Names

Code Name	Date	Remarks
ILONA	1942	Proposed invasion of Spain.
ISABELLA	November 1940	Proposed invasion of Portugal as an extension of Operation *FELIX*.
JUDAS	October 1944	Disarmament and capture of Bulgarian troops after the surrender of Bulgaria.
JUNO	June 1940	Naval operations around Norway.
KAMELIE	1942	Planned occupation of Corsica.
KATHLEEN	1940	Proposed invasion of Ireland.
KLABAUTERMANN	July 1942	"HOBGOBLIN," torpedo boat operations on Lake Lagoda in the Soviet Union.
KLETTE I	October 1942	"BURR," antipartisan offensives in the Kletnya-Mamakerka region of Russia.
KLETTE II	15 January–9 February 1943	Same as Operation *KLETTE I*.
KÖNIGSBERG	Winter 1942	Battle line established west of Moscow.
KONSERVEN	31 August 1939	"CANNED GOODS," dead German political prisoners dressed in Polish uniforms as part of the cover for Operation HIMMLER.
KONSTANTIN	September 1943	Occupation of Italian-held territory in the Balkans following Italy's surrender.
KOPENHAGEN	September 1943	"COPENHAGEN," German plans to seize the Mt. Cenis Pass as part of *ACHSE*.
KORALLE	1944	"CORAL," see Operation *NEPTUN*.
KORMORAN	22 May–20 June 1942	"CORMORANT," antipartisan offensive in the Borisov-Lepel region of Byelorussia.
KREML	May–June 1942	"KREMLIN," deception operations in the Soviet Union.
KREUZOTTER	5 August 1044	"VIPER," antiguerrilla operations in central and northern Greece.
KUGELBLITZ	22 February–8 March 1943	"LIGHTENING BALL," antipartisan offensive in the Surazh region of Byelorussia.
KUGELBLITZ	Late 1943	Antipartisan operations in Yugoslavia.
LACHSFANG	Summer-Fall 1942	"SALMON TRAP," proposed joint offensive with Finland against the Kandalaksha and Belomorsk regions of Russia.
LEHRGANG	11–17 August 1943	"COURSE OF INSTRUCTION," evacuation of German troops from Sicily to the Italian mainland.
LEOPARD	12–16 November 1943	"LEOPARD," German attack on the island of Leros.

Axis Code Names

Code Name	Date	Remarks
LEUTHEN	1945	Deployment of training units to combat zones (other than the *Volkssturm* and training divisions already committed to combat).
LILA	27 November 1942	"LILAC," occupation of Toulon, France, and the seizure of the French fleet, after Allied Operation TORCH.
LOGE	1940	"THEATER BOX," code name for London during Battle of Britain.
LONG JOHN	November 1943	Planned assassination of Stalin and Churchill at Teheran, Iran.
LÜTTICH	August 1944	Proposed counteroffensive to throw the Allies back off the Continent.
MAIGEWITTER	Mid–May 1943	"MAY THUNDERSTORM," anti-partisan offensive in the Polotsk lowlands of Byelorussia.
MAIGEWITTER	April 1944	"MAY THUNDERSTORM," anti-partisan offensive in Yugoslavia, Albania, and northern Greece.
MARGARETHE I	19 March 1944	Occupation of Hungary.
MARGARETHE II	1944	Planned occupation of Romania.
MARITA	6 April 1941	Invasion of Yugoslavia and Greece.
MERKUR	20 May 1941	"MERCURY," airborne and sea landings, Crete.
MICKEY MAUS	15 October 1944	"MICKEY MOUSE," the kidnapping of the son of Hungarian regent Miklós Horthy by SS commandos.
MITTELMEER	December 1940–January 1941	"MEDITERRANEAN SEA," air operations in that area.
MOONLIGHT SONATA	14 November 1940	*Luftwaffe* night attack on Coventry, England.
MOORBRAND	Mid–1942	"SWAMP FIRE," operation to destroy the Pogostye salient on the eastern front.
MORASTFIEBER	Early 1942	"MARSH FEVER," antipartisan offensive in Russia.
MORGENLUFT	15 February 1943	"MORNING AIR," *Afrika Korps* attack on Gafsa, Tunisia, following *FRÜHLINGS-WIND*.
MORGENRÖTE	4 February 1944	"DAWN," initial counteroffensive against the Anzio beachhead.
MÜNCHEN	19–31 March 1942	"MUNICH," antipartisan offensive in the Yelnya-Dorogobuzh region of Russia.
NACHBARHILFE	19 May–19 June 1943	"GOOD NEIGHBOR," antipartisan offensive in the Kletnya-Mamakerka region of Russia.

Axis Code Names

Code Name	Date	Remarks
NAUMBERG	June 1940	Proposed amphibious landings at Lyngen Fjord, Norway, for the relief of Narvik.
NEPTUN	1944	"NEPTUNE," antipartisan/antiguerrilla operations on Aegean and Adriatic islands.
NORD	1941	"NORTH," first code name for invasion of Norway.
NORDLICHT	Fall 1942	"NORTHERN LIGHTS," proposed offensive against Leningrad.
NORDMARK	February 1940	"NORTHERN BORDER," operation by battleships *Gneisenau* and *Scharnhorst* to raid British convoys between Norway and the Shetlands.
NORDPOL	1942–1944	"NORTH POLE," German control of British and Dutch intelligence networks in Belgium and Holland.
NORDWIND	31 December 1944	"NORTH WIND," last German ground offensive of the war in northern Alsace.
OCHSENKOPF	26 February 1943	"OX HEAD," operation to extend the Tunis bridgehead by capturing Beja and Medjez- el-Bab.
OLDENBURG	June 1941	Economic plan to exploit occupied Soviet territory.
OLIVENERNTE	January 1943	"OLIVE HARVEST," proposed operation to capture Medjez-el-Bab, Tunisia.
ORKAN	Mid–1942	"TORNADO," proposed operation to eliminate the Sukhinichi salient in the Soviet Union.
OTTO	1937–1938	Plans for the annexation of Austria.
OTTO	October 1940–May 1941	The *Wehrmacht's* program for improving road and rail facilities leading toward the Soviet border.
PANTHER	Late 1943	Antiguerrilla offensive in northern Greece.
PANTHER	1943–1944	Northern half of the projected East Wall.
PARKPLATZ	Spring 1943	"PARKING LOT," with Finland, planned offensive to capture Leningrad.
PASTORIUS	12 June 1942	Failed sabotage mission in the United States by German agents.
PAUKENSCHLAG	Early 1942	"DRUMBEAT," U-boat attacks on U.S shipping off the North American coast.
POLARFUCHS	July 1941	"POLAR FOX," ground offensive from Norway into the northern Soviet Union as part of *BARBAROSSA*.
POLARFUCHS	1943	Plans for the invasion of Sweden.
RAUBTIER	15 March 1942	"BEAST OF PREY," operation against Volkhov pocket in the Soviet Union.

Code Name	Date	Remarks
REGENBOGEN	31 December 1942	"RAINBOW," attack by the *Lutzow* and *Hipper* on Allied northern convoys.
REGENSCHAUER	April 1943	"RAIN SHOWER," antipartisan offensive in the Ushachi region of Byelorussia.
REINHARD	1942–1943	The systematic annihilation of the Jews in the General Government of Poland. Named after Heydrich.
RENTIER	February–March 1944	"REINDEER," antiguerrilla operation in northern Greece.
RHEIN	1939	Early code name for Operation *DANZIG*.
RHEINGOLD	January 1942	"RHINE GOLD," calling up previously deferred men to form six new divisions.
RHEINÜBUNG	21–27 May 1941	"RHINE EXERCISE," Atlantic raid by the *Bismarck* and *Prinz Eugen.*
RICHARD	1937–38	Plans for possible war with a Communist Spain.
ROLAND	17 June 1943	Proposed offensive against the Voronezh Front during final stages of the battle of Kursk.
ROLLBAHN	1943–1944	"HIGHWAY," fortification line paralleling the Leningrad-Chudovo highway.
RÖSLEIN	July–August 1944	Antiguerrilla operations in northern Greece and Albania.
RÖSSELSPRUNG	5–7 July 1942	"KNIGHT'S JUMP," attack on Allied convoy PQ-17.
RÖSSELSPRUNG	25 May 1944	Surprise airborne raid on Tito's headquarters.
ROT	June 1940	"RED," second half of the battle of France.
RÜBEZAHL	12 August 1944	Antipartisan offensive in Yugoslavia.
SCHAMIL	1942	Proposed airborne drop on Maikop oil fields in the Caucasus.
SCHILD UND SCHWERT	1944	"SHIELD AND SWORD," proposed Army Group North offensive in the Ukraine.
SCHLINGPFLANZE	October 1942	"VINE," proposed operation to widen the corridor to the Demyansk pocket in the Soviet Union.
SCHNEESTURM	Late 1943	"SNOWSTORM," antipartisan offensive in Yugoslavia.
SCHUTZWALL	1944	"BASTION," fortification line south of Ivalo, Finland.
SCHWARZ	May–June 1943	"BLACK," offensive against the Četniks in Yugoslavia.

Axis Code Names

Code Name	Date	Remarks
SCHWARZ	9 September 1943	Military takeover of Italy after its surrender; part of *ACHSE*.
SEELÖWE	Late 1940	"SEA LION," planned invasion of Britain.
SEYDLITZ	2 July 1942	Offensive west of Sychevka in the Soviet Union.
SIEGFRIED	July 1942	Advance by the center of Army Group South from Kharkov to Stalingrad.
SILBERFUCHS	May–June 1941	"SILVER FOX," troop buildup in Finland in preparation for Operation *BARBAROSSA*.
SILBERFUCHS	1 July–24 November 1941	With Finland, offensive in Lapland and Finland toward Murmansk, Russia.
SILBERSTREIF	May–July 1943	"SILVER STREAK," propaganda campaign to increase Soviet desertions.
SONNENBLUME	January–February 1941	"SUNFLOWER," movement of German troops to North Africa.
SONNENWENDE	7–13 January 1945	"SOLSTICE," attempt of the Nineteenth Army to break out of the Colmar pocket.
SONNENWENDE	16 February 1945	"SOLSTICE," last offensive of the *Wehrmacht* on the Eastern Front, near Stargard.
STEINADLER	July 1944	"ROCK EAGLE," antipartisan offensive in Yugoslavia, Albania, and northern Greece.
STETTIN	June 1938	Naval forces covering the land occupation of the Memel region of Lithuania.
STÖRFANG	7 June 1942	"STURGEON CATCH," the attack against Sevastopol.
STÖSSER	16 December 1944	"SPARROWHAWK," airborne operation part of Operation *WACHT AM RHEIN*.
STRAFE	6 April 1941	"PUNISHMENT," air attacks on Belgrade.
STUDENT	1943	Plans to take over Italian facilities in the event of Italy's surrender. Named after *Generaloberst* Kurt Student.
STUDIE ENGLAND	May 1940	Plans for the invasion of England drawn up by the German naval war staff.
STUDIE NORD	December 1939	"STUDY NORTH," plans for the occupation of Norway.
STURMBOCK	1944	"BATTERING RAM," fortification line west of Karesuando, Norway.
STURMFLUT	19–22 February 1943	"STORM FLOOD," *Afrika Korps* operation in the Kasserine Pass and the Sbiba gap in Tunisia.
TAIFUN	2 October 1941	"TYPHOON," ground offensive against Moscow.

Axis Code Names

Code Name	Date	Remarks
TANNENBERG	1940	Hitler's field headquarters in the Black Forest.
TANNE OST	September 1944	"FIR TREE EAST," landing on Suursaari Island in the Gulf of Finland.
TANNE WEST	1944	"FIR TREE WEST," planned occupation of the Aland Islands in the Gulf of Bothnia.
TAUBENSCHLAG	October 1942	"DOVECOTE," projected attacks against Toropets in the Soviet Union.
THESEUS	1942	Proposed operation into Libya.
TIGER	15 June 1940	German First Army attack through the Maginot Line.
TRAJAN	1943–1944	Romanian fortification line near Iasi.
TRAPPENJAGD	8 May 1942	"BUSTARD HUNT," operation on the Kerch Peninsula in the Crimea.
TREUBRUCH	October 1944	"INFIDELITY," occupation of Bulgarian-occupied territory after Bulgaria's surrender to the Allies.
TROJANISCHES PFERD	19 March 1944	"TROJAN HORSE," occupation of Budapest as part of Operation *MARGARETHE*.
VENEZIA	26 May 1942	"VENICE," *Afrika Korps* attack at Gazala.
WACHT AM RHEIN	16 December 1944	"WATCH ON THE RHINE," ground offensive in Belgium and Luxembourg aimed at Antwerp. Known in the West as Battle of the Bulge.
WALKÜRE	20 July 1944	"VALKYRIE," unsuccessful plot to assassinate Hitler.
WEISS	Early 1943	"WHITE," with Italy, operations against the Četniks and partisans in Croatia.
WERWOLF	1942	"WEREWOLF," Hitler's headquarters near Vinnitsa, Ukraine.
WESERÜBUNG	8 April 1940	"WESER EXERCISE," naval operations for the invasion of Denmark and Norway.
—NORD		—Invasion of Norway.
—SUD		—Invasion of Denmark.
WIESENGRUND	June 1942	"MEADOWLAND," planned occupation of the Rybatchi Peninsula.
WILHELM	10 June 1942	"WILLIAM," operation against the Volchansk salient.
WILLI	July 1940	Plot to kidnap the Duke of Windsor, the former King Edward VIII, who abdicated in 1936.
WINKELRIED	27 October 1942	Substitute for Operation *SCHLINGPFLANZE*.

Axis Code Names

Code Name	Date	Remarks
WINTERGEWITTER	12 December 1942	"WINTER STORM," ground offensive to relieve Stalingrad.
WIRBELWIND	11 August 1942	"WHIRLWIND," operation to pinch off part of the Red Army's Sukhinichi salient.
WOLF	1944	Ground offensive in northern Greece.
WOLFSSCHANZE	1944	"WOLF'S LAIR," Hitler's headquarters near Rastenburg, East Prussia.
WOLFSSCHLUCHT	June 1940	"WOLF'S GORGE," Hitler's headquarters in Givet, Belgium.
WOTAN	Fall 1943	"WODEN," southern half of projected East Wall.
WUNDERLAND I	Summer 1942	"WONDERLAND," German naval operations against Soviet Arctic sea routes.
WUNDERLAND II	Summer 1943	German naval operations against Soviet Arctic sea routes.
Z-PLAN	1939	Plan to match Britain's naval power.
ZITADELLE	5 July 1943	"CITADEL," ground offensive around the Kursk salient.
ZITRONELLA	7 September 1943	Reoccupation of Spitzbergen Island.

Compiled by John Beatty and William Van Husen

Appendix E

Selected Bibliography

If the study of military history is to be thorough, the student must examine more than the surface of the subject. Actual military events occupy only one portion of the total picture. The student must explore as well the diplomacy, economy, philosophy, psychology, and sociology behind any major war, as well as the people and their governments.

The true work of history further includes the critical examination of sources, documents, standard books, artifacts, and general reference works. Yet no work as concise as an encyclopedia, involving limited availability of space, can explore all avenues of history or provide all possible, relevent facts. In this volume, the editors and the various contributors have made critical choices as to what was most important, what could be included, and what had to be omitted. The contributors have provided their own interpretations of the historical events involved. Those readers desiring further detailed factual and analytical treatments are invited to pursue their interests in the excellent references provided at the end of each article.

The following selected bibliography is a list of books by writers and historians who used a variety of sources, including interviews with participants and research in American, British, Canadian, French, German, Polish, and Soviet archives. The books listed here are recommended as worthy of reading by students of history wishing to delve further into the many and varied aspects of World War II. This bibliography is organized into eight sections: general references, official histories, and a section for each of the six major sections of the encyclopedia.

In addition to the books in this bibliography, several excellent general reference works provide useful sources for further research. Among these are the various editions of *Jane's Fighting Ships* and *Jane's All the World's Aircraft;* the *Encyclopedia of 20th-Century Warfare;* the Time-Life series *The Second World War;* and the *Encyclopedia Britannica.* The interested reader can also consult several popular and scholarly periodicals that deal with military history in general and World War II in particular. These include the *Journal of Military History; MHQ: The Quarterly Journal of Military History; Military History* magazine; and *World War II* magazine.

GENERAL REFERENCES

Churchill, Winston S., *Closing the Ring: The Second World War,* Vol. V (Boston: 1952).

———, *The Gathering Storm: The Second World War,* Vol. I (Boston: 1948).

———, *The Grand Alliance: The Second World War,* Vol. III (Boston: 1950).

———, *The Hinge of Fate: The Second World War,* Vol. IV (Boston: 1951).

———, *Their Finest Hour: The Second World War,* Vol. II (Boston: 1949).

———, *Triumph and Tragedy: The Second World War,* Vol. VI (Boston: 1953).

Dear, I.C.B., and M.R.D. Foot (eds.), *The Oxford Companion to the Second World War* (New York: 1995).

Dziewanowski, M.K., *War at Any Price: World War II in Europe, 1939–1945* (Englewood Cliffs, New Jersey: 1991).

Ellis, John, *The World War II Fact Book* (London: 1993).

Fuller, J.F.C., *The Second World War 1939–1945:*

A Strategical and Tactical History (London: 1948).

Griess, Thomas E. (ed.), *The Second World War: Europe and the Mediterranean: The West Point Military History Series* (Wayne, New Jersey: 1984).

Jones, James, *WWII* (New York: 1975).

Keegan, John, *The Battle for History: Re-Fighting World War II* (New York: 1995).

———, *The Second World War* (New York: 1990).

———, *The Times Atlas of the Second World War* (New York: 1989).

Liddell Hart, B.H., *History of the Second World War* (London: 1970).

McCormick, Ken, and Hamilton Darby Perry, *Images of War: The Artist's Vision of World War II* (New York: 1990).

Mercer, Derrik (ed.), *The Chronicle of the Second World War* (London: 1990).

Michil, Henri, *The Second World War* (New York: 1975).

Nye, Wilbur S. [editor of a guide to and selection from a group of studies prepared by more than 200 German officers entitled] *World War II German Military Studies,* 14 vols. (New York: 1979).

Shirer, William L., *The Rise and Fall of the Third Reich* (New York: 1959).

Sulzberger, C.L., *World War II* (Boston: 1987).

Touras, Peter G., *The Great Patriotic War* (London: 1992).

Wright, Gordon, *The Ordeal of Total War, 1939–1945* (New York: 1968).

Young, Peter, *The World Almanac of World War II* (New York: 1986).

OFFICIAL HISTORIES—AUSTRALIA

Herington, John, *Air Power Over Europe, 1944–45: Australia in the War of 1939–45* (Canberra: 1963).

———, *Air War Against Germany and Italy, 1939–1943: Australia in the War of 1939–45* (Canberra: 1954).

Long, Gavin, *To Benghazi: Australia in the War of 1939–45* (Canberra: 1952).

———, *Greece, Crete, and Syria: Australia in the War of 1939–45* (Canberra: 1953).

Maughan, Barton, *Tobruk and El Alamein: Australia in the War of 1939–45* (Canberra: 1967).

OFFICIAL HISTORIES—CANADA

Nicholson, G.W.L., *The Canadians in Italy,* *1943–1945: Official History of the Canadian Army in the Second World War* (Ottawa: 1956).

Stacey, C.P., *The Canadian Army, 1939–1945: An Official Historical Summary* (Ottawa: 1948).

———, *The Victory Campaign, The Operations in Northwest Europe, 1944–1945: Official History of the Canadian Army in the Second World War* (Ottawa: 1960).

OFFICIAL HISTORIES—GERMANY

Boog, Horst (ed.), *The Conduct of the Air War in the Second World War: Studies in Military History* (issued by the German Research Institute for Military History) (Oxford, England: 1992).

Deist, Wilhelm, et al., *The Buildup of German Aggression: Germany and the Second World War* (issued by the German Research Institute for Military History) (Oxford, England: 1990).

Maier, Klaus A., et al, *Germany's Initial Conquests in Europe: Germany and the Second World War* (issued by the German Research Institute for Military History) (Oxford, England: 1991).

Reinhardt, Klaus, *Moscow—The Turning Point: The Failure of Hitler's Strategy in the Winter of 1941–42: Studies in Military History* (issued by the German Research Institute for Military History) (Oxford, England: 1992).

Schramm, Percy E. (ed.), *Kriegstagebuch des Oberkommandos der Wehrmacht,* 8 vols. (Munich: 1982).

Schreiber, Gerhard, et al., *The Mediterranean, Southeast Europe, and North Africa, 1939–1941: Germany and the Second World War* (issued by the German Research Institute for Military History) (Oxford, England: 1990).

Steiger, Rudolf, *Armour Tactics in the Second World War—Panzer Army Campaigns of 1939–41 in German War Diaries: Studies in Military History* (issued by the German Research Institute for Military History) (Oxford, England: 1991).

Wegner, Bernd, *Two Roads to Moscow: From the Hitler-Stalin Pact to Operation Barbarossa: Studies in Military History* (issued by the German Research Institute for Military History) (Oxford, England: 1993).

OFFICIAL HISTORIES—INDIA

Bharucha, P.C., *The North African Campaign, 1940–1943: Indian Armed Forces in World War II* (New Delhi: 1956).

Pal, Dharm, *Campaign in Italy, 1943–1945: Indian Armed Forces in World War II* (New Delhi: 1961).

———, *Campaign in Western Asia (Including Iraq, Syria, Iran, and Paiforce): Indian Armed Forces in World War II* (New Delhi: 1957).

OFFICIAL HISTORIES—NEW ZEALAND

Davin, D.M., *Crete: New Zealand Official War Histories* (Wellington: 1953).

Kay, R.L., *Italy, from Cassino to Trieste: New Zealand Official War Histories* (Wellington: 1967).

McClymont, W.G., *To Greece: New Zealand Official War Histories* (Wellington: 1959).

Murphy, W.E., *The Relief of Tobruk: New Zealand Official War Histories* (Wellington: 1961).

Phillips, N.C., *Italy—Sangro to Cassino: New Zealand Official War Histories* (Wellington: 1957).

Scoullar, J.L., *Battle for Egypt: The Summer of 1942: New Zealand Official War Histories* (Wellington: 1955).

Stevens, W.G., *Bardia to Enfidaville: New Zealand Official War Histories* (Wellington: 1962).

Walker, Ronald, *Alam Halfa and Alamein: New Zealand Official War Histories* (Wellington: 1967).

OFFICIAL HISTORIES—SOVIET UNION

History of the Great Patriotic War of the Soviet Union, 1941– 1945, 6 vols. (Moscow: 1961–1965).

OFFICIAL HISTORIES—UNITED KINGDOM

Butler, James R.M., *Grand Strategy: September 1939–June 1941: United Kingdom Military Series* (London: 1957).

Collier, Basil, *The Defence of the United Kingdom: United Kingdom Military Series* (London: 1957).

Derry, Thomas K., *The Campaign in Norway: United Kingdom Military Series* (London: 1952).

Ehrman, John, *Grand Strategy: August 1943 to September 1944: United Kingdom Military Series* (London: 1956).

———, *Grand Strategy: October 1944 to August 1945: United Kingdom Military Series* (London: 1956).

Ellis, Lionel F., *Victory in the West: The Battle of Normandy: United Kingdom Military Series* (London: 1962).

———, *Victory in the West: Defeat of Germany: United Kingdom Military Series* (London: 1969).

———, *The War in France and Flanders, 1939–1940: United Kingdom Military Series* (London: 1953).

Gibbs, Norman H., *Grand Strategy: 1933 to September 1939: United Kingdom Military Series* (London: n.d.).

Gwyer, J.M.A., and J.R.M. Butler, *Grand Strategy: June 1941 to August 1942: United Kingdom Military Series* (London: 1964).

Hinsley, F.H., et al., *British Intelligence in the Second World War: Its Influence on Strategy and Operations: United Kingdom Military Series*, 4 vols. (London: 1979–1988).

Howard, Michael, *British Intelligence in the Second World War: Volume 5, Strategic Deception: United Kingdom Military Series* (London: 1991).

———, *Grand Strategy: August 1942–August 1943: United Kingdom Military Series* (London: 1970).

Playfair, I.S.O., et al., *The Mediterranean and the Middle East: British Forces Reach Their Lowest Ebb—September 1941 to September 1942: United Kingdom Military Series* (London: 1960).

———, *The Mediterranean and the Middle East: The Destruction of the Axis Forces in Africa, 1942–1943: United Kingdom Military Series* (London: 1968).

———, *The Mediterranean and the Middle East: The Early Successes Against Italy—to May 1941: United Kingdom Military Series* (London: 1954).

———, *The Mediterranean and the Middle East: The Germans Come to the Help of Their Ally—1941: United Kingdom Military Series* (London: 1956).

Richards, Denis, and Hillary St.G. Saunders, *The Fight Avails: The Royal Air Force, 1939–1945* (London: 1954).

———, *The Fight at Odds: The Royal Air Force, 1939–1945* (London: 1953).

———, *The Fight is Won: The Royal Air Force, 1939–1945* (London: 1954).

Roskill, Stephen W., *The War at Sea 1939–1945:*

The Defensive: United Kingdom Military Series (London: 1954).

———, *The War at Sea 1939–1945: 1st June 1944 to 14 August 1945: United Kingdom Military Series* (London: 1961).

———, *The War at Sea 1939–1945: The Offensive: United Kingdom Military Series* (London: 1960).

———, *The War at Sea 1939–1945: The Period of Balance: United Kingdom Military Series* (London: 1956).

Webster, Charles, and Arthur Noble Frankland, *The Strategic Air Offensive Against Germany, 1939–1945: Annexes and Appendices: United Kingdom Military Series* (London: 1961).

———, *The Strategic Air Offensive Against Germany, 1939–1945: Endeavor: United Kingdom Military Series* (London: 1961).

———, *The Strategic Air Offensive Against Germany, 1939–1945: Preparation: United Kingdom Military Series* (London: 1961).

———, *The Strategic Air Offensive Against Germany, 1939–1945: Victory: United Kingdom Military Series* (London: 1961).

OFFICIAL HISTORIES—UNITED STATES

Blumenson, Martin, *Breakout and Pursuit: The United States Army in World War II* (Washington, D.C.: 1961).

———, *Salerno to Cassino: The United States Army in World War II* (Washington, D.C.: 1969).

Clarke, Jeffrey J., and Robert Ross Smith, *Riviera to the Rhine: The United States Army in World War II* (Washington, D.C.: 1993).

Cole, Hugh M., *The Ardennes: Battle of the Bulge: The United States Army in World War II* (Washington, D.C.: 1965).

———, *The Lorraine Campaign: The United States Army in World War II* (Washington, D.C.: 1950).

Craven, Wesley Frank, and James Lea Cate (eds.), *Europe—Argument to V-E Day, January 1944 to May 1945: The Army Air Forces in World War II* (Chicago: 1951).

———, *Europe—Torch to Pointblank, August 1942 to December 1943: The Army Air Forces in World War II* (Chicago: 1949).

———, *Men and Planes: The Army Air Forces in World War II* (Chicago: 1958).

———, *Plans and Early Operations, January 1939 to August 1942: The Army Air Forces in World War II* (Chicago: 1948).

Fisher, Ernest F., *Cassino to the Alps: The United States Army in World War II* (Washington, D.C.: 1977).

Garland, Albert N., and Howard McGraw Smyth, *Sicily and the Surrender of Italy: The United States Army in World War II* (Washington, D.C.: 1965).

Greenfield, Kent H., R.R. Palmer, and Bell I. Wiley, *The Organization of Ground Combat Troops: United States Army in World War II: Army Ground Forces* (Washington, D.C.: 1947).

Harrison, Gordon A., *Cross-Channel Attack: The United States Army in World War II* (Washington, D.C.: 1951).

Howe, George F., *Northwest Africa: Seizing the Initiative in the West: The United States Army in World War II* (Washington, D.C.: 1957).

Lee, Ulysses, *The Employment of Negro Troops: The United States Army in World War II* (Washington, D.C.: 1966).

Leighton, Richard M., and Robert W. Coakley, *Global Logistics and Strategy, 1940–1943: The United States Army in World War II* (Washington, D.C.: 1955).

MacDonald, Charles B., *The Last Offensive: The United States Army in World War II* (Washington, D.C.: 1973).

———, *The Siegfried Line Campaign: The United States Army in World War II* (Washington, D.C.: 1963).

MacDonald, Charles B., and Sidney T. Mathews, *Three Battles—Arnaville, Altuzzo, and Schmidt: The United States Army in World War II* (Washington, D.C.: 1952).

Matloff, Maurice, and Edwin M. Snell, *Strategic Planning for Coalition Warfare, 1941–1942: The United States Army in World War II* (Washington, D.C.: 1953).

———, *Strategic Planning for Coalition Warfare, 1943–1944: The United States Army in World War II* (Washington, D.C.: 1959).

Morison, Samuel Eliot, *The Atlantic Battle Won: History of the United States Naval Operations in World War II*, Vol. X (Boston: 1956).

———, *The Battle of the Atlantic: History of the United States Naval Operations in World War II*, Vol. I (Boston: 1947).

———, *The Invasion of France and Germany: History of the United States Naval Operations in World War II*, Vol. XI (Boston: 1957).

———, *Operations in North African Waters: History of the United States Naval Operations in World War II*, Vol. II (Boston: 1948).

————, *Sicily–Salerno–Anzio: History of the United States Naval Operations in World War II,* Vol. IX (Boston: 1955).

————, *Supplement and General Index: History of the United States Naval Operations in World War II,* Vol. XV (Washington, D.C.: 1962).

Pogue, Forrest C., *The Supreme Command: United States Army in World War II* (Washington, D.C.: 1954).

Ruppenthal, Ronald G., *Logistical Support of the Armies: United States Army in World War II,* 2 vols. (Washington, D.C.: 1953, 1959).

Treadwell, Mattie E., *The Women's Army Corps: The United States Army in World War II* (Washington, D.C.: 1954).

Vail Motter, T.H., *The Persian Corridor and Aid to Russia: The United States Army in World War II* (Washington, D.C.: 1952).

Watson, Mark S., *Chief of Staff: Prewar Planning and Preparation: The United States Army in World War II* (Washington, D.C.: 1950).

SOCIAL AND POLITICAL ISSUES AND EVENTS

Allied Control Authority for Germany, *Trial of the Major War Criminals Before the International Military Tribunal, Nuremberg, 14 November 1945–10 October 1946,* 42 vols. (Nuremberg, 1949).

Armstrong, Anne, *Unconditional Surrender: The Impact of the Casablanca Policy Upon World War II* (New Brunswick, New Jersey: 1961).

Backer, John H., *The Decision to Divide Germany* (Durham, North Carolina: 1978).

Bailey, K.G., *Dachau* (London: 1961).

Bailey, Thomas A., and Paul B. Ryan, *Hitler vs. Roosevelt: The Undeclared Naval War* (New York: 1979).

Bennet, Jeremy, *British Broadcasting and the Danish Resistance Movement* (Cambridge, England: 1966).

Bergh, Hendrik van, *Die Wahrheit über Katyn* (Berg am See, Germany: 1986).

Borsody, Gordon, *The Triumph of Tyranny: The Nazi and Soviet Conquest of Central Europe* (London: 1960).

Bosch, William J., *Judgement on Nuremberg* (Chapel Hill, North Carolina: 1970).

Bracher, Karl Dietrich, *The German Dictatorship* (New York: 1970).

Bradley, John, *Lidice: Sacrificial Village* (New York: 1972).

Brinkley, David, *Washington Goes to War* (New York: 1988).

Bry, Gesarhard, *Resistance: Recollections from the Nazi Years* (West Orange, New Jersey: 1979).

Buchheim, Hans et al., *Anatomy of the SS State* (New York: 1968).

Calvocoressi, Peter, and Guy Wint, *Nuremberg* (New York: 1948).

————, *Total War* (London: 1990).

Combs, Jerald A., *The History of American Foreign Policy* (New York: 1986).

Compton, James V., *The Swastika and the Eagle: Hitler, the United States, and the Origins of the Second World War* (London: 1968).

Dallin, Alexander, *German Rule in Russia* (New York: 1957).

Dallin, David J., *The Big Three: The United States, Britain, Russia* (New Haven, Connecticut: 1945).

Dank, Milton, *The French Against the French: Collaboration and Resistance* (Philadelphia: 1974).

Davidson, Eugene, *The Trial of the Germans* (New York: 1967).

Davis, Forrest, and E.K. Lindley, *How War Came: An American White Paper from the Fall of France to Pearl Harbor* (New York: 1942).

Dawidowicz, Lucy, *The War Against the Jews* (New York: 1975).

Deakin, Frederick W., *The Brutal Friendship: Mussolini, Hitler, and the Fall of Italian Fascism* (New York: 1962).

Deane, John R., *The Strange Alliance: The Story of Our Efforts at Wartime Cooperation with Russia* (New York: 1947).

Deborin, Grigorii, *The Second World War: A Politico-Military Survey* (New York: 1964).

Delzell, Charles F., *Mussolini's Enemies: The Italian Anti-Fascist Movement* (Princeton, New Jersey: 1961).

Deutsch, Harold C., *Hitler and His Generals* (Minneapolis: 1974).

Divine, Robert A., *Reluctant Belligerent: American Entry into World War II* (New York: 1965).

Donnison, Frank S.V., *Civil Affairs and Military Government* (London: 1966).

Dulles, Allen W., *Germany's Underground* (New York: 1947).

————, *The Secret Surrender* (New York: 1966).

Friedlander, Saul, *Prelude to Downfall: Hitler and the United States, 1939–1941* (London: 1967).

Funk, Authur Layton, *Politics of TORCH* (Lawrence, Kansas: 1974).

Gallo, Max, *The Night of the Long Knives* (New York: 1972).

Gantenbein, James W. (ed.), *Documentary Background of World War II, 1931–1941* (New York: 1948).

Graf, John R., *Survey of the American Economy, 1940–1946* (New York: 1947).

Grant, Neil, *The German-Soviet Pact* (New York: 1975).

Hart, Scott, *Washington at War, 1941–1945* (New York: 1970).

Healy, D., *The Curtain Falls: The Story of Socialism in Eastern Europe* (London: 1951).

Hoehling, Adolf A., *America's Road to War 1939–1941* (London: 1970).

Hoffmann, Peter, *The History of the German Resistance* (Cambridge, Massachusetts: 1977).

Jong, Louis de, *The German Fifth Column in the Second World War* (Chicago: 1956).

Jordan, Z., *The Oder-Neisse Line* (London: 1952).

Kamenetsky, Igor, *Secret Nazi Plans for Eastern Europe: A Study of Lebensraum Policies* (New York: 1961).

Kecskemeti, Paul, *Strategic Surrender: The Politics of Victory and Defeat* (Stanford, California: 1958).

Kendall, Alan, *Their Finest Hour: An Evocative Memoir of the British People in Wartime, 1939–1945* (London: 1972).

Kennan, George F., *Russia and the West Under Lenin and Stalin* (Boston: 1960).

Kraus, Jens, *Oradour-Sur-Glâne* (New York: 1969).

Langer, William, and S.E. Gleason, *Challenge to Isolation, 1937–1940* (New York: 1952).

Langer, William L, and S. Everett Gleason, *The Undeclared War, 1940–1941* (New York: 1953).

Librach, Jan, *The Rise of the Soviet Empire* (New York: 1964).

Lukas, Richard, *Forgotten Holocaust: The Poles Under German Occupation, 1939–1944* (Lexington, Kentucky: 1986).

Manchester, William, *The Arms of Krupp, 1578–1968* (New York: 1968).

Manvell, Roger, *The Conspirators: 20 July 1944* (New York: 1971).

Morgenthau, Henry G., *Germany Is Our Problem* (New York: 1945).

Mosley, P.E. (ed.), *The Soviet Union, 1922–1962* (New York: 1963).

Murphy, Robert, *Diplomat Among Warriors* (New York: 1964).

Naumann, Bernd, *Auschwitz* (New York: 1960).

Parkinson, Roger, *Peace for Our Time: Munich to Dunkirk—The Inside Story* (London: 1971).

Pratt, Fletcher, *America and Total War* (New York: 1941).

Pritchard, R. John, *Reichstag Fire: Ashes of Democracy* (New York: 1972).

Rhodes, Anthony R.E., *The Vatican in the Age of Dictators, 1922–1945* (London: 1973).

Rose, Lisle A., *After Yalta* (New York: 1973).

Rostow, W.W., *The Dynamics of Soviet Policy* (Cambridge, Massachusetts: 1953).

Rozek, Edward J., *Allied Wartime Diplomacy* (New York: 1958). [Revealing materials are contained in the wartime correspondence among the Big Three. See the two volumes entitled *Correspondence Between the Chairman of the Council of Ministers of the USSR and the President of the USA and the Prime Minister of Great Britain During the Great Patriotic War of 1941–1945*].

Schlabrendorff, Fabian von, *The Secret War Against Hitler* (New York: 1965).

Shirer, William L., *Berlin Diary* (London: 1940).

Smith, Gaddis, *American Diplomacy During the Second World War, 1941–1945* (New York: 1967).

Taylor, Lawrence, *The Trial of the Germans* (New York: 1981).

Taylor, Telford, *Sword & Swastika: Generals and Nazis in the Third Reich* (Chicago: 1952).

Terkel, Studs, *The Good War* (New York: 1984).

Tobias, Fritz, *The Reichstag Fire* (New York: 1964).

Tolstoy, Nikolai, *Night of the Long Knives* (New York: 1972).

U.S. Government, *Trials of War Criminals Before the Nuremberg Military Tribunals,* 15 vols. (Washington, D.C.: 1951–1952).

U.S. House of Representatives, *Report of the Select Committee on the Katyn Forest Massacre* (82nd Congress: 1951–1952).

Wolf, R.K., *The Balkans in Our Time* (Cambridge, Massachusetts: 1956).

Woodward, Ernest L., *British Foreign Policy in the Second World War* (London: 1962).

Wykes, Alan, *The Nuremberg Rallies* (New York: 1970).

Young, Roland A., *Congressional Politics in the Second World War* (New York: 1956).

Zawodny, Janusz, *Death in the Forest* (South Bend, Indiana: 1962).

Ziemke, Earl F., *The U.S. Army in the Occupation of Germany* (Washington, D.C.: 1975).

Leaders and Individuals

Alexander, Harold R.L.G., *The Alexander Memoirs, 1940–1945* (New York: 1961).

Ambrose, Stephen, *Eisenhower—1890–1952* (New York: 1985).

Ambrose, Stephen E., *The Supreme Commander: The War Years of General Dwight D. Eisenhower* (New York: 1970).

Amort, Cestmir, and I.M. Jedlicka, *The Canaris File* (London: 1970).

Andrus, Burton C., *I Was the Nuremberg Jailer* (New York: 1969).

Arnold Henry H., *Global Mission* (New York: 1949).

Baker, E.C.R., *The Fighter Aces of the R.A.F.* (London: 1962).

Balck, Hermann, *Ordnung im Chaos: Erinnerungen 1893–1948* (Osnabrück, Germany: 1980).

Barnett, Correlli, *The Desert Generals* (London: 1982).

Barnett, Correlli (ed.), *Hitler's Generals* (New York: 1989).

Beneš, Eduard, *Memoirs of Dr. Eduard Beneš, From Munich to New War and New Victory* (London: 1954).

Bialer, Seweryn (ed.), *Stalin and His Generals* (New York: 1984).

Blumenson, Martin, *Mark Clark* (New York: 1984).

Blumenson, Martin (ed.), *The Patton Papers*, 2 vols. (Boston: 1974).

Blumentritt, Günther, *Von Rundstedt: The Soldier and the Man* (London: 1963).

Boldt, Gerhard, *Hitler: The Last Ten Days* (London: 1973).

Bradley, Omar, *A Soldier's Story* (New York: 1951).

Bryant, Arthur, *Triumph in the West: A History of the War Years Based on the Diaries of Field Marshal Lord Alanbrooke, Chief of the Imperial General Staff* (Garden City, New Jersey: 1959).

———, *Turn of the Tide: A History of the War Years Based on the Diaries of Field Marshal Lord Alanbrooke, Chief of the Imperial General Staff* (Garden City, New Jersey: 1957).

Buell, Thomas B., *Master of Sea Power: A Biography of Fleet Admiral Ernest J. King* (New York: 1980).

Butcher, Harry C., *My Three Years with Eisenhower* (New York: 1946).

Carver, Michael (ed.), *The War Lords: Military Commanders of the Twentieth Century* (Boston: 1976).

Chaney, Otto P., *Zhukov* (Norman, Oklahoma: 1971).

Charmley, John, *Churchill—The End of Glory: A Political Biography* (New York: 1993).

Ciano, Galeazzo, *Ciano's Diary* (London and Toronto: 1947).

Collins, J. Lawton, *Lightning Joe: An Autobiography* (Baton Rouge, Louisiana: 1979).

Connell, John, *A Biography of Field Marshal Sir Claude Auchinleck* (London: 1959).

Constable, Trevor J., and Raymond F. Toliver, *Fighter Aces* (New York: 1965).

Cunningham, Andrew B., *A Sailor's Odyssey* (London: 1951).

Deakin, F.W., and G.R. Story, *The Case of Richard Sorge* (London: 1966).

Dedijer, Vladimir, *Tito* (New York: 1952).

D'Este, Carlo, *Patton: A Genius for War* (New York: 1995).

De Gaulle, Charles, *The War Memoirs of Charles de Gaulle,* 3 vols. (New York: 1958–1960).

De Guingand, Sir Francis, *Generals at War* (London: 1964).

Dönitz, Karl, *Ten Years and Twenty Days* (New York: 1959).

Draskovich, S.M., *Tito, Moscow's Trojan Horse* (Chicago: 1957).

Eisenhower, Dwight D., *Crusade in Europe* (New York: 1948).

Esseme, H., *Patton: A Study in Command* (New York: 1974).

Farago, Landislas, *Patton: Ordeal and Triumph* (New York: 1964).

Farrar-Hockley, Anthony H., *Student* (New York: 1973).

Feis, Herbert, *Churchill, Roosevelt, and Stalin: The War They Waged and the Peace They Sought* (Princeton: 1957).

Fest, Joachim C., *Hitler* (New York: 1973).

Ford, Corey, *Donovan of the O.S.S.* (Boston: 1970).

Fraser, David, *Alanbrooke* (London: 1982).

———, *Knight's Cross: A Life of Field Marshal Erwin Rommel* (London: 1993).

Gale, Richard N., *Call to Arms: An Autobiography* (London: 1968).

Galland, Adolf, *The First and the Last* (New York: 1954).

Gavin, James M., *On to Berlin: Battles of an Airborne Commander, 1943–1946* (New York: 1978).

Gibson, Hugh (ed.), *The Ciano Diaries 1939–1943* (New York: 1945).

Gilbert, Martin, *Winston S. Churchill, Road to Victory, 1941– 1945* (London: 1986).

Goebbels, Josef, *The Diaries of Josef Goebbels* (London: 1948).

Goodspeed, D.J., *Ludendorff* (Boston: 1966).

Görlitz, Walter, *Paulus and Stalingrad: A Life of Field Marshal Friedrich Paulus* (London: 1963).

Guderian, Heinz, *Panzer Leader* (New York: 1952).

Halder, Franz, *Hitler as Warlord* (London: 1950).

Hamilton, Nigel, *Master of the Battlefield: Monty's War Years 1942–1944* (New York: 1983).

———, *Monty: The Making of a General* (New York: 1981).

Harris, Arthur, *Bomber Offensive* (London: 1947).

Hitler, Adolf, *Mein Kampf* (Boston: 1943).

Hobbs, Joseph (ed.), *Dear General: Eisenhower's War Time Letters to Marshall* (London: 1960).

Hopkins, Harry L., and R.E. Sherwood (eds.), *The White House Papers of Harry L. Hopkins* (London: 1948).

Horrocks, Brian, *Corps Commander* (New York: 1978).

Höss, Rudolf, *Commandant of Auschwitz* (London: 1953).

Howarth, Stephen (ed.), *Men of War: Green Naval Leaders of World War II* (New York: 1993).

Hull, Cordell, *Memoirs* (New York: 1948).

Infield, Glenn B., *Skorzeny: Hitler's Commando* (London: 1981).

Irving, David, *The Rise and Fall of the Luftwaffe: The Life of Field Marshal Erhard Milch* (Boston: 1973).

———, *The Trail of the Fox* (New York: 1977).

Ismay, Hastings L., *The Memoirs of General the Lord Ismay* (London: 1960).

Jackson, W.G.F., *Alexander of Tunis as a Military Commander* (New York: 1971).

Johnson, J.E., *Wing Leader* (New York: 1957).

Keegan, John, *Guderian* (New York: 1973).

Keegan, John (ed.), *Churchill's Generals* (New York: 1991).

Keitel, Wilhelm, *The Memoirs of Field Marshal Keitel* (New York: 1966.

Kesselring, Albert, *A Soldier's Record* (New York: 1954).

Keyes, Elizabeth M., *Geoffrey Keyes, V.C., M.C.* (London: 1956).

King, Ernest J., and W.M. Whithill, *Fleet Admiral King: A Naval Record* (New York: 1952).

Kramarz, Joachim, *Staffenberg* (New York: 1967).

Lang, Jochen von, *The Secretary: Martin Bormann* (New York: 1979).

Larrabee, Eric, *Commander in Chief: Franklin Roosevelt, His Lieutenants, and Their War* (New York: 1987).

Laval, Pierre, *Diary* (New York: 1948).

Leahy, William D., *I Was There: The Personal Story of the Chief of Staff to Presidents Roosevelt and Truman, Based on His Notes and Diaries Made at the Time* (London: 1950).

Lecouture, Jean, *De Gaulle: The Rebel 1940–1944* (New York: 1991).

Ledwidge, Bernard, *De Gaulle* (New York: 1982).

Lee, Asher, *Göring: Air Leader* (New York: 1972).

Lewin, Ronald, *The Chief: Field Marshal Lord Wavell, Commander in Chief and Viceroy, 1939–1947* (London: 1962).

Liddell Hart, Basil H., *The German Generals Talk* (New York: 1948).

Liddell Hart, Basil H. (ed.), *The Rommel Papers* (New York: 1953).

Lowenheim, Francis L., Harold D. Langley, and Manfred Jones (eds.), *Roosevelt and Churchill: Their Secret Wartime Correspondence* (New York: 1975).

McCullough, David, *Truman* (New York: 1992).

Mannerheim, Carl G., *Memoirs* (London: 1954).

Mauldin, Bill, *Up Front* (New York: 1945).

Mellenthin, F.W. von, *German Generals of World War II: As I Saw Them* (Norman, Oklahoma: 1977).

Montgomery, Bernard, *The Memoirs of Field Marshal the Viscount Montgomery of Alamein* (New York: 1958).

———, *Normandy to the Baltic* (Boston: 1948).

Morgan, Frederick E., *COSSAC's Memoirs: Overture to Overlord* (London: 1951).

Mosley, Leonard, *The Reich Marshal: A Biography of Hermann Göring* (New York: 1974).

O'Donnell, James P., *The Bunker: The History of the Reich Chancellory Group* (Boston: 1978).

Papen, Franz von, *Memoirs* (New York: 1953).

Patton, George S., *War As I Knew It* (Boston: 1947).

Picker, Henry, *Hitler's Table Talk* (London: 1953).

Pogue, Forrest C., *George C. Marshall: Education of a General, 1880–1939* (New York: 1963).

———, *George C. Marshall: Ordeal and Hope, 1939– 1942* (New York: 1966).

———, *George C. Marshall: Organizer of Victory, 1943–1945* (New York: 1973).

Pyle, Ernest Taylor, *Brave Men* (New York: 1944).

Raeder, Erich, *My Life* (Annapolis, Maryland: 1960).

Rees, John R. (ed), *The Mind of Rudolf Hess* (New York: 1948).

Ribbentrop, Joachim von, *The Ribbentrop Memoirs* (London: 1953).

Ridgway, Matthew B., *Soldier: The Memoirs of Matthew B. Ridgway* (New York: 1956).

Ryan, Stephan, *Pétain the Soldier* (New York: 1969).

Salisbury-Jones, Guy, *So Full a Glory: A Biography of Marshal de Lattre de Tassigny* (London: 1954).

Schacht, Hjalmar, *Confessions of an Old Wizard* (Boston: 1956).

Schellenberg, Walter, *The Schellenberg Memoirs* (London: 1956).

Schmidt, Matthais, *Albert Speer: The End of a Myth* (London: 1984).

Schoenbrun, David, *The Three Lives of Charles De Gaulle* (New York: 1965).

Seaton, Albert, *Stalin as Military Commander* (New York: 1976).

Seitz, Albert, *Mihailovic: Hoax or Hero?* (Columbus, Ohio: 1953).

Sherwood, Robert E., *Roosevelt and Hopkins* (New York: 1956).

Shukman, Harold (ed.), *Stalin's Generals* (New York: 1993).

Smith, Walter Bedell, *Eisenhower's Six Great Decisions: Europe 1944–1945* (New York: 1956).

Speer, Albert, *Inside the Third Reich: Memoirs* (New York: 1970).

Spiller, Roger, *American Military Leaders* (New York: 1989).

Steinhoff, Johannes, *The Final Hours: A German Jet Pilot Plots Against Göring* (Baltimore: 1977).

Stevenson, William K., *A Man Called Intrepid* (New York: 1976).

Tedder, Arthur W., *With Prejudice: The War Memoirs of Marshal of the Royal Air Force, Lord Tedder* (Boston: 1966).

Toland, John, *Adolf Hitler* (New York: 1976).

Tremain, Rose, *Stalin* (New York: 1975).

Truscott, Lucian K., *Command Missions* (New York: 1954).

Ulam, Adam B., *Stalin: The Man and His Era* (New York: 1973).

Vasilevsky, Alexander, *A Lifelong Cause* (Moscow: 1981).

Vitukhin, Igor, *Soviet Generals Recall World War II* (New York: 1981).

Weygand, Maxime, *Recall to Service: The Memoirs of General Maxime Weygard* (London: 1952).

Whiting, Charles, *Skorzeny* (New York: 1972).

Wighton, Charles, *Heydrich: Hitler's Most Evil Henchman* (London: 1962).

Zhukov, Georgy, *The Memoirs of Marshal Zhukov* (New York: 1971).

UNITS AND ORGANIZATIONS

Adelman, Robert H., and George Walton, *The Devil's Brigade* (Philadelphia: 1966).

Allen, Robert S., *Lucky Forward: The History of Patton's Third U.S. Army* (New York: 1947).

Alsop, Stewart, and Thomas Bradem, *SUB ROSA: The OSS and American Espionage* (New York: 1964).

Ambrose, Stephen E., *Citizen Soldiers: The U.S. Army from the Normandy Beaches to the Bulge to the Surrender of Germany* (New York: 1997).

Auphan, Paul, and Hervé Cras, *The French Navy in World War II* (Annapolis: 1959).

Billingham, Elizabeth, *America's First Two Years: The Study of American Volunteers in Britain, 1939–1941* (London: 1942).

Blair, Clay, *Ridgway's Paratroopers: The American Airborne in World War II* (Garden City, New Jersey: 1985).

Blumbach, Werner, *The Life and Death of the Luftwaffe* (New York: 1960).

Bragadin, Marc Antonio, *The Italian Navy in World War II* (Annapolis, Maryland: 1957).

Cookridge, E.H., *Inside the SOE* (London: 1966).

Cooper, Matthew, *The German Army, 1933–1945, Its Political and Military Failure* (Chelsea, England: 1990).

Creveld, Martin van, *Fighting Power: German and U.S. Army Performance, 1939–1945* (Westport, Connecticut: 1982).

De Gaulle, Charles, *The Army of the Future* (Philadelphia: 1941).

Delarue, Jacques, *The History of the Gestapo* (London: 1964).

Edwards, Roger, *German Airborne Troops 1936–1945* (London: 1974).

Elstob, Peter, *Condor Legion* (New York: 1973).

English, John, *The Canadian Army and the Normandy Campaign: A Study of Failure in High Command* (New York: 1991).

Ferguson, Bernard, *The Watery Maze: The Story of Combined Operations* (New York: 1961).

Fuller, Jean Overton, *The German Penetration of SOE France, 1941–1944* (London: 1975).

Furr, Arthur, *Democracy's Negroes: A Book of Facts Concerning the Activities of Negroes in World War II* (Boston: 1947).

Galland, Adolf, *The First and The Last: The Rise and Fall of the German Fighter Forces, 1938–1945* (New York: 1954).

Gillie, Mildred H., *Forging the Thunderbolt: A History of the Development of the Armored Force* (Harrisburg, Pennsylvania: 1947).

Golovko, Arseni, *With the Fleet* (Moscow: 1979).

Görlitz, Walter, *History of the German General Staff, 1657–1945* (New York: 1953).

Hardesty, Von, *Red Phoenix: The Rise of Soviet Airpower, 1941–1945* (Washington, D.C.: 1991).

Her Majesty's Stationery Office, *German Order of Battle, 1944,* reprinted with an introduction by Ian V. Hogg (London: 1994.

———, *The Rise and Fall of the German Air Force* (London: 1948).

Hoffmann, Joachim, *Die Geschichte der Wlassow-Armee* (Freiburg, Germany: 1986).

———, *Die Ostlegionen 1941–1942* (Freiburg, Germany: 1986).

Höhne, Heinz, *The Order of the Death's Head: The Story of Hitler's SS* (New York: 1970).

Humble, Richard, *Hitler's High Seas Fleet* (New York: 1971).

Hurkula, John, *The Fighting First Division* (New York: 1958).

Irving, David, *The Rise and Fall of the Luftwaffe* (London: 1973).

Isakov, Ivan S., *The Red Fleet in the Second World War* (London: 1947).

Keegan, John, *Waffen SS: The Asphalt Soldiers* (New York: 1970).

Kerr, Walter B., *The Russian Army: Its Men, Its Leaders, and Its Battles* (London: 1944).

Killen, John, *A History of the Luftwaffe* (Garden City, 1964).

Koch, Hansjoachim W., *The Hitler Youth: Origins and Development, 1922–45* (New York: 1976).

Lattre de Tassigny, Jean de, *The History of the French First Army* (London: 1952).

Leach, Barry, *German General Staff* (New York: 1973).

Lee, Asher, *The Soviet Air Force* (New York: 1950).

Le Masson, Henri, *The French Navy* (London: 1969).

Macksey, Kenneth J., *Panzer Division, The Mailed Fist* (New York: 1968).

Manvell, Roger, *SS and Gestapo: Rule by Terror* (New York: 1969).

Mollo, Andrew, *The Armed Forces of World War II: Uniforms, Insignia, and Organization* (London: 1981).

Moynahan, Brian, *Claws of the Bear: The History of the Red Army from the Revolution to the Present* (New York: 1989).

North, John, *Europe 1944–45: The Achievement of the 21st Army Group* (London: 1953).

O'Ballance, Edgar, *The Red Army* (New York: 1964).

Porten, Edward von der, *The German Navy in World War II* (New York: 1969).

Preston, Anthony, and John Batchelor, *The Navies of World War II* (London: 1976).

Rust, Eric, *Naval Officers Under Hitler: The Story of Crew 34* (New York: 1991).

Sargent, Frederic O., *Night Fighters: An Official History of the 415 Night Fighter Squadron* (Madison, Wisconsin: 1946).

Seth, Ronald, *Jackals of the Reich: The Story of the British Free Corps* (London: 1972).

Stanton, Shelby, *Order of Battle, U.S. Army, World War II* (Novato, California: 1984).

Tucker, G.N., *A History of the Royal Canadian Navy* (Ottawa: 1952).

U.S. War Department, *TM-E 30–451 Handbook on German Military Forces* (Washington, D.C.: 1945), reprinted (Baton Rouge: 1990).

Wagner, Ray (ed.), *The Soviet Air Force in World*

War II: The Official History (New York: 1973).

Young, Peter, *Commando* (New York: 1969).

Zamoyski, Adam, *The Forgotten Few: The Polish Air Force in the Second World War* (New York: 1995).

WEAPONS AND EQUIPMENT

Baldwin, Ralph B., *The Deadly Fuze: Secret Weapon of World War II* (San Rafael, California: 1979).

Ballard, Robert D., *The Discovery of the Bismarck* (New York: 1990).

Barnes, Gladeon M., *Weapons of World War II* (New York: 1977).

Brown, David, *Warship Losses, 1939–1945* (New York: 1995).

Campbell, John, *Naval Weapons of World War II* (New York: 1985).

Chamberlain, Peter, and Chris Ellis, *British and American Tanks of World War II* (New York: 1969).

Dornberger, Walter, *V-2* (London: 1954).

Forty, George, *World War Two Tanks* (London: 1995).

Green, William, *Famous Bombers of the Second World War,* 2 vols. (London: 1959–60).

Gunston, Bill, *Aircraft of the Soviet Union* (London: 1983).

Hogg, Ian V., *British and American Artillery of World War 2* (London: 1978).

———, *The Encyclopedia of Infantry Weapons of World War II* (London: 1977).

———, *German Artillery of World War Two* (London: 1975).

Hogg, Ian V. (ed.), *The Americal Arsenal* (New York: 1996).

Hunnicutt, E.P., *Sherman: A History of the American Medium Tank* (Belmont, California: 1978).

Jablonski, Edward, *Flying Fortress* (Garden City, New Jersey: 1965).

Kirk, Johan, and Robert Young, *Great Weapons of World War II* (New York: 1961).

Macksey, Kenneth, *Tank Force: Allied Armor in World War II* (New York: 1970).

Macksey, Kenneth, John Milsom, *Russian Tanks 1900–1970* (New York: 1970).

Mason, David, *U-Boat: The Secret Menace* (New York: 1968).

McLean, Donald B., *Illustrated Arsenal of the Third Reich* (Wickenburg, Arizona: 1973).

Morris, Eric, Christopher Chant, Curt Johnson, and H.P. Willmont, *Weapons and Warfare of the Twentieth Century* (Secaucus, New Jersey: 1976).

Orgill, Douglas, *T-34: Russian Armor* (New York: 1971).

Poolman, Kenneth, *Allied Submarines of World War Two* (New York: 1990).

Rhodes, Richard, *The Making of the Atomic Bomb* (New York: 1986).

Senger und Etterlin, F.M., *German Tanks of World War II* (Harrisburg, Pennsylvania: 1969).

Stanford, Alfred B., *Force Mulberry: The Planning and Installation of the Artificial Harbor Off U.S. Beaches in World War II* (New York: 1951).

Stephens, Frederick J., *Edged Weapons of the Third Reich, 1933–1945* (London: 1972).

Swanborough, Gordon, *United States Military Aircraft Since 1909* (New York: 1963).

Taylor, Frank J., and Larson Wright, *Democracy's Air Arsenal* (New York: 1947).

Taylor, John W.R., *Combat Aircraft of the World from 1909 to the Present* (New York: 1969).

Thetford, Owen, *Aircraft of the Royal Air Force Since 1918* (London: 1957).

Wagner, Ray, *American Combat Planes* (Garden City, New Jersey: 1968).

Weal, Elke C., John A. Weal, and Richard F. Barker, *Combat Aircraft of World War Two* (New York: 1977).

Weeks, John, *Infantry Weapons* (New York: 1971).

Whitley, M.J., *German Capital Ships of World War Two* (New York: 1989).

STRATEGY, TACTICS, AND OPERATIONAL TECHNIQUES

Anders, Władysław, *Hitler's Defeat in Russia* (Chicago: 1953).

Bailey, Jonathan B.A., *Field Artillery and Firepower* (Oxford, England: 1989).

Beesley, Patrick, *Very Special Intelligence: The Story of the Admiralty's Operations Intelligence Center, 1939–1945* (Garden City, New Jersey: 1978).

Bidwell, Shelford, *Gunners at War: A Tactical Study of the Royal Artillery in the Twentieth Century* (London: 1970).

Bidwell, Shelford, and Dominick Graham, *Fire-Power: British Army Weapons and Theories of War, 1904–1945* (London: 1982).

Brown, Anthony Cave, *Bodyguard of Lies* (New York: 1975).

Butler, J.R.M., *Grand Strategy* (London: 1957).

Clausewitz, Carl von, *On War,* edited and

translated by Michael Howard and Peter Paret (Princeton, New Jersey: 1976).

Cruickshank, Charles, *Deception in World War II* (New York: 1980).

———, *The Fourth Arm: Psychological Warfare 1938–1945* (London: 1977).

Dickens, Gerald C., *Bombing and Strategy: The Fallacy of Total War* (London: 1947).

Dixon, Aubrey C., and Otto Heilbronn, *Communist Guerrilla Warfare* (New York: 1955).

English, John A., *On Infantry* (New York: 1981).

Farago, Ladislas, *The Game of Foxes: The Untold Story of German Espionage in the United States and Great Britain During World War II* (New York: 1971).

Fuller, J.F.C., *Armored Warfare* (Harrisburg, Pennsylvania: 1943).

———, *Conduct of War, 1789–1961* (New York: 1961).

Gavin, James M., *Airborne Warfare* (Washington, D.C.: 1947).

Glantz, David M., *Soviet Military Deception in the Second World War* (London: 1989).

Gordon, Don, *Electronic Warfare* (New York: 1981).

Greenfield, Kent Roberts (ed.), *Command Decisions* (Washington, D.C.: 1960).

Gudmundsson, Bruce I., *On Artillery* (Westport, Connecticut: 1993).

Hogg, Ian V., *Barrage: The Guns in Action* (New York: 1970).

House, Jonathan M., *Toward Combined Arms Warfare: A Survey of 20th-Century Tactics, Doctrine, and Organization* (Fort Leavenworth, Kansas: 1984).

Kahn, David, *The Code Breakers* (New York: 1967).

———, *Hitler's Spies* (New York: 1978).

———, *Seizing the Enigma: The Race to Break the German U-Boat Codes* (Boston: 1991).

Kemp, Paul, *Friend or Foe: Friendly Fire at Sea, 1939–1945* (London: 1995).

Leach, Barry A., *German Strategy Against Russia, 1939–1941* (Oxford, England: 1973).

Lewin, Ronald, *Ultra Goes to War* (New York: 1978).

MacDonald, Charles B., *Airborne* (New York: 1970).

McFarland, Stephen L., *America's Pursuit of Precision Bombing* (Washington, D.C.: 1995).

Marshall, S.L.A., *Men Against Fire* (New York: 1947).

Masterman, J.C., *The Double-Cross System in War from 1939–1945* (New Haven, Connecticut: 1972).

Messenger, Charles, *The Blitzkrieg Story* (New York: 1976).

Pile, Frederick, *Ack Ack: Britain's Defense Against Air Attack During the Second World War* (London: 1949).

Tedder, Arthur W., *Air Power in War* (London: 1948).

Trevor-Roper, H.R., *Blitzkrieg to Defeat: Hitler's War Directives 1939–1945* (New York: 1964).

Van der Rhoer, Edward, *Deadly Magic: An Account of Communications Intelligence in World War II* (London: 1978).

Warren, John C., *Airborne Operations in World War II: European Theater* (Washington, D.C.: 1956).

Watts, Anthony, *The U-Boat Hunters* (New York: 1976).

Weeks, John, *Men Against Tanks: A History of Anti-Tank Warfare* (New York: 1975).

Weigley, Russell F., *The American Way of War* (Bloomington, Indiana: 1977).

Wilt, Alan F., *The Atlantic Wall: Hitler's Defense in the West, 1941–1945* (Ames, Iowa: 1975).

Winterbotham, F.W., *The Ultra Secret* (New York: 1974).

Zabecki, David T., *Steel Wind: Colonel Georg Bruchmüller and the Birth of Modern Artillery* (Westport, Connecticut: 1994).

BATTLES, CAMPAIGNS, AND OPERATIONS

Allen, Kenneth, *Battle of the Atlantic* (London: 1973).

Ambrose, Stephen E., *Pegasus Bridge, June 6, 1944* (New York: 1985).

Ambrose, Stephen H., *D-Day, June 6, 1944. The Climactic Battle of World War II* (New York: 1994).

———, *Eisenhower and Berlin, 1945: The Decision to Halt at the Elbe* (New York: 1967).

Bekker, Cajus, *The Luftwaffe War Diaries* (Garden City, New Jersey: 1968).

———, *Verdammte See: Ein Kriegstagebuch der Deutschen Marine 1939–1945* (Munich, Germany: 1971).

Ben Arie, Katriel, *Die Schlacht bei Monte Cassino 1944* (Freiburg, Germany: 1986).

Bennett, Ralph, *Ultra in the West: The Normandy Campaign 1944–45* (New York: 1979).

Bishop, Edward, *Their Finest Hour: The Story of the Battle of Britain 1940* (New York: 1968).

Blau, George E., *The German Campaign in the Balkans* (Washington, D.C.: 1953).

Blond, Georges, *Ordeal Below Zero: The Heroic Story of the Arctic Convoys in World War II* (New York: 1956).

Blumenson, Martin, *Anzio: The Gamble that Failed* (New York: 1963).

———, *Kasserine Pass* (Cambridge, Massachusetts: 1967).

———, *Sicily: Whose Victory?* (New York: 1968).

Bonn, Keith E., *When the Odds Were Even: The Vosges Mountains Campaign, October 1944–January 1945* (Novato, California: 1994).

Bradford, Ernle, *Siege: Malta 1940–1943* (London: 1985).

Caidin, Martin, *The Tigers are Burning* (New York: 1974).

Carse, Robert A., *A Cold Corner of Hell: The Story of the Murmansk Convoys, 1941–1945* (New York: 1969).

Carver, Michael, *El Alamein* (London: 1962).

Chamberlain, Peter, and Chris Ellis, *Afrika Korps: German Operations in the Western Desert, 1941–42* (Stanford, California: 1962).

Chew, Allen F., *The White Death: The Epic of the Soviet-Finnish Winter War* (Lansing, Michigan: 1971).

Chuikov, Vasily, *The Battle for Stalingrad* (New York: 1964).

———, *The Fall of Berlin* (New York: 1968).

Clark, Alan, *Barbarossa: The Russian-German Conflict 1941–1945* (London: 1965).

Coffey, Thomas M., *Decision Over Schweinfurt. The U.S. Eighth Air Force Battle for Daylight Bombing* (New York: 1977).

Condon, Richard W., *The Winter War: Russia Against Finland* (New York: 1972).

Deighton, Len, *Fighter: The True Story of the Battle of Britain* (New York: 1977).

Deschner, Günther, *Warsaw Rising* (New York: 1972).

D'Este, Carlo, *The Battle for Sicily, 1943* (New York: 1991).

Eisenhower, Dwight D., *Report by the Supreme Commander to the Combined Chiefs of Staff on the Operations in Europe of the Allied Expeditionary Force, 6 June 1944–8 May 1945* (Washington and London: 1945).

Elstob, Peter, *Bastogne: The Road Block* (New York: 1968).

———, *The Battle of the Reichswald* (New York: 1970).

Erickson, John, *The Road to Berlin* (Boulder, Colorado: 1983).

———, *The Road to Stalingrad: Stalin's War with Germany* (New York: 1975).

Essame, H., *Normandy Bridgehead* (New York: 1970).

Fadeev, Alexander A., *Leningrad in the Days of the Blockade* (Westport, Connecticut: 1971).

Farrar-Hockley, Anthony, *Airborne Carpet: Operation Market Garden* (New York: 1969).

FitzGibbon, Constantine, *London's Burning* (New York: 1970).

Fleming, Peter, *Operation Sea Lion* (New York: 1957).

Garliński, Józef, *Poland in the Second World War* (London: 1985).

Graham, Dominick, *Cassino* (New York: 1970).

Graham, Dominick, and Shelford Bidwell, *Tug of War: The Battle for Italy 1943–1945* (London: 1986).

Hastings, Max, *Bomber Command* (London: 1989).

———, *Overlord* (London: 1985).

Hessler, Gunter, *The U-Boat War in the Atlantic, 1939–1945* (New York: 1989).

Hoffmann, Joachim, *Kaukasien 1942/43* (Freiburg, Germany: 1991).

Holmes, Richard, *Bir Hakim: Desert Citadel* (New York: 1971).

Horne, Alistair, *To Lose a Battle: France 1940* (Boston: 1969).

Hough, Richard, *The Longest Battle: The War at Sea, 1939–1945* (New York: 1986).

Irving, David, *The Destruction of Dresden* (London: 1963).

Jackson, W.F.G., *The Battle for North Africa* (New York: 1975).

Jacobsen, Jans, and Jurgen Rohwer (eds.), *Decisive Battles of World War II: The German View* (London: 1965).

Jones, Vincent, *Operation Torch: Anglo-American Invasion of North Africa* (New York: 1972).

Jukes, Geoffrey, *The Defense of Moscow* (New York: 1970).

———, *Kursk: The Clash of Armour* (New York: 1968).

Keegan, John, *Barbarossa: Invasion of Russia 1941* (New York: 1970).

———, *Six Armies in Normandy* (London: 1982).

Kennedy, Robert M., *The German Campaign in Poland (1939)* (Washington, D.C.: 1956).

Kieser, Egbert, *Hitler on the Doorstep: Operation "Sea Lion": The Germans Plan to Invade Britain, 1940* (London: 1997).

Kurzman, Dan, *Blood and Water: Sabotaging Hitler's Bomb* (New York: 1997).

Liss, Ulrich, *Westfront, 1939–1940* (Neckargemuend, Germany: 1959).

Lord, Walter, *The Miracle at Dunkirk* (New York: 1983).

Lucas, James, and James Barker, *The Battle of Normandy: The Falaise Gap* (New York: 1978).

MacDonald, Charles B., *A Time for Trumpets: The Untold Story of the Battle of the Bulge* (New York: 1985).

McFarland, Stephen L. and Wesley P. Newton, *To Command the Sky: The Battle for Air Superiority Over Germany, 1942– 1944* (New York: 1991).

Macintyre, Donald, *The Naval War Against Hitler* (New York: 1971).

Macksey, Kenneth, *Afrika Korps* (New York: 1972).

———, *Beda Fomm: The Classic Victory* (New York: 1971).

Manstein, Erich von, *Lost Victories* (Chicago: 1958).

Marshall, S.L.A., *Night Drop: The American Airborne Invasion of Normandy* (Boston: 1962).

Mason, David, *Breakout: Drive to the Seine* (New York: 1968).

———, *Raid on St. Nazaire* (New York: 1970).

———, *Salerno: Foothold in Europe* (New York: 1972).

Mellenthin, F.W. von, *Panzer Battles* (Norman, Oklahoma: 1956).

Middlebrook, Martin, *Convoy* (New York: 1976).

Montagu, Ewen, *The Man Who Never Was* (New York: 1954).

Moulton, James Louis, *A Study of Warfare in Three Dimensions: The Norwegian Campaign of 1940* (Athens, Ohio: 1967).

Mrazek, James E., *The Fall of Eben Emael* (Washington, D.C.: 1971).

Muller, Richard, *The German Air War in Russia* (Baltimore: 1992).

Parotkin, Ivan, *The Battle of Kursk* (Moscow: 1974).

Pitt, Barrie, *The Crucible of War: Western Desert 1941* (London: 1980).

———, *The Crucible of War: The Year of Alamein 1942* (London: 1982).

Potter, John D., *Fiasco: The Break-Out of the German Battleships* (London: 1970).

Raeder, Erich, *Struggle for the Sea* (London: 1959).

Ruge, Friedrich, *Der Seekrieg 1939–1945* (Stuttgart, Germany: 1954).

Rutherford, Ward, *Kasserine: Baptism of Fire* (New York: 1970).

Ryan, Cornelius, *A Bridge Too Far* (New York: 1974).

———, *The Last Battle* (New York: 1966).

———, *The Longest Day: June 6, 1944* (New York: 1959).

Salisbury, Harrison E., *The 900 Days: The Seige of Leningrad* (New York: 1969).

Schroeter, Heniz, *Stalingrad* (New York: 1958).

Seaton, Albert, *The Battle for Moscow, 1941– 1942* (New York: 1971).

———, *The Russo-German War, 1941–1945* (New York: 1971).

Shtemenko, S.M., *The Last Six Months* (New York: 1977).

Spidel, Hans, *Invasion 1944: Rommel and the Normandy Campaign* (New York: 1968).

Steenbeek, Wilhelmina, *Rotterdam: Invasion of Holland* (New York: 1973).

Steward, Ian McDougall, *The Struggle for Crete, 20 May-June 1941* (Oxford, England: 1966).

Stock, James, *Rhine Crossing* (New York: 1973).

Stock, James W., *Tobruk: The Siege* (New York: 1973).

Sweetman, John, *Ploeşti: Oil Strike* (New York: 1974).

———, *Schweinfurt: Disaster in the Skies* (New York: 1971).

Toland, John, *Battle: The Story of the Bulge* (New York: 1959).

———, *The Last 100 Days* (New York: 1965).

Trevelyan, Raleigh, *Rome '44* (New York: 1981).

Turney, Alfred, *Disaster at Moscow* (London: 1971).

Villa, Brian L., *Unauthorized Action: Mountbatten and the Dieppe Raid* (New York: 1989).

Vormann, Nikolaus von, *Der Feldzug 1939 in Polen: Die Operation des Heeres* (Weissenburg, Germany: 1958).

Wegmüller, Hans, *Die Abwehr der Invasion* (Freiburg, Germany: 1986).

Weigley, Russell F., *Eisenhower's Lieutenants: The Campaigns of France and Germany, 1944–45* (Bloomington, Indiana: 1981).

Westphal, Siegfried, *The German Army in the West* (London: 1951).

Whaley, Barton, *Codeword Barbarossa* (Boston: 1973).

Wheeler, Mark C., *Britain and the War for Yugoslavia 1940–1943* (Boulder, Colorado: 1980).

Williams, John, *France: Summer 1940* (New York: 1969).

Wilmont, Chester, *The Struggle for Europe* (London: 1952).

Wolff, Leon, *Low-Level Mission* (Garden City, New Jersey: 1957).

Woodhouse, C.M., *The Struggle for Greece 1941–1949* (London: 1976).

Wykes, Alan, *The Siege of Leningrad: Epic of Survival* (New York: 1970).

Ziemke, Earl F., *Battle for Berlin: End of the Third Reich* (New York: 1968).

———, *The German Northern Theater of Operations, 1940–1945* (Washington, D.C.: 1960).

———, *Stalingrad to Berlin: The German Defeat in the East* (Washington, D.C.: 1968).

Ziemke, Earl F., and Magna Bauer, *Moscow to Stalingrad: Decision in the East* (Washington, D.C.: 1987).

Indexes

A Word About the Indexes

World War II was a vast series of complex and interlocking events. Many of the topics listed in both the Index of Military Units and Warships and the General Index, therefore, are related in various ways.

Every topic with an article in the main body of the encyclopedia has a key entry in the General Index. Some topics, depending on the importance of their relationship to other topics, may also be listed again as a subheading of another topic. The Red Orchestra, for example, has its own main entry in the index, but it also is listed as a subheading of Opposition to Hitler.

All governmental organizations that have their own articles, such as MI-5 and the OSS, likewise have main entries in the General Index. Governmental organizations that do not have articles, such as the British War Cabinet, the American Office of War Mobilization, and the German People's Court, are listed as subheadings under the wartime government of each country.

It is impossible for an encyclopedia of this nature to have a separate article for every battle, operation, and combat action of the war. Those battles not having articles in the book are grouped as logically as possible as subheadings of the appropriate campaign or other larger combat action. Many of the air raids conducted against German cities, for example, have articles and are listed separately in the General Index. Those not having articles are listed under Germany, air campaign. The Siegfried Line campaign has its own article, as do the battles for Aachen, Arnhem, the Hürtgen Forest, and Schmidt—which were all part of the campaign. They all have main entries in the index. The capture of Bitburg, the crossing of the Prüm River, and Operation QUEEN do not have articles. All mention of those actions are grouped in the General Index under Siegfried Line campaign.

All references to items and models of military equipment are listed in the General Index. This includes all mention of warships by their class or type. Individual warships by name, however, are treated as military units and are listed under their respective navies in the Index of Military Units and Warships.

Some specialized military units, like the Rangers, the Commandos, and the Gurkhas, have articles and are, therefore, listed in the General Index. For the sake of completeness, they are also listed with their respective armies in the Index of Military Units and Warships.

Index of Military Units and Warships

The military, naval, and air units in this index are listed in the hierarchical order of military standard organizations. Within a given echelon of command, units are listed numerically and then alphabetically. For example, the three American army divisions with a numerical designation of "1st" are listed in the order 1st Armored Division, 1st Cavalry Division, 1st Infantry Division. Although there are slight variations from country to country, the army units are generally organized as follows: major commands and forces, army groups (fronts in the case of the Soviet Union), armies, corps, divisions, brigades, regiments, battalions, and companies. Functional organizations and technical branches of service, such as the American Army Nurse Corps, Corps of Engineers, Ordnance Corps, and Signal Corps, are listed in alphabetical order after the last operational unit. *Waffen-SS* units are grouped separately after the German army.

Navy units are organized as follows: major commands, fleets, forces, squadrons, flotillas, and groups. Warships are listed by category alphabetically and alphabetically within each category. The designations of air force units reflect the biggest differences from country to country. Air force units generally are listed in the following order: major commands, air forces, air divisions, wings, groups, and squadrons. For the British Royal Air Force, the order is reversed for groups and wings. For the German Air Force, the order is air fleet (*Luftflotte*), air corps (*Fliegerkorps*) and parachute corps, air division (*Fliegerdivision*) and parachute division, wing (*Geschwader*), group (*Gruppe*), and regiment. Military academies, schools, and colleges are listed at the end of this index by country and alphabetically within the country.

Page references to encyclopedia entries appear in bold type. M=map. P=photograph. T=table.

Air Forces

Air Forces

Germany (*Luftwaffe*—Third *Reich*) *(continued)*

Luftwaffenbefehlshaber Mitte, 1648

First Parachute Army, 514, 1357, 1367, 1513, 1561, 1640

First *Luftflotte,* 370

Second *Luftflotte,* 370–71, 467, 595, 1382, 1407, 1435–36, 1576, 1583, 1607

Third *Luftflotte,* 505–06, 1407, 1600

Fourth *Luftflotte,* 393, 467, 1390, 1436, 1456, 1550, 1719

Fifth *Luftflotte,* 1407

Sixth *Luftflotte,* 327, 1413, 1549–50

Luftflotte Reich, 1362

I *Fliegerkorps,* 1403

II *Fliegerkorps,* 1403, 1546

II Parachute *Korps,* 1562, 1641

III *Flak Korps,* 1362

V *Fliegerkorps,* 327, 1546

VIII *Fliegerkorps,* 467, 1177, 1436, 1440, 1676, 1701

X *Fliegerkorps,* 1574, 1576, 1606

XI *Fliegerkorps,* 305, 1125, 1436

XII *Fliegerkorps,* 1648

1st Parachute Division, 1359, 1527, 1585, 1666

2nd Parachute Division, 1404–05

3rd *Fliegerdivision,* 1403

3rd Parachute Division, 1603

4th Parachute Division, 1358

5th *Fliegerdivision,* 327

5th Parachute Division, 240, 1384, 1603, 1658

6th Parachute Division, 1641

7th *Fliegerdivision,* 514, 1125, 1674

7th Parachute Division, 1436, 1471–72, 1595, 1641, 1643, 1647

16th *Flakdivision,* 1403

16th *Luftwaffe* Field Division, 1416

22nd Parachute Division

Jagdgeschwader 7, 510

Jagdgeschwader 26, 312, 510

Jagdgeschwader 27, 595

Jagdgeschwader 44, 224, 510

Jagdgeschwader 52, 244, 463, 510

Jagdgeschwader 77, 510

Jagdgeschwader 300, 463

Jagdgruppe 51, 419

Jagdgruppe 53, 419

Jagdgruppe 88, 419, 695

Jagdverband 44, 312, 510

Kampfgruppe 40, 1188

Kampfgruppe 88, 695

Kampfgruppe 100, 1407, 1435

Kampfgruppe z.b. V.1, 1124

Trägergruppe 186, 892

1st Parachute Regiment, 1437

2nd Parachute Regiment, 1437

3rd Parachute Regiment, 1437

4th Parachute Regiment, 1668

6th Parachute Regiment, 1357, 1671

General Göring Regiment, 1124

Sturmregiment, 1437

Flugmeldehelferinnen, 200

Seenotdienst, 1165

Great Britain (Royal Air Force [RAF]), 154, 199, 283, 284–85, 336–37, 387–89, 398, 441–42, 454–55, 498, 503, 518–19, 527–28, 534, **576–80**, 586, 588, 597–98, 670–71, 750, 814, 862–64, 870–73, 961–63, 965, 973–75, 992–93, 1006, 1019, 1033, 1124, 1142, 1147, 1161–64, 1165, 1167, 1199, 1200, 1203, 1219, 1239–41, 1261, 1272, 1287–88, 1376, 1395, 1449, 1460, 1467

Air Council, 576, 1405

Army Cooperation Command, 1427

Balloon Command, 577

Bomber Command, 318, 336–37, 389, 454–55, 576–80, 591, 862–64, 870, 1164, 1200, 1227, 1240, 1244, 1266–69, 1289, 1393–94, 1397, 1416, 1426, 1427–28, 1479, 1499, 1505–09, 1514, 1532, 1562, 1618–19, 1625, 1647–49

Light Night Striking Force, 228

Pathfinder Force (PFF), 228, 1244, 1499

Coastal Command, 283, 497, 577–80, 711, 713, 863–64, 963, 1086, 1147, 1165, 1370, 1427–28, 1432, 1575

Fighter Command, 221, 283, 284–85, 318, 342, 388, 442, 577–80, 670–71, 713, 870, 1165, 1181–82, 1290, 1393, 1405–9, 1428

Maintenance Command, 577

Reserve Command, 577

Training Command, 577

Allied Expeditionary Air Forces, 537, 579–80, 1658

Mediterranean Allied Air Forces (MAAF), 288, 1495, 1585, 1587

Northwest African Air Forces, 597–98, 1288

Middle East Air Forces, 243, 518, 597

Allied Second Tactical Air Force, 264, 388, 579, 1350, 1415–16, 1442, 1480

Desert Air Force, 264, 1501

Combined Airlift Task Force, 1395–96

No. 1 Bomber Group, 1499

No. 5 Bomber Group, 336, 1227, 1244

No. 6 Bomber Group, 581

No. 8 Bomber (Pathfinder) Group, 1227, 1244, 1499, 1647

No. 11 Fighter Group, 388, 441–42, 577, 1165, 1182, 1408, 1449

No. 12 Fighter Group, 388, 442

No. 83 Group, 1416

No. 2 Fighter Wing, 495

No. 125 Wing, 364

No. 140 Wing, 1350

No. 1 Squadron, 527

No. 17 Squadron, 382

No. 21 Squadron, 1350

No. 23 Squadron, 221

No. 33 Squadron, 443

No. 43 Squadron, 527

No. 47 Squadron, 592

Frankforce, 1389
Layforce, 384, 765
Gideon Force, 555, 616
Small Scale Raiding Force, 765
No. 2 Commando, 1428
No. 3 Commando, 303, 512, 752, 1428, 1448
No. 4 Commando, 303, 752, 1428, 1448, 1672
No. 6 Commando, 303, 1428
No. 7 Commando, 767
No. 8 Commando, 384, 767
No. 9 Commando, 1358
No. 11 Scottish Commando, 371, 767
No. 43 Commando, 1358
No. 62 Commando, 765
"Popski's Private Army," 448–49, 697
Special Boat Squadron, 766

Greece, 440, **627**
East Macedonia Army, 1376
Epris Army, 627, 1377
West Macedonia Army, 1377
3rd Mountain Brigade, 627
Royal Guard, 627
Sacred Company, 627

Greenland, 78, **627–28**, 1735
Northeast Greenland Sledge Patrol, 628

Hungary, 543, **628–29**
First Army, 556, 1409–10, 1535
Second Army, 362, 638, 1455, 1534, 1727
Third Army, 1377, 1534, 1741
2nd Motor Car Brigade, 543

India, **629–30**, 630P, 685–87, 1049
4th Division, 412, 437, 629–30, 686, 1379, 1464,
    1527, 1585, 1587, 1680–81, 1682, 1689–90,
    1710, 1712, 1714
5th Division, 629, 1464, 1577–78
8th Division, 629–30, 1525, 1667–68
10th Division, 629–30, 1452, 1529, 1578, 1706
5th Infantry Brigade, 1706
9th Infantry Brigade, 1501, 1714
10th Infantry Brigade, 1501
17th Infantry Brigade, 1668
29th Infantry Brigade, 1577–78
43rd Gurkha Brigade, 629
Peshawar Brigade, 437

Italy, **630–32**, 819–20, 1011–12, 1020, 1143
Commando Supremo, 1542
Italian Expeditionary Force, 726
First Army, 577, 1570–71, 1609, 1717
Second Army, 212, 1377, 1741
Fourth Army, 480
Sixth Army, 1677
Eighth Army, 638, 1425, 1703
Ninth Army, 440
Tenth Army, 283, 437, 1385–86, 1605, 1680
XX Armored Corps, 1474, 1571, 1578
XXI Corps, 1571, 1682, 1712
Acqui Division, 1351
Ariete Armored Division, 1473, 1500–02, 1578, 1655,
    1682, 1689, 1713

Brescia Division, 1578
Centauro Armored Division, 1541
Cirene Division, 1680
Firenze Division, 1351
Giovani Fascisti Division, 1571
Littorio Armored Division, 1473, 1578
Livorno Division, 1678
Murge Division, 1743
Perugia Division, 1351
Sabratha Division, 1655
Savoi Granadiers Division, 1464
Taurinense Division, 1351
Trento Division, 1578
Trieste Division, 1474, 1500, 1502, 1578, 1607
Venezia Division, 1351
1st Libyan Division, 1681
2nd Libyan Division, 1680
222nd Coastal Division, 1664
7th *Bersaglieri* Regiment, 1578
Raggruppamento Sahariano, 1571
Savoia Cavalleria, 1179

Italian Social Republic, **632–33**
Guardia Nazionale Repubblicana (National Republican
    Guards), 633
Italia Division, 633
Littorio Division, 633
Monterosa Division, 633
San Marco Division, 633

Latvia, 224
Lithuania, 464
Malta
King's Own Malta Regiment, 1567
Royal Malta Artillery, 1566–67

Netherlands, 555, **614–15**, 1594–96
Army Air Service, 582, 1594–95
Air Defense Headquarters, 582
I Corps, 1595
II Corps, 1594
III Corps, 1594
IV Corps, 1594
Princess Irene's Motorized Brigade Group, 615

New Zealand, **633–34**, 1142
New Zealand Expeditionary Force, 534
New Zealand Forces Overseas, 633
Australia-New Zealand Corps (ANZAC), 232
New Zealand Corps, 1527, 1571, 1585
2nd Infantry Division, 633, 696, 1436, 1473, 1527,
    1577–78, 1637, 1655, 1667–68, 1682,
    1712–13
5th Brigade, 634
22nd Battalion, 1437
28th Maori Battalion, 634
Royal New Zealand Artillery, 440

Norway, 73, 297, 479, **634–35**, 1143
Landstorm, 634
Landvärn, 634
1st Division, 634
2nd Division, 634
3rd Division, 634

Armies

Union of Soviet Socialist Republics (Red Army)

(continued)

44th Division, 1705, 1736

51st Perekop Rifle Brigade, 425

58th Guards Rifle Division, 63

123rd Division, 1570

163rd Division, 1705, 1736

1st Artillery Antitank Brigade, 425

23rd Mechanized Brigade, 425

133rd Mechanized Brigade, 425

Women's Reserve Rifle Regiment, 201

Soviet Military Medical Service, 1230–31

United States of America (U.S. Army), 107, 624, **643–47**, 788, 804–05, 809–10, 824–27, 896–97, 977, 993–94, 999, 1015–19, 1020, 1119–22, 1142, 1151, 1162, 1172–73, 1190, 1208–09, 1216

Army General Headquarters (GHQ), 398, 646

Army Air Corps. *See* Air Forces, United States of America

Army Air Service, 596

Armored Force, 253, 276, 335, 444, 645, 1120

Army Ground Forces, 260, 264, 277, 349, 355, 398–99, 644, 646–47, 825, 1658

Army Air Forces. *See* Air Forces, United States of America

Army Service Forces, 355, 499–500, 647

Services of Supply, 263, 499, 646–47. *See also* Army Service Forces

American Expeditionary Force (1917–18), 299, 416, 443

Army Northern Ireland Forces, 752

U.S. Constabulary, 335

1st Army Group, 399

"First U.S. Army Group," 1485–86

6th Army Group, 276, 774, 1349, 1363, 1366, 1426–27, 1497, 1499, 1533, 1596–98

12th Army Group, 63, 238–39, 349, 537, 774, 1066, 1349, 1363–65, 1405, 1426, 1479–81, 1485, 1493, 1597, 1588, 1603, 1660, 1683–84

15th Army Group, 262, 1357, 1636, 1638, 1664, 1677–79, 1725

18th Army Group, 214, 1288, 1609, 1717

First Army, 239, 240, 275, 349, 423, 446, 478, 537, 1349, 1363–66, 1415–16, 1479–80, 1492, 1493, 1513, 1536, 1557, 1588, 1599, 1602–03, 1643–44, 1651, 1657, 1672–73, 1683

First Allied Airborne Army, 243, 1160, 1723

Second Army, 303

Third Army, 239, 240, 262, 290, 292, 310, 334, 349, 355, 444–46, 531, 547, 557, 621, 765, 1256–57, 1349, 1363–65, 1366, 1375, 1384–85, 1405, 1426, 1443–44, 1479, 1485, 1493, 1496–97, 1513, 1532–33, 1556–60, 1579–81, 1588, 1592, 1596, 1603, 1644–45, 1657, 1660, 1660–61, 1683–84

Fourth Army, 394, 443, 739

Fifth Army, 260–62, 305, 356, 408, 478, 530–31, 604, 634, 652, 673, 680, 745, 1357, 1360–61, 1516–18, 1524–27, 1539–40, 1585–87, 1609, 1614, 1636, 1638, 1663–67, 1669, 1725–26

Sixth Army, 262, 550

Seventh Army, 239, 260–61, 273, 276, 290, 443, 444, 745, 1426–27, 1493, 1495–97, 1513, 1533, 1596–98, 1645, 1677–79

Eighth Army, 468, 495, 537, 547, 652

Ninth Army, 239, 275, 494–95, 1363–64, 1405, 1514, 1640–41, 1643–44, 1651, 1683, 1723

Fifteenth Army, 317–18, 446, 1651

I Corps, 243, 438

I Airborne Corps, 335

I Armored Corps, 253, 444

II Corps, 214, 238, 260, 303, 393, 1361, 1402, 1475, 1516–18, 1527, 1541–42, 1571, 1608–09, 1638–39, 1669, 1717

III Corps, 248, 537, 1651

IV Corps, 443, 604, 1516

IV Armored Corps, 547

V Corps, 317–18, 1364, 1491, 1536–37, 1657, 1672–73, 1684

VI Corps, 261, 335, 393–94, 531, 1358–61, 1426, 1495–96, 1514, 1516, 1525–27, 1533, 1539, 1587, 1596–98, 1663–67, 1725–26

VII Corps, 263–64, 289, 315, 1349, 1350, 1491, 1493, 1536, 1588, 1603, 1644, 1657–60, 1672, 1683–84

VIII Corps, 413–14, 1185, 1364, 1404–05, 1493, 1536, 1603, 1657, 1659–60, 1660–61, 1662, 1684

X Corps, 211, 349, 652

XI Corps, 303

XII Corps, 289–90, 310, 495, 558, 1557–60, 1580, 1592–93, 1684

XIV Corps, 443

XV Corps, 1479–80, 1557–59, 1588, 1596–98, 1603

XVI Corps, 1651

XVIII Airborne Corps, 467–68, 1160, 1651, 1684, 1723

XIX Corps, 398, 1350, 1651, 1657, 1683

XX Corps, 547, 1557–60, 1580–81

XXI Corps, 1427

XXII Corps, 335

XXIII Corps, 537

8th Service Command, 547

1st Provisional Airborne Task Force, 304, 1495–96

1st Armored Division, 253, 335, 444, 897, 1120, 1358–61, 1716

   Combat Command A, 1360, 1541–42

   Combat Command B, 1638

   Combat Command C, 1542

1st Cavalry Division, 644, 646

1st Infantry Division, 211, 239, 355, 398, 434, 477, 655, 1349–50, 1402, 1475, 1537, 1600–01, 1657, 1659, 1683–84

General Index

Page references to encyclopedia entries appear in bold type. M=map. P=photograph. T=table.

U.S., **824–27**, 852T
  self-propelled guns
    M-7B1 105mm, 825P, 827
    M-12 155mm, 827
    M-37 105mm, 827
    M-40 155mm, 827
    M-41 155mm, 827
  towed guns
    M-1 155mm, 826–27
    M-1 240mm, 827
    M-1A1 75mm, 827
    M-1A1 155mm, 813
    M-2 8-inch, 827
    M-2A1 105mm, 645, 808, 813, 826–27, 826P
    M-3 105mm, 827
    M-101A1 105mm, 827
    M-114A1 155mm, 827
ASDIC. *See* sonar
Asquith, Prime Minister Herbert, 257
Association of the United States Army (AUSA), 240
Atlantic Campaign, 48, 157, 170, 353, 360, 456, 463,
    515, 578, 582, 588, 591, 700, 714–16, 725,
    734, 799, 801, 858, 866, 893–94, 929, 936,
    1041, 1082, 1085–86, 1086, 1088, 1151,
    1187–90, 1189P, 1193, 1259, 1262, 1269–
    72, 1276, 1282, 1314M, **1369–74**, 1428–35,
    1445, 1467, 1538, 1548, 1577, 1700. *See also*
    Alten Fjord; *Altmark; Atlantis;* Barents Sea;
    Bismarck; Channel Dash; Convoy battle in
    the North Channel; Convoy battle off
    Portugal; Convoy PQ-17; Convoy PQ-18;
    Convoys HX-229 and SC-122; Dakar;
    German Raiders; Granville Raid; North
    Cape; Platte River; Scapa Flow; Operation
    DRUMBEAT; Operation DYNAMO
  Murmansk run, 1041, 1277, 1380–81, 1468, 1610–
    11
Atlantic Charter, 9, **15–16**, 48, 52, 169, 172, 193, 196,
    335, 733, 1269
Atlantic Wall (*Atlantikwall*), 36, 68, 471, 747, **1173–74**,
    1193, 1598
Atlantis, raids, 469, **1374**, 1503–05
Atlee, Prime Minister Clement, 9, 51, **218–19**, 219P,
    231, 259, 267, 427, 661
Atwood, Lee, 871
Aubrial, Admiral Gabriel, 719
Auchinleck, Field Marshal Sir Claude, **219–20**, 220P,
    232, 267, 283, 305, 468, 512, 1352, 1500,
    1502, 1594, 1606–07, 1655, 1682, 1690–91,
    1711, 1713, 1714–15
Aulock, Colonel Andreas, 1661
Auphan, Admiral Paul, 720
Auschwitz. *See* concentration camps
Austria, campaign (1945), 324, **1374–75**. *See also* Vienna
Austrian-German Pact (1936), 8
Austro-Hungarian Empire, 117, 161
Auxiliary Territorial Service (ATS), 199, 377, **648–49**,
    649P, 709. *See also* women in the military,
    Britain

Avranche, counterattack. *See* Mortain
Axis Pact, **16–17**, 52–54, 188, 260, 431, 647
Axis Sally. *See* Gillars, Mildred E.
Axmann, Artur, 485
Azana, Manuel, 1697
Azzam, Abdul Rahman Pasha, 14

B
Baalsrud, Jan, 152
Babi-Yar, massacre, **18**, 81, 1546
Bach-Zalewski, *SS-Obergruppenführer* Erich von dem,
    784, 1733–34, 1734P
Bacherer, Colonel Rudolf, 1661
Baden, Prince Max von, 196, 394
Bader, Group Captain Douglas, **221**, 285, 388, 577
Badoglio, Marshal Pietro, 188–90, 212, **221–22**, 252,
    293, 326, 496, 540, 1271, 1351, 1477–78,
    1519, 1524, 1539
Baedecker air raids, **1376**
  Bath, 1376
  Canterbury, 1376
  Exeter, 1376
  Newcastle, 1376
  Norwich, 1376
  Sunderland, 1376
  York, 1376
Bagnold, Major Ralph A., 696
Bagramyan, General Ivan K., **222**, 1413
BAGRATION, Operation. *See* Byelorussia, campaign
Baker, Staff Sergeant George, **222**, 482, 737
Baker, Newton D., 475
Baker, Roy S., 167
Baker, Lieutenant Vernon J., 656
Bakirtzis, Euripidis, 1522
Bakopoulos, General Nikos, 1376
Bakunin, Mikhail, 40
Balbo, Italo, 188
Balck, General of Panzer Troops Hermann, **222–23**, 409,
    1254, 1424–25, 1559, 1580, 1665–66, 1719
Balck, Lieutenant General William, 222
Baldwin, Stanley, 253
Balkan Pact (1934), 647
Balkan War (1912–1913), 412, 494
Balkans, campaign (1941), 242, 392, 447, 494, 496,
    657, 680, 1230, 1263, 1275, 1290, 1316M,
    1376–78. *See also* Belgrade
  Skopje, capture of, 494
Balkans, campaign (1944-45), 1317M, **1378–79**
Balodis, Jánis, **223–24**,
Baltic states, **18–21**, 67, 116, 191, 506, 618, 677,
    1341M, 1482, 1553, 1691, 1736–37
  Estonia
    Estonian Fascist coup (1935), 400
  Latvia, 271
    Latvian War of Independence (1919–20), 223
Bank of International Settlements (BIS), 204
BARBAROSSA, Operation, 37, 42, 53, 90, 95, 192,
    235, 278, 333, 366, 375, 402, 404, 411, 418,
    425, 447, 463, 465, 479, 480, 569, 588, 640,

bomber aircraft

Soviet *(continued)*
Pe-2, 593, 869, 972, 1150, 1466
Pe-8, 869
Sb-2, 868, 1126, 1465–66
Su-2, 869
Tb-3, 592, 1126
Tu-2, 869
Tu-4, 870
U-2, 870, 1466
Yer-2, 869
U.S., **870–73**, 890T
A-20 Havoc, 870, 873, 1151
A-26 Invader, 873
B-17 Flying Fortress, 288, 299, 532, 597, 787, 864, 868, 869, 870–71, 872P, 1127, 1151, 1165, 1267, 1394, 1435, 1457, 1498, 1505–06, 1532, 1586, 1640, 1673–74
B-24 Liberator, 511, 578, 864, 870–71, 872P, 1086, 1127, 1151, 1267–68, 1457, 1506, 1628, 1723
B-25 Mitchell, 417, 864, 870–71, 1151
B-26 Marauder, 870–71, 1151, 1558, 1586
B-29 Super Fortress, 282, 599, 787, 870, 966, 1150–51
Bonaparte, Napoleon, 1047
Bonesteel, Colonel Charles H., 369
Bong, Major Richard, 571
Bonhoeffer, Pastor Dietrich, 136–37, **235–36**, 1186
Bonhoeffer, Karl, 235
Bonhoeffer, Sabine, 236
Bono Marshal Emilio de, 189–90, 1477
Bonomi, Inavoe, 190
book burning, **30–31**, 31P
books
Air Power in War, 519
All Quiet on the Western Front, 465
Americans Betrayed: Politics of the Japanese Evacuation, 739
Army Flyer, 288
The Army of the Future, 313
The Art of War, 1221
Back Home, 554
The Battle of France, 1489
Bomber Offensive, 337
Brave Men, 457
Carve Her Name with Pride, 516
Combat Commander, 335
The Command of the Air, 184, 1199
Commander in Chief, 476
Crusade in Europe, 194
To the Dark Men of Our Age, 297
This Flying Game, 288
The Future War, 492
The Gulag Archipelago, 36
The Halder Diaries, 333
Here is Your War, 456
Hitler as Warlord, 333
Die Hitlerjugend, 484

Infantrie greift an, 471
The Influence of Sea Power upon History, 476
Inside Hitler's Headquarters, 548
La Silence de la Mer, 151
Lectures on Field Service Regulations, 308
The Man Who Never Was, 1581–82
Man's Hope, 401
Mein Kampf, 13, 24, 69, 81, 108, **114–15**, 123, 339, 353
Men Against Fire, 407
Military History of the Western World, 309
The Myth of the Twentieth Century, 478
Neither Fear nor Hope, 490
Night, 83
Nuremberg and Vietnam: An American Tragedy, 518
OKW War Diary, 1409
Orbit of Satan, 251
Our Armoured Forces, 407
Panzer Battles, 410
Panzer Leader, 330
Protocols of the Elders of Zion, 2, 122
The Rise and Fall of the Third Reich, 491
See Here, Private Hargrove, 738
Skyways, 417
The Socialist Decision, 521
Soviet Military Strategy, 499
Star Spangled Banter, 409
Theory and Practice of Hell, 44
Towards Armageddon, 308
Twelve Legions of Angles, 285
Up Front, 409, 554
U.S. Army in World War II (series), 407
Victory Through Air Power, 490
Winged Defense, 417
Winged Warfare, 288
With Prejudice, 519
Borghese, Prince Junio Valerio, **236**, 633, 1354
Boris III, Tsar of Bulgaria, **236**, 414
Bőr-Komorowski, Lieutenant General Taduesz, 154, **236**, 600, 1634, 1732–35, 1734P
Bormann, Martin, 69, 91–94, 186, **237–38**, 237P, 281, 323, 340, 680, 707, 780
Borowietz, Major General Wilibald, 1571
Bottai, Giuseppi, 188–90
Bourret, General V., 816
Bousquet, René, 179–80
Boxer Rebellion, 371, 385
Bracher, Karl Dietrich, 8, 129
Bradley, General Omar N., 63, **238–40**, 239P, 275, 276, 318, 349, 355, 393, 458, 477–78, 537, 774, 1173, 1179, 1349, 1363–64, 1405, 1479–81, 1485, 1579, 1588, 1599, 1602–03, 1609, 1621, 1642, 1651, 1657, 1660, 1683–84
Brandenberger, General Erich, **240–41**, 1362, 1384, 1513
Brandenburg Division, 569, **657–58**, 694, 1264, 1470, 1577, 1594–95
Bau-und-Lehrkompanie Brandenburg, 1594
Kustenjägers, 657, 694, 1470

Caen, battle, 239, 423, 1179, 1338M, **1415–17**, 1491–92, 1602, 1657
  Bourquébus Ridge, 1417
  CHARNWOOD, Operation, 1416–17
  EPSOM, Operation, 414, 1415–17
  GOODWOOD, Operation, 1417, 1492, 1602–03, 1657–58
Cairncross, John, 701
Cairo Conference. *See* conferences, Allied
Calabria, battle, 1337M, **1417–18**, 1574
Cameron, Lieutenant Donald, **250**, 453, 1355
Camp X, **660**, 702
Campbell, Brigadier John C., **250**
Campbell, Lieutenant General Levin H., 1066
Campbell-Bannerman, Henry, 257
Campioni, Admiral Inigo, 1417–18
Canaris, Admiral Wilhelm, 236, **250–51**, 280, 341, 484, 569, 722–25, 1481, 1515, 1582
Capra, Frank, 143
Carls, Admiral Rolf, 1616
Carol II, King of Romania, 216, **251**, 414
Carpenter, Chaplain Charles I., 1184
carpet bombing, **1179**, 1657
Carr, Wilbur J., 368
Carré, Mathilde L., 233, **251**
carrier-borne aircraft
  British, 711, **891–92**, 909–10T
    Albacore, 1572
    Fulmar, 891, 1574
    Roc, 891
    Sea Gladiator, 891, 962, 1565
    Sea Hurricane, 891
    Seafire, 891
    Skua, 891
    Swordfish, 268, 891, 892P, 1418, 1424, 1566, 1572, 1574, 1708–09
  German, **892–93**, 911T
    Bf-109T, 892
    Fi-167, 892
    Ju-87C, 892
  Italian, **892–93**, 911T
    Re.2001, 893
  U.S., **893–94**, 909–10T
    F-4F, 891, 893–94, 962
    FM-1, 893–94
    TBF Avenger, 893–94
    TBM Avenger, 893–94
Carton de Wiart, Lieutenant General Sir Adrian, **251–52**
Cartwright, Marjorie, 86
Caruso, Pietro, 15
Casablanca Conference. *See* conferences, Allied
Cassino. *See* Gustav-Cassino Line, campaign; Monte Cassino, battle
Castellano, General Giuseppi, 190
casualty figures, **32-34**
CATAPULT, Operation. *See* Mers el Kébir
Catlos, General Ferdinand, **252**
Catroux, General Georges, 1706–07

Caucasus, campaign, 324, 375, 392, 400, 403, 638, 860, 1235, 1275–77, 1319M, **1418–22**, 1425, 1440–41, 1451, 1470, 1547, 1548, 1691, 1694–95, 1701, 1726, 1738
  Maykop, capture of, 1420
  Nalchik, battle, 1421
  Ordzhonikidze, battle, 1421
  Tuapse, battle, 1235
Cavagnari, Admiral Domenico, 188
Cavallero, Marshal Count Ugo, 189, 212, **252–53**, 483, 1577
cavalry operations, **1179–81**, 1180P
Caviglia, Marshal Enrico, 189
Céline, Louis-Ferdinand, 38
Celles, battle, 553, 1312M, **1422–23**, 1365
censorship, **34–36**, 1190
Central Intelligence Agency (CIA), 141–42, 152, 282, 287, 498, 693, 701–02, 747
Cernlli, Enrico, 483
Četniks, 76, 414, 523, 648, **660–61**, 750, 767, 1741–42
"chaff." *See* radar
Chaffee, Major General Adna R., **253**, 625, 645, 1120
Chain, Dr. Ernst B., 1148
CHAIN HOME, 548–49, 1067–68, 1147, 1161, 1163, **1181–82**, 1181P, 1219, 1318M, 1406
CHAIN HOME LOW, 549, 1068, 1318M, 1406
Chamberlain, Austen, 111, 253, 290
Chamberlain, Houston Stewart, 22, 122, **253**
Chamberlain, Joseph, 253
Chamberlain, Prime Minister Neville, 12–14, 108, 116–20, 117P, 182–83, 218, 226, **253–54**, 258, 265, 290, 351, 391, 557, 658, 1520, 1538, 1630, 1691, 1699
Channel Dash, battle, 725, 1315M, **1423–24**, 1735
Channel Islands, **36**, 622, 668, 747, 1520, 1599
chaplain support operations, 386, **1182–86**
Chapman, Edie ("Zig Zag"), 701
Charlemagne, 1349
Chatfield, Lord, 182
Chelmno. *See* concentration camps
chemical warfare deterrence, **36–37**, 1382–83, 1477. *See also* Bari; Ethiopia
Chennault, Major General Claire L., 534
Cherevichenko, General N.T., 1646
Chernyakovsky, General Ivan D., **254–55**, 254P, 538, 601, 1413, 1510, 1634–35
Cherwell, Lord. *See* Lindemann, Frederick
Cheshire, Group Captain Leonard, **255**, 255P
Chevallerie, General Kurt von der, 1496
Chiang Kai-shek, 47, 49, 252, 489, 541
Chicherin, Gerogy, 146
Chilton, Robert, 975
Chir River, battle, 223, 1346M, **1424–25**, 1703
Chkalov, V.K., 592
Choltitz, General Dietrich von, **255–56**, 1621–23, 1658–59
Christian X, King of Denmark, 148, **256**, 628, 1447
Christiansen, Major General James G., 399
Chruściel, Colonel Antoni, 1732–33

Falkenhorst, Colonel General Nikolaus von. **296**, 500, 1604, 1617
Falklands War (1982), 311, 687
Fall GELB (Case YELLOW), Operation, 1259, 1387–90, 1486, 1594, 1633
   Sichelschnitt, 1387
Fall WEISS (Case WHITE), Operation. *See* Poland, invasion of
Farinacci, Roberto, 190
Farley, James, 474
Farūq, 'Abd al-'Aziz, King of Egypt, **296–97**, 615
Fascism, 4, 13, 57, **65–66**, 103, 121–24, 165, 189–90, 222, 430–31, 452, 540, 631, 642, 650–51, 1476, 1697
   Brigate Nere (Black Brigades), 633
   Fascio di Combattimento, 430
fast attack boats, 981–82T
   Britain, 961
   Germany, 1469–70, 1503
   Italy, 1469, 1567
   Soviet, 1468–69
   U.S., 961
Faulhaber, Cardinal Michael von, **297**
FBI. *See* wartime government, United States
Feder, Gottfried, 706
Fedjuninsky, Colonel General I.I., 59
Fedorenko, Colonel General Yakov N., 640, 1727
Fegelein, Hermann, 428
Fehn, General Gustav, 575–76
Felber, General Hans, 1513
FELIX, Operation, 53, **1481–82**
Fermi, Enrico, 112
Ferrandis, Major, 595
Fichte, Johann G., 122
Fiebeg, Major General Martin, 1641
fighter aircraft
   Belgian
      Renard R-36, 576
   British, **961–63**, 983T, 1031–33, 1037T
      Beaufighter, 962–63, 1147, 1240, 1436, 1453
      Blenheim, 962
      Bulldog, 221
      Defiant, 962
      Fury, 1147
      Gamecock, 221
      Gladiator, 443, 962, 1464, 1520
      Hurricane, 284, 302, 442, 443, 527, 578, 670, 869, 961–62, 965–66, 969, 970, 973, 1163–64, 1182, 1406–08, 1566
      Meteor. *See* jet aircraft, British
      Mosquito, 961–63, 1069, 1449
      Spitfire, 221, 284, 310, 342, 442, 578, 670–71, 711, 891, 961–62, 965–66, 969, 970, 973, 1147, 1163–64, 1182, 1399–1400, 1405–08, 1424, 1449, 1453, 1566, 1576, 1665
      Tempest, 963, 1449
      Typhoon, 963, 1449
      Whirlwind, 963
   French, **963–64**, 984T

      MB-152, 583, 964
      D.520, 964
      H-75A, 964
      M.S.405, 972
      M.S.406, 964, 972
      Potez 63, 583
      Potez 631, 964
      P-36, 463, 964
      VG-33, 964
   German, **964–68**, 985T, 1031–33, 1037T
      Ar-68, 965
      Bf-109, 221, 224, 325, 392, 405, 412, 443, 512, 587, 595, 670, 695, 798, 892–93, 961, 964, 965–66, 970, 972, 973, 1164, 1182, 1397, 1407, 1453, 1465–66, 1501, 1508
      Bf-110, 443, 588, 961, 966, 972, 992, 1164, 1219, 1240, 1398, 1407, 1648
      Do-217, 967
      Do-335, 967
      FW-190, 517, 595, 864, 866, 964, 965–66, 970–71, 1148, 1398, 1453, 1466, 1508
      He-51, 694–95, 970
      He-162. *See* jet aircraft
      He-219, 966–67, 1148
      Ju-88, 965–66, 1219, 1240, 1397, 1648
      Me-163, 412, 589, 964, 968, 1148
      Me-209, 412
      Me-262. *See* jet aircraft, German
      Me-410, 966
      Ta-152, 517, 964, 966
      Ta-312, 517
   Italian, **968–70**, 986T
      Ba.65, 969
      CR.32, 969, 970, 1464
      CR.42, 969, 1464
      G.50 bis, 969
      G.55, 633, 969
      MC.200, 969
      MC.202, 969, 1501
      MC.205, 633, 969
      Re.2001, 969
      Re.2001 (naval version) 798, 893
      Re.2002, 969
      Re.2005, 969–70
   Japanese
      Ki-27, 970
   Polish
      P-7, 591
      P-11, 495, 591
   Soviet, **970–72**, 987T
      BI-1, 972, 1072
      I-15, 970, 1465–66
      I-16, 970, 1465–66
      I-153, 970, 1465–66
      La-5, 970, 1466
      La-7, 970, 972
      LaGG-3, 970, 1465
      MiG-1, 331, 415
      MiG-3, 331, 415, 970, 1465

Life, 444, 1202
National Geographic, 389
Neue Blätter für den Sozialismus, 520–21
Newsweek, 503
Signal, 738
Joyce, William, **364**, 364P, 657
JUBILEE, Operation. *See* Dieppe
JUDGEMENT, Operation. *See* Taranto
JUGGLER, Operation. *See* Regensburg, air raids
Juin, General Alphonse, **364**, 383, 1487, 1525, 1527, 1587, 1597
Juliana, Princess of the Netherlands, 553
July plot against Hitler, 137, 238, 251, 308, 321, 329, 333, 347, 376, 418, 420, 438–39, 447, 472, 483, 485, 505, 515, 548, 556, 561, 570, 695, 725, 762, 1186, 1603. *See also* Hitler, opposition to
Jung, Edgar, 470

K

Kaganovich, L.M., 592
Kähler, Commander Otto, 1503–04
Kahr, Gustav *Ritter* von, 22–23, 129
Kaiser, Henry J., **365**, 800
Kaltenbrunner, *SS-Obergruppenführer* Ernst, 91–94, 229, **365–66**, 365P, 755, 759
Kaminev, Leo, 41
Kamiński, Mieczysław, 1733
Kammhuber, Lieutenant General Josef, **366**, 1219, 1506, 1648
Kammhuber Line, 1069, **1219–20**, 1240, 1506
  Benito, ground approach procedure, 1648
  Seeburg table, 1240
Kammler, *SS-Brigadeführer* Heinz, 1723
Kane, Colonel John R., 1628
Kaplan, Chaim, 1730
Kapp, Dr. Wolfgang, 98, 722
Kapp-Lüttwitz *Putsch,* **98**, 197, 394, 485, 650, 679, 722
Kappler, Herbert, 15
Karaszewicz-Tokarzewski, Major General Michał, 600
Karl I, Austro-Hungarian Emperor, 162
Kartalis, George, 1523
Kartveli, Alexander, 490, 973
Kasiski, Frederich, 1193
Kassa, Ras, 1477
Kasserine Pass, battle, 211, 293, 444, 552, 1333M, 1475, **1541–43**, 1576, 1608, 1717
Katukov, General Mikhail, 1635
Katyń Forest massacre, 75, 93, **99–100**, 133–34, 154, 228, 493, 601, 637
Katzelnelson, Yitzhak, 82
Kauffman, Lieutenant Commander Draper, 778
Kauffman, Henrik, 1447
Kaupitsch, Major General Leonhard, 1447
Kearny Incident, **100**, 158, 171, 733
Keegan, John, 746
Keitel, Field Marshal Wilhelm, 29, 43, 91–94, 140, 338, 346, 360, **366–67**, 367P, 680, 742–44, 1211, 1515, 1602, 1616–17, 1633

Keller, Helen, 31
Kellogg-Briand Pact, **100–01**
Kemal, Mustafa, 627
Kemp, Anthony, 1564
Kemp, P.K., 120
Kempf, General Werner, 1450, 1456, 1550–51
Kennan, George F., **367–69**, 1278
Keough, Vernon, 670
Kerckhoffs, Auguste, 1193
Kerserovic, Dragutin, 660
Kesselring, Field Marshal Albert, 15, 64, 364, **369–71**, 370P, 438, 541, 552, 575, 595, 1257–61, 1435–36, 1513–14, 1516, 1525, 1527, 1539–40, 1541–42, 1576, 1577, 1582–84, 1585–87, 1637, 1664–67, 1677–79, 1716
Ketes, Major General Geoffrey, 1638–39
Keyes, Lieutenant Colonel Geoffrey C.T., **371**, 1543
Keyes, Admiral of the Fleet Sir Roger, **371**, 455, 667, 668, 766, 1543, 1661
Keyes Raid, **1543**
Keynes, John Maynard, 12, 167
KGB. *See* wartime government, Soviet
Kharkov, battle, 235, 375, 403, 447, 491, 507, 521, 1319M, 1345M, **1543–45**, 1727
  FRIEDERICUS, Operation, 1545
Khozin, General M.S., 411
Khripin, General Vasily, 594
Khrushchev, Nikita S., 156, 324, **371–372**, 401, 420, 426, 507, 538, 544, 564
Khrulev, General Andrei, 770
Kiev, battle (1941), 247, 480, 507, 1345M, 1543, **1545–47**, 1693
Kiffer, Raoul, 233
Kimmel, Admiral Husband, 733–34
King, Vice Admiral E.L.S., 1706
King, Fleet Admiral Ernest J., 218P, 279, **373–374**, 373P, 477, 508, 733–34, 1458
King, Chaplain William E., 1185
King, William L. Mackenzie, Prime Minister of Canada, 57, **374**, 400, 611
Kinloch, Lieutenant Commander D.C., 1381
Kinzel, Major General Eberhard, 316, 1514
Kinzel, Lieutenant Commander Manfred, 1434
Kirchner, General Friederich, 1459
Kirk, Admiral Alan G., **374**, 736
Kirk, Alexander, 368
Kirkman, Brigadier Sidney, 815
Kirov, Sergei M., 144
Kirponos, General Mikhail, 639, 1546
Kissinger, Henry, 1278
Kleeberg, Major General Franciszek, **375**, 1632
Kleinkampfverbände (KKV), **694**, 1264, 1577
Kleist, Field Marshal Paul Ludwig Ewald von, 329, **375–76**, 375P, 400, 480, 1377, 1389, 1420–21, 1425, 1456, 1459, 1487, 1545–46, 1646, 1720, 1741
Klimov, Vladimir, 592
Klingenberg, Fritz, 784
Klintzsch, Hans Ulrich, 772

Lovat, Lord. *See* Fraser, Simon C.

Love, Nancy Harkness, 787

Love, Major Robert, 787

Lovett, Robert, 596

Low Countries, campaign (1945), 1336M, **1560–62**
    AMHERST, Operation, 1561
    Delfzijl Pocket, battle, 1562
    Grebbe Line, battle, 1562
    Kapelsche Veer, battle, 1561
    PLUNDER, Operation, 1561, 1723

Low, David, 233, **393**

Low, Rear Admiral Francis S., 734

Löwenfeld, Captain Wilfried, 722

Löwenheim, Walter, 135

Lowry, Rear Admiral Frank J., 736, 1358

Lubbe, Marinus van der, 147

Lubbock, Dr. Isaac, 1069

Lucas, James, 1515

Lucas, Major General John P., **393–94**, 531, 736, 1357–
    61, 1525–26, 1667

Lucht, Lieutenant General Walter, 1513

Ludendorff, Erich, 22–24, 122, 163, **394**, 1645

Lueger, Karl, 345

Lumsden, Lieutenant General Herbert, 1473, 1502

Lütjens, Vice Admiral Günther, **394–95**, 395P, 1399–
    1402

Lutsky, M., 156

Lüttwitz, Lieutenant General Heinrich von, 1383–84

Lüttwitz, Lieutenant General Smilo von, 1641

Lüttwitz, General Walther *Freiherr* von, 98, 679

Lutze, Viktor, **305**

Lynn, Vera M., **395**

Lyster, Rear Admiral A.L. St.G, 1708

Lyton Commission, 106

M

MacArthur, General of the Army Douglas, 243, 263,
    282, 292, 313, 373, 477, 734, 746

MacDonald, Ramsay, 8, 218

Mach, Dr. Ernst, 1149

Mack, Captain P., 1573

Mackensen, Colonel General Eberhard von, **400**, 1358–
    61, 1456, 1646

MacKinder, Halford J., 107

Macksey, Major General P.J., 1594

Maclean, Donald, 701

MacNarney, General Joseph T., 5

Macon, Major General Robert C., 1661

Macridis, Roy C., 123–24

Maczek, Lieutenant General Stanisław, 400

Mae, Dr. Hjalmar, **400**

Maercker, General Ludwig, 548

Maffey, John, 1476

Maginot, Andre, **400–01**, 1225

Maginot Line, battle, 386, 603, 1327M, **1563–64**

Maginot Line, defensive installation, 142, 191, 295, 400,
    449, 618–19, 816, 821, 1008, 1174, 1125,
    1175, 1327M, 1387, 1486–87, 1570, 1596,
    1683

Magrin-Vernerey, Lieutenant Colonel, 679

Magruder, Peyton M., 873

Mahan, Admiral Alfred Thayer, 476

Malenkov, Georgy M., **401**, 705

Malinkovsky, Marshal of the Soviet Union Rodion Y.,
    401, 1378, 1443, 1451, 1534–35, 1635,
    1720

Malmédy, massacre, 278, 448, 784, 1312M, 1385,
    1564–65

Malraux, André, **401**, 1699

Malta, air campaign, 230, 324, 442, 581, 713, 726,
    1337M, **1565–67**, 1568, 1577, 1609, 1614,
    1714–15
    HERCULES, Operation, 370

Malta, relief convoys, 268, 397, 500, 700, 727, 796,
    1337M, 1432, 1566, **1568–70**, 1608, 1685,
    1686–87
    HALBRED, convoy, 1569
    HARPOON, convoy, 1566, 1569
    HATS, convoy, 1568
    PEDESTAL, convoy (WS-21S), 700, 796, 1337M,
        1567–68, 1567P, 1569, 1576
    PORTCULLIS, convoy, 1569
    STONEHENGE, convoy, 1569
    SUBSTANCE, convoy, 1569
    VIGOROUS, convoy, 1566, 1569

Maltzen, Ago *Freiherr* von, 146

Mamedoff, Andrew, 670

Mamsurov, General, 769

Manchester, air raids, 1213

Mancinelli, General Giuseppe, 1571

Manella, General Patassi, 1710

MANHATTAN Project, **112**, 249, 291, 327–28, 439,
    529, 600, 1148, 1151

Manic, Bora, 660

Mann, Thomas, 31, 1376

Mannerheim, Marshal Carl G., **402**, 411, 617–18,
    1482–83, 1552, 1553, 1555, 1570, 1737

Mannerheim Line, battle, 439, 617, 1326M, **1570**,
    1705, 1737

Mannerini, General Alberto, 1571

Mannock, Major Edward C., 570

Manstein, Field Marshal Erich von, 187, 346, 401, **402–
    03**, 418, 447, 480, 539, 556, 638, 1259,
    1412, 1424–25, 1439–40, 1450–52, 1456,
    1486, 1544, 1548, 1550, 1676, 1703, 1719–
    20

Manteuffel, General Hasso von, **403–04**, 1362–64,
    1483–84, 1512, 1558, 1593, 1662

manuals, military
    France
        *Instruction Générale sur le Tir de l'Artillerie
            (General Instructions for the Fire of Artillery),*
            816
    Germany
        *Army Manual 487, Command and Combat of the
            Combined Arms* (*Heeresdienstvorschrift 487,
            Führung und Gefecht der verbundenen Waffen,*
            "DAS FuG), 1176

75, 276, 293, 304P, 306, 324, 325, 330, 352, 362, 371, 387, 388, 397, **421–24**, 422P, 424, 434, 440, 444, 493, 520, 535, 613, 615, 774, 815, 1160, 1173, 1197–98, 1261, 1262, 1271, 1349, 1352–53, 1356, 1363–64, 1366–68, 1396–97, 1416–17, 1448, 1472–74, 1475, 1480–81, 1491–93, 1513–14, 1525, 1536, 1541–42, 1557, 1561–62, 1571, 1599, 1602, 1607–09, 1642, 1655–56, 1657, 1663, 1667–68, 1677, 1679, 1684, 1717, 1723

Montgomery, David, 422

Montgomery, Elizabeth (Carver), 422

Montherlant, Henry de, 38

Moon, Rear Admiral Don P., 736

Moore, Brigadier General James E., 495

Morgan, Lieutenant General Sir Frederick, **424**

Morgen, Konrad, 761

Morgenthau, Henry J. Jr., 90, 116, 356, **424–25**

Morgenthau Plan, 4, **116**, 356, 424, 529

Morison, Samuel Elliot, 734

Morshead, Lieutenant General Sir Leslie J., **425**, 602, 1689, 1711

Mortain, battle, 376, 1177, 1271, 1276, 1338M, 1479, 1493, **1588–89**, 1603

Moscow, battle, 192, 235, 325, 350, 378, 404, 465, 470, 491, 499, 500, 541, 563–64, 595, 641, 823, 1126, 1162, 1275, 1277, 1296, 1345M, 1545, 1547, 1554, 1582, **1589–91**, 1645–46, 1693, 1728–29

    Vyazma, Soviet airborne landings, 1590

Moscow Declaration (1943), 91, 1374

Moskalenko, Colonel General Kirill S. **425–26**

Mosley, Sir Oswald, 364, 417, **426**, 701

Mosley, Raymond, 474

Moulin, Jean, 151, **426–27**, 674

mountain operations, **1234–35**

Mountbatten, Vice Admiral Lord Louis, 49, 246, 252, 361, 384, **427**, 550, 667, 668, 1447, 1581–82, 1612, 1661

MULBERRY. *See* artificial harbors

Müller, Lieutenant General Friederich-Wilhelm, 1511

Müller, *SS-Gruppenführer* Heinrich, **427–28**

Müller, Hermann, 98, 197, 486

Müller, Josef, 136

Müller, Bishop Ludwig, 135

Mulugeta, Ras, 1477

Munich Crisis and Agreement, 12–14, 30, 75, 108, **116–120**, 117P, 161–63, 164, 227, 254, 258, 265, 270, 290, 333, 351, 368, 429, 556, 1353, 1699

Murcia, Major, 595

Murphy, Lieutenant Audie, **428–29**, 428P

Murphy, Justice Frank, 740

Murphy, Ambassador Robert D., 272, 553, 1612, 1614

Murray, Rear Admiral L.W., 715

Murrow, Edward R., **429**

Muselier, Admiral Emile, 718, 720

Mussolini, Alessandro, 429

Mussolini, Benito, 8, 13, 16, 57, 117P, 121–22, 125–26, 157, 197, 212, 221, 252, 254, 258, 260, 279, 290, 326, 412, **429–32**, 451, 454, 476, 483, 488, 489, 540, 556, 589–90, 621, 700, 797, 859, 1199, 1249, 1265, 1275–76, 1353, 1377, 1379, 1385, 1476, 1524, 1548, 1574–76, 1605, 1614, 1677, 1697–98

    conferences, Axis, 52–54

    fascism, 65–66

    Italian wartime government, 188–90

    Italian wartime strategy, 1403, 1680, 1715

    Latern Treaty, 103

    Munich Crisis, 116–20, 1353

    overthrow of, 268, 293, 1351, 1539, 1679, 1716

    rescue of, 496, 514, 632, 1010

    execution of, 432, 633

Mussolini, Rosa, 429

Muth, Carl, 487

Myers, Brigadier E.C.W., 1522

N

Nacht und Nebel (Night and Fog), 43, **121**, 367

Nahas, Mustafa, 296

Nancy, battle, 207, 262, 1328M, **1592–93**

    Arracourt, battle, 1593

Narodnyy Kommissariat Vnutrenniakh Del (NKVD), 89, 99, 153, 192, 228, 325, 426, 470, 529, 531, 637, 641, 672, **705–06**, 749, 755, 768–70, 1071, 1072, 1190, 1217, 1261, 1280–81, 1420, 1553, 1583, 1732, 1739

    OO-NKVD, 705

    Osnaz, 705, 769

Narvik, battle, 219, 277, 297, 332, 404, 621, 636, 680, 712, 719, 933, 1340M, 1543, **1593–94**, 1617

Nasi, General Guglielmo, 483, 1465

Nassau-Weilburg, Grand Duchess Charlotte von, 74–75, **433**

Nassau-Weilburg, Prince Felix, 433

Nassau-Weilburg, Prince Jean, 433

Nasser, Gamal Abdul, 14, 290, 615

National Association of German Officers, 679

National Catholic Community Servics, 779

National Committee to Save the Jews in Occupied Europe, 182

National Council for the Prevention of War, 96

National Inter-Professional Purge Commission, 38

National Jewish Welfare Board, 779, 1183

national redoubt, **121**, 487, 496, 553, 1375

National Security Act (1947), 298

National Socialism, 4, 57, 64, 66, 80, 114, **121–24**, 142, 234, 297, 434, 467, 478, 524, 677, 723, 1185, 1194, 1212, 1273, 1691, 1724

National Socialist Civil Service Act (1933), 73

National Socialist German Workers' Party (NSDAP), 5, 8, 12, 22, 73, 80, 92, 94, 122, 131–32, 135, 186–87, 198, 226, 237, 246, 270, 278, 291, 294, 301, 304, 305, 306, 307, 320, 322, 339–40, 341–42, 343, 345–47, 353, 395,

Polbin, Lieutenant I.S., 1466
Polikarpov, N.N., 592
Poling, Lieutenant Clark V., **299**
Polish Corridor, **140–41**, 1629
Polish-Soviet Agreement (1941), 213, 461, 561
Political Warfare Executive (PWE), 143, **750–51**, 767, 1217
Pollack, Ben, 416
Polryshkin, Colonel A.I., 594
Pölzl, Klara, 345
Pompidou, Georges, President of France, 526
Popov, Dusko ("Tricycle"), 701
Popov, Colonel General Markian M., **453–54**, 639, 1456, 1550
Portal, Air Chief Marshal Sir Charles, 268P, 336, **454–55**, 518, 576, 1509
Portes, Countess Helene de, 466
Posner, Gerald, 142
Potsdam Conference. *See* conferences, Allied
Poulsen, Ib, 628
Poulsson, Lieutenant Jens, 1604
Pound, Admiral Sir Dudley P., **455–56**, 455P, 1460
Powell, General Colin, 656
Powell, Squadron Leader Peter, 670
Pradzynski, Ignacy, 1654
Pratt, Admiral William V., 799
Preddy, Major George E., 975
Prételat, General André, 1564
Preuss, Joachim, 100
Previsi, General Prenk, **456**
Preysing, Monsignor, 452
Prezzolini, Guiseppi, 65
Price, Ward, 68
Pridham-Wippell, Vice Admiral H.D., 1572–73
Priebke, Erich, 15
Prien, Lieutenant Commander Günther, **456**, 1085, 1429–30, 1669–71
Primo de Rivera y Orbaneja, General Miguel, 300
principles of war, 406, **1246–47**, 1255
Prior, General Willem, **456**
Prioux, General René, 1388
prisoner of war operations, 1141, 1182, 1204, 1216, **1247–50**, 1248P
  Camp Gordon, Georgia, 1206
  Oflag IVb, 221
  Oflag IVc, 664
  Oflag XIIIb, 1532
  Stalag Luft I, 310
  Stalag Luft III, 1205
Probst, Christoph, 487, 785
Pröhl, Ilse, 339
propaganda, **141–44**, 1250
proximity fuze, 801, 803, 804, **1065–66**, 1069, 1073, 1123, 1150, 1161
Psaros, Dimitrios, 1522
psychological operations, 143, 345, **1250–52**
Punitive Expedition in Mexico (1914), 385, 398, 414, 443, 444, 494, 498, 530
  Vera Cruz, landings (1914), 360, 398

Purchase, Bentley, 1581
purges, Soviet, 90, 100, 115, **144–45**, 191–92, 228, 247, 324, 368, 378, 381, 401, 448, 470, 491, 506, 521, 522, 531, 532, 538, 541, 544, 562, 593, 595, 705, 730–32, 769, 860, 1088, 1171, 1173, 1465, 1692, 1737, 1741
Pyle, Ernest, **456–57**

Q

Q-ships, 929
Quesada, Lieutenant General Elwood, **458–59**, 502
Quisling, Vidkun, 38–39, 152–53, 332, **459–60**, 459P, 500, 520, 1616–18

R

Raczkiewicz, Władysław, President of Poland, **461**
Raczyński, Ambassador Edward, **461**
radar, 268, 281, 283, 284–85, 302, 308, 366, 391, 442, 461, 500, 524, 548, 577, 594, 596, 710–12, 714, 717, 718, 727–28, 734, 799, 803–04, 854, 858, 859, 896, 899, 900, 901, 902, 903, 905, 930, 932, 933, 934, 935, 936, 961, 962, 1065, **1067–69**, 1091, 1122, 1148, 1149, 1150, 1151, 1161–62, 1165, 1181–82, 1188–89, 1200, 1203, 1237–38, 1259, 1262, 1270, 1282–85, 1370, 1373, 1393, 1400, 1405–08, 1435, 1449–50, 1506, 1532, 1572, 1574, 1610–11, 1627, 1740
  Airborne Intercept (AI), 1067–68, 1239, 1436
  "Battle of the Beams," 1203
  Boozer, 1068, 1240
  "chaff," 1162, 1203, 1219, 1499
  Flensburg (FuG-227), 1069, 1240
  Freya, 1068, 1219, 1466
  FuMB radar warning device, 1430
  Gee, 1068, 1240, 1244, 1267, 1427
  H2S, 1068–69, 1240, 1244, 1507, 1625, 1648–49
  H2S/H2X, 1244
  Knickebein, 1068, 1203, 1436
  Lichtenstein (Fu-220), 966–67, 1068P, 1069, 1203, 1240, 1648
  Metox, 1087
  Micro-H, 1244
  Monica, 1068–69, 1240
  Naxos (FuG-350), 1069, 1240
  Neptun, 1069, 1240
  Oboe, 1068, 1240, 1244, 1267, 1507, 1625, 1648–49
  Rebecca-Eureka, 1068
  Serrate, 1240
  Type 291, 1069
  "window," 1162, 1203, 1219, 1394, 1507, 1532
  Würzburg, 1069, 1219, 1410–11, 1648
  X-Gerät, 1435–36
Radio Free Europe, 141
Radio Liberty, 141
Radio Orange, 74
Radium Institute, 600
Radu, General, 638

Raeder, Grand Admiral Erich, 28, 42, 87–88, 91–94,
185P, 280, 370, 404, **461–63**, 462P, 587,
694, 713, 722–25, 742, 797, 1000, 1084–85,
1232–34, 1244–45, 1264, 1369–70, 1372,
1382, 1390, 1399, 1409, 1423, 1467, 1616–
17, 1626, 1674–75, 1738
Rahn, Rudolf von, 190, 1705
RAINBOW plans, **1253**, 1679
Rall, Major Günther, **463**
Ramcke, General Hermann, 1404–05
Ramsay, Admiral Sir Bertram, **463–64**, 546, 736, 1357,
1462–63, 1599, 1678
Rangers, 271, 531, 657, 668, **752–53**, 778, 1266, 1360,
1448, 1600, 1663–64
1st Ranger Battalion, 271, 752, 1358, 1448
2nd Ranger Battalion, 271, 752
3rd Ranger Battalion, 752, 1358, 1669
4th Ranger Battalion, 271, 752, 1358
5th Ranger Battalion, 752
6th Ranger Battalion, 752
Rankin, Jeanette, 194
Rantzau, Lieutenant General Heinrich von, 1651
Rapallo Treaty, 115, **146**, 160
Rapido River, battle, 261–62, 1255, 1311M, 1525–26,
1638–39
Raskova, Marina, 392
Rasch, *SS-Brigadeführer* Dr. Otto, 671
Rasp, Siegfried, 1513
Raštikis, General Stasys, 381, **464**
Rath, Ernst vom, 101, 328
Rathenau, Field Marshal Walther von, 146, **464**
Ratzel, Friederich, 107
Raubal, Geli, 242
Ravenstein, Major General Johann, 1605
Reagan, Ronald, 282
reconnaissance and observation aircraft
Germany
He-70, 695
He-99, 695
Fi-156 *Storch,* 892, 1229, 1519
Red Army. *See* Army, Soviet (Index of Military Units)
Red Ball Express, 1223, **1253–54**
Red Cross, 229, 255, 351, 410, **753–54**, 754P, 788,
1250
Red Orchestra (*Rote Kapelle*), 135, 528, **754**
Reeves, Admiral J.M., 799
Regensburg, air raids, 532, 597, 873, 975, 1330M, 1398,
1508, 1624, **1639–40**
Reichenau, Field Marshal Walther von, 446–47, **464**,
742–44, 1388–90, 1460, 1481, 1646
Reichl, Major Joachim, 1727
Reichssicherheitshauptamt (RSHA—*Reich* Main Security
Office), 45, 66–67, 89, 91–94, 229, 291,
341–42, 365, 453, 484, 570, 683, **754–55**,
760, 763
Department IV B4, 291
Department VI, 484
Reichstag fire, 80, **146–48**, 147P, 323, 346
Reichswald, battle, 1344M, 1513, **1640–42**, 1643

Reichwein, Adolf, 137
Reinfarth, *SS-Gruppenführer* Heinz, 1733
REINHARD, *Aktion,* 47, 67
Reinhardt, Major General Emil F., 63, 63P
Reinhardt, Colonel General Georg-Hans, 98, **464–65**,
1377, 1389, 1412, 1487, 1511
Reinstein, Jacques, 369
Reitsch, Hanna, **465**, 999
Remagen Bridge, battle, 248, 286, 496, 537, 1033, 1057,
1255, 1331M, 1513, **1642**, 1644
Remarque, Erich Maria, **465**
Remer, Colonel Otto, 1384
Remy, Colonel Gilbert Renault, 150
Rendulic, Colonel General Lothar, **465–66**, 1511
Renner, Karl, 1724
Renthe-Fink, Dr. Cecil, 1447
Reparations Commission, 168
reprisals, 42, **148**, 151
Republic of Salò. *See* Italian Social Republic
Republican National Guard, 190
resistance, 1404
Albanian, 355
Anti-Fascist Council of National Liberation, 355
Zogist Resistance Army, 456
Belgian
Mouvement National Royaliste, 1356
Czech, 232, 434, 1444
Czech National Committee, 758
Defense of the Nation (*Obrana Naroda*), 232
Danish, **148–49**, 235, 1257, 1350–51, 1447
Freedom Council, 148
Information (press service), 148
French, **149–52**, 179, 255, 272, 299, 314, 401, 426,
480, 482, 659, 774, 1256, 1271, 1497,
1621–22
Armée Secèrte, 151, 674
Bureau Central de Reseignment et d'Action (BCRA),
151, **658–59**, 698
Bureau d'Opérations Aériennes, 151, **658–59**
Centre d'Opération de Parachutage, 151
Centurie, 150
Ceux de la Libération-Vengaence, 150
Ceux de la Résistance, 150
Cohors Asturies, 150
Combat, 150, 698
Comité National Français (CNF), 150, 674
Confrérie Notre-Dame, 150
Conseil National de la Résistance (CNR), 151, 426
Défense de la France, 150
Fana, 150
Forces Françaises de l'Intérieur (FFI), 150, 378,
559, 621–22, **674–75**, 699, 1496–97,
1621
Franc-Tireur, 150
Francs-Tireurs et Partisans Français, 151, 674
Front National, 150–51
Libération-Nord, 150, 698
Libération-Sud, 150, 698
L'Humanité (newspaper), 151

submarines *(continued)*
  U.S., **1090–92**, 1005T, 1122–24
    Gato-class, 1091
    O-class, 1091
    R-class, 1091
    S-class, 1091
submarine warfare, 546, 1149, 1187–90, **1282–88**
  Pillenwerfer, 1285
  Schnorchel, 1087, 1285, 1370, 1372
Sucharski, Major Henryk, 1736
Sudetenland, 13, 118–19, 162, **163–64**, 227, 254, 346,
    358, 569
Suez Crisis (1956), 259, 290
Suhard, Cardinal, 178
Sukhoi, P.O., 592
Sullivan, John L., 508
Sümmermann, Major General Max, 575
Sun Tzu, 1191
Suner, Ramon Serrano, 53, 642
Suomussalmi, battle, 1326M, 1570, **1704–05**, 1737
Supreme Headquarters Allied Expeditionary Force
    (SHAEF), 247–48, 311, 514, **774–76**, 1257,
    1271, 1425, 1499, 1514, 1536, 1559, 1643
  Chief of Staff, Supreme Allied Command (COSSAC),
    424, 774
SUSSEX, Operation, 746
Swaythling, Lady Jean. *See* Knox, Jean M.
Sweeny, Charles, 670
Swinton, Lieutenant Colonel E.D., 605
Świrski, Vice Admiral Jerzy, **515**
Syria, campaign, 14, 77, 275, 314, 549, 630, 1530,
    1705–07
  Damascus, occupation of, 1706
  EXPORTER, Operation, 1706
Szabo, Violette, **515–16**, 516P
Szálasi, Ferenc, 1535
Szeptycki, General Stanisław, 1653
Szilard, Leo, 112
Szylling, Lieutenant General Antoni, **516**, 1630

T
TACTICAL AIR SUPPORT, **1287–88**, 1666
Taft, William Howard, President of the United States, 511
TAIFUN (TYPHOON), Operation. *See* Moscow
Tanguy, Henri ("Colonel Rol"), 1622
Tank, Kurt, **517**
tanks
  British, **1107–09**, 1131T
    Cavalier, 1109
    Centaur, 1109, 1118
    Churchill, 613, 649P, 976, 1108–09, 1118, 1449
    Comet, 1109
    Cromwell, 1109, 1118
    Cruiser, 1108P, 1109
    Crusader, 1109, 1118
    Locust, 993
    Matilda, 1107–08, 1113, 1115, 1118, 1379,
        1502P, 1680, 1690, 1711, 1712P
    Mark-VI, 1107, 1118

    Sherman Firefly, 555, 1109, 1122
    Tetrach, 993, 1107
    Valentine, 813, 1108, 1115, 1118
  Canadian
    Ram, 613, 810, 813, 977
  Czechoslovakian
    LT-35, 1113
    LT-38, 1113
  French, **1109–10**, 1132T
    Char B1, 620, 1109, 1110P
    Char FCM2c-bis, 1109–10
    Hotchkiss H-39, 619, 1110
    Renault FT-17, 295, 619, 1110
    Renault R-35, 1110
    St. Chamond, 295
    Somua S-35, 619, 1110
  German, **1111–14**, 1133T
    PzKpfw-35(t), 1113
    PzKpfw-38(t), 803, 1113, 1119
    PzKpfw-I, 807, 1111, 1112P
    PzKpfw-II, 816, 1111–12, 1119
    PzKpfw-III, 976, 1111–13, 1111P, 1119, 1352,
        1500, 1502
    PzKpfw-IV, 611, 803, 817, 1108P, 1111–13, 1119,
        1352, 1488, 1500, 1502
    PzKpfw-V Panther, 808, 1116, 1122, 1148, 1534,
        1549, 1550
    PzKpfw-VI Tiger, 555, 806, 808, 1113–14, 1113P,
        1116, 1122, 1148, 1542, 1549
    PzKpfw-VIB Tiger II (*Königtiger*), 1114, 1148
  Italian
    Fiat L.33, 610
  Polish, **1114–15**, 1134T
    7TP, 1114
    TK, 1114
    TKS, 1114
    Vickers Mk-E, 1114
    Whippet, 635
  Soviet, **1115–17**, 1135T
    BT-5, 1115–16
    IS-1, 808, 1117, 1150
    IS-2, 1114, 1117
    IS-3, 1117
    KV-1, 1112, 1115, 1117, 1150, 1727
    KV-85, 1117
    SKM, 1117
    T-26, 1115
    T-27, 1115
    T-28, 1115–16
    T-32, 1117
    T-34, 193, 479, 564, 638, 640–41, 803, 806, 808,
        1112, 1114, 1115–17, 1116P, 1119, 1150,
        1298, 1589, 1695, 1727
    T-35, 1117
    T-37, 1115
    T-38, 1115
    T-40, 1116
    T-60, 1116
    T-70, 808, 1116, 1119

T-80, 1116
T-100, 1117
Special, **1117–19**, 1121, 1204
  Centaur variants
    armored bulldozer, 1118
  Chaffee variants
    M-19 SP AA gun, 1118
  Churchill variants
    armored recovery vehicle (ARV), 1118
    armored vehicle Royal Engineers (AVRE),
      1118
    beach armored recovery vehicle (BARV), 1118
    Crocodile (flamethrower), 976–77, 1118, 1148
  Cromwell variants
    Prong, 1118
  Crusader variants
    Tank AA, 1118
  Goliath, remote-controlled mini-tank, 1734
  Hobby's Funnies, 348, 1118, 1167
  Mark VI variants
    Light Tank AA Mark I, 1118
    Light Tank AA Mark II, 1118
  Matilda variants
    Canal Defense Light (CDL), 1118
  pneumatic dummy tank, 1118
  PzKpfw-II variants
    Schwimm-Panzer, 1119, 1675
  PzKpfw-III variants
    *Unterwasser-Panzer-*III, 1119, 1675
  PzKpfw-IV variants
    *Flakpanzer-*IV, 1119
    *Unterwasser-Panzer-*IV, 1119
  Sherman variants
    Crab, 1118
    duplex drive (DD), 1118, 1709
    flamethrower, 1118, 1122
    Rhino, 1659
    rocket launcher, 1073, 1073P, 1118, 1122
  T-70 variants
    SU-37 SP AA gun, 1119
  Valentine variants
    duplex drive (DD), 1118
    Snake, 1118
    Scorpion, 1118
U.S., **1119–22**, 1136T
  M-1 combat car, 1120
  M-2 combat car, 1120
  M-2A1 medium tank, 1120
  M-2A4 light tank, 1120
  M-3 Stuart, 1115, 1120–21
  M-3 Lee/Grant, 810, 1115, 1352, 1500, 1578
  M-4 Sherman, 827, 977, 1073P, 1109, 1115, 1118,
    1121–22, 1121P, 1384, 1415, 1473, 1542,
    1607
  M-5 Stuart, 977, 1120
  M-6 heavy tank, 1122
  M-22 Locust, 1120
  M-24 Chaffee, 827, 1118, 1120
  M-26 Pershing, 805, 1122

TANNENBAUM, Operation, 126
Tannenbergbund, 163
Taranto, air raid, 268, 711, 796, 891, 1347M, 1520,
    1574, 1605, **1708–09**
Taylor, A.J.P., 1224, 1490
Taylor, Brigadier General George A., 1350
Taylor, Lieutenant General Maxwell D., 396, **517–18**,
    1367, 1664
Taylor, Brigadier General Telford, 14, 116, **518**
Taylor, William E.G., 670
Tedder, Air Chief Marshal Sir Arthur W., 455, **518–19**,
    563P, 1415, 1609, 1677–78
Teheran Conference. *See* conferences, Allied
Templer, Lieutenant General Sir Gerald, **519**
Tennant, Captain W.G., 1462
10th Light Flotilla, Italian, 236, 657, 694, 728, **777**,
    1088, 1265, 1354–55, 1576
Terboven, Josef, 152, **519–20**, 1618
Terkel, Studs, 83
Teruzzi, Attilio, 483
Teutonia Order, 684
Thälmann, Ernst, 135
Thapa, Subedar Lalbahadur, 686
theaters of operations, Allied
  Atlantic Theater, **1369–74**
  Caribbean Defense Command, 215
  China-Burma-India (CBI) Theater, 389, 550, 1000,
    1128
  European Theater of Operations (ETO), 215, 263,
    272, 276, 407, 458, 561, 652, 655, 663, 745,
    774–76, 778, 788, 861, 862, 890, 893, 936,
    963, 977, 999, 1033, 1122, 1165–66, 1193,
    1239, 1497, 1614, 1680
  Mediterranean Theater of Operations (MTO), 210,
    268, 435, 468, 554, 598, 736, 745, 774,
    1382, 1497
  Pacific Theater, 746, 860, 1239, 1282
Theresienstadt. *See* Holocaust
Thiel, Dr. Walter, 1055, 1070, 1624
Thirty Years' War (1618–1648), 12
Thoholte, *General der Artillerie* Karl, 825
Thoma, Lieutenant General Wilhelm von, **520**, 575,
    1474
Thomas, Lieutenant Colonel Kurt, 680
Thomas, *SS-Brigadeführer* Max, 671
Thomas, Norman, 96
Thompson, J.J., 235
Thorne, Lieutenant General Andrew, 1484–85
Thyssen, Fritz, **520**
TIGER, exercise, 961, **1709–10**
Tillich, Paul, **520–21**
Timmerman, Lieutenant Karl, 286, 1642
Timoshenko, Marshal of the Soviet Union Semen K.,
    411, **521**, 562, 592, 639–40, 770, 823,
    1544–46, 1570, 1646, 1687, 1727, 1736
Tippelskirch, General Kurt, 1513
Tiso, Joseph, 162–63, **521**
Tito, Marshal (Josip Broz), 58, 76, 355, 414, 448, 450,
    465, 494, 498, **521–24**, 660–61, 750, 768,

underwater demolition teams (UDTs), **778–79**, 1167, 1265–66

uniforms, **1141–43**

Union of Soviet Socialist Republics. *See* Soviet Union

United Nations (UN), 4, 48, 50–52, 53, 61–62, 83, 104–05, **172–76**, 249, 355–56, 358, 368, 501, 529, 545, 557, 1269

  U.N. Atomic Energy Commission, 225

  U.N. Commission for the Investigation of War Crimes, 91

  U.N. Genocide Convention, 94

  U.N. Relief and Recovery Administration, 34, 424

  U.N. Security Council, 229, 315

United Services Organization (USO), **779**

Unrug, Vice Admiral Jozef, **533**, 729, 1630

Upham, Captain Charles H., **534**, 534P

Urbanowicz, Wing Commander Witold, **534**

Uren, Ormond, 767

Urquhart, Major General Robert E., **534–35**, 535P, 1367–68

Ustaša, 57–58, 447–48, 647, **779**, 1741–42

Ustinov, Colonel General Dimitri F., **535–36**

V

V-weapons, 548, 747, 1061T, 1164, 1266

  "Oslo Report," 1625

  V-1 buzz bomb, 416, 579, 591, 801, 866, 963, 1033, 1055–57, 1055P, 1065, 1071, 1148, 1276, 1290, 1357, 1442–43, 1449–50, 1492, 1722–23

  V-2 guided missile, 154, 242, 283, 1055–57, 1070, 1071, 1148, 1257, 1276, 1290, 1357, 1442–43, 1449, 1624–25, 1642, 1722

V-1/V-2 offensive, 37, 342, 792, 1056, 1357, 1441–43, 1449–50, 1492, **1722–23**

Vabre, Professor Donnedieu de, 91

Valera, Eamon de, 125

VALKYRIE, Operation. *See* July plot against Hitler

Valle, General Giuseppi, 188

Van Fleet, Major General James A., **537–38**, 1404, 1651

Vandenberg, Lieutenant General Hoyt S., **537**

Vansittart, Robert, 13

VARSITY, Operation, 1160, 1344M, **1723–24**

Vashugin, Nikolai, 640

Vasilevsky, Marshal of the Soviet Union Aleksandr M., 491, 507, **538**, 538P, 770–72, 1413, 1702

Vatutin, General Nikolai F., 538, **538–39**, 539P, 564, 1412, 1450–51, 1549–50, 1702, 1719, 1728

Vauban, Sebastien le Prestre de, 1404

VE Day, 1511, 1515

Vecchi, Cesare De, 189

Venables, Commander A.G., 1567

Venlo incident, 484

Verdilhac, General Raoul de, 1705–06

Veress, General Ljos, 1534

Vernon, Lieutenant D., 1410

Versailles Treaty. *See* Treaty of Versailles

Vershigora, P., 155

Vessey, Lieutenant John, **539**

Veterans of Foreign Wars (VFW), 203

veterinary services, **1293–94**

Vian, Rear Admiral Sir Phillip, **539–40**, 540P, 1356, 1576, 1685, 1686, 1700

Vichy France (1940–1944), 6, 10, 14, 39, 74, 76–77, 149–52, **177–80**, 178P, 234, 271, 272, 275–76, 278, 293, 313–15, 364, 384, 385, 552, 621, 674, 680, 703, 718–21, 745, 1007, 1270, 1445–46, 1490, 1530, 1608, 1611, 1612, 1614, 1705–07, 1716–17

  Armistice Army, 179, 383, 622, 1142

  French Volunteer Legion, 179

  Légion Française de Combats, 179

  Marine Nationale, 718–20

  Milice Française, 39, 179, 272

  Paris Protocols, 271

  Riom trials, 178, 270, 313, 466

  Service d'Ordre Légionnaire (SOL), 179

  Service de Travail Obligatorie (STO), 179, 698

Victor Emmanuel III, King of Italy, 66, 188–90, 212, 222, 326, 430, 483, **540–41**, 1351, 1353, 1539, 1679

Victoria, Queen of Great Britain, 1047

Victory Program. *See* strategy, Anglo/American

Vidussoni, Aldo, 189

Vienna, capture of, 770, 1342M, 1375, **1724–25**

Vietinghoff genannt Scheel, Colonel General Heinrich von, **541**, 1361, 1516, 1524–27, 1585, 1636–37, 1664–66, 1725

Vietnam War

  American phase (1965–1973), 14, 207, 339, 350, 539, 553, 658, 827, 873, 1039, 1127, 1150, 1266

  French phase (1945–1954), 622, 680

Vigenere, Blaise de, 1192

Vigerie, General François d'Astier de la, 583

Vigon, General Juan, 1481

Villa, Pancho, 444, 494

Vinci, Leonardo da, 999

Vlasov, Lieutenant General Andrei A., 43, **541–42**, 757–58, 1250, 1546

Voice of America, 141

Volchkov, Lieutenant Colonel A.F., 91

Volkmann, General Helmuth, 695

Volkov, M.I., 592

Volkssturm, 707, **780–81**, 1392, 1533, 1636, 1642

Voltaire, 31

Volturno River, battle, 1525, 1638, **1725–26**

Voronezh, battle, 235, 254, 322, 362, 1319M, 1701, **1726–28**

Voronov, Marshal of the Soviet Union Nikolai N., **542–43**, 542P, 770, 822

Vörös, Colonel General Janos, **543**, 1535

Voroshilov, Marshal of the Soviet Union Kliment Y., 144, 506, **543–44**, 543P, 563, 705, 770, 1117

Vyazma-Bryansk, battle, 1345M, 1589, **1728–29**

W

WAAC. *See* Women's Auxiliary Army Corps

Woodward, Vernon, 581
World Bank, 207, 368, 424
World War I (1914–1918), 6, 12, 14, 22, 36, 59, 60, 65,
  68, 79, 85, 90, 96, 98, 104, 113, 114, 117,
  124, 125, 127, 139, 140, 144, 146, 158, 161,
  163, 165–68, 169, 172, 177, 184, 187, 194,
  196, 198, 199, 204, 208, 209, 210, 211, 212,
  214, 216, 217, 218, 219, 222, 225, 226, 230,
  232, 233, 243, 245, 246, 248, 250, 252,
  254–55, 256, 257, 262, 263, 265, 267, 270,
  272, 275, 276, 277, 278, 280, 281, 283, 289,
  290, 292, 294, 296, 299, 305, 306, 308, 311,
  317, 318, 319, 321, 322, 324, 327, 330, 334,
  335, 336, 337, 338, 339, 341, 344, 345, 349,
  351, 353, 354, 355, 356, 358, 360, 361, 362,
  364, 366, 371, 374, 377, 382, 383, 385, 386,
  390, 392, 393, 395, 397, 398, 404, 404, 405,
  407, 411, 412, 414, 415, 416, 417, 420, 421,
  424, 425, 426, 427, 436, 437, 438, 440, 441,
  443, 444, 448, 449, 461, 463, 464, 465, 466,
  468, 469, 470, 474, 476, 478, 480, 482, 485,
  488, 489, 491, 492, 494, 497, 499, 505, 510,
  511, 514, 518, 519, 520, 521, 522, 524, 525,
  526, 527, 528, 529, 530, 531, 537, 538, 539,
  540, 546, 548, 551, 552, 553, 556, 557, 559,
  561, 562, 571, 584, 601, 603, 604, 606–09,
  610, 611, 613, 614, 615, 619, 622, 625–26,
  628, 630, 643–44, 648, 651, 660–61, 670,
  686, 699, 701, 708, 709, 711–12, 716, 717,
  718, 723–25, 726, 742, 762, 795, 799, 813,
  816, 817, 818, 820, 824, 825, 827, 854, 859,
  862, 870, 894, 896–98, 898, 902, 903, 929,
  934, 935, 960, 999, 1005, 1007–08, 1011,
  1012, 1016–18, 1047–48, 1051–53, 1065,
  1070, 1081, 1082, 1084–85, 1088–89,
  1090–91, 1110, 1115, 1122, 1142–43, 1149,
  1157–59, 1161, 1166, 1168, 1171, 1172,
  1175, 1186, 1187, 1190, 1192, 1199, 1203,
  1207, 1214, 1217, 1225–26, 1232–34, 1236,
  1246, 1259, 1263, 1265, 1267, 1270–71,
  1273–74, 1277, 1282–83, 1295, 1370–71,
  1404, 1405, 1411, 1415, 1459, 1487, 1499,
  1563, 1616, 1652–53, 1670, 1674, 1724
  Artois, battle (1915), 449
  Baltic islands, landings (1917), 1039
  Cambrai, battle (1917), 308, 605, 1175–76
  Champagne-Marne, battle (1918), 398, 498
  Dardanelles, campaign (1915), 500, 1455
  Gallipoli landings and campaign (1915–1916), 601,
    666–78, 1039, 1167, 1358, 1489, 1521,
    1587, 1677
  Jutland, battle (1916), 317, 455
  Malmaison, battle (1917), 319
  Marne, battle (1914), 446, 449, 619, 1488
  Masurian Lakes, battle (1914), 344, 394, 402
  Meuse-Argonne, battle (1918), 398, 444, 547, 1159,
    1176, 1537, 1557
  Neuve Chapelle, battle (1916), 345
  Passchendaele, battle (1917), 360, 1536

Plan XVII, 1258, 1487
St. Mihiel, battle (1918), 437, 444, 477, 547, 1176
Somme, battle (1916), 345, 390, 605
Tannenberg, battle (1914), 344, 394
Verdun, battle (1916), 400, 402, 446, 449–50, 515,
  619, 1225, 1488, 1557
Vimy Ridge, battle (1917), 360
Ypres, first battle (1914), 345
Ypres, third battle (1917), 345
Zeebrugge, raid, (1918), 667
Wrangel, General P.N., 541
WREN. *See* Women in the military, Britain; Women's
  Royal Enlisted Navy
Wright, Orville, 299
WRNS. *See* Women's Royal Naval Service
WUNDERLAND (WONDERLAND) I and II,
  Operations, **1738–40**

X

XX Committee, 319, 409, 421, **792**, 1191

Y

Yad Vashem, 83
Yakovlev, Aleksandr, 592, 970
Yalta Conference. *See* conferences, Allied
Yeager, Major Charles, **559**
Yefremov, General Mikhail, 1590
Yegorov, General Alexander, 1653–54
Yeltsin, Boris, 99
Yeo-Thomas, Wing Commander Forest F., **559**
Yeremenko, Marshal Andrei I., 222, 454, 526, 539, **559–
  60**, 640, 1412, 1441, 1702, 1729
Yorck, Peter von, 137
York, Sergeant Alvin, 1159
Young, Lieutenant Frederick, 685
Young, Owen, 204
Young Men's Christian Association (YMCA), 779
Young Plan, **204**, 513
Young Women's Christian Association (YWCA), 779
Yugoslavia, invasion of, 57, 76, 414, 450, 465, 494, 551,
  647, 660, 685, 750, 1263
  Operation "25," 1741
  Skopje, capture of, 494
Yugoslavia, national liberation war, 57–58, 523, 648,
  1317M, **1741–44**
  "Long March," Tito's, 1742
  RÖSSELSPRUNG, Operation, 1743
  SCHWARTZ, Operation, 1743
  WEISS, Operation, 1742

Z

Zaitsev, Vasily, 1702
Zakharov, General Matvei, 1413
Zaleski, August, Polish Foreign Minister, **561**
Zangen, General Gustav-Adolf von, 1651
Zauditu, Empress of Ethiopia, 1476
Zehender, *SS-Brigadeführer* August, 1411
Zeitzler, General of *Panzer* Troops Kurt, 187, **561**, 1695
Zemke, Colonel Hubert, 310, **561–62**